UNIVERSITY CASEBOOK SERIES®

CONTRACT LAW AND ITS APPLICATION

NINTH EDITION

DANIEL J. BUSSEL
Professor of Law
University of California, Los Angeles

FOUNDATION
PRESS

University Casebook Series is a trademark registered in the U.S. Patent and Trademark Office.

© 1971, 1977, 1983, 1988, 1994, 1999 FOUNDATION PRESS
© 2007, 2011 THOMSON REUTERS/FOUNDATION PRESS
© 2016 LEG, Inc. d/b/a West Academic
    444 Cedar Street, Suite 700
    St. Paul, MN 55101
    1-877-888-1330

Printed in the United States of America

ISBN: 978-1-68328-206-8

PREFACE TO THE NINTH EDITION

Twenty-five years in, for me, teaching first-year Contracts remains a joy. It is the perfect introduction to American law: There is doctrine, of course, but doctrine that evolves with the temper of the times. The cases are factually accessible to novices, but introduce them to a commercial world from which most of them have been largely sheltered thus far, having lived within households and at universities, but which, for most of them, will dominate their professional lives going forward. Contracts is a body of law embedded deep within a legal system that has shaped it and supplemented it, and which it in turn shapes and supplements, providing a window into that legal system without peer. From a skills perspective, it provides rich fodder for reading and applying both case law and statute law, drafting, counseling and advocacy. As noted in the Introduction, it has both a past and a future, and remains relevant to lawyers and clients.

Structurally this NINTH EDITION follows the mold of its immediate predecessors which is proven in the classroom. I begin with the thirty-thousand foot overview framed by Arthur Rosett's brilliant introductory hypothetical *Best v. Southland*, followed by an in-depth unit on contract interpretation—the major theme of the book. Then a long unit on remedies with its strong economic orientation, followed by the rest of the traditional canon. Remedies and performance issues—where all the real action is—receive the greatest emphasis.

The classic cases still work but I have introduced a few key new cases in some areas. Moreover, notes are updated throughout with examples, case summaries and questions that reflect the complicated, interrelated, technology-laden, diverse and evolving society we find ourselves in. One consequence of the resistance of contract doctrine to change over the last generation has been the increasing relevance of countervailing forces: The explosion in positive law regulating contractual and commercial relationships, of course, but more recently also, renewed interest in, developments in, and judicial and academic concern about, restitution and arbitration as alternatives to traditional contract remedies. Integrating the controversial THIRD RESTATEMENT OF RESTITUTION, and the developing case law relying on unconcionability doctrine as a mechanism to regulate arbitration are the most significant doctrinal innovations reflected in this NINTH EDITION. In addition, based on feedback from adopters and students, I have included a second Appendix consisting of selected sections of the RESTATEMENT, SECOND, CONTRACTS.

I am very grateful to Michael Morris-Nussbaum, UCLA School of Law Class of 2017 and Maxwell Michael, UCLA School of Law Class of 2018, for providing excellent research and editorial assistance for this NINTH EDITION. Once again, as on so many prior projects my staff assistant, Tal Grietzer, prepared a camera-ready manuscript of these materials through the miracle of modern desk-top publishing.

His efforts, skill and care made timely publication possible. A newer member of our faculty support group, Jessica Blatchley, also played an indispensable role in preparing the manuscript for publication, and I look forward eagerly to working with her again in the future. I also owe thanks to my law partners at Klee, Tuchin, Bogdanoff & Stern LLP for their indulgence and support of my academic work, and, of course, to the UCLA School of Law, its administration, its faculty, and the marvelously resourceful and helpful law librarians at the UCLA Hugh & Hazel Darling Law Library. My greatest debt, however, will always be to my greatly missed friend, colleague and mentor Arthur Rosett whose mind and spirit still infuse this work.

Los Angeles, California   D.J.B.
August 10, 2016

For Raquelle de la Rocha

ACKNOWLEDGMENTS

We gratefully acknowledge the permission extended to reprint excerpts from the following works:

ALBERT D. ANGEL, *The Use of Arbitration Clauses as a Means for the Resolution of Impasses Arising in the Negotiation of, or During the Life of, Long-Term Contractual Relationships*, 28 Bus. Law. 589 (1973). Copyright 1973 by the American Bar Association.

ABA Model Rules of Professional Conduct. Copyright 2009 by the American Bar Association.

STEPHEN M. BAINBRIDGE, *Exclusive Merger Agreements and Lock-Ups in Negotiated Corporate Acquisitions*, 75 MINN.L.REV. 239, 246 (1990).

PHYLLIS T. BOOKSPAN and MAXINE KLINE, *On Mirrors and Gavels: A Chronicle of How Menopause Was Used as a Legal Defense Against Women*, 32 IND. L. REV. 1267 (1999).

JOHN BREEN, *The Lost Volume Seller and Lost Profits Under 2-708(2): A Conceptual and Linguistic Critique*, 50 U. MIAMI L. REV. 779 (1996).

DANIEL J. BUSSEL, *Liability for Concurrent Breach of Contract*, 73 WASH. U.L.Q. 91 (1995).

ARTHUR L. CORBIN, *Corbin on Contracts* (1964)

ARTHUR L. CORBIN, *The Parol Evidence Rule*, 53 Yale L.J. 603 (1944). Copyright 1944, Yale Law Journal. Reprinted by permission of The Yale Law Journal Company and Fred B. Rothman & Company.

DAN B. DOBBS, REMEDIES: DAMAGES, EQUITY, RESTITUTION (2d ed. 1993).

TERRENCE M. DUNN, *The Franchisor's Control Over the Transfer of a Franchise*, 27 FRANCHISE L.J. 233, 233 (2008).

ANTHONY T. KRONMAN, *Specific Performance*, 45 U.CHI.L.REV. 351 (1978).

ANTHONY LIN, Attorney, *9/11 Fee Called 'Shocking, Unconscionable,'* N.Y. L.J. (Aug. 29, 2006). Reprinted by permission ALM Properties, Inc. © 2006. All rights reserved. Further duplication without permission is prohibited.

NORA LOCKWOOD TOOHER, *Two German Entrepreneurs* Win $ 255 Million, LAWYERS WEEKLY USA (Sept. 22, 2004). Reprinted with permission from *Lawyers* USA. Please visit our website at www.lawyersusaonline.com.

JONATHAN T. MOLOT, *A Market in Litigation Risk*,
76 U. CHI. L. REV. 367 (2009).

HARVEY S. PERLMAN, *Interference with Contract and Other Economic Expectancies: A Clash of Tort and Contract Doctrine*,
49 U. CHI. L. REV. 61, 128-29 (1982).

RESTATEMENT (SECOND) CONTRACTS. Copyright 1981 by the American Law Institute. Reproduced with permission. All rights reserved.

RESTATEMENT (SECOND) TORTS. Copyright 1963, 1965, 1977, 1979, 1981, 1982, 1984, 1986, 1987, 1989, 1991, 1992, 1994, 1995, 1998, 2002, 2005, 2006, 2010 by the American Law Institute. Reproduced with permission. All rights reserved.

KEITH ROWLEY, *You Asked For It You Got It … Toy Yoda*,
3 NEV.L.J. 526 (2003).

STEVEN SEIDENBERG, *International Arbitration Loses Its Grip*,
ABA JOURNAL (Apr. 2010).

W. DAVID SLAWSON, *Standard Form Contracts and Democratic Control of Law Making Power*, 84 Harv. L. Rev. 529 (1971).

RICHARD SUSSKIND, THE END OF LAWYERS? (Oxford 2008).

UNIFORM COMMERCIAL CODE. Copyright 2010 by the American Law Institute and the National Conference of Commissioners on Uniform State Laws. Reproduced with permission. All rights reserved.

ANTHONY JON WATERS, *The Property in the Promise: A Study of the Third Party Beneficiary Rule*, 98 HARV. L. REV. 1109 (1985).

JAMES J. WHITE & DAVID A. PETERS, *A Footnote for Jack Dawson*,
100 MICH. L. REV. 1954, 1966, 1971-72 (2002).

JESSE WILSON, *Punishing Contract Breakers:* Whiten v. Pilot Insurance *and the Sea Change in Canadian Law*, 10 AUCKLAND U.L.REV. 61 (2004).

Summary of Contents

TABLE OF CONTENTS

Introduction   1

Chapter 1

DEFINING CONTRACT: WHAT PROMISES ARE LEGALLY ENFORCEABLE AND WHY? 13

Chapter 2

Chapter 3

Chapter 4

SOCIETALLY IMPOSED LIMITS ON PROMISE

Chapter 5

Chapter 6

Chapter 7

Chapter 8

PERFORMANCE AND BREACH 727

Chapter 9

TABLE OF CASES

Principal cases are in **bold** type. Non-principal cases
are in roman type. References are to pages.

UNIVERSITY CASEBOOK SERIES®

CONTRACT LAW AND ITS APPLICATION

NINTH EDITION

INTRODUCTION

This Casebook introduces contract law to first-year American law students. The materials and the teaching method reflect the special structure of the legal system and legal education in the United States. The study of contract law has been central to the first-year law curriculum since Christopher Columbus Langdell developed "the case method" in the 19th century. The case method has dominated American legal education for more than four generations. Contracts was the first case method course, and remains the only required first year course in every accredited law school.

Contract law has both a past and a future. A subject with such a long history might be rather cut and dried, with few mysteries left to be fathomed. In fact, a rather rigid set of doctrines and rules did develop in contract law during the nineteenth and early twentieth centuries. This formalism supported the values, educational approach, and political structures of that period. By the second quarter of the 20th century, however, scholars and judges expressed increasing doubt whether that universal and abstract logical style reflects the commercial realities contract law must deal with and whether that style of reasoning helps or hinders the resolution of specific cases.

Gradually, the hard crust of traditional rules was broken by new approaches. While the classical rules continue to exert an influence (and students therefore must learn them), contract law today displays continuing vigor and growth. This new contract law is more specific and contextual. For example, labor and employment law, the law of partnerships, corporations, and other business organizations, and enterprise liability for products are all based on contracts, as are the professional relationships between lawyers and their clients and health care providers and their patients. It may be more accurate to say today that there are a number of bodies of law for different kinds of contracts, although these distinct bodies of law do share some general approaches.

The Central Themes of Contract Law

Contract law describes how and when society uses the authority of law to enforce private agreements. This core subject matter sets Contracts apart from other first-year courses. Property, for example, considers how society uses law to recognize people's interests in possessing things to the exclusion of other persons. Torts examines those non-contractual occasions when a person is legally obligated to compensate another for violating that other person's legally recognized interests. Criminal law considers the use of punishment to enforce rules of social behavior. The courses in procedure focus on the processes used by courts to protect all of these interests.

1

Inevitably, these compartments of the law are to some extent artificial and overlap. For example, when the law recognizes an agreement as enforceable, it creates a kind of property. The law will enforce the owner's claims to exclusive possession of those rights and usually will allow the contract-owner to sell them to a third person. Those who interfere with a contractual relationship may be liable in tort or punished criminally for their behavior. The procedural system frequently serves as a limiting factor on the enforcement the law gives to a private agreement. Unless there is a practical way to assert a claim and an effective remedy for the redress of valid claims, the abstract rights declared by the law do not mean much. The hard fact is that the law is indeed a "seamless web": a subject-matter with neither a simple, easily identifiable pattern, nor a single appropriate point to begin its study.

This Casebook attempts to impose some order on the field of contract law by identifying the following broad themes into which specific issues can be sorted in the study of the subject.

(1) *Contract as a Concept and as an Institution.* What promises are legally enforceable and why?

(2) *Formation.* How are binding agreements made? At what point in time do contract principles restrain the parties' freedom of action?

(3) *Performance and Breach.* On what basis does a lawyer determine the extent to which a contractual obligation has been performed or breached? To what degree does this determination assign factual and legal meanings to the terms the parties have explicitly or tacitly undertaken through their relationship? And to what extent does the law for societal reasons decide whether there has been performance or breach by imposing terms on the parties' relationship, regardless of their intentions?

(4) *Remedies.* What legal relief is available to a party dissatisfied with how an agreement is working out? In what situations and to what extent are these remedies essential, helpful, irrelevant, or useless?

(5) *Contract as Property.* Can a party transfer an interest in a contract to someone else as a house or a car might be sold? How far can parties to a contract go in creating rights and liabilities in third persons? When are outsiders prevented from interfering with contractual relationships?

(6) *Contract and Social Control.* To what extent is a contract more than a private matter, of significance not only to the parties who made it? When must a contract's legal recognition and performance be regulated to protect community interests?

These six themes form the core of the study of contract law.

This Casebook in Outline

This Casebook consists of nine chapters in addition to this Introduction and the Appendix, which reprints relevant sections from Articles 1 and 2 of the Uniform Commercial Code and the Restatement (Second) of Contracts.

Chapter One looks generally at the concept of promises, how they are given meaning in law, and the circumstances that will lead a lawyer to say that a promise is unenforceable.

Chapter Two introduces the crucial question of remedies. If contracts are legally enforceable promises, we must examine with care what "legally enforceable" means.

Chapter Three builds on the remedial framework discussed in Chapter Two. It examines four distinct ways that the law counterbalances the shortcomings of the basic contract remedies described earlier. When confronted by doctrine that deals unsatisfactorily with an important problem, one common response is to create a distinct set of rules under a different label and let judges decide which rules apply when. Thus, we find an alternative set of restitutionary remedies that mitigates hardships arising out of the denial of relief under the basic contract remedial scheme. Or, in aggravated cases, courts may lift the matter bodily out of the conceptual framework of contract and give it the more hospitable label of tort. This adjustment in nomenclature makes new and more generous damage rules available. Third, courts in many situations permit parties to pre-plan appropriate remedies through liquidated damages clauses. Finally, parties may contract their way out of the law courts altogether by arbitration agreements that empower a new set of tribunals applying a distinct set of rules.

Chapter Four looks at the limits placed on contract by legal rules that may not be varied by agreement.

Chapter Five introduces related limits on contract that flow from failures of the agreement process itself. One strong justification for enforcement of agreements is the obligated party's assent to the agreement. When the reality of that assent becomes dubious, legal enforcement of the ensuing contract may weaken.

Chapter Six examines one kind of promise our law has found particularly important and worthy of enforcement, the bargained-for exchange. The concept of the bargain forms the foundation of the doctrine of consideration, which is theoretically central to much American contract law. This chapter will also look at some of the other theories of contract enforceability that supplement and compete with consideration.

Chapter Seven looks at the process of contract making. It asks when and how people become bound by their promises.

Chapter Eight assumes a contract has been validly formed and examines how the law responds to events after formation. How do people satisfy the obligation to perform their contracts and what kinds of deviations will be considered a breach?

Chapter Nine asks a different sort of question. It looks at the contract from the perspective of persons other than those who made the original agreement. To what extent does the existence of a contract affect others' rights?

Is There a Law of Contracts?

This Casebook assumes that it is useful to act as though there is a body of learning that can be described as the law of contracts. This assumption is not obvious: The law of sales is very different from the law of employment agreements, and both are very different from the law of insurance contracts. But the similarities are as important as the differences and suggest an underlying set of shared doctrinal ideas.

The unity of contract law is also limited by its history and growth as a judge-made body of rules. Most contract law doctrines in common law countries originated in the reasons given by judges in deciding specific cases. Only gradually and imperfectly have those reasons accumulated and become reconciled into coherent doctrine. The study of contract law in an English-speaking law school is grounded on the examination of judicial decisions. In most of the rest of the world a civil law tradition relies heavily on the exposition of a logical structure of rules derived from a few axiomatic propositions and embodied in a code.

Deriving general principles out of specific cases decisions is difficult at best. Until a case arises, there may be no rule on a particular point. When the facts shift just a bit, it is difficult to apply that rule to the altered circumstances. It can be difficult to tell from a judicial opinion what is the general principle and what are the exceptions and limitations that generalities are always subject to. The law of contract presents the challenge of learning a body of rules that is weak on systematics, full of gaps, and likely to offer more than one principle that might be applied to the case.

The unity of contract law is challenged in yet another way. The common law of contracts began in the royal courts of England. Although there were several such courts and the competition among them sometimes led to divergent statements of the law, general consistency was assured by the recognized hierarchy of authority. For more than 200 years in the United States, contract has been primarily a matter of state, rather than federal, law. While most states recognized the same authorities and basic rules of law, there were notable variations and conflicts. As the United States developed a single national economy a century ago, the pressures to reconcile the diverse strands of state contract law became very strong. Today there are few major points of conflict in the law of contracts of most American states. The economic situation is changing rapidly again, however, as increasingly interdependent world markets increase the likelihood that a transaction will cross national borders, raising international law and choice of law questions.

The emergence of a global economy has an important effect on agreement behavior. People do business together but do not share the same linguistic and cultural tradition or legal regime. The meaning of words, the implications of actions, and the content of applicable legal rules become more difficult to determine. Because the laws of the contracting parties' nations may be different, parties in negotiating a contract must establish a shared legal framework for the transaction. The growth of international transactions has led to important international commercial law in the form of treaties and conventions. This book will provide excerpts from two such sources, the United Nations Convention on Contracts for the International Sale of Goods, and the UNIDROIT Principles of International Commercial Contracts to provide a glimpse of this emerging body of global law.

Contracts Litigation in the United States

We study contract law primarily by examining how doctrine has developed over time in the decisions of appellate courts. The jurisprudential approach of Legal Realism teaches that the law-in-fact is not found so much in high-flown statements of abstract doctrine and rules, but pragmatically is discovered in terms of what a court will do in a concrete case. As Justice Holmes taught, the law is what a court will make a bad person do in a specific situation. The case method is itself, however, subject to a number of pragmatic limits. Few cases are appealed to the higher courts, and most contracts disputes are resolved without anyone going to any court. How can one resolve these cases based on assumptions about what some appellate court (that will never hear the matter) would decide?

In recent years, many more serious contracts disputes have been resolved by arbitration and alternative dispute resolution than by the courts, but precise numbers are hard to find. Moreover, of those contracts cases that remain within the state and federal court systems, a tiny and ever decreasing percentage appear to be resolved by trials or appeals. *See* Marc Galanter, *The Vanishing Trial: An Examination of Trials and Related Matters in Federal and State Courts*, 1 J. Empirical Legal Stud. 459 (2004). One may glean some idea of the baseline of contract litigation by looking at statistics developed by the *Civil Justice Survey of State Courts, 2005* published by the Bureau of Justice Statistics (Dec. 2008).

This study examined a sample of cases from the courts of general jurisdiction in the 75 largest counties in the United States and extrapolated a national picture from that sample. The 2005 data suggest that about one million contract suits were filed in state courts, representing more than half the civil lawsuits filed in the nation. "Lawsuit" is defined to exclude a very large number of judicial proceedings that are not truly contested litigation, such as the probate of decedent estates and other domestic relations matters. Of course, it also excludes the very large number of criminal and juvenile proceedings and the supervision of persons of impaired mental capacity. It also excludes a relatively small number of contract disputes that are filed in federal courts (about 30,000 in recent years). The federal cases include cases in which the United States is a party and some very large commercial disputes but are only a very small fraction of the total.

More than half the plaintiffs bringing suit were individuals; businesses brought 43% of the cases; and the rest were initiated by government agencies and hospitals. Almost 60% of the defendants were businesses. Individuals usually were the plaintiffs and businesses the defendants in claims of fraud, breach of lease agreements, and employment complaints. These types of cases made up about 30% of the total number of contract suits. Another 30% of the contract cases tried in state courts in 2005 were complaints made by a seller of goods that the buyer had failed to pay the price for the goods delivered. In most cases there was at least one third party plaintiff or defendant named in addition to the primary parties.

How were the contracts disputes that reached the courts disposed of? Two-thirds were settled or dismissed by agreement, transferred, or referred to arbitration. In another 26% of the cases, a default judgment was granted when the defendant failed to appear in court. Only 2.2% were disposed of by trial on the merits. Only one case in a thousand was resolved by jury verdict. The trend since 1992 has been towards far fewer contracts cases and fewer jury trials. In 2005, only 3,474 contracts trials occurred in the 75 largest counties in the United States (down from 9,744 in 1992), and juries adjudicated only 1,250 of these cases. Many contracts cases are resolved in a few months by default, settlement, dismissal or summary judgment. The small number of cases resolved by trial are likely to take over two years to resolve. Even among the relatively few contracts cases tried, profound conceptual issues are rarely involved. Remember as you read the many appellate decisions in this Casebook that it is a very rare contract dispute that winds its way up to a court of appeals or state Supreme Court. Few contract disputes result in lawsuits, few lawsuits go to judgment in the trial court, few of these are appealed, and only a small fraction of these wind up as reported appellate cases.

The Tools Used by Law Students

This Casebook will introduce you to types of primary legal texts that will be tools for much of your professional activity and a tradition of interpretation, a different set of ways to give meaning to those text. The primary legal materials include cases (that is, judicial decisions in contract disputes) and statutes (that is, rules of law enacted by a legislature). Judicial opinions and statutes are quite different from the kinds of texts used earlier in your education.

(1) *The Case.* In most American jurisdictions, contract law is common law, which means that it is judge-made case law. There is, for example, in most states no single statute to which one can turn for an authoritative statement of the total law of contract formation. Where statutes do exist, they take on meaning largely as a result of being interpreted by courts on a case-by-case basis. While the primacy of judge-made contract law is far less true today than it once was, it is still largely so.

Contract law, therefore, did not emerge as the product of one keen analytic mind or of one lawgiver who synthesized a coherent and consistent set of principles. Rather, contract law accumulated slowly over the centuries as judges decided specific tough cases and gave reasons for their decisions. Such principles as emerged grew out of the facts of particular disputes at given times and places, and were not deduced from a set of logical axioms. Law developed through such a process is never complete and never final.

Time corrodes most things: Some of the cases and statutes in this book are centuries old, and yet retain that wonderful quality of continuing to make sense. Other decisions and rules, while sensible when made, may seem out of tune with the contemporary world and current values. The security provided by a good decision is not eternal; sooner or later the question will be brought up again and must be seriously reconsidered.

This book is built primarily out of appellate court decisions, yet there are limits on the usefulness of appellate cases as a teaching tool. In the Anglo–American system of justice, appellate court consideration of cases is supposed to be based on the facts found in the trial court by the judge or jury. Unlike Continental European practice, American law permits little appellate review of the evidence. The appellate court is generally required to assume that the facts are those found by the lower court. Because their studies emphasize appellate cases, first-year students can lose sight of the basic indeterminacy and open-ended nature of most factual inquiries. These characteristics of fact-finding can be lost in well-intentioned pedagogical efforts to build final principles on assumed and certain hypothetical facts. Yet as Judge Jerome Frank teaches on p. 61, "Perhaps nine-tenths of legal uncertainty is caused by uncertainty as to what courts will find, on conflicting evidence, to be the facts of cases." From the moment of first contact with a client, a lawyer's greatest difficulty is likely to be determining what in fact happened, or at least what are the important parts of what happened.

To derive law from decisions in past cases, the lawyer must analyze the facts of the case with precision. If facts remain indeterminate, it is difficult to tell whether a case that comes along is like an earlier one, and therefore whether it should be governed by the same rule of law. On the other hand, too rigid a sense of the relevant reduces the flexibility offered by a system where like cases are decided alike. The capacity to see new fact patterns in familiar circumstances is needed if legal institutions are to deal with emerging realities through common law problem solving. Often the tension is between two truths, two plausible ways of describing the same disorderly reality.

Some of the cases in this book were decided many centuries ago; others are very recent. The older cases are often included to introduce you to basic principles that form a baseline so accepted that there are no recent cases in which the parties thought them worth arguing about. Sometimes the Casebook includes older authorities that struggle with past problems that have influenced the shape of current doctrine even though the specific problem itself is no longer a current one because of a changed legal or business environment. Some of these cases were decided by wise and famous judges, others by men unknown to us except for their opinions. Some were decided in large commercial centers, others by judges in rural communities. Most are decisions of American courts, but a few are from English courts.

That these decisions are collected here as a means of teaching contract law indicates two central values of the common law: reason and precedent.

The practice of writing judicial opinions reflects one aspect of justice: justice is reasoned decision, reaching the right conclusion in a case so that the rightness of the result is articulated in terms that can be understood by other people. Many of the cases in this book may seem easy now, but they were tough for the judges who faced the problem for the first time. Many of these cases could have been decided more than one way. Beginning law students sometimes cynically view every judicial opinion as an after-the-fact rationalization for a decision made on an unstated arbitrary basis. But most judges are not so disingenuous. Judicial opinions, like all human activities, are subject to foibles and fallibilities, whims, and prejudices. Judges are the products of their time, their class, and their community. Their views reflect the biases and sensibilities of those backgrounds. Some mornings they get up on the wrong side of the bed and don't seem to be able to do anything right. But on other days they find it possible to "live greatly in the law." Their faith in the force of reason is at the core of the common law view.

The value that the common law places on precedent means that judicial opinions are relied upon as authority in deciding new cases. This reflects another aspect of justice: justice is treating like things alike. If two people are in the same position, they should be treated equally. Rules of social conduct should apply to all members of the community so that all will know the consequences of particular conduct and can plan their behavior accordingly. A judicial opinion provides a guide for deciding similar situations similarly. "What is fair to do in this case is clear. We shall treat these parties the way we treated those other parties with the same problem before." Since no two cases are ever exactly alike, the problem, of course, is determining similarity.

This legal principle of following precedent is called *stare decisis,* the force of decision. It gives predictability to court-resolution of cases and ties the decision of one case to the decision of others. A lawyer advising a client can examine the relevant cases and predict what is likely to happen if the dispute ends up in court. Reliance on precedent often is a conservative force in the law, obstructing change in the name of following past practice. It may also be a very creative force in the law, drawing on experience to solve new problems.

The use of judicial opinions as a form of legal authority has implications for the relationship among courts. The courts in every state are organized in a familiar pyramid, and the legal correctness of decisions of lower courts may be reviewed by courts higher up the pyramid until they reach a court at the pinnacle that announces the rules for the whole system. Not only does a court follow its own past decisions, it is expected to follow the law announced by higher courts within its system.

It is easy to overstate the binding force of case authority, for in most jurisdictions later judges are bound to follow only what higher courts **decide,** not what those courts **say.** Courts decide cases, they do not announce rules. When a later court finds an earlier decision inapplicable, it will distinguish the earlier case by indicating how this case differs and why the result, therefore, should be different.

The process of deciding cases is essentially one of persuasion. Lawyers try to persuade judges that this case is like that case and quite distinguishable from the other case. The centrality of persuasiveness means that in practice, a court faced with a novel case will look to see how other courts dealt with the issue even if those courts are in another jurisdiction or lower in the pyramid. Thus, within a court system, precedent may bind a later court to follow an earlier decision that it may disagree with, but the influence of precedent is more often based on the earlier decision's persuasiveness.

(2) *The Statute.* A century ago few statutes dealt with contract law. But the common law process proved too slow, episodic, and uncertain to keep up with rapid social and commercial changes. Unaided, it could not meet the needs of a complex modern economy set in a global market. Early in the 20th century this country, following the example set a short time earlier in England, began to enact sweeping statutes governing the sale of goods, the carriage of goods by sea, commercial paper, and negotiable instruments.

This movement was facilitated in America by the National Conference of Commissioners on Uniform State Laws (NCCUSL), which through the drafting of model statutes sought to bring consistency in the law throughout the United States in place of the vagaries of separate, sometimes archaic, state laws. NCCUSL updated and brought together a number of previously adopted model uniform laws dealing with commercial problems in the Uniform Commercial Code (UCC), first promulgated by NCCUSL in the 1950s and subsequently enacted into law by all 50 state legislatures. We shall repeatedly refer to the UCC in this book, especially Article 2 which deals with the sale of goods. The 2000 Official Text of Article 2 of the UCC (promulgated earlier in substantially the same form as the 1978 Official Text and adopted with only relatively minor local variations) presently constitutes the law governing sales of goods throughout the United States notwithstanding NCCUSL's subsequent promulgation of a controversial 2003 Official Text that was never enacted and subsequently withdrawn. In a few places we refer to the now-withdrawn 2003 Proposed Text and its proposed solutions to persistent problems that have arisen under the Official Text that remains in force.

Sections of Article 2 are set forth at places in the book for study with the topic a particular section deals with. To indicate the overall structure of this code, most of the key sections of the Official Text of Article 2 are reprinted in Appendix I. Although Article 2 by its terms applies only to contracts for the sale of goods, it has sometimes been influential in cases involving other kinds of contracts governed by general common law principles.

In 1986, the United States ratified the United Nations Convention on Contracts for the International Sale of Goods (CISG). The CISG provides the authoritative rules of law for that growing number of sales agreements that are international in character. Many provisions of the CISG resemble those of the UCC. In other cases, the representatives of the many nations that participated in creating the CISG drew upon rules taken primarily from other legal systems in the world, or in a few cases have introduced novel approaches to familiar problems.

(3) *Restatements.* As NCCUSL was framing model statutes to remedy some of the incompleteness, inconsistency, and uncertainty of case law, another distinguished body, the American Law Institute (ALI), took a different approach to the same problem. The ALI undertook to restate common law principles in a structured and logical way, weeding out ill-conceived and incoherent "rules" and local variations and collecting in one place a complete and reasoned view of the law. The product of these efforts has been a series of Restatements of the Law in such subjects as contracts, torts, trusts, property, agency, and restitution.

The Restatement of Contracts has been tremendously influential in the eighty years since it first appeared, but remember that the Restatement is not a statute. It is not "the law"; it has authority only to the extent that it is persuasive. Moreover, the Restatement has a major shortcoming in that its tidy presentation of general and symmetrical rules offers seductive security that does not square with the common law's emphasis on the specific facts in a particular controversy. The Restatement is a useful tool, but one that must be approached with some caution. The ALI completed its Second Restatement of Contracts (the current one) in 1979 and relevant sections are excerpted in Appendix II after the UCC.

The original Restatement of Contracts was very much a product of the dominant attitudes of its time. It reflected the thinking of the two magnificent scholars who were its major drafters, Professors Samuel Williston and Arthur Corbin. These scholars were great organizers and treatise writers. We live now in less self-confident times, in which doctrinal answers rarely find universal acceptance. Nevertheless the Second Restatement, to which we will refer throughout this book, remains helpful in explaining the structure of doctrine. The Second Restatement draws heavily on the UCC and related statutory changes.

(4) *Treatises.* Many of the great legal systems of the world rely upon treatises by authoritative scholars as the basic exposition of the law. The common law has been mightily influenced by learned authors from Bracton and Glanville to Coke, Blackstone, and Kent. During the formative period of our country's history, its judges learned the law from those giants, and their thoughts continue to be important to those who wish to learn how the law got where it is. Today's judges similarly grew up on Williston and Corbin. You may find Corbin's or Williston's multivolume treatises on contract law of help in exploring a point exhaustively. Beware of flooding yourself with masses of detail that may prove hard to put together or absorb.

(5) *The Hypothetical Case.* The beginning and the end of the matter is reasoned persuasion. Real disputes are the primary source of argument and decision, but lawyers have always depended heavily on the hypothetical fact situation as a basis for analogy and logical inference. Certainly one of the best ways to learn how to be a lawyer is to moot cases with classmates. Change the facts of a case in the book slightly and then argue why the change should or should not affect the decision. Only by arguing it out can one learn what kinds of distinctions *do* make a difference to lawyers and what kinds *should* make a difference. The questions after most of the cases in this book are designed to provide help in framing such hypotheticals.

Many beginning students assume that contract law can be reduced to a clear and consistent set of rules that can be applied to resolve all problems that arise. Some of the materials in this book do emphasize the rules and will help the student to learn to use conventional rules to resolve the kinds of situations in which they can be useful. Before very long, however, you are likely to make the vexing discovery that there are limits to the capacity of simple rules to resolve the problems. The circumstances may be special and not seem to fit the rule. The rule may be too general to give much guidance, but when one tries to frame a more specific rule, it quickly becomes too complex and exceptional situations keep arising in which the rule does not work well. Other interests demand to be considered that are not reflected in the rule. What is sometimes most troubling is that there are several competing rules, each with a claim to be applied, each leading toward a different result. The job may appear to be to separate the "right" rule from the "wrong" rule, but both rules seem right in a sense. It all depends on how one sees the situation and which aspect of it is most important, which value seems most central. Resolving such issues is a much more tangled task than stating the rule and applying it. In the end, an answer may be reached, but all doubts still are not resolved. There is still something to be said for the other side of the question. The difficulty is that there are too many conflicting answers and no simple way to ultimately decide among them. The only way to resolve the matter is by cutting off the messy ends that do not fit the solution, by repressing recognition of the validity of the other viewpoint.

This can be a frustrating experience for a law student, but it is the common fate of lawyers and judges. Operating in the face of persistent doubt and uncertainty can be threatening and lead some students to become skeptical whether there are any correct answers. Sometime during the first year many students become sufficiently distressed to suspect that finding the law is just a game, that the judges and professors merely follow their own whims and respond to their prejudices, self-interests, and backgrounds. Central to the lawyer's faith is recognition that these techniques and tools also may have the capacity to lead to the best available resolutions of some kinds of human problems. The matters may be persistently problematic, the answers arrived at may remain subject to cogent challenge, the route to resolution may be uncertain and tortuous, but in the end, there is only the limited comfort that, despite its limits, the answer is the best available to us here and now.

To help you prepare for class, this Casebook provides Questions and Notes every few pages. Pause after reading a case and see whether you can answer the questions. Sometimes one cannot give an answer because something is missing. Other questions simply may have no answer. A primary goal of this course is to teach aspiring lawyers to give meaning to a legal text by connecting factual circumstances with rules stating a legal value.

Try to write a simple paragraph answer to a question after a case and then have a friend read and comment on your answer. Pick a reader who will be critical of your writing style and clarity as well as your thinking, although the two are obviously connected. You need not pick another law student; someone not studying law may be a better test of your powers of clear explanation.

A short cogent answer to a question may be more challenging to produce than a complex and technical brief or contract. Yet writing a coherent paragraph analyzing a legal question is an essential lawyer's skill. Because people believe that you possess that skill, someday they will place their trust in you and pay you a fee for your services. As you write such a paragraph you are likely to find that what seemed the obvious answer no longer makes sense. Cheer up, that's often the first step toward a better answer.

CHAPTER 1

DEFINING CONTRACT: WHAT PROMISES ARE LEGALLY ENFORCEABLE AND WHY?

I. THEORIES OF PROMISSORY LIABILITY

There is no perfect reported case to begin a course in contract law. Judges rarely write opinions with the needs of law students uppermost in their minds. Nonetheless, a good case provides the best vehicle for class discussion. So we present the fictitious case of *Best v. Southland*, the opinions in which have been written by a court composed of frustrated Contracts professors.

Best Construction Co. v. Southland Construction Co.

Supreme Court of Southland, 2017.
57 Sthld. 362.

■ ROBQUIST, C.J. Southland Construction Company ("Southland"), the defendant in the trial court, appeals from the grant of summary judgment against it in this contract action brought by Best Construction Company ("Best"). The complaint alleges that Southland's failure to provide Best with 50,000 square feet of ¾ inch waterproof concrete-form plywood panels, as it had promised, was a breach of an enforceable contract causing damages to Best in the amount of $5,000. The trial court found that the pleadings raised no material issues of fact requiring trial and that Southland's promise gave rise to an enforceable contract which Southland totally failed to perform. It therefore granted summary judgment to Best for the $5,000 damages it claimed.

Best and Southland have been engaged in the construction business in and around Southland City for many years. Both use large quantities of construction grade plywood, including the ¾ inch waterproof concrete-form plywood in question. Both companies maintain inventories of these items, which they purchase from plywood mills in carload lots of approximately 50,000 square feet per car. Plywood purchased this way is, of course, substantially less expensive than if purchased in smaller quantities from a local lumber yard.

On June 11, 2005, Best's general superintendent discovered that its supply of concrete-form plywood was far short of what it would need on the Security Bank job it was about to start. Only an insignificant inventory was available in Best's warehouse. Management was advised of the problem, and G.H. Burke, Best's vice president and purchasing manager, immediately ordered two carloads from a mill in the State of Washington at a price of $290 per thousand feet, delivered at Southland City.

This order did not solve Best's problem, however, because delivery from the mill could not be expected for six to eight weeks and construction was due to start on the foundation of the 20–story Security Bank building within ten days. Best could have purchased the plywood it needed for immediate delivery from various local lumber yards, but only at the local warehouse price of about $360 per thousand feet.

Rather than incur this expense, Burke, on June 12, sought to borrow the plywood from other local construction companies. All of these companies maintain inventories of standard items. They are business competitors, but from time to time they help each other meet unexpected shortages if they conveniently can. Burke's first call was to A.H. Stevens, vice president of defendant, Southland. According to the uncontroverted affidavits submitted in support of Best's motion for summary judgment, Burke described Best's shortage to Stevens and was told that Southland had recently received three carloads of the needed plywood and had an inventory far in excess of its foreseeable short-term needs. Burke and Stevens thereupon agreed that Best would send its trucks to Southland's warehouse during the next three weeks, beginning on June 22, to pick up not more than 50,000 square feet of plywood as Best needed it on the job. In return, Burke promised to return the same quantity of similar plywood and have its employees re-pile it in Southland's warehouse as soon as its carload shipments arrived. Stevens reminded Burke that "one good turn deserves another" and that he was helping out in the expectation that "Best would bail Southland out next time." Burke assured Stevens that Best would make every effort to meet Southland's inventory problem the next time one developed.

On June 19, Burke received a call from Stevens, who reported that Coastal Lumber Company, a retail supply yard, had offered Southland $352 per thousand square feet for its entire inventory of ¾ inch plywood. Coastal needed the material at once to fill pressing commitments to its local customers caused by a careless over-booking of orders by one of its sales representatives. Under the circumstances, Stevens said it was obvious that Southland couldn't be expected to go through with the loan to Best.

During the last half of June, plywood prices advanced sharply. Improved economic conditions in the construction industry had increased demand and new governmental conservation regulations on lumbering in national forests threatened to make supplies scarcer and more expensive. Burke tried in vain to find another contractor willing to help him out with a loan and finally purchased the needed plywood on June 20 from local lumber yards. The price from these sources had advanced to $390 per thousand square feet from the $360 price on June 12, when he had made his arrangement with Southland. Thus Best had to pay $1,500 more than if it would have had it purchased the plywood locally a week earlier instead of relying on Southland's promise of a loan. It claimed $5,000 as damages, however, basing that claim on the $100 per thousand difference between the $390 it had to pay locally and the $290 cost to it of the carload plywood with which it would have repaid Southland's loan. The $5,000 was awarded to Best by the court below.

The initial question raised by this contract claim is whether Southland promised Best that it would lend Best the plywood that it needed. Restatement, Second, Contracts § 1 states that a contract is **"a promise or a set of promises for the breach of which the law gives a remedy or the performance of which the law in some way recognizes as a duty."** Contract law is indeed limited to the enforcement of promises.

The court below assumed that Southland made a promise. No reasonable person would interpret the conversation between Stevens and Burke as anything other than a request for an assurance that Southland would furnish the plywood Best needed, and the voluntary and conscious giving of that assurance by Stevens. That satisfies every recognized definition of promise, including the following language of § 2(1) of the Restatement (Second) of Contracts: **"A promise is a manifestation of intention to act or refrain from acting in a specified way, so made as to justify a promisee in understanding that a commitment has been made."** Totally absent are such promise-destroying elements as illusoriness, vagueness, duress, lack of capacity, frivolity, fraud and mistake.

But the fact that Southland promised Best does not settle the matter. For implicit in the Restatement's § 1 reference to contracts as "promises that the law will enforce" is the proposition that all promises are not enforceable. Is Southland's such an unenforceable promise?

This was a transaction between businesspersons in a serious business context. We can quickly disregard such categories of nonenforceability as polite social commitments and family housekeeping arrangements which the law has felt are too trivial to bother with or too sensitive to meddle with. We can also disregard promises tainted by illegality. But we cannot so easily disregard that broad category of promises that are unenforceable because not "paid for," *i.e.*, gift promises. For better or worse, the law of contracts—after a long period of groping for a base—settled on the bargain as the core of enforceability, and the essence of a bargain is *exchange*.

Thus except in a relatively few special situations that need not concern us here, unless a promisor asks for and receives a sufficient price for the performance contained in his promise, the law will not hold him to it. The doctrine requiring a price is called consideration. As Blackstone put it in the eighteenth century:

> A consideration of some sort or other is so absolutely necessary to the forming of a contract that a *nudum pactum,* or agreement to do or pay anything on one side, without any compensation on the other, is totally void in law; and a man cannot be compelled to perform it. As if one man promises to give another 100£, here there is nothing contracted for or given on the one side, and therefore there is nothing binding on the other. And, however a man may or may not be bound to perform it, in honour or conscience, which the municipal laws do not take upon them to decide; certainly those municipal laws will not compel the execution of what he had no visible inducement to engage for; and therefore our law has adopted the maxim of the civil law, that *ex nudo pacto non oritur actio.*

2 BLACKSTONE'S COMMENTARIES 445 (1765).

The modern statement of this basic principle is to be found in § 71 of the Restatement which reads as follows:

---

§ 71 Requirement of Exchange; Types of Exchange.

(1) To constitute consideration, a performance or a return promise must be bargained for.

(2) A performance or return promise is bargained for if it is sought by the promisor in exchange for his promise and is given by the promisee in exchange for that promise.

(3) The performance may consist of

   (a) an act other than a promise, or

   (b) a forbearance, or

   (c) the creation, modification or destruction of a legal relation.

(4) The performance or return promise may be given to the promisor or to some other person. It may be given by the promisee or by some other person.

Whether there was consideration for Southland's promise would seem at first glance to be easily answered in the affirmative because this promise was made in a commercial setting, where bargain is the norm. It is safe to infer that a promise made in a business setting is motivated by expectation of beneficial gain. But every businessperson's requested price for a promise does not automatically qualify as a sufficient price to make that promise legally enforceable. Although the law is reluctant to question the adequacy of consideration, there must be at least *some* determinable value attached to a definitely requested price before it can qualify. And where the price asked is—as it was here by Southland—a return assurance by the other party, that assurance must in turn qualify as a true promise if it is to have legal value.

In the case before us we have an excellent example of such a nonqualifying price. What did Southland expect from the assurance by Best that it requested as the price for its promise of a loan of plywood? Clearly it expected nothing more than the creation in Best of good will—or of moral obligation—that would influence Best to be equally generous and cooperative if Southland subsequently needed similar help. But such a hope can hardly be dignified by the term consideration. The books are full of cases in which it has been consistently held that mere requested expressions of appreciation or a warm glow generated in the breast of a gift promisor, or the promisor's desire to demonstrate love and affection, or the creation of a moral obligation by an unselfish act are not sufficient to constitute consideration. Best's sweeping statement about reciprocating in the future (for what? in what quantities? for how long? under what circumstances?) cannot be dignified with the title "promise." If Southland had loaned the plywood to Best and had subsequently demanded a specific return loan from Best and Best had refused the request, could Best have been held in breach of an enforceable promise? To ask this question is to answer it.

Southland's promise to lend plywood to Best must be held to be unenforceable because it is without sufficient consideration. The grant summary judgment to respondent by the court below is reversed and that court is directed to dismiss the complaint.

■ KENTHOM, J. I concur in the majority's conclusion that the court below erred in granting the motion for summary judgment, but I must express my concern over the labored reasoning employed to reach that conclusion. In my view, the central issue is whether the communications between the parties contained a real promise, or as some of my colleagues would put it, whether there is an enforceable promise.

The majority notes that not all voluntary, serious and definite commitments, *i.e.*, promises, are enforceable and that "after a long period of groping" the law has come to insist that a promise must be part of a bargain and exchange (as those terms are given meaning in the doctrine of consideration) to be enforced as a contract.

It is distressing to think that so important a matter as the enforcement of promises is merely the result of historical accident or of mindless "groping." Doctrine—the ordered body of principle and rule—is a vital dimension of the law, but we should not apply it mechanically. We must be aware of its uses and limits and not reach out to use it in cases where it obscures, rather than explains, the basis of decision. My colleagues distinguish between enforceable and unenforceable promises.

To me the term promise always implies a commitment and when its use is appropriate it always implies legal enforceability. If the conduct does not imply a commitment, it should not be called a promise.

The majority tells us that bargained-for promises are enforceable, but it fails to tell us why *only* bargained-for promises are enforceable. Certainly when stated in such extreme form the doctrine of consideration becomes an *ipse dixit*: Southland's promise is unenforceable because the law does not enforce such promises. In extreme form the doctrine can be understood to suggest that the law will not enforce unbargained-for promises even if they are serious and sensible and have a powerful legitimate claim for enforcement. Moreover, this approach focuses all attention on what was given for the promise, treating the issue of enforceability as a matter that is independent of the promise itself.

The root of the difficulty is the majority's distinction between non-promises and unenforceable promises. This distinction adds nothing but confusion to an already overly confused area. A better approach would be to look at all the facts and circumstances surrounding promissory language in one analytical operation to see whether that language objectively implies a serious and sensible voluntary commitment by the promisor in a context in which society permits private persons to make binding promises. If the words themselves imply no substantial commitment or are so conditioned that the promise is illusory, there is no contract. If there was no voluntary intelligent act because of duress, lack of capacity, or fraud, there is no contract if the victimized party elects to avoid it. If we find that the promise was to act illegally or that it was an arrangement—trivial or otherwise—outside the area where the law allows people to bind themselves by their promises, there is no contract. And there is no contract, if the behavior claimed to be contractual lacks the clear inducing motive to commitment that separates the serious promise from just talk, impulsive statement, social or family arrangement, or improvident "gift" promise subsequently repented. If we find a serious and sensible commitment and none of the mentioned constraints are present, we give it the legal force of a contract.

We are asked to decide whether Southland's statement to Best was a serious promise. I agree with the majority that Southland's words were definitely promissory. But seen in their total context, Southland's statements provide too slender a basis for finding so rigid a commitment as Best seeks to enforce here. At most they amount to a casual accommodation. They lack the formality, specificity, and deliberation that mark the intentional promise. This conclusion is strengthened by the absence of any significant price paid by Best for Southland's offer to lend plywood. But rather than endow that one factor with the talismanic significance it is given by the majority, I reach the same result on the common sense basis that there was simply no binding commitment intended by the parties in this case.

■ KAGAMAYOR, J. I dissent. The majority dismisses by its reference to "special situations that need not concern us here" precisely such a special situation as is presented by this case. That special situation is covered by the Restatement which states:

§ 90 Promise Reasonably Inducing Action or Forbearance.

A promise which the promisor should reasonably expect to induce action or forbearance on the part of the promisee or a third person and which does induce such action or forbearance is binding if injustice can be avoided only by enforcement of the promise. The remedy granted for breach may be limited as justice requires.

Best's reliance on Southland's promise meets all of the tests set out in § 90. Best had every reason to rely, it did so rely to its damage, and injustice can now be avoided only by reimbursing Best for the loss caused by its justifiable reliance.

It is true that there is authority holding that this doctrine should be used only to protect innocents who have trustingly relied on promises to make a gift. The parties involved here would scarcely qualify as "innocents," nor is the gift aspect all that clear. But modern cases that follow the Restatement emphasize the degree to which obligations created by reliance can arise in a commercial setting.

By permitting Southland to escape on a "no consideration" technicality from an explicit promise to lend plywood to Best, we encourage conduct that will significantly impair the utility of promise in our economy. We should not be so willing to destroy sensible commercial relationships by insisting on legal niceties. If Southland had agreed to lend Best the plywood if Best paid or promised to pay $10, would that make Southland's promise more enforceable? If one is to believe the majority, the answer must be "yes." That, I submit, reduces contracting and commercial relations to a game with arbitrary and senseless rules. It revives the long discredited formalism of the common law which centuries ago gave magical enforcing power to language over substance. The consideration doctrine even today makes sense as a recognition of the central place of bargain in contract transactions. It loses that meaning when converted into an arid formalism.

The arrangement between Southland and Best was a serious and sensible arrangement between two businesses. Such arrangements should be strongly encouraged by protecting reliance on them. In this case, Best's reliance amounted to the difference between the price at which it could have purchased the required plywood from a local source at the time Southland agreed to lend it, and what it had to pay such a source when Southland reneged on its promise—namely $1,500. This recovery is $3,500 less than that claimed by Best and awarded by the court below, namely the $5,000 representing the difference between Best's $290 cost of replacement plywood from the mill and the $390 Best had to pay locally when Southland reneged on its promise to lend. I would remand with instructions to award Best $1,500 in reliance damages.

■ O'SOUTER, J., dissenting. The majority and concurring opinions spin fine already overrefined rules of contract liability. They conclude that defendant Southland is not liable for the substantial losses it has inflicted upon plaintiff, Best, by its deliberate acts. Nowhere do the majority or concurring opinions explain why contract should be a special island of immunity separated from the basic principles of human justice which declare that a wrongdoer is liable for injuries proximately caused by its acts, whether willful or negligent. Our Civil Code has long provided in § 1708: "Every person is bound, without contract, to abstain from injuring the person or property of another or infringing upon any of his or her rights." To the same effect is § 3281 of the Civil Code, which for over a century has provided: "Every person who suffers detriment from the unlawful act or omission of another, may recover from the person in fault a compensation therefor in money, which is called damages."

Courts should recognize that failure to perform as promised may give rise to a cause of action under remedial tort concepts as well as under more restrictive concepts of promissory liability. Indeed, this recognition is a cornerstone of modern liability for defective products as well as professional malpractice. In both cases liability measured by tort standards arises regularly out of an essentially contractual relationship.

Contract liability is merely a subspecies of general civil liability for injury. Promises may give rise to liability for harm caused just as broader social obligations may create a basis for compensation to those injured by breach of a legal duty. An ironic consequence of the majority's rigid adherence to synthetic categories of tort and contract is that those who commit no conscious wrong, but merely fail to meet a standard of care of which they may be only dimly aware, are subject to broad liability for consequences provided for negligence. In contrast, those who solemnly and deliberately undertake a promissory obligation which they willfully breach without a shadow of an excuse are held to liability for a much narrower range of consequences or, as in this case, may be exonerated from all liability. Surely this result is irrational and should be avoided by casting aside the conceptual artificialities that engendered it.

Anglo–American law during part of its history has tended to see tort and contract as two watertight compartments. Perhaps the pattern originated in the peculiarities of ancient common law procedure and forms of action. For at least three centuries, common law distinguished claims based on a promise, recognized in the writ of assumpsit, from other forms of trespass. This distinction undoubtedly was reinforced by the special history of American legal education. Since the days of

Dean Christopher Columbus Langdell of the Harvard Law School more than a century ago, the first-year curriculum has treasured as its crowning jewel a Contracts course using the case method. Great treatises by professors Williston and Corbin and the monumental Restatements of Contracts of the American Law Institute have reinforced this tendency. The distinction is embedded in the organization of the West Publishing Company digest system that influences the way lawyers think and perceive problems. Everyone knows that contract law is found under one set of key numbers and tort law is found under another. Legal systems in most other advanced nations do not place such great emphasis on the distinction between tort and contract, and it is an open secret that our law, when pressed by a tough case, ignores it as well.

The appropriate factors for deciding whether defendant should be liable to plaintiff in this case are traditional and clear: (a) the extent to which the transaction was intended to affect the plaintiff, (b) the foreseeability of harm to the plaintiff, (c) the degree of certainty that the plaintiff suffered injury, (d) the closeness of the connection between the defendant's conduct and the injury suffered, (e) the moral blame attached to the defendant's conduct, and (f) the policy of preventing future harm.

Since this case should be returned to the lower court for trial under appropriate standards, it is not necessary to anticipate its outcome. Nonetheless, it seems obvious that plaintiff has a substantial claim deserving trial and the majority errs in dismissing this action.

■ OHNO, J., dissenting. I cannot join the Chief Justice's opinion because it goes around in circles. First it defines contract in terms of legally enforceable promises and then uses this definition to decide whether this particular promise should be legally enforced. Nor can I join my sister Kagamayor in dissent, for she too reasons circularly when she proposes that promises should be legally enforced if they induce reasonable reliance. It is plain that the reasonableness of required reliance (especially in commercial contexts) must depend in large part on whether the promisee could confidently expect to enforce the reliance-inducing promise in court.

All this shows the folly of seeking some logically exclusive syllogism that will define the concept of contract with completeness and precision. We must not forget that the life of the law is not logic, but, as Holmes taught, experience. In my experience the legal conclusion that a contract exists is likely to rest less on whether some set of mechanical elements have been satisfied than on whether the transaction is—as Judge Cardozo so eloquently put it in *Wood v. Lucy, Lady Duff-Gordon*, 222 N.Y. 88 (1917)—"'instinct with an obligation,' when viewed as a whole and through the eyes of the community in which it was made." The existence of a contract the law should enforce is not determined by abstract rules, but by the fact of agreement as discerned in their particular context by the peers of those who made the deal.

The Uniform Commercial Code, which our legislature has adopted as the law of this state, recognizes this truth in defining "Contract" in § 1–201(12) to mean **"the total legal obligation which results from the parties' agreement as affected by this Act and any other applicable rules of law."** "Agreement" is similarly defined in UCC § 1–201(3) to mean the **"bargain of the parties in fact as found in their language or by implication from other circumstances including course of dealing or usage of trade or course of performance* * *."** In other words, contract is found in the total context of the transaction by looking at the deal in its full setting.

The Chief Justice leads us up to the correct answer, and I join so much of his opinion as recognizes that contract depends on promises and exchange. We should start from the assumption that when people make solemn promises the law will expect that they keep them, for social order and peace rest upon the reliability of people's undertakings, voluntarily assumed. And since, of course, not all words or acts that may look like promises are sufficiently promissory in substance to deserve the law's attention, we look for other clues. Surely two kinds of promises deserving enforcement are: (a) those that reasonable persons regularly rely upon, and (b) those that sensible people think are worth paying for. When something significant has been exchanged for a promise, it would be unjust to let the promisor retain the benefit but repudiate the promise for which he has been paid. The concepts of reliance and consideration have these common sense roots and it is in this spirit that they should be applied.

Let us apply common sense to the facts of this case. The Chief Justice correctly finds in his opinion that Southland promised to lend the plywood in question to Best. Moreover, it is recognized that this promise was part of an exchange, although it is found that this exchange of promises does not provide adequate "consideration" because Best's return assurance involved nothing more than a sense of "moral obligation" and a "vague hope." Therefore, the majority concludes, the case is to be dismissed on the pleadings as a matter of law, and Best is not entitled to a trial to demonstrate the existence of a binding contract.

The majority may feel confident that Best's assurance of reciprocity was of insufficient value to serve as adequate consideration, but I wonder how many hardheaded and practical businesspersons would share that view. Every businessperson knows that the goodwill of those with whom you deal repeatedly, the ability to call upon them for help when needed, and the prize of high reputation built from such cooperative behavior, are the most valuable assets that a businessperson can gain. Moreover, they are readily convertible over time into hard cash. The majority may view Best's assurances through the hard and flinty eyesight cultivated in lawyers from their first day in law school, but the law promises the parties an opportunity at trial to persuade their peers to a more sensible view.

The majority's cynical hardness has another apparent flaw; it simply fails to explain Southland's behavior. Adopting the majority's perspective, we must look upon Southland as a cold-blooded, profit-maximizing entrepreneur. It is, in any event, hardly a charitable organization. So if it did not consider Best's promise of reciprocity to be of value to it, why did it promise the loan in the first place? Certainly, the fact that it freely made a valuable promise in apparent exchange for the assurance of future cooperation must create some issue of fact precluding both summary judgment or dismissal of Best's claim of a binding contract created by the exchange of valuable promises. The case should go back for a trial on these vital questions.

QUESTIONS

1. Why is there any question in this case? Shouldn't all promises be kept? Isn't it always wrong to break your word? If breaking a promise is wrong and causes harm, shouldn't the law require the wrongdoer to perform its promise?

2. On the other hand, why should any court be concerned with this transaction? Do people keep promises only if they will have to pay damages if they don't? Why do bad people keep promises? How much does the possibility that, after years of litigation, the defendant will have to pay damages add?

3. Would you feel more strongly that Southland's promise should be enforced if it had been put in writing?

4. Suppose that Southland agreed to sell the lumber rather than lend it. Same result? Would there be any question of consideration for Chief Justice Robquist? Should sales be enforceable but not loans?

5. If Stevens of Southland had called Burke of Best fifteen minutes after he had agreed to lend the plywood and said: "Sorry, I've changed my mind," would there have been anything for Best to complain about? If Best had delivered a $100 check to Southland for its promise to lend plywood, and fifteen minutes later Southland reneged but sent the check back undeposited, would Best have a valid complaint?

6. Do we want to encourage transactions of this sort? If so, how can we best do so? What is the likely impact on future social behavior if this case comes out one way or the other?

7. Would this case look the same if Burke had just found Southland on the internet and they had never done business together before? What is the relevance of the fact that they have a course of dealings over the years?

8. How significant to the decision of this case should be the general practices of the construction business in Southland City? If all of these companies customarily help each other out from time to time, isn't Southland's promise a firmer basis for reliance than it might otherwise be?

9. In this case Southland could accommodate Best only by forgoing a very valuable opportunity to sell the plywood at a handsome profit. Would you feel the same about the case if this element were absent? Suppose Southland has no good reason at all for not letting Best take the plywood. Suppose their refusal to fulfill the deal was based on spite or competitive zeal.

10. If Best were to win this case, what would the appropriate remedy be? If Best had a legal right to the plywood, why didn't it just send its workers and truck over to Southland's yard and pick up its plywood? Should the judge order Southland to lend Best the plywood as promised?

11. If Southland is to be ordered to pay damages in this case, how should they be measured?

12. In this case the price of plywood increased sharply during the transaction. Suppose the price of plywood remained constant. Would Best have a claim for damages if Southland failed to perform?

13. How much will it cost Best to bring this lawsuit? If it recovers a judgment, will it be awarded the real costs of the suit? If it is very expensive to assert claims and to defend them in court, how will people's promissory behavior be affected?

DRAFTING EXERCISE

Imagine that you are the attorney for Best in its case against Southland and that you are preparing the complaint and perhaps an accompanying motion for summary judgment. You now have the benefit of knowing what these judges think about at least some of the stories you might tell.

A. Write a memorandum to the file of no more than two pages outlining the story you plan to tell on Best's behalf.

B. Write instructions to the fact investigator of no more than two pages telling her what facts to look for in her interviews with the client and witnesses and in her general effort to scrounge around.

HISTORICAL NOTE: WHAT IS THE COMMON LAW?

The common law historically refers to the law administered by the ancient English Royal Courts of Justice at Westminster. Following the Norman Conquest of England, the King's power and the jurisdiction of the Royal Courts were restricted by the power of competing institutions. These included the courts of the Church, the manorial courts of the barons and other feudal overlords, the mercantile courts and a variety of independent local courts for cities, boroughs, and fairs. English political and legal history from the 11th to the 19th century is largely the stormy story of the gradual expansion and domination of secular national authority, epitomized by the King, over ecclesiastical, feudal, and local rivals.

The jurisdiction of the Royal Courts was limited to suits based upon certain clearly defined forms of action. Until the 19th century, a person who wanted to sue would have to obtain a writ from the Chancellor's office based upon a form of action that fit the facts of his case. If there were no writs for this kind of a complaint, no suit could be brought. Each form of action carried with it its own set of remedies, its own rules of evidence and proof, and even its own mode of trial (battle, ordeal, trial by oath, jury). The basic Royal Court writs were related to the two essential interests of the King as chief feudal overlord; they were concerned primarily with land and keeping the peace.

Before the commercial age—apart from land transactions—few of the disputes we would classify as contract cases were within the purview of the Royal Courts. Some contract suits were heard by the mercantile courts and others by the ecclesiastical courts. Church courts were involved because one basic ground for the enforcement of promises was the religious obligation to keep oaths and to speak the truth. This development was stunted when those courts were ousted from jurisdiction early in the long fight between King and Church.

Some contracts, particularly those under seal, for a sum certain, or for specified goods, could be heard in the Royal Courts under a writ of debt or detinue or a writ of covenant. These forms of action grew out of real property law and were inadequate to meet the needs of claimants involved in commercial contracts. Among the disadvantages of using the forms of action of debt and detinue was that the defendant could demand a trial by wager of law. The lawsuit would be decided by a number of persons swearing to the justice of one party's cause, rather than by an impartial jury based upon evidence. Such swearers became too readily available in the market.

Covenant and debt contributed to contract law, but most modern contract law developed through the other major basis of royal jurisdiction, the obligation to keep the peace. The tool with which this was done was the writ of trespass, a wonderfully flexible writ, whose descendants include not only the modern law of contracts, but torts and criminal law as well.

Originally the writ of trespass was directed at injuries by forcible breaches of the peace, but by the 13th century one form of the writ became available in cases of non-violent trespass. It was labeled "trespass on the special case." Under it, a person might be liable for acting carelessly and causing injury to another. By the 14th century it was held that if a person undertook to do a particular act and performed it badly, recovery for ensuing injury could be had in trespass on the special case. The central concept was that the defendant had undertaken to act properly, and the central allegation in the writ, by which the form of action came to be known, was the Latin word "*assumpsit*," meaning "he undertook." Note that in this early form the action might describe either a claim of negligence (tort) or breach of promise (contract).

Gradually, the two divided, and by the 16th century assumpsit was clearly understood to be a contractual action. Also in the 16th century England's commercial and economic situation began changing radically, and the pressures for legal tools to meet the needs of the new age increased. Assumpsit, like all actions in trespass, was subject to trial by jury, not ordeal or wager of law, and thus it was preferred. Early requirements that the undertaking be explicit were diluted by the courts' increased willingness to imply the promise. The last major barrier was broken in *Slade's Case* (1602) where the King's Bench held: "Every contract executory imports in itself an assumpsit, for when one agrees to pay money or to deliver anything, thereby he assumes or promises to pay or deliver it."

By this process the common law gained a basis for the enforcement of promises independent of semi-religious conceptions of the sanctity of promises. While the secular footing of the law is now firmly established, it remains difficult to articulate in one or two sentences **why** promises are enforceable in our law.

II. PROMISES THAT LACK COMMITMENT

The judges in *Best v. Southland* all agree that a contract requires at a minimum some language or other behavior that is promissory—that communicates a serious commitment to future action or inaction on the part of at least one of the parties. These elements of futurity and commitment distinguish contracts from legal relationships created by property concepts or general obligations imposed by tort.

These defining characteristics of contract exclude those communications that import only flimsy or spurious commitments of future action or inaction. For example, "I promise to lend you the plywood unless I change my mind" is not a promise because the statement itself negates firm commitment. Yet, no promises in the real world are absolute; futurity itself conditions every promise on the passage of time. The fact that a promise is conditioned by some contingency need not deprive the commitment of substance unless the likelihood of performance becomes so remote as to be valueless or the limiting event is so within the unbridled discretion of the promisor ("I will paint your house if I feel like it") that no sensible person will deem it worthy of reliance.

Legal treatises label such statements illusory promises, a classification that includes both those promises that are conditioned by limitations so large they swallow the committing force of the promise and those promises conditioned on fanciful or highly unlikely events. The line between the real and the illusory is sometimes a difficult one to draw. Many promises are conditioned on acts or events over which the promisor has no control, but they nonetheless look, feel, and taste like serious deals.

You might think that identifying a promise is essentially a matter of the presence of particular words or symbols, such as, "I promise." The definition of a promise in § 2 of the Restatement, Second, Contracts, p. 15, focuses on the impact of the promise on the promisee. A promise is a "manifestation of intention to act ... so made as to justify a promisee in understanding that a commitment has been made." You can tell whether something is a promise only by reference to its social, as opposed to its formal, content. The Restatement definition opens the process to promises that are unspoken but implied from acts of the promisor or the social context in which the promisor operates. Emphasizing what the promisor implies leads us to focus on the intention of the promisor. As the emphasis shifts to how the promisee, society, or the judge understands the promisor's behavior, social custom and social expectations are applied to contract quite independently of what this particular promisor meant. In this way the process of interpretation and implication of meaning blends seamlessly into the process of legislation and the construction of social obligations in law.

A.   CONDITIONAL AND ILLUSORY PROMISES

De Los Santos v. Great Western Sugar Co.
Nebraska Supreme Court, 1984.
217 Neb. 282, 348 N.W.2d 842.

■ CAMBRIDGE, D.J.

This is an appeal by plaintiff of a summary judgment entered by the trial court in favor of the defendant in an action for breach of contract.

...

This appeal centers around the following provision contained in the "Hauling Contract" executed by the plaintiff and the defendant in October 1980:

> The Contractor [i.e., plaintiff] shall transport in the Contractor's trucks *such tonnage of beets as may be loaded by the Company* [i.e., defendant] from piles at the beet receiving stations of the Company, and unload said beets at such factory or factories as may be designated by the Company. The term of this contract shall be from October 1, 1980, until February 15, 1981. (Emphasis supplied.)

The plaintiff, as an independent contractor, was obligated under the "Hauling Contract" to furnish certain insurance, suitable trucks and equipment, and all necessary labor, maintenance, fuel, and licenses required for his operations thereunder, and the compensation which he was to receive for his services was based solely upon the amount of beets which he transported, the rate per ton varying with the length of the haul.

It is undisputed that upon executing the hauling contract the plaintiff knew that the defendant had executed identical such contracts with other independent truckers who would also be hauling the defendant's beets and that the plaintiff would therefore transport on his trucks only "such tonnage of beets as may be loaded by" the defendant upon the plaintiff's trucks, not all of the beets "as may be loaded by" the defendant from piles at the defendant's beet receiving stations. The plaintiff had been transporting beets under the contract for approximately 2 months when, in early December 1980, the defendant informed the plaintiff that his services would no longer be needed. The plaintiff does not claim that he was entitled to transport all of the beets, but he does contend that he was entitled to continue to haul until all of the beets had been transported to the factory, that the defendant did not allow him to do so, and that the defendant thereby wrongfully terminated the hauling contract, causing the plaintiff loss of profits, forced sale of his trucks at a loss, and other damages to be proved on trial. In his petition the plaintiff predicated his action against the defendant upon the hauling contract. The defendant in its amended answer thereto alleged, among other defenses not relevant to the disposition of this appeal, that the defendant was not obligated under the contract to allow the plaintiff to haul any particular amount of tonnage and that its determination that it would no longer require the plaintiff's services was a determination which was within the defendant's discretion under the terms of the contract....

Considering the words contained therein together with the aforesaid undisputed facts known to both the plaintiff and the defendant when they executed the hauling contract, it is clear that neither the plaintiff nor the defendant intended to or did, either in fact or law, promise to transport a specific quantity of beets or promise to transport beets during a specific period of time. The term of the contract set forth therein, i.e., October 1, 1980, until February 15, 1981, did not constitute a promise, but merely established the period of time during which the promises which were contained in the contract would be in effect. Although the plaintiff made a number of promises in the hauling contract, all centered around the plaintiff's promise to transport beets as loaded by the defendant on the plaintiff's trucks during the period of October 1, 1980, through February 15, 1981, the defendant made no promises at all other than the promise to pay for the transportation of those beets which were in fact loaded by the defendant onto the trucks of the plaintiff during that period. An agreement which depends upon the wish, will, or pleasure of one of the parties is unenforceable....

Where a promisor agrees to purchase services from the promisee on a per unit basis, but the agreement specifies no quantity and the parties did not intend that the promisor should take all of his needs from the promisee, there is no enforceable agreement, and the promisor is not obligated to accept any services from the promisee and may terminate the relationship at any time without liability other than to pay for the services accepted. The fact that the promisor has accepted services from the promisee in the past under such an agreement does not furnish the consideration necessary to require the promisor to accept such services in the future under the agreement. Nor does the specification in such an agreement of the period of time during which it will be operative impose an obligation that is not already present under the agreement. Applying the foregoing to this case, it is apparent that the right of the defendant to control the amount of beets loaded onto the plaintiff's trucks was in effect a right to terminate the contract at any time, and this rendered the contract as to its unexecuted portions void for want of mutuality. In the absence of a specification of quantity, the defendant had no obligation to use any of the plaintiff's services, and the defendant's decision to cease using those services after a certain point is not actionable.

The plaintiff contends that prior actions of the defendant constituted a course of conduct which caused the plaintiff to justifiably believe that the defendant would permit the plaintiff to haul beets until all of the same had been transported from the receiving stations to the factory. The Restatement (Second) of Contracts § 223 provides:

> (1) A course of dealing is a sequence of previous conduct between the parties to an agreement which is fairly to be regarded as establishing a common basis of understanding for interpreting their expressions and other conduct.

> (2) Unless otherwise agreed, a course of dealing between the parties gives meaning to or supplements or qualifies their agreement.

That principle of law is of no avail to the plaintiff in this case. The evidence is undisputed that prior to the plaintiff's execution of the hauling contract of October 1980, there had been no similar course of dealing between the plaintiff and the defendant and that the course of dealing had between the defendant and other parties in preceding years, as well as for the year 1980, clearly established that independent truckers such as the plaintiff who had less seniority than others with hauling contracts were let go prior to completion of the beet haul.

...

Affirmed.

QUESTIONS

1. Why did the parties make this agreement? What purpose did it serve? Did this agreement serve its function for Great Western? Did it serve its function for Mr. De Los Santos if it is not judicially enforceable?

2. Does this decision mean that there never was a time when Mr. De Los Santos and Great Western had a contract? Suppose that after Mr. De Los Santos has carried loads of beets for two months, Great Western refused to pay him. Could the sugar company avoid payment on grounds that there was no contract? Suppose the Company loaded a truck full of beets and Mr. De Los Santos took them away but failed to deliver them at the sugar refinery. Could he avoid Great Western's claim for damages on grounds that there was no contract?

3. Suppose Mr. De Los Santos fails to show up and Great Western can't find another driver. Would Mr. De Los Santos be liable for damages? Suppose the weather is terrible and Mr. De Los Santos tells Great Western, "I can carry beets tomorrow, but only at twice the contract price."

4. Suppose Great Western has lots of beets to haul but won't give Mr. De Los Santos any because the dispatcher has a personal feud with him. Is there an implied promise of fairness that would give Mr. De Los Santos a claim?

Mattei v. Hopper

California Supreme Court, 1958.
51 Cal.2d 119, 330 P.2d 625.

■ SPENCE, J.

Plaintiff brought this action for damages after defendant allegedly breached a contract by failing to convey her real property in accordance with the terms of a deposit receipt which the parties had executed. After a trial without a jury, the court concluded that the agreement was "illusory" and lacking in "mutuality." From the judgment accordingly entered in favor of defendant, plaintiff appeals.

Plaintiff was a real estate developer. He was planning to construct a shopping center on a tract adjacent to defendant's land. For several months, a real estate agent attempted to negotiate a sale of defendant's property under terms agreeable to both parties. After several of plaintiff's proposals had been rejected by defendant because of the inadequacy of the price offered, defendant submitted an offer. Plaintiff accepted on the same day.

The parties' written agreement was evidenced on a form supplied by the real estate agent, commonly known as a deposit receipt. Under its terms, plaintiff was required to deposit $1,000 of the total purchase price of $57,500 with the real estate agent, and was given 120 days to "examine the title and consummate the purchase." At the expiration of that period, the balance of the price was "due and payable upon tender of a good and sufficient deed of the property sold." The concluding paragraph of the deposit receipt provided: "Subject to Coldwell Banker & Company obtaining leases satisfactory to the purchaser." This clause and the 120–day period were desired by plaintiff as a means for arranging satisfactory leases of the shopping center buildings prior to the time he was finally committed to pay the balance of the purchase price and to take title to defendant's property.

Plaintiff took the first step in complying with the agreement by turning over the $1,000 deposit to the real estate agent. While he was in the process of securing the leases and before the 120 days had elapsed, defendant's attorney notified plaintiff that defendant would not sell her land under the terms contained in the deposit receipt. Thereafter, defendant was informed that satisfactory leases had been obtained and that plaintiff had offered to pay the balance of the purchase price. Defendant failed to tender the deed as provided in the deposit receipt.

Initially, defendant's thesis that the deposit receipt constituted no more than an offer by her, which could only be accepted by plaintiff notifying her that all of the desired leases had been obtained and were satisfactory to him, must be rejected. Nowhere does the agreement mention the necessity of any such notice. Nor does the provision making the agreement "subject to" plaintiff's securing "satisfactory" leases necessarily constitute a condition to the existence of a contract. Rather, the whole purchase receipt and this particular clause must be read as merely making plaintiff's performance dependent on the obtaining of "satisfactory" leases. Thus a contract arose, and plaintiff was given the power and privilege to terminate it in the event he did not obtain such leases....

However, the inclusion of this clause, specifying that leases "satisfactory" to plaintiff must be secured before he would be bound to perform, raises the basic question whether the consideration supporting the contract was thereby vitiated. When the parties attempt, as here, to make a contract where promises are exchanged as the consideration, the promises must be mutual in obligation. In other words, for the contract to bind either party, both must have assumed some legal obligations. Without this mutuality of obligation, the agreement lacks consideration and no enforceable contract has been created. Or, if one of the promises leaves a party free to perform or to withdraw from the agreement at his own unrestricted pleasure, the promise is deemed illusory and it provides no consideration. Whether these problems are couched in terms of mutuality of obligation or the illusory nature of a promise, the underlying issue is the same—consideration.

While contracts making the duty of performance of one of the parties conditional upon his satisfaction would seem to give him wide latitude in avoiding any obligation and thus present serious consideration problems, such "satisfaction" clauses have been given effect. They have been divided into two primary categories and have been accorded different treatment on that basis. First, in those contracts where the condition calls for satisfaction as to commercial value or quality, operative fitness, or mechanical utility, dissatisfaction cannot be claimed arbitrarily, unreasonably, or capriciously and the standard of a reasonable person is used in determining whether satisfaction has been received.... However, it would seem that the factors involved in determining whether a lease is satisfactory to the lessor are too numerous and varied to permit the application of a reasonable man standard as envisioned by this line of cases. Illustrative of some of the factors which would have to be considered in this case are the duration of the leases, their provisions for renewal options, if any, their covenants and restrictions, the amounts of the rentals, the financial responsibility of the lessees, and the character of the lessees' businesses.

This multiplicity of factors which must be considered in evaluating a lease shows that this case more appropriately falls within the second line of authorities dealing with "satisfaction" clauses, being those involving fancy, taste, or judgment. Where the question is one of judgment, the promisor's determination that he is not satisfied, when made in good faith, has been held to be a defense to an action on the contract. Although these decisions do not expressly discuss the issues of mutuality of obligation or illusory promises, they necessarily imply that the promisor's duty to exercise his judgment in good faith is an adequate consideration to support the contract. None of these cases voided the contracts on the ground that they were illusory or lacking in mutuality of obligation....

...

If the foregoing cases and other authorities were the only ones relevant, there would be little doubt that the deposit receipt here should not be deemed illusory or lacking in mutuality of obligation because it contained the "satisfaction" clause. However, language in two recent cases led the trial court to the contrary conclusion. The first case, *Lawrence Block Co. v. Palston*, stated that the following two conditions placed in an offer to buy an apartment building would have made the resulting contract illusory: "O.P.A. Rent statements to be approved by Buyer" and "Subject to buyer's inspection and approval of all apartments." These provisions were said to give the purchaser "unrestricted discretion" in deciding whether he would be bound to the contract and to provide no "standard" which could be used in compelling him to perform. However, this language was not necessary to the decision....

The other case, *Pruitt v. Fontana*, presented a similar situation. The court concluded that the written instrument with a provision making the sale of land subject to the covenants and easements being "approved by the buyers" was illusory. It employed both the reasoning and language of *Lawrence Block Co.* in deciding that this clause provided no "objective criterion" preventing the buyers from exercising an "unrestricted subjective discretion" in deciding whether they would be bound. But again, this language was not necessary to the result reached. The buyers in *Pruitt* refused to approve all of the easements of record, and the parties entered into a new and different oral agreement....

While the language in these two cases might be dismissed as mere *dicta*, the fact that the trial court relied thereon requires us to examine the reasoning employed. Both courts were concerned with finding an objective standard by which they could compel performance. This view apparently stems from the statement in *Lawrence Block Co.* that "The standard 'as to the satisfaction of a reasonable person' does not apply where the performance involves a matter dependent on judgment." By making this assertion without any qualification, the court necessarily implied that there is no other standard available. Of course, this entirely disregards those cases which have upheld "satisfaction" clauses dependent on the exercise of judgment. In such cases, the criterion becomes one of good faith. Insofar as the language in *Lawrence Block Co.* and *Pruitt* represented a departure from the established rules governing "satisfaction" clauses, they are hereby disapproved.

We conclude that the contract here was neither illusory nor lacking in mutuality of obligation because the parties inserted a provision in their contract making plaintiff's performance dependent on his satisfaction with the leases to be obtained by him.

The judgment is reversed.

QUESTIONS AND NOTES

1. The courts in this case and in *De Los Santos*, refer to the parties by their roles in the trial court as "plaintiff" and "defendant." This style contributes to the rather abstract tone of the opinion and may confuse readers. Mr. Mattei was a real estate developer; Ms. Hopper owned the property in question. Who brought this suit, Mr. Mattei or Ms. Hopper? In whose favor was the case decided in the trial court? Who wins on appeal? What will happen to the case after the appellate court decision? For example, is Mr. Mattei now entitled to the damages he asks, or will there have to be a further trial?

2. Does the likelihood that the "good faith" standard will be difficult to enforce against Mr. Mattei suggest that Ms. Hopper was given nothing of value for her promise to sell her land? Or does the contract give Ms. Hopper something of value and some security of expectation, although Mr. Mattei's power to get out of the deal is broad?

3. Prior to their divorce, Tom Clancy, the best-selling author, and his wife, Wanda King, entered into a partnership agreement establishing a joint venture named "Tom Clancy's Op-Center" for various book projects. After the couple divorced, Clancy sought to terminate the Op-Center venture in his discretion as managing partner of the joint venture. King sued alleging the termination was invalid. The court found that in exercising his rights under the partnership agreement, Clancy "only needed to act in good faith toward his business partners, even if such actions actually were adverse to the interests of [the partnership]." King proffered evidence that Clancy only wanted to end the Op-Center series in order to deprive her of financial benefits. The court in *Clancy v. King*, 954 A.2d 1092 (Md. 2008) drew on the hit comedy *Seinfeld* ("The Wig Master") (NBC original television broadcast Apr. 4, 1996) to illustrate the limitation the good faith requirement places on the exercise of otherwise discretionary contractual right. In the episode, Jerry purchased a "returnable" jacket at a men's clothing shop. The following discussion took place:

> Jerry: Excuse me, I'd like to return this jacket.
>
> Clerk: Certainly. May I ask why?
>
> Jerry: For spite.

Clerk: Spite?

Jerry: That's right. I don't care for the salesman that sold it to me.

Clerk: I don't think you can return an item for spite.

Jerry: What do you mean?

Clerk: Well, if there was some problem with the garment. If it were unsatisfactory in some way, then we could do it for you, but I'm afraid spite doesn't fit into any of our conditions for a refund.

Jerry: That's ridiculous, I want to return it. What's the difference what the reason is?

Clerk: Let me speak with the manager ... excuse me ... Bob!

(walks over to the manager and whispers)

Bob: What seems to be the problem?

Jerry: Well, I want to return this jacket and she asked me why and I said for spite and now she won't take it back.

Bob: That's true. You can't return an item based purely on spite.

Jerry: Well, so fine then ... then I don't want it and then that's why I'm returning it.

Bob: Well you already said spite so....

Jerry: But I changed my mind.

Bob: No, you said spite. Too late.'

The court wrote:

"In attempting to exercise his contractual discretion out of 'spite,' Jerry breached his duty to act in good faith towards the other party to the contract. Jerry would have been authorized to return the jacket if, in his good faith opinion, it did not fit or was not an attractive jacket. He may not return the jacket, however, for the sole purpose of denying to the other party the value of the contract. Jerry's *post hoc* rationalization that he was returning the jacket because he did not 'want it' was rejected properly by Bob as not credible."

So Clancy could wind-down Op-Center for any other reason, regardless of the financial effect on King, but not simply because he wanted to hurt his ex-wife financially. Nor could he simply rely on some other reason, or no reason at all, as a pretext if his true motivation was spite. The *Clancy* court remanded the case for a factual determination on these matters.

4. Suppose Mr. Mattei didn't want to go through with the transaction with Hopper, but as his lawyer you advise him that he has a good faith duty to try and procure satisfactory leases for the shopping center. How would you respond if Mr. Mattei asked what he had to do to satisfy that obligation? Note that a counseling lawyer's

interpretation of a promise may depend heavily on the lawyer's prediction of (a) how a judge might interpret the promise, and (b) how an advocate at trial will go about proving non-performance of the promise, as well as (c) how the lawyer reads the terms of the promise itself.

5. What does Justice Spence mean on p. 34, where he dismissed what the courts said in two older cases as "mere *dicta*"? What does he mean when he says that the earlier cases are "hereby disapproved"?

In many legal systems around the world, judges' written decisions are stated in a very formal, often syllogistic, style that is intended to delineate the "grounds" or basis in law for the decision. The dominant style in the English-speaking world is quite different. Appellate decisions were, and in a few cases still are, rendered orally in a rather discursive narrative style, sometimes immediately after the judges have deliberated and decided the case. Unlike the practice in most of the world, it is common in English-speaking courts for the decision of a multi-judge court to be delivered by an individual judge, not as an anonymous, collective decision. Indeed, as you will soon read in the cases that follow, other judges on the panel are likely to add their personal views separately when they disagree with the court's outcome (dissenting opinion) or with its reasoning (concurring opinion).

In other legal systems with highly structured logical forms of decision it may be a rather straightforward matter to identify the "grounds" for the decision (although the reader often may be left with the suspicion that the grounds given are an after-the-fact rationalization for the decision rather than the motivating reason that led to it). In the English-speaking style it is likely that the more candid the judge is in describing the mental process that led to the result, the more difficult it will be to extract an easily generalizable principle of law from it. The term *dicta* is frequently used in contrast to the "holding" of a judicial decision to indicate that some things a court says are central to the decision and other matters are merely commentary or supportive. When a court refers to another judicial statement as *dicta*, it usually is disapproving of that statement and denying its binding force on the case being decided.

Sylvan Crest Sand & Gravel Co. v. United States

United States Court of Appeals, Second Circuit, 1945.
150 F.2d 642.

■ SWAN, J. This is an action for damages for breach of four alleged contracts under each of which the plaintiff was to deliver trap rock to an airport project "as required" and in accordance with delivery instructions to be given by the defendant.

The breach alleged was the defendant's refusal to request or accept delivery within a reasonable time after the date of the contracts, thereby depriving the plaintiff of profits it would have made in the amount of $10,000.... Upon the pleadings, consisting of complaint, answer and reply, the defendant moved to dismiss the action for failure of the complaint to state a claim or, in the alternative, to grant summary judgment for the defendant on the ground that no genuine issue exists as to any material fact. The contracts in suit were introduced as exhibits at the hearing on the motion. Summary judgment for the defendant was granted on the theory that the defendant's reservation of an unrestricted power of cancellation caused the alleged contracts to be wholly illusory as binding obligations. The plaintiff has appealed.

The plaintiff owned and operated a trap rock quarry in Trumbull, Conn. Through the Treasury Department, acting by its State Procurement Office in Connecticut, the United States invited bids on trap rock needed for the Mollison Airport, Bridgeport, Conn. The plaintiff submitted four bids for different sized screenings of trap rock and each bid was accepted by the Assistant State Procurement Officer on June 29, 1937. The four documents are substantially alike and it will suffice to describe one of them. It is a printed government form, with the blank spaces filled in in typewriting, consisting of a single sheet bearing the heading:

"Invitation, Bid, and Acceptance"

"(Short Form Contract)"

Below the heading, under the subheadings, follow in order the "Invitation," the "Bid," and the "Acceptance by the Government." The Invitation, signed by a State Procurement Officer, states that "Sealed bids in triplicate, subject to the conditions on the reverse hereof, will be received at this office * * * for furnishing supplies * * * for delivery at WP 2752—Mollison Airport, Bridgeport, Ct." Then come typed provisions which, so far as material, are as follows:

> Item No. 1. ½" Trap Rock to pass the following screening test * * * approx. 4000 tons, unit price $2.00 amount $8000. To be delivered to project as required. Delivery to start immediately. Communicate with W.J. Scott, Supt. W.P.A. Branch Office, 147 Canon Street, Bridgeport, Ct., for definite delivery instructions. Cancellation by the Procurement Division may be effected at any time.

The Bid, signed by the plaintiff, provides that

> In compliance with the above invitation for bids, and subject to all of the conditions thereof, the undersigned offers, and agrees, if this bid be accepted * * * to furnish any or all of the items upon which prices are quoted, at the prices set opposite each item, delivered at the point(s) as specified, * * *.

The Acceptance, besides its date and the signature of an Assistant State Procurement Officer, contains only the words "Accepted as to items numbered 1." The printing on the reverse side of the sheet under the heading "Conditions" and "Instructions to Contracting Officers" clearly indicates that the parties supposed they were entering into an enforcible contract. For example, Condition 3 states that "in case of default of the contractor" the government may procure the articles from other sources and hold the contractor liable for any excess in cost; and Condition 4 provides that "if the contractor refuses or fails to make deliveries * * * within the time specified * * * the Government may by written notice terminate the right of the contractor to proceed with deliveries * * *." The Instructions to Contracting Officers also presupposes the making of a valid contract; No. 2 reads:

> Although this form meets the requirements of a formal contract (R.S. 3744), if the execution of a formal contract with bond is contemplated, U.S. Standard Forms 31 and 32 should be used.

No one can read the document as a whole without concluding that the parties intended a contract to result from the Bid and the Government's Acceptance. If the United States did not so intend, it certainly set a skillful trap for unwary bidders. No such purpose should be attributed to the government. In construing the document the presumption should be indulged that both parties were acting in good faith.

Although the Acceptance contains no promissory words, it is conceded that a promise by the defendant to pay the stated price for rock delivered is to be implied. Since no precise time for delivery was specified, the implication is that delivery within a reasonable time was contemplated. This is corroborated by the express provision that the rock was "to be delivered to the project as required. Delivery to start immediately." There is also to be implied a promise to give delivery instructions; nothing in the language of the contracts indicates that performance by the plaintiff was to be conditional upon the exercise of the defendant's discretion in giving such instructions. A more reasonable interpretation is that the defendant was placed under an obligation to give instructions for delivery from time to time when trap rock was required at the project. Such were the duties of the defendant, unless the cancellation clause precludes such a construction of the document.

Beyond question the plaintiff made a promise to deliver rock at a stated price; and if the United States were suing for its breach the question would be whether the "acceptance" by the United States operated as a sufficient consideration to make the plaintiff's promise binding. Since the United States is the defendant the question is whether it made any promise that has been broken. Its "acceptance" should be interpreted as a reasonable business man would have understood it. Surely it would not have been understood thus: "We accept your offer and bind you to your promise to deliver, but we do not promise either to take the rock or pay the price." The reservation of a power to effect cancellation at any time meant something different from this. We believe that the reasonable interpretation of the document is as follows: "We accept your offer to deliver within a reasonable time, and we promise to take the rock and pay the price unless we give you notice of cancellation within a reasonable time." Only on such an interpretation is the United States justified in expecting the plaintiff to prepare for performance and to remain ready and willing to deliver. Even so, the bidder is taking a great risk and the United States has an advantage. It is not "good faith" for the United States to insist upon more than this. It is certain that the United States intended to bind the bidder to a "contract," and that the bidder thought that the "acceptance" of his bid made a "contract." A reasonable interpretation of the language used gives effect to their mutual intention. Consequently we cannot accept the contention that the defendant's power of cancellation was unrestricted and could be exercised merely by failure to give delivery orders. The words "cancellation may be effected at any time" imply affirmative action, namely, the giving of notice of intent to cancel. The defendant itself so construed the clause by giving notice of cancellation on July 11, 1939, as alleged in its answer. While the phrase "at any time" should be liberally construed, it means much less than "forever." If taken literally, it would mean that after the defendant had given instructions for delivery and the plaintiff had tendered delivery in accordance therewith, or even after delivery had actually been made, the defendant could refuse to accept and when sued for the price give notice of cancellation of the contract. Such an interpretation would be not only unjust and unreasonable, but would make nugatory the entire contract, contrary to the intention of the parties, if it be assumed that the United States was acting in good faith in accepting the plaintiff's bid. The words should be so construed as to support the contract and not render illusory the promises of both parties. This can be accomplished by interpolating the word "reasonable," as is often done with respect to indefinite time clauses. Hence the agreement obligated the defendant to give delivery instructions or notice of cancellation within a reasonable time after the date of its "acceptance." This constituted consideration for the plaintiff's promise to deliver in accordance with delivery instructions, and made the agreement a valid contract.

It must be conceded that the cases dealing with agreements in which one party has reserved to himself an option to cancel are not entirely harmonious. Where the option is completely unrestricted some courts say that the party having the option has promised nothing and the contract is void for lack of mutuality. These cases have been criticized by competent text writers and the latter case cited by this court "with distinct lack of warmth," as Judge Clark noted in *Bushwick-Decatur Motors v. Ford Motor Co.* But where, as in the case at bar, the option to cancel "does not wholly defeat consideration," the agreement is not *nudum pactum*. A promise is not made illusory by the fact that the promisor has an option between two alternatives, if each alternative would be sufficient consideration if it alone were bargained for. As we have construed the agreement the United States promised by implication to take and pay for the trap rock or give notice of cancellation within a reasonable time. The alternative of giving notice was not difficult of performance, but it was a sufficient consideration to support the contract.

The judgment is reversed and the cause remanded for trial.

QUESTIONS

1. Does Judge Swan decide that there was an enforceable contract here?

2. The court interprets the cancellation clause to be restricted by an implied promise to give notice of cancellation within a reasonable time. Do you agree with the court that the implication of such a promise on the government's part is the interpretation a reasonable businessperson would have made in this circumstance?

3. If the government contract form read "cancellable without notice for any reason at any time—reasonable or not—within the next 20 years," would a supplier like Sylvan Crest Sand as readily accept such an order? Would it think that it had made a contract if it did accept it? Would the result in *Sylvan Crest* have been the same if this had been the language requiring interpretation?

4. Was the United States bound because it had "promised by implication," or had it "promised by implication" because it was bound?

5. If the government abandoned construction of the airport and hence needed no rock (*i.e.*, it didn't buy rock from anyone else), would its failure to give Sylvan Crest notice be a breach? If the government's power of cancellation were unrestricted, would there be any contract at all? Must the answers to these two questions be necessarily reconcilable?

Wood v. Lucy, Lady Duff-Gordon

New York Court of Appeals, 1917.
222 N.Y. 88, 118 N.E. 214.

■ CARDOZO, J. The defendant styles herself "a creator of fashions." Her favor helps a sale. Manufacturers of dresses, millinery, and like articles are glad to pay for a certificate of her approval. The things which she designs, fabrics, parasols, and what not, have a new value in the public mind when issued in her name. She employed the plaintiff to help her to turn this vogue into money. He was to have the exclusive right, subject always to her approval, to place her indorsements on the designs of others. He was also to have the exclusive right to place her own designs on sale, or to license others to market them. In return she was to have one-half of "all profits and revenues" derived from any contracts he might make. The exclusive right was to last at least one year from April 1, 1915, and thereafter from year to year unless terminated by notice of 90 days. The plaintiff says that he kept the contract on his part, and that the defendant broke it. She placed her indorsement on fabrics, dresses, and millinery without his knowledge, and withheld the profits. He sues her for the damages, and the case comes here on demurrer.

The agreement of employment is signed by both parties. It has a wealth of recitals. The defendant insists, however, that it lacks the elements of a contract. She says that the plaintiff does not bind himself to anything. It is true that he does not promise in so many words that he will use reasonable efforts to place the defendant's indorsements and market her designs. We think, however, that such a promise is fairly to be implied. The law has outgrown its primitive stage of formalism when the precise word was the sovereign talisman, and every slip was fatal. It takes a broader view today. A promise may be lacking, and yet the whole writing may be "instinct with an obligation," imperfectly expressed (Scott, J., in *McCall Co. v. Wright*, 133 App.Div. 62). If that is so, there is a contract.

The implication of a promise here finds support in many circumstances. The defendant gave an exclusive privilege. She was to have no right for at least a year to place her own indorsements or market her own designs except through the agency of the plaintiff. The acceptance of the exclusive agency was an assumption of its duties. Many other terms of the agreement point the same way. We are told at the outset by way of recital that:

> "The said Otis F. Wood possesses a business organization adapted to the placing of such indorsements as the said Lucy, Lady Duff–Gordon, has approved."

The implication is that the plaintiff's business organization will be used for the purpose for which it is adapted. But the terms of the defendant's compensation are even more significant. Her sole compensation for the grant of an exclusive agency is to be one-half of all the profits resulting from the plaintiff's efforts. Unless he gave his efforts, she could never get anything. Without an implied promise, the transaction cannot have such business "efficacy, as both parties must have intended that at all events it should have." Bowen, L.J., in *The Moorcock*, 14 P.D. 64, 68. But the contract does not stop there. The plaintiff goes on to promise that he will account monthly for all moneys received by him, and that he will take out all such patents and copyrights and trademarks as may in his judgment be necessary to protect the rights and articles affected by the agreement. It is true, of course, as the Appellate Division has said, that if he was under no duty to try to market designs or to place certificates of indorsement, his promise to account for profits or take out copyrights would be valueless. But in determining the intention of the parties the promise has a value. It helps to enforce the conclusion that the plaintiff had some duties. His promise to pay the defendant one-half of the profits and revenues resulting from the exclusive agency and to render accounts monthly was a promise to use reasonable efforts to bring profits and revenues into existence. For this conclusion the authorities are ample.

The judgment of the Appellate Division should be reversed, and the order of the Special Term affirmed, with costs in the Appellate Division and in this court.

QUESTIONS

1. The problem in this case is whether there was consideration to bind Lady Lucy to her promise. Is this a problem of interpretation?

2. Did Wood promise to make sales, did he promise to use reasonable efforts, or did he and Lady Lucy merely agree that so long as he used reasonable efforts his exclusive agency could not be taken away from him? Is the lack of an express promise here just a matter of imperfect expression, as Judge Cardozo suggests, or is the substance of the deal uncertain? Imagine that we interrupted Wood and Lady Lucy while negotiating this agency agreement and asked them what they thought. Do you think that each had a clear intention regarding Wood's obligations at that time? Do you think that their intentions were identical? If not, was there a contract?

3. Reverse the parties in the case by supposing that Lady Lucy (having scrupulously kept the agreement on her part) sued Wood on the ground that he had not used reasonable efforts to market her "favor." Would the court be as apt to find the implied promise by Wood that it found here? How could Lady Lucy prove that Wood's efforts were less than reasonable and how much business she had lost because of Wood's lack of diligence? What information would she need?

4. There are thousands of "exclusive dealership" contracts made every year. How would you draft such an agreement so that you wouldn't have to rely on a Cardozo to find a contract? What kind of information would you want from your client and from the other party? Remember that such a contract must be acceptable to both parties. See UCC § 2–306(2).

B. Lewis Productions v. Angelou

U.S. District Court, S.D.N.Y., 2005.
2005 WL 1138474.

■ MUKASEY, D.J. Plaintiff B. Lewis Productions, Inc. (BLP) sues defendant Maya Angelou for breach of contract and breach of the duty of good faith and fair dealing. For the reasons set forth below, [Angelou's motion for summary judgment is] denied.

I.

. . .

B. Factual History

Butch Lewis is the president and sole owner of BLP. BLP's business consists primarily of promoting boxing and other sports and entertainment events. Defendant Maya Angelou, a resident of North Carolina, is a renowned poet. Hallmark Cards, Incorporated, a Missouri corporation, manufactures greeting cards and related products. In this action, BLP claims that Angelou breached an agreement in which she granted BLP the exclusive right to exploit her original literary works for publication in greeting cards and similar products. Angelou claims that no enforceable contract existed.

Lewis and Angelou became acquainted in early 1994 when, at Lewis's request, Angelou visited Mike Tyson at an Indiana prison. At that meeting, Angelou and Lewis discussed how she might reach a broader base of readers by publishing her works in greeting cards. Several months after this initial meeting, Lewis met with Angelou at her North Carolina home to discuss a potential collaboration between Angelou and BLP to market Angelou's works to greeting card companies. In November 1994, Lewis and Angelou signed a "letter agreement" that established what the letter called a "Joint Venture" to publish Angelou's writings in greeting cards and other media forms. The letter agreement, dated November 22, 1994 and signed by both parties, reads as follows:

> This letter agreement made between B. LEWIS PRODUCTIONS, INC. (BLP) with offices at 250 West 57th Street, New York, N.Y. 10019 and MAYA ANGELOU (ANGELOU) whose address is 2720 Reynolda Road, Suite # 1, Winston-Salem, NC 27106, sets forth the understandings of the parties with reference to the following:
>
> 1. The parties will enter into a Joint Venture (Venture), wherein ANGELOU will exclusively contribute original literary works (Property) to the Venture and BLP will seek to exploit the rights for publishing of said Property in all media forms including, but not limited to greeting cards, stationery and calendars, etc.
>
> 2. BLP will contribute all the capital necessary to fund the operation of the Venture.

3. ANGELOU will contribute, on an exclusive basis, original literary works to the Venture after consultations with and mutual agreement of Butch Lewis, who will be the managing partner of the Venture.

4. The Venture shall own the copyrights to all of ANGELOU's contributions to the Venture.

> (a) If any of the subject copyrights do not produce any income for a consecutive five (5) year period as a result of the exploitation referred to [in] paragraph 1 herein then the ownership of these copyrights shall revert to Angelou exclusively.

5. The name of the Venture shall be mutually agreed upon.

6. Gross Revenue shall be distributed and applied in the following order:

> (a) Return of BLP's capital contribution.
>
> (b) Reimbursement of any and all expenses of the Venture.
>
> (c) Balance (net profits) to be shared equally between BLP and ANGELOU.
>
> (d) ANGELOU shall have the right at any time, upon reasonable notice, to inspect all records including but not limited to the financial records of the Venture.

This Agreement shall be binding upon the parties until a more formal detailed agreement is signed.

In late 1994, BLP began to market Angelou's work to Hallmark and several other greeting card companies. Lewis began to negotiate a license agreement with Hallmark on Angelou's behalf. When Hallmark asked Lewis for confirmation that he was indeed authorized to act on Angelou's behalf, on June 19, 1996, Lewis sent Hallmark a letter signed by Angelou that stated:

> This will confirm that BUTCH LEWIS PRODUCTIONS, INC. (BLP) has the exclusive right to represent DR. MAYA ANGELOU for the exploitation of her work product in the area of greeting cards, stationery, calendars, etc. as per the contract executed by BLP and Dr. Angelou dated November 22, 1994 which is still in full force and effect.

BLP declined to send Hallmark the November 22, 1994 agreement itself because Lewis wanted to keep its terms confidential.

In March 1997, after extended negotiations, Hallmark sent BLP a license agreement for the use of Angelou's future exclusive works which would have paid her and BLP 9% of gross revenues from sales of licensed products, with a $50,000 advance payment and a guaranteed minimum $100,000 in royalties. Angelou's greeting cards would be administered through Hallmark's Ethnic Business Center. Also in March 1997, Lewis and Angelou encountered one another at an event in Las Vegas, where Angelou saw Lewis, who is black, punctuate a conversation with white people by grabbing his crotch. After she witnessed Lewis's behavior, Angelou "burned up his ears." She claims that she told him that the "venture" between them was off, and that she no longer wanted to work with him. Lewis denies that Angelou made any such comment at the time.

However, when Lewis forwarded the Hallmark license agreement to Angelou, she did not sign it, and later told her literary agent Helen Brann to "start putting a little cold water on the prospect of this deal with Hallmark." After meeting with Lewis and his associate Joy Farrell, Brann sent a letter to Lewis on May 5, 1997, informing him "that it is not going to work out now for Dr. Maya Angelou to make any deal with Hallmark Cards." In her letter, Brann cited Angelou's commitment to Random House as the publisher of all of Angelou's "major work" as a reason for not proceeding with Hallmark. Brann noted that "[n]either Dr. Angelou nor I like to say never, and I suppose that sometime in the future we might all figure out a way, in cooperation with Random House and Hallmark and us, to launch some kind of greeting card program, but this year is definitely not the year to contemplate such a move."

Lewis claims that at a later meeting in 1997, Angelou told him that she would sign the licensing agreement with Hallmark "after the New Year," and that in February 1998, she told him she was planning to sign the agreement "as soon as she [got] everything off her table." However Angelou did not sign the Hallmark licensing agreement,[2] and according to Lewis's associate Farrell, when Farrell left BLP in mid-1998, in her opinion the deal was "dead," and the project was over. Additionally, because Hallmark did not hear from Lewis after it sent him the licensing agreement in 1997, Hallmark executives eventually concluded that the collaboration between BLP and Angelou was "dead."

Hallmark wrote Angelou's agent Brann in March 1998 to inquire whether Angelou was still interested in pursuing a program of greeting cards, stating that its "discussions with Mr. Lewis ended in early 1997 when he could not deliver a program." Brann responded that Angelou was not interested in entering into an agreement with Hallmark at that time. However, in June 1999, Angelou's close friend Amelia Parker, who was acquainted with an executive at Hallmark, convinced Angelou to have lunch with Hallmark executives at the company's St. Louis headquarters when Angelou was in town for an unrelated speaking engagement. Angelou was encouraged by this meeting and decided to try to arrange a licensing deal with Hallmark.

Simultaneously, Angelou sought to assure that her ties to Lewis were severed. On June 16, 1999 Angelou's North Carolina counsel sent a letter to BLP stating that "any business relationship that you may have had or contemplated pursuant to a letter dated November 22, 1994 from you to Dr. Angelou, has been terminated." Lewis claims that he never received this letter, and that as far as he was concerned, the November 1994 letter agreement was still in force in 1999. According to Lewis,

---

2. Angelou declined also to sign a more formal version of the November 22, 1994 letter agreement between her and BLP that Lewis forwarded to her in 1997.

he contacted Angelou in 1999 about the Hallmark licensing agreement and she put him off again; at this point Lewis stopped trying to communicate with Angelou about Hallmark, and instead kept abreast of her views on the matter by communicating with her close friend Bob Brown, who did not tell Lewis that the "venture" had been terminated. Lewis learned that Hallmark and Angelou had reached an agreement without his assistance when he saw a press release about the deal in November 2000.

On June 28, 2000, after more than a year of negotiations and discussions, Hallmark and Angelou signed a licensing agreement which featured a sliding royalty scale based on net revenues, guaranteed Angelou a minimum payment of $2 million, and gave her a $1 million advance. This agreement allowed Hallmark to use Angelou's previously published work as well as future works she would create for the project; additionally, the marketing of Angelou's products would not be restricted to ethnic consumers.

II.

In her motion for summary judgment, Angelou claims that as a matter of law, no bilateral contract existed between her and BLP because the Agreement was vague, indefinite, and lacking in essential terms.

A. Definiteness and Essential Terms

"In order for an agreement to be enforced, it must be sufficiently 'definite and explicit so [that the parties'] intention may be ascertained to a reasonable degree of certainty.'" *Best Brands Beverage, Inc. v. Falstaff Brewing Corp.* (2d Cir.1987); *see also* 1 Corbin on Contracts § 4.1 ("A court cannot enforce a contract unless it can determine what it is. It is not enough that the parties think that they have made a contract. They must have expressed their intentions in a manner that is capable of being understood. It is not even enough that they have actually agreed, if their expressions, when interpreted in the light of accompanying factors and circumstances, are not such that the court can determine what the terms of the agreement are.").

Moreover, an agreement cannot be enforced if it lacks essential terms, and if the court is unable to supply such missing terms in a reasonable fashion that is consistent with the parties' intent. *Best Brands*; *see also* Restatement (Second) of Contracts § 204 (1981) ("When the parties to a bargain sufficiently defined to be a contract have not agreed with respect to a term which is essential to a determination of their rights and duties, a term which is reasonable in the circumstances is supplied by the court.").

A court may not "rewrite the contract and impose liabilities not bargained for." *A/S Atlantica v. Moran Towing & Transp. Co.* (2d Cir.1974). However, New York and North Carolina courts are reluctant to strike down contracts for indefiniteness.

Courts are cautioned not to turn the requirements of definiteness and essential terms into a fetish, because

> at some point virtually every agreement can be said to have a degree of indefiniteness, and if the doctrine is applied with a heavy hand it may defeat the reasonable expectations of the parties in entering into a contract. While there must be a manifestation of mutual assent to essential terms, parties also should be held to their promises and courts should not be pedantic or meticulous in interpreting contract expressions.

Cobble Hill Nursing Home, Inc. v. Henry & Warren Corp. (N.Y.1989).

A term is essential if "it seriously affects the rights and obligations of the parties and there is a significant evidentiary dispute as to its content." *Ginsberg Machine Co. v. J. & H. Label Processing Corp.* (2d Cir.1965). Terms that may be considered essential in any agreement include the price to be paid, the work to be done, and the time of performance. See 1 Williston on Contracts § 4.18. When a court encounters indefinite terms, but finds that the parties did intend to form a contract, as the court found in its first decision in this case, the court then must attempt to "attach a sufficiently definite meaning to [the] bargain." 1 Williston § 4.18. A court should be especially willing to do so if the plaintiff has fully or partly performed under the agreement "since the performance may either remove the uncertainty or militate in favor of recovery even if the uncertainty continues." *Id.* (citing Restatement (Second) of Contracts § 34)); *see also* 1 Corbin § 4.1 ("The fact that one [party], with the knowledge and approval of the other, has begun performance is nearly always evidence that [the parties] regard the contract as consummated and intend to be bound thereby.").

Of course, the court may not make a contract for the parties. However, because the parties in this case did intend a contract, the court is obligated to fill any gaps their Agreement contains, if it reasonably is able to do so. Voiding an agreement for lack of essential terms "is a step that courts should take only in rare and extreme circumstances." *Shann v. Dunk* (2d Cir.1996).

Angelou claims that the Agreement in this case is unenforceable because it lacks multiple essential terms. She notes that the Agreement does not specify or describe: what "original literary works" she would be contributing to the project; whether these literary works would be new or chosen from her previously published works; the quantity of works Angelou was to produce; when she was to contribute these works; the duration of the Agreement; or the extent of BLP's substantive or financial obligations under the Agreement. Further, Angelou argues that the Agreement's designation of BLP's right to exploit Angelou's work in "all media forms" is overbroad and does not express the parties' intent, because this provision would have affected Angelou's agreement with her literary publisher Random

House. As explained below, these allegedly indefinite or missing terms are capable of reasonable interpretation.

1. Price

The general rule is that price is "an essential ingredient" of every contract, and that a compensation clause is enforceable only if payment can be determined from the agreement without any "further expression by the parties." Angelou notes that the Agreement does not state how much capital, if any, BLP was obligated to contribute to the project, and argues that this constitutes a failure to specify the essential term of price. The Agreement does state, however, that BLP will contribute "all the capital necessary." The Agreement further specifies how gross revenue generated by the "Venture" was to be distributed: BLP's capital is returned, any of the Venture's expenses are reimbursed, and any net profits are shared equally between BLP and Angelou. There is at least a material question of fact as to whether this payment and distribution scheme was sufficiently definite. BLP was obligated under the Agreement to contribute "all" capital—an arrangement with a meaning that arguably is capable of enforcement. Moreover, the capital necessary to a "Venture" of the sort at issue here would be modest, if indeed any capital expenditures would have been necessary. Even expense items were likely to be limited to funds required to produce greeting card mock-ups, postage, and perhaps some travel.

If Angelou had signed the Hallmark license agreement that Lewis had negotiated on her behalf, and if revenue had been generated from Angelou's line of greeting cards, the Agreement between BLP and Angelou would have provided clear guidelines for distribution of that revenue. A compensation clause need not specify dollar figures to be definite.

BLP's part performance too shows that the parties had a meeting of the minds on the financial aspects of the Agreement. BLP paid all initial expenses as Lewis began to negotiate licensing deals with various greeting card companies, and Angelou raised no objection during that time.

The price terms of the Agreement are capable of reasonable interpretation, and therefore arguably are sufficiently definite for enforcement.

2. Duration

Angelou claims also that the Agreement's lack of a duration term renders it too vague for enforcement. Indeed, in his deposition, Lewis admitted that "[t]here was no time set" on the Agreement. The parties dispute whether the Agreement's copyright provision contains an implicit duration term. However, the court need decide this issue because the Agreement's lack of a duration term is not material.

Under both New York and North Carolina law, a duration clause is not necessary in a contract for services. If such a contract makes no provision for duration, the contract is presumed to be terminable at will. If the Agreement between Angelou and BLP is viewed not as a joint venture but as a simple bilateral contract, BLP was contracting for Angelou's services as a writer and Angelou was contracting for BLP's services as a marketer of her work; under this view, the Agreement is a contract for services that need not contain a provision for duration, and may be terminated at will.[5]

3. Subject Matter

Angelou argues that the Agreement insufficiently defined the works she would supply to the project and the form in which her works would be exploited. The Agreement provides that Angelou will "exclusively contribute original literary works (Property) to the Venture and BLP will seek to exploit the rights for publishing of said Property in all media forms including, but not limited to greeting cards, stationery and calendars, etc." The Agreement adds that Angelou will contribute, "on an exclusive basis, original literary works to the Venture after consultations with and mutual agreement of Butch Lewis, who will be the managing partner of the Venture."

BLP claims that the Agreement's subject matter was sufficiently definite because the Agreement stated that the details of the work would be mutually agreed upon, and could not be finalized until a licensing agreement with a specific greeting card company had been reached. Angelou claims that this admission confirms her argument that the Agreement was merely an "agreement to agree," and not a binding Agreement in and of itself. The parties understood that they were agreeing to work together to publish Angelou's writings in greeting cards, and potentially in related media forms such as calendars and stationery. The details of the arrangement would become final as individual projects were undertaken. When the Agreement was signed, there was a meeting of the minds as to its subject matter, and given the expressed intent of the parties, the court reasonably would be able to supply missing details, if necessary. Any omitted details are not material.

Again, BLP partially performed under the Agreement when it procured from Hallmark at least a draft that proposed the licensing of Angelou's writings for use in greeting cards and related products. Although Angelou did not enter into this deal, neither did she question the propriety of BLP's discussions with Hallmark, or suggest that her obligations under the Agreement were too indefinite to validate those discussions. BLP's part performance thus helps to resolve uncertainty about the Agreement's subject matter—if there was any such uncertainty to begin with. *See* 1

---

5. Again, because Angelou has not moved for summary judgment on the issue of termination, the court expresses no opinion on the issue of whether the Agreement here was terminated, and if it was, what repercussions such termination would have on BLP's claim against Angelou.

Corbin § 4.1 ("[T]he argument that a particular agreement is too indefinite to constitute a contract frequently is an afterthought excuse for attacking an agreement that failed for reasons other than the indefiniteness."). Although defined in broad strokes, the Agreement's subject matter was not so indefinite as to constitute "rare and extreme" circumstances justifying invalidation of a binding contract intended by both parties.

B. Duty of Good Faith and Fair Dealing

The above discussion of missing essential terms intersects with the issue of whether the parties here owed one another an obligation of good faith and fair dealing. New York and North Carolina courts have held that every contract contains an implied covenant of good faith and fair dealing, in which each party agrees not to injure the rights of the other to receive benefits under that agreement. In this case, BLP argues that each party's duty of good faith and fair dealing served to supply any missing terms relating to their respective obligations under the Agreement, and that Angelou breached her implied covenant of good faith when she failed to contribute any works to the project. Angelou counters that this claim duplicates BLP's breach of contract claim, and that the duty of good faith and fair dealing may not be used to force her into obligations she never intended to assume.

1. Duty of Good Faith and Missing Terms

Then-Judge Cardozo's opinion in *Wood v. Lucy, Lady Duff Gordon*, underpins the analysis here. In that case, the defendant Lady Duff Gordon, a self-styled "creator of fashions," agreed with the plaintiff Otis Wood that he would have the exclusive right, subject to her approval, to sell her designs, to license others to market them, and to place her endorsement on the designs of others. As Cardozo phrased it, "[s]he employed the plaintiff to turn this vogue into money." Under the agreement, Lady Duff Gordon was to receive one half of "all profits and revenues" derived from contracts made by the defendant involving her work. The defendant sued Lady Duff Gordon, claiming that she had placed her endorsement on various products without his knowledge and kept the profits for herself. Lady Duff Gordon claimed in response that the original agreement between herself and Wood was unenforceable and illusory because it failed to specify Wood's obligation to sell and market her designs.

The facts here strongly resemble those in Cardozo's classic. As in that case, we have here an artistic defendant, a 50-50 arrangement to market her creations, and an alleged behind-the-back breach, with Ms. Angelou cast as a Lady Duff Gordon for the modern age.

In *Wood*, the Court held that although the contract between the parties did not spell out each party's obligations,

[t]he law has outgrown its primitive stage of formalism when the precise word was the sovereign talisman, and every slip was fatal. It takes a broader view today. A promise may be lacking, and yet the whole writing may be instinct with an obligation, imperfectly expressed. If that is so, there is a contract.

The Court found the implication of a binding promise between the parties from numerous aspects of the agreement. Lady Duff Gordon gave Wood the "exclusive" right to market her creations; she must have expected him to perform, because her business would have ceased to exist without him. Additionally, Lady Duff Gordon's sole compensation was to be one-half of the profits: Therefore unless Wood made reasonable efforts under the agreement, she could recover nothing under its terms, defeating the "business efficacy" that both parties must have desired when they made the agreement. The contract between Wood and Lady Duff Gordon was upheld, and generated a body of law in which the duty of good faith upheld binding agreements with scant details. 2 Corbin § 5.27 ("The finding of implied promises is more common today than in the era before the *Wood* case. Courts recognize that if the parties intend a contract, rather than a nullity, implying promises to avoid the finding of illusoriness or indefiniteness protects the reasonable expectation of the parties engendered by the agreement.").

Angelou claims that the Agreement is unenforceable because it fails to define either party's obligations. She argues that the Agreement does not specify a quantity of work to be supplied by her, nor does it state what effort BLP was required to expend in furtherance of the Agreement. According to Angelou, the Agreement was so vague that she could have complied with its terms and never provided any work to the project; similarly, BLP could have complied simply by making a few telephone inquiries. Indeed, both Lewis and Angelou testified that Angelou was under no obligation to provide any works to the project. Perhaps, but consider what might have occurred if Angelou had accepted some version of the proposal that Hallmark made to BLP. If Angelou had failed thereafter to contribute some works, but had published other works on her own that could have been used in greeting cards, BLP might have sued for damages stemming from Angelou's nonperformance.

As was the case in *Wood*, it appears that the parties here intended to form a binding contract. Deficiencies or gaps in the Agreement regarding the parties' obligations may be filled by the obligation of good faith that each incurred upon signing it. As in *Wood*, the profit-sharing arrangement between the parties here meant that Angelou and BLP had nothing to gain from the Agreement if either failed to perform or gave minimal effort. Therefore we must assume that each party arguably had an obligation to make "reasonable efforts" in furtherance of the Agreement in order to vindicate the "business efficacy" that both parties must have contemplated when they entered the Agreement.

Angelou cites *Ginsberg* for the proposition that some contractual voids are too great to fill by implication. In *Ginsberg*, an oral contract followed by an exchange of letters between two businessmen for an exclusive agency in the selling of machine labels was found unenforceable for lack of any duration term in the agreement and other important omissions. The *Ginsberg* Court acknowledged *Wood*'s "classic principle," but found too many terms missing, and held that "the risk of ensnaring a party in a set of contractual obligations that he never knowingly assumed [wa]s too serious."

In this case, the evidence shows that Lewis and Angelou agreed on the terms of the contract and on the meaning of those terms. Angelou and BLP never argued over the substance of the Agreement, and as Lewis marketed the Angelou project to greeting card companies, Angelou never protested. To the contrary, she signed a confirmation of the Agreement on June 19, 1996, which was sent to Hallmark. Angelou did eventually refuse to deal with BLP, but this decision was not motivated by any contractual dispute. Angelou testified that she did not like the mock-ups of the greeting cards that BLP presented to her, that she was disgusted by Lewis's behavior at the event in Las Vegas, and that she felt it was morally wrong to compromise her relationship with Random House by publishing her work elsewhere. None of these reservations had anything to do with the terms of the contract Angelou signed with BLP. Angelou articulated no concerns about the nature or scope of the Agreement, and did not complain that she had been ensnared into contractual obligations she had unknowingly assumed. Angelou's plight does not resemble that of the merchant in *Ginsberg* who made an oral contract and signed an informal letter confirming a vague arrangement. Her case more closely parallels that of Lady Duff Gordon, who signed a binding agreement that she later came to regret.

The repeated use of the language of exclusivity in the dealings between Angelou and BLP is further evidence that each party had a good faith obligation to perform under the Agreement. The Agreement twice uses the word "exclusive" in describing Angelou's contributions to the "Venture"— "Angelou will exclusively contribute original literary works," and "Angelou will contribute, on an exclusive basis, original literary works"—and in the letter sent by Angelou and BLP to Hallmark on June 19, 1996, Angelou stated that BLP had the "exclusive right" to represent her "for the exploitation of her work product in the area of greeting cards, stationery, calendars, etc." This court held previously that the parties did not contemplate an exclusive agency in their Agreement—instead, they set out to form a joint venture, but did so improperly. Lewis denied repeatedly that he was Angelou's exclusive agent, and instead insisted that the two were "partners." But even if the arrangement Angelou and Lewis entered into could not be described as an agency, the Agreement and the June 19, 1996 confirmation letter both show that the parties intended to work with one another on the greeting card project, and Angelou promised that she would provide her work for use in greeting cards exclusively to BLP. This language is further evidence that the parties assumed that each would act in good faith to further the Agreement. As in *Wood*, "[w]e are not to suppose that one party was to be placed at the mercy of the other"; rather, Angelou committed to work only with BLP to accomplish her contractual goal, and trusted that BLP would fulfill his obligations under the Agreement.

As discussed above, and bearing in mind that the court must construe all evidence in the light most favorable to the nonmoving party, the Agreement at least arguably contains most if not all required essential terms for enforcement. Any remaining vagueness or uncertainty regarding the parties' obligations may be found immaterial, because the parties' reciprocal duty of good faith under the Agreement ensured that they would make reasonable efforts to perform.

NOTES AND QUESTIONS

1. Dr. Maya Angelou (1928-2014) was a highly regarded literary figure and civil rights activist. Her major works include her first novel, *I Know Why the Caged Bird Sings* (1970). She wrote and delivered her poem *On the Pulse of The Morning* at President Bill Clinton's first inauguration. Butch Lewis (1946-2011) managed and promoted prominent boxers including Leon and Michael Spinks. Judge Michael Mukasey went on to become Attorney General of the United States under President George W. Bush.

2. Do you agree that Dr. Angelou and Lady Lucy are similarly situated here? Who do you think has the stronger claim for enforcement Wood or BLP? If you were to distinguish the two cases on what basis would you do so representing Dr. Angelou? How about if you were representing BLP?

3. The subsequent settlement of this lawsuit gave rise to further litigation between these parties. Lewis eventually settled for a lump sum payment of $456,019 plus 1.25% of future net revenues from Hallmark. In *B. Lewis Prods. v. Angelou*, 2008 U.S. Dist. WL1826486 (S.D.N.Y Apr. 22, 2008), the court dismissed BLP's complaint that it had been defrauded in the settlement negotiations. Under the terms of the settlement, BLP accepted future royalties from Hallmark in satisfaction of its claim against Angelou, but Angelou had already accepted (but failed to disclose) an advance from Hallmark that had the effect of reducing future royalties payable to BLP. Concluding that BLP is "a sophisticated player who was on notice of the existence of the [agreement between Hallmark and Angelou] and its impact on Angelou's past and future payments from Hallmark," the court held that BLP's reliance on Angelou's silence was not reasonable: Angelou could keep her undisclosed advance, and BLP's royalties under the settlement would be accordingly reduced.

DRAFTING EXERCISE

Your senior partner has just been consulted by A.H. Stevens, who told him of the conversations described on p. 14. The partner is inclined to advise Southland that there is no enforceable contract for reasons stated in Chief Justice Robquist's opinion, but he solicits your opinion. On the basis of what you have read in *B. Lewis Productions, Wood, Sylvan Crest, Mattei,* and *De Los Santos,* what advice would you give Southland? Prepare a memorandum of no more than two pages addressed to your partner and reacting to his preliminary view.

B. CONTEXT THAT SUGGESTS NO COMMITMENT—FUN AND GAMES

Things are not always what they seem, and what looks and sounds like a voluntary and serious expression of intent sometimes is recognized to be nothing of the sort. An actor on the stage may swear and bind himself by great oaths with impunity. Children may play "store" and buy and sell vast quantities of imaginary goods in transactions that would not give any judge much pause (unless the judge happened to be an eight-year-old playmate). When the children grow up and play in bars it may be harder to tell play from business, but the line remains a real one nonetheless. The rule is clear: One party cannot convert what both parties knew was only a joke into a serious transaction simply by claiming on it. But what if the claimant states that *she* wasn't joking and didn't think the other party was? Still no contract because if one party is joking there is no "meeting of the minds"? Or if one party jokes, does he do so at his peril?

Keller v. Holderman

Michigan Supreme Court, 1863.
11 Mich. 248.

Action by Holderman against Keller upon a check for $300 drawn by Keller upon a banker at Niles, and not honored. The cause was tried without a jury, and the Circuit Judge found as facts, that the check was given for an old silver watch, worth about $15, which Keller took and kept till the day of trial, when he offered to return it to the plaintiff, who refused to receive it. The whole transaction was a frolic and banter—the plaintiff not expecting to sell, nor the defendant intending to buy the watch at the sum for which the check was drawn. The defendant when he drew the check had no money in the banker's hands, and had intended to insert a condition in the check that would prevent his being liable upon it; but as he had failed to do so, and had retained the watch, the Judge held him liable, and judgment was rendered against him for the amount of the check.

■ MARTIN, CH. J. When the court below found as a fact that "the whole transaction between the parties was a *frolic and a banter,* the plaintiff not expecting to sell, nor the defendant intending to buy the watch at the sum for which the check was drawn," the conclusion should have been that no contract was ever made by the parties, and the finding should have been that no cause of action existed upon the check to the plaintiff.

The judgment is reversed with costs of this court and of the court below.

The other Justices concurred.

QUESTIONS

1. For Chief Judge Martin the case was easy: the trial court made a factual finding and the judgment was inconsistent with that finding. But how did the trial judge know that this was a "frolic and a banter"?

Comment *c* to Restatement (Second) of Contracts § 18 states: "If one party is deceived and has no reason to know of the joke, the law takes the joker at his word." But, undoubtedly, Holderman testified that the bargain was serious, while Keller insisted that it was all a joke. How is a judge or jury supposed to decide such controversies? What's a poor trier of fact to do?

What facts recited in the opinion suggest that Holderman believed Keller to be serious? What facts suggest that Holderman believed Keller to be jesting? What facts suggest that Holderman had reason to believe that Keller was serious? What facts suggest that Holderman had reason to believe that Keller was only jesting? Are there any additional facts that you can imagine that the trier of fact might have found persuasive?

2. How did the court know that the old silver watch was worth about $15? Is that how much Keller would be willing to pay for it? Is that how much Holderman would be willing to sell it for? Does it matter if there are people in the world who would pay $300 for the watch?

Brown v. Finney

Pennsylvania Supreme Court, 1866.
53 Pa. 373.

[Robert Finney brought an action of assumpsit against William Brown in the Court of Common Pleas of Allegheny County for breach of a contract for the delivery in Cincinnati of 100,000 bushels of coal. Trial was before a jury, which delivered a verdict of $2000 for the plaintiff, Finney. The defendant, Brown, appealed to this court, claiming that the trial judge misled the jury in his instructions on the law that the jury was to apply to the case.]

■ THOMPSON, J. The testimony shows that the plaintiff and defendant accidentally met at a restaurant or refreshment saloon, not on business, but accidentally, to procure refreshment. Several others were present, and the defendant being an extensive coal dealer, the conversation turned to the price of coal, and eventually the price at which it could be delivered per bushel at Cincinnati. The defendant alleged he could deliver it there at the price it was selling at Pittsburgh, at sixteen cents per bushel. The plaintiff,—the witness McKee thought,—bantered him about delivering coal there to him at that price, but the defendant said he could and would. Finney said he would take 100,000 bushels, and called for pen, ink and paper to write a contract. Brown said the barges to be used in transporting the coal were to be returned in good order, reasonable wear and tear excepted, and he must have $10 a day for each after a proper time had elapsed for the plaintiff to unload and return them. He further said the coal must be [paid for in] cash. The plaintiff said, "Certainly," and commenced writing a check, one of the plaintiff's party handing him a stamp. Brown then remarked, "Never mind that, I'll have the papers drawn up tomorrow." The matter proceeded no further then, but on the next day or next but one, the plaintiff with one or two of those who were of his party at the saloon, called on the defendant to consummate the writings, but disputes arising, the contract was never put in writing, and the plaintiff not long thereafter sued on the contract as complete at the first interview, and recovered $2000 damages.

... "Either party," said the learned judge [in his instructions to the jury], "in making a contract, can make it conditional or dependent on being reduced to writing before becoming binding upon him, so that he may see its terms in a definite shape; but this must be a condition or one of the conditions of the contract itself or reservation on his part on entering into it." Here ... a complete contract [is] assumed, and the necessity for a reservation or condition to prevent it being binding as a contract. This assumes the question at issue by requiring reservations and conditions to prevent the contract going into effect, which without them would be complete. But this would not be necessary where the terms of the contract were not all agreed upon. Such reservations or conditions would be out of place then. Whether a contract had been completed in the case in hand was the essential question of the case, and when instructions were given based upon an assumed complete contract the jury were, doubtless, misled. It needs no reservations or provisoes in a case where all the essential terms are not agreed upon but postponed to another time, for the assent of the contracting minds is wanting.... The transaction looks like what McKee thought it was, a bantering proposition by the plaintiff to the defendant, and wanting the intention to contract. There was certainly testimony on this point—the time, place and circumstances tended to show it, and it should have been clearly put to the jury to say whether, under the testimony, there was a contract or not. It is not every loose conversation that is to be turned into a contract, although the parties may seem to agree. A man is not to be snapped up for an unintended proposition made when he has no reason to suppose anybody wants to accept what he proposes. When people meet to do business they are presumed to mean what they propose, and expect to be taken up; but a proposition made and accepted where no expectation of contracting exists, should be carefully weighed with all the circumstances when the question of assent at the time comes to be questioned, as here. We do not intend to intimate any opinion on the merits of this controversy, but for the reasons given we think it ought to go to another jury. We see nothing else in the case which calls for notice or correction.

Judgment reversed, and a *venire de novo* awarded.

QUESTIONS AND NOTES

1. The issue on appeal in this case is the correctness of the trial judge's instructions to the jury. The jury trial system divides the function of the jury to decide questions of fact from the function of the judge to decide matters of law. After the testimony of witnesses and other proof has been presented to the jury, the trial judge frames the factual issues by instructing the jury on the relevant issues of law. The jury is expected to decide the ultimate issues of liability in conformity with the judge's instructions, but there is little direct review of the jury's findings. While the jury is supposed to follow the law, it is left a lot of room in practice to reach what it thinks is a just and sensible result.

Jury instructions also describe a division of function between the trial court and the reviewing appellate court. Trial judges generally accept the jury's findings as binding within broad limits. A trial judge may order judgment notwithstanding the verdict (JNOV) only if the judge believes that no reasonable jury could have found as it did consistent with the legal instructions given. A trial judge, however, may without giving judgment for one party or the other order a new trial in the interests of justice if he believes that the jury verdict is against the weight of the evidence. Appellate courts are even less free to second guess jury factfinding. The judge's instructions are freely reviewable on appeal as questions of law, but the appellate court should not reverse on the facts, unless no substantial evidence supports the jury's verdict. Nonetheless, the reviewing court may reach quite far to find a legal error in the instructions and reverse a questionable result on this ground.

2. Now that the trial judge has a second chance, what instruction should he give in view of the Pennsylvania Supreme Court's decision?

3. Like Holderman, Finney had to prove that he in fact believed and had reason to believe the other party to be serious. What facts recited in the opinion suggest that Finney believed Brown to be serious and what facts suggest that Finney had reason to believe Brown to be serious?

4. Professor Keith Rowley examines the doctrine relating to "promises" made in jest in *You Asked For It You Got It ... Toy Yoda*, 3 NEV. L.J. 526 (2003). He describes the following complaint filed in Florida Circuit Court: "Former Hooters waitress Jodee Berry sued her ex-employer for breaching its promise to award a new Toyota to the winner of an April 2001 sales contest. Berry alleged that her manager, Jared Blair, told the waitresses at the Hooters where she worked at the time that whoever sold the most beer at each participating location during April 2001 would be entered in a drawing, the winner of which would receive a new Toyota. As the contest progressed, Blair allegedly told the waitresses that he did not know whether the winner would receive a Toyota car, truck, or van, but that she would have to pay any registration fees on the vehicle. In early May, Blair informed Berry that she had won the contest. He proceeded to blindfold her and lead her to the restaurant's parking lot. Waiting for her there was not a Toyota car, truck, or van, but a doll of the character Yoda from the Star Wars movies—a 'toy Yoda.' Blair laughed. Berry did not."

Should Berry or Blair have the last laugh?

III. INTERPRETATION OF VAGUE AND INDEFINITE PROMISES

One vital aspect of the arrangement between Best and Southland was: What did the parties intend and what reasonable expectations might have been created by the language they used? There is no question what *words* the parties said to each other; that was admitted. But what was the total meaning of what they said?

Southland was to "lend" plywood to Best, certainly, but did the parties agree that the transfer of the plywood was to go ahead under any and all circumstances?

Was Southland to let Best have the plywood even if Southland unexpectedly got a job for which it needed it itself? Was Southland bound to supply the plywood even if its yard was struck by lightning and its own lumber all burned? Was it to let Best have the lumber even at the sacrifice of a profit from an unexpected opportunity to sell it to someone else? Or was the promise merely to lend the plywood, so long as it was just inventory for which Southland itself had no pressing immediate need?

Questions like this go to the heart of this and most contract problems. It is often difficult to determine what risks have been assumed by each of the parties when they made the deal. The question is begged by the proposition that it is the intent of the parties when they made the contract that governs. Of course, people are free to make agreements, and the law will lend its power to enforce the obligations people voluntarily assume by their contracts. But how do judges determine that intent?

At the outset the interpreter must deal with variations in what is meant by "intent" and "agreement." At one end of the spectrum is the view that an agreement is a shared mental state by two parties. The interpretive search is for indications of the psychological, internal, subjective state of mind that they shared. At the other extreme is the view that an agreement has little to do with the subjective state of mind of the parties. An agreement is an objective, external, observable reality. This perspective emphasizes the extent to which the contract is not only the concern of the parties, but also will be importantly relied on by third parties who will act, change their relations, and expend wealth on the basis of it. Consider the banker approached to lend money to one of the parties to finance performance of the contract. The banker needs to assess the risks and potential costs of the agreement and determine what it means objectively. The banker can't practically inquire into what the parties had in mind; she needs to interpret the contract on the basis of its objective content. In the real world both perspectives will make a claim on the interpreter. It is because the contract reflects the parties' subjective intention that the agreement is considered worthy of the law's enforcing attention. At the same time, the needs of commerce demand that contracts consist of objective and ascertainable behavior that a third person can observe, place in context, and depend upon. In practice, the law sometimes gives prominence to an objective theory of contracts, and at other times it applies a more subjective approach. Often courts and legislatures blend both perspectives and leave it to the interpreter to work the conflict out in a particular case.

For Justice Holmes and a great many other lawyers, the potential discontinuity between a judge's interpretation and the parties' subjective intent is not only inevitable but appropriate:

> I do not suppose that you could prove, for purposes of construction as distinguished from avoidance, an oral declaration or even an agreement that words in a dispositive instrument making sense as they stand should have a different

meaning from the common one: for instance, that the parties to a contract orally agreed that when they wrote five hundred feet it should mean one hundred inches, or that Bunker Hill Monument should signify Old South Church. On the other hand, when you have the security of a local or class custom or habit of speech, it may be presumed that the writer conforms to the usage of his place or class when that is what a normal person in his situation would do....

Oliver Wendell Holmes, Jr., *The Theory of Legal Interpretation*, 12 HARV. L. REV. 417, 420 (1899).

■ JEROME FRANK, J. in *Zell v. American Seating Co.*, 138 F.2d 641 (2d Cir. 1943):

The policy of stern refusal to consider subjective intention, prevalent in the centralized common law courts of that period, later gave way; in the latter part of the 18th and the early part of the 19th century, the recession from that policy went far, and there was much talk of the "meeting of the minds" in the formation of contracts, of giving effect to the actual "will" of the contracting parties. The obstacles to learning that actual intention have, more recently, induced a partial reversion to the older view. Today a court generally restricts its attention to the outward behavior of the parties: the meaning of their acts is not what either party or both parties intended but the meaning which a "reasonable man" puts on those acts; the expression of mutual assent, not the assent itself, is usually the essential element. We now speak of "externality," insisting on judicial consideration of only those manifestations of intention which are public ("open to the scrutiny and knowledge of the community") and not private ("secreted in the heart" of a person). This objective approach is of great value, for a legal system can be more effectively administered if legal rights and obligations ordinarily attach only to overt conduct....

But we should not demand too much of this concept of "objectivity"; like all useful concepts it becomes a thought-muddler if its limitations are disregarded. We can largely rid ourselves of concern with the subjective reactions of the parties; when, however, we test their public behavior by inquiring how it appears to the "reasonable man," we must recognize, unless we wish to fool ourselves, that although one area of subjectivity has been conquered, another remains unsubdued.... We say that "the objective viewpoint of a third person is used." But where do we find that "objective" third person? We ask judges or juries to discover that "objective viewpoint"—through their own subjective processes. Being but human, their beliefs cannot be objectified, in the sense of being standardized. Doubtless, there is some moderate approximation to objectivity, that is, to uniformity of beliefs, among judges—men with substantially similar training—although less than is sometimes supposed. But no one can seriously maintain that such uniformity exists among the multitude of jurymen, men with the greatest conceivable variety of training and background. When juries try cases, objectivity is largely a mirage; most of the objectivity inheres in the words of the "reasonable man" standard which the judges, often futilely, admonish juries to apply to the evidence. Certain aspects of subjectivity common to all men seem to have been successfully eliminated in the field of science through the "relativity theory"—which might better be called the "anti-relativity" or "absolute" theory. But equal success has not attended the anti-relativity or objective theory in the legal field. Perhaps nine-tenths of legal uncertainty is caused by uncertainty as to what courts will find, on conflicting evidence, to be the facts of cases.

Once a basic interpretive stance is established, several other levels of difficulty immediately become apparent.

A.   WORDS ARE AMBIGUOUS

The ambiguity of words, their capacity to express different meanings and their way of taking on differing shades of meaning all constrain a party's (and his lawyer's) capacity to express intentions and expectations unambiguously. Words are slippery tools and are often subject to more than one meaning. It is almost always possible to find an obscurity or ambiguity in the meaning of the most common phrases. Sometimes the variant meanings will seem farfetched, and the suggestion that a phrase has a surprising meaning sounds like a lawyer's pettifogging game designed to let a party slip out of his obligation. But, often there is genuine uncertainty about how to best resolve ambiguities in an agreement. The uncertainty is likely to be particularly acute when an agreement consists of an informal conversation or letters between the parties rather than formal writings drafted by their lawyers. Businesspeople do not negotiate each word as diplomats drafting a treaty. Many contracts outline the deal in rather general terms and do not bother to state the assumptions "everybody knows" or provide a dictionary defining each term used.

Dictionaries may purport to assign and describe the precise meaning of words, but usage often varies from dictionary definitions. Some such deviations may be peculiar to an individual; others reflect group, trade, or community usage not found in standard dictionaries. Moreover dictionaries do not insist that there is a single correct meaning for each word. Justice Holmes poetically described the relationship between words and meanings in *Towne v. Eisner*, 245 U.S. 418, 425 (1918), in concluding that "income" in a revenue act did not necessarily mean the same as "income" in the Sixteenth Amendment: "A word is not a crystal, transparent and unchanged; it is the skin of a living thought and may vary greatly in color and content according to the circumstances and the time in which it is used."

Interpretation may be difficult, but courts are not without resources. The obvious first place to look for meaning is to the words of the contract itself. Some potential meanings will seem obvious, and it is easier to persuade a judge or jury that the contract means what it says, or, conversely, that a far-fetched or silly meaning is not likely to be the correct or attractive one. Nonetheless, there is plenty of room for variant interpretations.

When the words used seem plain, there is an understandable inclination to apply the plain meaning and foreclose lawyers' games designed to persuade that up means down. But words do not generally have a "plain meaning" divorced from the context and circumstances in which they are used. Hence, UCC § 1–201(11) defines contract as "the total legal obligation which results from the parties' agreement as affected by this Act and any other applicable rules of law." And UCC § 1–201(3) defines agreement as "the bargain of the parties in fact as found in their language or by the implication from other circumstances including course of dealing or usage of trade or course of performance...."

Not only are words slippery tools at best, but people (even lawyers) often fail to spell out what to them is "obvious." No matter how long and complex a writing may be, therefore, it inevitably is drafted against a background of unexpressed assumptions by the parties as to what they are doing, what its words mean, and what its consequences might be in the numberless contingencies that might occur.

To identify these special or unstated terms in any given agreement, one must look at its language in the context of the community and the trade within which it was made. What do words like these, actions like these, agreements of this sort connote in *this* community, within *this* business, to persons situated as *these* persons were?

The importance of linguistic context is already familiar to you from your daily life. It will be brought home to you when you take breaks from law school and try to explain to friends and relatives around the family dinner table what you have been doing this year. You are learning a new language and are beginning to give familiar words some very special meanings. The contagion of legal rhetoric will enable you to speak so that no non-lawyer will be able to grasp what you are saying. After you graduate from law school, people will hire you to deal with documents and transactions in which ordinary people are confounded by lawyers' talk. By nurturing its own unique modes of expression the profession creates a market for its services. Outsiders have to hire us to understand what is going on.

Linguistic particularity is presented in starkest form in communications between persons from two countries where different languages are spoken. Around the world, and to a growing extent, business crosses national borders. How does one interpret the meaning of communications between persons who speak different languages, especially when neither of them is speaking in his native tongue? The case that follows illustrates the possibilities. It involves a sales agent in New York, who apparently speaks German as well as English, selling chickens to a Swiss corporation acting as an agent for the former Czechoslovak government. The negotiations occurred in conversations in New York, transatlantic cables, and telephone calls that apparently were in both English and German. Viewed in terms of the subjective intent of the parties, it is very hard to determine what they had in mind in using the word "chicken." Viewed objectively, the interpretive issues are even more puzzling, for it is clear that there are many communities involved in this transaction, and the meaning attached to "chicken" differs in different communities. How does a judge searching for a single viewpoint from which to decide the case choose among the possibilities? Are we searching for the objective meaning of the word as used by chicken sellers in New York, New Jersey, and Chicago, European chicken wholesalers, chicken regulators in the U.S. Department of Agriculture, or cheeky, Czech, chicken chewers from Cheb?

————

Frigaliment Importing Co. v. B.N.S. International Sales Corp.
U.S. District Court, S.D.N.Y., 1960.
190 F.Supp. 116.

■ FRIENDLY, J. The issue is, what is chicken? Plaintiff says "chicken" means a young chicken, suitable for broiling and frying. Defendant says "chicken" means any bird of that genus that meets contract specifications on weight and quality, including what it calls "stewing chicken" and plaintiff pejoratively terms "fowl." Dictionaries give both meanings, as well as some others not relevant here. To support its [definition], plaintiff sends a number of volleys over the net; defendant essays to return them and adds a few serves of its own. Assuming that both parties were acting in good faith, the case nicely illustrates Holmes' remark "that the making of a contract depends not on the agreement of two minds in one intention, but on the agreement of two sets of external signs—not on the parties' having *meant* the same thing but on their having *said* the same thing." *The Path of the Law*. I have concluded that plaintiff has not sustained its burden of persuasion that the contract used "chicken" in the narrower sense.

The action is for breach of the warranty that goods sold shall correspond to the description. Two contracts are in suit. In the first, dated May 2, 1957, defendant, a New York sales corporation, confirmed the sale to plaintiff, a Swiss corporation, of

"US Fresh Frozen Chicken, Grade A, Government Inspected, Eviscerated 2½–3 lbs. and 1½–2 lbs. each all chicken individually wrapped in cryovac, packed in secured fiber cartons or wooden boxes, suitable for export

75,000 lbs. 2½–3 lbs.   @$33.00

25,000 lbs. 1½–2 lbs.   @$36.50

per 100 lbs. FAS New York

scheduled May 10, 1957 pursuant to instructions from Penson & Co., New York."

The second contract, also dated May 2, 1957, was identical save that only 50,000 lbs. of the heavier "chicken" were called for, the price of the smaller birds was $37 per 100 lbs., and shipment was scheduled for May 30. The initial shipment under the first contract was short but the balance was shipped on May 17. When the initial shipment arrived in Switzerland, plaintiff found, on May 28, that the 2½–3 lbs. birds were not young chicken suitable for broiling and frying but stewing chicken or "fowl"; indeed, many of the cartons and bags plainly so indicated. Protests ensued. Nevertheless, shipment under the second contract was made on May 29, the 2½–3 lbs. birds again being stewing chicken. Defendant stopped the transportation of these at Rotterdam.

Since the word "chicken" standing alone is ambiguous, I turn first to see whether the contract itself offers any aid to its interpretation. Plaintiff says the 1½–2 lbs. birds necessarily had to be young chicken since the old birds do not come in that size, hence the 2½–3 lbs. birds must likewise be young. This is unpersuasive—a contract for "apples" of two different sizes could be filled with different kinds of apples even though only one species came in both sizes. Defendant notes that the contract called not simply for chicken but for "US Fresh Frozen Chicken, Grade A, Government Inspected." It says the contract thereby incorporated by reference the Department of Agriculture's regulations, which favor its interpretation; I shall return to this after reviewing plaintiff's other contentions.

The first hinges on an exchange of cablegrams which preceded execution of the formal contracts. The negotiations leading up to the contracts were conducted in New York between defendant's secretary, Ernest R. Bauer, and a Mr. Stovicek, who was in New York for the Czechoslovak government at the World Trade Fair. A few days after meeting Bauer at the fair, Stovicek telephoned and inquired whether defendant would be interested in exporting poultry to Switzerland. Bauer then met with Stovicek, who showed him a cable from plaintiff dated April 26, 1957, announcing that they "are buyer" of 25,000 lbs. of chicken 2½–3 lbs. weight, Cryovac packed, grade A Government inspected, at a price up to 33¢ per pound, for shipment on May 10, to be confirmed by the following morning, and were interested in further offerings. After testing the market for price, Bauer accepted, and Stovicek sent a confirmation that evening. Plaintiff stresses that, although these and subsequent cables between plaintiff and defendant, which laid the basis for the additional quantities under the first and for all of the second contract, were predominantly in German, they used the English word "chicken"; it claims this was done because it understood "chicken" meant young chicken whereas the German word, "Huhn," included both "Brathuhn" (broilers) and "Suppenhuhn" (stewing chicken), and that defendant, whose officers were thoroughly conversant with German, should have realized this. Whatever force this argument might otherwise have is largely drained away by Bauer's testimony that he asked Stovicek what kind of chickens were wanted, received the answer "any kind of chickens," and then, in German, asked whether the cable meant "Huhn" and received an affirmative response. Plaintiff attacks this as contrary to what Bauer testified on his deposition in March, 1959, and also on the ground that Stovicek had no authority to interpret the meaning of the cable. The first contention would be persuasive if sustained by the record, since Bauer was free at the trial from the threat of contradiction by Stovicek as he was not at the time of the deposition; however, review of the deposition does not convince me of the claimed inconsistency. As to the second contention, it may well be that Stovicek lacked authority to commit plaintiff for prices or delivery dates other than those specified in the cable; but plaintiff cannot at the same time rely on its cable to Stovicek as its dictionary to the meaning of the contract and repudiate the interpretation given the dictionary by the man in whose hands it was put. Plaintiff's reliance on the fact that the contract forms contain the words "through the intermediary of:", with the blank not filled as negating agency, is wholly unpersuasive; the purpose of this clause was to permit filling in the name of an intermediary to whom a commission would be payable, not to blot out what had been the fact.

Plaintiff's next contention is that there was a definite trade usage that "chicken" meant "young chicken." Defendant showed that it was only beginning in the poultry trade in 1957, thereby bringing itself within the principle that "when one of the parties is not a member of the trade or other circle, his acceptance of the standard must be made to appear" by proving either that he had actual knowledge of the usage or that the usage is "so generally known in the community that his actual individual knowledge of it may be inferred." Here there was no proof of actual knowledge of the alleged usage; indeed, it is quite plain that defendant's belief was to the contrary. In order to meet the alternative requirement, the law of New York demands a showing that "the usage is of so long continuance, so well established, so notorious, so universal and so reasonable in itself, as that the presumption is violent that the parties contracted with reference to it, and made it a part of their agreement." *Walls v. Bailey* (N.Y.1872).

Plaintiff endeavored to establish such a usage by the testimony of three witnesses and certain other evidence. Strasser, resident buyer in New York for a large chain of Swiss cooperatives, testified that "on chicken I would definitely understand a broiler." However, the force of this testimony was considerably weakened by the fact that in his own transactions the witness, a careful businessman, protected himself by using "broiler" when that was what he wanted and "fowl" when he wished older birds. Indeed, there are some indications, dating back to a remark of Lord Mansfield, *Edie v. East India Co.*, 2 Burr. 1216, 1222 (1761), that no credit should be given "witnesses to usage, who could not adduce instances in verification." 7 Wigmore, Evidence (3d ed. 1940), § 1954. While Wigmore thinks this goes too far, a witness' consistent failure to rely on the alleged usage deprives his opinion testimony of much of its effect. Niesielowski, an officer of one of the companies that had furnished the stewing chicken to defendant, testified that "chicken" meant "the male species of the poultry industry. That could be a broiler, a fryer or a roaster," but not a stewing chicken; however, he also testified that upon receiving defendant's inquiry for "chickens," he asked whether the desire was for "fowl or frying chickens" and, in fact, supplied fowl, although taking the precaution of asking defendant, a day or two after plaintiff's acceptance of the contracts in suit, to change its confirmation of its order from "chickens," as defendant had originally prepared it, to "stewing chickens." Dates, an employee of Urner–Barry Company, which publishes a daily market report on the poultry trade, gave it as his view that the trade meaning of "chicken" was "broilers and fryers." In addition to this opinion testimony, plaintiff relied on the fact that the Urner–Barry service, the Journal of Commerce, and Weinberg Bros. & Co. of Chicago, a large supplier of poultry, published quotations in a manner which, in one way or another, distinguish between "chicken," comprising broilers, fryers and certain other categories, and "fowl," which, Bauer acknowledged, included stewing chickens. This material would be impressive if there were nothing to the contrary. However, there was, as will now be seen.

Defendant's witness Weininger, who operates a chicken eviscerating plant in New Jersey, testified "Chicken is everything except a goose, a duck, and a turkey. Everything is a chicken, but then you have to say, you have to specify which category you want or that you are talking about." Its witness Fox said that in the trade "chicken" would encompass all the various classifications. Sadina, who conducts a food inspection service, testified that he would consider any bird coming within the classes of "chicken" in the Department of Agriculture's regulations to be a chicken. The specifications approved by the General Services Administration include fowl as well as broilers and fryers under the classification "chickens." Statistics of the Institute of American Poultry Industries use the phrases "Young chickens" and "Mature chickens," under the general heading "Total chickens." and the Department of Agriculture's daily and weekly price reports avoid use of the word "chicken" without specification.

Defendant advances several other points which it claims affirmatively support its construction. Primary among these is the regulation of the Department of Agriculture, 7 C.F.R. §§ 70.300–70.370, entitled, "Grading and Inspection of Poultry and Edible Products Thereof." and in particular § 70.301 which recited:

Chickens. The following are the various classes of chickens:

(a) Broiler or fryer * * *

(b) Roaster * * *

(c) Capon * * *

(d) Stag * * *

(e) Hen or stewing chicken or fowl * * *

(f) Cock or old rooster * * *

Defendant argues, as previously noted, that the contract incorporated these regulations by reference. Plaintiff answers that the contract provision related simply to grade and Government inspection and did not incorporate the Government definition of "chicken," and also that the definition in the Regulations is ignored in the trade. However, the latter contention was contradicted by Weininger and Sadina; and there is force in defendant's argument that the contract made the regulations a dictionary, particularly since the reference to Government grading was already in plaintiff's initial cable to Stovicek.

Defendant makes a further argument based on the impossibility of its obtaining broilers and fryers at the 33¢ price offered by plaintiff for the 2½–3 lbs. birds. There is no substantial dispute that, in late April, 1957 the price for 2½–3 lbs. broilers was between 35¢ and 37¢ per pound, and that when defendant entered into the contracts, it was well aware of this and intended to fill them by supplying fowl in these weights. It claims that plaintiff must likewise have known the market since plaintiff had reserved shipping space on April 23, three days before plaintiff's cable to Stovicek, or, at least, that Stovicek was chargeable with such knowledge. It is scarcely an answer to say, as plaintiff does in its brief, that the 33¢ price offered [for] the 2½–3 lbs. "chickens" was closer to the prevailing 35¢ price for broilers than to the 30¢ at which defendant procured fowl. Plaintiff must have expected defendant to make some profit—certainly it could not have expected defendant deliberately to incur a loss.

Finally, defendant relies on conduct by the plaintiff after the first shipment had been received. On May 28 plaintiff sent two cables complaining that the larger birds in the first shipment constituted "fowl." Defendant answered with a cable refusing to recognize plaintiff's objection and announcing "We have today ready for shipment 50,000 lbs. chicken 2½–3 lbs. 25,000 lbs. broilers 1½–2 lbs.," these being the goods procured for shipment under the second contract, and asked immediate answer "whether we are to ship this merchandise to you and whether you will accept the merchandise." After several other cable exchanges, plaintiff replied on May 29 "Confirm again that merchandise is to be shipped since resold by us if not enough pursuant to contract chickens are shipped the missing quantity is to be shipped within ten days stop we resold to our customers pursuant to your contract chickens grade A you have to deliver us said merchandise we again state that we shall make you fully responsible for all resulting costs."[2] Defendant argues that if plaintiff was sincere in thinking it was entitled to young chickens, plaintiff would not have allowed the shipment under the second contract to go forward, since the distinction between broilers and chickens drawn in defendant's cablegram must have made it clear that the larger birds would not be broilers. However, plaintiff answers that the cables show plaintiff was insisting on delivery of young chickens and that defendant shipped old ones at its peril. Defendant's point would be highly relevant on another disputed issue—whether if liability were established, the measure of damages should be the difference in market value of broilers and stewing chicken in New York or the larger difference in Europe, but I cannot give it weight on the issue of interpretation. Defendant points out also that plaintiff proceeded to deliver some of the larger birds in Europe, describing them as "poulets"; defendant argues that it was only when plaintiff's customers complained about this that plaintiff developed the idea that "chicken" meant "young chicken." There is little force in this in view of plaintiff's immediate and consistent protests.

When all the evidence is reviewed, it is clear that defendant believed it could comply with the contracts by delivering stewing chicken in the 2½–3 lbs. size. Defendant's subjective intent would not be significant if this did not coincide with an objective meaning of "chicken." Here it did coincide with one of the dictionary meanings, with the definition in the Department of Agriculture Regulations to which the contract made at least oblique reference, with at least some usage in the trade, with the realities of the market, and with what plaintiff's spokesman had said. Plaintiff asserts it to be equally plain that plaintiff's own subjective intent was to obtain broilers and fryers; the only evidence against this is the material as to market prices and this may not have been sufficiently brought home. In any event it is unnecessary to determine that issue. For plaintiff has the burden of showing that "chicken" was used in the narrower rather than in the broader sense, and this it has not sustained.

This opinion constitutes the Court's findings of fact and conclusions of law. Judgment shall be entered dismissing the complaint with costs.

---

2. These cables were in German; "chicken," "broilers" and, on some occasions, "fowl," were in English.

QUESTIONS AND NOTES

1. List the specific sources of information that Judge Friendly turns to in order to uncover the meaning of "chicken." Which sources does Judge Friendly find persuasive and which unpersuasive? What reasons does he give for his treatment of the various sources? Do you agree with Judge Friendly's assessment? How might you have anticipated Judge Friendly's assessment were you the lawyer telling the story?

2. In concluding that the plaintiff has not sustained its burden of persuasion that the contract used "chicken" in the narrower sense, did Judge Friendly conclude that there is no contract in this case?

3. Since both parties to this litigation were corporations, how can they be said to have "meant" or "intended" anything? Is it actually Bauer and Stovicek's intent that is important? Should the court then be more concerned with whether Bauer is new to the business and not whether B.N.S. "was only beginning in the poultry trade"? Suppose Bauer was new in the trade, but that the sole shareholder, president and director of B.N.S. had been in the business for 30 years. In short, what does a corporation intend apart from what its agents and employees intend?

4. The meaning of the German phrase "*beteiligt werden*" was the $255 million question in *Buettner v. Bertelsmann AG* (Cal. Super. Ct. Sta. Barbara Cty) (Dec. 11, 2003) described below in an excerpt from *Lawyers Weekly USA*:[*]

> Two German entrepreneurs last month were awarded a minimum of 209.3 million Euros (worth $254.6 million as of the Dec. 11 verdict) in a complex lawsuit in which two German businessmen claimed they were cheated out of their equity stake in a European joint venture between Bertelsmann AG and America Online. Jan Henric Buettner, 39, and Andreas von Blottnitz, 38, helped Bertelsmann set up a 1995 joint venture to establish AOL Europe. They claimed that Bertelsmann and its former chief executive, Thomas Middelhoff, promised them partial ownership of the online venture company. When Bertelsmann sold its 50 percent share in the venture to AOL Time Warner in 2000 for $6.75 billion, however, Beuttner and von Blottnitz received nothing. In the early 1990s, Buettner and von Blottnitz were both rising young stars in the emergent European online media market. They founded a consulting firm in 1994, and were recruited by Middelhoff—then head of Bertelsmann's multimedia and corporate development— to help develop the company's new media/Internet strategy. According to their complaint, the plaintiffs had no interest in being employees of Bertelsmann, but agreed to work for Middelhoff in return for a

---

[*] Nora Lockwood Tooher, *Two German Entrepreneurs Win $ 255 Million*, LAWYERS WEEKLY USA (Sept. 22, 2004). Reprinted with permission from *Lawyers* USA. Please visit our website at www.lawyersusaonline.com.

"significant equity position" in the company's Internet operation. Price said that the plaintiffs turned down job prospects with Microsoft and other companies because their agreement with Bertelsmann meant that they would get equity and manage the company's online venture business. Despite repeated requests, the complaint alleges, Middelhoff refused to provide the plaintiffs with what they said was a 49 percent agreed-upon equity interest in Bertelsmann's online media venture company. After Bertelsmann sold its 50 percent interest in AOL Europe, the dispute moved to California, home of the two plaintiffs.

Because of the disagreement over what exactly Bertelsmann promised the plaintiffs, the company's contract with the two men was one of the most critical pieces of evidence in the trial. There was, however, a major catch: The contract was in German. Both sides hired translators to tell jurors exactly what the contract promised the plaintiffs. And both translators told jurors something different. The plaintiffs' translator testified that the phrase *beteiligt werden* in the contract expressed the plaintiffs' request for equity. The expert testified that this interpretation of the words was supported by the fact that it referred to *beteiligt werden* in a *gesellschaft*. The accepted translation of *gesellschaft* is a company.

Not so, said the defense. "The actual contract itself— if you read German, which none of the jurors or the judge did— referred to a specific executive incentive compensation plan," [the defendant's counsel] Murray said. He also said that the defense's translator, a United Nations translator, was more qualified to translate the contract than the plaintiff's expert, a professor of German literature at Stanford University. To counteract the defense translator's testimony, [plaintiff's counsel] Price said he was able to get German businesspeople and Bertelsmann executives to testify that the same phrase used in other documents meant equity. "Jurors found compelling evidence that these words *beteiligt werden* mean equity," Price said. But defense counsel Murray said the debate over the contract wording was simply one example of why the case never should have been tried in the United States in the first place. "Jurors did their best," he said. "But how do you determine who is right and who is wrong about the translation of words when you read nothing of the language yourself?"

B.   NO CONTRACT IS COMPLETE

The institution of contract may be based on unrealistic expectations about human capacity to plan for the future. A substantial criticism of American contract law and practice is that it often fails to recognize its limits and provides inadequate support for the parties to deal with these limits. The assumption seems to be that if the drafters are skilled enough, if they negotiate long enough, if the document is worked over until it discusses every contingency, then all will be well. In fact no contract can ever hope to be complete and to deal comprehensively with every aspect of the transaction. There will always be gaps to be filled in.

C.   INTENTION IS A FICTION

In some cases the problem may lie more in the uncertainty of or conflicts between the parties' intentions, rather than in the imprecision of the words used to express them. Contract rhetoric assumes that there is an intention that lies behind the expression of the agreement by the parties. In reality, people will have no intention regarding a subject that never crossed their conscious minds, and they may have conflicting intentions about other matters within the scope of their "agreement."

D.   OBJECTIVE MANIFESTATION OF ASSENT ALSO IS A FICTION

Contracting parties' intentions are not fully formed much less congruent on all aspects of a transaction. This factual limitation on intention provides a strong reason for insisting that the meaning of a contract depends on the objective manifestations of assent. But assigning objective meaning to an agreement also is likely to be a fiction in which the "reasonable person" ends up strongly resembling the judge or juror who must decide the case. In short, courts are likely to insist that an agreement means what the court thinks it ought to mean. If a society is homogeneous and shares a strong common set of values, there is likely to be a high level of certainty on the objective meaning of external manifestations. If the deal is between strangers, if the deal is novel, or if it concerns matters as to which there is limited social consensus, the objective meaning will be to that extent uncertain. That is the common situation today, as trade and communications tie people all over the world together, and as even national consensus on crucial social assumptions seems more elusive.

E.   TIME WASHES AWAY ALL THINGS

The institution of contract is based on the assumption that a contract is made at one point in time and continues to control the parties thereafter. This assumption leads courts to retrospectively cast meaning on the parties' agreement. As we shall see in Chapter Eight, it also weakens the contract in the face of supervening events that demand reconsideration and modification of the deal. Time and tide wash away meaning and agreement. All contracts contain the element of futurity, but we can only plan for what we can imagine. As time flows, it is likely to bring changes the parties did not foresee or plan for and will change the values and interests that underlie the contract.

F.   MANY CONTRACTS ARE BEST LEFT INCOMPLETE DELIBERATELY

Lawyers must balance their desire for precision and pressures to agree. A lawyer's job is not to kill a deal that a (presumably well-advised) client wants. Nor should the lawyer unnecessarily prolong the process by raising technical drafting concerns and worries about unlikely contingencies. The result is that the contract often papers over disagreement with ambiguity or omission.

Some American lawyers believe that good drafting requires that all contingencies should be specified and provided for as precisely as possible. An appreciation of all knowable risks and careful drafting certainly is to be encouraged, but this approach is over-optimistic in assuming that it is possible to fully specify every contingency. It is not only impractical but also bad economics to attempt to provide for *every* contingency. Why spend all that time and energy worrying about remote contingencies? In any event, even the best lawyer cannot provide with precision for unimagined risks and must depend upon later interpretation by the parties and, if necessary, a court.

Consider, by contrast, the view that observers have attributed to Japanese practice. Accepting the indeterminacy of the future, the Japanese are said to conceive of a contract as establishing a relationship and a commitment mutually to pursue solutions to problems as they arise. Words cannot be made to do what people cannot; the unknowable remains so no matter how detailed the contract. What is written establishes the nature of the relationship, but it must be supplemented with sensible elements of good will to resolve problems when they arise by a process of harmonious accommodation.

What goes on in fact in American contract practice is often more like the Japanese than the American conception of what ought to be. Use of such terms as "interpretation" or "implication" to describe what a court does emphasizes the primary importance of what the court thinks the parties meant. As the search for intention becomes increasingly hypothetical, it becomes indistinguishable from other kinds of rule-making and standard-fixing: a decision not of what the parties actually meant, but of what the parties to a contract like this one *should* mean in the opinion of the court. Inevitably this is apt to boil down in some cases to what the court thinks *it* would have meant in the situation before it.

But why should one expect anything different? A court, like the parties before it, does what it must in interpreting what is written and unwritten in the face of what happened but was not expected. The inevitable limits on cognition and verbal expression must be taken into account in any sensible view of contract as a social tool.

G.   THE LAWYER AS INTERPRETER

A lawyer plays many different roles, and his perspective as an interpreter will depend on his role.

The *counselor* advising a client as to the meaning of an agreement is a very conservative creature. She is on the lookout for any conceivable source of trouble in order that the client may be forewarned. It means relatively little to her that a majority of the State Supreme Court is likely to adopt a favorable view of an ambiguous agreement. As a practical matter, such vindication will come too late to enable the client to avoid disaster. The counselor's job is to keep the client out of trouble.

Similarly, the *drafter's* perspective is basically one of avoidance and caution. By use of all the tools available he must devise a document that is likely to be interpreted to mean what the client wants it to mean (a job complicated by the likely circumstance that the client isn't really sure what it wants in any detail). While a counselor often must advise on the basis of an agreement as it stands, the drafter is in a position to draft himself out of perceived problems. Moreover, the drafter often must deal with a counterpart, the person drafting for the other side who is trying to protect *her* client. These positions are not inevitably hostile. If the deal is sensible and carefully thought out, then a lucid exposition is most likely to be in both sides' interests. The drafter's job can present fascinating creative opportunities. When done well, drafting is not merely a matter of riveting sections of boilerplate into place but of stretching the spare outline of the agreement reached by the parties to cover the body of a coherent working relationship.

The *advocate's* perspective, of course, is very different. She must take the agreement as written, along with the existence of a serious dispute between the parties concerning its operation. Her job is to find persuasive arguments for the client's position and counters for the arguments she anticipates from the other side. She hopes to find previously decided cases that support her arguments. From the advocate's viewpoint, it is almost a complete answer to say that the court has previously determined that her interpretation is correct; after all, that court is her immediate audience.

The cases that you are studying should help you to operate effectively in all of these areas, even though they are all products of litigation. In litigation the question "What is the agreement reached by the parties?" is considered entirely from the perspective of a court assessing the post-formation conduct of parties to a contract. Cases decided from this viewpoint supply the major part of the material on which a lawyer must base his strategy in practically all of the roles that he must play. This is because—in the final analysis—the effective meaning of any contract is what a court will say it is.

H. POSITIVE LAW SOMETIMES DETERMINES MEANING

Beyond what the parties expressly said, beyond what they are deemed to have said by implication, and beyond the community and trade usage context that give meaning to an agreement, a lawyer must also consider the terms that society for its own reasons imposes on the parties to an agreement. Modern contracts are increasingly governed by a complex web of government regulation ranging from such statutes as the Uniform Commercial Code, labor codes, and tax codes, to administrative regulations, rules, and guidelines. Contracts setting the terms of employment of workers, of issuance of securities to capitalize a business, of the sale of products to customers, or of a promotional campaign to encourage sales simply cannot be understood without detailed examination of the host of pertinent statutes, rules, and regulations now on the books.

I. CONSTRUCTING A COHERENT, PERSUASIVE INTERPRETATION

Each of the sources of meaning that we have considered—the express terms of an agreement, the implied terms, custom and usage, and the terms imposed by the law through statute or regulation—contributes to the definition of the "total legal obligation which results from the parties' agreement." It is that total meaning which a lawyer must always seek.

To an unjustifiable extent the law has treated the process of seeking the total meaning as if it were composed of a set of watertight compartments: defining the words, interpreting the meaning of groups of words based on the context, implying and constructing meanings that the parties have not made explicit, testing the terms used against trade usage, looking to custom in the community, ferreting out special meanings the parties may have established in the course of their dealings, imposing meaning on the agreement for social purposes, and so on. In fact, one can do all of these things to the same contract term at the same time—and one often does so. One cannot consider interpretation of an element of the agreement, such as its express terms, in isolation from consideration of all of the other elements. The agreement must be seen as a coherent entity composed of all of these.

The maddening thing about this complex process is that one is likely to be led to very different results depending on which element of the agreement (the words, context, custom, social needs, etc.) one permits to be dominant in the interpretive process. Nothing in the literature will help the lawyer or judge very much in choosing among competing modes of interpretation. In a particular situation some approaches will make sense while others will seem silly. One must wrestle with those that make sense and hope that one's feel for the situation is similar to that of the judge who will decide the case.

———

ARTHUR L. CORBIN, *OFFER AND ACCEPTANCE, AND SOME OF THE RESULTING LEGAL RELATIONS,* 26 YALE L.J. 169 (1917). AS REVISED BY THE AUTHOR FOR PUBLICATION IN SELECTED READINGS ON THE LAW OF CONTRACTS 170, 197 (1931):

Parties are bound by the reasonable meaning of what they said and not by what they thought. ... It may be said that the purpose of the rule is to carry out the intentions of the parties in the great majority of cases; but it seems better to say that its purpose is to secure the fulfillment of the promisee's reasonable expectations as induced by the promisor's act. In the law of contract as in the law of tort, men are expected to live up to the standard of the reasonably prudent man. If the expressions of the parties are capable of two different and equally reasonable interpretations, and neither one negligently misled the other, there is no contract. The same is true if both are equally negligent. If they integrate their agreement in specific words, they are bound in accordance with the meaning given to those words by the court.

The legal relations consequent upon offer and acceptance are not wholly dependent, even upon the reasonable meaning of the words and acts of the parties. The law determines these relations in the light of subsequent circumstances, these often being totally unforeseen by the parties. In such cases it is sometimes said that the law will create that relation which the parties would have intended had they foreseen. The fact is, however, that the decision will depend upon the notions of the court as to policy, welfare, justice, right and wrong, such notions often being inarticulate and subconscious.

———

GLANVILLE WILLIAMS, *LANGUAGE AND THE LAW*, 61 L.Q. REV. 71, 401 (1945):

It has already been remarked that the Courts will generally enforce consequences logically implied in the language of contracts, wills, statutes, and other legal documents and transactions. The point now to be noticed is that the legal doctrine of implied terms goes much farther than this. Judges are accustomed to read into documents and transactions many terms that are not logically implied in them. As an academic matter, non-logical implications may be classified into three kinds: (i) of terms that the parties (the plural shall throughout include the singular) probably had in mind but did not trouble to express; (ii) of terms that the parties, whether or not they actually had them in mind would probably have expressed if the question had been brought to their attention; and (iii) of terms that the parties, whether or not they had them in mind or would have expressed them if they had foreseen the difficulty, are implied by the Court because of the Court's view of fairness or policy or in consequence of rules of law. Of these three kinds of non-logical implications (i) is an effort to arrive at actual intention; (ii) is an effort to arrive at hypothetical or conditional intention—the intention that the parties would have had if they had foreseen the difficulty; (iii) is not concerned with the intention of the parties except to the extent that the term implied by the Court may be excluded by an expression of positive intention to the contrary.

———

Berg v. Hudesman
Washington Supreme Court, 1990.
115 Wash.2d 657, 801 P.2d 222.

■ BRACHTENBACH, J. This suit concerns a 99–year ground lease. The main issue is the meaning of the rent payment clause. The trial court granted summary judgment to the landlord, held that the lease was not ambiguous, determined the meaning of the rental clause, and awarded back rent to the landlord based upon the trial court's interpretation of the rental clause. By unpublished opinion, the Court of Appeals affirmed in the main but remanded for determination of certain facts which existed at the inception of the lease. We reverse the trial court, modify the Court of Appeals opinion, and remand for trial.

The ground lease, executed in 1959, terminates in 2058. The ground tenant, defendant, removed a residence from the property, as allowed by the lease agreement, and constructed a commercial building on the land. This commercial building was originally leased to Safeway Stores for 15 years. Upon Safeway's removal, the tenant converted the building to a small shopping center which was subleased to a number of tenants during the period at issue.

In August 1987, the landlord brought the present suit, contending that for several years the defendant incorrectly calculated the rent due the landlord under the ground lease.

As will be seen, the rent due the landlord under the ground lease is calculated with respect to what constitutes "gross rentals" from the subtenants and what may be deducted therefrom to ascertain "net rentals." "Net rentals" is the amount to which a formula set out in the ground lease applies for division of income between the landlord and the tenant, the parties in this suit.

The lease contains the following provision:

(3) Rental. The rental shall be Five Thousand and No/100 Dollars ($5,000.00) per year, payable in advance on or before the 19th day of October, 1959, of each year during the term of this lease. Receipt of Five Thousand and No/100 Dollars ($5,000.00) paid as rental for the first year of said term is hereby acknowledged. It is expressly provided that on the first of the month in which the annual rent falls due, Lessee, prior to paying the annual rental of $5,000.00, each year during the term hereof, commencing with the fifteenth (15) year, shall refer to the then current United States Consumer Price Index (all items) as compiled by the Bureau of Labor Statistics of the United States Department of Labor (1947–1949 = 100). If such index reading at date hereof reflects an increase or decrease in the purchasing power of the United States Dollar equal to five percent (5%) or more, the minimum rent payment hereunder shall be proportionately increased or decreased to the end that rent payments are annually adjusted to maintain the same purchasing power they represented at date hereof, provided that the total increase or decrease above or below the original rental of $5,000.00 per year shall in no event exceed three percent (3%) multiplied by the number of years of said term which shall have expired. In the event the said Consumer Price Index is modified or replaced, the comparable effective cost of living index published by the United States Department of Labor or other Federal agency shall be employed using reasonable and accepted conversion factors as necessary.

In addition to the above mentioned rental, Lessee shall pay ten (10%) per cent of net rentals received after the third year of said term from tenants of any buildings constructed on said property. If Lessee uses or enters into any agreement for the use of said property or any portion thereof for parking or thoroughfare purposes for the benefit of any business conducted in a building or buildings on other property, a portion of any such building or buildings shall be assumed to be on the above described property for the purpose of computing rental hereto. Said portion shall be in the same proportion as the area of the above described property used for such purposes bears to the total area used for building, parking and thoroughfare purposes for the benefit of such business. Net rentals shall be defined as gross rentals from the actual tenants, less payments made for taxes and assessments, insurance on said premises, management fees not to exceed five (5%) per cent of gross rentals and real estate commissions not to exceed five (5%) per cent of the gross rentals for the first ten (10) years and two-and-a-half (2½%) per cent of the gross rentals thereafter, and depreciation actually taken for income tax purposes.

Commencing with the sixteenth (16) year after completion of the first building constructed on said property, the rental shall be as computed above, or it shall be fifty (50%) per cent of net rentals, whichever is greater.

Lessor shall have the right each year for a period of ten (10) consecutive working days selected by them to audit those books of Lessee pertaining to rentals received by Lessee from such tenants.

In broad terms, the question posed is the interpretation of the subject lease....

It is deceptively simple to state the purpose of a court in interpreting a contract. "The cardinal rule with which all interpretation begins is that its purpose is to ascertain the intention of the parties." Corbin, *The Interpretation of Words and the Parol Evidence Rule*, 50 Cornell L.Q. 161, 162 (1965); 4 S. Williston, Contracts § 601, at 306 (3d ed. 1961).

As would be expected, problems of contract interpretation have long been a source of judicial opinion. The subject has produced thousands of cases, numerous texts and countless commentaries. A study of these materials, including Washington cases, leads us to concur with the observation: "[T]he rules produced by accumulated decisions as to how such discovery [of the parties' intention] shall be conducted often overlap and sometimes produce hindrance rather than help, while reconciliation of all cases is a task neither possible nor worth the effort * * *." *Nicoll v. Pittsvein Coal Co.*, 269 F. 968, 971 (2d Cir.1920).

In approaching contract interpretation, every court should heed the strong words of Corbin:

[I]t can hardly be insisted on too often or too vigorously that language at its best is always a defective and uncertain instrument, that words do not define themselves, that terms and sentences in a contract, a deed, or a will do not apply themselves to external objects and performances, that the meaning of such terms and sentences consists of the ideas that they induce in the mind of some individual person who uses or hears or reads them, and that seldom in a litigated case do the words of a contract convey one identical meaning to the two contracting parties or to third persons.

3 A. Corbin, Contracts § 536 (1960). Holmes was more poetic:

A word is not a crystal, transparent and unchanged; it is the skin of a living thought and may vary greatly in color and content according to the circumstances and the time in which it is used.

A second major point applicable to contract interpretation is that the various principles of interpretation should not be applied as absolutes. They "are to be taken as suggestive working rules only * * *. They will be harmful if they are taken as dogmatic directions that must be followed, or if they mislead us into thinking that language has only one meaning, the one absolutely correct." Various efforts have been made to compile a set of rules of contract interpretation. Patterson, *The Interpretation and Construction of Contracts*, 64 Colum.L.Rev. 833, 852 (1964) (listing ten "standard maxims" of contract interpretation); Restatement (Second) of Contracts § 202 (1981) (listing rules in aid of interpretation). Each set of rules is subject to Corbin's caution. "There is some doubt whether they [maxims of interpretation] have reliable guidance value for judges, or are merely justifications for decisions arrived at on other grounds, which may or may not be revealed in the opinion." Patterson, 64 Colum.L.Rev. at 852.

With the above observations in mind we turn to the central issue of contract interpretation in this case. There remains to be discussed the interpretation issue which presents the greatest difficulty. If the disputed language is written, will the proponent of one meaning be permitted to aid his cause by verbal testimony? If so, what is the permissible range such testimony can take? On these important details the Washington cases are in confusion.

There are cases in which the court examined the circumstances surrounding the execution of a writing as an aid to its interpretation and sustained the admissibility of the pertinent evidence even though the writing might on its face be unambiguous. The position taken in these cases is the one endorsed by Professors Corbin and Williston and by the Restatement of Contracts. It is the only approach which can consistently yield interpretations likely to coincide with the meanings the parties contemplated.

There are other cases in which the court indicated that it will not look beyond the four corners of a contract writing unless what appears within those four corners is ambiguous. The reason is variously stated as an interpretation principle, or as an application of the parol evidence rule. Neither reason is persuasive....

Despite the accuracy of the conclusion that seldom will any word or phrase carry only a single meaning which is readily discernible by any reader, this court on occasion has embraced the "plain meaning rule." The Plain Meaning Rule states that if a writing, or the term in question, appears to be plain and unambiguous on its face, its meaning must be determined from the four corners of the instrument without resort to extrinsic evidence of any nature. In following this rule, this court has held that only if a contract is ambiguous on its face will the court look to evidence of the parties' intent as shown by the contract as a whole, its subject matter and objective, the circumstances of its making, the subsequent conduct of the parties, and the reasonableness of their interpretations.

The instant case presents a clear opportunity for this court to resolve the long-standing confusion engendered by inconsistent holdings in this area.

We now hold that extrinsic evidence is admissible as to the entire circumstances under which the contract was made, as an aid in ascertaining the parties' intent. We adopt the Restatement (Second) of Contracts §§ 212, 214(c) (1981). Section 212 provides:

(1) The interpretation of an integrated agreement is directed to the meaning of the terms of the writing or writings in the light of the circumstances, in accordance with the rules stated in this Chapter.

(2) A question of interpretation of an integrated agreement is to be determined by the trier of fact if it depends on the credibility of extrinsic evidence or on a choice among reasonable inferences to be drawn from extrinsic evidence. Otherwise a question of interpretation of an integrated agreement is to be determined as a question of law.

As explained in comment *b* to this section:

It is sometimes said that extrinsic evidence cannot change the plain meaning of a writing, but meaning can almost never be plain except in a context. Accordingly, the rule stated in Subsection (1) is not limited to cases where it is determined that the language used is ambiguous. Any determination of meaning or ambiguity should only be made in the light of the relevant evidence of the situation and relations of the parties, the subject matter of the transaction, preliminary negotiations and statements made therein, usages of trade, and the course of dealing between the parties.

This court's line of cases which includes *Stender v. Twin City Foods, Inc.,* [*infra*], is in line with the Restatement and is in line with ascertaining the parties' actual intent.

In discerning the parties' intent, subsequent conduct of the contracting parties may be of aid, and the reasonableness of the parties' respective interpretations may also be a factor in interpreting a written contract.

We thus reject the theory that ambiguity in the meaning of contract language must exist before evidence of the surrounding circumstances is admissible. Cases to the contrary are overruled.

Another issue involving interpretation which may be relevant in this case concerns the possibility that language used in the lease is technical or constitutes terms of art. If so, the general rule is that such language is to be given its technical meaning when used in a transaction within its technical field....

... In light of our adoption of the context rule for interpreting written contracts in accord with the parties' intent, the summary judgment in favor of the landlord must be reversed and this matter must be remanded for trial. As noted, the trial court refused to consider evidence as to the circumstances surrounding the contract under the now disapproved "plain meaning rule." As explained hereafter, there are material questions of fact remaining as to the intent of the contracting parties and interpretation of the ground lease.

The lease in this case well illustrates why extrinsic evidence is necessary to assist the court in interpreting words and applying them to the actual events in order to ascertain and implement the intentions of the parties.

The lease provides for a possible alternative computation of rent commencing with the 16th year. The record discloses that the original tenant's sublease, the Safeway Stores lease, was for 15 years. The parties had no dispute as to rent calculation during those 15 years. The Safeway lease is relevant because the rental clause calls for a different formula "[c]ommencing with the sixteenth (16) year after completion of the first building constructed on said property." That lease (which constitutes extrinsic evidence) is not in the record and was not considered by the trial court. How do the terms of the original lease bear on the meaning and purpose of the different rent formula in the ground lease which comes into operation at the end of that sublease?

"Gross rentals" is the starting point for determining the division between the landlord and the tenant, but the term "gross rentals" is not defined. What did the parties intend to be the meaning of that phrase? The trial court held the term included "all amounts received from subtenants of the shopping center." Under this interpretation the ground tenant is out of pocket 50 percent of the reimbursement from the subtenants. For example, if the ground tenant pays out $10,000 for common area maintenance and is reimbursed that $10,000 by a subtenant, he is then whole, but under the trial court's holding, he must pay $5,000 to the landlord.

In actual operation, according to the record, in 1 year actual common maintenance expenses paid by the ground tenant were $28,952.78. By reimbursement from subtenants the ground tenant is made whole, i.e., he neither loses nor gains. But under the landlord's interpretation, adopted by the trial court, the tenant must (1) include $28,952.78 in gross rents, and (2) cannot deduct those actual expenses to calculate net rentals against which the 50 percent rental formula is applied. Therefore, the tenant must pay $14,476.39 to the landlord.

Given this result, if the trial court determines the language is subject to two possible constructions, it should apply the following principle: When a provision is subject to two possible constructions, one of which would make the contract unreasonable and imprudent and the other of which would make it reasonable and just, we will adopt the latter interpretation.

In contrast to the trial court's interpretation of the lease, the Court of Appeals held that if such expenses had been paid directly by a subtenant, they were not gross rentals. The Court of Appeals held that so long as reimbursements were of the exact same nature as those paid by the original subtenants they were not gross rentals.

Apparently the Court of Appeals divined the intent of the parties for 99 years from the terms of the first 15–year sublease, but modified that by excluding direct payments by subtenants to the extent that the landlord would have to include such direct payments within his income for federal income tax purposes. We find no support in the record that the treatment of a money item was to be governed by federal income tax law. We note that when income tax law was relevant, it was expressly so provided, e.g., the deduction for depreciation in arriving at "net rental" referred to "depreciation actually taken for income tax purposes." (As an aside, we note that even that specificity could create a problem of interpretation if the tax deduction allowed by Internal Revenue Service were different from that actually taken.)

Adding to the problem of interpretation of the parties' lease, the language "gross rentals from actual tenants" requires reference to rental income from the subtenants. The only sublease in the record provides for the subtenant to pay a proportionate share of specified expenses, including operating expenses and expenses of maintaining common areas of the shopping center. However, the sublease specifically states that such proportionate share is "in addition to the rent." What is the effect of the subleases' characterization of income?

Further questions remain. Under the lease definition of "net rentals," the ground tenant could deduct from the proportionate share paid by subtenants those amounts representing taxes and insurance, but not amounts paid out of pocket for common area maintenance and operation. The amount reimbursed to the ground tenant is significant, e.g., $28,952.78 in the rent year ending in October 1987. The trial court even included within gross rentals interest paid to the ground tenant on funds held by the property manager before rent was due the landlord. These facts seem to require application of the principle noted above that the court should take into account "the reasonableness of respective interpretations advocated by the parties." *Stender v. Twin City Foods, Inc.*, 82 Wash.2d 250, 254 (1973).

Continuing the interpretation confusion is the fact that the lease provides that its term shall be 99 years. Paragraph 3 provides: "The rental shall be Five Thousand and No/100 Dollars ($5,000.00) per year * * * of each year during the term of this lease." The lease later describes the $5,000 as "minimum rent payment hereunder" with an adjustment consistent with the Consumer Price Index.

The lease goes on to provide that "[i]n addition to the above mentioned rental," there shall be paid a percentage of net rent after the third year. Thus, from the third year through the 15th year, it is clear that the $5,000 is paid in addition to the specified percentage of net rentals. The problem arises from the language applicable to the 16th year and subsequent years. It provides that the rental shall be "as computed above" (i.e., the adjusted $5,000 plus 10 percent of net rentals) or "it shall be fifty (50%) per cent of net rentals, whichever is greater." The obvious question is whether the minimum rent is in addition to the 50 percent or is no longer to be considered. Preceding the 50 percent language the lease provides in two separate paragraphs that the $5,000, as adjusted, shall be paid "each year during the term hereof." The lease defines the "term" as 99 years. If the rent is to be calculated under the phrase "or it shall be fifty (50%) per cent of net rentals," without the additional minimum rent, there is a conflict with the provision that the $5,000, as adjusted, shall be paid every year during the 99–year term.

Avoidance of this conflict presents another problem, however. If $5,000 is to be paid every year during the lease term, in addition to a percentage of net rentals, then the language applicable to the 16th year and thereafter seems to make no sense. That is, $5,000 (as adjusted) plus 10 percent of net rentals would be compared to $5,000 (as adjusted) plus 50 percent of net rentals.

Another significant question of intent and meaning arises from the listing of permissible deductions from gross rentals to arrive at net rentals. This question exists even under the landlord's contention that the only deductions from gross rentals are those defined in the lease. The question comes from the authorization to deduct "real estate commissions not to exceed five (5%) per cent of the gross rentals for the first ten (10) years and two-and-a-half (2½%) per cent of the gross rentals thereafter." The landlord contends that the limitation for deductible real estate commissions refers to the years of the master lease. That is, during the first 10 years of the 99–year term, the ground tenant can deduct up to 5 percent of the gross rentals for real estate commissions and only 2½ percent for the remaining 89 years. The ground tenant argues that this limitation refers to the length of the terms of the subleases. Thus, if, in the 20th year of the master lease, there was negotiated a 15–year sublease, the ground tenant could deduct up to 5 percent of the gross rent for real estate commissions from that particular lease for 10 years and up to 2½ percent for the remaining 5 years. Again, the differences in the respective contentions are significant. In the lease year ending in October 1986, the ground tenant paid and deducted real estate commissions of $30,141; the landlord's interpretation allowed only $5,067.78.

A major point of dispute is how to arrive at "net rentals" for the 50/50 percent division after the 15th year. Stated again, the lease provides that at that time: "[T]he rental shall be as computed above, or it shall be fifty (50%) per cent of net rentals, whichever is greater." The phrase "as computed above" can only refer to the preceding paragraph which calls for the minimum $5,000, as adjusted, plus 10 percent of the net rentals. "Net rentals" is defined as "gross rentals [undefined] from the actual tenants, less payments made for taxes and assessments, insurance on said premises, management fees not to exceed five (5%) per cent of gross rentals and real estate commissions * * * [as above described], and depreciation actually taken for income tax purposes."

The question is whether the phrase "net rentals" to which the 50 percent applies means the same as is defined in the preceding paragraph and particularly whether the deductions from gross rentals are limited to those authorized in arriving at the sum to which the "10 percent of net rentals" is applied. What the parties intended is not clear. When calculating the sum to which the 10 percent applies, after the 15th year, reference is made to the methodology of the preceding paragraph. The 50 percent calculation is preceded by the word "or" and "net rentals" is not referenced to the preceding paragraph as it is in the first part of the sentence. The ground tenant argues that the change from a $5,000 adjusted minimum plus 10 percent of the defined net rentals to 50 percent of undefined net rentals necessarily means that the parties intended a different formula to arrive at a 50/50 percent division of net rentals. He supports his position with the fact that this change in formula coincided with the termination of the known term of the 15–year lease of the first subtenant, that the ground tenant's improvements represent two-thirds of the assessed value of the land and improvements, and that the interpretation and intent he advances is that commonly understood by those operating within the realm of long-term ground leases. This latter point is supported by affidavits from persons with knowledge of such standards.

From accountings in the record, the tenant constructs a model of net incomes to each party under the landlord's theory. In his worst scenario the landlord in 1 year nets $63,280 and the tenant $1,160. In the best year for the tenant, his figures show $80,108 to the landlord and $59,106 to the tenant. The tenant contends that over a 5–year period the average net return is 77 percent to the landlord and 23 percent to the tenant. By setting forth the tenant's contentions on this point we do not mean to imply that they are correct or factually established. What the illustrations do raise is the initial question whether the parties in fact did intend such results. If they did so intend, so be it. However, if it is determined that was not their intent, then the court must determine a more reasonable interpretation from all the circumstances.

In conclusion, it is apparent from our analysis of the contract language that there are certain ambiguities appearing on the face of the lease instrument. Lest there be any doubt as to our holding, we expressly state that we are not implicitly applying the "plain meaning rule." Whether or not ambiguity is apparent from the face of a contract, evidence of the circumstances of the making of the contract is admissible. We reject the plain meaning rule and expressly adopt the context rule as the applicable rule for ascertaining the parties' intent and interpreting written contracts.

The trial court is reversed and the matter remanded for proceedings consistent with this opinion.

QUESTIONS AND NOTES

1. This case involves the interpretation of the rent clause in a 99-year lease. Those making an agreement with a term greatly exceeding their life expectancies may provide for future contingencies as best they can, but their ability to do so inevitably will be limited. In this case the lease fixes a base rent ($5,000) that is to increase after 15 years to reflect changes in the Consumer Price Index, reflecting inflation. In addition, the tenant is to pay 10% of "net rentals" it receives from those to whom it sublets the property. It seems safe to assume that this percentage rent was larger than the base rent, certainly during the 15-year term when the property was leased to a supermarket. Thirty years later the parties find themselves in a dispute over the meaning of this clause. To what sources might the trial court turn on retrial to find out what the clause means? How available is each kind of evidence likely to be after more than 30 years?

2. What is wrong with this rent clause that creates the need for interpretation? Sometimes interpretation is needed because the parties failed to deal with a situation. Interpretation fills in gaps. Sometimes interpretation is needed because the parties did not express themselves clearly and it is necessary to figure out what the words mean. It may be that they made a typographical or grammatical mistake that interferes with understanding. We all use familiar words in unclear or incorrect ways and only realize the problem when someone points out the obscurity or when a situation arises that demands we think more precisely about the terms used. Some people may think they speak with perfect precision, but few approach this goal. Indeed, for most purposes it wouldn't be worth the time and effort to sharpen each statement until it is as precise as possible. Instead, we interject "You know what I mean?" in every other sentence and move ahead. Such attempts at precision are likely to be futile in any event; in the real world we often only appreciate the problems *after* they arise, not by anticipation.

Other times interpretation is necessary because the parties each think the contract term has an unambiguous meaning, but they differ on what that meaning is. In this case the claim might be that the terms defining gross rent and net rent are ambiguous and might mean any one of several things, or the claim might be that the contract defines the terms in inconsistent ways in different parts of the document, or it might be that the narrow meaning of the words used produces a nonsensical result as is shown by the parties' practices for more than 30 years. Finally, there apparently were some judges in Washington, at least until this decision, who believed that words and sentences have a single plain meaning and that the job of the judge is to determine and apply the words on the page without consideration of any confusing context.

3. Who drafted this troublesome clause? In a portion of this opinion omitted here, the court states that the lease was drafted by the landlord's attorney and re-cites the ancient canon that ambiguous contract terms are to be interpreted against the party who drafted them. This idea is sometimes referred to by the Latin term *contra proferendum.* That principle sounds sensible enough, but in this case both sides were represented by counsel in a large transaction, and the dispute focuses on the central term of the agreement, a rent clause, that both sides presumably focused on and negotiated. Weren't the tenant and his lawyer just as responsible for getting the rent term right as the landlord? Didn't these clients pay these lawyers to draft them a lease? If the lawyers draft an inadequate rent term, shouldn't they be liable for their clients' losses? After all, if you hire a surgeon to remove your appendix and she doesn't do it correctly, you may have a claim for malpractice.

4. In *Hearst Communications, Inc. v. Seattle Times Co.*, 154 Wash.2d 493 (2005), the Washington Supreme Court acknowledged that notwithstanding *Berg*'s empha-sis on context, including relevant extrinsic evidence, Washington continued to adhere to the objective theory of contract: The goal of the interpretive process is "to determine the parties' intent by focusing on the objective manifestations in the agreement, rather than on the unexpressed subjective intent of the parties." *Id.* at 503. Can you reconcile the objective theory of contract with *Berg*'s methodology for contract interpretation?

CHAPTER 2

REMEDIES: HOW THE LAW ENFORCES PROMISES

How society enforces a promise is intimately related to *why* promises are enforced. Through the complexities of contract enforcement runs a simple principle: The basic source of contract obligations is the undertaking of the promisor to the promisee. When the promisee's expectation is disappointed, its remedy is based on the value of the promised performance to the promisee. As Oliver Wendell Holmes, Jr., put it in THE COMMON LAW 234–37 (Howe ed., 1963):

> The only universal consequence of a legally binding promise is that the law makes the promisor pay damages if the promised event does not come to pass. In every case it leaves him free from interference until the time for fulfillment has gone by, and therefore free to break his contract if he chooses.... When a man commits a tort, he incurs, by force of the law, a liability to damages, measured by certain rules. When a man makes a contract, he incurs, by force of the law, a liability to damages, unless a certain promised event comes to pass. But, unlike the case of torts, as the contract is by mutual consent, the parties themselves, expressly or by implication, fix the rule by which the damages are to be measured. The old law seems to have regarded it as technically in the election of the promisor to perform or to pay damages. It is true that, as people when contracting contemplate performance, not breach, they commonly say little or nothing as to what shall happen in the latter event, and the common rules have been worked out by common sense, which has established what the parties probably would have said if they had spoken about the matter....

If promise-enforcement stemmed from a high value on the moral quality of keeping one's word, those who break their promises would be seen as morally deficient and deserving punishment. Breach of contract might be treated as a crime and subject to heavy afflictive sanctions. At the very least, an emphasis on promise-keeping might lead to a set of remedies which would force people to keep their promises and in which court orders to a breaching party to perform would play a large role. What more obvious and accurate reflection of this moral imperative would there be than for the judges in *Best v. Southland* to order Southland to deliver the plywood to Best?

The law, however, does not treat contract breach as a moral fault or a crime or an occasion for punitive damages, even when the harm is clear and the failure to perform deliberate. Why does the law attach no great stigma to those who fail to keep their promises? The social values underlying this attitude are not hard to find.

Modern capitalist society places a high value on producing material goods and facilitating profitable market exchange. Business planning, the rational allocation of resources, and the extension of credit all depend on contracting in risky situations. Because it is desirable that people contract, it is important that the law not erect discouragingly high barriers that would make it too hard to get out of contracts that turn sour. The material plenty of modern life is said to depend on cheap contract.

These assumptions can be challenged on many levels. Some may doubt whether the heavy emphasis on material plenty is socially healthy. Others may wonder why we should encourage economic activity by those who will only commit themselves if assured that they can bug out if things don't work to their liking. Others question whether the marginal gain from such economic activity offsets the great loss and dislocation from disappointed contract expectations caused by letting promisors breach without penalty. Such issues are worthy of extended discussion, but they cannot be resolved definitively in this course. See Seana V. Shiffrin, *The Divergence of Contract and Promise*, 120 HARV. L. REV. 708 (2007).

In any event, American law generally does not make people perform their promises, but instead awards money damages as a substitute for the promised performance. None of the judges in *Best v. Southland* considers ordering Southland to deliver the plywood to Best. Instead, Best seeks a sum of money that will compensate it for the loss of that promised performance. Very soon you will become aware that money damages often are an imperfect substitute for performance. A general characteristic of contract law is that it leaves disappointed parties inadequately compensated for their losses when the other side fails to perform. One source of this inadequacy is that the rules governing contract damages fail to recognize or, by making proof difficult, severely limit the disappointed party's ability to recover many actual losses. Another important limit on the usefulness of giving damages as a substitute for performance is the uncertainty and other costs of collecting damages.

A prevailing plaintiff is not guaranteed payment of court-assessed damages. If the defendant does not voluntarily pay a court judgment, the plaintiff (now a "judgment creditor") may cause the sheriff to levy upon and seize the defendant's property, which the sheriff will then sell, subject to any prior liens, paying the plaintiff only after deducting his own fees out of the proceeds. But the judgment debtor may have no property to seize in the jurisdiction, or the property he has may be exempt from execution under the law. In many cases, a judgment amounts to no more than a hunting license, but the rules of the hunt are limiting, there is often little game in the forest, and there are likely to be other hunters after the same quarry. The net result is that often even after a full and final adjudication of a breach of a contractual promise, there will be no *effective* legal remedy. Nor is the judgment, even if collected, likely to fully compensate the injured party for the out-of-pocket expenses of hiring an attorney or for the market interest lost on the money paid late. In short, the law is surprisingly tender to contract breakers.

Remedies awarded for breach of promise primarily vindicate narrow economic interests. Compensation usually is limited to out-of-pocket and market losses. Why should nonviolent larceny be punished, but those who breach faith by failing to perform their promises only pay economic damages? Penal sanctions are not reserved only for shocking or depraved behavior. Traffic regulations are enforced by fines and incarceration, as well as the generous damage rules of tort law. What value choices justify treating these rules as subject to such heavy sanctions but being so tender to promise breakers?

The standard approach to contract remedies tends to treat all kinds of promises alike. This produces an analysis that makes sense for promises strongly grounded in purely economic calculations (isolated sales transactions are the model) but unsatisfying for contracts that have strong non-economic dimensions. The law does recognize non-economic injuries in limited cases when it finds that the parties contemplated mental distress as a foreseeable consequence of breach. Mental suffering damages have been applied to funeral directors who breach the funeral contract by dumping the body unceremonially on the floor or mixing the loved one's ashes with those of unknown persons. In general, however, this approach is rarely and narrowly applied. Many of the cases that are likely to be most troubling regarding contract remedies involve relationships with duration, reliance by parties on the continued performance of the promise, or strong emotional elements that are crucial to the motivation of the agreement. Yet there seems to be little inclination to follow a general principle that contract law should consider such elements in every case.

This Chapter repeatedly points out the weaknesses of contract remedies and how frequently disappointed contract makers are undercompensated for their losses by contract law. In the next Chapter, we will examine how the law tries to make up for these weaknesses and reaches out for more adequate remedies. In the end, you are likely to remain somewhat disappointed. When it is said that someone has a legal right, that statement in effect is a prediction that a court will award a remedy. In general, people who feel the other side has not performed a contract want what is coming to them, not just an impressive piece of paper proclaiming that they are right. If there is no effective remedy for its violation, a legal right remains, at least to lawyers and clients, a rather abstract value.

At the same time, do not fall too soon into the lawyer's tendency of identifying all remedies with court remedies. The law reflects deep social values that have their own strong sanctioning power. By telling people what is right and wrong, the law leads most people to do the right thing. Rebecca Stone, *Contracts from the Internal Point of View*, 117 COLUM. L. REV. ___ (2017). It is less the fear of damages than the commitment to social values that leads people to honor their obligations. Our behavior is influenced by nonlegal community and group sanctions and the fear of loss of reputation. This is particularly true of contracts because most contracts are not isolated deals between strangers. Most bargains are business transactions among people whose lives and livelihoods depend on developing relationships that enable them to engage in profitable deals. This course emphasizes legal remedies, but the law may operate best when its values and community values are so closely aligned that relatively weak legal remedies are sufficient to motivate compliance.

■ PARSONS, C.J. in *Frye v. Hubbell*, 74 N.H. 358, 374 (1907):

One may be morally bound to do precisely in terms as he agrees; but he is legally bound to do, as a practical proposition, whatever the theory may be, only what he can be compelled by law to do. The common law does not compel men to do as they agree. It gives damages for the failure to perform legal or contractual duties, but except in a few instances only can the specific performance of the contract be enforced. If A owes B a promissory note, no form of action is known by which B can compel A to pay it when due. If A does not pay as promised, in an action of assumpsit B can recover damages because of the breach of A's promise. Since the abolition of imprisonment for debt, the law does not take any steps to compel A to pay the damages. A's property, if he has any subject to execution, the law will seize and apply on B's damages. So that the most that A, who owes B a note, can be legally compelled to do is to suffer his property to be applied to pay B's damages. As to permit this is all A can be compelled to do, it is all that he is legally bound to do. The law does not prohibit his breach of his contract, but leaves him free to break it if he chooses, giving the other party the remedy of damages. The damages the law awards for the non-payment of money is interest, and for the expense of obtaining judgment and execution costs. If costs always equal the expense of litigation, if interest is always full recompense for delayed payment, and if an execution is always equivalent to money in hand then a present part payment of a debt in cash is in fact never beneficial to the creditor or detrimental to the debtor, and can never be a consideration for a discharge of the balance. Whatever the conclusions of scholastic logic, as men having some acquaintance with affairs, judges are bound to know that none of these propositions are always, if ever true.

QUESTION

Is Chief Justice Parsons suggesting that the law of contract is a reed so weak that a sensible person will rely on it only as a last resort?

I.   PUNITIVE SANCTIONS

White v. Benkowski

Wisconsin Supreme Court, 1967.
37 Wis.2d 285, 155 N.W.2d 74.

This case involves a neighborhood squabble between two adjacent property owners.

Prior to November 28, 1962, Virgil and Gwynneth White, the plaintiffs, were desirous of purchasing a home in Oak Creek. Unfortunately, the particular home that the Whites were interested in was without a water supply. Despite this fact, the Whites purchased the home.

The adjacent home was owned and occupied by Paul and Ruth Benkowski, the defendants. The Benkowskis had a well in their yard which had piping that connected with the Whites' home.

On November 28, 1962, the Whites and Benkowskis entered into a written agreement wherein the Benkowskis promised to supply water to the White home for ten years or until an earlier date when either water was supplied by the municipality, the well became inadequate, or the Whites drilled their own well. The Whites promised to pay $3 a month for the water and one-half the cost of any future repairs or maintenance that the Benkowski well might require. As part of the transaction, but not included in the written agreement, the Whites gave the Benkowskis $400 which was used to purchase and install a new pump and an additional tank that would increase the capacity of the well.

Initially, the relationship between the new neighbors was friendly. With the passing of time, however, their relationship deteriorated and the neighbors actually became hostile. In 1964, the water supply, which was controlled by the Benkowskis, was intermittently shut off. Mrs. White kept a record of the dates and durations that her water supply was not operative. Her record showed that the water was shut off on the following occasions:

(1) March 5, 1964, from 7:10 p.m. to 7:25 p.m.

(2) March 9, 1964, from 3:40 p.m. to 4:00 p.m.

(3) March 11, 1964, from 6:00 p.m. to 6:15 p.m.

(4) June 10, 1964, from 6:20 p.m. to 7:03 p.m.

The record also discloses that the water was shut off completely or partially for varying lengths of time on July 1, 6, 7, and 17, 1964, and on November 25, 1964.

Mr. Benkowski claimed that the water was shut off either to allow accumulated sand in the pipes to settle or to remind the Whites that their use of the water was excessive. Mr. White claimed that the Benkowskis breached their contract by shutting off the water.

Following the date when the water was last shut off (November 25, 1964), the Whites commenced an action to recover compensatory and punitive damages for an alleged violation of the agreement to supply water. A jury trial was held....

Before the case was submitted to the jury, the defendants moved to strike the verdict's punitive-damage question. The court reserved its ruling on the motion. The jury returned a verdict which found that the Benkowskis maliciously shut off the Whites' water supply for harassment purposes. Compensatory damages were set at $10 and punitive damages at $2,000. On motions after verdict, the court reduced the compensatory award to $1 and granted defendants' motion to strike the punitive-damage question and answer.

■ WILKIE, J. Two issues are raised on this appeal.

1. Was the trial court correct in reducing the award of compensatory damages from $10 to $1?

2. Are punitive damages available in actions for breach of contract?

Reduction of Jury Award

The evidence of damage adduced during the trial here was that the water supply had been shut off during several short periods. Three incidents of inconvenience resulting from these shut-offs were detailed by the plaintiffs. Mrs. White testified that the lack of water in the bathroom on one occasion caused an odor and that on two other occasions she was forced to take her children to a neighbor's home to bathe them. Based on this evidence, the court instructed the jury that:

> * * * in an action for a breach of contract the plaintiff is entitled to such damages as shall have been sustained by him which resulted naturally and directly from the breach if you find that the defendants did in fact breach the contract. Such damages include pecuniary loss and inconvenience suffered as a natural result of the breach and are called compensatory damages. In this case the plaintiffs have proved no pecuniary damages which you or the Court could compute. In a situation where there has been a breach of contract which you find to have damaged the plaintiff but for which the plaintiffs have proven no actual damages, the plaintiffs may recover nominal damages.

By nominal damages is meant trivial—a trivial sum of money.

Plaintiffs did not object to this instruction. In the trial court's decision on motions after verdict it states that the court so instructed the jury because, based on the fact that the plaintiffs paid for services they did not receive, their loss in proportion to the contract rate was approximately 25 cents. This rationale indicates that the court disregarded or overlooked Mrs. White's testimony of inconvenience. In viewing the evidence most favorable to the plaintiffs, there was some injury. The plaintiffs are not required to ascertain their damages with mathematical precision, but rather the trier of fact must set damages at a reasonable amount. Notwithstanding this instruction, the jury set the plaintiffs' damages at $10. The court was in error in reducing that amount to $1.

Punitive Damages

"If a man shall steal an ox, or a sheep, and kill it, or sell it; he shall restore five oxen for an ox, and four sheep for a sheep."

Over one hundred years ago this court held that, under proper circumstances, a plaintiff was entitled to recover exemplary or punitive damages.

Kink v. Combs is the most recent case in this state which deals with the practice of permitting punitive damages. In *Kink* the court relied on *Fuchs v. Kupper* and re-affirmed its adherence to the rule of punitive damages.

In Wisconsin compensatory damages are given to make whole the damage or injury suffered by the injured party. On the other hand, punitive damages are given

* * * on the basis of punishment to the injured party not because he has been injured, which injury has been compensated with compensatory damages, but to punish the wrongdoer for his malice and to deter others from like conduct.

Thus we reach the question of whether the plaintiffs are entitled to punitive damages for a breach of the water agreement.

The overwhelming weight of authority supports the proposition that punitive damages are not recoverable in actions for breach of contract. In CHITTY ON CONTRACTS, the author states that the right to receive punitive damages for breach of contract is now confined to the single case of damages for breach of a promise to marry.

Simpson states:

Although damages in excess of compensation for loss are in some instances permitted in tort actions by way of punishment * * * in contract actions the damages recoverable are limited to compensation for pecuniary loss sustained by the breach.

Corbin states that as a general rule punitive damages are not recoverable for breach of contract.

In Wisconsin, the early case of *Gordon v. Brewster* involved the breach of an employment contract. The trial court instructed the jury that if the nonperformance of the contract was attributable to the defendant's wrongful act of discharging the plaintiff, then that would go to increase the damages sustained. On appeal, this court said that the instruction was unfortunate and might have led the jurors to suppose that they could give something more than actual compensation in a breach of contract case. We find no Wisconsin case in which breach of contract (other than breach of promise to marry) has led to the award of punitive damages.

Persuasive authority from other jurisdictions supports the proposition (without exception) that punitive damages are not available in breach of contract actions. This is true even if the breach, as in the instant case, is willful.

Although it is well recognized that breach of a contractual duty may be a tort, in such situations the contract creates the relation out of which grows the duty to use care in the performance of a responsibility prescribed by the contract. Not so here. No tort was pleaded or proved.

Reversed in part by reinstating the jury verdict relating to compensatory damages and otherwise affirmed. Costs to appellant.

QUESTIONS AND NOTES

1. Wasn't it a tort for the Benkowskis to maliciously turn off the Whites' water? Did this case come out this way merely because the Whites' lawyer drafted his pleadings incorrectly?

2. Apart from "the overwhelming weight of authority," the Wisconsin Supreme Court doesn't offer a persuasive explanation why contract damages are limited to "compensation." Are the reasons that justify the rule so apparent that they need not be identified and discussed? Even if the Court were unwilling to punish breach by exemplary damages in general, why didn't it consider treating a willful or malicious failure to perform differently from a failure despite a good faith try? Why not two sets of sanctions—a tough one for nasty, willful contract breakers and a softer one for those who innocently or negligently fail to perform?

3. If a major purpose of providing official support to promises is to encourage reliance on them because they are important to the functioning of our network of relationships, why not simply impose heavy penalties on those who breach such promises?

4. The source of the Benkowskis' legal obligation is their promise to the Whites, whereas the source of the obligation not to jaywalk or to park in certain places is a statute or regulation. Does the source of the obligation provide a basis for imposing different responses to failure? When we seek to bind ourselves specially through promise, is the commitment less intense or less compelling than obedience to the general commands of government? We fine jaywalkers and parking violators. Are these more serious breaches of the peace than the Benkowskis maliciously cutting off the White family's water?

5. If Chisler orders goods from Victim and promises to pay for them although he does not intend to do so, he is guilty of a form of theft if he makes off with the goods. Same result if Chisler decides after delivery not to pay for the goods? If not, why not?

6. Behavior that breaches a contract may also be a crime, though it is not the contract breach that makes the behavior criminal. For example, if a trusted bookkeeper embezzles her employer's funds, she is obviously in breach of her employment contract. She may also be subject to criminal prosecution, but not because she breached a contract. While this approach is an almost implicit assumption in our legal system, other legal systems treat certain breaches of promise as themselves criminal offenses. Consider § 422 of the Canadian Criminal Code:

CRIMINAL CODE, R.S.C. § 422 (1985) (CAN.):

(1) Every one who willfully breaks a contract, knowing or having reasonable cause to believe that the probable consequences of doing so, whether alone or in combination with others, will be

(a) to endanger human life,

(b) to cause serious bodily injury,

(c) to expose valuable property, real or personal, to destruction or serious injury,

(d) to deprive the inhabitants of a city or place, or part thereof, wholly or to a great extent, of their supply of light, power, gas or water, or

(e) to delay or prevent the running of any locomotive engine, tender, freight or passenger train or car, on a railway that is a common carrier

is guilty of

(f) an indictable offence and is liable to imprisonment for a term not exceeding five years, or

(g) an offence punishable on summary conviction.

(2) [Omitted. It excludes labor disputes from this section.]

(3) No proceedings shall be instituted under this section without the consent of the Attorney General.

7. For a comparative perspective on the common law rule barring recovery of punitive damages in most contract claims, see Jesse Wilson, *Punishing Contract*

Breakers: Whiten v. Pilot Insurance *and the Sea Change in Canadian Law*, 10 AUCK-LAND U. L. REV. 61 (2004), which notes that Canada and New Zealand have recently abandoned the common law rule and compares the practices in England, Australia, and the United States, which at least nominally adhere to it.

II.   SPECIFIC PERFORMANCE

A legal system unwilling to impose criminal penalties or punitive damages for breach of promise nonetheless may be sufficiently committed to the concept of promise to require the breaching party to render the promised performance. Requiring the breaching party to perform specifically is the closest the law can come to giving the promisee precisely the performance purchased. If a deal is a deal, shouldn't breaching parties be routinely ordered by the State to perform their part of the bargain? If they are not, it is natural to wonder why.

One objection to such a seemingly simple solution is that in most cases the exact performance that was bargained for cannot be rendered subsequent to breach, if only because performance later can never be the equivalent of performance at the earlier date specified in the contract. This difference, of course, might be compensated for by also ordering the breaching party to pay a sum of money to the nonbreaching party to compensate her for any loss suffered by the late performance. This, however, is likely to prove a clumsy way to handle a great many breaches. For example, when an undelivered performance can easily be procured by the nonbreaching party from some other source, as in the case of nondelivery of standard merchandise readily available elsewhere, there would seem to be little point in ordering performance by the breaching party. The simple solution in such a case is to compensate the nonbreaching party by awarding her a money judgment to cover whatever losses she suffers in the substitute purchase.

Another shortcoming of specific performance is that such an order may require subsequent court action to enforce it (a hearing or hearings leading to contempt citations), and thus is costly to employ. Many times a breach occurs because the breaching party is unable to perform and thus ordering him to perform is a futile gesture. Moreover, ordering a defendant to perform under threat of imprisonment implicates long-standing public policy against imprisonment for debt, or—in the case of contracts of employment—against forced labor.

For these and other less logical reasons, Anglo–American jurisprudence has long held that specific performance is available only as an extraordinary remedy when the award of money damages would be "inadequate."

Northern Delaware Industrial Dev. Corp. v. E.W. Bliss Co.

Delaware Court of Chancery, 1968.
245 A.2d 431.

■ MARVEL, VICE CHANCELLOR. Plaintiffs and defendant are parties to a contract dated May 26th, 1966, under the terms of which defendant agreed to furnish all labor, services, materials and equipment necessary to expand and modernize a steel fabricating plant owned by the plaintiff Phoenix Steel Corporation at Claymont, Delaware. A massive undertaking is called for in the contract, the total price for the work to be performed by the defendant being set in the contract at $27,500,000 and the area of contract performance extending over a plant site of approximately sixty acres.

Work on the project has not progressed as rapidly as contemplated in the contract and what plaintiffs now seek is an order compelling defendant to requisition 300 more workmen for a night shift, thus requiring defendant to put on the job, as it allegedly contracted to do, the number of men required to make up a full second shift at the Phoenix plant site during the period when one of the Phoenix mills must be shut down in order that its modernization may be carried out under the contract. And while the present record is sparse, there seems to be no doubt but that defendant has fallen behind the work completion schedules set forth in such contract. What plaintiffs apparently seek is a speeding up of work at the site by means of a court-ordered requisitioning by defendant of more laborers.

The basis for plaintiffs' application for equitable relief is found in a work proposal made by defendant's prime subcontractor, Noble J. Dick, Inc., to the Bliss Company, the terms of which are made part of the contract between plaintiffs and defendant. Such proposal stipulates inter alia:

T. Working Schedule

All work is quoted on a normal 40 hour basis—5 days per week except for necessary service tie-ins. The only additional premium time included is that required during the shut-down of #1 mill when two turn-week work is contemplated.

According to plaintiffs, the phrase "two turn-week work" is a term used in the steel industry to designate the employment of day and night shifts over a full seven day work week, and defendant does not deny this. Plaintiffs therefor reason that inasmuch as at or about the time of the filing of the complaint defendant was operating one shift at the site ranging in size from 192 to 337 workers per day, whereas paragraph "T" above referred to contemplates two daily shifts, that they are entitled to a court order directing defendant to employ not less than 300 construction workers on each of two shifts, seven days per week. Plaintiffs seek other relief, including damages, but consideration of such other requested relief will be deferred for the present. Defendants earlier moved for dismissal or a stay because the parties are allegedly contractually bound to arbitrate their differences.

However, the sole matter now for decision is a question raised by the Court at argument on defendant's motion, namely whether or not this Court should exercise its jurisdiction to grant plaintiffs' application for an order for specific performance of an alleged contractual right to have more workers placed on the massive construction project here involved, and order the requisitioning of 300 workers[1] for a night shift, this being the number of laborers deemed by plaintiffs to be appropriate properly to bring about prompt completion of the job at hand.

On the basis of the record before me, viewed in the light of the applicable law, I am satisfied that this Court should not, as a result of granting plaintiffs' prayer for specific performance of an alleged term of a building contract, become committed to supervising the carrying out of a massive, complex, and unfinished construction contract, a result which would necessarily follow as a consequence of ordering defendant to requisition laborers as prayed for. Parenthetically, it is noted that if such laborers are in fact available (which appears not to be the case), their presence at the Claymont site might well impede rather than advance the orderly completion of the steel mill renovation work now under way.

It is not that a court of equity is without jurisdiction in a proper case to order the completion of an expressly designed and largely completed construction project, particularly where the undertaking to construct is tied in with a contract for the sale of land and the construction in question is largely finished. Furthermore, this is not a case which calls for a building plan so precisely definite as to make compliance therewith subject to effective judicial supervision, but rather an attempt to have the Court as the result of ordering a builder to speed up general work by hiring a night shift of employees (a proposal which was merely "contemplated" by the subcontractor, Dick) to become deeply involved in supervision of a complex construction project located on plaintiffs' property.

The point is that a court of equity should not order specific performance of any building contract in a situation in which it would be impractical to carry out such an

---

1. Nowhere in the contract here in issue, however, does defendant undertake to supply any specific number of laborers.

order, unless there are special circumstances or the public interest is directly involved.[2] In the case of *City Stores v. Ammerman* (D.C.D.C.) which plaintiffs cite to support their application, specific performance was sought of an agreement which contemplated that plaintiff would become a tenant in a designated section of a shopping center to be constructed by defendant. The plans for such center were quite definite and the court was obviously impressed by the fact that unless the relief sought were to be granted, plaintiff would lose out on a promised opportunity to share in the expected profits of a shopping center located in a burgeoning North Virginia suburb. The ruling while perhaps correct under the circumstances of the case has no application here.

I conclude that to grant specific performance, as prayed for by plaintiffs, would be inappropriate in view of the imprecision of the contract provision relied upon and the impracticability if not impossibility of effective enforcement by the Court of a mandatory order designed to keep a specific number of men on the job at the site of a steel mill which is undergoing extensive modernization and expansion. If plaintiffs have sustained loss as a result of actionable building delays on defendant's part at the Phoenix plant at Claymont, they may, at an appropriate time, resort to law for a fixing of their claimed damages.

On notice, an application may be made for the entry of an order of dismissal of this action insofar as it seeks an order for specific performance of the Dick proposal "T", or, in the alternative, for the removal of such cause of action to a court of competent jurisdiction.

QUESTIONS AND NOTES

1. Isn't an ounce of prevention worth a pound of cure? Consider the effects of this $27.5 million project on the economy of Claymont, Delaware. Will damages be able to compensate for the losses that will be suffered by the steel company in lost sales, the workers in lost wages, and the entire community in lost wealth due to the delay in performance?

2. The traditional view is that an order for specific performance can only be justified if money damages fail to put the injured party in as good a position as he would have been had the contract been performed. So long as a court is able to identify a

---

2. *See also* 4 Pomeroy, *Equity Jurisprudence* § 1402 which notes the English exceptions to the rule that specific performance of a construction contract generally will not be ordered except where: (1) the contract is defined and certain, (2) the defendant has contracted to construct a defined project on his own land, (3) the defendant has agreed to build on lands acquired from plaintiff, and (4) there has been a part performance so that defendant is enjoying the benefits in specie.

substitute in the market and to calculate, with some certainty, money damages on the basis of that substitute, money damages are considered adequate relief.

What matters in measuring money damages is the amount, refinement, and reliability of the available information about substitutes for the subject matter of the breached contract. "When the relevant information is thin and unreliable, there is a substantial risk that an award of money damages will either exceed or fall short of the promisee's actual loss. Of course this risk can always be reduced—but only at great cost when reliable information is difficult to obtain. Conversely, when there is a great deal of consumer behavior generating abundant and highly dependable information about substitutes, the risk of error in measuring the promisee's loss may be reduced at a much smaller cost. In asserting that the subject matter of a particular contract is unique and has no established market value, a court is really saying that it cannot obtain, at reasonable cost, enough information about substitutes to permit it to calculate an award of money damages without imposing an unacceptably high risk of undercompensation on the injured promisee. Conceived in this way, the uniqueness test seems economically sound." Anthony T. Kronman, *Specific Performance*, 45 U. CHI. L. REV. 351, 362 (1978).

3. The implications for economic efficiency of making specific performance more readily available are uncertain. A party entering a contract might pay the other side to limit recourse to specific performance in the event of breach. Or breaching promisors might "bribe" promisees to release them from specifically performing and thus incurring costs greater than the value of the promised performance to the promisee. This suggests that so long as applicable law allows parties to "contract around" equitable remedies, efficient allocation of resources will not be affected by the use of equitable over legal remedies. Consider on the other hand this Reporter's Note to Chapter 16 (Remedies) of the Restatement (Second) of Contracts:

> . . .
>
> The important role that the institution of contract plays in the economy has drawn the attention of economists to the law of contract remedies. In classic economic theory the mechanism of exchange resulting from bargain is essential to the voluntary reallocation of goods, labor and other resources in a socially desirable manner. However, a party may err in calculating the net benefit to be expected from the performance of a bargain, or circumstances may so change as to disappoint his expectations. A contract that he once thought would be profitable may therefore become unprofitable for him. If the contract is still profitable for the other party, however, a question arises as to whether the reluctant party should be compelled to perform. The answer provided by at least some economic analysis tends to confirm the traditional response of common-law judges in dealing with this question.

The traditional goal of the law of contract remedies has not been compulsion of the promisor to perform his promise but compensation of the promisee for the loss resulting from breach. "Willful" breaches have not been distinguished from other breaches, punitive damages have not been awarded for breach of contract, and specific performance has not been granted where compensation in damages is an adequate substitute for the injured party. In general, therefore, a party may find it advantageous to refuse to perform a contract if he will still have a net gain after he has fully compensated the injured party for the resulting loss.

This traditional response is not without its shortcomings. Its focus on the pecuniary aspects of breach fails to take account of notions of the sanctity of contract and the resulting moral obligation to honor one's promises. The analysis of breach of contract in purely economic terms assumes an ability to measure value with a certainty that is not often possible in the judicial process. The analysis also ignores the "transaction costs" inherent in the bargaining process and in the resolution of disputes, a defect that is especially significant where the amount in controversy is small. However, the main thrust of the preceding economic analysis lends some support to traditional contract doctrine in this area.

4. Compare the appropriateness of an order of specific performance that requires that a contractor hire three hundred more workers with one that requires completion of the construction project on or before the date specified in the contract.

5. Supervision of a decree for specific performance of the construction project conceivably could entail an extensive and long-term involvement by the court and, in any event, management responsibilities beyond that required to execute a money judgment through a typical sheriff's sale. Yet courts have for centuries been involved in the kind of long-term supervision which construction of the steel plant might require. Probating estates, supervising trusts, and administering bankruptcies can often be matters of great complexity, commitment and duration. Courts are so regularly involved in these matters that we notice nothing unusual if a court must oversee the operation of an airline, retail chain, or gambling casino.

Is the supervision of the construction of the steel plant pursuant to a decree for specific performance somehow illegitimate because of the absence of a complex statutory framework? Is the supervision of a construction project ill-advised because of the court's lack of expertise? How much do courts know about running an airline or casino-hotel in bankruptcy proceedings or about the value and marketing of an art collection included in a large estate?

HISTORICAL NOTE: LAW AND EQUITY

Discussions of specific performance are likely to rely heavily on aphorisms sprinkled around the opinion which distinguish between "courts of equity" and "courts of law." "Equity will not compel specific performance of an agreement to lend money" because a breach "can always be fully compensated by damages." And "[t]he fact that a party can avail himself of a remedy in a court of law will not preclude him from obtaining relief in a court of equity...." One might ask who "equity" is and why does it have a court of its own where someone can obtain "relief" different from the "remedy" available in a court of law? Why does our legal system claim that money damages are the rule for contract cases and specific performance the exception, while most other legal systems in the world at least claim the opposite? (Be aware that whatever different legal systems claim, in most practical situations courts around the world tend to come out in about the same place.)

Many legal concepts simply make no sense without an appreciation of the historic experience out of which they grew. Law tends to be rationalistic in argument and format, but as Holmes taught, "the life of the law is not logic, but experience." Times change, revolutions wash away institutions, but the old spirit often lives on in the new. Without some familiarity with the historical experience, you are doomed to remain forever puzzled by the law's major features.

From the time of the great Roman lawyers onward, a distinction has been drawn between the substantive content of legal rules and the procedural rules that govern legal process. Most legal education for two millennia (including your own) has emphasized the conceptual structure of abstract substantive rules in isolation from, and in preference to, the grubby details of procedure. From either a practical or an historic perspective, however, the distinction is artificial and, if anything, it is procedure that determines substance, rather than the other way around. Justice Robert Jackson, the last U.S. Supreme Court Justice to learn law in a lawyer's office rather than a law school, stated the historic truth when he observed that the substantive law often grows in the interstices of procedure.

Specific performance is not a favored remedy at common law because historically this procedure was associated with a set of courts and political officials who competed for power with common law judges. To bring an action in one of the King's Courts in England before the 19th century reforms, the plaintiff would have to obtain a writ from the Office of the Lord Chancellor, known as Chancery, by showing that the claim fell into the increasingly technical definitions of claims cognizable by a royal court. In medieval times the Lord Chancellor usually was a clerk, in both connotations of that term. He was a literate administrator, able to keep files and write documents in an age in which those skills were scarce. He possessed those skills because he was a cleric, a churchman, and frequently the King's confessor. It was the job of the Chancellor to decide whether cases fit in the conventional categories and occasionally to open a new category when circumstances required it. The motivation to open new categories of claims was not merely administrative. As the King's confessor, the keeper of the royal conscience, the Chancellor was open to claims of right based on the King's obligation to do justice. When the remedies of the law failed to provide justice, the Chancellor would do equity and provide relief.

The Chancellor's Court or "the court of equity" started as an interstitial forum limited to hearing "suits in equity" when "the legal remedy" (that is, the remedy provided by the common law courts) was inadequate. The Chancellor's view of what he could do and why he could do it was more open-ended than that of the judges sitting as common law courts. Chancellor's courts were heavily influenced by canon law and, like Church courts, ordered defendants to act personally for the good of their souls. Equitable decrees directed a defendant to do or not to do something. A disobedient defendant could be fined and imprisoned for contempt.

By contrast, the common law courts seldom ordered the defendant to do anything. The King's central interests were land and military order in the countryside. A common law judgment characteristically declared that the plaintiff recover from the defendant a sum of money. If a judgment debtor did not pay voluntarily, his real and personal property were subject to seizure and sale by the sheriff, who began as the King's resident military officer in the county. If no assets could be identified and seized, the common law court could do no more—the judgment went unsatisfied. The commands issued by the common law court thus typically were addressed to royal officers to execute against the defendant's property, not directly to defendants.

During the Tudor and Stuart revolutions of the 16th and 17th centuries, the medieval order was replaced by an increasingly centralized national state. The limiting jurisdictional concepts of the common law proved a constraint not only on judges but upon kings. The Crown and its bureaucratic servants became stronger and eventually claimed the right to rule absolutely without the restraints of law and its cumbersome procedures. In time, the law and professional lawyers became a major political group opposing this new royal power. Judges and Chancellors competed for power, and the common law and equity each insisted on its primacy. In the end, King James I determined that the Chancellor would prevail if his jurisdiction were properly invoked, but that first recourse must be to the common law. Equity would not act in cases properly cognizable at law; if damages provided an adequate remedy, the Chancellor would not intervene.

In the 19th century the separate court systems of law and equity were abolished along with the forms of action in England and most American states. Delaware maintains one of the few separate equity courts in the nation. Elsewhere, there is one court of general jurisdiction in all civil cases. But lawyers' habits die hard when they have the weight of so many generations behind them. On any given Monday morning in most large cities, one is likely to discover that some of the judges sitting in the courthouse are hearing "legal motions," while others preside over a separate "writs and receivers' department" or a courtroom with some other arcane title where equitable relief is granted. Moreover, the forms of action may be dead, but you are likely to learn when you enter practice to separate your contract claims from those sounding in tort, to keep the basic contract claim (special assumpsit) separate from the "common counts," and otherwise imitate in practice distinctions the law claims to have abandoned long before your great grandfather was born.

The very mention of specific performance triggers in the minds of judges and lawyers alike special labels, special rules, and even special feelings. To some degree, this response simply reflects the continued state of the law. Both the Second Restatement and the Uniform Commercial Code preserve the remedial hierarchy and measure requests for specific performance by standards that, by and large, were first developed in the English courts of equity. While the drafters desired to foster "a more liberal attitude" (UCC § 2–716, Comment 1), they preserved the old bottom line: Specific performance shall be granted only if legal remedies fail in their purpose.

━━━━━

American Broadcasting Companies v. Wolf

New York Court of Appeals, 1981.
52 N.Y.2d 394, 438 N.Y.S.2d 482, 420 N.E.2d 363.

■ COOKE, C.J. This case provides an interesting insight into the fierce competition in the television industry for popular performers and favorable ratings. It requires legal resolution of a rather novel employment imbroglio.

The issue is whether plaintiff American Broadcasting Companies, Incorporated (ABC), is entitled to equitable relief against defendant Warner Wolf, a New York City sportscaster, because of Wolf's breach of a good faith negotiation provision of a now expired broadcasting contract with ABC. In the present circumstances, it is concluded that the equitable relief sought by plaintiff—which would have the effect of forcing Wolf off the air—may not be granted.

I

Warner Wolf, a sportscaster who has developed a rather colorful and unique on-the-air personality, had been employed by ABC since 1976. In February, 1978, ABC and Wolf entered into an employment agreement which, following exercise of renewal option, was to terminate on March 5, 1980. The contract contained a clause, known as a good-faith negotiation and first-refusal provision, that is at the crux of this litigation:

> You agree, if we so elect, during the last ninety (90) days prior to the expiration of the extended term of this agreement, to enter into good faith negotiations with us for the extension of this agreement on mutually agreeable terms. You further agree that for the first forty-five (45) days of this renegotiation period, you will not negotiate for your services with any other person or company other than WABC–TV or ABC. In the event we are unable to reach an agreement for an extension by the expiration of the extended term hereof, you agree that you will not accept, in any market for a period of three (3) months following expiration of the extended term of this agreement, any offer of employment as a sportscaster, sports news reporter, commentator, program host, or analyst in broadcasting (including television, cable television, pay television and radio) without first giving us, in writing, an opportunity to employ you on substantially similar terms and you agree to enter into an agreement with us on such terms.

Under this provision, Wolf was bound to negotiate in good faith with ABC for the 90–day period from December 6, 1979 through March 4, 1980. For the first 45 days, December 6 through January 19, the negotiation with ABC was to be exclusive. Following expiration of the 90–day negotiating period and the contract on March 5, 1980, Wolf was required, before *accepting* any other offer, to afford ABC a right of first refusal; he could comply with this provision either by refraining from accepting another offer or by first tendering the offer to ABC. The first-refusal period expired on June 3, 1980 and on June 4 Wolf was free to accept any job opportunity, without obligation to ABC.

Wolf first met with ABC executives in September, 1979 to discuss the terms of a renewal contract. Counterproposals were exchanged, and the parties agreed to finalize the matter by October 15. Meanwhile, unbeknownst to ABC, Wolf met with representatives of CBS in early October. Wolf related his employment requirements and also discussed the first refusal-good faith negotiation clause of his ABC contract. Wolf furnished CBS a copy of that portion of the ABC agreement. On October 12, ABC officials and Wolf met, but were unable to reach agreement on a renewal contract. A few days later, on October 16 Wolf again discussed employment possibilities with CBS.

Not until January 2, 1980 did ABC again contact Wolf. At that time, ABC expressed its willingness to meet substantially all of his demands. Wolf rejected the offer, however, citing ABC's delay in communicating with him and his desire to explore his options in light of the impending expiration of the 45–day exclusive negotiation period.

On February 1, 1980, after termination of that exclusive period, Wolf and CBS orally agreed on the terms of Wolf's employment as sportscaster for WCBS–TV, a CBS-owned affiliate in New York. During the next two days, CBS informed Wolf that it had prepared two agreements and divided his annual compensation between the two: one covered his services as an on-the-air sportscaster, and the other was an off-the-air production agreement for sports specials Wolf was to produce. The production agreement contained an exclusivity clause which barred Wolf from performing "services of any nature for" or permitting the use of his "name, likeness, voice or endorsement by, any person, firm or corporation" during the term of the agreement, unless CBS consented. The contract had an effective date of March 6, 1980.

Wolf signed the CBS production agreement on February 4, 1980. At the same time, CBS agreed in writing, in consideration of $100 received from Wolf, to hold open an offer of employment to Wolf as sportscaster until June 4, 1980, the date on which Wolf became free from ABC's right of first refusal. The next day, February 5, Wolf submitted a letter of resignation to ABC.

Representatives of ABC met with Wolf on February 6 and made various offers and promises that Wolf rejected. Wolf informed ABC that they had delayed negotiations with him and downgraded his worth. He stated he had no future with the company. He told the officials he had made a "gentlemen's agreement" and would leave ABC on March 5. Later in February, Wolf and ABC agreed that Wolf would continue to appear on the air during a portion of the first-refusal period, from March 6 until May 28.[1]

ABC commenced this action on May 6, 1980, by which time Wolf's move to CBS had become public knowledge. The complaint alleged that Wolf, induced by CBS breached both the good-faith negotiation and first-refusal provisions of his contract with ABC. ABC sought specific enforcement of its right of first refusal and an injunction against Wolf's employment as a sportscaster with CBS.

After a trial, Supreme Court found no breach of the contract, and went on to note that, in any event, equitable relief would be inappropriate. A divided Appellate Division, while concluding that Wolf had breached both the good-faith negotiation and first-refusal provisions, nonetheless affirmed on the ground that equitable intervention was unwarranted. There should be an affirmance.

II

Initially, we agree with the Appellate Division that defendant Wolf breached his obligation to negotiate in good faith with ABC from December, 1979 through March, 1980. When Wolf signed the production agreement with CBS on February 4, 1980, he obligated himself not to render services "of any nature" to any person, firm or corporation on and after March 6, 1980. Quite simply, then, beginning on February

---

1. The agreement also provided that on or after June 4, 1980 Wolf was free to "accept an offer of employment with anyone of [his] choosing and immediately begin performing on air services." The parties agreed that their rights and obligations under the original employment contract were in no way affected by the extension of employment.

4 Wolf was unable to extend his contract with ABC; his contract with CBS precluded him from legally serving ABC in any capacity after March 5. Given Wolf's existing obligation to CBS, any negotiations he engaged in with ABC, without the consent of CBS, after February 4 were meaningless and could not have been in good faith.

At the same time, there is no basis in the record for the Appellate Division's conclusion that Wolf violated the first-refusal provision by entering into an oral sportscasting contract with CBS on February 4. The first-refusal provision required Wolf, for a period of 90 days after termination of the ABC agreement, either to refrain from accepting an offer of employment or to first submit the offer to ABC for its consideration. By its own terms, the right of first refusal did not apply to offers accepted by Wolf prior to the March 5 termination of the ABC employment contract. It is apparent, therefore, that Wolf could not have breached the right of first refusal by accepting an offer during the term of his employment with ABC. Rather, his conduct violates only the good-faith negotiation clause of the contract. The question is whether this breach entitled ABC to injunctive relief that would bar Wolf from continued employment at CBS. To resolve this issue, it is necessary to trace the principles of specific performance applicable to personal service contracts.

III

-A-

Courts of equity historically have refused to order an individual to perform a contract for personal services. Originally this rule evolved because of the inherent difficulties courts would encounter in supervising the performance of uniquely personal efforts.[4] During the Civil War era, there emerged a more compelling reason for not directing the performance of personal services: the Thirteenth Amendment's prohibition of involuntary servitude. It has been strongly suggested that

---

4. The New York Court of Chancery in *De Rivafinoli v. Corsetti* (4 Paige Chs. 264, 270) eloquently articulated the traditional rationale for refusing affirmative enforcement of personal service contracts:

> I am not aware that any officer of this court has that perfect knowledge of the Italian language, or possesses that exquisite sensibility in the auricular nerve which is necessary to understand, and to enjoy with a proper zest, the peculiar beauties of the Italian opera, so fascinating to the fashionable world. There might be some difficulty, therefore, even if the defendant was compelled to sing under the direction and in the presence of a master in chancery, in ascertaining whether he performed his engagement according to its spirit and intent. It would also be very difficult for the master to determine what effect coercion might produce upon the defendant's singing, especially in the livelier airs; although the fear of imprisonment would unquestionably deepen his seriousness in the graver parts of the drama. But one thing at least is certain; his songs will be neither comic, or even semi-serious, while he remains confined in that dismal cage, the debtor's prison of New York.

judicial compulsion of services would violate the express command of that amendment. For practical, policy and constitutional reasons, therefore, courts continue to decline to affirmatively enforce employment contracts.

Over the years, however, in certain narrowly tailored situations, the law fashioned other remedies for failure to perform an employment agreement. Thus, where an employee refuses to render services to an employer in violation of an existing contract, and the services are unique or extraordinary, an injunction may issue to prevent the employee from furnishing those services to another person for the duration of the contract. Such "negative enforcement" was initially available only when the employee had expressly stipulated not to compete with the employer for the term of the engagement. Later cases permitted injunctive relief where the circumstances justified implication of a negative covenant. In these situations, an injunction is warranted because the employee either expressly or by clear implication agreed not to work elsewhere for the period of his contract. And, since the services must be unique before negative enforcement will be granted, irreparable harm will befall the employer should the employee be permitted to labor for a competitor.

-B-

After a personal service contract terminates, the availability of equitable relief against the former employee diminishes appreciably. Since the period of service has expired, it is impossible to decree affirmative or negative specific performance. Only if the employee has expressly agreed not to compete with the employer following the term of the contract, or is threatening to disclose trade secrets or commit another tortious act, is injunctive relief generally available at the behest of the employer. Even where there is an express anticompetitive covenant, however, it will be rigorously examined and specifically enforced only if it satisfies certain established requirements. Indeed, a court normally will not decree specific enforcement of an employee's anticompetitive covenant unless necessary to protect the trade secrets, customer lists or good will of the employer's business, or perhaps when the employer is exposed to special harm because of the unique nature of the employee's services.[6] And, an otherwise valid covenant will not be enforced if it is unreasonable in time, space or scope or would operate in a harsh or oppressive manner. There is, in short, general judicial disfavor of anticompetitive covenants contained in employment contracts.

---

6. Although an employee's anticompetitive covenant may be enforceable where the employee's services were special or unique no New York case has been found where enforcement has been granted, following termination of the employment contract, solely on the basis of the uniqueness of the services.

Underlying the strict approach to enforcement of these covenants is the notion that, once the term of an employment agreement has expired, the general public policy favoring robust and uninhibited competition should not give way merely because a particular employer wishes to insulate himself from competition. Important, too, are the "powerful considerations of public policy which militate against sanctioning the loss of a man's livelihood." At the same time, the employer is entitled to protection from unfair or illegal conduct that causes economic injury. The rules governing enforcement of anticompetitive covenants and the availability of equitable relief after termination of employment are designed to foster these interests of the employer without impairing the employee's ability to earn a living or the general competitive mold of society.

-C-

Specific enforcement of personal service contracts thus turns initially upon whether the term of employment has expired. If the employee refuses to perform during the period of employment, was furnishing unique services, has expressly or by clear implication agreed not to compete for the duration of the contract and the employer is exposed to irreparable injury, it may be appropriate to restrain the employee from competing until the agreement expires. Once the employment contract has terminated, by contrast, equitable relief is potentially available only to prevent injury from unfair competition or similar tortious behavior or to enforce an express and valid anticompetitive covenant. In the absence of such circumstances, the general policy of unfettered competition should prevail.

IV

Applying these principles, it is apparent that ABC's request for injunctive relief must fail. There is no existing employment agreement between the parties; the original contract terminated in March, 1980. Thus, the negative enforcement that might be appropriate during the term of employment is unwarranted here. Nor is there an express anticompetitive covenant that defendant Wolf is violating, or any claim of special injury from tortious conduct such as exploitation of trade secrets. In short, ABC seeks to premise equitable relief after termination of the employment upon a simple, albeit serious, breach of a general contract negotiation clause. To grant an injunction in that situation would be to unduly interfere with an individual's livelihood and to inhibit free competition where there is no corresponding injury to the employer other than the loss of a competitive edge. Indeed, if relief were granted here, any breach of an employment contract provision relating to renewal negotiations logically would serve as the basis for an open-ended restraint upon the employee's ability to earn a living should he ultimately choose not to extend his employment. Our public policy, which favors the free exchange of goods and services through established market mechanisms, dictates otherwise.

Equally unavailing is ABC's request that the court create a noncompetitive covenant by implication. Although in a proper case an implied-in-fact covenant not to compete for the term of employment may be found to exist, anticompetitive covenants covering the postemployment period will not be implied.[9] Indeed, even an express covenant will be scrutinized and enforced only in accordance with established principles.

This is not to say that ABC has not been damaged in some fashion or that Wolf should escape responsibility for the breach of his good-faith negotiation obligation. Rather, we merely conclude that ABC is not entitled to equitable relief. Because of the unique circumstances presented, however, this decision is without prejudice to ABC's right to pursue relief in the form of monetary damages, if it be so advised.

Accordingly, the order of the Appellate Division should be affirmed.

■ FUCHSBERG, J. (dissenting).

I agree with all the members of this court, as had all the Justices at the Appellate Division, that the defendant Wolf breached his undisputed obligation to negotiate in good faith for renewal of his contract with ABC. Where we part company is in the majority's unwillingness to mold an equitable decree, even one more limited than the harsh one the plaintiff proposed, to right the wrong.

Central to the disposition of this case is the first-refusal provision. Its terms are worth recounting. They plainly provide that, in the 90–day period immediately succeeding the termination of his ABC contract, before Wolf could accept a position as sportscaster with another company, he first had to afford ABC the opportunity to engage him on like terms. True, he was not required to entertain offers, whether from ABC or anyone else, during that period. In that event he, of course, would be off the air for that 90 days, during which ABC could attempt to orient its listeners from Wolf to his successor. On the other hand, if Wolf wished to continue to broadcast actively during the 90 days, ABC's right of first refusal put it in a position to make sure that Wolf was not doing so for a competitor. One way or the other, however labeled, the total effect of the first refusal agreement was that of an express conditional covenant under which Wolf could be restricted from appearing on the air other than for ABC for the 90–day posttermination period.

One need not be in the broadcasting business to understand that the restriction ABC bargained for, and Wolf granted, when they entered into the original employment contract was not inconsequential. The earnings of broadcasting companies are directly related to the "ratings" they receive. This, in turn, is at least in part dependent on the popularity of personalities like Wolf. It therefore was to ABC's

9. Of course, as discussed, tortious interference with the employer's business by a former employee may sometimes be enjoined absent a noncompetitive covenant.

advantage, once Wolf came into its employ, especially since he was new to the New York market, that it enhance his popularity by featuring, advertising and otherwise promoting him. This meant that the loyalty of at least part of the station's listening audience would become identified with Wolf, thus enhancing his potential value to competitors, as witness the fact that, in place of the $250,000 he was receiving during his last year with ABC, he was able to command $400,000 to $450,000 per annum in his CBS "deal." A reasonable opportunity during which ABC could cope with such an assault on its good will had to be behind the clause in question.

Moreover, it is undisputed that, when in late February Wolf executed the contract for an extension of employment during the 90–day hiatus for which the parties had bargained, ABC had every right to expect that Wolf had not already committed himself to an exclusivity provision in a producer's contract with CBS in violation of the good-faith negotiation clause. Surely, had ABC been aware of this gross breach, had it not been duped into giving an uninformed consent, it would not have agreed to serve as a self-destructive vehicle for the further enhancement of Wolf's potential for taking his ABC-earned following with him.

In the face of these considerations, the majority rationalizes its position of powerlessness to grant equitable relief by choosing to interpret the contract as though there were no restrictive covenant, express or implied. However, as demonstrated, there is, in fact, an express three-month negative covenant which, because of Wolf's misconduct, ABC was effectively denied the opportunity to exercise. Enforcement of this covenant, by enjoining Wolf from broadcasting for a three-month period, would depart from no entrenched legal precedent. Rather, it would accord with equity's boasted flexibility.

QUESTIONS AND NOTES

1. Should ABC take up the Court of Appeals on its invitation to seek monetary damages? What sort of damages will it be able to prove?

2. While many American jurisdictions, like New York, will enforce covenants not to compete in employment contracts that are limited in time and scope in at least some circumstances, *see also* Restatement (Second) § 186, some states, notably California, do not. *See, e.g., Edwards v. Arthur Andersen LLP*, 189 P.3d 285 (Cal. 2008). California courts invalidate such covenants in light of California's public policy favoring open competition and trade. *See Hill Med. Corp. v. Wycoff*, 103 Cal. Rptr. 2d 779 (Ct. App. 2001). Some commentators have linked the economic vitality of California's Silicon Valley to non-enforcement of covenants not to compete, noting that the California rule facilitates the movement of talent and dissemination of knowledge from established firms to start-ups and competitors, encouraging innovation. Ronald Gilson, *The Legal Infrastructure of High Technology Industrial Districts:*

Silicon Valley, Route 128, and Covenants Not to Compete, 74 N.Y.U. L. REV. 575 (1999). But even California enforces "reasonable" covenants not to compete when executed in connection with the sale of the goodwill of a business or the dissolution of a partnership. *See, e.g., Alliant Ins. Servs., Inc. v. Gaddy*, 72 Cal. Rptr. 3d 259 (Ct. App. 2008).

———————

The decision below illustrates a modern trend to more liberally award specific performance to remedy certain contract breaches. Even though these cases proclaim a greater receptivity toward specific performance, the judges who write these opinions, like the lawyers who practice before them and the drafters of the Restatement and the UCC, think in terms of the remedial hierarchy established by the Chancery courts and even criticize its effects by presupposing that it is correct.

Walgreen Co. v. Sara Creek Property Co.

United States Court of Appeals, Seventh Circuit, 1992.
966 F.2d 273.

■ POSNER, J.

This appeal from the grant of a permanent injunction raises fundamental issues concerning the propriety of injunctive relief. The essential facts are simple. Walgreen has operated a pharmacy in the Southgate Mall in Milwaukee since its opening in 1951. Its current lease, signed in 1971 and carrying a 30-year, 6-month term, contains, as had the only previous lease, a clause in which the landlord, Sara Creek, promises not to lease space in the mall to anyone else who wants to operate a pharmacy or a store containing a pharmacy.

In 1990, fearful that its largest tenant—what in real estate parlance is called the "anchor tenant"—having gone broke was about to close its store, Sara Creek informed Walgreen that it intended to buy out the anchor tenant and install in its place a discount store operated by Phar-Mor Corporation, a "deep discount" chain, rather than, like Walgreen, just a "discount" chain. Phar-Mor's store would occupy 100,000 square feet, of which 12,000 would be occupied by a pharmacy the same size as Walgreen's. The entrances to the two stores would be within a couple of hundred feet of each other.

Walgreen filed this diversity suit for breach of contract against Sara Creek and Phar-Mor and asked for an injunction against Sara Creek's letting the anchor premises to Phar-Mor. After an evidentiary hearing, the judge found a breach of Walgreen's lease and entered a permanent injunction against Sara Creek's letting the anchor tenant premises to Phar-Mor until the expiration of Walgreen's lease. He did this over the defendants' objection that Walgreen had failed to show that its remedy at law—damages—for the breach of the exclusivity clause was inadequate. Sara Creek had put on an expert witness who testified that Walgreen's damages could be readily estimated, and Walgreen had countered with evidence from its employees that its damages would be very difficult to compute, among other reasons because they included intangibles such as loss of goodwill.

Sara Creek reminds us that damages are the norm in breach of contract as in other cases. Many breaches, it points out, are "efficient" in the sense that they allow resources to be moved into a more valuable use. Perhaps this is one—the value of Phar-Mor's occupancy of the anchor premises may exceed the cost to Walgreen of facing increased competition. If so, society will be better off if Walgreen is paid its damages, equal to that cost, and Phar-Mor is allowed to move in rather than being kept out by an injunction. That is why injunctions are not granted as a matter of course, but only when the plaintiff's damages remedy is inadequate. Walgreen's is not, Sara Creek argues; the projection of business losses due to increased competition is a routine exercise in calculation. Damages representing either the present value of lost future profits or (what should be the equivalent) the diminution in the value of the leasehold have either been awarded or deemed the proper remedy in a number of reported cases for breach of an exclusivity clause in a shopping-center lease. Why, Sara Creek asks, should they not be adequate here?

Sara Creek makes a beguiling argument that contains much truth, but we do not think it should carry the day. For if, as just noted, damages have been awarded in some cases of breach of an exclusivity clause in a shopping-center lease, injunctions have been issued in others. The choice between remedies requires a balancing of the costs and benefits of the alternatives. The task of striking the balance is for the trial judge, subject to deferential appellate review in recognition of its particularistic, judgmental, fact-bound character. As we said in an appeal from a grant of a preliminary injunction—but the point is applicable to review of a permanent injunction as well—"The question for us [appellate judges] is whether the [district] judge exceeded the bounds of permissible choice in the circumstances, not what we would have done if we had been in his shoes." *Roland Machinery Co. v. Dresser Industries, Inc.,* 749 F.2d 380, 390 (7th Cir.1984).

The plaintiff who seeks an injunction has the burden of persuasion—damages are the norm, so the plaintiff must show why his case is abnormal. But when, as in this case, the issue is whether to grant a permanent injunction, not whether to grant a temporary one, the burden is to show that damages are inadequate, not that the denial of the injunction will work irreparable harm. "Irreparable" in the injunction context means not rectifiable by the entry of a final judgment. It has nothing to do with whether to grant a permanent injunction, which, in the usual case anyway, *is* the final judgment. The use of "irreparable harm" or "irreparable injury" as synonyms for inadequate remedy at law is a confusing usage. It should be avoided.

The benefits of substituting an injunction for damages are twofold. First, it shifts the burden of determining the cost of the defendant's conduct from the court to the parties. If it is true that Walgreen's damages are smaller than the gain to Sara Creek from allowing a second pharmacy into the shopping mall, then there must be a price for dissolving the injunction that will make both parties better off. Thus, the effect of upholding the injunction would be to substitute for the costly processes of forensic fact determination the less costly processes of private negotiation. Second, a premise of our free-market system, and the lesson of experience here and abroad as well, is that prices and costs are more accurately determined by the market than by government. A battle of experts is a less reliable method of determining the actual cost to Walgreen of facing new competition than negotiations between Walgreen and Sara Creek over the price at which Walgreen would feel adequately compensated for having to face that competition.

That is the benefit side of injunctive relief but there is a cost side as well. Many injunctions require continuing supervision by the court, and that is costly. A request for specific performance (a form of mandatory injunction) of a franchise agreement was refused on this ground in *North American Financial Group, Ltd. v. S.M.R. Enterprises, Inc.*; see Edward Yorio, *Contract Enforcement: Specific Performance and Injunctions* § 3.3.2 (1989). This ground was also stressed in *Rental Development Corp. v. Lavery*, a case involving a lease. Some injunctions are problematic because they impose costs on third parties. A more subtle cost of injunctive relief arises from the situation that economists call "bilateral monopoly," in which two parties can deal only with each other: the situation that an injunction creates. The sole seller of widgets selling to the sole buyer of that product would be an example. But so will be the situation confronting Walgreen and Sara Creek if the injunction is upheld. Walgreen can "sell" its injunctive right only to Sara Creek, and Sara Creek can "buy" Walgreen's surrender of its right to enjoin the leasing of the anchor tenant's space to Phar-Mor only from Walgreen. The lack of alternatives in bilateral monopoly creates a bargaining range, and the costs of negotiating to a point within that range may be high. Suppose the cost to Walgreen of facing the competition of Phar-Mor at the Southgate Mall would be $1 million, and the benefit to Sara Creek of leasing to Phar-Mor would be $2 million. Then at any price between those figures for a waiver of Walgreen's injunctive right both parties would be better off, and we expect parties to bargain around a judicial assignment of legal rights if the assignment is inefficient. R.H. Coase, *The Problem of Social Cost*, 3 J. Law & Econ. 1 (1960). But each of the parties would like to engross as much of the bargaining range as possible—Walgreen to press the price toward $2 million, Sara Creek to depress it toward $1 million. With so much at stake, both parties will have an incentive to devote substantial resources of time and money to the negotiation process. The process may even break down, if one or both parties want to create for future use a reputation as a hard bargainer; and if it does break down, the injunction will have brought about an inefficient result. All these are in one form or another costs of the injunctive process that can be avoided by substituting damages.

The costs and benefits of the damages remedy are the mirror of those of the injunctive remedy. The damages remedy avoids the cost of continuing supervision and third-party effects, and the cost of bilateral monopoly as well. It imposes costs of its own, however, in the form of diminished accuracy in the determination of value, on the one hand, and of the parties' expenditures on preparing and presenting evidence of damages, and the time of the court in evaluating the evidence, on the other.

The weighing up of all these costs and benefits is the analytical procedure that is or at least should be employed by a judge asked to enter a permanent injunction, with the understanding that if the balance is even the injunction should be withheld. The judge is not required to explicate every detail of the analysis and he did not do so here, but as long we are satisfied that his approach is broadly consistent with a proper analysis we shall affirm; and we are satisfied here. The determination of Walgreen's damages would have been costly in forensic resources and inescapably inaccurate. The lease had ten years to run. So Walgreen would have had to project its sales revenues and costs over the next ten years, and then project the impact on those figures of Phar-Mor's competition, and then discount that impact to present value. All but the last step would have been fraught with uncertainty.

We may have given too little weight to such uncertainties in *American Dairy Queen Corp. v. Brown-Port Co.,* but in that case the district judge had found that the remedy at law was adequate in the circumstances and the movant had failed to make its best argument for inadequacy in the district court. It is difficult to forecast the profitability of a retail store over a decade, let alone to assess the impact of a particular competitor on that profitability over that period. Of course one can hire an expert to make such predictions, Glen A. Stankee, *Econometric Forecasting of Lost Profits: Using High Technology to Compute Commercial Damages,* 61 Fla.B.J. 83 (1987), and if injunctive relief is infeasible the expert's testimony may provide a tolerable basis for an award of damages. We cited cases in which damages have been awarded for the breach of an exclusivity clause in a shopping-center lease. But they are awarded in such circumstances not because anyone thinks them a clairvoyant forecast but because it is better to give a wronged person a crude remedy than none at all. It is the same theory on which damages are awarded for a disfiguring injury. No one thinks such injuries readily monetizable, but a crude estimate is better than letting the wrongdoer get off scot-free (which, not incidentally, would encourage more such injuries). Sara Creek presented evidence of what happened (very little) to Walgreen when Phar-Mor moved into other shopping malls in which Walgreen has a pharmacy, and it was on the right track in putting in comparative evidence. But there was a serious question whether the other malls were actually comparable to the Southgate Mall, so we cannot conclude, in the face of the district judge's contrary conclusion, that the existence of comparative evidence dissolved the difficulties of computing damages in this case. Sara Creek complains that the judge refused to compel Walgreen to produce all the data that Sara Creek needed to demonstrate the feasibility of forecasting Walgreen's damages. Walgreen resisted, on grounds of the confidentiality of the data and the cost of producing the massive data that Sara Creek sought. Those are legitimate grounds; and the cost (broadly conceived) they expose of pretrial discovery, in turn presaging complexity at trial, is itself a cost of the damages remedy that injunctive relief saves.

Damages are not always costly to compute, or difficult to compute accurately. In the standard case of a seller's breach of a contract for the sale of goods where the buyer covers by purchasing the same product in the market, damages are readily calculable by subtracting the contract price from the market price and multiplying by the quantity specified in the contract. But this is not such a case and here damages would be a costly and inaccurate remedy; and on the other side of the balance some of the costs of an injunction are absent and the cost that is present seems low. The injunction here, like one enforcing a covenant not to compete (standardly enforced by injunction), is a simple negative injunction—Sara Creek is not to lease space in the Southgate Mall to Phar-Mor during the term of Walgreen's lease—and the costs of judicial supervision and enforcement should be negligible. There is no contention that the injunction will harm an *unrepresented* third party. It may harm Phar-Mor but that harm will be reflected in Sara Creek's offer to Walgreen to dissolve the injunction. (Anyway Phar-Mor *is* a party.) The injunction may also, it is true, harm potential customers of Phar-Mor—people who would prefer to shop at a deep-discount store than an ordinary discount store—but their preferences, too, are registered indirectly. The more business Phar-Mor would have, the more rent it will be willing to pay Sara Creek, and therefore the more Sara Creek will be willing to pay Walgreen to dissolve the injunction.

The only substantial cost of the injunction in this case is that it may set off a round of negotiations between the parties. In some cases, illustrated by *Boomer v. Atlantic Cement Co.*, this consideration alone would be enough to warrant the denial of injunctive relief. The defendant's factory was emitting cement dust that caused the plaintiffs harm monetized at less than $200,000, and the only way to abate the harm would have been to close down the factory, which had cost $45 million to build. An injunction against the nuisance could therefore have created a huge bargaining range (could, not would, because it is unclear what the current value of the factory was), and the costs of negotiating to a point within it might have been immense. If the market value of the factory was actually $45 million, the plaintiffs would be tempted to hold out for a price to dissolve the injunction in the tens of millions and the factory would be tempted to refuse to pay anything more than a few hundred thousand dollars. Negotiations would be unlikely to break down completely, given such a bargaining range, but they might well be protracted and costly. There is nothing so dramatic here. Sara Creek does not argue that it will have to close the mall if enjoined from leasing to Phar-Mor. Phar-Mor is not the only potential anchor tenant. *Liza Danielle, Inc. v. Jamko, Inc.*, on which Sara Creek relies, presented the converse case where the grant of the injunction would have forced an existing tenant to close its store.

To summarize, the judge did not exceed the bounds of reasonable judgment in concluding that the costs (including forgone benefits) of the damages remedy would exceed the costs (including forgone benefits) of an injunction. We need not consider whether, as intimated by Walgreen, exclusivity clauses in shopping-center leases should be considered presumptively enforceable by injunctions. Although we have described the choice between legal and equitable remedies as one for case-by-case determination, the courts have sometimes picked out categories of cases in which injunctive relief is made the norm. The best-known example is specific performance of contracts for the sale of real property. Anthony T. Kronman, *Specific Performance*, 45 U.Chi.L.Rev. 351, 355 and n. 20 (1978). The rule that specific performance will be ordered in such cases as a matter of course is a generalization of the considerations discussed above. Because of the absence of a fully liquid market in real property and the frequent presence of subjective values (many a homeowner, for example, would not sell his house for its market value), the calculation of damages is difficult; and since an order of specific performance to convey a piece of property does not create a continuing relation between the parties, the costs of supervision and enforcement if specific performance is ordered are slight. The exclusivity clause in Walgreen's lease relates to real estate, but we hesitate to suggest that every contract involving real estate should be enforceable as a matter of course by injunctions. Suppose Sara Creek had covenanted to keep the entrance to Walgreen's store free of ice and snow, and breached the covenant. An injunction would require continuing supervision, and it would be easy enough if the injunction were denied for Walgreen to hire its own ice and snow remover and charge the cost to Sara Creek. On the other hand, injunctions to enforce exclusivity clauses are quite likely to be justifiable by just the considerations present here—damages are difficult to estimate with any accuracy and the injunction is a one-shot remedy requiring no continuing judicial involvement. So there is an argument for making injunctive relief presumptively appropriate in such cases, but we need not decide in this case how strong an argument.

AFFIRMED.

QUESTIONS AND NOTES

1. The unenacted 2003 Draft of UCC Article 2 provides:

§ 2–716. Specific Performance.

(1) Specific performance may be decreed if the goods or the agreed performance of the party in breach of contract are unique or in other proper circumstances. In a contract other than a consumer contract, specific performance may be decreed if the parties have agreed to that remedy. However, even if the parties agree to specific performance, specific performance may not be decreed if the breaching party's sole remaining contractual obligation is the payment of money.

(2) The decree for specific performance may include terms and conditions as to payment of the price, damages, or other relief as the court considers just.

Note that this proposed model law differs from current law by expressly permitting parties to commercial contracts to contract for the remedy of specific performance. Should parties be permitted to contract for specific performance in the event of breach even if that remedy would not otherwise be proper? What about the costs to third parties, other social and legal values and the judicial system itself discussed in *Walgreen*? When would a seller of goods ever need or agree to specific performance?

2. Judge Posner in *Walgreen* notes that "courts have sometimes picked out categories of cases in which injunctive relief is made the norm." He identifies contracts involving the transfer of real estate as one such area where courts have categorically determined that equitable relief is presumptively available—even if on specific facts it seems likely that damages could be calculated with reasonable certainty. Another such area is contracts for the sale of "unique" goods. UCC 2-716. Difficulties in valuing unique property and the lack of fully adequate market substitutes support the common law presumption that specific performance is generally appropriate in such cases. Anthony T. Kronman, *Specific Performance*, 45 U.CHI.L.REV. 351 (1978).

III. COMPENSATORY DAMAGES

The basic remedy for breach of contract is an award of damages that gives the injured party the financial equivalent of performance. When a person makes a promise, he undertakes to give the promisee the promised performance or a sum of money that will place the promisee in the same economic position he would have been in had the promise been performed. Thus, the amount of money to which a promisee is entitled if the promise is not kept is defined by the promise. In this sense, the remedy for breach is as much a creature of the parties' agreement as the other terms of the promise.

The basic scheme is easy enough to illustrate. Suppose that Southland had promised to sell Best one carload of plywood for $15,000 but failed to deliver. Assume that on the delivery date the market price had risen to $20,000. Obviously, the disappointed Best could obtain the return of any money paid toward the purchase price and would be excused from paying the rest of the price of the contract. But if Best is to receive the full financial equivalent of performance, it must also be given a sum of money equal to however much more it would have cost on the delivery date to go into the market and buy the plywood elsewhere. The basic formula is that the disappointed buyer is entitled to both the difference between contract price and market price and to the cost of finding a new source of supply. This simple concept can be expressed as: $(M-K) + I = D$, where M is the market price, K is the contract price, I is incidental costs incurred on account of the breach, and D is the total damages.

This straightforward example suggests some important points about damage rules in contract law. First, the difference between contract price and market price fails to compensate Best for its sense of injury or the bother resulting from the failure of performance. Second, if the plywood is readily available elsewhere and its market price has remained constant, Best can obtain the equivalent of performance merely by going into the market and buying the plywood at current market prices. When the market can supply plywood at or near the contract price, Best's money damages will ordinarily be very small or nothing at all.

As attention shifts from the simple case of the disappointed buyer in a sale of goods contract to other contract situations, the factors which must be taken into account in determining how to give the injured party the financial equivalent of performance may shift. Damage rules assume, as one might predict, a somewhat different shape and sound in different contexts, as you shall see as you study cases involving the sale of goods, personal services, and construction. As you progress through cases that describe the basic scheme, keep in mind that at the core some version of the market minus contract (M-K) theme replicates itself in all contexts, and that in operation the rules are modest both in terms of the interest they protect and the damages they award.

One limitation on all contract damages is the principle that an injured party cannot collect those damages it might have avoided by reasonable action on its part after it knew of the breach. This is called the rule of avoidable consequences or, more commonly but less accurately, the duty to mitigate damages. This rule usually is justified in terms of causation: the damage claimed was caused by the unreasonable action or inaction of the injured party rather than the breach itself. Consider the manufacturer that does not receive delivery of raw materials needed to continue operation. If the goods are available elsewhere, the manufacturer should obtain them on the open market and thus limit its loss; it may not shutter its plant and claim all resulting losses. Damages are limited to the contract-market differential. While this limitation is usually referred to as the duty to mitigate damages, it is not a duty in the conventional legal sense. The disappointed buyer does not breach an obligation by failing to go to market, but it may not recover damages for losses which it failed to take reasonable actions to avoid.

Damages are designed to put the injured party in the same position it would have been in if the contract had been performed by both parties. This leads to another limit on recovery: the monetary remedy must be reduced by any amount that the injured plaintiff saved by not being required to complete its performance of the contract. A disappointed buyer, therefore, does not receive the market price of the promised goods, what it will cost to go into the market to buy them. Instead, the buyer receives only the difference between that market price and what is "saved" because the breach excused the buyer from having to perform its promise to pay the contract price for the goods.

The concept of savings resulting from a breach merges in many situations with the concept of savings made possible by mitigation. If a buyer has not paid the full contract price, the amount it has not yet paid must of course be deducted from any claim based on the market price of the goods contracted for. If its obligation under the contract is to render performance other than payment of money, the value of the performance it now not only does not have to make, but must stop making, must similarly be deducted. The rationale is that it can now use what is "saved" and it is expected to do so, if possible, in such a way as to obtain its full value.

This simple structure based on giving the disappointed party the financial equivalent of the promised performance is supplemented in a number of situations by two other approaches to compensation for breach of contract. Sometimes, as our original illustration from *Best v. Southland* suggests, the disappointed party may have made a partial advance payment or expended time and materials in performance of its obligations under the agreement before the other party's breach. In that case, the injured party will want its money back; it will seek the return of what it has expended in reliance on the other side's promise. Compensation for expenditures in reliance can be important even in situations when there has been no change in market price and therefore no damages are recoverable to provide the financial equivalent of performance. In addition, the disappointed party may have conferred benefits on the other side that it wants restored to it. These three elements overlap in many ways and all may be present in the same situation. All derive from the concept of compensatory damages, but they are often treated by scholars and courts as if they were three distinct "interests." The distinction may help the student analyze problems, but it becomes potentially misleading if the three interests are understood to be exclusive and competitive rather than complementary or alternative ways of describing the same general approach. The Restatement (Second) of Contracts develops this distinction as follows:

§ 344. Purposes of Remedies.

Judicial remedies under the rules stated in this Restatement serve to protect one or more of the following interests of a promisee:

(a) his "expectation interest," which is his interest in having the benefit of his bargain by being put in as good a position as he would have been in had the contract been performed,

(b) his "reliance interest," which is his interest in being reimbursed for loss caused by reliance on the contract by being put in as good a position as he would have been in had the contract not been made, or

(c) his "restitution interest," which is his interest in having restored to him any benefit that he has conferred on the other party.

COMMENT:

a. Three Interests. The law of contract remedies implements the policy in favor of allowing individuals to order their own affairs by making legally enforceable promises. Ordinarily, when a court concludes that there has been a breach of contract, it enforces the broken promise by protecting the expectation that the injured party had when he made the contract. It does this by attempting to put him in as good a position as he would have been in had the contract been performed, that is, had there been no breach. The interest protected in this way is called the "expectation interest." It is sometimes said to give the injured party the "benefit of the bargain." This is not, however, the only interest that may be protected.

The promisee may have changed his position in reliance on the contract by, for example, incurring expenses in preparing to perform, in performing, or in foregoing opportunities to make other contracts. In that case, the court may recognize a claim based on his reliance rather than on his expectation. It does this by attempting to put him back in the position in which he would have been had the contract not been made. The interest protected in this way is called "reliance interest." Although it may be equal to the expectation interest, it is ordinarily smaller because it does not include the injured party's lost profit.

In some situations a court will recognize yet a third interest and grant relief to prevent unjust enrichment. This may be done if a party has not only changed his own position in reliance on the contract but has also conferred a benefit on the other party by, for example, making a part payment or furnishing services under the contract. The court may then require the other party to disgorge the benefit that he has received by returning it to the party who conferred it. The interest of the claimant protected in this way is called the "restitution interest." Although it may be equal to the expectation or reliance interest, it is ordinarily smaller because it includes neither the injured party's lost profit nor that part of his expenditures in reliance that resulted in no benefit to the other party.

The interests described in this Section are not inflexible limits on relief and in situations in which a court grants such relief as justice requires, the relief may not correspond precisely to any of these interests....

§ 347. Measure of Damages in General.

Subject to the limitations stated in §§ 350–53, the injured party has a right to damages based on his expectation interest as measured by

(a) the loss in the value to him of the other party's performance caused by its failure or deficiency, plus

(b) any other loss, including incidental or consequential loss, caused by the breach, less

(c) any cost or other loss that he has avoided by not having to perform.

COMMENT:

a. Expectation Interest. Contract damages are ordinarily based on the injured party's expectation interest and are intended to give him the benefit of his bargain by awarding him a sum of money that will, to the extent possible, put him in as good a position as he would have been in had the contract been performed....

A.   THE FINANCIAL EQUIVALENT OF PERFORMANCE

Thorne v. White

District of Columbia Municipal Court of Appeals, 1954.
103 A.2d 579.

■ QUINN, J. Appellant, hereinafter referred to as Thorne, contracted to put a new roof on appellee's residence and to make certain repairs in connection therewith for the sum of $225. Pursuant to the contract, Thorne delivered certain materials to the job and began work. Within a few hours the work was discontinued because of inclement weather. Thorne never returned to the job and a few days later had his materials hauled away. White then entered into an agreement with the Koons Roofing Company to have the work completed at a cost of $582.26. This was $357.26 more than the amount of Thorne's contract. He sued Thorne for that difference alleging breach of contract. The court, hearing the case without a jury, ruled in favor of White, and Thorne brings this appeal.

We find no error in the trial court's ruling that Thorne had breached the contract. He testified that he had not completed the work because White had ordered him to discontinue, but White denied ever having made such a statement. Thus, the issue as to the breach of contract was clearly one of fact. There was ample support in the evidence to sustain the court's finding.

The aspect of the case which gives us more concern is the question of damages. White was awarded a judgment for $357.26, which amount represents the difference between the contract price with Thorne and the amount paid to the Koons Company for the completion of the work. This sum would be the correct measure of damages, provided the second contract did not call for additional work not contemplated by nor included in the first one. This is in accord with the general rule that a party damaged by a breach may only recover for losses which are the natural consequence and proximate result of that breach. Damages are awarded for the purpose of compensation and the injured party should not be placed in a better position than he would have been in had no breach occurred. In cases such as the present one the successful plaintiff should only be allowed to recover what it has cost him to complete the same work, over and above the original contract price.

In the instant case the trial court found that the two roofing contracts were substantially the same and that the damages were therefore the amount by which Koons' contract exceeded Thorne's price. We rule that such a holding was error. Besides the large difference between the two contract prices, the evidence was that Thorne's contract called for a 4–ply roof, while the second contract was for what was in effect a 5–ply roof; that Thorne was merely to put a new roof over the old one, while the Koons Company entirely removed the old roof; and that several additional items were provided for under the second contract not called for in the first. A representative of the Koons Company testified that these additional items added to the cost of their contract. As the evidence clearly shows that White received more from the Koons Company than he was to receive from Thorne, we think an improper measure of damages was applied.

Reversed with instructions to grant a new trial on the issue of damages.

QUESTIONS

1. Why did Koons put on a more expensive roof? If Thorne's promised job would have resulted in a leaky roof, how is White to be given the financial equivalent of performance? By giving him enough to buy another lousy roof or enough to have the job done right?

2. How should White's damages be established at the new trial? Did Thorne promise a 4–ply roof or a serviceable roof? What if the court finds that only a 5–ply roof would serve? What evidence is there likely to be on that question?

3. How did Judge Quinn determine whether the agreement with Koons was a "substitute" for Thorne's promised performance?

DRAFTING EXERCISE

Imagine you are representing one of the parties (either Thorne or White, your choice) on remand and are preparing for the retrial on damages.

A. Outline the direct examination of your client.

B. Outline the cross-examination of the adverse party.

---

1. Expectation Interest

Freund v. Washington Square Press
New York Court of Appeals, 1974.
34 N.Y.2d 379, 357 N.Y.S.2d 857.

■ SAMUEL RABIN, J. In this action for breach of a publishing contract, we must decide what damages are recoverable for defendant's failure to publish plaintiff's manuscript. In 1965, plaintiff, an author and a college teacher, and defendant, Washington Square Press, Inc., entered into a written agreement which, in relevant part, provided as follows. Plaintiff ("author") granted defendant ("publisher") exclusive rights to publish and sell in book form plaintiff's work on modern drama. Upon plaintiff's delivery of the manuscript, defendant agreed to complete payment of a nonreturnable $2,000 "advance." Thereafter, if defendant deemed the manuscript not "suitable for publication," it had the right to terminate the agreement by written notice within 60 days of delivery. Unless so terminated, defendant agreed to publish the work in hardbound edition within 18 months and afterwards in paperbound edition. The contract further provided that defendant would pay royalties to plaintiff, based upon specified percentages of sales. (For example, plaintiff was to receive 10%

of the retail price of the first 10,000 copies sold in the continental United States.) If defendant failed to publish within 18 months, the contract provided that "this agreement shall terminate and the rights herein granted to the Publisher shall revert to the Author. In such event all payments theretofore made to the Author shall belong to the Author without prejudice to any other remedies which the Author may have." The contract also provided that controversies were to be determined pursuant to the New York simplified procedure for court determination of disputes (CPLR 3031–3037, Consol.Laws, c. 8).

Plaintiff performed by delivering his manuscript to defendant and was paid his $2,000 advance. Defendant thereafter merged with another publisher and ceased publishing in hardbound. Although defendant did not exercise its 60–day right to terminate, it has refused to publish the manuscript in any form.

Plaintiff commenced the instant action pursuant to the simplified procedure practice and initially sought specific performance of the contract. The Trial Term Justice denied specific performance but, finding a valid contract and a breach by defendant, set the matter down for trial on the issue of monetary damages, if any, sustained by the plaintiff. At trial, plaintiff sought to prove: (1) delay of his academic promotion; (2) loss of royalties which would have been earned; and (3) the cost of publication if plaintiff had made his own arrangements to publish. The trial court found that plaintiff had been promoted despite defendant's failure to publish, and that there was no evidence that the breach had caused any delay. Recovery of lost royalties was denied without discussion. The court found, however, that the cost of hardcover publication to plaintiff was the natural and probable consequence of the breach and, based upon expert testimony, awarded $10,000 to cover this cost. It denied recovery of the expenses of paperbound publication on the ground that plaintiff's proof was conjectural.

The Appellate Division, (3 to 2) affirmed, finding that the cost of publication was the proper measure of damages. In support of its conclusion, the majority analogized to the construction contract situation where the cost of completion may be the proper measure of damages for a builder's failure to complete a house or for use of wrong materials. The dissent concluded that the cost of publication is not an appropriate measure of damages and consequently, that plaintiff may recover nominal damages only. We agree with the dissent. In so concluding, we look to the basic purpose of damage recovery and the nature and effect of the parties' contract.

It is axiomatic that, except where punitive damages are allowable, the law awards damages for breach of contract to compensate for injury caused by the breach—injury which was foreseeable, i.e., reasonably within the contemplation of the parties, at the time the contract was entered into. Money damages are substitutional relief designed in theory "to put the injured party in as good a position as he would have been put by full performance of the contract, at the least cost to the defendant and without charging him with harms that he had no sufficient reason to foresee when he made the contract." (5 Corbin, Contracts, § 1002, pp. 31–32; 11 Williston, Contracts [3d ed.], § 1338, p. 198.) In other words, so far as possible, the law attempts to secure to the injured party the benefit of his bargain, subject to the limitations that the injury—whether it be losses suffered or gains prevented—was foreseeable, and that the amount of damages claimed be measurable with a reasonable degree of certainty and, of course, adequately proven. But it is equally fundamental that the injured party should not recover more from the breach than he would have gained had the contract been fully performed.

Measurement of damages in this case according to the cost of publication to the plaintiff would confer greater advantage than performance of the contract would have entailed to plaintiff and would place him in a far better position than he would have occupied had the defendant fully performed. Such measurement bears no relation to compensation for plaintiff's actual loss or anticipated profit. Far beyond compensating plaintiff for the interests he had in the defendant's performance of the contract—whether restitution, reliance or expectation, an award of the cost of publication would enrich plaintiff at defendant's expense.

Pursuant to the contract, plaintiff delivered his manuscript to the defendant. In doing so, he conferred a value on the defendant which, upon defendant's breach, was required to be restored to him. Special Term, in addition to ordering a trial on the issue of damages, ordered defendant to return the manuscript to plaintiff and plaintiff's restitution interest in the contract was thereby protected.

At the trial on the issue of damages, plaintiff alleged no reliance losses suffered in performing the contract or in making necessary preparations to perform. Had such losses, if foreseeable and ascertainable, been incurred, plaintiff would have been entitled to compensation for them.

As for plaintiff's expectation interest in the contract, it was basically two-fold—the "advance" and the royalties. (To be sure, plaintiff may have expected to enjoy whatever notoriety, prestige or other benefits that might have attended publication, but even if these expectations were compensable, plaintiff did not attempt at trial to place a monetary value on them.) There is no dispute that plaintiff's expectancy in the "advance" was fulfilled—he has received his $2,000. His expectancy interest in the royalties—the profit he stood to gain from sale of the published book—while theoretically compensable, was speculative. Although this work is not plaintiff's first, at trial he provided no stable foundation for a reasonable estimate of royalties he would have earned had defendant not breached its promise to publish. In these circumstances, his claim for royalties falls for uncertainty.

Since the damages which would have compensated plaintiff for anticipated royalties were not proved with the required certainty, we agree with the dissent in the Appellate Division that nominal damages alone are recoverable. Though these are damages in name only and not at all compensatory, they are nevertheless awarded as a formal vindication of plaintiff's legal right to compensation which has not been given a sufficiently certain monetary valuation.

In our view, the analogy by the majority in the Appellate Division to the construction contract situation was inapposite. In the typical construction contract, the owner agrees to pay money or other consideration to a builder and expects, under the contract, to receive a completed building in return. The value of the promised performance to the owner is the properly constructed building. In this case, unlike the typical construction contract, the value to plaintiff of the promised performance—publication—was a percentage of sales of the books published and not the books themselves. Had the plaintiff contracted for the printing, binding and delivery of a number of hardbound copies of his manuscript, to be sold or disposed of as he wished, then perhaps the construction analogy, and measurement of damages by the cost of replacement or completion, would have some application.

Here, however, the specific value to plaintiff of the promised publication was the royalties he stood to receive from defendant's sales of the published book. Essentially, publication represented what it would have cost the defendant to confer that value upon the plaintiff, and, by its breach, defendant saved that cost. The error by the courts below was in measuring damages not by the value to plaintiff of the promised performance but by the cost of that performance to defendant. Damages are not measured, however, by what the defaulting party saved by the breach, but by the natural and probable consequences of the breach *to the plaintiff.* In this case, the consequence to plaintiff of defendant's failure to publish is that he is prevented from realizing the gains promised by the contract—the royalties. But, as we have stated, the amount of royalties plaintiff would have realized was not ascertained with adequate certainty and, as a consequence, plaintiff may recover nominal damages only.

Accordingly, the order of the Appellate Division should be modified to the extent of reducing the damage award of $10,000 for the cost of publication to six cents, but with costs and disbursements to the plaintiff.

QUESTIONS AND NOTES

1. By breaching this contract, the defendant publisher saved the expenses of publication, less what it would have realized net from selling the books. So in this case the breaching defendant ends up better off economically by breaching than by performing, while the injured plaintiff receives only nominal damages.

2. Did the court give Freund the financial equivalent of performance? Why doesn't Freund have a claim for his lost royalties? Might Freund have done better on a reliance damages or restitution theory? Does the publisher "returning" the

manuscript place Freund in the position he would have been in had there been no contract?

3. Why should uncertainties in calculating damages work against the injured plaintiff rather than the breaching the defendant? Isn't it the defendant's fault that we find ourselves in a circumstance where calculating damages is so difficult and speculative?

Sullivan v. O'Connor

Massachusetts Supreme Judicial Court, 1973.
363 Mass. 579, 296 N.E.2d 183.

■ KAPLAN, J. The plaintiff patient secured a jury verdict of $13,500 against the defendant surgeon for breach of contract in respect to an operation upon the plaintiff's nose. The substituted consolidated bill of exceptions presents questions about the correctness of the judge's instructions on the issue of damages.

The declaration was in two counts. In the first count, the plaintiff alleged that she, as patient, entered into a contract with the defendant, a surgeon, wherein the defendant promised to perform plastic surgery on her nose and thereby to enhance her beauty and improve her appearance; that he performed the surgery but failed to achieve the promised result; rather the result of the surgery was to disfigure and deform her nose, to cause her pain in body and mind, and to subject her to other damage and expense. The second count, based on the same transaction, was in the conventional form for malpractice, charging that the defendant had been guilty of negligence in performing the surgery. Answering, the defendant entered a general denial.

On the plaintiff's demand, the case was tried by jury. At the close of the evidence, the judge put to the jury, as special questions, the issues of liability under the two counts, and instructed them accordingly. The jury returned a verdict for the plaintiff on the contract count, and for the defendant on the negligence count. The judge then instructed the jury on the issue of damages.

As background to the instructions and the parties' exceptions, we mention certain facts as the jury could find them. The plaintiff was a professional entertainer, and this was known to the defendant. The agreement was as alleged in the declaration. More particularly, judging from exhibits, the plaintiff's nose had been straight, but long and prominent; the defendant undertook by two operations to reduce its prominence and somewhat to shorten it, thus making it more pleasing in relation to the plaintiff's other features. Actually the plaintiff was obliged to undergo three operations, and her appearance was worsened. Her nose now had a concave line to about the midpoint, at which it became bulbous; viewed frontally, the nose from bridge to midpoint was flattened and broadened, and the two sides of the tip had lost symmetry. This configuration evidently could not be improved by further surgery. The plaintiff did not demonstrate, however, that her change of appearance had resulted in loss of employment. Payments by the plaintiff covering the defendant's fee and hospital expenses were stipulated at $622.65.

The judge instructed the jury, first, that the plaintiff was entitled to recover her out-of-pocket expenses incident to the operations. Second, she could recover the damages flowing directly, naturally, proximately, and foreseeably from the defendant's breach of promise. These would comprehend damages for any disfigurement of the plaintiff's nose—that is, any change of appearance for the worse—including the effects of the consciousness of such disfigurement on the plaintiff's mind, and in this connection the jury should consider the nature of the plaintiff's profession. Also consequent upon the defendant's breach, and compensable, were the pain and suffering involved in the third operation, but not in the first two. As there was no proof that any loss of earnings by the plaintiff resulted from the breach, that element should not enter into the calculation of damages.

By his exceptions the defendant contends that the judge erred in allowing the jury to take into account anything but the plaintiff's out-of-pocket expenses (presumably at the stipulated amount). The defendant excepted to the judge's refusal of his request for a general charge to that effect, and, more specifically, to the judge's refusal of a charge that the plaintiff could not recover for pain and suffering connected with the third operation or for impairment of the plaintiff's appearance and associated mental distress.

The plaintiff on her part excepted to the judge's refusal of a request to charge that the plaintiff could recover the difference in value between the nose as promised and the nose as it appeared after the operations. However, the plaintiff in her brief expressly waives this exception and others made by her in case this court overrules the defendant's exceptions; thus she would be content to hold the jury's verdict in her favor.

We conclude that the defendant's exceptions should be overruled.

It has been suggested on occasion that agreements between patients and physicians by which the physician undertakes to effect a cure or to bring about a given result should be declared unenforceable on grounds of public policy. But there are many decisions recognizing and enforcing such contracts, and the law of Massachusetts has treated them as valid, although we have had no decision meeting head on the contention that they should be denied legal sanction. These causes of action are, however, considered a little suspect, and thus we find courts straining sometimes to read the pleadings as sounding only in tort for negligence, and not in contract for breach of promise, despite sedulous efforts by the pleaders to pursue the latter theory.

It is not hard to see why the courts should be unenthusiastic or skeptical about the contract theory. Considering the uncertainties of medical science and the variations in the physical and psychological conditions of individual patients, doctors can seldom in good faith promise specific results. Therefore it is unlikely that physicians of even average integrity will in fact make such promises. Statements of opinion by the physician with some optimistic coloring are a different thing, and may indeed have therapeutic value. But patients may transform such statements into firm promises in their own minds, especially when they have been disappointed in the event, and testify in that sense to sympathetic juries.[2] If actions for breach of promise can be readily maintained, doctors, so it is said, will be frightened into practising "defensive medicine." On the other hand, if these actions were outlawed, leaving only the possibility of suits for malpractice, there is fear that the public might be exposed to the enticements of charlatans, and confidence in the profession might ultimately be shaken. The law has taken the middle of the road position of allowing actions based on alleged contract, but insisting on clear proof. Instructions to the jury may well stress this requirement and point to tests of truth, such as the complexity or difficulty of an operation as bearing on the probability that a given result was promised.

If an action on the basis of contract is allowed, we have next the question of the measure of damages to be applied where liability is found. Some cases have taken the simple view that the promise by the physician is to be treated like an ordinary commercial promise, and accordingly that the successful plaintiff is entitled to a standard measure of recovery for breach of contract — "compensatory" ("expectancy") damages, an amount intended to put the plaintiff in the position he would be in if the contract had been performed, or, presumably, at the plaintiff's election, "restitution" damages, an amount corresponding to any benefit conferred by the plaintiff upon the defendant in the performance of the contract disrupted by the defendant's breach. Thus in *Hawkins v. McGee*, 84 N.H. 114, the defendant doctor was taken to have promised the plaintiff to convert his damaged hand by means of an operation into a good or perfect hand, but the doctor so operated as to damage the hand still further. The court, following the usual expectancy formula, would have asked the jury to estimate and award to the plaintiff the difference between the value of a good or perfect hand, as promised, and the value of the hand after the operation.

---

2. Judicial skepticism about whether a promise was in fact made derives also from the possibility that the truth has been tortured to give the plaintiff the advantage of the longer period of limitations sometimes available for actions on contract as distinguished from those in tort or for malpractice.

(The same formula would apply, although the dollar result would be less, if the operation had neither worsened nor improved the condition of the hand.) If the plaintiff had not yet paid the doctor his fee, that amount would be deducted from the recovery. There could be no recovery for the pain and suffering of the operation, since that detriment would have been incurred even if the operation had been successful; one can say that this detriment was not "caused" by the breach. But where the plaintiff by reason of the operation was put to more pain than he would have had to endure, had the doctor performed as promised, he should be compensated for that difference as a proper part of his expectancy recovery. It may be noted that on an alternative count for malpractice the plaintiff in the *Hawkins* case had been nonsuited; but on ordinary principles this could not affect the contract claim, for it is hardly a defence to a breach of contract that the promisor acted innocently and without negligence. The New Hampshire court further refined the *Hawkins* analysis in *McQuaid v. Michou*, 85 N.H. 299, all in the direction of treating the patient-physician cases on the ordinary footing of expectancy.

Other cases, including a number in New York, without distinctly repudiating the *Hawkins* type of analysis, have indicated that a different and generally more lenient measure of damages is to be applied in patient-physician actions based on breach of alleged special agreements to effect a cure, attain a stated result, or employ a given medical method. This measure is expressed in somewhat variant ways, but the substance is that the plaintiff is to recover any expenditures made by him and for other detriment (usually not specifically described in the opinions) following proximately and foreseeably upon the defendant's failure to carry out his promise. This, be it noted, is not a "restitution" measure, for it is not limited to restoration of the benefit conferred on the defendant (the fee paid) but includes other expenditures, for example, amounts paid for medicine and nurses; so also it would seem according to its logic to take in damages for any worsening of the plaintiff's condition due to the breach. Nor is it an "expectancy" measure, for it does not appear to contemplate recovery of the whole difference in value between the condition as promised and the condition actually resulting from the treatment. Rather the tendency of the formulation is to put the plaintiff back in the position he occupied just before the parties entered upon the agreement, to compensate him for the detriments he suffered in reliance upon the agreement. This kind of intermediate pattern of recovery for breach of contract is discussed in the suggestive article by Fuller and Perdue, *The Reliance Interest in Contract Damages*, where the authors show that, although not attaining the currency of the standard measures, a "reliance" measure has for special reasons been applied by the courts in a variety of settings, including noncommercial settings.

For breach of the patient-physician agreements under consideration, a recovery limited to restitution seems plainly too meager, if the agreements are to be enforced at all. On the other hand, an expectancy recovery may well be excessive. The factors, already mentioned, which have made the cause of action somewhat suspect, also suggest moderation as to the breadth of the recovery that should be permitted. Where, as in the case at bar and in a number of the reported cases, the doctor has been absolved of negligence by the trier, an expectancy measure may be thought harsh. We should recall here that the fee paid by the patient to the doctor for the alleged promise would usually be quite disproportionate to the putative expectancy recovery. To attempt, moreover, to put a value on the condition that would or might have resulted, had the treatment succeeded as promised, may sometimes put an exceptional strain on the imagination of the fact finder. As a general consideration, Fuller and Perdue argue that the reasons for granting damages for broken promises to the extent of the expectancy are at their strongest when the promises are made in a business context, when they have to do with the production or distribution of goods or the allocation of functions in the market place; they become weaker as the context shifts from a commercial to a noncommercial field.

There is much to be said, then, for applying a reliance measure to the present facts, and we have only to add that our cases are not unreceptive to the use of that formula in special situations. We have, however, had no previous occasion to apply it to patient-physician cases.[5]

The question of recovery on a reliance basis for pain and suffering or mental distress requires further attention. We find expressions in the decisions that pain

---

5. In *Mt. Pleasant Stable Co. v. Steinberg*, 238 Mass. 567, the plaintiff company agreed to supply teams of horses at agreed rates as required from day to day by the defendant for his business. To prepare itself to fulfil the contract and in reliance on it, the plaintiff bought two "Cliest" horses at a certain price. When the defendant repudiated the contract, the plaintiff sold the horses at a loss and in its action for breach claimed the loss as an element of damages. The court properly held that the plaintiff was not entitled to this item as it was also claiming (and recovering) its lost profits (expectancy) on the contract as a whole. *Cf.* Noble v. Ames Mfg. Co., 112 Mass. 492. (The loss on sale of the horses is analogous to the pain and suffering for which the patient would be disallowed a recovery in *Hawkins v. McGee*, 84 N.H. 114, because he was claiming and recovering expectancy damages.) The court in the *Mt. Pleasant* case referred, however, to *Pond v. Harris*, 113 Mass. 114, as a contrasting situation where the expectancy could not be fairly determined. There the defendant had wrongfully revoked an agreement to arbitrate a dispute with the plaintiff (this was before such agreements were made specifically enforceable). In an action for the breach, the plaintiff was held entitled to recover for his preparations for the arbitration which had been rendered useless and a waste, including the plaintiff's time and trouble and his expenditures for counsel and witness. The context apparently was commercial but reliance elements were held compensable when there was no fair way of estimating an expectancy. A noncommercial example is *Smith v. Sherman*, 4 Cush. 408, 413–414, suggesting that a conventional recovery for breach of promise of marriage included a recompense for various efforts and expenditures by the plaintiff preparatory to the promised wedding.

and suffering (or the like) are simply not compensable in actions for breach of contract. The defendant seemingly espouses this proposition in the present case. True, if the buyer under a contract for the purchase of a lot of merchandise, in suing for the seller's breach, should claim damages for mental anguish caused by his disappointment in the transaction, he would not succeed; he would be told, perhaps, that the asserted psychological injury was not fairly foreseeable by the defendant as a probable consequence of the breach of such a business contract. But there is no general rule barring such items of damage in actions for breach of contract. It is all a question of the subject matter and background of the contract, and when the contract calls for an operation on the person of the plaintiff, psychological as well as physical injury may be expected to figure somewhere in the recovery, depending on the particular circumstances.

Again, it is said in a few of the New York cases, concerned with the classification of actions for statute of limitations purposes, that the absence of allegations demanding recovery for pain and suffering is characteristic of a contract claim by a patient against a physician, that such allegations rather belong in a claim for malpractice. These remarks seem unduly sweeping. Suffering or distress resulting from the breach going beyond that which was envisaged by the treatment as agreed, should be compensable on the same ground as the worsening of the patient's conditions because of the breach. Indeed it can be argued that the very suffering or distress "contracted for"—that which would have been incurred if the treatment achieved the promised result—should also be compensable on the theory underlying the New York cases. For that suffering is "wasted" if the treatment fails. Otherwise stated, compensation for this waste is arguably required in order to complete the restoration of the status quo ante.

In the light of the foregoing discussion, all the defendant's exceptions fail: the plaintiff was not confined to the recovery of her out-of-pocket expenditures; she was entitled to recover also for the worsening of her condition, and for the pain and suffering and mental distress involved in the third operation. These items were compensable on either an expectancy or a reliance view. We might have been required to elect between the two views if the pain and suffering connected with the first two operations contemplated by the agreement, or the whole difference in value between the present and the promised conditions, were being claimed as elements of damage. But the plaintiff waives her possible claim to the former element, and to so much of the latter as represents the difference in value between the promised condition and the condition before the operations.

Plaintiff's exceptions waived.

Defendant's exceptions overruled.

QUESTIONS AND NOTES

1. In this case the jury found for Ms. Sullivan on the contract claim and for Dr. O'Connor on the negligence claim. Can these two verdicts be reconciled?

2. How do the contracts damages awarded in this case differ from medical malpractice damages in tort? Should they differ?

3. As a result of this decision, Ms. Sullivan, by recovering in contract, avoids having to prove negligence or similar fault on the part of the doctor and has the benefit of the more generous contract statute of limitations. She also recovers tort-like damages for pain and suffering as contract damages. In such a case why would a plaintiff ever sue in tort?

4. Murphy injures his back in the workplace and consults an orthopedic surgeon, Dr. Implicito, who recommends spinal bone graft surgery. After explaining the various risks of the surgery including the potential failure of a graft to properly fuse, Implicito informs Murphy that the surgery can be performed with his own bone material grafted from another part of his skeleton ("autograft") or with material from a cadaver ("allograft"). Murphy who has a morbid fear of death, dying and cadavers, emphatically rejects the allograft option but agrees to hire Dr. Implicito to perform the autograft procedure. The surgery is performed but the Dr. Implicito uses cadaver material rather than an autograft. Murphy's spine falls to fuse properly and a second doctor performs another autograft procedure to correct his unfused spinal graft. The second doctor after congratulating Murphy on the apparent success of the second operation, informs him that although it made no difference in the outcome of the first procedure (which by all accounts was competently performed in accordance with all applicable medical standards) in fact the first procedure had been an allograft (which has now been removed) rather than an autograft. Murphy is furious and suffers emotional trauma in the form of nightmares and constant morbid thoughts. Murphy sues Dr. Implicito for breach of contract. Should Murphy win? What are his damages? *See Murphy v. Implicito*, 392 N.J. Super. 245 (2007).

---

2. Reliance Interest

Anglia Television Ltd. v. Reed

Court of Appeal, Civil Division, 1971.
[1972] 1 Q.B. 60, [1971] All E.R. 690.

■ LORD DENNING, MASTER OF THE ROLLS. Anglia Television Ltd. were minded in 1968 to make a film of a play for television entitled *The Man in the Wood*. It portrayed an American married to an English woman. The American has an adventure in an

English wood. The film was to last for 90 minutes. Anglia Television made many arrangements in advance. They arranged for a place where the play was to be filmed. They employed a director, a designer and a stage manager, and so forth. They involved themselves in much expense. All this was done before they got the leading man. They required a strong actor capable of holding the play together. He was to be on the scene the whole time. Anglia Television eventually found the man. He was Mr. Robert Reed, an American who has a very high reputation as an actor. He was very suitable for this part. By telephone conversation on 30th August 1968 it was agreed by Mr. Reed through his agent that he would come to England and be available between 9th September and 11th October 1968 to rehearse and play in this film. He was to get a performance fee of £1,050, living expenses of £100 a week, his first class fares to and from the United States, and so forth. It was all subject to the permit of the Ministry of Labour for him to come here. That was duly given on 2nd September 1968. So the contract was concluded. But unfortunately there was some muddle with the bookings. It appears that Mr. Reed's agent had already booked him in America for some other play. So on 3rd September 1968 the agent said that Mr. Reed would not come to England to perform in this play. He repudiated his contract. Anglia Television tried hard to find a substitute but could not do so. So on 11th September they accepted his repudiation. They abandoned the proposed film. They gave notice to the people whom they had engaged and so forth.

Anglia Television then sued Mr. Reed for damages. He did not dispute his liability, but a question arose as to the damages. Anglia Television do not claim their profit. They cannot say what their profit would have been on this contract if Mr. Reed had come here and performed it. So, instead of claim for loss of profits, they claim for the wasted expenditure. They had incurred the director's fees, the designer's fees, the stage manager's and assistant manager's fees, and so on. It comes in all to £2,750. Anglia Television say that all that money was wasted because Mr. Reed did not perform his contract.

Mr. Reed's advisers take a point of law. They submit that Anglia Television cannot recover for expenditure incurred *before* the contract was concluded with Mr. Reed. They can only recover the expenditure *after* the contract was concluded. They say that the expenditure *after* the contract was only £854.65, and that is all that Anglia Television can recover. The master rejected that contention; he held that Anglia Television could recover the whole £2,750; and now Mr. Reed appeals to this court.

Counsel for Mr. Reed has referred us to the recent unreported case of *Perestrello & Compania Limitada v. United Paint Co. Ltd. (No. 2)*, in which Thesiger, J., quoted the words of Lord Tindal, CJ, in 1835 in *Hodges v. Earl of Litchfield*:

> "The expenses preliminary to the contract ought not to be allowed. The party enters into them for his own benefit at a time when it is uncertain whether there will be any contract or not."

Thesiger, J., applied those words, saying: "In my judgment pre-contract expenditure, though thrown away, is not recoverable ..."

I cannot accept the proposition as stated. It seems to me that a plaintiff in such a case as this had an election: he can either claim for his loss of profits; or for his wasted expenditure. But he must elect between them. He cannot claim both. If he has not suffered any loss of profits—or if he cannot prove what his profits would have been—he can claim in the alternative the expenditure which has been thrown away, that is, wasted, by reason of the breach....

If the plaintiff claims the wasted expenditure, he is not limited to the expenditure incurred *after* the contract was concluded. He can claim also the expenditure incurred *before* the contract, provided that it was such as would reasonably be in the contemplation of the parties as likely to be wasted if the contract was broken. Applying that principle here, it is plain that, when Mr. Reed entered into this contract, he must have known perfectly well that much expenditure had already been incurred on director's fees and the like. He must have contemplated—or, at any rate, it is reasonably to be imputed to him—that if he broke his contract, all that expenditure would be wasted, whether or not it was incurred before or after the contract. He must pay damages for all the expenditure so wasted and thrown away. This view is supported by the recent decision of Brightman, J., in *Lloyd v. Stanbury*. There was a contract for the sale of land. In anticipation of the contract—and before it was concluded—the purchaser went to much expense in moving a caravan to the site and in getting his furniture there. The seller afterwards entered into a contract to sell the land to the purchaser, but afterwards broke his contract. The land had not increased in value, so the purchaser could not claim for any loss of profit. But Brightman, J., held that he could recover the cost of moving the caravan and furniture, because it was "within the contemplation of the parties when the contract was signed." That decision is in accord with correct principle, namely, that wasted expenditure can be recovered when it is wasted by reason of the defendant's breach of contract. It is true that, if the defendant had never entered into the contract, he would not be liable, and the expenditure would have been incurred by the plaintiff without redress; but, the defendant having made his contract and broken it, it does not lie in his mouth to say he is not liable, when it was because of his breach that the expenditure has been wasted.

I think the master was quite right and this appeal should be dismissed.

QUESTIONS AND NOTES

1. Anglia Television recovers its outlays on the whole project to make *The Man in the Wood*. Can this result be explained in terms of the three interests described in Restatement, Second, § 344? Anglia conferred no benefit on Reed, so the available options are the expectancy and the reliance interests. In what sense does the award of these outlays give Anglia the financial equivalent of performance? How can it be claimed that Anglia was relying on Reed in making outlays before it had a contract with him?

2. What is the significance of the fact that Anglia abandoned the project?

3. What might Lord Denning mean when he says that Anglia Television couldn't find a substitute? Was Robert Reed the only actor in the world who could play the role?

4. Compare Lord Denning's analysis of wasted pre-contractual expenditures in *Anglia Television* with Judge Richard Posner's analysis of the recoverability of fixed overhead expenses in *Autotrol Corp. v. Continental Water Sys. Corp.*, 918 F.2d 689 (7th Cir. 1990):

> The question of the proper treatment of overhead expenses arises more frequently in cases in which the plaintiff is seeking not the expenses themselves — they have not been incurred — but the price of a contract that has not yet been fully performed, and the defendant asks that the overhead expenses assigned by the plaintiff on the uncompleted portion of the contract be deducted, on the theory that they were saved by the breach and therefore that their inclusion would exaggerate the plaintiff's loss. The proper analysis of that case is symmetrical with the proper analysis of our case. If the plaintiff can either cut his overhead expenses or recover them in a substitute contract, then he indeed has not lost them as a result of the breach and they should not be figured in his damages. But if he cannot do either of these things — if in other words these really are fixed costs — then the breach gives him no scope to economize and there should be no deduction.
>
> The breach in this case of course occurred after the overhead expenses were incurred. This sequence meant that the breach, far from enabling those expenses to be covered in a substitute contract, converted them from a bookkeeping entry into a loss, because it was too late for the plaintiff to make the substitute contract that would have enabled the plaintiff to recover the expenses. If there had been a contract price, therefore, the jury would not have been entitled to subtract the overhead expenses from it in figuring Autotrol's damages. The only thing to be subtracted would be expenses not yet incurred, and therefore saved by the breach. But there was no contract price. Autotrol was not selling something to Continental; they were joint venturers. That made figuring profits difficult and the implicit theory of the damages award is that Autotrol would have had zero profits on the venture, and is thus conservative. The defendants do not deny

that Autotrol would have done well enough on the contract to cover the overhead expenses allocated to it, and with that concession Autotrol's case is complete.

The assumption of zero profits is based on the rule of Texas law "that the loss of anticipated profits from a new business is too speculative and conjectural to support a recovery of damages." Were it not for that rule Autotrol would not be seeking reliance damages, but instead expectation damages, and the issue of overhead expenses to which we have been devoting such complex attention would be simplified.

5. Alfred Thompson Denning (1899-1999) was one of the greatest English judges of the 20th century, perhaps of all time. He had a distinguished, but at times controversial, appellate career as a law lord sitting in the House of Lords (predecessor to the current Supreme Court of the United Kingdom) and as Master of Rolls, the senior appellate judge on the Court of Appeal, the second highest court in the British system. Note the discursive quality of Lord Denning's *Anglia Television* opinion which reflects traditional English appellate practice featuring extemporaneous *seriatim* oral rulings by impressively bewigged lords bedecked in scarlet robes immediately following often extended oral argument by counsel. Appellate practice in the United States relies predominantly on more formal and elaborate written briefs by the parties and written opinions of the court. American appellate courts commonly dispense with oral argument altogether in many less difficult matters, and rarely, if ever, make oral rulings on the merits from the bench.

———

3. Restitution Interest

A court may also award contract damages based on an injured party's restitution interest to restore to the injured party any value that it may have conferred on the breaching party. This concept of restitutionary damages stems from the same fundamental idea as the alternative body of restitution doctrine we will study in Chapter Three. The distinction, however, is important. Here, the restitutionary interest describes a type of contract damages. In Chapter Three, restitution (also known as quantum meruit or unjust enrichment) constitutes an alternative doctrinal basis for recovery often available in contexts where no action for breach of contract can be supported or where standard contract doctrine yields a less favorable recovery.

■ PETERS, C.J. in *Bernstein v. Nemeyer*, 213 Conn. 665, 673-74 (1990):

When a court grants [the remedy of restitution] for breach, the party in breach is required to account for a benefit that has been conferred on him by the injured party * * *. In contrast to cases in which the court grants specific performance or awards damages as a remedy for breach, the effort is not to enforce the promise by protecting the injured party's expectation or reliance interest, but to prevent unjust enrichment of the party in breach by protecting the injured party's restitution interest. The objective is not to put the injured party in as good a position as he would have been in if the contract had been performed, nor even to put the injured party back in the position he would have been in if the contract had not been made; it is, rather, to put the party in breach back in the position he would have been in if the contract had not been made. E. A. Farnsworth, Contracts (1982) § 12.19. When an injured party seeks an award of money to protect his restitutionary interest, any award "may as justice requires be measured by either (a) the reasonable value to the other party of what he received * * * or (b) the extent to which the other party's property has been increased in value or his other interests advanced." Restatement (Second) of Contracts § 371 (1981).

———

Contract doctrine favors expectation and reliance interest remedies, and contract damages based on a restitutionary interest have been rarely awarded. But recently some commentators, drawing some support from the new Restatement (Third) of Restitution, and criticizing the under-compensatory effect of the traditional rules, have urged a renewed emphasis on disgorgement by the breaching party as a measure of contract damages. Steve Thel & Peter Siegelman, *You Do Have to Keep Your Promises: A Disgorgement Theory of Contract Remedies*, 52 WM. & MARY L. REV. 1181 (2011). Restitution as an alternative to contract damages (rather than a measure of recovery in contract itself), however, remains a far more common approach in practice, as we shall see in Chapter Three.

B. AVOIDABLE CONSEQUENCES

Rockingham County v. Luten Bridge Co.
United States Court of Appeals, Fourth Circuit, 1929.
35 F.2d 301.

■ PARKER, J. This was an action at law instituted in the court below by the Luten Bridge Company, as plaintiff, to recover of Rockingham County, North Carolina, an amount alleged to be due under a contract for the construction of a bridge. The county admits the execution and breach of the contract, but contends that notice of cancellation was given the bridge company before the erection of the bridge was commenced, and that it is liable only for the damages which the company would have sustained, if it had abandoned construction at that time. The judge below refused to strike out an answer filed by certain members of the board of commissioners of the county, admitting liability in accordance with the prayer of the complaint, allowed this pleading to be introduced in evidence as the answer of the county, excluded evidence offered by the county in support of its contentions as to notice of cancellation and damages, and instructed a verdict for plaintiff for the full amount of its claim. From judgment on this verdict the county has appealed.

As the county now admits the execution and validity of the contract, and the breach on its part, the ultimate question in the case is one as to the measure of plaintiff's recovery....

... [W]e do not think that, after the county had given notice, while the contract was still executory, that it did not desire the bridge built and would not pay for it, plaintiff could proceed to build it and recover the contract price. It is true that the county had no right to rescind the contract, and the notice given plaintiff amounted to a breach on its part; but, after plaintiff had received notice of the breach, it was its duty to do nothing to increase the damages flowing therefrom. If A enters into a binding contract to build a house for B, B, of course, has no right to rescind the contract without A's consent. But if, before the house is built, he decides that he does not want it, and notifies A to that effect, A has no right to proceed with the building and thus pile up damages. His remedy is to treat the contract as broken when he receives the notice, and sue for the recovery of such damages as he may have sustained from the breach, including any profit which he would have realized upon performance, as well as any other losses which may have resulted to him. In the case at bar, the county decided not to build the road of which the bridge was to be a part, and did not build it. The bridge, built in the midst of the forest, is of no value to the county because of this change of circumstances. When, therefore, the county gave notice to the plaintiff that it would not proceed with the project, plaintiff should have desisted from further work. It had no right thus to pile up damages by proceeding with the erection of a useless bridge.

The contrary view was expressed by Lord Cockburn in *Frost v. Knight*, L.R. 7 Ex. 111, but, as pointed out by Prof. Williston (Williston on Contracts, vol. 3, p. 2347), it is not in harmony with the decisions in this country. The American rule and the reasons supporting it are well stated by Prof. Williston as follows:

> There is a line of cases running back to 1845 which holds that after an absolute repudiation or refusal to perform by one party to a contract, the other party cannot continue to perform and recover damages based on full performance. This rule is only a particular application of the general rule of damages that a plaintiff cannot hold a defendant liable for damages which need not have been incurred; or, as it is often stated, the plaintiff must, so far as he can without loss to himself, mitigate the damages caused by the defendant's wrongful act. The application of this rule to the matter in question is obvious. If a man engages to have work done, and afterwards repudiates his contract before the work has been

begun or when it has been only partially done, it is inflicting damage on the defendant without benefit to the plaintiff to allow the latter to insist on proceeding with the contract. The work may be useless to the defendant, and yet he would be forced to pay the full contract price. On the other hand, the plaintiff is interested only in the profit he will make out of the contract. If he receives this it is equally advantageous for him to use his time otherwise.

The leading case on the subject in this country is the New York case of *Clark v. Marsiglia*, 1 Denio (N.Y.) 317. In that case defendant had employed plaintiff to paint certain pictures for him, but countermanded the order before the work was finished. Plaintiff, however, went on and completed the work and sued for the contract price. In reversing a judgment for plaintiff, the court said:

> The plaintiff was allowed to recover as though there had been no countermand of the order; and in this the court erred. The defendant, by requiring the plaintiff to stop work upon the paintings, violated his contract, and thereby incurred a liability to pay such damages as the plaintiff should sustain. Such damages would include a recompense for the labor done and materials used, and such further sum in damages as might, upon legal principles, be assessed for the breach of the contract; but the plaintiff had no right, by obstinately persisting in the work, to make the penalty upon the defendant greater than it would otherwise have been.

... It follows that there was error in directing a verdict for plaintiff for the full amount of its claim. The measure of plaintiff's damage, upon its appearing that notice was duly given not to build the bridge, is an amount sufficient to compensate plaintiff for labor and materials expended and expense incurred in the part performance of the contract, prior to its repudiation, plus the profit which would have been realized if it had been carried out in accordance with its terms.

Reversed.

QUESTIONS AND NOTES

1. Why are some county commissioners admitting liability to Luten Bridge Co. and other commissioners seeking to strike the admission? If the county commission was divided and some were in favor of canceling the bridge project, while others were urging its completion, what would you advise Luten Bridge Co. to do?

2. In this case, the builder could not continue to build after being told not to. This makes good sense. And so long as the builder gets the full profit that it would have made on the job if it had been permitted to complete that job, there's no reason for it to complain.

But what about the laborers who were counting on the job with Luten Bridge Co.? Will they be paid their wages? The only way Luten Bridge can be made whole by paying it only its lost profit is if it "saves" the workers' wages. Does the county owe the workers a duty? One might say that the costs of the breach are borne not by the breaching promisor and not by the promisee, whose profits are protected, but by those who lose because of the breach when the parties to the contract "save" their wages.

3. What about the time now available to it because of the County's breach? If the bridge company immediately took another bridge job on which it made a tremendous profit, should this be used to reduce its damages against the County? Does this depend on how many bridge jobs the company could handle at one time? Suppose it lost money on the second job?

If the court is committed to making breach as cheap as possible, why doesn't it really make Luten Bridge use its time well? Wouldn't it make economic sense to subtract from Luten's lost profit that profit that Luten might have earned had it put to work those resources "freed up" as a result of Rockingham County's breach?

4. The bridge to nowhere made famous in this case still stands. Subsequently connected to roads on each end in 1968, in 2003 the bridge closed to vehicular traffic, but it remains open to pedestrians and supports a sewer main. Barak Richman, Jordi Weinstock & Jason Mehta, *A Bridge, A Tax Revolt, and the Struggle to Industrialize: The Story and Legacy of* Rockingham County v. Luten Bridge Co., 84 N.C. L. REV. 1841 (2006).

DRAFTING EXERCISE

Imagine that you are the attorney for Rockingham County preparing for trial. Assuming that damages are the only issue that will be litigated, write instructions of no more than two pages to the fact investigator telling her what facts to look for (in files, records, and interviews with witnesses). Make certain to include useful illustrations and some explanation of why particular facts might be important.

Sutherland v. Wyer
Maine Supreme Judicial Court, 1877.
67 Me. 64.

■ VIRGIN, J. The plaintiff contracted with the defendants to "play first old man and character business, at the Portland museum, and to do all things requisite and necessary to any and all performances which" the defendants "shall designate, and to conform strictly to all the rules and regulations of said theatre," for thirty-six weeks, commencing on Sept. 6, 1875, at thirty-five dollars per week; and the defendants agreed "to pay him thirty-five dollars for every week of public theatrical representations during said season." By one of the rules mentioned, the defendants "reserved the right to discharge any person who may have imposed on them by engaging for a position which, in their judgment, he is incompetent to fill properly."

The plaintiff entered upon his service under the contract, at the time mentioned therein, and continued to perform the theatrical characterizations assigned to him, without any suggestion of incompetency, and to receive the stipulated weekly salary, until the end of the eighteenth week; when he was discharged by the defendants, as they contended before the jury for incompetency under the rule; but, as the plaintiff there contended, for the reason that he declined to accept twenty-four dollars per week during the remainder of his term of service.

Three days after his discharge and before the expiration of the nineteenth week, the plaintiff commenced this action to recover damages for the defendants' breach of the contract. The action was not premature. The contract was entire and indivisible. The performance of it had been commenced, and the plaintiff been discharged and thereby been prevented from the further execution of it; and the action was not brought until after the discharge and consequent breach. The doctrine of *Daniels v. Newton*, 114 Mass. 530, is not opposed to this. Neither do the defendants insist that the action was prematurely commenced; but they contend that the verdict should be set aside as being against the weight of evidence.

The verdict was for the plaintiff. The jury must, therefore, have found the real cause of his discharge to be his refusal to consent to the proposed reduction of his salary. The evidence upon this point was quite conflicting. Considering that all the company were notified, at the same time, that their respective salaries would be reduced one-third, without assigning any such cause as incompetency; that no suggestion of the plaintiff's incompetency was ever made to him, prior to his discharge; and that his written discharge was equally silent upon that subject, we fail to find sufficient reason for disturbing the verdict upon this ground of the motion, especially since the jury might well find as they did on this branch of the case, provided they believed the testimony in behalf of the plaintiff.

There are several classes of cases founded both in tort and in contract, wherein the plaintiff is entitled to recover, not only the damages actually sustained when the action was commenced, or at the time of the trial, but also whatever the evidence proves he will be likely to suffer thereafter from the same cause. Among the torts coming within this rule, are personal injuries caused by the wrongful acts or negligence of others. The injury continuing beyond the time of trial, the future as well as the past is to be considered, since no other action can be maintained. So in cases of contract the performance of which is to extend through a period of time which has not elapsed when the breach is made and the action brought therefor and the trial had. Among these are actions on bonds or unsealed contracts stipulating for the support of persons during their natural life.

The contract in controversy falls within the same rule. Although, as practically construed by the parties, the salary was payable weekly, still, when the plaintiff was peremptorily discharged from all further service during the remainder of the season, such discharge conferred upon him the right to treat the contract as entirely at an end, and to bring his action to recover damages for the breach. In such action he is entitled to a just recompense for the actual injury sustained by the illegal discharge. Prima facie, such recompense would be the stipulated wages for the remaining eighteen weeks. This, however, would not necessarily be the sum which he would be entitled to; for in cases of contract as well as of tort, it is generally incumbent upon an injured party to do whatever he reasonably can, and to improve all reasonable and proper opportunities to lessen the injury. The plaintiff could not be justified in lying idle after the breach; but he was bound to use ordinary diligence in securing employment elsewhere, during the remainder of the term; and whatever sum he actually earned or might have earned by the use of reasonable diligence, should be deducted from the amount of the unpaid stipulated wages. And this balance with interest thereon should be the amount of the verdict. Applying the rule mentioned, the verdict will be found too large.

By the plaintiff's own testimony, he received only $60, from all sources after his discharge—$25 in February and $35 from the 10th to the 20th of April, at Booth's. His last engagement was for eight weeks, commencing April 10, which he abandoned on the 20th, thus voluntarily omitting an opportunity to earn $57, prior to the expiration of his engagement with the defendants, when the law required him to improve such an opportunity, if reasonable and proper. We think he should have continued the last engagement until May 6, instead of abandoning it and urging a trial in April, especially inasmuch as he could have obtained a trial in May, just as well. The instructions taken together were as favorable to the defendants as they were entitled to.

If, therefore, the plaintiff will remit $57, he may have judgment for the balance of the verdict; otherwise the entry must be verdict set aside and new trial granted.

Parker v. Twentieth Century–Fox Film Corp.

California Supreme Court, 1970.

3 Cal.3d 176, 89 Cal.Rptr. 737, 474 P.2d 689.

■ BURKE, J. Defendant Twentieth Century–Fox Film Corporation appeals from a summary judgment granting to plaintiff the recovery of agreed compensation under a written contract for her services as an actress in a motion picture. As will appear, we have concluded that the trial court correctly ruled in plaintiff's favor and that the judgment should be affirmed.

Plaintiff is well known as an actress, and in the contract between plaintiff and defendant is sometimes referred to as the "Artist." Under the contract, dated August 6, 1965, plaintiff was to play the female lead in defendant's contemplated production of a motion picture entitled "Bloomer Girl." The contract provided that defendant would pay plaintiff a minimum "guaranteed compensation" of $53,571.42 per week for 14 weeks commencing May 23, 1966, for a total of $750,000. Prior to May 1966 defendant decided not to produce the picture and by a letter dated April 4, 1966, it notified plaintiff of that decision and that it would not "comply with our obligations to you under" the written contract.

By the same letter and with the professed purpose "to avoid any damage to you," defendant instead offered to employ plaintiff as the leading actress in another film tentatively entitled "Big Country, Big Man" (hereinafter, "Big Country"). The compensation offered was identical, as were 31 of the 34 numbered provisions or articles of the original contract.[1] Unlike "Bloomer Girl," however, which was to have been a musical production, "Big Country" was a dramatic "western type" movie. "Bloomer Girl" was to have been filmed in California; "Big Country" was to be produced in Australia. Also, certain terms in the proffered contract varied from those of the original.[2] Plaintiff was given one week within which to accept; she did

---

1. Among the identical provisions was the following found in the last paragraph of Article 2 of the original contract: "We [defendant] shall not be obligated to utilize your [plaintiff's] services in or in connection with the Photoplay hereunder, our sole obligation, subject to the terms and conditions of this Agreement, being to pay you the guaranteed compensation herein provided for."

2. Article 29 of the original contract specified that plaintiff approved the director already chosen for "Bloomer Girl" and that in case he failed to act as director plaintiff was to have approval rights of any substitute director. Article 31 provided that plaintiff was to have the right of approval of the "Bloomer Girl" dance director, and Article 32 gave her the right of approval of the screen play.

Defendant's letter of April 4 to plaintiff, which contained both defendant's notice of breach of the "Bloomer Girl" contract and offer of the lead in "Big Country," eliminated or impaired each of those rights. It read in part as follows: "The terms and conditions of our offer of employment are identical to those set forth in the 'BLOOMER GIRL' Agreement, Articles 1 through 34 and Exhibit A to the Agreement, except as follows:

1. Article 31 of said Agreement will not be included in any contract of employment regarding 'BIG COUNTRY, BIG MAN' as it is not a musical and it thus will not need a dance director.

2. In the 'BLOOMER GIRL' agreement, in Articles 29 and 32, you were given certain director and screenplay approvals and you had preapproved certain matters. Since there

not, and the offer lapsed. Plaintiff then commenced this action seeking recovery of the agreed guaranteed compensation.

The complaint sets forth two causes of action. The first is for money due under the contract; the second, based upon the same allegations as the first, is for damages resulting from defendant's breach of contract. Defendant in its answer admits the existence and validity of the contract, that plaintiff complied with all the conditions, covenants and promises and stood ready to complete the performance, and that defendant breached and "anticipatorily repudiated" the contract. It denies, however, that any money is due to plaintiff either under the contract or as a result of its breach, and pleads as an affirmative defense to both causes of action plaintiff's allegedly deliberate failure to mitigate damages, asserting that she unreasonably refused to accept its offer of the leading role in "Big Country."

Plaintiff moved for summary judgment under Code of Civil Procedure section 437c, the motion was granted, and summary judgment for $750,000 plus interest was entered in plaintiff's favor. This appeal by defendant followed.

The familiar rules are that the matter to be determined by the trial court on a motion for summary judgment is whether facts have been presented which give rise to a triable factual issue. The court may not pass upon the issue itself. Summary judgment is proper only if the affidavits or declarations in support of the moving party would be sufficient to sustain a judgment in his favor and his opponent does not by affidavit show facts sufficient to present a triable issue of fact. The affidavits of the moving party are strictly construed, and doubts as to the propriety of summary judgment should be resolved against granting the motion. Such summary procedure is drastic and should be used with caution so that it does not become a substitute for the open trial method of determining facts. The moving party cannot depend upon allegations in his own pleadings to cure deficient affidavits, nor can his adversary rely upon his own pleadings in lieu or in support of affidavits in opposition to a motion; however, a party can rely on his adversary's pleadings to establish facts not contained in his own affidavits. Also, the court may consider facts stipulated to by the parties and facts which are properly the subject of judicial notice.

---

simply is insufficient time to negotiate with you regarding your choice of director and regarding the screen play and since you already expressed an interest in performing the role in 'BIG COUNTRY, BIG MAN,' we must exclude from our offer of employment in 'BIG COUNTRY, BIG MAN' any approval rights as are contained in said Articles 29 and 32; however, we shall consult with you respecting the director to be selected to direct the photoplay and will further consult with you with respect to the screenplay and any revisions or changes therein, provided, however, that if we fail to agree * * * the decision of * * * [defendant] with respect to the selection of a director and to revisions and changes in the said screenplay shall be binding upon the parties to said agreement.

As stated, defendant's sole defense to this action which resulted from its deliberate breach of contract is that in rejecting defendant's substitute offer of employment plaintiff unreasonably refused to mitigate damages.

The general rule is that the measure of recovery by a wrongfully discharged employee is the amount of salary agreed upon for the period of service, less the amount which the employer affirmatively proves the employee has earned or with reasonable effort might have earned from other employment. However, before projected earnings from other employment opportunities not sought or accepted by the discharged employee can be applied in mitigation, the employer must show that the other employment was comparable, or substantially similar, to that of which the employee has been deprived; the employee's rejection of or failure to seek other available employment of a different or inferior kind may not be resorted to in order to mitigate damages.

In the present case defendant has raised no issue of *reasonableness of efforts* by plaintiff to obtain other employment; the sole issue is whether plaintiff's refusal of defendant's substitute offer of "Big Country" may be used in mitigation. Nor, if the "Big Country" offer was of employment different or inferior when compared with the original "Bloomer Girl" employment, is there an issue as to whether or not plaintiff acted reasonably in refusing the substitute offer. Despite defendant's arguments to the contrary, no case cited or which our research has discovered holds or suggests that reasonableness is an element of a wrongfully discharged employee's option to reject, or fail to seek, different or inferior employment lest the possible earnings therefrom be charged against him in mitigation of damages.[5]

Applying the foregoing rules to the record in the present case, with all intendments in favor of the party opposing the summary judgment motion—here,

---

5. Instead, in each case the reasonableness referred to was that of the efforts of the employee to obtain other employment that was not different or inferior; his right to reject the latter was declared as an unqualified rule of law. Thus, *Gonzales v. Internat. Assn. of Machinists* holds that the trial court correctly instructed the jury that plaintiff union member, a machinist, was required to make "such *efforts* as the average [member of his union] desiring employment would make at that particular time and place" (italics added); but, further, that the court *properly rejected defendant's offer of proof of the availability of other kinds of employment* at the same or higher pay than plaintiff usually received and all outside the jurisdiction of his union, as plaintiff could not be required to accept different employment or a nonunion job.

In *Harris v. Nat. Union, etc., Cooks* and *Stewards*, the issues were stated to be, inter alia, whether comparable employment was open to each plaintiff employee, and if so whether each plaintiff made a *reasonable effort* to secure such employment. It was held that the trial court properly *sustained an objection to an offer to prove a custom of accepting a job in a lower rank* when work in the higher rank was not available, as "The duty of mitigation of damages * * * does not require the plaintiff 'to seek or to accept other employment of a different or inferior kind.'" (254 P.2d at 676.) ...

defendant—it is clear that the trial court correctly ruled that plaintiff's failure to accept defendant's tendered substitute employment could not be applied in mitigation of damages because the offer of the "Big Country" lead was of employment both different and inferior, and that no factual dispute was presented on that issue. The mere circumstance that "Bloomer Girl" was to be a musical review calling upon plaintiff's talents as a dancer as well as an actress, and was to be produced in the City of Los Angeles, whereas "Big Country" was a straight dramatic role in a "Western Type" story taking place in an opal mine in Australia, demonstrates the difference in kind between the two employments; the female lead as a dramatic actress in a western style motion picture can by no stretch of imagination be considered the equivalent of or substantially similar to the lead in a song-and-dance production.

Additionally, the substitute "Big Country" offer proposed to eliminate or impair the director and screenplay approvals accorded to plaintiff under the original "Bloomer Girl" contract (see fn. 2, ante), and thus constituted an offer of inferior employment. No expertise or judicial notice is required in order to hold that the deprivation or infringement of an employee's rights held under an original employment contract converts the available "other employment" relied upon by the employer to mitigate damages, into inferior employment which the employee need not seek or accept.

Statements found in affidavits submitted by defendant in opposition to plaintiff's summary judgment motion, to the effect that the "Big Country" offer was not of employment different from or inferior to that under the "Bloomer Girl" contract, merely repeat the allegations of defendant's answer to the complaint in this action, constitute only conclusionary assertions with respect to undisputed facts, and do not give rise to a triable factual issue so as to defeat the motion for summary judgment.

In view of the determination that defendant failed to present any facts showing the existence of a factual issue with respect to its sole defense—plaintiff's rejection of its substitute employment offer in mitigation of damages—we need not consider plaintiff's further contention that for various reasons, including the provisions of the original contract set forth in footnote 1, *ante*, plaintiff was excused from attempting to mitigate damages.

The judgment is affirmed.

■ SULLIVAN, ACTING CHIEF JUSTICE (dissenting). The basic question in this case is whether or not plaintiff acted reasonably in rejecting defendant's offer of alternate employment. The answer depends upon whether that offer (starring in "Big Country, Big Man") was an offer of work that was substantially similar to her former

employment (starring in "Bloomer Girl") or of work that was of a different or inferior kind. To my mind this is a factual issue which the trial court should not have
determined on a motion for summary judgment. The majority have not only repeated this error but have compounded it by applying the rules governing mitigation
of damages in the employer-employee context in a misleading fashion. Accordingly,
I respectfully dissent.

The familiar rule requiring a plaintiff in a tort or contract action to mitigate damages embodies notions of fairness and socially responsible behavior which are
fundamental to our jurisprudence. Most broadly stated, it precludes the recovery of
damages which, through the exercise of due diligence, could have been avoided.
Thus, in essence, it is a rule requiring reasonable conduct in commercial affairs. This
general principle governs the obligations of an employee after his employer has
wrongfully repudiated or terminated the employment contract. Rather than permitting the employee simply to remain idle during the balance of the contract period,
the law requires him to make a reasonable effort to secure other employment.[1] He is
not obliged, however, to seek or accept any and all types of work which may be available. Only work which is in the same field and which is of the same quality need be
accepted.[2]

Over the years the courts have employed various phrases to define the type of
employment which the employee, upon his wrongful discharge, is under an obligation to accept. Thus in California alone it has been held that he must accept
employment which is "substantially similar"; "comparable employment"; employment "in the same general line of the first employment"; "equivalent to his prior
position"; "employment in a similar capacity"; employment which is "not * * * of
a different or inferior kind * * *."

For reasons which are unexplained, the majority cite several of these cases yet
select from among the various judicial formulations which contain one particular
phrase, "Not of a different or inferior kind," with which to analyze this case. I have

---

1. The issue is generally discussed in terms of a duty on the part of the employee to minimize
loss. The practice is long established and there is little reason to change despite Judge Cardozo's
observation of its subtle inaccuracy. "The servant is free to accept employment or reject it according to his uncensored pleasure. What is meant by the supposed duty is merely this: That if
he unreasonably reject, he will not be heard to say that the loss of wages from then on shall be
deemed the jural consequence of the earlier discharge. He has broken the chain of causation, and
loss resulting to him thereafter is suffered through his own act." (*McClelland v. Climax Hosiery
Mills* (1930) 252 N.Y. 347, 359, concurring opinion.)

2. This qualification of the rule seems to reflect the simple and humane attitude that it is too
severe to demand of a person that he attempt to find and perform work for which he has no
training or experience. Many of the older cases hold that one need not accept work in an inferior
rank or position nor work which is more menial or arduous. This suggests that the rule may have
had its origin in the bourgeois fear of resubmergence in lower economic classes.

discovered no historical or theoretical reason to adopt this phrase, which is simply a negative restatement of the affirmative standards set out in the above cases, as the exclusive standard. Indeed, its emergence is an example of the dubious phenomenon of the law responding not to rational judicial choice or changing social conditions, but to unrecognized changes in the language of opinions or legal treatises. However, the phrase is a serviceable one and my concern is not with its use as the standard but rather with what I consider its distortion.

The relevant language excuses acceptance only of employment which is of a *different kind*. It has never been the law that the mere existence of *differences between two jobs in the same field* is sufficient, as a matter of law, to excuse an employee wrongfully discharged from one from accepting the other in order to mitigate damages. Such an approach would effectively eliminate any obligation of an employee to attempt to minimize damage arising from a wrongful discharge. The only alternative job offer an employee would be required to accept would be an offer of his former job by his former employer.

Although the majority appear to hold that there was a difference "in kind" between the employment offered plaintiff in "Bloomer Girl" and that offered in "Big Country," an examination of the opinion makes crystal clear that the majority merely point out differences between the two *films* (an obvious circumstance) and then apodictically assert that these constitute a difference in the *kind of employment*. The entire rationale of the majority boils down to this: that the "*mere circumstances*" that "Bloomer Girl" was to be a musical review while "Big Country" was a straight drama "demonstrates the difference in kind" since a female lead in a western is not "the equivalent of or substantially similar to" a lead in a musical. This is merely attempting to prove the proposition by repeating it. It shows that the vehicles for the display of the star's talents are different but it does not prove that her employment as a star in such vehicles is of necessity different *in kind* and either inferior or superior.

I believe that the approach taken by the majority (a superficial listing of differences with no attempt to assess their significance) may subvert a valuable legal doctrine.[5] The inquiry in cases such as this should not be whether differences between the two jobs exist (there will always be differences) but whether the differences which are present are substantial enough to constitute differences in the

---

5. The values of the doctrine of mitigation of damages in this context are that it minimizes the unnecessary personal and social (e.g., nonproductive use of labor, litigation) costs of contractual failure. If a wrongfully discharged employee can, through his own action and without suffering financial or psychological loss in the process, reduce the damages accruing from the breach of contract, the most sensible policy is to require him to do so. I fear the majority opinion will encourage precisely opposite conduct.

kind of employment or, alternatively, whether they render the substitute work employment of an *inferior kind.*

It seems to me that *this* inquiry involves, in the instant case at least, factual determinations which are improper on a motion for summary judgment. Resolving whether or not one job is substantially similar to another or whether, on the other hand, it is of a different or inferior kind, will often (as here) require a critical appraisal of the similarities and differences between them in light of the importance of these differences to the employee. This necessitates a weighing of the evidence, and it is precisely this undertaking which is forbidden on summary judgment.

This is not to say that summary judgment would never be available in an action by an employee in which the employer raises the defense of failure to mitigate damages. No case has come to my attention, however, in which summary judgment has been granted on the issue of whether an employee was obliged to accept available alternate employment. Nevertheless, there may well be cases in which the substitute employment is so manifestly of a dissimilar or inferior sort, the declarations of the plaintiff so complete and those of the defendant so conclusionary and inadequate that no factual issues exist for which a trial is required. This, however, is not such a case.

It is not intuitively obvious, to me at least, that the leading female role in a dramatic motion picture is a radically different endeavor from the leading female role in a musical comedy film. Nor is it plain to me that the rather qualified rights of director and screenplay approval contained in the first contract are highly significant matters either in the entertainment industry in general or to this plaintiff in particular. Certainly, none of the declarations introduced by plaintiff in support of her motion shed any light on these issues.[6] Nor do they attempt to explain why she declined the offer of starring in "Big Country, Big Man." Nevertheless, the trial court

---

6. Plaintiff's declaration states simply that she has not received any payment from defendant under the "Bloomer Girl" contract and that the only persons authorized to collect money for her are her attorney and her agent.

The declaration of Herman Citron, plaintiff's theatrical agent, alleges that prior to the formation of the "Bloomer Girl" contract he discussed with Richard Zanuck, defendant's vice president, the conditions under which plaintiff might be interested in doing "Big Country"; that it was Zanuck who informed him of Fox's decision to cancel production of "Bloomer Girl" and queried him as to plaintiff's continued interest in "Big Country"; that he informed Zanuck that plaintiff was shocked by the decision, had turned down other offers because of her commitment to defendant for "Bloomer Girl" and was not interested in "Big Country." It further alleges that "Bloomer Girl" was to have been a musical review which would have given plaintiff an opportunity to exhibit her talent as a dancer as well as an actress and that "Big Country" was a straight dramatic role; the former to have been produced in California, the latter in Australia. Citron's declaration concludes by stating that he has not received any payment from defendant for plaintiff under the "Bloomer Girl" contract.

granted the motion, declaring that these approval rights were "critical" and that their elimination altered "the essential nature of the employment."

In the instant case, there was nothing properly before the trial court by which the importance of the approval rights could be ascertained, much less evaluated. Thus, in order to grant the motion for summary judgment, the trial court misused judicial notice. In upholding the summary judgment, the majority here rely upon per se rules which distort the process of determining whether or not an employee is obliged to accept particular employment in mitigation of damages.

I believe that the judgment should be reversed so that the issue of whether or not the offer of the lead role in "Big Country, Big Man" was of employment comparable to that of the lead role in "Bloomer Girl" may be determined at trial....

QUESTIONS AND NOTES

1. Ms. Parker is best known by her stage name, Shirley MacLaine. Her filmography includes scores of pictures of all genres: dramas, westerns, comedies, and musicals. But she danced in only a small minority of those films. Were her roles in those other films necessarily "different and inferior" to those she danced in—even the one in which she earned her Best Actress Academy Award (*Terms of Endearment*)? Does the majority opinion in this case properly apply the summary judgment standard it adopts? That is, do the affidavits establish that no reasonable jury could find that the second movie role is not different or inferior employment to the first?

2. Does someone have to do business with a dirty contract breaker to avoid consequences? Suppose Fox repudiated the contract with Parker not to abandon the project but to hire Parker's younger arch-rival, Jennifer Lawrence? Suppose further that the deal with J-Law fell through and Fox re-extended the offer to Parker. Would Parker forfeit any right to damages if she refused a second, identical offer by Fox to do *Bloomer Girl*, even though now she neither trusts nor wants to work for Fox?

3. Consider the uncertainties facing a counselor advising an employee soon after breach by the employer. If you advise the worker to take another job, the earnings on that job are likely to reduce damages. Yet if you advise the worker that the available work is different and inferior, you run the risk that if a court later disagrees with your guess, damages will be reduced anyway by what the worker might have earned.

Benjamin Neuman's declaration states that he is plaintiff's attorney; that after receiving notice of defendant's breach he requested Citron to make every effort to obtain other suitable employment for plaintiff; that he (Neuman) rejected defendant's offer to settle for $400,000 and that he has not received any payment from defendant for plaintiff under the "Bloomer Girl" contract. It also sets forth correspondence between Neuman and Fox which culminated in Fox's final rejection of plaintiff's demand for full payment.

In such a situation isn't any sensible counselor going to advise the worker to take any job that comes along and seems roughly similar to the old one?

4. Compare the mitigation standard in *Parker* with that applied in *In re World-Com, Inc.*, 361 B.R. 675 (Bankr. S.D.N.Y. 2007). Michael Jordan (of Chicago Bulls fame) and MCI entered into a 10-year $20 million endorsement agreement in 1995. In 2002 MCI filed for bankruptcy. In 2003 Jordan filed a claim against MCI seeking $2 million for each of the years 2002, 2003, 2004, and 2005. MCI argued it was under no obligation to pay for contract years 2004 and 2005 because Jordan failed to mitigate damages by not pursuing other endorsement opportunities. Jordan re-plied (not unlike Parker) that he acted reasonably when he chose not to pursue other endorsement deals. But unlike the California Supreme Court, the *WorldCom* court held that Jordan's blanket claim that seeking another endorsement deal could dilute the value of his endorsement or damage his reputation was not convincing. The court reasoned that replacing the MCI deal with another endorsement would main-tain the status quo, not dilute Jordan's endorsement value. The court did not find any support for the proposition that making a new endorsement would harm Jor-dan's reputation. Aren't the differences between various firms who might wish to promote themselves with Michael Jordan's endorsement at least as great as the dif-ferences between *Bloomer Girl* and *Big Country Big Man*? Should Jordan have to endorse other firms' products and services to mitigate damages because of MCI's breach?

---

5 ARTHUR L. CORBIN, CORBIN ON CONTRACTS, § 1095, AT 517–19 (1964):[*]

The rule as to avoidable consequences is applicable in this situation for the rea-son that the employee's privilege to earn wages under a new employer is directly due to his discharge by the first employer. The discharge causes injury, but it also sets free valuable time for use in other service. This is true, and the rule is applicable, only in case the new service that the employee can obtain is of a kind that he could not properly have performed if the employer had not discharged him from the first contract.

If a discharged employee engages in business instead of working for wages, the profits that he makes in such an enterprise have been held to be deductible from the amount to which he would otherwise be entitled as damages. It is very doubtful whether such a deduction should ever be allowed. Even if the enterprise is of such a character that the employee could not have engaged in it except for the fact of his discharge, the business risks are such that he cannot reasonably be expected to incur them; and if he chooses to engage in the business, investing capital therein, the risk

---

[*] Copyright 1964. Printed with the permission of the West Publishing Co.

of gain or loss should be his. Whether or not he goes into another business or makes a gain or loss therein, his damages should be measured by the wages promised less what he could earn by reasonable effort in a similar position of employment.

It has frequently been said that the employee is under a "duty" to mitigate damages by looking for other work and accepting it if it can be obtained. Accurately speaking, however, this is not the case. It makes no difference whatever whether the employee actually uses the time that is set free for his use by the employer's discharge or does not use it. His recoverable damages are exactly the same in either case. He is legally privileged to throw away his time if he so desires.

The burden of proof is on the employer to show that similar employment could be obtained by reasonable effort. Any serious doubt as to whether the obtainable service is similar in a sufficient degree to that required by the broken contract is resolved against the employer.

There are cases in which a wrongful discharge by an employer causes other injury to the employee than the mere loss of money wages. The discharge may cause loss of opportunity to learn a trade or to acquire a valuable reputation. If such injury is caused and the employer had reason to foresee such an injury at the time that the contract of employment was made, damages are recoverable for such a consequential injury if its amount in money can be proved with a reasonable degree of certainty. The agreed wages may themselves be uncertain in amount, as where the amount to be paid for the service consisted in commissions on business to be done or in a share of the profits to be made. The employee is not refused a remedy because of this kind of uncertainty, but in his evidence he must lay a substantial basis for making an estimate of the amount that he would have received under the contract, had there been no discharge.

UNIFORM COMMERCIAL CODE:

§ 2-708. Seller's Damages for Non-acceptance or Repudiation.

(1) Subject to subsection (2) and to the provisions of this Article with respect to proof of market price (Section 2-723), the measure of damages for non-acceptance or repudiation by the buyer is the difference between the market price at the time and place for tender and the unpaid contract price together with any incidental damages provided in this Article (Section 2-710), but less expenses saved in consequence of the buyer's breach.

(2) If the measure of damages provided in subsection (1) is inadequate to put the seller in as good a position as performance would have done then the measure of damages is the profit (including reasonable overhead) which the seller would have made from full performance by the buyer, together with

any incidental damages provided in this Article (Section 2–710), due allowance for cost reasonably incurred and due credit for payments or proceeds of resale.

Neri v. Retail Marine Corp.

New York Court of Appeals, 1972.
30 N.Y.2d 393, 334 N.Y.S.2d 165, 285 N.E.2d 311.

■ GIBSON, J. The appeal concerns the right of a retail dealer to recover loss of profits and incidental damages upon the buyer's repudiation of a contract governed by the Uniform Commercial Code. This is, indeed, the correct measure of damage in an appropriate case and to this extent the code (§ 2–708, subsection [2]), effected a substantial change from prior law, whereby damages were ordinarily limited to "the difference between the contract price and the market or current price." Upon the record before us, the courts below erred in declining to give effect to the new statute and so the order appealed from must be reversed.

The plaintiffs contracted to purchase from defendant a new boat of a specified model for the price of $12,587.40, against which they made a deposit of $40. They shortly increased the deposit to $4,250 in consideration of the defendant dealer's agreement to arrange with the manufacturer for immediate delivery on the basis of "a firm sale," instead of the delivery within approximately four to six weeks originally specified. Some six days after the date of the contract plaintiffs' lawyer sent to defendant a letter rescinding the sales contract for the reason that plaintiff Neri was about to undergo hospitalization and surgery, in consequence of which, according to the letter, it would be "impossible for Mr. Neri to make any payments." The boat had already been ordered from the manufacturer and was delivered to defendant at or before the time the attorney's letter was received. Defendant declined to refund plaintiffs' deposit and this action to recover it was commenced. Defendant counterclaimed, alleging plaintiffs' breach of the contract and defendant's resultant damage in the amount of $4,250, for which sum defendant demanded judgment. Upon motion, defendant had summary judgment on the issue of liability tendered by its counterclaim; and Special Term directed an assessment of damages, upon which it would be determined whether plaintiffs were entitled to the return of any portion of their down payment.

Upon the trial so directed, it was shown that the boat ordered and received by defendant in accordance with plaintiffs' contract of purchase was sold some four months later to another buyer for the same price as that negotiated with plaintiffs. From this proof the plaintiffs argue that defendant's loss on its contract was recouped, while defendant argues that but for plaintiffs' default, it would have sold two boats and have earned two profits instead of one. Defendant proved, without contradiction, that its profit on the sale under the contract in suit would have been $2,579 and that during the period the boat remained unsold incidental expenses aggregating $674 for storage, upkeep, finance charges and insurance were incurred. Additionally, defendant proved and sought to recover attorneys' fees of $1,250.

The trial court found "untenable" defendant's claim for loss of profit, inasmuch as the boat was later sold for the same price that plaintiffs had contracted to pay; found, too, that defendant had failed to prove any incidental damages; further found "that the terms of section 2–718, subsection 2(b), of the Uniform Commercial Code are applicable and same make adequate and fair provision to place the sellers in as good a position as performance would have done" and, in accordance with paragraph (b) of subsection (2) thus relied upon, awarded defendant $500 upon its counterclaim and directed that plaintiffs recover the balance of their deposit, amounting to $3,750. The ensuing judgment was affirmed, without opinion, at the Appellate Division, and defendant's appeal to this court was taken by our leave.

The issue is governed in the first instance by section 2–718 of the Uniform Commercial Code which provides, among other things, that the buyer, despite his breach, may have restitution of the amount by which his payment exceeds: (a) reasonable liquidated damages stipulated by the contract or (b) absent such stipulation, 20% of the value of the buyer's total performance or $500, whichever is smaller (§ 2–718, subsection [2], pars. [a], [b]). As above noted, the trial court awarded defendant an offset in the amount of $500 under paragraph (b) and directed restitution to plaintiffs of the balance. Section 2–718, however, establishes, in paragraph (a) of subsection (3), an alternative right of offset in favor of the seller, as follows: "(3) The buyer's right to restitution under subsection (2) is subject to offset to the extent that the seller establishes (a) a right to recover damages under the provisions of this Article other than subsection (1)."

Among "the provisions of this Article other than subsection (1)" are those to be found in section 2–708, which the courts below did not apply. Subsection (1) of that section provides that "the measure of damages for non-acceptance or repudiation by the buyer is the difference between the market price at the time and place for tender and the unpaid contract price together with any incidental damages provided in this Article (Section 2–710), but less expenses saved in consequence of the buyer's breach." However, this provision is made expressly subject to subsection (2), providing: "(2) If the measure of damages provided in subsection (1) is inadequate to put the seller in as good a position as performance would have done then the measure of damages is the profit (including reasonable overhead) which the seller would have made from full performance by the buyer, together with any incidental damages provided in this Article (Section 2–710), due allowance for costs reasonably incurred and due credit for payments or proceeds of resale."

It is evident, first, that this retail seller is entitled to its profit and, second, that the last sentence of subsection (2), as hereinbefore quoted, referring to "due credit for payments or proceeds of resale" is inapplicable to this retail sales contract. Closely parallel to the factual situation now before us is that hypothesized by Dean Hawkland as illustrative of the operation of the rules:

> Thus, if a private party agrees to sell his automobile to a buyer for $2,000, a breach by the buyer would cause the seller no loss (except incidental damages, i.e., expense of a new sale) if the seller was able to sell the automobile to another buyer for $2,000. But the situation is different with dealers having an unlimited supply of standard-priced goods. Thus, if an automobile dealer agrees to sell a car to a buyer at the standard price of $2,000, a breach by the buyer injures the dealer, even though he is able to sell the automobile to another for $2,000. If the dealer has an inexhaustible supply of cars, the resale to replace the breaching buyer costs the dealer a sale, because, had the breaching buyer performed, the dealer would have made two sales instead of one. The buyer's breach, in such a case, depletes the dealer's sales to the extent of one, and the measure of damages should be the dealer's profit on one sale....

It follows that plaintiffs are entitled to restitution of the sum of $4,250 paid by them on account of the contract price less an offset to defendant in the amount of $3,253 on account of its lost profit of $2,579 and its incidental damages of $674.

QUESTIONS AND NOTES

1. Isn't a "middleman" seller's damage almost always his "lost profit"? What is he in business for—to dispose of one lot of goods or to make as many sales as he can? Does the fact, then, that he can sell an article again after he has lost its first sale make him whole? Couldn't he have made the second sale, too, thus making two profits, if the first buyer hadn't breached? How can he possibly "avoid consequences"?

2. Assume Retail Marine, after Neri's breach, had sold the boat that Neri had contracted for to another dealer at cost and then claimed the difference between contract and its resale price. Would you feel better about the result if the court gave Retail Marine that difference?

3. UCC § 2-708(2) appears to require "due credit for payment or proceeds of resale" in calculating lost profit damages. If the resale price equals the contract price, doesn't duly crediting sale proceeds eliminate any damages? *See* John Breen, *The Lost Volume Seller and Lost Profits Under 2-708(2): A Conceptual and Linguistic Critique*, 50 U. MIAMI L. REV. 779 (1996).

4. What if the market price actually went up during the period? Does Retail Marine still suffer loss of profit anticipated on its sale to Neri?

5. Recall *Rockingham County v. Luten Bridge Company*, p. 139. If Luten Bridge Company had stopped construction of the bridge when notified of the county's repudiation, would the damages that it should receive be influenced by its efforts to mitigate damages in seeking alternative work? Is the answer the same whether Luten Bridge Company is just old man Luten who can only build one bridge at a time or a large firm able to manage twenty projects at the same time?

6. It is unclear whether retailers in competitive markets actually suffer lost profits from buyers' wrongful refusals to accept and pay for goods in the absence of a change in market price. The problem of the "lost volume seller" has long been a favorite analytical exercise for economists and their fellow travelers in the legal academy. For a summary of the various approaches to the problem see Robert Scott, *The Case for Market Damages: Revisiting the Lost Profits Puzzle*, 57 U. CHI. L. REV. 1155 (1990).

C. FORESEEABILITY: CONSEQUENTIAL DAMAGES AND THE EFFECT OF PROCEDURAL RULES ON CONTRACT DAMAGES

A major theme throughout your legal education will be the interrelation of substantive rules of liability and the procedural rules which establish how disputes are heard and resolved. Procedural rules often determine the reality and the content of substantive rules. Traditional pleading rules and habits have had a particularly substantial impact on contract damage rules. As a matter of pleading, some kinds of damages need only be stated generally to be recoverable. The plaintiff merely pleads a cause of action and then demands judgment in the sum of X-dollars, without having to specify just how that figure was computed. Under such an allegation, plaintiff may proceed to prove its damages for those kinds of losses that are always available under such a claim.

These damages are referred to as general damages, and the rationale for allowing them is that it is clearly foreseeable that this type of damage will occur if the contract is breached, despite the best efforts of the injured party to avoid them. There is no need under the pleading rules to give the defendant notice as to these damages because everyone knows such elements are part of the story. The difference between market and contract price in the sale of goods case is an example of a loss that can always be proved under a general damage pleading.

But there are other kinds of losses that a plaintiff may recover only if it pleads them specially in a specific allegation. These are called special damages and are typified by the consequential damage a disappointed party suffers, such as a loss of customers or lost profits or damages to property caused by a breach.

Whether a particular item of damages is general or special is primarily a matter of custom and can only be answered with assurance in any given case by looking to see how such matters are pled in the relevant jurisdiction. But these pleading habits are too deeply ingrained in the law to be ignored, and they continue to be applied under modern pleading rules. *See, e.g.*, FED. R. CIV. P. 9(g).

Our tradition of trial by jury in civil cases also has influenced the development of contract damage rules. Historically, questions of damages were treated primarily as issues of fact to be decided by the jury, rather than matters of law for the trial judge. Appellate courts came to discuss damage issues relatively late in history and still do so only rarely. The first few paragraphs of Baron Alderson's opinion in *Hadley v. Baxendale*, which follows, reflect that as late as 1854 it was felt necessary to defend the idea that an appellate court should announce rules to guide the jury in such matters.

Although there is no longer any dispute that damage computations are the appropriate subject for legal rules, useful statements of such rules are still hard to find. One major reason is the procedural context in which these questions are likely to arise. The issue of damages is left to the jury, and the instructions the trial judge will give the jury are likely to be vague and general. Under typical procedural rules, the jury does not state how it arrived at its damage award; its verdict typically announces merely, "We find for the plaintiff in the sum of X dollars." In most cases, there will be a variety of evidence that the jury was free to accept or reject in deciding a case and in computing damages. Moreover, the common experience is that the jury's computations are very mysterious things, and the arithmetic often will not match precisely any obvious view of the evidence. The appellate court called upon to review such a verdict will likely be unable to determine how the jury computed the damages and whether it used an appropriate legal standard.

Even if it appears that something is wrong somewhere with the jury's computations, the court is often reluctant to intervene and send the case back for a new trial that may cost more than the dollar difference between the jury's verdict and correctly computed damages. Practically speaking most appellate courts leave damages to the rough judgment of the finder of fact except in the most egregious cases.

OLIVER WENDELL HOLMES, JR., THE COMMON LAW 236 (HOWE ED., 1963):

A more practical advantage in looking at a contract as the taking of a risk is to be found in the light which it throws upon the measure of damages. If a breach of contract were regarded in the same light as a tort, it would seem that if, in the course of performance of the contract the promisor should be notified of any particular consequence which would result from its not being performed, he should be held liable for that consequence in the event of non-performance. Such a suggestion has been made. But it has not been accepted as the law. On the contrary, according to the opinion of a very able judge, which seems to be generally followed, notice, even at the time of making the contract, of special circumstances out of which special damages would arise in case of breach, is not sufficient unless the assumption of that risk is to be taken as having fairly entered into the contract.

Hadley v. Baxendale

Court of Exchequer, 1854.
9 Exch. 341, 156 Eng.Rep. 145.

At the trial before Crompton, J., at the last Gloucester Assizes, it appeared that the plaintiffs carried on an extensive business as millers at Gloucester; and that on the 11th of May, their mill was stopped by a breakage of the crank shaft by which the mill was worked. The steam-engine was manufactured by Messrs. Joyce & Co., the engineers, at Greenwich, and it became necessary to send the shaft as a pattern for a new one to Greenwich. The fracture was discovered on the 12th, and on the 13th the plaintiffs sent one of their servants to the office of the defendants, who are the well-known carriers trading under the name of Pickford & Co., for the purpose of having the shaft carried to Greenwich. The plaintiffs' servant told the clerk that the mill was stopped, and that the shaft must be sent immediately; and in answer to the inquiry when the shaft would be taken, the answer was, that if it was sent up by twelve o'clock any day, it would be delivered at Greenwich on the following day. On the following day the shaft was taken by the defendants, before noon, for the purpose of being conveyed to Greenwich, and the sum of 2*l.* 4*s.* was paid for its carriage for the whole distance; at the same time the defendants' clerk was told that a special entry, if required, should be made to hasten its delivery. The delivery of the shaft at Greenwich was delayed by some neglect; and the consequence was, that the plaintiffs did not receive the new shaft for several days after they would otherwise have done, and the working of their mill was thereby delayed, and they thereby lost the profits they would otherwise have received.

On the part of the defendants, it was objected that these damages were too remote, and that the defendants were not liable with respect to them. The learned Judge left the case generally to the jury, who found a verdict with £25 damages beyond the amount paid into Court.

Whateley, in last Michaelmas Term, obtained a rule nisi for a new trial, on the ground of misdirection.

■ ALDERSON, B. We think that there ought to be a new trial in this case; but, in so doing, we deem it to be expedient and necessary to state explicitly the rule which the Judge, at the next trial, ought, in our opinion, to direct the jury to be governed by when they estimate the damages.

It is, indeed, of the last importance that we should do this; for, if the jury are left without any definite rule to guide them, it will, in such cases as these, manifestly lead to the greatest injustice. The Courts have done this on several occasions; and, in *Blake v. Midland Railway Company*, 18 Q.B. 93, the Court granted a new trial on this very ground, that the rule had not been definitely laid down to the jury by the learned Judge at Nisi Prius.

"There are certain established rules," this Court says, in *Alder v. Keighley*, 15 M. & W. 117, "according to which the jury ought to find." And the Court, in that case, adds: "and here there is a clear rule, that the amount which would have been received if the contract had been kept, is the measure of damages if the contract is broken."

Now we think the proper rule in such a case as the present is this:—Where two parties have made a contract which one of them has broken, the damages which the other party ought to receive in respect of such breach of contract should be such as may fairly and reasonably be considered either arising naturally, i.e., according to the usual course of things, from such breach of contract itself, or such as may reasonably be supposed to have been in the contemplation of both parties, at the time they made the contract, as the probable result of the breach of it. Now, if the special circumstances under which the contract was actually made were communicated by the plaintiffs to the defendants, and thus known to both parties, the damages resulting from the breach of such a contract, which they would reasonably contemplate, would be the amount of injury which would ordinarily follow from a breach of contract under these special circumstances so known and communicated. But, on the other hand, if these special circumstances were wholly unknown to the party breaking the contract, he, at the most, could only be supposed to have had in his contemplation the amount of injury which would arise generally, and in the great multitude of cases not affected by any special circumstances, from such a breach of contract.

For, had the special circumstances been known, the parties might have specially provided for the breach of contract by special terms as to the damages in that case; and of this advantage it would be very unjust to deprive them. Now the above principles are those by which we think the jury ought to be guided in estimating the damages arising out of any breach of contract. It is said, that other cases such as breaches of contract in the nonpayment of money, or in the not making a good title to land, are to be treated as exceptions from this, and as governed by a conventional rule. But as, in such cases, both parties must be supposed to be cognizant of that well-known rule, these cases may, we think, be more properly classed under the rule above enunciated as to cases under known special circumstances, because there both parties may reasonably be presumed to contemplate the estimation of the amount of damages according to the conventional rule. Now, in the present case, if we are to apply the principles above laid down, we find that the only circumstances here communicated by the plaintiffs to the defendants at the time the contract was made, were, that the article to be carried was the broken shaft of a mill, and that the plaintiffs were the millers of that mill.

But how do these circumstances shew reasonably that the profits of the mill must be stopped by an unreasonable delay in the delivery of the broken shaft by the carrier to the third person? Suppose the plaintiffs had another shaft in their possession put up or putting up at the time, and that they only wished to send back the broken shaft to the engineer who made it; it is clear that this would be quite consistent with the above circumstances, and yet the unreasonable delay in the delivery would have no effect upon the intermediate profits of the mill. Or, again, suppose that, at the time of the delivery to the carrier, the machinery of the mill had been in other respects defective, then, also, the same results would follow. Here it is true that the shaft was actually sent back to serve as a model for a new one, and that the want of a new one was the only cause of the stoppage of the mill, and that the loss of profits really arose from not sending down the new shaft in proper time, and that this arose from the delay in delivering the broken one to serve as a model. But it is obvious that, in the great multitude of cases of millers sending off broken shafts to third persons by a carrier under ordinary circumstances, such consequences would not, in all probability, have occurred; and these special circumstances were here never communicated by the plaintiffs to the defendants. It follows therefore, that the loss of profits here cannot reasonably be considered such a consequence of the breach of contract as could have been fairly and reasonably contemplated by both the parties when they made this contract. For such loss would neither have flowed naturally from the breach of this contract in the great multitude of such cases occurring under ordinary circumstances, nor were the special circumstances, which, perhaps, would have made it a reasonable and natural consequence of such breach of contract, communicated to or known by the defendants. The Judge ought, therefore, to have told the jury that, upon the facts then before them they ought not to take the loss of profits into consideration at all in estimating the damages. There must therefore be a new trial in this case.

Rule absolute.

QUESTIONS AND NOTES

1. If the plaintiff cannot recover for the "lost profits" caused by the mill's shutdown for the period of the delayed delivery, what damages can it recover? Does a crankshaft have a pure use-value as such? If not, what general damages can be said to flow from a breach such as this one?

2. If Hadley's employee had served notice, would Hadley have made its case that special circumstance had been communicated and that it was therefore entitled to consequential damages? Were *Hadley* litigated today, would comment *f* to Restatement (Second) of Contracts § 351 justify the same outcome?

> *f. Other Limitations on Damages.* It is not always in the interest of justice to require the party in breach to pay damages for all of the foreseeable loss that he has caused. There are unusual instances in which it appears from the circumstances either that the parties assumed that one of them would not bear the risk of a particular loss or that, although there was no such assumption, it would be unjust to put the risk on that party. One such circumstance is an extreme disproportion between the loss and the price charged by the party whose liability for that loss is in question. The fact that the price is relatively small suggests that it was not intended to cover the risk of such liability. Another such circumstance is an informality of dealing, including the absence of a detailed written contract, which indicates that there was no careful attempt to allocate all of the risks. The fact that the parties did not attempt to delineate with precision all of the risks justifies a court in attempting to allocate them fairly. The limitations dealt with in this Section are more likely to be imposed in connection with contracts that do not arise in a commercial setting. Typical examples of limitations imposed on damages under this discretionary power involve the denial of recovery for loss of profits and the restriction of damages to loss incurred in reliance on the contract. Sometimes these limits are covertly imposed, by means of an especially demanding requirement of foreseeability or of certainty. The rule stated in this Section recognizes that what is done in such cases is the imposition of a limitation in the interests of justice.

3. The facts recited in the case report state that the carrier's failure to deliver the shaft on time was the result of some neglect. Why couldn't Hadley have recovered on a tort theory? Suppose that the defendant was an expert shaft engineer who carelessly repaired the shaft. Would you be more likely to say either "that's a tort" or at least that losses from careless repair were in the contemplation of the parties?

4. The defining limits placed upon contract damages by the rule in *Hadley v. Baxendale* was timely, for this case arose as the industrial revolution was transforming life in England. The case can be understood in historical context as a mark of the ascendency of the capitalist class, which was heavily dependent on limited liability of new corporate enterprises for their contracts to enable capitalists to calculate with greater assurance the expected return on their investments. More specifically, *Hadley* is a carrier case and announces a rule highly important to the various new means of communications and transportation that were emerging. Post, telegraph, railroads and steamships were making cheap mass communications possible. But a common carrier cannot routinely carry parcels and letters bearing penny stamps for great distances if loss of the item carried might impose liability for all conceivable consequences. The burden of loss is more efficiently shifted to insurance obtained by the shipper, who knows of and can protect itself against such losses. *Hadley* thus moved the law of damages into a new age in which the liabilities of enterprises in general, and of carriers in particular, for consequences of the contract breach were held to manageable levels.

Globe Refining Co. v. Landa Cotton Oil Co.

Supreme Court of the United States, 1903.
190 U.S. 540, 23 S.Ct. 754, 47 L.Ed. 1171.

■ MR. JUSTICE HOLMES delivered the opinion of the Court:

This is an action of contract brought by the plaintiff in error, a Kentucky corporation, against the defendant in error, a Texas corporation, for breach of a contract to sell and deliver crude oil. The defendant excepted to certain allegations of damage, and pleaded that the damages had been claimed and magnified fraudulently for the purpose of giving the United States circuit court jurisdiction, when in truth they were less than $2,000. The judge sustained the exceptions. He also tried the question of jurisdiction before hearing the merits, refused the plaintiff a jury, found that the plea was sustained, and dismissed the cause. The plaintiff excepted to all the rulings and action of the court, and brings the case here by writ of error. If the rulings and findings were right, there is no question that the judge was right in dismissing the suit; but the grounds upon which he went are re-examinable here.

The contract was made through a broker, it would seem by writing, and, at all events, was admitted to be correctly stated in the following letter:

Dallas, Texas, 7/30/97. Landa Oil Company, New Braunfels, Texas.

Gentlemen:

Referring to the exchange of our telegrams to-day, we have sold for your account to the Globe Refining Company, Louisville, Kentucky, ten (10) tanks prime crude C/S oil at the price of 15¾ cents per gallon of 7½ pounds, f.o.b. buyers' tank at your mill. Weights and quality guaranteed.

Terms: Sight draft without exchange b/ldg. attached. Sellers paying commission.

Shipment: Part last half August and balance first half September. Shipping instructions to be furnished by the Globe Refining Company.

Yours truly,

Thomas & Green, as Broker

Having this contract before us, we proceed to consider the allegations of special damage over and above the difference between the contract price of the oil and the price at the time of the breach, which was the measure adopted by the judge. These allegations must be read with care, for it is obvious that the pleader has gone as far as he dared to go, and to the verge of anything that could be justified under the contract, if not beyond.

It is alleged that it was agreed and understood that the plaintiff would send its tank cars to the defendant's mills, and that the defendant promptly would fill them with oil (so far, simply following the contract), and that the plaintiff sent tanks. "In order to do this, the plaintiff was under the necessity of obligating itself unconditionally to the railroad company (and of which the defendant had notice) to pay to it for the transportation of the cars from said Louisville to said New Braunfels in the sum of $900," which sum plaintiff had to pay, "and was incurred as an advancement on said oil contract." This is the first item. The last words quoted mean only that the sum paid would have been allowed by the railroad as part payment of the return charges had the tanks been filled and sent back over the same road.

Next it is alleged that the defendant, contemplating a breach of the contract, caused the plaintiff to send its cars a thousand miles, at a cost of $1,000; that defendant canceled its contract on the 2d of September, but did not notify the plaintiff until the 14th, when, if the plaintiff had known of the cancellation, it would have been supplying itself from other sources; that plaintiff (no doubt defendant is meant) did so wilfully and maliciously, causing an unnecessary loss of $2,000.

Next it is alleged that, by reason of the breach of contract and want of notice, plaintiff lost the use of its tanks for thirty days,—a loss estimated at $700 more. Next it is alleged that the plaintiff had arranged with its own customers to furnish the oil in question within a certain time, which contemplated sharp compliance with the contract by the defendant; "all of which facts, as above stated were well known to the defendant and defendant had contracted to that end with the plaintiff." This item is put at $740, with $1,000 more for loss of customers, credit, and reputation. Finally, at the end of the petition, it is alleged generally that it was known to defendant, and in contemplation of the contract, that plaintiff would have to send tanks at great expense from distant points, and that plaintiff "was required to pay additional freight in order to rearrange the destination of the various tanks and other points." Then it is alleged that by reason of the defendant's breach, the plaintiff had to pay $350 additional freight.

Whatever may be the scope of the allegations which we have quoted, it will be seen that none of the items was contemplated expressly by the words of the bargain. Those words are before us in writing, and go no further than to contemplate that when the deliveries were to take place the buyer's tanks should be at the defendant's mill. Under such circumstances the question is suggested how far the express terms of a writing, admitted to be complete, can be enlarged by averment and oral evidence; and, if they can be enlarged in that way, what averments are sufficient. When a man commits a tort, he incurs, by force of the law, a liability to damages, measured by certain rules. When a man makes a contract, he incurs, by force of the law, a liability to damages, unless a certain promised event comes to pass. But, unlike the case of torts, as the contract is by mutual consent, the parties themselves, expressly or by implication, fix the rule by which the damages are to be measured. The old law seems to have regarded it as technically in the election of the promisor to perform or to pay damages. It is true that, as people when contracting contemplate performance, not breach, they commonly say little or nothing as to what shall happen in the latter event, and the common rules have been worked out by common sense, which has established what the parties probably would have said if they had spoken about the matter. But a man never can be absolutely certain of performing any contract when the time of performance arrives, and, in many cases, he obviously is taking the risk of an event which is wholly, or to an appreciable extent, beyond his control. The extent of liability in such cases is likely to be within his contemplation, and, whether it is or not, should be worked out on terms which it fairly may be presumed he would have assented to if they had been presented to his mind. For instance, in the present case, the defendant's mill and all its oil might have been burned before the time came for delivery. Such a misfortune would not have been an excuse, although probably it would have prevented performance of the contract. If a contract is broken, the measure of damages generally is the same, whatever the cause of the breach. We have to consider, therefore, what the plaintiff would have been entitled to recover in that case, and that depends on what liability the defendant fairly may be supposed to have assumed consciously, or to have warranted the plaintiff reasonably to suppose that it assumed, when the contract was made.

This point of view is taken by implication in the rule that "a person can only be held to be responsible for such consequences as may be reasonably supposed to be in the contemplation of the parties at the time of making the contract." The suggestion thrown out by Bramwell, B., in *Gee v. Lancashire & Y.R. Co.*, 6 Hurlst. & N. 211, 218, that perhaps notice after the contract was made and before breach would be enough, is not accepted by the later decisions. The consequences must be contemplated at the time of the making of the contract.

The question arises, then, What is sufficient to show that the consequences were in contemplation of the parties, in the sense of the vendor taking the risk? It has been held that it may be proved by oral evidence when the contract is in writing. But, in the language quoted, with seeming approbation, by Blackburn, J., from Mayne on Damages, 2d ed. 10, in *Elbinger Actien-Gesellschafft v. Armstrong*, L.R. 9 Q.B. 473, 478, "it may be asked, with great deference, whether the mere fact of such consequences being communicated to the other party will be sufficient, without going on to show that he was told that he would be answerable for them, and consented to undertake such a liability." Mr. Justice Willes answered this question, so far as it was in his power, in *British Columbia & V.I. Spar, Lumber, & Saw-Mill Co. v. Nettleship*, L.R. 3 C.P. 499, 500:

> I am disposed to take the narrow view that one of two contracting parties ought not to be allowed to obtain an advantage which he has not paid for. * * * If that [a liability for the full profits that might be made by machinery which the defendant was transporting, if the plaintiff's trade should prove successful and without a rival] had been presented to the mind of the ship owner at the time of making the contract, as the basis upon which he was contracting, he would at once have rejected it. And though he knew, from the shippers, the use they intended to make of the articles, it could not be contended that the mere fact of knowledge, without more, would be a reason for imposing upon him a greater degree of liability than would otherwise have been cast upon him. To my mind, that leads to the inevitable conclusion that the mere fact of knowledge cannot increase the liability. The knowledge must be brought home to the party sought to be charged, under such circumstances that he must know that the person he contracts with reasonably believes that he accepts the contract with the special condition attached to it.

It may be said with safety that mere notice to a seller of some interest or probable action of the buyer is not enough necessarily and as matter of law to charge the seller with special damage on that account if he fails to deliver the goods. With that established, we recur to the allegations. With regard to the first, it is obvious that the plaintiff was free to bring its tanks from where it liked,—a thousand miles away or an adjoining yard,—so far as the contract was concerned. The allegation hardly amounts to saying that the defendant had notice that the plaintiff was likely to send its cars from a distance. It is not alleged that the defendant had notice that the plaintiff had to bind itself to pay $900, at the time when the contract was made, and it nowhere is alleged that the defendant assumed any liability in respect of this uncertain element of charge. The same observations may be made with regard to the claim for loss of use of the tanks and to the final allegations as to sending the tanks from distant points. It is true that this last was alleged to have been in contemplation of the contract, if we give the plaintiff the benefit of the doubt in construing a somewhat confused sentence. But, having the contract before us, we can see that this ambiguous expression cannot be taken to mean more than notice, and notice of a fact which would depend upon the accidents of the future.

It is to be said further, with regard to the foregoing items, that they were the expenses which the plaintiff was willing to incur for performance. If it had received the oil, there were deductions from any profit which the plaintiff would have made. But, if it gets the difference between the contract price and the market price, it gets what represents the value of the oil in its hands, and to allow these items in addition would be making the defendant pay twice for the same thing.

It must not be forgotten that we are dealing with pleadings, not evidence, and with pleadings which, as we have said, evidently put the plaintiff's case as high as it possibly can be put. There are no inferences to be drawn, and therefore cases like *Hammond v. Bussey*, L.R. 20 Q.B.Div. 79, do not apply. It is a simple question of allegations which, by declining to amend, the plaintiff has admitted that it cannot reinforce. This consideration applies with special force to the attempt to hold the defendant liable for the breach of the plaintiff's contract with third persons. The allegation is that the fact that the plaintiff had contracts over was well known to the defendant, and that "defendant had contracted to that end with the plaintiff." Whether, if we were sitting as a jury, this would warrant an inference that the defendant assumed an additional liability, we need not consider. It is enough to say that it does not allege the conclusion of fact so definitely that it must be assumed to be true. With the contract before us it is in a high degree improbable that any such conclusion could have been made good.

The only other allegation needing to be dealt with is that the defendant maliciously caused the plaintiff to send the tanks a thousand miles, contemplating a breach of its contract. So far as this item has not been answered by what has been said, it is necessary only to add a few words. The fact alleged has no relation to the time of the contract. Therefore it cannot affect the damages, the measure of which was fixed at that time. The motive for the breach commonly is immaterial in an action on the contract. It is in this case. Whether, under any circumstances, it might give rise to an action of tort, is not material here.

The allowance of the exceptions made the trial of the plea superfluous. If the question of fact was to be tried as to whether the amount of damages that fairly could be claimed was sufficient to give the court jurisdiction, the court had authority to try it. In coming to his conclusion, apart from what was apparent on the face of the pleadings, the judge no doubt was influenced largely by a letter from the plaintiff to the defendant, inclosing an itemized bill for $1,021.28. This letter suggested no further claim except for "any additional mileage we may have to pay." Of course, if the judge accepted the plaintiff's own view of its case as expressed here, the pretence of jurisdiction was at an end. Some attempt was made to make out this was an offer of compromise, and inadmissible. But the letter did not purport to be anything of the sort; it was an out and out adverse demand.

Judgment affirmed.

QUESTIONS AND NOTES

1. The price of the oil in this case was quoted "F.O.B." or "free-on-board." This means that the seller was obligated under this contract to load the oil on buyer's railroad cars and that the contract price therefore included the price of the goods plus the cost of lading. The cost of transportation from seller's mill to buyer's place of business was not included in the price and was the buyer's responsibility. Other common sale terms are "F.A.S." or "free-along-side" which indicates that lading and shipping are both buyer's responsibility and the price includes only the cost of the goods themselves which are to be delivered alongside buyer's ship, truck or car, and "C&F" or "cost of goods and freight" which indicates that the seller will deliver the goods to buyer at its place of business and the price includes cost of goods, lading and shipping. See UCC §§ 2–319, 2–320.

2. Was other cottonseed oil available to the buyer at or near New Braunfels? If so, and if it refused to buy it, choosing instead to bring its tank cars back to Louisville empty, was its inability to collect for freight and car rental due to lack of "notice" to seller that it was sending cars to New Braunfels, or to its failure to mitigate damages by making a substitute purchase so as to put the cars to use?

3. What is buyer's "cost" on this oil? If it is the F.O.B. mill price plus transportation to his place of business, does giving him the cost of additional transportation to and from the next available source of oil give him a double recovery?

4. If Justice Holmes had adopted the following formula as the measure of damages in the case—"The difference between the cost of oil at New Braunfels plus transportation to Louisville and the cost of oil at the nearest available market plus transportation to Louisville, plus so much of the transport already paid by the buyer as was rendered useless by the seller's breach"—would he have equally well disposed of most of the elements of buyer's claimed damages?

5. Is this decision consistent with UCC § 2–715 reproduced below?

UNIFORM COMMERCIAL CODE:

§ 2–715. Buyer's Incidental and Consequential Damages.

(1) Incidental damages resulting from the seller's breach include expenses reasonably incurred in inspection, receipt, transportation and care and custody of goods rightfully rejected, any commercially reasonable charges, expenses or commissions in connection with effecting cover and any other reasonable expense incident to the delay or other breach.

(2) Consequential damages resulting from the seller's breach include

    (a) any loss resulting from general or particular requirements and needs of which the seller at the time of contracting had reason to know and which could not reasonably be prevented by cover or otherwise; and

    (b) injury to person or property proximately resulting from any breach of warranty.

Postal Instant Press v. Sealy

California Court of Appeal, 1996.
43 Cal.App.4th 1704, 51 Cal.Rptr.2d 365.

■ JOHNSON, J. Defendants appeal from a judgment in favor of plaintiff for breach of a franchise agreement. In what apparently is a case of first impression not only in California but the entire nation we consider whether a franchisee's failure to timely pay some past royalty fees entitles a franchisor to both terminate the franchise agreement and receive an award of over seven years in "future lost royalties." We conclude the franchisee's breach was not the "proximate" or "natural and direct" cause of the franchisor's loss of future royalties in this case. Furthermore, in the circumstances of this case, these damages are "excessive," "oppressive," and "disproportionate" to the loss. Accordingly we hold these lost future royalties are not a proper element of contract damages in the circumstances of this case.

I. FACTS AND PROCEEDINGS BELOW

Respondent and plaintiff Postal Instant Press, Inc. (PIP) is an internationally known franchisor of printing businesses. In 1979 PIP entered into a 20–year franchise agreement with appellants and defendants, Sue and Steve Sealy (collectively the Sealys). PIP agreed to provide its trademark and certain services to the Sealys in exchange for royalty fees of 6 percent of gross revenues and advertising fees of 1 percent of gross. According to the franchise agreement the Sealys were to pay these fees to PIP monthly.

Among its other terms, the lengthy franchise agreement also lists a number of possible failures on the part of the franchisee, any one of which would constitute a "material breach." In the event the franchisee commits a "material breach" the franchisor is entitled to "[t]erminate this Agreement, and thereafter bring such action * * * and to recover such damages, including but not limited to the benefit of its bargain hereunder * * * ." One of these "material breaches" is any failure to make a monthly royalty or advertising fee within ten days after notice it is unpaid.

This 20–year franchise agreement remained in effect for almost 13 years. In the late 1980's, however, the Sealys failed to timely make several of their monthly royalty and advertising fee payments. The Sealys paid some of these fees late and PIP negotiated a note with the Sealys covering other overdue payments. Then in 1991, the Sealys again failed to make several of these regular payments and fell delinquent on the note as well. Ultimately, on January 22, 1992, PIP declared the overdue payments for past royalties constituted a material breach and sent the Sealys a termination letter. In pertinent part this letter advises the Sealys:

> You are no longer authorized to hold yourself out as a Postal Instant Press ("PIP") franchisee, to hold out your business as a PIP store, to conduct business under the PIP name, to perform any act that might tend to give the public the impression that you are operating a PIP Store, to use any of the PIP trade and service marks * * *.

Elsewhere this termination letter warns the Sealys to "Cease * * * Immediately" conducting any operation as a print shop and refers to a noncompete clause found in Paragraph VIII of the agreement. (Respondent concedes this "non-compete" clause is invalid under public policy and does not seek to enforce it in this case).

One month later, on February 28, 1992, PIP filed a breach of contract action against the Sealys. In this action, PIP sought $77,300 in unpaid past royalties (including the sum which had been reduced to a note) along with interest, attorney fees and costs. In addition, the franchisor sought "future royalties and payments for the remaining unfulfilled term of the Franchise Agreement in the principal amount of at least $495,699."

After a bench trial, the court awarded PIP a total of $432,510.35 plus prejudgment interest, attorney fees, and expenses and costs. The court measured the expectation damage award according to unpaid royalty and advertising fund contributions from the date of termination through the remainder of the contract term, a period of seven and one-half years. Based upon defendants' sales history, sales figures from 1990 and 1991 were averaged and, without applying any inflation or growth factor, PIP deducted its incremental costs of performance and discounted the amount to present value or $301,334. Thus, the "estimated future profits" damages represent over two-thirds of the total judgment.

Appellants do not dispute the portion of the judgment representing damages for past royalty and advertising fees they owe and thus those damages are not a part of this appeal. However, appellants do challenge the trial court's award of unpaid future royalty and advertising fees for the remaining term of the Franchise Agreement, a period of almost eight years. This portion of the award is $301,344 and is the subject of this appeal.

II.
BREACH OF CONTRACT DAMAGES FOR "LOST FUTURE EXPECTED PROFITS" ARE LIMITED TO THOSE THE LOSS OF WHICH ARE "PROXIMATELY CAUSED" AND A "NATURAL AND DIRECT CONSEQUENCE" OF THE DEFENDANT'S BREACH ITSELF

Under general contract principles, when one party breaches a contract the other party ordinarily is entitled to damages sufficient to make that party "whole," that is, enough to place the non-breaching party in the same position as if the breach had not occurred. This includes future profits the breach prevented the non-breaching party from earning at least to the extent those future profits can be estimated with reasonable certainty.

The trial court ruled that under these general contract principles PIP was entitled to estimated future royalties this franchisor would have earned in the coming year. This period extended from the time its franchisee, the Sealys, breached the franchise contract by failing to timely make certain royalty payments until the end of the term of this contract, a duration of almost eight years. We disagree. In so ruling, the trial court overlooked an important limitation embedded in the general rule.

Under contract principles, the non-breaching party is entitled to recover only those damages, including lost future profits, which are "proximately caused" by the specific breach. 1 Witkin, Summary of California Law (9th ed.), Contracts, § 815 ["It is essential to establish a causal connection between the breach and the damages sought."] Or, to put it another way, the breaching party is only liable to place the non-breaching party in the same position as if the specific breach had not occurred. Or, to phrase it still a third way, the breaching party is only responsible to give the non-breaching party the benefit of the bargain to the extent the specific breach deprived that party of its bargain.

In the context of franchisor-franchisee relationships, this principle is illustrated by cases from other jurisdictions awarding parties future profits when the breach itself prevented the party from earning those profits. In most of these cases it is the franchisor who breached and the franchisee who is collecting damages. For example, if the franchisor wrongfully terminates the franchise, courts have held the franchisee entitled to the future profits it would have earned had the franchise remained in effect. Similarly, if the franchisor fails to provide clear title to its trademark so the franchisee cannot sell the franchised product or service, courts have held the franchisee is entitled to the profits it would have earned on sales of that product or service during the term of the franchise agreement. Once again, if the franchisor wrongfully terminates a product line, courts have awarded the franchisee the future profits it would have earned on sales of the discontinued product.

In the above cases, it is easy to determine the lost profits were a "natural and direct consequence of the breach." Because the franchisor in these cases committed breaches which directly prevented the franchisee from earning the profits it reasonably could have expected to have earned under the contract, the franchisee is entitled to those lost profits as damages. Notably, however, at least one appellate court refused to award lost future profits in a franchise context because it deemed such damages too speculative.

As mentioned earlier, we have found no cases in any jurisdiction, however, holding "lost future profit" damages for the type of breach involved in the instant case. Here the franchisee breached the franchise contract by failing to timely make some past royalty payments. There is a "natural and direct" causal connection between the franchisee's breaches and the loss of those past royalty payments. As a direct result of these breaches the franchisor lost those past royalty payments. To be made "whole" or in the other terminology, to gain the "benefit of its bargain" the franchisor must receive those past, unpaid royalty payments.

But the franchisee's failure to timely make these past royalty payments is not a "natural and direct" cause of the franchisor's failure to receive future royalty payments. Indeed the franchisor could have remained entitled to those future royalties for the full term of the franchise contract even if it sued to collect the past payments. Nothing in the franchisee's failure to pay past royalties in any sense prevented the franchisor from earning and receiving its future royalty payments. No, it was the franchisor's own decision to terminate the franchise agreement that deprived it of its entitlement to those future royalty payments. At worst, if the franchisor had not terminated the franchise agreement it might have been required to sue again or perhaps again and again to compel the franchisee to pay those future royalties in a timely fashion as those royalties accrued. (However, given the strong lesson the Sealys would have learned in having to pay PIP's attorney fees as well as interest and costs, it seems highly unlikely they would have ever again been late in making their royalty payments after losing this, the first collection action brought against them.)[3]

---

3. At oral argument, PIP's counsel argued the franchisor did not have the option of retaining the Sealys as franchisees and suing them in the future should they fail to make subsequent royalty payments. In his argument, counsel appeared to imply once it filed this action to recover these particular unpaid past royalty payments "basic contract principles" would prohibit PIP from filing suit to recover later unpaid royalty payments owed under the same contract.

Our research suggests the contrary proposition is well settled in contract law.

PIP points to several California cases in which courts have awarded lost future profits in other contexts. But in none of these was the defendant's breach a mere failure to pay moneys owed for past performance. Instead they involved total failures to perform at all.

For example, in *Hollywood Cleaning & Pressing Co. v. Hollywood Laundry Service, Inc.* (1932), the defendant contracted to promote a cleaning service and subcontract exclusively with plaintiff for a ten-year period, then stopped performing at all after a short time. The breach was total and akin to those involved in the franchise cases discussed above where the franchisor wrongfully terminates the franchise or closes down a product line. So it is not surprising the California Supreme Court allowed the plaintiff to recover future profits it was prevented from earning as a direct result of defendant's breach.

Another case PIP cites follows a similar scenario. In *Gold Min. & Water Co. v. Swinerton* (1943), a lessor granted a lessee the right to extract minerals from a tract of land in return for a royalty based on the minerals extracted. Shortly thereafter, the lessor denied the lessee's request to assign the lease. The lessee then repudiated the lease and refused to perform. The California Supreme Court allowed the plaintiff lessor to recover its lost future profits, in this case the royalty payments it would have earned on the extracted minerals had the lessee performed. But once again the defendant's breach was a total failure to perform under the contract which directly prevented the plaintiff from earning those royalty payments. The lessee's breach in *Gold Mining* was not his failure to make one or more of the periodic royalty payments he would have owed the lessor if he had performed his contractual duty to extract minerals. Instead his breach was his failure to perform his duty to extract the minerals in the first place. So once again this case is no authority for awarding future lost profits as a penalty for failing to timely pay past profits.

Not only is this a case of first impression, but it is difficult to locate close analogies.[4] However, a franchise bears many similarities to a license and the relationship

---

The franchise agreement in this case establishes an executory contract. The franchisee receives a benefit each month—use of the franchisor's trademark and services—and pays for that benefit each month. When the franchisee fails to pay for one month's benefit the franchisor can sue to recover the unpaid payment for that month without losing its right to provide future benefits and sue again should the franchisee once again fail to pay for those later benefits. Even "[w]here one party to an executory contract repudiates it and refuses any longer to be bound by it, the injured party has the right to elect to * * * keep the contract alive for the benefit of both parties, being and keeping himself at all times ready, willing, and able to perform his part of the contract, and at the time fixed by the contract for performance, sue and recover according to the terms of the contract * * *." (Armstrong v. Illinois Bankers Life Ass'n. (1940); Williston on Contracts, supra, 695.)

4. Although the cases are distinguishable on the facts, we observe two other courts expressed reluctance to award future royalties to franchisors once their franchisees lost the trademark and

between franchisor and franchisee is similar to that of licensor and licensee. So it is instructive to find a California court held a non-breaching party's decision to terminate a license because of the other party's breach also terminated the licensee's duty to pay future royalties under the license. (*Fageol & Tate v. Baird–Bailhache Co.* (1931)). In that case, the court held:

> The provision for the termination of the contract upon default of the licensee was for the benefit of the licensors. Upon default of the licensee, the licensors could either terminate the contract by giving the thirty-day notice therein provided for or they could elect to continue the contract in force and insist on the payment of the royalties as they accrued. They could not do both * * *. The license of the appellant to manufacture and sell the patented articles ceased * * * and their obligation to pay future royalties ceased as well.

Likewise in the instant case, once PIP terminated the Franchise Agreement the right of the Sealys to sell their printing services as a PIP franchise ceased, and so it would seem "their obligation to pay future royalties ceased as well."

We conclude the Sealys' breach in failing to timely pay past royalties and advertising fees was not a "proximate" or "natural and direct" cause of PIP's loss of future royalties and advertising fees. Failing to make those payments did not prevent PIP from receiving royalties on future revenues the Sealys' produced under the Franchise Agreement. It was only when PIP elected to terminate that agreement that it ended the Sealys' ability to produce revenues as a PIP franchisee and also ended its own right to collect royalties on those revenues. Accordingly, these future profits are not a form of damages to which PIP is entitled for this particular breach of the franchise agreement. At the same time, we wish to make it clear we are not holding franchisors can never collect lost future royalties for franchisees' breaches of the franchise agreement. That entitlement depends on the nature of the breach and whether the breach itself prevents the franchisor from earning those future royalties.

---

other benefits to which they had been entitled under the franchise agreement. In *In re Arthur Treacher's Franchisee Litigation* (3d Cir.1982), a franchisor terminated a franchise and then sued to enjoin a franchisee from continued use of the trademark. By the time the case reached the appellate state the franchisee had agreed to give up the trademark and other franchise benefits. The Third Circuit then held, "Since [defendant] is no longer an Arthur Treacher's franchisee using Arthur Treacher's trademark, it should no longer be required to pay royalties."

III.

EVEN IF APPELLANTS' BREACH WAS THE CAUSE OF PIP'S LOSING SOME FUTURE ROYALTY PAYMENTS, IT IS INAPPROPRIATE TO AWARD LOST FUTURE PROFITS WHERE IT WOULD RESULT IN DAMAGES WHICH ARE UNREASONABLE, UNCONSCIONABLE AND OPPRESSIVE

As a second independent and sufficient rationale[5] for our reversal of the trial court's "lost future profits" award, we conclude it would violate the statutory and

---

5. Because we reverse the "future lost profits" award on the two grounds discussed in this opinion, we need not consider whether this award also runs afoul of a third limitation on such awards. The law allows the award of lost future profits only when courts can calculate their amount with some degree of certainty.

In the present case, the trial court found that degree of certainty in a straightforward projection of past experience to the seven and a half years remaining on the franchise contract. The court based this projection on the Sealy's gross income for the 1990–1991 period. It multiplied this gross by the royalty fee of 6 percent and the advertising fee of 1 percent to arrive at an annual lost royalty figure. The court then multiplied that annual lost royalty amount by the number of years remaining on the franchise contract.

At first blush, the very simplicity of this calculation appears to support a finding it is possible to estimate "lost future profits" in this case with the requisite certainty. But upon closer examination this simple formula may be an oversimplification. In order to estimate what PIP stands to lose in the form of lost future profits after it terminated the Sealys' franchise requires a court to consider a complex equation of imponderables. It takes a great deal of courage if not daring to venture a guess as to the gross profits a PIP outlet is likely to earn seven—or five or even three— years hence in a field as volatile as printing and reproduction. By the time this franchise term runs out "desktop publishing," the "information superhighway," the "paperless office," and like developments already may have transformed the industry in which the PIP stores and like operations strive to operate. This case arises in a field where the short term future to say nothing of the medium and long term future is almost uniquely unpredictable.

But the major imponderable in estimating how much net profit PIP will lose over the next seven years resulted from PIP's election to terminate the franchise agreement and thus to release PIP to open a new outlet directly across the street from the Sealys' print store. Or it could open a "mega store" a few blocks away with advanced equipment and services which drew customers from a broad territory including the Sealy print store. In either event, the Sealys could lose most or all of their business—and gross revenues—to another PIP franchise or two. Meanwhile PIP would be receiving royalty payments from its new franchisees on the business which used to go to the Sealys but now went to the competing PIP outlets. To the extent it received these royalty payments PIP would not experience net "lost profits" from the Sealys' departure from the PIP fold. Conversely, to the extent PIP already had received a "lost profits" damage award from the Sealys, the corporation would receive double profits on the income its new franchisee managed to attract from the Sealys.

Whether and when PIP chooses to award a franchise to open a store or mega store which will compete with the Sealys' establishment is almost entirely in PIP's control. The franchisor is free to do so from the moment it cancels the agreement. It has little incentive to install a new franchise, however, until it has won its award of "future lost profits" from the disenfranchised franchisee, assuming the courts allow such an award. Once the franchisor has that award in its

common law prohibition of damages which are "unreasonable, unconscionable or grossly oppressive."

This prohibition is found in Civil Code section 3359. "Damages must, in all cases, be reasonable, and where an obligation of any kind appears to create a right to unconscionable and grossly oppressive damages, contrary to substantial justice, no more than reasonable damages can be recovered." The limitation applies to contract as well as tort damages. The Restatement contains a similar limitation which applies specifically to contract damages. This one recognizes the potential of "future lost profit" awards in particular to produce excessive compensation for the plaintiff. "A court may limit damages for foreseeable loss by excluding recovery for loss of profits, * * * if it concludes that in the circumstances justice so requires in order to avoid disproportionate compensation." (Restatement 2d Contracts § 351(3).)

In our view, PIP's entitlement to recover its past unpaid royalties, along with attorneys fees and costs, along with its right to immediately install a new franchisee in what formerly had been the Sealys' exclusive territory provides it with a full measure of "reasonable" damages. But a further award of "lost future royalties" provides PIP with "disproportionate compensation" which is "unreasonable" and an "unconscionable" and "grossly oppressive" imposition on its franchisee, the Sealys. To do so is "contrary to substantial justice" between franchisors and franchisees in general and this franchisor and this franchisee in particular. Damages of this nature and in this amount distort the relationship between the breach and its remedy and seriously disturb the balance between franchisor and franchisee and between creditor and debtor. In essence, allowing "lost future profits" damages in

---

pocket, it has nothing to lose from vigorously seeking out someone interested in opening a franchise store right next door to its former franchisee. Any dollar that new franchisee turns over to the franchisor in the form of a royalty payment is a dollar of extra profit for that franchisor, since it already has received its expected royalty payments for that franchise territory in the form of a "lost future profits" award from the court.

It follows that a franchisor, such as PIP, would have every reason to wait until after it received the "lost future profits" award before doing anything which someone might construe as an attempt to install a competitor to its former franchisee. For, if it does so before trial the franchisor would risk losing its "future lost profits" damages. So it is hardly surprising the Sealys failed to introduce evidence PIP had awarded a competing franchise or was about to or even had done anything suggesting it might be considering that option. Moreover, short of finding and tendering its own competition, the Sealys had no way of mitigating the "lost future profits" damages they might be inflicting on PIP.

This court recognizes these difficulties in arriving at an estimate of net "lost future royalties" in which we can have any confidence. However, we need not and do not address the issue whether the extreme instability of the print shop market and especially the franchisor's absolute control over the "competing franchisee" variable combine to render any estimate of net future lost royalties so speculative as to preclude an award of such damages.

these circumstances would place a bludgeon in the hands of franchisors in contract disputes with their franchisees.

The relationship between franchisor and franchisee is a significant issue, and growing more important each year. As recently explained, "Franchising is rapidly becoming the dominant mode of distributing goods and services in the United States. According to the International Franchise Association, one out of every twelve businesses in the United States is a franchise. In addition, franchise systems now employ over eight million people and account for approximately forty-one percent of retail sales in the United States. Even conservative estimates predict that franchised businesses will be responsible for over fifty percent of retail sales by the year 2000."

Although franchise agreements are commercial contracts they exhibit many of the attributes of consumer contracts. The relationship between franchisor and franchisee is characterized by a prevailing, although not universal, inequality of economic resources between the contracting parties. Franchisees typically, but not always, are small businessmen or businesswomen or people like the Sealys seeking to make the transition from being wage earners and for whom the franchise is their very first business. Franchisors typically, but not always, are large corporations. The agreements themselves tend to reflect this gross bargaining disparity. Usually they are form contracts the franchisor prepared and offered to franchisees on a take-or-leave-it basis. Among other typical terms, these agreements often allow the franchisor to terminate the agreement or refuse to renew for virtually any reason, including the desire to give a franchisor-owned outlet the prime territory the franchisee presently occupies.

Some courts and commentators have stressed the bargaining disparity between franchisors and franchisees is so great[8] that franchise agreements exhibit many of the attributes of an adhesion contract and some of the terms of those contracts may be unconscionable. "Franchising involves the unequal bargaining power of franchisors and franchisees and therefore carries within itself the seeds of abuse. Before the relationship is established, abuse is threatened by the franchisor's use of contracts

---

8. A comment PIP's counsel made at oral argument underscores this franchisee's lack of bargaining power. The court asked why any prospective franchisee would sign an agreement with PIP if the contract were construed to give PIP up to twenty years of "lost future profits" for a failure to timely make a royalty payment or for a similar "material breach." PIP's counsel responded there were lots of people earning $6 an hour in the labor force who would welcome the opportunity to sign such an agreement in order to gain the chance for the much higher earnings available to successful PIP franchisees. (This evidently was a reference to the Sealys, since there are indications in the record Mr. Sealy was working for $6 an hour prior to becoming a PIP franchisee.)

of adhesion presented on a take-it-or-leave-it basis. Indeed such contracts are some-times so one-sided, with all the obligations on the franchisee and none on the franchisor, as not to be legally enforceable."

The "lost future profits" award PIP seeks in this case dramatically expands the already enormous bargaining gap between this franchisor and this franchisee. PIP argues it is entitled to these damages because the failure to timely make one or more royalty payments constitutes a "material breach" under the contract. The franchise agreement further provides any "material breach," in turn, entitles the franchisor to terminate the contract and collect the "benefit of the bargain," which in PIP's view means all the future royalty fees the franchisor could expect to receive from this franchisee for the remaining term of the contract. Thus, under PIP's view, had the Sealys failed to timely make their first royalty payment PIP would have been entitled to declare a breach, terminate the franchise agreement and collect 20 years of estimated future royalty payments from the newly disenfranchised franchisees, the Sealys.[9]

For reasons explained in section II, we do not construe the franchise agreement as permitting this form of damages as part of the franchisor's "benefit of the bar-gain" when it elects to terminate the franchise because a franchisee failed to timely make some past royalty payments. As pointed out in this earlier section, in the con-text of a franchise arrangement "future lost profits" are not a result of the franchisee's breach in failing to timely pay royalties but of the franchisor's election to cancel the franchise agreement. Consequently, the receipt of "lost future royalty payments" is not part of the bargain to which the franchise agreement entitles the franchisor when it terminates for this type of breach.

But even assuming this contract is properly construed to call for an award of "lost future royalty payments" after PIP terminated the Sealys' franchise for non-payment of past royalties, we conclude such an award would be "excessive" and "unconscionable" and "oppressive" within the meaning of Civil Code section 3359. Furthermore, it would provide PIP with "disproportionate compensation" within the meaning of Restatement 2nd Contracts section 351(3).

---

9. The terms of this Franchise Agreement, if fully enforced, would have been even more draco-nian. As noted earlier, the Agreement contained a "no compete" clause which precluded the Sealys from continuing in the printshop business. Were that term enforced along with the "lost future royalties" award, the Sealys would have been required to pay a judgment calculated as a percentage of the gross receipts they no longer were allowed to earn, even if they did so without the PIP trademark or other franchise benefits. Meanwhile PIP would have been able to install a new franchisee, perhaps in the Sealys' abandoned location, and receive a second royalty on the same business which formerly would have gone to the Sealys but now was coming to its new franchisee.

To sanction such an award in this case would so unbalance the relationship between franchisors and franchisees as to threaten to convert every franchise agreement allowing such damages into an unconscionable and oppressive contract. Imagine the position of a small-business person operating a franchise involved in some minor contract dispute with the franchisor during the 20–year term of the agreement. Don't do exactly everything the way the franchisor demands and the franchisee risks declaration of a "material breach" backed up by the whip of a giant "lost future profits" award. Such an award would leave the franchisee enslaved for five or ten or twenty years working primarily for the franchisor's benefit but without its trademark or other services. Franchisors would seldom have to apply that whip, of course. It would be enough to crack it now and then to keep their franchisees in line. This is nearly the definition of oppression. And, a specie of damage award which produces this degree of imbalance between a franchisor and his franchisees is clearly "oppressive" as well as "excessive."

For this second independent and sufficient reason, we also are compelled to reverse the trial court's award of "lost future profits" damages (in this case future royalty and advertising fee payments.)

CONCLUSION

Although we find compelling reasons for reversing the "lost future profits" award in this case, we emphasize the limits of our holding. We are not holding a trial court can never appropriately award some "lost future profits" to a franchisor. In a future case, the breach may be of a type which directly causes the franchisor to lose future profits independent of the franchisor's own termination of the franchise agreement. Furthermore, the amount of the award may be of a size which is neither "excessive" nor "oppressive" nor "disproportionate to the loss." What we do hold, however, is that a "lost future profits" award to a franchisor must satisfy all of these conditions—just as would such an award to any other party. Furthermore, we conclude the franchisor-franchisee relationship introduces some special considerations in determining whether the conditions are met. As detailed above, those considerations include the lengthy term of such agreements, the franchisor's power to terminate the franchise and substitute a new franchisee, and the typical imbalance between the parties.[10]

---

10. We also stress we do not adopt a position the Sealys' counsel advocated at oral argument. He pressed for a rule which would allow franchisees to terminate the franchise agreement almost at will subject only to forfeiture of the "security deposit" and payment of past unpaid royalties, if any.

The Sealys' counsel justified this as a market oriented solution. He argued franchisees would only give up their rights to the franchise trademark and other services when those "benefits" no longer were worth the franchise fee because it had become a "dying" franchise system. (He further claimed PIP is such a "dying" system, because of changes in technology and market

DISPOSITION

The judgment is reversed insofar as it awards expectancy damages in the form of estimated future lost profits (franchise royalty and advertising fee payments) and the cause remanded for further proceedings consistent with this opinion. In all other respects, the judgment is affirmed. Appellants to recover their costs on appeal.

NOTE

Consider the following critique of *Sealy* in *Moran Indus. v. Mr. Transmission of Chattanooga*, 2010 U.S. Dist. LEXIS 71753 (E.D. Tenn. 2010):

> The court's decision in *Sealy* has come under scrutiny from courts and commentators alike in recent years. *See e.g.*, Robert L. Ebe, David L. Steinberg, & Brett R. Waxdeck, *Radisson and the Potential Demise of the Sealy-Barnes-Hinton Rule*, 27 FRANCHISE L.J. 3, 5 (2007). Some courts ... have adhered to the reasoning expressed in *Sealy*....
>
> However, other courts have rejected the *Sealy* reasoning. For example, in *American Speedy Printing Centers, Inc. v. AM Marketing, Inc.* the Sixth Circuit affirmed the district court's award of $115,616.12 in lost future profits/royalties. In response to the franchisee's argument that the franchisor was requesting inconsistent remedies, the Sixth Circuit disagreed:
>
>> We agree with the district court and find that [the franchisor] requests consistent remedies. . . . It is clear from the plain language of both the franchise agreement and the complaint filed in this action that by the time [the franchisor] filed the complaint, it had already terminated the agreement in response to [the franchisee's] breach. [The franchisor] seeks injunctive relief to stop [the franchisee] from using its marks or holding itself out as a

---

conditions.) In his view, it is unfair and uneconomic to force franchisees to remain linked to a sinking franchisor by requiring them to continue paying royalty fees if they elect to terminate the franchise agreement. It is better for the economy to permit strong franchisees to swim away on their own to operate as independent businesses rather than sinking with the rest of the system. If required to continue paying royalties for unnecessary and possibly counterproductive trademarks and services, even the stronger franchisees may not be able to survive.

This is an interesting argument but one which we do not adopt in this opinion. For whatever reason, the Sealys' counsel argued for a principle far broader than needed to resolve the instant case. Here we have a franchise agreement the franchisor, not the franchisee elected to terminate, instead of maintaining the franchise and filing a debt collection action for unpaid royalties. The franchisor cited the franchisee's failure to timely make some past royalty payments as the "material breach" justifying this termination. Under these circumstances, it is unnecessary for this court to consider what "future lost profits" damages might be appropriate where a franchisee rather than the franchisor unilaterally terminates the agreement.

franchise owner, and monetary compensation in the form of lost profits/royalties for defendants' actual breach of the agreement that has already occurred—entirely consistent remedies for separate and distinct injuries. The assignment of error is without merit.

Applying Michigan law, the Sixth Circuit determined that the franchisor's future lost royalties were not too speculative and could be awarded because the franchisor "is entitled to all damages necessary to be put in a position equivalent to that in which it would find itself if the agreement continued in effect for the full twenty years."

* * *

In their 2007 law review article on the subject, Radisson *and the Potential Demise of the* Sealy-Barnes-Hinton *Rule*, the authors summarize the "lack of consensus" in courts regarding a franchisor's right to future lost royalties and then argue:

> that what we call the *Sealy/Barnes/Hinton* rule does not make sense. That rule, which basically allows future damages if the franchisee, but not the franchisor, terminates (even if the franchisee has committed continuing uncured breaches), elevates form over substance by failing to properly analyze proximate causation and, in many cases, properly apply principles of mitigation to avoid excessive damages. We suggest instead an approach more consistent with basic contract principles under which future lost profit damages should be available if, at the time of contracting, the parties might reasonably have foreseen that such losses would be the probable result of the franchisee's breach. However, whether or not the agreement granted the franchisee an exclusive territory, a franchisor should not recover lost profits that the franchisee proves could have been either avoided by installing a replacement franchisee or otherwise mitigated.

The approach the authors believe follows basic principles of contract law more faithfully is outlined by the district court in *Radisson Hotels Int'l, Inc. v. Majestic Towers, Inc.*, a case involving breach of a hotel franchise agreement. In that case the franchise agreement contained a liquidated damages clause outlining damages that the franchisee would bear if the franchisor terminated the agreement due to the fault of the franchisee. The court analyzed the *Sealy* decision and distinguished the hotel franchise agreement from the agreement at issue in *Sealy*. In contrast to the agreement in *Sealy*, the hotel franchise agreement specifically contemplated liquidated damages based on the franchisor's termination of the agreement due to the franchisee's failure to pay royalties. In addition, however, the court noted in a footnote:

Alternatively, this Court believes that the *Sealy* decision is mistaken.... The *Sealy* court based its proximate cause analysis on a single case involving a licensor-licensee relationship decided by another intermediate California appellate court in 1931. In this Court's view, the *Sealy* Court's holding that a franchisor has no remedy but to sue the franchisee over and over again as lost royalties accrue is simply untenable.... the Court believes that where a franchisee breaches a contract and demonstrates that is it unable or unwilling to meet its obligations, lost future profits are a proximate result of the breach because the franchisee's actions are a "substantial factor in bringing about that loss or damage." Thus, this Court does not find *Sealy* to be persuasive.

Eastern Air Lines v. McDonnell Douglas Corp.

United States Court of Appeals, Fifth Circuit, 1976.
532 F.2d 957.

[This suit by an airline against an aircraft manufacturer was based on the late delivery of commercial airplanes due to diversion of resources into military production associated with the Vietnam War. The Court of Appeals vacated and remanded the trial court's judgment for the airline and discussed the question of damages as follows:]

V. The Determination of Eastern's Damages

During the six-week damages phase of this bifurcated trial, the jury was confronted with a staggering array of highly technical evidence concerning the lost profits, surplus pilot expenses, wasted pilot training and rescheduling costs which Eastern alleges it suffered as a result of the delivery delays. The complexity of the airline business and its special sensitivity to economic and market fluctuations made the determination of Eastern's lost profits especially difficult. This is best reflected, perhaps, by the extreme variation between the estimates provided by the parties' experts. Eastern's primary witness on the damages issue, Mr. Wemple, estimated that the delivery delays caused the airline to lose $23,400,000 in profits. McDonnell's expert, Mr. Simat, on the other hand, estimated that Eastern saved at least $1,294,000 because the planes were not delivered on time.[111] Throughout the damages trial, therefore, each side undertook extensive cross-examination of the other's witnesses in an effort to account for this $24,600,000 discrepancy.

---

111. Mr. Simat estimated that, as a result of late deliveries, Eastern suffered a loss in operating profit of at most $0.3 million. This loss, in Mr. Simat's view, was more than offset by the added costs of capital Eastern would have incurred in order to obtain and pay for the Douglas aircraft.

At trial and on appeal, McDonnell has vigorously contested several of the basic assumptions underlying Eastern's estimate of its damages. McDonnell relies on the established proposition that an expert's opinion as to lost profits and other damages must be predicated on assumptions which have a reasonable basis in the evidence.

It is not enough, however, that several of Wemple's assumptions may be open to question.[112] Instead, the issue is whether the probative value of the expert's testimony was so slight that it should not have been submitted to the jury.[113] A jury's award of damages, therefore, may have adequate support in the evidence even though an expert's assumptions and methodology may not have been the only permissible ones for determining damages.

Rather than anticipate the relitigation of this issue, we pretermit any assessment of the Wemple testimony. We do, however, make several suggestions which the District Court may consider in the event that a retrial of Eastern's damages claims becomes necessary. In our view, the trial judge is obliged to scrutinize most carefully unusually technical or complicated expert testimony. A court must be mindful of the particular difficulties that can arise when a plaintiff resorts, in Judge Friendly's words, "to an array of figures conveying a delusive impression of exactness in an area where a jury's common sense is less available than usual to protect it." *Herman Schwabe, Inc. v. United Shoe Machinery Corp.*, 2 Cir., 1962.

These added costs, which were not considered by Mr. Wemple, were estimated as being over $1.6 million.

112. McDonnell's primary contention is that there is no basis in the evidence for Mr. Wemple's assumption that the 3 per cent increase in capacity which would have resulted from timely deliveries would have been matched by an equivalent increase in passenger traffic. However, McDonnell also argues that Wemple's use of "system wide average passenger yields" overstated the gross revenues which Eastern would have received because the airline's yields on Douglas jets were substantially lower than the system average. McDonnell contends further that Wemple assigned additional passenger traffic and revenue to Eastern's shuttle services when, in fact, all passengers desiring to use this service were being accommodated. Another Wemple assumption challenged by McDonnell is that 20 per cent of Eastern's costs ($164.5 million) would not have increased at all even if the Douglas planes had been delivered on time. McDonnell also claims that it was speculative for Wemple to assume that Eastern would have derived extra cargo income on a percentage basis equivalent to the assumed increase in passengers. Finally McDonnell attacks Wemple's failure to deduct from Eastern's estimated lost profits the cost of financing those aircraft which were purchased rather than leased.

113. Both *Terrell* and *Greene* were actions brought under the Sherman Act. The proof of damages in private anti-trust suits is significantly less arduous than is usually the case in other actions. Therefore, our reliance on *Terrell* and *Greene* should not be taken as indicating that in this case, Eastern must not be held to the traditional rule against speculative or conjectural estimates of damages in contract actions. See *Center Chemical Co. v. Avril, Inc.*, 5 Cir., 1968.

The District Court must do more than merely weigh the probative value of an expert's testimony considered as a whole. Where practical, a trial judge should exclude particular assumptions or other aspects of an expert's testimony which considered individually do not meet the "minimum of probative value." This more detailed scrutiny is necessary because some telling errors may become virtually unreviewable once the jury has returned its verdict.

In this case, for example, Wemple should have considered whether Eastern's estimated loss of profits was reduced by the cost of financing those planes which were purchased rather than leased. McDonnell argues that this was an error which overstated the airline's lost profits by $1.6 million. However, because Eastern was awarded only 85 per cent of the damages estimated by Wemple, it cannot be said that McDonnell's cross-examination did not bring this point home to the jury. In complicated or technical cases, therefore, an expert's testimony should be cleansed of unsupportable assumptions or clear errors which have less than the minimum of probative value. This would reduce the possibility of a confused jury and an arbitrary verdict.

Finally, we note that the District Court has the discretion to call an expert witness on its own. The unusual difficulty of estimating a major airline's lost profits resulting from extensive delays stretching over a period of three years and involving 90 jet aircraft suggests to us that the jury might benefit from the testimony of a neutral expert in this case. Because a court-appointed witness would be unconcerned with either promoting or attacking a particular estimate of Eastern's damages, he could provide an objective insight into the $24.5 million difference of opinion between the parties' experts. Indeed, the mere presence of a neutral expert may have, in Judge Prettyman's phrase, "a great tranquilizing effect" on the experts retained by Eastern and McDonnell.

QUESTIONS AND NOTES

1. Given the $24 million range in Eastern's damages based on the conflicting expert testimony, why aren't the damages considered too speculative? Does testimony by "experts" who disagree wildly render the damage calculation more or less speculative than it would otherwise be? Compare *Eastern Air Lines* with *Freund* and *Sealy*.

2. Knowing the great difficulty in measuring damages resulting from late delivery (and the even greater difficulty of obtaining specific performance), what might you advise Eastern to have done?

3. Are there special problems associated with the Fifth Circuit's suggestion to the District Court regarding the appointment of a neutral expert?

4. Since *Eastern Air Lines* was decided, the Supreme Court has tightened the rules on the admission of expert testimony in federal trials to ensure that the methodology or technique employed by the expert is generally accepted in the relevant discipline. *See Daubert v. Merrell Dow Pharmaceuticals*, 509 U.S. 579 (1993). Nevertheless, concerns about the probative value and integrity of partisan expert testimony proffered on damages issues in complex cases have only increased. *See* Hill, Hogan, Karam & Langvardt, *Increasing Complexity and Partisanship in Business Damages Expert Testimony: The Need for a Modified Trial Regime in Quantification of Damages*, 11 U. PA. J. BUS. L. 297 (2009).

CHAPTER 3

COUNTERVAILING INFLUENCES ON CONTRACT REMEDIES

If the basic remedies described in Chapter Two were the whole story, the law of contract damages would be simple, but stringent. The basic remedies are not the whole story because when tested by real cases they produce too many unsatisfactory results both for parties planning transactions and for courts trying to reach a just resolution in a particular dispute. An aggrieved party with a legitimate claim may be left with no damages remedy (or six cents in nominal damages) notwithstanding an apparently significant loss. At the other extreme, if the grant of consequential damages becomes too liberal, the risks of contract increase and prices rise.

Four ways out of contract remedies problems that are worthy of note will be considered in this Chapter. First, the potential of contract damages to deny justified relief is limited by the presence of an alternative set of restitutionary remedies. Second, in aggravated cases courts may lift the matter bodily out of the conceptual framework of contract and give it the more hospitable label of tort, making new and more generous damage rules available. Third, in many situations the parties may preplan appropriate remedies by liquidated damages clauses. Finally, parties may contract out of the law courts altogether by arbitration agreements that empower a new set of tribunals applying distinct rules.

A characteristic of judge-made law is that principles emerge slowly as experience accretes in deciding disputes day by day. In any dispute worth fighting about, there will be two sides to the story. Sometimes one side will be more compelling and sometimes the other, and so the common law contains divergent, if not discordant, strains. Two or more lines of decision may emerge. Sometimes an appellate court will definitively decide that one is the law and the other is not. More often the courts will try to minimize the inconsistencies, reconciling the cases and distinguishing the factors that lead toward different results. Very often contradictions are resolved by announcing two separate principles, erecting a high wall between them and scoffing at naive questions that suggest that there is a connection. It is not enough, therefore, to learn the basic scheme we have described for contract damages. One must also be aware of the available alternatives should basic contract doctrine lead in undesirable directions.

I.   RESTITUTION

One ancient alternative set of remedies to those provided by the rules of contract damages is known by a variety of names, including restitution, unjust enrichment, the common counts, general assumpsit, quasi-contract, or *quantum meruit*.

Damages and specific performance in theory give the injured party the promised performance either directly (specific performance) or by substituting its financial equivalent (damages). Both seek to put the injured party in the position it would have been in had the contract been performed. But this expectancy of performance is not the only interest protected in contract transactions. A party may pay in advance or expend money, time and material in performing its part of the contract. If a breach occurs and the transaction collapses, such a party may just want its money back or compensation for what it has expended in part performance. In such a case, the injured party seeks to be restored to the position it would have been in had there never been a contract, instead of damages to provide the financial equivalent of performance of the contract. Such claims look backwards in time to the parties' positions before entering into their contract, rather than toward their expected future positions after the contract is fulfilled by performance.

Some of these expenditures may have directly benefitted the breaching party, and the injured party will feel entitled to compensation measured by this unjust enrichment. But it may be that the injured party's action in reliance on the promise has produced no obvious benefit to the breaching party; nonetheless, the injured party deserves compensation for its justified reliance. Although the distinctions between these three interests (expectancy, restitution and reliance) were recognized as long ago as Aristotle, the common law made no clear choice among them. Early decisions can be found that apply sometimes one and sometimes another in a promissory situation. As we have already noted, the legal measures of damages have always been vague and the computation of damages treated largely as a question of fact for the jury.

Modern American contract law continues to emphasize the expectancy interest, seeking to give the injured party the financial equivalent of performance. Sometimes outlays in reliance are used as a substitute measure of expectancy damages, particularly when it appears that full performance would not have yielded a profit for the plaintiff. In addition, the law has allowed the injured party to elect alternative restitutionary forms of relief if it wants to.

Some of the confusion concerning restitution is traceable to the use of the same Latin phrase, *quantum meruit*, to describe two different kinds of claims. The original use was to recover the reasonable value of goods (*quantum valebant*) or services (*quantum meruit*) delivered pursuant to defendant's explicit request and express or implied in fact promise to pay the reasonable value (instead of a specific price) of what was to be delivered. A car owner's request to the mechanic to "fix the car," with no agreement on price, implies a promise to pay the reasonable value of the work the mechanic does on the car. In modern usage quantum meruit has come to be commonly used to include actions for both goods and for services.

The second meaning of quantum meruit arose when the common law courts appropriated the substance of the equitable remedy of restitution by asserting that every contract included a fictional promise that if the contract were breached, the breaching party would pay the value of any performance rendered by the non-breaching party. Take a builder who lays the foundation and puts the frame and roof on a house before the owner wrongfully terminates the contract. The builder may sue in quantum meruit for the value of work, instead of his damages. If the job was difficult and the anticipated profits lost by the breach were low, the wronged party is likely to prefer being paid the fair value of the partial performance rather than damages. As generations passed, implied promises to pay measurable value conferred became increasingly fictitious and were used to force disgorgement in situations that were not contractual in any realistic sense. This fiction, sometimes called "quasi contract," provided judges with a flexible tool to do justice but muddied the conceptual stream of the law to the chagrin of law professors and the dismay of students.

By a comparatively recent expansion of quasi contract theory, the restitutionary remedy became available in many states to breaching parties as well as innocent ones when the value of the partial performance before breach significantly exceeded the non-breaching party's damages. Return to our example, but now suppose that the builder rather than the owner breached after the foundation, frame, and roof are in place. The homeowner never promised to pay for a foundation, frame, or roof, as such; he promised only to pay for a house. Nevertheless, the builder may be permitted to maintain a quantum meruit action for the value to the owner of the work done to the extent it exceeds the owner's damage from the breach. To do otherwise would unjustly enrich the owner by the reduced cost of building his house that results from the builder's abortive efforts.

American law has come to recognize restitution, or quasi contract, as a distinct body of legal rules. Be warned that the area is not subject to easy conceptual analysis; rules are confusing, and there are substantial inconsistencies and variations among different jurisdictions. Fortunately, casebooks do not have to be conceptually neat. This book will not attempt to reconcile the divergent positions taken by courts in various states and by scholarly authorities.

As Professor Dan Dobbs observes in his three volume treatise:

> Most generalizations about restitution are trustworthy only so long as they are not very meaningful, and meaningful only so long as they are not very trustworthy. There are, however, some core ideas.... Restitution is a simple word but a difficult subject, partly because restitutionary ideas appear in many guises.

DAN B. DOBBS, REMEDIES: DAMAGES, EQUITY, RESTITUTION 551 (2d ed. 1993).

———

At this point in your studies, a few general principles will suffice.

(1) In most jurisdictions, the restitutionary claim is stated by a "common count," alleging an implied promise to pay quantum meruit separate and apart from the allegation of an express contract. This claim can stand without inevitable inconsistency alongside a claim for contract damages based on the allegation of breach of an express agreement. The two claims will be considered by the court in the same lawsuit but remain distinct in theory and practice. The "common count" or restitutionary claim usually is pleaded separately from the contract claim. A plaintiff may recover under a contract theory for damages or in restitution, but not both.

Restitutionary recovery and contract damages are calculated in different ways, and in a given case one may yield a significantly larger recovery for the plaintiff. Plaintiffs are likely to plead both theories and finally elect the one that promises the greatest reward. The point in the lawsuit when the election must be made varies among jurisdictions.

(2) The basic measure of restitutionary recovery is the value of the benefit plaintiff conferred on defendant. But there are usually conflicting possible measures of "value." For example, should the value of the part performance be measured by the contract price or by a fair market price? In most cases involving a plaintiff who is not in breach itself, the courts generally presume that a fair market value measure is appropriate. The question of under what circumstances the contract price may serve as a limit on restitutionary recovery for a party not in breach is controversial. The weight of judicial authority, however, denies the breaching party the protection of the contract it has violated in at least some circumstances, particularly if the innocent plaintiff would otherwise suffer a loss under the terms of the contract.

Thus, restitution will be attractive to a non-breaching party that has put more value into performance than is likely to be awarded as contract damages. In other words, restitution is a preferred remedy for the innocent party to a losing contract because it allows the loser to get out of the deal without the loss it would have suffered if it had performed the contract.

Note that this somewhat anomalous result has been the subject of much scholarly criticism, particularly over the last 20 years. Although the Restatement

(Second) of Contracts § 373(1), promulgated in 1979, nevertheless embraces this result, the Restatement (Third) of Restitution §§ 37-38 (2011) expressly criticizes and rejects this rule, limiting even the non-breaching party in restitution to a recovery based on contract price. It remains to be seen whether the courts will follow this newer approach. *See* William J. Woodward, Jr., *Restitution Without Context: An Examination of the Losing Contract Problem in the Restatement (Third) of Restitution*, in BRAUCHER *et al.*, REVISITING THE CONTRACTS SCHOLARSHIP OF STEWART MACAULEY (Hart 2013) (critiquing new approach of Restatement (Third) of Restitution and suggesting that "the proponents of change have not met their normative burden, and that the courts who have worked in the thicket of relational contracts are more likely to have got it 'right' than the theorists."). Even under the older Restatement (Second) of Contracts view, however, recovery is limited in the case where restitution is sought by a non-breaching party who has fully performed its end of the bargain. Restatement (Second) of Contracts § 373(2). In such a case, the plaintiff, although innocent, is not permitted to claim that the performance was worth more than the price agreed upon. The obligation of the breaching party is considered a liquidated debt which is the limit of recovery on either a contract or a restitution claim. So, for example, a seller who delivers goods and then sues for breach when the buyer fails to pay may recover only the contract price and may not claim that the goods were worth more on the market.

Note that under any view, when a *breaching* party is claiming, its recovery is definitely limited by the contract price. This just makes good sense, for otherwise (if prices have risen sharply) the breaching party would recover more by breaching the contract than it would by performing.

(3) The value of the part performance may be measured in terms of the benefit received by the defendant (the extent of unjust enrichment), or by the value of what the plaintiff put out (the extent of reliance). These two measurements need not produce the same result. In a personal service contract, for example, the value of the plaintiff's services on the labor market may be much more than the benefit received by the defendant in respect of those services, particularly if the performance was not satisfactory. The market value of home renovation services, for example, commonly exceeds any resulting increase in the market value of the home renovated. Less commonly, services may in particular cases result in a windfall profit from the perspective of the employer greatly exceeding the market wage when viewed. While there is less uniformity than might be wished, a sound general statement is that courts take into account which party has breached. When restitution in a contract transaction is sought by a non-breaching plaintiff, the value will generally be measured by the market value of the goods or services provided by the plaintiff. When restitution is sought by a party in breach, the value will generally be limited to the lesser of the benefit received by the defendant and the market value of the services.

(4) The use of the term *value* covers and frequently obscures a number of issues that lie in the borderland between law and accounting. For example, is the value of a plaintiff's past performance to be limited by its out of pocket costs? What allowance, if any, is to be made for direct and indirect overhead, profit, or return on invested capital? To the extent that market value is used, which market is referred to? Remember that restitution is sought after *part* performance. On what market are partially excavated cellars, houses without walls or roofs, or two-thirds of a well-drafted will sold? Judges tend to become very confused by such issues, and the few opinions that are reported provide little reliable guidance.

RESTATEMENT, SECOND, CONTRACTS:

§ 370. Requirement That Benefit Be Conferred.

A party is entitled to restitution under the rules stated in this Restatement only to the extent that he has conferred a benefit on the other party by way of part performance or reliance.

COMMENT:

a. Meaning of Requirement. A party's restitution interest is his interest in having restored to him any benefit that he has conferred on the other party. See § 344(2). Restitution is, therefore, available to a party only to the extent that he has conferred a benefit on the other party. The benefit may result from the transfer of property or from services, including forbearance. See Restatement of Restitution § 1, Comment *b*. The benefit is ordinarily conferred by performance by the party seeking restitution, and receipt by the other party of performance that he bargained for is regarded as a benefit. However, a benefit may also be conferred if the party seeking restitution relies on the contract in some other way, as where he makes improvements on property that does not ultimately become his. However, a party's expenditures in preparation for performance that do not confer a benefit on the other party do not give rise to a restitution interest.... If, for example, the performance consists of the manufacture and delivery of goods and the buyer wrongfully prevents its completion, the seller is not entitled to restitution because no benefit has been conferred on the buyer.... The injured party may, however, have an action for damages, including one for recovery based on his reliance interest (§ 349). The requirement of this Section is generally satisfied if a benefit has been conferred, and it is immaterial that it was later lost, destroyed or squandered....

§ 371. Measure of Restitution Interest.

If a sum of money is awarded to protect a party's restitution interest, it may as justice requires be measured by either

(a) the reasonable value to the other party of what he received in terms of what it would have cost him to obtain it from a person in the claimant's position, or

(b) the extent to which the other party's property has been increased in value or his other interests advanced.

COMMENT:

a. Measurement of Benefit. Under the rules stated in §§ 344 and 370, a party who is liable in restitution for a sum of money must pay an amount equal to the benefit that has been conferred upon him. If the benefit consists simply of a sum of money received by the party from whom restitution is sought, there is no difficulty in determining this amount. If the benefit consists of something else, however, such as services or property, its measurement in terms of money may pose serious problems....

An especially important choice is that between the reasonable value to a party of what he received in terms of what it would have cost him to obtain it from a person in the claimant's position and the addition to the wealth of that party as measured by the extent to which his property has been increased in value or his other interests advanced. In practice, the first measure is usually based on the market price of such a substitute. Under the rule stated in this Section, the court has considerable discretion in making the choice between these two measures of benefit. Under either choice, the court may properly consider the purposes of the recipient of the benefit when he made the contract, even if those purposes were later frustrated or abandoned.

b. Choice of Measure. The reasonable value to the party against whom restitution is sought (Paragraph (a)) is ordinarily less than the cost to the party seeking restitution, since his expenditures are excluded to the extent that they conferred no benefit. See Comment *a* to § 344. Nor can the party against whom restitution is sought reduce the amount for which he may himself be liable by subtracting such expenditures from the amount of the benefit that he has received.... The reasonable value to the party from whom restitution is sought (Paragraph (a)), is, however, usually greater than the addition to his wealth (Paragraph (b)). If this is so, a party seeking restitution for part performance is commonly allowed the more generous measure of reasonable value, unless that measure is unduly difficult to apply, except when he is in breach (§ 374).... In the case of services rendered in an emergency or to save life, however, restitution based on addition to wealth will greatly exceed that based on expense saved and recovery is invariably limited to the smaller amount.... In the case of services rendered to a third party as the intended beneficiary of a gift promise, restitution from the promisee based on his enrichment is generally not susceptible of measurement and recovery based on reasonable value is appropriate.

§ 373. Restitution When Other Party Is in Breach.

(1) Subject to the rule stated in Subsection (2), on a breach by nonperformance that gives rise to a claim for damages for total breach or on a repudiation, the injured party is entitled to restitution for any benefit that he has conferred on the other party by way of part performance or reliance.

(2) The injured party has no right to restitution if he has performed all of his duties under the contract and no performance by the other party remains due other than payment of a definite sum of money for that performance.

COMMENT:

. . .

b. *When Contract Price Is a Limit.* The rule stated in Subsection (1) is subject to an important exception. If, after one party has fully performed his part of the contract, the other party then refuses to pay a definite sum of money that has been fixed as the price for that performance, the injured party is barred from recovery of a greater sum as restitution under the rule stated in Subsection (2). Since he is entitled to recover the price in full together with interest, he has a remedy that protects his expectation interest by giving him the very thing that he was promised. Even if he asserts that the benefit he conferred on the other party exceeds the price fixed by the contract, justice does not require that he have the right to recover this larger sum in restitution. To give him that right would impose on the court the burden of measuring the benefit in terms of money in spite of the fact that this has already been done by the parties themselves when they made their contract.... If, however, the performance to be rendered by the party in breach is something other than the payment of a definite sum in money, this burden is less of an imposition on the court since, even if damages were sought by the injured party, the court would have to measure the value to him of the performance due from the party in breach. The clearest case occurs where the injured party has paid the full price in money for the performance that the party in breach has subsequently failed to render. To allow restitution of the sum paid in that case imposes no burden of measurement on the court and relieves it of the burden that it would have if damages were awarded of measuring the value to the injured party of the performance due from the party in breach....

d. Losing Contracts. An injured party who has performed in part will usually prefer to seek damages based on his expectation interest (§ 347) instead of a sum of money based on his restitution interest because such damages include his net profit and will give him a larger recovery. Even if he cannot prove what his net profit would have been, he will ordinarily seek damages based on his reliance interest (§ 348), since this will compensate him for all of his expenditures, regardless of whether they resulted in a benefit to the party in breach. See Comment *a* to § 344. In the case of a contract on which he would have sustained a loss instead of having made a profit, however, his restitution interest may give him a larger recovery than would damages on either basis. The right of the injured party under a losing contract to a greater amount in restitution than he could have recovered in damages has engendered much controversy. The rules stated in this Section give him that right. He is entitled to such recovery even if the contract price is stated in terms of a rate per unit of work and the recovery exceeds that rate. There are, however, two important limitations. The first limitation is one that is applicable to any claim for restitution: the party in breach is liable only to the extent that he has benefitted from the injured party's performance. If he has, for example, taken advantage of the injured party's part performance by having the rest of the work completed after his breach, the extent of his benefit is easy to measure in terms of the reasonable value of the injured party's performance.... If, however, he has abandoned the project and not completed the work, that measurement will be more difficult.... In that situation, the court may exercise its sound discretion in choosing between the two measures stated in § 371. In doing so it will take account of all the circumstances including the observance by the parties of standards of good faith and fair dealing during any negotiations leading up to the rupture of contractual relations (§ 208)....

Mooney v. York Iron Co.

Michigan Supreme Court, 1890.
82 Mich. 263, 46 N.W. 376.

■ CAHILL, J. The plaintiffs brought an action in justice court to recover an amount claimed to be due them for work and labor performed in sinking a mining shaft for the defendant. The plaintiffs recovered a judgment in justice court, and the defendant appealed, when the plaintiffs again had judgment, and the case is brought to this court on writ of error.

The case made by the plaintiffs is that they made a contract with defendant through Capt. Florada, who was at the time superintendent of the defendant company, by which they were to sink a shaft 8 by 11 feet, down to the "ledge," and timber the same up; plaintiffs to furnish everything, and to be paid $10 per foot. They claimed that they sunk the shaft to the "ledge," and had timbered it to within 8 or 10 inches of the "ledge," when they were stopped in their work by Capt. Carlin, who, as they claim, had immediate charge of the mining operations for the defendant. They claim the right to recover for the work actually done by them under the *quantum meruit* on the ground that they were prevented by the defendant, without fault on their part, from performing the contract.

The case was submitted to the jury by the circuit judge upon this theory, and the jury were instructed as follows: "It is the law that if an employer terminates a contract without any fault on the part of the employee or contractor, that then the employee or contractor may sue upon the contract to recover damages, or he may sue in *assumpsit* upon the common counts, as they are called—the *quantum meruit*— to recover what his services were worth. That does not mean what they were worth to the employer. It is the fair value; that is, the value of work and labor. Of course, the main question is first as to whether the contract was performed up to that time by the plaintiffs. If it was not, then the defendant had the right to stop the work, and discharge them, and they could not recover."

Now comes the question as to the discharge. That depends upon two witnesses, as I remember the testimony; that is, Capt. Carlin and the plaintiff Mooney. I understand all the testimony there is upon that point is given by these two men. Mooney says that Capt. Carlin "told us to stop and take the timbers up." Mr. Carlin denies it. The burden of proof is upon the plaintiffs in the case, so that if you find that the contract was performed up to that time by the plaintiffs but still that they were not discharged, but stopped the contract without being discharged, then they cannot recover in this case at all. If that were the case, then the plaintiffs could recover only upon the ground that their work had been of value to the defendant.

Counsel for defendant objects to that part of the above charge in which the court said "the plaintiffs might recover upon a *quantum meruit* what their services were worth; that this does not mean what they were worth to the defendant, but the fair value of the work and labor"; and it is claimed that the true basis of recovery in such cases is not the value of the work and labor, but of the product of the work and labor. We think the circuit judge adopted the correct rule. If the plaintiffs had abandoned the work, without being directed to do so by the defendant, and the defendant had appropriated the work to its own use, the rule contended for by defendant's counsel would have been correct. That rule was recognized, and clearly stated by the circuit judge in his charge. But where, as in this case, the plaintiffs are prevented from performing the contract, they are entitled to recover if at all what their work and labor is worth, whether it was of value to the defendant or not.

... The judgment is affirmed, with costs.

QUESTIONS

Assume that the ledge to which Mooney was to dig was fifty feet down, so that the contract price was $500 at ten dollars per foot. Further assume that it cost Mooney a uniform amount to dig each foot and that his costs were seven dollars per foot. Finally, assume that there is a market for holes in Michigan in 1890 and that the current price for holes of this sort on the Michigan Hole Exchange, where lots of holes are traded every day, is twelve dollars per foot.

a. Suppose Mooney never shows up for the job. What would York Iron's damages be? Would York Iron have a claim for restitution?

b. Suppose Mooney shows up to do the job, but York won't let him dig. What are Mooney's damages? Would Mooney have a claim for restitution?

c. Suppose instead that Mooney digs down forty feet and then is thrown off the job wrongfully. What are Mooney's damages? Would Mooney have a claim for restitution? How would it be measured?

d. Suppose that the contract was a loser for Mooney; that is, the contract price is ten dollars a foot, but his costs turn out to be higher than expected, and it is costing him eleven dollars a foot to dig through heavy clay. After Mooney digs forty feet down, York wrongfully throws him off the job. Now what are Mooney's damages? What would the restitutionary recovery be?

e. Now suppose that after digging down forty feet, Mooney walks off the job in frustration but without legal excuse. Would Mooney be able to maintain a successful action for contract damages? Might Mooney have a good claim for restitution? How would that claim be measured? Does Mooney's recovery depend on whether York completes the project or just lets Mooney's hole sit there? If Mooney recovers in these circumstances, won't that encourage people with losing contracts to walk off after partial performance and then sue for restitution?

Sparks v. Gustafson

Alaska Supreme Court, 1988.
750 P.2d 338.

■ MATTHEWS, J.

FACTS AND PROCEEDINGS

The decedent, Robert Sparks, Sr., and the plaintiff, Ernie Gustafson, were personal friends and business associates for many years. In 1980 Sparks purchased a one-half interest in the Nome Center Building. Gustafson managed the building for Sparks without charge until Sparks died on March 1, 1981. Thereafter Gustafson continued to manage the building and collect rents on behalf of Sparks, Sr.'s estate, with the knowledge and approval of the executor, Robert Sparks, Jr. Gustafson did not request any compensation for his services.

Under Gustafson's management, Nome Center operated at a loss. The Estate deposited $10,000 in a Nome Center account to cover operating expenses, but the amount was not sufficient to meet the necessary costs of insurance, mortgage payments, utility bills, and repairs. Gustafson often paid Nome Center expenses out of his own pocket. Maintenance and remodeling work were performed by Gustafson, using in part his own funds. Although he mailed monthly reports of the Nome Center's income and expenses, these reports did not include all of his own expenditures.

In February, 1982, the Estate signed a document entitled "purchase agreement" which indicated that Gustafson had purchased the building from the Estate, and would assume the deed of trust as soon as the purchase details could be worked out. However, no purchase details were ever agreed upon. The Estate sold the building to a third party in February, 1983, and Gustafson ceased to manage the property at that time.

On July 14, 1983, Gustafson and his business corporation, Nome Business Venture, Inc., filed suit against the Estate and the executor in Nome, claiming that the defendants breached an oral agreement to sell the Nome Center Building to Gustafson. Plaintiffs subsequently filed an amended complaint which further alleged that Gustafson was entitled to recover for funds and services that he expended on the building under a statutory or equitable lien theory. Defendants filed an answer and counterclaimed for an accounting of all monies collected and expended on the building.

At trial the superior court found that Gustafson had no enforceable lien. The court also concluded that it would be inequitable to allow the Estate to retain the benefits that Gustafson had conferred upon Nome Center at his own expense. The court ordered the Estate to pay Gustafson $65,706.07 in compensation for the services and improvements that he conferred upon the Estate during his two years of managing the Nome Center Building. This appeal followed.

II. DISCUSSION ON THE MERITS:
UNJUST ENRICHMENT

Rule

Unjust enrichment exists where the defendant has received a benefit from the plaintiff and it would be inequitable for defendant to retain the benefit without compensating plaintiff for its value. Sparks claims that plaintiffs failed to prove either element of unjust enrichment: first, that the Estate received any benefit from plaintiffs, and second, that if a benefit was received then its retention would be unjust.

0 argument

A person confers a benefit upon another if he gives the other some interest in money, land or possessions; performs services beneficial to or at the request of the other; satisfies a debt of the other; or in any way adds to the other's advantage. In this case Gustafson made substantial repairs and improvements to the Nome Center, provided management services that kept Nome Center operating, and paid debts incurred by Nome Center, all arguably on the Estate's behalf. There is no question that Gustafson conferred a benefit upon the Estate.

test

facts

Even where a person has conferred a benefit upon another, however, he is entitled to compensation only if it would be just and equitable to require compensation under the circumstances. Courts will allow the defendant to retain a benefit without compensating plaintiff in several situations, one of which is relevant to the case at hand: where the benefit was given gratuitously without expectation of payment. Appellants argue that this situation is present in the case before us.

2nd rule

This court has not yet addressed the circumstances which give rise to a finding of gratuitous intent. A good discussion of this issue in the context of a decedent's estate can be found in *Kershaw v. Tracy Collins Bank & Trust Co.* (Utah 1977). In that case the decedent's best friend provided a variety of services to the decedent's widow, including chauffeuring, buying groceries, running errands, and performing minor repair work. The court looked at the extent of the services provided to the widow, the closeness of the relationship between the parties, and the fact that the plaintiff never sought compensation until after the widow died. The court found that the widow had not been unjustly enriched, since plaintiff's services were not necessary for the widow's existence and were of the sort which could reasonably be expected from a long time friend.

2nd test

In this case there was a similarly close relationship between the plaintiff and the decedent. It appears that Gustafson managed the Nome Center Building for the decedent without requesting compensation, in recognition of many long years of friendship and business association together. At trial, the executor testified that he thought Gustafson would continue to manage the building for two years after Sparks' death out of the goodness of his heart, without expectation of payment. Gustafson never requested compensation for his services during his tenure as the Nome Center manager for the Estate. The closeness of the parties' relationship and

facts

Gustafson's failure to request compensation in a timely manner suggest that Gustafson offered his services to the Estate gratuitously.

issue

However, the services that Gustafson performed for the Estate were not the sort which one would ordinarily expect to receive from a friend as a mere gratuity. Gustafson spent approximately five hours a day for two years collecting rents for Nome Center, soliciting new tenants, making repairs and improvements, paying utility, insurance and mortgage bills out of his own pocket when rental income fell short of expenses, and performing other general maintenance and management services for the Estate. These are the types of extensive business services for which one would ordinarily expect to be paid. We therefore agree with the trial court that Gustafson's services were not offered gratuitously.

Determining facts

holding

Sparks argues that a distinction should be made between remodeling expenses and those which were for maintenance and general management. He argues that the remodeling expenditures were made solely to benefit Gustafson. This argument, however, was not raised below. Indeed, Sparks argued that if Gustafson had established any claim for relief his damages should be limited to $62,706.07. "If the court finds any of Plaintiff's theories supported by evidence, Defendant's damage theory [that damages are limited to $62,506.07] is the only correct basis for an award of damages." The court followed this suggestion, adding only one $3,200 item which is not presently in dispute. Since Sparks' damage theory was accepted by the trial court (with the exception of $3,200), Sparks has waived his right to contend that a further breakdown of damages should have been made. While "plain error" is an exception to the rule of waiver, it does not exist here. Sparks' argument that the remodeling expenses did not benefit the Estate is facially incorrect since at least some of the rental income which the Estate received is directly related to the remodeling expenditures.

The judgment of the superior court is AFFIRMED.

QUESTIONS

1. Would the court come to the same conclusion if there were no evidence of a Purchase Agreement between Gustafson and the Sparks Estate?

2. Was there a contract to provide services in this case? What if Gustafson had stopped managing the building? Could the Sparks Estate have obtained damages? What if Gustafson had failed to properly maintain the roof and it collapsed under the weight of the first snowfall in 1982?

3. In *Chodos v. West Publishing Co.*, 292 F.3d 992 (9th Cir. 2002) (*Chodos I*), the court faced a claim from Rafael Chodos, a well-regarded California lawyer, who,

pursuant to a standard Author Agreement similar to that in *Freund,* p. 124, had labored for 3600 hours over three years on a 1247 page legal treatise that the publisher subsequently determined it would not publish because of weak projected sales and other commercial criteria. The publisher admitted that the quality and literary merit of the treatise were otherwise satisfactory. The court found that the publisher's termination rights under the Author Agreement were limited to good faith determinations that the work was unworthy of publication for quality or literary reasons, but not commercial considerations. Chodos's claim for lost future royalties, the only compensation provided for in the Author Agreement, however, was disallowed as speculative. The court nevertheless permitted Chodos to pursue a claim "off the contract" in restitution for the *quantum meruit* of his services as an author. The Ninth Circuit ultimately affirmed a jury award of $300,000 to Chodos on this theory, but rejected Chodos's claim to be compensated at his standard hourly rate as an attorney for the 3600 hours of work on the manuscript. *Chodos v. West Publishing Co.*, 92 Fed. Appx. 471 (9th Cir. 2004) (*Chodos II*). Would Freund similarly have been entitled to recover on a restitution theory?

Britton v. Turner

New Hampshire Supreme Court of Judicature, 1834.
6 N.H. 481.

Assumpsit, for work and labor, performed by the plaintiff, in the service of the defendant, from March 9, 1831, to December 27, 1831.

The declaration contained the common counts, and among them a count in quantum meruit, for the labor, averring it to be worth $100.

At the trial in the C.C. Pleas, the plaintiff proved the performance of the labor as set forth in the declaration.

The defense was that it was performed under a special contract; that the plaintiff agreed to work one year, from some time in March, 1831, to March, 1832, and that the defendant was to pay him for said year's labor the sum of $120; and the defendant offered evidence tending to show that such was the contract under which the work was done. Evidence was also offered to show that the plaintiff left the defendant's service without his consent, and it was contended by the defendant that the plaintiff had no good cause for not continuing in his employment. There was no evidence offered of any damage arising from the plaintiff's departure, farther than was to be inferred from his nonfulfillment of the entire contract.

The court instructed the jury that, if they were satisfied from the evidence that the labor was performed under a contract to labor a year, for the sum of $120, and if they were satisfied that the plaintiff labored only the time specified in the declaration, and then left the defendant's service, against his consent, and without any good cause, yet the plaintiff was entitled to recover, under his quantum meruit count, as much as the labor he performed was reasonably worth, and under this direction the jury gave a verdict for the plaintiff for the sum of $95.

The defendant excepted to the instructions thus given to the jury.

■ PARKER, J., delivered the opinion of the court.

It may be assumed that the labor performed by the plaintiff, and for which he seeks to recover a compensation in this action, was commenced under a special contract to labor for the defendant the term of one year, for the sum of $120, and that the plaintiff has labored but a portion of that time, and has voluntarily failed to complete the entire contract.

It is clear then, that he is not entitled to recover upon the contract itself, because the service, which was to entitle him to the sum agreed upon, has never been performed.

But the question arises: Can the plaintiff, under these circumstances, recover a reasonable sum for the service he has actually performed, under the count in quantum meruit? Upon this, and questions of a similar nature, the decisions to be found in the books are not easily reconciled. It has been held, upon contracts of this kind for labor to be performed at a specified price, that the party who voluntarily fails to fulfil the contract by performing the whole labor contracted for, is not entitled to recover anything for the labor actually performed, however much he may have done toward the performance; and this has been considered the settled rule of law upon this subject.

That such rule in its operation may be very unequal, not to say unjust, is apparent. A party who contracts to perform certain specified labor, and who breaks his contract in the first instance, without any attempt to perform it, can only be made liable to pay the damages which the other party has sustained by reason of such nonperformance, which in many instances may be trifling; whereas a party who in good faith has entered upon the performance of his contract, and nearly completed it, and then abandoned the further performance, —although the other party has had the full benefit of all that has been done, and has perhaps sustained no actual damage, —is in fact subjected to a loss of all which has been performed, in the nature of damages for the nonfulfilment of the remainder, upon the technical rule, that the contract must be fully performed in order to [support] a recovery of any part of the compensation.

By the operation of this rule, then, the party who attempts performance may be placed in a much worse situation than he who wholly disregards his contract, and the other party may receive much more, by the breach of the contract, than the injury which he has sustained by such breach, and more than he could be entitled to were he seeking to recover damages by an action.

The case before us presents an illustration. Had the plaintiff in this case never entered upon the performance of his contract, the damage could not probably have been greater than some small expense and trouble incurred in procuring another to do the labor which he had contracted to perform. But having entered upon the performance, and labored nine and a half months, the value of which labor to the defendant as found by the jury is $95, if the defendant can succeed in this defence, he in fact receives nearly five sixths of the value of a whole year's labor, by reason of the breach of contract by the plaintiff, a sum not only utterly disproportionate to any probable, not to say possible damage which could have resulted from the neglect of the plaintiff to continue the remaining two and a half months, but altogether beyond any damage which could have been recovered by the defendant, had the plaintiff done nothing towards the fulfilment of his contract.

... It is said that where a party contracts to perform certain work, and to furnish materials, as, for instance, to build a house, and the work is done, but with some variations from the mode prescribed by the contract, yet if the other party has the benefit of the labor and materials he should be bound to pay so much as they are reasonably worth....

Those cases are not to be distinguished, in principle, from the present, unless it be in the circumstance that where the party has contracted to furnish materials, and do certain labor, as to build a house in a specified manner, if it is not done according to the contract, the party for whom it is built may refuse to receive it,—elect to take no benefit from what has been performed; and therefore if he does receive, he shall be bound to pay the value—whereas in a contract for labor, merely, from day to day, the party is continually receiving the benefit of the contract under an expectation that it will be fulfilled, and cannot upon the breach of it have an election to refuse to receive what has been done, and thus discharge himself from payment. But we think this difference in the nature of the contracts does not justify the application of a different rule in relation to them.

The party who contracts for labor merely, for a certain period, does so with full knowledge that he must, from the nature of the case, be accepting part performance from day to day, if the other party commences the performance, and with knowledge also that the other may eventually fail of completing the entire term.

If under such circumstances he actually receives a benefit from the labor performed, over and above the damage occasioned by the failure to complete, there is as much reason why he should pay the reasonable worth of what has thus been done for his benefit, as there is when he enters and occupies the house which has been built for him, but not according to the stipulations of the contract, and which he perhaps enters, not because he is satisfied with what has been done, but because circumstances compel him to accept it such as it is, that he should pay for the value of the house.

... If then the party stipulates in the outset to receive part performance from time to time, with a knowledge that the whole may not be completed, we see no reason why he should not equally be holden to pay for the amount of value received, as where he afterwards takes the benefit of what has been done, with a knowledge that the whole which was contracted for has not been performed. In neither case has the contract been performed. In neither can an action be sustained on the original contract. In both the party has assented to receive what is done. The only difference is, that in the one case the assent is prior, with a knowledge that all may not be performed, in the other it is subsequent, with a knowledge that the whole has not been accomplished.

We have no hesitation in holding that the same rule should be applied to both classes of cases, especially as the operation of the rule will be to make the party who has failed to fulfill his contract liable to such amount of damages as the other party has sustained, instead of subjecting him to an entire loss for a partial failure, and thus making the amount received in many cases wholly disproportionate to the injury. It is as "hard upon the plaintiff to preclude him from recovering at all, because he has failed as to part of his entire undertaking," where his contract is to labor for a certain period, as it can be in any other description of contract, provided the defendant has received a benefit and value from the labor actually performed.

We hold, then, that where a party undertakes to pay upon a special contract for the performance of labor, or the furnishing of materials, he is not to be charged upon such special agreement until the money is earned according to the terms of it, and where the parties have made an express contract the law will not imply and raise a contract different from that which the parties have entered into, except upon some further transaction between the parties.

In case of a failure to perform such special contract, by the default of the party contracting to do the service, if the money is not due by the terms of the special agreement he is not entitled to recover for his labor, or for the materials furnished, unless the other party receives what has been done, or furnished, and upon the whole case derives a benefit from it.

But if, where a contract is made of such a character, a party actually receives labor, or materials, and thereby derives a benefit and advantage, over and above the damage which has resulted from the breach of the contract by the other party, the labor actually done, and the value received, furnish a new consideration, and the law thereupon raises a promise to pay to the extent of the reasonable worth of such excess. This may be considered as making a new case, one not within the original agreement, and the party is entitled to "recover on his new case, for the work done, not as agreed, but yet accepted by the defendant." 1 Dane's Abr. 224.

If on such failure to perform the whole, the nature of the contract be such that the employer can reject what has been done, and refuse to receive any benefit from the part performance, he is entitled so to do, and in such case is not liable to be charged, unless he has before assented to and accepted of what has been done, however much the other party may have done towards the performance. He has in such case received nothing, and having contracted to receive nothing but the entire matter contracted for, he is not bound to pay, because his express promise was only to pay on receiving the whole, and having actually received nothing the law cannot and ought not to raise an implied promise to pay. But where the party receives value—takes and uses the materials, or has advantage from the labor, he is liable to pay the reasonable worth of what he has received. And the rule is the same whether it was received and accepted by the assent of the party prior to the breach, under a contract by which, from its nature, he was to receive labor from time to time until the completion of the whole contract; or whether it was received and accepted by an assent subsequent to the performance of all which was in fact done. If he received it under such circumstances as precluded him from rejecting it afterward, that does not alter the case—it has still been received by his assent.

In fact we think the technical reasoning, that the performance of the whole labor is a condition precedent, and the right to recover anything dependent upon it; that the contract being entire there can be no apportionment; and that there being an express contract no other can be implied, even upon the subsequent performance of service,—is not properly applicable to this species of contract, where a beneficial service has been actually performed; for we have abundant reason to believe, that the general understanding of the community is that the hired laborer shall be entitled to compensation for the service actually performed, though he does not continue the entire term contracted for, and such contracts must be presumed to be made with reference to that understanding, unless an express stipulation shows the contrary.

Where a beneficial service has been performed and received, therefore, under contracts of this kind, the mutual agreements cannot be considered as going to the whole of the consideration, so as to make them mutual conditions the one precedent to the other, without a specific proviso to that effect.

It is easy, if parties so choose, to provide by an express agreement that nothing shall be earned, if the laborer leaves his employer without having performed the whole service contemplated, and then there can be no pretence for a recovery if he voluntarily deserts the service before the expiration of the time.

The amount, however, for which the employer ought to be charged, where the laborer abandons his contract, is only the reasonable worth or the amount of advantage he receives upon the whole transaction; and, in estimating the value of the labor, the contract price for the service cannot be exceeded.

If a person makes a contract fairly he is entitled to have it fully performed; and if this is not done he is entitled to damages. He may maintain a suit to recover the amount of damages sustained by the nonperformance.

Rule

The benefit and advantage which the party takes by the labor, therefore, is the amount of value which he receives, if any, after deducting the amount of damage; and if he elects to put this in defense he is entitled so to do, and the implied promise which the law will raise, in such case, is to pay such amount of the stipulated price for the whole labor, as remains after deducting what it would cost to procure a completion of the residue of the service, and also any damage which has been sustained by reason of the nonfulfillment of the contract. If in such case it be found that the damages are equal to or greater than the amount of the labor performed, so that the employer, having a right to the full performance of the contract, has not upon the whole case received a beneficial service, the plaintiff cannot recover.

policy

This rule, by binding the employer to pay the value of the service he actually receives, and the laborer to answer to damages where he does not complete the entire contract, will leave no temptation to the former to drive the laborer from his service, near the close of his term, by ill treatment, in order to escape from payment, nor to the latter to desert his service before the stipulated time, without a sufficient reason; and it will in most instances settle the whole controversy in one action, and prevent a multiplicity of suits and cross-actions.

... Judgment on the verdict.

QUESTIONS AND NOTES

1. In early agricultural economies, labor contracts were commonly seasonal or annual. Both the worker and the farmer only see cash at harvest time when the crop is sold. The worker must stay on the job through harvest to earn cash compensation. The contract is entire in the sense that it is a single contract for service for the whole agricultural season from planting through harvest, not a series of divisible claims for each hour, week, or month worked. Modern labor codes create a statutory claim for the worker to compensation for time worked before quitting. This case imaginatively expanded restitutionary concepts to work social justice a century before those labor codes were enacted and before the industrial revolution caused labor markets generally to shift away from annual or seasonal contracts to an employment-at-will structure. For a fascinating historical look at how these legal, social and economic

changes were presaged by *Britton,* see Robert W. Gordon, Britton v. Turner*: A Signpost on the Crooked Road to "Freedom" in the Employment Contract,* 26 HAWAII L. REV. 423 (2004) *expanded and reprinted in* CONTRACT STORIES (Baird, ed. Foundation Press 2007).

2. We aren't told in this case what kind of labor Britton performed. The jury returned a verdict that awarded him very close to the pro rata portion of the annual contract rate for the nine months worked. But one imagines that if we are talking about agricultural labor in New England that almost all the employee's effort would be expended between April and October and in particular in August and September during the Fall harvest. Should that affect the proper restitutionary recovery? Justice Parker limits restitutionary recovery to the amount that the injured employer benefitted over and beyond the damages suffered by the employee's breach in quitting in the middle of the job. How would the worker show that value other than by hours of labor expended in his employer's service? Is it enough for the worker to show that he came to work every day, or would he have to show that his work was productive?

———

RESTATEMENT, SECOND, CONTRACTS:

§ 374. *Restitution in Favor of Party in Breach.*

(1) Subject to the rule stated in Subsection (2), if a party justifiably refuses to perform on the ground that his remaining duties of performance have been discharged by the other party's breach, the party in breach is entitled to restitution for any benefit that he has conferred by way of part performance or reliance in excess of the loss that he has caused by his own breach.

(2) To the extent that, under the manifested assent of the parties, a party's performance is to be retained in the case of breach, that party is not entitled to restitution if the value of the performance as liquidated damages is reasonable in the light of the anticipated or actual loss caused by the breach and the difficulties of proof of loss.

COMMENT:

b. Measurement of Benefit. If the party in breach seeks restitution of money that he has paid, no problem arises in measuring the benefit to the other party.... If, however, he seeks to recover a sum of money that represents the benefit of services rendered to the other party, measurement of the benefit is more difficult. Since the party seeking restitution is responsible for posing the problem of measurement of benefit, doubts will be resolved against him and his recovery will not exceed the less generous of the two measures stated in § 371, that of the other party's increase in wealth.... If no value can be put on this, he cannot recover.... Although the contract price is evidence of the benefit, it is not conclusive. However, in no case will the party in breach be allowed to recover more than a ratable portion of the total contract price where such a portion can be determined.

A party who intentionally furnishes services or builds a building that is materially different from what he promised is properly regarded as having acted officiously and not in part performance of his promise and will be denied recovery on that ground even if his performance was of some benefit to the other party. This is not the case, however, if the other party has accepted or agreed to accept the substitute performance....

United States for Use of Palmer Constr. v. Cal State Electric

United States Court of Appeals, Ninth Circuit, 1991.
940 F.2d 1260.

■ FERNANDEZ, J. This case presents a clash of principles at the interface between the law of expressed contracts and the law of quasi contracts. Here, Cal State Electric, Inc. (CSE) entered into a contract with Palmer Construction, Inc. (Palmer). Palmer breached its contract, and after a trial the district court found that CSE should pay damages and attorneys fees to Palmer. CSE appealed the final judgment arising out of that somewhat jarring result. We agree that the judgment is in error and reverse.

BACKGROUND FACTS

CSE entered into a prime contract with the U.S. Army Corps of Engineers to construct the STS Power Plant at Vandenburg Air Force Base in California. CSE then entered into a contract with Palmer in which a portion of the work was subcontracted to the latter entity. The contract price for Palmer's work was to be $220,162. Due to agreed extra work, an additional $14,975 was added to the contract price for a total of $235,137.

Palmer commenced work but, after completing a portion of the job, Palmer breached. There is no doubt about that. By the time of the breach Palmer had supplied some goods and services which the district court found to have a value of $204,845.26. Against the sum, CSE had already paid Palmer a total of $114,758.98, and after Palmer's breach CSE was required to expend the further sum of $126,673.56 in order to complete the work that Palmer had contracted to do.

CSE had, thus, paid out a total of $241,432.54 in order to obtain a job that it had contracted to get from Palmer at a price of $235,137. Therefore, CSE had suffered damages in the amount of $6,295.54. The district court so found.

However, rather than leaving matters where they stood, the district court went on to reflect on the fact that since the value of Palmer's work was $204,845.26 and it had only received $114,758.98, it was entitled to reimbursement for the rest of those services, less the "damage" done to CSE. The result of that calculation, after also giving CSE prejudgment interest of $1,468.88, was a net sum due to Palmer of $82,321.86 plus attorneys fees.

Not surprisingly, CSE, the innocent party, expressed its chagrin at a result that required it to pay additional sums to Palmer plus attorneys fees. It argues that this was caused by a misapplication of legal principles. We agree.

DISCUSSION

A. The Measure and Allocation of Damages.

The question which faces us on this appeal is one of some jurisprudential complexity. It has engaged the attention of commentators for many years. As a matter of pure contract law it is generally true that if two individuals enter into a contract and one breaches, the breaching party cannot obtain a recovery from the innocent party. Rather, if the innocent party has suffered, a recovery against the party in breach is generally accorded. In building contracts "[t]he measure of damages * * * is the reasonable cost * * * to finish the work in accordance with the contract."

On the other hand, if the breaching party has conferred a benefit upon the innocent party rather than a detriment, it would unjustly enrich the innocent party and unduly punish the breaching party if the latter received nothing for its services. Quasi contract principles will supply the remedy for that.

These policies appear to conflict to some extent, so anyone who considers them must reconcile their opposing tendencies. When faced with these propositions, the commentators have resolved them by stating that the breaching party is entitled to the reasonable value of its services less any damages caused by the breach. They have added that the breaching party should not, in any event, be able to recover more than the contract price, or perhaps even a ratable part of that contract price. Williston puts it as follows: The true measure of quasi contractual recovery, where the performance is incomplete but readily remediable, is the unpaid contract price less the cost of completion and other additional harm to the defendant except that it must never exceed the benefit actually received by him. This is the net benefit by which the defendant is enriched.

While this phraseology is somewhat more complex, it can readily be seen that the effect is to preclude a recovery by the breaching party which will cause the innocent party to pay more than the contract price itself.[2] The Restatement is in accord with this approach, for while it, too, allows for recovery for part performance, it indicates that the amount of that recovery is not only limited to the extent that the innocent party's gain exceeded its loss, but is also limited to no more than a ratable portion of the total contract price.

It is interesting to observe that treatise illustrations of the application of these principles demonstrate that the innocent party never winds up paying a total that is more than the contract price itself. That is sensible. Were it otherwise, there would be a powerful inducement to breach rather than complete any contract which did *policy* not turn out to be profitable. By doing so, the ultimate loss of the bargain would be shifted from the breaching party to the innocent party, which is precisely what would occur in the case at hand if the district court's judgment stands.

Palmer has referred us to cases from our and other circuits but not one of them stands for the proposition that an innocent party must pay more than the contract price for the goods or services it sought.

Moreover, if the breaching party were permitted to recover an amount that leaves the innocent party paying more than the contract price for the goods and services contracted for, that would cause an increase in the loss to the innocent party on account of the breach and would offset the additional amount demanded by the breaching party. However, no such paraphrastic principles are needed if the cost to the innocent party for the goods and services contracted for is limited to the contract price itself. The breaching party would then be required to pay damages for excess costs imposed upon the innocent party.

It is, therefore, apparent that the district court erred when it offset the damages *holding* to CSE against the raw value of the work done by Palmer, with the result that CSE was ordered to absorb the loss that Palmer incurred by entering into a contract which turned out to be unprofitable to it. Instead, when it became apparent that Palmer's breach actually cost CSE $6,295.54 more than the contract price, CSE should have been awarded its damages and Palmer should have recovered nothing.[3]

---

2. In the case at hand, for example, the mathematics would come out as follows: (a) contract price—$235,137.00; (b) unpaid portion—$120,378.02; (c) cost of completion—$126,673.56; (b)-(c) = $6,295.54, which is exactly the damage to CSE and which leaves no quasi contractual recovery for Palmer.

3. Of course, if CSE had not previously paid out $114,758.98 to Palmer, there could have been some amount due to Palmer. That is the situation that has usually been illustrated by the commentators. But payment had been made. Far from being entitled to recover more, Palmer should have been ordered to disgorge part of what it already had received.

B. Attorneys Fees.

The contract between CSE and Palmer provided for an award of attorneys fees to the prevailing party. Given that, we apply the law of California to the contract. That law approves of the enforcement of attorneys fee provisions. Cal.Civ.Code § 1717. The district court recognized that but, because it considered Palmer to be the prevailing party, fees were awarded to Palmer. In light of our decision on the merits, that was an error. On the contrary, fees should have been awarded to CSE. On remand, the amount of those fees must be determined.

CONCLUSION

It is possible to syncretize the principles which require people to carry out their contracts and those which prevent people from unjustly retaining benefits conferred upon them. In other words it is possible to reach a just result in cases which involve both principles. We hold that where, as here, the innocent party has paid more than the contract price for the goods and services ordered from the breaching party, the innocent party may recover the overage from the breaching party. The breaching party may not obtain a quasi contractual recovery from the innocent party. In short, the innocent party is not unjustly enriched when it receives what it bargained for and pays no more than the contract price.

CSE is therefore entitled to recover the sum of $6,295.24 plus prejudgment interest of $1,478.88 from Palmer. CSE is also entitled to recover attorneys fees and costs for its litigation expenses in the district court, as well as its costs on appeal.

■ REINHARDT, J., concurring:

I concur in Judge Fernandez's fine opinion harmonizing various principles of law. However, I do not think the problem is nearly as complicated as it appears. All that is required is a little common sense.

In the rush of dealing with an overwhelming daily calendar, the district judge made a simple error, as we all do from time to time. She could have applied the two formulas that she utilized and reached the right result. The error occurred because she applied them in the wrong order. These things happen.

Conceptually, it is easy to see the error that results when the damages formula is applied first and the quantum meruit formula second. Under that approach, the damages included in the damage formula are not the total damages CSE will incur — they fail to include the quantum meruit payment, which has not yet been calculated, but which it will be required to pay. Thus, if both formulas are to be utilized, CSE's damages cannot properly be determined until after the quantum meruit calculation is performed. Otherwise, we may end up, as we did here, with the non-breaching party having to pay more than the contract price.

Alt   Rule

On the other hand, when the quantum meruit theory is applied first, we determine at the outset that Palmer would be entitled to an additional payment of $90,086.28 for the work actually performed. If we then required that the additional amount be paid, Palmer's total payment would be $204,845.26. Instead, however, we proceed to step 2—the determination of CSE's actual damages. We then find that if CSE is required to pay Palmer the unpaid amount of $90,086.28, and thus the total amount of $204,845.26, the total cost to CSE for the job would be $331,521.82—since CSE was also required to pay a third party the sum of $126,673.56 to finish the job. Because the contract price was only $235,137.00, the damages to CSE would be $96,384.82. However, we next subtract from CSE's damages the $90,086.28 that it theoretically owes Palmer in quantum meruit (but need not pay because it is less than Palmer owes). As a result, we find that CSE's actual damages are reduced to the correct amount—$6,295.54. Voilà!

All this mathematical exercise proves is that if the district judge had applied the two theories in the proper order, she would have come to the correct result. Thus express contract law and quantum meruit doctrines can be harmonized and live together happily ever after.

Judge Fernandez's learned approach certainly provides a more intellectual explanation of clashing legal principles. It also provides a simpler and preferable method of calculating damages. The only purpose of this concurrence is to show that from a practical and mathematical standpoint the two legal principles discussed in Judge Fernandez's opinion are not in conflict.

The elementary rules that emerge from both of our analyses are relatively simple. When the party performing the work breaches the contract, it may nevertheless recover all or a portion of the value of the services it has actually rendered, but only under certain circumstances. The breaching party may not recover any amount which, when added to the amount previously paid it, and the amount paid or owing to any party whose services are used to complete the job, would cause the contract price to be exceeded. As Judge Fernandez's opinion clearly states, the contract price represents a ceiling on the amount the non-breaching party may be required to pay—in toto. Similarly, regardless of the value of the work performed by the breaching party, if the amount the non-breaching party must pay to a third party to finish the job, when added to the amount it has already paid to the breaching party, exceeds the contract price, the non-breaching party may recover the excess amount from the breaching party as damages. Thus, depending on the amount already paid the breaching party, the value of the labors it has performed, and the amount required to finish the job, the same breach may result in a recovery by either the breaching or non-breaching party. Who recovers is not a function of who breaches—what matters is who has already paid how much to whom for what.

Finally, I want to emphasize that it is not necessary to utilize the two-step process illustrated at the beginning of this separate opinion. One step will do. However, all the figures must be calculated first. It will then be possible to apply the applicable legal principles to that set of figures and determine who owes how much to whom.

QUESTIONS AND NOTES

1. Note the apparent confusion judges experience in computing contract damages and *quantum meruit*. Absurdly, the trial judge became sufficiently confused to reach the conclusion that the non-breaching party should be required to pay $323,754.40 ($241,432.54 in payments to contractors plus $82,321.86 "quantum meruit") to get the job done (even though the total contract price was $235,137) and be required to pay the defaulting subcontractor's attorney's fees to boot! Part of the problem here is that many of those who go to law school and go on to become judges are arithmetically challenged. Part of the problem is that the judges are trying to juggle damages and restitutionary relief in one calculation.

2. In this case the plaintiff, Palmer, was clearly in breach, and the court found that its recovery should be limited to "the contract price, or perhaps a ratable part of that contract price." Suppose that Palmer was not the breaching party and that, despite the problems with this job, it stuck to its promise and carried the project almost to completion at a cost of over $350,000 before CSE threw it off the job. In that circumstance should the contract price be a ceiling on Palmer's claim to recover the reasonable value of its performance? *See* Note, pp. 190-195.

3. Note that the court awarded CSE attorney's fees. The usual "American rule" is that each party must bear its own attorney's fees. But the American rule has been changed by statute in some situations, notably in certain civil rights cases under the Equal Access to Justice Act. Moreover, many contracts provide that the prevailing party is entitled to collect its attorney's fees from the breaching party in any action on the contract. Attorney's fees may be very substantial indeed and must have greatly exceeded the $6,295.54 in damages ultimately awarded in *Palmer Construction*. When a party in breach successfully persuades a court that it is entitled to compensation despite its breach, should it be awarded attorney's fees as the prevailing party under a contractual attorney's fees provision in a contract which it has itself breached? In this case the ultimate outcome was determined by recognizing substantial claims each side had against the other. In such a case how does a court determine who the prevailing party is?

4. Plaintiffs in restitution that are not breaching parties are entitled to more generous damage rules than the plaintiff in *Palmer Construction*. When, in relatively rare cases, restitution is measured by the defendant's benefit rather than the plaintiff's

loss, plaintiffs may recover an element of profit. More commonly, however, plaintiff's restitutionary recovery is measured by the value that the plaintiff gave. DAN B. DOBBS, REMEDIES: DAMAGES, EQUITY, RESTITUTION § 12.1 (2d ed. 1993). The traditional rule disallows recovery of profits in *quantum meruit* measured in this way, although all direct and indirect costs, including "overhead," may properly form part of the recovery. The line between profits and costs can often be very fuzzy. In practice, "profits" may sometimes be awarded in recognition of the fact that market values may include an element of profit for the seller or as a surrogate for indirect costs that may be difficult to quantify otherwise. *Aniero Concrete Co. v. Aetna Cas. and Sur. Co.*, 301 F. Supp. 2d 302 (S.D.N.Y. 2004) ("Under a *quantum meruit* claim, a building contractor may recover its actual job costs for work, labor and services performed and material furnished, plus an allowance for overhead and profit."). *See also U.S. ex rel. Maris Equip. Co. v. Morganti*, 163 F. Supp. 2d 174 (E.D.N.Y. 2001) (noting that overhead and profit have frequently been awarded on a *quantum meruit* basis in construction contract cases); *but see Petropoulos v. Lubienski*, 152 A.2d 801 (Md. 1959) (no positive profit awarded in *quantum meruit*). The Fourth Circuit while noting "profits *per se* have no place in a *quantum meruit* recovery," went on to find that profits "may be considered, however, to the extent that they may have a bearing upon assessing the reasonable value of the aggrieved party's performance." *W.F. Magann Corp. v. Diamond Mfg. Co.*, 775 F.2d 1202, 1208 (4th Cir. 1985).

Watson v. Wood Dimension
California Court of Appeal, 1989.
209 Cal.App.3d 1359, 257 Cal.Rptr. 816.

■ SONENSHINE, J. Wood Dimension, Inc. (WDI), appeals an adverse judgment awarding L. Dale Watson $155,955.85 in damages plus interest, costs and attorney fees....

I

WDI manufactures stereo speakers for resale by sound system companies. A major customer for several years, Fisher Corporation was an enormous asset, its orders accounting for 30 to 50 percent of WDI's business. Fisher ceased purchasing from WDI in early 1982. The loss was a serious financial detriment for WDI; regaining Fisher as a customer, which it was unable to do by itself, was of vital importance.

Gene Hedlund, president of WDI, and Dale Watson had known each other for many years. In early 1983, Hedlund's desire to reacquire Fisher's business surfaced in conversation with Watson. Watson was socially acquainted with Ira Horon, Fisher's general manager and vice president.

The possibility arose of utilizing Watson's relationship with Horon to reacquire Fisher's business. WDI might indeed double its production if Fisher were to require the same volume of components as it had earlier.

Realizing the potential if Watson were successful, WDI originally offered him five percent of all Fisher orders. However, as conceded by the parties, they eventually orally agreed upon a three percent commission.

WDI and Watson were unable to agree on specific terms for a written version of their agreement, in particular the termination provision. When Hedlund announced, "I wouldn't cheat you out of your commission—Let's shake hands," they did just that and agreed a writing was unnecessary.

Horon came to Palm Springs approximately once a month for relaxation. Watson frequently met him at the airport and joined him for golf and dinner. Pursuant to his agreement with Hedlund, Watson was to maintain these activities, generally wining and dining Horon with a view to introducing him to Hedlund at the propitious moment. All went well and, in April, the [alliance] was cemented; Fisher again became a customer of WDI. Watson continued to entertain Horon and to collect his three percent commission on Fisher orders through 1983.

In early 1984, WDI unilaterally attempted to reduce Watson's commission to two percent and, on May 15, Watson was summarily terminated. Watson's friendship with Horon endured until the latter's death in January 1985; his commissions did not. Fisher continued to place orders with WDI, accounting for almost $10,000,000 in business to WDI through July 1985.

Watson filed a complaint for damages based on oral contract, open book account, quantum meruit, and fraud. At trial, the court indicated it would probably be necessary to appoint a referee to assess the voluminous accounting records should a determination of commissions due after date of termination become necessary. Evidence was presented on liability first, although the court later announced it would not rule on the issue until after receipt of the referee's report. Extensive argument ensued concerning the "cutoff" date applicable for payment of commissions to Watson. The court ordered additional briefing and set another hearing date.

Thereafter, the court appointed Judicial Arbitration Service to examine the relevant documents and to make specified determinations. Watson had compiled, from the WDI invoices, a listing of all Fisher invoices from April 1983 through July 1985, including total dollar amounts, commissions due to Watson, and amounts received against those totals. Hedlund objected to those documents being included in the referee's "packet." The court stated, "Then I'll revise my ruling. Just provide the invoices and the other records which you have produced to the referee."

The referee held a hearing, examined the records and produced his report, which embraced the summaries presented by Watson. He found $241,314.34 due and owing to Watson through July 15, 1985. This amount was the cumulative total of the monthly commissions payable to Watson beginning on the date of his termination.

Following receipt of the referee's report, the court entertained argument, accepted a further brief from WDI, and took the matter under submission. In its statement of decision, the court awarded Watson $155,955.84, the amount appearing on the referee's report as cumulative commissions due as of December 15, 1984. The court found the parties agreed to an employment relationship requiring Watson to "regain the previously lost Fisher account for [WDI] in exchange for 3 percent of the sales." The attempt to reduce their arrangement to writing, the failure to agree on termination provisions, and the eventual "handshake" treatment of the dilemma were outlined. The court then stated: "Absent an agreement on termination and attendant compensation, the Court has concluded that under the circumstances of this case, plaintiff is entitled to the reasonable value of the services he performed." The statement noted there was no discussion of reduction of the percent to be paid, the length of time the commission would be paid, or when it would be paid, i.e., "on orders placed, orders shipped or orders paid. The only testimony bearing on the subject was to the effect that orders were anticipated by defendants up to four months prior to receipt."

In determining the reasonable value of Watson's services, the court weighed the factors favoring each party. It then concluded awarding commissions through December 15, 1984, provided Watson "with reasonable compensation for placing the account with Wood Dimension and yet does not compensate him beyond a point when he could no longer influence placement of the account." WDI's motion for new trial was denied.

. . .

III

There is no dispute the parties had a valid oral agreement for a three percent commission to Watson on all Fisher orders. However, there was no meeting of the minds regarding compensation at the time of a cessation of Watson's relationship with WDI; because they could not agree on a termination plan, they essentially ignored the possibility. When the possibility became a reality, there was no formula for terminating the right to commissions as well as the employment.

WDI objects to any award of commissions based on sales made to Fisher after Watson's termination. Watson argues because he was the procuring cause of the Fisher involvement with WDI, he is essentially entitled to commissions for the life of that relationship. Recognizing the inequity inherent in either extreme, the court balanced the factors favoring each party and awarded post-termination commissions for a reasonable period of time based on quantum meruit.

Although California sanctions the payment of commissions, after termination and pursuant to an oral agreement where the salesperson is the procuring cause of a particular sale, we are not cited to a California case dealing with the precise issue presented here. Watson was not the usual commissioned salesperson; he did not solicit customers or place orders for specific products. His value to WDI was his relationship with Horon and the possibility of reacquiring and maintaining the lucrative Fisher business. Thus, it is the business relationship in its entirety which Watson delivered to WDI, not merely one or more orders.

Federal appellate courts have relied on quantum meruit to find that one who procures an ongoing business relationship, as opposed to single order transactions, is entitled to compensation for a "reasonable" time after termination. In *U.S. Controls Corp. v. Windle* (7th Cir.1975), Windle met with two other men, Rose and Schantz, to discuss forming a new business. Windle had important connections at Whirlpool Corporation to whom he introduced the other two men. Rose and Schantz incorporated U.S. Controls and, without notice to Windle, eventually designed and marketed an item desired by Whirlpool and for which it issued purchase orders. The court awarded Windle reasonable compensation for his earlier services on the basis of quantum meruit. Because the majority of the U.S. Controls business was furnishing its products to Whirlpool, the court examined the profits over a period of time and awarded two and one-half percent of those profits for two years. The reviewing court agreed the majority of U.S. Control's business arose from "initial contacts and introductions" made by Windle; and Windle was entitled to reasonable compensation for his services. "Further, the trial court limited Windle's compensation to the sales for the first two years. This appears to have been a reasonable cutoff date, although Controls had additional sales * * *."

In *Richer v. Khoury Bros., Inc.* (7th Cir.1965), the court determined "[p]laintiff as the procuring cause of the sales, under the agreement of the parties * * * [was] entitled to commissions notwithstanding the fact that the sales were made or consummated subsequent to the termination of the plaintiff's services." There, plaintiff induced certain mail order companies to insert descriptions of his employer's furniture and then received commissions on orders from the catalogue. After he had procured advertisements in several yet-to-be issued catalogues, he was terminated. The court found him entitled to commissions through the life of the catalogues.

In each instance, it was necessary to compensate plaintiff for a reasonable period of time beyond his termination or alliance with the defendant. And it mattered not whether the plaintiff personally obtained or "wrote" the orders. That is clearly what the court attempted to accomplish here. It considered the earlier and devastating loss of the Fisher account, WDI's strong desire to reinstate the account and demonstrated inability to do so itself, Watson's relationship with Horon which he used for WDI's advantage, and WDI's realization of over $9,000,000 in new business after Watson delivered the Fisher account. On the other side of the balance was WDI's retention of the account without assistance from Watson coupled with the death of Horon in January 1985, removing his ability to influence Fisher. The court concluded Watson was entitled to compensation after termination until mid-December 1984. We find the quantum meruit standard applied by the court eminently fair.

Contrary to WDI's contention, use of the commission totals calculated at three percent was not an impermissible use of a contract term for quantum meruit recovery. The court may consider the price agreed upon by the parties "as a criterion in ascertaining the reasonable value of services performed."

Moreover, the amount of the damages relates to the three percent commission agreed upon, but only in the context of what the reasonable value of Watson's services was to WDI for procuring the WDI/Fisher relationship. The reasonable value of those services was not a daily dollar amount for taking Horon golfing—it was the value of the benefit received by WDI. "California law allows evidence of the value of a benefit conferred to prove reasonable value."[6] And evidence of the benefit to WDI was voluminous—regaining and continuing to receive Fisher's business which accounted for up to one-half of WDI's production and almost $10,000,000 through July 1985....

. . .

VI
WATSON'S APPEAL

Watson argues he should have been awarded, at a minimum, three percent of the orders generated from Fisher through the entire accounting period, i.e., through July 1985, because he was the "procuring cause" of the ongoing relationship established between Fisher and WDI. He suggests we modify the judgment to reflect this amount or, in the alternative, remand the matter to the trial judge and/or a referee for this determination.[10]

---

6. The court specifically announced it was "not following some mechanical or mathematical formula, but attempting to determine what dollar figure constitutes the reasonable value of the services plaintiff performed." Although the testimony of the WDI principals was in conflict, the anticipated future needs of Fisher were communicated to WDI far in advance of receipt of Fisher's actual purchase orders. As a consequence, there was a "lag time" of many months between Fisher's notice to prepare for an upcoming order and WDI's invoicing and shipment. While not an element of the referee's report, the court considered this factor as well in determining the reasonable compensation due Watson.

10. Watson relies upon the following statement by the court at the hearing on WDI's motion for new trial, a year after trial.

As discussed in Section III, *ante*, we agree the compensation awarded was reasonable under the circumstances. The trial court strived for a fair determination of the "cutoff" point—that point in time when Watson no longer had any influence over Fisher's procurement policies and Fisher's continued reordering, while set in motion by Watson, would depend upon WDI's product and service.

Judgment affirmed. Each party to bear its own costs.

QUESTIONS AND NOTES

1. The uncertainty in this case did not concern the sales that formed the basis of the claim for commissions. The referee examined voluminous records and calculated WDI's sales to Fisher quite precisely. The uncertainty concerned the term of the agreement between the parties, that is, how long Watson was to receive a commission on WDI's sales to Fisher. Did the parties intend that Watson would collect commissions so long as Fisher ordered, so long as Watson played golf with Fisher's general manager, or so long as Fisher's orders were fairly traceable to Watson's efforts? If the parties failed to reach agreement on this crucial matter, what can the court do?

2. In what sense is the court's decision here one in *quantum meruit*? Can three percent of the revenues from the Fisher business be the fair market value of Watson's "services"? Is playing golf and happily sharing meals with your buddy "worth" upwards of $300,000? Is awarding Watson this sum placing the parties back in the position they were in before making this contract, or is it the financial equivalent of performance?

Certainly it's not a traditional case in any respect. But probably because of the numbers involved and that you have plaintiff who was retained or at least in some way hired to bring a certain customer to your company. He performed.

And in fact the accounting showed that because of that, during the accounting period some $9-million of gross business was brought to the company. In any situation where you have that volume you're going to have substantial commissions involved. And your people want to pay something like 24 or $25,000. "In weighing all those factors [in the statement of decisions] the court was simply trying to some to the reasonable value of the services rendered. I may be off the mark on the reasonable value, but in my view, I'm probably low."

I think that you look at that line of cases, although not in California, that talk about commissions going on for the life of the contract or the life of the involvement between Fisher—Fisher and Wood Dimensions—I think that the Appellate Court might adopt that line of cases for California. I couldn't find any California case that goes that far. Obviously counsel couldn't either. But certainly the individual is entitled to compensation for the amount of gross business he brought the company.

So I decided it on the reasonable value of the services rendered, weighing all the factors I thought were brought in. * * * The testimony was very clear that his primary function was to bring back the Fisher contract, and that the company was in dire straits without it.

II. TORT ALTERNATIVES

If contract remedies produce unacceptably low recovery courts may sometimes label the matter a "tort" and then award damages they think just in the circumstances. We observe this happening in a variety of situations. Claims by consumers against sellers that may be problematic on a warranty theory become "products liability" suits; claims against health care providers are commonly brought on "medical malpractice" rather than on contract theories; and suits against insurance companies that fail to provide the insured with the protection provided in the insurance contract become "bad faith" claims.

All complex legal systems divide problems into conventional analytic categories. Books are indexed, cases catalogued, and law school class hours subdivided in terms of conventional categories. You have one course in Contracts, another in Torts, and a third in Procedure. By the end of this year you will have a sense of the slot in which a particular problem belongs.

Civil justice requires persons who harm others by breaking legal obligations to compensate the injured party. This is both simple justice and necessary for social peace. Our legal system, like most others, distinguishes between injuries flowing from breach of an obligation specially assumed through a promise (contract) and those from breach of an obligation generally imposed by society without regard to any agreement (tort). These categories do not describe islands in the law; tort and contract often overlap. If the two overlap, why care whether liability is based in tort or contract? Indeed contracts and torts are separate legal categories in the common law largely on account of procedural considerations in earlier times that have little continuing relevance. Nevertheless, the distinction has stuck. Part of the reason is that the available remedies and the measure of damages are quite different in tort than they are in contract. Similarly, the process of proof at trial and the evidence that must be produced are likely to differ in the two classes of cases. An understanding of the relationship between tort and contract is illuminated by an appreciation of the past, and it helps to anticipate the future development of the law. Many of the most significant contract law problems seem to involve the gray area between tort and contract. Consumer warranties, socially regulated contracts, and form and mass contracts, to name just a few, are situations in which the law in the long run seems likely to move away from emphasis on the agreement aspects of the transaction to put greater weight on the general obligations of persons who enter those sorts of transactions.

Hargrave v. Oki Nursery

United States Court of Appeals, Second Circuit, 1980.
636 F.2d 897.

■ NICKERSON, DISTRICT JUDGE. ...

Plaintiff Long Island Vineyards, Inc., is a New York corporation of which plaintiff Hargrave is president. Plaintiffs operate a vineyard in Suffolk County, New York, and make wine from the grapes they produce. Oki is a California corporation with its main office in Sacramento and grows and sells nursery stocks including wine grape vines. The complaint, brought in the Supreme Court of the State of New York, Suffolk County, asserts six claims against Oki. The first alleges that during 1973 and 1974 Oki represented to plaintiffs that vines purchased from Oki would be healthy, free of disease, and suitable for wine production, that plaintiffs relied on the representations and in May 1974 purchased vines from Oki, that the representations were knowingly false, and that the vines sold to plaintiffs were diseased and incapable of bearing fruit of adequate quality or quantity for plaintiffs' commercial wine production.

... Oki argues that no "tortious act" has been alleged in the complaint since plaintiffs, by applying the fraud label, may not convert a claim for breach of a contractual representation into a tort claim....

The law of torts and the law of contracts are said to protect different interests. A plaintiff may recover in contract because the defendant has made an agreement, and the law thinks it desirable that he be held to that agreement. Tort liability is imposed on the basis of some social policy that disapproves the infliction of a specific kind of harm irrespective of any agreement. Specifically the law of fraud seeks to protect against injury those who rely to their detriment on the deliberately dishonest statements of another.

Thus, it does not follow that because acts constitute a breach of contract they cannot also give rise to liability in tort. Where the conduct alleged breaches a legal duty which exists "independent of contractual relations between the parties" a plaintiff may sue in tort.... If the only interest at stake is that of holding the defendant to a promise, the courts have said that the plaintiff may not transmogrify the contract claim into one for tort.... But if in addition there is an interest in protecting the plaintiff from other kinds of harm, the plaintiff may recover in tort whether or not he has a valid claim for breach of contract.

In the present case the complaint sets forth all the elements of an action in tort for fraudulent representations, namely, "representation of a material existing fact, falsity, *scienter,* deception and injury." Oki is alleged to have knowingly misrepresented the material existing fact that the vines were healthy. Plaintiffs assert they relied on the misrepresentations, paid for the vines, and sustained injury because they were in fact diseased. These allegations state a claim for fraud, and if Oki indeed made the fraudulent representations it "is subject to liability *in tort* whether the agreement is enforcible or not."

The court need not consider plaintiffs' other contentions.

The order is reversed.

QUESTIONS AND NOTES

1. If the complaint was filed in the Supreme Court of New York (Suffolk County), how did the appeal end up in the United States Court of Appeals for the Second Circuit before a federal district judge?

2. Does the distinction made by Judge Nickerson between the law of torts and the law of contracts explain why punitive damages are available for tort claims but not for contract claims? Does this case suggest that tort, like restitution, provides an alternative that is not necessarily exclusive of familiar contract recovery?

3. In what sense is the harm which tort law redresses "irrespective of any agreement" if, as the opinion indicates, fraud focuses ultimately on the "statements of another"? To put the question differently, how can the legal duty that is a predicate to tort liability exist "independent of contractual relations between the parties" when the duty seems to arise out of the promissory relationship?

4. Did the Benkowskis have a legal duty "irrespective of any agreement" to provide uninterrupted water service to the Whites? *See* p. 91. Was there a legal duty grounded in tort that arose out of the promissory relationship?

5. The elements of proof will be different for fraud and for breach of contract. How will Hargrave show, for example, that Oki intended at the time the contract was made to sell inferior vines? Will such proof be needed to show contract breach? Will it be needed to show fraud? Suppose Oki learned of the vines' deficiencies after the contract was formed but before it was performed. Finally, suppose all Hargrave can prove is that the vines as delivered were inferior.

Decker v. Browning–Ferris Indus. of Colorado

Colorado Supreme Court, 1997.
931 P.2d 436.

■ JUSTICE KIRSHBAUM delivered the Opinion of the Court.

In *Decker v. Browning–Ferris Industries of Colorado, Inc.*, and *Castillo v. Browning–Ferris Industries of Colorado, Inc.*, the court of appeals determined, inter alia, that plaintiffs-petitioners Thomas H. Decker (Decker) and Jose Castillo (Castillo) could not recover damages in tort from their employer, defendant-respondent Browning-Ferris Industries of Colorado, Inc. (BFI), for breach of an express covenant of good faith and fair dealing because no such tort exists in Colorado in the employment context. The court of appeals also remanded both cases to the trial court for new trials on damages because it could not determine from the special verdict forms and instructions on damages whether the juries had based their awards on the tort claims. Having granted certiorari to review the propriety of the court of appeals' decisions, we affirm in part, reverse in part, and remand the cases to the court of appeals with directions.

I

A

In June 1985, Decker obtained a position as a trash removal truck driver's helper with BFI. Decker was hired by Anthony Vagneur (Vagneur), the manager of BFI's Aspen, Colorado, district (the Aspen District), and was assigned to work in that district. In 1985, Decker earned a wage of $7.75 per hour.

Decker was subsequently promoted to the position of trash removal truck driver, which position Decker held for approximately five years. Decker received each pay increase for which he was eligible during his employment with BFI. In 1990, Vagneur wrote a letter to Decker informing Decker that he would receive a "discretionary" $400 bonus, congratulating Decker "on having a successful winter season with BFI," and stating that BFI appreciated Decker's work. The letter contained a statement that BFI "look[ed] forward to a long and lasting relationship" with Decker.

Vagneur was Decker's immediate supervisor until January 1991, when BFI discharged Vagneur and replaced him with Gerald P. Vandervelde (Vandervelde). In August 1991, Vandervelde terminated Decker's employment for the stated reason that Decker worked too slowly. At this time Decker earned a wage of $11.50 per hour. After his discharge from BFI, Decker obtained employment for a period of time as a truck driver for a newspaper company, earning $95 per day without benefits. Decker subsequently opened a restaurant using retirement funds accumulated during his employment at BFI as well as money borrowed from family members. At the time of trial, the restaurant was not profitable.

B

Castillo was hired by Vagneur in 1989 as a trash removal truck driver's helper for BFI in BFI's Aspen district. During the course of his employment, Castillo was promoted to the position of driver and received approximately five pay raises. In 1990 Castillo received a letter from Vagneur congratulating Castillo on a "successful winter season with BFI," expressing BFI's appreciation for Castillo's work, informing Castillo of his entitlement to a "discretionary" $400 bonus, and containing a statement that BFI looked forward to a "long and lasting relationship" with Castillo. In May 1991, Castillo broke his ankle while performing duties at BFI and reported the injury to BFI's workers' compensation physician. Castillo ultimately received workers' compensation benefits for this injury. In June 1991, Castillo obtained permission from his physician to return to BFI with the restriction that he perform only light duties. In August 1991 Vandervelde terminated Castillo's employment on the stated ground that Castillo was working too slowly. After his employment at BFI was terminated, Castillo twice underwent surgery on his ankle. In December 1992, he worked for ten days as a dishwasher at a restaurant. He obtained a full-time position with another company in March 1993, earning a wage of $8.00 per hour with no benefits. At the time of trial, Castillo was still employed by that company.

C

In early 1992, Decker and Castillo filed separate civil actions in the trial court against BFI. Because both Decker and Castillo were represented by the same counsel and had been discharged under similar circumstances from their employment with BFI, their complaints were identical in many respects. Decker and Castillo alleged, inter alia, that they had been discharged in violation of a progressive disciplinary policy adopted by Vagneur—a claim for wrongful discharge which sounded in contract. Decker and Castillo subsequently filed amended complaints against BFI which contained an additional claim of "breach of covenant of good faith and fair dealing" based on alleged express promises by BFI management that they would be treated fairly. Although the amended complaints characterized this as a contract claim, the amended complaints requested compensatory, noneconomic and punitive damages with respect to this claim.

Castillo's action was tried first. At trial, Vagneur testified that he had personally promised to treat Castillo fairly. During the instruction conference, BFI objected to the instructions and special verdict forms which would permit the jury to award punitive damages on the breach of covenant of good faith and fair dealing claim. BFI argued that this claim sounded in contract, and punitive damages are not available for a breach of contract. The trial court held that while the covenant of good faith and fair dealing may have had its origins in contract law, its breach constituted a tort and could thus properly support an award of punitive damages. Aside from this one objection to the submission of punitive damages, BFI raised no other objection concerning the covenant of good faith and fair dealing claim, either as to the instruction defining its elements or to the special verdict form which permitted the jury to award damages for "inconvenience and emotional stress" in the event of its breach. At closing arguments, neither party made any distinction between contract and tort theories concerning the claim for breach of express covenant of good faith and fair dealing, but merely discussed whether BFI had breached its promises of fair treatment to Castillo. The jury returned a verdict in favor of Castillo and against BFI. The jury determined that BFI had adopted a personnel policy concerning discipline and termination and had breached that policy. The jury also determined that BFI had promised fair treatment to Castillo in its employment decisions and had breached that promise as well. The jury awarded Castillo $33,500 in damages for lost income, determined that BFI's breach of covenant of good faith and fair dealing was attended by circumstances of willful and wanton conduct by BFI, and awarded Castillo punitive damages in the amount of $11,500. The jury did not award Castillo damages for inconvenience or emotional stress. BFI did not file any post-trial motions. With respect to Decker's claims, BFI expressly stipulated at trial that it had promised to treat Decker fairly. BFI also raised the same objections concerning punitive damages that it had raised in Castillo's case, and the trial court likewise denied them for the same reasons. The parties similarly never raised the contract/tort distinction before the jury, but merely discussed whether BFI had breached its promises of fair treatment to Decker. The jury returned a verdict in favor of Decker and against BFI on the breach of disciplinary policy and breach of covenant of good faith and fair dealing claims. As in Castillo's case, the jury found that BFI had terminated Decker in violation of both its progressive disciplinary policy and its express promise of fair treatment. The jury also found that BFI had willfully and wantonly breached its promises of good faith and fair dealing. The jury awarded Decker $600,000 in damages for lost income, $80,000 in damages for inconvenience and emotional stress, and an additional $680,000 in punitive damages on the claim of breach of covenant of good faith and fair dealing. BFI filed post-trial motions which focused largely on the matter of the punitive damage award. BFI adopted the trial court's characterization of the covenant of good faith and fair dealing claim as a tort, and stipulated that the claim had been tried as a tort. BFI argued that Colorado did not recognize a tort claim for breach of an express covenant of good faith and fair dealing in the employment context.

D

BFI appealed both cases. Throughout the appellate proceedings before this court and the court of appeals, the parties have referred to the breach of disciplinary policy claim as the "contract" claim, and the breach of express covenant of good faith and fair dealing claim as the "tort" claim. The primary issue presented which the parties framed for the court of appeals was whether Colorado recognized a tort claim for breach of an express covenant of good faith and fair dealing in the employment context. In Decker's case, the court of appeals accepted the parties' characterizations of the breach of disciplinary policy claim as a contract claim and the breach of covenant of good faith and fair dealing claim as a tort claim. The court of appeals affirmed the jury's determination of liability on the breach of contract claim, but determined that because Colorado does not recognize a tort claim in the employment context for breach of covenant of good faith and fair dealing, the trial court erroneously allowed the jury to consider that claim. The court of appeals concluded that in the absence of a viable tort claim, the awards for punitive damages and noneconomic damages must be vacated. The court of appeals held that the punitive damage award could not be based upon the breach of the progressive disciplinary policy claim because it was a contract claim. With respect to the award of noneconomic damages, the court observed that while damages for "mental suffering" are sometimes recoverable for willful and wanton breach of contract, the jury in this case was not requested to find willful and wanton breach of the progressive disciplinary policy. The court of appeals also determined that the award of noneconomic damages was improper because noneconomic damages may be awarded in a breach of contract action only for "mental suffering," and the jury instructions allowed the jury to consider future noneconomic losses as well as inconvenience and emotional stress. The court of appeals noted that Decker could on retrial seek damages for mental suffering for breach of contract if he proved that BFI's breach of the progressive disciplinary policy was willful or wanton. In setting aside the award of $600,000 for lost income, the court of appeals concluded that it was impossible to discern from the special verdict form under which theory the lost income was awarded, and that it must be presumed that BFI had been prejudiced by the special verdict form.

The court of appeals employed an identical analysis in Castillo's appeal. It held that Colorado does not recognize a tort claim for breach of covenant of good faith and fair dealing in the context of employment relations, and set aside the jury's award of punitive damages based on that claim. It also affirmed the jury's verdict on liability for breach of the progressive disciplinary policy, but held that the award of economic damages had to be vacated because it was impossible to determine whether it had been awarded under the proper contract theory or the improper tort theory. The court of appeals thus remanded both cases for new trials on damages.

II

Decker and Castillo argue that tort claims for breach of express covenant of good faith and fair dealing are cognizable in Colorado in the employment context. We reject this argument.

* * *

2

We have recognized in the context of insurance contracts that a party to such an agreement may recover damages in tort for breach of an implied covenant of good faith and fair dealing. An insurer's tort liability for breach of an implied duty of good faith and fair dealing arises from the nature of the insurance contract as well as from the relationship between the insurer and the insured. In contrast to a party who seeks to secure commercial advantage in the context of a general commercial contract, an insured who enters into a contract of insurance seeks to obtain "financial security and protection against calamity." Because an insurer's bad faith refusal to pay valid claims defeats the very purpose of the insurance contract, a special duty is imposed upon an insurer to deal in good faith with an insured. This "quasi-fiduciary" relationship between an insurer and an insured is thus based in part on this special contract. In addition, when an insured suffers a loss, the insured becomes "particularly vulnerable" to the insurer. For example, an insurer may delay payment of a claim to the insured in the hope of settling for an amount less than what might be due under the contract. Thus the implied covenant of good faith and fair dealing in the context of insurance contracts also arises from the heightened reliance necessarily placed by an insured on the insurer.

Decker and Castillo suggest that an employment relationship possesses many of the characteristics found in the relationship between an insurer and an insured in support of their argument that a covenant of good faith and fair dealing should be imposed in the former context. The insurance analogy has been rejected by several courts.

There are certain parallels between insurance and employment contexts. An insurance contract protects the insured from such calamities as medical emergencies and accidental property damage. An employment contract is of even greater significance to an employee because it provides the means for the employee to meet his or her basic needs. Thus both insurance and employment contracts afford financial security to the insured and the employee, respectively. However, the positions of insureds and of employees who suffer harm as a result of unreasonable conduct are not always similar. A wrongfully discharged employee may be able to obtain alternative employment and must make reasonable attempts to do so to mitigate damages. Unreasonably discharged employees who are not able to secure alternative employment may recover damages for lost income.[7] In contrast, an insured whose valid claim for coverage has been denied in bad faith has no recourse in the marketplace. No other insurance company will assume responsibility for the insured's losses. It is also noteworthy that the interests of insureds and insurers may conflict. An insurer has an incentive to delay payment of a valid claim in the hope of settling for an amount less than the sum owed pursuant to the policy. In contrast, employees as well as employers generally seek to promote the business interests of the employer. Of course, the possibility of arbitrary and unreasonable treatment by an employer

---

7. Of course, a wrongfully discharged employee may suffer injuries not compensable by contract damages, such as foreclosure of a mortgage on a home because of the owner employee's inability to make required payments.

always exists—a phenomenon which can not be prevented by reliance on the dynamics of the marketplace.

Some courts have applied rationales developed in insurance contract cases to recognize a tort claim for breach of covenant of good faith and fair dealing in employment cases. In *K Mart Corp. v. Ponsock*, 103 Nev. 39 (1987), the plaintiff was employed by the defendant as a forklift driver. The defendant consistently characterized the plaintiff as an excellent employee. The plaintiff's retirement benefits were due to vest after the plaintiff had been employed for ten years. A few months before the plaintiff's retirement benefits were due to vest, the plaintiff was terminated by the defendant, allegedly for applying paint to the battery cover of the forklift which he operated. The plaintiff, without securing permission from his supervisor, had applied paint from a can he discovered earlier in the day to the battery cover in order to remedy the deteriorating condition of that cover. When asked by a maintenance worker to remove the paint, the plaintiff complied. The plaintiff was reprimanded by a supervisor for his conduct, and his "separation report" provided that he had been terminated for defacing company property with misappropriated merchandise (the paint) on company time. A jury determined that the defendant had in reality terminated the plaintiff in order to avoid paying the plaintiff's retirement benefits. The court concluded that the plaintiff was entitled to tort damages reasoning that the employee was highly economically dependent upon the employer and vulnerable to the employer's abuse because of that dependency. The court determined that the particular employment relationship at issue was similar to the relationship between an insured and an insurer because the plaintiff specially relied on the defendant's apparent commitment to retain the plaintiff until retirement.

The court limited its holding to the particular factual circumstances of the case as follows: "The special relationships of trust between this employer and this employee under this contract under this type of abusive and arbitrary dismissal cries out for relief and for a remedy beyond that traditionally flowing from breach of contract." In *D'Angelo v. Gardner*, 107 Nev. 704 (1991), the Supreme Court of Nevada distinguished *Ponsock* in holding that a plaintiff employee was not entitled to an award of tort damages, comparing the facts of that case to the facts of *Ponsock* and describing *Ponsock* as "the exemplar for that narrow class of cases in which, because of the relationship of employer to employee, the offending conduct 'goes well beyond the bounds of ordinary liability for breach of contract.'"

In view of these cases, it is not clear that the rationales supporting recognition of the tort of breach of covenant of good faith and fair dealing in the context of insurance contracts require recognition of a tort claim for bad faith breach of an express covenant of good faith and fair dealing in the employment context.

3

However, we conclude that a tort claim for breach of covenant of good faith and fair dealing need not be recognized in the employment context because we have previously recognized the existence a tort claim for wrongful discharge in violation of public policy. That claim, as well as tort claims for bad faith breach of insurance contracts, are firmly grounded in legislative or other public policy declarations thus insuring that all interested parties are aware of the scope of the relevant duty....

It is thus apparent that the torts of wrongful discharge in violation of public policy and bad faith breach of the implied covenant of good faith and fair dealing inherent in insurance contracts are based on administrative or legislative declarations of public policy. As a result, employers and insurers have notice of the scope of their duties to their employees and insureds. No parallel declarations of public policy have been articulated by the General Assembly or other governmental institutions with respect to the employment context. In the absence of such declarations of public policy, there is no appropriate basis upon which to ground a tort of breach of an express covenant of good faith and fair dealing in employment contracts. To the extent the contents of employment contracts and insurance contracts are similar, the tort of wrongful termination of an employment contract in violation of public policy represents an appropriate analog to the tort of bad faith breach of the implied covenant of good faith and fair dealing of an insurance contract.

III

For the foregoing reasons, we decline to recognize the existence in this jurisdiction of a tort claim for breach of an express covenant of good faith and fair dealing in employment contracts. However, we have concluded that the claims for breach of express covenant of good faith and fair dealing asserted by Decker and Castillo sound in contract, not in tort. We therefore address issues respecting the damage awards in these cases.

A

Decker and Castillo assert that the court of appeals erred in reversing the judgments of punitive damages entered by the trial court. We reject this argument.

In *Mortgage Finance, Inc. v. Podleski* (Colo.1987), we emphasized that the law of torts and the law of contracts reflect different policies and, therefore, recognize different remedies. The law of contracts does not seek to compel performance of a contract by punishing a breach, but rather to compensate the promisee for losses sustained as a result of a breach. The law of torts is premised upon legal duties imposed by law. Breach of such legal duties can, in certain circumstances, justify the imposition of exemplary damages in order to punish the defendant and deter others from similar conduct in the future.

Here, as in *Podleski*, we are faced with conduct which amounts to a breach of contract, and "no tort claim was before the trial court at the conclusion of the trial." Under such circumstances, the awards of punitive damages must be vacated, as the court of appeals determined.

B

Decker and Castillo argue that the court of appeals erroneously reversed the juries' verdicts awarding them economic damages. We agree.

... [A]lthough the special verdict forms require the juries to reach separate liability determinations with respect to the breach of progressive disciplinary policy and breach of covenant of good faith and fair dealing claims, such forms do not require the juries to distinguish between the two claims when determining whether damages for lost income, inconvenience and emotional stress should be awarded. In each case, the special verdict form provides that if the jury finds BFI liable on either claim, the jury should "state the amount of lost income, if any, suffered * * * ." In addition, the special verdict forms allowed the juries to award damages for "inconvenience and emotional stress" if they answered "yes" to liability on either the breach of disciplinary policy or breach of covenant of good faith and fair dealing claim.

The court of appeals concluded that it was "impossible" to discern whether the awards for economic damages were based on the proper breach of disciplinary policy claim or the improper breach of covenant of good faith and fair dealing claim. However, as we have observed, in each case both the claim for breach of the progressive disciplinary policy and the claim for breach of express covenant of good faith and fair dealing were pled, tried, and found by the jury to be breaches of an express contractual obligation. The juries' calculations of economic damages in these cases were limited by the instructions to "back pay, loss of future pay and loss of benefits," which are appropriate economic damages designed to put the wrongfully discharged employee in the same position he or she would have been in had the employer not breach the employment contract. Under the circumstances of these cases, we conclude that the juries' awards of economic damages to Decker and to Castillo should be affirmed.

C

Decker argues that in the event that we should refuse to recognize a tort claim for breach of express covenant of good faith and fair dealing, we should treat the jury's findings on that claim as a finding that BFI's breach of contract was attended by willful and wanton conduct and thereby uphold the jury's award of $80,000 in noneconomic damages. We agree.

The special verdict form submitted to the jury authorized an award of punitive damages if the jury found "with respect to Thomas Decker's claim for breach of the covenant of good faith and fair dealing, that the injury, if any, was attended by circumstances of willful and wanton conduct by BFI." The jury found that BFI's conduct in firing Decker was willful and wanton.

Although we have concluded that the juries' awards of punitive damages must be vacated, the jury's special verdict with respect to Decker's claims establishes that the jury found that BFI breached an express contractual obligation to Decker and that such breach was characterized by willful and wanton conduct. Damages for "mental suffering" are recoverable on a breach of contract claim when the breach is accompanied by willful and wanton conduct and when the damages are a natural and proximate consequence of such conduct. Here, the jury awarded noneconomic damages specifically for "inconvenience and emotional stress" caused in part by BFI's breach of its promise of fair treatment. Thus, the award of $80,000 in noneconomic damages for BFI's willful and wanton breach of its express covenant of good faith and fair dealing is proper under Colorado law, and must be upheld.

D

Because the court of appeals reversed all of the damage awards against BFI, it did not address BFI's claim that the jury's award of $600,000 to Decker in lost wages was excessive. As noted in part I(A), at the time of his discharge Decker earned a wage of $11.50 per hour. Considering the testimony of Decker's economic expert in the light most favorable to Decker as the verdict winner, it is clear that the jury's award of $600,000 in economic damages includes a substantial amount for front pay, or lost future wages.

Thus, while we affirm the jury's finding that BFI is liable to Decker for economic damages, we remand Decker's case to the court of appeals for consideration of BFI's arguments challenging the amount of the jury's award of economic damages in that case.

QUESTIONS AND NOTES

1. In most jurisdictions, covenants of good faith and fair dealing are implied in all contracts, and, in general, this obligation cannot be waived or disclaimed. In this sense the "covenant" is an obligation imposed by law rather than one voluntarily assumed, and on this basis injured parties have argued that bad faith conduct in the course of contractual performance may give rise to tort remedies. In most contexts and most jurisdictions these attempts have been rebuffed. Ordinarily, bad faith breach of contract will give rise only to ordinary contract remedies. Do you agree with this position? Why not punish bad faith behavior in connection with contractual performance?

2. Recall Justice O'Souter's opinion in *Best v. Southland*, p. 20. O'Souter argues that courts should generally view failure to perform as promised as giving rise to tort remedies and notes that they indeed do so in certain contexts. His argument draws heavily on GRANT GILMORE, THE DEATH OF CONTRACT (1974) a scholarly *tour d'force* which traced the history of contract law back to its roots in trespass and projected that contract and tort might be in incipiently recombining. And indeed in the 1970s and 1980s, California appeared to be leading the way towards generally assimilating contract and tort remedies by creating a tort action for negligent interference with prospective economic advantage (a tort that sounds very much like negligent breach of contract) in a widely-commented upon case, *J'Aire Corp. v. Gregory*, 24 Cal. 3d 799 (1979). *J'Aire* awarded the plaintiff, a commercial tenant, compensation for lost profits based on unreasonable construction delays on the landlord's property. *See also People Express Airlines v. Consolidated Rail Corp.*, 100 N.J. 246 (1985) (imposing tort liability on railroad for economic losses arising out of plaintiff airline's flight cancellations necessitated by gas leak from railway tank car). Moreover, the California Supreme Court of this era also had started down the road of generally authorizing punitive damages as a remedy for bad-faith breach of a commercial contract in another much-commented upon case, *Seaman's Direct Buying Service v. Standard Oil Co. of California.*, 36 Cal. 3d 752 (1984).

But the predicted demise of contract law proved at best premature. These developments in the California case law were criticized, cut short, and sharply limited in the 1990s. In *Freeman & Mills v. Belcher Oil Co.*, 11 Cal. 4th 85 (1995), the California Supreme Court overruled *Seaman's*. The California Supreme Court also appears to have sharply limited *J'Aire*, in *Aas v. Superior Court of San Diego County (William Lyon Co., Real Party-In-Interest)*, 24 Cal. 4th 627 (2000). In *Aas*, the Court rejected a claim for recovery of economic losses in a negligence action in a home construction case in the absence of personal injury or physical property damage asserting:

> Any construction defect can diminish the value of a house. But the difference between price paid and value received, and deviations from standards of quality that have not resulted in property damage or personal injury, are primarily the domain of contract and warranty law or the law of fraud, rather than of negligence. In actions for negligence, a manufacturer's liability is limited to damages for physical injuries; no recovery is allowed for economic loss alone. This general principle, the so-called economic loss rule, is the primary obstacle to plaintiffs' claim.

Id. at 636. The bottom line appears to be that "prospective economic advantage" remains compensable in California only under the more restrictive traditional contract doctrines, and this includes the rule that punitive damages are not available in contract except in cases where an independent tort cause of action exists (generally based on property damage or personal injury or fraud) or where a unique special relationship exists, such as that between insurer and insured.

3. Perhaps the most salient difference between contract and tort is the nature of the injuries usually sought to be redressed. Contract focuses on protecting economic expectancies. Tort focuses on compensating personal injuries. Does this difference support the remedial distinctions between tort and contract? Do these distinctions make sense when the nature of the injury is the loss of a job? Why does the *Decker* court award the plaintiff $80,000 in non-economic damages after rejecting his tort theory?

Jarvis v. Swans Tours Ltd.

Court of Appeal, Civil Division, 1973.
[1973] 1 Q.B. 233.

■ LORD DENNING. The plaintiff, Mr. Jarvis, is a solicitor employed by a local authority at Barking. In 1969 he was minded to go for Christmas to Switzerland. He was looking forward to a ski-ing holiday. It is his one fortnight's holiday in the year. He prefers it in the winter rather than in the summer.

Mr. Jarvis read a brochure issued by Swans Tours, Ltd. He was much attracted by the description of Mörlialp, Giswil, Central Switzerland. I will not read the whole of it, but just pick out some of the principal attractions:

> HOUSE PARTY CENTRE with special resident host * * * MÖRLIALP is a most wonderful little resort on a sunny plateau * * * Up there you will find yourself in the midst of beautiful alpine scenery, which in winter becomes a wonderland of sun, snow and ice, with a wide variety of fine ski-runs, a skating-rink and an exhilarating toboggan run * * * Why did we choose the Hotel Krone ... mainly and most of all, because of the GEMUTLICHKEIT and friendly welcome you will receive from Herr and Frau Weibel * * * The Hotel Krone has its own Alphütte Bar which will be open several evenings a week * * * No doubt you will be in for a great time, when you book this houseparty holiday * * * Mr. Weibel, the charming owner, speaks English.

On the same page, in a special yellow box, it was said:

> SWANS HOUSEPARTY IN MÖRLIALP. *All these Houseparty arrangements are included in the price of your holiday.* Welcome party on arrival. Afternoon tea and cake for 7 days. Swiss Dinner by candlelight. Fondue-party. Yodler evening. Chali farewell party in the "Alphütte Bar." Service of representative.

Alongside on the same page there was a special note about ski-packs:

> "Hire of Skis, Sticks and Boots * * * 12 days £11·10."

In August 1969, on the faith of that brochure, Mr. Jarvis booked a 15 day holiday, with ski-pack. The total charge was £63·45, including Christmas supplement. He was to fly from Gatwick to Zurich on 20th December 1969 and return on 3rd January 1970.

The plaintiff went on the holiday, but he was very disappointed. He was a man of about 35 and he expected to be one of a houseparty of some 30 or so people. Instead, he found there were only 13 during the first week. In the second week there was no houseparty at all. He was the only person there. Mr. Weibel could not speak English. So there was Mr. Jarvis, in the second week, in his hotel with no houseparty at all, and no one could speak English, except himself. He was very disappointed, too, with the ski-ing. It was some distance away at Giswil. There were no ordinary length skis. There were only miniskis, about 3 ft. long. So he did not get his ski-ing as he wanted to. In the second week he did get some longer skis for a couple of days, but then, because of the boots, his feet got rubbed and he could not continue even with the long skis. So his ski-ing holiday, from his point of view, was pretty well ruined.

There were many other matters, too. They appear trivial when they are set down in writing, but I have no doubt they loomed large in Mr. Jarvis's mind, when coupled with the other disappointments. He did not have the nice Swiss cakes which he was hoping for. The only cakes for tea were potato crisps and little dry nutcakes. The yodler evening consisted of one man from the locality who came in his working clothes for a little while, and sang four or five songs very quickly. The "Alphütte Bar" was an unoccupied annexe which was only open one evening. There was a representative, Mrs. Storr, there during the first week, but she was not there during the second week. The matter was summed up by the learned judge:

> * * * during the first week he got a holiday in Switzerland which was to some extent inferior * * * and, as to the second week he got a holiday which was very largely inferior [to what he was led to expect].

What is the legal position? I think that the statements in the brochure were representations or warranties. The breaches of them give Mr. Jarvis a right to damages. It is not necessary to decide whether they were representations or warranties; because, since the Misrepresentation Act of 1967, there is a remedy in damages for misrepresentation as well as for breach of warranty.

The one question in the case is: what is the amount of damages? The judge seems to have taken the difference in value between what he paid for and what he got. He said that he intended to give "the difference between the two values and no other damages" under any other head. He thought that Mr. Jarvis had got half of what he paid for. So the judge gave him half the amount which he had paid, namely, £31·72. Mr. Jarvis appeals to this court. He says that the damages ought to have been much more.

What is the right way of assessing damages? It has often been said that on a breach of contract damages cannot be given for mental distress. Thus in *Hamlin v. Great Northern Railway Co.*, Pollock, C.B., said that damages cannot be given "for the disappointment of mind occasioned by the breach of contract." And in *Hobbs v. London & South Western Railway Co.*, Mellor, J., said that–

> * * * for the mere inconvenience, such as annoyance and loss of temper, or vexation, or for being disappointed in a particular thing which you have set your mind upon, without real physical inconvenience resulting, you cannot recover damages.

The courts in those days only allowed the plaintiff to recover damages if he suffered physical inconvenience, such as, having to walk five miles home, as in Hobbs's case; or to live in an overcrowded house: see *Bailey v. Bullock*.

I think that those limitations are out of date. In a proper case damages for mental distress can be recovered in contract, just as damages for shock can be recovered in *rule* tort. One such case is a contract for a holiday, or any other contract to provide entertainment and enjoyment. If the contracting party breaks his contract, damages can be given for the disappointment, the distress, the upset and frustration caused by the breach. I know that it is difficult to assess in terms of money, but it is no more difficult than the assessment which the courts have to make every day in personal injury cases for loss of amenities. Take the present case. Mr. Jarvis has only a fortnight's holiday in the year. He books it far ahead, and looks forward to it all that time. He ought to be compensated for the loss of it.

A good illustration was given by Edmund Davies L.J. in the course of the argument. He put the case of a man who has taken a ticket for Glyndbourne. It is the only night on which he can get there. He hires a car to take him. The car does not turn up. His damages are not limited to the mere cost of the ticket. He is entitled to general damages for the disappointment he has suffered and the loss of the entertainment which he should have had. Here, Mr. Jarvis's fortnight's winter holiday has been a grave disappointment. It is true that he was conveyed to Switzerland and back and had meals and bed in the hotel. But that is not what he went for. He went to enjoy himself with all the facilities which the defendants said he would have. He is entitled to damages for the lack of those facilities, and for his loss of enjoyment.

A similar case occurred in 1951. It was *Stedman v. Swan's Tours*. A holiday-maker was awarded damages because he did not get the bedroom and the accommodation which he was promised. The county court judge awarded him £13·15s. This court increased it to £50.

I think the judge was in error in taking the sum paid for the holiday, £63·45, and halving it. The right measure of damages is to compensate him for the loss of entertainment and enjoyment which he was promised, and which he did not get. Looking at the matter quite broadly, I think the damages in this case should be the sum of £125. I would allow the appeal accordingly.

[Concurring opinions of EDMUND DAVIES and STEPHENSON L.J.'S are omitted.]

Recall: *Sullivan v. O'Connor*, p. 128.

QUESTIONS AND NOTES

1. It appears that Mr. Jarvis stayed at Mörlialp for the two weeks of his tour. Should he be able to recover for all his disappointments, or should his recovery be offset by the damages he could have avoided by telephoning for a taxi on the second day and moving to a better hotel?

2. This was Mr. Jarvis' only vacation for the year. Would the result have been the same if Jarvis' employer gave him six weeks vacation per year? Does Swans Tours have to ask all potential tour participants how important their vacation is to them?

3. Jarvis paid £63.45 for his holiday and was allowed £125 for his disappointment. In what sense is this the financial equivalent of performance? Is a £63 vacation that lives up to expectations worth £125? If Jarvis' one fortnight of vacation per year is so valuable to him, why did he book such a cheap tour? Didn't he assume the risk?

4. The *Wall Street Journal* reported on February 9, 1989 that thousands of German tourists sue tour operators each year for "defective travel" or "loss of pleasure on holiday" when their holiday is damaged by dirt, insects, seasickness, or inadequate hotel rooms. German judges use a schedule of fixed damages in such cases that provides, for instance, that if the brochure promises a heated swimming pool and the pool is cold the client may claim 5% of the tour price, a room without a bathroom is likely to be awarded 15% to 20% and food that tastes terrible 20% to 30%. Lack of promised facilities for nude sunbathing can be worth up to 20%.

On April 25, 1991, the Local Court (Amtsgericht) of Mönchengladbach, Germany, issued the following judgment (Az.: 5 ä C 106/91):

Statement of Facts

Plaintiff booked a vacation on Menorca, Hotel La Calata, with the defendant tour operator for himself and his life companion (*Lebensgefährtin*) from August 15 to 29, 1990 for the price of DM 3,078.00. The accommodation was to be a double room with a double bed. Plaintiff alleges that after arrival at the hotel he discovered that instead of a double bed, the room contained two unattached twin beds. Plaintiff claims that his sleeping and cohabitation habits were severely impaired from the first night. He was unable to enjoy the peaceful and harmonious experience of falling asleep and cohabitating with his companion during the whole two-week vacation period, because the twin beds, which were standing on slippery tiles, separated at the slightest motion. Harmonious cohabitation was completely impossible.

Plaintiff demands recovery of damages for vacation time that was wasted, in the amount of 20% of the vacation expenses. The anticipated recreational value, the relaxation, and the hoped for harmony with his life companion was substantially impaired. This led to peevishness, dissatisfaction, and annoyance displayed by him and by his life companion. Thus the recreational value of their vacation suffered.

Plaintiff moves that defendant be ordered to pay him DM 615.50, plus interest from September 11, 1990.

Defendant asks for the dismissal of the action....

Reasons for the decision

In any case, upon the merits, this claim is without sufficient basis.

Plaintiff does not explain in detail why his specific cohabitation habits require a double bed fixed to each other. This point needs not be further developed, though, because the particular habits of the plaintiff are not important. What is important is whether the beds were unsuitable for the average traveler. But the beds were appropriate. The Court is aware of several generally known and usual variations for performing sexual intercourse, which can indeed be practiced on a single bed to the satisfaction of all participants. Thus, Plaintiff did not have to spend his vacation completely without the private life he so desired.

Even if one concedes that Plaintiff's special cohabitation practices require a double bed, there is no breach in the performance of the vacation contract, because the fault could have been removed immediately. That is to say, when a fault can be remedied easily, the traveler is expected to do so on his own, so that the full vacation benefits can be realized and no claim for damages exists.

Plaintiff presented the court a photograph of the beds in question. In this photo one can see that the mattresses lie on a solid frame which obviously is made of metal. The two metal frames quickly could have been joined with a strong cord. It may be that the plaintiff did not have such a cord with him, but it could have been purchased inexpensively. Until a suitable cord was acquired, Plaintiff could have availed himself of his trouser belt for instance, because this was certainly not needed in its original function at that moment ...

Aha!

III. LIQUIDATED DAMAGES

Remedies are as much a product of the agreement as other performance terms. Freedom of contract would suggest that the parties have the power to eliminate future confusion or difficulties over the damages to be awarded in the event of a breach by providing in the contract either an amount or a formula for calculating them. Nevertheless, for centuries the courts affixed the label of "penalty" to such contract provisions and often refused to enforce them. More recently the law has increasingly recognized the propriety of parties contracting their way out of remedies problems. If the contract provision is considered reasonable it will be described as "liquidated damages" and will be honored by a court. The consequences of attaching the labels are clear: reasonable liquidated damages will be enforced, and penalties will be disregarded. How does a lawyer determine which is which when drafting a contract? She does the best she can with the clues available, always uncomfortably aware of the fact that hindsight causes many a judge to view as a penalty that which the parties saw as a reasonable damage estimate at the time they made their contract.

Lake River Corp. v. Carborundum Co.

United States Court of Appeals, Seventh Circuit, 1985.
769 F.2d 1284.

■ POSNER, J.

This diversity suit between Lake River Corporation and Carborundum Company requires us to consider questions of Illinois commercial law, and in particular to explore the fuzzy line between penalty clauses and liquidated-damages clauses.

Carborundum manufactures "Ferro Carbo," an abrasive powder used in making steel. To serve its midwestern customers better, Carborundum made a contract with Lake River by which the latter agreed to provide distribution services in its warehouse in Illinois. Lake River would receive Ferro Carbo in bulk from Carborundum, "bag" it, and ship the bagged product to Carborundum's customers. The Ferro Carbo would remain Carborundum's property until delivered to the customers.

Carborundum insisted that Lake River install a new bagging system to handle the contract. In order to be sure of being able to recover the cost of the new system ($89,000) and make a profit of 20 percent of the contract price, Lake River insisted on the following minimum-quantity guarantee:

> In consideration of the special equipment [i.e., the new bagging system] to be acquired and furnished by LAKE-RIVER for handling the product, CARBORUNDUM

shall, during the initial three-year term of this Agreement, ship to LAKE–RIVER for bagging a minimum quantity of [22,500 tons]. If, at the end of the three-year term, this minimum quantity shall not have been shipped, LAKE–RIVER shall invoice CARBO-RUNDUM at the then prevailing rates for the difference between the quantity bagged and the minimum guaranteed.

If Carborundum had shipped the full minimum quantity that it guaranteed, it would have owed Lake River roughly $533,000 under the contract.

After the contract was signed in 1979, the demand for domestic steel, and with it the demand for Ferro Carbo, plummeted, and Carborundum failed to ship the guaranteed amount. When the contract expired late in 1982, Carborundum had shipped only 12,000 of the 22,500 tons it had guaranteed. Lake River had bagged the 12,000 tons and had billed Carborundum for this bagging, and Carborundum had paid, but by virtue of the formula in the minimum-guarantee clause Carborundum still owed Lake River $241,000—the contract price of $533,000 if the full amount of Ferro Carbo had been shipped, minus what Carborundum had paid for the bagging of the quantity it had shipped.

When Lake River demanded payment of this amount, Carborundum refused, on the ground that the formula imposed a penalty. At the time, Lake River had in its warehouse 500 tons of bagged Ferro Carbo, having a market value of $269,000, which it refused to release unless Carborundum paid the $241,000 due under the formula. Lake River did offer to sell the bagged product and place the proceeds in escrow until its dispute with Carborundum over the enforceability of the formula was resolved, but Carborundum rejected the offer and trucked in bagged Ferro Carbo from the East to serve its customers in Illinois, at an additional cost of $31,000.

Lake River brought this suit for $241,000, which it claims as liquidated damages. Carborundum counterclaimed for the value of the bagged Ferro Carbo when Lake River impounded it and the additional cost of serving the customers affected by the impounding. The theory of the counterclaim is that the impounding was a conversion, and not as Lake River contends the assertion of a lien. The district judge, after a bench trial, gave judgment for both parties. Carborundum ended up roughly $42,000 to the good: $269,000 + $31,000 − $241,000 − $17,000, the last figure representing prejudgment interest on Lake River's damages. (We have rounded off all dollar figures to the nearest thousand.) Both parties have appealed.

The hardest issue in the case is whether the formula in the minimum-guarantee clause imposes a penalty for breach of contract or is merely an effort to liquidate damages. Deep as the hostility to penalty clauses runs in the common law, we still might be inclined to question, if we thought ourselves free to do so, whether a modern court should refuse to enforce a penalty clause where the signator is a substantial corporation, well able to avoid improvident commitments. Penalty clauses provide an earnest of performance. The clause here enhanced Carborundum's credibility in promising to ship the minimum amount guaranteed by showing that it was willing to pay the full contract price even if it failed to ship anything. On the other side it can be pointed out that by raising the cost of a breach of contract to the contract breaker, a penalty clause increases the risk to his other creditors; increases (what is the same thing and more, because bankruptcy imposes "deadweight" social costs) the risk of bankruptcy; and could amplify the business cycle by increasing the number of bankruptcies in bad times, which is when contracts are most likely to be broken. But since little effort is made to prevent businessmen from assuming risks, these reasons are no better than makeweights.

A better argument is that a penalty clause may discourage efficient as well as inefficient breaches of contract. Suppose a breach would cost the promisee $12,000 in actual damages but would yield the promisor $20,000 in additional profits. Then there would be a net social gain from breach. After being fully compensated for his loss the promisee would be no worse off than if the contract had been performed, while the promisor would be better off by $8,000. But now suppose the contract contains a penalty clause under which the promisor if he breaks his promise must pay the promisee $25,000. The promisor will be discouraged from breaking the contract, since $25,000, the penalty, is greater than $20,000, the profits of the breach; and a transaction that would have increased value will be forgone.

On this view, since compensatory damages should be sufficient to deter inefficient breaches (that is, breaches that cost the victim more than the gain to the contract breaker), penal damages could have no effect other than to deter some efficient breaches. But this overlooks the earlier point that the willingness to agree to a penalty clause is a way of making the promisor and his promise credible and may therefore be essential to inducing some value-maximizing contracts to be made. It also overlooks the more important point that the parties (always assuming they are fully competent) will, in deciding whether to include a penalty clause in their contract, weigh the gains against the costs—costs that include the possibility of discouraging an efficient breach somewhere down the road—and will include the clause only if the benefits exceed those costs as well as all other costs.

On this view the refusal to enforce penalty clauses is (at best) paternalistic—and it seems odd that courts should display parental solicitude for large corporations. But however this may be, we must be on guard to avoid importing our own ideas of sound public policy into an area where our proper judicial role is more than usually deferential. The responsibility for making innovations in the common law of Illinois rests with the courts of Illinois, and not with the federal courts in Illinois. And like every other state, Illinois, untroubled by academic skepticism of the wisdom of refusing to enforce penalty clauses against sophisticated promisors, continues steadfastly to insist on the distinction between penalties and liquidated damages. To be valid under Illinois law a liquidation of damages must be a reasonable estimate at the time of contracting of the likely damages from breach, and the need for estimation at that time must be shown by reference to the likely difficulty of measuring the actual damages from a breach of contract after the breach occurs. If damages would be easy to determine then, or if the estimate greatly exceeds a reasonable upper estimate of what the damages are likely to be, it is a penalty.

Mindful that Illinois courts resolve doubtful cases in favor of classification as a penalty, we conclude that the damage formula in this case is a penalty and not a liquidation of damages, because it is designed always to assure Lake River more than its actual damages. The formula—full contract price minus the amount already invoiced to Carborundum—is invariant to the gravity of the breach. When a contract specifies a single sum in damages for any and all breaches even though it is apparent that all are not of the same gravity, the specification is not a reasonable effort to estimate damages; and when in addition the fixed sum greatly exceeds the actual damages likely to be inflicted by a minor breach, its character as a penalty becomes unmistakable. This case is within the gravitational field of these principles even though the minimum-guarantee clause does not fix a single sum as damages.

Suppose to begin with that the breach occurs the day after Lake River buys its new bagging system for $89,000 and before Carborundum ships any Ferro Carbo. Carborundum would owe Lake River $533,000. Since Lake River would have incurred at that point a total cost of only $89,000, its net gain from the breach would be $444,000. This is more than four times the profit of $107,000 (20 percent of the contract price of $533,000) that Lake River expected to make from the contract if it had been performed: a huge windfall.

Next suppose (as actually happened here) that breach occurs when 55 percent of the Ferro Carbo has been shipped. Lake River would already have received $293,000 from Carborundum. To see what its costs then would have been (as estimated at the time of contracting), first subtract Lake River's anticipated profit on the contract of $107,000 from the total contract price of $533,000. The difference—Lake River's total cost of performance—is $426,000. Of this, $89,000 is the cost of the new bagging system, a fixed cost. The rest ($426,000 – $89,000 = $337,000) presumably consists of variable costs that are roughly proportional to the amount of Ferro Carbo bagged; there is no indication of any other fixed costs. Assume, therefore, that if Lake River bagged 55 percent of the contractually agreed quantity, it incurred in doing so 55 percent of its variable costs, or $185,000.

When this is added to the cost of the new bagging system, assumed for the moment to be worthless except in connection with the contract, the total cost of performance to Lake River is $274,000. Hence a breach that occurred after 55 percent of contractual performance was complete would be expected to yield Lake

River a modest profit of $19,000 ($293,000 – $274,000). But now add the "liqui-
dated damages" of $241,000 that Lake River claims, and the result is a total gain
from the breach of $260,000, which is almost two and a half times the profit that
Lake River expected to gain if there was no breach. And this ignores any use value
or salvage value of the new bagging system, which is the property of Lake River—
though admittedly it also ignores the time value of money; Lake River paid $89,000
for that system before receiving any revenue from the contract.

To complete the picture, assume that the breach had not occurred till performance was 90 percent complete. Then the "liquidated damages" clause would not
be so one-sided, but it would be one-sided. Carborundum would have paid $480,000
for bagging. Against this, Lake River would have incurred its fixed cost of $89,000
plus 90 percent of its variable costs of $337,000, or $303,000. Its total costs would
thus be $392,000, and its net profit $88,000. But on top of this it would be entitled
to "liquidated damages" of $53,000, for a total profit of $141,000—more than 30
percent more than its expected profit of $107,000 if there was no breach.

The reason for these results is that most of the costs to Lake River of performing
the contract are saved if the contract is broken, and this saving is not reflected in the
damage formula. As a result, at whatever point in the life of the contract a breach
occurs, the damage formula gives Lake River more than its lost profits from the
breach—dramatically more if the breach occurs at the beginning of the contract;
tapering off at the end, it is true. Still, over the interval between the beginning of
Lake River's performance and nearly the end, the clause could be expected to generate profits ranging from 400 percent of the expected contract profits to 130
percent of those profits. And this is on the assumption that the bagging system has
no value apart from the contract. If it were worth only $20,000 to Lake River, the
range would be 434 percent to 150 percent.

Lake River argues that it would never get as much as the formula suggests, because it would be required to mitigate its damages. This is a dubious argument on
several grounds. First, mitigation of damages is a doctrine of the law of court-assessed damages, while the point of a liquidated-damages clause is to substitute party
assessment; and that point is blunted, and the certainty that liquidated-damages
clauses are designed to give the process of assessing damages impaired, if a defendant can force the plaintiff to take less than the damages specified in the clause, on
the ground that the plaintiff could have avoided some of them. It would seem therefore that the clause in this case should be read to eliminate any duty of mitigation,
that what Lake River is doing is attempting to rewrite the clause to make it more
reasonable, and that since actually the clause is designed to give Lake River the full
damages it would incur from breach (and more) even if it made no effort to find a
substitute use for the equipment that it bought to perform the contract, this is just

one more piece of evidence that it is a penalty clause rather than a liquidated-damages clause.

But in any event mitigation would not mitigate the penal character of this clause. If Carborundum did not ship the guaranteed minimum quantity, the reason was likely to be—the reason was—that the steel industry had fallen on hard times and the demand for Ferro Carbo was therefore down. In these circumstances Lake River would have little prospect of finding a substitute contract that would yield it significant profits to set off against the full contract price, which is the method by which it proposes to take account of mitigation. At argument Lake River suggested that it might at least have been able to sell the new bagging equipment to someone for something, and the figure $40,000 was proposed. If the breach occurred on the first day when performance under the contract was due and Lake River promptly sold the bagging equipment for $40,000, its liquidated damages would fall to $493,000. But by the same token its costs would fall to $49,000. Its profit would still be $444,000, which as we said was more than 400 percent of its expected profit on the contract. The penal component would be unaffected.

With the penalty clause in this case compare the liquidated-damages clause in *Arduini v. Board of Education,* which is representative of such clauses upheld in Illinois. The plaintiff was a public school teacher whose contract provided that if he resigned before the end of the school year he would be docked 4 percent of his salary. This was a modest fraction of the contract price. And the cost to the school of an untimely resignation would be difficult to measure. Since that cost would be greater the more senior and experienced the teacher was, the fact that the liquidated damages would be greater the higher the teacher's salary did not make the clause arbitrary. Even the fact that the liquidated damages were the same whether the teacher resigned at the beginning, the middle, or the end of the school year was not arbitrary, for it was unclear how the amount of actual damages would vary with the time of resignation. Although one might think that the earlier the teacher resigned the greater the damage to the school would be, the school might find it easier to hire a replacement for the whole year or a great part of it than to bring in a replacement at the last minute to grade the exams left behind by the resigning teacher. Here, in contrast, it is apparent from the face of the contract that the damages provided for by the "liquidated damages" clause are grossly disproportionate to any probable loss and penalize some breaches much more heavily than others regardless of relative cost.

We do not mean by this discussion to cast a cloud of doubt over the "take or pay" clauses that are a common feature of contracts between natural gas pipeline companies and their customers. Such clauses require the customer, in consideration of the pipeline's extending its line to his premises, to take a certain amount of gas at a specified price—and if he fails to take it to pay the full price anyway. The resemblance to the minimum-guarantee clause in the present case is obvious, but perhaps quite superficial. Neither party has mentioned take-or-pay clauses, and we can find no case where such a clause was even challenged as a penalty clause—though in one case it was argued that such a clause made the damages unreasonably low. If, as appears not to be the case here but would often be the case in supplying natural gas, a supplier's fixed costs were a very large fraction of his total costs, a take-or-pay clause might well be a reasonable liquidation of damages. In the limit, if all the supplier's costs were incurred before he began supplying the customer, the contract revenues would be an excellent measure of the damages from breach. But in this case, the supplier (Lake River, viewed as a supplier of bagging services to Carborundum) incurred only a fraction of its costs before performance began, and the interruption of performance generated a considerable cost saving that is not reflected in the damage formula.

The fact that the damage formula is invalid does not deprive Lake River of a remedy. The parties did not contract explicitly with reference to the measure of damages if the agreed-on damage formula was invalidated, but all this means is that the victim of the breach is entitled to his common law damages. In this case that would be the unpaid contract price of $241,000 minus the costs that Lake River saved by not having to complete the contract (the variable costs on the other 45 percent of the Ferro Carbo that it never had to bag). The case must be remanded to the district judge to fix these damages.

QUESTIONS AND NOTES

1. Judge Posner says that on remand Lake River will be permitted to prove damages based on the contract price less savings (variable costs saved). Should it alternatively be permitted to recover its outlays in reliance less the present market value of the machinery it purchased? Recall *Anglia Television v. Reed*, p. 134. Which measure will yield a larger damages award?

2. The doctrinal and policy concerns in *Lake River,* and in most reported liquidated damage cases, are whether the liquidated damages are set too high, overcompensate the injured party, encourage inefficient over-performance, and therefore run afoul of the penalty doctrine. Historically there has been scant concern in the courts about liquidated damages that are set so low that they operate as a limitation on liability. As a general doctrinal matter limitations on liability are enforceable in accordance with their terms, unless they are so extreme as to systematically deny an injured party any practical remedy or otherwise operate in an unconscionable manner. UCC-2-719. But as a matter of contract design (as opposed

to doctrine) unreasonably low liquidated damages can raise the concern of encouraging inefficient breach. In one well known experiment, Uri Gneezy & Aldo Rustichini, *A Fine is a Price*, 29 J. LEG. STUD. 1 (2000), the researchers found that the number of late pick-ups from child care centers **doubled** after a small monetary penalty for each instance of late pick-up was introduced. Viewing payment of a small fine as an option, parents had less compunction about violating their contractual commitment to timely pick up their children. So, ironically, they breached more often after the introduction of the small monetary penalty than they did when there was no penalty at all. Going further, in three interesting studies conducted over the internet by Tess Wilkinson-Ryan, *Do Liquidated Damages Encourage Breach?: A Psychological Experiment*, 108 MICH. L. REV. 633 (2010), the research showed that liquidated damages (even those set at a slightly punitive level) had the effect of encouraging efficient breach as compared to a control condition where no liquidated amount was fixed in the parties' agreement.

California & Hawaiian Sugar Co. v. Sun Ship
United States Court of Appeals, Ninth Circuit, 1987.
794 F.2d 1433, as modified, 811 F.2d 1264.

■ NOONAN, J.

. . .

C and H is an agricultural cooperative owned by fourteen sugar plantations in Hawaii. Its business consists in transporting raw sugar—the crushed cane in the form of coarse brown crystal—to its refinery in Crockett, California. Roughly one million tons a year of sugar are harvested in Hawaii. A small portion is refined there; the bulk goes to Crockett. The refined sugar—the white stuff—is sold by C and H to groceries for home consumption and to the soft drink and cereal companies that are its industrial customers.

To conduct its business, C and H has an imperative need for assured carriage for the raw sugar from the islands. Sugar is a seasonal crop, with 70 percent of the harvest occurring between April and October, while almost nothing is harvestable during December and January. Consequently, transportation must not only be available, but seasonably available. Storage capacity in Hawaii accommodates not more than a quarter of the crop. Left stored on the ground or left unharvested, sugar suffers the loss of sucrose and goes to waste. Shipping ready and able to carry the raw sugar is a priority for C and H.

In 1979 C and H was notified that Matson Navigation Company, which had been supplying the bulk of the necessary shipping, was withdrawing its services as of January 1981. While C and H had some ships at its disposal, it found a pressing need for a large new vessel, to be in service at the height of the sugar season in 1981. It decided to commission the building of a kind of hybrid—a tug of catamaran design with two hulls and, joined to the tug, a barge with a wedge which would lock between the two pontoons of the tug, producing an "integrated tug barge." In Hawaiian, the barge and the entire vessel were each described as a Mocababoo or push boat.

C and H relied on the architectural advice of the New York firm, J.J. Henry. It solicited bids from shipyards, indicating as an essential term a "preferred delivery date" of June 1981. It decided to accept Sun's offer to build the barge and Halter's offer to build the tug.

In the fall of 1979 C and H entered into negotiations with Sun on the precise terms of the contract. Each company was represented by a vice-president with managerial responsibility in the area of negotiation; each company had a team of negotiators; each company had the advice of counsel in drafting the agreement that was signed on November 14, 1979. This agreement was entitled "Contract for the Construction of One Oceangoing Barge for California and Hawaiian Sugar Company By Sun Ship, Inc." The "Whereas" clause of the contract identified C and H as the Purchaser, and Sun as the Contractor; it identified "one non-self-propelled oceangoing barge" as the Vessel that Purchaser was buying from Contractor. Article I provided that Contractor would deliver the Vessel on June 30, 1981. The contract price was $25,405,000.

Under Article I of the agreement, Sun was entitled to an extension of the delivery date for the usual types of force majeure and for "unavailability of the Tug to Contractor for joining to the Vessel, where it is determined that Contractor has complied with all obligations under the Interface Agreement." (The Interface Agreement, executed the same day between C and H, Sun, and Halter provided that Sun would connect the barge with the tug.) Article 17 "Delivery" provided that "the Vessel shall be offered for delivery fully and completely connected with the Tug." Article 8, "Liquidated Damages for Delay in Delivery" provided that if "Delivery of the Vessel" was not made on "the Delivery Date" of June 30, 1981, Sun would pay C and H "as per-day liquidated damages, and not as a penalty" a sum described as "a reasonable measure of the damages"—$17,000 per day.

On the same date C and H entered into an agreement with Halter to purchase "one oceangoing catamaran tug boat" for $20,350,000. The tug (the "Vessel" of that contract) was to be delivered on April 30, 1981 at Sun's shipyard. Liquidated damages of $10,000 per day were provided for Halter's failure to deliver.

Halter did not complete the tug until July 15, 1982. Sun did not complete the barge until March 16, 1982. Tug and barge were finally connected under C and H's direction in mid-July 1982 and christened the *Moku Pahu*. C and H settled its claim against Halter. Although Sun paid C and H $17,000 per day from June 30, 1981 until January 10, 1982, it ultimately denied liability for any damages, and this lawsuit resulted.

ANALYSIS

Sun contends that its obligation was to deliver the barge connected to the tug on the delivery date of June 30, 1981 and that only the failure to deliver the integrated hybrid would have triggered the liquidated damage clause. It is true that Article 17 creates some ambiguity by specifying that the Vessel is to be "offered for delivery completely connected with the Tug." The case of the barge being ready while the tug was not, is not explicitly considered. Nonetheless, the meaning of "Vessel" is completely unambiguous. From the "Whereas" clause to the articles of the agreement dealing with insurance, liens, and title, "the Vessel" is the barge. It would require the court to rewrite the contract to find that "the Vessel" in Article 8 on liquidated damages does not mean the barge. The article takes effect on failure to deliver "the Vessel"—that is, the barge.

Sun contends, however, that on such a reading of the contract, the $17,000 per day is a penalty, not to be enforced by the court. The barge, Sun points out, was useless to C and H without the tug. Unconnected, the barge was worse than useless—it was an expensive liability. C and H did not want the barge by itself. To get $17,000 per day as "damages" for failure to provide an unwanted and unusable craft is, Sun says, to exact a penalty. C and H seeks to be "paid according to the tenour of the bond"; it "craves the law." And if C and H sticks to the letter of the bond, it must like Shylock end by losing; a court of justice will not be so vindictive. Breach of contract entitles the wronged party only to fair compensation.

Seductive as Sun's argument is, it does not carry the day. Represented by sophisticated representatives, C and H and Sun reached the agreement that $17,000 a day was the reasonable measure of the loss C and H would suffer if the barge was not ready. Of course they assumed that the tug would be ready. But in reasonable anticipation of the damages that would occur if the tug was ready and the barge was not, Article 8 was adopted. As the parties foresaw the situation, C and H would have a tug waiting connection but no barge and so no shipping. The anticipated damages were what might be expected if C and H could not transport the Hawaiian sugar crop at the height of the season. Those damages were clearly before both parties. As Joe Kleschick, Sun's chief negotiator, testified, he had "a vision" of a "mountain of sugar piling up in Hawaii"—a vision that C and H conjured up in negotiating the damage clause. Given the anticipated impact on C and H's raw sugar and on C and H's ability to meet the demands of its grocery and industrial customers if the sugar could not be transported, liquidated damages of $17,000 a day were completely reasonable.

The situation as it developed was different from the anticipation. The barge was not ready but neither was the tug. C and H was in fact able to find other shipping. The crop did not rot. The customers were not left sugarless. Sun argues that, measured by the actual damages suffered, the liquidated damages were penal.

We look to Pennsylvania law for guidance. Although no Pennsylvania case is squarely on point, it is probable that Pennsylvania would interpret the contract as a sale of goods governed by the Uniform Commercial Code. The governing statute provides that liquidated damages are considered reasonable "in the light of anticipated or actual harm." 12A Pa.Cons.Stat.Ann. 2–718(1) (Purdon 1970) (Pennsylvania's adoption of the Uniform Commercial Code).

The choice of the disjunctive appears to be deliberate. The language chosen is in harmony with the Restatement (Second) of Contracts § 356 (1979), which permits liquidated damages in the light of the anticipated or actual loss caused by the breach and the difficulties of proof of loss. Section 356, Comment b declares explicitly: "Furthermore, the amount fixed is reasonable to the extent that it approximates the loss anticipated at the time of the making of the contract, even though it may not approximate the actual loss."

Despite the statutory disjunctive and the Restatement's apparent blessing of it, the question is not settled by these authorities which must be read in the light of common law principles already established and accepted in Pennsylvania. Prior to the adoption of the Uniform Commercial Code, Pennsylvania enforced liquidated damage clauses that its courts labeled as nonpenal, but equitable considerations relating to the actual harm incurred were taken into account along with the difficulty of proving damages if a liquidated damage clause was rejected. We do not believe that the U.C.C. overrode this line of reasoning. Indeed, in a lower court case, decided after the U.C.C.'s enactment, it was stated that if liquidated damages appear unreasonable in light of the harm suffered, "the contractual provision will be voided as a penalty." *Unit Vending Corp. v. Tobin Enterprises*, 194 Pa.Super. 470, 473 (1961). That case, however, is not on all fours with our case: Unit Vending involved an adhesion contract between parties of unequal bargaining power; the unfair contract was characterized by the court as "a clever attempt to secure both the penny and the cake" by the party with superior strength. Mechanically to read it as Pennsylvania law governing this case would be a mistake. The case, however, does show that Pennsylvania courts, like courts elsewhere, attempt to interpret the governing statute humanely and equitably.

The Restatement § 356 Comment b, after accepting anticipated damages as a measure, goes on to say that if the difficulty of proof of loss is slight, then actual damage may be the measure of reasonableness: "If, to take an extreme case, it is clear that no loss at all has occurred, a provision fixing a substantial sum as damages is unenforceable. See Illustration 4." Illustration 4 is a case of a contractor, A, agreeing to build B's race track by a specific date and to pay B $1,000 a day for every day's delay. A delays a month, but B does not get permission to operate the track for that month, so B suffers no loss. In that event, the Restatement characterizes the $1,000 per day as an unenforceable penalty. Sun contends that it is in the position of A: no actual loss was suffered by C and H because C and H had no tug to mate with the barge.

This argument restates in a new form Sun's basic contention that the liquidated damage clause was meant to operate only if the integrated tug barge was not delivered. The argument has been rejected by us as a misinterpretation of the contract. But in its new guise it gains appeal. If Illustration 4 is the present case, Sun is home scot-free. The Restatement, however, deals with a case where the defaulting contractor was alone in his default. We deal with a case of concurrent defaults. If we were to be so literal-minded as to follow the Restatement here, we would have to conclude that because both parties were in default, C and H suffered no damage until one party performed. Not until the barge was ready in March 1982 could C and H hold Halter for damages, and then only for the period after that date. The continued default of both parties would operate to take each of them off the hook. That cannot be the law.

Sun objects that Halter had a more absolute obligation to deliver than Sun did. Halter did not have to deliver the integrated tug, only the tug itself; it was not excused by Sun's default. Hence the spectacle of two defaulting contractors causing no damages would not be presented here. But Sun's objection does not meet the point that Halter's unexcused delivery would, on Sun's theory, have generated no damages. The tug by itself would have been no use to C and H.

We conclude, therefore, that in this case of concurrent causation each defaulting contractor is liable for the breach and for the substantial damages which the joint breach occasions. Sun is a substantial cause of the damages flowing from the lack of the integrated tug; Sun cannot be absolved by the absence of the tug.

Sun has a final argument. Even on the assumption that it is liable as a substantial cause of the breach of contract, Sun contends that the actual damages suffered by C and H for lack of the integrated tug boat were slight. Actual damages were found by the district court to consist of "interest on progress payments, unfavorable terms of conversion to long-term financing, and additional labor expense." No dollar amount was determined by the district court in finding that these damages "bore a reasonable relationship to the amount liquidated in the Barge Contract."

The dollar value of the damages found by the district judge is, to judge from C and H's own computation, as follows:

Additional Construction Interest	$1,486,000
Added Payments to J.J. Henry	161,000
Added Vessel Operating Expenses	73,000
C and H Employee Costs	109,000
	$1,829,000

But "actual damages" have no meaning if the actual savings of C and H due to the nondelivery of the integrated tug barge are not subtracted. It was clearly erroneous for the district judge to exclude these savings from his finding. These savings, again according to C and H's own computation, were:

Transportation savings	$ 525,000
Lay-up costs	$ 936,000
	$ 1,461,000

The net actual damages suffered by C and H were $368,000. As a matter of law, Sun contends that the liquidated damages are unreasonably disproportionate to the net actual damages.

C and H urges on us the precedent of *Bellefonte Borough Authority v. Gateway Equipment & Supply Co.*, 442 Pa. 492 (1971), forfeiting a bid bond of $45,000 on the failure of a contractor to perform a municipal contract, even though the loss to the municipality was $1,000; the disproportion was 45 to 1. But that decision is not decisive here. It did not purport to apply the Uniform Commercial Code. Rules appropriate for bids to the government are sufficiently different from those applicable between private parties to prevent instant adoption of this precedent. A fuller look at relevant contract law is appropriate.

Litigation has blurred the line between a proper and a penal clause, and the distinction is "not an easy one to draw in practice." *Lake River Corp. v. Carborundum Co.*, 769 F.2d 1284, 1290 (7th Cir.1985) (per Posner, J.). But the desire of courts to avoid the enforcement of penalties should not obscure common law principles followed in Pennsylvania. Contracts are contracts because they contain enforceable promises, and absent some overriding public policy, those promises are to be enforced. "Where each of the parties is content to take the risk of its turning out in a particular way" why should one "be released from the contract, if there were no misrepresentation or other want of fair dealing?" *Ashcom v. Smith*, 2 Pen. & W. 211, 218–219 (Pa.1830) (per Gibson, C.J.). Promising to pay damages of a fixed amount, the parties normally have a much better sense of what damages can occur. Courts must be reluctant to override their judgment. Where damages are real but difficult to prove, injustice will be done the injured party if the court substitutes the requirements of judicial proof for the parties' own informed agreement as to what is a reasonable measure of damages. Pennsylvania acknowledges that a seller is bound to pay consequential damages if the seller had reason to know of the buyer's special circumstances. The liquidated damage clause here functions in lieu of a court's determination of the consequential damages suffered by C and H.

These principles inform a leading common law case in the field, *Clydebank Engineering & Shipbuilding Co. v. Yzquierdo y Castaneda*, 1905 A.C. 6. The defendant shipyard had agreed to pay 500 pounds per week per vessel for delay in the delivery of four torpedo boat destroyers to the Spanish Navy in 1897. The shipyard pointed out that had the destroyers been delivered on schedule they would have been sunk with the rest of the Spanish Navy by the Americans in 1898. The House of Lords found the defense unpersuasive. To prove damages the whole administration of the Spanish Navy would have had to have been investigated. The House of Lords refused to undertake such a difficult investigation when the parties had made an honest effort in advance to set in monetary terms what the lack of the destroyers would mean to Spain.

C and H is not the Spanish Navy, but the exact damages caused its manifold operations by lack of the integrated tug boat are equally difficult of ascertainment. Proof of its loss is difficult—as difficult, perhaps, as proof of loss would have been if the sugar crop had been delivered late because shipping was missing. Whatever the loss, the parties had promised each other that $17,000 per day was a reasonable measure. The court must decline to substitute the requirements of judicial proof for the parties' own conclusion. The *Moku Pahu*, available on June 30, 1981, was a great prize, capable of multiple employments and enlarging the uses of the entire C and H fleet. When sophisticated parties with bargaining parity have agreed what lack of this prize would mean, and it is now difficult to measure what the lack did mean, the court will uphold the parties' bargain. C and H is entitled to keep the liquidated damages of $3,298,000 it has already received and to receive additional liquidated damages of $1,105,000 with interest thereon, less setoffs determined by the district court.

. . .

AFFIRMED.

QUESTIONS AND NOTES

1. In this case C & H's damages for late delivery of the barge are easy to compute in precisely the way the court did compute them. If the barge is delivered late, the loss will be however much it costs to "cover" by hiring other transportation for the sugar, less the savings from not having to operate the barge. Only if one assumes that there is no alternative transport available between Hawaii and California, a highly unlikely supposition, would there be any difficulty in calculating damages.

Assuming that this is so, should the law allow the parties to fix damages by whatever measure they choose? That is, if C & H, for its own reasons, wants to motivate Sun Ship to perform on time so it sets liquidated damages at $17,000 per day and Sun Ship freely agrees to this arrangement, why should the rest of us care? Putting the matter in slightly different form, should the law insist that contract damages be displaced by liquidated damages clauses only when it is difficult to compute actual damages or the rule in *Hadley v. Baxendale* is likely to foreclose the injured party from recovering losses actually suffered?

2. Is it efficient to hold Sun Ship liable for damages under circumstances where prompt performance would be costly to it and yet result in no economic benefit to C & H in light of Halter's continuing delay?

3. Given that neither the barge nor the tug were ready on time, if there were no liquidated damages clause, could Sun Ship, the barge builder, and Halter, the tug manufacturer, each point at the other and claim that its breach did not cause the damages, but that it was the other party's fault? What does the court mean when it holds "each defaulting contractor ... liable ... for the substantial damages which the joint breach occasions"? Aren't there actually separate breaches of independent contracts here rather than a joint breach? For a thorough analysis of the problem of allocating damages between Halter and Sun Ship, see Daniel J. Bussel, *Liability for Concurrent Breach of Contract*, 73 WASH. U. L.Q. 97 (1995).

4. The Court of Appeals affirmed the award of $4,403,000 in liquidated damages to C & H when the actual damages suffered were less than a tenth that amount, a mere $368,000. How disproportionate must the loss be from the actual damages before a court will attach the label "penalty" and invalidate the contract clause?

Compare the following statement by Judge Van Oosterhout in a similar situation in *Southwest Engineering Co. v. United States*, 341 F.2d 998, 1003 (8th Cir. 1965):

> When parties have by their contract agreed upon a liquidated damages provision as a reasonable forecast of just compensation for breach of contract and damages are difficult to estimate accurately, such provision should be enforced. If in the course of subsequent developments, damages prove to be greater than those stipulated, the party entitled to damages is bound by the liquidated damages agreement. It is not unfair to hold the contractor performing the work to such agreement if by reason of later developments damages prove to be less or nonexistent. Each party by entering into such contractual provision took a calculated risk and is bound by reasonable contractual provisions pertaining to liquidated damages.

Doesn't this approach eliminate the actual harm prong of the penalty doctrine? Consider, on the other hand, the dissenting judge's view on a liquidated damages clause when there is no actual harm in *Barrie School v. Patch*, 933 A.2d 382, 396, 404 (Md. 2007) (dissenting):

> It does not follow that merely because a contract contains a liquidated damages clause, which facially is not punitive, upon breach, damages in the amount stipulated automatically will be awarded to the non-breaching party….[W]here the non-breaching party has suffered no damages, or relatively insignificant damages in comparison to the stipulated sum, due to the breach…that fact must be taken into account.

The majority in *Barrie* this case, nevertheless, ruled that the validity of a liquidated damages clause is to be determined by "looking to the stipulated loss at the time of the contract's formation, and not the actual losses resulting from breach." It found the fact that the plaintiff suffered no actual damages irrelevant to the validity of the clause. Should actual damages be relevant to whether the liquidated damage clause operates as a penalty?

5. Even assuming that non-delivery of the barge could reasonably be anticipated to result in spoilage of the sugar crop, how could $17,000 per day have been a reasonable estimate of this future harm from Sun Ship's breach? Consider whether it was likely that damages would run at the same rate whether it was sugar season or not. Consider how the estimated harm from non-delivery of the tug could be only $10,000 per day if $17,000 per day was the reasonable estimate of harm from non-delivery of the barge.

WEST'S ANN. CALIFORNIA CIVIL CODE:

§ 1671. Validity; Standards for Determination; Applicability of Section.

(a) This section does not apply in any case where another statute expressly applicable to the contract prescribes the rules or standard for determining the validity of a provision in the contract liquidating the damages for the breach of the contract.

(b) Except as provided in subdivision (c), a provision in a contract liquidating the damages for the breach of the contract is valid unless the party seeking to invalidate the provision establishes that the provision was unreasonable under the circumstances existing at the time the contract was made.

(c) The validity of a liquidated damages provision shall be determined under subdivision (d) and not under subdivision (b) where the liquidated damages are sought to be recovered from either:

(1) A party to a contract for the retail purchase, or rental, by such party of personal property or services, primarily for the party's personal, family, or household purposes; or

(2) A party to a lease of real property for use as a dwelling by the party or those dependent upon the party for support.

(d) In the cases described in subdivision (c), a provision in a contract liquidating damages for the breach of the contract is void except that the parties to such a contract may agree therein upon an amount which shall be presumed to be the amount of damage sustained by a breach thereof, when, from the nature of the case, it would be impracticable or extremely difficult to fix the actual damage.

IV. ARBITRATION

We have seen that the law recognizes that parties possess at least limited power to define the remedies available for breach of their agreement. To the extent liquidated damages provisions are enforced, parties can tailor the remedial aspects of their relationship when the rules of law fail to meet their special needs. Another common device that can be used to the same end is the arbitration clause, which substitutes a decision by an arbitrator selected by the parties for the judgment of a court. The spotty history of arbitration clauses at common law is traced by Judge Jerome Frank in the excerpt that follows.

■ FRANK, J. in *Kulukundis Shipping Co. v. Amtorg Trading Corp.*, 126 F.2d 978, 982–85 (2d Cir. 1942):

In considering these contentions in the light of the precedents, it is necessary to take into account the history of the judicial attitude towards arbitration: The English courts, while giving full effect to agreements to submit controversies to arbitration after they had ripened into arbitrators' awards, would—over a long period beginning at the end of the 17th century—do little or nothing to prevent or make irksome the breach of such agreements when they were still executory.[5] Prior to 1687, such a breach could be made costly: a penal bond given to abide the result of an arbitration

---

5. The early English history of enforcement of executory arbitration agreements is not too clear. Arbitration was used by the medieval guilds and in early maritime transactions. Some persons trace an influence back to Roman law, doubtless itself affected by Greek law; others discern the influence of ecclesiastical law.

had a real bite, since a breach of the bond's condition led to a judgment for the amount of the penalty. It was so held in 1609 in *Vynior's Case*, 8 Coke Rep. 81b. To be sure, Coke there, in a dictum, citing precedents, dilated on the inherent revocability of the authority given to an arbitrator; such a revocation was not too important, however, if it resulted in a stiff judgment on a penal bond. But the Statute of Fines and Penalties (8 & 9 Wm. III c. 11, § 8), enacted in 1687, provided that in an action on any bond given for performance of agreements, while judgment would be entered for the penalty, execution should issue only for the damages actually sustained. Coke's dictum as to revocability, uttered seventy-eight years earlier, now took on a new significance, as it was now held that for breach of an undertaking to arbitrate the damages were only nominal. Recognizing the effect of the impact of this statute on executory arbitration agreements, Parliament, eleven years later, enacted a statute, 9 Wm. III c. 15 (1698), designed to remedy the situation by providing that, if an agreement to arbitrate so provided, it could be made a "rule of court" (i.e., a court order), in which event it became irrevocable, and one who revoked it would be subject to punishment for contempt of court; but the submission was revocable until such a rule of court had been obtained. This statute, limited in scope, was narrowly construed and was of little help. The ordinary executory arbitration agreement thus lost all real efficacy since it was not specifically enforceable in equity, and was held not to constitute the basis of a plea in bar in, or a stay of, a suit on the original cause of action. In admiralty, the rulings were much the same.

It has been well said that "the legal mind must assign some reason in order to decide anything with spiritual quiet." And so, by way of rationalization, it became fashionable in the middle of the 18th century to say that such agreements were against public policy because they "oust the jurisdiction" of the courts. But that was a quaint explanation, inasmuch as an award, under an arbitration agreement, enforced both at law and in equity, was no less an ouster; and the same was true of releases and covenants not to sue, which were given full effect. Moreover, the agreement to arbitrate was not illegal, since suit could be maintained for its breach. Here was a clear instance of what Holmes called a "right" to break a contract and to substitute payment of damages for non-performance; as, in this type of case, the damages were only nominal, that "right" was indeed meaningful.

An effort has been made to justify this judicial hostility to the executory arbitration agreement on the ground that arbitrations, if unsupervised by the courts, are undesirable, and that legislation was needed to make possible such supervision. But if that was the reason for unfriendliness to such executory agreements, then the courts should also have refused to aid arbitrations when they ripened into awards. And what the English courts, especially the equity courts, did in other contexts, shows that, if they had had the will, they could have devised means of protecting parties to arbitrations. Instead, they restrictively interpreted successive statutes intended to give effect to executory arbitrations. No similar hostility was displayed by the Scotch courts. Lord Campbell explained the English attitude as due to the desire of the judges, at a time when their salaries came largely from fees, to avoid loss of income. Indignation has been voiced at this suggestion; perhaps it is unjustified. Perhaps the true explanation is the hypnotic power of the phrase, "oust the jurisdiction." Give a bad dogma a good name and its bite may become as bad as its bark.

In 1855, in *Scott v. Avery*, 5 H.C.L. 811, the tide seemed to have turned. There it was held that if a policy made an award of damages by arbitrators a condition precedent to a suit on the policy, a failure to submit to arbitration would preclude such a suit, even if the policy left to the arbitrators the consideration of all the elements of liability. But, despite later legislation, the hostility of the English courts to executory arbitrations resumed somewhat after *Scott v. Avery*, and seems never to have been entirely dissipated.

That English attitude was largely taken over in the 19th century by most courts in this country. Indeed, in general, they would not go as far as *Scott v. Avery*, and continued to use the "ouster of jurisdiction" concept: An executory agreement to arbitrate would not be given specific performance or furnish the basis of a stay of proceedings on the original cause of action. Nor would it be given effect as a plea in bar, except in limited instances, i.e., in the case of an agreement expressly or impliedly making it a condition precedent to litigation that there be an award determining some preliminary question of subsidiary fact upon which any liability was to be contingent. In the case of broader executory agreements, no more than nominal damages would be given for a breach.

Generally speaking, then, the courts of this country were unfriendly to executory arbitration agreements. The lower federal courts, feeling bound to comply with the precedents, nevertheless became critical of this judicial hostility. There were intimations in the Supreme Court that perhaps the old view might be abandoned, but in the cases hinting at that newer attitude the issue was not raised. Effective state arbitration statutes were enacted beginning with the New York Statute of 1920.

Forty-nine states and the District of Columbia have adopted arbitration statutes modeled on either the 1955 Uniform Arbitration Act promulgated by the National Commissioners on Uniform State Laws, or its successor, the 2000 Revised Uniform Arbitration Act. 7 U.L.A. § 1 *et seq.* In addition, the Federal Arbitration Act, 9 U.S.C. § 1 *et seq.*, embodying a federal policy favoring arbitration in matters touching on interstate commerce, broadly preempts state laws denying or limiting enforcement of contractual arbitration provisions.

Arbitration has long been the dominant means of enforcing collective bargaining agreements, including resolving labor contract grievances and disputes. In addition, a large and steadily increasing portion of commercial agreements contain arbitration clauses that remove dispute resolution from the courts. Many major institutions (and some entire industries) insist on arbitration clauses in all their agreements. Industries with strong trade associations often provide arbitration procedures for the resolution of disputes involving members and their customers, including, notably, the securities industry. Many construction contracts are based on the standard forms of the American Institute of Architects, which provide for arbitration of all disputes. Increasingly, standard form sales documents will include an arbitration provision among the "boiler plate" printed clauses. In international transactions, arbitration clauses provide a convenient way to avoid foreign and potentially hostile court systems. The United States and 155 other nations (including all our major trading partners) have acceded to the UN Convention on the Recognition and Enforcement of Foreign Arbitral Awards, popularly known as the New York Convention. The New York Convention greatly simplifies, and therefore promotes, the use of arbitration in international transactions by making the enforcement of an arbitration award simpler and often more certain than the enforcement of a foreign court judgment.

Arbitration is primarily a mechanism for the resolution of disputes that may arise in the future. It can also, however, substitute for contract preplanning if the parties cannot agree in advance on how to deal with a known contract issue. Instead of specifying the rights and liabilities of the parties in a given situation, the parties may authorize an arbitrator to declare their rights should the situation require. Used in this way, the arbitration clause may tend to swallow up the substantive provisions of the contract.

ALBERT D. ANGEL, THE USE OF ARBITRATION CLAUSES AS A MEANS FOR THE RESOLUTION OF IMPASSES ARISING IN THE NEGOTIATION OF, OR DURING THE LIFE OF, LONG-TERM CONTRACTUAL RELATIONSHIPS, 28 BUS. LAW. 589, 590–92 (1973):[*]

Where the parties are negotiating a long-term relationship, an impasse or delay caused by excessively detailed provision drafting can destroy the aura of good feeling previously carefully constructed and nurtured. Joint ventures, and many license and acquisition agreement negotiations, find the parties like prospective marriage partners. They are skittish enough without having to consider what they will do when they argue or want a divorce at some future date. Counsel often risks losing a favorable opportunity for his client if he insists on negotiating detailed contract provisions

---

to cover contingencies beyond both parties' control which may or may not occur in the future. An arbitration clause properly drafted can provide a vehicle for resolution of such matters if they arise and avoid bogging down negotiations. For example, a new process being licensed may have one or two known uses which can adequately be dealt with in the agreement. But both parties may sincerely believe that other uses will develop during the course of the agreement. The licensee naturally wishes complete assurance that he will be free to use the process in this projected new manner paying a just royalty. The licensor often wishes to encourage search for new applications for its process but fears inadequate compensation. There are a number of ways to resolve such impasses. But one which you should consider is an arbitration provision which provides for third party resolution of disputes as to royalty rate for new applications should the parties be unable to resolve the matter between themselves. Similarly, arbitration clauses can be used as safety valves where fears develop that a royalty rate, presently satisfactory, will prove destructive after future market price erosion, or process or product obsolescence.

Arbitration clauses can also be used in those situations where the prospective partners *know* they are going to clash and wish outside expert assistance. For example, in one recent acquisition negotiation involving a United States company as purchaser and an Italian seller, the purchaser was willing to pay a specified price per share only if earnings proved to be as represented. As many of you may know, one cannot determine what many Italian or other companies are earning by looking at their balance sheets or tax returns. Often several sets of books are kept. And so the parties agreed that each would retain a U.S. based accounting firm to audit and recast the Italian company's books. If both accounting firms could agree on the treatment of a particular item under U.S. accounting principles, there would be no problem. But if they could not, they were authorized to choose a third firm from an agreed list whose determination would be final.

If the parties had attempted to draft provisions to determine which of the many conflicting U.S. accounting principles would apply in several dozen different situations, they would have never been able to leave the negotiating table. This unusual arbitration clause avoided this problem. It also served the very important purpose of avoiding a situation where the principals would be calling into question each other's principles. The agreement provided for insulation of the clients from these often arcane disputes.

Arbitration clauses can also be useful in assisting parties to resolve disputes which arise in the course of a projected long-term collaboration without souring that relationship. Anyone who has ever engaged in international negotiations knows that "face" is important ... to nearly all nationalities. (Indeed, I would venture to guess that more prospective mergers between two U.S. companies founder because of problems of "face" and "status" among the executives of the prospective partners than one might suspect from press reports.) We can learn from the Japanese and Chinese in this respect.

In a recent article in *The Business Lawyer*, the author noted that

In Japan a person who asserts rigid legal rights is thought to be "inflexible" and selfish. The businessman never introduces a lawyer into a domestic business conference. Introduction of a lawyer into a business conference is thought to be an unfriendly act, an act equal to an explicit threat of litigation.

The author concludes that the Japanese feel that every practical problem should be solved by mutual compromise and accommodation, "regardless of formal rights and obligations."

Those who have engaged in negotiating sessions with the mainland Chinese have found that "* * * the Chinese will go to great lengths to avoid any kind of formal arbitration over the disagreements, problems and tensions which eventually arise in international business. All Chinese contracts have a clause requiring disagreements be settled through 'friendly negotiations' first, before arbitration."

All this is contrary to the instinct of many U.S. counsel not engaged in international practice. Many U.S. counsel insist upon an arbitration provision providing that arbitration can be speedily invoked with a prompt judicially enforceable decision to follow. But in long-term relationships such as joint ventures, where many future dispute areas can be identified which may be important yet not go to the heart of the relationship, a simple arbitration proceeding, resulting in a clear victory or defeat, may prove too destructive. Any victory will be pyrrhic if it makes future cooperation problematical.

In such circumstances, whether international or domestic relationships are involved, counsel should seriously consider contractual vehicles that allow parties to reason together. For example, there are joint venture agreements which provide that where there are disputes which the operational representatives of each party cannot resolve, they are to call in senior management members of the parent companies to arbitrate or mediate the dispute informally. Some agreements have provided for several layers of this type of informal arbitration—internal appeals courts which may dissipate the heat of the moment. I should emphasize that these are circumstances where preservation of the relationship between the parties is of profound importance. Thus, efforts at inter-party resolution are institutionalized by the agreement which requires that the party resort to this before turning to more traditional and formal arbitration proceedings. Those of you familiar with labor-management disputes will note the similarity of the foregoing contract provisions with grievance mechanisms. The analogy is well taken. The important characteristic here is the provision of a system to which the parties may resort without loss of "face." In effect, these agreements provide that joint venture managers must turn to avuncular senior management for help in resolving disputes before proceeding further. Although one might think that this is what they would do in any event, providing for this procedure in the agreement has been found most constructive where the heat of the moment obscures reason.

It is interesting to note that the laws of several countries permit parties to statutory arbitrations to request the legally appointed arbitrator or mediator to conciliate before arriving at a decision. These proceedings, as well as the informal internal arbitrations I have just described, are much more subtle than the head-chopping, calendar-busting settlement sessions some counsel have suffered through in crowded courts. However, they share this in common: a strong incentive to the parties to settle the dispute is the recognition that failure will result in a formal win-lose decision. In long-term relationships, as in marriage, it is often wise to forego clear-cut victories or defeats.

―――――――

Buckeye Check Cashing v. Cardegna

Supreme Court of the United States, 2006.
126 S.Ct. 1204.

■ SCALIA, J., delivered the opinion of the Court.

We decide whether a court or an arbitrator should consider the claim that a contract containing an arbitration provision is void for illegality.

I

Respondents John Cardegna and Donna Reuter entered into various deferred-payment transactions with petitioner Buckeye Check Cashing (Buckeye), in which they received cash in exchange for a personal check in the amount of the cash plus a finance charge. For each separate transaction they signed a "Deferred Deposit and Disclosure Agreement" (Agreement), which included the following arbitration provisions:

> "1. *Arbitration Disclosure* By signing this Agreement, you agree that i[f] a dispute of any kind arises out of this Agreement or your application therefore or any instrument relating thereto, th[e]n either you or we or third-parties involved can choose to have that dispute resolved by binding arbitration as set forth in Paragraph 2 below ....

> 2. *Arbitration Provisions* Any claim, dispute, or controversy ... arising from or relating to this Agreement ... or the validity, enforceability, or scope of this Arbitration Provision or the entire Agreement (collectively 'Claim'), shall be resolved, upon the election of you or us or said third-parties, by binding arbitration .... This arbitration Agreement is made pursuant to a transaction involving interstate commerce, and shall be governed

by the Federal Arbitration Act ('FAA'). The arbitrator shall apply applicable substantive law constraint *[sic]* with the FAA and applicable statu[t]es of limitations and shall honor claims of privilege recognized by law ... ."

Respondents brought this putative class action in Florida state court, alleging that Buckeye charged usurious interest rates and that the Agreement violated various Florida lending and consumer-protection laws, rendering it criminal on its face. Buckeye moved to compel arbitration. The trial court denied the motion, holding that a court rather than an arbitrator should resolve a claim that a contract is illegal and void *ab initio*. The District Court of Appeal of Florida for the Fourth District reversed, holding that because respondents did not challenge the arbitration provision itself, but instead claimed that the entire contract was void, the agreement to arbitrate was enforceable, and the question of the contract's legality should go to the arbitrator.

Respondents appealed, and the Florida Supreme Court reversed, reasoning that to enforce an agreement to arbitrate in a contract challenged as unlawful "'could breathe life into a contract that not only violates state law, but also is criminal in nature....'"

II

A

To overcome judicial resistance to arbitration, Congress enacted the Federal Arbitration Act (FAA). Section 2 embodies the national policy favoring arbitration and places arbitration agreements on equal footing with all other contracts:

"A written provision in ... a contract ... to settle by arbitration a controversy thereafter arising out of such contract ... or an agreement in writing to submit to arbitration an existing controversy arising out of such a contract ... shall be valid, irrevocable, and enforceable, save upon such grounds as exist at law or in equity for the revocation of any contract."

Challenges to the validity of arbitration agreements "upon such grounds as exist at law or in equity for the revocation of any contract" can be divided into two types. One type challenges specifically the validity of the agreement to arbitrate. The other challenges the contract as a whole, either on a ground that directly affects the entire agreement (*e.g.,* the agreement was fraudulently induced), or on the ground that the illegality of one of the contract's provisions renders the whole contract invalid.[1] Respondents' claim is of this second type. The crux of the complaint is that the

---

1. The issue of the contract's validity is different from the issue of whether any agreement between the alleged obligor and obligee was ever concluded. Our opinion today addresses only the former, and does not speak to the issue decided in the cases cited by respondents (and by the Florida Supreme Court), which hold that it is for courts to decide whether the alleged obligor

contract as a whole (including its arbitration provision) is rendered invalid by the usurious finance charge.

In *Prima Paint Corp. v. Flood & Conklin Mfg. Co.*, we addressed the question of who—court or arbitrator—decides these two types of challenges. The issue in the case was "whether a claim of fraud in the inducement of the entire contract is to be resolved by the federal court, or whether the matter is to be referred to the arbitrators." *Id.*, at 402. Guided by § 4 of the FAA,[2] we held that "if the claim is fraud in the inducement of the arbitration clause itself—an issue which goes to the making of the agreement to arbitrate—the federal court may proceed to adjudicate it. But the statutory language does not permit the federal court to consider claims of fraud in the inducement of the contract generally." *Id.*, at 403-404. We rejected the view that the question of "severability" was one of state law, so that if state law held the arbitration provision not to be severable a challenge to the contract as a whole would be decided by the court.

Subsequently, in *Southland Corp.*, we held that the FAA "create[d] a body of federal substantive law," which was "applicable in state and federal court." 465 U.S., at 12. We rejected the view that state law could bar enforcement of § 2, even in the context of state-law claims brought in state court.

B

Prima Paint and *Southland* answer the question presented here by establishing three propositions. First, as a matter of substantive federal arbitration law, an arbitration provision is severable from the remainder of the contract. Second, unless the challenge is to the arbitration clause itself, the issue of the contract's validity is considered by the arbitrator in the first instance. Third, this arbitration law applies in state as well as federal courts. The parties have not requested, and we do not undertake, reconsideration of those holdings. Applying them to this case, we conclude that because respondents challenge the Agreement, but not specifically its arbitration provisions, those provisions are enforceable apart from the remainder of the contract. The challenge should therefore be considered by an arbitrator, not a court.

---

ever signed the contract, whether the signor lacked authority to commit the alleged principal, and whether the signor lacked the mental capacity to assent.

2. In pertinent part, § 4 reads:

"A party aggrieved by the alleged failure, neglect, or refusal of another to arbitrate under a written agreement for arbitration may petition any United States district court [with jurisdiction] ... for an order directing that such arbitration proceed in a manner provided for in such agreement ... .[U]pon being satisfied that the making of the agreement for arbitration or the failure to comply therewith is not in issue, the court shall make an order directing the parties to proceed to arbitration in accordance with the terms of the agreement ... ."

In declining to apply *Prima Paint's* rule of severability, the Florida Supreme Court relied on the distinction between void and voidable contracts. "Florida public policy and contract law," it concluded, permit "no severable, or salvageable, parts of a contract found illegal and void under Florida law. *Prima Paint* makes this conclusion irrelevant. That case rejected application of state severability rules to the arbitration agreement *without discussing* whether the challenge at issue would have rendered the contract void or voidable. Indeed, the opinion expressly disclaimed any need to decide what state-law remedy was available (though Justice Black's dissent *asserted* that state law rendered the contract void). Likewise in *Southland,* which arose in state court, we did not ask whether the several challenges made there— fraud, misrepresentation, breach of contract, breach of fiduciary duty, and violation of the California Franchise Investment Law—would render the contract void or voidable. We simply rejected the proposition that the enforceability of the arbitration agreement turned on the state legislature's judgment concerning the forum for enforcement of the state-law cause of action. So also here, we cannot accept the Florida Supreme Court's conclusion that enforceability of the arbitration agreement should turn on "Florida public policy and contract law."

. . .

Respondents point to the language of § 2, which renders "valid, irrevocable, and enforceable" "a written provision in" or "an agreement in writing to submit to arbitration an existing controversy arising out of" a "contract." Since, respondents argue, the only arbitration agreements to which § 2 applies are those involving a "contract," and since an agreement void *ab initio* under state law is not a "contract," there is no "written provision" in or "controversy arising out of" a "contract," to which § 2 can apply. This argument echoes Justice Black's dissent in *Prima Paint:* "Sections 2 and 3 of the Act assume the existence of a valid contract. They merely provide for enforcement where such a valid contract exists." 388 U.S., at 412-413. We do not read "contract" so narrowly. The word appears four times in § 2. Its last appearance is in the final clause, which allows a challenge to an arbitration provision "upon such grounds as exist at law or in equity for the revocation of any *contract.*" (Emphasis added.) There can be no doubt that "contract" as used this last time must include contracts that later prove to be void. Otherwise, the grounds for revocation would be limited to those that rendered a contract voidable—which would mean (implausibly) that an arbitration agreement could be challenged as voidable but not as void. Because the sentence's final use of "contract" so obviously includes putative contracts, we will not read the same word earlier in the same sentence to have a more narrow meaning.[3] We note that neither

---

3. Our more natural reading is confirmed by the use of the word "contract" elsewhere in the United States Code to refer to putative agreements, regardless of whether they are legal. For

Prima Paint nor *Southland* lends support to respondents' reading; as we have discussed, neither case turned on whether the challenge at issue would render the contract voidable or void.

. . .

It is true, as respondents assert, that the *Prima Paint* rule permits a court to enforce an arbitration agreement in a contract that the arbitrator later finds to be void. But it is equally true that respondents' approach permits a court to deny effect to an arbitration provision in a contract that the court later finds to be perfectly enforceable. *Prima Paint* resolved this conundrum—and resolved it in favor of the separate enforceability of arbitration provisions. We reaffirm today that, regardless of whether the challenge is brought in federal or state court, a challenge to the validity of the contract as a whole, and not specifically to the arbitration clause, must go to the arbitrator.

The judgment of the Florida Supreme Court is reversed, and the case is remanded for further proceedings not inconsistent with this opinion.

It is so ordered.

■ THOMAS, J., dissenting.

[Omitted].

NOTES

1. In spite of, or perhaps because of, the strong pro-arbitration stance adopted by the Supreme Court, the impartiality of arbitrators designated in consumer contracts has come under attack. Notoriously, arbitrators employed in consumer debt-collection cases, especially credit card cases, are overwhelmingly likely to find in favor of the creditor (*i.e.* card issuer) and against the consumer in processing disputes. In 2009, the Minnesota Attorney General sued the National Arbitration Forum (NAF), the nation's largest arbitration firm, alleging that the NAF was concealing its financial ties to collection agencies and credit card companies. The NAF is controlled by Accretive LLC, a private "hedge fund" that also controls major debt collection firms. The NAF was designated as the arbitrator in numerous credit card agreements in which Accretive's affiliates served as the debt collectors. The NAF's affiliation with Accretive, coupled with Accretive's control of large debt collectors, raised concerns about the NAF's impartiality in arbitrating credit card disputes in

---

instance, the Sherman Act, as amended, states that "[e]very contract, combination ..., or conspiracy in restraint of trade ... is hereby declared to be illegal." Under respondents' reading of "contract," a bewildering circularity would result: A contract illegal because it was in restraint of trade would not be a "contract" at all, and thus the statutory prohibition would not apply.

which its affiliates were interested. *See* Complaint, *Swanson v. National Arbitration Forum*, Case No. 27CV0918550 (D. Minn. July 14, 2009). After the filing of this Complaint, the NAF entered into a settlement with the Minnesota authorities under which it agreed it would no longer arbitrate consumer credit card disputes. *Firm Agrees to End Role in Arbitrating Card Debt*, N.Y. TIMES, July 20, 2009, at B8. At about the same time, the American Arbitration Association (AAA) also agreed to cease arbitrating disputes between customers and credit card companies. Robin Sidel & Amol Sharma, *Credit Card Disputes Tossed Into Disarray*, WALL ST. J., July 22, 2009, at A1. In a press release, the Minnesota authorities asserted in connection with the *Swanson* case:

> This is a classic case of the little guy getting stepped on by fine print contracts. The company tells consumers, the public, courts, and the government that it is independent and operates like an impartial court system. In fact, it has extensive ties to the collection industry—ties that it hides from the public.

National Arbitration Forum Barred from Credit Card and Consumer Arbitrations Under Agreement with Attorney General Swanson (July 20, 2009) (available at http://www.ag.state.mn.us/). The concerns were in part addressed by the federal Consumer Financial Protection Bureau (CFPB) created under the Dodd-Frank Wall Street Reform and Consumer Protection Act, Pub. L. No. 111-203, 124 Stat. 1376 (2010). After a long period of study the CFPB has recently promulgated new proposed rules regulating the scope, use and enforcement of mandatory pre-dispute arbitration clauses in consumer financial agreements under its regulatory purview. 12 CFR § 1040 (May 5, 2016). This rule is highly controversial and is likely to be tested in the courts should it become final in the summer of 2017 as is presently anticipated.

2. Most of the world sharply distinguishes between the arbitration of commercial disputes between businesses (which is strongly favored) and the arbitration of disputes involving private individuals in the role of employee or consumer. Mandatory pre-dispute arbitration clauses in consumer and employment agreements are either prohibited or regulated in these non-U.S. jurisdictions. Thomas J. Stipanowich, *The Third Arbitration Trilogy*, AM. REV. INT'L ARB. 323, 407-421 (2011) (discussing EU, UK, Canada, Japan, Brazil and New Zealand law). Set in this global context the federal prohibition of such regulation under the Supreme Court's expansive reading of the hundred-year-old Federal Arbitration Act can be fairly characterized as anomalous. But the United States default mechanism for ***adjudication*** of such individual disputes is also highly anomalous. No other nation employs jury trials, contingent fee arrangements and liberal class action procedures in the way they are available in most American jurisdictions.

3. *Buckeye Check Cashing* effectively permits a check cashing firm allegedly extracting criminally usurious interest and violating various consumer protection statutes as a matter of routine business practice to insulate itself not only from courts and juries, but also from a statewide class action procedure. That procedure permits small claimants to aggregate their claims and obtain class-wide relief in circumstances where it is uneconomic for individuals to assert individual claims because the amounts at stake are too small on an individual basis to justify the costs of litigation. The use of arbitration clauses to effectively preclude consumer class action litigation has been a matter of continuing controversy. The California Supreme Court took the position that enforcement of arbitration clauses expressly precluding class action type relief in such circumstances is unconscionable as a matter of California law. The Supreme Court of the United States, however, construed the Federal Arbitration Act to require a different result in the following case.

AT&T Mobility v. Concepcion
Supreme Court of the United States, 2011.
533 U.S. 333.

■ Scalia, J., delivered the opinion of the Court, in which Roberts, C.J., and Kennedy, Thomas, and Alito, JJ., joined. Thomas, J., filed a concurring opinion. Breyer, J., filed a dissenting opinion, in which Ginsburg, Sotomayor, and Kagan, JJ., joined.

Section 2 of the Federal Arbitration Act (FAA) makes agreements to arbitrate "valid, irrevocable, and enforceable, save upon such grounds as exist at law or in equity for the revocation of any contract." 9 U.S.C. § 2. We consider whether the FAA prohibits States from conditioning the enforceability of certain arbitration agreements on the availability of classwide arbitration procedures.

I

In February 2002, Vincent and Liza Concepcion entered into an agreement for the sale and servicing of cellular telephones with AT & T Mobility. The contract provided for arbitration of all disputes between the parties, but required that claims be brought in the parties' "individual capacity, and not as a plaintiff or class member in any purported class or representative proceeding."[2] The agreement authorized AT&T to make unilateral amendments, which it did to the arbitration provision on several occasions. The version at issue in this case reflects revisions made in December 2006, which the parties agree are controlling.

---

2. That provision further states that "the arbitrator may not consolidate more than one person's claims, and may not otherwise preside over any form of a representative or class proceeding."

The revised agreement provides that customers may initiate dispute proceedings by completing a one-page Notice of Dispute form available on AT&T's Web site. AT&T may then offer to settle the claim; if it does not, or if the dispute is not resolved within 30 days, the customer may invoke arbitration by filing a separate Demand for Arbitration, also available on AT&T's Web site. In the event the parties proceed to arbitration, the agreement specifies that AT&T must pay all costs for nonfrivolous claims; that arbitration must take place in the county in which the customer is billed; that, for claims of $10,000 or less, the customer may choose whether the arbitration proceeds in person, by telephone, or based only on submissions; that either party may bring a claim in small claims court in lieu of arbitration; and that the arbitrator may award any form of individual relief, including injunctions and presumably punitive damages. The agreement, moreover, denies AT&T any ability to seek reimbursement of its attorney's fees, and, in the event that a customer receives an arbitration award greater than AT&T's last written settlement offer, requires AT&T to pay a $7,500 minimum recovery and twice the amount of the claimant's attorney's fees.[3]

The Concepcions purchased AT&T service, which was advertised as including the provision of free phones; they were not charged for the phones, but they were charged $30.22 in sales tax based on the phones' retail value. In March 2006, the Concepcions filed a complaint against AT&T in the Southern District of California. The complaint was later consolidated with a putative class action alleging, among other things, that AT&T had engaged in false advertising and fraud by charging sales tax on phones it advertised as free.

In March 2008, AT&T moved to compel arbitration under the terms of its contract with the Concepcions. The Concepcions opposed the motion, contending that the arbitration agreement was unconscionable and unlawfully exculpatory under California law because it disallowed classwide procedures. The District Court denied AT&T's motion. It described AT&T's arbitration agreement favorably, noting, for example, that the informal dispute-resolution process was "quick, easy to use" and likely to "promp[t] full or ... even excess payment to the customer *without* the need to arbitrate or litigate"; that the $7,500 premium functioned as "a substantial inducement for the consumer to pursue the claim in arbitration" if a dispute was not resolved informally; and that consumers who were members of a class would likely be worse off. Nevertheless, relying on the California Supreme Court's decision in *Discover Bank v. Superior Court* (Cal. 2005), the court found that the arbitration provision was unconscionable because AT&T had not shown that bilateral arbitration adequately substituted for the deterrent effects of class actions.

---

3. The guaranteed minimum recovery was increased in 2009 to $10,000.

The Ninth Circuit affirmed, also finding the provision unconscionable under California law as announced in *Discover Bank*. It also held that the *Discover Bank* rule was not preempted by the FAA because that rule was simply "a refinement of the unconscionability analysis applicable to contracts generally in California." In response to AT&T's argument that the Concepcions' interpretation of California law discriminated against arbitration, the Ninth Circuit rejected the contention that "'class proceedings will reduce the efficiency and expeditiousness of arbitration'" and noted that "'*Discover Bank* placed arbitration agreements with class action waivers on the *exact same footing* as contracts that bar class action litigation outside the context of arbitration.'"

II

The FAA was enacted in 1925 in response to widespread judicial hostility to arbitration agreements. See *Hall Street Associates, L.L.C. v. Mattel, Inc.* (U.S. 2008). Section 2, the "primary substantive provision of the Act," *Moses H. Cone Memorial Hospital* (U.S. 1983), provides, in relevant part, as follows:

> "A written provision in any maritime transaction or a contract evidencing a transaction involving commerce to settle by arbitration a controversy thereafter arising out of such contract or transaction ... shall be valid, irrevocable, and enforceable, save upon such grounds as exist at law or in equity for the revocation of any contract." 9 U.S.C. § 2.

We have described this provision as reflecting both a "liberal federal policy favoring arbitration," *Moses H. Cone* and the "fundamental principle that arbitration is a matter of contract," *Rent–A–Center* (U.S. 2010). In line with these principles, courts must place arbitration agreements on an equal footing with other contracts, *Buckeye Check Cashing v. Cardegna* (U.S. 2006), and enforce them according to their terms, *Volt Information Sciences, Inc.* (U.S.1989).

The final phrase of § 2, however, permits arbitration agreements to be declared unenforceable "upon such grounds as exist at law or in equity for the revocation of any contract." This saving clause permits agreements to arbitrate to be invalidated by "generally applicable contract defenses, such as fraud, duress, or unconscionability," but not by defenses that apply only to arbitration or that derive their meaning from the fact that an agreement to arbitrate is at issue. The question in this case is whether § 2 preempts California's rule classifying most collective-arbitration waivers in consumer contracts as unconscionable. We refer to this rule as the *Discover Bank* rule.

Under California law, courts may refuse to enforce any contract found "to have been unconscionable at the time it was made," or may "limit the application of any unconscionable clause." Cal. Civ.Code Ann. § 1670.5(a). A finding of unconscionability requires "a 'procedural' and a 'substantive' element, the former focusing on 'oppression' or 'surprise' due to unequal bargaining power, the latter on 'overly harsh' or 'one-sided' results." *Armendariz v. Foundation Health Pyschcare Servs., Inc.* (Cal. 2000); accord, *Discover Bank.*

In *Discover Bank,* the California Supreme Court applied this framework to class-action waivers in arbitration agreements and held as follows:

> "[W]hen the waiver is found in a consumer contract of adhesion in a setting in which disputes between the contracting parties predictably involve small amounts of damages, and when it is alleged that the party with the superior bargaining power has carried out a scheme to deliberately cheat large numbers of consumers out of individually small sums of money, then ... the waiver becomes in practice the exemption of the party 'from responsibility for [its] own fraud, or willful injury to the person or property of another.' Under these circumstances, such waivers are unconscionable under California law and should not be enforced."

California courts have frequently applied this rule to find arbitration agreements unconscionable.

III

A

The Concepcions argue that the *Discover Bank* rule, given its origins in California's unconscionability doctrine and California's policy against exculpation, is a ground that "exist[s] at law or in equity for the revocation of any contract" under FAA § 2. Moreover, they argue that even if we construe the *Discover Bank* rule as a prohibition on collective-action waivers rather than simply an application of unconscionability, the rule would still be applicable to all dispute-resolution contracts, since California prohibits waivers of class litigation as well.

When state law prohibits outright the arbitration of a particular type of claim, the analysis is straightforward: The conflicting rule is displaced by the FAA. But the inquiry becomes more complex when a doctrine normally thought to be generally applicable, such as duress or, as relevant here, unconscionability, is alleged to have been applied in a fashion that disfavors arbitration. In *Perry v. Thomas* (U.S.1987), for example, we noted that the FAA's preemptive effect might extend even to grounds traditionally thought to exist "'at law or in equity for the revocation of any contract.'" We said that a court may not "rely on the uniqueness of an agreement to arbitrate as a basis for a state-law holding that enforcement would be unconscionable, for this would enable the court to effect what ... the state legislature cannot."

An obvious illustration of this point would be a case finding unconscionable or unenforceable as against public policy consumer arbitration agreements that fail to provide for judicially monitored discovery. The rationalizations for such a holding are neither difficult to imagine nor different in kind from those articulated in *Discover Bank*. A court might reason that no consumer would knowingly waive his right to full discovery, as this would enable companies to hide their wrongdoing. Or the court might simply say that such agreements are exculpatory—restricting discovery would be of greater benefit to the company than the consumer, since the former is more likely to be sued than to sue. See *Discover Bank* (arguing that class waivers are similarly one-sided). And, the reasoning would continue, because such a rule applies the general principle of unconscionability or public-policy disapproval of exculpatory agreements, it is applicable to "any" contract and thus preserved by § 2 of the FAA. In practice, of course, the rule would have a disproportionate impact on arbitration agreements; but it would presumably apply to contracts purporting to restrict discovery in litigation as well.

Other examples are easy to imagine. The same argument might apply to a rule classifying as unconscionable arbitration agreements that fail to abide by the Federal Rules of Evidence, or that disallow an ultimate disposition by a jury (perhaps termed "a panel of twelve lay arbitrators" to help avoid preemption). Such examples are not fanciful, since the judicial hostility towards arbitration that prompted the FAA had manifested itself in "a great variety" of "devices and formulas" declaring arbitration against public policy. And although these statistics are not definitive, it is worth noting that California's courts have been more likely to hold contracts to arbitrate unconscionable than other contracts. Broome, *An Unconscionable Applicable of the Unconscionability Doctrine: How the California Courts are Circumventing the Federal Arbitration Act*, 3 HASTINGS BUS. L.J. 39, 54, 66 (2006); Randall, *Judicial Attitudes Toward Arbitration and the Resurgence of Unconscionability*, 52 BUFFALO L.REV. 185, 186–187 (2004).

The Concepcions suggest that all this is just a parade of horribles, and no genuine worry. "Rules aimed at destroying arbitration" or "demanding procedures incompatible with arbitration," they concede, "would be preempted by the FAA because they cannot sensibly be reconciled with Section 2." The "grounds" available under § 2's saving clause, they admit, "should not be construed to include a State's mere preference for procedures that are incompatible with arbitration and 'would wholly eviscerate arbitration agreements.'"

We largely agree. Although § 2's saving clause preserves generally applicable contract defenses, nothing in it suggests an intent to preserve state-law rules that stand as an obstacle to the accomplishment of the FAA's objectives. As we have said, a federal statute's saving clause " 'cannot in reason be construed as [allowing] a common law right, the continued existence of which would be absolutely inconsistent with the provisions of the act. In other words, the act cannot be held to destroy itself.' " *American Telephone & Telegraph Co.* (U.S.1998).

We differ with the Concepcions only in the application of this analysis to the matter before us. We do not agree that rules requiring judicially monitored discovery or adherence to the Federal Rules of Evidence are "a far cry from this case." The overarching purpose of the FAA, evident in the text of §§ 2, 3, and 4, is to ensure the enforcement of arbitration agreements according to their terms so as to facilitate streamlined proceedings. Requiring the availability of classwide arbitration interferes with fundamental attributes of arbitration and thus creates a scheme inconsistent with the FAA.

B

The "principal purpose" of the FAA is to "ensur[e] that private arbitration agreements are enforced according to their terms." *Volt*; see also *Stolt–Nielsen S.A.* (U.S. 2010). This purpose is readily apparent from the FAA's text. Section 2 makes arbitration agreements "valid, irrevocable, and enforceable" as written (subject, of course, to the saving clause); § 3 requires courts to stay litigation of arbitral claims pending arbitration of those claims "in accordance with the terms of the agreement"; and § 4 requires courts to compel arbitration "in accordance with the terms of the agreement" upon the motion of either party to the agreement (assuming that the "making of the arbitration agreement or the failure ... to perform the same" is not at issue). In light of these provisions, we have held that parties may agree to limit the issues subject to arbitration, *Mitsubishi Motors Corp.* (U.S.1985), to arbitrate according to specific rules, *Volt*, and to limit *with whom* a party will arbitrate its disputes, *Stolt–Nielsen*.

The point of affording parties discretion in designing arbitration processes is to allow for efficient, streamlined procedures tailored to the type of dispute. It can be specified, for example, that the decisionmaker be a specialist in the relevant field, or that proceedings be kept confidential to protect trade secrets. And the informality of arbitral proceedings is itself desirable, reducing the cost and increasing the speed of dispute resolution.

The dissent quotes *Dean Witter Reynolds Inc. v. Byrd* (U.S.1985), as " 'reject[ing] the suggestion that the overriding goal of the Arbitration Act was to promote the expeditious resolution of claims.' " That is greatly misleading. After saying (accurately enough) that "the overriding goal of the Arbitration Act was [not] to promote the expeditious resolution of claims," but to "ensure judicial enforcement of privately made agreements to arbitrate," *Dean Witter* went on to explain: "This is not to say that Congress was blind to the potential benefit of the legislation for expedited resolution of disputes. Far from it ...." It then quotes a House Report saying that "the costliness and delays of litigation ... can be largely eliminated by agreements for arbitration." The concluding paragraph of this part of its discussion begins as follows:

"We therefore are not persuaded by the argument that the conflict between two goals of the Arbitration Act—enforcement of private agreements and encouragement of efficient and speedy dispute resolution—must be resolved in favor of the latter in order to realize the intent of the drafters."

In the present case, of course, those "two goals" do not conflict—and it is the dissent's view that would frustrate *both* of them.

Contrary to the dissent's view, our cases place it beyond dispute that the FAA was designed to promote arbitration. They have repeatedly described the Act as "embod[ying] [a] national policy favoring arbitration," *Buckeye Check Cashing*, and "a liberal federal policy favoring arbitration agreements, notwithstanding any state substantive or procedural policies to the contrary," *Moses H. Cone*; see also *Hall Street Assocs.* Thus, in *Preston v. Ferrer*, holding preempted a state-law rule requiring exhaustion of administrative remedies before arbitration, we said: "A prime objective of an agreement to arbitrate is to achieve 'streamlined proceedings and expeditious results,' " which objective would be "frustrated" by requiring a dispute to be heard by an agency first. That rule, we said, would "at the least, hinder speedy resolution of the controversy."[5]

California's *Discover Bank* rule similarly interferes with arbitration. Although the rule does not *require* classwide arbitration, it allows any party to a consumer contract to demand it *ex post*. The rule is limited to adhesion contracts, *Discover Bank*, but the times in which consumer contracts were anything other than adhesive are long past.[6] The rule also requires that damages be predictably small, and that the consumer allege a scheme to cheat consumers. *Discover Bank*. The former requirement, however, is toothless and malleable (the Ninth Circuit has held that damages of $4,000 are sufficiently small, and the latter has no limiting effect, as all that is

_____

5. Relying upon nothing more indicative of congressional understanding than statements of witnesses in committee hearings and a press release of Secretary of Commerce Herbert Hoover, the dissent suggests that Congress "thought that arbitration would be used primarily where merchants sought to resolve disputes of fact ... [and] possessed roughly equivalent bargaining power." *Post*, at 6. Such a limitation appears nowhere in the text of the FAA and has been explicitly rejected by our cases. "Relationships between securities dealers and investors, for example, may involve unequal bargaining power, but we [have] nevertheless held ... that agreements to arbitrate in that context are enforceable." *Gilmer* (U.S. 1991) (allowing arbitration of claims arising under the Age Discrimination in Employment Act of 1967 despite allegations of unequal bargaining power between employers and employees). Of course the dissent's disquisition on legislative history fails to note that it contains nothing—not even the testimony of a stray witness in committee hearings—that contemplates the existence of class arbitration.

6. Of course States remain free to take steps addressing the concerns that attend contracts of adhesion—for example, requiring class-action-waiver provisions in adhesive arbitration agreements to be highlighted. Such steps cannot, however, conflict with the FAA or frustrate its purpose to ensure that private arbitration agreements are enforced according to their terms.

required is an allegation. Consumers remain free to bring and resolve their disputes on a bilateral basis under *Discover Bank,* and some may well do so; but there is little incentive for lawyers to arbitrate on behalf of individuals when they may do so for a class and reap far higher fees in the process. And faced with inevitable class arbitration, companies would have less incentive to continue resolving potentially duplicative claims on an individual basis.

Although we have had little occasion to examine classwide arbitration, our decision in *Stolt–Nielsen* is instructive. In that case we held that an arbitration panel exceeded its power under § 10(a)(4) of the FAA by imposing class procedures based on policy judgments rather than the arbitration agreement itself or some background principle of contract law that would affect its interpretation. We then held that the agreement at issue, which was silent on the question of class procedures, could not be interpreted to allow them because the "changes brought about by the shift from bilateral arbitration to class-action arbitration" are "fundamental." This is obvious as a structural matter: Classwide arbitration includes absent parties, necessitating additional and different procedures and involving higher stakes. Confidentiality becomes more difficult. And while it is theoretically possible to select an arbitrator with some expertise relevant to the class-certification question, arbitrators are not generally knowledgeable in the often-dominant procedural aspects of certification, such as the protection of absent parties. The conclusion follows that class arbitration, to the extent it is manufactured by *Discover Bank* rather than consensual, is inconsistent with the FAA.

First, the switch from bilateral to class arbitration sacrifices the principal advantage of arbitration—its informality—and makes the process slower, more costly, and more likely to generate procedural morass than final judgment. "In bilateral arbitration, parties forgo the procedural rigor and appellate review of the courts in order to realize the benefits of private dispute resolution: lower costs, greater efficiency and speed, and the ability to choose expert adjudicators to resolve specialized disputes." But before an arbitrator may decide the merits of a claim in classwide procedures, he must first decide, for example, whether the class itself may be certified, whether the named parties are sufficiently representative and typical, and how discovery for the class should be conducted. A cursory comparison of bilateral and class arbitration illustrates the difference. According to the American Arbitration Association (AAA), the average consumer arbitration between January and August 2007 resulted in a disposition on the merits in six months, four months if the arbitration was conducted by documents only. AAA, Analysis of the AAA's Consumer Arbitration Caseload. As of September 2009, the AAA had opened 283 class arbitrations. Of those, 121 remained active, and 162 had been settled, withdrawn, or dismissed. Not a single one, however, had resulted in a final award on the merits. Brief for AAA as *Amicus Curiae* in *Stolt–Nielsen.* For those cases that were no longer active, the median time from filing to settlement, withdrawal, or dismissal—not judgment on the merits—was 583 days, and the mean was 630 days.[7]

Second, class arbitration *requires* procedural formality. The AAA's rules governing class arbitrations mimic the Federal Rules of Civil Procedure for class litigation. Compare AAA, Supplementary Rules for Class Arbitrations (2003) with Fed. Rule Civ. Proc. 23. And while parties can alter those procedures by contract, an alternative is not obvious. If procedures are too informal, absent class members would not be bound by the arbitration. For a class-action money judgment to bind absentees in litigation, class representatives must at all times adequately represent absent class members, and absent members must be afforded notice, an opportunity to be heard, and a right to opt out of the class. At least this amount of process would presumably be required for absent parties to be bound by the results of arbitration.

We find it unlikely that in passing the FAA Congress meant to leave the disposition of these procedural requirements to an arbitrator. Indeed, class arbitration was not even envisioned by Congress when it passed the FAA in 1925; as the California Supreme Court admitted in *Discover Bank,* class arbitration is a "relatively recent development." And it is at the very least odd to think that an arbitrator would be entrusted with ensuring that third parties' due process rights are satisfied.

Third, class arbitration greatly increases risks to defendants. Informal procedures do of course have a cost: The absence of multilayered review makes it more likely that errors will go uncorrected. Defendants are willing to accept the costs of these errors in arbitration, since their impact is limited to the size of individual disputes, and presumably outweighed by savings from avoiding the courts. But when damages allegedly owed to tens of thousands of potential claimants are aggregated and decided at once, the risk of an error will often become unacceptable. Faced with even a small chance of a devastating loss, defendants will be pressured into settling questionable claims. Other courts have noted the risk of "in terrorem" settlements that class actions entail, and class arbitration would be no different.

Arbitration is poorly suited to the higher stakes of class litigation. In litigation, a defendant may appeal a certification decision on an interlocutory basis and, if unsuccessful, may appeal from a final judgment as well. Questions of law are reviewed *de novo* and questions of fact for clear error. In contrast, 9 U.S.C. § 10 allows a court to vacate an arbitral award *only* where the award "was procured by corruption, fraud, or undue means"; "there was evident partiality or corruption in the arbitrators"; "the arbitrators were guilty of misconduct in refusing to postpone the hearing

---

7. The dissent claims that class arbitration should be compared to class litigation, not bilateral arbitration. Whether arbitrating a class is more desirable than litigating one, however, is not relevant. A State cannot defend a rule requiring arbitration-by-jury by saying that parties will still prefer it to trial-by-jury.

... or in refusing to hear evidence pertinent and material to the controversy[,] or of any other misbehavior by which the rights of any party have been prejudiced"; or if the "arbitrators exceeded their powers, or so imperfectly executed them that a mutual, final, and definite award ... was not made." The AAA rules do authorize judicial review of certification decisions, but this review is unlikely to have much effect given these limitations; review under § 10 focuses on misconduct rather than mistake. And parties may not contractually expand the grounds or nature of judicial review. *Hall Street Assocs.* We find it hard to believe that defendants would bet the company with no effective means of review, and even harder to believe that Congress would have intended to allow state courts to force such a decision.[8]

The Concepcions contend that because parties may and sometimes do agree to aggregation, class procedures are not necessarily incompatible with arbitration. But the same could be said about procedures that the Concepcions admit States may not superimpose on arbitration: Parties *could* agree to arbitrate pursuant to the Federal Rules of Civil Procedure, or pursuant to a discovery process rivaling that in litigation. Arbitration is a matter of contract, and the FAA requires courts to honor parties' expectations. *Rent-A-Center.* But what the parties in the aforementioned examples would have agreed to is not arbitration as envisioned by the FAA, lacks its benefits, and therefore may not be required by state law.

The dissent claims that class proceedings are necessary to prosecute small-dollar claims that might otherwise slip through the legal system. But States cannot require a procedure that is inconsistent with the FAA, even if it is desirable for unrelated reasons. Moreover, the claim here was most unlikely to go unresolved. As noted earlier, the arbitration agreement provides that AT & T will pay claimants a minimum of $7,500 and twice their attorney's fees if they obtain an arbitration award greater than AT & T's last settlement offer. The District Court found this scheme sufficient to provide incentive for the individual prosecution of meritorious claims that are not immediately settled, and the Ninth Circuit admitted that aggrieved customers who filed claims would be "essentially guarantee[d]" to be made whole. Indeed, the District Court concluded that the Concepcions were *better off* under their arbitration agreement with AT & T than they would have been as participants in a class action, which "could take months, if not years, and which may

---

8. The dissent cites three large arbitration awards (none of which stems from classwide arbitration) as evidence that parties are willing to submit large claims before an arbitrator. Those examples might be in point if it could be established that the size of the arbitral dispute was predictable when the arbitration agreement was entered. Otherwise, all the cases prove is that arbitrators can give huge awards—which we have never doubted. The point is that in class-action arbitration huge awards (with limited judicial review) will be entirely predictable, thus rendering arbitration unattractive. It is not reasonably deniable that requiring consumer disputes to be arbitrated on a classwide basis will have a substantial deterrent effect on incentives to arbitrate.

merely yield an opportunity to submit a claim for recovery of a small percentage of a few dollars."

* * *

Because it "stands as an obstacle to the accomplishment and execution of the full purposes and objectives of Congress," California's *Discover Bank* rule is preempted by the FAA. The judgment of the Ninth Circuit is reversed, and the case is remanded for further proceedings consistent with this opinion.

It is so ordered.

■ THOMAS, J., concurring opinion.

I write separately to explain how I would find that limit in the FAA's text. As I would read it, the FAA requires that an agreement to arbitrate be enforced unless a party successfully challenges the formation of the arbitration agreement, such as by proving fraud or duress. 9 U.S.C. §§ 2, 4. Under this reading, I would reverse the Court of Appeals because a district court cannot follow both the FAA and the *Discover Bank* rule, which does not relate to defects in the making of an agreement.

* * *

■ BREYER, J., dissenting opinion.
* * *

I

The California law in question consists of an authoritative state-court interpretation of two provisions of the California Civil Code. The first provision makes unlawful all contracts "which have for their object, directly or in-directly, to exempt anyone from responsibility for his own ... violation of law." § 1668. The second provision authorizes courts to "limit the application of any unconscionable clause" in a contract so "as to avoid any unconscionable result." § 1670.5(a).

The specific rule of state law in question consists of the California Supreme Court's application of these principles to hold that "some" (but not "all") "class action waivers" in consumer contracts are exculpatory and unconscionable under California "law." In particular, in *Discover Bank* the California Supreme Court stated that, when a class-action waiver

> "is found in a consumer contract of adhesion in a setting in which disputes between the contracting parties predictably involve small amounts of damages, and when it is alleged that the party with the superior bargaining power has carried out a scheme to deliberately cheat large numbers of consumers out of individually small sums of money, then ... the waiver becomes in practice the exemption of the party 'from responsibility for [its] own fraud, or willful injury to the person or property of another.'"

In such a circumstance, the "waivers are unconscionable under California law and should not be enforced."

The *Discover Bank* rule does not create a "blanket policy in California against class action waivers in the consumer context." Instead, it represents the "application of a more general [unconscionability] principle." Courts applying California law have enforced class-action waivers where they satisfy general unconscionability standards. And even when they fail, the parties remain free to devise other dispute mechanisms, including informal mechanisms, that, in context, will not prove unconscionable. See *Volt Information Sciences* (U.S.1989).

II

A

The *Discover Bank* rule is consistent with the federal Act's language. It "applies equally to class action litigation waivers in contracts without arbitration agreements as it does to class arbitration waivers in contracts with such agreements." Linguistically speaking, it falls directly within the scope of the Act's exception permitting courts to refuse to enforce arbitration agreements on grounds that exist "for the revocation of *any* contract." 9 U.S.C. § 2 (emphasis added). The majority agrees.

B

The *Discover Bank* rule is also consistent with the basic "purpose behind" the Act. We have described that purpose as one of "ensur[ing] judicial enforcement" of arbitration agreements. *Marine Transit Corp.* (U.S.1932) ("'The purpose of this bill is to make *valid and enforceable* agreements for arbitration'" (quoting H.R.Rep. No. 96, 68th Cong., 1st Sess., 1 (1924); emphasis added)); 65 Cong. Rec.1931 (1924) ("It creates no new legislation, grants no new rights, except a remedy to enforce an agreement in commercial contracts and in admiralty contracts"). As is well known, prior to the federal Act, many courts expressed hostility to arbitration, for example by refusing to order specific performance of agreements to arbitrate. The Act sought to eliminate that hostility by placing agreements to arbitrate "'*upon the same footing as other contracts.*'" *Scherk v. Alberto–Culver Co.* (U.S.1974) (emphasis added).

Congress was fully aware that arbitration could provide procedural and cost advantages. The House Report emphasized the "appropriate[ness]" of making arbitration agreements enforceable "at this time when there is so much agitation against the costliness and delays of litigation." *Id.,* at 2. And this Court has acknowledged that parties may enter into arbitration agreements in order to expedite the resolution of disputes.

But we have also cautioned against thinking that Congress' primary objective was to guarantee these particular procedural advantages. Rather, that primary objective was to secure the "enforcement" of agreements to arbitrate. *Dean Witter* (we "reject the suggestion that the overriding goal of the Arbitration Act was to promote the expeditious resolution of claims"); *id.* ("[T]he intent of Congress" requires us to apply the terms of the Act without regard to whether the result would be "possibly inefficient"); cf. *id.* (acknowledging that "expedited resolution of disputes" might lead parties to prefer arbitration). The relevant Senate Report points to the Act's basic purpose when it says that "[t]he purpose of the [Act] is *clearly set forth in section 2,*" S.Rep. No. 536, at 2 (emphasis added), namely, the section that says that an arbitration agreement "shall be valid, irrevocable, and enforceable, save upon such grounds as exist at law or in equity for the revocation of any contract," 9 U.S.C. § 2.

Thus, insofar as we seek to implement Congress' intent, we should think more than twice before invalidating a state law that does just what § 2 requires, namely, puts agreements to arbitrate and agreements to litigate "upon the same footing."

III

The majority's contrary view (that *Discover Bank* stands as an "obstacle" to the accomplishment of the federal law's objective) rests primarily upon its claims that the *Discover Bank* rule increases the complexity of arbitration procedures, thereby discouraging parties from entering into arbitration agreements, and to that extent discriminating in practice against arbitration. These claims are not well founded.

For one thing, a state rule of law that would sometimes set aside as unconscionable a contract term that forbids class arbitration is not (as the majority claims) like a rule that would require "ultimate disposition by a jury" or "judicially monitored discovery" or use of "the Federal Rules of Evidence." Unlike the majority's examples, class arbitration is consistent with the use of arbitration. It is a form of arbitration that is well known in California and followed elsewhere. American Arbitration Association (AAA), Supplementary Rules for Class Arbitrations (2003); JAMS, The Resolution Experts, Class Action Procedures (2009). Indeed, the AAA has told us that it has found class arbitration to be "a fair, balanced, and efficient means of resolving class disputes." Brief for AAA as *Amicus Curiae* in *Stolt–Nielsen S.A.* (hereinafter AAA *Amicus* Brief). And unlike the majority's examples, the *Discover Bank* rule imposes equivalent limitations on litigation; hence it cannot fairly be characterized as a targeted attack on arbitration.

Where does the majority get its contrary idea—that individual, rather than class, arbitration is a "fundamental attribut[e]" of arbitration? The majority does not explain. And it is unlikely to be able to trace its present view to the history of the arbitration statute itself.

When Congress enacted the Act, arbitration procedures had not yet been fully developed. Insofar as Congress considered detailed forms of arbitration at all, it may well have thought that arbitration would be used primarily where merchants sought to resolve disputes of fact, not law, under the customs of their industries, where the parties possessed roughly equivalent bargaining power. This last mentioned feature of the history—roughly equivalent bargaining power—suggests, if anything, that California's statute is consistent with, and indeed may help to further, the objectives that Congress had in mind.

Regardless, if neither the history nor present practice suggests that class arbitration is fundamentally incompatible with arbitration itself, then on what basis can the majority hold California's law pre-empted?

For another thing, the majority's argument that the *Discover Bank* rule will discourage arbitration rests critically upon the wrong comparison. The majority compares the complexity of class arbitration with that of bilateral arbitration. And it finds the former more complex. See *ibid*. But, if incentives are at issue, the *relevant* comparison is not "arbitration with arbitration" but a comparison between class arbitration and judicial class actions. After all, in respect to the relevant set of contracts, the *Discover Bank* rule similarly and equally sets aside clauses that forbid class procedures—whether arbitration procedures or ordinary judicial procedures are at issue.

Why would a typical defendant (say, a business) prefer a judicial class action to class arbitration? AAA statistics "suggest that class arbitration proceedings take more time than the average commercial arbitration, but may take *less time* than the average class action in court." AAA *Amicus* Brief (emphasis added). Data from California courts confirm that class arbitrations can take considerably less time than in-court proceedings in which class certification is sought. And a single class proceeding is surely more efficient than thousands of separate proceedings for identical claims. Thus, if speedy resolution of disputes were all that mattered, then the *Discover Bank* rule would reinforce, not obstruct, that objective of the Act.

The majority's related claim that the *Discover Bank* rule will discourage the use of arbitration because "[a]rbitration is poorly suited to ... higher stakes" lacks empirical support. *Ante,* at 16. Indeed, the majority provides no convincing reason to believe that parties are unwilling to submit High-Stake disputes to Arbitration. and There are numerous counterexamples. Loftus, *Rivals Resolve Dispute Over Drug*, WSJ, Apr. 16, 2011 (discussing $500 million settlement in dispute submitted to arbitration); Ziobro, *Kraft Seeks Arbitration In Fight With Starbucks Over Distribution*, WSJ, Nov. 30, 2010 (describing initiation of an arbitration in which the payout "could be higher" than $1.5 billion); Markoff, *Software Arbitration Ruling Gives I.B.M. $833 Million From Fujitsu*, N.Y. Times, Nov. 30, 1988 (describing both companies as "pleased with the ruling" resolving a licensing dispute).

Further, even though contract defenses, *e.g.,* duress and unconscionability, slow down the dispute resolution process, federal arbitration law normally leaves such matters to the States. *Rent–A–Center* (2010) (arbitration agreements "may be invalidated by 'generally applicable contract defenses'"). A provision in a contract of adhesion (for example, requiring a consumer to decide very quickly whether to pursue a claim) might increase the speed and efficiency of arbitrating a dispute, but the State can forbid it. See, *e.g., Hayes v. Oakridge Home* (Ohio 2009) ("Unconscionability is a ground for revocation of an arbitration agreement"); *In re Poly–America* (Tex.2008) ("Unconscionable contracts, however—whether relating to arbitration or not—are unenforceable under Texas law"). The *Discover Bank* rule amounts to a variation on this theme. California is free to define unconscionability as it sees fit, and its common law is of no federal concern so long as the State does not adopt a special rule that disfavors arbitration.

Because California applies the same legal principles to address the unconscionability of class arbitration waivers as it does to address the unconscionability of any other contractual provision, the merits of class proceedings should not factor into our decision. If California had applied its law of duress to void an arbitration agreement, would it matter if the procedures in the coerced agreement were efficient?

Regardless, the majority highlights the disadvantages of class arbitrations, as it sees them. But class proceedings have countervailing advantages. In general agreements that forbid the consolidation of claims can lead small-dollar claimants to abandon their claims rather than to litigate. I suspect that it is true even here, for as the Court of Appeals recognized, AT & T can avoid the $7,500 payout (the payout that supposedly makes the Concepcions' arbitration worthwhile) simply by paying the claim's face value, such that "the maximum gain to a customer for the hassle of arbitrating a $30.22 dispute is still just $30.22."

What rational lawyer would have signed on to represent the Concepcions in litigation for the possibility of fees stemming from a $30.22 claim? See, *e.g., Carnegie v. Household Int'l, Inc.* (C.A.7 2004) ("The *realistic* alternative to a class action is not 17 million individual suits, but zero individual suits, as only a lunatic or a fanatic sues for $30"). In California's perfectly rational view, nonclass arbitration over such sums will also sometimes have the effect of depriving claimants of their claims (say, for example, where claiming the $30.22 were to involve filling out many forms that require technical legal knowledge or waiting at great length while a call is placed on hold). *Discover Bank* sets forth circumstances in which the California courts believe that the terms of consumer contracts can be manipulated to insulate an agreement's author from liability for its own frauds by "deliberately cheat[ing] large numbers of consumers out of individually small sums of money." Why is this kind of decision—weighing the pros and cons of all class proceedings alike—not California's to make?

Finally, the majority can find no meaningful support for its views in this Court's precedent. The federal Act has been in force for nearly a century. We have decided dozens of cases about its requirements. We have reached results that authorize complex arbitration procedures. We have upheld nondiscriminatory state laws that slow down arbitration proceedings. But we have not, to my knowledge, applied the Act to strike down a state statute that treats arbitrations on par with judicial and administrative proceedings.

At the same time, we have repeatedly referred to the Act's basic objective as assuring that courts treat arbitration agreements "like all other contracts." *Buckeye Check Cashing* (U.S. 2006). And we have recognized that "[t]o immunize an arbitration agreement from judicial challenge" on grounds applicable to all other contracts "would be to elevate it over other forms of contract." *Prima Paint Corp.* (U.S. 1967); see also *Marchant v. Mead–Morrison Mfg. Co.* (NY 1929) (Cardozo, C.J.) ("Courts are not at liberty to shirk the process of [contractual] construction under the empire of a belief that arbitration is beneficent any more than they may shirk it if their belief happens to be the contrary"); Cohen & Dayton, 12 VA. L.REV., at 276 (the Act "is no infringement upon the right of each State to decide for itself what contracts shall or shall not exist under its laws").

These cases do not concern the merits and demerits of class actions; they concern equal treatment of arbitration contracts and other contracts. Since it is the latter question that is at issue here, I am not surprised that the majority can find no meaningful precedent supporting its decision.

NOTE

Pursuant to the Dodd-Frank Act, the federal Consumer Financial Protection Bureau has formally proposed a rule regulating mandatory pre-dispute arbitration clauses, 12 CFR § 1040 (May 5, 2016) that, if it becomes final, will effectively reverse the Concepcion result in credit card agreements and other consumer financial contracts (but not cell-phone agreements or other non-financial consumer contracts) within its jurisdiction that are entered into more than 180 days after the effective date of the final regulation. The rule as proposed would require those subject to CFPB regulation to afford class action remedies to consumers as a matter of federal law.

———————

Arbitration can be seen as providing primarily a special forum for the resolution of disputes. As such, it may be useful to avoid the delay, expense, publicity, and complexity of court litigation. But its implications may be much broader. Under an arbitration clause, not only is the arbitrator substituted for the judge, but a different and simpler set of procedural and evidence rules may be substituted for those provided by the statutory law. In its broadest forms, arbitrators are not only freed from the constraints of the procedural codes, but are also free to decide disputes on the basis of their own sense of justice without constraint by the substantive rules established by the law. Under American arbitration law the courts generally give great deference to arbitrators and decline to review the legal merits of their decisions. A classic statement of this approach, now over a century old, indicates the breadth of this view:

ANDREWS, J. in *Fudickar v. Guardian Mutual Life Ins. Co.*, 62 N.Y. 392, 399–400 (1875):

The arbitrator is a judge appointed by the parties; he is by their consent invested with judicial functions in the particular case; he is to determine the right as between the parties in respect to the matter submitted, and all questions of fact or law upon which the right depends are, under a general submission, deemed to be referred to him for decision. The court possesses no general supervisory power over awards, and if arbitrators keep within their jurisdiction their award will not be set aside because they have erred in judgment either upon the facts or the law. If courts should assume to rejudge the decision of arbitrators upon the merits, the value of this method of settling controversies would be destroyed, and an award instead of being a final determination of a controversy would become but one of the steps in its progress. The courts in this State have adhered with great steadiness to the general rule that awards will not be opened for errors of law or fact on the part of the arbitrator.

———

Arbitration gives the parties power to opt out of the substantive and procedural rules established by the law and to bind themselves by their agreement to a different set of rules. However, the courts may insist that this "opting out of the law" is effective only if it is the result of a clear and unambiguous exercise of the power to make agreements. In some modern settings, even this agreement process becomes attenuated. For example, when a worker takes a job in a factory covered by a collective bargaining agreement, he takes with the job the remedial and substantive law structure created by the collective bargaining agreement between the union and the employer, and, particularly, the arbitration clause included in that agreement. It is doubtful, however, whether the individual worker has any opportunity to read, negotiate, or consent to that agreement. He takes it as he finds it. So does the fast food franchisee presented with a package agreement by the franchisor. Their position is quite similar to that of most Americans who are covered by medical insurance plans that provide for arbitration of disputes. The employee, the franchisee, the insured, and others subject to such "contractual" relationships find themselves bound into a private system of law that may be very different from that created by legislatures and the courts.

Sims v. Siegelson

New York Supreme Court, Appellate Division, 1998.
246 A.D.2d 374, 668 N.Y.S.2d 20.

■ Per Curiam.

Judgment, Supreme Court, New York County, entered June 26, 1995, which, to the extent appealed from, granted the petition to the extent of vacating an award made by an arbitration panel of respondent-intervenor-appellant Diamond Dealers Club ("DDC") in favor of respondent Krischer and against petitioner in the amount of $37,371.00 and permanently enjoining DDC from enforcing that award, and denied Krischer's cross motion to dismiss the petition and confirm said award, unanimously reversed, on the law, with costs, the petition denied and the cross motion to confirm the award granted, together with a 15% surcharge and interest. The Clerk is directed to enter judgment accordingly.

Petitioner Sims and respondent Krischer are both members of respondent DDC, an organization whose members are in the business of buying and selling precious gems. Pursuant to the DDC bylaws and the individual membership agreements, each member agrees to be bound by the bylaws and to arbitrate all disputes with other members arising out of the diamond business before a DDC arbitration panel. The bylaws also provide that each member is personally responsible for transactions with other members whether he conducts business personally, as a member of a partnership or through a corporation, and further require that members withdrawing from a partnership or corporation must immediately notify the DDC executive offices.

The underlying dispute arose as a result of an August 1994 sale of diamonds from Krischer to David Sims, petitioner's son, who had previously been employed by petitioner's corporation, S & H Diamond Corp. David Sims purchased the diamonds on behalf of his new corporation, Diamond Way Corp. ("Diamond Way"). According to Krischer however, at the time of the purchase on consignment, David Sims represented that he was still associated with his father's diamond business.

Shortly thereafter, Diamond Way's diamond inventory was allegedly stolen, resulting in its filing for bankruptcy. Since Diamond Way owed substantial amounts to various creditors who were members of DDC, an arbitration hearing before a DDC arbitration panel was scheduled for October 25, 1994. Petitioner was notified by letter that claims filed by Krischer and three other members would be heard before an arbitration panel on that date. Petitioner appeared at the hearing and testified in opposition to the claims, as did David Sims. The arbitrator ruled in favor of Krischer and the three other claimants, stating in pertinent part: "After much consideration, the Arbitrators have come to the conclusion that the onus and responsibility falls upon Edward Sims to make good for his son, David Sims to ... Sam Krischer—$37,371.00."

Petitioner commenced the instant proceeding to vacate the arbitration award primarily on the ground that the arbitration clause signed by all DDC members did not obligate him to arbitrate disputes between himself and his son's bankrupt corporation, Diamond Way, with which he denied any connection. The IAS court[*] agreed, finding no business connection between petitioner and Diamond Way, and that a 1987 guaranty petitioner had executed for his son's debts had expired before the transaction at issue occurred. The court rejected the notion that "one generation is liable for the debts of another."

We reverse and grant respondents' motion to confirm the DDC's arbitration award. CPLR 7501 instructs that courts should not "pass upon the merits of the dispute" raised in an arbitration proceeding. Indeed, judicial review is so circumspect that an arbitrator's award will not be set aside even though the arbitrator misconstrues or disregards the agreement, or misapplies substantive rules of law, unless it violates strong public policy or is totally irrational. Rather, a party who has been served with a notice to arbitrate, or who has participated in the arbitration, may seek vacatur only on the grounds that the "the rights of that party were prejudiced by corruption, fraud or misconduct in procuring the award, partiality of an arbitrator, that the arbitrator exceeded his power or failed to make a final and definite award, or a procedural failure that was not waived (CPLR 7511, subd [b], par 1)."

The IAS court failed to identify any statutory ground supporting vacatur, and we conclude that none exists. Petitioner's allegations of misconduct and partiality by DDC are baseless and require no discussion. The IAS court's determination was apparently based on the rationale that holding petitioner liable for his son's debt was an act in excess of the arbitrators' powers or was simply irrational. However, considerable evidence existed to support the award. Petitioner and his son were, at one time, selling diamonds for the same corporation, rendering each of them personally liable for its obligations pursuant to DDC rules. Petitioner never notified DDC of his withdrawal from that enterprise, which is also required by DDC rules. Moreover, petitioner had executed a guaranty for his son's debts as a condition for his son's admission to DDC, and according to Krischer, David Sims represented that he was still affiliated with his father's business. Although respondents apparently concede that a DDC resolution (not bylaw) limits the duration of such guarantees to five years, ample evidence existed for the arbitrators to rationally conclude that a continuing business relationship existed between petitioner and David Sims.

---

[*] EDITOR'S NOTE: "IAS Court" refers to a New York procedure pursuant to which civil matters are assigned to a single Supreme Court Justice for all purposes at the trial level. "IAS" is an acronym for "Individual Assignment System."

In any event, respondents are correct in arguing that any inquiry into these factual and legal determinations of the arbitrators is prohibited. Thus, even if we disagreed with the conclusion of the arbitrator, as did the IAS court, vacatur would be improper. An arbitrator "may do justice as he sees it, applying his own sense of law and equity to the facts as he finds them to be and making an award reflecting the spirit rather than the letter of the agreement."

Petitioner's claims that the award should be vacated due to DDC's non-compliance with the procedures of Article 75 was waived by his participation in the arbitration proceeding without objection (CPLR 7511[b][1][iv]). Similarly waived by his participation is petitioner's claim that there was no agreement to arbitrate this dispute (CPLR 7511[b][2][ii]). Petitioner's assertions that he was duped into attending the arbitration hearing, and thereafter refused to participate in it, are belied by the contents of the notice of arbitration letter sent to him, and his signature on the hearing attendance sheet, respectively. Nor has petitioner demonstrated he was prejudiced by the alleged procedural irregularities.

Since no basis exists to vacate the award, Krischer's cross motion to confirm the arbitration award is granted, including his request for an additional 15% surcharge, which he properly calculates as $5,605. DDC's rules permit recovery of a 15% surcharge when a party is forced to seek judicial confirmation of an arbitration award in their favor. Accordingly, Krischer is entitled to judgment in the amount of $42,976, plus interest.

QUESTIONS AND NOTES

1. Does *Sims* mean that arbitrators can make up their own rules in deciding contract issues? Could an arbitrator, for example, decide to award damages in *Freund v. Washington Square Press*, p. 124, where there was insufficient evidence for the damages to be calculated with certainty?

2. The principal justification for the delegation of such power to arbitrators is that the parties chose arbitration to resolve their disputes. But do you really choose to submit an unknown future dispute to arbitration by signing a form contract? Anyone who has worked as a member of a labor union or bought insurance is likely bound to arbitrate any disputes arising from the contract, whether they were aware of this fact or not. Does this sort of consent justify exercise of almost unappealable decision-making power over health care or employment issues to an arbitrator?

3. What does the New York statute mean when it authorizes a court to vacate an arbitral decision if the arbitrator "exceeded his powers"? How does the court determine if this were the case? What if the arbitrator gave no explanation for his decision?

Hall Street Associates v. Mattel

Supreme Court of the United States, 2008.
552 U.S. 576.

■ JUSTICE SOUTER delivered the Opinion of the Court.

The Federal Arbitration Act (FAA or Act), provides for expedited judicial review to confirm, vacate, or modify arbitration awards. The question here is whether statutory grounds for prompt vacatur and modification may be supplemented by contract. We hold that the statutory grounds are exclusive.

I

This case began as a lease dispute between landlord, petitioner Hall Street Associates, LLC, and tenant, respondent Mattel, Inc. The property was used for many years as a manufacturing site, and the leases provided that the tenant would indemnify the landlord for any costs resulting from the failure of the tenant or its predecessor lessees to follow environmental laws while using the premises.

Tests of the property's well water in 1998 showed high levels of trichloroethylene (TCE), the apparent residue of manufacturing discharges by Mattel's predecessors between 1951 and 1980. After the Oregon Department of Environmental Quality (DEQ) discovered even more pollutants, Mattel stopped drawing from the well and, along with one of its predecessors, signed a consent order with the DEQ providing for cleanup of the site.

After Mattel gave notice of intent to terminate the lease in 2001, Hall Street filed this suit, contesting Mattel's right to vacate on the date it gave, and claiming that the lease obliged Mattel to indemnify Hall Street for costs of cleaning up the TCE, among other things. Following a bench trial, Mattel won on the termination issue, and after an unsuccessful try at mediating the indemnification claim, the parties proposed to submit to arbitration. The District Court was amenable, and the parties drew up an arbitration agreement, which the court approved and entered as an order. One paragraph of the agreement provided that

> "[t]he United States District Court for the District of Oregon may enter judgment upon any award, either by confirming the award or by vacating, modifying or correcting the award. The Court shall vacate, modify or correct any award: (i) where the arbitrator's findings of facts are not supported by substantial evidence, or (ii) where the arbitrator's conclusions of law are erroneous."

Arbitration took place, and the arbitrator decided for Mattel. In particular, he held that no indemnification was due, because the lease obligation to follow all applicable federal, state, and local environmental laws did not require compliance with the testing requirements of the Oregon Drinking Water Quality Act (Oregon Act); that Act the arbitrator characterized as dealing with human health as distinct from environmental contamination.

Hall Street then filed a District Court Motion for Order Vacating, Modifying And/Or Correcting the arbitration decision on the ground that failing to treat the Oregon Act as an applicable environmental law under the terms of the lease was legal error. The District Court agreed, vacated the award, and remanded for further consideration by the arbitrator. The court expressly invoked the standard of review chosen by the parties in the arbitration agreement, which included review for legal error, and cited *LaPine Technology Corp. v. Kyocera Corp.*, for the proposition that the FAA leaves the parties "free ... to draft a contract that sets rules for arbitration and dictates an alternative standard of review."

On remand, the arbitrator followed the District Court's ruling that the Oregon Act was an applicable environmental law and amended the decision to favor Hall Street. This time, each party sought modification, and again the District Court applied the parties' stipulated standard of review for legal error, correcting the arbitrator's calculation of interest but otherwise upholding the award. Each party then appealed to the Court of Appeals for the Ninth Circuit, where Mattel switched horses and contended that the Ninth Circuit's recent en banc action overruling *LaPine* in *Kyocera Corp. v. Prudential-Bache Trade Servs., Inc.*, left the arbitration agreement's provision for judicial review of legal error unenforceable. Hall Street countered that *Kyocera* (the later one) was distinguishable, and that the agreement's judicial review provision was not severable from the submission to arbitration.

The Ninth Circuit reversed in favor of Mattel in holding that, "[u]nder *Kyocera* the terms of the arbitration agreement controlling the mode of judicial review are unenforceable and severable." The Circuit instructed the District Court on remand to

> "return to the application to confirm the original arbitration award (not the subsequent award revised after reversal), and ... confirm that award, unless ... the award should be vacated on the grounds allowable under 9 U.S.C. § 10, or modified or corrected under the grounds allowable under 9 U.S.C. § 11."

After the District Court again held for Hall Street and the Ninth Circuit again reversed[1] we granted certiorari to decide whether the grounds for vacatur and modification provided by §§ 10 and 11 of the FAA are exclusive.

II

Congress enacted the FAA to replace judicial indisposition to arbitration with a "national policy favoring [it] and plac[ing] arbitration agreements on equal footing with all other contracts." *Buckeye Check Cashing v. Cardegna*. As for jurisdiction

---

1. On remand, the District Court vacated the arbitration award, because it supposedly rested on an implausible interpretation of the lease and thus exceeded the arbitrator's powers, in violation of 9 U.S.C. § 10. Mattel appealed, and the Ninth Circuit reversed, holding that implausibility is not a valid ground for vacating or correcting an award under § 10 or § 11.

over controversies touching arbitration, the Act does nothing, being "something of an anomaly in the field of federal-court jurisdiction" in bestowing no federal jurisdiction but rather requiring an independent jurisdictional basis.[2] But in cases falling within a court's jurisdiction, the Act makes contracts to arbitrate "valid, irrevocable, and enforceable," so long as their subject involves "commerce." And this is so whether an agreement has a broad reach or goes just to one dispute, and whether enforcement be sought in state court or federal.

The Act also supplies mechanisms for enforcing arbitration awards: a judicial decree confirming an award, an order vacating it, or an order modifying or correcting it. §§ 9-11. An application for any of these orders will get streamlined treatment as a motion, obviating the separate contract action that would usually be necessary to enforce or tinker with an arbitral award in court. § 6. Under the terms of § 9, a court "must" confirm an arbitration award "unless" it is vacated, modified, or corrected "as prescribed" in §§ 10 and 11. Section 10 lists grounds for vacating an award, while § 11 names those for modifying or correcting one.[4]

The Courts of Appeals have split over the exclusiveness of these statutory grounds when parties take the FAA shortcut to confirm, vacate, or modify an award, with some saying the recitations are exclusive, and others regarding them as mere threshold provisions open to expansion by agreement. As mentioned already, when this litigation started, the Ninth Circuit was on the threshold side of the split from which it later departed *en banc* in favor of the exclusivity view, *see Kyocera*, which it

---

2. Because the FAA is not jurisdictional, there is no merit in the argument that enforcing the arbitration agreement's judicial review provision would create federal jurisdiction by private contract. The issue is entirely about the scope of judicial review permissible under the FAA.

4. Title 9 U.S.C. § 10(a) provides: "(a) In any of the following cases the United States court in and for the district wherein the award was made may make an order vacating the award upon the application of any party to the arbitration—"(1) where the award was procured by corruption, fraud, or undue means; "(2) where there was evident partiality or corruption in the arbitrators, or either of them; "(3) where the arbitrators were guilty of misconduct in refusing to postpone the hearing, upon sufficient cause shown, or in refusing to hear evidence pertinent and material to the controversy; or of any other misbehavior by which the rights of any party have been prejudiced; or "(4) where the arbitrators exceeded their powers, or so imperfectly executed them that a mutual, final, and definite award upon the subject matter submitted was not made." Title 9 U.S.C. § 11 (2000 ed.) provides: "In either of the following cases the United States court in and for the district wherein the award was made may make an order modifying or correcting the award upon the application of any party to the arbitration—"(a) Where there was an evident material miscalculation of figures or an evident material mistake in the description of any person, thing, or property referred to in the award. "(b) Where the arbitrators have awarded upon a matter not submitted to them, unless it is a matter not affecting the merits of the decision upon the matter submitted. "(c) Where the award is imperfect in matter of form not affecting the merits of the controversy. "The order may modify and correct the award, so as to effect the intent thereof and promote justice between the parties."

followed in this case. We now hold that §§ 10 and 11 respectively provide the FAA's exclusive grounds for expedited vacatur and modification. *holding*

III

Hall Street makes two main efforts to show that the grounds set out for vacating or modifying an award are not exclusive, taking the position, first, that expandable judicial review authority has been accepted as the law since *Wilko v. Swan* (1953). This, however, was not what *Wilko* decided, which was that § 14 of the Securities Act of 1933 voided any agreement to arbitrate claims of violations of that Act, a holding since overruled by *Rodriguez de Quijas v. Shearson/American Express, Inc.* (1989). Although it is true that the Court's discussion includes some language arguably favoring Hall Street's position, arguable is as far as it goes. *△ argument*

The *Wilko* Court was explaining that arbitration would undercut the Securities Act's buyer protections when it remarked (citing FAA § 10) that "[p]ower to vacate an [arbitration] award is limited," and went on to say that "the interpretations of the law by the arbitrators in contrast to manifest disregard [of the law] are not subject, in the federal courts, to judicial review for error in interpretation." Hall Street reads this statement as recognizing "manifest disregard of the law" as a further ground for *vacatur* on top of those listed in § 10, and some Circuits have read it the same way. Hall Street sees this supposed addition to § 10 as the camel's nose: if judges can add grounds to vacate (or modify), so can contracting parties. *△ argument*

But this is too much for *Wilko* to bear. Quite apart from its leap from a supposed judicial expansion by interpretation to a private expansion by contract, Hall Street overlooks the fact that the statement it relies on expressly rejects just what Hall Street asks for here, general review for an arbitrator's legal errors. Then there is the vagueness of *Wilko*'s phrasing. Maybe the term "manifest disregard" was meant to name a new ground for review, but maybe it merely referred to the § 10 grounds collectively, rather than adding to them. *See, e.g., Mitsubishi Motors Corp. v. Soler Chrysler-Plymouth, Inc.* (1985) (Stevens, J., dissenting) ("Arbitration awards are only reviewable for manifest disregard of the law"). Or, as some courts have thought, "manifest disregard" may have been shorthand for § 10(a)(3) or § 10(a)(4), the subsections authorizing *vacatur* when the arbitrators were "guilty of misconduct" or "exceeded their powers." We, when speaking as a Court, have merely taken the *Wilko* language as we found it, with out embellishment, *see First Options of Chicago, Inc. v. Kaplan* (1995), and now that its meaning is implicated, we see no reason to accord it the significance that Hall Street urges. *SC Argument*

Second, Hall Street says that the agreement to review for legal error ought to prevail simply because arbitration is a creature of contract, and the FAA is "motivated, first and foremost, by a congressional desire to enforce agreements into which parties ha[ve] entered." *Dean Witter Reynolds Inc. v. Byrd* (1985). But, again, we *△ argument* think the argument comes up short. Hall Street is certainly right that the FAA lets parties tailor some, even many features of arbitration by contract, including the way arbitrators are chosen, what their qualifications should be, which issues are arbitrable, along with procedure and choice of substantive law. But to rest this case on the general policy of treating arbitration agreements as enforceable as such would be to beg the question, which is whether the FAA has textual features at odds with enforcing a contract to expand judicial review following the arbitration.

To that particular question we think the answer is yes, that the text compels a reading of the §§ 10 and 11 categories as exclusive. To begin with, even if we assumed §§ 10 and 11 could be supplemented to some extent, it would stretch basic interpretive principles to expand the stated grounds to the point of evidentiary and legal review generally. Sections 10 and 11, after all, address egregious departures from the parties' agreed-upon arbitration: "corruption," "fraud," "evident partiality," "misconduct," "misbehavior," "exceed[ing]. . . powers," "evident material miscalculation," "evident material mistake," "award[s] upon a matter not submitted;" the only ground with any softer focus is "imperfect[ions]," and a court may correct those only if they go to "[a] matter of form not affecting the merits." Given this emphasis on extreme arbitral conduct, the old rule of ejusdem generis has an implicit lesson to teach here. Under that rule, when a statute sets out a series of specific items ending with a general term, that general term is confined to covering subjects comparable to the specifics it follows. Since a general term included in the text is normally so limited, then surely a statute with no textual hook for expansion cannot authorize contracting parties to supplement review for specific instances of outrageous conduct with review for just any legal error. "Fraud" and a mistake of law are not cut from the same cloth.

That aside, expanding the detailed categories would rub too much against the grain of the § 9 language, where provision for judicial confirmation carries no hint of flexibility. On application for an order confirming the arbitration award, the court "must grant" the order "unless the award is vacated, modified, or corrected as prescribed in sections 10 and 11 of this title." There is nothing malleable about "must grant," which unequivocally tells courts to grant confirmation in all cases, except when one of the "prescribed" exceptions applies. This does not sound remotely like a provision meant to tell a court what to do just in case the parties say nothing else.[6]

---

6. Hall Street claims that § 9 supports its position, because it allows a court to confirm an award only "[i]f the parties in their agreement have agreed that a judgment of the court shall be entered upon the award made pursuant to the arbitration." Hall Street argues that this language "expresses Congress's intent that a court must enforce the agreement of the parties as to whether, and under what circumstances, a judgment shall be entered." Reply Brief for Petitioner 5. It is a peculiar argument, converting agreement as a necessary condition for judicial enforcement into a sufficient condition for a court to bar enforcement. And the text is otherwise problematical for

In fact, anyone who thinks Congress might have understood § 9 as a default provision should turn back to § 5 for an example of what Congress thought a default provision would look like:

> "[i]f in the agreement provision be made for a method of naming or appointing an arbitrator. . . such method shall be followed; but if no method be provided therein, or if a method be provided and any party thereto shall fail to avail himself of such method, . . . then upon the application of either party to the controversy the court shall designate and appoint an arbitrator. . . ."

"[I]f no method be provided" is a far cry from "must grant . . . unless" in § 9.

Instead of fighting the text, it makes more sense to see the three provisions, §§ 9-11, as substantiating a national policy favoring arbitration with just the limited review needed to maintain arbitration's essential virtue of resolving disputes straightaway. Any other reading opens the door to the

full-bore legal and evidentiary appeals that can "rende[r] informal arbitration merely a prelude to a more cumbersome and time-consuming judicial review process," *Kyocera*; and bring arbitration theory to grief in post-arbitration process.

Nor is *Dean Witter* to the contrary, as Hall Street claims it to be. *Dean Witter* held that state-law claims subject to an agreement to arbitrate could not be remitted to a district court considering a related, nonarbitrable federal claim; the state-law claims were to go to arbitration immediately. Despite the opinion's language "reject[ing] the suggestion that the overriding goal of the [FAA] was to promote the expeditious resolution of claims," the holding mandated immediate enforcement of an arbitration agreement; the Court was merely trying to explain that the inefficiency and difficulty of conducting simultaneous arbitration and federal-court litigation was not a good enough reason to defer the arbitration.

When all these arguments based on prior legal authority are done with, Hall Street and Mattel remain at odds over what happens next. Hall Street and its *amici* say parties will flee from arbitration if expanded review is not open to them. One of Mattel's amici foresees flight from the courts if it is. We do not know who, if anyone, is right, and so cannot say whether the exclusivity reading of the statute is more of a

---

Hall Street: § 9 says that if the parties have agreed to judicial enforcement, the court "must grant" confirmation unless grounds for vacatur or modification exist under § 10 or § 11. The sentence nowhere predicates the court's judicial action on the parties' having agreed to specific standards; if anything, it suggests that, so long as the parties contemplated judicial enforcement, the court must undertake such enforcement under the statutory criteria. In any case, the arbitration agreement here did not specifically predicate entry of judgment on adherence to its judicial-review standard. To the extent Hall Street argues otherwise, it contests not the meaning of the FAA but the Ninth Circuit's severability analysis, upon which it did not seek certiorari.

threat to the popularity of arbitrators or to that of courts. But whatever the consequences of our holding, the statutory text gives us no business to expand the
statutory grounds.[7]

IV

In holding that §§ 10 and 11 provide exclusive regimes for the review provided
by the statute, we do not purport to say that they exclude more searching review
based on authority outside the statute as well. The FAA is not the only way into
court for parties wanting review of arbitration awards: they may contemplate enforcement under state statutory or common law, for example, where judicial review
of different scope is arguable. But here we speak only to the scope of the expeditious
judicial review under §§ 9, 10, and 11, deciding nothing about other possible avenues
for judicial enforcement of arbitration awards.

Although one such avenue is now claimed to be revealed in the procedural history of this case, no claim to it was presented when the case arrived on our doorstep,
and no reason then appeared to us for treating this as anything but an FAA case.
There was never any question about meeting the FAA § 2 requirement that the
leases from which the dispute arose be contracts "involving commerce." 9 U.S.C.
§ 2; *Allied-Bruce Terminix Cos. v. Dobson* (1995) (§ 2 "exercise[s] Congress' commerce power to the full"). Nor is there any doubt now that the parties at least had
the FAA in mind at the outset; the arbitration agreement even incorporates FAA §
7, empowering arbitrators to compel attendance of witnesses.

---

7. The history of the FAA is consistent with our conclusion. The text of the FAA was based upon
that of New York's arbitration statute. *See* S. Rep. No. 536, 68th Cong., 1st Sess., 3 (1924) ("The
bill . . . follows the lines of the New York arbitration law enacted in 1920 . . ."). The New York
Arbitration Law incorporated pre-existing provisions of the New York Code of Civil Procedure.
Section 2373 of the code said that, upon application by a party for a confirmation order, "the
court must grant such an order, unless the award is vacated, modified, or corrected, as prescribed
by the next two sections." 2 N. Y. Ann. Code Civ. Proc. (Stover 6th ed. 1902) (herein after
Stover). The subsequent sections gave grounds for vacatur and modification or correction virtually identical to the 9 U.S.C. §§ 10 and 11 grounds. *See* 2 Stover §§§§ 2374, 2375. In a brief
submitted to the House and Senate Subcommittees of the Committees on the Judiciary, Julius
Henry Cohen, one of the primary drafters of both the 1920 New York Act and the proposed
FAA, said, "The grounds for vacating, modifying, or correcting an award are limited. If the
award [meets a condition of § 10], then and then only the award may be vacated. . . . If there was
[an error under § 11], then and then only it may be modified or corrected . . . ." The House
Report similarly recognized that an "award may . . . be entered as a judgment, subject to attack
by the other party for fraud and corruption and similar undue influence, or for palpable error in
form." In a contemporaneous campaign for the promulgation of a uniform state arbitration law,
Cohen contrasted the New York Act with the Illinois Arbitration and Awards Act of 1917, which
required an arbitrator, at the request of either party, to submit any question of law arising during
arbitration to judicial determination.

While it is true that the agreement does not expressly invoke FAA § 9, § 10, or § 11, and none of the various motions to vacate or modify the award expressly said that the parties were relying on the FAA, the District Court apparently thought it was applying the FAA when it alluded to the Act in quoting *LaPine*, for the then-unexceptional proposition that "'[f]ederal courts can expand their review of an arbitration award beyond the FAA's grounds, when . . . the parties have so agreed.'" And the Ninth Circuit, for its part, seemed to take it as a given that the District Court's direct and prompt examination of the award depended on the FAA; it found the expanded-review provision unenforceable under *Kyocera* and remanded for confirmation of the original award "unless the district court determines that the award should be vacated on the grounds allowable under 9 U.S.C. § 10, or modified or corrected under the grounds allowable under 9 U.S.C. § 11." In the petition for certiorari and the principal briefing before us, the parties acted on the same premise. *See, e.g.,* Pet. for Cert. 27 ("This Court should accept review to resolve this important issue of statutory construction under the FAA"); Brief for Petitioner 16 ("Because arbitration provisions providing for judicial review of arbitration awards for legal error are consistent with the goals and policies of the FAA and employ a standard of review which district courts regularly apply in a variety of contexts, those provisions are entitled to enforcement under the FAA").

One unusual feature, however, prompted some of us to question whether the case should be approached another way. The arbitration agreement was entered into in the course of district court litigation, was submitted to the District Court as a request to deviate from the standard sequence of trial procedure, and was adopted by the District Court as an order. Hence a question raised by this Court at oral argument: should the agreement be treated as an exercise of the District Court's authority to manage its cases under Federal Rules of Civil Procedure 16? *See, e.g.,* Tr. of Oral Arg. 11-12. Supplemental briefing at the Court's behest joined issue on the question, and it appears that Hall Street suggested something along these lines in the Court of Appeals, which did not address the suggestion.

We are, however, in no position to address the question now, beyond noting the claim of relevant case management authority independent of the FAA. The parties' supplemental arguments on the subject in this Court implicate issues of waiver and the relation of the FAA both to Rule 16 and the Alternative Dispute Resolution Act of 1998, none of which has been considered previously in this litigation, or could be well addressed for the first time here. We express no opinion on these matters beyond leaving them open for Hall Street to press on remand. If the Court of Appeals finds they are open, the court may consider whether the District Court's authority to manage litigation independently warranted that court's order on the mode of resolving the indemnification issues remaining in this case.

* * *

Although we agree with the Ninth Circuit that the FAA confines its expedited judicial review to the grounds listed in 9 U.S.C. §§ 10 and 11, we vacate the judgment and remand the case for proceedings consistent with this opinion.

It is so ordered.

■ JUSTICE STEVENS, dissenting.

May parties to an ongoing lawsuit agree to submit their dispute to arbitration subject to the caveat that the trial judge should refuse to enforce an award that rests on an erroneous conclusion of law? Prior to Congress' enactment of the Federal Arbitration Act (FAA or Act) in 1925, the answer to that question would surely have been "Yes."[1] Today, however, the Court holds that the FAA does not merely authorize the vacation or enforcement of awards on specified grounds, but also forbids enforcement of perfectly reasonable judicial review provisions in arbitration agreements fairly negotiated by the parties and approved by the district court. Because this result conflicts with the primary purpose of the FAA and ignores the historical context in which the Act was passed, I respectfully dissent.

Prior to the passage of the FAA, American courts were generally hostile to arbitration. They refused, with rare exceptions, to order specific enforcement of executory agreements to arbitrate. Section 2 of the FAA responded to this hostility by making written arbitration agreements "valid, irrevocable, and enforceable." This section, which is the centerpiece of the FAA, reflects Congress' main goal in passing the legislation: "to abrogate the general common-law rule against specific enforcement of arb itration agreements," *Southland Corp. v. Keating* (1984) (Stevens, J., concurring in part and dissenting in part), and to "ensur[e] that private arbitration agreements are enforced according to their terms," *Volt Information Sciences, Inc. v. Board of Trustees of Leland Stanford Junior Univ.* (1989). Given this settled understanding of the core purpose of the FAA, the interests favoring enforceability of parties' arbitration agreements are stronger today than before the FAA was enacted. As such, there is more—and certainly not less—reason to give effect to parties' fairly negotiated decisions to provide for judicial review of arbitration awards for errors of law.

Petitioner filed this rather complex action in an Oregon state court. Based on the diverse citizenship of the parties, respondent removed the case to federal court. More than three years later, and after some issues had been resolved, the parties sought and obtained the District Court's approval of their agreement to arbitrate

---

1. *See* Kleine v. Catara, 14 F. Cas. 732, 735, F. Cas. No. 7869 (C. C.D. Mass. 1814) ("If the parties wish to reserve the law for the decision of the court, they may stipulate to that effect in the submission; they may restrain or enlarge its operation as they please") (Story, J.).

the remaining issues subject to de novo judicial review. They neither requested, nor suggested that the FAA authorized, any "expedited" disposition of their case. Because the arbitrator made a rather glaring error of law, the judge refused to affirm his award until after that error was corrected. The Ninth Circuit reversed.

This Court now agrees with the Ninth Circuit's (most recent) interpretation of the FAA as setting forth the exclusive grounds for modification or vacation of an arbitration award under the statute. As I read the Court's opinion, it identifies two possible reasons for reaching this result: (1) a supposed *quid pro quo* bargain between Congress and litigants that conditions expedited federal enforcement of arbitration awards on acceptance of a statutory limit on the scope of judicial review of such awards; and (2) an assumption that Congress intended to include the words "and no other" in the grounds specified in §§ 10 and 11 for the vacatur and modification of awards. Neither reason is persuasive.

While § 9 of the FAA imposes a 1-year limit on the time in which any party to an arbitration may apply for confirmation of an award, the statute does not require that the application be given expedited treatment. Of course, the premise of the entire statute is an assumption that the arbitration process may be more expeditious and less costly than ordinary litigation, but that is a reason for interpreting the statute liberally to favor the parties' use of arbitration. An unnecessary refusal to enforce a perfectly reasonable category of arbitration agreements defeats the primary purpose of the statute.

That purpose also provides a sufficient response to the Court's reliance on statutory text. It is true that a wooden application of "the old rule of ejusdem generis," might support an inference that the categories listed in §§ 10 and 11 are exclusive, but the literal text does not compel that reading—a reading that is flatly inconsistent with the overriding interest in effectuating the clearly expressed intent of the contracting parties. A listing of grounds that must always be available to contracting parties simply does not speak to the question whether they may agree to additional grounds for judicial review.

Moreover, in light of the historical context and the broader purpose of the FAA, §§ 10 and 11 are best understood as a shield meant to protect parties from hostile courts, not a sword with which to cut down parties' "valid, irrevocable and enforceable" agreements to arbitrate their disputes subject to judicial review for errors of law.[3] § 2.

---

3. In the years before the passage of the FAA, arbitration awards were subject to thorough and broad judicial review. In §§ 10 and 11 of the FAA, Congress significantly limited the grounds for judicial vacatur or modification of such awards in order to protect arbitration awards from hostile and meddlesome courts.

Even if I thought the narrow issue presented in this case were as debatable as the conflict among the courts of appeals suggests, I would rely on a presumption of overriding importance to resolve the debate and rule in favor of petitioner's position that the FAA permits the statutory grounds for vacatur and modification of an award to be supplemented by contract. A decision "not to regulate" the terms of an agreement that does not even arguably offend any public policy whatsoever, "is adequately justified by a presumption in favor of freedom." *FCC v. Beach Communications, Inc.* (1993) (Stevens, J., concurring in judgment).

Accordingly, while I agree that the judgment of the Court of Appeals must be set aside, and that there may be additional avenues available for judicial enforcement of parties' fairly negotiated review provisions, I respectfully dissent from the Court's interpretation of the FAA, and would direct the Court of Appeals to affirm the judgment of the District Court enforcing the arbitrator's final award.

■ JUSTICE BREYER, dissenting.

[Omitted].

QUESTIONS AND NOTES

1. While the speed and efficiency of arbitration are often touted by its proponents, large and complex arbitrations frequently take years to resolve, and, particularly in high stakes cases, arbitration can often be more expensive than traditional litigation, primarily because judges tend to limit the length of hearings to a greater degree than do arbitrators. *See* Thomas Stipanowich, *Rethinking American Arbitration*, 63 IND. L.J. at 484 (1988). For many years now, arbitration has been the preferred form of dispute resolution in international transactions. But as international arbitration has come to increasingly resemble American-style litigation, but without appellate review, that may be changing. The ABA JOURNAL recently reported that: "A growing number of businesses appear to be turning away from arbitration and resolving their international commercial disputes the old-fashioned way—in the courts. In a targeted survey of corporate counsel published in 2006 by the School of International Arbitration at Queen Mary, University of London, only 11 percent of in-house counsel said they preferred litigation to settle international disputes. In a follow-up survey conducted two years later, that figure rose to 41 percent—only slightly less than the number who prefer international arbitration." Steven Seidenberg, *International Arbitration Loses Its Grip*, ABA JOURNAL (Apr. 2010). One important persistent advantage to arbitration over adjudication in the international arena is that arbitral awards are more easily enforced in many parts of the world under the New York Convention, *see* Note, p. 257, than are foreign court judgments.

2. How can Hall Street's consent to arbitrate subject to appellate review be deemed consent to arbitrate without appellate review? Would Hall Street have had any better luck challenging the contractual arbitration clause prior to the completion of the arbitration?

3. Do repeat players have a greater or lesser structural advantage in arbitration than in traditional litigation? In thinking about this question, consider that arbitrators are compensated by the parties, are generally free from appellate review, and are not bound to follow precedent or give reasons for their decisions. Under what circumstances would you prefer to litigate before an arbitrator rather than a judge or jury?

4. While *Hall Street* does not on its face disavow *Wilko*'s *dicta* permitting a court to vacate an award that issues in "manifest disregard of the law," following *Hall Street* some courts have found that even "manifest disregard of the law" is no longer a basis to vacate because of the Court's holding in *Hall Street* that the statutory grounds for review are exclusive. Those grounds do not expressly include "manifest disregard of the law." *See, e.g., Frazier v. CitiFinancial Corp.*, 604 F.3d 1313 (11th Cir. 2010); *Citigroup Global Markets v. Bacon*, 562 F.3d 349 (5th Cir. 2009). The Ninth Circuit, however, has found, notwithstanding *Hall Street,* that arbitral awards may still be vacated if "completely irrational" or "the arbitrators recognized the applicable law and then ignored it." *Lagstein v. Certain Underwriters at Lloyds, London*, 607 F.3d 634 (9th Cir. 2010).

CHAPTER 4

SOCIETALLY IMPOSED LIMITS ON PROMISE

I. POSITIVE LAW AS A LIMIT ON CONTRACT

The parties' promises create legal rights and obligations that the state enforces through the courts. In this sense, contract-making is a kind of lawmaking. How does the law the parties make for themselves by their agreements fit in with the larger system of law binding on everyone?

The legal system often supports private contracts and sometimes defers to them. UCC § 1-302 for instance, states a general principle that "the effect of provisions of this Act may be varied by agreement," provided however that "[t]he obligations of good faith, diligence, reasonableness and care prescribed by this Act may not be disclaimed by agreement." Subject to these exceptions, therefore, the UCC provides a background law, sometimes referred to as "default rules," that applies only if the parties do not agree on other rules for themselves.

But many laws or regulations are mandatory rather than merely "default rules." A contract does not exclude the regulatory power of the state to order behavior. Some contracts are illegal, and others are unenforceable because they contravene clear public policies embodied in specific laws. Contract law will not enforce an agreement to sell illegal narcotics, nor one to fix prices. In these examples, making or performing the contract is a crime and the parties to the agreement may be fined or imprisoned. In other cases, the state does not go that far. It declares that a promise is unenforceable but not punishable. For example, in some states unlicensed building contractors cannot recover against homeowners who refuse to pay as provided in the agreement. Sometimes the label of "illegality" is undoubtedly intended to channel behavior and to discourage undesirable transactions. Sometimes this is less clear, and it appears that the court's primary concern is its unwillingness to become involved in a messy or distasteful situation. In every case, the label indicates a judgment that the autonomy of the parties to fix their own rules should be limited based on social or public rulemaking.

As the regulatory state has expanded into a modern-day Leviathan, the sheer quantity of positive legislation impinging on contractual relations has exploded. Thus, employment contracts are constrained by a host of labor and tax laws that impose many obligations on employers that they would never have agreed to accept and deny or limit enforcement to otherwise bargained-for terms. Everyday contractual relations with financial institutions are framed with reference to an equally imposing assortment of banking, tax, and securities regulation. Environmental, homeland security, consumer protection, antitrust, safety regulations, to name but a few areas of modern regulatory legislation, expressly constrain the enforcement and content of contracts all the time in many or most contexts and circumstances. Comprehensively delineating the scope and content of such legislation in a first-year Contracts course is impossible. Such legislation and regulation will form the heart of many of the advanced statutory courses in the upper-level law school curriculum. But to paraphrase John Donne, contract law is not an island entire of itself, it is a part of the main body of the law, and, inevitably, in the course of counseling clients and practicing law, one must understand the applicable constraints that legislation imposes upon contracting parties.

For centuries the common law has also refused to enforce those bargained-for promises thought to contravene public policy. Courts will not aid an assassin in collecting his blood money. Even if the refusal does not meaningfully deter homicide, it is inappropriate to make the judicial process available in support of such an agreement. Defining public policy for these purposes historically was mostly a matter of judicial development. Judges decided, for example, that it was contrary to public policy to restrain trade or impair family relations; courts wouldn't help even if someone had paid good money for a promise to do something contrary to these policies. Today public policy is most often manifested in legislation. Statutes regulate credit and consumer transactions and the licensing of trades and professions. When a statute does not directly control the issue, judges will often point to the existence or absence of related legislation as support for a judicial declaration of public policy.

The following cases offer illustrations of this form of judicial activity. What makes judges hostile to these transactions? Are community interests furthered by the refusal to enforce the promises made?

McConnell v. Commonwealth Pictures Corp.

New York Court of Appeals, 1960.
7 N.Y.2d 465, 166 N.E.2d 494, 199 N.Y.S.2d 483.

■ DESMOND, C.J. ... Plaintiff sues for an accounting. Defendant had agreed in writing that, if plaintiff should succeed in negotiating a contract with a motion picture producer whereby defendant would get the distribution rights for certain motion pictures, defendant would pay plaintiff $10,000 on execution of the contract between defendant and the producer, and would thereafter pay plaintiff a stated percentage of defendant's gross receipts from distribution of the pictures. Plaintiff negotiated the distribution rights for defendant and defendant paid plaintiff the promised $10,000 but later refused to pay him the commissions or to give him an accounting of profits.

Defendant's answer contains, besides certain denials and counterclaims not now before us, two affirmative defenses the sufficiency of which we must decide. In these defenses it is asserted that plaintiff, without the knowledge of defendant or of the producer, procured the distribution rights by bribing a representative of the producer and that plaintiff agreed to pay and did pay to that representative as a bribe the $10,000 which defendant paid plaintiff. The courts below (despite a strong dissent in the Appellate Division) held that the defenses were insufficient to defeat plaintiff's suit. Special Term's opinion said that, since the agreement sued upon between plaintiff and defendant was not in itself illegal, plaintiff's right to be paid for performing it could not be defeated by a showing that he had misconducted himself in carrying it out. The court found a substantial difference between this and the performance of an illegal contract. We take a different view. Proper and consistent application of a prime and long-settled public policy closes the doors of our courts to those who sue to collect the rewards of corruption.

New York's policy has been frequently and emphatically announced in the decisions. "It is the settled law of this State (and probably of every other State) that a party to an illegal contract cannot ask a court of law to help him carry out his illegal object, nor can such a person plead or prove in any court a case in which he, as a basis for his claim, must show forth his illegal purpose," *Stone v. Freeman,* 298 N.Y. 268, 271, citing the leading cases. The money plaintiff sues for was the fruit of an admitted crime and "no court should be required to serve as paymaster of the wages of crime." Id. And it makes no difference that defendant has no title to the money since the court's concern "is not with the position of the defendant" but with the question of whether "a recovery by the plaintiff should be denied for the sake of public interests," a question which is one "of public policy in the administration of the law." *Flegenheimer v. Brogan,* 284 N.Y. 268, 272. That public policy is the one described in *Riggs v. Palmer:*

No one shall be permitted to profit by his own fraud, or to take advantage of his own wrong, or to found any claim upon his own iniquity, or to acquire property by his own crime. These maxims are dictated by public policy, have their foundation in universal law administered in all civilized countries, and have nowhere been superseded by statutes.

We must either repudiate those statements of public policy or uphold these challenged defenses. It is true that some of the leading decisions were in suits on intrinsically illegal contracts but the rule fails of its purpose unless it covers a case like the one at bar. Here, as in *Stone v. Freeman*, the money sued for was (assuming the truth of the defenses) "the fruit of an admitted crime." To allow this plaintiff to collect his commissions would be to let him "profit by his own fraud, or to take advantage of his own wrong, or to found a claim upon his own iniquity, or to acquire property by his own crime" (*Riggs v. Palmer*). The issue is not whether the acts alleged in the defenses would constitute the crime of commercial bribery under section 439 of the Penal Law, although it appears that they would. "A seller cannot recover the price of goods sold where he has paid a commission to an agent of the purchaser; neither could the agent recover the commission, even at common law and before the enactment of section [439] of the Penal Law" (Judge Crane in *Reiner v. North American Newspaper Alliance*, 259 N.Y. 250, 261)....

We are not working here with narrow questions of technical law. We are applying fundamental concepts of morality and fair dealing not to be weakened by exceptions. So far as precedent is necessary, we can rely on *Sirkin v. Fourteenth Street Store*, and *Reiner v. North American Newspaper Alliance*. *Sirkin* is the case closest to ours and shows that, whatever be the law in other jurisdictions, we in New York deny awards for the corrupt performance of contracts even though in essence the contracts are not illegal. Sirkin had sued for the price of goods sold and delivered to defendant. Held to be good was a defense which charged that plaintiff seller had paid a secret commission to an agent of defendant purchaser. There cannot be any difference in principle between that situation and the present one where plaintiff (it is alleged) contracted to buy motion-picture rights for defendant but performed his covenant only by bribing the seller's agent. In the *Reiner* case, likewise, the plaintiff had fully performed the services required by his agreement with the defendant but was denied a recovery because his performance had involved and included "fraud and deception" practiced not on defendant but on a third party. It is beside the point that the present plaintiff on the trial might be able to prove a prima facie case without the bribery being exposed. On the whole case (again assuming that the defenses speak the truth) the disclosed situation would be within the rule of our precedents forbidding court assistance to bribers.

It is argued that a reversal here means that the doing of any small illegality in the performance of an otherwise lawful contract will deprive the doer of all rights, with the result that the other party will get a windfall and there will be great injustice. Our ruling does not go as far as that. It is not every minor wrongdoing in the course of contract performance that will insulate the other party from liability for work done or goods furnished. There must at least be a direct connection between the illegal *rule* transaction and the obligation sued upon. Connection is a matter of degree. Some illegalities are merely incidental to the contract sued on. We cannot now, any more than in our past decisions, announce what will be the results of all the kinds of corruption, minor and major, essential and peripheral. All we are doing here is labeling the conduct described in these defenses as gross corruption depriving plaintiff of all right of access to the courts of New York State. Consistent with public morality and settled public policy, we hold that a party will be denied recovery even on a contract valid on its face, if it appears that he has resorted to gravely immoral and illegal con- *rule* duct in accomplishing its performance.

Perhaps this application of the principle represents a distinct step beyond *Sirkin* and *Reiner* in the sense that we are here barring recovery under a contract which in itself is entirely legal. But if this be an extension, public policy supports it. We point out that our holding is limited to cases in which the illegal performance of a contract originally valid takes the form of commercial bribery or similar conduct and in which *rule* the illegality is central to or a dominant part of the plaintiff's whole course of conduct in performance of the contract.

There is no pertinence here of the rule which makes such defenses unavailable to one who is a mere depository or escrow-that is, one who is holding money or goods for one of the parties without himself being a party to the transaction sued upon. That exception is used when, in execution or satisfaction of an illegal transaction, one of the parties thereto turns over money or property to a third person (not a party to the illegal deal) for the use of one who is a party. In our case there were two parties only plaintiff and defendant. There is no third person holding money or property.

The sufficiency of defendant's counterclaim (for the return of its $10,000) was litigated below but it is not before us on this appeal.

The order appealed from should be reversed, with costs, the certified question answered in the negative, and plaintiff's motion, insofar as it attacks the sufficiency of the two separate defenses, should be denied.

■ FROESSEL, J. (dissenting). Plaintiff sues for an accounting and related relief under a clearly lawful contract, whereby defendant agreed to make certain payments in connection with plaintiff's negotiation, on behalf of defendant, of an agreement with Universal Pictures Company, Inc., for distribution rights with respect to 40 western feature films and 4 serial motion pictures. The payments agreed upon were $10,000 upon the execution of a contract with Universal, and 20% of all the gross receipts received by defendant from the distribution of said pictures after defendant had re-couped the amount of $100,000 from 60% of the gross receipts. Upon negotiation of the distribution rights, defendant paid plaintiff said sum of $10,000, but thereafter declined upon demand to pay plaintiff any further moneys.

Two defenses set forth in the answer were stricken below. The first defense al-leged that plaintiff secured the Universal contract as a result of influencing an agent of Universal and United World Films, Inc., to cause United to execute the contract with defendant, for which he paid the agent $10,000, in claimed violation of section 439 of the Penal Law. The second defense reiterated the allegations of the first, and alleged that the enforcement of the contract would be contrary to public policy. These allegations are denied, except of course as they are deemed admitted as a matter of law by challenging their legal sufficiency. It is to be noted that defendant does not charge that its own agent was bribed or that its contract with plaintiff con-templates any illegal act. Moreover, neither the answer nor the affidavit in opposition suggests that Universal or United has in anywise questioned the distri-bution contract or that defendant has not enjoyed the full fruits thereof.

The narrow question before us as framed by Special Term is "whether the un-lawful acts imputed to the plaintiff in performance are fatal to recovery under a lawful contract." We agree with the courts below "that recovery for services under a valid agreement may be had, notwithstanding that the plaintiff has in the course of their rendition committed illegal acts." This was implicit in our holding in *Chesebrough v. Conover*, and it was so squarely held in *Dunham v. Hastings Pavement Co.*, where the court correctly stated the applicable rule of law as follows:

Precedent

> If the contract contemplated legal service, and that alone, we do not think that it would be rendered illegal by the fact that the plaintiff did illegal acts in its performance. The question is and continues, was the contract in fact for the per-formance of illegal service? If it was not, then it is valid and can be enforced.

This is not a case where the contract *sued upon* is intrinsically illegal; or was *pro-cured* by the commission of a crime; or where a beneficiary under a will murdered his ancestor in order to obtain the speedy enjoyment of his property. In the *Sirkin* case, so heavily relied upon by the majority, the plaintiff obtained the very contract he was seeking to enforce by paying secret commissions to defendant's own pur-chasing agent. In *Merchants' Line v. Baltimore & Ohio R. Co.*, we pointed out that in *Sirkin* "the plaintiff reached and bribed the man who made *the contract under which he was seeking to recover*" (emphasis supplied). In *Morgan Munitions Supply Co. v. Studebaker Corp.*, we likewise cited the *Sirkin* case for the proposition that "a con-tract *procured by* the commission of a crime is unenforceable even if executed" (emphasis supplied).

In the instant case, the contract which plaintiff is seeking to enforce is perfectly valid, and it was not intended or even contemplated that plaintiff would perform the contract by illegal or corrupt means. Having received and retained the full benefits of plaintiff's performance, defendant now seeks to "inject into" its contract with plaintiff, "which was fair and legal in itself, the illegal feature of the other independent transaction." *Messersmith v. American Fidelity Co.* This court is now adopting a rule that a party may retain the benefits of, but escape his obligations under, a wholly lawful contract if the other party commits some illegal act not contemplated nor necessary under the contract. By way of a single illustration, an owner may thus avoid paying his contractor for the cost of erecting a building because the contractor gave an inspector a sum of money to expedite an inspection.

The majority opinion seeks to distinguish between "major" and "minor" illegality and "direct" and "peripheral" corruption. It decides this case on the ground that the manner in which plaintiff performed his admittedly valid contract with defendant was "gravely immoral and illegal." Such distinctions are neither workable nor sanctioned by authority. If a contract was lawfully made, and did not contemplate wrongdoing, it is enforcible; if, on the other hand, it was procured by the commission of a crime, or was in fact for the performance of illegal services, it is not enforcible. These are the criteria distinguishing enforcible from unenforcible contracts not "nice" distinctions between degrees of illegality and immorality in the performance of lawful contracts, or whether the illegal act of performance was "directly" or "peripherally" related to the main contract.

Moreover, a reversal here would be contrary to the spirit, if not the letter, of our holding in *Southwestern Shipping Corp. v. National City Bank*. The broad proposition for which that case stands is that a party unconnected with an illegal agreement should not be permitted to reap a windfall by pleading the illegality of that agreement, to which he was a stranger. There, the contract between the plaintiff and the bank was entirely lawful, and the bank attempted to avoid the consequences of its breach of contract and negligence by asserting the illegality of a different contract between plaintiff and a third party. Here, the contract between plaintiff and defendant was perfectly legal, and defendant is seeking to avoid its obligations under the contract of which it has reaped the benefits for some 12 years by asserting the illegality of a different and subsequent agreement between plaintiff and a third party. This it should not be permitted to do.

The order appealed from should be affirmed, with costs, and the question certified answered in the affirmative.

■ VAN VOORHIS, J. (dissenting). Public morals and fair dealing are likely to be advanced by limiting rather than by enlarging the rule that is being extended to the facts of this case. This rule is grounded on considerations of public policy. Courts will not intervene between thieves to compel them to divide the spoils. But in a situation like the present, it seems to me that the effect of this decision will not be to restrain the corrupt influencing of agents, employees or servants but to encourage misappropriation of funds and breaches of faith between persons who do not stand in corrupt relationships with one another. The public interest is not served best by decisions which put a premium on taking unconscionable advantage of such situations, or which drive the enforcement of obligations of this kind underground. I concur in the dissenting opinion by Judge Froessel.

QUESTIONS AND NOTES

1. Chief Judge Desmond and Judge Froessel are bound by the same precedents and the same factual record on appeal. Review each opinion and compare their treatment of the following issues: What questions does each judge think that the court must answer? What does each judge think that the earlier cases mean—that is, what do the prior cases tell him is the law? Do the judges agree which public policy is at issue? What is the source of that public policy? What does each judge think the court must do to further that public policy? Where does Chief Judge Desmond find the "fundamental concepts of morality and fair dealing not to be weakened by exceptions" that he refers to on p. 302?

2. Suppose that Seller, in order to deliver goods to Buyer on time, speeds to the place of delivery in violation of the speed limit. Is Buyer excused from accepting the goods and paying for them? If Buyer only learns of the speeding violation after accepting the goods but before paying for them, can Buyer keep the goods but refuse to pay for them? If McConnell had asked, would the court have forced Commonwealth to give up its distribution rights and all the profits made as of the time of litigation?

3. Can Universal/United refuse to continue its distribution contract with Commonwealth because that contract was tainted in its procurement? If "yes," did claimant McConnell earn the commission he claimed?

4. Who benefits from the court's decision in this case: crooks, people who do business with crooks, or pharisees who have crooks do their dirty work for them? Who would have benefited if the court had affirmed the decision below?

5. Is it unethical for a lawyer to draft a contract that contravenes public policy? To what sanctions, if any, should the lawyer be subject? On what does your answer depend?

6. Reconcile (if you can) *McConnell* to a later New York case, *XLO Concrete Corp. v. Rivergate Corp.*, 634 N.E.2d 158 (N.Y. 1994). In *XLO*, the plaintiff subcontractor, XLO, sued to enforce a written contract with the defendant general contractor, Rivergate, to pour the concrete superstructure of a project in Manhattan. XLO was a member of the "Club," an arrangement among four New York City

organized crime families and seven concrete construction companies. The Club chose which concrete companies would get which jobs and rigged the bidding to ensure that the chosen firm would win. Presumably this bid-rigging system inflated the price of concrete construction work in New York by eliminating true competitive bidding. The Club allocated the Rivergate project to XLO, which then negotiated a contract with the defendant. The defendant (like all general contractors in New York) had full knowledge of the Club and its rules. XLO completed the work as agreed, but the defendant refused to pay. The defendant contended that "the contract at issue is so integrally related to an antitrust conspiracy ... that it is void and unenforceable as a matter of law." The court rejected this contention, holding that "a contract which is legal on its face and does not call for unlawful conduct in its performance is not voidable simply because it resulted from an antitrust conspiracy." The court stated that "courts should avoid upholding antitrust defenses in contract cases where doing so would work a substantial forfeiture on one party while unjustly enriching the other."

RESTATEMENT, SECOND, CONTRACTS:

§ 178. When a Term Is Unenforceable on Grounds of Public Policy.

(1) A promise or other term of an agreement is unenforceable on grounds of public policy if legislation provides that it is unenforceable or the interest in its enforcement is clearly outweighed in the circumstances by a public policy against the enforcement of such terms.

(2) In weighing the interest in the enforcement of a term, account is taken of

    (a) the parties' justified expectations,

    (b) any forfeiture that would result if enforcement were denied, and

    (c) any special public interest in the enforcement of the particular term.

(3) In weighing a public policy against enforcement of a term, account is taken of

    (a) the strength of that policy as manifested by legislation or judicial decisions,

    (b) the likelihood that a refusal to enforce the term will further that policy,

    (c) the seriousness of any misconduct involved and the extent to which it was deliberate, and

    (d) the directness of the connection between that misconduct and the term.

§ 179 Bases of Public Policies Against Enforcement.

A public policy against the enforcement of promises or other terms may be derived by the court from

(a) legislation relevant to such a policy, or

(b) the need to protect some aspect of the public welfare, as is the case for the judicial policies against, for example,

    (i) restraint of trade,

    (ii) impairment of family relations, and

    (iii) interference with other protected interests.

QUESTIONS AND NOTES

1. Reconsider *McConnell,* p. 301, in light of REST. (2d) §§ 178-79. Do the factors in the balancing test set out in the Restatement lead you to the majority or the dissenting judges' conclusions? Are these factors helpful in your analysis?

2. Note that Chief Judge Desmond expressly relied on principles of public policy predating New York's commercial bribery statute, N.Y. Penal Code § 439. Presumably these principles fall within Rest. 2d § 179(b)(iii), unlawful interference with a protected interest, the protected interest being the fiduciary relationship between Universal and the Universal employee corrupted by McConnell's bribe. What other sort of interests are worthy of this kind of protection, and how far does the protection go? Note the tension between the judicial policy against "restraint of trade" and the judicial policy against "interference with protected interests." In *McConnell,* interfering with another firm's employees violates public policy. But in other situations, public policy in favor of competition may privilege firms to interfere with their competitors' employees by recruiting them away. California, for example, has a particularly strong public policy in favor of open competition. Accordingly, unlike the situation in New York, *see ABC v. Wolf,* p. 104, the general rule in California is that covenants not to compete executed by employees are void. Cal. Civ. Code § 16600 ("Except as provided in this chapter, every contract by which anyone is restrained from engaging in a lawful profession, trade, or business of any kind is to that extent void."). There are two narrow exceptions to this rule, where a person sells the goodwill of a business and executes a covenant not to compete with the buyer, and where a partner agrees not to compete in anticipation of dissolution of a partnership. Cal. Civ. Code § 16601-16602. But otherwise the general rule applies. *Edwards v. Arthur Anderson LLP,* 44 Cal.4th 937 (2008). The tension between protection of existing legal and economic relationships and the promotion of free competition will resurface in Chapter Nine when we discuss tortious interference with contractual relations.

Perhaps the most difficult area for courts in deriving and applying public policy exceptions to contract enforcement is on the basis that the agreement "impair[s] family relationships." REST. (2d) § 179(b)(ii). The problem, of course, is that the nature and content of family relationships in our society is both rapidly evolving and controversial. Reliance on precedent can be hazardous in this area, as the case below suggests.

In re Marriage of Pendleton and Fireman

California Supreme Court, 2000.
24 Cal.4th 39.

■ BAXTER, J.. We are asked to decide whether a premarital agreement in which the parties to be married waive the right to spousal support in case of dissolution is enforceable.[1] The Court of Appeal held that such agreements are enforceable. It is not necessary to decide in this case whether all such agreements are enforceable regardless of the circumstances of the parties at the time enforcement is sought. We conclude that no policy of this state makes an agreement like that entered into by the parties to this action per se unenforceable, and affirm the judgment of the Court of Appeal.

I. BACKGROUND

Candace Pendleton and Barry I. Fireman married on July 13, 1991. On July 1, 1991, they had executed a premarital agreement which provided, inter alia: "[B]oth parties now and forever waive, in the event of a dissolution of the marriage, all rights to any type of spousal support or child support from the other; ..." The agreement acknowledged that each party had been represented by independent counsel in the negotiation and preparation of the agreement, that counsel had advised each of the meaning and legal consequences of the agreement, and that each party had read and understood the agreement and its legal consequences. Their respective counsel certified that this had been done and that their clients understood the meaning and legal consequences of the agreement and executed it freely and voluntarily.

---

1. The right to spousal support is statutory. Family Code section 4330, subdivision (a), provides: "In a judgment of dissolution of marriage or legal separation of the parties, the court may order a party to pay for the support of the other party an amount, for a period of time, that the court determines is just and reasonable, based on the standard of living established during the marriage, taking into consideration the circumstances as provided in Chapter 2 (commencing with Section 4320)."

The couple separated in 1995, and on April 3, 1996, Candace filed a petition for dissolution of the marriage and subsequently sought spousal support. Candace acknowledged the existence of a premarital agreement in a declaration that accompanied her request for spousal support, stating that she was then investigating its validity. At the time the dissolution petition was filed, each party had a net worth of approximately $2.5 million. Candace, who had two children from a prior marriage, held a master's degree and was an aspiring writer. Barry, who held a doctorate in pharmacology and a law degree, was a businessman with ownership interests in numerous companies and business ventures. Candace declared that her monthly gross income was $5,772, consisting of $1,352 in Social Security benefits for two children from a prior marriage, $2,000 from a brokerage account, and $2,420 in rental income. Her net monthly income was $4,233.

Barry sought to strike the pleading seeking support or to have a separate trial on the validity of the prenuptial agreement. The court denied the motion for separate trial, concluding that discovery on the issue of validity would overlap that on other issues and would not result in saving time or litigation costs. The court ruled that the waiver of spousal support was against public policy and thus was unenforceable,[2]

---

2. The order explained: "Assuming arguendo that the validity and enforceability of the waiver of spousal support provision of the parties' prenuptial agreement can be tested in a motion to strike, the court denied this motion on the ground that a waiver of spousal support in a premarital agreement is void and unenforceable as against California public policy. The court is persuaded that the legislative history of the statute dealing with the permissible subjects of premarital agreements indicated that the Legislature intended to omit a provision in the California version of the Uniform Premarital Agreement Act (UPAA) that allowed for a premarital waiver of spousal support.

"The court is further persuaded that the pre-UPAA cases that hold that premarital agreements that diminish or waive a party's obligation to pay spousal support to the other party to the marriage are unenforceable as against public policy and would continue to be so held after the passage of the UPAA. At least one purpose of a policy that a spousal support waiver will be unenforceable in this state is to protect the state, not just a party to the marriage. A person's financial circumstances can change markedly from those found just prior to that person's marriage. A valid premarital spousal support waiver could produce spouses who at the time of their marriage have assets and earning capacity to support themselves without spousal support, but by the time of the dissolution of their marriages may be unable to support themselves and in need of financial support. The state has an interest in having such needy spouses supported by their spouses if possible. Just as the state has a serious fiscal interest in not paying for support of children if there is a parent with the capacity to support that parent's children, the state has a fiscal interest in seeing that it not be forced to support needy former spouses if the non-needy former spouse is able to contribute to the support of the needy former spouse and if ordering the payment of such support is warranted, pursuant to the principles of Family Code § 4320. Thus the same principles and policies that underlie the public policy against permitting a binding waiver of child support would apply to premarital waivers of spousal support."

noted that the couple had maintained a lifestyle in the high $20,000 to $32,000 per month range, and ordered Barry to pay temporary spousal support of $8,500 per month.

On Barry's appeal, the Court of Appeal reversed the order for temporary spousal support. The Court of Appeal acknowledged that the Legislature had deleted subdivision (a)(4) from section 3 of the Uniform Premarital Agreement Act (Uniform Act) prior to adopting the act in 1985. The omitted subdivision would have expressly permitted the parties to a premarital agreement to contract with respect to modification or elimination of spousal support. The Court of Appeal concluded, however, that the Legislature intended to leave the question of whether spousal support waivers in premarital agreements violate public policy to the courts and that there was presently no authority governing the public policy question. In reaching the latter conclusion, the court reasoned that the question had not been reconsidered after the adoption of the Family Law Act of 1969, which repealed the law permitting divorce only on a showing of fault, or in light of current law that gives both spouses equal control over management and control of community property and mandates equal division on dissolution. In the view of the Court of Appeal, the current state of family law is one that "should not per se prohibit premarital spousal support waivers or limitations. All the protection the parties need is expressly provided by the California [version of the Uniform] Act." The Court of Appeal therefore remanded the matter to the trial court which, in the belief that such waivers were per se unenforceable, had not determined whether this agreement was enforceable under the rules set forth in section 1615 and the policies underlying the Uniform Act and the California version thereof.[4]

---

4. Section 1615:

    (a) A premarital agreement is not enforceable if the party against whom enforcement is sought proves either of the following:

        (1) That party did not execute the agreement voluntarily.

        (2) The agreement was unconscionable when it was executed and, before execution of the agreement, all of the following applied to that party:

            (A)   That party was not provided a fair and reasonable disclosure of the property or financial obligations of the other party.

            (B)   That party did not voluntarily and expressly waive, in writing, any right to disclosure of the property or financial obligations of the other party beyond the disclosure provided.

            (C)   That party did not have, or reasonably could not have had, an adequate knowledge of the property or financial obligations of the other party.

    (b) An issue of unconscionability of a premarital agreement shall be decided by the court as a matter of law."

II. DISCUSSION

Article 2 of the California Uniform Premarital Agreement Act governs premarital agreements. A premarital agreement is "an agreement between prospective spouses made in contemplation of marriage and to be effective upon marriage." Section 1612 specifies the permissible objects of a premarital agreement:

"(a) Parties to a premarital agreement may contract with respect to all of the following:

(1) The rights and obligations of each of the parties in any of the property of either or both of them whenever and wherever acquired or located.

(2) The right to buy, sell, use, transfer, exchange, abandon, lease, consume, expend, assign, create a security interest in, mortgage, encumber, dispose of, or otherwise manage and control property.

(3) The disposition of property upon separation, marital dissolution, death, or the occurrence or nonoccurrence of any other event.

(4) The making of a will, trust, or other arrangement to carry out the provisions of the agreement.

(5) The ownership rights in and disposition of the death benefit from a life insurance policy.

(6) The choice of law governing the construction of the agreement.

(7) Any other matter, including their personal rights and obligations, not in violation of public policy or a statute imposing a criminal penalty.

(b) The right of a child to support may not be adversely affected by a premarital agreement."

As noted, *ante*, the California version of the Uniform Act omits subdivision (a)(4) of section 3 of the Uniform Act. When first introduced on March 7, 1985, Senate Bill No. 1143, the California version of the Uniform Act, included subdivision (a)(4), and thus listed among the permissible subjects of a premarital agreement "the modification or elimination of spousal support." The spousal support waiver provision was deleted by amendment. The amendment of Senate Bill 1143 that deleted subdivision (a)(4) simultaneously deleted a provision, subdivision (b) of section 6 of the Uniform Act, which provided: "If a provision of a premarital agreement modifies or eliminates spousal support and that modification or elimination causes one party to the agreement to be eligible for support under a program of public assistance at the time of separation or marital dissolution, a court, notwithstanding the terms of the agreement, may require the other party to provide support to the extent necessary to avoid that eligibility." As enacted, Senate Bill 1143 became Civil Code former section 5315, now Family Code section 1612.

The Court of Appeal held that neither the Legislature's deletion from the legislation of express authorization for premarital waivers of spousal support, nor past cases refusing to enforce waivers of spousal support, preclude such waivers today. The court reasoned that the legislative history of section 1612 suggested that, in omitting subdivision (a)(4) of the Uniform Act, the Legislature intended to leave the enforceability of spousal support waivers to the courts. It found support for that conclusion in two reports by the Assembly Subcommittee on Administration of Justice. The first was prepared for an August 19, 1985, hearing on Senate Bill 1143. Senate Bill 1143 repealed prior statutory law governing premarital agreements and enacted the Uniform Act. In the first report staff advised that California courts did not permit enforcement of premarital agreements on spousal support and recommended deletion "to allow California case law to continue to prevail on the issue of spousal support in premarital agreements."

The second report, prepared after the amendment passed, stated that as a result of the amendment "California case law would ... prevail on the issue of spousal support in premarital agreements. There is a split in authority among the states as to whether a premarital agreement may control on the issue of spousal support. Some states, such as California, do not permit a premarital agreement to control this issue. See *In re Marriage of Dawley*, 17 Cal.3d 342 (1976), in which the court notes that the enforcement of provisions in premarital contracts to waive or limit spousal support rights is barred because such provisions are considered promotive of divorce." The Court of Appeal understood this history to mean that the Legislature recognized that enforceability of spousal support waivers is a question for the courts, not the Legislature.

At the time the California version of the Uniform Act was adopted, this court had held that agreements waiving the right to spousal support were unenforceable as being against public policy if the waiver would promote or encourage dissolution. This court had held in *In re Marriage of Higgason*, speaking of both spousal support and property division, that to be valid, premarital agreements must be made "in contemplation that the marriage relation will continue until the parties are separated by death. Contracts which facilitate divorce or separation by providing for a settlement only in the event of such an occurrence are void as against public policy. Insofar as an antenuptial agreement relates to the disposition of the property of the respective parties, and does not seek to alter support obligations imposed by law, it will be upheld." At issue in *Higgason* was an agreement in which both husband and wife waived all interest in the property of the other party as well as the right to support. The court concluded that a purported waiver was invalid as against public policy insofar as the agreement sought to alter the wife's statutory obligation to support the husband during marriage. The court also held that the agreement did not preclude exercise of the court's discretionary power to award postdissolution support. Although the basis for the latter holding is not made clear in the opinion, it appears to be that married persons assume, by means of the marriage contract, an obligation for support that continues throughout the lifetime of the parties regardless of whether they live together or apart, and any agreement to waive that obligation is also unenforceable.

When the issue of enforceability of premarital agreements next arose in *In re Marriage of Dawley* (1976), where the parties had agreed before marriage that the earnings and property acquired during marriage would be held as separate property, the court concluded that *Higgason* had misstated the law in stating that premarital agreements must be made in contemplation that the marriage would continue throughout the lifetime of the parties and disapproved that *Higgason* dictum. We also explained that, apart from *Higgason*, "California courts have uniformly held that contracts offend the state policy favoring marriage only" if, objectively viewed, by its terms the contract promotes dissolution of marriage. We noted in *Dawley* that in two cases provisions in agreements that waived or limited spousal support rights had been invalidated on the basis that they promoted divorce, while other provisions containing property divisions were enforced; but *Dawley* did not endorse or otherwise approve those decisions. Notably, in *Dawley* we did not distinguish premarital agreements governing property rights and those governing spousal support. Our discussion of the enforceability of premarital agreements in no way suggested that spousal support waivers were per se unenforceable. The rule we stated was: "[A]n antenuptial agreement violates the state policy favoring marriage only insofar as its terms encourage or promote dissolution." [5]

The parties have not called our attention to any legislative history other than the two legislative reports, the latter of which did not accurately state the holding of this court in *Dawley*,[6] and neither of which adequately explains the legislative purpose in

---

5. *Dawley* also observed that use of the term "facilitate" in past cases describing unenforceable premarital agreements was misleading, since any such agreement could be said to facilitate dissolution by making a dissolution proceeding shorter and less expensive. Speaking in the context of a property agreement, we said that "public policy does not render property agreements unenforceable merely because such agreements simplify the division of marital property: it is only when the agreement encourages or promotes dissolution that it offends the public policy to foster and protect marriage."

6. Candace asks the court to take judicial notice of copies of: (1) a letter dated August 14, 1985, to Assemblyman Lloyd G. Connelly, from the Family Law Section of the State Bar of California opposing the inclusion in Senate Bill 1143 of authorization for premarital waivers of spousal support; (2) a June 6, 1985, letter to the same effect to Senator Robert Beverly; (3) various sections of the New Jersey version of the Uniform Premarital Agreement Act; and (4) former section 159 of the Civil Code, as originally enacted in 1872 and repealed in 1969.

omitting subdivision (a)(4). Two possible interpretations of the Legislature's intent in omitting express authority for premarital waivers of spousal support come to mind. The Legislature may have intended to deny couples the right to enter into any premarital agreement regarding spousal support by adopting what the committee report erroneously described as the existing case law under which premarital waivers would be per se unenforceable. Alternatively, the Legislature may have concluded that policy governing spousal support agreements, having been established by the court in the past, should continue to evolve in the court.

The public policy under which waivers of spousal support once were held unenforceable was explained in *Loveren v. Loveren* (1895): "'The authorities are uniform in holding that any contract between the parties having for its object the dissolution of the marriage contract, or *facilitating that result*, such as an agreement by the defendant in a pending action for divorce to withdraw his or her opposition and to make no defense, is void as *contra bonos mores*'; and that courts 'will esteem it their duty to interfere, *upon their own motion*, whenever it appears the dissolution is sought to be effected by the connivance or collusion of the parties.'" Another concern was that a man should not be able to contract before marriage against the liability to his wife that he would incur should he commit offenses against the wife during the marriage. The rule those decisions implemented found its origin in the common law, but the policy had been declared by the Legislature in 1872 with the adoption of the Civil Code. Former section 159 of the Civil Code then provided: "A husband and wife cannot, by any contract with each other, alter their legal relations, except as to property, ... and except that they may agree to an immediate separation, and may make provision for the support of either of them and of their children during such separation."[8]

Barry suggests, and we agree, that changes in the law governing the spousal relation warrant reexamination of the assumptions and policy underlying the refusal to enforce waivers of spousal support. We may not do so, however, if the Legislature

---

The first two items, although bearing a Legislative Intent Service stamp, are not certified copies and it is not apparent that either was considered by the Legislature when Senate Bill 1143 was considered. There is no basis for an assumption that such letters reflect legislative intent. Judicial notice may be taken of the law of another state. However, that law was not enacted until 1988 and thus is not relevant to legislative intent in this state. We therefore deny the request for judicial notice.

The position of the Women Lawyers' Association of Los Angeles was made clear to the Legislature in the subcommittee report discussed herein which quoted parts of it. That report listed the Family Law Section of the State Bar as a supporter of Senate Bill 1143, a position that later changed, as reflected in the referenced letter. The request for judicial notice of former section 159 of the Civil Code is granted.

8. At that time, the court was empowered to award support to a wife to whom a divorce was granted and could also award maintenance even if the divorce was denied.

intends that section 1612 control the permissible subjects of a premarital agreement and that public policy with respect to waiver of spousal support no longer be governed by the common law subject to reconsideration and development by the courts.

(1) It is clear that the Legislature understood that the omission of authorization for premarital waivers of spousal support in section 1612 would leave the law as it was in 1985. The subcommittee reports reflect that understanding. We do not agree with respondent and the dissent, however, that in so doing the Legislature thereby abrogated the role of the courts in developing the law governing premarital waivers of spousal support. We will not presume that the Legislature intended that the law remain static. It would be unreasonable to assume that the Legislature intended the common law of the 19th century to govern the marital relationship in the 21st century. The most reasonable understanding of the Legislature's purpose when it omitted subdivision (a)(4) is that it was satisfied with the evolution of the common law governing premarital waivers of spousal support and intended to permit that evolution to continue. Had the Legislature intended to forbid spousal support waivers, it is logical to assume that it would have done so by expressly including spousal support in subdivision (b) of section 1612, which reads: "The right of a child to support may not be adversely affected by a premarital agreement." We agree with the Court of Appeal, therefore, that the court is free to reexamine the assumptions that underlie the common law rule that premarital spousal support waivers promote dissolution and for that reason contravene public policy. (2) Having done so, we also agree with the Court of Appeal that the common law policy, based on assumptions that dissolution of marriage is contrary to public policy and that premarital waivers of spousal support may promote dissolution, is anachronistic.

Some 41 jurisdictions have already abandoned the common law restrictions on premarital waivers of spousal support. In 21 jurisdictions, premarital waivers of spousal support are authorized by statutes that either adopt all or substantially all of the provisions of the Uniform Act. One jurisdiction (New York) had other statutory authorization for such waivers, and in another 18 the right to enforce a premarital waiver of spousal support exists pursuant to judicial decision.

The changes in public policy and the attitude toward marriage, already reflected in *Dawley*, are made manifest by contrasting the current statutory treatment of marriage and premarital agreements with an early decision of the Oregon Supreme Court that reflects the 19th-century view of public policy regarding marriage. "The welfare of society is so deeply interested in the preservation of the marriage relation, and so fraught with evil is regarded whatever is calculated to impair its usefulness, or designed to terminate it, that it has long been the settled policy of the law to guard and maintain it with a watchful vigilance. Although marriage, in the eye of the law, is a civil contract, unlike any other civil contract, it cannot be rescinded or annulled by consent of the parties to it. By mutual consent, if the parties are of the proper age and capacity, the marriage relation may be created and receive the sanction of the law, but it cannot dissolve or terminate it. That high office can only be performed by a court of competent jurisdiction, for some specified cause prescribed by law, upon proof taken in a suit for that purpose. The good order and well being of society, as well as the laws of this state, require this. And so strict and careful are courts in the administration of this justice, out of regard for the public morals and the general welfare of society, that they will esteem it their duty to interfere upon their own motions whenever it appears the dissolution is sought to be effected by the conniv-ance or collusion of the parties; and all contrivances or agreements, having for their object the termination of the marriage contract, or designed to facilitate or procure it, will be declared illegal and void as against public policy.... '... And when the mar-riage relation has been assumed, it is equally the policy of the law to sustain and uphold it. It, therefore, holds all contracts void which contemplate or provide for the future separation of the parties....'" *Phillips v. Thorp,* 10 Or. at 495-496.

California statutory law of the time reflected these policies and values. In 1872, divorce could be granted only on the grounds of adultery, extreme cruelty, willful desertion, willful neglect, habitual intemperance, or conviction of a felony, and could be denied on grounds, inter alia, of connivance or collusion-the "corrupt con-sent" by one party to the other's commission of an act constituting cause for divorce or an agreement between the parties that one should commit, appear to commit, or represent to the court that one had committed such an act. The husband had exclu-sive control of the community property with "absolute power of disposition (other than testamentary) as he ha[d] of his separate estate" and a wife could not contract for the payment of money. The court was empowered to order the husband to pay alimony on divorce if the divorce was granted for an offense of the husband, but had no power to order a wife to pay alimony.

The assumptions underlying the refusal to enforce premarital waivers of spousal support were that the state had a vital interest in and should act to ensure the per-manency of the marriage relation, and that this interest was undermined by such waivers, assumptions reflected in statutory law governing marriage, dissolution, and property rights. In *Dawley,* however, we emphasized that only agreements that on their face promote dissolution violate the public policy favoring marriage. We rec-ognized there that contemporary attitudes toward the marriage relationship are more pragmatic: "In recent years, however, an increasing number of couples have executed antenuptial agreements in order to structure their legal relationship in a manner more suited to their needs and values. Neither the reordering of property rights to fit the needs and desires of the couple, nor realistic planning that takes ac-count of the possibility of dissolution, offends the public policy favoring and protecting marriage. It is only when the terms of an agreement go further-when they promote and encourage dissolution, and thereby threaten to induce the destruction of a marriage that might otherwise endure-that such terms offend public policy." *Dawley*, 17 Cal.3d at 358.

Both public attitude and contemporary official policy have changed substantially over the past century. Public policy continues to favor and encourage marriage, but it now acknowledges that lifetime commitment is no longer the norm. When legitimate grounds for dissolution exist, dissolution does not contravene public policy, but is the preferred solution. The adoption of the California Uniform Premarital Agreement Act itself reflects recognition that permanency is no longer a dominant characteristic of modern marriage. The Family Law Act of 1969 permitted, and now the Family Code permits, no-fault dissolution. A stipulation governing division of community property, once held in reliance on *Phillips v. Thorp* to be collusive and to violate public policy, today is expressly allowed, encouraged, and no longer condemned as facilitating dissolution. Spouses who are separated have long been permitted to contract with regard to division of property and to include provisions for spousal support on dissolution, even when community property was evenly divided and thus the division was not consideration for the modification of spousal support rights. The right of husband and wife to agree in writing to separate and provide for spousal support both during separation and on dissolution of the marriage continues to be expressly recognized by statute.

Legal recognition also has been given to the changing position of married women who, in increasing numbers, are employed outside the home and have been given equal right to management of the property of the community as well as primary right to manage businesses they are operating. Public policy toward spousal support has also changed. While spouses must support each other during marriage, the court has been given greater discretion in marital dissolutions to deny spousal support altogether or to limit such support in an amount and duration that reflects the ability of both parties in contemporary unions to provide for their own needs. The changing attitudes are reflected in the 1969 repeal of former section 139 of the Civil Code, which authorized the court to award lifetime support if a divorce was based on an offense of the husband. The underlying theory, we explained was then "'that the husband entered upon an obligation which bound him to support his wife during the period of their joint lives, that by his own wrong he has forced her to sever the relation which enabled her to compel the performance of this duty, and that he is required to make compensation for the offense committed by him which has deprived her of the benefit of the obligation.'" *Webber v. Webber* (1948) 33 Cal.2d 153, 157-158. Today, however, a court ordering spousal support must consider, inter alia, "[t]he goal that the supported party shall be self-supporting within a reasonable period of time." The law has thus progressed from a rule that entitled some women to lifelong alimony as a condition of the marital contract of support to one that entitles either spouse to postdissolution support for only so long as necessary to become self-supporting.

These changes in the relationship between spouses and support obligations in particular, accurately described by the Court of Appeal as "dramatic" and by a legal commentator as a "sea change" (Ellman, *The Theory of Alimony* (1989) 77 Cal. L.Rev. 1, 7), clearly warrant reassessment of what remains of the rule that premarital waivers of spousal support may promote dissolution and, if they do so, are unenforceable. Public policy, to the extent that it is reflected in these legislative acts, no longer reflects concern that premarital waivers of property rights threaten the marriage relationship. Section 1612 expressly permits the parties to contract with regard to numerous property rights, including "[t]he disposition of property upon separation, marital dissolution, death, or the occurrence or nonoccurrence of any other event." No basis appears on which to distinguish premarital waivers of spousal support from agreements governing property rights insofar as either has a potential for promoting dissolution. As the Court of Appeal recognized, today the availability of an enforceable premarital agreement "may in fact encourage rather than discourage marriage." We agree with the Court of Appeal, therefore, that, when entered into voluntarily by parties who are aware of the effect of the agreement, a premarital waiver of spousal support does not offend contemporary public policy. Such agreements are, therefore, permitted under section 1612, subdivision (a)(7), which authorizes the parties to contract in a premarital agreement regarding "[a]ny other matter, including their personal rights and obligations, not in violation of public policy or a statute imposing a criminal penalty."

We need not decide here whether circumstances existing at the time enforcement of a waiver of spousal support is sought might make enforcement unjust.[12] It is enough to conclude here that no public policy is violated by permitting enforcement of a waiver of spousal support executed by intelligent, well-educated persons, each of whom appears to be self-sufficient in property and earning ability, and both of whom have the advice of counsel regarding their rights and obligations as marital partners at the time they execute the waiver. Such a waiver does not violate public policy and is not per se unenforceable as the trial court believed.

III. DISPOSITION

The judgment of the Court of Appeal is affirmed.

Werdegar, J., Chin, J., Brown, J., Hastings, J., concurred.

---

12. The Legislature may, of course, limit the right to enter into premarital waivers of spousal support and/or specify the circumstances in which enforcement should be denied.

■ MOSK, J. and ACTING C.J.: I concur in the result.

The relevant statute provides that premarital agreements may concern any subject that does not violate public policy or a statute imposing a criminal penalty. When a statute's words are "clear and unambiguous our inquiry ends. There is no need for judicial construction and a court may not indulge in it." (*Diamond Multimedia Systems, Inc. v. Superior Court* (1999) 19 Cal.4th 1036, 1047.) That is true here. Any lingering question whether the Legislature intended to omit premarital spousal support agreements from the scope of Family Code section 1612 is dispelled by subdivision (b), which prohibits premarital agreements to waive or reduce child support. Had the Legislature desired to prohibit spousal support agreements, it could have added a few words similar to those of subdivision (b).

Clearly, the parties did not conspire to violate the criminal law. The only question is whether their premarital agreement violated public policy. I agree with the majority that it did not.

■ KENNARD, J.: I dissent.

In *In re Marriage of Higgason*, this court unanimously held that premarital agreements waiving spousal support in the event of separation or dissolution of the marriage violate California's public policy and are therefore invalid, leaving it to the trial court to determine at the time of separation or dissolution whether to award spousal support. Three years later, in *In re Marriage of Dawley* (1976), this court, again unanimously, came to the same conclusion. Our Legislature was fully aware of these decisions when in 1985, in adopting provisions of the Uniform Premarital Agreement Act, it chose to omit the act's provision allowing premarital waiver of spousal support, thus affirming the decisional law of this state that such waivers violate public policy.

In overruling by judicial fiat the Legislature's decision to continue this state's prohibition against premarital waivers of spousal support, the majority has (1) invaded the legislative domain, (2) invalidated a legislative decision reflecting sound public policy, and (3) failed to articulate an intelligible standard to guide members of the bench and bar in determining whether a premarital waiver of spousal support is or will be enforceable.

I cannot and do not join the majority in its usurpation of legislative powers. Any change in the law at issue should come from the Legislature, not the judiciary.

I

California statutory law generally imposes an obligation to support one's spouse.

In 1985, California became one of the first states to adopt provisions of the Uniform Premarital Agreement Act. Uniform acts are drafted by the National

Conference of Commissioners on Uniform State Laws "to promote uniformity in state law, on all subjects where uniformity is desirable and practicable, by voluntary action of each state government."

On March 7, 1985, Senate Bill No. 1143 was introduced in our Legislature. The bill proposed adopting the Uniform Premarital Agreement Act in its entirety. On August 28, 1985, however, the bill was amended to *delete* these two provisions of the act:

> Section 3, subdivision (a)(4), allowing spousal support to be modified or eliminated through premarital agreements[1] and Section 6, subdivision (b), providing that if, as a result of having entered into an a premarital agreement waiving spousal support, a spouse at the time of separation or marital dissolution becomes impoverished and eligible for public assistance, then a court retains the authority to award support "to the extent necessary to avoid that eligibility."[2]

When the Legislature deleted these two provisions from Senate Bill No. 1143, two decisions of this court, *In re Marriage of Higgason* and *In re Marriage of Dawley*, had held roughly a decade earlier that premarital agreements waiving spousal support violated California's public policy and were therefore invalid. At the time of the deletion and until today's decision by the majority, it was the trial court that determined whether to award spousal support, depending on the circumstances existing at the time of separation or dissolution of the marriage. (See Fam. Code, § 4320 [circumstances trial court should consider in awarding spousal support].)

---

1. Section 3 of the Uniform Premarital Agreement Act provides: "(a) Parties to a premarital agreement may contract with respect to: (1) the rights and obligations of each of the parties in any of the property of either or both of them whenever and wherever acquired or located; (2) the right to buy, sell, use, transfer, exchange, abandon, lease, consume, expend, assign, create a security interest in, mortgage, encumber, dispose of, or otherwise manage and control property; (3) the disposition of property upon separation, marital dissolution, death, or the occurrence or nonoccurrence of any other event; *(4) the modification or elimination of spousal support;* (5) the making of a will, trust, or other arrangement to carry out the provisions of the agreement; (6) the ownership rights in and disposition of the death benefit from a life insurance policy; (7) the choice of law governing the construction of the agreement; and (8) any other matter, including their personal rights and obligations, not in violation of public policy or a statute imposing a criminal penalty. (b) The right of a child to support may not be adversely affected by a premarital agreement."

2. Section 6, subdivision (b) of the Uniform Premarital Agreement Act states: "If a provision of a premarital agreement modifies or eliminates spousal support and that modification or elimination causes one party to the agreement to be eligible for support under a program of public assistance at the time of separation or marital dissolution, a court, notwithstanding the terms of the agreement, may require the other party to provide support to the extent necessary to avoid that eligibility."

Does the Legislature's deletion of the provision allowing premarital waivers of spousal support establish its intent to preclude such waivers? The answer is "yes," as I explain below.

On point is this court's decision in *Kusior v. Silver* (1960). There, as here, the Legislature was considering the adoption of a uniform act. There, the Legislature had refused to enact into law a provision of the Uniform Act on Blood Tests to Determine Paternity allowing blood tests to show that the husband was not the father of the child. There, as here, California decisional law was contrary to the proposed provision.

This court in *Kusior* observed that "[s]tatutes are to be interpreted by assuming that the Legislature was aware of the existing judicial decisions." We then held that in omitting from its adoption of the uniform act at issue a provision directly at odds with this state's decisional law, the Legislature's omission "must be deemed" an intent to approve and retain the decisional law. Similarly, here the Legislature's express rejection of the Uniform Premarital Agreement Act's provision allowing premarital spousal support waivers, in the face of decisional law to the contrary, "must be deemed" an intent to approve and retain the existing law. (See also *Estate of Sanders* (1992) 2 Cal.App.4th 462, 473-474 ["'[t]he rejection by the Legislature of a specific provision contained in an act as originally introduced is most persuasive to the conclusion that the act should not be construed to include the omitted provision'"].)

This court's decision in *Kusior* is dispositive here. Under the reasoning of that decision, our Legislature's express rejection of the proposed uniform law provision allowing waivers of spousal support was a decision to approve and retain California's rule prohibiting such waivers. By now deciding that premarital spousal support waivers do not violate California's public policy, the majority has invaded the legislative domain, judicially enacting in substance a provision that the Legislature intended to reject, and judicially abrogating the rule that the Legislature intended to retain.

II

Our Legislature's decision not to enact into law the Uniform Premarital Agreement Act's provision allowing premarital waivers of spousal support, while adopting other provisions of the act, reflects sound public policy.

Such waivers do not allow for changed circumstances between execution of the premarital agreement and separation or dissolution of the marriage. An agreement equitable at the time of the marriage may later become inequitable and unjust. For example, the health, earning capacity, or financial resources of a spouse may change markedly during the marriage, especially one that is lengthy. An elderly spouse or one in poor health may be left destitute. The earning capacity of a spouse may be impaired by the obligations of caring for children produced by a marriage of short duration. After the marriage one spouse may elect to give up his or her career to raise the children of the marriage or to move to another location in the interest of furthering the career of the other spouse. And a spouse may substantially deplete his or her financial resources to advance the other spouse's education, training, or career during the marriage.[3]

These considerations are reflected in the Legislature's enactment of Family Code section 4320, which sets forth spousal support guidelines for the trial courts.[4]

---

3. The issues I address here are not presented in *In re Marriage of Bonds* (2000) 24 Cal.4th 1 (*Bonds*), a unanimous decision of this court filed simultaneously with this decision, although both concern premarital agreements and both require interpretation of the Uniform Premarital Agreement Act. The main issue in *Bonds* is whether one spouse voluntarily entered into the premarital agreement, an issue not presented here. Also, the focus of the dispute in *Bonds* appears to be the premarital waiver of community property rights, not spousal support. This distinction is crucial because the Legislature, when it enacted the Uniform Premarital Agreement Act, deliberately omitted the provision authorizing spousal support waivers while approving and enacting the provision authorizing waivers of community property rights.

The Legislature's decision to permit waiver of community property rights, but not spousal support, may be explained on policy grounds. A spouse who has waived community property rights, but not spousal support, retains effective protection against a sudden, drastic, and inequitable loss of income resulting from dissolution of marriage, and may have recourse either to former community property or to separate property to enforce a spousal support order (Fam. Code, § 4338). By contrast, a spouse who has lost the right to spousal support may well have no recourse except public assistance. Thus, the inequities that may result from premarital spousal support waivers are much graver than those that may result from a premarital waiver of community property rights.

4. Family Code section 4320 provides: "In ordering spousal support under this part, the court shall consider all of the following circumstances: (a) The extent to which the earning capacity of each party is sufficient to maintain the standard of living established during the marriage, taking into account all of the following: (1) The marketable skills of the supported party; the job market for those skills; the time and expenses required for the supported party to acquire the appropriate education or training to develop those skills; and the possible need for retraining or education to acquire other, more marketable skills or employment. (2) The extent to which the supported party's present or future earning capacity is impaired by periods of unemployment that were incurred during the marriage to permit the supported party to devote time to domestic duties. (b) The extent to which the supported party contributed to the attainment of an education, training, a career position, or a license by the supporting party. (c) The ability to pay of the supporting party, taking into account the supporting party's earning capacity, earned and unearned income, assets, and standard of living. (d) The needs of each party based on the standard of living established during the marriage. (e) The obligations and assets, including the separate property, of each party. (f) The duration of the marriage. (g) The ability of the supported party to engage in gainful employment without unduly interfering with the interests of dependent children in the custody of the party. (h) The age and health of the parties .... (i) The immediate and specific tax consequences to each party. (j) The balance of the hardships to each party. (k) The goal that the supported party shall be self-supporting within a reasonable period of time.... [A] 'reasonable

They are also reflected in the Legislature's express declarations that spousal support is a "serious legal obligation[ ]" and that it "is the policy of the State of California" to "ensure fair and sufficient" spousal support awards. In rejecting the proposed provision to allow premarital waivers of spousal support, the Legislature must have recognized the serious potential for injustice at the time of dissolution of marriage.

That concern was succinctly expressed in a letter the Women Lawyers' Association of Los Angeles wrote on June 6, 1985 to Elihu Harris, the Chair of the Assembly Judiciary Committee, stating its opposition to that part of Senate Bill No. 1143 proposing adoption of the Uniform Premarital Agreement Act's provision allowing premarital waivers of spousal support: "The bill would change existing California law, which does not enforce premarital waivers of spousal support, to allow such waivers under certain conditions. Current California law allows spouses to waive spousal support only at the time of separation, when they are much more aware of what they have contributed to and sacrificed for the marriage as well as their prospects for self-support following the separation. California law regards the duty to support one's spouse as an essential incident of marriage and refuses to confer the benefits of marriage on those who would avoid this obligation. Although numerous states have adopted the Uniform Premarital Agreement Act, California's position represents sounder public policy and should not be sacrificed to achieve uniformity."

In a letter to the Legislature on August 14, 1985, the Family Law Section of the State Bar of California echoed that concern. In opposing the proposed provision allowing premarital waivers of spousal support, the Family Law Section warned that such an enactment "would be a major change in California law" and "a great step backward in terms of assuring that the financial consequences of a dissolution of marriage are borne by both spouses in an equitable manner."

In sharp contrast to the thoughtful action by the Legislature, which after the letters quoted above deleted the proposed provision allowing premarital waivers of spousal support, the majority ignores the significant public policy considerations that prompted the Legislature to retain our existing law prohibiting such waivers.

---

period of time' for purposes of this section generally shall be one-half the length of the marriage. However, nothing in this section is intended to limit the court's discretion to order support for a greater or lesser length of time, based on any of the other factors listed in this section ... and the circumstances of the parties. (*l*) Any other factors the court determines are just and equitable." Section 4320 applies to spousal support upon legal separation or dissolution of the marriage.

III

After repudiating the existing law of this state prohibiting all premarital waivers of spousal support, the majority abdicates its responsibility to articulate guidelines for the bench and bar explaining when, if ever, such waivers are enforceable. The majority declares that it will *not* decide "whether all such agreements [premarital agreements waiving spousal support] are enforceable regardless of the circumstances of the parties at the time enforcement is sought" and that it will *not* decide "whether circumstances existing at the time enforcement of a waiver of spousal support is sought might make enforcement unjust."

Given the majority's "holding" that such provisions may or may not be enforceable depending upon circumstances the majority refuses to discuss, what guidance is there for attorneys preparing a premarital agreement to decide whether to include a waiver of spousal support? And what guidance is there for trial courts in determining the enforceability of such agreements? If enforcement of a premarital waiver of spousal support results in a spouse's becoming eligible for public assistance, should the trial court order spousal support limited to the amount necessary to avoid such eligibility, as provided for in the Uniform Premarital Agreement Act? Or should the trial court in that instance continue to apply the considerations the Legislature has specified in Family Code section 4320? The majority's silence on these important questions does a disservice to the public, the bar, and the bench.

I would reverse the judgment of the Court of Appeal.

QUESTIONS AND NOTES

1. Notwithstanding this attempt byp "intelligent, well-educated persons, each of whom appears to be self-sufficient in property and earning ability, and both of whom have the advice of counsel regarding their rights and obligations as marital partners," to specify their respective rights and obligations upon dissolution in a formal written premarital agreement, Candace Pendleton and Barry Fireman's divorce proceedings generated two subsequent unpublished California Court of Appeal decisions relating to property division. *In toto*, their divorce proceedings lasted twice as long as their 42 month marriage. What does that teach you about the limits of one's ability to plan through premarital agreements?

2. The enforceability of waivers of spousal support remains controversial in California. Following the California Supreme Court's decision in *Marriage of Pendleton*, the California legislature amended Family Code § 1612 to provide:

(c) Any provision in a premarital agreement regarding spousal support, including, but not limited to, a waiver of it, is not enforceable if the party against whom enforcement of the spousal support provision is sought was not represented by independent counsel at the time the agreement containing the provision was signed, or if the provision regarding spousal support is unconscionable at the time of enforcement. An otherwise unenforceable provision in a premarital agreement regarding spousal support may not become enforceable solely because the party against whom enforcement is sought was represented by independent counsel.

In *In re Marriage of Rosendale*, 119 Cal. App. 4th 1202 (2004), *review granted and opinion depublished*, 2004 Cal. LEXIS 9655, *appeal dismissed*, 31 Cal. Rptr. 3d 95 (2005), the California Court of Appeal described the situation it faced as follows:

> A man and a woman entered into a premarital agreement shortly before their marriage. Eight years later, the woman was in a life-shattering automobile accident. At one point pronounced dead, the woman survived the accident. However, she suffered brain damage, internal injuries and numerous broken bones. She underwent fifteen reconstructive surgeries and is slated to have many more. A couple of years after the accident, her husband decided to move on. He filed a petition for dissolution of marriage ... [and] sought a determination that the waiver of spousal support [in the premarital agreement] was enforceable.

The Court of Appeal denied enforcement of the spousal support waiver on the ground that enforcement would be unconscionable given the spouses' circumstances at the time of the dissolution, even though the premarital agreement in question (i) pre-dated the post-*Pendleton* amendment codified in Family Code § 1612(c) and (ii) did not appear to be unconscionable at the time it was executed. The California Supreme Court granted a petition for review but thereafter dismissed the appeal without addressing the case on the merits. As a matter of California procedure, dismissal of the appeal after a grant of review leaves the judgment below intact, but it negates the precedential force of the Court of Appeal opinion. What does *Rosendale* teach you about the limits of one's ability to plan through premarital agreements? More recently, the California Court of Appeal refused to apply *Pendleton* to a prenuptial agreement executed in 1985, prior to California's adoption of the Uniform Premarital Agreement Act, asserting that as of the time of the agreement, California law was clear that spousal support waivers were per se unenforceable. *In re Marriage of Melissa*, 212 Cal. App. 4th 598, *review denied*, 2013 Cal. LEXIS 2281 (2013). Should the obligations of the parties to a premarital agreement be assessed by reference to the state of the law at the time of the agreement or at the time of enforcement? If public policy that would have been a bar to enforcement at the time the agreement was made no longer applies hasn't the obstacle to the enforcement of the agreement been removed? If at the time of enforcement, the agreement violates then existing public policy shouldn't the court refuse enforcement? How can a court today even know what public policy would or would not have permitted 30 years ago? Isn't it hard enough to figure out what public policy today is? Isn't the real issue, as set out by the California legislature in amended section 1612(c), what is just as between the parties today given the agreement between them *and* the other relevant circumstances as they exist at the time of dissolution?

II.   RELATIONSHIPS THAT LIMIT AND GIVE MEANING TO PROMISES

Our legal system gives high priority to the enforcement of contracts, and this supports basic social and political values. We place a great value on individual autonomy, choice, and voluntary association as the basis of human relationship. Individualism, rationalism, and democracy all connote a large role for personal choices. But of course, for most people in most places and during most of human history, those choices simply were not available. Status, class, caste, and gender have determined the content of most human relationships, not choice. Today most people are more insistent on the primacy of choice, but perhaps in consequence we face real uncertainty regarding the content of some of the most intimate human relationships. Recall the changing nature of the marital relationship discussed in *Marriage of Pendleton*, p. 309. Society is unsure how to structure such relationships by consent and how power and obligation within the family should be organized. We also are unsure who should do the organizing. To what extent should the state set the rules, and when should it be tolerant of other rules the parties may agree to among themselves?

We are often obligated even when we do not promise. Some agreements are outside of contract and are not legally enforceable because they grow out of a relationship that has a predefined content, a status. That status may be dominant, as in the case of marriage, even though the law has only imperfectly defined its content. Family members, for example, rightly feel special obligations toward one another. Our sense of commitment is likely to extend more broadly to those whose lives touch ours. Relationships may not only precede promises and impose obligations outside of promise, but may also exclude legally binding promises and deprive those in the relationship from the capacity to organize their dealings by binding promises to one another.

Tenet v. Doe

Supreme Court of the United States, 2005.
544 U.S. 1.

■ REHNQUIST, C.J. delivered the opinion of the Court.

In *Totten v. United States,* 92 U.S. 105 (1876), we held that public policy forbade a self-styled Civil War spy from suing the United States to enforce its obligations under their secret espionage agreement. Respondents here, alleged former Cold War spies, filed suit against the United States and the Director of the Central Intelligence Agency (CIA), asserting estoppel and due process claims for the CIA's alleged failure to provide respondents with the assistance it had promised in return for their espionage services. Finding that *Totten* did not bar respondents' suit, the District Court and the Court of Appeals for the Ninth Circuit held that the case could proceed. We reverse because this holding contravenes the longstanding rule, announced more than a century ago in *Totten,* prohibiting suits against the Government based on covert espionage agreements.

Respondents, a husband and wife who use the fictitious names John and Jane Doe, brought suit in the United States District Court for the Western District of Washington.[1] According to respondents, they were formerly citizens of a foreign country that at the time was considered to be an enemy of the United States, and John Doe was a high-ranking diplomat for the country. After respondents expressed interest in defecting to the United States, CIA agents persuaded them to remain at their posts and conduct espionage for the United States for a specified period of time, promising in return that the Government "would arrange for travel to the United States and ensure financial and personal security for life." After "carrying out their end of the bargain" by completing years of purportedly high-risk, valuable espionage services, respondents defected (under new names and false backgrounds) and became United States citizens, with the Government's help. The CIA designated respondents with "PL-110" status and began providing financial assistance and personal security.[2]

---

1. The Government has neither confirmed nor denied any of respondents' allegations. We therefore describe the facts as asserted in respondents' second amended complaint. They are, of course, no more than allegations.

2. While the Government neither confirms nor denies that respondents are part of any "PL-110" program, the parties agree this reference is to a provision enacted [as part of the Central Intelligence Agency Act of 1949]. This provision allows a limited number of aliens and members of their immediate families per year to be admitted to the United States for permanent residence, regardless of their admissibility under the immigration laws, upon a determination by the Director of the CIA, the Attorney General, and the Commissioner of Immigration that admission of the particular alien "is in the interest of national security or essential to the furtherance of the

With the CIA's help, respondent John Doe obtained employment in the State of Washington. As his salary increased, the CIA decreased his living stipend until, at some point, he agreed to a discontinuation of benefits while he was working. Years later, in 1997, John Doe was laid off after a corporate merger. Because John Doe was unable to find new employment as a result of CIA restrictions on the type of jobs he could hold, respondents contacted the CIA for financial assistance.[3] Denied such assistance by the CIA, they claim they are unable to properly provide for themselves. Thus, they are faced with the prospect of either returning to their home country (where they say they face extreme sanctions), or remaining in the United States in their present circumstances.

Respondents assert, among other things, that the CIA violated their procedural and substantive due process rights by denying them support and by failing to provide them with a fair internal process for reviewing their claims. They seek injunctive relief ordering the CIA to resume monthly financial support pending further agency review. They also request a declaratory judgment stating that the CIA failed to provide a constitutionally adequate review process, and detailing the minimal process the agency must provide. Finally, respondents seek a mandamus order requiring the CIA to adopt agency procedures, to give them fair review, and to provide them with security and financial assistance.

The Government moved to dismiss the complaint, principally on the ground that *Totten* bars respondents' suit. The District Court dismissed some of respondents' claims but denied the Government's *Totten* objection, ruling that the due process claims could proceed. After minimal discovery, the Government renewed its motion to dismiss based on *Totten,* and it moved for summary judgment on respondents' due process claims. Apparently construing the complaint as also raising an estoppel claim, the District Court denied the Government's motions, ruled again that *Totten* did not bar respondents' claims, and found there were genuine issues of material fact warranting a trial on respondents' due process and estoppel claims. The District Court certified an order for interlocutory appeal ....

---

national intelligence mission." § 403h. However, nothing in this statute, nor anything in the redacted CIA regulations and related materials respondents cite, represents an enforceable legal commitment by the CIA to provide support to spies that may be admitted into the United States under § 403h.

3. Respondents document their alleged series of contacts with the CIA. For instance, respondents allegedly received a letter from the CIA in June 1997, expressing regret that the agency no longer had funds available to provide assistance. Later, respondents claim they were told the agency determined "the benefits previously provided were adequate for the services rendered." Although the CIA apparently did not disclose to respondents the agency's appeals process, respondents were permitted to appeal the initial determination both to the Director of the CIA and to a panel of former agency officials called the Helms Panel; both appeals were denied.

In *Totten,* the administrator of William A. Lloyd's estate brought suit against the United States to recover compensation for services that Lloyd allegedly rendered as a spy during the Civil War. Lloyd purportedly entered into a contract with President Lincoln in July 1861 to spy behind Confederate lines on troop placement and fort plans, for which he was to be paid $200 a month. The lower court had found that Lloyd performed on the contract but did not receive full compensation. After concluding with "no difficulty," that the President had the authority to bind the United States to contracts with secret agents, we observed that the very essence of the alleged contract between Lloyd and the Government was that it was secret, and had to remain so:

> "The service stipulated by the contract was a secret service; the information sought was to be obtained clandestinely, and was to be communicated privately; the employment and the service were to be equally concealed. Both employer and agent must have understood that the lips of the other were to be for ever sealed respecting the relation of either to the matter. This condition of the engagement was implied from the nature of the employment, and is implied in all secret employments of the government in time of war, or upon matters affecting our foreign relations, where a disclosure of the service might compromise or embarrass our government in its public duties, or endanger the person or injure the character of the agent."

Thus, we thought it entirely incompatible with the nature of such a contract that a former spy could bring suit to enforce it.

We think the Court of Appeals was quite wrong in holding that *Totten* does not require dismissal of respondents' claims. That court, and respondents here, reasoned first that *Totten* developed merely a contract rule, prohibiting breach-of-contract claims seeking to enforce the terms of espionage agreements but not barring claims based on due process or estoppel theories. In fact, *Totten* was not so limited: "[P]ublic policy forbids the maintenance of *any suit* in a court of justice, the trial of which would inevitably lead to the disclosure of matters which the law itself regards as confidential." (emphasis added); [and, "The secrecy which such contracts impose precludes *any action* for their enforcement." (emphasis added)]. No matter the clothing in which alleged spies dress their claims, *Totten* precludes judicial review in cases such as respondents' where success depends upon the existence of their secret espionage relationship with the Government.

Relying mainly on *United States v. Reynolds,* 345 U.S. 1 (1953), the Court of Appeals also claimed that *Totten* has been recast simply as an early expression of the evidentiary "state secrets" privilege, rather than a categorical bar to their claims. *Reynolds* involved a wrongful-death action brought under the Federal Tort Claims Act by the widows of three civilians who died in the crash of a military B-29 aircraft.

In the course of discovery, the plaintiffs sought certain investigation- related documents, which the Government said contained "highly secret," privileged military information. We recognized "the privilege against revealing military secrets, a privilege which is well established in the law of evidence," and we set out a balancing approach for courts to apply in resolving Government claims of privilege. We ultimately concluded that the Government was entitled to the privilege in that case.

When invoking the "well established" state secrets privilege, we indeed looked to *Totten.* See also Brief for United States in *United States v. Reynolds* (citing *Totten* in support of a military secrets privilege). But that in no way signaled our retreat from *Totten's* broader holding that lawsuits premised on alleged espionage agreements are altogether forbidden. Indeed, our opinion in *Reynolds* refutes this very suggestion: Citing *Totten* as a case "where the very subject matter of the action, a contract to perform espionage, was a matter of state secret," we declared that such a case was to be "dismissed *on the pleadings without ever reaching the question of evidence,* since it was so obvious that the action should never prevail over the privilege." (emphasis added).

In a later case, we again credited the more sweeping holding in *Totten,* thus confirming its continued validity. See *Weinberger v. Catholic Action of Haw./Peace Ed. Project* (citing *Totten* in holding that "whether or not the Navy has complied with [the National Environmental Policy Act of 1969] 'to the fullest extent possible' is beyond judicial scrutiny in this case," where, "[d]ue to national security reasons," the Navy could "neither admit nor deny" the fact that was central to the suit, *i.e.,* "that it propose[d] to store nuclear weapons" at a facility). *Reynolds* therefore cannot plausibly be read to have replaced the categorical *Totten* bar with the balancing of the state secrets evidentiary privilege in the distinct class of cases that depend upon clandestine spy relationships.

Nor does *Webster v. Doe,* 486 U.S. 592 (1988), support respondents' claim. There, we held that [the National Security Act of 1947], may not be read to exclude judicial review of the constitutional claims made by a former CIA employee for alleged discrimination. In reaching that conclusion, we noted the "'serious constitutional question' that would arise if a federal statute were construed to deny any judicial forum for a colorable constitutional claim." But there is an obvious difference, for purposes of *Totten,* between a suit brought by an acknowledged (though covert) employee of the CIA and one filed by an alleged former spy. Only in the latter scenario is *Totten's* core concern implicated: preventing the existence of the plaintiff's relationship with the Government from being revealed.[5] That is why the

---

5. The Court of Appeals apparently believed that the plaintiff's relationship with the CIA *was* secret in *Webster,* just as in this case. It is true that the plaintiff in *Webster* proceeded under a pseudonym because "his status as a CIA employee cannot be publicly acknowledged." Brief for

CIA regularly entertains Title VII claims concerning the hiring and promotion of its employees, as we noted in *Webster*, yet *Totten* has long barred suits such as respondents'.

There is, in short, no basis for respondents' and the Court of Appeals' view that the *Totten* bar has been reduced to an example of the state secrets privilege.

We adhere to *Totten*. The state secrets privilege and the more frequent use of *in camera* judicial proceedings simply cannot provide the absolute protection we found necessary in enunciating the *Totten* rule. The possibility that a suit may proceed and an espionage relationship may be revealed, if the state secrets privilege is found not to apply, is unacceptable: "Even a small chance that some court will order disclosure of a source's identity could well impair intelligence gathering and cause sources to 'close up like a clam.'" Forcing the Government to litigate these claims would also make it vulnerable to "graymail," *i.e.,* individual lawsuits brought to induce the CIA to settle a case (or prevent its filing) out of fear that any effort to litigate the action would reveal classified information that may undermine ongoing covert operations. And requiring the Government to invoke the privilege on a case-by-case basis risks the perception that it is either confirming or denying relationships with individual plaintiffs.

The judgment of the Court of Appeals is reversed.

■ STEVENS, J., concurring. [omitted].

■ SCALIA, J., concurring. [omitted].

Woods v. Fifth-Third Union Trust Co.
Ohio Court of Appeals, 1936.
54 Ohio App. 303, 6 N.E.2d 987.

■ MATTHEWS, J. This is an appeal on questions of law from the court of common pleas of Hamilton county.

The appellant, John C. Woods, was the son of Susan L.B. Woods, and filed this action against the executor of her last will to recover for personal services rendered by him during the six years immediately preceding her death.

United States in *Webster v. Doe.* But the fact that the plaintiff in *Webster* kept his *identity* secret did not mean that the employment *relationship* between him and the CIA was not known and admitted by the CIA.

The decedent, Susan L.B. Woods, during that period lived at the Hotel Alms, and the appellant lived with his family about one mile distant therefrom. The services, so far as the evidence shows, consisted in personal attention and in assisting her in managing her property, consisting apparently of securities of the value of about $80,000.

At the close of the plaintiff's evidence the court sustained the defendant's motion for an instructed verdict. The court overruled the plaintiff's motion for a new trial and entered judgment on the verdict.

The appeal presents for determination the question whether the court erred in sustaining the motion for an instructed verdict.

We are of [the] opinion that no promise, implied in law or fact, arises from the performance of personal services by a son for the benefit of his mother, regardless of whether they are living together as a part of the same household. The relation of parent and child is so close that the implication arises that whatever service the one renders to the other, the same is performed without expectation of compensation on the part of the one rendering the service.

The common experience of mankind is that a son in rendering such service does it because of the moral duty which he owes to his mother.

While a son owes no legal duty to perform gratuitous personal service for his mother who is financially able to pay, it is commonly recognized that the performance of such service springs from other motives than the desire for material gain. There are duties of imperfect obligation not enforceable at law that govern the relation of parent and child in such matters. Personal attention and service rendered by one to the other usually result from the recognition of such duties, or from the sheer desire to be of service, and do not arise from the purpose of creating a legal obligation. Therefore, the implication is that there was no intention to create a legal obligation by words and acts passing between them.

No implied promise arising by the performance on the one hand, and the receipt of the benefit thereof on the other, there must be additional evidence of an intention to contract if a legal obligation to compensate is to attach. There must be an express promise made under such circumstances as to manifest an intention of contracting. And it is not sufficient that the evidence of such a promise is such that reasonable minds could reasonably draw different conclusions therefrom on the subject, which is the general rule in the ordinary civil action, as decided in the case of *Hamden Lodge v. Ohio Fuel Gas Co.*, 127 Ohio St. 469. In this sort of a case the evidence of a promise made under such circumstances as to manifest an intention to contract must be clear and convincing.

Now what is the evidence of an express promise made with the intention of assuming a legal obligation to pay for these personal services?

Facts

One witness testified that she had heard testatrix say that her son "was to be paid for his services"; another said that he had heard her say that "her son John was taking care of her business and that he would be paid for his services." Three witnesses testified that they had heard the testatrix say to her son, the plaintiff, when he did things for her, "that she would pay him for everything he did." And this was all the evidence on that subject.

Now considering the surrounding circumstances, can it be said as a matter of law that this is not clear and convincing evidence?

Promissory language does not under all circumstances manifest an intent to contract. In 1 Williston on Contracts (Revised Ed.) 36 and 37, it is said:

> Consequently, if both parties indicate that their words are merely in joke, no contract will be formed. So where words appropriate to an offer are used evidently merely as a boast or explosion of wrath so that no reasonable person would be justified in taking them literally, no contract will result from an acceptance. But if, under the circumstances, a reasonable person would understand the words used as importing that the speaker promised to do something if given a requested exchange therefor, it is immaterial what intention the offeror may have had.

In *New York Trust Co. v. Island Oil & Transport Corporation* the court said:

> However, the form of utterance chosen is never final; it is always possible to show that the parties did not intend to perform what they said they would, as, for example that the transaction is a joke (*Keller v. Holderman*); or that it arose in relations between the members of a family which forbade it. It is quite true that contracts depend upon the meaning which the law imputes to the utterances, not upon what the parties actually intended; but, in ascertaining what meaning to impute, the circumstances in which the words are used is always relevant and usually indispensable. The standard is what a normally constituted person would have understood them to mean, when used in their actual setting.

Of course, if a reasonable person would understand the words used as importing a promise with contractual intent to do something, the secret intent of the person uttering the words would be of no legal significance. But in determining whether a reasonable person would so understand the words, all the circumstances must be taken into consideration.

We have here words used by a mother to her son. She needed his attention and had natural claims to it. She had an estate and unless she provided otherwise by will he would inherit half of it. She had a complete legal right to entirely disinherit him, and his neglect of her might have caused her to exercise that right.

She stated on many occasions that he would be paid or that she would pay him for everything he did. Did that language clearly and convincingly indicate any particular mode of compensation? Did it indicate contractual and not testamentary provision, or the benefit he would receive on intestacy? According to all the dictionaries there is no specific method necessarily conveyed in the meaning of the word "pay." The only essential meaning conveyed is that of recompense or compensation. The duty discharged may be either a legal or moral one. Illustrating the meaning Webster says: "Hence, to compensate justly; to requite according to merit; to reward or punish as required; to retort or retaliate on."

It seems to us clear as a matter of law that the use of such language by a mother to her son under the circumstances cannot be said to prove a contract between them by clear and convincing evidence. It proves an intention "to requite according to merit; to reward or punish as required." The intent disclosed by such language is fully satisfied by adequate provision in a will. That the son did not regard it as a contract requiring satisfaction during the mother's lifetime is demonstrated by the fact that no demand was ever made by him during her lifetime, and the claim now asserted extends over the entire period allowed by the statute of limitations. If a contract existed, he allowed half of his claim to become barred by lapse of time.

With reference to such language between members of a family, this court, in *Arns, Ex'r v. Disser* said:

> Giving the declarations here their full force and effect, they are but expressions of gratitude, and an intention to do something for Disser, all of which she did by deeding him the blacksmith shop property and providing the bequest for him in the first will she executed (though she later revoked this bequest) and in furnishing him a home with free board.

> We are unable to find any expression or any conduct that would furnish clear and convincing proof of an express contract on the part of Disser to perform the services for compensation, or on the part of Mrs. Arns, when accepting the services, that she was to pay for them.

In the case at bar the evidence shows that the plaintiff received far more by the provisions of the will than the amount claimed. It is true that his sister was given one-half of the estate. The fact does not in any way detract from the fact that he was given more than his claim. The motives for the testamentary provisions are immaterial, as is also a comparison of them.

For these reasons, the judgment is affirmed.

QUESTIONS AND NOTES

1. If Ms. Woods' son, were a house painter and he painted his mother's house after she said he would be paid for his services, would his claim for the reasonable value of such a paint job receive the same treatment from the court as did the claim for his management services in this case? Suppose John Woods were a professional property manager? Same result if John Woods were not Susan Woods' son but merely an old friend?

2. If John managed his mother's affairs for a year and then brought suit for the reasonable value of his services when she refused his demand for payment, what result?

3. Lawyers, doctors, and investment advisors are frequently subjected to people seeking advice in a social setting. Sometimes you can turn away these requests with the suggestion that they telephone you at the office next Monday morning, but sometimes you can't. When your friend, the orthodontist, seeks your advice about his complex tax problems during the third set of your Sunday tennis game, can you recover for the value of your legal services? Does your answer depend on how good a friend he is? Doesn't living in a world made up of families, friends, and communities imply that we will do things for each other without expecting payment in return from other members of our little community? Does your answer regarding the orthodontist's tax advice depend on whether he takes care of your children's teeth and how much he charges?

4. Is the court saying that Mrs. Woods did not make an enforceable promise or that she made one but performed it in full? Suppose that she had cut John off in her will without a cent. Same result here?

5. What result if Susan Woods' promise to John had been for a specific amount, e.g., to pay John $5,000 on her death for his property management services during her lifetime, and she had cut him off without a cent?

6. Social mores regarding care of elderly family members have evolved substantially since the time of *Woods*, but the issue of when family duty leaves off and contract begins remains with us. *Caregiving in the United States* (2015), a study sponsored by the National Alliance for Caregiving and the American Association of Retired Persons, estimates that 34.2 million American adults provide unpaid care to elderly and disabled adult relatives. The "typical" caregiver is a 52-year old married woman with some college education who reports providing on average 24.4 hours of care per week for her widowed mother. Forty-eight percent of caregivers furnishing more than 20 hours of care weekly were employed in addition to giving care. Caregivers overall averaged 34.7 hours per week at their jobs. The median household income of those furnishing more than 20 hours of care weekly was $45,700.

Nearly one-quarter of caregivers provide 41 or more hours per week of unpaid care. Rachel Emma Silverman, *Who Will Mind Mom? Check Her Contract*, WALL ST. J., Sept. 7, 2006, at D1, reports on an increasing trend for families with elderly dependents to enter into written "caregiver contracts." One force driving this trend is the Medicaid program. Medicaid is "means-tested," and payments under the caregiver contract, by reducing the dependent person's assets, may allow the dependent to qualify for government-paid healthcare under the Medicaid program. But many advisors, noting the difficulty in enforcing informal compensation arrangements such as that alleged in *Woods*, recommend formal written caregiver contracts specifically to avoid squabbles and will contests among caregiving and non-caregiving heirs and to provide a clear legal basis to compensate children and other relatives who devote significant time, effort, and money to the care of dependent elderly relatives. Nevertheless, as one California lawyer, Michael Gilfix, remarked to the *Wall Street Journal*, a certain stigma and resistance to contracting in this realm remains: "People are still uncomfortable with the idea that you are paying your kids."

Favrot v. Barnes

Louisiana Court of Appeals, 1976.
332 So.2d 873, rev'd on other grounds, 339 So.2d 843 (1976).

■ REDMANN, J. An ex-husband appeals from an alimony award as unwarranted and, alternatively, excessive....

ENTITLEMENT

This prospective husband and wife, in middle age, had each been married before. They executed a pre-marital agreement stipulating separateness of property. We first reject the husband's argument that the agreement's waiver by each of every "claim to the property" of the other in case of divorce or death is a waiver of alimony. If public policy were to allow such a waiver, this agreement does not constitute one. Alimony to a divorced wife is not a "claim to the property" of the husband; it is a claim against the husband, limited by his "income."

The spouses had other pre-marital discussions in which, at the husband's instance, they agreed to limit sexual intercourse to about once a week. The husband asserts, as divorce-causing fault, that the wife did not keep this agreement but sought coitus thrice daily. The wife testifies she kept their agreement despite her frustration at not being "permitted" at other times even to touch her husband.

We reject the view that a pre-marital understanding can repeal or amend the nature of marital obligations as declared by C.C. 119: "The husband and wife owe to each other mutually, fidelity, support and assistance." Marriage obliges the spouses to fulfill "the reasonable and normal sex desires of each other." It is this abiding sexual relationship which characterizes a contract as marriage, rather than, e.g., domestic employer-employee, or landlord-tenant. Persons may indeed agree to live in the same building in some relationship other than marriage. But that is not what our litigants did. They married.

The law does not authorize contractual modification of the "conjugal association" except "[i]n relation to property," C.C. 2325. C.C. 2327 prohibits alteration of marriage like that agreed to here which the wife allegedly breached: "Neither can husband and wife derogate by their matrimonial agreement from the rights resulting from the power of the husband over the person of his wife * * *." Nor—because the rights over the person are largely mutual, C.C. 119 and La. Const. art. 1 sec. 3—can their matrimonial agreement derogate from the power of the wife over the person of her husband.

The fault here alleged by the husband is not, in law, any fault.

The husband also finds fault in the wife's not having sufficiently disciplined her daughter by a previous marriage. There appears to have been a personality conflict between husband and daughter, which resulted in the wife's awesome decision to send her teen-age daughter out of her home to placate the husband. The daughter was away from home for almost all of the last year and a half of the marriage. The wife's behavior regarding her daughter was far from fault towards the husband.

We find no fault which would defeat the ex-wife's entitlement to alimony.

Set aside and remanded.

QUESTIONS AND NOTES

1. The husband here asserts breach of a premarital agreement as grounds for reducing or eliminating his alimony obligation upon divorce. Compare *Marriage of Pendleton*, p. 309. Why enforce waivers of spousal support but not allow its forfeiture for breach of this agreement?

2. What if the disappointed spouse wants the contract enforced, not terminated. Could the husband have sued for an injunction or specific performance of this agreement? If he were injured by the wife's breach, could he recover damages for her failure to keep the bargain? In other legal cultures courts may be more willing to intervene to enforce agreements between spouses and to protect the dependent spouse even on intimate aspects of marriage. For several millennia Jewish law enforced by rabbinic courts has been prepared to enforce the rights of the wife to food, clothing, and sexual relations, as the following news story from the *San Diego Tribune* of December 20, 1979, indicates:

ISRAELI COURT ORDERS MAN TO PERFORM SEXUAL "DUTIES"

TEL AVIV, Israel (UPI)—A rabbinical court has handed down a landmark judgment ordering a 32-year-old man to perform his conjugal duties or pay 36 grains of silver a week until he does so, an Israeli news report said.

Ruling the man "rebellious" against religious law for refusing to have sexual relations with his wife, the three rabbis decreed the countdown start with the handing down of the judgment Tuesday, the Maariv newspaper said.

If the husband disobeys the rabbinical court, the woman will be eligible for a divorce, with the silver accruing over the period added to the alimony settlement. There are 43.5 grains of silver in an ounce.

The court summoned the couple to a hearing based on the wife's complaint. The woman described her husband's behavior toward her in every other way as "exemplary."

But the husband was quoted as having told the rabbis "I am fed up with her" when he was asked to explain why he refused to have relations with his wife.

Rabbinical courts have sole jurisdiction over marriages and divorces in Israel.

3. While the traditional marriage contract in our society is at best vague on the nature and scope of the parties' sexual obligations to one another, it's pretty clear that extramarital affairs generally violate the deal. What if the parties negotiate a liquidated damages provision to enforce the obligation to "forsake all others"? In *Diosado v. Diosado*, 97 Cal. App. 4th 470 (2002), the parties had an express written contract that imposed liquidated damages of $50,000 for each extramarital affair. When the husband cheated nevertheless, the wife not only filed for divorce, but also sued to collect her damages. The California Court of Appeal rejected her damage claim as "contrary to public policy underlying the no-fault provisions for dissolution of marriage. ... [*Pendleton*, p. 309] provides no authority for enforceability of an agreement between spouses to pay damages in the event one party engages in sexual infidelity."

4. In *Favrot* the agreement between spouses related to their sexual relations. Suppose a husband and wife agree during marriage that the wife will give the husband all but $100 a week of her take-home pay to apply to household expenses and his clothing and entertainment. If the wife fails to perform, what legal redress is available to the disappointed husband? It is clear that in most states the parties could separate and the husband could demand spousal support with the court's help, but will a court intervene if the spouses stay together? The answer in our culture is likely to be that courts do not intervene in the agreements of partners to an existing marriage. But the reasons for this judicial reluctance are less clear. It may be, as some opinions suggest, that these arrangements are not contracts, are not supported by consideration, or are not intended to be enforceable. Or it may be that courts abstain out of concern for the privacy and sanctity of the family, which might be damaged by outside intervention in these delicate matters. Or it may be that courts stay out of these problems because they fear that their capacity to do other important tasks would be hurt if the courts were flooded with squabbles between spouses and between parents and children. Yet questions of domestic support are very important to society. The courts enforce other less important classes of contract: Why should these agreements be outside the realm of enforceable contract?

————

Maglica v. Maglica

California Court of Appeal, 1998.
66 Cal.App.4th 442, 78 Cal.Rptr.2d 101.

■ SILLS, PRESIDING JUSTICE.

I. INTRODUCTION

This case forces us to confront the legal doctrine known as "quantum meruit" in the context of a case about an unmarried couple who lived together and worked in a business solely owned by one of them. Quantum meruit is a Latin phrase, meaning "as much as he deserves," and is based on the idea that someone should get paid for beneficial goods or services which he or she bestows on another.

The trial judge instructed the jury that the reasonable value of the plaintiff's services was either the value of what it would have cost the defendant to obtain those services from someone else or the "value by which" he had "benefitted [sic] as a result" of those services. The instruction allowed the jury to reach a whopping number in favor of the plaintiff—$84 million—because of the tremendous growth in the value of the business over the years.

As we explain later, the finding that the couple had no contract in the first place is itself somewhat suspect because certain jury instructions did not accurately convey the law concerning implied-in-fact contracts. However, assuming that there was indeed no contract, the quantum meruit award cannot stand. The legal test for recovery in quantum meruit is not the value of the benefit, but value of the services (assuming, of course, that the services were beneficial to the recipient in the first place). In this case the failure to appreciate that fine distinction meant a big difference. People who work for businesses for a period of years and then walk away with $84 million do so because they have acquired some equity in the business, not because $84 million dollars is the going rate for the services of even the most workaholic manager. In substance, the court was allowing the jury to value the plaintiff's services as if she had made a sweetheart stock option dealСyet such a deal was precisely what the jury found she did not make. So the $84 million judgment cannot stand.

On the other hand, plaintiff was hindered in her ability to prove the existence of an implied-in-fact contract by a series of jury instructions which may have misled the jury about certain of the factors which bear on such contracts. The instructions were insufficiently qualified. They told the jury flat out that such facts as a couple's living together or holding themselves out as husband and wife or sharing a common surname did not mean that they had any agreement to share assets. That is not exactly correct. Such factors can, indeed, when taken together with other facts and in context, show the existence of an implied-in-fact contract. At most the jury instructions should have said that such factors do not by themselves necessarily show an implied-in-fact contract. Accordingly, when the case is retried, the plaintiff will have another chance to prove that she indeed had a deal for a share of equity in the defendant's business.

II. FACTS

The important facts in this case may be briefly stated. Anthony Maglica, a Croatian immigrant, founded his own machine shop business, Mag Instrument, in 1955. He got divorced in 1971 and kept the business. That year he met Claire Halasz, an interior designer. They got on famously, and lived together, holding themselves out as man and wifeChence Claire began using the name Claire MaglicaCbut never actually got married. And, while Claire worked side by side building the business, Anthony never agreedCor at least the jury found Anthony never agreedCto give Claire a share of the business. When the business was incorporated in 1974 all shares went into Anthony's name. Anthony was the president and Claire was the secretary. They were paid equal salaries from the business after incorporation. In 1978 the business began manufacturing flashlights, and, thanks in part to some great ideas and hard work on Claire's part (for example, coming out with a purse-sized flashlight in colors), the business boomed. Mag Instrument is now worth hundreds of millions of dollars.

In 1992 Claire discovered that Anthony was trying to transfer stock to his children but not her, and the couple split up in October. In June 1993 Claire sued Anthony for, among other things, breach of contract, breach of partnership agreement, fraud, breach of fiduciary duty and quantum meruit. The case came to trial in the spring of 1994. The jury awarded $84 million for the breach of fiduciary duty and quantum meruit causes of action, finding that $84 million was the reasonable value of Claire's services.

III. DISCUSSION

A. The Jury's Finding That There Was No Agreement To Hold Property for One Another Meant There Was No Breach of Fiduciary Duty

Preliminarily we must deal with the problem of fiduciary duty, as it was an alternative basis for the jury's award. We cannot, however, affirm the judgment on this basis because it is at odds with the jury's factual finding that Anthony never agreed to give Claire a share of his business. Having found factually that there was no contract, the jury could not legally conclude that Anthony breached a fiduciary duty.

The reason is that fiduciary duties are either imposed by law or are undertaken by agreement, and neither way of establishing the existence of a fiduciary duty applies here. As to the former, the fact that Claire and Anthony remained unmarried during their relationship is dispositive. California specifically abolished the idea of a "common law marriage" in 1895 and that, if it is not too harsh to say it, was clearly the substance of Claire and Anthony's relationship. They had a common law marriage. As our Supreme Court said in *Elden*, "[f]ormally married couples are granted significant rights and bear important responsibilities toward one another which are not shared by those who cohabit without marriage." The court noted, in that context, that a variety of statutes impose rights and obligations on married people. One set of such imposed rights and obligations, for example, is Family Code sections 1100 through 1103, which both establish a fiduciary duty between spouses with regard to the management and control of community assets and provide for remedies for a breach of that duty.

It would be contrary to what our Supreme Court said in *Elden* and to the evident policy of the law to promote formal (as distinct from common law) marriage to impose fiduciary duties based on a common law marriage. Indeed, in the context of this case the potential for anomalous results is readily apparent. For example, in family law matters involving dissolution of marriage, punitive damages are not available to remedy breaches of fiduciary duty in the management and control of community property (though there are, of course, other remedies). Punitive damages, however, are sometimes available in other breach of fiduciary duty cases. It is unthinkable, given California's abolition of common law marriage, that an unmarried, cohabiting partner should have a more powerful remedy than a spouse.

That leaves contract, and the jury found there was no contract. Claire, despite the closeness of their relationship, never entrusted her property to Anthony; she only rendered services. And without entrustment of property, or an oral agreement to purchase property together, there can be no fiduciary relationship no matter how "confidential" a relationship between an unmarried, cohabiting couple. Indeed, as the *Toney* decision points out, it takes clear and convincing evidence of such entrustment or an agreement to buy property together to overcome the presumption of titleCand, as previously mentioned, there is no dispute that title to the stock of Mag Instrument was taken solely in Anthony's name. Here, because the jury affirmatively found there were no such agreements, we need not even address the question of whether the evidence was "clear and convincing."

B. Quantum Meruit Allows Recovery For the Value of Beneficial Services, Not The Value By Which Someone Benefits From Those Services

The absence of a contract between Claire and Anthony, however, would not preclude her recovery in quantum meruit: As every first year law student knows or should know, recovery in quantum meruit does not require a contract.

The classic formulation concerning the measure of recovery in quantum meruit is found in *Palmer v. Gregg.* Justice Mosk, writing for the court, said: "The measure of recovery in quantum meruit is the reasonable value of the services rendered provided they were of direct benefit to the defendant."

The underlying idea behind quantum meruit is the law's distaste for unjust enrichment. If one has received a benefit which one may not justly retain, one should "restore the aggrieved party to his [or her] former position by return of the thing or its equivalent in money." The idea that one must be benefited by the goods and services bestowed is thus integral to recovery in quantum meruit; hence courts have always required that the plaintiff have bestowed some benefit on the defendant as a prerequisite to recovery.

But the threshold requirement that there be a benefit from the services can lead to confusion, as it did in the case before us. It is one thing to require that the defendant be benefited by services, it is quite another to measure the reasonable value of those services by the value by which the defendant was "benefited" as a result of them. Contract price and the reasonable value of services rendered are two separate things; sometimes the reasonable value of services exceeds a contract price. And sometimes it does not.

At root, allowing quantum meruit recovery based on "resulting benefit" of services rather than the reasonable value of beneficial services affords the plaintiff the best of both contractual and quasi-contractual recovery. Resulting benefit is an open-ended standard, which, as we have mentioned earlier, can result in the plaintiff obtaining recovery amounting to de facto ownership in a business all out of reasonable relation to the value of services rendered. After all, a particular service timely rendered can have, as Androcles was once pleasantly surprised to discover in the case of a particular lion, disproportionate value to what it would cost on the open market.

The facts in this court's decision in *Passante v. McWilliam* illustrate the point nicely. In *Passante*, the attorney for a fledgling baseball card company gratuitously arranged a needed loan for $100,000 at a crucial point in the company's history;

because the loan was made the company survived and a grateful board promised the attorney a three percent equity interest in the company. The company eventually became worth more than a quarter of a billion dollars, resulting in the attorney claiming $33 million for his efforts in arranging but a single loan. This court would later conclude, because of the attorney's duty to the company as an attorney, that the promise was unenforceable. Interestingly enough, however, the one cause of action the plaintiff in *Passante* did not sue on was quantum meruit; while this court opined that the attorney should certainly get paid "something" for his efforts, a $33 million recovery in quantum meruit would have been too much. Had the services been bargained for, the going price would likely have been simply a reasonable finder's fee.

The jury instruction given here allows the value of services to depend on their impact on a defendant's business rather than their reasonable value. True, the services must be of benefit if there is to be any recovery at all; even so, the benefit is not necessarily related to the reasonable value of a particular set of services. Sometimes luck, sometimes the impact of others makes the difference. Some enterprises are successful; others less so. Allowing recovery based on resulting benefit would mean the law imposes an exchange of equity for services, and that can result in a windfallCas in the present caseCor a serious shortfall in others. Equity-for-service compensation packages are extraordinary in the labor market, and always the result of specific bargaining. To impose such a measure of recovery would make a deal for the parties that they did not make themselves. If courts cannot use quantum meruit to change the terms of a contract which the parties did make, it follows that neither can they use quantum meruit to impose a highly generous and extraordinary contract that the parties did not make.

The cases relied on by Claire for an equity measure of the value of her services are inapposite. [In the omitted portion of the opinion, the court distinguishes several cases cited by plaintiff.] *Watson v. Wood Dimension, Inc.* is a little closer, because it allowed a recovery based on a contemplated commission. But it is still off the mark because the commission was specifically agreed to by the parties.

In *Wood Dimension* a stereo speaker manufacturer hired the friend of a lost customer to wine and dine the customer's general manager. The parties orally agreed that the friend would be paid three percent commission, but they didn't agree on how long the commission might extend after the plaintiff was terminated from employment. As this court noted, there is no reason a court may not consider an agreed price when ascertaining the reasonable value of services. Of course, in the case before us, there was no agreement and no agreed price.

The same applies to the attorney contingent fee cases, of which *Cazares v. Saenz* features most prominently in Claire's argument. As in *Watson*, a recovery that what was a share of an enterprise passed muster because the parties had already agreed to such valuation. In *Cazares* it was a standard one-third contingency fee which had to be shared between the attorneys who made that deal with the client and other attorneys with whom they later associated. "Fortunately, when an attorney partially performs on a contingency fee contract," said the court, "we already have the parties' agreement as to what was a reasonable fee for the entire case."

Telling the jury that it could measure the value of Claire's services by "[t]he value by which Defendant has benefited as a result of [her] services" was error. It allowed the jury to value Claire's services as having bought her a de facto ownership interest in a business whose owner never agreed to give her an interest. On remand, that part of the jury instruction must be dropped.

D. Certain Jury Instructions May Have Misled the Jury Into Finding There Was No Implied Contract When In Fact There Was One

As we have shown, the quantum meruit damage award cannot stand in the wake of the jury's finding that Claire and Anthony had no agreement to share the equity in Anthony's business. But the validity of that very finding itself is challenged in Claire's protective cross-appeal, where she attacks a series of five jury instructions, specially drafted and proffered by Anthony. These instructions are set out in the margin.[11] We agree with Claire that it was error for the trial court to give three of these five instructions.[12] The three instructions are so infelicitously worded that they might have misled the jury into concluding that evidence which can indeed support a finding of an implied contract could not.

---

11. Here are the five:

    1. NO CONTRACT RESULTS FROM PARTIES HOLDING THEMSELVES OUT AS HUSBAND AND WIFE. You cannot find an agreement to share property or form a partnership from the fact that the parties held themselves out as husband and wife. The fact that unmarried persons live together as husband and wife and share a surname does not mean that they have any agreement to share earnings or assets.

    2. NO IMPLIED CONTRACT FROM LIVING TOGETHER. You cannot find an implied contract to share property or form a partnership simply from the fact that the parties lived together[.]

    3. CREATION OF AN IMPLIED CONTRACT.... The fact the parties are living together does not change any of the requirements for finding an express or implied contract between the parties.

    4. COMPANIONSHIP DOES NOT CONSTITUTE CONSIDERATION. Providing services such as a constant companion and confidant does not constitute the consideration required by law to support a contract to share property, does not support any right of recovery and such services are not otherwise compensable.

    5. OBLIGATIONS IMPOSED BY LEGAL MARRIAGE. In California, there are various obligations imposed upon parties who become legally and formally married. These obligations do not arise under the law merely by living together without a formal and legal marriage.

12. The third and fifth instructions in footnote 11 are simple truisms.

The problem with the three instructions is this: They isolate three uncontested facts about the case: (1) living together, (2) holding out to others as husband and wife, (3) providing services "such as" being a constant companion and confidantCand, seriatim, tell the jury that these facts definitely do not mean there was an implied contract. True, none of these facts by themselves and alone necessarily compel the conclusion that there was an implied contract. But that does not mean that these facts cannot, in conjunction with all the facts and circumstances of the case, establish an implied contract. In point of fact, they can.

Unlike the "quasi-contractual" quantum meruit theory which operates without an actual agreement of the parties, an implied-in-fact contract entails an actual contract, but one manifested in conduct rather than expressed in words.[14]

In *Alderson v. Alderson* (1986) 180 Cal.App.3d 450, 461, the court observed that a number of factors, including

- direct testimony of an agreement;

- holding out socially as husband and wife;

- the woman and her children taking the man's surname;

- pooling of finances to purchase a number of joint rental properties;

- joint decision-making in rental property purchases;

- rendering bookkeeping services for, paying the bills on, and collecting the rents of, those joint rental properties; and

- the nature of title taken in those rental properties

could all support a finding there was an implied agreement to share the rental property acquisitions equally.

We certainly do not say that living together, holding out as husband and wife, and being a companion and confidant, even taken together, are sufficient in and of themselves to show an implied agreement to divide the equity in a business owned by one of the couple. However, *Alderson* clearly shows that such facts, together with

---

14. Because an implied in fact contract can be found where there is no expression of agreement in words, the line between an implied in fact contract and recovery in quantum meruit—where there may be no actual agreement at all—is fuzzy indeed. We will not attempt, in dicta, to clear up that fuzziness here. Suffice to say that because quantum meruit is a theory which implies a promise to pay for services as a matter of law for reasons of justice, while implied in fact contracts are predicated on actual agreements, albeit not ones expressed in words, recovery in quantum meruit is necessarily a different theory than recovery on an implied in fact contract. Neither do we address the quantum of proof necessary to support recovery on a quantum meruit theory or attempt to divine the dividing line between services which may be so gratuitously volunteered under circumstances in which there can be no reasonable expectation of payment and services which do qualify for recovery in quantum meruit. These matters have not been briefed and may be left for another day.

others bearing more directly on the business and the way the parties treated the equity and proceeds of the business, can be part of a series of facts which do show such an agreement. The vice of the three instructions here is that they affirmatively suggested that living together, holding out, and companionship could not, as a matter of law, even be part of the support for a finding of an implied agreement. That meant the jury could have completely omitted these facts when considering the other factors which might also have borne on whether there was an implied contract.

On remand, the three instructions should not be given. The jury should be told, rather, that while the facts that a couple live together, hold themselves out as married, and act as companions and confidants toward each other do not, by themselves, show an implied agreement to share property, those facts, when taken together and in conjunction with other facts bearing more directly on the alleged arrangement to share property, can show an implied agreement to share property.

DISPOSITION

The judgment is reversed. The case is remanded for a new trial. At the new trial the jury instructions identified in this opinion as erroneous shall not be given. In the interest of justice both sides will bear their own costs on appeal.

QUESTIONS AND NOTES

1. Few would question that two people like the Maglicas, who lived together for over 20 years, shared their lives as well as a surname. They made a home, worked together, had sexual relations, raised children, ate and traveled together, shared friends, felt that they were a couple, and were thought of as such by others. Under these circumstances, is it plausible that the Maglicas impliedly agreed that Claire would be compensated for performing certain domestic duties and personal services by obtaining equity in Tony's business? Is it more or less plausible that the Maglicas entered into a business partnership agreement? Can one "impliedly" grant an equity interest in a corporation? Or is Claire's claim really the same as if she were a divorcing dependent spouse rather than a business partner?

2. Should the court assume that couples who live together for years, hold themselves out to the community as married, and raise children intend marriage-like obligations? If such parties intend such consequences, why don't they pay the state $23 and get married?

3. What will happen in this case upon remand to the trial court? If you were plaintiff's counsel, what kind of details would you look for to weave into your story at trial? What would the trier of fact need to see and hear in order to come to the conclusion that the Maglicas did enter into an agreement? How would her remedy

be calculated if she proves an implied contract? What remedy would she have if she cannot prove an implied contract?

4. Couples cohabiting for companionship or love have widely varying expectations. Some are affianced and in "trial marriages" that the partners expect will ripen into legal marriages, or terminate, within a relatively short period of time. Others may involve older widowed or divorced partners who have already raised children in past legal marriages with others, and seek long term mutual support, but choose not to marry to preserve separate Social Security, pension or medical benefits, or to maintain financial separateness for reasons of inheritance or other family reasons. Others (including many college students) may be in more temporary dating relationships but find it convenient to temporarily share a household to reduce expenses. And some are in committed long-term relationships in which they live together, pool finances, bear and raise children, and participate in community life as a traditional two-parent family but without legally marrying. Most are likely to be uncertain precisely how they feel at any one point in time. Moreover relationships evolve. A couple may begin living together on one set of assumptions but find that over time their relationship evolves into another type altogether. It is safe to suggest that every couple has its ups and downs, sometimes feeling very close and sometimes very distant. How should a court decide what the agreement, implied or expressed, consists of? Should the warm sharing statements of sunny days override other indications of a desire to maintain separateness?

5. The incidence of heterosexual couples living together without marriage has exploded over the last 50 years. In 1960 the US Census reported 500,000 such couples. According to the US Census' Current Population Survey, in 2012, 7.6 million unmarried heterosexual couples (constituting 6.5% of the total adult US population) shared a household. In addition about 500,000 same-sex couples were reported. There is every indication that this trend towards cohabitation without marriage will continue or perhaps even accelerate given demographic trends including the changing ethnic composition of the population and the decline of older cohorts that tend not to form such households. Indeed, married heterosexual couples now constitute less than half of all households in the United States. Few couples, married or not, enter into express contracts that purport to govern the financial aspects of their relationships or their termination. How can contract law better respond to the formation and dissolution of these multifarious personal relationships? Is it capable of doing so?

6. If you had asked the Maglicas in 1971, 1981, and 1991 what kind of a deal they had, would you have gotten the same answer? If you had asked Ms. Maglica would you have gotten the same answer that you would have gotten from Mr. Maglica? Which deal is binding, or are they all binding?

7. Much of the pressure in these cases seems to be for an explicit written agreement. Will lovers eschewing marriage write such agreements? If such agreements are drafted, will they be likely to redress gender and other inequalities between the parties, or will they more often aggravate typical male-female imbalance in society? One dilemma associated with encouraging people to solve social problems by contract is that negotiated contracts tend to work to the advantage of the strong, and the product therefore tends to aggravate imbalances in bargaining strength between the parties rather than equalize them.

8. Professor Cynthia Bowman in *Unmarried Couples, Law and Public Policy* (Oxford 2010) surveys the legal, historical, sociological, and comparative law landscape relating to non-marital relationships. She notes that the United States has lagged behind such nations as Canada, the United Kingdom and the Netherlands in developing legal structures to protect dependent partners in non-marital relationships. She proposes that states adopt "a multifaceted legal regime under which a heterosexual couple initially may choose between marrying or entering into a domestic partnership that extends the rights and obligations of marriage unless they execute a contract between them to avoid these consequences. If they do not do so, after two years or the birth of a child, this quasi-marriage status would be imposed on them unless they specifically opt-out by agreement." *Id.* at 8. Are the reforms Bowman proposes necessary? Are they sufficient? Why not protect all dependent spouses, married and unmarried, without regard to any phony agreements they get pushed into signing? That is, deal with the substantive inequality that permeates the structure of our society by changing the rules!

9. Few laws or decisions define the content of the marital relation beyond general statements about mutual obligations of respect, fidelity, and support. Each couple over time gives content to its own marriage, and, as long as the couple remains joined, the law does not attempt to define its union. There has been increasing interest in recent years in agreements between spouses that define their rights and duties toward each other. The subject matter of these agreements is likely to include the allocation of responsibility for household tasks and child-raising, matters of primary concern to society and its continuity. Should courts entertain suits to enforce such agreements? Suppose a husband agrees to do his share of the housework and child-care chores, neglects his duties, and spends weekends in front of the TV with six-packs of beer. How should a court react to a wife's contract claim for damages or specific performance?

III. SOCIAL REGULATION OF LAWYER-CLIENT CONTRACTS

Consider the legal aspects of the contracts under which you (or your employer) will be compensated for your professional services after you graduate. Lawyer retention agreements are a special subset of the more general category of personal service contracts.

Lawyers' retention agreements are subject to special rules and are naturally of special interest to law students. Given the nature of legal services, performance is often difficult to define precisely in terms of quantity and quality. As in other contexts, contract doctrine adjusts in light of such circumstances.

The major theme of this section is the extent to which relationships between attorneys and clients should be a matter of contract. How much freedom should society recognize for lawyers and clients to define the terms of their relationship, the price of the attorney's services, the scope of employment, and other definitions of their mutual obligations? There are many reasons to constrict the range of contract terms for attorney employment. Lawyers are professionals, and the obligations we bear our clients are fixed by traditional professional standards. Ethical rules and statutes reinforce these traditions and further limit lawyers' freedom to agree to different terms.

Most clients and most attorneys do not bargain on an equal footing: Contracts are the lawyer's turf. Few clients come to lawyers before a crisis situation has arisen. The average American consults a lawyer only once or twice in a lifetime. Sometimes the first interview is in a jail holding cell. Even when the meeting is not under such extreme constraints, it commonly occurs because the client's spouse has just left home and cleaned out the bank accounts on the way; a family member has died, and tangled legal and financial affairs must be attended to in the face of overwhelming grief; or some other trauma has brought home to the client the unwelcome awareness that a lawyer is needed. In those situations the client may be forced to negotiate terms of retention with the lawyer from a position of gross disadvantage.

A. A LAWYER'S TALE

Paula Harding was four years out of law school. Six months ago she had left Gibson, Austin & Cromwell LLP to hang out her shingle as a labor and employment lawyer in California. Those early months in solo law practice were hard, although referrals from her old firm paid the rent while Paula worked to build her practice.

Ted Olsen was a college classmate and had been co-president with Paula of the Student Council during their senior year. While Paula had been in law school and slaving at Gibson, Austin & Cromwell, back on the East Coast Ted became the hottest young man in e-commerce. He had an uncanny ability to drive traffic to websites through what he called an "integrated packaging approach." The technique required a programmer's skills, but also finesse and imagination in developing a unique approach for each application.

Ted texted Paula to say he was coming to California and wanted to have lunch. Over lunch Ted explained that he was talking to Amalgamated Consolidated Enterprises (ACE), a giant conglomerate in just about every kind of business. ACE saw the potential in Ted's integrated packaging approach not only for its own websites, but also for those of its many business customers. ACE wanted Ted to head up this new operation in a newly formed ACE subsidiary.

Prior to Ted and Paula's lunch, ACE's president had offered Ted a three-year contract which he said would contain "the works" in the way of fringe benefits, with a total potential value, including stock options and bonuses, of more than $5,000,000.

Paula and Ted talked long into the afternoon, examining all the angles of Ted's position, the new business, the ACE contract, Ted's place in the organization, the effect of the move on his existing business relationships, and the changes it implied for his tax and estate planning. Ted asked Paula to be his lawyer "for the whole situation" and Paula of course was very excited to land her first major client on her own. Ted agreed to send Paula a retainer and pay for Paula's services on an hourly basis. Later that afternoon Paula prepared the following letter which she emailed to Ted:

November 18, 2015

Dear Ted:

You have asked me to represent you in the matter of your negotiations for an employment contract with Amalgamated Consolidated Enterprises. The scope of the representation will include negotiations with the prospective employer (if you so desire), preparation and review of the contract and any collateral agreements that may be required, and an examination of the retirement and other fringe benefits.

You will pay me an initial fee of $5,000 and at the conclusion of the matter I will bill you on the basis of services actually performed, crediting you with the $5,000 down payment. I will bill you from time to time for out-of-pocket disbursements for which you will be responsible.

If the above meets with your understanding, please sign on the copy of this letter in the space indicated below, return it to me with the initial fee, and this shall constitute the agreement between us.

Very truly yours,

Paula Harding

Accepted and Agreed:

_____

Ted Olsen

When Ted got back to his office the next day he opened up the attachment, raised an eyebrow at the $5,000 "initial fee," shrugged, printed it out, signed it, and returned it to Paula with his check for $5,000.

QUESTIONS

What ambiguities exist in Paula's retainer letter? What would you change? What provisions are missing?

B.   THE ATTORNEY'S RETAINER AGREEMENT

Retainer agreements often are in the form of an accepted or acknowledged letter, although some types of legal employment and fees, for example those of bankruptcy counsel whose fees are paid from the estate, must follow a prescribed form and be approved by the court. Beyond reciting that the attorney has been retained, the retainer letter may be extremely sketchy and can be a fertile source of dispute. The scope of the work to be done often is vaguely described and provides an inadequate standard against which performance can be measured. Particularly when the fee is either fixed or contingent on recovery, questions may arise as to just how much the lawyer is expected to do to earn the fee. It is important for the lawyer to make all appropriate disclosures and seek waivers of any conflicts of interest at the very beginning of the lawyer-client relationship, and a good retainer letter will accomplish those objectives as well as furnishing a written contractual basis for the collection of the attorney's fee and expenses. When lawyers practice in large firms, the process of client intake, including conflict checks, negotiating waivers, making disclosures, defining the proper scope of work, and providing adequate assurance of payment can be involved and complex processes involving intake committee approvals and compliance with procedures mandated by the firm and its malpractice carrier to limit liability and avoid future disputes. Client intake procedures in such firms may also be heavily influenced by the firm's internal compensation practices including the allocation of "credit" to individual for the origination and management of cases and clients.

At the other extreme, in a substantial number of situations involving lawyers practicing in less bureaucratic settings, the lawyer may have no written agreement with the client. This practice has come under increasing attack from critics both within and outside the legal profession. Many states now require a written agreement when the lawyer is working for a contingent fee and, as the California statutes below indicate, the requirement of a written agreement is becoming more general.

WEST'S ANN. CALIFORNIA BUSINESS AND PROFESSIONS CODE:

§ 6147. *Contingency fee contracts; duplicate copy; contents; effect of noncompliance; recovery of workers' compensation benefits.*

(a) An attorney who contracts to represent a client on a contingency fee basis shall, at the time the contract is entered into, provide a duplicate copy of the contract, signed by both the attorney and the client, or the client's guardian or representative, to the client, or to the client's guardian or representative. The contract shall be in writing and shall include, but is not limited to, all of the following:

(1) A statement of the contingency fee rate which the client and attorney have agreed upon.

(2) A statement as to how disbursements and costs incurred in connection with the prosecution or settlement of the claim will affect the contingency fee and the client's recovery.

(3) A statement as to what extent, if any, the client could be required to pay any compensation to the attorney for related matters that arise out of their relationship not covered by their contingency fee contract. This may include any amounts collected for the plaintiff by the attorney.

(4) Unless the claim is subject to the provisions of Section 6146, a statement that the fee is not set by law but is negotiable between attorney and client.

(5) If the claim is subject to the provisions of Section 6146, a statement that the rates set forth in that section are the maximum limits for the contingency fee agreement, and that the attorney and client may negotiate a lower rate.

(b) Failure to comply with any provision of this section renders the agreement voidable at the option of the plaintiff, and the attorney shall thereupon be entitled to collect a reasonable fee.

...

§ 6148. Contracts for services in cases not coming within § 6147; bills rendered by attorney; contents; failure to comply.

(a) In any case not coming within Section 6147 in which it is reasonably foreseeable that total expense to a client, including attorney fees, will exceed one thousand dollars ($1,000), the contract for services in the case shall be in writing. At the time the contract is entered into, the attorney shall provide a duplicate copy of the contract signed by both the attorney and the client, or the client's guardian or representative, to the client or to the client's guardian or representative. The written contract shall contain all of the following:

   (1) Any basis of compensation including, but not limited to, hourly rates, statutory fees or flat fees, and other standard rates, fees, and charges applicable to the case.

   (2) The general nature of the legal services to be provided to the client.

   (3) The respective responsibilities of the attorney and the client as to the performance of the contract.

(b) All bills rendered by an attorney to a client shall clearly state the basis thereof. Bills for the fee portion of the bill shall include the amount, rate, basis for calculation, or other method of determination of the attorney's fees and costs. Bills for the cost and expense portion of the bill shall clearly identify the costs and expenses incurred and the amount of the costs and expenses. Upon request by the client, the attorney shall provide a bill to the client no later than 10 days following the request unless the attorney has provided a bill to the client within 31 days prior to the request, in which case the attorney may provide a bill to the client no later than 31 days following the date the most recent bill was provided. The client is entitled to make similar requests at intervals of no less than 30 days following the initial request. In providing responses to client requests for billing information, the attorney may use billing data that is currently effective on the date of the request, or, if any fees or costs to that date cannot be accurately determined, they shall be described and estimated.

(c) Failure to comply with any provision of this section renders the agreement voidable at the option of the client, and the attorney shall, upon the agreement being voided, be entitled to collect a reasonable fee.

(d) This section shall not apply to any of the following:

(1) Services rendered in an emergency to avoid foreseeable prejudice to the rights or interests of the client or where a writing is otherwise impractical.

(2) An arrangement as to the fee implied by the fact that the attorney's services are of the same general kind as previously rendered to and paid for by the client.

(3) If the client knowingly states in writing, after full disclosure of this section, that a writing concerning fees is not required.

(4) If the client is a corporation.

...

The retainer agreement serves several distinct functions: It establishes (a) the authority of the lawyer to act as agent and attorney of the client; (b) the scope of the work to be done; (c) the basis for compensation; (d) disclosure and consent to certain types of conflicting interests or concurrent representations that would otherwise violate the rules of professional responsibility; and (e) other terms governing the relationship, ranging from termination to dispute resolution.

In addition to a license from the state, a lawyer needs authority from the client to act on the client's behalf. Admission to the bar does not authorize lawyers to intervene officiously in the affairs of others. The source of this authority is the mandate of the client, which establishes a relationship between the lawyer as agent and the client as principal. In some modern situations it may be difficult to tell whether the client or the lawyer is really in charge, particularly when the attorney is assigned by a court or public agency to represent the client or when the client is a large anonymous class which the lawyer has created by the pleader's sleight of hand. Whatever the practical problems may be, there is no conceptual difficulty here. The attorney's authority to act is created and defined by the client's agreement to retain the lawyer, subject to limitations imposed by law.

Lawyer's fees typically are set on one of three bases:

(a) *Fixed Fee:* Under this approach, a set price is placed on a given service: $200 to draft a deed; $20,000 to brief and argue an appeal; $2,500 to examine a complex set of documents. In many jurisdictions minimum or suggested fee schedules for various services used to be established by bar associations or court rule. In 1976 the Supreme Court of the United States held in *Goldfarb v. Virginia State Bar* that bar fee schedules violate the antitrust laws, at least when they are mandatory and enforced against the lawyer. For some special kinds of service, such as worker's compensation, social security or veterans' benefits proceedings before administrative agencies, the lawyer's fee may be regulated by state or federal statute.

(b) *Time Charges:* For most complex legal matters, it is difficult when the lawyer is retained to estimate how much effort may be required. From the lawyer's point of view the most important factor in setting the fee usually is the time to be invested in the job and the extent to which it will tie up office resources. The retainer agreement, therefore, is likely to state that services will be billed on the basis of time spent at agreed hourly rates plus reimbursement of expenses.

Paula Harding's letter to Ted Olsen is an example of such an agreement, but note that, like many agreements you will encounter in actual practice, it gives no clear idea of how much the client will be charged for any given service, nor does it clearly indicate what the "initial fee" of $5,000 covers. For example, if ACE terminates discussions with Ted two days after he retains Paula and before she does anything on his behalf, does she get to keep the $5,000? Is it a minimum fee or a form of security deposit?

(c) *Contingent Fees:* Sometimes, particularly when lawyers represent plaintiffs suing for damages, legal fees may be calculated as a percentage of the amount recovered. This may be advantageous from the client's viewpoint since the fee, if any, is dependent on the result obtained and the benefit gained by the client. If there is no recovery, the lawyer receives nothing. In any event, the client need not pay for the services until there is a recovery, which is an important benefit to a client who lacks funds to retain counsel otherwise. Contingent fee arrangements may be subject to abuse, however, and a number of jurisdictions seek to control the percentage fee the lawyer may receive and otherwise supervise the relationship. Few nations outside the United States permit such arrangements, and in this country contingent fees are permissible only in some situations. In particular, contingent fees are generally useful only when the lawyer's efforts will produce a fund of money out of which the fee will be paid; although, certain institutional clients and their lawyers are increasingly experimenting with contingent fees based on successful defense of monetary claims. Contingent fees are inappropriate when a lawyer represents a defendant in a suit seeking nonmonetary relief (at least in the absence of a fee-shifting statute like the Equal Access to Justice Act, 5 U.S.C. § 504; 28 U.S.C. § 2412) and are generally considered unethical in divorce or criminal cases.

The bases for computing lawyers' charges reflects at least five different views of lawyers' work and relationship to the client and society.

The lawyer as the client's aristocratic friend in court. The Anglo-American legal profession once sharply distinguished courtroom lawyers from office counselors. This bifurcation is still present in the profession in England, which has two separate kinds of lawyers, barristers and solicitors. Time has diluted, but not eliminated, the kinds of distinctions between barristers, who are courtroom advocates, and solicitors, who are office counselors and drafters.

The barrister started as a gentleman friend of the client in Royal Court. Class and connections, blended artistically with a smooth and persuasive articulateness rather than rigorous education, were required for entry into the profession. Barristers were called to the bar after having attended a set number of dinner sessions at the Inns of Court. Direct pedagogy was diluted with food, fellowship, and good claret. The barrister gives counsel to the client and presents the client's case to the Court, but the gentleman barrister does not work for the client. It remains unethical in England for the barrister to have direct financial dealings with the client. The client must be introduced to the barrister by a solicitor, and dealings between them are mediated by the solicitor. The barrister's fee started as a gratuity from the solicitor, and to this day it is not negotiated personally by the barrister, but by a clerk who handles the barrister's office administration. The barrister has no contractual claim for the fee enforceable against the client. The class assumptions underlying this structure do not fit very well in contemporary American life, but the continuity of these practices in the United Kingdom testifies to the viability of structures other than contract to organize professional relationships.

The lawyer as an artisan. Not all providers of legal services have an aristocratic professional origin. Solicitors start out as skilled servants of aristocrats. One part of this branch of the profession grew out of estate agents who managed the property and personal business affairs of the wealthy, while their employers devoted their time to military, political, ecclesiastical, and other cultural pursuits. These solicitors would draft written instruments dealing with property. Solicitors learned their professions as articled clerks, apprenticed early in their teens for lengthy on-the-job training, culminating in lectures and an examination at a professional institute. As Gilbert and Sullivan teach us, as the young lawyer moved up from office boy to junior clerk, "I served the writs with a smile so bland, and I copied all the letters in a big round hand." Viewed this way, solicitors were artisans who had a special set of skills to sell. They produced documents and agreements, just as shoemakers produced shoes. This view of their function would suggest compensation on a fixed-fee basis for each of their units of production. While these products traditionally were hand-crafted by lawyer-artisans individually for each client, new technologies and market structures have commoditized many of these sorts of legal services. Either through computer software or outsourcing of legal services, an increasing share of what used to be the work of highly skilled individual lawyers can be produced and marketed more efficiently on a mass basis. Certainly this is the case in many areas of consumer law. But even businesses are increasingly relying on technology and outsourcing rather than traditional law firms in meeting their routine legal needs.

Richard Susskind provocatively predicts that technology and outsourcing will radi-cally reshape the market for legal services in the 21st century into a very small market for extremely specialized services provided on a traditional basis, and a much larger market in which a relatively small number of lawyers do not provide directly, but rather organize the provision of, routine services for almost all clients by less highly skilled persons (perhaps in less developed countries) working at lower wages, and, increasingly, computers. RICHARD SUSSKIND, THE END OF LAWYERS? (Oxford 2008).

The lawyer as wage worker. There is another way of looking at solicitors serving their powerful clients. Such relationships often were long-standing and persisted for generations as a firm of solicitors grew from youth to age serving a landed family's interests. These solicitors might be seen as a kind of high status servant, continually employed to advance the family's interests, rather than as an artisan selling individual scraps of paper. As such, their compensation would be measured by a wage, salary, or other periodic retainer.

In America today, a growing number of lawyers work on a salary basis for a single client. This reflects the increase in large organizations that have created their own legal departments to service their needs full-time instead of hiring outside lawyers. Corporations, government agencies, universities all are likely to have salaried em-ployees working as house counsel this way. In addition, law practice, which two generations ago was dominated by single practitioners and office sharing lawyers working together, has now become dominated by large law firms that may employ thousands of attorneys. The senior members of the firm are partners and share in the profits of their activities, but most of the lawyers working for the firm will be associates, or salaried workers, who do not directly charge the client for their ser-vices. Instead, the firm charges the client and pays the associate a salary that is independent of the fees charged to clients. Indeed many of the partners of such a firm may have very limited management responsibility and may function as highly-compensated employees with a profit-sharing arrangement rather than as owners of the firm.

The lawyer as the client's co-venturer. In the American experience the lawyer may play a broader role in the client's affairs than just a courtroom advocate or skilled drafter. Lawyers advise clients on the wisdom and potential tax, business and legal consequences of contemplated ventures and negotiate the terms of the deal. Some-times their fees may not be in cash or based on time worked or documents produced, but in the form of an interest in the enterprise, a piece of the action. Lawyers are most commonly their client's co-venturers in another way, for as was mentioned, our system permits contingent fees to enhance access to legal services for clients with a valuable claim but no cash for lawyers' fees.

The lawyer as a public utility. If lawyers are providers of a necessary public service, then the prices and terms of their service may be fixed by law or regulation. Indeed, in most communities the organized bar claims just such a function to regulate and discipline members. In addition, there has been growing recognition that in many common situations the availability of legal services is a right of the client. The source of this right may be constitutional, for example, when a person charged with a serious crime claims the right of assistance of counsel, or it may be part of a governmental program to provide legal services to all persons, as is the case of some legal aid programs organized by the state and federal governments. The consequences of this public utility view are clear: the lawyer's tie to the client is based on the contract to only a very limited degree.

C.   ATTORNEY-CLIENT CONTRACTS AND REASONABLE VALUE

ABA MODEL RULES OF PROFESSIONAL CONDUCT

Rule 1.5 Fees.

(a) A lawyer's fee shall be reasonable. The factors to be considered in determining the reasonableness of a fee include the following:

   (1) the time and labor required, the novelty and difficulty of the questions involved, and the skill requisite to perform the legal service properly;

   (2) the likelihood, if apparent to the client, that the acceptance of the particular employment will preclude other employment by the lawyer;

   (3) the fee customarily charged in the locality for similar legal services;

   (4) the amount involved and the results obtained;

   (5) the time limitations imposed by the client or by the circumstances;

   (6) the nature and length of the professional relationship with the client;

   (7) the experience, reputation, and ability of the lawyer or lawyers performing the services; and

   (8) whether the fee is fixed or contingent.

(b) When the lawyer has not regularly represented the client, the basis or rate of the fee shall be communicated to the client, preferably in writing, before or within a reasonable time after commencing the representation.

(c) A fee may be contingent on the outcome of the matter for which the service is rendered, except in a matter in which a contingent fee is prohibited by paragraph (d) or other law. A contingent fee agreement shall be in writing and shall state the method by which the fee is to be determined, including the percentage or percentages that shall accrue to the lawyer in the event of settlement, trial or appeal, litigation and other expenses to be deducted from the recovery, and whether such expenses are to be deducted before or after the contingent fee is calculated. Upon conclusion of a contingent fee matter, the lawyer shall provide the client with a written statement stating the outcome of the matter and, if there is a recovery, showing the remittance to the client and the method of its determination.

(d) A lawyer shall not enter into an arrangement for, charge, or collect:

(1) any fee in a domestic relations matter, the payment or amount of which is contingent upon the securing of a divorce or upon the amount of alimony or support, or property settlement in lieu thereof; or

(2) a contingent fee for representing a defendant in a criminal case.

(e) A division of fee between lawyers who are not in the same firm may be made only if:

(1) the division is in proportion to the services performed by each lawyer or, by written agreement with the client, each lawyer assumes joint responsibility for the representation;

(2) the client is advised of and does not object to the participation of all the lawyers involved; and

(3) the total fee is reasonable.

Consider this *New York Law Journal* report concerning a dispute over legal fees incurred by the family of a victim of the 9/11 terrorist attack on the World Trade Center:

Laura Balemian, whose husband Edward J. Mardovich died in the World Trade Center, received one of the largest awards paid out by the September 11th Victim Compensation Fund: $6.7 million.

But she in turn paid out what is almost certainly the highest legal fee. While the vast majority of victims were represented before the fund pro bono or for a nominal fee, Balemian paid her lawyer, Thomas J. Troiano, a one-third contingent fee, or over $2 million.

The propriety of Troiano's fee is now before the courts. A guardian appointed by the Suffolk County Surrogate's Court in New York, where Mardovich's estate is in probate, last year challenged the fee as excessive and not in the best interests of Balemian's four children. Troiano responded earlier this year by suing Balemian in Manhattan federal court for declaratory judgment approving his fees.

The situation is an uncomfortable one for trial lawyers' groups, who normally support contingent fee arrangements but went to extraordinary lengths to avoid being seen as profiting from the terrorist attacks.

Kenneth R. Feinberg, the special master who oversaw the fund's distribution of some $7 billion, submitted an April 21 affidavit in the federal case in which he called Troiano's fee "shocking and unconscionable" in light of the fund's purpose and its guidelines recommending attorney fees be kept under 5 percent.

"In my experience of presiding over the processing and award determinations of some 7,400 claims, of conducting hundreds of individual hearings within the Program, and of meeting with thousands of families and victims in large and small groups, I have never learned of a legal fee even approaching the fee sought in this case," Feinberg wrote.

But Troiano, who declined to be interviewed for this article, said in court documents responding to Feinberg's affidavit that Balemian's large award, which was increased from an initial presumptive award of $1.1 million, justified the contingent fee.

"Fund statistics show that lesser attorneys—or perhaps those who were marginally incentivized by the meager 5 percent fee recommended by the Special Master—achieved results that pale in comparison to the award [Troiano] obtained for [Balemian]," the lawyer said.

"If anything is 'shocking and unconscionable' it is that, due to unabashed greed, Defendant now (more than two years after having ratified the Retainer Agreement) seeks disgorgement of fees earned by Plaintiff from the hard work, at significant personal sacrifice, he rendered for the benefit of Defendant and her children."

At the time of his death, Mardovich was the 42-year-old president of Euro Brokers, an interdealer brokerage that had offices on the 84th floor of the World Trade Center's South Tower. The firm lost 61 of its 65 employees in the terrorist attack.

According to his federal complaint, Troiano, 62, had never represented Mardovich or his wife before but was a longtime friend and neighbor in their North Shore Long Island community. He claims that, in the days after Sept. 11, a "frightened and confused" Balemian reached out to him and asked him to assist her with the legal issues arising from the death of her husband, who left no will.

"She told him that he was the only person she trusted to handle such matters," Troiano's complaint states. "She told him that Edward Mardovich had told her that if anything ever happened to him, she should turn to Tom Troiano for help."

Troiano claims he took charge of all of the family's legal affairs, including locating and consolidating money in Mardovich's various accounts, finding a suitable financial planner and resolving the deceased's partnership interest in several racehorses.

For essentially becoming the Mardovich family lawyer, Troiano said he never asked for nor received any payment. But he did have Balemian sign a retainer agreement on Oct. 15, 2001. (She was Ms. Mardovich at the time. She married Robert Balemian in April 2002).

The agreement states the one-third fee will be contingent on a recovery in possible lawsuits against, among others, the airlines, Osama bin Laden, the Taliban regime of Afghanistan, New York City as well as "any other legal, governmental, quasi-governmental or non-profit agency responsible for the September 11, 2001 crash or any recoverable claims resulting after the September 11, 2001 destruction of the World Trade Center."

Congress created the compensation fund on Sept. 22, 2001, as part of the Air Transportation Safety and Systems Stabilization Act. Feinberg was appointed special master in November 2001, and the fund's rules were initially published in December of that year. In return for receiving compensation from the fund, claimants waived their rights to sue the airlines. Over 97 percent of affected families ultimately participated in the fund.

Troiano claims he explored all possible avenues of recovery for Balemian, including tort litigation. He said he spent one year monitoring the fund's activities and talked regularly to other participating lawyers in order to figure out how to maximize an award from the fund. He retained Conrad Berenson, a Baruch College economist, to draft a report on Mardovich's future earning potential.

This report was submitted to the fund with other records on March 14, 2003. Three months later, Balemian was notified she would receive a presumptive award of $1,087,420, based on estimated losses of $3,931,497 minus insurance offsets $2,844,256. She was given the option of requesting a hearing.

Troiano claims he urged Balemian to contest the award, which she did. He represented her at an August 13, 2003, hearing, calling as witnesses Berenson and the chief financial officer of Euro Brokers.

On Sept. 30, 2003, Balemian was notified that her final award would be $6,656,151, based on estimated losses of $9,500,408 minus insurance offsets. Troiano was paid his fee in January 2004.

In his court papers, Troiano called the final award an "astounding" result and stressed his skill and legal acumen. "Rather than greedily seeking disgorgement from Troiano," one of his filings states, "[Balemian] ought to be happily praising his extraordinary efforts, which yielded a lifetime of security for [her] and her children."

Balemian's lawyer, Kevin P. Simmons of Syosset, N.Y.'s Simmons, Jannace & Stagg, said his client was not claiming that Troiano did not do a good job.

"He obviously did," said Simmons. "The question is how much is that worth."

Despite the 5 percent guideline, the fund's rules defer to state law with regard to attorney's fees. But in an interview with the New York Law Journal last week, Feinberg challenged the notion that skillful advocacy played a role in the size of victims' awards.

"I find it difficult to understand how any lawyer can request a 30 percent fee for simply filing a claim with the 9/11 fund," he said. "It's a nonadversarial process where the special master was working with families and family lawyers to find a way to legitimately give them this money."

Hearings that led to higher awards were a routine part of the process, said Feinberg. In his affidavit, he noted that 68 percent of the claims involving deaths had a hearing at which evidence was presented.

Steven Lubet, a legal ethics professor at Northwestern University School of Law, said courts have been divided on what factors to consider in weighing the appropriateness of contingent-fee arrangements. He said some courts had taken a strict contract approach, going with the clear language of the retainer agreement.

But Lubet said other courts have taken the view that "contingent fees need to be contingent on something." These courts, he said, generally look at whether the lawyer taking the case is running a risk of nonrecovery.

Simmons said that, given the nature of the fund, Troiano had run no risk at all. "There was absolutely no chance that it would be zero," said Simmons.

ANTHONY LIN, *Attorney's 9/11 Fee Called 'Shocking, Unconscionable,'* N.Y. L.J. (Aug. 29, 2006).[*]

QUESTION

Broglio is arrested for extortion and contacts Walton to represent him. Walton agrees to represent Broglio for a non-refundable fixed fee of $15,000. Is this a reasonable fee? Only about half of all felony arrests result in the filing of a criminal complaint. What if Walton calls the district attorney to discuss the case and learns he has already decided to drop the charges against Broglio? On the other hand, what if Broglio is charged with a felony and demands a jury trial that consumes six months of Walton's time even before the appeals that will carry the case all the way to the Supreme Court in the hopes of obtaining reversal and yet another jury trial? What if Walton is known as the best criminal defense lawyer in the area? Could Broglio have shopped around for a better deal? What were his real choices as he sat in the holding cell? What if Broglio fires Walton shortly after agreeing to the $15,000 retainer, and Walton therefore performs no services on Broglio's behalf? Compare *Walton v. Broglio*, 52 Cal. App. 3d 400 (1975) with *Matter of Cooperman*, 83 N.Y.2d 465 (1994).

CHAPTER 5

PROMISES TAINTED BY FAILURES OF VOLUNTARY ASSENT

Contract is intimately associated with private autonomy: the idea that people should be free to order their own affairs by agreement. Private autonomy presupposes free and voluntary commitment. Some statements that appear promissory in form nonetheless are unenforceable because they are not voluntarily and intelligently made. "Promises" uttered by someone without capacity, exacted through duress, or induced by fraud or essential mistake are not deserving of respect and enforcement.

These tests are administered in a commonsense fashion, and without great difficulty, to decide that the promise of a woman who has a gun held to her head should not be enforced. Similarly, no one would suggest treating the promise of a four-year-old or a mental incompetent like that of a normal adult for purposes of contract law, or that the victim of a fraud must render a promised performance to the person who is bilking him. But these clear cases quickly shade off into more troublesome ones.

Part of the trouble lies in uncertainty over the philosophical and psychological assumptions behind our concept of assent: a faith in the human qualities of consciousness and intention, voluntariness, and free will. Modern psychology challenges these assumptions by emphasizing the ambivalence and ambiguity that marks most human behavior. People act out of unconscious motives of which they are at best imperfectly aware; they are required to act in the face of persistent and irreconcilable conflict; their apparent intention masks mixed and inconsistent desires.

In interpreting a contract, the judge gives it a sensible meaning in light of the background assumptions of the parties when they agreed. But the very term *assumptions* suggests a process that is less than conscious and focused. One does not often consciously consider what one assumes.

Concerns about the reality of human intention are in tension with the law's emphasis on mutual assent as an essential element of agreement. It is all very well to talk about agreement as a "meeting of the minds." But when do such meetings occur and who serves as witness to the event? No contract of any complexity is ever complete in the sense that the parties have explicitly stated and provided for all the circumstances and eventualities that might affect its performance. Many implied terms of an agreement were not in anyone's mind when the parties made their deal.

This obvious truth casts doubt on those terms as the product of voluntary and intelligent assent. Assume the writing evidencing the agreement is silent as to the material provision (the one the parties are now fighting about) and that it is clear that the parties never consciously thought about this provision. Suppose the contract does contain a clause on the subject, but it is also clear that the parties entering the agreement weren't paying attention. People often sign papers without reading them; all of us do so some of the time. How should the law handle these obvious non-assent situations?

The bases for non-enforcement discussed in this Chapter are intertwined. In some cases, particularly those that emphasize lack of capacity, there appears to be something wrong with the promisor that sets this person apart from other people and leads us to be less willing to accord the same legal weight to this person's promises given to other people's promises. In other cases, particularly those labeled fraud and duress, the focus is on the behavior of the promisee, rather than nature of the promisor. The promise is of questionable enforceability because the promisee did something improper to induce the promise. In a third group of cases, those tagged as "unconscionability" cases, or misunderstandings, the heart of the problem is the oppressive nature of the bargaining process and the promise itself. Yet underlying all of these cases is a concern that the values exchanged in the transaction are grossly unequal. As this inequality in substantive values exchanged increases, concern grows and we wonder why the promisor would enter into such a strange bargain. This leads us to examine critically whether the promisor was a normal adult, whether the promisee induced the peculiar deal by fraud or force, whether the bargaining was marred by fine print or incomprehensible language, or whether the whole deal was just a big misunderstanding.

Note that the capacity of the promisor, the behavior of the promisee, the form of the bargaining, and the substantive fairness of the deal are cumulative factors. People of limited capacity are more easily taken advantage of, particularly when the bargaining process does not bring forcefully to their attention what they are committing themselves to. Conversely, we are less concerned about lawyers who fail to read the fine print they presumably are trained to understand. Finally, note that the substantive unfairness of the bargain is an overriding concern. We do not worry too much about enforcing sensible contracts for necessities by persons of very limited capacity to contract if the price and terms of the contracts are fair.

I.   LACK OF CAPACITY

Emphasis on voluntary assent as an element in contract necessarily implies that the promisor possesses the capacity to use reason. This requirement is easy enough to apply in extreme cases, as §§ 12 and 15 of the Restatement, Second, Contracts suggest.

RESTATEMENT, SECOND, CONTRACTS:

§ 12. Capacity to Contract.

(1) No one can be bound by contract who has not legal capacity to incur at least voidable contractual duties. Capacity to contract may be partial and its existence in respect of a particular transaction may depend upon the nature of the transaction or upon other circumstances.

(2) A natural person who manifests assent to a transaction has full legal capacity to incur contractual duties thereby unless he is

   (a) under guardianship, or

   (b) an infant, or

   (c) mentally ill or defective, or

   (d) intoxicated.

§ 15. Mental Illness or Defect.

(1) A person incurs only voidable contractual duties by entering into a transaction if by reason of mental illness or defect

   (a) he is unable to understand in a reasonable manner the nature and consequences of the transaction, or

   (b) he is unable to act in a reasonable manner in relation to the transaction and the other party has reason to know of his condition.

(2) Where the contract is made on fair terms and the other party is without knowledge of the mental illness or defect, the power of avoidance under Subsection (1) terminates to the extent that the contract has been so performed in whole or in part or the circumstances have so changed that avoidance would be unjust. In such a case a court may grant relief as justice requires.

As with the insanity defense in the criminal law, the traditional doctrine of mental capacity to contract fits uneasily with modern medical views of mental illness.

Moreover, concepts of infancy have been modified and challenged, and the age of majority has been lowered. It is easy to state general rules in these situations. Children and people with very impaired mental functions are different and are not held to the same obligations as the rest of the community. But notice how difficult it can be to apply this sensible approach in specific cases. When you look at all but the most extreme situation in detail, you are likely to find some reason to become skeptical whether this person is so different as to be relieved of liability. After all, millions of people in the community have serious mental disabilities, tens of millions more are functionally illiterate, and many businesspersons conduct business after a liquid lunch that impairs judgment.

Two distinctions have been useful to courts faced with thorny questions of capacity. One distinguishes between those transactions in which the promisor is so lacking in capacity to contract that the deal is totally *void* and those which are *voidable*, that is, the disabled promisor may choose to avoid the transaction although prima facie a legal obligation is created. The second distinction is drawn between incapacities that affect a promisor's power to enter *any* transaction and those that affect the promisor's capacity to act reasonably with respect to a *particular* transaction.

Whether the distinctions make sense or not, they allow courts to work their way through tough cases, avoiding contracts in which the agreement is unjust to the disabled party, but enforcing sensible deals by not so sensible people when the promisee has relied or partly performed to his detriment without reason to know of the promisor's incapacity.

Ortelere v. Teachers' Retirement Board of New York

New York Court of Appeals, 1969.
25 N.Y.2d 196, 303 N.Y.S.2d 362, 250 N.E.2d 460.

■ BREITEL, J. This appeal involves the revocability of an election of benefits under a public employees' retirement system and suggests the need for a renewed examination of the kinds of mental incompetency which may render voidable the exercise of contractual rights. The particular issue arises on the evidently unwise and foolhardy selection of benefits by a 60–year–old teacher, on leave for mental illness and suffering from cerebral arteriosclerosis, after service as a public schoolteacher and participation in a public retirement system for over 40 years. The teacher died a little less than two months after making her election of maximum benefits, payable to her during her life, thus causing the entire reserve to fall in. She left surviving her husband of 38 years of marriage and two grown children.

There is no doubt that any retirement system depends for its soundness on an actuarial experience based on the purely prospective selections of benefits and mortality rates among the covered group, and that retrospective or adverse selection after the fact would be destructive of a sound system. It is also true that members of retirement systems are free to make choices which to others may seem unwise or foolhardy. The issue here is narrower than any suggested by these basic principles. It is whether an otherwise irrevocable election may be avoided for incapacity because of known mental illness which resulted in the election when, except in the barest actuarial sense, the system would sustain no unfavorable consequences.   *Issue*

The husband and executor of Grace W. Ortelere, the deceased New York City schoolteacher, sues to set aside her application for retirement without option, in the event of her death. It is alleged that Mrs. Ortelere, on February 11, 1965, two months before her death from natural causes, was not mentally competent to execute a retirement application. By this application, effective the next day, she elected the maximum retirement allowance. She thus revoked her earlier election of benefits under which she named her husband a beneficiary of the unexhausted reserve upon her death. Selection of the maximum allowance extinguished all interests upon her death.

Following a nonjury trial in Supreme Court, it was held that Grace Ortelere had been mentally incompetent at the time of her February 11 application, thus rendering it "null and void and of no legal effect." The Appellate Division, by a divided court, reversed the judgment of the Supreme Court and held that, as a matter of law, there was insufficient proof of mental incompetency as to this transaction.

Mrs. Ortelere's mental illness, indeed, psychosis, is undisputed. It is not seriously disputable, however, that she had complete cognitive judgment or awareness when she made her selection. A modern understanding of mental illness, however,   *policy* suggests that incapacity to contract or exercise contractual rights may exist, because of volitional and affective impediments or disruptions in the personality, despite the intellectual or cognitive ability to understand. It will be recognized as the civil law parallel to the question of criminal responsibility which has been the recent concern of so many and has resulted in statutory and decisional changes in the criminal law.

Mrs. Ortelere, an elementary schoolteacher since 1924, suffered a "nervous breakdown" in March, 1964 and went on a leave of absence expiring February 5, 1965. She was then 60 years old and had been happily married for 38 years. On July 1, 1964 she came under the care of Dr. D'Angelo, a psychiatrist, who diagnosed her breakdown as involutional psychosis, melancholia type. Dr. D'Angelo prescribed, and for about six weeks decedent underwent, tranquilizer and shock therapy. Although moderately successful, the therapy was not continued since it was suspected that she also suffered from cerebral arteriosclerosis, an ailment later confirmed. However, the psychiatrist continued to see her at monthly intervals until March, 1965. On March 28, 1965 she was hospitalized after collapsing at home from an aneurysm. She died 10 days later; the cause of death was "Cerebral thrombosis due to H[ypertensive] H[eart] D[isease]."

As a teacher she had been a member of the Teachers' Retirement System of the City of New York. This entitled her to certain annuity and pension rights, preretirement death benefits, and empowered her to exercise various options concerning the payment of her retirement allowance.

Some years before, on June 28, 1958, she had executed a "Selection of Benefits under Option One" naming her husband as beneficiary of the unexhausted reserve. Under this option upon retirement her allowance would be less by way of periodic retirement allowances, but if she died before receipt of her full reserve the balance of the reserve would be payable to her husband. On June 16, 1960, two years later, she had designated her husband as beneficiary of her service death benefits in the event of her death prior to retirement.

Then on February 11, 1965, when her leave of absence had just expired and she was still under treatment, she executed a retirement application, the one here involved, selecting the maximum retirement allowance payable during her lifetime with nothing payable on or after death. She also, at this time, borrowed from the system the maximum cash withdrawal permitted, namely, $8,760. Three days earlier she had written the board, stating that she intended to retire on February 12 or 15 or as soon as she received "the information I need in order to decide whether to take an option or maximum allowance." She then listed eight specific questions, reflecting great understanding of the retirement system, concerning the various alternatives available. An extremely detailed reply was sent, by letter of February 15, 1965, although by that date it was technically impossible for her to change her selection. However, the board's chief clerk, before whom Mrs. Ortelere executed the application, testified that the questions were "answered verbally by me on February 11th." Her retirement reserve totalled $62,165 (after deducting the $8,760 withdrawal), and the difference between electing the maximum retirement allowance (no option) and the allowance under "option one" was $901 per year or $75 per month. That is, had the teacher selected "option one" she would have received an annual allowance of $4,494 or $375 per month, while if no option had been selected she would have received an annual allowance of $5,395 or $450 per month. Had she not withdrawn the cash the annual figures would be $5,247 and $6,148 respectively.

Following her taking a leave of absence for her condition, Mrs. Ortelere had become very depressed and was unable to care for herself. As a result, her husband gave up his electrician's job, in which he earned $222 per week, to stay home and take care of her on a full-time basis. She left their home only when he accompanied her. Although he took her to the Retirement Board on February 11, 1965, he did not know why she went, and did not question her for fear "she'd start crying hysterically that I was scolding her. That's the way she was. And I wouldn't upset her."

The Orteleres were in quite modest circumstances. They owned their own home, valued at $20,000, and had $8,000 in a savings account. They also owned some farm land worth about $5,000. Under these circumstances, as revealed in this record, retirement for both of the Orteleres or the survivor of them had to be provided, as a practical matter, largely out of Mrs. Ortelere's retirement benefits.

According to Dr. D'Angelo, the psychiatrist who treated her, Mrs. Ortelere never improved enough to "warrant my sending her back [to teaching]." A physician for the Board of Education examined her on February 2, 1965 to determine her fitness to return to teaching. Although not a psychiatrist but rather a specialist in internal medicine, this physician "judged that she had apparently recovered from the depression" and that she appeared rational. However, before allowing her to return to teaching, a report was requested from Dr. D'Angelo concerning her condition. It is notable that the Medical Division of the Board of Education on February 24, 1965 requested that Mrs. Ortelere report to the board's "panel psychiatrist" on March 11, 1965.

Dr. D'Angelo stated "[a]t no time since she was under my care was she ever mentally competent"; that "[m]entally she couldn't make a decision of any kind, actually, of any kind, small or large." He also described how involutional melancholia affects the judgment process:

> They can't think rationally, no matter what the situation is. They will even tell you "I used to be able to think of anything and make any decision. Now," they say, "even getting up, I don't know whether I should get up or whether I should stay in bed." Or, "I don't even know how to make a slice of toast any more." Everything is impossible to decide, and everything is too great an effort to even think of doing. They just don't have the effort, actually, because their nervous breakdown drains them of all their physical energies.

While the psychiatrist used terms referring to "rationality," it is quite evident that Mrs. Ortelere's psychopathology did not lend itself to a classification under the legal test of irrationality. It is undoubtedly, for this reason, that the Appellate Division was unable to accept his testimony and the trial court's finding of irrationality in the light of the prevailing rules as they have been formulated.

The well-established rule is that contracts of a mentally incompetent person who has not been adjudicated insane are voidable. Even where the contract has been partly or fully performed it will still be avoided upon restoration of the *status quo*.

Traditionally, in this State and elsewhere, contractual mental capacity has been measured by what is largely a cognitive test. Under this standard the "inquiry" is whether the mind was "so affected as to render him wholly and absolutely incompetent to comprehend and understand the nature of the transaction." A requirement that the party also be able to make a rational judgment concerning the particular transaction qualified the cognitive test. Conversely, it is also well recognized that contractual ability would be affected by insane delusions intimately related to the particular transaction.

These traditional standards governing competency to contract were formulated when psychiatric knowledge was quite primitive. They fail to account for one who by reason of mental illness is unable to control his conduct even though his cognitive ability seems unimpaired. When these standards were evolving it was thought that all the mental faculties were simultaneously affected by mental illness. This is no longer the prevailing view.

Of course, the greatest movement in revamping legal notions of mental responsibility has occurred in the criminal law. The nineteenth century cognitive test embraced in the *M'Naghten* rules has long been criticized and changed by statute and decision in many jurisdictions.

While the policy considerations for the criminal law and the civil law are different, both share in common the premise that policy considerations must be based on a sound understanding of the human mind and, therefore, its illnesses. Hence, because the cognitive rules are, for the most part, too restrictive and rest on a false factual basis they must be re-examined. Once it is understood that, accepting plaintiff's proof, Mrs. Ortelere was psychotic and because of that psychosis could have been incapable of making a voluntary selection of her retirement system benefits, there is an issue that a modern jurisprudence should not exclude, merely because her mind could pass a "cognition" test based on nineteenth century psychology.

There has also been some movement on the civil law side to achieve a modern posture. For the most part, the movement has been glacial and has been disguised under traditional formulations. Various devices have been used to avoid unacceptable results under the old rules by finding unfairness or overreaching in order to avoid transactions.

It is quite significant that Restatement, 2d, Contracts, states the modern rule on competency to contract. This is in evident recognition, and the Reporter's Notes support this inference, that, regardless of how the cases formulated their reasoning, the old cognitive test no longer explains the results. Thus, the new Restatement section reads: "(1) A person incurs only voidable contractual duties by entering into a transaction if by reason of mental illness or defect * * * (b) he is unable to act in a reasonable manner in relation to the transaction and the other party has reason to know of his condition." (Restatement, 2d, Contracts § 18.) (See, also, Allen, Ferster, Weihofen, Mental Impairment and Legal Incompetency, p. 253 [Recommendation b] and pp. 260–282; and Note, 57 Mich.L.Rev. 1020, supra, where it is recommended "that a complete test for contractual incapacity should provide protection to those persons whose contracts are merely uncontrolled reactions to their mental illness, as well as for those who could not understand the nature and consequences of their actions." *policy*

The avoidance of duties under an agreement entered into by those who have done so by reason of mental illness, but who have understanding, depends on balancing competing policy considerations. There must be stability in contractual relations and protection of the expectations of parties who bargain in good faith. On the other hand, it is also desirable to protect persons who may understand the nature of the transaction but who, due to mental illness, cannot control their conduct. Hence, there should be relief only if the other party knew or was put on notice as to the contractor's mental illness. Thus, the Restatement provision for avoidance contemplates that "the other party has reason to know" of the mental illness.

When, however, the other party is without knowledge of the contractor's mental illness and the agreement is made on fair terms, the proposed Restatement rule is: "The power of avoidance under subsection (1) terminates to the extent that the contract has been so performed in whole or in part or the circumstances have so changed that avoidance would be inequitable. In such a case a court may grant relief on such equitable terms as the situation requires." *rule*

The system was, or should have been, fully aware of Mrs. Ortelere's condition. They, or the Board of Education, knew of her leave of absence for medical reasons and the resort to staff psychiatrists by the Board of Education. Hence, the other of the conditions for avoidance is satisfied. *application*

Lastly, there are no significant changes of position by the system other than those that flow from the barest actuarial consequences of benefit selection.

Nor should one ignore that in the relationship between retirement system and member, and especially in a public system, there is not involved a commercial, let alone an ordinary commercial, transaction. Instead the nature of the system and its announced goal is the protection of its members and those in whom its members have an interest. It is not a sound scheme which would permit 40 years of contribution and participation in the system to be nullified by a one-instant act committed by one known to be mentally ill. This is especially true if there would be no substantial harm to the system if the act were avoided. On the record none may gainsay that her selection of a "no option" retirement while under psychiatric care, ill with cerebral arteriosclerosis, aged 60, and with a family in which she had always manifested concern, was so unwise and foolhardy that a factfinder might conclude that it was explainable only as a product of psychosis. *argument*

On this analysis it is not difficult to see that plaintiff's evidence was sufficient to sustain a finding that, when she acted as she did on February 11, 1965, she did so solely as a result of serious mental illness, namely, psychosis. Of course, nothing less serious than medically classified psychosis should suffice or else few contracts would be invulnerable to some kind of psychological attack. Mrs. Ortelere's psychiatrist testified quite flatly that as an involutional melancholiac in depression she was incapable of making a voluntary "rational" decision. Of course, as noted earlier, the trial court's finding and perhaps some of the testimony attempted to fit into the rubrics of the traditional rules. For that reason rather than reinstatement of the judgment at Trial Term there should be a new trial under the proper standards frankly considered and applied.

Accordingly, the order of the Appellate Division should be reversed, without costs, and the action remanded to Special Term for a new trial.

■ JASEN, J. (dissenting). Where there has been no previous adjudication of incompetency, the burden of proving mental incompetence is upon the party alleging it. I agree with the majority at the Appellate Division that the plaintiff, the husband of the decedent, failed to sustain the burden incumbent upon him of proving deceased's incompetence.

The evidence conclusively establishes that the decedent, at the time she made her application to retire, understood not only that she was retiring, but also that she had selected the maximum payment during her lifetime.

Indeed, the letter written by the deceased to the Teachers' Retirement System prior to her retirement demonstrates her full mental capacity to understand and to decide whether to take an option or the maximum allowance. The full text of the letter reads as follows:

> February 8, 1965
>
> Gentlemen:
>
> I would like to retire on Feb. 12 or Feb. 15. In other words, just as soon as possible after I receive the information I need in order to decide whether to take an option or maximum allowance. Following are the questions I would like to have answered:
>
> 1. What is my "average" five-year salary?
>
> 2. What is my maximum allowance?
>
> 3. I am 60 years old. If I select option four-a with a beneficiary (female) 27 years younger, what is my allowance?
>
> 4. If I select four-a on the pension part only, and take the maximum annuity, what is my allowance?
>
> 5. If I take a loan of 89% of my year's salary before retirement, what would my maximum allowance be?
>
> 6. If I take a loan of $5,000 before retiring, and select option four-a on both the pension and annuity, what would my allowance be?

7. What is my total service credit? I have been on a leave without pay since Oct. 26, 1964.

8. What is the "factor" used for calculating option four-a with the above beneficiary?

Thank you for your promptness in making the necessary calculations. I will come to your office on Thursday afternoon of this week.

It seems clear that this detailed, explicit and extremely pertinent list of queries reveals a mind fully in command of the salient features of the Teachers' Retirement System. Certainly, it cannot be said that the decedent could possess sufficient capacity to compose a letter indicating such a comprehensive understanding of the retirement system, and yet lack the capacity to understand the answers.

As I read the record, the evidence establishes that the decedent's election to receive maximum payments was predicated on the need for a higher income to support two retired persons—her husband and herself. Since the only source of income available to decedent and her husband was decedent's retirement pay, the additional payment of $75 per month which she would receive by electing the maximal payment was a necessity. Indeed, the additional payments represented an increase of 20% over the benefits payable under option 1. Under these circumstances, an election of maximal income during decedent's lifetime was not only a rational, but a necessary decision.

Further indication of decedent's knowledge of the financial needs of her family is evidenced by the fact that she took a loan for the maximal amount ($8,760) permitted by the retirement system, at the time she made application for retirement.

Moreover, there is nothing in the record to indicate that the decedent had any warning, premonition, knowledge or indication at the time of retirement that her life expectancy was, in any way, reduced by her condition.

Decedent's election of the maximum retirement benefits, therefore, was not so contrary to her best interests so as to create an inference of her mental incompetence.

Indeed, concerning election of options under a retirement system, it has been held: "Even where no previous election has been made, the court must make the election for an incompetent which would be in accordance with what would have been his manifest and reasonable choice if he were sane, and, in the absence of convincing evidence that the incompetent would have made a different selection, it is *presumed that he would have chosen the option yielding the largest returns in his lifetime.*" (*Schwartzberg v. Teachers' Retirement Bd.*; emphasis supplied.)

Nor can I agree with the majority's view that the traditional rules governing competency to contract "are, for the most part, too restrictive and rest on a false factual basis."

The issue confronting the courts concerning mental capacity to contract is under what circumstances and conditions should a party be relieved of contractual obligations freely entered. This is peculiarly a legal decision, although, of course, available medical knowledge forms a datum which influences the legal choice. It is common knowledge that the present state of psychiatric knowledge is inadequate to provide a fixed rule for each and every type of mental disorder. Thus, the generally accepted rules which have evolved to determine mental responsibility are general enough in application to encompass all types of mental disorders, and phrased in a manner which can be understood and practically applied by juries composed of laymen.

The generally accepted test of mental competency to contract which has thus evolved is whether the party attempting to avoid the contract was capable of understanding and appreciating the nature and consequences of the particular act or transaction which he challenges. This rule represents a balance struck between policies to protect the security of transactions between individuals and freedom of contract on the one hand, and protection of those mentally handicapped on the other hand. In my opinion, this rule has proven workable in practice and fair in result. A broad range of evidence including psychiatric testimony is admissible under the existing rules to establish a party's mental condition. In the final analysis, the lay jury will infer the state of the party's mind from his observed behavior as indicated by the evidence presented at trial. Each juror instinctively judges what is normal and what is abnormal conduct from his own experience, and the generally accepted test harmonizes the competing policy considerations with human experience to achieve the fairest result in the greatest number of cases.

As in every situation where the law must draw a line between liability and nonliability, between responsibility and nonresponsibility, there will be borderline cases, and injustices may occur by deciding erroneously that an individual belongs on one side of the line or the other. To minimize the chances of such injustices occurring, the line should be drawn as clearly as possible.

The Appellate Division correctly found that the deceased was capable of understanding the nature and effect of her retirement benefits, and exercised rational judgment in electing to receive the maximum allowance during her lifetime. I fear that the majority's refinement of the generally accepted rules will prove unworkable in practice, and make many contracts vulnerable to psychological attack. Any benefit to those who understand what they are doing, but are unable to exercise self-discipline, will be outweighed by frivolous claims which will burden our courts and undermine the security of contracts. The reasonable expectations of those who innocently deal with persons who appear rational and who understand what they are doing should be protected.

Accordingly, I would affirm the order appealed from.

QUESTIONS AND NOTES

1. Ms. Ortelere had "complete cognitive judgment or awareness" when she made her contract but suffered under "volitional or affective impediments." But many, if not most, human acts are the products of irrational, perhaps pathological, unconscious drives. Can the legal system of contract survive if its assumptions as to the capacity for rational volitional activity are undermined?

2. Judge Breitel insists that "nothing less serious than medically classified psychosis should suffice [to justify invalidating a contract on the basis of mental illness] or else few contracts would be invulnerable to some kind of psychological attack." Does this encourage too great a reliance on psychiatric diagnosis? Psychiatrists often differ on the diagnosis of particular patients and may disagree on the existence and nature of mental illness. Dr. D'Angelo, for instance, found Ms. Ortelere to be suffering from "involutional psychosis, melancholia type." Yet the existence of such a condition, which was generally linked to menopause, is at best dubious. In 1980, the American Psychiatric Association eliminated the classification of involutional melancholia from the authoritative listing of psychiatric nomenclature, The Diagnostic and Statistical Manual of Mental Disorders. *See* Phyllis T. Bookspan and Maxine Kline, *On Mirrors and Gavels: A Chronicle of How Menopause Was Used as a Legal Defense Against Women*, 32 IND. L. REV. 1267, 1285-86 (1999) (criticizing pre-1980 practice of diagnosing menopausal women as suffering from involutional melancholia and noting that "[m]edical professionals developed careers around the physical and emotional disorders of menopause. When called to the courtroom, their testimony was replete with scientific sounding jargon that the court frequently asked them to translate into lay terms. When this was done, the records reveal that their testimony amounted to little more than stereotyped, folkloric conclusions."). Should psychiatry's evolving views of Ms. Ortelere's probable condition affect the legal decision in *Ortelere*?

3. In *Ortelere* it was relatively easy for the court to give relief to the plaintiff. The defendant was a huge retirement fund to which the deceased wife of the rather poor plaintiff had contributed for forty years. By avoiding Ms. Ortelere's election, the court restored the parties to the positions they were in before she acted. But suppose that while depressed, Ms. Ortelere contracted to paint her entire apartment a dark shade of blue. Should she be privileged to avoid the contract? If the painter had done the job, would you excuse Ms. Ortelere from paying? If the contract were not so bizarre (the purchase of a big automobile or a large life insurance policy), would you treat it differently? Do your reactions turn on her psychiatric diagnosis or on other factors?

4. The plaintiff in this suit is Mr. Ortelere, whose mental capacity is not in question. Recall that Mr. Ortelere drove Ms. Ortelere down to the Board of Education that fateful day. What was he doing while his mentally ill wife was upstairs changing her retirement plan? Driving around the block in search of a parking space? Why didn't he stop her? Why didn't he warn the Board of Education? Should he now be allowed to avoid the consequences of his failure to prevent his wife from acting improvidently?

5. After the Board becomes aware of Ms. Ortelere's psychiatric condition, should they refuse to honor any election she makes even though she is not under any form of legal guardianship? Can they?

6. Suppose that the evidence at trial disclosed that the Orteleres had fought for 42 years and, as the letter quoted in the dissenting opinion perhaps suggests, she specifically intended to "cut him off" in favor of their daughter. Would it matter on those facts that she suffered from involutional psychosis, melancholia type?

7. Some evidence in the record below suggested that Ms. Ortelere had recovered from her nervous breakdown. Recall that Ms. Ortelere retired only after her disability leave was terminated. She had been examined by a Board of Education physician who found that she had fully recovered and was able to resume her duties. This physician testified that Ms. Ortelere's "depression and nervousness followed a heart attack had by her husband and his large losses in the stock market" and that "she had shaken off her worries concerning the stocks" and "felt that she could return to [teaching] without any trouble." He went on to relate that she said that "she had had her house redecorated, that she shopped, that she had been seeing friends and playing cards, that she went and visited her daughter and her grandchildren, and that she had done some painting of pictures." Ms. Ortelere was "quite alert, by which I would mean that she answered my questions ... without any hesitation, and that she did not contradict herself. She didn't appear at all depressed. Neither did she appear euphoric—with her head in the clouds. She didn't claim that everything was perfect." Both the trial court and the Court of Appeals ignored this testimony. But who seems more credible to you: the Board of Education physician or Dr. D'Angelo? And if the psychiatrists disagree about the existence and extent of her depression, what basis is there for finding that the now-deceased Ms. Ortelere lacked mental capacity to contract?

8. Suppose that Ms. Ortelere did not die soon after retirement but that at age 98 she was still going strong. Should the pension fund be able to discontinue payments at the maximum allowance rate on the ground that she lacked mental capacity at the time she made her election?

9. If you represented the Board of Education *during* this litigation, what story would you try to tell a trier of fact? What circumstantial evidence would you be interested in learning about?

10. If you represented the Board of Education *after* the litigation, what procedures would you recommend to avoid future disputes with the Mr. Orteleres of this world? Would the recommended procedures be something that you would have wanted to include, in some fashion or another, in your story to the trier of fact?

NOTE ON THE LEGAL CAPACITY OF NON-ENGLISH SPEAKING AND ILLITERATE PERSONS

According to the 2003 National Assessment of Adult Literacy, approximately 30 million adult Americans, 14% of the adult population, lack basic English language literacy skills. Those adults could not read and understand information in short commonplace prose texts or simple documents. An additional 50-60 million American adults lack the skills necessary to perform moderately challenging literacy activities. Only 13% of American adults were assessed as "proficient" in literacy skills. In light of this problem, should the rules of contract law be modified? Do all these people have limited legal capacity to make enforceable agreements?

Traditionally, the answer has been that an inability to read and write in English is not a legal disability for purposes of contract law. Absent fraud or other overreaching by their counterparties, those not literate in English are nevertheless bound by the terms of the written English-language contracts they manifest assent to. It is the responsibility (say the courts) of those not literate in English to have written agreements read to them or explained to them if they do not wish to be bound by terms that they are not aware of. Indeed, given the vast numbers of people with limited English language ability who have always lived and worked in the United States, the rule could hardly be otherwise.

In *Morales v. Sun Constructors*, 541 F.3d 218 (3d Cir. 2008), the court stated that "[i]n the absence of fraud, the fact that an offeree cannot read, write, speak, or understand the English language is immaterial to whether an English-language agreement the offeree executes is enforceable." *See also Am. Heritage Life Ins. Co. v. Lang*, 321 F.3d 533, 538 (5th Cir. 2003) (holding that since "[i]t is a widely accepted principle of contracts that one who signs or accepts a written instrument will normally be bound in accordance with its written terms," the defendant, "illiterate or not, would be bound" by the agreement); *Scrutu v. Int'l Student Exch.*, 523 F. Supp. 2d 1313, 1320 (S.D. Ala. 2007) ("[A] person who signs an instrument despite an inability to read cannot avoid the effect of his signature if he has neither asked to have the instrument read nor inquired as to its contents."); *Golden State Trading v. Wayne Electro Sys.*, 889 N.Y.S.2d 72 (N.Y. App. Div. 2009) (holding that the plaintiff company "may not rely on its president's inability to speak English to invalidate the contracts"); *Holcomb v. TWR Express*, 782 N.Y.S.2d 840, (N.Y. App. Div. 2004)

("'A party who executes a contract is presumed to know its contents and to assent to them.' An inability to understand the English language, without more, is insufficient to avoid this general rule. A person who is illiterate in the English language is not automatically excused from complying with the terms of a contract simply because he or she could not read it."); *Mason v. Acceptance Loan Co.*, 850 So.2d 289 (Ala. 2002) ("Conditions such as illiteracy and a lack of education do not make one 'insane' or otherwise deprive one of the ability to contract.").

Obviously, in many circumstances, it will be infeasible for someone illiterate in English to have a document read to him or translated before he signs it. Illiteracy in English is a significant handicap in our society, but an inability to enter into a binding contract is only likely to make matters worse for illiterate persons.

More broadly, we are all in some sense functionally illiterate given the practical realities of modern life and the complexity of modern contracts. We all constantly face situations where we execute contracts we have not read and the specific provisions of which we have only limited, or no, awareness. There may be good reasons to enforce the terms of such contracts as written even in the absence of any real assent. On the other hand, in some cases there may be good reasons to challenge contract law's casual assumption that execution of a writing is a sufficient basis to bind the parties to all its terms notwithstanding overwhelming evidence of a complete lack of understanding of those terms by one or both parties.

II. DURESS

S.P. Dunham & Co. v. Kudra
New Jersey Superior Court, Appellate Division, 1957.
44 N.J.Super. 565, 131 A.2d 306.

■ CLAPP, S.J.A.D. Plaintiff, S.P. Dunham & Company, sued defendants for the restitution of $3,232.55 paid them allegedly under business compulsion. The trial court, sitting without a jury, gave judgment for the plaintiff in the amount stated. Defendants appeal.

Plaintiff has for over a century operated a department store in Trenton. For some three years it had leased its fur department to a concessionaire, Elmer A. Hurwitz & Co., but the business of the department was so conducted as to appear to customers to have been a part of plaintiff's operations. During these three years fur coats, left by customers with Hurwitz for storage and cleaning were turned over by him to the defendants Kudra who stored and cleaned them pursuant to an agreement with Hurwitz. Plaintiff knew something of Hurwitz' arrangement with Kudra.

In November 1955 Hurwitz went bankrupt and Dunham thereupon cancelled his concession. However, winter was coming on, and Dunham's customers wanted their coats. On November 23, 1955 Kudra had possession of 412 garments, on which Hurwitz owed Kudra $622.50. This sum plaintiff offered to pay Kudra in return for the garments. But Hurwitz owed Kudra an additional $3,232.55 with respect to other garments that had been delivered back to customers during the preceding two years; and on November 23, Kudra announced that the 412 coats would not be turned over unless plaintiff paid the total sum of $3,855.05. One of the owners of Dunham, much upset, asked Kudra for a few days to think the matter over and consult with counsel. Apparently at about that time, the temperature had dropped to 15 degrees; many substantial customers of the store demanded their coats. When both owners of Dunham then sought to negotiate further, Kudra came up with the proposition that it would deliver the garments directly to plaintiff's customers without charge to the plaintiff, if plaintiff would turn over their names; not only would plaintiff thus place the names of customers in the hands of a competitor in the fur business, but Kudra apparently proposed to bill them directly for Hurwitz' total charges on the coats, which totalled some $4,000. Plaintiff flatly rejected this proposition and on November 29 yielded to Kudra's original demand, paying the $3,855.05. Allegedly, three days later it sought the return of $3,232.55 and on December 15 commenced this action.

Plaintiff seeks the restitution of the $3,232.55 on the ground that the money was paid to defendants, not voluntarily, but under a species of duress, sometimes known as "business compulsion." It claims that defendants, taking advantage of its plight, sought to squeeze it between their own improper demands and the complaints of its customers. Indeed, the predicament in which it was placed was so embarrassing a matter that one of the owners of the store, apprehensive of a serious impairment in its good will, himself spent hours in the fur department talking to customers. There is little doubt but that the pressure which defendants brought to bear upon the plaintiff was an inducing, indeed the sole cause of its payment of the $3,232.55.

A slight examination of the subject will demonstrate that the law of duress is in the process of development. 5 Williston, Contracts (Rev. ed. 1937), § 1603; Dawson, "Economic Duress—An Essay in Perspective," 45 Mich.L.Rev. 253 (1947); Dalzell, "Duress by Economic Pressure," 20 No.Car.L.Rev. 237, 341 (1942). Thus in New Jersey, after some conflicting decisions on the point, our courts have finally rejected the objective test, namely, that duress is irremediable unless it is of such severity as to overcome the will of a person of ordinary firmness; the test now is

Subjective Test (handwritten margin note)

simply this—has the person complaining been constrained to do what he otherwise would not have done?

Apropos of this, attention may be directed to a point brought up by the respondent. It has repeatedly been held in our cases that a person cannot claim to have made a payment under duress if, before he made the payment, there was available to him an immediate and adequate remedy in the courts to test or resist it. This harsh rule has been rejected by the Restatement, Contracts, § 493, Illustrations 8, 9, and also by Williston. Williston points out that:

old rule (handwritten margin note)

> the only reason which could be given for such a rule is that a threat of this sort should not terrify a person of "ordinary firmness." But, though such statements are still repeated, the rule is artificial and, so far as it would require a person threatened with injury necessarily to endure the injury because the law provides a remedy for it, cannot be accepted.

Now that New Jersey in *Rubenstein v. Rubenstein* has definitely repudiated the standard of "ordinary firmness," there may be little reason to retain the other rule; the criterion perhaps should be solely whether the will of the victim was really overborne. An attempt has been made to justify the rule stated, upon the ground that the person exerting the duress has relied on the payment made to him by the victim, and having relied, he should be protected. But why should the law have such a tender regard for a wrongdoer? Relief by way of restitution puts no undue burden upon him; he is not subjected to damages for his wrong, but merely called upon to give back that which he forced from his victim. The court granting restitution should have an easy conscience in the matter.

argument (handwritten margin note)

However, we need not pass upon this more fundamental question. If we accept the rule as stated in our cases, we must still ask ourselves whether the plaintiff had a "complete and adequate remedy" enabling it to recover the coats for its customers and avoid the payment of the $3,232.55. Or did it have merely a "questionable" or uncertain remedy? Redress by way of replevin was suggested on the oral argument. But plaintiff, by way of reply, said first that it was questionable whether it had the standing to maintain an action of replevin, since the owners of the coats had delivered them to Hurwitz and Hurwitz in turn had handed them over to defendants pursuant to his agreement with them; in fact, defendants say in their brief that "Dunham had no control over the return of these coats by Kudra." We pass the question as to whether plaintiff had the standing to maintain the action. And we may also pass the second question raised by plaintiff in that regard, namely, whether the remedy in replevin was entirely adequate in view of Kudra's right to prevent the delivery of the goods by putting up a redelivery bond. It might be said in this latter connection that the action on such a bond "'would not have afforded the plaintiff the relief to which he was entitled, the immediate possession of his property; he would have been compelled to exchange [the] property for a right of action against these defendants'" on the redelivery bond.

Passing those two questions, we come to plaintiff's third contention, namely, that there was no adequate remedy here through any form of litigation. Plaintiff, faced with the clamoring demands of its customers, plainly did not want it brought home to each of them at that juncture that its competitors, the defendants, were in fact attending to the storing and cleaning of her coat. We think a public suit at that time did not constitute adequate relief.

We turn now to defendants' principal argument, which seems to be that they should not be chargeable by plaintiff with "the duress * * * it itself had long ago prepared." They rely on the fact that plaintiff for three years during the summer months had lent Hurwitz money "in the neighborhood of $2,000, $1,500"; and they claim that, though these amounts were paid back in September each year, plaintiff should have known of Hurwitz' financial difficulties. The argument seems to be that plaintiff itself caused defendants to exert the duress. The point is without the slightest substance.

Next, defendants seem to argue, referring to the early common-law doctrine of "duress of goods," that under our present concepts of "business compulsion" redress could be had by the plaintiff here only if it had been compelled to pay out money in order to recover its own property. There is nothing to this point either. The law today does not take such a narrow view of the matter, if indeed it ever did.

Further, defendants contend that the plaintiff cannot have been under duress since, for six days, it had an opportunity to deliberate and consult with its own counsel. These are matters which should be taken into account in determining whether in fact the plaintiff made the payment voluntarily and whether the pressure of defendants' demands still subsisted after deliberation and consultation; but they do not of themselves preclude relief.

Again it is urged that one person (Dunham) cannot claim to have been placed under duress if he pays money to the defendants for the relief of another person (i.e., its customers). We need not refer to the law on the subject, because it is apparent that Dunham paid the $3,232.55 for the relief of itself from an injury to its own good will.

... [W]e might refer to the trial court's concluding remarks below: "it (defendant's conduct) is one of the things I prefer not to * * * have to live with in the community. I couldn't justify it."

Affirmed.

QUESTIONS AND NOTES

1. Was S.P. Dunham & Co. under duress in the same sense as a man who makes an agreement with a gun against his head? If the market supply of nuts and bolts needed by a manufacturer for production is short and it agrees to pay a 30% bonus to get what it needs, may it later resist an action for the price because of duress?

2. To what extent does the term duress describe the necessity or the availability of choice to one party, rather than the moral repugnance of the conduct used by another party? Did Dunham recover in this case because it didn't consent to the contract as a result of duress, or did it recover because Kudra's behavior is one of the things the judge would "prefer not to * * * have to live with in the community"?

3. Kudra's claim appears to be without legal foundation, that is, Dunham was clearly not liable for the amount Hurwitz owed Kudra on the other coats. Suppose Kudra did have a valid claim but enforced it by very tough tactics, threats, and withholding the coats. Wouldn't Dunham be just as subject to duress and have just as little choice whether to comply? Would the result in a suit by Dunham to recover the money it paid under duress be the same?

4. Peter is wrongfully arrested by the police, who have confused him with another person with a similar name. He is held in a cell for 18 hours and then released only after he signs a form that releases any civil claim he may have for false arrest against the police. Is the release enforceable in a later suit Peter brings against the police?

5. May a lawyer threaten to refer a matter to criminal prosecution unless the potential defendant pays a claim asserted by the lawyer's client? May a lawyer threaten to turn an adverse party in to Immigration and Customs Enforcement unless the adverse party drops his suit? Consider Cal. R. Prof. Conduct 5–100(a):

> A member shall not threaten to present criminal, administrative or disciplinary charges to obtain an advantage in a civil dispute.

Note that in July and September of 2010, the State Bar of California adopted new Rules of Professional Conduct, which have been submitted to the Supreme Court of California for approval. This rule, which will become Rule 3.10, will not be affected by the revisions.

Selmer Co. v. Blakeslee–Midwest Co.

United States Court of Appeals, Seventh Circuit, 1983.
704 F.2d 924.

■ POSNER, J. This appeal by the plaintiff from summary judgment for the defendants in a diversity case requires us to consider the meaning, under Wisconsin contract law, of "economic duress" as a defense to a settlement of a contract dispute.

On this appeal, we must take as true the following facts. The plaintiff, Selmer, agreed to act as a subcontractor on a construction project for which the defendant Blakeslee–Midwest Prestressed Concrete Company was the general contractor. Under the contract between Blakeslee–Midwest and Selmer, Selmer was to receive $210,000 for erecting prestressed concrete materials supplied to it by Blakeslee–Midwest. Blakeslee–Midwest failed to fulfill its contractual obligations; among other things, it was tardy in supplying Selmer with the prestressed concrete materials. Selmer could have terminated the contract without penalty but instead agreed orally with Blakeslee–Midwest to complete its work, provided Blakeslee–Midwest would pay Selmer for the extra costs of completion due to Blakeslee–Midwest's defaults. When the job was completed, Selmer demanded payment of $120,000. Blakeslee–Midwest offered $67,000 and refused to budge from this offer. Selmer, because it was in desperate financial straits, accepted the offer.

Two and a half years later Selmer brought this suit against Blakeslee–Midwest (the other defendants' liability, being derivative from Blakeslee–Midwest's, does not require separate consideration), claiming that its extra costs had amounted to $150,000 ($120,000 being merely a settlement offer), and asking for that amount minus the $67,000 it had received, plus consequential and punitive damages. Although Selmer, presumably in order to be able to claim such damages, describes this as a tort rather than a contract action, it seems really to be a suit on Blakeslee–Midwest's alleged oral promise to reimburse Selmer in full for the extra costs of completing the original contract after Blakeslee–Midwest defaulted. But the characterization is unimportant. Selmer concedes that, whatever its suit is, it is barred by the settlement agreement if, as the district court held, that agreement is valid. The only question is whether there is a triable issue as to whether the settlement agreement is invalid because procured by "economic duress."

If you extract a promise by means of a threat, the promise is unenforceable. This is not, as so often stated, because such a promise is involuntary, unless "involuntary" is a conclusion rather than the description of a mental state. If the threat is ferocious ("your money or your life") and believed, the victim may be desperately eager to fend it off with a promise. Such promises are made unenforceable in order to discourage threats by making them less profitable. The fundamental issue in a duress case is therefore not the victim's state of mind but whether the statement that induced the promise is the kind of offer to deal that we want to discourage, and hence that we call a "threat." Selmer argues that Blakeslee–Midwest said to it in effect, "give up $53,000 of your claim for extras [$120,000 minus $67,000], or you will get nothing." This has the verbal form of a threat but is easily recast as a promise innocuous on its face—"I promise to pay you $67,000 for a release of your claim." There is a practical argument against treating such a statement as a threat: it will make an inference of duress inescapable in any negotiation where one party makes an offer from which it refuses to budge, for the other party will always be able to argue that he settled only because there was a (figurative) gun at his head. It would not matter whether the party refusing to budge was the payor like Blakeslee–Midwest or the promisor like Selmer. If Selmer had refused to complete the job without being paid exorbitantly for the extras and Blakeslee–Midwest had complied with this demand because financial catastrophe would have loomed if Selmer had walked off the job, we would have the same case. A vast number of contract settlements would be subject to being ripped open upon an allegation of duress if Selmer's argument were accepted.

Sensitive—maybe oversensitive—to this danger, the older cases held that a threat not to honor a contract could not be considered duress. But the principle was not absolute, as is shown by *Alaska Packers' Ass'n v. Domenico*, 117 Fed. 99 (9th Cir.1902). Sailors and fishermen (the libelants) "agreed in writing, for a certain stated compensation, to render their services to the appellant in remote waters where the season for conducting fishing operations is extremely short, and in which enterprise the appellant had a large amount of money invested; and, after having entered upon the discharge of their contract, and at a time when it was impossible for the appellant to secure other men in their places, the libelants, without any valid cause, absolutely refused to continue the services they were under contract to perform unless the appellant would consent to pay them more money." The appellant agreed, but later reneged, and the libelants sued. They lost; the court refused to enforce the new agreement. Although the technical ground of decision was the absence of fresh consideration for the modified agreement, it seems apparent both from the quoted language and from a reference on the same page to coercion that the court's underlying concern was that the modified agreement had been procured by duress in the form of the threat to break the original contract.

Alaska Packers' Ass'n shows that because the legal remedies for breach of contract are not always adequate, a refusal to honor a contract may force the other party to the contract to surrender his rights—in *Alaska Packers' Ass'n,* the appellant's right to the libelants' labor at the agreed wage. It undermines the institution of contract to allow a contract party to use the threat of breach to get the contract modified in his favor not because anything has happened to require modification in the mutual interest of the parties but simply because the other party, unless he knuckles under to the threat, will incur costs for which he will have no adequate legal remedy. If contractual protections are illusory, people will be reluctant to make contracts. Allowing contract modifications to be voided in circumstances such as those in *Alaska Packers' Ass'n* assures prospective contract parties that signing a contract is not stepping into a trap, and by thus encouraging people to make contracts promotes the efficient allocation of resources.

Capps v. Georgia Pac. Corp., 253 Or. 248 (1969), illustrates the principle of *Alaska Packers' Ass'n* in the context of settling contract disputes. The defendant promised to give the plaintiff, as a commission for finding a suitable lessee for a piece of real estate, 5 percent of the total rental plus one half of the first month's rent. The plaintiff found a suitable lessee and the lease was signed. Under the terms of the commission arrangement the defendant owed the plaintiff $157,000, but he paid only $5,000, and got a release from the plaintiff of the rest. The plaintiff later sued for the balance of the $157,000, alleging that when requesting payment of the agreed-upon commission he had "informed Defendant that due to Plaintiff's adverse financial condition, he was in danger of immediately losing other personal property through repossession and foreclosure unless funds from Defendant were immediately made available for the purpose of paying these creditors." But "Defendant, through its agent * * *, advised Plaintiff that though he was entitled to the sums demanded in Plaintiff's Complaint, unless he signed the purported release set forth in Defendant's Answer, Plaintiff would receive no part thereof, inasmuch as Defendant had extensive resources and powerful and brilliant attorneys who would and could prevent Plaintiff in any subsequent legal proceeding from obtaining payment of all or any portion of said sums." We can disregard the reference to the defendant's "powerful and brilliant attorneys" yet agree with the Oregon Supreme Court that the confluence of the plaintiff's necessitous financial condition, the defendant's acknowledged indebtedness for the full $157,000, and the settlement of the indebtedness for less than 3 cents on the dollar—with no suggestion that the defendant did not have the money to pay the debt in full—showed duress. The case did not involve the settlement of a genuine dispute, but, as in *Alaska Packers' Ass'n,* an attempt to exploit the contract promisee's lack of an adequate legal remedy.

Although *Capps* is not a Wisconsin case, we have no reason to think that Wisconsin courts would reach a different result. But the only feature that the present case shares with *Capps* is that the plaintiff was in financial difficulties. Since Blakeslee–Midwest did not acknowledge that it owed Selmer $120,000, and since the settlement exceeded 50 percent of Selmer's demand, the terms of the settlement are not unreasonable on their face, as in *Capps*. Thus the question is starkly posed whether financial difficulty can by itself justify setting aside a settlement on grounds of duress. It cannot. "The mere stress of business conditions will not constitute duress where the defendant was not responsible for the conditions." The adverse

Policy

effect on the finality of settlements and hence on the willingness of parties to settle their contract disputes without litigation would be great if the cash needs of one party were alone enough to entitle him to a trial on the validity of the settlement. In particular, people who desperately wanted to settle for cash—who simply could not afford to litigate—would be unable to settle, because they could not enter into a *binding* settlement; being desperate, they could always get it set aside later on grounds of duress. It is a detriment, not a benefit, to one's long-run interests not to be able to make a binding commitment.

policy

Matters stand differently when the complaining party's financial distress is due to the other party's conduct. Although Selmer claims that it was the extra expense caused by Blakeslee-Midwest's breaches of the original contract that put it in a financial vise, it could have walked away from the contract without loss or penalty

argument

when Blakeslee-Midwest broke the contract. Selmer was not forced by its contract to remain on the job, and was not prevented by circumstances from walking away from the contract, as the appellant in *Alaska Packers' Ass'n* had been; it stayed on the job for extra pay. We do not know why Selmer was unable to weather the crisis that arose when Blakeslee-Midwest refused to pay $120,000 for Selmer's extra expenses—whether Selmer was undercapitalized or overborrowed or what—but Blakeslee-Midwest cannot be held responsible for whatever it was that made Selmer so necessitous, when, as we have said, Selmer need not have embarked on the extended contract.

argument

To assimilate this case to one of the conventional categories of duress Selmer argues that Blakeslee-Midwest withheld $21,000 in "retainage" in order to force Selmer to settle the dispute over the extras, and in thus withholding Selmer's property was guilty of "duress of goods," rather than merely of a refusal to settle a contract dispute. Many construction contracts, including this one, allow the payor to retain 10 percent of any advance payments due under the contract as security for the contractor's completing the job. At the completion of the job the amount retained must of course be paid the contractor. To have held the retainage back with no justification at all, merely to force Selmer to yield on its dispute over the extras, might well have been duress, since Blakeslee-Midwest is alleged to have known of Selmer's desperate circumstances.

argument

The precise allegation concerning retainage, however, is that Blakeslee-Midwest's take-it-or-leave-it offer of $67,000 included the retainage of $21,000. Since the retainage was 10 percent of the contract price, Selmer must have received 90 percent of the price, or $189,000, and that plus $67,000 would equal $256,000. But Selmer in fact received a total of $280,000 from Blakeslee-Midwest. As this must have included the retainage, the retainage allegation was discredited and so did not create a triable issue. It might of course have been duress for Blakeslee-Midwest to say to Selmer, "we will give you your retainage of $21,000 plus $67,000 if and only if you abandon your claim for any additional extra payments," but that is not Selmer's contention. It says it was offered $67,000 including the retainage—not that it was offered $88,000—and this is inconsistent with the uncontradicted evidence that the entire contract price of $210,000 was paid plus the $67,000 in extras. Moreover, Selmer waived its subcontractor's lien, indicating it had been paid in full. This waiver, incidentally, was signed after Selmer received the $67,000 it claims to have accepted under duress. This is additional evidence that Selmer was not acting under duress when it made the settlement that years later it tried to repudiate.

Affirmed.

QUESTIONS AND NOTES

1. In this case Judge Posner finds no triable issue of fact on the question of duress. What evidence would Selmer have to submit to create an issue for trial?

2. How would Judge Clapp have decided *Selmer v. Blakeslee-Midwest*? How would Judge Posner have decided *S.P. Dunham v. Kudra*?

3. Would Judge Posner have reached the same result if Selmer had brought suit three days after the deal instead of two years later?

4. Entrepreneur buys a well in the desert, the only water within 200 miles. Cattle-driver arrives with his thirsty herd, and Entrepreneur demands $1.00 per gallon for water. Cattle-driver says "You've got me" and pays, then sues to recover. Is this duress so he gets his money back? Or is this free enterprise, freedom of contract, and the law of supply and demand, in which case he doesn't get his money back?

5. Consider the same Entrepreneur and the same well, but this time Human arrives after her car breaks down and she has walked 15 miles in the desert sun. Human is almost dead of thirst. Entrepreneur says, "$10,000 a glass." Human replies, "I promise." Can Human later resist Entrepreneur's suit to collect on grounds of duress? Does it make any difference if Human is very rich and can afford to spend millions?

6. An interesting situation involving duress of a highly emotional sort is described in the *Los Angeles Times* (Dec. 7, 1971):

> A Los Angeles businessman signed a three page contract to give a $10,000 wedding present to a young man if he married someone other than his daughter within five years and stayed married for at least one year. The young man did so. Now the father does not want to pay and has filed suit to have the contract voided. One of the attorneys involved states that the businessman is Jewish and does not want to have his daughter marry outside the faith, and the young man with whom he contracted is a Baptist and was dating his daughter.

The suit to avoid the contract is based on the claim that the young man involved caused the father great mental anguish in threatening to persuade his daughter to live with him, and that the father was "under duress, measured in terms of his social, economic, religious and political background" when he signed the contract.

In the classic language of an examination question, who wins and why?

Andreini v. Hultgren

Utah Supreme Court, 1993.
860 P.2d 916.

■ ZIMMERMAN, J.

On May 5, 1987, Andreini entered Holy Cross Hospital and underwent surgery on his right knee. Dr. R. David Beck, an orthopedic surgeon, performed the operation. He was assisted by Dr. Bruce Hultgren, an anesthesiologist, and several nurses employed by Holy Cross. On May 6, 1987, while still in the hospital, Andreini noticed a "pins and needles" sensation in both hands. While it is unclear from the record exactly when he noticed additional symptoms, by May 19, 1987, the date of discharge, Andreini exhibited noticeable atrophy of both hands. His discharge summary indicated that he had sustained a bilateral ulnar neuropathy, a deterioration of the nerves extending from his arms into both hands. However, the discharge summary did not suggest a cause. Andreini contends that none of the doctors or nurses made this diagnosis known to him prior to his discharge, and that, when he became aware of the diagnosis during his discharge, no one offered an explanation as to its meaning. Andreini claims that Beck told him his condition was probably the result of lying in bed or that it could be due to "heredity" or his "physical structure."

On July 2, 1987, Andreini visited Dr. Nathaniel M. Nord, who informed him that he had suffered a compression paralysis of both hands. Nord, however, did not express an opinion as to the cause. After Nord reported his findings to Beck, Beck suggested to Andreini that a second surgery be performed to correct the condition. Beck said that he would ask the hospital to waive its charges for the corrective surgery and that he would allow Andreini to make payments to cover his fee. The surgery was scheduled for July 9, 1987.

Approximately one week before the scheduled operation, a nurse apparently not associated with defendants told Andreini that the compression paralysis in his hands might have resulted from the improper strapping of his wrists during surgery. Andreini claims this was the first time he became aware that improper strapping was a possible cause of his injury.

On July 9th, Andreini arrived at Holy Cross Hospital and was prepared for surgery. At some point between one-half to one hour before surgery was to begin, a Holy Cross employee presented Andreini with a release form and asked him to sign it. Andreini refused. The employee then arranged to have Beck talk to Andreini by phone. Beck told Andreini that he would not perform the surgery unless Andreini released both him and Holy Cross from future liability. Although visibly upset, Andreini signed the form and underwent the operation. The procedure was unsuccessful. Andreini has lost most of the dexterity in his hands and cannot perform any activity that requires grasping or holding.

With respect to the claims against Beck and Holy Cross, the court found that Andreini had released both parties from liability and, as a matter of law, had not signed the form under duress. Andreini now appeals.

Finally, we address Andreini's contention that the trial court erred when it dismissed his complaint against Beck and Holy Cross. The trial court reasoned that "the release executed by the plaintiff on July 9, 1987 released any of plaintiff's claims that he may have then had or thereafter had against Dr. Beck, the Holy Cross Hospital and its personnel." Andreini admits to signing the release form but claims that he did so under duress and therefore is not bound by its terms. He argues that he has adduced sufficient facts to entitle him to take this issue to the jury.

With respect to the legal standard for duress, the parties direct us to two Utah cases, *Heglar Ranch, Inc. v. Stillman* and *Fox v. Piercey* (1951), and to sections 175 and 176 of the Restatement (Second) of Contracts. The court order granting summary judgment against Holy Cross and Beck similarly relies on concepts from both of these cases and the Second Restatement. However, the *Heglar-Fox* standard for duress differs significantly from the Second Restatement standard, and the parties' arguments before this court reveal considerable confusion as to the appropriate legal standard for determining duress. Therefore, we take this occasion to review the law in this area and to clarify the legal standard to be applied in Utah.

Our 1951 decision in *Fox* was the first Utah case to discuss extensively the legal concept of duress. In that case, after tracing the evolution of the common law standard for duress, we adopted the then "modern rule," which was essentially the rather general rule articulated in the Restatement (First) of Contracts. Under that view, to invalidate a contract for duress, the alleged victim must show that the perpetrator committed "a wrongful act or threat which actually puts the victim in such fear as to compel him to act against his will." In *Heglar*, decided in 1980, we quoted this formulation of the duress standard from *Fox* and used it to resolve the issue then before us. However, we did not examine the vitality of that articulation of duress or its underlying concepts.

Two years later, in *Horgan v. Industrial Design Corp.*, we said that the *Heglar-Fox* formulation is "not a rigid rule based on precise elements that must be satisfied in every case," but rather is "a general definition to be applied flexibly to the distinct facts of each case." We noted that the law of duress had since broadened, which made it difficult to arrive at a clear-cut definition of duress. Nonetheless, we held that a critical factor in determining whether an alleged victim had suffered duress was whether he or she "had no other viable alternative."

Between our decisions in *Fox* and *Horgan*, the Restatement drafters largely abandoned the First Restatement's formulation of duress that we had adopted in *Fox* and followed in *Heglar* because the formulation was too general to be of much guidance to courts and parties. The drafters articulated a new test that, among other things, divided the "wrongful act" requirement into two distinct parts: duress by physical compulsion and duress by improper threat. The drafters defined the latter by adopting carefully crafted legal elements drawn from the case law of many courts. See Restatement (Second) of Contracts §§ 174–76 (1979). The drafters omitted the requirement that the perpetrator's actions "must arouse such fear as precludes a party from exercising free will and judgment" because "of its vagueness and impracticality." Id. § 175 cmt. b. They reasoned, "It is enough if the threat actually induces assent * * * on the part of one who has no reasonable alternative."

We agree with this reasoning and explicitly adopt the legal standards of duress set forth in sections 175 and 176 of the Restatement (Second) of Contracts. Our decision today is not as much a break with the past as a clarification that the Utah law of duress accords with the now prevalent view. In *Horgan*, we distanced ourselves from *Fox's* formulation and in that case, moved toward the Second Restatement position. We note that the results reached in *Fox* and *Heglar* would have been the same under the Second Restatement formulation.

For the purposes of the instant case, we consider only those sections of the Restatement necessary to determine whether the trial court erred in finding no question of material fact as to whether Andreini signed the release under duress. Section 175(1) states that a contract may be voided "[i]f a party's manifestation of assent is induced by an improper threat by the other party that leaves the victim no reasonable alternative." Section 176 sets forth when a threat is "improper":

> (1) A threat is improper if
>
>> (d) the threat is a breach of the duty of good faith and fair dealing under a contract with the recipient.
>
> (2) A threat is improper if the resulting exchange is not on fair terms, and
>
>> (b) the effectiveness of the threat in inducing the manifestation of assent is significantly increased by prior unfair dealing by the party making the threat....

Andreini argues that he has put into issue sufficient material facts to raise a jury question as to whether Beck's threat not to perform the corrective surgery was a breach of the duty of good faith and fair dealing and therefore constituted an improper threat. He also argues that he has raised a jury question as to whether he had any reasonable alternatives to signing the release. By making these arguments, Andreini hopes to meet the requirements established in sections 175(1) and 176(1)(d) of the Restatement, which would allow him to void the release.

We first consider if Andreini adduced sufficient material facts as to whether defendants made an improper threat by breaching the duty of good faith and fair dealing. Under section 176(1)(d) of the Restatement, the breach of the duty of good faith and fair dealing must be "under a contract with the recipient." Therefore, to find a breach of the duty of good faith and fair dealing, there must be some type of preexisting contractual relationship. This is consistent with our case law. Andreini, however, does not explicitly allege that he and defendants entered into a contract before he was presented with and later signed the release. Consequently, Andreini may not rely on an alleged breach of good faith and fair dealing to claim duress for the first time on appeal.

However, Andreini does make an argument that, fairly construed, appears to constitute an improper threat under section 176(2)(b) of the Restatement. Under this provision, an improper threat may be found when (i) "the resulting exchange is not on fair terms," and (ii) "the effectiveness of the threat in inducing the manifestation of assent is significantly increased by prior unfair dealing by the party making the threat." Restatement (Second) of Contracts § 176(2)(b) (1979). Andreini argues that Beck improperly induced him into signing the release by promising that the corrective surgery would fully restore the use of his hands. He avers that prior to entering the hospital for the corrective surgery, Beck told him that patients with similar injuries had recovered 50% use within two weeks and 100% use within two months as a result of surgery similar to that proposed. Andreini also points to language in the release itself suggesting full recovery: "I, EUGENE R. ANDREINI, will receive surgery to correct ulnar nerve palsy * * *." This evidence is sufficient to establish the legal possibility that the "resulting exchange"—defendants' unfulfilled promise to correct Andreini's injury exchanged for Andreini's release of all claims against defendants—is "not on fair terms" within the meaning of section 176(2) of the Restatement.

However, to avoid summary judgment under section 176(2)(b)'s formulation of an "improper threat," there must also be sufficient evidence to raise a factual issue as to whether defendants had engaged in unfair dealing and whether this significantly increased the impropriety of their threat. Andreini argues that defendants acted in bad faith by promising him that the corrective surgery would result in his full recovery while neglecting to inform him until just prior to surgery that he would have to waive any claims he might have against them.

Viewing the evidence in the light most favorable to Andreini, there is sufficient evidence to take this argument to the jury. We have already recited the evidence suggesting that defendants promised Andreini full recovery, and in Andreini's deposition, he testifies that he was not told until after he had been placed in a gown, shaved, and prepared for surgery that he would have to relinquish his rights. Andreini also testified that defendants were purposely noncommittal about the paralysis in his hands and its possible causes, even after Dr. Nord diagnosed his condition as compression paralysis. Moreover, Andreini averred that when he signed the release, his hands "were getting progressively worse" and "seemed to get worse each day." An expert affidavit submitted by Andreini indicates that time was, in fact, crucial to his recovery and suggests that Beck may have been aware that immediate surgery was necessary. Dr. Masud Seyal stated in the affidavit that "[a]fter the onset of Andreini's bilateral ulnar neuropathy, as diagnosed by R. David Beck, prompt surgical intervention was the recommended procedure" and the two-month delay "in performing the nerve transposition on July 9, 1987, likely denied Mr. Andreini a more substantial recovery."

Based on this evidence, a jury could find that defendants engaged in unfair dealing that significantly increased the effectiveness of their threat to refuse to undertake the corrective surgery. This conclusion is consistent with the Restatement's official commentary. Comment "f" states that section 176(2)(b) "is concerned with cases in which the party making the threat has by unfair dealing achieved an advantage over the recipient that makes his [or her] threat unusually effective. Typical examples involve manipulative conduct during the bargaining stage that leaves one person at the mercy of the other."

Having determined that Andreini has adduced sufficient facts to raise a jury question as to whether defendants made an improper threat, we now consider if Andreini has mustered sufficient facts as to whether he had any reasonable alternatives to signing the release. Again, viewing the evidence in the light most favorable to Andreini, we think that a jury could find that Andreini had no reasonable alternatives under the attendant circumstances. We acknowledge, as the trial court found, that Andreini could have left the hospital and that he was not in a life-threatening situation. However, there is evidence from which a jury could find that his alternatives were not reasonable. As mentioned earlier, Andreini averred that he was aware that his hands were getting progressively worse each day when he was confronted with the release and an expert affidavit suggests that immediate corrective surgery was indeed necessary to prevent further irreversible damage. When Andreini initially refused to sign the release, Beck allegedly told him that if he did not sign, Beck was "going to play hard ball" with him, which Andreini took to mean that defendants would not provide the corrective surgery regardless of who would pay for it.

This evidence is sufficient to convince us that while Andreini may have had alternatives to signing the release form, there is a question of material fact as to whether those alternatives were reasonable.

We note that this analysis is also consistent with the comments to the Second Restatement. First, contrary to the trial court's apparent reasoning, the Restatement recognizes that the victim does not need to be in a life-threatening situation for a jury to find that there were no reasonable alternatives. Comment "a" to section 175 states, "Courts originally restricted duress to threats involving loss of life, mayhem or imprisonment, but these restrictions have been greatly relaxed and, in order to constitute duress, the threat need only be improper * * *." Second, the Restatement notes that duress can often result from situations in which time is of the essence, a factor that the trial court in the instant case seems to have overlooked. Comment "b" to section 175 observes that the reasonable alternative "standard is a practical one under which account must be taken of the exigencies in which the victim finds himself."

Therefore, we hold that Andreini has adduced sufficient evidence to raise an issue of fact as to whether defendants' actions in procuring the release constituted an improper threat and whether Andreini had any reasonable alternatives to signing it. Consequently, Andreini has raised a jury question as to whether he signed the release under duress by improper threat under sections 175(1) and 176(2)(b) of the Restatement.

In sum, the trial court erred in (i) finding no material issues of fact with respect to whether Andreini knew he had suffered a legal injury within the applicable limitation period, (ii) interpreting the Utah Health Care Malpractice Act to bar his claim for failure to timely request prelitigation review, and (iii) finding no material issues of fact with respect to whether Andreini signed the release under duress. We therefore reverse both summary judgments and remand the matter for further proceedings consistent with this opinion.

QUESTION

What do you think the jury will find on remand? Representing Dr. Beck and Holy Cross before a jury, do you really want to rely on a release obtained in this way?

RESTATEMENT, SECOND, CONTRACTS:

§ 175. When Duress By Threat Makes A Contract Voidable.

(1) If a party's manifestation of assent is induced by an improper threat by the other party that leaves the victim no reasonable alternative, the contract is voidable by the victim.

(2) If a party's manifestation of assent is induced by one who is not a party to the transaction, the contract is voidable by the victim unless the other party to the transaction in good faith and without reason to know of the duress either gives value or relies materially on the transaction.

§ 176. When A Threat Is Improper.

(1) A threat is improper if

    (a) what is threatened is a crime or a tort, or the threat itself would be a crime or a tort if it resulted in obtaining property,

    (b) what is threatened is a criminal prosecution,

    (c) what is threatened is the use of civil process and the threat is made in bad faith, or

    (d) the threat is a breach of the duty of good faith and fair dealing under a contract with the recipient.

(2) A threat is improper if the resulting exchange is not on fair terms, and

    (a) the threatened act would harm the recipient and would not significantly benefit the party making the threat,

    (b) the effectiveness of the threat in inducing the manifestation of assent is significantly increased by prior unfair dealing by the party making the threat, or

    (c) what is threatened is otherwise a use of power for illegitimate ends.

III. CONTRACTS OF ADHESION AND UNJUST TERMS

Lack of assent has been one significant element in the law of unconscionable contracts. Today's consumer has little realistic opportunity to negotiate or even fully understand and assent to the standard terms of many contracts. These are mass transactions in which the individual deals with a large and sophisticated seller of goods or services.

———————

W. DAVID SLAWSON, STANDARD FORM CONTRACTS AND DEMOCRATIC CONTROL OF LAW MAKING POWER, 84 HARV. L. REV. 529, 529–32 (1971):[*]

Standard form contracts probably account for more than ninety-nine percent of all contracts now made. Most persons have difficulty remembering the last time they contracted other than by standard form; except for casual oral agreements, they probably never have. But if they are active, they contract by standard form several times a day. Parking lot and theater tickets, package receipts, department store charge slips and gas station credit card purchase slips are all standard form contracts.

Moreover, standard forms have come to dominate more than just routine transactions. For individuals, if not quite yet for corporations, form contracts are in common use for even such important matters as insurance, leases, deeds, mortgages, automobile purchases, and all of the various forms of consumer credit....

The predominance of standard forms is the best evidence of their necessity. They are characteristic of a mass production society and an integral part of it. They provide information and enforce order. A typical automobile insurance policy, for example, informs the policyholder how to conduct himself should he become involved in an accident or other kind of occurrence from which liability of the kind covered may arise. It enforces all or a part of such conduct by the sanction of denying insurance protection unless it is performed. These services are essential, and if they are to be provided at reasonable cost, they must be standardized and mass-produced like other goods and services in an industrial economy. The need for order could, in theory, be fully satisfied by officially drafted rules—by laws in the traditional sense. One of the beliefs by which our society is organized, however, is that at least some lawmaking is better accomplished in a decentralized manner. We therefore prefer that the economy be controlled privately to a large extent, and private control today means control largely by standard form.

... The extreme specialization of function of modern life requires that we contract with each other too frequently to take the time to reach even a mildly complicated agreement every time we do, and the complexity of modern life and modern law combine to demand that even minor agreements usually be complicated....

———————

* Copyright 1971, Harvard Law Review.

KARL N. LLEWELLYN, *THE COMMON LAW TRADITION* 362 (1960):

The impetus to the form-pad is clear, for any business unit: by standardizing terms, and by standardizing even the spot on the form where any individually dickered term appears, one saves all the time and skill otherwise needed to dig out and record the meaning of variant language; one makes check-up, totaling, follow-through, etc., into routine operations; one has duplicates (in many colors) available for the administration of a multidepartment business; and so on more. The content of the standardized terms accumulates experience, it avoids or reduces legal risks and also confers all kinds of operating leeways and advantages, all without need of either consulting counsel from instance to instance or of bargaining with the other parties. Not to be overlooked, either, is the tailoring of the crude misfitting hand-me-down pattern of the "general law" "in the absence of agreement" to the particular detailed working needs of your own line of business—whether apartment rentals, stock brokerage, international grain trade, installment selling of appliances, flour milling, sugar beet raising, or insurance....

Note the extent in the following material that the elements of substantive unfairness of terms and inadequate manifestations of assent contribute to the conclusion that the agreement is unconscionable and unenforceable.

ADDISON MUELLER, *CONTRACTS OF FRUSTRATION*, 78 YALE L.J. 576, 578–581 (1969):

Two factors combine to bring about the modern consumer's lack of effective legal power when he buys a product which is faulty but does not cause physical injury. Both of them stem from the fact that he is a little man in the scheme of things. First, there is an all-pervasive difficulty: our machinery of justice is simply not designed for easy use by the average citizen with a minor claim of any kind. If anything, it is designed to discourage him. He is not apt to know a lawyer and he does not particularly want to know one.[13] And if he does muster up his courage and finds a lawyer, he will almost surely discover that his small claim is of no interest to that lawyer unless he is prepared to guarantee what to him will seem a preposterous sum. Even in those localities where small claims courts are supposed to be readily available, the use of the law remains a mysterious and a frightening prospect for the

---

13. [I]t seems to me that at bottom of the popular hatred of lawyers is the black cloud in which the lawyers operate. It is a darkness compounded of an unknown language, intricate procedures, esoteric learning, and the trouble that occasions their presence. The layman approaches the lawyer reluctantly; it is strange; it may bite; it usually does. Mellinkoff, Review, 15 U.C.L.A. L. Rev. 1075, 1076 (1968).

average citizen. It is especially frightening for the below-average citizen, for "the poor man looks upon the law as an enemy, not as a friend. For him the law is always taking something away."

The unavailability of simple process handicaps the little man regardless of the nature of his small claim, and it is handicap enough. But when he claims as a consumer against a seller, he encounters a second difficulty. Unless his claim is based on accidental injury to person or property caused by a defective product and is thus eligible for relief in tort, he claims in contract and must use a deck of doctrine that is stacked against him.

Most of his losing cards are colored "freedom of contract." Contract (says the jurisprudence) is a voluntary association, and the parties are therefore free within broad limits to adopt such terms as they see fit. The reasonably equal bargaining power that is manifestly required to support this basic principle is presumed,[17] as is the fact that parties to a written agreement know, or ought to know, the terms of their agreement. The ultimate consumer faced with a defective appliance or product, is almost sure to find that his seller has taken full advantage of these presumptions. He will discover that the printed contract that he "made" with his dealer contained one or more variously labeled terms and conditions designed by lawyers to give the dealer and everyone above him in the distribution pipeline maximum protection against consumer claims. He has, in short, entered into what we have come to call a contract of adhesion. Professor Patterson, who coined the phrase in 1919 in an article discussing life insurance policies, described such a contract as one "drawn up by the insurer, and the insured, who merely 'adheres' to it, has little choice as to its terms." In less elegant but no less accurate language, a contract of adhesion is a contract that sticks the helpless consumer with standard form clauses that he might not have agreed to if he had actually had free choice.

Some of this printed boilerplate is apt to come in an envelope containing assorted other literature that is sealed in the carton or is taped to the chassis of the purchased equipment. In consequence it is seldom seen by the buyer until after delivery. Clearly, then, the buyer might persuasively claim that he cannot be bound by it because he never accepted it as part of his bargain. But it would make little practical difference if he not only saw it but read it and even understood it before his purchase. The result of an attempt on his part to reject it would be no purchase; it would be a rare and imaginative dealer indeed (to say nothing of a rare and imaginative customer) who would act in so non-institutional a fashion as to agree to a special warranty arrangement. Even if a dealer were willing to do so, his action would almost

---

17. Perhaps the neatest, though oblique, expression of this presumption is the "rule" that the law will not question the adequacy of consideration. The presumption is, of course, rebuttable. See 1 A. Corbin, Contracts § 127, at 541 (1964).

surely be held not to have involved the deeper pockets of the supplier or the manu-facturer of the product.[21] And though theoretically the buyer could go elsewhere and buy from a merchant who did not so limit his obligations, he would almost certainly find that all competing goods were similarly limited.[22] So to turn the matter on the buyer's lack of knowledge would simply put dealers to the useless task of saying, "Look at this," before they say, "Sign here." A requirement that full disclosure be made concerning terms that can in fact be accepted or rejected is a meaningful and important element of contract law. But standard disclaimers and limitation of rem-edy clauses[23] such as make up the bulk of the printed boilerplate in contracts for the sale of consumer goods are not such choice-offering terms. The problem with such clauses is not lack of notice but lack of consumer power to bargain about them. The problem is that they are parts of contracts of adhesion.

Williams v. Walker–Thomas Furniture Co.

United States Court of Appeals, District of Columbia Circuit, 1965.
121 U.S.App.D.C. 315, 350 F.2d 445.

■ J. SKELLY WRIGHT, C.J. Appellee, Walker–Thomas Furniture Company, operates a retail furniture store in the District of Columbia. During the period from 1957 to 1962 each appellant in these cases purchased a number of household items from Walker–Thomas, for which payment was to be made in installments. The terms of each purchase were contained in a printed form contract which set forth the value of the purchased item and purported to lease the item to appellant for a stipulated

---

21. Manufacturers' warranties usually state explicitly that a dealer is not authorized to alter or make additional warranties on behalf of the manufacturer. Such limitations should at least be given effect against a claim over by a dealer who is held to such altered or additional obligation by his customer. Whether a consumer should be entitled to claim directly against the manufac-turer in such a case depends on whether an agency relationship (express or apparent) can reasonably be spelled out. The problem ties into that arising when a dealer warrants that a prod-uct is fit for a use not reasonably encompassed by the nature of the product. In such a case, a remote seller's defense of no privity to a consumer claim based on product failure under the stress of such special use makes some sense.

22. The clause limiting remedy to repair or replacement is now as much a fixture in business literature as those old friends the force majeure clause, the offer subject to prior sale and ac-ceptance clause, and standard invocations of the parol evidence rule. The feeling about them is that they—like so much contractual language—can do no harm and might do some good.

23. Broad disclaimers of warranty are frowned upon by the UCC; limitations of remedy, on the other hand, are encouraged, Compare UCC § 2–316 (exclusion or modification of warranties) with §§ 2–718 (liquidation or limitation of damages) and 2–719 (contractual modification or lim-itation of remedy).

monthly rent payment. The contract then provided, in substance, that title would remain in Walker–Thomas until the total of all the monthly payments made equaled the stated value of the item, at which time appellants could take title. In the event of a default in the payment of any monthly installment, Walker–Thomas could repossess the item.

The contract further provided that "the amount of each periodical installment payment to be made by [purchaser] to the Company under this present lease shall be inclusive of and not in addition to the amount of each installment payment to be made by [purchaser] under such prior leases, bills or accounts; *and all payments now and hereafter made by [purchaser] shall be credited pro rata on all outstanding leases, bills and accounts* due the Company by [purchaser] at the time each such payment is made." Emphasis added. The effect of this rather obscure provision was to keep a balance due on every item purchased until the balance due on all items, whenever purchased, was liquidated. As a result, the debt incurred at the time of purchase of each item was secured by the right to repossess all the items previously purchased by the same purchaser, and each new item purchased automatically became subject to a security interest arising out of the previous dealings.

On May 12, 1962, appellant Thorne purchased an item described as a Daveno, three tables, and two lamps, having total stated value of $391.10. Shortly thereafter, he defaulted on his monthly payments and appellee sought to replevy all the items purchased since the first transaction in 1958. Similarly, on April 17, 1962, appellant Williams bought a stereo set of stated value of $514.95.[1] She too defaulted shortly thereafter, and appellee sought to replevy all the items purchased since December, 1957. The Court of General Sessions granted judgment for appellee. The District of Columbia Court of Appeals affirmed, and we granted appellants' motion for leave to appeal to this court.

Appellants' principal contention, rejected by both the trial and the appellate courts below, is that these contracts, or at least some of them, are unconscionable and, hence, not enforceable. In its opinion in *Williams v. Walker–Thomas Furniture Company*, 198 A.2d 914, 916 (1964), the District of Columbia Court of Appeals explained its rejection of this contention as follows:

> Appellant's second argument presents a more serious question. The record reveals that prior to the last purchase appellant had reduced the balance in her account to $164. The last purchase, a stereo set, raised the balance due to $678. Significantly, at the time of this and the preceding purchases, appellee was aware of appellant's financial position. The reverse side of the stereo contract listed

---

1. At the time of this purchase her account showed a balance of $164 still owing from her prior purchases. The total of all the purchases made over the years in question came to $1,800. The total payments amounted to $1,400.

the name of appellant's social worker and her $218 monthly stipend from the government. Nevertheless, with full knowledge that appellant had to feed, clothe and support both herself and seven children on this amount, appellee sold her a $514 stereo set.

We cannot condemn too strongly appellee's conduct. It raises serious questions of sharp practice and irresponsible business dealings. A review of the legislation in the District of Columbia affecting retail sales and the pertinent decisions of the highest court in this jurisdiction disclose, however, no ground upon which this court can declare the contracts in question contrary to public policy. We note that were the Maryland Retail Installment Sales Act, Art. 83, §§ 128–153, or its equivalent, in force in the District of Columbia, we could grant appellant appropriate relief. We think Congress should consider corrective legislation to protect the public from such exploitive contracts as were utilized in the case at bar.

We do not agree that the court lacked the power to refuse enforcement to contracts found to be unconscionable. In other jurisdictions, it has been held as a matter of common law that unconscionable contracts are not enforceable. While no decision of this court so holding has been found, the notion that an unconscionable bargain should not be given full enforcement is by no means novel. In *Scott v. United States*, 79 U.S. (12 Wall.) 443, 445 (1870), the Supreme Court stated:

> * * * If a contract be unreasonable and unconscionable, but not void for fraud, a court of law will give to the party who sues for its breach damages, not according to its letter, but only such as he is equitably entitled to. * * * "

Since we have never adopted or rejected such a rule, the question here presented is actually one of first impression.

Congress has recently enacted the Uniform Commercial Code, which specifically provides that the court may refuse to enforce a contract which it finds to be unconscionable at the time it was made. 28 D.C.Code § 2–302 (Supp. IV 1965). The enactment of this section, which occurred subsequent to the contracts here in suit, does not mean that the common law of the District of Columbia was otherwise at the time of enactment nor does it preclude the court from adopting a similar rule in the exercise of its powers to develop the common law for the District of Columbia. In fact, in view of the absence of prior authority on the point, we consider the congressional adoption of § 2–302 persuasive authority for following the rationale of the cases from which the section is explicitly derived. Accordingly, we hold that where the element of unconscionability is present at the time a contract is made, the contract should not be enforced.

Unconscionability has generally been recognized to include an absence of meaningful choice on the part of one of the parties together with contract terms which are unreasonably favorable to the other party. Whether a meaningful choice is present in a particular case can only be determined by consideration of all the circumstances surrounding the transaction. In many cases the meaningfulness of the choice is negated by a gross inequality of bargaining power. The manner in which the contract *rule* was entered is also relevant to this consideration. Did each party to the contract, considering his obvious education or lack of it, have a reasonable opportunity to understand the terms of the contract, or were the important terms hidden in a maze of fine print and minimized by deceptive sales practices? Ordinarily, one who signs an agreement without full knowledge of its terms might be held to assume the risk that he has entered a one-sided bargain. But when a party of little bargaining power, and hence little real choice, signs a commercially unreasonable contract with little or no knowledge of its terms, it is hardly likely that his consent, or even an objective manifestation of his consent, was ever given to all the terms. In such a case the usual rule *holding* that the terms of the agreement are not to be questioned should be abandoned and the court should consider whether the terms of the contract are so unfair that enforcement should be withheld.

In determining reasonableness or fairness, the primary concern must be with the terms of the contract considered in light of the circumstances existing when the contract was made. The test is not simple, nor can it be mechanically applied. The terms *rule* are to be considered "in the light of the general commercial background and the commercial needs of the particular trade or case." Corbin suggests the test as being whether the terms are "so extreme as to appear unconscionable according to the *test* mores and business practices of the time and place." We think this formulation correctly states the test to be applied in those cases where no meaningful choice was exercised upon entering the contract.

Because the trial court and the appellate court did not feel that enforcement could be refused, no findings were made on the possible unconscionability of the contracts in these cases. Since the record is not sufficient for our deciding the issue as a matter of law, the cases must be remanded to the trial court for further proceedings.

So ordered.

■ DANAHER, CIRCUIT JUDGE (dissenting). The District of Columbia Court of Appeals obviously was as unhappy about the situation here presented as any of us can possibly be. Its opinion in the *Williams* case, quoted in the majority text, concludes: "We think Congress should consider corrective legislation to protect the public from such exploitive contracts as were utilized in the case at bar."

My view is thus summed up by an able court which made no finding that there had actually been sharp practice. Rather the appellant seems to have known precisely where she stood.

There are many aspects of public policy here involved. What is a luxury to some may seem an outright necessity to others. Is public oversight to be required of the expenditures of relief funds? A washing machine, *e.g.*, in the hands of a relief client might become a fruitful source of income. Many relief clients may well need credit, and certain business establishments will take long chances on the sale of items, expecting their pricing policies will afford a degree of protection commensurate with the risk. Perhaps a remedy when necessary will be found within the provisions of the "Loan Shark" law, D.C.Code §§ 26–601 *et seq.* (1961).

I mention such matters only to emphasize the desirability of a cautious approach to any such problem, particularly since the law for so long has allowed parties such great latitude in making their own contracts. I dare say there must annually be thousands upon thousands of installment credit transactions in this jurisdiction, and one can only speculate as to the effect the decision in these cases will have.

I join the District of Columbia Court of Appeals in its disposition of the issues.

QUESTIONS AND NOTES

1. The security agreement Ora Lee Williams agreed to in this case contained what is referred to in the trade as a cross-collateral clause. Today such clauses are regulated under a wide variety of consumer protection legislation and, to some extent, the federal Bankruptcy Code. *See* Uniform Consumer Credit Code §§ 3.302–3.303. What is there about this contract that is unconscionable? Is it unconscionable because Ms. Williams didn't understand what it said? Is it unconscionable because it was on a printed form with fine print? Is it unconscionable because Ms. Williams was poor? Was on public relief? Had no real opportunity to negotiate? Is it unconscionable because cross-collateral clauses are generally unjustified by business risks or inherently unfair? Is it unconscionable because it is wrong to sell a woman with seven minor children to support that is relying on public assistance a $514 stereo set?

2. Didn't Ms. Williams have meaningful choices such as (a) not buying the stereo set until she had cash, (b) borrowing money elsewhere, (c) doing without a stereo? Should Ms. Williams be held less responsible for her contractual obligations than other adults not on public relief?

3. In drafting a form agreement, isn't a lawyer justified in loading it with clauses favorable to her client? If the lawyer thinks a particular clause probably is unenforceable because a court is likely to hold it unconscionable, she has an obligation to advise her client of this probability. If the client nonetheless wants the clause included, does the lawyer violate her professional obligations in acceding? What can the lawyer do in this situation?

4. Is this decision or UCC § 2–302 generally likely to increase or decrease the availability of consumer goods to the poor?

5. While recognizing that the legal power of government may be needed to protect consumers from unfair terms in contracts for sale of goods, UCC § 2–302 suffers from two related weaknesses: (a) The amorphous doctrine does not give clear guidance what kinds of contract terms are impermissible; and (b) the concept relies on court interpretation through a long series of lawsuits. Professor Arthur Leff aptly described these problems in his article *Unconscionability and the Crowd—Consumers and the Common Law Tradition*, 31 U. PITT. L. REV. 349 (1970), which is a response to an early defense of § 2–302 by Professor John Murray:

> In order to establish the unenforceability of any particular provision, in any particular jurisdiction, there will have to be at least one lawsuit, with the relatively high transaction costs (especially relative to the amount at issue) of that law-reform technique. Now, what happens after that first lawsuit? Take a case like *Williams*. In that case the court remanded for a finding whether a cross-collateral clause, allowing the seller to repossess all items ever bought from it by the buyer, upon default in payment for the most recently purchased item, was "unconscionable." Let us assume that on remand that it is decided that, at least where the buyer is a lady on relief with seven children, such a clause is unenforceable. What's the seller's next move? Why to "distinguish the case," of course. Perhaps the next thing to do is make the clause clearer, maybe to make it read: "Caution: if you don't pay for what you just bought we may be able to take back whatever we ever sold you." Well, now we've got a new case for case-by-case development. O.K., let's assume that the seller loses that one too, perhaps because the apparent assent was not "verified" (in Professor Murray's terms) because the buyer did not have, in the "relevant geographic market," any alternative to such a clause when buying what he bought, or any functional equivalent of it (to make which finding the court must also decide, under Professor Murray's approach, what the "relevant product market" is). Fine. We've just had two little internal antitrust suits, (under § 2–302(2), I assume), one on relevant geographical markets and one on functional equivalence, and the seller has lost again. But, of course, the next seller who wants to use a clause like the first seller ought not be daunted. After all, if his neighborhood or product is different, it's a whole new ball game.

> . . .

> To cut this short, the problem is not with Professor Murray's criteria, but with the common-law tradition itself when sought to be used to regulate the quality of transactions on a case-by-case basis, each one of which is economically trivial (so that you need free legal help for the consumer, and the seller can almost always avoid nasty precedent by an early surrender or settlement), and

each one of which depends upon several doses of "the total context of the fact situation" and "copious examination of the manifestations of the parties and the surrounding circumstances followed by a balancing effort." Wouldn't it be easier and far more effective, if one finds these cross-collateral clauses, or some others, offensive in consumer transactions, just to face one's conclusion and regulate them out of existence, in a manner no lawyer could conscientiously avoid? Wouldn't it be better, finally, to face the political problems and pass a statute that deals with cross-collateral clauses, negotiable-note and waiver-of-defense financing, abusive collection devices, a wide panoply of quasi-crooked marketing devices, and so on, and maybe even gross overpricing (on analogy to the civil-law *laesio enormis* progeny) and tuck in, along with private causes of action for the victims, an administrative enforcement arm to police these repetitive nasty practices (and perhaps get compensation for the whole class of bilked consumers theretofore identifiably bilked)? Isn't there some economy of scale in that approach? Remember, the idea is to change as many nasty forms and practices as possible, not merely to add to the glorious common law tradition of eventually coping. Wouldn't more be changed by explicit positive law, administratively interpreted and enforced, than by the feed-back from easily distinguishable, easily stallable, exceedingly expensive cases?

6. Form contracts resemble legislation in that they are standardized rules imposed on a particular transaction and not bargained for in each case. But legislation carries the legitimacy and imprimatur of the government. Why should the interests of the parties be determined by words on a privately drafted form no one reads? An alternative would be to enact a consumer sales code that would displace the fine print with statutory provisions that have been thought through with seller and consumer interests in mind. Beginning a generation ago, both Congress and State legislatures adopted a number of consumer protection statutes with particular emphasis on warranty and credit terms. Most of these laws concentrate on requiring disclosure of the terms of the transaction to the consumer or on providing remedies to consumers who have been victimized by unfair or deceptive sales and credit practices. Some of these laws have gone beyond notification and remedies and have directly outlawed certain abusive contract provisions. The Uniform Consumer Credit Code, which has been adopted by nine states, deals with the substance of a number of lender practices that are subject to abuse, such as wage assignments, confession of judgment clauses, and, as was noted in question 1, cross-collateral clauses. Acting under the Magnuson–Moss Federal Trade Commission Improvements Act, 15 U.S.C. § 2301 et seq., the Federal Trade Commission has adopted regulations that substantially limit holder-in-due-course defenses, wage assignments, confessions of judgment, security interests in household goods, and waivers of property exemptions.

7. Notwithstanding UCC § 2-302 and other more specific sorts of consumer protection legislation, exploitive transactions not unlike that discussed in *Williams v. Walker-Thomas Furniture Co.* remain common in America's cities. The very profitable "rent-to-own" business has managed to escape consumer credit regulation targeted at some perceived abuses on the ground that it leases consumer products rather than sells them on credit. The practices of a leading firm in that industry, Rent-A-Center, first came to national attention in a newspaper exposé, Alix M. Friedman, *Peddling Dreams: A Marketing Giant Uses Its Sales Prowess to Profit on Poverty*, WALL ST. J. SEPT. 22, 1993, at A1. The *Wall Street Journal* reported that Rent-A-Center, which leases consumer electronics, furniture, and other household goods to both urban and rural poor, was the conglomerate Thorn EMI's most profitable business, earning margins more than double those of conventional retailers. Rent-A-Center's success was based on onerous lease terms that amounted to "heads I win, tails you lose." If the consumer made all the weekly payments required under the lease, she effectively purchased the goods on credit with an implicit interest rate of over 200%. If, as was far more likely, she returned the goods or defaulted, Rent-A-Center would repossess the goods and relet them on similar terms again and again, reaping even greater profits. One Rent-A-Center customer explained to the *Wall Street Journal* that she leased a new microwave oven from Rent-A-Center *after* suffering a particularly humiliating repossession of her refrigerator, couch, and other household goods because she needed the oven and "I felt like there was nowhere else to go."

What does outlawing a particular term of a consumer contract like cross-collateralization accomplish when the Ms. Williamses of the world need microwave ovens they can't afford, have nowhere else to go, and Rent-A-Center can set prices and lease rates at levels so exorbitant that it is even more profitable for it to collect a few payments and repossess and relet the oven than it is to collect contractual payments equivalent to earning 200% interest annually?

K.D. v. Educational Testing Service

New York County Supreme Court, 1976.
87 Misc.2d 657, 386 N.Y.S.2d 747.

■ FRAIMAN, J. This is a motion to dismiss the complaint, pursuant to CPLR Rule 3211(a) paras. 1, 7 and subd. (c) on the grounds that there is a defense founded upon documentary evidence and that the complaint fails to state a cause of action.

Plaintiff is a 37 year old college graduate, having entered college at the age of 32. Seeking to attend law school, he took the Law School Admission Test (LSAT) twice within a four month period in 1973–74. Defendant is a non-profit corporation engaged in the business of preparing and administering various well-known educational tests, including the LSAT, for use by colleges and graduate schools throughout the nation. It has administered the LSAT since 1954. The LSAT is an objective test designed to measure general aptitude for the study of law of candidates seeking admission to law school. It consists of approximately 130 so-called multiple choice questions and it also has a section of about 70 questions of a similar nature designed to test writing ability. Defendant administers the LSAT for the Law School Admissions Council (LSAC), a non-profit membership association of graduate schools of law. The LSAC sets policy for administration of the examinations and the reporting of scores.

Test scores play an important role in determining whether a candidate will be admitted to law school. To insure that they accurately reflect the candidate's own effort, the administration of the tests are carefully monitored, and after they are scored, individual scores are checked by computer against any previous scores by the same candidate. Where an increase of more than 150 points (out of a total of 800) is found, defendant conducts an investigation before the candidate's score is reported to the law schools.

Each candidate who applies to take the LSAT is sent a booklet entitled "Law School Admissions Bulletin" and a registration form. Upon receipt of the completed form, defendant sends the candidate an admission card to take the examination on a specified date at a designated testing center. The registration form requires the applicant to write out in longhand the following statement and to sign it:

> * * * I accept the conditions set forth in the Bulletin concerning the administration of the test and the reporting of information to law schools.

Plaintiff took the examination in December 1973 and again in April 1974. Before each examination, he was sent a copy of the Bulletin and completed in his own handwriting the statement above on his registration forms. The Bulletins received by plaintiff each contained the following language under the heading "Scores Cancelled by ETS":

> We are concerned with reporting only valid scores. On rare occasions, misconduct * * * or circumstances beyond the candidate's control * * * may render scores invalid. If doubts are raised about your score because of these or other circumstances, we will expect you to cooperate in our investigation. We reserve the right to cancel any test score if, in our sole opinion, there is adequate reason to question its validity. Before exercising this right, we will offer you an opportunity to take the test again at no additional fee.

> If we cancel a score, we will notify the law schools that received, or were to receive, the scores as well as the schools receiving subsequent reports.

On his December, 1973 examination plaintiff received a score of 399 on the LSAT portion and 26 on the writing ability portion. His April, 1974 LSAT score was 637, or 238 points higher, and his writing ability score was 62. The 238 point discrepancy between the two LSAT scores prompted an investigation by defendant which disclosed striking similarities between plaintiff's answers and the answers of one "KL," the candidate seated adjacent to plaintiff. Plaintiff answered 39 of the 130 multiple choice questions on the LSAT portion of the test incorrectly. Of these, 27 were the same incorrect answers as those selected by KL. The significance of this correlation is made evident from an analysis by defendant of the answer sheets of ten other candidates taking the same LSAT who obtained scores in the same range as plaintiff and KL. Comparing their incorrect answers with plaintiff's, discloses that, on average, there were only 7 incorrect responses identical to plaintiff's. Of the ten other answer sheets analyzed, the most incorrect responses on any one answer sheet which were identical to those of plaintiff was 11. A comparison and analysis of plaintiff's writing ability answer sheet with KL's and the ten other candidates disclosed a similar result.[*]

On the basis of the foregoing, defendant wrote to plaintiff requesting that he furnish any information which he believed was relevant to his questioned scores. In addition, he was offered an opportunity to take the examination again at a regularly scheduled time at no cost. If he elected to do so, and his retest score came within 50 points of the questioned score, defendant stated that the questioned score would be forwarded to the law schools. On the other hand, if the retest score failed to confirm the questioned score, or if plaintiff refused to take the retest, defendant indicated that it would cancel the questioned score and notify the law schools that plaintiff's score was cancelled "due to serious doubt as to [its] authenticity."

---

[*] The scores of KL, who was unknown to plaintiff, were not questioned because he had achieved scores in the same range as those on the April, 1974 examination on two prior occasions on which he took the LSAT.

In response to this letter, plaintiff submitted a sworn statement that he did not cheat on the examination. However, he refused to take a retest. He then commenced the instant action for a declaratory judgment and an injunction restraining defendant from cancelling his April, 1974 test score; from notifying the law schools that this action was taken because of the score's doubtful authenticity; and compelling defendant to report the April, 1974 score to the law schools as a valid score.

In support of its motion to dismiss the complaint, defendant alleges that plaintiff is barred by the contract he entered into when he agreed on his registration forms to accept the conditions set forth in the Bulletin concerning the administration of the test and the reporting of results to the law schools. Defendant contends that its actions are in full accord with the following provisions in the Bulletin:

> We reserve the right to cancel any test score if, in our sole opinion, there is adequate reason to question its validity * * *. If we cancel a score, we will notify the law schools that * * * were to receive the score * * *.

We turn now to a consideration of that portion of the injunctive relief sought by plaintiff wherein he seeks to restrain defendant from cancelling his April, 1974 test scores and to compel it to forward the scores to the law schools. As noted above, the right to cancel any test score if in its opinion there was adequate reason to question its validity was expressly reserved to itself by defendant in the Bulletin, and plaintiff accepted that as well as all other conditions set forth in the Bulletin when he completed his registration form. Nevertheless, plaintiff contends that he is not bound by his agreement, because, he argues, his contract with defendant is a contract of adhesion, and therefore void. A contract of adhesion is one entered into between parties with unequal bargaining power. They are typically standard contracts which are offered by the party with strong bargaining power to the weaker party on a take it or leave it basis. The instant agreement would appear to fit this description. Almost every accredited law school in the United States requires a candidate for admission to take the LSAT. Thus, when plaintiff decided to attend law school he had no alternative but to accept the standard conditions fixed by defendant for all test takers. Plaintiff could neither contract with a party other than defendant to take a law school aptitude test, since no such entity exists, or indicate to defendant that the terms contained in the Bulletin were not acceptable to him. In the latter case it is clear that if he had done so he would not have been permitted to take the examination.

However, while plaintiff's description of the agreement herein as a contract of adhesion may be justified, his conclusion that it is therefore void, is not. Where the court finds that an agreement is a contract of adhesion, effort will frequently be made to protect the weaker party from the agreement's harsher terms by a variety of pretexts, while still keeping the elementary rules of the law of contracts intact. Kessler, "Contracts of Adhesion—Some Thoughts about Freedom of Contract," 43

Colum.L.Rev. 629 (1943). The Court may, for example, find the obnoxious clause "ambiguous," even where no ambiguity exists, and then construe it against its author; or it may find the clause to be against public policy and declare it unenforceable; or finally, the court may hold that although the offending clause prohibits a recovery by plaintiff *ex contractu,* it does not prohibit a recovery in tort.

Thus, the issue in the instant case is whether the clause reserving to defendant itself the right to cancel plaintiff's test score if there is a question about its validity, and requiring him to take a retest in such event, is so unfair and unreasonable that the court, having found it a part of a contract of adhesion, will disregard it by means of one or more of the pretexts above. The issue as thus stated must be answered in the negative. To the extent that defendant can accurately predict the aptitude of a candidate for law school by means of its test results, it performs a highly valuable service not only to the law schools but to the public as well. Moreover, the accuracy of its predictions is defendant's sole stock in trade. The less accurate as a forecaster its tests are, the less value they have to the law schools. Thus, if defendant reasonably believed that the test scores of plaintiff as scored on the April, 1974 test, did not accurately reflect his aptitude for law school, it acted within its right to protect its own image as well as its obligation to the schools who are its clients in cancelling plaintiff's scores and requiring him to take a retest....

In the instant case, the evidence that plaintiff did not achieve his scores on the April, 1974 LSAT unaided was sufficient to justify the action contemplated by defendant. Moreover, its offer of a free retest under normal testing conditions with the understanding that it would forward plaintiff's April, 1974 scores if the retest score came within 50 points of the earlier scores was eminently fair and reasonable under the circumstances. Finally, with respect to plaintiff's claim that defendant's actions violated the Due Process clause of the Constitution, it is sufficient to note that the 14th Amendment is applicable only to state action and not private action and hence is not relevant here. Even if it were, the court finds no basis to conclude that plaintiff was not afforded due process.

For all the foregoing reasons, the motion to dismiss so much of the complaint as seeks to enjoin defendant from cancelling plaintiff's April, 1974 test scores, and to compel it to forward those scores to the law schools is granted.

NOTE

Scoring changes in the LSAT have obscured the dramatic improvement in KD's performance on the test. In his first attempt, KD scored in the 13th percentile. Miraculously, on the second attempt, KD was in the 92nd percentile.

Armendariz v. Foundation Health Psychcare Services

Supreme Court of California, 2000.
24 Cal. 4th 83.

■ MOSK, J.

In this case, we consider a number of issues related to the validity of a mandatory employment arbitration agreement, i.e., an agreement by an employee to arbitrate wrongful termination or employment discrimination claims rather than filing suit in court, which an employer imposes on a prospective or current employee as a condition of employment. The employees in this case claim that employees may not be compelled to arbitrate antidiscrimination claims brought under the California Fair Employment and Housing Act (FEHA). We conclude that such claims are in fact arbitrable *if* the arbitration permits an employee to vindicate his or her statutory rights. As explained, in order for such vindication to occur, the arbitration must meet certain minimum requirements, including neutrality of the arbitrator, the provision of adequate discovery, a written decision that will permit a limited form of judicial review, and limitations on the costs of arbitration.

The employees further claim that several provisions of the arbitration agreement are unconscionable, both because they fail to meet these minimum requirements and because the arbitration agreement is not bilateral. We conclude that the agreement possesses a damages limitation that is contrary to public policy, and that it is unconscionably unilateral.

Finally, the employees contend that the presence of these unconscionable provisions renders the entire arbitration agreement unenforceable. The employer argues that even if some of the provisions are unconscionable or contrary to public policy, the proper remedy is to strike or restrict those clauses pursuant to Civil Code section 1670.5, and to enforce the rest of the arbitration agreement. The trial court chose the employees' preferred solution of refusing to enforce the arbitration agreement, but the Court of Appeal sided with the employer and enforced the agreement minus the one provision it found unconscionable. We conclude, for reasons explained below, that the arbitration agreement is unenforceable and that therefore the Court of Appeal's judgment must be reversed.

I. STATEMENT OF FACTS AND PROCEDURAL ISSUES

Marybeth Armendariz and Dolores Olague-Rodgers (hereafter the employees) filed a complaint for wrongful termination against their former employer, Foundation Health Psychcare Services, Inc. (hereafter the employer). The complaint and certain documents filed in support of the employer's petition to compel arbitration provide us with the basic factual background of this case. In July and August of 1995, the employer hired the employees in the "Provider Relations Group" and they were later given supervisory positions with annual salaries of $38,000. On June 20, 1996, they were informed that their positions were "being eliminated" and that they were "being terminated." During their year of employment, they claim that their supervisors and coworkers engaged in sexually based harassment and discrimination. The employees alleged that they were "terminated ... because of their perceived and/or actual sexual orientation (heterosexual)."

Both employees had filled out and signed employment application forms, which included an arbitration clause pertaining to any future claim of wrongful termination. Later, they executed a separate employment arbitration agreement, containing the same arbitration clause. The clause states in full: "I agree as a condition of my employment, that in the event my employment is terminated, and I contend that such termination was wrongful or otherwise in violation of the conditions of employment or was in violation of any express or implied condition, term or covenant of employment, whether founded in fact or in law, including but not limited to the covenant of good faith and fair dealing, or otherwise in violation of any of my rights, I and Employer agree to submit any such matter to binding arbitration pursuant to the provisions of title 9 of Part III of the California Code of Civil Procedure, commencing at section 1280 et seq. or any successor or replacement statutes. I and Employer further expressly agree that in any such arbitration, my exclusive remedies for violation of the terms, conditions or covenants of employment shall be limited to a sum equal to the wages I would have earned from the date of any discharge until the date of the arbitration award. I understand that I shall not be entitled to any other remedy, at law or in equity, including but not limited to reinstatement and/or injunctive relief."

The employees' complaint against the employer alleges a cause of action for violation of the FEHA[1] and three additional causes of action for wrongful termination based on tort and contract theories of recovery. The complaint sought general damages, punitive damages, injunctive relief, and the recovery of attorney fees and costs of suit.

The employer countered by filing a motion for an order to compel arbitration pursuant to Code of Civil Procedure section 1281.2. The parties submitted declarations in support of, and in opposition to, the motion. Relying on *Stirlen v. Supercuts, Inc.*, the trial court denied the motion on the ground that the arbitration provision in question was an unconscionable contract. The trial court first found that the arbitration agreement was an "adhesion contract." It also found that several of the provisions of the contract are "so one-sided as to 'shock the conscience.'" In particular, it singled out the fact that only employees who file claims against an employer are required to arbitrate their claims, but not vice versa. Second, the agreement limits damages to backpay, precluding damages available for statutory

---

1. Same-sex harassment has been held to be unlawful under the FEHA.

antidiscrimination claims and tort damages, such as punitive damages. The trial court also mentioned the supposed lack of discovery under the arbitration agreement. It concluded: "Given the overall unfairness of the provision," this was not an appropriate case for striking the unlawful provisions of the arbitration agreement; instead it invalidated the entire agreement.

After the employer filed a timely appeal, the Court of Appeal reversed. The court concluded that the contract was indeed one of adhesion and that the damages provision was unconscionable and contrary to public policy. But for reasons elaborated below, the Court of Appeal held, contrary to the trial court, that the rest of the arbitration agreement should be enforced. It also determined that because the agreement incorporated the California Arbitration Act (CAA), adequate discovery, pursuant to Code of Civil Procedure section 1283.05, was available.

We granted review.

II. DISCUSSION

...

D. Unconscionability of the Arbitration Agreement

1.   General Principles of Unconscionability

... In this section, we will consider objections to arbitration that apply more generally to any type of arbitration imposed on the employee by the employer as a condition of employment, regardless of the type of claim being arbitrated. These objections fall under the rubric of "unconscionability."

We explained the judicially created doctrine of unconscionability in *Scissor-Tail*. Unconscionability analysis begins with an inquiry into whether the contract is one of adhesion. "The term [contract of adhesion] signifies a standardized contract, which, imposed and drafted by the party of superior bargaining strength, relegates to the subscribing party only the opportunity to adhere to the contract or reject it." (*Neal v. State Farm Ins. Cos.* (1961)). If the contract is adhesive, the court must then determine whether "other factors are present which, under established legal rules— legislative or judicial—operate to render it [unenforceable]." (*Scissor-Tail*.) "Generally speaking, there are two judicially imposed limitations on the enforcement of adhesion contracts or provisions thereof. The first is that such a contract or provision which does not fall within the reasonable expectations of the weaker or 'adhering' party will not be enforced against him. The second—a principle of equity applicable to all contracts generally—is that a contract or provision, even if consistent with the reasonable expectations of the parties, will be denied enforcement if, considered in its context, it is unduly oppressive or 'unconscionable.'" Subsequent cases have referred to both the "reasonable expectations" and the "oppressive" limitations as being aspects of unconscionability. (See *A & M Produce Co. v. FMC Corp.* (1982)).

In 1979, the Legislature enacted Civil Code section 1670.5, which codified the principle that a court can refuse to enforce an unconscionable provision in a contract. As section 1670.5, subdivision (a) states: "If the court as a matter of law finds the contract or any clause of the contract to have been unconscionable at the time it was made the court may refuse to enforce the contract, or it may enforce the remainder of the contract without the unconscionable clause, or it may so limit the application of any unconscionable clause as to avoid any unconscionable result." Because unconscionability is a reason for refusing to enforce contracts generally, it is also a valid reason for refusing to enforce an arbitration agreement under Code of Civil Procedure section 1281, which, as noted, provides that arbitration agreements are "valid, enforceable and irrevocable, save upon such grounds as exist [at law or in equity] for the revocation of any contract." The United States Supreme Court, in interpreting the same language found in section 2 of the FAA, recognized that "generally applicable contract defenses, such as fraud, duress, or *unconscionability, may* be applied to invalidate arbitration agreements...." (*Doctor's Associates, Inc. v. Casarotto,* italics added.)

As explained in *A & M Produce Co.,* "unconscionability has both a 'procedural' and a 'substantive' element," the former focusing on "oppression" or "surprise" due to unequal bargaining power, the latter on "overly harsh" or "one-sided" results. "The prevailing view is that [procedural and substantive unconscionability] must both be present in order for a court to exercise its discretion to refuse to enforce a contract or clause under the doctrine of unconscionability." (*Stirlen v. Supercuts, Inc.*) But they need not be present in the same degree. "Essentially a sliding scale is invoked which disregards the regularity of the procedural process of the contract formation, that creates the terms, in proportion to the greater harshness or unreasonableness of the substantive terms themselves." (15 Williston on Contracts (3d ed. 1972) § 1763A; see also *A & M Produce Co.*) In other words, the more substantively oppressive the contract term, the less evidence of procedural unconscionability is required to come to the conclusion that the term is unenforceable, and vice versa.

2. Unconscionability and Mandatory Employment Arbitration

Applying the above principles to this case, we first determine whether the arbitration agreement is adhesive. There is little dispute that it is. It was imposed on employees as a condition of employment and there was no opportunity to negotiate.

Moreover, in the case of preemployment arbitration contracts, the economic pressure exerted by employers on all but the most sought-after employees may be particularly acute, for the arbitration agreement stands between the employee and necessary employment, and few employees are in a position to refuse a job because of an arbitration requirement. While arbitration may have its advantages in terms of greater expedition, informality, and lower cost, it also has, from the employee's point of view, potential disadvantages: waiver of a right to a jury trial, limited discovery, and limited judicial review. Various studies show that arbitration is advantageous to employers not only because it reduces the costs of litigation, but also because it reduces the size of the award that an employee is likely to get, particularly if the employer is a "repeat player" in the arbitration system. (Bingham, *Employment Arbitration: The Repeat Player Effect* (1997) 1 Employee Rts. & Employment Policy J. 189; Schwartz, *supra,* 1997 Wis. L.Rev. at pp. 60-61.) It is perhaps for this reason that it is almost invariably the employer who seeks to compel arbitration. (See Schwartz, *supra,* 1997 Wis. L.Rev. at pp. 60-63.)

Arbitration is favored in this state as a voluntary means of resolving disputes, and this voluntariness has been its bedrock justification. As we stated recently: "[P]olicies favoring the efficiency of private arbitration as a means of dispute resolution must sometimes yield to its fundamentally contractual nature, and to the attendant requirement that arbitration shall proceed as the parties themselves have agreed." (*Vandenberg v. Superior Court.*) Given the lack of choice and the potential disadvantages that even a fair arbitration system can harbor for employees, we must be particularly attuned to claims that employers with superior bargaining power have imposed one-sided, substantively unconscionable terms as part of an arbitration agreement. "Private arbitration may resolve disputes faster and cheaper than judicial proceedings. Private arbitration, however, may also become an instrument of injustice imposed on a 'take it or leave it' basis. The courts must distinguish the former from the latter, to ensure that private arbitration systems resolve disputes not only with speed and economy but also with fairness." (*Engalla* (Kennard, J., concurring)). With this in mind, we turn to the employees' specific unconscionability claims.

Aside from FEHA issues discussed in the previous part of this opinion, the employees contend that the agreement is substantively unconscionable because it requires only employees to arbitrate their wrongful termination claims against the employer, but does not require the employer to arbitrate claims it may have against the employees. In asserting that this lack of mutuality is unconscionable, they rely primarily on the opinion of the Court of Appeal in *Stirlen*. The employee in that case was hired as a vice-president and chief financial officer; his employment contract provided for arbitration "'in the event there is any dispute arising out of [the employee's] employment with the Company,'" including "the termination of that employment." The agreement specifically excluded certain types of disputes from the scope of arbitration, including those relating to the protection of the employer's intellectual and other property and the enforcement of a postemployment covenant not to compete, which were to be litigated in state or federal court. The employee was to waive the right to challenge the jurisdiction of such a court. The arbitration agreement further provided that the damages available would be limited to "'the amount of actual damages for breach of contract, less any proper offset for mitigation of such damages.'" When an arbitration claim was filed, payments of any salary or benefits were to cease "'without penalty to the Company,'" pending the outcome of the arbitration.

The *Stirlen* court concluded that the agreement was one of adhesion, even though the employee in question was a high-level executive, because of the lack of opportunity to negotiate. The court then concluded that the arbitration agreement was substantively unconscionable. The court relied in part on *Saika v. Gold* (1996), in which the court had refused to enforce a provision in an arbitration agreement between a doctor and a patient that would allow a "trial de novo" if the arbitrator's award was $25,000 or greater. The *Saika* court reasoned that such a clause was tantamount to making arbitration binding when the patient lost the arbitration but not binding if the patient won a significant money judgment. *Stirlen* concluded that the Supercuts agreement lacked even the "modicum of bilaterality" that was present in *Saika*. The employee pursuing claims against the employer had to bear not only with the inherent shortcomings of arbitration—limited discovery, limited judicial review, limited procedural protections—but also significant damage limitations imposed by the arbitration agreement. The employer, on the other hand, in pursuing its claims, was not subject to these disadvantageous limitations and had written into the agreement special advantages, such as a waiver of jurisdictional objections by the employee if sued by the employer.

The *Stirlen* court did not hold that all lack of mutuality in a contract of adhesion was invalid. "We agree a contract can provide a 'margin of safety' that provides the party with superior bargaining strength a type of extra protection for which it has a legitimate commercial need without being unconscionable. However, unless the 'business realities' that create the special need for such an advantage are explained in the contract itself, which is not the case here, it must be factually established." The *Stirlen* court found no "business reality" to justify the lack of mutuality, concluding that the terms of the arbitration clause were "so extreme as to appear unconscionable according to the mores and business practices of the time and place."

The court in *Kinney v. United HealthCare Services, Inc.* (1999), came to the same conclusion with respect to an arbitration agreement to compel the employee, but not the employer, to submit claims to arbitration. As the *Kinney* court stated: "Faced with the issue of whether a unilateral obligation to arbitrate is unconscionable, we conclude that it is. The party who is required to submit his or her claims to arbitration [forgoes] the right, otherwise guaranteed by the federal and state Constitutions, to have those claims tried before a jury. Further, except in extraordinary circumstances, that party has no avenue of review for an adverse decision, even if that decision is based on an error of fact or law that appears on the face of the ruling and results in substantial injustice to that party. By contrast, the party requiring the other to waive these rights retains all of the benefits and protections the right to a judicial forum provides. Given the basic and substantial nature of the rights at issue, we find that the unilateral obligation to arbitrate is itself so one-sided as to be substantively unconscionable." The court also found that certain terms of the arbitration agreement—limits to discovery and caps on compensatory and punitive damages—"heightened" its unconscionability.

We conclude that *Stirlen* and *Kinney* are correct in requiring this "modicum of bilaterality" in an arbitration agreement. Given the disadvantages that may exist for plaintiffs arbitrating disputes, it is unfairly one-sided for an employer with superior bargaining power to impose arbitration on the employee as plaintiff but not to accept such limitations when it seeks to prosecute a claim against the employee, without at least some reasonable justification for such one-sidedness based on "business realities." As has been recognized "'unconscionability turns not only on a "one-sided" result, but also on an absence of "justification" for it.'" If the arbitration system established by the employer is indeed fair, then the employer as well as the employee should be willing to submit claims to arbitration. Without reasonable justification for this lack of mutuality, arbitration appears less as a forum for neutral dispute resolution and more as a means of maximizing employer advantage. Arbitration was not intended for this purpose.

The employer cites a number of cases that have held that a lack of mutuality in an arbitration agreement does not render the contract illusory as long as the employer agrees to be bound by the arbitration of employment disputes. We agree that such lack of mutuality does not render the contract illusory, i.e., lacking in mutual consideration. We conclude, rather, that in the context of an arbitration agreement imposed by the employer on the employee, such a one-sided term is unconscionable. Although parties are free to contract for asymmetrical remedies and arbitration clauses of varying scope, *Stirlen* and *Kinney* are correct that the doctrine of unconscionability limits the extent to which a stronger party may, through a contract of adhesion, impose the arbitration forum on the weaker party without accepting that forum for itself.

... We disagree that enforcing "a modicum of bilaterality" in arbitration agreements singles out arbitration for suspect status. The *Stirlen* court correctly rejected a similar criticism: "Some California courts have been [loath] to apply the doctrine of unconscionability articulated in *Scissor-Tail* to arbitration agreements subject to the FAA on the ground that the opinion in that case 'weav[es] together principles of adhesion contracts and state statutes governing the neutrality of arbitrators,' and the United States Supreme Court has taught 'that a court may not rely upon any-thing that is unique to an agreement to arbitrate when assessing unconscionability of an agreement governed by the FAA.' (*Heily v. Superior Court* (1988)). However, while the *form* of unconscionability involved in *Scissor-Tail* related to arbitration—the nonneutrality of the arbitrator—the fundamental principles set forth by the Supreme Court in that case relate to unconscionability in general, not simply to arbitration agreements."

We agree with the *Stirlen* court that the ordinary principles of unconscionability may manifest themselves in forms peculiar to the arbitration context. One such form is an agreement requiring arbitration only for the claims of the weaker party but a choice of forums for the claims of the stronger party. The application of this principle to arbitration does not disfavor arbitration. It is no disparagement of arbitration to acknowledge that it has, as noted, both advantages and disadvantages. The perceived advantages of the judicial forum for plaintiffs include the availability of discovery and the fact that courts and juries are viewed as more likely to adhere to the law and less likely than arbitrators to "split the difference" between the two sides, thereby lowering damages awards for plaintiffs. (See Haig, *Corporate Counsel's Guide: Development Report on Cost-Effective Management of Corporate Litigation* (July 1999) 610 PLI/Lit. 177, 186-187 ["a company that believes it has a strong legal and factual position may want to avoid arbitration, with its tendency to 'split the difference,' in favor of a judicial forum where it may be more likely to win a clear-cut victory"]; see also Schwartz, *supra,* 1997 Wisc.L.Rev. at pp. 64-65.) An employer may accordingly consider courts to be a forum superior to arbitration when it comes to vindicating its own contractual and statutory rights, or may consider it advantageous to have a choice of arbitration or litigation when determining how best to pursue a claim against an employee. It does not disfavor arbitration to hold that an employer may not impose a system of arbitration on an employee that seeks to maximize the advantages and minimize the disadvantages of arbitration for itself at the employee's expense. On the contrary, a unilateral arbitration agreement imposed by the employer without reasonable justification reflects the very mistrust of arbitration that has been repudiated by the United States Supreme Court in *Doctors' Associates, Inc. v. Casarotto* and other cases. We emphasize that if an employer does have reasonable justification for the arrangement—i.e., a justification grounded in something other than the employer's desire to maximize its advantage based on the perceived superiority of the judicial forum—such an agreement would not be unconscionable. Without such justification, we must assume that it is.

Applying these principles to the present case, we note the arbitration agreement was limited in scope to employee claims regarding wrongful termination. Although it did not expressly authorize litigation of the employer's claims against the employee, as was the case in *Stirlen* and *Kinney,* such was the clear implication of the agreement. Obviously, the lack of mutuality can be manifested as much by what the agreement does not provide as by what it does. (Cf. *24 Hour Fitness, Inc. v. Superior Court* (1998) [employee arbitration clause in personnel handbook found not to be unconscionable where it pertains to "'any dispute aris[ing] from your employment'"].)

This is not to say that an arbitration clause must mandate the arbitration of all claims between employer and employee in order to avoid invalidation on grounds of unconscionability. Indeed, as the employer points out, the present arbitration agreement does not require arbitration of all conceivable claims that an employee might have against an employer, only wrongful termination claims. But an arbitration agreement imposed in an adhesive context lacks basic fairness and mutuality if it requires one contracting party, but not the other, to arbitrate all claims arising out of the same transaction or occurrence or series of transactions or occurrences. The arbitration agreement in this case lacks mutuality in this sense because it requires the arbitration of employee—but not employer—claims arising out of a wrongful termination. An employee terminated for stealing trade secrets, for example, must arbitrate his or her wrongful termination claim under the agreement while the employer has no corresponding obligation to arbitrate its trade secrets claim against the employee.

The unconscionable one-sidedness of the arbitration agreement is compounded in this case by the fact that it does not permit the full recovery of damages for employees, while placing no such restriction on the employer. Even if the limitation on FEHA damages is severed as contrary to public policy, the arbitration clause in the present case still does not permit full recovery of ordinary contract damages. The arbitration agreement specifies that damages are to be limited to the amount of back-pay lost up until the time of arbitration. This provision excludes damages for prospective future earnings, so-called "front pay," a common and often substantial component of contractual damages in a wrongful termination case. (See 4 Wilcox, Cal. Employment Law (2000) § 60.08 [b], p. 60-102 and [b][iii], p. 60-97.) The employer, on the other hand, is bound by no comparable limitation should it pursue a claim against its employees.

The employer in this case, as well as the Court of Appeal, claim the lack of mutuality was based on the realities of the employees' place in the organizational hierarchy. As the Court of Appeal stated: "We ... observe that the wording of the agreement most likely resulted from the employees' position within the organization and may reflect the fact that the parties did not foresee the possibility of any dispute arising from employment that was not initiated by the employee. Plaintiffs were lower-level supervisory employees, without the sort of access to proprietary information or control over corporate finances that might lead to an employer suit against them."

The fact that it is unlikely an employer will bring claims against a particular type of employee is not, ultimately, a justification for a unilateral arbitration agreement. It provides no reason for categorically exempting employer claims, however rare, from mandatory arbitration. Although an employer may be able, in a future case, to justify a unilateral arbitration agreement, the employer in the present case has not done so.

E. Severability of Unconscionable Provisions

The employees contend that the presence of various unconscionable provisions or provisions contrary to public policy leads to the conclusion that the arbitration agreement as a whole cannot be enforced. The employer contends that, insofar as there are unconscionable provisions, they should be severed and the rest of the agreement enforced.

As noted, Civil Code section 1670.5, subdivision (a) provides that "[i]f the court as a matter of law finds the contract or any clause of the contract to have been unconscionable at the time it was made the court may refuse to enforce the contract, or it may enforce the remainder of the contract without the unconscionable clause, or it may so limit the application of any unconscionable clause as to avoid any unconscionable result." Comment 2 of the Legislative Committee comment on section 1670.5, incorporating the comments from the Uniform Commercial Code, states: "Under this section the court, in its discretion, may refuse to enforce the contract as a whole if it is permeated by the unconscionability, or it may strike any single clause or group of clauses which are so tainted or which are contrary to the essential purpose of the agreement, or it may simply limit unconscionable clauses so as to avoid unconscionable results."

Thus, the statute appears to give a trial court some discretion as to whether to sever or restrict the unconscionable provision or whether to refuse to enforce the entire agreement. But it also appears to contemplate the latter course only when an agreement is "permeated" by unconscionability. We could discover no published cases in California that address directly the question of when a trial court abuses its discretion by refusing to enforce an entire agreement, as the trial court did in this case, nor precisely what it means for an agreement to be "permeated" by unconscionability. But there is a good deal of statutory and case law discussing the related question of when it is proper to sever *illegal* contract terms—a subject to which we will now turn.

Civil Code section 1598 states that "[w]here a contract has but a single object, and such object is unlawful, whether in whole or in part, or wholly impossible of performance, or so vaguely expressed as to be wholly unascertainable, the entire contract is void." Section 1599 states that "[w]here a contract has several distinct objects, of which one at least is lawful, and one at least is unlawful, in whole or in part, the contract is void as to the latter and valid as to the rest." In *Keene v. Harling* (1964), we elaborated on those provisions: "'Whether a contract is entire or separable depends upon its language and subject matter, and this question is one of construction to be determined by the court according to the intention of the parties. If the contract is divisible, the first part may stand, although the latter is illegal. It has long been the rule in this state that 'When the transaction is of such a nature that the good part of the consideration can be separated from that which is bad, the Courts will make the distinction, for the ... law ... [divides] according to common reason; and having made that void that is against law, lets the rest stand.'" ([S]ee also *Birbrower, Montalbano, Condon & Frank v. Superior Court* (1998) [holding severable legal from illegal portions of attorney fee agreement].)

... Two reasons for severing or restricting illegal terms rather than voiding the entire contract appear implicit in case law. The first is to prevent parties from gaining undeserved benefit or suffering undeserved detriment as a result of voiding the entire agreement—particularly when there has been full or partial performance of the contract. Second, more generally, the doctrine of severance attempts to conserve a contractual relationship if to do so would not be condoning an illegal scheme. The overarching inquiry is whether "'the interests of justice ... would be furthered'" by severance. (*Beynon v. Garden Grove Medical Group* (1980)). Moreover, courts must have the *capacity* to cure the unlawful contract through severance or restriction of the offending clause, which, as discussed below, is not invariably the case.

The basic principles of severability that emerge from Civil Code section 1599 and the case law of illegal contracts appear fully applicable to the doctrine of unconscionability. Courts are to look to the various purposes of the contract. If the central purpose of the contract is tainted with illegality, then the contract as a whole cannot be enforced. If the illegality is collateral to the main purpose of the contract, and the illegal provision can be extirpated from the contract by means of severance or restriction, then such severance and restriction are appropriate. That Civil Code section 1670.5 follows this basic model is suggested by the Legislative Committee comment quoted above, which talks in terms of contracts not being enforced if "permeated" by unconscionability, and of clauses being severed if "so tainted or ... contrary to the essential purpose of the agreement." (Leg. Com. com., *supra*).

In this case, two factors weigh against severance of the unlawful provisions. First, the arbitration agreement contains more than one unlawful provision; it has both an unlawful damages provision and an unconscionably unilateral arbitration clause. Such multiple defects indicate a systematic effort to impose arbitration on an employee not simply as an alternative to litigation, but as an inferior forum that works to the employer's advantage. In other words, given the multiple unlawful provisions, the trial court did not abuse its discretion in concluding that the arbitration agreement is permeated by an unlawful purpose.[13]

Second, in the case of the agreement's lack of mutuality, such permeation is indicated by the fact that there is no single provision a court can strike or restrict in order to remove the unconscionable taint from the agreement. Rather, the court would have to, in effect, reform the contract, not through severance or restriction, but by augmenting it with additional terms. Civil Code section 1670.5 does not authorize such reformation by augmentation, nor does the arbitration statute. Code of Civil Procedure section 1281.2 authorizes the court to refuse arbitration if grounds for revocation exist, not to reform the agreement to make it lawful. Nor do courts have any such power under their inherent, limited authority to reform contracts. Because a court is unable to cure this unconscionability through severance or restriction, and is not permitted to cure it through reformation and augmentation, it must void the entire agreement.

... The approach described above is consistent with our holding in *Scissor-Tail*. In that case, we found an arbitration agreement to be unconscionable because the agreement provided for an arbitrator likely to be biased in favor of the party imposing the agreement. We nonetheless recognized that "[t]he parties have indeed agreed to arbitrate" and that there is a "strong public policy of this state in favor of resolving disputes by arbitration." (*Ibid.*) The court found a way out of this dilemma through the CAA, specifically Code of Civil Procedure section 1281.6, which provides in part: "If the arbitration agreement does not provide a method for appointing

---

13. We need not decide whether the unlawful damages provision in this arbitration agreement, by itself, would be sufficient to warrant a court's refusal to enforce that agreement. We note, however, that in the analogous case of overly broad covenants not to compete, courts have tended to invalidate rather than restrict such covenants when it appears they were drafted in bad faith, i.e., with a knowledge of their illegality. The reason for this rule is that if such bad faith restrictive covenants are enforced, then "employers are encouraged to overreach; if the covenant they draft is overbroad then the court [will redraft] it for them." This reasoning applies with equal force to arbitration agreements that limit damages to be obtained from challenging the violation of unwaivable statutory rights. An employer will not be deterred from routinely inserting such a deliberately illegal clause into the arbitration agreements it mandates for its employees if it knows that the worst penalty for such illegality is the severance of the clause after the employee has litigated the matter. In that sense, the enforcement of a form arbitration agreement containing such a clause drafted in bad faith would be condoning, or at least not discouraging, an illegal scheme, and severance would be disfavored unless it were for some other reason in the interests of justice. The refusal to enforce such a clause is also consistent with the rule that a party may waive its right to arbitration through bad faith or willful misconduct. Because we resolve this case on other grounds, we need not decide whether the state of the law with respect to damages limitations was sufficiently clear at the time the arbitration agreement was signed to lead to the conclusion that this damages clause was drafted in bad faith.

an arbitrator, the parties to the agreement who seek arbitration and against whom arbitration is sought may agree on a method of appointing an arbitrator and that method shall be followed. In the absence of an agreed method, or if the agreed method fails or for any reason cannot be followed, or when an arbitrator appointed fails to act and his or her successor has not been appointed, the court, on petition of a party to the arbitration agreement, shall appoint the arbitrator." Citing this provision, the court stated: "We therefore conclude that upon remand the trial court should afford the parties a reasonable opportunity to agree on a suitable arbitrator and, failing such agreement, the court should on petition of either party appoint the arbitrator." Other cases, both before and after *Scissor-Tail,* have also held that the part of an arbitration clause providing for a less-than-neutral arbitration forum is severable from the rest of the clause.

... The employer also points to two cases in which unconscionably one-sided provisions in arbitration agreements were severed and the agreement enforced. *Saika,* as discussed, involved an arbitration agreement with a provision that would make the arbitration nonbinding if the arbitration award were $25,000 or greater. In *Beynon v. Garden Grove Medical Group*, a provision of the arbitration agreement gave one party, but not the other, the option of rejecting the arbitrator's decision. The courts in both instances concluded, in *Saika* implicitly, in *Beynon* explicitly, that the offending clause was severable from the rest of the arbitration agreement.

The provisions in these two cases are different from the one-sided arbitration provision at issue in this case in at least two important respects. First, the one-sidedness in the above two cases was confined to single provisions regarding the rights of the parties after an arbitration award was made, not a provision affecting the scope of the arbitration. As such, the unconscionability could be cured by severing the unlawful provisions. Second, in both cases, the arguments against severance were made by the party that had imposed the unconscionable provision in order to prevent enforcement of an arbitration award against it, and the failure to sever would have had the effect of accomplishing the precise unlawful purpose of that provision—the invalidation of the arbitration award. As discussed, courts will generally sever illegal provisions and enforce a contract when nonenforcement will lead to an undeserved benefit or detriment to one of the parties that would not further the interests of justice. In *Beynon* and *Saika,* the interests of justice would obviously not have been furthered by nonenforcement. The same considerations are not found in the present case.

■ BROWN, J., Concurring.

[Omitted].

QUESTIONS AND NOTES

1. What practical difference would it make if the arbitration clause in *Armendariz* were expanded to include all claims arising out of the employment relationship, not just wrongful termination claims? Is there any realistic chance that an employer will sue fired employees that had been earning annual salaries of $38,000? How does a procedure that is "unconscionable" suddenly become acceptable if employers agreed to submit their nonexistent and noncollectable claims to that same process? Why should the employee's right to a jury trial in a court of law on her sexual harassment claim turn on that?

2. What would you advise Foundation Health (and other employers) to do regarding its employment contracts in the wake of *Armendariz*?

3. Reconsider the unconscionability attack on Thomas Troiano's attorney's fee discussed in the *New York Law Journal* excerpt reprinted at p. 360 in light of this passage from a California Court of Appeal decision finding that Bank of America's $3 per item charge for returned checks (which cost the Bank far less than $1 per item to process) as applied to grocery stores and other large volume check customers was not unconscionable:

> Judicial review of one service fee charged by one bank is an entirely inappropriate method of overseeing bank service fees....
>
> This case implicates a question of economic policy: whether service fees charged by banks are too high and should be regulated. "It is primarily a legislative and not a judicial function to determine economic policy." We agree with *Jacobs v. Citibank, N.A.* (1984) 61 N.Y.2d 869, 871–72, a case involving [No Sufficient Funds] fees, which concluded, "To grant the relief requested by plaintiffs would be to impose a limit on the amount Federally chartered banks can charge for processing overdrafts. This is a task more properly left to the Comptroller of the Currency who has decided that '[a]ll charges to customers should be arrived at by each bank on a competitive basis.'"

California Grocers Ass'n v. Bank of America, 22 Cal. App. 4th 205, 218 (1994).

Don't lawyers provide legal services in a market at least as competitive as the market for checking accounts? Throughout the economic system, oligopolists charge prices that exceed cost by large percentages. Is it unconscionable for an airline to charge one customer $1,500 for the same seat that another bought the week before (or the day after) for $99? Or for a software manufacturer to charge hundreds of dollars for a product with a marginal cost of pennies per unit? In short, can a finding of unconscionability be based on excessive price alone?

4. Can you reconcile the application of the unconscionability doctrine in this case with the Supreme Court's construction of the Federal Arbitration Act in *Concepcion*, p. 266, *supra*?

IV. FRAUD AND MISREPRESENTATION

The line between fraudulent misrepresentation and legitimate sales talk is often a thin one. How naive can a buyer legitimately claim to be? Does a seller have to disclose all of the weaknesses in his product when he is trying to make a sale or only give honest answers to a customer's questions? The line has been blurred even more as legal liability has expanded from cases of deliberate and knowing falsehood with intent to deceive, to statements not known to be false in which the utterer was negligent in not discovering their falsity, to innocent misrepresentation by statements which the utterer reasonably believed true but which are false. In this progression the laws of misrepresentation and fraud blend into concepts of warranty and liability for goods that fail to meet description.

A variety of distinctions are made in describing the difference we all feel between selling and swindling, between puffing and lying. Some distinctions are made between representations of fact and promises or between facts and opinions. Different kinds of sellers are burdened with different levels of responsibility along the following spectrum:

a. *Caveat Emptor.* It is the buyer's job to examine the goods and ask questions and the seller's job to sell. It is a normal part of market behavior for sellers to exaggerate, puff, and leave out unpleasant bits of information, even if that makes what is said misleading.

b. *The Duty to Give an Honest Answer.* A seller is not permitted to lie and must believe that what he tells the buyer is correct, but the seller is not liable if it turns out to be wrong.

c. *The Duty to Give an Accurate Answer.* A seller must be correct in what is said but is under no obligation to volunteer information.

d. *The Duty to Give a Complete Answer.* A seller is obligated to give truthful and complete answers to questions asked but need not point out matters not raised by the buyer.

e. *The Duty to Disclose.* A seller is obligated to disclose, without need for an inquiry, relevant information known to it that might bear on the buyer's decision.

f. *The Duty to Investigate.* A seller is obliged to conduct a complete and accurate investigation and to disclose fully all material information without being asked by the buyer.

Note the extent to which it makes a difference to you whether buyer and seller are:

a. people in the same line of business.

b. both merchants, although not necessarily in the same trade.

c. consumers.

d. gullible, simple people with no business experience.

Also note the difference it makes to you whether the object being bought and sold is:

a. a used car.

b. a painting or object of art.

c. a diamond.

d. a house.

e. a stock, bond, or other financial asset.

f. food.

g. medicine.

━━━━━━━━━

■ Learned Hand, D. J., in *Vulcan Metals Co. v. Simmons Mfg. Co.*, 248 Fed. 853, 856 (2d Cir. 1918):

When the parties are so situated that the buyer may reasonably rely upon the expression of the seller's opinion, it is no excuse to give a false one. And so it makes much difference whether the parties stand "on an equality." For example, we should treat very differently the expressed opinion of a chemist to a layman about the properties of a composition from the same opinion between chemist and chemist, when the buyer had full opportunity to examine. The reason of the rule lies, we think, in this: There are some kinds of talk which no sensible man takes seriously, and if he does he suffers from his credulity. If we were all scrupulously honest, it would not be so; but, as it is, neither party usually believes what the seller says about his own opinions, and each knows it. Such statements, like the claims of campaign managers before election, are rather designed to allay the suspicion which would attend their absence than to be understood as having any relation to objective truth. It is quite true that they induce a compliant temper in the buyer, but it is by a much more subtle process than through the acceptance of his claims for his wares.

━━━━━━━━━

Stambovsky v. Ackley

New York Supreme Court, Appellate Division, 1991.
169 A.D.2d 254, 572 N.Y.S.2d 672.

■ RUBIN, J. Plaintiff, to his horror, discovered that the house he had recently contracted to purchase was widely reputed to be possessed by poltergeists, reportedly seen by defendant seller and members of her family on numerous occasions over the last nine years. Plaintiff promptly commenced this action seeking rescission of the contract of sale. Supreme Court reluctantly dismissed the complaint, holding that plaintiff has no remedy at law in this jurisdiction.

The unusual facts of this case, as disclosed by the record, clearly warrant a grant of equitable relief to the buyer who, as a resident of New York City, cannot be expected to have any familiarity with the folklore of the Village of Nyack. Not being a "local," plaintiff could not readily learn that the home he had contracted to purchase is haunted. Whether the source of the spectral apparitions seen by defendant seller are parapsychic or psychogenic, having reported their presence in both a national publication (*Readers' Digest*) and the local press (in 1977 and 1982, respectively), defendant is estopped to deny their existence and, as a matter of law, the house is haunted. More to the point, however, no divination is required to conclude that it is defendant's promotional efforts in publicizing her close encounters with these spirits which fostered the home's reputation in the community. In 1989, the house was included in a five-home walking tour of Nyack and described in a November 27th newspaper article as "a riverfront Victorian (with ghost)." The impact of the reputation thus created goes to the very essence of the bargain between the parties, greatly impairing both the value of the property and its potential for resale. The extent of this impairment may be presumed for the purpose of reviewing the disposition of this motion to dismiss the cause of action for rescission and represents merely an issue of fact for resolution at trial.

While I agree with [the trial court] that the real estate broker, as agent for the seller, is under no duty to disclose to a potential buyer the phantasmal reputation of the premises and that, in his pursuit of a legal remedy for fraudulent misrepresentation against the seller, plaintiff hasn't a ghost of a chance, I am nevertheless moved by the spirit of equity to allow the buyer to seek rescission of the contract of sale and recovery of his downpayment. New York law fails to recognize any remedy for damages incurred as a result of the seller's mere silence, applying instead the strict rule of *caveat emptor*. Therefore, the theoretical basis for granting relief, even under the extraordinary facts of this case, is elusive if not ephemeral.

"Pity me not but lend thy serious hearing to what I shall unfold."

William Shakespeare, *Hamlet*, Act I, Scene V [Ghost].

From the perspective of a person in the position of plaintiff herein, a very practical problem arises with respect to the discovery of a paranormal phenomenon: "Who you gonna' call?" as the title song to the movie *Ghostbusters* asks. Applying the strict rule of *caveat emptor* to a contract involving a house possessed by poltergeists conjures up visions of a psychic or medium routinely accompanying the structural engineer and Terminix man on an inspection of every home subject to a contract of sale. It portends that the prudent attorney will establish an escrow account lest the subject of the transaction come back to haunt him and his client—or pray that his malpractice insurance coverage extends to supernatural disasters. In the interest of avoiding such untenable consequences, the notion that a haunting is a condition which can and should be ascertained upon reasonable inspection of the premises is a hobgoblin which should be exorcised from the body of legal precedent and laid quietly to rest.

It has been suggested by a leading authority that the ancient rule which holds that mere non-disclosure does not constitute actionable misrepresentation "finds proper application in cases where the fact undisclosed is patent, or the plaintiff has equal opportunities for obtaining information which he may be expected to utilize, or the defendant has no reason to think that he is acting under any misapprehension" (Prosser, Law of Torts § 106, at 696 [4th ed., 1971]). However, with respect to transactions in real estate, New York adheres to the doctrine of *caveat emptor* and imposes no duty upon the vendor to disclose any information concerning the premises unless there is a confidential or fiduciary relationship between the parties or some conduct on the part of the seller which constitutes "active concealment." Normally, some affirmative misrepresentation or partial disclosure is required to impose upon the seller a duty to communicate undisclosed conditions affecting the premises.

Caveat emptor is not so all-encompassing a doctrine of common law as to render every act of non-disclosure immune from redress, whether legal or equitable. "In regard to the necessity of giving information which has not been asked, the rule differs somewhat at law and in equity, and while the law courts would permit no recovery of damages against a vendor, because of mere concealment of facts under certain circumstances, yet if the vendee refused to complete the contract because of the concealment of a material fact on the part of the other, equity would refuse to compel him so to do, because equity only compels the specific performance of a contract which is fair and open, and in regard to which all material matters known to each have been communicated to the other." Even as a principle of law, long before exceptions were embodied in statute law, the doctrine was held inapplicable to contagion among animals, adulteration of food, and insolvency of a maker of a promissory note and of a tenant substituted for another under a lease. Common law is not moribund. *Ex facto jus oritur* (law arises out of facts). Where fairness and common sense dictate that an exception should be created, the evolution of the law should not be stifled by rigid application of a legal maxim.

The doctrine of *caveat emptor* requires that a buyer act prudently to assess the fitness and value of his purchase and operates to bar the purchaser who fails to exercise due care from seeking the equitable remedy of rescission. For the purposes of the instant motion to dismiss the action pursuant to CPLR 3211(a)(7), plaintiff is entitled to every favorable inference which may reasonably be drawn from the pleadings, specifically, in this instance, that he met his obligation to conduct an inspection of the premises and a search of available public records with respect to title. It should be apparent, however, that the most meticulous inspection and the search would not reveal the presence of poltergeists at the premises or unearth the property's ghoulish reputation in the community. Therefore, there is no sound policy reason to deny plaintiff relief for failing to discover a state of affairs which the most prudent purchaser would not be expected to even contemplate.

The case law in this jurisdiction dealing with the duty of a vendor of real property to disclose information to the buyer is distinguishable from the matter under review. The most salient distinction is that existing cases invariably deal with the physical condition of the premises, defects in title, liens against the property, expenses or income and other factors affecting its operation. No case has been brought to this court's attention in which the property value was impaired as the result of the reputation created by information disseminated to the public by the seller (or, for that matter, as a result of possession by poltergeists).

Where a condition which has been created by the seller materially impairs the value of the contract and is peculiarly within the knowledge of the seller or unlikely to be discovered by a prudent purchaser exercising due care with respect to the subject transaction, nondisclosure constitutes a basis for rescission as a matter of equity. Any other outcome places upon the buyer not merely the obligation to exercise care in his purchase but rather to be omniscient with respect to any fact which may affect the bargain. No practical purpose is served by imposing such a burden upon a purchaser. To the contrary, it encourages predatory business practice and offends the principle that equity will suffer no wrong to be without a remedy.

Defendant's contention that the contract of sale, particularly the merger or "as is" clause, bars recovery of the buyer's deposit is unavailing. Even an express disclaimer will not be given effect where the facts are peculiarly within the knowledge of the party invoking it. Moreover, a fair reading of the merger clause reveals that it expressly disclaims only representations made with respect to the physical condition of the premises and merely makes general reference to representations concerning "any other matter or things affecting or relating to the aforesaid premises." As broad as this language may be, a reasonable interpretation is that its effect is limited to tangible or physical matters and does not extend to paranormal phenomena. Finally, if the language of the contract is to be construed as broadly as defendant urges to encompass the presence of poltergeists in the house, it cannot be said that she has delivered the premises "vacant" in accordance with her obligation under the provisions of the contract rider.

To the extent New York law may be said to require something more than "mere concealment" to apply even the equitable remedy of rescission, the case of *Junius Construction Corporation v. Cohen*, while not precisely on point, provides some guidance. In that case, the seller disclosed that an official map indicated two as yet unopened streets which were planned for construction at the edges of the parcel. What was not disclosed was that the same map indicated a third street which, if opened, would divide the plot in half. The court held that, while the seller was under no duty to mention the planned streets at all, having undertaken to disclose two of them, he was obliged to reveal the third.

In the case at bar, defendant seller deliberately fostered the public belief that her home was possessed. Having undertaken to inform the public at large, to whom she has no legal relationship, about the supernatural occurrences on her property, she may be said to owe no less a duty to her contract vendee. It has been remarked that the occasional modern cases which permit a seller to take unfair advantage of a buyer's ignorance so long as he is not actively misled are "singularly unappetizing" (Prosser, Law of Torts § 106, at 696 [4th ed. 1971]). Where, as here, the seller not only takes unfair advantage of the buyer's ignorance but has created and perpetuated a condition about which he is unlikely to even inquire, enforcement of the contract (in whole or in part) is offensive to the court's sense of equity. Application of the remedy of rescission, within the bounds of the narrow exception to the doctrine of *caveat emptor* set forth herein, is entirely appropriate to relieve the unwitting purchaser from the consequences of a most unnatural bargain.

All concur except MILONAS, J.P. and SMITH, J., who dissent in an opinion by SMITH, J.

■ SMITH, JUSTICE (dissenting).

I would affirm the dismissal of the complaint by the motion court.

Plaintiff seeks to rescind his contract to purchase defendant Ackley's residential property and recover his down payment. Plaintiff alleges that Ackley and her real estate broker, defendant Ellis Realty, made material misrepresentations of the property in that they failed to disclose that Ackley believed that the house was haunted by poltergeists. Moreover, Ackley shared this belief with her community and the general public through articles published in *Reader's Digest* (1977) and the local newspaper (1982). In November 1989, approximately two months after the parties entered into the contract of sale but subsequent to the scheduled October 2, 1989 closing, the house was included in a five-house walking tour and again described in the local newspaper as being haunted.

Prior to closing, plaintiff learned of this reputation and unsuccessfully sought to rescind the $650,000 contract of sale and obtain return of his $32,500 down payment without resort to litigation. The plaintiff then commenced this action for that relief and alleged that he would not have entered into the contract had he been so advised and that as a result of the alleged poltergeist activity, the market value and resaleability of the property was greatly diminished. Defendant Ackley has counterclaimed for specific performance.

It is settled law in New York that the seller of real property is under no duty to speak when the parties deal at arm's length. The mere silence of the seller, without some act or conduct which deceived the purchaser, does not amount to a concealment that is actionable as a fraud. The buyer has the duty to satisfy himself as to the quality of his bargain pursuant to the doctrine of *caveat emptor*, which in New York State still applies to real estate transactions.

London v. Courduff (1988).

The parties herein were represented by counsel and dealt at arm's length. This is evidenced by the contract of sale which, *inter alia*, contained various riders and a specific provision that all prior understandings and agreements between the parties were merged into the contract, that the contract completely expressed their full agreement and that neither had relied upon any statement by anyone else not set forth in the contract. There is no allegation that defendants, by some specific act, other than the failure to speak, deceived the plaintiff. Nevertheless, a cause of action may be sufficiently stated where there is a confidential or fiduciary relationship creating a duty to disclose and there was a failure to disclose a material fact, calculated to induce a false belief. However, plaintiff herein has not alleged and there is [a] basis for concluding that a confidential or fiduciary relationship existed between these parties to an arm's length transaction such as to give rise to a duty to disclose. In addition, there is no allegation that defendants thwarted plaintiff's efforts to fulfill his responsibilities fixed by the doctrine of *caveat emptor*. Finally, if the doctrine of *caveat emptor* is to be discarded, it should be for a reason more substantive than a poltergeist. The existence of a poltergeist is no more binding upon the defendants than it is upon this court.

QUESTIONS AND NOTES

1. Do Justices Rubin and Smith agree on the meaning of *caveat emptor?* The meaning of *caveat emptor* is unclear, beyond its basic sense that the risk of defects in the property or the seller's title, except to the extent expressly represented on warranted to the contrary, are placed on buyers. Both judges acknowledge that it is the

law of New York for the purchase of real estate. Of what need the buyer beware? Would the buyer's claim for return of the down payment because of misrepresentation be stronger if seller had affirmatively stated "There are no ghosts around here"? If seller had arranged for the ghosts to vacate during the period the buyer is inspecting, would that be fraud? If the buyer retained an exorcist who failed to detect ghosts the seller has often encountered, would Justice Smith leave the risk entirely with the buyer? If the seller had been aware that there was a dangerous accumulation of radon gas in the basement that can cause fatal ailments to occupants of the house, but buyer's inspection failed to disclose the problem, would Justice Smith approve of the seller keeping silent?

2. The procedural setting of this case on appeal is somewhat unusual. The trial court dismissed the complaint, finding no issues of fact requiring trial. Buyer's allegation that the house was reputedly haunted and that this condition adversely affects its resale value therefore must be accepted as true. How might buyer prove these matters at trial?

3. As a matter of common sense, and ignoring almost a thousand years of history, do you think that a lesser burden of proof should be imposed on a buyer who wishes to call a deal off and obtain return of the down payment than should be demanded of the same buyer when seeking to recover damages from the seller because of the misrepresentation by silence? Should these burdens be different from that imposed on the seller who seeks to obtain a judicial order directing the buyer to specifically perform the contract by buying the property?

Cushman v. Kirby

Vermont Supreme Court, 1987.
148 Vt. 571, 536 A.2d 550.

■ DOOLEY, J. This is an appeal by the defendants-sellers of a home from a judgment entered, after a jury verdict in favor of the plaintiffs-buyers, in a suit for misrepresentation. We affirm.

In the spring of 1984, the plaintiffs, Lynn and Julie Cushman, entered into negotiations with the defendants, Gregory and Elizabeth Kirby, for the purchase of a single-family home in the Town of Waltham. After viewing the premises on two occasions, and agreeing on a purchase price of $102,500, the parties executed a purchase and sale agreement in April, 1984. The real property was conveyed by defendants to plaintiffs on June 12, 1984, for the agreed upon price.

Two months later, plaintiffs brought an action for misrepresentation claiming defendants had, during the course of negotiations, represented that there was good quality well water available on the land suitable for all household uses, when in fact the available well water was not of good quality. Trial by jury resulted in a verdict for plaintiffs in the amount of $6,600....

... Through the offices of a realtor, plaintiffs briefly viewed the property once in the summer of 1983, and again in March of 1984. During the second visit, which was a much more thorough tour of the house, they discovered an apparatus for a water treatment system in the basement. Since the apparatus was labelled "water conditioner," plaintiffs inquired from defendants: "What kind of water do you have?" Mrs. Kirby answered: "It's good. It's fine. It's a little hard, but the system downstairs takes care of it." Mr. Kirby, who was present during this exchange, remained silent. Satisfied with the representation that the water was simply hard, plaintiffs inquired no further about water quality.

While moving into the home after closing, plaintiffs first discovered that the well water was in fact sulfur water that smelled strongly of rotten eggs. Dismayed by this discovery, plaintiffs contacted Mrs. Kirby, who responded by stating that she forgot to tell plaintiffs that the basement water treatment system needed "Clorox." She said that when the "Clorox" level is too low, the water smells and tastes bad.

Following Mrs. Kirby's instruction, plaintiffs added "Clorox" to the system. Rather than solving the problem, the "Clorox" made the water taste like sulfur and chlorine. They then consulted a plumber, who confirmed that they had sulfur water, and explained that sulfur water is not the same as hard water. The plumber testified that hard water is a condition caused by calcium, which does not require treatment for drinking, or cause foul taste or smell, as does sulfur water. The plumber also informed plaintiffs that it would cost at least $1,000 to rehabilitate the existing system—exclusive of labor, regular maintenance, and repair costs. He also testified that even with a properly operating system, the end result would be treated sulfur water, which even defendants testified would bring the water only to a "tolerable level of drinkability."

Based on advice from their plumber, as well as information received from other people who were not satisfied with similar sulfur filtration systems, plaintiffs determined that the most cost-effective, long-term solution to their sulfur water problem was to join with two other neighbors and hookup to the Vergennes city water supply. Thereafter, they accomplished the hookup for a cost of approximately $5,000, plus annual water bills.

I.

Defendants' first argument is that, because of the absence of any evidence that either defendant made any affirmative misrepresentation to plaintiffs concerning water quality, the trial court erroneously denied their motions for directed verdicts. The premise of this argument is that the legal standard applicable to their conduct requires that they must have made intentional misrepresentations of existing fact before either of them could be held liable for fraud. We disagree.

This Court stated in *Crompton v. Beedle* that: Where one has full information and represents that he has, if he discloses a part of his information only, and by words or conduct leads the one with whom he contracts to believe that he has made a full disclosure and does this with intent to deceive and overreach and to prevent investigation, he is guilty of fraud against which equity will relieve, if his words and conduct in consequence of reliance upon them bring about the result which he desires. We think that, regardless of whether Mrs. Kirby's statement was actually false, and known by her to be false when it was made, the standard of conduct applicable to her was that stated in *Crompton*.

On review of the propriety of a denial of a directed verdict, this Court will view the evidence in the light most favorable to the nonmoving party, exclusive of any modifying evidence....

Mrs. Kirby testified that at the time of the sale to the Cushmans, she was aware that the well water on the property contained sulfur to an extent requiring treatment to make it of tolerable quality. It was also uncontroverted that, despite her knowledge of the presence of sulfur in the water, Mrs. Kirby represented to the Cushmans, in response to inquiries about water quality, that the water on the property was "a little hard," but that the water treatment equipment in the basement would take care of it. There was no evidence that either defendant ever disclosed the presence of sulfur in the water. The plaintiffs testified that they relied on the truth of Mrs. Kirby's statements about the extent of the water problem when they decided to buy the house.

This evidence makes out a case of actionable fraud, under the standard of *Crompton*, sufficient to carry the case to the jury. It follows that it was not error to deny Mrs. Kirby's motion for directed verdict.

A somewhat different standard of conduct applies to Mr. Kirby, however, since he made no affirmative representations to plaintiffs about the quality of water. The claim for fraud against him was based exclusively on his silence while in the company of plaintiffs and Mrs. Kirby when she made the statements about water quality referred to above.

"Silence alone is insufficient to constitute fraud unless there is a duty to speak." *Cheever v. Albro* (1980). In *Cheever*, we concluded that the party sued for fraud had such a duty to speak based on "superior knowledge and means of knowledge" over the plaintiff, as well as certain contract language relevant to the disputed transaction. Although *Cheever* involved the sale of a corporation, rather than real estate, we think that a duty to speak based on the superior knowledge of a seller is equally present where the relationship of the parties is that of vendor and purchaser of real estate. As stated by one court: Where material facts are accessible to the vendor only, and he knows them not to be within the reach of the diligent attention, observation and judgment of the purchaser, the vendor [of real estate] is bound to disclose such facts and make them known to the purchaser.

Mr. Kirby testified that he was aware of the sulfur in the water at the time of the sale. He also testified that he had assisted in maintaining the water treatment system, that he had a working knowledge of the system, and that he understood the system was designed to treat sulfur in the water. Thus, by his own testimony, Mr. Kirby was fully cognizant of the quality of the water, and no question of fact existed as to his state of mind regarding this issue. Mr. Kirby further testified that he heard Mrs. Kirby represent to the plaintiffs that the water equipment took care of the "hard water" problem. As such, the only question of fact at issue with respect to Mr. Kirby's liability was whether his wife's representation constituted fraud. This is because if Mrs. Kirby's statement amounted to an inadequate disclosure constituting a misrepresentation, then, Mr. Kirby, based on his own knowledge, and his position as a seller of the property, had an affirmative duty to speak. This duty existed as a matter of law. The jury found Mrs. Kirby's statement to be a misrepresentation. Given the resolution of this sole factual issue, in conjunction with his own testimony, Mr. Kirby had a duty to speak, yet he remained silent. Under the circumstances of the present case, this silence constituted a misrepresentation.

Mr. Kirby's liability hinged on the determination of the factual issue of whether Mrs. Kirby's representation to the plaintiffs amounted to a misrepresentation, which was a question clearly within the province of the jury. Therefore, the trial court correctly denied Mr. Kirby's motion for directed verdict.

* * *

III.

Defendants' remaining argument is that the court's instruction on damages was erroneous. Defendants requested that the court instruct that plaintiffs were entitled to recover at most the cost of repairs to the treatment system. Instead, the court charged that it is a jury question whether repairs to the treatment system would fully and adequately accomplish the goal of placing plaintiffs in the same position in which they would have been had the property been sold as represented—with good quality water. If so, the court charged, the measure of damages suggested by defendants would be the maximum recovery. If not, the proper measure of damages is the difference in value of the property as represented and the value of the property as it actually existed.

In general, a party seeking damages for fraud is entitled to "recover such damages ... as will compensate him for the loss or injury actually sustained and place him *rule = expectation*

in the same position that he would have occupied had he not been defrauded." *Larochelle v. Komery* (1969). The precise measure of damages that will provide the defrauded party with the benefit of his bargain, however, depends on "the facts and circumstances surrounding the fraud, and the nature and extent of the injury suffered by the defrauded party."

If the injury is temporary in the sense that restoration can cure the harm, the reasonable cost of repair may serve the need and provide adequate and fair compensation. If the damage is permanent and beyond full repair, the variance in value of the property before and after the injury often affords the better guide to a just award. It all depends upon the character of the property and the nature and extent of the injury. The court's charge appropriately tracked the rule... Furthermore, there was ample evidence in the record to support the jury's conclusion that the fraud in this case could not be adequately remedied by repair of the water treatment system. The court's damage instruction was not error, and the damage award must stand.

Affirmed.

QUESTIONS AND NOTES

1. Didn't the Cushmans have an opportunity to turn on the tap and taste the water or to hire an expert home inspector to smell it for them? Put yourself in the kitchen with the Kirbys and Cushmans. Ms. Kirby has just said that when the system isn't working right the water tastes and smells bad. Wouldn't that arouse your curiosity enough to ask her if she had a spare glass so you could try it out?

2. The problem in this case could be cured effectively by hooking up to the city water system for $5,000. Would you be as comfortable with this result if three water experts had testified that the only way to deal with this problem would be either to install a fancy reverse osmosis distillation system for $75,000 or to bring in city water at a roughly equivalent net present value cost?

V. MISUNDERSTANDING AND MISTAKE

If a party to a contract is mistaken as to what the other party is offering to buy or sell, it is easy to say that she should not be held to her promise because she really never consented to the deal she appears to have made. But the term *mistake* can cover a bewilderingly diverse conglomeration of fact situations with very different legal significance. How can we distinguish between the cases in which the contract should be enforced, even if it proves to be a bad bargain for one party who claims she made a mistake, and those cases in which her performance should be excused? It is safe to say that the law's answer to this question is very garbled. Mistake is one of the most confused and puzzling areas of contract law, but a faint path through the morass can be discerned.

(1) *Mistake in Business Judgment.* One of the parties to almost every contract can, after the fact, be said to have made a mistake in judgment. Contract is a tool for bargain and exchange, and every sale involves a guess by each party as to the value of what he is bargaining for. Not infrequently, then, a month after the exchange one of the parties will think he made a good deal, and the other will think he made a mistake in selling so cheaply or in paying so much. Obviously, this alone does not excuse performance.

(2) *Mistake in Integration.* In other cases, the parties reach an agreement, but it goes astray in the process of writing it down. A slip of the tongue, or carelessness in typing up the agreement, may result in a writing that does not reflect the understanding. The law governing these cases is clear; the parties have a contract, albeit imperfectly expressed. The remedy for this kind of mistake, once a court is convinced that a scrivener's error has occurred, is to reform the contract to express accurately the intention of the parties.

Stare v. Tate

California Court of Appeal, 1971.
21 Cal.App.3d 432, 98 Cal.Rptr. 264.

■ KAUS, P.J. Plaintiff appeals from an adverse judgment in an action to reform a property settlement agreement with her former husband, the defendant, and to enforce the agreement as reformed.

FACTS

The agreement in question was signed by both parties on February 21, 1968. It was the culmination of protracted negotiations which had been going on for several years. Both sides were represented by counsel at all times.

In the negotiations both sides apparently agreed that the community property was to be evenly divided. They did not agree, however, on the value of certain items and on the community property status of certain stocks which stood in the husband's name alone.

These disagreements centered principally on items which, it was understood, were to be retained by the husband.

In particular the wife, Joan, had an *idée fixe* that certain real property (the "Holt" property) which she and the husband, Tim, owned as tenants in common with his brother, was worth $550,000. The husband's valuation was somewhere between $425,000 and $450,000. Joan had very little evidence on which to base her contention: First, there was a statement by Tim's parents when they had owned the property that it was worth about $550,000; second, a former attorney of Tim's had, in 1966, written a letter to Joan's attorney which contained a settlement offer based upon a value of $550,000.[3]

The second important area of disagreement centered on the ownership of stock in a family corporation and the proper basis for its valuation. In all Tim owned 25,500 shares. Of these he had owned 5000 shares long before he married Joan. Joan realized that any claim that these 5000 shares were community property was tenuous, at best. Similarly, on his part, Tim conceded that a block of 7500 shares was community property. Another block of 5000 shares was, according to Joan, given to her and Tim as a wedding present by his parents. Yet another block of 8000 shares was, again according to Joan, given to both her and Tim as a present during their marriage. The shares were, however, in Tim's name alone and he denied that the community had any interest in them.

The book value of the shares was a little less than $7.00 per share. Joan claimed that the fair market value was, however, $1.50 per share over the book value and that Tim should "buy" her community interest in the shares at that value.

To sum up: If Joan was correct with respect to the value of the Holt property, her community property interest in it was about $25,000 higher than Tim conceded; if she were to succeed on her contentions with respect to the stock, Tim would have had to pay her roughly $40,000 more than he was willing.

In January 1968, Joan's attorney prepared a document entitled "SECOND PROPOSAL FOR A BASIS OF SETTLEMENT—TATE v. TATE" which, among other things, arrived at a suggested figure of $70,081.85 for the value of

---

3. Based on the $550,000 figure, taking into account several encumbrances and the fact that the community only owned a fifty percent interest in the property, the attorney arrived at an equity of $60,000. As will be seen, about fifteen months later the equity based on the $550,000 figure was worth, roughly, $120,000. The record does not indicate why there was such a big change in such a relatively short time. Presumably, at least part of it is due to payments on the encumbrances.

Joan's share in the Holt property. This value was arrived at by a computation set forth in the proposal. It is copied in the footnote.[4]

It is obvious that Joan's attorney arrived at the figure of $70,081.85 for the community equity in the property only by making two substantial errors. First, the net value after deducting the encumbrances from the asserted gross value of $550,000 is $241,637.01, not $141,637.01; second, one-half of $241,637.01 is substantially more than $70,081.85. The correct figure for the equity should have been $120,818.50 or, roughly $50,000 more.

The mistake did not escape Tim's accountant who discovered it while helping Tim's attorney in preparing a counter-offer. He brought it to the attention of the attorney who, in his own words, reacted as follows:

> I told him that I had been arguing with [the wife's attorney] to use the value that was on the—on the real property tax statement, but I knew that that was low and [he] would never go for it, that the appraisal had been $425,000.00 when the building had been purchased by said owners, and I thought that until we got it, that we would use something like a $450,000.00 value, and he said, 'Fine.' It is my recollection that I said to him, 'You know, you might as well use the figure that Walker has there because his mistake is a hundred thousand dollars and we value it at a hundred thousand dollars less, so it is basically the same thing, so give it a $70,000.00 equity,' and that is what he did and that is how it came about.

A counter-offer was then submitted to Joan and her lawyer. It lists all of the community assets, with the property in question being valued at $70,082.00, rounding up the erroneous figure in Joan's offer to the nearest dollar. There can be no reasonable doubt that the counter-offer was prepared in a way designed to minimize the danger that Joan or her attorney would discover the mistake. While all other encumbered properties are listed at an agreed gross value, with encumbrances shown as a deduction therefrom, the only figure that appears next to the Holt property is the equity!

The counter-offer said nothing about attorneys' fees. One of its terms was that Joan would assume a note of not quite $11,000. It was based on only 7500 shares of the family corporation's stock being community property and a valuation at book. In other words, it represented a demand for total surrender by Joan on the two major items in dispute.

---

4. "888 East Holt Avenue, Pomona
      (Note: value as per previous offer)
           Total value...................... $550,000.00
           Less encumbrance .... −308,362.99
           Net value 141,637.01
      One-half community....................$70,081.85"

Based on the figures in the counter-offer Tim would have received substantially more in assets than Joan. This difference was to be made up by a cash payment of $46,534.

On February 16, 1968, the parties and their attorneys had a settlement conference. The counter-offer was the basis for the discussion. There was no mention that the figure of $70,082 for the equity in the Holt property was based on an agreed value of $550,000 or any other figure. In the discussion it was agreed that the husband was to assume the liability on the $11,000.00 note and was to pay Joan's attorney $7,500, a figure somewhat smaller than counsel's time charges up till then. The result of all this give and take was that the cash payment from Tim to Joan was to be reduced to $40,000.

A few days later a formal agreement was signed. It simply recites who was to get what, without ascribing any value to any of the properties. It also provides for the $40,000 cash payment. Sometime in March 1968, Joan obtained a divorce.

The mistake might never have come to light had not Tim desired to have that exquisite last word. A few days after Joan had obtained the divorce he mailed her a copy of the offer which contained the errant computation. On top of the page he wrote with evident satisfaction: "PLEASE NOTE $100,000.00 MISTAKE IN YOUR FIGURES. * * *" The present action was filed exactly one month later.

Tim testified that he did not learn of the arithmetical error until after the property settlement agreement was signed. The record contains no evidence to the contrary.

DISCUSSION

There is really no substantial conflict in the evidence and it is hard to understand how the trial court could do anything but grant Joan's prayer for relief.

Section 3399 of the Civil Code provides: "When, through fraud or a mutual mistake of the parties, *or a mistake of one party, which the other at the time knew or suspected,* a written contract does not truly express the intention of the parties, it may be revised on the application of a party aggrieved, so as to express that intention, so far as it can be done without prejudice to rights acquired by third persons, in good faith and for value." (Italics added.)

Clearly there was a mistake, Joan and her attorney thinking that a $550,000 value resulted in a community equity of about $70,000. The mistake was known to Tim's former attorney who swept it under the rug in the counter-offer by setting forth just the equity, instead of the value minus encumbrances, as he did with respect to other properties. True, he apparently justified this to himself morally by the fact that the value which Tim had been claiming all along resulted in a $70,000 equity, but he never drew the other side's attention to the fact that the counter-offer was based on Tim's previous position on the value of the Holt property. Joan and her attorney were, of course, quite satisfied in believing that Tim had surrendered his point on Holt since she was to abandon her position with respect to the ownership of 13,000 shares and the method of valuing of the entire block of 20,500 shares. Inasmuch as the error was discovered by Tim's attorney, it is, of course, no defense that it was negligently made by Joan's attorney. Nor was the defense based on any such theory. Rather what the defense proceeded to do was to isolate the problem of the correct valuation of the Holt property from all others that were on the table during the final settlement negotiations, by offering proof that it was worth no more than an amount which would result in the $70,000 equity. The trial court clearly went along with this approach, permitted Tim to prove the value of the Holt property by expert testimony and other means, found that the property was worth no more than $425,000, that Joan had received an equitable division of the community property "and that no reformation is required for said reason."

Joan's counsel at all times resisted this compartmentalization of the issues that divided the parties before the property settlement agreement was signed. He was, of course, quite correct. If it is the law that reformation in this case can only be had if the trial court felt that the division of community property was fair, how could it possibly make such a finding based only on the value of the Holt property? As noted, Joan's extremely tenable position with respect to the stock would, if sustained, have been worth about $40,000, while the fight over the Holt property meant only $25,000. How did the trial court take into account the fact that Joan waived alimony? What the court did, in effect, was to retry just one of the many issues that could have arisen in a litigated divorce, to find that she would not have prevailed on that issue and to conclude from that that the entire property settlement agreement was fair.

This approach was wholly wrong. It ignores that the parties had settled their claims, thereby giving up any right to have a court determine them. That goes for Tim, as well as for Joan. The only legitimate question which was before the trial court was whether the settlement agreement should be reformed to express Joan's intent which was known to Tim who also knew, through his attorney, that the instrument did not express it.

Counsel for Tim argues, as defendants in these cases usually do, that Tim never intended to enter into a settlement based on the $550,000 figure and that a court of equity cannot make a new contract for the parties, whether a mistake is unilateral or bilateral. The law is, however, more subtle in that it estops the party who knows of the plaintiff's mistake from claiming that his intent differs from what he leads the other to believe it is. In *Eagle Indem. Co. v. Industrial Acc. Com.*, 92 Cal.App.2d 222, an insurer knew that a certain policy did not provide for certain coverage, and that the insured thought it did. It was held that the policy was subject to reformation according to the insured's intent. "Petitioner argues that the commission by ordering reformation of the policy created a new contract for the parties. Of course, reformation cannot be ordered so as to create a new and different contract for the parties but where, as here, the case falls within the language of Civil Code, section 3399, '[w]hen, through * * * a mistake of one party, which the other * * * knew or suspected, a written contract does not truly express the intention of the parties * * *' *' *' *' *' the contract which was intended by the party acting under unilateral mistake known or suspected by the other, is, as a matter of law, the contract of the parties. * * *'" Indeed, in view of the express wording of section 3399 of the Civil Code any other rule would thwart the legislative intent.

The rule that the party who misleads another is estopped from claiming that the contract is anything but what the other is led to believe, appears to be quite generally accepted. Citing many cases from other jurisdictions and noting no contrary authority Corbin says: "Reformation may be a proper remedy even though the mistake is not mutual. If one of the parties mistakenly believes that the writing is a correct integration of that to which he had expressed his assent and the other party knows that it is not, reformation may be decreed. The conduct of the other party in permitting the first to execute the erroneous writing and later attempting to enforce it may be regarded as fraudulent; but it is enough to justify reformation that he knows the terms proposed by the first party and the meaning thereof and leads that party reasonably to believe that he too assents to those terms. This makes a contract; and the writing may be reformed to accord with it. The fact that the first party was negligent in failing to observe that the writing does not express what he has assented to does not deprive him of this remedy. The ground for estoppel is against the other and non-mistaken party, not against the mistaken party even though he is negligent." (3 Corbin on Contracts, § 614) The rule is also in accord with the Restatement of Contracts.[8]

Therefore the fact stressed over and over again by defendant, that he never affirmatively assented to a $550,000 valuation, is quite immaterial.

The trial court made a number of detailed findings, some of which are quite evidentiary and argumentative, which are attacked as being without support in the

---

8. The rule is stated in section 505 of the Restatement. In comment (a) it said: " * * * Reformation where it is available for mutual mistake precludes a power of avoidance of the contract. On the other hand, where a reformation is based on mistake of one party and fraud of the other the defrauded party has also as an alternative the power of avoidance." In 42 Cal.Jur.2d "Reformation" section 31, the authors cite the Restatement comment for the proposition that "knowledge or reason on the part of one party to suspect that the other's intention is something different from that which the writing expresses affords ground for reformation, but not for avoidance." No cases are cited to support this startling announcement which rests, of course, on a misreading of the Restatement.

evidence. There is no need to discuss all of them, since several only relate to the basic misconception that Tim's lack of affirmative assent to the higher value vitiates Joan's right to reformation. We only discuss those which, if founded on evidence, might support the judgment.

The court found four different times that plaintiff knew that the counter-offer was not based on the $550,000 value. There just is nothing in the record to support that finding. Even if we attach no sinister significance to the fact that the counter-offer did not set forth the value on which the $70,000 equity depended and on the fact that no value was mentioned during the negotiations of February 16, 1968, we are still left with a plaintiff who mistakenly believed that her valuation had been accepted and a defendant who knew of that belief.[9]

The court found that Joan would have entered into the property settlement agreement if she had not obtained the acceptance of the $550,000 valuation. This, of course, is a far cry from finding that she would have settled if she had known that the settlement was based on $450,000. In any event there is nothing whatever in the record to support the finding. Tim argues that the finding is justified by Joan's knowledge he would not accept her $550,000 figure. As we have shown that finding is not supported in the evidence. The finding is thus based solely on conjecture. Settlement negotiations of the kind that were had between the parties are usually nothing but a high stake game of poker. Since it appears that each was holding the cards close to the vest, it does not appear possible to determine judicially who was bluffing. Finally we have found no case which indicates that it matters what Joan would have done had Tim been more frank. By permitting her to enter into the contract in the belief that he had accepted her $550,000 value, he simply took the risk that if she discovered the mistake and sought judicial redress, the contract would be enforced on the terms which she mistakenly thought she had already received.

The court found that Tim did not conceal any item of community property and that he disclosed the "nature, description and value" of all the items. What Tim concealed, however, was his discovery of the error or errors, which concealment, or to put it more charitably, which lack of disclosure is the nub of this litigation.

---

9. Above we suggested that Tim's attorney possibly justified his actions morally by the fact that the figure in the counter offer was based on, as he put it, "something like a $450,000 value." Actually the offer was not based on such a value but on, to be precise, a value of $448,526.99. If Tim's attorney also spotted the mistake which Joan's attorney made when dividing $141,637.01 by 2 and coming up with $70,081.85, it becomes rather obvious that he was not making an offer based on $450,000, but rather thought to lull Joan by repeating the mathematical error. In fairness, however, it should be noted that the evidence is susceptible of the interpretation that the attorney knew of the $100,000 mistake, but not of the other. It seems unlikely, however, that the latter escaped the attention of the accountant.

The case was fully tried and, as we said at the outset of our discussion, the record supports nothing but a judgment for the plaintiff as prayed.

QUESTIONS AND NOTES

1. Note that in this case Ms. Tate is granted reformation of the contract, which is then enforced against Mr. Tate. This result is justified because Mr. Tate and his lawyer knew of her error. Suppose the lawyer and Mr. Tate had not been aware of the mistake. What remedies, if any, would Ms. Tate be entitled to: relief from enforcement of the contract, rescission, reformation?

2. What should Mr. Tate's lawyer have done when he became aware of the mistake? Suppose the lawyer advised Mr. Tate of the mistake and counseled him not to take unfair advantage of his poor ex-wife, but Mr. Tate just laughed. Would his attorney be free under the Rules of Professional Conduct to say anything to Ms. Tate or her lawyer? What could he do? Consider the following ethics opinion:

ABA STANDING COMMITTEE ON ETHICS AND PROFESSIONAL RESPONSIBILITY, INFORMAL OPINION 86–1518 (FEB. 9, 1986)

A and B, with the assistance of their lawyers, have negotiated a commercial contract. After deliberation with counsel, A ultimately acquiesced in the final provision insisted upon by B, previously in dispute between the parties and without which B would have refused to come to overall agreement. However, A's lawyer discovered that the final draft of the contract typed in the office of B's lawyer did not contain the provision which had been in dispute. The Committee has been asked to give its opinion as to the ethical duty of A's lawyer in that circumstance.

The Committee considers this situation to involve merely a scrivener's error, not an intentional change in position by the other party. A meeting of the minds has already occurred. The Committee concludes that the error is appropriate for correction between the lawyers without client consultation.[19]

A's lawyer does not have a duty to advise A of the error pursuant to any obligation of communication under Rule 1.4 of the ABA Model Rules of Professional Conduct (1983). "The guiding principle is that the lawyer should fulfill reasonable client expectations for information consistent with the duty to act in

---

19. Assuming for purposes of discussion that the error is "information relating to [the] representation," under Rule 1.6 disclosure would be "impliedly authorized in order to carry out the representation." The Comment to Rule 1.6 points out that a lawyer has implied authority to make "a disclosure that facilitates a satisfactory conclusion"—in this case completing the commercial contract already agreed upon and left to the lawyers to memorialize. We do not here reach the issue of the lawyer's duty if the client wishes to exploit the error.

the client's best interests and the client's overall requirements as to the character of representation." Comment to Rule 1.4. In this circumstance there is no "informed decision," in the language of Rule 1.4, that A needs to make; the decision on the contract has already been made by the client. Furthermore, the Comment to Rule 1.2 points out that the lawyer may decide the "technical" means to be employed to carry out the objective of the representation, without consultation with the client.

The client does not have a right to take unfair advantage of the error. The client's right pursuant to Rule 1.2 to expect committed and dedicated representation is not unlimited. Indeed, for A's lawyer to suggest that A has an opportunity to capitalize on the clerical error, unrecognized by B and B's lawyer, might raise a serious question of the violation of the duty of A's lawyer under Rule 1.2(d) not to counsel the client to engage in, or assist the client in, conduct the lawyer knows is fraudulent. In addition, Rule 4.1(b) admonishes the lawyer not knowingly to fail to disclose a material fact to a third person when disclosure is necessary to avoid assisting a fraudulent act by a client, and Rule 8.4(c) prohibits the lawyer from engaging in conduct involving dishonesty, fraud, deceit, or misrepresentation.

The result would be the same under the predecessor ABA Model Code of Professional Responsibility (1969, revised 1980). While EC 7–8 teaches that a lawyer should use best efforts to ensure that the client's decisions are made after the client has been informed of relevant considerations, and EC 9–2 charges the lawyer with fully and promptly informing the client of material developments, the scrivener's error is neither a relevant consideration nor a material development and therefore does not establish an opportunity for a client's decision. The duty of zealous representation in DR 7–101 is limited to lawful objectives. See DR 7–102. Rule 1.2 evolved from DR 7–102(A)(7), which prohibits a lawyer from counseling or assisting the client in conduct known to be fraudulent. See also DR 1–102(A)(4), the precursor of Rule 8.4(c), prohibiting the lawyer from engaging in conduct involving dishonesty, fraud, deceit, or misrepresentation.

The standards governing the ethical dilemmas faced by Mr. Tate's lawyer will not be affected by the new Rules of Professional Conduct currently under consideration in California.f

3. Suppose no lawyers were involved. Would Mr. Tate or his non-lawyer advisor be able to take advantage of the other side's apparent miscalculation?

4. If you see an item in a store bearing a price tag that appears very low, are you free to buy the goods? Must you point out the low price and ask the storeowner whether he means it? If you don't ask, can the storeowner recover the goods later on a claim of mistake? Better yet, can the storeowner later prove that you had reason to know

there was a mistake and therefore reform the contract and make you pay the higher price for the goods?

---

(3) *Mistake in Performance.* A third kind of mistake is likely not to involve a contract at all. Sometimes one party in his performance exceeds the agreement. The question then arises whether he is entitled to compensation for the services he has rendered in the mistaken belief that they were required under a contract. The attendant at the filling station who thought you said, "fill it up," and did so when you only asked for $10 worth, may not have a contract with you because of the misunderstanding, but she wants to be paid for the tankful of gasoline. So does the paver who was supposed to put a new driveway in front of your neighbor's house but repaves your broken old driveway instead. These are traditional cases for relief, but not under a contract theory. Equitable, restitutionary, and "quasi-contract" principles are available to provide compensation and prevent unjust enrichment in at least the more outrageous of these cases.

(4) *Misunderstandings.* In some cases the error occurs somewhere in the communications between the parties. The language reasonably used by one party to refer to something is reasonably understood by the other party as referring to something else; the parties are simply not talking about the same thing. In fact, no agreement is reached in these cases, and the likely conclusion is that there is no contract because none was ever made.

RESTATEMENT, SECOND, CONTRACTS:

§ 20. Effect of Misunderstanding.

(1) There is no manifestation of mutual assent to an exchange if the parties attach materially different meanings to their manifestations and

    (a) neither party knows or has reason to know the meaning attached by the other; or

    (b) each party knows or each party has reason to know the meaning attached by the other.

(2) The manifestations of the parties are operative in accordance with the meaning attached to them by one of the parties if

    (a) that party does not know of any different meaning attached by the other, and the other knows the meaning attached by the first party; or

    (b) that party has no reason to know of any different meaning attached by the other, and the other has reason to know the meaning attached by the first party.

§ 201. Whose Meaning Prevails.

(1) Where the parties have attached the same meaning to a promise or agreement or a term thereof, it is interpreted in accordance with that meaning.

(2) Where the parties have attached different meanings to a promise or agreement or a term thereof, it is interpreted in accordance with the meaning attached by one of them if at the time the agreement was made

    (a) that party did not know of any different meaning attached by the other, and the other knew the meaning attached by the first party; or

    (b) that party had no reason to know of any different meaning attached by the other, and the other had reason to know the meaning attached by the first party.

(3) Except as stated in this Section, neither party is bound by the meaning attached by the other, even though the result may be a failure of mutual assent.

Raffles v. Wichelhaus

Court of Exchequer, 1864.
2 Hurl. & C. 906.

Declaration.—For that it was agreed between the plaintiff and the defendants, to wit, at Liverpool, that the plaintiff should sell to the defendants, and the defendants buy of the plaintiff, certain goods, to wit, 125 bales of Surat cotton, guarantied middling fair merchant's Dhollorah, to arrive ex "Peerless" from Bombay; and that the cotton should be taken from the quay, and that the defendants would pay the plaintiff for the same at a certain rate, to wit, at the rate of 17¼ d. per pound, within a certain time then agreed upon after the arrival of the said goods in England.— *Averments*: that the said goods did arrive by the said ship from Bombay in England, to wit, Liverpool, and the plaintiff was then and there ready and willing and offered to deliver the said goods to the defendants, & c. *Breach*: that the defendants refused to accept the said goods or pay the plaintiff for them.

Plea.—That the said ship mentioned in the said agreement was meant and intended by the defendants to be the ship called the "Peerless," which sailed from Bombay, to wit, in October; and that the plaintiff was not ready and willing and did not offer to deliver to the defendants any bales of cotton which arrived by the last-mentioned ship, but instead thereof was only ready and willing and offered to deliver to the defendants 125 bales of Surat cotton which arrived by another and different ship, which was also called the "Peerless," and which sailed from Bombay, to wit, in December.

Demurrer, and joinder therein.

Milward, in support of the demurrer.—The contract was for the sale of a number of bales of cotton of a particular description, which the plaintiff was ready to deliver. It is immaterial by what ship the cotton was to arrive, so that it was a ship called the "Peerless." The words "to arrive ex 'Peerless,'" only mean that if the vessel is lost on the voyage, the contract is to be at an end. [POLLOCK, C.B.—It would be a question for the jury whether both parties meant the same ship called the "Peerless."] That would be so if the contract was for the sale of a ship called the "Peerless;" but it is for the sale of cotton on board a ship of that name. [POLLOCK, C.B.—The defendant only bought that cotton which was to arrive by a particular ship. It may as well be said, that if there is a contract for the purchase of certain goods in warehouse A., that is satisfied by the delivery of goods of the same description in warehouse B.] In that case there would be goods in both warehouses; here it does not appear that the plaintiff had any goods on board the other "Peerless." [MARTIN, B.—It is imposing on the defendant a contract different from that which he entered into. POLLOCK, C.B.—It is like a contract for the purchase of wine coming from a particular estate in France or Spain, where there are two estates of that name.] The defendant has no right to contradict by parol evidence a written contract good upon the face of it. He does not impute misrepresentation or fraud, but only says that he fancied the ship was a different one. Intention is of no avail, unless stated at the time of the contract. [POLLOCK, C.B.—One vessel sailed in October and the other in December.] The time of sailing is no part of the contract.

Mellish (Cohen with him), in support of the plea.—There is nothing on the face of the contract to show that any particular ship called the "Peerless" was meant; but the moment it appears that two ships called the "Peerless" were about to sail from Bombay there is a latent ambiguity, and parol evidence may be given for the purpose of showing that the defendant meant one "Peerless" and the plaintiff another. That being so, there was no consensus ad idem, and therefore no binding contract. He was then stopped by the Court.

PER CURIAM. There must be judgment for the defendants.

QUESTIONS AND NOTES

1. Most of this report consists of the argument among counsel (Milward, Mellish, and Cohen) and the judges (Chief Baron Pollock and Baron Martin). What was the court's opinion in this case?

2. If there were not two ships named *Peerless* involved in this case, but the goods merely arrived two months late, would the court find that the buyer had to accept the goods anyway? Would the court be likely to find no binding contract?

3. The significance of there being two ships named *Peerless* may relate to the scheduled arrival dates of the ships and the buyer's position as a cotton merchant who resells the cotton in anticipation of its arrival. If there were two ships named *Peerless* and they arrived at Liverpool fifteen minutes apart, would it make any difference if seller meant one ship and buyer was thinking of the other? Suppose buyer was a consumer of raw cotton who maintained a warehouse full of inventory for his manufacturing operation so that, whether this shipment arrived in October or December, it could be expected to sit in the inventory for many months before being used. Wouldn't there be just as much of a misunderstanding in either of these circumstances? Would the contract be enforced?

---

(5) *Mistake in Basic Assumptions.* The preceding kinds of mistake are relatively noncontroversial. The law's major problem with contract mistake arises in those situations where an agreement apparently is reached, and the language is correctly recorded, but the parties were mistaken in the sense that some of the relevant assumptions upon which the deal was based were incorrect.

Imagine the situation in which A sells B a pebble which they both believe to be a diamond; or A sells B a diamond which they both believe to be a pretty pebble. At least on the surface there is no misunderstanding in this case because both parties are referring to the same rock. The mistake is in their assumption, which may be tacit or explicit, as to the nature of the rock, diamond, or pretty pebble. If the mistake is entertained by only one of the parties, as when one believes the stone to be a diamond and the other knows that it is a pebble, the situation begins to look like a misunderstanding at best, and like fraud at worst. The line here between legitimate, shrewd business dealing and fraud by nondisclosure is a fine one. Recall also the fine line between legitimate sales enthusiasm and fraudulent misrepresentation we have just considered in the preceding subsection and notice the overtones of mistake it contains.

Beachcomber Coins v. Boskett

New Jersey Superior Court, Appellate Division, 1979.
166 N.J.Super. 442, 400 A.2d 78.

■ CONFORD, P. J. A. D. Plaintiff, a retail dealer in coins, brought an action for rescission of a purchase by it from defendant for $500 of a dime purportedly minted in 1916 at Denver. Defendant is a part-time coin dealer. Plaintiff asserts a mutual mistake of fact as to the genuineness of the coin as Denver-minted, such a coin being a rarity and therefore having a market value greatly in excess of its normal monetary worth. Plaintiff's evidence at trial that the "D" on the coin signifying Denver mint-age was counterfeited is not disputed by defendant. Although at trial defendant disputed that the coin tendered back to him by plaintiff was the one he sold, the implicit trial finding is to the contrary, and that issue is not raised on appeal.

The trial judge, sitting without a jury, held for defendant on the ground that the customary "coin dealing procedures" were for a dealer purchasing a coin to make his own investigation of the genuineness of the coin and to "assume the risk" of his purchase if his investigation is faulty. The judge conceded that the evidence demonstrated satisfaction of the ordinary requisites of the rule of rescission for mutual mistake of fact that both parties act under a mistake of fact and that the fact be "central" (material) to the making of the contract. The proofs were that the seller had himself acquired this coin and two others of minor value for a total of $450 and that his representative had told the purchaser that he would not sell the dime for less than $500. The principal of plaintiff firm spent from 15 to 45 minutes in close examination of the coin before purchasing it. Soon thereafter he received an offer of $700 for the coin subject to certification of its genuineness by the American Numismatic Society. That organization labeled it a counterfeit, and as a result plaintiff instituted the present action.

The evidence and trial judge's findings establish this as a classic case of rescission for mutual mistake of fact. As a general rule,

> * * * where parties on entering into a transaction that affects their contractual relations are both under a mistake regarding a fact assumed by them as the basis on which they entered into the transaction, it is voidable by either party if enforcement of it would be materially more onerous to him than it would have been had the fact been as the parties believed it to be.

Restatement, Contracts § 502 (1932).[1]

By way of example, the Restatement posits the following: "A contracts to sell to B a specific bar of silver before them. The parties supposed that the bar is sterling. It has, however, a much larger admixture of base metal. The contract is voidable by B."

Moreover, "negligent failure of a party to know or to discover the facts as to which both parties are under a mistake does not preclude rescission or reformation on account thereof." Restatement, [Contracts] § 502. The law of New Jersey is in

---

1. No substantial change in the rule was effected by Restatement, Contracts 2d, § 294(1).... This provides:

> (1) Where a mistake of both parties at the time a contract was made has a material effect on the agreed exchange of performances, the contract is voidable by the adversely affected party unless he bears the risk of the mistake under the rule stated in § 296.

The exceptions in § 296 are not here applicable.

accord. *See Riviere v. Berla* (1918). In the *Riviere* case relief was denied only because the parties could not be restored to the status quo ante. In the present case they can be. It is undisputed that both parties believed that the coin was a genuine Denver-minted one. The mistake was mutual in that both parties were laboring under the same misapprehension as to this particular, essential fact. The price asked and paid was directly based on that assumption. That plaintiff may have been negligent in his inspection of the coin (a point not expressly found but implied by the trial judge) does not, as noted above, bar its claim for rescission.

Defendant's contention that plaintiff assumed the risk that the coin might be of greater or lesser value than that paid is not supported by the evidence. It is well established that a party to a contract can assume the risk of being mistaken as to the value of the thing sold. The Restatement states the rule this way:

> Where the parties know that there is doubt in regard to a certain matter and contract on that assumption, the contract is not rendered voidable because one is disappointed in the hope that the facts accord with his wishes. The risk of the existence of the doubtful fact is then assumed as one of the elements of the bargain.

Restatement, Contracts § 502, Comment *f*.

However, for the stated rule to apply, the parties must be conscious that the pertinent fact may not be true and make their agreement at the risk of that possibility. In this case both parties were certain that the coin was genuine. They so testified. Plaintiff's principal thought so after his inspection, and defendant would not have paid nearly $450 for it otherwise. A different case would be presented if the seller were uncertain either of the genuineness of the coin or of its value if genuine, and had accepted the expert buyer's judgment on these matters.

The trial judge's rationale of custom of the trade is not supported by the evidence. It depended upon the testimony of plaintiff's expert witness who on cross-examination as to the "procedure" on the purchase by a dealer of a rare coin, stated that the dealer would check it with magnification and then "normally send it to the American Numismatic Certification Service for certification." This testimony does not in our opinion establish that practice as a usage of trade "having such regularity of observance in a * * * trade as to justify an expectation that it will be observed with respect to the transaction in question," within the intent of the Uniform Commercial Code [§ 1–205(2)].[2]

The cited code provision contemplates that the trade usage is so prevalent as to warrant the conclusion that the parties contracted with reference to, and intended

---

2. Note, also, that evidence of a trade usage is not admissible unless the offering party gives the other party advance notice to prevent unfair surprise. Plaintiff received no notice that the judge intended to decide this case on the basis of the alleged trade usage.

their agreement to be governed by it. Our reading of the testimony does not indicate any basis for findings either that this was a trade usage within the Code definition at all or that these parties in fact accepted it as such to the extent that they were agreeing that because of it the sale was an "as is" transaction. Indeed, the same witness testified there was a "normal policy" among coin dealers throughout the United States of a "return privilege" for altered coins.

The foregoing conclusions make it unnecessary for us to discuss plaintiff's alternative contention that the contract was "unenforceable" because it constituted an illegal contract to purchase a counterfeit coin. We regard that position as devoid of merit.

Reversed.

QUESTIONS AND NOTES

1. The defendant sold the coin to the plaintiff for $500 and then the plaintiff quickly found a buyer for $700. If the defendant testified at trial that the fair market value of the coin was $700, but he sold it for $500 because he was not sure that the coin was genuine, what result?

2. Can the defendant prevent this type of problem in the future by posting a sign or adding a clause to the sales contract that all sales are final and all risks are assumed by the buyer?

3. What if the Seller were not a coin-dealer? Would the coin-dealer Buyer still have a right to return the coin and get its money back?

4. Does the defendant now have a cause of action against whoever sold him the counterfeit coin?

Lenawee County Board of Health v. Messerly

Michigan Supreme Court, 1982.
417 Mich. 17, 331 N.W.2d 203.

■ RYAN, J. In March of 1977, Carl and Nancy Pickles, appellees, purchased from appellants, William and Martha Messerly, a 600–square–foot tract of land upon which is located a three-unit apartment building. Shortly after the transaction was closed, the Lenawee County Board of Health condemned the property and obtained a permanent injunction which prohibits human habitation on the premises until the defective sewage system is brought into conformance with the Lenawee County sanitation code.

We are required to determine whether appellees should prevail in their attempt to avoid this land contract on the basis of mutual mistake and failure of consideration. We conclude that the parties did entertain a mutual misapprehension of fact, but that the circumstances of this case do not warrant rescission.

I

The trial court found that, prior to this transfer, the Messerlys' predecessor in title, Mr. Bloom, had installed a septic tank on the property without a permit and in violation of the applicable health code....

... After inspecting the property, Mr. and Mrs. Pickles executed a new land contract with the Messerlys on March 21, 1977. It provided for a purchase price of $25,500. A clause was added to the end of the land contract form which provides:

> "17. Purchaser has examined this property and agrees to accept same in its present condition. There are no other or additional written or oral understandings."

Five or six days later, when the Pickleses went to introduce themselves to the tenants, they discovered raw sewage seeping out of the ground. Tests conducted by a sanitation expert indicated the inadequacy of the sewage system. The Lenawee County Board of Health subsequently condemned the property and initiated this lawsuit in the Lenawee Circuit Court against the Messerlys as land contract vendors, and the Pickleses, as vendees, to obtain a permanent injunction proscribing human habitation of the premises until the property was brought into conformance with the Lenawee County sanitation code. The injunction was granted, and the Lenawee County Board of Health was permitted to withdraw from the lawsuit by stipulation of the parties.

After a bench trial, the court concluded that the Pickleses had no cause of action against either the Messerlys or the Barneses as there was no fraud or misrepresentation. This ruling was predicated on the trial judge's conclusion that none of the parties knew of Mr. Bloom's earlier transgression or of the resultant problem with the septic system until it was discovered by the Pickleses, and that the sanitation problem was not caused by any of the parties. The trial court held that the property was purchased "as is," after inspection and, accordingly, its "negative * * * value cannot be blamed upon an innocent seller." Foreclosure was ordered against the Pickleses, together with a judgment against them in the amount of $25,943.09.

Mr. and Mrs. Pickles appealed from the adverse judgment. The Court of Appeals unanimously affirmed the trial court's ruling with respect to Mr. and Mrs. Barnes but, in a two-to-one decision, reversed the finding of no cause of action on the Pickleses' claims against the Messerlys. It concluded that the mutual mistake between the Messerlys and the Pickleses went to a basic, as opposed to a collateral, element of the contract, and that the parties intended to transfer income-producing rental property but, in actuality, the vendees paid $25,500 for an asset without value.

We granted the Messerlys' application for leave to appeal.

II

We must decide initially whether there was a mistaken belief entertained by one or both parties to the contract in dispute and, if so, the resultant legal significance.

A contractual mistake "is a belief that is not in accord with the facts." 1 Restatement Contracts, 2d, § 151. The erroneous belief of one or both of the parties must relate to a fact in existence at the time the contract is executed. That is to say, the belief which is found to be in error may not be, in substance, a prediction as to a future occurrence or non-occurrence.

The Court of Appeals concluded, after a *de novo* review of the record, that the parties were mistaken as to the income-producing capacity of the property in question. We agree. The vendors and the vendees each believed that the property transferred could be utilized as income-generating rental property. All of the parties subsequently learned that, in fact, the property was unsuitable for any residential use.

Appellants assert that there was no mistake in the contractual sense because the defect in the sewage system did not arise until after the contract was executed. The appellees respond that the Messerlys are confusing the date of the inception of the defect with the date upon which the defect was discovered.

This is essentially a factual dispute which the trial court failed to resolve directly. Nevertheless, we are empowered to draw factual inferences from the facts found by the trial court.

An examination of the record reveals that the septic system was defective prior to the date on which the land contract was executed. The Messerlys' grantor installed a nonconforming septic system without a permit prior to the transfer of the property to the Messerlys in 1971. Moreover, virtually undisputed testimony indicates that, assuming ideal soil conditions, 2,500 square feet of property is necessary to support a sewage system adequate to serve a three-family dwelling. Likewise, 750 square feet is mandated for a one-family home. Thus, the division of the parcel and sale of one acre of the property by Mr. and Mrs. Barnes in 1976 made it impossible to remedy the already illegal septic system within the confines of the 600–square-foot parcel.

Appellants do not dispute these underlying facts which give rise to an inference contrary to their contentions.

Having determined that when these parties entered into the land contract they were laboring under a mutual mistake of fact, we now direct our attention to a determination of the legal significance of that finding.

A contract may be rescinded because of a mutual misapprehension of the parties, but this remedy is granted only in the sound discretion of the court. Appellants argue that the parties' mistake relates only to the quality or value of the real estate transferred, and that such mistakes are collateral to the agreement and do not justify rescission, citing *A & M Land Development Co. v. Miller*, 354 Mich. 681 (1959).

In that case, the plaintiff was the purchaser of 91 lots of real property. It sought partial rescission of the land contract when it was frustrated in its attempts to develop 42 of the lots because it could not obtain permits from the county health department to install septic tanks on these lots. This Court refused to allow rescission because the mistake, whether mutual or unilateral, related only to the value of the property.

There was here no mistake as to the form or substance of the contract between the parties, or the description of the property constituting the subject matter. The situation involved is not at all analogous to that presented in *Scott v. Grow*, 301 Mich. 226 (1942). There the plaintiff sought relief by way of reformation of a deed on the ground that the instrument of conveyance had not been drawn in accordance with the intention and agreement of the parties. It was held that the bill of complaint stated a case for the granting of equitable relief by way of reformation. In the case at bar plaintiff received the property for which it contracted. The fact that it may be of less value than the purchaser expected at the time of the transaction is not a sufficient basis for the granting of equitable relief, neither fraud nor reliance on misrepresentation of material facts having been established.

Appellees contend, on the other hand, that in this case the parties were mistaken as to the very nature of the character of the consideration and claim that the pervasive and essential quality of this mistake renders rescission appropriate. They cite in support of that view *Sherwood v. Walker*, 66 Mich. 568 (1887), the famous "barren cow" case. In that case, the parties agreed to the sale and purchase of a cow which was thought to be barren, but which was, in reality, with calf. When the seller discovered the fertile condition of his cow, he refused to deliver her. In permitting rescission, the Court stated:

> It seems to me, however, in the case made by this record, that the mistake or misapprehension of the parties went to the whole substance of the agreement. If the cow was a breeder, she was worth at least $750; if barren, she was worth not over $80. The parties would not have made the contract of sale except upon the understanding and belief that she was incapable of breeding, and of no use as a cow. It is true she is now the identical animal that they thought her to be

when the contract was made; there is no mistake as to the identity of the creature. Yet the mistake was not of the mere quality of the animal, but went to the
very nature of the thing. A barren cow is substantially a different creature than
a breeding one. There is as much difference between them for all purposes of
use as there is between an ox and a cow that is capable of breeding and giving
milk. If the mutual mistake had simply related to the fact whether she was with
calf or not for one season, then it might have been a good sale; but the mistake
affected the character of the animal for all time, and for her present and ultimate
use. She was not in fact the animal, or the kind of animal, the defendants intended to sell or the plaintiff to buy. She was not a barren cow, and, if this fact
had been known, there would have been no contract. The mistake affected the
substance of the whole consideration, and it must be considered that there was
no contract to sell or sale of the cow as she actually was. The thing sold and
bought had in fact no existence. She was sold as a beef creature would be sold;
she is in fact a breeding cow, and a valuable one.

The court should have instructed the jury that if they found that the cow
was sold, or contracted to be sold, upon the understanding of both parties that
she was barren, and useless for the purpose of breeding, and that in fact she was
not barren, but capable of breeding, then the defendants had a right to rescind,
and to refuse to deliver, and the verdict should be in their favor.

As the parties suggest, the foregoing precedent arguably distinguishes mistakes
affecting the essence of the consideration from those which go to its quality or value,
affording relief on a per se basis for the former but not the latter.

However, the distinctions which may be drawn from *Sherwood* and *A & M Land
Development Co.* do not provide a satisfactory analysis of the nature of a mistake sufficient to invalidate a contract. Often, a mistake relates to an underlying factual
assumption which, when discovered, directly affects value, but simultaneously and
materially affects the essence of the contractual consideration. It is disingenuous to
label such a mistake collateral.

Appellant and appellee both mistakenly believed that the property which was
the subject of their land contract would generate income as rental property. The fact
that it could not be used for human habitation deprived the property of its income-earning potential and rendered it less valuable. However, this mistake, while
directly and dramatically affecting the property's value, cannot accurately be characterized as collateral because it also affects the very essence of the consideration.
"The thing sold and bought [income generating rental property] had in fact no existence."

We find that the inexact and confusing distinction between contractual mistakes
running to value and those touching the substance of the consideration serves only
as an impediment to a clear and helpful analysis for the equitable resolution of cases

in which mistake is alleged and proven. Accordingly, the holdings of *A & M Land Development Co.* and *Sherwood* with respect to the material or collateral nature of a mistake are limited to the facts of those cases.

Instead, we think the better-reasoned approach is a case-by-case analysis whereby rescission is indicated when the mistaken belief relates to a basic assumption of the parties upon which the contract is made, and which materially affects the agreed performances of the parties.[11] Rescission is not available, however, to relieve a party who has assumed the risk of loss in connection with the mistake.[12]

All of the parties to this contract erroneously assumed that the property transferred by the vendors to the vendees was suitable for human habitation and could be utilized to generate rental income. The fundamental nature of these assumptions is indicated by the fact that their invalidity changed the character of the property transferred, thereby frustrating, indeed precluding, Mr. and Mrs. Pickles' intended use of the real estate. Although the Pickleses are disadvantaged by enforcement of the contract, performance is advantageous to the Messerlys, as the property at issue is less valuable absent its income-earning potential. Nothing short of rescission can remedy the mistake. Thus, the parties' mistake as to a basic assumption materially affects the agreed performances of the parties.

---

11. The parties have invited our attention to the first edition of the Restatement of Contracts in their briefs, and the Court of Appeals cites to that edition in its opinion. However, the second edition was published subsequent to the issuance of the lower court opinion and the filing of the briefs with this Court. Thus, we take it upon ourselves to refer to the latest edition to aid us in our resolution of this case.

Section 152 delineates the legal significance of a mistake.

> *§ 152. When Mistake of Both Parties Makes a Contract Voidable.*
>
> (1) Where a mistake of both parties at the time a contract was made as to a basic assumption on which the contract was made has a material effect on the agreed exchange of performances, the contract is voidable by the adversely affected party unless he bears the risk of the mistake under the rule stated in § 154.
>
> (2) In determining whether the mistake has a material effect on the agreed exchange of performances, account is taken of any relief by way of reformation, restitution, or otherwise.

12.   *§ 154. When a Party Bears the Risk of a Mistake.*

A party bears the risk of a mistake when

(a) the risk is allocated to him by agreement of the parties, or

(b) he is aware, at the time the contract is made, that he has only limited knowledge with respect to the facts to which the mistake relates but treats his limited knowledge as sufficient, or

(c) the risk is allocated to him by the court on the ground that it is reasonable in the circumstances to do so.

Despite the significance of the mistake made by the parties, we reverse the Court of Appeals because we conclude that equity does not justify the remedy sought by Mr. and Mrs. Pickles.

Rescission is an equitable remedy which is granted only in the sound discretion of the court. A court need not grant rescission in every case in which the mutual mistake relates to a basic assumption and materially affects the agreed performance of the parties.

In cases of mistake by two equally innocent parties, we are required, in the exercise of our equitable powers, to determine which blameless party should assume the loss resulting from the misapprehension they shared. Normally that can only be done by drawing upon our "own notions of what is reasonable and just under all the surrounding circumstances."

Equity suggests that, in this case, the risk should be allocated to the purchasers. We are guided to that conclusion, in part, by the standards announced in § 154 of the Restatement of Contracts 2d, for determining when a party bears the risk of mistake. See fn. 12. Section 154(a) suggests that the court should look first to whether the parties have agreed to the allocation of the risk between themselves. While there is no express assumption in the contract by either party of the risk of the property becoming uninhabitable, there was indeed some agreed allocation of the risk to the vendees by the incorporation of an "as is" clause into the contract which, we repeat, provided:

> "Purchaser has examined this property and agrees to accept same in its present condition. There are no other or additional written or oral understandings."

That is a persuasive indication that the parties considered that, as between them, such risk as related to the "present condition" of the property should lie with the purchaser. If the "as is" clause is to have any meaning at all, it must be interpreted to refer to those defects which were unknown at the time that the contract was executed. Thus, the parties themselves assigned the risk of loss to Mr. and Mrs. Pickles.

We conclude that Mr. and Mrs. Pickles are not entitled to the equitable remedy of rescission and, accordingly, reverse the decision of the Court of Appeals.

QUESTIONS AND NOTES

1. What was the mistake that the Pickleses assert justifies rescission and avoidance of the contract? Was this a unilateral or a mutual mistake, or either or neither? Frame a description of the circumstances in this case that will fit each of these categories.

2. On what basis does the court conclude that the burden of this mistake was allocated to the Pickleses? What is the significance of the "as is" clause, the concept of *caveat emptor,* the existence of an opportunity to inspect? Weren't the Messerlys under a comparable obligation to be aware of the status of their cesspool, whether their property was habitable under health regulations, and whether the property they were selling in fact could be rented without violating the law? If they were under an obligation to know about the state of the sanitary facilities in the apartment house they rented to others, why weren't they under an obligation to disclose this information to potential buyers like the Pickleses?

3. Why does the court in this case place the burden of mutual mistake on the buyer, while in *Beachcomber Coins* the burden is placed on the seller? Is there any way to reconcile these cases?

4. Consider the following factors that may be of help in deciding when to relieve a party from liability for a promise grounded on mistaken assumptions:

a. Was the mistake the fault of the mistaken party?

b. Is there a basis other than fault for allocating the risk to one side or the other? Are there grounds for saying one side either bought or was paid to assume this risk, that one side is in a better position to prevent it, to bear it, to distribute it?

c. Are there reasons to say that one side took advantage of the other? Was the relying party operating in good faith? Are there shades of fraud and unconscionability?

d. Can the contract be "rescinded" and the parties restored to the *status quo ante?*

Another type of mistake in assumptions involves erroneous assumptions as to future events. Mistakes of this kind also sometimes affect enforceability of an otherwise valid contract. This subject is covered in conjunction with Supervening Events, p. 757.

VI. RELEASE

The allocation of the risks of mistakes in assumptions is likely to arise in particularly dramatic form in situations where an injured party settles a claim and gives the liable party a release or when a party about to engage in a risky activity gives a release of potential liability to induce another to allow the activity to take place. In both situations there are strong reasons to allow the release to operate to allocate the risks or to settle the liability finally. In both situations, however, subsequent information may disclose that the parties were fundamentally mistaken when they agreed to the release. Two powerful interests (now) collide, and the result may be difficult to predict.

WEST'S ANN. CALIFORNIA CIVIL CODE:

§ 1541. Extinction of Obligations.

Obligation Extinguished by Release. An obligation is extinguished by a release therefrom given to the debtor by the creditor, upon a new consideration, or in writing, with or without new consideration.

§ 1542. General Release; Extent.

A general release does not extend to claims which the creditor does not know or suspect to exist in his or her favor at the time of executing the release, which if known by him or her must have materially affected his or her settlement with the debtor.

Olsen v. Breeze

California Court of Appeal, 1996
48 Cal.App.4th 608, 55 Cal.Rptr.2d 818

■ PUGLIA, PRESIDING JUSTICE. This appeal concerns the legality of a release from liability required as a condition for purchasing, renting, or obtaining service on ski bindings. For reasons hereafter discussed, we shall conclude the use of such releases in the ski industry does not violate either state unfair competition laws or the Consumers Legal Remedies Act.

I

Plaintiff, Philip A. Olsen, is an attorney and "avid recreational skier" who for many years has represented in personal injury litigation plaintiffs who sustained injuries skiing. In December 1993, plaintiff took his skis to a shop operated by defendant Breeze, Inc. (Breeze) to be serviced, including the adjustment of his ski bindings. As a condition for the return of his equipment, plaintiff was required to sign a form which described the risks of skiing and released Breeze from any liability for injury resulting from use of the equipment, including injury caused by negligence, breach of warranty, or product defect.[1] He refused to sign the form and was denied return of his equipment.

The requirement of a release by Breeze is consistent with industry custom. Ski equipment distributors throughout the state offer indemnity to retail and service outlets in the event of injury caused by the failure of ski bindings to release properly but only if the retailer or service provider has obtained the customer's signature on a release form supplied by the distributor, or one substantially similar thereto. This form is a release of liability, similar to that used by Breeze, often absolving both the retailer/service provider and the distributor from legal liability for injuries caused by failure of the equipment.

Plaintiff initiated this action on behalf of himself and all others in the State who own or seek to rent or purchase ski bindings of various brands. Named as defendants are six ski equipment distributors, Salomon/North America, Inc. (Salomon), Head Sports, Inc. (Head), Raichle–Molitor, USA, Inc. (Raichle), Geze Sports Products (Geze), Marker USA, Inc. (Marker), and Atomic Ski USA, Inc. (Atomic), who are alleged to supply "all, or substantially all," the ski bindings sold and rented in the state of California. Also named as defendants are Trimont Land Company (Trimont), the operator of two ski areas in Northern California, Breeze, a retailer/service provider and a class of all others situated similarly to either Trimont or Breeze. The trial court denied plaintiff's motion to certify a defendant class as alleged. Plaintiff does not challenge this ruling on appeal.

The complaint contains two causes of action. The first cause of action alleges violation of the Consumers Legal Remedies Act (CLRA). The second cause of action alleges unfair competition. Plaintiff alleges it is unlawful and unconscionable for defendants to require customers to sign releases of liability as a condition for obtaining goods or services. The CLRA cause of action is stated on behalf of a plaintiff class, while the unfair competition claim is stated on behalf of plaintiff alone. In addition to the two separately stated causes of action, the complaint contains two counts seeking, respectively, declaratory and injunctive relief.

Based on the modified releases, the various defendants moved for summary adjudication of the unfair competition cause of action and for a determination the

---

1. The release reads in relevant part:

I hereby release from any legal liability Breeze, Inc. (dba Breeze Ski Rentals) and its owners, agents and employees from any and all liability for damage and injury or death to myself or to any person or property resulting from the selection, installation, adjustment, maintenance or use of this equipment and for any claim based upon negligence, breach of warranty, contract, claim or product defect, or other legal theory, accepting myself, the full responsibility for any and all such damages or injury which may result.

CLRA claim is without merit. The superior court granted these motions as to all defendants except Head and Raichle and entered judgments of dismissal. Plaintiff appeals from these judgments.

The matter proceeded to trial before the court without a jury as to Head and Raichle. The court granted the motion of these defendants to vary the order of proof, permitting the issues whether Head adequately modified its release and whether Raichle is no longer in a position to modify its release to conform to California law to be tried first. Head presented evidence that it changed its release form and communicated this change to its retail outlets. Raichle presented evidence that it is no longer authorized to distribute ski bindings in California. Head and Raichle moved for judgment. The superior court granted the motions and entered judgments of dismissal. Plaintiff also appeals from these judgments.

II

We address first plaintiff's unfair competition cause of action. Business and Professions Code section 17200 defines unfair competition as "any unlawful, unfair or fraudulent business act or practice * * *." "The 'unlawful' practices prohibited by section 17200 are any practices forbidden by law, be it civil or criminal, federal, state, or municipal, statutory, regulatory, or court made. It is not necessary that the predicate law provide for private civil enforcement. As our Supreme Court put it, section 17200 'borrows' violations of other laws and treats them as unlawful practices independently actionable under section 17200 et seq. 'Unfair' simply means any practice whose harm to the victim outweighs its benefits. 'Fraudulent,' as used in the statute, does not refer to the common law tort of fraud but only requires a showing members of the public "are likely to be deceived."

Plaintiff contends the second cause of action states several forms of unfair competition associated with defendants' use of general releases, to wit: (1) imposing unenforceable contract terms; (2) using release forms likely to mislead the public; (3) causing the public to sign agreements they are not likely to understand; and (4) holding themselves out as competent while refusing to accept responsibility for their actions. Plaintiff argues the superior court erred in granting summary adjudication to Salomon, Breeze, Trimont, Atomic, and Marker as these defendants failed to negate all forms of unfair competition alleged.

Of the four categories of unfair competition relied upon by plaintiff, only the first, imposing unenforceable contract terms, requires more than a brief comment. In *People v. McKale*, the court concluded it was unfair competition for a mobile home park operator to require tenants to sign rules and regulations containing unlawful terms. Notwithstanding the defendant's argument that these rules and regulations were not being enforced, the court explained: "When a mobilehome park operator requires tenants to sign park rules and regulations which the park is prohibited by law from enforcing, those tenants are likely to be deceived, and allegations of unfair competition based thereon are sufficient to withstand demurrer."

In *Baker Pacific*, the court held void as against public policy a release required as a condition of employment which contained terms violative of Civil Code section 1668. Civil Code section 1668 declares violative of public policy contracts which "have for their object, directly or indirectly, to exempt anyone from the responsibility for his own fraud, or willful injury to the person or property of another, or violation of law, whether willful or negligent * * *." Pursuant to the release at issue in *Baker Pacific*, a subscribing employee undertook to assume "all risks" of exposure to asbestos, covenanted not to sue "for, from and against any and all liability whatsoever," and waived "any and all claims of every nature" relating to asbestos exposure. The court concluded this language "clearly includes a release from liability for fraud and intentional acts and thus on its face violates the public policy as set forth in Civil Code section 1668."

Baker Pacific is inapposite. That decision rests on the existence of a public interest in the employer-employee relationship. Where the public interest is implicated, an agreement exempting a party from responsibility for negligence is void as against public policy.

When the public interest is not implicated, private parties are free among themselves to shift a risk elsewhere than where the law would otherwise place it. Such agreements, in the context of sporting or recreational activities, have consistently been enforced. In *Westlye*, we held the public interest does not preclude enforcement of an agreement to bar claims for negligent adjustment of ski bindings.

Plaintiff's reliance on *Westlye*, as it relates to strict liability claims, is also misplaced. Assuming defendants were under a legal obligation to modify their releases in accordance with *Westlye*, nearly all did so during the pendency of this proceeding. For example, the original release of Salomon included "any claim based upon negligence, breach of warranty, contract, claim of product defect or other legal theory." As modified, the release reads, "any claim based upon negligence, breach of warranty, contract, or other legal theory." Atomic, whose original release did not mention product defect or strict liability, added language reading: "This document is a legally binding contract which is in[t]ended to provide a comprehensive release of liability, but is not intended to assert any claims or defenses which are prohibited by law."

The lone exception is Marker, whose modified release encompasses all claims based on "negligence, breach of warranty, strict products liability or any other legal theories." However, Marker's modified release also states: "This document * * * is intended to provide a comprehensive release of liability, but it is not intended to assert any claims of defenses which are prohibited by law. The specific rights of the parties may vary from state to state."

Plaintiff contends the modified releases are unlawful despite these changes because they are ambiguous regarding product defect or strict liability claims. Plaintiff insists defendants' releases must expressly exclude such claims. As we shall explain, post, defendants are under no duty to outline in their releases the details of their customers' legal rights. As long as the releases do not expressly include strict liability claims or, alternatively, do exclude claims prohibited by law, which in this state would embrace strict liability claims, they comply with the decision in *Westlye*.

Plaintiff argues that modification to comply with *Westlye* does not preclude injunctive relief to prohibit repetition of past misconduct. Defendants concede an injunction may be issued to prevent recurrence of past misconduct. However, even assuming the use of the old releases was actionable, Business and Professions Code section 17203 provides a court "may" enjoin any person who has engaged in unfair competition. The trial court presumably chose not to exercise this power and we find no abuse of discretion under the circumstances.

We now consider plaintiff's theory the releases are unlawful because they are unconscionable. Plaintiff argues the agreements skiers are required to sign are contracts of adhesion which are objectively unreasonable under the circumstances presented. Specifically, he cites the sweeping use of releases in the ski industry and the unreasonableness of shifting the risk of injury away from the only party in a position to protect against it.

Assuming the doctrine of unconscionability may be used affirmatively as the predicate of an unfair competition claim, it is inapplicable here. Unconscionable agreements typically involve contractual provisions which operate in a harsh and one-sided manner without any justification. They have both a procedural and a substantive element. "The procedural element focuses on two factors: oppression and surprise. Oppression arises from an inequality of bargaining power which results in no real negotiation and an absence of meaningful choice. Surprise involves the extent to which the terms of the bargain are hidden in a 'prolix printed form' drafted by a party in a superior bargaining position. Substantive unconscionability inquires into whether the one-sidedness of an agreement is objectively justified. This component is tied to procedural unconscionability and requires a balancing test, such that "the greater the unfair surprise or inequality of bargaining power, the less unreasonable the risk reallocation which will be tolerated.'"

For purposes of defendants' summary adjudication motions, we consider the evidence in the light most favorable to plaintiff. Based on this evidence, and the reasonable inferences which may be drawn therefrom, the ultimate question of unconscionability is one of law which we consider de novo.

There is nothing inherently unreasonable in skiers agreeing with ski equipment distributors or service providers to allocate to skiers the risk of injury from failure of a ski binding to release properly. Skiers already assume the risks inherent in the sport. The releases at issue deal with risks associated with negligent acts which increase the risks inherent in skiing. Furthermore, consumers are not denied a meaningful choice by virtue of the common use of releases. Their choice to ski already exposes them to a number of risks inherent in that activity. Skiing, like other athletic or recreational pursuits, however beneficial, is not an essential activity.

Furthermore, even assuming an inequality of bargaining power, there is no credible evidence release agreements are a surprise to skiers. The agreements themselves are short and the pertinent release language is as prominent as other language in the form. There is no evidence defendants conceal or misrepresent the language of the release in order to obscure its effect. Given the prevalence of releases in sporting and recreational activities, the failure of defendants to utilize releases of liability would be the greater surprise.

This is not to say that under appropriate circumstances we would not find a broadly or vaguely worded release unconscionable. However, such a determination must await those circumstances. Courts do not render advisory opinions. Courts deal with actual, not hypothetical, controversies. All we conclude here is that it is not unconscionable for ski equipment distributors and retailers to require and use the releases at issue as a condition for doing business with them.

We turn now to plaintiff's alternative theories of unfair competition. Plaintiff contends defendants' practices are likely to mislead the public regarding their legal rights and cause customers to sign releases they do not understand. However, the complaint alleges only that defendants require customers to sign releases. It alleges no conduct by which defendants mislead their customers or cause them to sign documents they do not comprehend. Nor has plaintiff presented any such evidence.

In order effectively to exculpate a tortfeasor from liability for future negligence or other misconduct, a release "must be clear, unambiguous and explicit in expressing the intent of the parties." "Such an agreement, read as a whole, must clearly notify the prospective releasor or indemnitor of the effect of signing the agreement." A release effective as to one type of misconduct may not be effective as to another.

The mere fact a release is not sufficiently clear to be enforceable under all conceivable circumstances does not render its use unfair competition. We are aware of no general duty owed by one contracting party to another to explain the other's legal rights in connection with the agreement. We will not presume a contracting party who is uncertain regarding the breadth of a release will interpret the document broadly and thereby forego relief which would otherwise be available. We assume contracting parties are aware of their legal rights or will seek competent legal assistance where necessary. It is pure speculation a party faced with a release which may or may not cover a given injury will forego the possibility of redress.

This does not change merely because the party obtaining a release of liability holds himself out as competent to perform the task in question. While it may be good business to stand behind one's work, this is not an obligation imposed by law absent other circumstances.

QUESTIONS AND NOTES

1. Should companies seeking release agreements like the ski binding manufacturers have a dual pricing system? If you release them of all liability, you can rent skis for $20, but if you wish to retain your right to sue, you must pay $100. Would anyone really pay $80 more just for an intangible right to sue?

2. If ski shops can agree with their customers that they will not be liable to the customer for negligently adjusted ski bindings, why shouldn't lawyers be able to agree with their clients that the lawyer will "do his best" but will not be liable for the negligent preparation of a legal document?

Leon v. Family Fitness Center

California Court of Appeal, 1998.
61 Cal.App.4th 1227, 71 Cal.Rptr.2d 923.

■ WORK, ACTING PRESIDING JUSTICE. Carlos Leon appeals a summary judgment entered in favor of Family Fitness Center, Inc. (Family Fitness) in his negligence action for personal injuries sustained when a bench collapsed beneath him while using the sauna at Family Fitness. Leon contends the trial court erroneously concluded there were no triable issues of material fact regarding whether the liability release contained in the retail installment contract he signed was legally adequate to exculpate Family Fitness from its own negligence and whether the release was obtained by fraud or overreaching in its inception. On de novo review, we conclude the purported release is neither sufficiently conspicuous nor unambiguous to insulate Family Fitness from liability to Leon for injuries received when its sauna bench collapsed. Accordingly, we reverse the judgment and remand the matter for further proceedings.

FACTUAL AND PROCEDURAL BACKGROUND

Carlos Leon signed a Club Membership Agreement (Retail Installment Contract) on June 1993 and thereafter became a member of Family Fitness. The membership agreement is a legal-length single sheet of paper covered with writing front and back. The front page is divided into two columns, with the right-hand column containing blanks for insertion of financial and "Federal Truth in Lending" data plus approximately 76 lines of text of varying sizes, some highlighted with bold print. The left-hand column contains approximately 90 lines of text undifferentiated as to size, with no highlighting and no paragraph headings or any other indication of its contents. The back of the agreement contains approximately 90 lines of text. The exculpatory clause is located at the bottom of the left-hand column of the front page and states the following:

> Buyer is aware that participation in a sport or physical exercise may result in accidents or injury, and Buyer assumes the risk connected with the participation in a sport or exercise and represents that Member is in good health and suffers from no physical impairment which would limit their use of FFC's facilities. Buyer acknowledges that FFC has not and will not render any medical services including medical diagnosis of Member's physical condition. Buyer specifically agrees that FFC, its officers, employees and agents shall not be liable for any claim, demand, cause of action of any kind whatsoever for, or on account of death, personal injury, property damage or loss of any kind resulting from or related to Member's use of the facilities or participation in any sport, exercise or activity within or without the club premises, and Buyer agrees to hold FFC harmless from same.

In January 1994, Leon sustained head injuries when a sauna bench on which he was lying collapsed beneath him at Family Fitness. After Leon filed an action for personal injuries against Family Fitness, the trial court granted summary judgment for Family Fitness based on its defense of release.

DISCUSSION

Summary judgment is proper only where there is no triable issue of material fact and the moving party is entitled to judgment as a matter of law. "On review of a summary judgment in favor of the defendant, we review the record de novo to determine whether the defendant has conclusively negated a necessary element of the plaintiff's case or demonstrated that under no hypothesis is there a material issue of fact that requires the process of trial." Although we must strictly construe the moving party's papers and liberally construe those of the opposing party, the latter bears the burden of showing triable issues of fact exist. We resolve all doubts in favor of the party opposing the judgment.

"An express release is not enforceable if it is not easily readable." [citations omitted] "Furthermore, the important operative language should be placed in a position which compels notice and must be distinguished from other sections of the document. A [layperson] should not be required to muddle through complex language to know that valuable, legal rights are being relinquished." [citations omitted] An exculpatory clause is unenforceable if not distinguished from other sections, if printed in the same typeface as the remainder of the document, and if not likely to attract attention because it is placed in the middle of a document. In other words, a release must not be buried in a lengthy document, hidden among other verbiage, or so encumbered with other provisions as to be difficult to find.

A.

The trial court found the exculpatory clause was sufficiently conspicuous, citing only that it is written in 8-point type as required for retail installment contracts by Civil Code section 1803.1 and stated in plain and simple language. Although print size is an important factor, it is not the only one to be considered in assessing the adequacy of a document as a release. The court failed to address specifically other relevant characteristics of the exculpatory clause—its size, form and location within the undifferentiated paragraph in which it appears. In fact, Civil Code section 1803.2 requires warnings to protect consumers' financial interests from potential hazards in retail installment contracts by providing notice in larger, bold-face type (14, 12 or 10 point). Clearly, Civil Code section 1803.1's perfunctory mandate that all retail installment sales contracts be at least in 8-point type, is not legislative acknowledgement that 8-point type alone is per se evidence of adequate conspicuousness so as to universally relieve a party of liability for its general negligence. Indeed, Civil Code section 1812.85 requires even a provision of lesser import, a cancellation clause in contracts for health services offered by facilities such as Family Fitness, to be at least 10-point boldface print.

Here, the release clause, although a separate paragraph, is in undifferentiated type located in the middle of a document. Although some other portions are printed in bold and in enlarged print, the releasing paragraph is not prefaced by a heading to alert the reader it is an exculpatory release, contains no bold lettering, and is in the same smaller font size as is most of the document. No physical characteristic distinguishes the exculpatory clause from the remainder of the document. The document itself is titled "Club Membership Agreement (Retail Installment Contract)" giving no notice to the reader it includes a release or waiver of liability. Of particular relevance, there is no language to alert a reader Family Fitness intended the release to exculpate it from claims based on its own negligence. Where such exculpation is sought, the release must contain specific words "clearly and explicitly expressing such intent."

To be valid and enforceable, a written release purporting to exculpate a tortfeasor from damage claims based on its future negligence or misconduct must clearly, unambiguously, and explicitly express this specific intent of the subscribing parties. "If a tortfeasor is to be released from such liability the language used 'must be clear, explicit and comprehensible in each of its essential details. Such an agreement, read as a whole, must clearly notify the prospective releasor or indemnitor of the effect of signing the agreement.'"

B.

The membership agreement signed by Leon is prefaced with an assumption of the risk statement. The general release is unobtrusively inserted thereafter. Although some courts have treated the two interchangeably others have separately analyzed the enforceability of either. Whether taken separately or analyzed as a whole, we conclude the general release statement is fatally ambiguous.

The Restatement Second of Torts states: "In order for the agreement to assume the risk to be effective, it must also appear that its terms were intended by both parties to apply to the particular conduct of the defendant which has caused the harm. Again, where the agreement is drawn by the defendant and the plaintiff passively accepts it, its terms will ordinarily be construed strictly against the defendant." (Rest., Torts, § 496B, com. d, p. 566.) In its most basic sense, assumption of risk means that one person, in advance, has given his express consent to relieve another of obligations toward himself, and to assume the chance of injury from a known risk arising from what the other defendant is to do or leave undone. The result is the other person is relieved of a legal duty to the plaintiff; and being under no duty, he cannot be charged with negligence solely based on the occurrence of the event anticipated.

Here, an individual who understandingly entered into the membership agreement at issue can be deemed to have waived any hazard known to relate to the use of the health club facilities. These hazards typically include the risk of a sprained ankle due to improper exercise or overexertion, a broken toe from a dropped weight, injuries due to malfunctioning exercise or sports equipment, or from slipping in the locker-room shower. On the other hand, no Family Fitness patron can be charged with realistically appreciating the risk of injury from simply reclining on a sauna bench. Because the collapse of a sauna bench when properly utilized is not a "known risk," we conclude Leon cannot be deemed to have assumed the risk of this incident as a matter of law.

C.

The Family Fitness membership agreement contained a general release or hold harmless provision as well. "Where a participant in an activity has expressly released the defendant from responsibility for the consequences of any act of negligence, the law imposes no requirement that the participant have had a specific knowledge of the particular risk which resulted in his death [or injury.] Not every possible specific act of negligence by the defendant must be spelled out in the agreement or discussed by the parties. Where a release of all liability for any act of negligence is given, the release applies to any such negligent act, whatever it may have been. It is only necessary that the act of negligence, which results in injury to the releaser, be reasonably related to the object or purpose for which the release is given." Here, Family Fitness's negligence was not reasonably related to the object or purpose for which the release was given, that is, as stated, injuries resulting from participating in sports or exercise rather than from merely reclining on the facility's furniture.

The objective purpose of the release Leon signed was to allow him to engage in fitness activities within the Family Fitness facilities. However, it was not this type of activity which led to his injury. Leon allegedly was lying on a fixed, non-movable, permanent bench in the sauna room. Injuries resulting during the proper use of the bench would no more be expected to be covered by the clause than those caused by the ceiling falling on his head or from a prat fall caused by a collapsing office chair. These incidents have no relation to an individual's participation in a health club's fitness regimen.

Further, the release is ineffective because, read as a whole, it does not clearly notify a customer of the effect of signing the agreement—it was not clear, unambiguous and explicit. The release begins with language that participation in a sport or physical exercise may result in accidents or injury, and buyer assumes the risk connected with the participation in such. The release is followed by a statement in large print and bold, capital letters: "MODERATION IS THE KEY TO A SUCCESSFUL FITNESS PROGRAM AND ALSO THE KEY TO PREVENTING INJURIES." Family Fitness placed the general waiver between these two statements which deal strictly with the risks inherent in an exercise or sports program without any mention that it was intended to insulate the proprietor from liability for injuries caused by its own negligence.

Reading the entire document leads to the inescapable conclusion the release does not clearly, explicitly and comprehensibly set forth to an ordinary person untrained in the law, such as Leon, that the intent and effect of the document is to release claims for his own personal injuries resulting from the enterprise's own negligent acts, regardless whether related to the sports or exercise activities it marketed.

QUESTIONS AND NOTES

1. The court distinguishes the collapse of the sauna bench from other "known risks" "inherent in an exercise or sports program." Is this helpful? What if a weight bench collapsed beneath Mr. Leon? Isn't this a "known risk" "inherent in an exercise or sports program"?

2. Reread the waiver on p. 467. Isn't it clear that Mr. Leon waived any claim arising from "Member's use of the facilities"? What more does Family Fitness need to say to have members waive liability for collapsing sauna benches?

3. Is working out at Family Fitness more necessary than skiing? Would the *Olsen* court have decided this case differently, given their statement that "[s]kiing, like other athletic or recreational pursuits, however beneficial, is not an essential activity"?

4. Consider California Civil Code § 1542 at p. 461. Doesn't this statute apply to both *Olsen* and *Leon*? In light of this statute, how can one ever effectively release claims prior to suffering any injury? Note that California courts permit parties to expressly waive the protections of § 1542 and that in fact such waivers are commonly included in forms of release. What is the point of a statute that prohibits release of unknown claims absent express waiver? Is it simply a trap for unwary releasees?

CHAPTER 6

CONSIDERATION: BARGAINS AND ACTION IN RELIANCE

I.   BARGAIN AND EXCHANGE

The law in English-speaking countries has focused on enforcing promises that are part of a bargained-for exchange. A bargained-for or purchased promise is supported by "consideration" and generally will be enforced. Consideration refers to "the element of exchange required for a contract [to be] enforceable as a bargain...." Comment *a*, Restatement, Second, Contracts § 71. Said another way, consideration is what the promisor asks for and receives in return for the promise.

Chief Justice Robquist on p. 16 first introduced you to the notion of consideration. This interest in enforcing bargained-for exchanges reflects the economic orientation of the common law. Bargained-for exchanges usually are market transactions that seek to reallocate resources profitably for the parties and therefore efficiently for society at large. Moreover, promises that are valuable enough to pay for are important enough to merit social protection and enforcement. Finally, when a promisee relies on a promise by paying for it, a sense of justice demands that the promisor should not be allowed to keep the benefit received for the promise without performing the obligation undertaken.

Two points should be made as we begin our study of consideration. First, as Chief Justice Robquist, pp. 13-17 makes clear, consideration doctrine has been around for a long time and has picked up bumps and barnacles over the generations. You will encounter divergent definitions of consideration in the case law. Many of these complications grow out of expectations that an exchange will be a symmetrical transaction in which the values on each side will be roughly equal. Recall the troubles you had early in Chapter One with cases like *Mattei v. Hopper*, p. 31, *Sylvan Crest Sand & Gravel Co. v. United States*, p. 36 and *Wood v. Lucy, Lady Duff-Gordon*, p. 40, because one side seemed to be putting much more into the deal than the other. This expectation is natural and, as you have already seen, continues to bother us even as we recognize exchanges of grossly disparate values. We will return to this expectation and the promises it engenders in Topic III, when we study the question of adequacy of consideration. Train yourself to look at consideration as a requirement that, to be enforceable, a promise must be part of a ***bargained-for exchange***. Viewed this way the notion is simple enough and remarkably useful as a predictor of contract enforceability. Avoid conceptualizations of consideration that suggest you look for benefits and detriments, not because there are not respectable authorities of former generations, and a few of the current generation, that use such language (you will find many such statements), but because this terminology is unhelpful in predicting how courts should decide cases. If you work at it, you will always find a detriment or a benefit. Unless that detriment or benefit was bargained-for, that is, unless it was the price for the promise, it will not be consideration.

Second, do not fall into the trap of viewing consideration as the exclusive mark of an enforceable promise. As Justice Kenthom pointed out in *Best v. Southland*, p. 17, everyone recognizes that bargained-for promises have a heavy claim to enforcement, but traditional doctrine fails to tell us why *only* bargained-for promises should be enforceable. Consideration has followed a path similar to other legal ideas as it has moved from being a factor that marked the enforceable promise to becoming the exclusive defining feature of an enforceable promise, to the role it plays today as the principal, but not exclusive, mark of contract enforceability. Later in this Chapter we will explore some of the competitors and supplements to consideration that Justice Kagamayor introduced you to on p. 19. Soon enough you will see the limits of the bargain notion. In the meantime, you should begin to develop the lawyer's suspicion (keep it a suspicion, not a certainty!) that when a promise is not bargained for, it may not be deemed serious or important enough in the law's eyes to be enforceable.

II.   BARGAIN PROMISES V. GIFT PROMISES

An unbargained-for promise, unless enforceable for some special reason, will be labeled a "gift promise" and will not be enforced. The term gift promise implies the conclusion of non-enforceability. It does not imply that the "gift" was motivated by love or benevolence. A promise that is not part of a bargain is presumptively not legally enforced, but that does not mean it is not a promise to be kept: family and personal relationships, business reputation, trust, moral probity, and self-esteem may dictate performance of a legally unenforceable gift promise.

Remember that we are talking about promises, not performances. The law's insistence that gift promises are not enforceable does not mean that a donor can reclaim a gift after making it. The crucial moment is delivery. An unperformed promise to make a gift of $100 can be withdrawn and will not be enforced, but once the $100 is delivered, it cannot be recalled.

The law leaves room in the definition of "delivery" for cases such as delivery of the key to a safety deposit box as delivery of the contents, or delivery of a document of title such as a deed or a car's "pink slip" or a bill of lading as delivery of the physical property (constructive or symbolic delivery). But prior to some physical delivery related to a promised gift, the promise can be withdrawn or repudiated.

———————

3 SAMUEL WILLISTON, WILLISTON ON CONTRACTS § 7:18 (RICHARD A. LORD ED.) (4TH ED. 2003):

If a benevolent man says to a tramp, "If you go around the corner to the clothing shop there, you may purchase an overcoat on my credit," no reasonable person would understand that the short walk was requested as the consideration for the promise; rather, the understanding would be that in the event of the tramp going to the shop the promisor would make him a gift. Yet the walk to the shop is in its nature capable of being consideration. It is a legal detriment to the tramp to take the walk, and the only reason why the walk is not consideration is because on a reasonable interpretation, it must be held that the walk was not requested as the price of the promise, but was merely a condition of a gratuitous promise.

It is often a difficult question to decide whether words of condition in a promise indicate a request for consideration or state a mere condition in a gratuitous promise. ... In close cases, whether the promisee has incurred a detriment on the faith of the promise or has conferred a benefit on the promisor in bringing about the condition, may control the outcome, for courts in such a case will naturally be loath to regard the promise as a mere gratuity and the detriment incurred or benefit conferred as merely a condition. It is therefore not surprising that courts, prodded by the drafters of the Restatement and the Restatement (Second), have offered increasing protection to promisees who incur detriment or confer a benefit on the faith of a promise. This helps to explain those cases where courts have enforced options to purchase land for which no consideration is given other than the promise to make an expensive examination of the property or title, when the promisee has incurred the expense or made valuable improvements. This same rationale underlies those decisions upholding promises to make provision by will in recognition of services to the promisor when the claimant, having fully performed, sues the estate. Some courts have also gone to great lengths to find an element of bargain in family settlements, a result focusing not only on the detriment undergone or benefit conferred but also encouraged by the strong public policy favoring family settlements. But in some cases, it is so clear that a conditional gift was intended that, despite the fact that the promisee has incurred detriment or the promisor obtained some minor benefit, the promise has been held unenforceable.

QUESTIONS AND NOTES

1. What makes Williston so certain that "on a reasonable construction it must be held that the [tramp's] walk was not requested as the price of the promise, but was merely a condition of a gratuitous promise"?

2. Is it so clear that the walk was of no benefit to the benevolent man or of no detriment to the tramp? If the benevolent man were to ask the tramp to mail a letter on the way to the clothing store, would mailing it be "consideration" or an additional "condition"? Should we even speak of "benefit" and "detriment" when Restatement, Second, Contracts § 71(2) (p. 16) provides that a "performance or return promise is bargained for if it is sought by the promisor in exchange for his promise and is given by the promisee in exchange for that promise"?

3. The law recognizes that gifts can serve a social purpose, *and* it affirms the validity of executed gifts. Is it not inconsistent to deny enforcement of promises to make gifts?

4. Are "free gift" offers based on conditions, such as buying 10 gallons of gas, opening a savings account, or visiting a new subdivision, ever intended to be generous acts? If not, are they gift promises at all? But are they requests to bargain?

5. Recall *Best v. Southland*, p. 13. Didn't Best promise to send its trucks to Southland's warehouse to pick up the plywood and to return and have its employees re-pile the wood when its shipment came in? Are these requested acts conditions on a gift promise by Southland or part of a bargained for exchange? Aren't they detrimental reliance, a burden to Best?

Reread: *Robquist, C.J.'s opinion in Best v. Southland*, p. 13.

NOTE ON THE EXCHANGE OF PROMISES

The idea of bargain reflected in the doctrine of consideration is relatively easy to understand when it refers to the present exchange of tangible objects or performances. It is easy to see that one party may give up a cow in immediate exchange for another's horse or that one party may undertake immediate performance as the price of the performance undertaken by the other. But when the bargain consists of the present exchange of promises to render future performances, the English common law's acceptance was not so readily forthcoming. It took centuries before the agreement consisting of a promise for a promise was generally seen as an exchange of things real enough to enforce—a conceptual difficulty paralleled, anthropologists tell us, in the development of a variety of cultures.

As feudalism receded, treating promises as things of value was inevitable because the most significant bargains in commercial societies involve exchanges over time. Do not lose sight of the fact that the person who bargains for and receives a promise is typically interested not in the promise as such, but in the expectation of receiving the performance that lies behind the words. Checks and securities are printed on very pretty paper, but few of us would assign to them the value we do if we were not confident of the performance they promise. Thus, a promise is consideration if the performance promised would be consideration if it alone were bargained for.

At the same time, for reasons that are not altogether clear or inevitable, promises may be consideration for a return promise if they are capable of being relied upon, without regard to whether they were in fact relied upon. Thus, if Jack promises Jill to sell her a car, delivery in 30 days, in exchange for Jill's promise to pay $5,000 at the time of delivery, a contract is formed at the moment the promises are exchanged, and neither party thereafter may withdraw. The respective promises justify reliance and the law treats them as things of value given in exchange in order to make the other party's promise enforceable. If a day, or even a minute, later Jack repudiates and is sued for breach of the agreement, he cannot defend on the basis that Jill did not significantly change her position by performing or otherwise relying upon the promise. In other words, the fact that the contract is wholly executory—the parties have neither begun performance, nor in any other way relied upon the promises—does not mean the promises exchanged are not supported by consideration and thus unenforceable. What inchoate justifications are there for the enforcement of unrelied upon mutual promises?

General Motors Corp. v. Michigan Dep't of Treasury

Supreme Court of Michigan, 2002.
466 Mich. 231, 644 N.W.2d 734.

■ WEAVER, J.

Plaintiff, General Motors Corporation (GM), appeals from the Court of Appeals decision that defendant, Department of Treasury, could impose use tax on the vehicle components and parts plaintiff provided to customers as part of plaintiff's goodwill adjustments policy. We reverse the decision of the Court of Appeals and hold that assessment of use tax on the goodwill adjustments was improper because they were taxed pursuant to the General Sales Tax Act when customers purchased vehicles at retail.

I

When customers purchase new GM automobiles, they are provided with a GM limited manufacturer's warranty. These limited manufacturer's warranties provide, in pertinent part, for the replacement of defective parts of the automobile under certain circumstances. They also generally provide coverage for an expressly stated length of time, subject to earlier expiration, if the vehicle is driven for a certain number of miles. The department acknowledges that parts provided under these limited warranties are not subject to use tax because the customers paid for the right to replacement parts under the warranties at the time of the retail sale.

In addition to the limited warranties, GM provides a more open-ended "goodwill" adjustment policy under which GM will, on a discretionary basis, pay for replacement parts for GM vehicles even after the limited warranty period has expired. Although not referred to by name as a "goodwill adjustment policy," notice of this policy is contained in the General Motors warranty manual provided to customers at the time of sale. In this regard, the manual provides:

> Should you ever encounter a problem during *or after* the warranty periods that is not resolved, talk to a member of dealer management. If the problem persists, follow the additional procedure outlined in "Owner Assistance," on page 16 of this booklet. [Emphasis added.]

The Owner Assistance section of the manual outlines a "Customer Satisfaction Procedure." It states that problems will "normally" be resolved by the dealer's sales or service departments.[3] However, if a concern is not resolved at that level, the manual recommends first discussing the problem with the dealership management. If the problem is not resolved by the dealer management, customers are told to contact GM directly. A customer dissatisfied with the outcome of the procedure may elect arbitration. The manual states that, while a customer is not bound to accept the result of the arbitration proceeding, GM will "generally" agree to be bound by

---

3. General Motors, in a bulletin to its dealers, directs them to make goodwill adjustments case by case "where special consideration is in order to enhance customer satisfaction and loyalty." GM provides the dealers with a recommended set of guidelines for goodwill policy adjustments to help them distinguish defects in materials and workmanship from defects caused by aging, physical damage, lack of proper maintenance, or owner abuse.

Testimony revealed that GM estimates the cost of, and establishes a budget reserve for, both warranty repairs and goodwill adjustments for the lifetime of every make and model of vehicle. Twice annually, GM internally audits both the cost of warranty repairs and that of the goodwill policy for each make and model of vehicle. A GM representative explained that the vehicle sales price is designed to recover all costs, including those associated with the goodwill adjustment policy, as well as to maintain profitability.

it even though it reserves the right to terminate its participation in the arbitration program.[4]

The department conducted an audit of GM's compliance with Michigan tax laws for the period of January 1, 1986, through December 31, 1992. As a result of the audit, the department assessed against GM use taxes and interest of $5.5 million on the vehicle components and parts provided by GM to customers as goodwill adjustments. The department had not previously assessed such a tax. During the audit period, GM customers in Michigan obtained $82 million in components and parts under the goodwill policy.

GM appealed the assessment to the Court of Claims. In pertinent part, GM alleged that the department lacked the statutory authority to impose use tax on goodwill adjustments because sales tax was imposed on the cost of the goodwill adjustments when vehicles were sold at retail. However, the Court of Claims disagreed with GM's position and granted summary disposition in favor of the department pursuant to MCR 2.116(C)(10), holding, in relevant part, that the transfer of parts under the goodwill program is subject to use tax. The Court of Appeals affirmed regarding this issue, concluding that "plaintiff's dealers were not obligated to provide all customers with goodwill adjustments" and, therefore, that the "value of the goodwill program was not included in the gross proceeds arising from the retail sales of plaintiff's vehicles." The Court of Appeals also emphasized its view that the purchasers of GM vehicles did not obtain "any enforceable rights in the goodwill program." We granted leave to appeal.

…

III

…

GM contends that the cost of its goodwill adjustments is exempt from use tax under § 4(1)(a) of the UTA. M.C.L. § 205.94(1)(a) provides that "[p]roperty sold in this state on which transaction a tax is paid under the general sales tax act" is exempt from the use tax "if the tax was due and paid on the retail sale to a consumer." Thus, our inquiry is whether "tax was due and paid" pursuant to the GTA on the cost of the goodwill adjustments when vehicles were sold at retail.

At the time of retail sale, GM customers receive an owner's manual. The manual invites customers to initiate a dialogue with the dealership when a defect arises, "during or after the warranty periods." The manual states the goal of resolving the

---

4. We note the possibility of arbitration merely to provide a comprehensive outline of the complaint resolution procedure. In light of our analysis, it is not necessary to consider whether the possibility of arbitration is a form of "consideration" in this case.

defect to the "customer's satisfaction." GM admits that its customers are not guaranteed that requested after-warranty goodwill adjustments will be made. Indeed, GM suggests its dealers negotiate with customers for copayment on goodwill adjustments case by case. Nevertheless, GM's goodwill policy is a promise to hear and address customer complaints even after the written warranty expires.

To have consideration there must be a bargained-for exchange. There must be "'a benefit on one side, or a detriment suffered, or service done on the other.'" *Plastray Corp. v. Cole,* 324 Mich. 433, 440 (1949). Courts do not generally inquire into the sufficiency of consideration. It has been said "[a] cent or a pepper corn, in legal estimation, would constitute a valuable consideration." *Whitney v. Stearns,* 16 Me. 394 (1839). The owner's manual provided at the time of sale invites customers to voice complaints even after the warranty period ends, with the goal of resolving the complaint to the customer's satisfaction. We hold that this opportunity for dialogue and possible resolution of complaints—even outside the warranty period—is a benefit flowing to purchasers of GM vehicles at the time of retail sale and, therefore, is consideration for the sale.[8] Therefore, replacement parts provided pursuant to the goodwill program are subject to the sales tax at the time of retail sale and are exempt from the use tax under § 4(1)(a) of the UTA.[9]

GM's promise pursuant to its goodwill adjustments policy, while discretionary with respect to whether there will be any "adjustment," is not discretionary regarding GM's obligation to act reasonably and in good faith in response to a customer complaint.[10] Reinforcing this contractual undertaking to act in good faith is ... Michigan's version of the Uniform Commercial Code. M.C.L. § 440.1203 provides that

---

8. While acknowledging that a customer pays for the goodwill program, the dissent "cannot fathom" that a customer would bargain for the opportunity to have postwarranty complaints addressed. This skepticism is inconsistent with this Court's traditional reluctance to question the sufficiency of consideration and is not justification to override the Legislature's expression of intent in UTA § 4(1)(a) to avoid the pyramiding of the sales and use taxes.

9. While not part of our dispositive analysis, it is noteworthy that GM audits the cost of the goodwill adjustment policy twice annually with the goal of recovering costs and maintaining profitability. A witness for the department acknowledged that GM uses the same method to account for the cost of warranty repairs and goodwill policy adjustments. It is evident that GM attempts to effectively include the cost of warranty repairs in the retail price of its vehicles. The record reflects that the cost of the goodwill adjustment policy is likewise included in the retail price of GM vehicles. A GM witness testified that "implicit in the price is the fact that we need to cover all the costs, and both policy and warranty are costs that are included...."

10. As stated by Professor Arthur Corbin:

> Promissory words are not nullified by making the promise conditional on some event within the promisor's own power, if at the same time the promisor impliedly promises to make a reasonable effort to bring the event about or to use good faith and honest judgment in determining whether or not it has in fact occurred.

"[e]very contract or duty within this act imposes an obligation of good faith in its performance or enforcement."[11] This means that, should GM not consider complaints under the goodwill adjustment policy in good faith, it can be sued.

The dissent agrees that a unilateral or discretionary promise could "constitute valid consideration." However, the dissent would decline to rule that GM's promise is valid consideration in part because GM's customers have "little if any" knowledge of the scope of GM's discretion. That it is unknown how liberally GM will exercise its discretion does not mean there is no discretion. In fact, it means there is discretion, i.e., a benefit to the consumer.[12] The dissent has fallen into the error of considering not merely if there is consideration, but its sufficiency. As we have stated, courts do not inquire into the adequacy of consideration to support a contract.[13] Thus, we conclude that the duty the goodwill policy imposes on GM to consider requests for redress in good faith is a valuable consideration that is worth far more than the legendary peppercorn.[14]

Moreover, the evidence indicates that for the period 1986-1992, plaintiff provided "goodwill" parts to customers of General Motors cars having an estimated value of $82 million. As the dissent itself recognizes, "the cost of ... [these] parts has been factored into the retail cost of the car...." If this is so, then such costs have been necessarily paid by the consumer at sale, i.e., a car otherwise valued at $9975 has been increased in price to $10,000 and the consumer has paid an additional $25 for the goodwill policy. Plaintiff, not being a charitable institution, must necessarily

---

11. Because the sale of a vehicle is the sale of a good, a contract for such a sale is subject to the Uniform Commercial Code.

12. We note that this is a greater right than the inherent ability to complain possessed by consumers generally. While a customer would typically have the practical ability to bring a complaint to the attention of a manufacturer, absent a contractual or other legal duty, the manufacturer would be free to simply ignore such complaints without giving them any consideration. However, because of its contractual undertaking for the goodwill policy, GM has a duty to consider such complaints in good faith.

13. This point is reinforced by Professor Samuel Williston:

It is an elementary and oft quoted principle that the law will not inquire into the adequacy of consideration so long as the consideration is otherwise valid to support a promise. By this is meant that so long as the requirement of a bargained-for benefit or detriment is satisfied, the fact that the relative value or worth of the exchange is unequal is irrelevant so that anything which fulfills the requirement of consideration will support a promise, regardless of the comparative value of the consideration and of the thing promised. The rule is almost as old as the doctrine of consideration itself.

14. In concluding that the goodwill program amounted to an illusory promise, the Court of Appeals referenced *Barbat v. M E Arden Co.,* for the proposition that "[a]n unenforceable promise cannot constitute consideration." However, that case is inapplicable because it involved a promised performance that was "unenforceable" because it was void as illegal.

have factored the cost of the goodwill policy into the cost of the car, and such cost must necessarily have been paid by the consumer. Further, it can be presumed that the consumer paid $25 because something of value passed. The automobile industry is sufficiently competitive that few companies can afford to tack costs onto their products for parts or services that are perceived as valueless by their consumers. Contrary to the dissent, we can easily envision a "rational, self-interested market participant" paying something for a benefit estimated to provide more than $13 million in annual benefits to consumers. Our interpretation of M.C.L. § 205.94(1)(a) does not constitute a "lax" interpretation of consideration as the dissent asserts. Rather, our interpretation is based on fundamental contract principles and reflects the realities of the marketplace.[15]

IV

Because the goodwill adjustment policy provides an opportunity for GM customers to seek redress of vehicle defects and because the policy is included in the retail price of GM vehicles and purchased at the time of retail sale, it is part of the consideration flowing to GM customers when they purchase a GM vehicle that is taxed pursuant to the GTA at retail sale. We reverse the decision of the Court of Appeals and remand this case to the Court of Claims for entry of judgment in favor of GM.

■ CAVANAGH, J. (dissenting).

I write separately to express my disagreement with the majority's conclusion that retail new car customers exchange consideration for goodwill policy parts when purchasing vehicles manufactured by plaintiff. Plaintiff has claimed its goodwill repair parts should not be subject to use tax because the costs are included in the price of the vehicle, which is subject to sales tax. Under M.C.L. § 205.94(1)(a), no use tax is owed on retail sales subject to sales tax. However, this exemption applies only if the parts are included in a "sale at retail," i.e., "a transaction by which the ownership of tangible personal property is transferred for consideration...." M.C.L. § 205.51(1)(b). Because I cannot agree that the goodwill parts are transferred for consideration, I must respectfully dissent.

---

15. The dissent asserts that "[m]erely because plaintiff proved through its accounting methods that it charges all consumers for costs associated with a program ..., I cannot conclude that 'consideration' was paid by purchasers...." If this statement does not set forth the very essence of "consideration," it is hard to know what the term means. Of course, we recognize that not *every* cost factored into the price of a manufacturer's product is exempt from use tax as a form of "consideration" to a customer. Costs that do not provide a benefit to a customer could not be consideration.

I

Plaintiff directs its dealers to make goodwill adjustments case by case "where special consideration is in order to enhance customer satisfaction and loyalty." Most dealers have the discretion to provide repair parts free or at a reduced rate to consumers after the original warranty expires. These repairs are provided to select customers who are unsatisfied with defective parts after the manufacturer's warranty expires.

Consumers are not given any general or specific information concerning the goodwill program and are informed in the warranty manual of their right to contact plaintiff after the manufacturer's warranty expires if they are dissatisfied with the dealer's offered resolution. The written warranty also indicates that arbitration proceedings may be an option.[3] In essence, the consumer is given an opportunity to ask for free repair parts, but has no legal right to any specific repair and knows nothing of the goodwill policy program in general, or of its specific terms. Though plaintiff may agree to subject itself to arbitration proceedings, consumers gain no legally enforceable right as a result of this program, a program purportedly "purchased" at the retail sale.

Consideration requires bargained-for legal detriment. I agree with the majority that a discretionary promise must be exercised in good faith and that the reasonable execution of such a promise may constitute valid consideration. *J.R. Watkins Co. v. Rich,* 254 Mich. 82, 84-85 (1931); *Wood v. Lucy, Lady Duff-Gordon,* 222 N.Y. 88 (1917). However, I am not convinced that plaintiff's good-faith exercise of its discretionary power is sufficient to permit a finding of bargained-for consideration in this instance. A party relying on the good-faith exercise of another's unilateral discretion generally has some knowledge of the scope of discretion involved and the potential benefits that might accrue. In this case, customers have little if any knowledge of what they allegedly bargained and paid for at the retail sale. I cannot fathom what rational, self-interested market participant would actually bargain for and purchase such a promise. If it came free with the purchase price, most would accept it, but almost no one would *buy* it.

Further, I am not sure that an arbitrator would have *any* reason to rule in favor of a customer if dissatisfaction actually resulted in an arbitration hearing. On the basis of the contract between the parties, the express warranty would have expired

---

3. Contrary to the implication by the majority, plaintiff's participation in arbitration is in no way guaranteed. While a consumer may always request arbitration, plaintiff reserves the right to refuse to participate. *See* 1990 Warranty and Owner Assistance Information for Buick New Cars ("GM will *generally* agree to be bound by the arbitrator's decision.... [GM] reserves the right to change eligibility limitations and/or to discontinue its participation in the program" [emphasis added]).

if a customer requested parts under the goodwill policy. The simple failure to purchase a supplemental warranty suggests plaintiff has absolutely no legal or good-faith *duty* to repair defective parts after the warranty expires. The presence of express promises (original warranty) and the opportunity to purchase supplemental promises (extended warranty) evidence the parties' intention that plaintiff escape liability for defects after the original warranty period expires. Because information concerning the terms of the goodwill policy is generally kept secret, I am not sure that a consumer could adequately plead his case to the arbitrator, assuming plaintiff agreed to participate. All a consumer is left with is the right to complain to plaintiff, and I believe it is a stretch to consider that sufficient consideration where such a right exists regardless of the goodwill policy. Therefore, I would hold that the goodwill policy adjustment program does not constitute valid consideration.[4]

Even so, I agree that the cost of the goodwill policy parts has been factored into the retail cost of the car, and to that extent the goodwill parts are subject both to use and sales tax. Unfortunately, because the use tax statute exempts only costs transferred for consideration in a retail sale, the Legislature essentially failed to avoid pyramiding taxes where costs are factored into a product, but are not actually part of the consideration paid.[5]

---

4. Like the majority, I respect the doctrine that generally prohibits courts from questioning the adequacy of consideration. Unfortunately, that doctrine is inapplicable here because absolutely no consideration for the goodwill parts passed between the parties at the retail sale. Merely because plaintiff proved through its accounting methods that it charges all consumers for costs associated with a program that results in free or discounted parts to some, I cannot conclude that "consideration" was paid by purchasers at the retail sale for goodwill parts. GM's $82 million worth of repairs, while certainly of value, simply cannot be regarded as legal consideration.

Further, the majority implies that any cost factored into the price of the car by GM should be exempt from use tax. If that were the case, no manufacturer would ever pay use tax because generally all costs work their way into the price of products. The statute as currently drafted does not provide an exclusion per se for all costs factored into product prices, only those for which consideration has passed at a retail sale. The majority also presumes that a customer can pinpoint the costs associated with a program it knows nothing of and buy the car in part on the basis of the promised value associated with the goodwill policy. The error lies in that assumption. We cannot assume market participants are making rationale choices when they lack sufficient knowledge of the goodwill policy. Neither GM nor the dealer bargains over this product with the consumer. GM keeps the terms and scope of the program confidential, thereby making it impossible for a consumer to pay for such a program with consideration. The majority's attempt to rebut my position ignores the foundational principles of consideration, i.e., bargained-for consideration is absent where "the action that the promisee took was *not induced* by the promise." Farnsworth, Contracts, (2d ed.), § 2.6, p. 52 (emphasis in original). In this case, plaintiff simply fails to give consumers an opportunity to be induced by the alleged benefit.

5. In an attempt to refute my position, the majority erroneously infers the following:

> [T]he dissent would decline to rule that GM's promise is valid consideration in part because GM's customers have "little if any" knowledge of the scope of GM's discretion. That it is

II

I suspect the most appropriate and forthright method to analyze the goodwill program for tax purposes would be to conceive of the parts as promotional or gratuitous items. Plaintiff grants adjustments "in order to enhance customer satisfaction and loyalty." In essence, the goodwill policy is a select form of advertising, i.e., a large scale version of the distribution of free pens and cups to conference participants or the provision of free pharmaceutical samples to physicians. Dealers probably grant the benefits of the discretionary goodwill program to those customers most likely to experience enhanced manufacturer loyalty. Because the program most resembles a marketing or customer satisfaction offer, and because there is no general statutory exemption for promotional items from use tax in Michigan,[6] I would permit defendant to assess use taxes, assuming it does so in a uniform fashion.

III

The majority permits a lax interpretation of consideration in order to bridge the gap between the text of the statute and the general desire to avoid duplicate taxation. While the end might be worthwhile, the method arguably creates an empty definition of consideration that could affect future bargainers. Rather than compensate for the legislative failure to exempt all product costs from use tax by watering down our understanding of consideration, I would hold that the repair parts are not included in the retail sale for which consideration is paid.

QUESTIONS

1. Is the problem in this case that GM's "promise" to consider requests for out-of-warranty service is a gift promise, or that it is illusory? Even if the promise lacked

---

unknown how liberally GM will exercise its discretion does not mean there is no discretion. In fact, it means there is discretion, i.e., a benefit to the consumer.

To clarify, I conclude that GM's parts cannot constitute valid consideration because the consumers did not bargain for, and were not induced to act because of, the goodwill policy in general or the parts in particular. Moreover, I agree that GM has discretion. In fact, GM has so much discretion that it would be impossible for consumers to bring an action claiming that discretion was exercised without good faith. The majority errs by inferring from my statement that describes a consumer's lack of knowledge concerning the scope of GM's discretion that the existence of discretion is itself dispositive of the inquiry.

6. MCL 205.94(1)(c) exempts from use tax certain promotional items, which include:

[P]romotional merchandise transferred pursuant to a redemption offer to a person located outside this state or any packaging material, *other than promotional merchandise,* acquired for use in fulfilling a redemption offer or rebate to a person located outside this state. [Emphasis added.]

meaningful commitment, is the subsequent performance of that promise by providing parts and service not covered by the express warranty best viewed as a gift, or as a part of GM's original bargain with the car buyer? Or is the provision of this service just a promotional expense intended to maintain GM's goodwill with the general public? In what sense is GM acting the part of the benevolent man in Professor Williston's story of the tramp?

2. If GM never informs the buyer or the public of its goodwill policy and the buyer does not otherwise know of it, how can the undisclosed "promise" to furnish goodwill parts be part of the original bargain?

3. If a buyer complains to his seller about the quality of goods delivered and the seller agrees to fix the problem without admitting contractual liability either for delivery of nonconforming goods or under a warranty, has the seller made a gift? Or is it simply an example of parties to a contract working out a dispute between themselves over their respective rights and obligations?

4. Why should the obligation to remit additional Michigan use tax on account of the provision of out-of-warranty parts and service depend upon whether there is a sentence on p. 16 in the Owner's Manual advising the buyer that if she can't work out an issue with the dealer she can contact someone at GM and if they can't resolve the matter, GM will generally agree to arbitrate the issue? Would the parts suddenly become taxable if the Owner's Manual said nothing more than "If you have a complaint, contact Customer Service at 1-800-GMOTORS"?

E.J. Baehr v. Penn–O–Tex Oil Corp.

Minnesota Supreme Court, 1960.
258 Minn. 533, 104 N.W.2d 661.

■ LOEVINGER, J. This is an action for rents which defendant is claimed to owe plaintiff because of possession and contract.

Plaintiff leased certain gasoline filling stations to one Kemp, doing business as Webb Oil Company, under written leases. Kemp was purchasing the business known as Webb Oil Company and certain related property from defendant. On account of these transactions and purchases of petroleum products, Kemp was heavily indebted to defendant. Kemp became unable to meet payments due to defendant and on December 10, 1955, gave defendant an assignment of accounts receivable and to become receivable, including those involving the plaintiff's filling stations. Thereafter, during the period involved here, defendant collected rents paid by the operators of the filling stations, received other payments made to Webb Oil Company, paid some of its debts at Kemp's direction out of these sums, and installed its agent in the office to run the business.

Plaintiff was in Florida when he received a letter dated December 28, 1955, from Kemp, stating that defendant had all of Kemp's assets tied up. A short time after this, plaintiff called defendant's agent to ask about payment of the filling station rents. Plaintiff was told "that Mr. Kemp's affairs were in a very mixed up form but that he would get them straightened out and mail me [plaintiff] my checks for the rent." Hearing nothing further, plaintiff wrote a letter to defendant asking what he had to do to get his rent checks and adding: "Or will I have to give it to an attorney to sue." Defendant replied by letter stating it was attempting to assist Kemp in keeping the business going, "but in no way are operating or taken possession." The letter denied knowledge of or responsibility for any rent due plaintiff. A week or 10 days after receiving this letter, plaintiff again called defendant and asked for his rent. Defendant's agent then said to plaintiff, "they [the company] were interested and that they would see that I [plaintiff] got my rent, and would take care of it, and they would work it out with the head office. * * * He said he would take it up with them and they would assure me my rent."

The rent was not paid, and in April or May 1956 plaintiff returned to Minneapolis from Florida. Soon after this plaintiff consulted a lawyer, and "shortly thereafter, as rapidly as the lawyer could get moving, a suit was started." On June 2, 1956, plaintiff sent defendant a letter advising that he was reentering and taking possession under the leases of the filling stations and because of failure to receive rent. On July 10, 1956, this suit was started for rents due on the filling stations for the period December 1, 1955, through June 2, 1956, upon the grounds that defendant was in possession of the stations and had contracted to pay the rent during this period.

The case was fully tried on all issues in the district court. At the conclusion of plaintiff's evidence, the court ruled that the evidence was conclusive that defendant neither took possession of the filling stations nor an assignment of Kemp's leases. Defendant then presented evidence on the issue of a contract to pay the rents, and this issue was submitted to the jury under proper instructions. The amount that would be due under such a contract was agreed upon; and the jury returned a verdict for plaintiff in that amount. Thereafter, the district court granted defendant's motion for judgment notwithstanding the verdict; and ordered a new trial in the event of reversal. Plaintiff appealed.

[The Court's rejection of plaintiff's first theory, that defendant was liable for the rents because of its possession of the land, is omitted.]

The issue whether there was a contract by defendant to pay plaintiff is more doubtful. Unfortunately, contract, like most of the basic terms constituting the intellectual tools of law, is conventionally defined in a circular fashion. By the most common definition, a contract is a promise or set of promises for the breach of which the law gives a remedy or the performance of which the law recognizes as a duty. This amounts to saying that a contract is a legally enforceable promise. But a promise is legally enforceable only if it is a contract. Thus nothing less than the whole body of applicable precedents suffices to define the term "contract."

Although the definition of contract does not help much in determining what expressions shall be held to impose legal obligations, it does direct attention to a promise as the starting point of inquiry. Both in popular and legal usage, a promise is an assurance, in whatever form of expression given, that a thing will or will not be done. While we must take care to distinguish between statements meant to express merely present intention and those meant to give an assurance as to a future event, this involves no more than the common difficulty of seeking precise meaning in the usually imprecise, and often careless, expressions of ordinary colloquy.

If we accept plaintiff's version of the statements made by defendant's agent, as we are required to do by the verdict, there was an unequivocal assurance given that the rents would be paid. This cannot be anything but a promise.

However, the fact that a promise was given does not necessarily mean that a contract was made. It is clear that not every promise is legally enforceable. Much of the vast body of law in the field of contracts is concerned with determining which promises should be legally enforced. On the one hand, in a civilized community men must be able to assume that those with whom they deal will carry out their undertakings according to reasonable expectations. On the other hand, it is neither practical nor reasonable to expect full performance of every assurance given, whether it be thoughtless, casual and gratuitous, or deliberately and seriously made.

The test that has been developed by the common law for determining the enforceability of promises is the doctrine of consideration. This is a crude and not altogether successful attempt to generalize the conditions under which promises will be legally enforced. Consideration requires that a contractual promise be the product of a bargain. However, in this usage, "bargain" does not mean an exchange of things of equivalent, or any, value. It means a negotiation resulting in the voluntary assumption of an obligation by one party upon condition of an act or forbearance by the other. Consideration thus insures that the promise enforced as a contract is not accidental, casual, or gratuitous, but has been uttered intentionally as the result of some deliberation, manifested by reciprocal bargaining or negotiation. In this view, the requirement of consideration is no mere technicality, historical anachronism, or arbitrary formality. It is an attempt to be as reasonable as we can in deciding which promises constitute contracts. Although the doctrine has been criticized, no satisfactory substitute has been suggested. It is noteworthy that the civil law has a corresponding doctrine of "causa" which, to the eye of a common-law lawyer, is not much different than consideration.

Consideration, as essential evidence of the parties' intent to create a legal obligation, must be something adopted and regarded by the parties as such. Thus, the same thing may be consideration or not, as it is dealt with by the parties. In substance, a contractual promise must be of the logical form: "If * * * (consideration is given) * * * then I promise that * * *." Of course, the substance may be expressed in any form of words, but essentially this is the logical structure of those promises enforced by the law as contracts.

Applying these principles to the present case, it appears that although defendant's agent made a promise to plaintiff, it was not in such circumstances that a contract was created. Plaintiff correctly states that an agreement of forbearance to sue may be sufficient consideration for a contract. Plaintiff further contends that his failure to institute suit immediately upon learning of Kemp's assignment to defendant permits an inference of an agreement to forbear from suit in consideration for defendant's assurance of payment of rents to plaintiff. This court has held that circumstantial evidence may support the inference of such an agreement to forbear. However, such an inference must rest upon something more than the mere failure to institute immediate suit. The difficulty with plaintiff's case is that there is no more than this.

Plaintiff's conversation with defendant's agent was about the middle of February 1956 while plaintiff was in Florida. Plaintiff returned to Minneapolis, which was his residence as well as the jurisdiction where defendant was found, about the latter part of April or the first of May 1956. Soon after this he consulted a lawyer, and suit was started "as rapidly as the lawyer could get moving." There is nothing in the evidence to suggest that plaintiff deferred initiating legal action any longer than suited his own personal convenience. There is nothing in the evidence to suggest that defendant sought any forbearance by plaintiff or thought that it was securing such action; nor is there any evidence that plaintiff's delay from the middle of February until April or May in undertaking legal action was related to defendant's promises. There is no evidence that either of the parties took defendant's assurances seriously or acted upon them in any way. There was, therefore, no consideration, and the promises did not amount to a contract. Since the district court was correct in ordering judgment entered for the defendant, notwithstanding the verdict, on this ground, it is unnecessary to consider other points relating to enforceability of the alleged contract.

Affirmed.

QUESTIONS AND NOTES

1. In an omitted portion of the opinion, the Court finds that Penn–O–Tex was neither in possession of nor operating Kemp's gas stations. Thus Baehr's claim for rent could be maintained only against Kemp under his lease, unless Penn–O–Tex had made an enforceable promise to Baehr that it would pay the rent. Didn't the Court find that Penn–O–Tex Oil, through its agent (who presumably had authority to act for it), promised during the telephone conversation with Mr. Baehr that the rent would be paid?

2. What was the agent's motive in assuring Baehr that the rent would be paid? What did Penn–O–Tex stand to gain if Baehr didn't bring suit to evict Kemp, the tenant, for nonpayment of the rent?

3. Statements that appear promissory may nevertheless lack sufficient substance to serve as the essential element of the bargain. So, "I promise you a million dollars if you promise to accept a million dollars" is not a bargain because the return commitment is a mirror that is customarily presumed to have no significance independent of the initial promise. Otherwise, any *nudum pactum* could be linguistically transformed into a bargain. Was the return commitment by Baehr roughly the equivalent of "I promise to accept the rent payments"?

4. If Penn–O–Tex's agent had explicitly asked Baehr to withhold legal action against Kemp for at least three months, promising to pay the rent if Kemp did not, and Baehr promised to so forebear, would the court have enforced Penn–O–Tex's promise to pay the rent? Why doesn't the court interpret the facts this way? Is it because at some fundamental level the court did not really believe that Penn–O–Tex had promised to pay the rent? Were there any express promissory words here?

III. ADEQUACY OF CONSIDERATION

There is common sense appeal to the idea that an important promise, and therefore a promise worthy of legal enforcement, is one for which someone paid something of significant value. But what kinds of prices are sufficient to be consideration? How do you determine whether a promise or performance is truly bargained for? Moreover, how do you decide whether one set of promises or performances was given in exchange for the other? The parties' statement of the bargain is an obvious starting point, but placing too much weight on a recital of exchange, reduces consideration to a formality. The gift promise becomes binding because of the promisee's reciprocal kiss; a valuable promise is exchanged for a penny.

Bear in mind that the law for many centuries has claimed that it cannot and should not weigh the relative values of the promise and the consideration given for it in determining the enforceability of the agreement. If serious and sensible people operating at arm's length considered it a desirable exchange, the law says it will look no further. Classically, this principle is stated: The law will not question the adequacy of consideration.

As Thomas Hobbes expressed this idea centuries ago: "The value of all things contracted for, is measured by the appetite of the contractors: and therefore the just value is that which they be contented to give." LEVIATHAN (1688).

Or as § 79 of the Restatement, Second, Contracts, puts it:

If the requirement of consideration is met [that something is bargained for, *see* § 71, *supra*], there is no additional requirement of

(a) a gain, advantage or benefit to the promisor or a loss, disadvantage, or detriment to the promisee; or

(b) equivalence in the values exchanged; or

(c) "mutuality of obligation."

Few exchanges are precisely equal, and value usually is left to the judgment of the bargainer. But in extreme situations the value of the consideration may become so slight that we begin to wonder whether anything was paid for the promise. Moreover, value cannot always be measured in simple monetary terms. If I think a crumby old painting, or a kooky new painting, is worth $250,000, that's my problem. Even in commercial situations, the rewards of a bargain may be subtle and not measured precisely in dollars. It may be good business or enhance one's prestige to make what looks like a terrible bargain that draws customers into your store, or helps you to sell something else, or keeps your idle productive capacity going or makes you look and feel like a prince. What was the value of Best's promise of reciprocity to Southland?

But we all become uncomfortable when the disparity between what is sold and what is paid becomes very great. Part of our discomfort arises from the sense that an unequal deal doesn't seem serious and sensible. Somebody is either out of his mind, or didn't understand what he was doing, or didn't voluntarily consent to this exchange.

In sum, the law generally presumes knowing and capable parties may determine the values involved in their serious and sensible transactions for themselves. Hence, if nothing else in the circumstances surrounding a deal looks out of line (no duress, no lack of capacity, no joke, no fraud, no mistake, etc.), the fact that the consideration appears relatively slight will not *in itself* invalidate the deal. Significant disparity in values may cause the court to take a closer look; that itself is an important effect.

But sometimes—in the course of the look—the disparity in price that was the look's stimulant somehow gets converted into the principal evidence supporting a conclusion that there was enough wrong with the deal to invalidate it.

Apfel v. Prudential–Bache Securities

New York Court of Appeals, 1993.
81 N.Y.2d 470, 616 N.E.2d 1095, 600 N.Y.S.2d 433.

■ SIMONS, J. Defendant, an investment bank, seeks to avoid an agreement to purchase plaintiffs' idea for issuing and selling municipal bonds. Its principal contention is that plaintiffs had no property right in the idea because it was not novel and, therefore, consideration for the contract was lacking. For reasons which follow, we conclude that a showing of novelty is not required to validate the contract. The decisive question is whether the idea had value, not whether it was novel.

I

In 1982, plaintiffs, an investment banker and a lawyer, approached defendant's predecessor with a proposal for issuing municipal securities through a system that eliminated paper certificates and allowed bonds to be sold, traded, and held exclusively by means of computerized "book entries." Initially, the parties signed a confidentiality agreement that allowed defendant to review the techniques as detailed in a 99–page summary. Nearly a month of negotiations followed before the parties entered into a sale agreement under which plaintiffs conveyed their rights to the techniques and certain trade names and defendant agreed to pay a stipulated rate based on its use of the techniques for a term from October 1982 to January 1988. Under the provisions of the contract, defendant's obligation to pay was to remain even if the techniques became public knowledge or standard practice in the industry and applications for patents and trademarks were denied. Plaintiffs asserted that they had not previously disclosed the techniques to anyone and they agreed to maintain them in confidence until they became public.

From 1982 until 1985, defendant implemented the contract, although the parties dispute whether amounts due were fully paid. Defendant actively encouraged bond issuers to use the computerized "book entry" system and, for at least the first year, was the sole underwriter in the industry employing such a system. However, in 1985, following a change in personnel, defendant refused to make any further payments. It maintained that the ideas conveyed by plaintiffs had been in the public domain at the time of the sale agreement and that what plaintiffs sold had never been theirs to sell. Defendant's attempts to patent the techniques proved unsuccessful. By 1985, investment banks were increasingly using computerized systems, and by 1990 such systems were handling 60% of the dollar volume of all new issues of municipal securities.

Plaintiffs commenced this litigation seeking $45 million in compensatory and punitive damages.

Supreme Court concluded that triable issues existed on the questions of whether defendant breached the contract by refusing to make payments and whether plaintiffs committed a breach by allegedly disclosing the techniques to another company. The court also found defendant had raised a triable issue on whether plaintiffs had partially waived their right to payment by forgoing certain claims to compensation. The remainder of the pleadings were found to be legally insufficient. Accordingly, the court dismissed all the causes of action except the first, which alleges breach of contract, and struck all defendant's defenses and counterclaims except those relating to breach of contract and the partial defense of waiver. The Appellate Division modified the order by reinstating defendant's claim that the sale agreement lacked consideration. It held that novelty was required before an idea could be valid consideration but concluded that the question was one of fact to be decided at trial. It also reinstated the cause of action for unjust enrichment, holding that the presence of an express contract did not foreclose recovery on a theory of quasi contract.

On this appeal, defendant's principal contention is that no contract existed between the parties because the sale agreement lacked consideration. Underlying that argument is its assertion that an idea cannot be legally sufficient consideration unless it is novel. Plaintiffs insist that their system was indeed novel, but contend that, in any event, novelty is not required to validate the contract at issue here.

II

Defendant's cross motion for summary judgment insofar as it sought to dismiss the first cause of action alleging breach of contract was properly denied. Additionally, plaintiffs' motion to dismiss the lack of consideration defenses and counterclaims should be granted.

Under the traditional principles of contract law, the parties to a contract are free to make their bargain, even if the consideration exchanged is grossly unequal or of dubious value. Absent fraud or unconscionability, the adequacy of consideration is not a proper subject for judicial scrutiny. It is enough that something of "real value in the eye of the law" was exchanged. The fact that the sellers may not have had a property right in what they sold does not, by itself, render the contract void for lack of consideration.

Manifestly, defendant received something of value here; its own conduct establishes that. After signing the confidentiality agreement, defendant thoroughly reviewed plaintiffs' system before buying it. Having done so, it was in the best position to know whether the idea had value. It decided to enter into the sale agreement and aggressively market the system to potential bond issuers. For at least a year, it was the only underwriter to use plaintiffs' "book entry" system for municipal bonds, and it handled millions of such bond transactions during that time. Having obtained full disclosure of the system, used it in advance of competitors, and received the associated benefits of precluding its disclosure to others, defendant can hardly claim now the idea had no value to its municipal securities business. Indeed, defendant acknowledges it made payments to plaintiffs under the sale agreement for more than two years, conduct that would belie any claim it might make that the idea was lacking in value or that it had actually been obtained from some other source before plaintiffs' disclosure.

Thus, defendant has failed to demonstrate on this record that the contract was void or to raise a triable issue of fact on lack of consideration.

III

Defendant's position rests on *Downey v. General Foods Corp.*, and *Soule v. Bon Ami Co.*, and similar decisions. It contends those cases establish an exception to traditional principles of contract law and require that the idea must be novel before it can constitute valid consideration for a contract. While our cases have discussed novelty as an element of an idea seller's claim, it is not a discrete supplemental requirement, but simply part of plaintiff's proof of either a proprietary interest in a claim based on a property theory or the validity of the consideration in a claim based on a contract theory.

In *Downey*, plaintiff submitted an idea for an advertising campaign. A short time later, defendant General Foods mounted a campaign that was similar to the one plaintiff had suggested and plaintiff sought damages in a complaint alleging several theories for recovery. We ordered the dismissal of the complaint on two separate grounds: first, the lack of novelty and, second, defendant's prior possession of the idea—i.e., its lack of novelty as to defendant. To the extent plaintiff's causes of action were grounded on assertions of a property right, we found that they were untenable "if the elements of novelty and originality [were] absent, since the property right in an idea is based upon these two elements." Second, we concluded that the defendant possessed plaintiff's ideas prior to plaintiff's disclosure. Thus, the ideas could have no value to defendant and could not supply consideration for any agreement between the parties.

In *Soule v. Bon Ami Co.*, plaintiff made an express contract with Bon Ami to disclose a way to increase profits. The idea consisted largely of a proposal to raise prices. The Appellate Division, in a frequently cited opinion, denied plaintiff any recovery, finding that the bargain lacked consideration because the idea was not novel. This Court affirmed but it did so on a different basis: it held that plaintiff had failed to show that profits resulted from the disclosure.

These decisions do not support defendant's contention that novelty is required in all cases involving disclosure of ideas. Indeed, we have explicitly held that it is not. *Downey*, *Soule* and cases in that line of decisions involve a distinct factual pattern: the buyer and seller contract for disclosure of the idea with payment based on use, but no separate postdisclosure contract for use of the idea has been made. Thus, they present the issue of whether the idea the buyer was using was, in fact, the seller's.

Such transactions pose two problems for the courts. On the one hand, how can sellers prove that the buyer obtained the idea from them, and nowhere else, and that the buyer's use of it thus constitutes misappropriation of property? Unlike tangible property, an idea lacks title and boundaries and cannot be rendered exclusive by the acts of the one who first thinks it. On the other hand, there is no equity in enforcing a seemingly valid contract when, in fact, it turns out upon disclosure that the buyer already possessed the idea. In such instances, the disclosure, though freely bargained for, is manifestly without value. A showing of novelty, at least novelty as to the buyer, addresses these two concerns. Novelty can then serve to establish both the attributes of ownership necessary for a property-based claim and the value of the consideration—the disclosure—necessary for contract-based claims.

There are no such concerns in a transaction such as the one before us. Defendant does not claim that it was aware of the idea before plaintiffs disclosed it but, rather, concedes that the idea came from them. When a seller's claim arises from a contract to use an idea entered into after the disclosure of the idea, the question is not whether the buyer misappropriated property from the seller, but whether the idea had value to the buyer and thus constitutes valid consideration. In such a case, the buyer knows what he or she is buying and has agreed that the idea has value, and the Court will not ordinarily go behind that determination. The lack of novelty, in and of itself, does not demonstrate a lack of value. To the contrary, the buyer may reap benefits from such a contract in a number of ways—for instance, by not having to expend resources pursuing the idea through other channels or by having a profit-making idea implemented sooner rather than later. The law of contracts would have to be substantially rewritten were we to allow buyers of fully disclosed ideas to disregard their obligation to pay simply because an idea could have been obtained from some other source or in some other way.

IV

Having found that defendant's counterclaims and defenses challenging the existence of a valid contract should be stricken, we further conclude that the Appellate Division erred in reinstating plaintiffs' seventh cause of action, which alleged unjust enrichment on a quasi-contract theory. The transaction is controlled by the express agreement of the parties and their rights and liabilities are to be determined solely on theories of breach of contract and the partial defense of waiver.

V

We have reviewed the remaining contentions of the parties and find them without merit.

Accordingly, the order of the Appellate Division should be modified, without costs, in accordance with this opinion, and, as so modified, affirmed, and the certified question answered in the negative.

QUESTION

Does the Court in this case refuse to question the adequacy of consideration, or having questioned it, does it find the consideration adequate?

Dyer v. National By-Products

Supreme Court of Iowa, 1986.
380 N.W.2d 732.

■ SCHULTZ, J. The determinative issue in this appeal is whether good faith forbearance to litigate a claim, which proves to be invalid and unfounded, is sufficient consideration to uphold a contract of settlement. The district court determined, as a matter of law, that consideration for the alleged settlement was lacking because the forborne claim was not a viable cause of action. We reverse and remand.

On October 29, 1981, Dale Dyer, an employee of National By-Products, lost his right foot in a job-related accident. Thereafter, the employer placed Dyer on a leave of absence at full pay from the date of his injury until August 16, 1982. At that time he returned to work as a foreman, the job he held prior to his injury. On March 11, 1983, the employer indefinitely laid off Dyer.

Dyer then filed the present lawsuit against his employer claiming that his discharge was a breach of an oral contract. He alleged that he in good faith believed that he had a valid claim against his employer for his personal injury. Further, Dyer claimed that his forbearance from litigating his claim was made in exchange for a promise from his employer that he would have lifetime employment. The employer specifically denied that it had offered a lifetime job to Dyer after his injury.

Following extensive discovery procedures, the employer filed a motion for summary judgment claiming there was no genuine factual issue and that it was entitled to judgment as a matter of law. The motion was resisted by Dyer. The district court sustained the employer's motion on the basis that: (1) no reciprocal promise to work for the employer for life was present, and (2) there was no forbearance of any viable cause of action, apparently on the ground that workers' compensation provided Dyer's sole remedy.

On appeal, Dyer claims that consideration for the alleged contract of lifetime employment was his forbearance from pursuing an action against his employer. Accordingly, he restricts his claim of error to the second reason advanced by the district court for granting summary judgment. Summary judgment is only proper when there is no genuine issue of any material fact. Dyer generally contends that an unresolved issue of material fact remains as to whether he reasonably and in good faith forbore from asserting a claim against his employer and his co-employees in exchange for the employer's alleged promise to employ him for life. Specifically, he asserts that the trial court erred because: (1) the court did not consider the reasonableness and good faith of his belief in the validity of the claim he forbore from asserting, and (2) the court considered the legal merits of the claim itself which Dyer forbore from asserting.

The employer, on the other hand, maintains that workers' compensation[1] benefits are Dyer's sole remedy for his injury and that his claim for damages is unfounded. It then urges that forbearance from asserting an unfounded claim cannot serve as consideration for a contract. For the purpose of this discussion, we shall assume that Dyer's tort action is clearly invalid and he had no basis for a tort suit against either his employer or his fellow employees. We recognize that the fact issue, as to whether Dyer in good faith believed that he had a cause of action based in tort against the employer, remains unresolved. The determinative issue before the district court and now on appeal is whether the lack of consideration for the alleged promise of lifetime employment has been established as a matter of law.

Preliminarily, we observe that the law favors the adjustment and settlement of controversies without resorting to court action. Compromise of a doubtful right asserted in good faith is sufficient consideration for a promise.

The more difficult problem is whether the settlement of an unfounded claim asserted in good faith is consideration for a contract of settlement. Professor Corbin presents a view favorable to Dyer's argument when he states:

[F]orbearance to press a claim, or a promise of such forbearance, may be a sufficient consideration even though the claim is wholly ill-founded. It may be

---

1. It is undisputed that the employee was covered under workers' compensation. The Iowa workers' compensation act states in pertinent part that:

The rights and remedies provided in this chapter * * * for an employee on account of injury * * * for which benefits under this chapter * * * are recoverable, shall be the exclusive and only rights and remedies of such employee * * * at common law or otherwise, on account of such injury * * * against:

(1) his or her employer * * *.

ill-founded because the facts are not what he supposes them to be, or because the existing facts do not have the legal operation that he supposes them to have. In either case, his forbearance may be a sufficient consideration, although under certain circumstances it is not. The fact that the claim is ill-founded is not in itself enough to prevent forbearance from being a sufficient consideration for a promise.

1 Corbin on Contracts § 140, at 595 (1963). Further, in the same section, it is noted that:

> The most generally prevailing, and probably the most satisfactory view is that forbearance is sufficient if there is any reasonable ground for the claimant's belief that it is just to try to enforce his claim. He must be asserting his claim "in good faith"; but this does not mean he must believe that his suit can be won. It means that he must not be making his claim or threatening suit for purposes of vexation, or in order to realize on its "nuisance value."

Indeed, we find support for the Corbin view in language contained in our cases.

The Restatement (Second) of Contracts § 74 (1979), supports the Corbin view and states:

(1) Forbearance to assert or the surrender of a claim or defense which proves to be invalid is not consideration unless

   (a) the claim or defense is in fact doubtful because of uncertainty as to the facts or the law, or

   (b) the forbearing or surrendering party believes that the claim or defense may be fairly determined to be valid.

COMMENT:

b. Requirement of good faith. The policy favoring compromise of disputed claims is clearest, perhaps, where a claim is surrendered at a time when it is uncertain whether it is valid or not. Even though the invalidity later becomes clear, the bargain is to be judged as it appeared to the parties at the time; if the claim was then doubtful, no inquiry is necessary as to their good faith. Even though the invalidity should have been clear at the time, the settlement of an honest dispute is upheld. But a mere assertion or denial of liability does not make a claim doubtful, and the fact that invalidity is obvious may indicate that it was known. In such cases Subsection (1)(b) requires a showing of good faith.

However, not all jurisdictions adhere to this view. Some courts require that the claim forborne must have some merit in fact or at law before it can provide consideration and these jurisdictions reject those claims that are obviously invalid.

In fact, we find language in our own case law that supports the view which is favorable to the employer in this case. Additionally, Professor Williston notes that:

> While there is a great divergence of opinion respecting the kind of forbearance which will constitute consideration, the weight of authority holds that although forbearance from suit on a clearly invalid claim is insufficient consideration for a promise, forbearance from suit on a claim of doubtful validity is sufficient consideration for a promise if there is a sincere belief in the validity of the claim.

1 Williston on Contracts § 135 (3rd ed. 1957).

We believe, however, that the better reasoned approach is that expressed in the Restatement (Second) of Contracts section 74. Even the above statement from Williston, although it may have been the state of the law in 1957, is a questionable assessment of the current law. In fact, most of the cases cited in the cumulative supplement to Williston follow the "good faith and reasonable" language. As noted before, as a matter of policy the law favors compromise and such policy would be defeated if a party could second guess his settlement and litigate the validity of the compromise. The requirement that the forbearing party assert the claim in good faith sufficiently protects the policy of law that favors the settlement of controversies. Our holdings which are to the contrary to this view are overruled.

In the present case, the invalidity of Dyer's claim against the employer does not foreclose him, as a matter of law, from asserting that his forbearance was consideration for the alleged contract of settlement. However, the issue of Dyer's good faith must still be examined. In so doing, the issue of the validity of Dyer's claim should not be entirely overlooked:

> Although the courts will not inquire into the validity of a claim which was compromised in good faith, there must generally be reasonable grounds for a belief in order for the court to be convinced that the belief was honestly entertained by the person who asserted it. Sufficient consideration requires more than the bald assertion by a claimant who has a claim, and to the extent that the validity or invalidity of a claim has a bearing upon whether there were reasonable grounds for believing in its possible validity, evidence of the validity or invalidity of a claim may be relevant to the issue of good faith.

We conclude that the evidence of the invalidity of the claim is relevant to show a lack of honest belief in the validity of the claim asserted or forborne.

Under the present state of the record, there remains a material fact as to whether Dyer's forbearance to assert his claim was in good faith. Summary judgment should not have been rendered against him. Accordingly, the case is reversed and remanded for further proceedings consistent with this opinion.

QUESTIONS AND NOTES

1. What kind of evidence does Dyer need to bring at trial to prove that his belief that he could bring suit against National By–Products was in "good faith and reasonable"? Isn't it more or less common knowledge that workers' compensation is the only method of recovery against an employer for "on the job" accidents? What is the likelihood that National By–Products actually promised Dyer lifetime employment in exchange for dropping a tort suit clearly barred by the workers' compensation statute?

2. Why is Baehr's forbearance from repossessing his property for nonpayment of rent (a slam-dunk cause of action) not consideration, while Dyer's forbearance from suing in tort may be, even though he has no cause of action as a matter of law? Certainly there is a procedural issue: Baehr's case is a review of judgment notwithstanding the jury verdict after trial, while Dyer's is a review of summary judgment. Baehr had the burden of showing there was sufficient evidence to uphold the jury verdict, while Dyer needed only to have a material issue of fact concerning the possible existence of the contract to escape summary judgment and go to trial. But is there a substantive issue that distinguishes the cases?

3. How can forbearance from bringing a meritless suit be consideration? Doesn't this encourage unscrupulous bullies to extract concessions by threatening meritless suits against those who are not legally savvy or lack the resources to defend?

GOOD FAITH, BEST EFFORTS, REQUIREMENT AND OUTPUT CONTRACTS

From Chapter One of this book you have seen contracts enforced notwithstanding that the obligations on one side may be substantially more onerous than those on the other. One common example of this is the requirements contract, where the seller agrees to provide all of the other party's requirements, but the buyer does not promise to have any requirements or to place any orders. Conversely, in an output contract, the buyer promises to buy all of its counterparty's output of an item, but the seller does not promise to have any output.

UNIFORM COMMERCIAL CODE:

§ 2–306. Output, Requirements and Exclusive Dealings.

(1) A term which measures the quantity by the output of the seller or the requirements of the buyer means such actual output or requirements as may occur in good faith, except that no quantity unreasonably disproportionate to any stated estimate or in the absence of a stated estimate to any normal or

otherwise comparable prior output or requirements may be tendered or demanded.

(2) A lawful agreement by either the seller or the buyer for exclusive dealing in the kind of goods concerned imposes unless otherwise agreed an obligation by the seller to use best efforts to supply the goods and by the buyer to use best efforts to promote their sale.

Feld v. Henry S. Levy & Sons

New York Court of Appeals, 1975.
37 N.Y.2d 466, 373 N.Y.S.2d 102, 335 N.E.2d 320.

■ COOKE, J. Plaintiff operates a business known as the Crushed Toast Company and defendant is engaged in the wholesale bread baking business. They entered into a written contract, as of June 19, 1968, in which defendant agreed to sell and plaintiff to purchase "all bread crumbs produced by the Seller in its factory at 115 Thames Street, Brooklyn, New York, during the period commencing June 19, 1968, and terminating June 18, 1969," the agreement to "be deemed automatically renewed thereafter for successive renewal periods of one year" with the right to either party to cancel by giving not less than six months notice to the other by certified mail. No notice of cancellation was served. Additionally, pursuant to a contract stipulation, a faithful performance bond was delivered by plaintiff at the inception of the contractual relationship, and a bond continuation certificate was later submitted for the yearly term commencing June 19, 1969.

Interestingly, the term "bread crumbs" does not refer to crumbs that may flake off bread; rather, they are a manufactured item, starting with stale or imperfectly appearing loaves and followed by removal of labels, processing through two grinders, the second of which effects a finer granulation, insertion into a drum in an oven for toasting and, finally, bagging of the finished product.

Subsequent to the making of the agreement, a substantial quantity of bread crumbs, said to be over 250 tons, were sold by defendant to plaintiff but defendant stopped crumb production on about May 15, 1969. There was proof by defendant's comptroller that the oven was too large to accommodate the drum, that it was stated that the operation was "very uneconomical," but after said date of cessation no steps were taken to obtain more economical equipment. The toasting oven was intentionally broken down, then partially rebuilt, then completely dismantled in the summer of 1969 and, thereafter, defendant used the space for a computer room. It appears, without dispute, that defendant indicated to plaintiff at different times that the former would resume bread crumb production if the contract price of 6 cents per pound be changed to 7 cents, and also that, after the crumb making machinery was dismantled, defendant sold the raw materials used in making crumbs to animal food manufacturers.

Special Term denied plaintiff's motion for summary judgment on the issue of liability and turned down defendant's counter-request for a summary judgment of dismissal. From the Appellate Division's order of affirmance, by a divided court, both parties appeal.

Defendant contends that the contract did not require defendant to manufacture bread crumbs, but merely to sell those it did, and, since none were produced after the demise of the oven, there was no duty to then deliver and, consequently from then on, no liability on its part. Agreements to sell all the goods or services a party may produce or perform to another party are commonly referred to as "output" contracts and they usually serve a useful commercial purpose in minimizing the burdens of product marketing. The Uniform Commercial Code rejects the ideas that an output contract is lacking in mutuality or that it is unenforceable because of indefiniteness in that a quantity for the term is not specified. Official Comment 2 to section 2–306 states in part: "Under this Article, a contract for output * * * is not too indefinite since it is held to mean the actual good faith output * * * of the particular party. Nor does such a contract lack mutuality of obligation since, under this section, the party who will determine quantity is required to operate his plant or conduct his business in good faith and according to commercial standards of fair dealing in the trade so that his output * * * will proximate a reasonably foreseeable figure."

The real issue in this case is whether the agreement carries with it an implication that defendant was obligated to continue to manufacture bread crumbs for the full term. Section 2–306 of the Uniform Commercial Code, entitled "Output, Requirements and Exclusive Dealings" provides:

(1) A term which measures the quantity by the output of the seller or the requirements of the buyer means such actual output or requirements as may occur in good faith, except that no quantity unreasonably disproportionate to any stated estimate or in the absence of a stated estimate to any normal or otherwise comparable prior output or requirements may be tendered or demanded.

(2) *A lawful agreement* by either the seller or the buyer *for exclusive dealing* in the kind of goods concerned *imposes* unless otherwise agreed an obligation *by the seller to use best efforts to supply the goods* and by the buyer to use best efforts to promote their sale. (Emphasis supplied.)

The Official Comment thereunder reads in part:

Subsection (2), on exclusive dealing, makes explicit the commercial rule embodied in this Act under which the parties to such contracts are held to have impliedly, even when not expressly, bound themselves to use reasonable diligence as well as good faith in their performance of the contract. * * * An exclusive dealing agreement brings into play all of the good faith aspects of the output and requirement problems of subsection (1). It also raises questions of insecurity and right to adequate assurance under this Article.

Section 2–306 is consistent with prior New York case law. Every contract of this type imposes an obligation of good faith in its performance (Uniform Commercial Code, § 1–203). Under the Uniform Commercial Code, the commercial background and intent must be read into the language of any agreement and good faith is demanded in the performance of that agreement and, under the decisions relating to output contracts, it is clearly the general rule that good faith cessation of production terminates any further obligations thereunder and excuses further performance by the party discontinuing production.

This is not a situation where defendant ceased its main operation of bread baking. Rather, defendant contends in a conclusory fashion that it was "uneconomical" or "economically not feasible" for it to continue to make bread crumbs. Although plaintiff observed in his motion papers that defendant claimed it was not economically feasible to make the crumbs, plaintiff did not admit that as a fact. In any event, "economic feasibility," an expression subject to many interpretations, would not be a precise or reliable test.

There are present here intertwined questions of fact, whether defendant performed in good faith and whether it stopped its manufacture of bread crumbs in good faith, neither of which can be resolved properly on this record. The seller's duty to remain in crumb production is a matter calling for a close scrutiny of its motives confined here by the papers to financial reasons. It is undisputed that defendant leveled its crumb making machinery only after plaintiff refused to agree to a price higher than that specified in the agreement and that it then sold the raw materials to manufacturers of animal food. There are before us no componential figures indicating the actual cost of the finished bread crumbs to defendant, statements as to the profits derived or the losses sustained, or data specifying the net or gross return realized from the animal food transactions.

The parties by their contract gave the right of cancellation to either by providing for a six months' notice to the other. The apparent purpose of such a stipulation was to provide an opportunity to either the seller or buyer to conclude their dealings in the event that the transactions were not as profitable or advantageous as desired or expected, or for any other reason. Correspondingly, such a notice would also furnish the receiver of it a chance to secure another outlet or source of supply, as the case might be. Short of such a cancellation, defendant was expected to continue to perform in good faith and could cease production of the bread crumbs, a single facet of its operation, only in good faith. Obviously, a bankruptcy or genuine imperiling of the very existence of its entire business caused by the production of the crumbs would warrant cessation of production of that item; the yield of less profit from its sale than expected would not. Since bread crumbs were but a part of defendant's enterprise and since there was a contractual right of cancellation, good faith required continued production until cancellation, even if there be no profit. In circumstances such as these and without more, defendant would be justified, in good faith, in ceasing production of the single item prior to cancellation only if its losses from continuance would be more than trivial, which, overall, is a question of fact.

The order of the Appellate Division should be affirmed, without costs.

QUESTIONS

1. What does the court understand Henry S. Levy & Sons' promise to mean? Can you state it better?

2. Assume you represent Henry S. Levy & Sons and now must prepare for trial. What kind of story will you tell? Specify the evidence you will look for.

Technical Assistance International v. United States

U.S. Court of Appeals, Federal Circuit, 1998.
150 F.3d 1369.

■ BRYSON, J. This case requires us to determine how much freedom the government has to vary its requirements when it enters into a requirements contract. The government entered into a requirements contract with Technical Assistance International, Inc., (TAI), pursuant to which TAI was to maintain and repair the Army's vehicle fleet at the White Sands Missile Range. The United States Court of Federal Claims held that when the government increased the rate at which it replaced the older vehicles in the fleet, and thus decreased its requirements for vehicle maintenance and repair services, the government violated its contractual obligations to TAI. We reverse.

I

In early 1992, the Army consolidated its fleet of general purpose vehicles at the White Sands Missile Range into the Interagency Fleet Management System. The Interagency Fleet Management System is a federal agency service program under which the General Services Administration (GSA) assumes ownership of and maintenance responsibilities for fleets of vehicles formerly owned and maintained by various federal agencies. The purpose of the program is to achieve economies of scale in the purchasing, management, and servicing of such fleets.

The average age of the vehicles in the Army's White Sands fleet before being transferred into the GSA program was eight years. One of the Army's goals in consolidating its fleet into the GSA program was to bring the fleet up to GSA standards, which call for vehicles to be replaced after three to six years of use (depending on vehicle type and mileage). Because GSA could not afford to replace all of the Army's old vehicles at once, it committed itself to bringing the Army's fleet up to its replacement standard over a five-year period. Of particular relevance to this case, GSA and the Army agreed that during the first year of consolidation, GSA would replace at least 30% of the vehicles eligible for replacement, and perhaps a higher percentage if it had the resources to do so.

GSA does not service and repair vehicles itself, but instead hires on-site contractors to perform those services. On November 15, 1991, GSA issued a bid solicitation for a requirements contract for the maintenance and repair of the White Sands vehicle fleet. As part of that solicitation, GSA prepared an estimate of the fleet's maintenance and repair needs, itemized by service types. Because GSA had not previously procured maintenance services for the White Sands fleet, it did not have any historic bid or price data to use in formulating the estimate. Instead, GSA based its estimate on a number of factors, including the number and types of vehicles in the fleet, the terrain and typical use of vehicles at White Sands, a review of GSA service contracts at similar sites, and GSA's commitment to replace at least 30% of the vehicles eligible for replacement during the first year of consolidation.

GSA awarded the contract to TAI on March 30, 1992. The contract term began on May 1, 1992, and was to run for one year, with two one-year options to renew at the government's discretion. Within two months of beginning performance, TAI projected that the work required for the White Sands fleet was going to fall considerably short of GSA's estimate. TAI submitted a request for an equitable adjustment based on the projected shortfall, as well as a certified claim for compensation based on a charge that GSA's contract estimate was prepared negligently. GSA denied the requested relief.

TAI subsequently filed suit in the Court of Federal Claims. The complaint alleged that TAI suffered damages as a result of the government's negligent estimate preparation. On cross-motions for summary judgment, the trial court ruled that the government had not been negligent in the preparation of its estimate, but the court nonetheless held that the government had breached its obligations under the contract and that TAI was entitled to relief.

In reaching its decision, the court relied on testimony from Virlene Griffin, the Group Leader of Operations for GSA's Fleet Maintenance Division, that during the first year of consolidation, GSA replaced more than twice the number of vehicles it had expected to replace. Ms. Griffin testified that there were a number of factors that resulted in the accelerated replacement rate, including the downsizing of GSA fleets at several nearby locations, the grant of permission from the Office of Management and Budget for GSA to acquire new cars through leasing as well as purchasing, and the delivery of new vehicles that had been ordered before the consolidation of the Army's fleet.

The court held that when a contractor enters into a requirements contract, it assumes only the risk of a change in requirements caused by to the "vagaries of user demand." The court regarded the accelerated rate at which GSA replaced the fleet's older cars to have been prompted by fleet surpluses at other locations, rather than by a change in the "indigenous needs" of the facility that TAI contracted to serve. The court reasoned that TAI had not assumed the risk that GSA would increase the rate of replacement of the White Sands fleet in the event other GSA fleets developed a surplus. For that reason, the court concluded that when the government reduced its requirements by increasing the replacement rate for the White Sands fleet, the government effected a constructive change in the contract and breached its contractual obligations to TAI.

II

A

A requirements contract is primarily designed to provide a buyer with flexibility in operating its business. The buyer is likely to enter into such a contract when its needs are unpredictable and it wishes to preserve for itself the freedom to determine its level of consumption and to conduct its operations according to its best business judgment. The buyer is generally accorded significant freedom in determining its requirements under a requirements contract because it has specifically bargained for such flexibility, in exchange for which it has usually agreed to pay a premium price for the goods or services to be provided.

Nevertheless, the law imposes some limits on the buyer, lest it be permitted to vary its requirements to such an extent that the seller is exposed to an undue risk of severe economic hardship.

The limitation on the buyer's freedom to vary its requirements is usually expressed as a duty to act in good faith.

A buyer acts in good faith if it has a valid business reason for varying its requirements other than dissatisfaction with the contract. "Bad faith" includes actions "motivated solely by a reassessment of the balance of advantages and disadvantages under the contract." That is, if the buyer "had second thoughts about the terms of the contract," and decreased its requirements in an attempt to avoid its obligations under the contract, the buyer is deemed to have endeavored to manipulate the contract and thus to have acted in bad faith.

The Uniform Commercial Code contains a separate restriction on the buyer's freedom to vary its requirements, see Uniform Commercial Code § 2–306(1) (buyer of goods cannot demand a quantity "unreasonably disproportionate to any stated estimates"), but it is unclear how much that additional restriction adds to the obligation of good faith. In any event, the Uniform Commercial Code is not binding with respect to government contracts, and we decline to adopt the Uniform Commercial Code standard here.

TAI argues that another limitation should restrict the government's ability to vary its requirements: A variation should not be permitted if it is occasioned by a decision on the part of the government that "materially alter[s] factors upon which the estimates are based." According to TAI, if the government makes any decisions that affect the factors that formed the basis for the contract estimate, the government must compensate the contractor for any losses it suffers as a result.

We reject TAI's proposed limitation, because it would severely hamper the government's ability to adjust its requirements in accordance with its true needs and thus would undermine the primary function of a requirements contract—to permit the government to operate its business according to its business judgment when its needs are uncertain or unpredictable. In essence, TAI's limitation would require the government to commit itself "to go through with whatever project generated the estimate of required quantity, no matter what happened over the life of the project," a result that has been clearly rejected by the long line of cases that have permitted buyers to discontinue their businesses and thereby eliminate their requirements altogether, as long as they do so in good faith.

In sum, we hold that the only limitation upon the government's ability to vary its requirements under a requirements contract is that it must do so in good faith. Our holding is in accord with numerous decisions from other courts. That rule has the benefit of simplicity, and it enables the government to take full advantage of the flexibility for which it has bargained. Of course, the seller can control the risk that a requirements contract may result in harsh consequences by incorporating minimum and maximum quantity terms, or other similar provisions, into the contract.

B

The party alleging a breach of contract bears the burden of proving the breach. Thus, in a requirements contract case in which the seller alleges that the buyer breached the contract by reducing its requirements, the burden of proof is on the seller to prove that the buyer acted in bad faith, for example, by reducing its requirements solely in order to avoid its obligations under the contract. In the absence of such a showing, the buyer will be presumed to have varied its requirements for valid business reasons, i.e., to have acted in good faith, and will not be liable for the change in requirements.

In the present case, TAI has neither alleged nor shown that the government altered its requirements in bad faith. The government introduced evidence that it had valid business reasons for incorporating available new vehicles into the White Sands fleet. Specifically, doing so enabled the government to "suffer less downtime" and resulted in "making a better fleet." TAI has not pointed to any evidence showing that the government's reduction in requirements was "motivated solely by a reassessment of the balance of advantages and disadvantages under the contract."

This case is very similar to *Southwest Natural Gas Co.* [*v. Oklahoma Portland Cement Co.*] in which the buyer in a requirements contract reduced its gas requirements as a result of having replaced an old, worn-out boiler with a new, more efficient boiler. The court concluded that the buyer did not breach the contract because it improved its plant "in good faith and in the exercise of prudent business judgment." In this case, there was uncontroverted evidence that the government increased the vehicle replacement rate in a similar attempt to improve its fleet. Because the government "had a business reason for deciding [to make use of available new vehicles] that was independent of the terms of the contract ... with [TAI]," the government acted in good faith. Accordingly, the government did not breach or constructively change its contract with TAI.

QUESTIONS AND NOTES

1. Note that the court expressly does not adopt the UCC rule for government contracts. If the court had applied UCC § 2–306 in this case, would the outcome have been different?

2. Notice that the trial court held that when a contractor enters into a requirements contract, it assumes only the risk of a change in requirements caused by the "vagaries of user demand," but the appellate court found no such limitation in the contract. Assume that TAI is willing to bear the risk of vagaries of user demand, but not the risk that the Government will alter the nature of the fleet or other risks that reflect changed circumstances at White Sands. How would you suggest it avoid bearing such risks in the future? What if it doesn't want to bear all the risk of vagaries of user demand?

IV. PAST CONSIDERATION — MORAL OBLIGATION

If a bargain is essential to an enforceable promise, a promise based on something that the promisor already has is obviously not enforceable. There can be no present exchange in such a circumstance and therefore, *a fortiori,* no consideration as defined by Restatement, Second, Contracts § 71. This logical point has caused difficulty in the law of contract, for many a promise is made out of gratitude or a feeling of obligation for what the promisee did for the promisor in the past. Whether such a promise should bind the promisor depends ultimately upon the reasons for holding promises to be binding.

Passante v. McWilliam
California Court of Appeal, 1997.
53 Cal.App.4th 1240, 62 Cal.Rptr.2d 298.

■ SILLS, PRESIDING JUSTICE. As someone once said, if you build it they will come. And by the same token, if you make a baseball card that can't be counterfeited, they will buy it. Which brings us to the case at hand.

In 1988 the Upper Deck Company was a rookie baseball card company with an idea for a better baseball card: one that had a hologram on it. Holograms protect credit cards from counterfeiting, and the promoters of the company thought they could protect baseball cards as well. By the 1990's the Upper Deck would become a major corporation whose value was at least a quarter of a billion dollars. Collecting baseball cards, like baseball itself, is big business.

But the outlook wasn't brilliant for the Upper Deck back in the summer of 1988. It lacked the funds for a $100,000 deposit it needed to buy some special paper by August 1, and without that deposit its contract with the major league baseball players association would have been jeopardized.

The Upper Deck's corporate attorney, Anthony Passante, then came through in the clutch. Passante found the money from the brother of his law partner, and, on the morning of July 29, had it wired to a company controlled by one of the directors. That evening, the directors of the company accepted the loan and, in gratitude, agreed among themselves that the corporate attorney should have three percent of the firm's stock. The rest is history. Instead of striking out, the Upper Deck struck it rich.

At this point, if we may be forgiven the mixed metaphor, we must change gears. No good deed goes unpunished. Anthony Passante never sought to collect the inchoate gift of stock, and later, the company just outright reneged on its promise. Passante sued for breach of oral contract, and the jury awarded him close to $33 million—the value of three percent of the Upper Deck at the time of trial in 1993.

The trial judge, however, granted a judgment notwithstanding the verdict, largely because he concluded that Passante had violated his ethical duty as a lawyer to his client. There was no dispute that Passante did not tell the board that it might want to consult with another lawyer before it made its promise. Nor did Passante advise the board of the complications which might arise from his being given three percent of the stock.

The board had a clear moral obligation to honor its promise to Passante. He had, as the baseball cliche goes, stepped up to the plate and homered on the Upper Deck's behalf. And if this court could enforce such moral obligations, we would advise the company even yet to pay something in honor of its promise.

But the trial judge was right. If the promise was bargained for, it was obtained in violation of Passante's ethical obligations as an attorney. If, on the other hand, it was not bargained for—as the record here clearly shows—it was gratuitous. It was therefore legally unenforceable, even though it might have moral force. We must therefore, with perhaps a degree of reluctance, affirm the judgment of the trial court.

FACTS AND PROCEDURAL HISTORY

The Upper Deck Company was formed in March 1988 to produce baseball cards with holograms. The initial directors were Paul Sumner, William Hemrick, Boris Korbel, Richard P. McWilliam, Angels' pitcher DeWayne Buice and Anthony Passante. Passante, who was already the personal attorney for Korbel and McWilliam, was appointed corporate attorney and secretary. McWilliam, an accountant with contacts to a number of investors, had the responsibility of obtaining start-up financing for the company. Passante made no investment in the company and owned no stock.

Upper Deck needed $100,000 to put on deposit with an Italian paper company by August 1, 1988, so the paper would be available for the inaugural run of baseball cards planned for December. Without the paper, the company risked losing its license with major league baseball.[2] However, as of July 26, 1988, the company had not obtained financing. To make matters worse, McWilliam was demanding more stock in return for the financing he was supposed to obtain. Board members instructed Passante to demand the return of McWilliam's 11 percent stock if he would not change his demands.

When Passante found out that McWilliam would not be coming up with the money, he told his law partner, Andy Prendiville that "there was really no hope for the company to make it." Prendiville asked Passante if he should talk to his brother, who was a doctor and might be able to make a loan of $100,000. Passante told Prendiville to call his brother, who said that he "was in a position to loan the money and

---

2. Because Passante prevailed with the jury on his contract claim, all reasonable conflicts and inferences are resolved in his favor. Accordingly, we assume, even though the evidence was in conflict on the point, that the $100,000 loan was vital to the survival of the company.

would do so." Both Passante and Prendiville spoke to Korbel concerning the availability of "those funds." They told Korbel "that the funds were available."

Korbel then requested that Passante come to a special board meeting to be held on the evening of July 29, 1988 "in order to talk to the other two shareholders about that loan." Korbel said he wanted the other shareholders to be a party to the loan. And, because the shareholders would be guaranteeing the repayment of the funds, Korbel "wanted to make sure that he had the agreement of his co-shareholders for that type of an arrangement."

Dr. Kevin Prendiville wired $100,000 to an account controlled by Korbel just a little after 11 a.m. on July 29, 1988, though Passante still understood that if the board did not approve the loan "it wasn't going to be made."

At the board meeting that evening, Passante told the assembled board members (assembled without notice to McWilliam) "about the availability of the funds." He asked them "if they would be interested in obtaining the money from Dr. Prendiville." The board members agreed.

The board members were "all quite excited about the availability of those funds." Korbel "brought up" the idea that the board should consider giving Passante some ownership interest if he got the loan, and Hemrick said, "Look, if you can get that money for us then I think you're entitled to three percent of the company." There was "general agreement" among the board members "that that would be the case." Passante said, "Okay. We'll do the loan," and then went back to his office.

Passante drafted a note which did not have an interest rate on it. However, at Korbel's insistence, an extra $10,000 was paid to Dr. Prendiville for the 90-day loan. The Upper Deck made its deposit.

The day after the deadline, the board members were "quite happy people." At a meeting held that day, the board members discussed how McWilliam's 11 percent would be divided; "it was determined" that Passante would receive 3 percent from McWilliam's 11 percent, and Korbel would receive the 8 percent balance.

Passante's three percent, however, was "to be held by Boris Korbel." The idea was that Korbel would hold Passante's interest in the company until McWilliam returned his stock certificate, and, when a new investor was brought in and new certificates were issued, Passante would receive his stock.

But the Upper Deck still needed financing, and, after an unsuccessful attempt to enlist a New York firm, Korbel told Passante that maybe McWilliam should be brought back into the company after all. Passante told Korbel that he "should do whatever he thought necessary to make the company go forward."

What Korbel thought necessary was to contact McWilliam. On August 31, 1988, Korbel told Passante about Korbel's conversation with McWilliam. McWilliam, it seemed, was "extremely upset" at Passante "because of what had occurred at the end of July." Accordingly, McWilliam would only "invest in Upper Deck" on the condition that Passante "not participate as an owner of the company." Korbel told Passante that "in order to get the company going" Korbel would hold Passante's three percent for him and "we wouldn't tell Mr. McWilliam or any of the other shareholders about this interest." After McWilliam "cool[ed] off" and everything was "smooth again," Korbel would discuss Passante's three percent interest and either "get a stock certificate representing that interest from the corporation," or Korbel would at least make sure Passante "obtained the benefit of that three percent through him" by way of profit distributions from the company.

In early fall McWilliam came back into the company; McWilliam soon brought in Richard Kughn, a Chicago investor. As a result, the shares of the company were redistributed, leaving Korbel, McWilliam and Kughn each with 26 percent. After Kughn made his investment, Passante was fired as corporate attorney because Kughn wanted the company represented by a large law firm.

In 1988 and early 1989, Korbel told Passante that he need not be concerned about the three percent—that Korbel "had it" and he "would take care of it" for Passante. In November 1990, however, at a restaurant in Orange, Korbel told Passante that he wasn't going to get his three percent. In essence, Kughn had been given Passante's three percent in the redistribution of stock occasioned by Kughn's investment.

The next month Passante filed this lawsuit. Andy Prendiville was also named as a plaintiff because Passante told him, after the August 2 meeting, that "because of his being so instrumental in obtaining the $100,000 loan" "half of whatever [Passante] got was his."

As set forth in his second amended complaint, Passante sued McWilliam for intentional interference with prospective advantage, negligent interference with economic relationship, bad faith, breach of fiduciary duty, bad faith denial of contract, conversion, intentional interference with contract, fraud, negligent misrepresentation, unjust enrichment, intentional fraudulent misrepresentation, and equitable estoppel. He sued Upper Deck for negligent interference with economic relationship, bad faith, bad faith denial of contract, conversion, unjust enrichment, intentional fraudulent misrepresentation, and equitable estoppel. He sued Boris Korbel for negligent interference with economic relationship, bad faith, breach of fiduciary duty, breach of oral contract, bad faith denial of contract, conversion, fraud, negligent misrepresentation, constructive trust, unjust enrichment, intentional fraudulent misrepresentation, and equitable estoppel.

Passante did not sue the Upper Deck for breach of oral contract.

All breach of fiduciary duty and intentional fraudulent misrepresentation claims were dismissed pursuant to sustained demurrers. The bad faith, fraud and negligent misrepresentation were dismissed pursuant to stipulation after the trial court refused, as a sanction for not having disclosed the identity of the witness during discovery, to allow Passante to present the testimony of Daniel Lybarger, a former controller of the Upper Deck, who would have testified that McWilliam actually knew that Passante had been given three percent of the company's stock.

After the close of the plaintiffs' case, the trial judge granted nonsuit motions which eliminated all remaining claims against McWilliam, the Upper Deck, and Korbel except the 11th cause of action for breach of fiduciary duty and imposition of a constructive trust against Korbel only. However, the trial judge also granted Passante's request to add a claim for breach of oral contract against the Upper Deck.

The claim against the Upper Deck and the claim against Korbel went to the jury. The jury found for Passante and awarded him some $32 million against Upper Deck and $1 million against Korbel. The Upper Deck then moved for a judgment notwithstanding the verdict or, alternatively, a new trial; the trial court granted both. The trial judge also determined that the sole remaining claim against Korbel was equitable in nature and, in a tentative decision issued July 2, 1993, gave judgment for Korbel on that claim, finding that there was no transaction between Korbel and Passante "which could serve as a basis for imposing a constructive trust."

Two formal judgments were filed August 3, 1993, one in favor of both the Upper Deck and McWilliam, the other in favor of Korbel on the equitable cause of action. Passante then filed this appeal from those judgments.

DISCUSSION

In his opening brief Passante asserts that "[a]n enforceable contract requires only a promise capable of being enforced and consideration to support the promise." As framed, the assertion is incomplete. Consideration must also be given in exchange for the promise. Past consideration cannot support a contract.

Cases relied on by Passante merely demonstrate the rule that the extinguishment of a preexisting obligation, or the rendering of past services with the expectation of future payment, constitute sufficient consideration for a contract....

As a matter of law, any claim by Passante for breach of contract necessarily founders on the rule that consideration must result from a bargain.

Thus if the stock promise was truly bargained for, then he had an obligation to the Upper Deck, as its counsel, to give the firm the opportunity to have separate counsel represent it in the course of that bargaining. The legal profession has certain rules regarding business transactions with clients. Rule 3–300 of the California Rules of Professional Conduct forbids members from entering "a business transaction with a client" without first advising the client "in writing that the client may seek the advice of an independent lawyer of the client's choice."

Here it is undisputed that Passante did not advise the Upper Deck of the need for independent counsel in connection with its promise, either in writing or even orally. Had he done so before the Upper Deck made its promise, the board of directors might or might not have been so enthusiastic about his finding the money as to give away three percent of the stock. In a business transaction with a client, notes our Supreme Court, a lawyer is obligated to give "his client 'all that reasonable advice against himself that he would have given him against a third person.'" Bargaining between the parties might have resulted in Passante settling for just a reasonable finder's fee. Independent counsel would likely have at least reminded the board members of the obvious—that a grant of stock to Passante might complicate future capital acquisition.

For better or worse, there is an inherent conflict of interest created by any situation in which the corporate attorney for a fledgling company in need of capital accepts stock as a reward for past service. As events in this case proved out, had the gift of 3 percent of the company's stock been completed, it would have made the subsequent capital acquisition much more difficult.

Passante's rejoinder to the ethics issue is, as we have noted, to point to the evidence that the stock was virtually thrust at him in return for what he had done. The terms were totally dictated by the Upper Deck board. And that is it, precisely. There was no bargaining.

But a close reading of the facts shows that the stock had not been bargained for in exchange for arranging the loan; Passante had already arranged the loan (even though the loan had not been formally accepted by the board) before the idea of giving him stock was ever brought up. There is no evidence that Passante had any expectation that he be given stock in return for arranging the $100,000 loan. Clearly, all of Passante's services had already been rendered by the time the idea of giving Passante some stock was proposed. As the court in *Dow* plainly stated, "if there was no expectation of payment by either party when the services were rendered, the promise is a mere promise to make a gift and not enforceable."

CONCLUSION

The promise of three percent of the stock was not a reward contract; it was Passante who first told Korbel that "funds were available." It was simply, to use a phrase usually associated with life insurance contracts, an inchoate gift—that is, an unenforceable promise from a grateful corporate board. Like the corporate resolution in *Dow*, it represented a moral obligation. And like the corporate resolution in *Dow*, it was legally unenforceable. (See Dow v. River Farms Co., 110 Cal.App.2d 403 (1952) [company executive rendered services without expectation of payment, thus subsequent promise by board to pay him $50,000 for those services as soon as the company became free of floating indebtedness was unenforceable].)[8]

QUESTIONS AND NOTES

1. *Passante* refers to Rule 3-300 of the California Rules of Professional Conduct. Under new Rules of Professional Conduct proposed by the State Bar of California this rule will be renumbered Rule 1.8.1 but will remain substantially unchanged.

2. Is the court saying there is no promise here, or that there is no consideration for the promise?

3. The court makes a fuss about Passante's lack of informing Upper Deck that it has a right to counsel before engaging in contractual relations with him. If the facts are as described (Passante arranged for the loan completely before the board decided to reward him for his efforts), would it have mattered if Passante immediately told the board of its right to independent counsel and followed it up with a written notice? What if Passante was Upper Deck's accountant rather than its attorney? Would he be entitled to three percent then?

4. Is the lesson of *Passante* not to be too proactive and instead to bargain expressly for every service rendered? Isn't it clear that if Passante had just said to the board, "If you promise to give me a three percent share of the company, I will find the funds to make the $100,000 payment" and the board accepted, a contract would have been formed and he would have been entitled to damages based on the value of three percent of the company?

5. Would the result of this case bother you more if Passante had spent a month calling in favors of all his friends and acquaintances and wining and dining new potential investors to arrange the loan? According to the reasoning of the court, would such facts change the outcome? Are there other grounds on which Passante could recover?

———————————

8. The question of what ethical duties apply when a client offers an attorney a gift has not been briefed and we do not address it. Passante's entire focus has been on enforcing the promise of stock as the fruit of a bargain, not as a completed gift.

Mills v. Wyman

Massachusetts Supreme Judicial Court, 1825.
20 Mass. (3 Pick.) 207.

This was an action of *assumpsit* brought to recover a compensation for the board, nursing, & c., of Levi Wyman, son of the defendant, from the 5th to the 20th of February, 1821. The plaintiff then lived at Hartford, in Connecticut; the defendant, at Shrewsbury, in this county. Levi Wyman, at the time when the services were rendered, was about 25 years of age, and had long ceased to be a member of his father's family. He was on his return from a voyage at sea, and being suddenly taken sick at Hartford, and being poor and in distress, was relieved by the plaintiff in the manner and to the extent above stated. On the 24th of February, after all the expenses had been incurred, the defendant wrote a letter to the plaintiff, promising to pay him such expenses. There was no consideration for this promise, except what grew out of the relation which subsisted between Levi Wyman and the defendant, and Howe, J., before whom the cause was tried in the Court of Common Pleas, thinking this not sufficient to support the action, directed a nonsuit. To this direction the plaintiff filed exceptions.

PARKER, C.J. General rules of law established for the protection and security of honest and fair-minded men, who may inconsiderately make promises without any equivalent, will sometimes screen men of a different character from engagements which they are bound *in foro conscientiae* to perform. This is a defect inherent in all human systems of legislation. The rule that a mere verbal promise, without any consideration, cannot be enforced by action, is universal in its application, and cannot be departed from to suit particular cases in which a refusal to perform such a promise may be disgraceful.

The promise declared on in this case appears to have been made without any legal consideration. The kindness and services towards the sick son of the defendant were not bestowed at his request. The son was in no respect under the care of the defendant. He was twenty-five years old, and had long left his father's family. On his return from a foreign country, he fell sick among strangers, and the plaintiff acted the part of the good Samaritan, giving him shelter and comfort until he died. The defendant, his father, on being informed of this event, influenced by a transient feeling of gratitude, promises in writing to pay the plaintiff for the expenses he had incurred. But he has determined to break this promise, and is willing to have his case appear on record as a strong example of particular injustice sometimes necessarily resulting from the operation of general rules.

It is said a moral obligation is a sufficient consideration to support an express promise; and some authorities lay down the rule thus broadly; but upon examination of the cases we are satisfied that the universality of the rule cannot be supported, and that there must have been some preexisting obligation, which has become inoperative by positive law, to form a basis for an effective promise. The cases of debts barred by the statute of limitations, of debts incurred by infants, of debts of bankrupts, are generally put for illustration of the rule. Express promises founded on such preexisting equitable obligations may be enforced; there is a good consideration for them; they merely remove an impediment created by law to the recovery of debts honestly due, but which public policy protects the debtors from being compelled to pay. In all these cases there was originally a *quid pro quo;* and according to the principles of natural justice the party receiving ought to pay; but the legislature has said he shall not be coerced; then comes the promise to pay the debt that is barred, the promise of the man to pay the debt of the infant, of the discharged bankrupt to restore to his creditor what by the law he had lost. In all these cases there is a moral obligation founded upon an antecedent valuable consideration. These promises therefore have a sound legal basis. They are not promises to pay something for nothing; not naked pacts; but the voluntary revival or creation of obligation which before existed in natural law, but which had been dispensed with, not for the benefit of the party obliged solely, but principally for the public convenience. If moral obligation, in its fullest sense, is a good substratum for an express promise, it is not easy to perceive why it is not equally good to support an implied promise. What a man ought to do, generally he ought to be made to do, whether he promise or refuse. But the law of society has left most of such obligations to the *interior* forum, as the tribunal of conscience has been aptly called. Is there not a moral obligation upon every son who has become affluent by means of the education and advantages bestowed upon him by his father, to relieve that father from pecuniary embarrassment, to promote his comfort and happiness, and even to share with him his riches, if thereby he will be made happy? And yet such a son may, with impunity, leave such a father in any degree of penury above that which will expose the community in which he dwells, to the danger of being obliged to preserve him from absolute want. Is not a wealthy father under strong moral obligation to advance the interest of an obedient, well disposed son, to furnish him with the means of acquiring and maintaining a becoming rank in life, to rescue him from the horrors of debt incurred by misfortune? Yet the law will uphold him in any degree of parsimony, short of that which would reduce his son to the necessity of seeking public charity.

Without doubt there are great interests of society which justify withholding the coercive arm of the law from these duties of imperfect obligation, as they are called; imperfect, not because they are less binding upon the conscience than those which are called perfect, but because the wisdom of the social law does not impose sanctions upon them.

A deliberate promise, in writing, made freely and without any mistake, one which may lead the party to whom it is made into contracts and expenses, cannot be broken without a violation of moral duty. But if there was nothing paid or promised for it, the law, perhaps, wisely, leaves the execution of it to the conscience of him who makes it. It is only when the party making the promise gains something, or he to whom it is made loses something, that the law gives the promise validity. And in the case of the promise of the adult to pay the debt of the infant, of the debtor discharged by the statute of limitations or bankruptcy, the principal is preserved by looking back to the origin of the transaction, where an equivalent is to be found. An exact equivalent is not required by the law; for there being a consideration, the parties are left to estimate its value: though here the courts of equity will step in to relieve from gross inadequacy between the consideration and the promise.

These principles are deduced from the general current of decided cases upon the subject as well as from the known maxims of the common law. The general position, that moral obligation is a sufficient consideration for an express promise, is to be limited in its application, to cases where at some time or other a good or valuable consideration has existed.

The cases of instruments under seal and certain mercantile contracts, in which considerations need not be proved, do not contradict the principles above suggested. The first import a consideration in themselves, and the second belong to a branch of the mercantile law, which has found it necessary to disregard the point of consideration in respect to instruments negotiable in their nature and essential to the interests of commerce.

For the foregoing reasons we are all of opinion that the nonsuit directed by the court of common pleas was right, and that judgment be entered thereon for costs for the defendant.

QUESTIONS AND NOTES

1. Chief Justice Parker says on p. 517, "What a man ought to do, generally he ought to be made to do, whether he promise or refuse." Do you agree? Even if there were no promise in this case, don't you think father Wyman should have compensated the stranger who kindly took care of his poor and distressed son during his last illness? Why does Chief Justice Parker feel compelled to reach a result he knows is unjust? Don't judges have power to do justice? Part of the answer is likely to be that somehow moral obligations are less worthy of enforcement than commercial obligations. You will encounter this attitude repeatedly in your studies, but it may remain a puzzle. Why should the law be so afraid of enforcing promises motivated by the feelings of the heart?

2. Chief Justice Parker points out that the law has always enforced promises supported by certain obligations unenforceable at law. The most common are promises

to pay debts barred by the statute of limitations, discharged in bankruptcy, or voidable because made by an infant or an incompetent. Do the principles of natural justice invoked by Chief Justice Parker satisfactorily distinguish such cases from the situation in *Mills v. Wyman*? Where should we look to find these principles and how can we tell whether they are as much in force today as they were in 1825?

Webb v. McGowin

Alabama Court of Appeals, 1935.
27 Ala.App. 82, 168 So. 196.

■ BRICKEN, PRESIDING JUDGE. This action is in assumpsit. The complaint as originally filed was amended. The demurrers to the complaint as amended were sustained, and because of this adverse ruling by the court the plaintiff took a nonsuit, and the assignment of errors on this appeal are predicated upon said action or ruling of the court.

A fair statement of the case presenting the questions for decision is set out in appellant's brief, which we adopt.

On the 3d day of August, 1925, appellant while in the employ of the W.T. Smith Lumber Company, a corporation, and acting within the scope of his employment, was engaged in clearing the upper floor of mill No. 2 of the company. While so engaged he was in the act of dropping a pine block from the upper floor of the mill to the ground below; this being the usual and ordinary way of clearing the floor, and it being the duty of the plaintiff in the course of his employment to so drop it. The block weighed about 75 pounds.

As appellant was in the act of dropping the block to the ground below, he was on the edge of the upper floor of the mill. As he started to turn the block loose so that it would drop to the ground, he saw J. Greeley McGowin, testator of the defendants, on the ground below and directly under where the block would have fallen had appellant turned it loose. Had he turned it loose it would have struck McGowin with such force as to have caused him serious bodily harm or death. Appellant could have remained safely on the upper floor of the mill by turning the block loose and allowing it to drop, but had he done this the block would have fallen on McGowin and caused him serious injuries or death. The only safe and reasonable way to prevent this was for appellant to hold to the block and divert its direction in falling from the place where McGowin was standing and the only safe way to divert it so as to prevent its coming into contact with McGowin was for appellant to fall with it to the ground below. Appellant did this, and by holding to the block and falling with it to the ground below, he diverted the course of its fall in such way that McGowin was not injured. In thus preventing the injuries to McGowin appellant himself received serious bodily injuries, resulting in his right leg being broken, the heel of his right foot torn off and his right arm broken. He was badly crippled for life and rendered unable to do physical or mental labor.

On September 1, 1925, in consideration of appellant having prevented him from sustaining death or serious bodily harm and in consideration of the injuries appellant had received, McGowin agreed with him to care for and maintain him for the remainder of appellant's life at the rate of $15 every two weeks from the time he sustained his injuries to and during the remainder of appellant's life; it being agreed that McGowin would pay this sum to appellant for his maintenance. Under the agreement McGowin paid or caused to be paid to appellant the sum so agreed on up until McGowin's death on January 1, 1934. After his death the payments were continued to and including January 27, 1934, at which time they were discontinued. Thereupon plaintiff brought suit to recover the unpaid installments accruing up to the time of the bringing of the suit.

The action was for the unpaid installments accruing after January 27, 1934, to the time of the suit.

The principal grounds of demurrer to the original and amended complaint are: (1) It states no cause of action; (2) its averments show the contract was without consideration; (3) it fails to allege that McGowin had, at or before the services were rendered, agreed to pay appellant for them; (4) the contract declared on is void under the statute of frauds.

1. The averments of the complaint show that appellant saved McGowin from death or grievous bodily harm. This was a material benefit to him of infinitely more value than any financial aid he could have received. Receiving this benefit, McGowin became morally bound to compensate appellant for the services rendered. Recognizing his moral obligation, he expressly agreed to pay appellant as alleged in the complaint and complied with this agreement up to the time of his death; a period of more than 8 years.

Had McGowin been accidentally poisoned and a physician, without his knowledge or request, had administered an antidote, thus saving his life, a subsequent promise by McGowin to pay the physician would have been valid. Likewise, McGowin's agreement as disclosed by the complaint to compensate appellant for saving him from death or grievous bodily injury is valid and enforceable.

Where the promisee cares for, improves, and preserves the property of the promisor, though done without his request, it is sufficient consideration for the promisor's subsequent agreement to pay for the service, because of the material benefit received....

In *Boothe v. Fitzpatrick*, 36 Vt. 681, the court held that a promise by defendant to pay for the past keeping of a bull which had escaped from defendant's premises and been cared for by plaintiff was valid, although there was no previous request, because the subsequent promise obviated that objection; it being equivalent to a previous request. On the same principle, had the promisee saved the promisor's life or his body from grievous harm, his subsequent promise to pay for the services rendered would have been valid. Such service would have been far more material than caring for his bull. Any holding that saving a man from death or grievous bodily harm is not a material benefit sufficient to uphold a subsequent promise to pay for the service, necessarily rests on the assumption that saving life and preservation of the body from harm have only a sentimental value. The converse of this is true. Life and preservation of the body have material, pecuniary values, measurable in dollars and cents. Because of this, physicians practice their profession charging for services rendered in saving life and curing the body of its ills, and surgeons perform operations. The same is true as to the law of negligence, authorizing the assessment of damages in personal injury cases based upon the extent of the injuries, earnings, and life expectancies of those injured.

In the business of life insurance, the value of a man's life is measured in dollars and cents according to his expectancy, the soundness of his body, and his ability to pay premiums. The same is true as to health and accident insurance.

It follows that if, as alleged in the complaint, appellant saved J. Greeley McGowin from death or grievous bodily harm, and McGowin subsequently agreed to pay him for the service rendered, it became a valid and enforceable contract.

2. It is well settled that a moral obligation is a sufficient consideration to support a subsequent promise to pay where the promisor has received a material benefit, although there was no original duty or liability resting on the promisor.... In the case of *State ex rel. Bayer v. Funk*, the court held that a moral obligation is a sufficient consideration to support an executory promise where the promisor has received an actual pecuniary or material benefit for which he subsequently expressly promised to pay.

The case at bar is clearly distinguishable from that class of cases where the consideration is a mere moral obligation or conscientious duty unconnected with receipt by promisor of benefits of a material or pecuniary nature. Here the promisor received a material benefit constituting a valid consideration for his promise.

3. Some authorities hold that, for a moral obligation to support a subsequent promise to pay, there must have existed a prior legal or equitable obligation, which for some reason had become unenforceable, but for which the promisor was still morally bound. This rule, however, is subject to qualification in those cases where the promisor, having received a material benefit from the promisee, is morally bound

to compensate him for the services rendered and in consideration of this obligation promises to pay. In such cases the subsequent promise to pay is an affirmance or ratification of the services rendered carrying with it the presumption that a previous request for the service was made....

Under the decisions above cited, McGowin's express promise to pay appellant for the services rendered was an affirmance or ratification of what appellant had done raising the presumption that the services had been rendered at McGowin's request.

From what has been said, we are of the opinion that the court below erred in the ruling complained of; that is to say, in sustaining the demurrer, and for this error the case is reversed and remanded.

Reversed and remanded.

■ SAMFORD, J. (concurring). The questions involved in this case are not free from doubt, and perhaps the strict letter of the rule, as stated by judges, though not always in accord, would bar a recovery by plaintiff, but following the principle announced by Chief Justice Marshall in *Hoffman v. Porter*, Fed.Cas. No. 6,577, 2 Brock. 156, 159, where he says, "I do not think that law ought to be separated from justice, where it is at most doubtful," I concur in the conclusions reached by the court.

QUESTIONS AND NOTES

1. If McGowin's son Floyd—grateful to Webb for saving his father's life—had made the promise instead of J. Greeley McGowin himself, would the Alabama court have followed *Mills v. Wyman?*

2. If McGowin during his lifetime, rather than his executor after his death, had refused to carry out the promise and had been sued, would the result have been different?

3. If McGowin had promised Webb $500,000 as a reward for his action, would the Alabama court have reached the same result as it did here? Would the $500,000 promise have been "without consideration"?

4. Judge Bricken stated, "It is well settled that a moral obligation is a sufficient consideration to support a subsequent promise to pay where the promisor has received a material benefit, although there was no original duty or liability resting on the promisor." Can this statement be reconciled with the holding in *Passante v. McWilliam?* If the Upper Deck board received a material benefit from Passante's work to secure funding for the company, isn't the moral obligation to compensate

Passante for performing that service sufficient to make its subsequent promise to give Passante three percent of the company enforceable?

RESTATEMENT, SECOND, CONTRACTS:

§ 86. Promise for Benefit Received.

(1) A promise made in recognition of a benefit previously received by the promisor from the promisee is binding to the extent necessary to prevent injustice.

(2) A promise is not binding under Subsection (1)

(a) if the promisee conferred the benefit as a gift or for other reasons the promisor has not been unjustly enriched; or

(b) to the extent that its value is disproportionate to the benefit.

COMMENT:

a. *"Past Consideration"; "Moral Obligation."* Enforcement of promises to pay for benefit received has sometimes been said to rest on "past consideration" or on the "moral obligation" of the promisor, and there are statutes in such terms in a few states. Those terms are not used here: "past consideration" is inconsistent with the meaning of consideration stated in § 71, and there seems to be no consensus as to what constitutes a "moral obligation." The mere fact of promise has been thought to create a moral obligation, but it is clear that not all promises are enforced. Nor are moral obligations based solely on gratitude or sentiment sufficient of themselves to support a subsequent promise.

ILLUSTRATION:

1. A gives emergency care to B's adult son while the son is sick and without funds far from home. B subsequently promises to reimburse A for his expenses. The promise is not binding under this Section.

WEST'S ANN. CALIFORNIA CIVIL CODE

§ 1606. Good Consideration; Legal or Moral Obligation.

How Far Legal or Moral Obligation Is a Good Consideration. An existing legal obligation resting upon the promisor, or a moral obligation originating in some benefit conferred upon the promisor, or prejudice suffered by the promisee, is also a good consideration for a promise, to an extent corresponding with the extent of the obligation, but no further or otherwise.

NEW YORK GENERAL OBLIGATIONS LAW (MCKINNEY 1978)

§ 5–1105. Written Promise Expressing Past Consideration.

A promise in writing and signed by the promisor or by his agent shall not be denied effect as a valid contractual obligation on the ground that consideration for the promise is past or executed, if the consideration is expressed in the writing and is proved to have been given or performed and would be a valid consideration but for the time when it was given or performed.

QUESTIONS

1. The Second Restatement § 86 tells us when a promise made in recognition of a past benefit is "binding," while California Civil Code § 1606 tells us to what extent the moral obligation based on past benefit is "good consideration," and New York General Obligations Law § 5–1105 says when such promises "shall not be denied effect as a valid contractual obligation" on that ground. What significance, if any, do you attach to these different formulations? Which one do you prefer?

2. If, as the California Court of Appeal suggests, p. 514, the Upper Deck's commitment to Passante was an attempt by the board to fulfill "a moral obligation," why doesn't California Civil Code § 1606 make the promise to Passante legally enforceable "to an extent corresponding with the extent of the [moral] obligation"?

DRAFTING EXERCISE

Write a short memorandum indicating how *Mills v. Wyman* and *Webb v. McGowin* would be decided under (i) Restatement, Second, Contracts § 86; (ii) Cal. Civil Code § 1606; and (iii) N.Y. Gen. Obligations Law § 5–1105.

V.   PREEXISTING DUTY

Can a promise to perform an act the promisor already is obligated to perform be consideration for another promise? In the abstract, the answer would appear to be no. The promisor is not getting anything for her promise; she would be entitled to the same performance without ever making the promise. But the answer is more complicated in some situations. Parties to an ongoing or executory contract may need to modify it during the course of performance. If Buyer agrees to permit Seller to increase the price for the goods because costs have risen between the time the contract was made and the date of delivery, what consideration does Seller provide for the modification? Seller has already promised to deliver the goods at the lower price. If Sarah owes Eli $100 on a past due debt, can she enforce a promise by Eli to accept $50 in satisfaction of the debt? What consideration has Eli received for his promise? Does it matter that the debt has been outstanding for years and Eli had long since resigned himself to the probability that it is uncollectable? The answer to questions like this must be flexible enough to permit contracts to be adjusted in the face of unforeseen circumstances and to permit good faith compromise of disputes but not so loose as to encourage extortion and chiseling by unscrupulous contractors.

A.   MODIFICATION OF AN ONGOING CONTRACT

Schwartzreich v. Bauman–Basch

New York Court of Appeals, 1921.
231 N.Y. 196, 131 N.E. 887.

■ CRANE, J. On the 31st day of August, 1917, the plaintiff entered into the following employment agreement with the defendant:

> Bauman–Basch, Inc.
> Coats & Wraps
> 31–33 East 32d Street
> New York
>
> Agreement entered into this 31st day of August, 1917, by and between Bauman–Basch, Inc., a domestic corporation, party of the first part, and Louis Schwartzreich, of the borough of Bronx, city of New York, party of the second part, witnesseth:
>
> The party of the first part does hereby employ the party of the second part, and the party of the second part agrees to enter the services of the party of the first part as a designer of coats and wraps.
>
> The employment herein shall commence on the 22d day of November, 1917, and shall continue for twelve months thereafter. The party of the second part shall receive a salary of ninety ($90.00) per week, payable weekly.
>
> The party of the second part shall devote his entire time and attention to the business of the party of the first part, and shall use his best energies and endeavors in the furtherance of its business.

In witness whereof, the party of the first part has caused its seal to be affixed hereto and these presents to be signed, and the party of the second part has hereunto set his hand and seal the day and year first above written.

Bauman–Basch, Inc.,
S. Bauman
Louis Schwartzreich.
In the presence of.

In October the plaintiff was offered more money by another concern. Mr. Bauman, an officer of the Bauman–Basch, Inc., says that in that month he heard that the plaintiff was going to leave and thereupon had with him the following conversation:

A. I called him in the office, and I asked him, "Is that true that you want to leave us?" and he said "Yes," and I said "Mr. Schwartzreich, how can you do that; you are under contract with us?" He said, "Somebody offered me more money." * * * I said, "How much do they offer you?" He said, "They offered him $115 a week." * * * I said, "I cannot get a designer now, and, in view of the fact that I have to send my sample line out on the road, I will give you a hundred dollars a week rather than to let you go." He said, "If you will give me $100, I will stay."

Thereupon Mr. Bauman dictated to his stenographer a new contract, dated October 17, 1917, in the exact words of the first contract and running for the same period, the salary being $100 a week, which contract was duly executed by the parties and witnessed. Duplicate originals were kept by the plaintiff and defendant.

Simultaneously with the signing of this new contract the plaintiff's copy of the old contract was either given to or left with Mr. Bauman. He testifies that the plaintiff gave him the paper but that he did not take it from him. The signatures to the old contract plaintiff tore off at the time according to Mr. Bauman.

The plaintiff's version as to the execution of the new contract is as follows:

A. I told Mr. Bauman that I have an offer from Scheer & Mayer of $110 a week, and I said to him: "Do you advise me as a friendly matter—will you advise me as a friendly matter what to do; you see I have a contract with you, and I should not accept the offer of $110 a week, and I ask you, as a matter of friendship, do you advise me to take it or not." At the minute he did not say anything, but the day afterwards he came to me in and he said "I will give you $100 a week, and I want you to stay with me.' I said: 'All right, I will accept it; it is very nice of you that you do that, and I appreciate it very much.'"

The plaintiff says that on the 17th of October, when the new contract was signed, he gave his copy of the old contract back to Mr. Bauman, who said: "You do not want this contract any more because the new one takes its place."

The plaintiff remained in the defendant's employ until the following December, when he was discharged. He brought this action under the contract of October 17th for his damages.

The defense, insisted upon through all the courts, is that there was no consideration for the new contract as the plaintiff was already bound under his agreement of
August 31, 1917, to do the same work for the same period at $90 a week.

The trial justice submitted to the jury the question whether there was a cancellation of the old contract and charged as follows:

> If you find that the $90 contract was prior to or at the time of the execution
> of the $100 contract canceled and revoked by the parties by their mutual con-
> sent, then it is your duty to find that there was a consideration for the making of
> the contract in suit, viz., the $100 contract, and, in that event, the plaintiff would
> be entitled to your verdict for such damages as you may find resulted proxi-
> mately, naturally, and necessarily in consequence of the plaintiff's discharge
> prior to the termination of the contract period of which I shall speak later on.

Defendant's counsel thereupon excepted to that portion of the charge in which
the court permitted the jury to find that the prior contract may have been canceled
simultaneously with the execution of the other agreement. Again the court said:

> The test question is whether by word or by act, either prior to or at the time
> of the signing of the $100 contract, these parties mutually agreed that the old
> contract from that instant should be null and void.

The jury having rendered a verdict for the plaintiff, the trial justice set it aside
and dismissed the complaint on the ground that there was not sufficient evidence
that the first contract was canceled to warrant the jury's findings.

The above quotations from the record show that a question of fact was presented
and that the evidence most favorable for the plaintiff would sustain a finding that the
first contract was destroyed, canceled, or abrogated by the consent of both parties.

The Appellate Term was right in reversing this ruling. Instead of granting a new
trial, however, it reinstated the verdict of the jury and the judgment for the plaintiff.
The question remains, therefore, whether the charge of the court, as above given,
was a correct statement of the law or whether on all the evidence in the plaintiff's
favor a cause of action was made out.

Can a contract of employment be set aside or terminated by the parties to it and
a new one made or substituted in its place? If so, is it competent to end the one and
make the other at the same time?

It has been repeatedly held that a promise made to induce a party to do that
which he is already bound by contract to perform is without consideration. But the
cases in this state, while enforcing this rule, also recognize that a contract may be
canceled by mutual consent and a new one made. Thus *Vanderbilt v. Schreyer* held
that it was no consideration for a guaranty that a party promise to do only that which
he was before legally bound to perform. This court stated, however:

It would doubtless be competent for parties to cancel an existing contract and make a new one to complete the same work at a different rate of compensation, but it seems that it would be essential to its validity that there should be a valid cancellation of the original contract....

In *Cosgray v. New England Piano Co.*, it was decided that where the plaintiff had bound himself to work for a year at $30 a week, there was no consideration for a promise thereafter made by the defendant that he should, notwithstanding, receive $1,800 a year. Here it will be noticed there was no termination of the first agreement which gave occasion for Bartlett, J., to say in the opinion: "The case might be different if the parties had, by word of mouth, agreed, wholly to abrogate and do away with a pre-existing written contract in regard to service and compensation, and had substituted for it another agreement."

Any change in an existing contract, such as a modification of the rate of compensation, or a supplemental agreement, must have a new consideration to support it. In such a case the contract is continued, not ended. Where, however, an existing contract is terminated by consent of both parties and a new one executed in its place and stead, we have a different situation and the mutual promises are again a consideration. Very little difference may appear in a mere change of compensation in an existing and continuing contract and a termination of one contract and the making of a new one for the same time and work, but at an increased compensation. There is, however, a marked difference in principle. Where the new contract gives any new privilege or advantage to the promis[or], a consideration has been recognized, though in the main it is the same contract.

If this which we are now holding were not the rule, parties having once made a contract would be prevented from changing it no matter how willing and desirous they might be to do so, unless the terms conferred an additional benefit to the promis[or].

All concede that an agreement may be rescinded by mutual consent and a new agreement made thereafter on any terms to which the parties may assent. Prof. Williston, in his work on Contracts, says (volume 1, § 130a): "A rescission followed shortly afterwards by a new agreement in regard to the same subject-matter would create the legal obligations provided in the subsequent agreement."

The same effect follows in our judgment from a new contract entered into at the same time the old one is destroyed and rescinded by mutual consent. The determining factor is the rescission by consent. Provided this is the expressed and acted upon intention, the time of the rescission, whether a moment before or at the same time as the making of the new contract, is unimportant.

The efforts of the courts to give a legal reason for holding good a promise to pay an additional compensation for the fulfillment of a pre-existing contract is commented upon in note upon *Abbott v. Doane* and the result reached is stated as follows: "The almost universal rule is that without any express rescission of the old contract the promise is made simply for additional compensation, making the new promise a mere *nudum pactum*."

As before stated, in this case we have an express rescission and a new contract.

There is no reason that we can see why the parties to a contract may not come together and agree to cancel and rescind an existing contract, making a new one in its place. We are also of the opinion that reason and authority support the conclusion that both transactions can take place at the same time.

For the reasons here stated, the charge of the trial court was correct, and the judgments of the Appellate Division and the Appellate Term should be affirmed, with costs.

■ MULLAN, J. Dissenting in the Appellate Term's opinion in the above case: *Schwartzreich v. Bauman–Basch*, 105 Misc. 214, 219, 172 N.Y.S. 683, 686 (N.Y. App. Term. 1918):

Of course it goes without saying that the parties *could* have canceled the old contract and subsequently have made a new one. It is equally plain that they observed the *formalities* usual in making a contract, that is to say, they performed all the necessary gestures, and gave promise for promise, and made what would have been, except for the rule of law under discussion, the clearest example of a good contract. But were the parties capable, at the time, of making that particular contract? The answer to that question depends upon the answer to the primary question whether, when the second contract was made, the first contract was at an end.

A true cancellation of a contract leaves the parties to it in *statu quo ante,* that is, it leaves them in the same situation, in respect of the subject matter of the canceled contract, as if they had never seen or heard of each other. An agreement to cancel a contract is itself just as truly a contract as the contract it terminates, and its effect is to put an end to the contract, not merely that the contractors may thereby be enabled to enter into another contract with each other, but to leave them in perfect freedom to refuse to enter into any further contractual relationship with each other. Now, it may be theoretically possible for parties to a contract genuinely to terminate it by agreement, thereby intending to be free to refuse to deal with each other again, and then immediately and genuinely to change their minds and remake the contract that was canceled, with a change of terms in favor of one party only. It is more reasonable, however, to assume that at least some few moments must elapse between the time when two given minds shall agree to cancel an existing contract, and the time when those same two minds shall decide to reinstate it, or again make one very like it. In the world of realities lightning-fast changes of the kind that must have taken place to make the second contract good do not occur, and I feel quite safe in saying dogmatically that no such sudden revulsion occurred here; nor, indeed, do I understand that such an absurdity is claimed. Can it be seriously urged that the defendant was willing that the plaintiff should have any moment of freedom from the old contract—such freedom, I mean, as to give the plaintiff the right to seek employment from some one other than the defendant? I think it is very clear that the parties never intended to be free from each other, and that the new contract was a mere substitution for the old one, and that is precisely what the rule that refuses validity to a promise to pay more for what the promisee is already obligated to do, was intended to prevent.

argument

There is nothing in this case that distinguishes it from the many cases in the books in which the ancient rule of law referred to was applied. The tearing up of one writing and the delivery of another writing in its stead are unimportant evidentiary details. Whenever the question of the rule's applicability has arisen, one contract has been in legal effect destroyed, and another contract, valid but for the rule, has been substituted for it. Quite obviously, the physical tearing of a piece of paper accomplishes nothing more than does an oral agreement to cancel. And I see no importance in the particular chronological order in which the various physical gestures occurred. Indeed, it seems to me that the entire argument of the appellant amounts to nothing more than a mere magnification of the value of immaterial details, and misses the real meaning and purpose of the doctrine we are dealing with. That the courts have shown no disposition to authorize any departure from the rule is shown in a comparatively recent case where it was said: "Thus, the only question presented in this case is whether a new promise by a party to do less than he has already agreed to do is a sufficient consideration for the promise of another party to do more than he is obliged to do. It seems to me that the negative answer to that question is so plain that there is no opportunity for doubt...."

QUESTIONS AND NOTES

1. Judges become suspicious when a second agreement requires a party to be paid more to do only what it was already obligated to do. They are hesitant to believe that a party would pay more for what it already had a right to for less. Even when they do not articulate this suspicion, they may adopt a presumption against the party seeking to enforce the agreement. "Prove to the court," judges seem to say, "that the other party freely and knowingly entered into this agreement. Tell a story that itself gives a good reason for not invoking the pre-existing duty rule."

Yet there is likely to be more than one version of what happened. Schwartzreich has his story, and Mr. Bauman has his. Which story, Schwartzreich's or Bauman-

Basch's, should the trier of fact have believed? What about the surrounding circumstances leads you to this conclusion? What additional information would you like to have were you the trier of fact?

2. The Court of Appeals places a great deal of weight on the largely ceremonial acts of surrendering and tearing the signatures off the old contract. These acts seem significant to the court for both doctrinal and credibility reasons. The court also seems to assume that parties intending to have a second agreement enforced would go through the right steps to announce this fact to the outside world. If the problem here is that Bauman is only consenting to the new agreement under duress, does the fact that Schwartzreich surrendered the old contract and tore off the parties' signatures necessarily support the conclusion that Bauman–Basch was not coerced? In fact, what else might Schwartzreich have done to make it appear that the parties intended to have the second agreement be enforceable?

3. It would appear under the most generous theory of damages that this lawsuit involved less than $1,000. Why did Bauman–Basch fight through jury trial and two levels of appeal? Does this persistence suggest that Bauman–Basch was really mad at Schwartzreich for ripping it off? Should its lawyer have advised it to continue fighting this case when it became clear that the costs of court proceedings would far exceed any possible judgment it might avoid even if ultimately vindicated?

Watkins & Son v. Carrig

New Hampshire Supreme Court, 1941.
21 A.2d 591, 91 N.H. 459.

Assumpsit, for work done. By a written contract between the parties the plaintiff agreed to excavate a cellar for the defendant for a stated price. Soon after the work was commenced solid rock was encountered. The plaintiff's manager notified the defendant, a meeting between them was held, and it was orally agreed that the plaintiff should remove the rock at a stipulated unit price about nine times greater than the unit price for excavating upon which the gross amount to be paid according to the written contract was calculated. The rock proved to constitute about two-thirds of the space to be excavated.

A referee found that the oral agreement "superseded" the written contract, and reported a verdict for the plaintiff based on the finding. To the acceptance of the report and an order of judgment thereon the defendant excepted. Further facts appear in the opinion.

■ ALLEN, CHIEF JUSTICE. ...

In the situation presented the plaintiff entered into a contractual obligation. Facts subsequently learned showed the obligation to be burdensome and the contract improvident. On insistent request by the plaintiff, the defendant granted relief from the burden by a promise to pay a special price which overcame the burden. The promise was not an assumption of the burden; the special price was fair and the defendant received reasonable value for it.

The issue whether the grant of relief constituted a valid contract is one of difficulty. The basic rule that a promise without consideration for it is invalid leads to its logical application that a promise to pay for what the promisor already has a right to receive from the promisee is invalid. The promisee's performance of an existing duty is no detriment to him, and hence nothing is given by him beyond what is already due the promisor. But the claim is here made that the original contract was rescinded, either in full or in respect to some of its terms, by mutual consent, and since any rescission mutually agreed upon is in itself a contract, the claim of a promise to pay for performance of a subsisting duty is unfounded. The terms of the contract of rescission are of course valid if the rescission is valid. The defendant's answer to this claim is well stated in this quotation from Williston, Contr., 2d Ed., § 130a: "But calling an agreement an agreement for rescission does not do away with the necessity of consideration, and when the agreement for rescission is coupled with a further agreement that the work provided for in the earlier agreement shall be completed and that the other party shall give more than he originally promised, the total effect of the second agreement is that one party promises to do exactly what he had previously bound himself to do, and the other party promises to give an additional compensation therefor."

With due respect for this eminent authority, the argument appears to clothe consideration with insistence of control beyond its proper demands. With full recognition of the legal worthlessness of a bare promise and of performance of a subsisting duty as a void consideration, a result accomplished by proper means is not necessarily bad because it would be bad if the means were improper or were not employed.

It is not perceived that the requirement of consideration is necessarily disregarded in spite of the net result of a promise to pay more for less, without additional obligation of the promisee. If the process in reaching such a result is inoffensive to the doctrine of consideration, the result does not become a naked promise. If in analysis of the transaction compliance with the elements of a valid contract may be found, it is hardly a perversion of principle to give the steps taken recognition. The result being reasonable, the means taken to reach it may be examined to determine their propriety.

In common understanding there is, importantly, a wide divergence between a bare promise and a promise in adjustment of a contractual promise already outstanding. A promise with no supporting consideration would upset well and long-established human interrelations if the law did not treat it as a vain thing. But parties to a valid contract generally understand that it is subject to any mutual action they may take in its performance. Changes to meet changes in circumstances and conditions should be valid if the law is to carry out its function and service by rules conformable with reasonable practices and understandings in matters of business and commerce.

Rescission in full or in modification being intended, it should be effective although the result benefits only one party and places a burden only on the other. It is the fact of rescission rather than the effect of it that determines its legal quality. The difference between a rescission unrelated to a new contract and one interdependent with a new contract, with the result the same in each case, signifies no failure of consideration in the latter case. The result, whatever it may be, is indecisive of the contractual character of the transaction. The steps taken being pointed out by the law, the result should not be held an idle one. Merger of the rescission and promise into one transaction does not destroy them as elements composing the transaction.

In another analysis of the transaction, more than a naked promise to pay more than the promisor owed appears. The promise was accompanied by the mutual understanding that the terms of the contract were to be modified. The conclusion follows that if the promisor had the right under the contract to have rock excavated at the same price as was to be paid for other material, he surrendered it. Conceding that the plaintiff did no more than the contract called for, yet if it was presented with a discharge from its duty, as an element of the transaction, by application of the law of gifts a completed discharge of a liability was validly effected. The form of statement by which one surrenders a right, if the law does not have special requirements for it, may be in any words showing the act to be one of making a present. The gift here was not of the promise to pay more, but of release of the plaintiff's duty to work for less. Whether it was, in its character and form, a gift to which the law attaches validity, is to be considered.

It is true that by the weight of authority an oral gift of a chose in action is legally ineffective, in respect to a transfer to one not the debtor. The relation between the creditor and the debtor is personal, and by common law the creditor's title is not assignable. So far as under equitable doctrines one may assign, as a present, the use and benefit of his intangible rights, a verbal statement of the transfer is ineffective. Williston, Conts., 1st Ed. But when a creditor releases his debtor, without full payment of the debt, no assignment is involved. The debt is extinguished, and if the release is in full or partial measure a present, the present is perfected. If the creditor agrees to take a part of the debt in full payment, and the part is paid, no exception to the need of consideration is apparent. The completed transaction is of a promise fulfilled. The debt is satisfied, according to the intention of the parties, and it is thought that the law should validate the action. The law has no policy that a creditor may not make voluntary and gratuitous concessions to his debtor. It is the everyday experience of business life, and is consistent with legal principle, and no rule of the law of evidence interposes to require proof of the present by other than oral testimony of it.

The argument for validity of the release is as strong as in the cases of a promise by a debtor to pay a debt barred by bankruptcy or by the statute of limitations. In such cases, while the cause of action survives, the debtor gives away his right not to be sued upon it, without receiving anything in return for the surrender. The ground upon which the cases are usually put, of a past consideration, or of one implied, is illogical, and in resting upon it they are anomalous. But upon the view of a release presented legal consistency is maintained.

Whether the gift to a debtor of an intangible right be termed a waiver, a surrender, an abandonment, or a release, seems broadly immaterial. Its nature, in yielding the right, or in forgiving the obligation, is determinative, rather than its appellation. There may be distinctions and discriminations in the required manner of their metaphysical delivery, but here. . . no symbolism or particular form of evidence is an essential of proof. The case is one of a simple relinquishment of a right pertaining to intangible personalty. The defendant intentionally and voluntarily yielded to a demand for a special price for excavating rock. In doing this he yielded his contract right to the price it provided. Whether or not he thought he had the right, he intended, and executed his intent, to make no claim of the right. The promise of a special price for excavating rock necessarily imported a release or waiver of any right by the contract to hold the plaintiff to the lower price the contract stipulated. In mutual understanding the parties agreed that the contract price was not to control. The contract right being freely surrendered, the issue of contract law whether the new promise is valid is not doubtful. If the totality of the transaction was a promise to pay more for less, there was in its inherent makeup a valid discharge of an obligation. Although the transaction was single, the element of discharge was distinct in precedence of the new promise.

The foregoing views are considered to meet the reasonable needs of standard and ethical practices of men in their business dealings with each other. Conceding that the plaintiff threatened to break its contract because it found the contract to be improvident, yet the defendant yielded to the threat without protest, excusing the plaintiff, and making a new arrangement. Not insisting on his rights but relinquishing them, fairly he should be held to the new arrangement. The law is a means to the end. It is not the law because it is the law, but because it is adapted and adaptable to establish and maintain reasonable order. If the phrase justice according to law were transposed into law according to justice, it would perhaps be more accurately expressive. In a case like this, of conflicting rules and authority, a result which is considered better to establish "fundamental justice and reasonableness," should be attained. It is not practical that the law should adopt all precepts of moral conduct, but it is desirable that its rules and principles should not run counter to them in the important conduct and transactions of life.

Exceptions overruled.

QUESTIONS AND NOTES

1. Chief Justice Allen, unlike Judge Crane in *Schwartzreich*, does not demand a ceremonial effort evidencing rescission of the first agreement. Why not? How does the court know that the bargain was not the product of duress?

2. Carrig's willingness to pay more for what he has a right to for less is described as a gift whose "appellation" ("a waiver, a surrender, an abandonment, or a release") is "immaterial." If Watkins had subsequently refused to perform the *second* contract, would the court still have talked "gift" and thus limited Carrig's damages to those based on that second contract's higher price?

3. The court seems to accept that Carrig acceded to Watkins' threat not to perform according to the terms of the first contract. Did Watkins originally agree to excavate that much rock? If not, did Carrig give up any rights? If so, was the fact that Carrig gave up a right acceptable because he did so without protest at the time? Isn't Carrig's unwillingness to pay the second contract's rate a properly lodged protest? Is it any less appropriate or timely than the protest that is implicit in an assertion of duress?

4. If the answer to Question 3 entails inquiry into the fairness of the adjustment made by the parties, can someone in Watkins' position threaten so long as the adjustment sought is a fair market exchange? How does this decision square with the doctrine of adequacy of consideration? Consider Comment c to Restatement, Second, Contracts § 73:

> **c.** *Contractual Duty to the Promisor.* Legal remedies for breach of contract ordinarily involve delay and expense and rarely put the promisee in fully as good a position as voluntary performance. It is therefore often to a promisee's advantage to offer a bonus to a recalcitrant promisor to induce performance without legal proceedings, and an unscrupulous promisor may threaten breach in order to obtain such a bonus. In extreme cases, a bargain for additional compensation under such circumstances may be voidable for duress.... And the lack of social utility in such bargains provides what modern justification there is for

the rule that performance of a contractual duty is not consideration for a new promise.

But the rule has not been limited to cases where there was a possibility of unfair pressure, and it has been much criticized as resting on scholastic logic. Slight variations of circumstance are commonly held to take a case out of the rule, particularly where the parties have made an equitable adjustment in the course of performance of a continuing contract....

5. Compare the last paragraph of Chief Justice Allen's opinion with the views of Chief Justice Parker in *Mills v. Wyman*, p. 516. Now write a short paragraph on the relation between law and morality. Does law override morality; does morality override law; how do the two illuminate each other?

Autotrol Corp. v. Continental Water Systems Corp.

United States Court of Appeals, Seventh Circuit, 1990.
918 F.2d 689.

■ POSNER, J. This is a diversity suit, primarily for breach of contract. The suit was tried to a jury, and the plaintiff, Autotrol Corporation, obtained a judgment of more than $1.5 million. The appeal raises a large number of issues, only a handful of which require discussion. So far as the remaining issues are concerned, it is enough to note that the district judge resolved most of them in a thoroughly satisfactory manner and that the others could not possibly have affected the outcome of the trial.

The contract provides that any dispute under it shall be resolved in accordance with the law of Texas. Neither party questions the validity of this choice-of-law stipulation but it is rather academic because there are no Texas cases on the hotly contested issues.

The contract, signed in May 1986, established a joint venture between Autotrol's controls division and Continental Water Systems Corporation to create a system for water purification based on a patented new technology, known as "electrodiarese," that Continental owned the exclusive right to exploit. Autotrol was to manufacture the control for the system and Continental the rest and both companies would sell the completed systems—Autotrol the large systems, Continental the small ones. There was an ambiguity, later to prove critical, about the dividing line between large and small.

Before production could begin, there had to be product specifications. These had not been completed when the contract was signed. Anticipating this possibility, the contract provided that when approved by both parties the specifications would be attached to, and thereby made a part of, the contract; and should the parties be "unable, in good faith, to agree upon the contents of the Products Specifications Schedule by June 30, 1986, either party hereto may elect to terminate this Agreement." On June 25 the parties agreed to extend this deadline to July 17. July 17 came and went and the product specifications had not been agreed upon but neither party exercised its right of termination. It was almost a year later, with the product specifications still not having been agreed upon, that Continental declared the contract terminated. That is the alleged breach. Meanwhile the other defendant, Olin Corporation, had acquired all the stock of Continental, and according to evidence that the jury reasonably could credit had decided that unless Autotrol acceded to the defendants' understanding of what the smallest system was that Autotrol was entitled to sell—which Autotrol refused to do—Autotrol would be encroaching on the segment of the market that Olin wanted to reserve for Continental.

The defendants argue that they were free to terminate the contract at any time after July 17, for any reason or no reason, without liability, provided only that the product specifications had not been finally agreed upon and attached to the contract as a schedule. Yet Continental encouraged Autotrol to continue working, which meant continue spending, on Autotrol's share of the project for many months after July 17—indeed, right up to the notice of termination—even though the product specifications had not been agreed upon. Autotrol does not argue that this encouragement was sufficiently promissory in form to support liability under a theory of promissory estoppel, on which see Restatement (Second) of Contracts § 89(c) and comment d (1981). But it does argue that, in conjunction with Autotrol's parallel forbearance to exercise its right of termination, Continental's encouragement supports an inference that the parties had modified the contract to waive Continental's right to terminate after July 17 for failure to agree on product specifications. This is assuming Continental had such a right, which Autotrol denies, thus giving it two grounds upon which to argue that there was a breach of contract. The jury found a breach but was not asked to indicate the ground, so we must affirm if either ground is supportable; as a matter of fact both are.

Under either of Autotrol's theories, once July 17 came and went Continental could not terminate the contract without liability—ever—even if the parties never did work out product specifications. At first acquaintance the argument is implausible. The parties could not go into production without such specifications. If they reached impasse after bargaining in good faith, would not either party be entitled to walk away from the contract without liability? Apparently not. The contract is deliberately asymmetrical with respect to termination after July 17 (June 30 in the original contract, before the date was extended). Until then either party can walk if the product specifications have not been agreed upon. After that Autotrol can walk until production commences but "Continental shall have no right to terminate this Agreement except as provided in" certain paragraphs of the contract that relate to specific (and immaterial) changed circumstances, such as bankruptcy, but not to failure to work out product specifications. Not only by encouraging Autotrol to continue working after July 17, but in the contract itself, Continental seems to have surrendered the right it would otherwise have had to terminate the contract upon the failure of an essential condition.

What sense can this make? The answer lies in the asymmetry of the parties' position. Continental controlled the patent on electrodiarese and if it abandoned the project, say by failing to agree on product specifications, Autotrol would be unable to go forward and would lose its investment. But if Autotrol abandoned the project Continental could always get another partner. Making the contract terminable by Autotrol but not by Continental gave Autotrol leverage to force Continental to license the patent to Autotrol on reasonable terms if Continental lost interest in the project.

If all this is wrong and Continental somehow retained an implicit right to terminate the contract without liability, even after July 17, provided that the parties were unable to agree upon product specifications, still the jury was entitled to find that the parties had modified the contract to forbid termination on this ground at least until such time as the need to agree on product specifications was urgent and agreement impossible. That deadline had not been reached when the defendants terminated—on a ground, moreover, that had nothing to do with product specifications, but rather with the division of the market for the product. The modification was supported by consideration; both parties benefited from relaxing the deadline, inasmuch as this allowed the project to proceed. Though oral, and somewhat vague about the duration of Continental's commitment, the modification was sufficiently definite to be enforceable, and an oral modification is enforceable under Texas law even if the contract forbids oral modifications, as this one did. The Texas approach is, by no means, idiosyncratic. For in most of the cases in which oral modifications are enforced in the face of prohibitory language in the contract the party seeking enforcement has relied on the modification; and an invitation to rely, here inferable from both statements and conduct of Continental, is the sort of waiver of a clause forbidding oral modifications that would be honored even under the Uniform Commercial Code, which makes such clauses expressly enforceable in contracts for the sale of goods.

[Damages discussion omitted here and excerpted in part at pp. 137-138]

We find no reversible error in the judgment, and it is therefore AFFIRMED.

QUESTIONS AND NOTES

1. Autotrol's contract had a clause expressly prohibiting oral modification of its terms. Why does the court have little problem allowing exactly that? Can you draft a contract that effectively prohibits oral modification? Shouldn't you be able to?

2. What consideration did Autotrol give for the oral modification? What consideration did Continental give?

———

UNIFORM COMMERCIAL CODE:

§ 2–209. Modification, Rescission and Waiver.

(1) An agreement modifying a contract within this Article needs no consideration to be binding.

(2) A signed agreement which excludes modification or rescission except by a signed writing cannot be otherwise modified or rescinded, but except as between merchants such a requirement on a form supplied by the merchant must be separately signed by the other party.

(3) The requirements of the statute of frauds section of this Article (Section 2–201) must be satisfied if the contract as modified is within its provisions.

(4) Although an attempt at modification or rescission does not satisfy the requirements of subsection (2) or (3) it can operate as a waiver.

(5) A party who has made a waiver affecting an executory portion of the contract may retract the waiver by reasonable notification received by the other party that strict performance will be required of any term waived, unless the retraction would be unjust in view of a material change of position in reliance on the waiver.

OFFICIAL COMMENTS:

1. This section seeks to protect and make effective all necessary and desirable modifications of sales contracts without regard to the technicalities which at present hamper such adjustments.

2. Subsection (1) provides that an agreement modifying a sales contract needs no consideration to be binding.

However, modifications made thereunder must meet the test of good faith imposed by this Act. The effective use of bad faith to escape performance on the original contract terms is barred, and the extortion of a "modification" without legitimate commercial reason is ineffective as a violation of the duty of good faith. Nor can a mere technical consideration support a modification made in bad faith.

RESTATEMENT, SECOND, CONTRACTS:

§ 89. Modifications of Executory Contract.

A promise modifying a duty under a contract not fully performed on either side is binding

(a) if the modification is fair and equitable in view of circumstances not anticipated by the parties when the contract was made; or

(b) to the extent provided by statute; or

(c) to the extent that justice requires enforcement in view of material change in position in reliance on the promise.

WEST'S ANN. CALIFORNIA CIVIL CODE:

§ 1697. Oral Contract [Modification of Verbal Contract.]

A contract not in writing may be modified in any respect by consent of the parties, in writing, without a new consideration, and is extinguished thereby to the extent of the modification.

§ 1698. Written Contract; Oral Agreement; Rules of Law [Modification of Written Contract.]

(a) A contract in writing may be modified by a contract in writing.

(b) A contract in writing may be modified by an oral agreement to the extent that the oral agreement is executed by the parties.

(c) Unless the contract otherwise expressly provides, a contract in writing may be modified by an oral agreement supported by new consideration. The statute of frauds (Section 1624) is required to be satisfied if the contract as modified is within its provisions.

(d) Nothing in this section precludes in an appropriate case the application of rules of law concerning estoppel, oral novation and substitution of a new agreement, rescission of a written contract by an oral agreement, waiver of a provision of a written contract, or oral independent collateral contracts.

UN CONVENTION ON CONTRACTS FOR THE INTERNATIONAL SALE OF GOODS:

Article 29.

(1) A contract may be modified or terminated by the mere agreement of the parties.

(2) A contract in writing which contains a provision requiring any modification or termination by agreement to be in writing may not be otherwise modified

or terminated by agreement. However, a party may be precluded by his conduct from asserting such a provision to the extent that the other party has relied on that conduct.

DRAFTING EXERCISE

CISG Article 29, UCC § 2–209 and Restatement, Second, Contracts § 89 represent modern attempts to deal with the modification of executory contracts. With the aim of showing the differences, if any, of these approaches when confronted with practical problems, apply these rules to *Schwartzreich v. Bauman–Basch* and *Watkins & Son v. Carrig.* (In fact, even today these cases would not be directly governed by UCC § 2–209 or CISG Art. 29 because they do not involve the sale of goods, or by the Second Restatement, which is persuasive rather than binding authority.) You are a law clerk for a judge confronted with both of these cases. Write a memorandum not more than three pages in length indicating the crucial elements in both of these cases under CISG Art. 29, UCC § 2–209 and Restatement, Second § 89 and how they should be resolved. Does one of these formulations provide you with superior guidance?

B.   SETTLEMENTS OF LIQUIDATED DEBTS AND CHECK–CASHING RULES

An ancient application of the pre-existing duty rule provides that a promise to pay a lesser amount is not consideration to discharge a greater outstanding debt. The rule announcing this result is often referred to as the doctrine of *Foakes v. Beer*, L.R. 9 A.C. 605 (1884), although its antecedents can be traced back to Lord Coke's dictum in *Pinnel's Case*, 77 Eng. Rep. 237 (C.P.1602). While seemingly far-reaching, the rule can be successfully invoked only if the debt is liquidated, undisputed, and matured, and even then can be escaped if the debtor's promise to pay the lesser sum is accompanied by any minor change in the terms of payment constituting a detriment to the debtor or by something more or different—the modern equivalent of Lord Coke's metaphorical suggestion that a "horse, hawk or robe" might in such cases be sufficient additional consideration. Indeed modifications of debts that reduce the principal owing are a commonplace in the commercial world. The fact that this rule has been so deliberately gutted undoubtedly reflects an uneasiness with the "logically compelled" results of the requirement of consideration in cases of claims settlement.

RESTATEMENT, SECOND, CONTRACTS:

§ 74. Settlement of Claims.

(1) Forbearance to assert or the surrender of a claim or defense which proves to be invalid is not consideration unless

    (a) the claim or defense is in fact doubtful because of uncertainty as to the facts or the law, or

    (b) the forbearing or surrendering party believes that the claim or defense may be fairly determined to be valid.

(2) The execution of a written instrument surrendering a claim or defense by one who is under no duty to execute it is consideration if the execution of the written instrument is bargained for even though he is not asserting the claim or defense and believes that no valid claim or defense exists.

COMMENTS:

b. Requirement of Good Faith. The policy favoring compromise of disputed claims is clearest, perhaps, where a claim is surrendered at a time when it is uncertain whether it is valid or not. Even though the invalidity later becomes clear, the bargain is to be judged as it appeared to the parties at the time; if the claim was then doubtful, no inquiry is necessary as to their good faith. Even though the invalidity should have been clear at the time, the settlement of an honest dispute is upheld. But a mere assertion or denial of liability does not make a claim doubtful, and the fact that invalidity is obvious may indicate that it was known. In such cases Subsection (1)(b) requires a showing of good faith.

c. Unliquidated Obligations. An undisputed obligation may be unliquidated, that is uncertain or disputed in amount. The settlement of such a claim is governed by the same principles as settlement of a claim the existence of which is doubtful or disputed. The payment of any definite sum of money on account of a single claim which is entirely unliquidated is consideration for a return promise. An admission by the obligor that a minimum amount is due does not liquidate the claim even partially unless he is contractually bound to the admission. But payment of less than is admittedly due may in some circumstances tend to show that a partial defense or offset was not asserted in good faith.

Payment of an obligation which is liquidated and undisputed is not consideration for a promise to surrender an unliquidated claim which is wholly distinct.... Whether in a particular case there is a single unliquidated claim or a combination of separate claims, some liquidated and some not, depends on the circumstances and the agreements of the parties. If there are no circumstances of unfair pressure or economic coercion and a disputed item is closely related to an undisputed item, the two are treated as making up a single unliquidated claim; and payment of the amount admittedly due can be consideration for a promise to surrender the entire claim.

ILLUSTRATION:

5. A owes B at least $4,280 on a logging contract. Additional items in the account are unliquidated, and some of them are the subject of honest dispute. A disputes B's right to all above $4,280 on grounds he knows to be untrue, and offers $4,000 in full settlement. A's payment of $4,000 is not consideration for B's promise to surrender his entire claim.

NOTE ON ACCORDS

When parties substitute a new contract for one previously made, the old contract is dead. But a full substitution may be unfair unless the new deal is performed. When one party compromises her advantage under the old contract to avoid a threatened breach, she will be stuck with a reduced claim without obtaining the bargained-for benefit of avoiding the burdens of suit. To solve this problem, the law has long provided a device labeled an *accord* that attempts to provide the best of two worlds: protection of the new deal as dominant over the old one, with retention of the old deal until the new deal is performed. This device can be used not only in situations where breach is threatened before performance is due, but also in cases where breach has occurred and a settlement agreement is made. In the process of providing such a device, the law—as might be expected—created a variety of new (and largely unnecessary) problems.

————————

RESTATEMENT, SECOND, CONTRACTS:

§ 281. Accord and Satisfaction.

(1) An accord is a contract under which an obligee promises to accept a stated performance in satisfaction of the obligor's existing duty. Performance of the accord discharges the original duty.

(2) Until performance of the accord, the original duty is suspended unless there is such a breach of the accord by the obligor as discharges the new duty of the obligee to accept the performance in satisfaction. If there is such a breach, the obligee may enforce either the original duty or any duty under the accord.

(3) Breach of the accord by the obligee does not discharge the original duty, but the obligor may maintain a suit for specific performance of the accord, in addition to any claim for damages for partial breach.

COMMENTS:

a. Nature of an Accord. An accord is a contract under which an obligee promises to accept a substituted performance in future satisfaction of the obligor's duty. Because an accord is a contract, it differs from a mere revocable offer by the obligee to accept a substituted performance in satisfaction of the duty.... The typical accord involves an exchange of promises (Illustration 1), although an accord may also take the form of an option contract. It is the essence of an accord that the original duty is not satisfied until the accord is performed, a result that is sometimes suggested by use of the term "executory accord." See Comment *e*.

b. Suspensory Effect. The accord entitles the obligor to a chance to render the substituted performance in satisfaction of the original duty. Under the rule stated in Subsection (2), the obligee's right to enforce that duty is suspended subject to the terms of the accord until the obligor has had that chance. If the obligor is under a duty to perform the accord, his performance discharges both his original duty and his duty under the accord.... If, however, there is such a breach of the accord by the obligor as discharges the obligee's duty under the accord to accept the stated performance in satisfaction, he is no longer bound by the accord. He may then choose between enforcement of the original duty and any duty under the accord....

ILLUSTRATIONS:

1. A owes B $10,000. They make a contract under which A promises to deliver to B a specific machine within 30 days and B promises to accept it in satisfaction of the debt. The contract is an accord. A's debt is suspended and is discharged if A delivers the machine within 30 days.

4. The facts being otherwise as stated in Illustration 1, A fails to deliver the machine within 30 days and tells B that he will not deliver it. B can enforce either the original $10,000 debt or the duty to deliver the machine.

COMMENT:

d. Validity of Accord. The enforceability of an accord is governed by the rules applicable to the enforceability of contracts in general. The obligee's promise to accept the substituted performance in satisfaction of the original duty may be supported by consideration because that performance differs significantly from that required by the original duty (§ 73) or because the original duty is in fact doubtful or is believed by the obligor to be so (§ 74).

It may also be supported by the obligor's reliance even in the absence of consideration (§ 90)....

ILLUSTRATION:

6. A contracts with B to have repairs made on A's house, no price being fixed. B sends A a bill for $1,000. A honestly disputes this amount and sends a letter explaining that he thinks the amount excessive and is enclosing a check for $800 as payment in full. B, after reading the letter, indorses the check and deposits it in his bank for collection. B is bound by an accord under which he promises to accept payment of the check as satisfaction of A's debt for repairs. The result is the same if, before indorsing the check, B adds the words "Accepted under protest as part payment." The result would be different, however, if B's claim were liquidated, undisputed and matured. See § 74.

COMMENT:

e. Substituted Contract Distinguished. Because the obligor's original duty is not satisfied until the accord is performed, an accord differs from a substituted contract, under which a promise of substituted performance is accepted in satisfaction of the original duty. See § 279. Whether a contract is an accord or a substituted contract is a question of interpretation.... In resolving doubts in this regard, a court is less likely to conclude that an obligee was willing to accept a mere promise in satisfaction of an original duty that was clear than in satisfaction of one that was doubtful. It is therefore less likely to find a substituted contract and more likely to find an accord if the original duty was one to pay money, if it was undisputed, if it was liquidated and if it was matured.

§ 279. Substituted Contract.

(1) A substituted contract is a contract that is itself accepted by the obligee in satisfaction of the obligor's existing duty.

(2) The substituted contract discharges the original duty and breach of the substituted contract by the obligor does not give the obligee a right to enforce the original duty.

COMMENT:

a. Nature and Effect of a Substituted Contract. A substituted contract is one that is itself accepted by the obligee in satisfaction of the original duty and thereby discharges it. A common type of substituted contract is one that contains a term that is inconsistent with a term of an earlier contract between the parties. If the parties intend the new contract to replace all of the provisions of the earlier contract, the contract is a substituted contract. If a substituted contract brings in a new party it is called a "novation" (§ 280).

ILLUSTRATION:

1. A is under a duty to deliver a tractor to B on July 1. On June 1, A offers to deliver a bulldozer to B on July 1 if B will accept his promise in satisfaction of A's duty to deliver the tractor, and B accepts. The contract is a substituted contract. A's duty to deliver the tractor is discharged. If A does not deliver the bulldozer, B can enforce the duty to deliver it but not the original duty to deliver the tractor.

COMMENT:

c. *Accord Distinguished.* Because the original duty is discharged regardless of whether the substituted contract is performed, a substituted contract differs from an accord, under which the original duty is discharged only if the accord is performed. See § 281. Whether a contract is a substituted contract or an accord is a question of interpretation.... In resolving doubts in this regard, a court is less likely to conclude that an obligee was willing to accept a mere promise in satisfaction of an original duty that was clear than in satisfaction of one that was doubtful. It will therefore be less likely to find a substituted contract and more likely to find an accord if the original duty was one to pay money, if it was undisputed, if it was liquidated and if it was matured. Compare Illustration 1 with Illustration 1 to § 281.

━━━━━━━

Johnson v. Utile

Nevada Supreme Court, 1970.
86 Nev. 593, 472 P.2d 335

■ MOWBRAY, J. This is a contract case arising from the sale of a 160–acre parcel of real property in Lyon County. The dispute centers about three wells located on the property.

1. THE FACTS.

In February 1967, Clarence Johnson and his wife, Glodean, who are the appellants, agreed to sell their property to Joe and Ann M. Utile, who are the respondents. The parties signed a "Deposit Receipt and Agreement of Sale," which provided in pertinent part:

"* * * Seller agrees to drill 16 inch well, same area, same depth as existing irrigation well. Well to be tested, minimum 24 hours, at between 1,000 and 1,200 GPM (gallons per minute). Seller agrees to drill and test well on or before close of escrow."

In 1 month to the day, on March 3, 1967, the parties signed their escrow instructions, which provided in pertinent part:

"(6) Sellers herein to drill and test a new well prior to close of escrow. Well to be 16 inches and in the same area and at the same depth as the existing well."

Approximately 1 month later, the Johnsons orally informed the Utiles that the existing well on the property, which had been drilled and used for some time (and which we shall designate as Well No. 1), was no longer operative and that, therefore, it was not to be considered included in the sale of the premises. The Utiles then consulted their attorney and resolved the matter by having him write the Johnsons a letter dated May 12, 1967, which provided in pertinent part:

"* * * (Y)our suggestion to leave your test pump and a gasoline-powered motor on the new well (Well No. 2) for and in consideration of the Utiles relinquishing any claim on the existing well (Well No. 1) would be satisfactory, provided that the equipment is in satisfactory operating condition, and, further, assuming that the new well has been tested and is capable of producing the amount of gallonage set out in the agreements referred to herein, and, of course that the pump and motor are capable of pumping the water in the desired amounts consistent with the gallonage rating of the well itself. * * *"

This arrangement appeared to satisfy the parties, and Mr. Johnson, who is a licensed well driller, proceeded to drill Well No 2. He drilled the well to a depth of 105 feet and testified that it produced, over a 24-hour period, from 1,000 to 1,200 gallons of water per minute. The Utiles took possession of the property in June. They claim that the well never produced more than 300 gallons of water per minute and that in September 1967 the well went dry. Thereafter, the Utiles drilled a third well (Well No. 3), which apparently is operative and satisfactory for all ostensible purposes.

The Utiles then commenced this action in the district court, seeking damages for (1) the loss of Well No. 1, (2) expenses incurred in attempting to repair Well No. 2 and for drilling Well No. 3, (3) seed loss due to water shortage, and (4) attorney's fees and costs. The district judge found in favor of the Utiles and awarded them damages as follows: (1) $3,200 for the loss of Well No. 1; (2) $419.15 for expenses incurred in attempting to make Well No. 2 operative; (3) $3,060 for the cost of Well No. 3; (4) $636 for seed loss; and (5) $1,500 for attorney's fees and costs. We affirm the judgment of the lower court and the damages awarded therein.

2. THE COMPROMISE AGREEMENT.

A. Executory accord or substituted contract.

The principal issue in this case will be resolved by our interpretation of counsel's letter to the Johnsons of May 12, 1967; i.e.: Was the proposed compromise agreement, which the Johnsons accepted, an executory accord or a substituted contract?

A compromise agreement is a contract whereby the parties, in an effort to resolve their differences over a claim, agree to an amicable settlement based upon mutual concessions. Compromise agreements are usually divided into two principal categories: One may be called an 'executory accord'; the other may be called a 'substituted contract.' If the compromise provides for the acceptance in the future of a stated performance in satisfaction of the claim, the contract is an 'executory accord.' If, on the other hand, the compromise agreement itself is accepted as a substitution for and extinguishment of the existing claim, then the compromise is a substituted contract. Or, to state it another way, an agreement that operates as a satisfaction of an antecedent claim only when performed is an executory accord, and an agreement that operates as an immediate substitution for and extinguishment of an antecedent claim is a substituted contract.

The distinction becomes vital in relation to the remedies available to the non-breaching party if and when the compromise agreement is broken. If an executory accord is breached, the nonbreaching party may sue either upon the original obligation or upon the compromise agreement. As stated in Restatement of Contracts s 417(c) (1932):

"If the debtor breaks such a contract the creditor has alternative rights. He can enforce either the original duty or the subsequent contract."

This is the prevailing view throughout the American jurisdictions.

B.   The Intent.

The determination of whether the compromise agreement is an executory accord or a substituted contract turns on the intent of the parties to it. As stated by Corbin, supra, § 1293, at 190:

It is frequently difficult to determine whether a new agreement is a substituted contract operating as an immediate discharge, or is an accord executory, the performance of which it is agreed shall operate as a future discharge. It is wholly a question of intention to be determined by the usual processes of interpretation, implication or construction.

In the instant case, the record shows that counsel's letter of May 12 and the Johnsons' acceptance by their subsequent conduct constituted an executory accord. Admittedly, the language of the Deposit Receipt and Agreement of Sale and the escrow instructions lacks clarity. Because of the ambiguity in the written documents, the district judge heard and considered the oral testimony of the parties, and he concluded as a result thereof that their initial agreement included not only an operating well (Well No. 1), but also the drilling of Well No. 2. A fair reading of counsel's May 12 letter supports the court's conclusion that the letter referred to an antecedent obligation, where the proposed compromise stated that the Utiles agreed to relinquish their claim to operating Well No. 1, 'provided that the equipment (on Well

No. 1) is in satisfactory operating condition, and, further, assuming that the new well (Well No. 2) has been tested and is capable of producing the amount of gallonage set out in the agreements * * *' (Emphasis added.) Such language supports the district judge's decision, in that the Utiles agreed to relinquish their right to Well No. 1 only after Well No. 2 had been drilled and had produced and operated satisfactorily.

C. The Breach.

The Utiles may recover damages for the loss of Well No. 1 only if the record supports the district judge's finding that the Johnsons breached the parties' compromise agreement by failing to produce Well No. 2, in that it was not "capable of producing the amount of gallonage set out in the agreements * * *"

Appellants argue on this point that their only duty with respect to Well No. 2 was to produce a well on the property that would test between 1,000 and 1,200 gallons of water per minute. Mr. Johnson testified that he conducted such a test, with satisfactory results. The Utiles, however, produced evidence that the well production never exceeded 300 gallons per minute and that in a comparatively short period of time it went dry. While there is a conflict in the record, there is sufficient evidence to support the district judge's finding that the parties bargained for something more than a mere test and truly intended that the well to be drilled, Well No. 2, should be capable of producing the specified gallonage over a reasonable period of time, if the well were to be of any value to the purchasers. This court may not disturb the finding of the lower court where there is evidence in the record to support it.

3. THE DAMAGES.

This court has reiterated on several occasions the well recognized rule that one who breaches a duty to another is liable for all damages naturally flowing from the wrongful breach.

Since we have ruled in the instant case that the compromise agreement of the parties was an executory accord, which was breached by the appellants, it follows that the plaintiffs-respondents were entitled to damages for the loss of Well No. 1, their expenses incurred in attempting to make Well No. 2 operative, the drilling of Well No. 3 to replace Well No. 2, and their seed loss due to lack of water, as well as their attorney's fees and costs. The record supports the damages awarded by the district judge, and we may not disturb the award on appeal.

The judgment is affirmed.

IFC Credit Corp. v. Bulk Petroleum Corp.

United States Court of Appeals, Seventh Circuit, 2005.
403 F.3d 869.

■ CUDAHY, J.

Plaintiff IFC Credit Corporation (IFC) brought suit alleging that Bulk Petroleum Corporation (Bulk) and its CEO, Darshan Dhaliwal, breached a lease agreement under which Bulk leased gasoline tanks and other equipment from IFC with an option to purchase them at the end of the lease. Bulk claims that the lease agreement has been concluded through an accord and satisfaction executed with the assignee of IFC's rights under the lease. The district court, through Magistrate Judge Aaron E. Goodstein, granted Bulk's motion for summary judgment, ruling that a valid accord and satisfaction had taken place. IFC now appeals that ruling, and we affirm.

I. FACTUAL BACKGROUND AND DISPOSITION BELOW

On or about June 21, 1995, Bulk and IFC entered into a series of agreements by which Bulk leased gasoline tanks and equipment from IFC to be used at various gas stations operated by Bulk. Under the terms of the agreements, Bulk was given an option to purchase the equipment at the end of the 72-month lease term. The purchase price was to be the greater of the fair market value of the equipment and $31,419.40, together with all applicable taxes. The lease documents also provided for extension of the lease term at a rate of $2,820.52 per month. The documents further required that any notices regarding the purchase of the equipment were to be sent to IFC at a designated address. Concurrent with the execution of the lease, Bulk's CEO, Darshan Dhaliwal, executed a personal guaranty of the agreements.

Less than two weeks later, on or about June 30, 1995, the Bulk lease was assigned by IFC to Finova Capital Corporation (Finova), giving Finova full right, title and interest in the lease, including the initial scheduled payments under the lease. Bulk's payments were to be sent to a Finova lockbox.

Beginning in November 2000, IFC's Patrick Witowski and Bulk's John Gerth engaged in negotiations concerning the termination of the lease and purchase of the equipment by Bulk. However, the two parties could not agree on a purchase price. On January 23, 2001, while these negotiations were ongoing, Finova notified Bulk in writing that all further negotiations regarding the purchase option were to be conducted with IFC (and with Witowski specifically). Finova then promptly filed for bankruptcy on March 7, 2001.

On June 18, 2001, Dhaliwal, who to that point had apparently not been involved in negotiations, sent a letter to Finova and a check for $31,419.40, made out to Finova Capital Corporation. The invoice attached to the check read "pay off lease 5613500," and the endorsement area on the back of the check stated "payment in full of lease and purchase option # 5613500." The accompanying letter from Dhaliwal stated that the check represented "payment in full of the lease and the purchase option" and that "[a]cceptance of this check represents full satisfaction of the obligation of Bulk Petroleum to Finova Capital Corporation." The letter concluded by stating that if Finova did not accept the check, then it should inform Bulk as to where it should ship the leased equipment back to Finova.

The parties dispute the exact date upon which IFC, via Witowski, received a copy of Dhaliwal's letter. They also dispute whether the letter and the check were sent together or separately, and whether the check was sent to Finova's "automated lockbox" rather than to its office (though the letter does not appear to have been sent to a P.O. Box address). In any event, it is undisputed that Witowski (and hence IFC) received a copy of the letter and the check via fax from Bulk on June 22, 2001. The check was negotiated three days later by Finova on June 25, 2001. Following negotiation of the check, IFC did not return the tendered money or claim that Finova had negotiated the check in error. Instead, IFC retained the tendered money, claiming that it constituted only partial satisfaction of Bulk's outstanding obligations under the agreement (which IFC reckoned to be in excess of $200,000). Bulk refused to make further payments, contending that its contractual obligations under the lease had been fulfilled upon acceptance and negotiation of the $31,419.40 check to Finova.

IFC filed this action on December 15, 2002, seeking to recover $207,961.88 (plus holdover rent) that it claims is owed by Bulk due to the breach of the lease agreement. IFC also sued Dahliwal based upon the personal guaranty he executed contemporaneously with the lease. On October 22, 2003, Bulk and Dahliwal filed a motion for summary judgment, contending that IFC's claim was barred by a valid accord and satisfaction. The district court granted Bulk and Dahliwal's motion, ruling that there was no remaining question of fact that defendants had met all the requirements of an accord and satisfaction under the relevant Uniform Commercial Code (UCC) provisions and Illinois law, and there was no evidence that the check was tendered in bad faith. (Apr. 5, 2004 Order.) IFC's appeal now comes before this Court. Since Bulk's tender met all the requirements of a valid accord and satisfaction, and above all since IFC did not return the tendered money or attempt to "undo" the transaction, we affirm.

. . .

III. DISCUSSION

Under both Illinois law and the relevant provisions of the UCC, an accord and satisfaction occurs when the "person against whom a claim is asserted proves that (i) that person in good faith tendered an instrument to the claimant as full satisfaction of the claim, (ii) the amount of the claim was unliquidated or subject to a bona fide dispute, and (iii) the claimant obtained payment of the instrument." [UCC § 3-311(a)]. *Accord Saichek v. Lupa* ("An accord and satisfaction is a contractual method of discharging a debt or claim. To constitute an accord and satisfaction there must be: (1) a bona fide dispute, (2) an unliquidated sum, (3) consideration, (4) a shared and mutual intent to compromise the claim, and (5) execution of the agreement."). Additionally, [UCC § 3-311(b)] requires that "the instrument or an accompanying written communication contain[ ] a conspicuous statement to the effect that the instrument was tendered as full satisfaction of the claim."

Clearly Bulk's tendered check and accompanying letter facially meet these criteria. The purchase price of the tanks was subject to a "bona fide dispute" (the parties could not agree on a price), the instrument and accompanying letter sent by Bulk contained highly "conspicuous statement[s]" that the check was tendered as full satisfaction of all obligations under the lease and purchase agreement, and Finova "obtained payment of the instrument" by negotiating the check on June 25, 2001. So far so good.

Paragraph (c) of section 3-311 adds a slight twist. It provides for an exception to these basic requirements which is designed to avoid inadvertent satisfaction of debts when a tender is sent to a large company. Under section (c), an otherwise valid tender to a claimant "organization" fails if "(i) within a reasonable time before the tender, the claimant sent a conspicuous statement to the person against whom the claim is asserted that communications concerning disputed debts, including an instrument tendered as full satisfaction of a debt, are to be sent to a *designated person, office, or place,* and (ii) the instrument or accompanying communication was not received by that designated person, office, or place." 3- 311(c) (emphasis added). This exception does not apply, however, if "within a *reasonable time before collection of the instrument* was initiated, the claimant or an agent of the claimant having direct responsibility with respect to the disputed obligation knew that the instrument was tendered in full satisfaction of the claim." 3-311(d) (emphasis added).

In the present case, assuming that IFC and Finova qualify as "organizations" so as to trigger the provisions of paragraph (c), Witowski was the acknowledged "designated person" responsible for conducting communications regarding the lease/purchase agreement, and Bulk sent the disputed check to Finova rather than to IFC or Witowski directly. Had no further communications taken place, this circumstance could have thwarted any attempted accord and satisfaction under section 3-311(c). However, it is undisputed that Witowski eventually received notice of Bulk's tender no later than June 22, 2001 three days before the check was cashed by Finova. The transaction here thus falls squarely within the provisions of section 3-311(d): regardless of any initial misdirection in making the tender, notice was given to the correct party within a reasonable time before collection of the instrument. The special exception contained in paragraph (c) does not apply, and Finova's negotiation of the check presumptively suffices to conclude a valid accord and satisfaction.

IFC objects that there is a material question of fact as to whether Bulk tendered its check in good faith. The UCC comment provides that "good faith" implies "not only honesty in fact, but the observance of reasonable commercial standards of fair dealing. The meaning of 'fair dealing' will depend upon the facts in the particular case." U.C.C. § 3-311, cmt. ¶ 4 (2002). Here, IFC alleges that Bulk's failure to send the check directly to Witowski and its mailing of the check and explanatory letter separately, taken together, indicate that Bulk was surreptitiously attempting to induce IFC into an inadvertent accord and satisfaction. On this score we note first that the parties hotly contest whether the letter and check were sent separately or together, and in any case IFC has waived this particular argument since it did not advance it below.

Moreover, IFC's allegations, even if credited, are probably not sufficient to obviate the tender in any event. Ordinarily the good faith requirement is violated where there is no bona fide mutual dispute concerning consideration, or the party tendering the payment affirmatively misleads the claimant. *See McMahon Food Corp. v. Burger Dairy Co.* (holding there was no good faith where debtor induces acceptance of payment by falsely leading creditor's agent to believe that creditor agreed to the terms of the payment). Here, by contrast, there was no misrepresentation or proactive deception; Bulk merely sent the check to the wrong party. Additionally, Bulk quickly notified Witowski of the tender verbally and via fax thereafter.

But in any event, IFC continues to retain the money sent to it by Bulk. This bare fact trumps any concerns we might have about the procedural specifics of the transaction itself. On the basis of this consideration alone IFC's claims must fail. Illinois courts have long held that, where there is a bona fide dispute as to the amount due, retention of a tender conspicuously identified as an accord and satisfaction effectively dooms a claimant's case. An Illinois appellate court has recently applied this principle to a case analogous to the one at bar. In *Bankers Leasing Association, Inc. v. Pranno,* the debtor sent the creditor a check conspicuously marked as being in full satisfaction of all outstanding debts and accompanied by a letter to the same effect. The creditor, with full knowledge of the dispute as to the amount of the debt, promptly cashed the check and, just as IFC/Finova has done in this case, attempted to characterize the transaction as only partial satisfaction of outstanding debts. The court rejected this argument, however, holding that a valid accord and satisfaction had occurred:

> When Pranno [the creditor] cashed the check, however, he knew there was a dispute. He knew the parties did not agree on what amount Bankers owed him .... Pranno may have tried to hedge what he was agreeing to by stating in an affidavit that the check satisfied only part of the dispute, but "If there is a bona fide dispute as to the amount due, it makes no difference that the creditor protests

that he does not accept the amount in full satisfaction. The creditor must either accept the payment with the condition or refuse."

Both the check and letter Bankers sent Pranno clearly indicated that by cashing the check, Pranno agreed that all claims between Bankers and Pranno would be satisfied. If Pranno did not agree to these terms, he should not have cashed the check.

Pranno, 224 Ill.Dec. 46, 681 N.E.2d at 34. IFC attempts to distinguish *Pranno* by pointing out that there the tendered check and the explanatory letter arrived together, while in this case they were (allegedly) sent separately. Once again, IFC has waived any argument to this effect, and in any case such a minor factual quibble is irrelevant to the principle articulated here. The recipient of a conspicuously-marked tender proposing an accord and satisfaction may not keep the tender and simultaneously contend that no accord and satisfaction occurred.

IV. CONCLUSION

In light of the foregoing, we AFFIRM the district court's grant of summary judgment in favor of defendants Bulk Petroleum and Darshan Dhaliwal.

The creation of the "accord" and its "satisfaction" are often discussed as if they occurred simultaneously. Accord and satisfaction are, however, independent (even if overlapping) events and are not necessarily simultaneous. For example, until the drawer's bank honors a check, there may be a period where there is an accord executory but not yet a satisfaction. In fact, what appears to be an accord executory may well be nothing more than an offer of an option contract, i.e., a creditor's offer which can be "accepted" only by delivery of the stated substitute performance by the debtor. Following this analysis the accord is, of course, no bar to an action by the offeror until it "is performed." Yet it does not necessarily follow that the offer can in every case be revoked before performance; arguments along the lines of Restatement, Second, Contracts §§ 45 and 90 may operate to limit the offeror's power of revocation.

If the arrangement between creditor and debtor is said to be a contract based on an exchange of promises, then either of two possible interpretations follow. The first is that new contract substitutes for the old obligation. The new agreement, in other words, will then be a satisfaction in itself. If this is the case, of course it can be pleaded by the debtor "in bar" to a suit by the creditor on the original obligation, an obligation that has been extinguished by the substituted agreement. What is more, even if the debtor does not perform this new agreement, the creditor will only be able to hold him on the new agreement; the old agreement will have been fully discharged.

Another possible interpretation, however, is that an accord has been formed which preserves the creditor's ability to sue on the original obligation if the debtor defaults on the new agreement. This is accomplished by finding that the new agreement consists of a promise by the debtor to perform a new obligation in return for the creditor's conditional promise to release the debtor from the old obligation if— and only if—the new obligation is performed. Under this view, there is no bar to the creditor's action on the old obligation *if the debtor defaults* on the new one because the old one is not extinguished until the new one is performed. The creditor can then pick either the old obligation or the broken new agreement as the basis for his suit.

Why all this ado about whether a debtor may use a valid "accord executory" as a "bar" to a creditor's suit in breach of that accord? All of the cases admit that the debtor can maintain an action for damages on the breached accord. If this is the case, doesn't a counterclaim by the debtor in the creditor's wrongful suit fully protect the debtor? Won't the damages on such a counterclaim put the debtor in as good a position, practically speaking, as if the accord were accepted "in bar"?

VI. ACTION IN RELIANCE

The most common form of action taken in reliance on a promise is the furnishing of consideration. In reliance on seller's promise to deliver the goods, buyer pays the purchase price. This is bargained for action in reliance. The payment is consideration, binding the seller to the promise to deliver the goods. The first thing for you to learn about action in reliance, therefore, is that it usually is bargained-for and therefore is not different from consideration and need not be treated as a distinct subject of analysis.

Sometimes the promisor does not explicitly request the other party to perform an action or make a return promise as the price of the promise, but nonetheless the promisee may rely on the promise by taking a variety of actions it otherwise would not take. The promisee may take substantial action in preparation of its own performance. It may commit resources and materials and expend large amounts of time and effort toward that performance. In most commercial situations this action in reliance is anticipated by both sides, and it is not hard to find that the promisee's performance of these actions is part of the exchange. Recall *Wood v. Lucy, Lady Duff-Gordon*, p. 40, or *Sylvan Crest Sand & Gravel Co. v. United States*, p. 36. There are situations, however, in which it is not so clear that the action or forbearance taken in reliance on the promise was requested as part of a bargained-for exchange.

This may suggest that the action was gratuitous (a gift) and not consideration. Recall *Baehr v. Penn–O–Tex Oil Corp.*, p. 486. Moreover, as we move away from business transactions to other contexts, such as family transactions, charitable subscriptions and the like, the intention of the promisor to bargain for the action in reliance becomes less clear. Recall Williston's tramp, p. 475. It may become strained in such situations to talk about the other party's action in reliance as "bargained-for."

A small, but distinct, body of doctrine has grown up to explain how unbargained-for action in reliance can make a promise enforceable. The conceptual handle that judges grabbed to explain this result is "estoppel." This term historically described an evidentiary concept that precluded a party who has led another to rely on the existence of a particular state of facts from then denying the truth of those facts. The idea is that you cannot make representations that lead the other side to believe something is true and to rely to its detriment on that belief, and then change your story and assert that that same thing is not true. Having induced reliance, the party is precluded from denying that the facts are as it has led the other side to believe. Using the term estoppel allows the court to avoid calling the party who switches stories a liar or a fraud by instead focusing on the preclusive effect of the other side's reliance. The term "promissory estoppel" is a label for the application of the estoppel idea to promises as opposed to facts. The classic statement of this concept is found in Section 90 of the Restatement, Second, Contracts.

RESTATEMENT, SECOND, CONTRACTS:

§ 90. Promise Reasonably Inducing Action or Forbearance.

(1) A promise which the promisor should reasonably expect to induce action or forbearance on the part of the promisee or a third person and which does induce such action or forbearance is binding if injustice can be avoided only by enforcement of the promise. The remedy granted for breach may be limited as justice requires.

Section 90's assumption that reliance on unperformed promises can result in unfairness and injustice is heavily dependent on the reasonableness of the action in reliance. In many common situations, the same facts that would support a conclusion that the reliance was reasonable also would support the inference that it was requested and, therefore, bargained-for. When unbargained-for action in reliance is claimed to be the basis for enforcing a promise, it often is reasonable for the court to find, as a matter of fact, that there was an implicit bargain arising out of the context of the parties' dealings.

As a result, many, if not most, cases decided under Section 90 could have been analyzed by the court in traditional consideration terms. Note how many of the cases that follow could have been dealt with by treating the reliance as consideration, simply by interpreting the promisor as impliedly requesting the acts of reliance by the promisee.

Reread: Kagamayor, J. in *Best v. Southland*, p. 19.

Ricketts v. Scothorn

Nebraska Supreme Court, 1898.
57 Neb. 51, 77 N.W. 365.

■ SULLIVAN, J. In the district court of Lancaster county the plaintiff, Katie Scothorn, recovered judgment against the defendant, Andrew D. Ricketts, as executor of the last will and testament of John C. Ricketts, deceased. The action was based upon a promissory note, of which the following is a copy: "May the first, 1891. I promise to pay to Katie Scothorn on demand, $2,000, to be at 6 per cent. per annum. J.C. Ricketts." In the petition the plaintiff alleges that the consideration for the execution of the note was that she should surrender her employment as bookkeeper for Mayer Bros., and cease to work for a living. She also alleges that the note was given to induce her to abandon her occupation, and that, relying on it, and on the annual interest, as a means of support, she gave up the employment in which she was then engaged. These allegations of the petition are denied by the administrator. The material facts are undisputed. They are as follows: John C. Ricketts, the maker of the note, was the grandfather of the plaintiff. Early in May—presumably on the day the note bears date—he called on her at the store where she was working. What transpired between them is thus described by Mr. Flodene, one of the plaintiff's witnesses:

> A. Well, the old gentleman came in there one morning about nine o'clock, probably a little before or a little after, but early in the morning, and he unbuttoned his vest, and took out a piece of paper in the shape of a note; that is the way it looked to me; and he says to Miss Scothorn, 'I have fixed out something that you have not got to work any-more.' He says, 'none of my grandchildren work, and you don't have to.'
>
> Q. Where was she?
>
> A. She took the piece of paper and kissed him, and kissed the old gentleman, and commenced to cry.

It seems Miss Scothorn immediately notified her employer of her intention to quit work, and that she did soon after abandon her occupation. The mother of the plaintiff was a witness, and testified that she had a conversation with her father, Mr. Ricketts, shortly after the note was executed, in which he informed her that he had given the note to the plaintiff to enable her to quit work; that none of his grandchildren worked, and he did not think she ought to. For something more than a year the plaintiff was without an occupation, but in September, 1892, with the consent of her grandfather, and by his assistance, she secured a position as bookkeeper with Messrs. Funke & Ogden. On June 8, 1894, Mr. Ricketts died. He had paid one year's interest on the note, and a short time before his death expressed regret that he had not been able to pay the balance. In the summer or fall of 1892 he stated to his daughter, Mrs. Scothorn, that if he could sell his farm in Ohio he would pay the note out of the proceeds. He at no time repudiated the obligation.

We quite agree with counsel for the defendant that upon this evidence there was nothing to submit to the jury, and that a verdict should have been directed peremptorily for one of the parties. The testimony of Flodene and Mrs. Scothorn, taken together, conclusively establishes the fact that the note was not given in consideration of the plaintiff pursuing, or agreeing to pursue, any particular line of conduct. There was no promise on the part of the plaintiff to do, or refrain from doing anything. Her right to the money promised in the note was not made to depend upon an abandonment of her employment with Mayer Bros., and future abstention from like service. Mr. Ricketts made no condition, requirement, or request. He exacted no quid pro quo. He gave the note as a gratuity, and looked for nothing in return. So far as the evidence discloses, it was his purpose to place the plaintiff in a position of independence, where she could work or remain idle, as she might choose. The abandonment of Miss Scothorn of her position as bookkeeper was altogether voluntary. It was not an act done in fulfillment of any contract obligation assumed when she accepted the note.

The instrument in suit, being given without any valuable consideration, was nothing more than a promise to make a gift in the future of the sum of money therein named. Ordinarily, such promises are not enforceable, even when put in the form of a promissory note. But it has often been held that an action on a note given to a church, college, or other like institution, upon the faith of which money has been expended or obligations incurred, could not be successfully defended on the ground of a want of consideration. In this class of cases the note in suit is nearly always spoken of as a gift or donation, but the decision is generally put on the ground that the expenditure of money or assumption of liability by the donee on the faith of the promise constitutes a valuable and sufficient consideration. It seems to us that the true reason is the preclusion of the defendant, under the doctrine of estoppel, to deny the consideration. Such seems to be the view of the matter taken by the supreme court of Iowa in the case of *Simpson Centenary College v. Tuttle*, 71 Iowa 596, where Rothrock, J., speaking for the court, said:

> Where a note, however, is based on a promise to give for the support of the objects referred to, it may still be open to this defense [want of consideration],

unless it shall appear that the donee has, prior to any revocation, entered into engagements, or made expenditures based on such promise, so that he must suffer loss or injury if the note is not paid. This is based on the equitable principle that, after allowing the donee to incur obligations on the faith that the note would be paid, the donor would be estopped from pleading want of consideration.

And in the case of *Reimensnyder v. Gans*, 110 Pa.St. 17, which was an action on a note given as a donation to a charitable object, the court said: "The fact is that, as we may see from the case of *Ryerss v. Trustees*, 33 Pa.St. 114, a contract of the kind here involved is enforceable rather by way of estoppel than on the ground of consideration in the original undertaking." It has been held that a note given in expectation of the payee performing certain services, but without any contract binding him to serve, will not support an action. But when the payee changes his position to his disadvantage in reliance on the promise, a right of action does arise.

Under the circumstances of this case, is there an equitable estoppel which ought to preclude the defendant from alleging that the note in controversy is lacking in one of the essential elements of a valid contract? We think there is. An estoppel in pais is defined to be "a right arising from acts, admissions, or conduct which have induced a change of position in accordance with the real or apparent intention of the party against whom they are alleged." Mr. Pomeroy has formulated the following definition:

> Equitable estoppel is the effect of the voluntary conduct of a party whereby he is absolutely precluded, both at law and in equity, from asserting rights which might, perhaps, have otherwise existed, either of property, of contract, or of remedy, as against another person who in good faith relied upon such conduct, and has been led thereby to change his position for the worse, and who on his part acquires some corresponding right, either of property, of contract, or of remedy.

2 Pom.Eq.Jur. 804. According to the undisputed proof, as shown by the record before us, the plaintiff was a working girl, holding a position in which she earned a salary of $10 per week. Her grandfather, desiring to put her in a position of independence, gave her the note, accompanying it with the remark that his other grandchildren did not work, and that she would not be obliged to work any longer. In effect, he suggested that she might abandon her employment, and rely in the future upon the bounty which he promised. He doubtless desired that she should give up her occupation, but, whether he did or not, it is entirely certain that he contemplated such action on her part as a reasonable and probable consequence of his gift. Having intentionally influenced the plaintiff to alter her position for the worse on the faith of the note being paid when due, it would be grossly inequitable to permit

argued

the maker, or his executor, to resist payment on the ground that the promise was given without consideration.

The petition charges the elements of an equitable estoppel, and the evidence conclusively establishes them. If errors intervened at the trial, they could not have been prejudicial. A verdict for the defendant would be unwarranted. The judgment is right and is affirmed.

QUESTIONS AND NOTES

1. Would Katie's action in reliance have been substantial enough to bind her grandfather if he, instead of his executor, had personally repudiated?

2. Was Grandpa bargaining for something in return for his promise—Katie not working—or simply providing equal treatment for his grandchildren? Did Katie give him his requested price for his promise?

3. What injustice can be avoided in this case only by enforcing Grandpa's promise?

4. Consider this case reported in Christian Nolan, *College Grad Sues Father to Recoup Tuition Costs*, Connecticut Law Tribune (June 29, 2010):

> [Dana Soderberg] persuaded [her father Howard] to enter into a written contract obligating him to pay her college tuition until she was 25, along with other school expenses such as textbooks, and her car insurance. As part of the agreement, Dana would make an effort to apply for student loans and Howard Soderberg would pay off those loans. Howard delivered on his word through March 24, 2007. But when it came time for Dana to begin her senior year at Southern Connecticut, Howard Soderberg refused to pay the bills. Dana finished up school and then filed a breach of contract lawsuit in New Haven Superior Court against her father for failing to pay for her senior year of college. . . [The court ruled] that father and daughter had a legitimate contract, that Dana proved to be the more credible party in the lawsuit, and that the father had breached the agreement. [D]amages totaled around $47,000, including the loan [Dana incurred], interest, attorney fees and missed car insurance payments.

Was Dad's promise a gift or a bargain? Assuming it was a gift, if Dad pays for three out of the four years of Dana's college and then decides she should finance the rest of her education herself, should he be able to retract his promise even though she has satisfied the conditions he initially laid down?

NOTE ON CHARITABLE SUBSCRIPTIONS

One classic form of gratuitous promise is the charitable pledge. Recognizing a strong public policy in favor of the enforcement of such promises and more generally in the support of private charity, courts have strained mightily to find either consideration or unbargained-for reliance in these situations in order to enforce such gift promises against the reneging donor, or more commonly, her estate.

"Consideration" has been found in the form of the subscriptions of others which are often tenuously said to have been induced by the reneging donor's promise or in the agreement of the charity to memorialize the donor's name. *Allegheny College v. National Chautauqua County Bank of Jamestown*, 246 N.Y. 369 (1927) (Cardozo, C.J.). Other courts, apparently reluctant to find a bargain where so obviously a gift is intended, seize on promissory estoppel as a basis for enforcement. In many situations, a charitable beneficiary does make commitments to third parties in the expectation that pledges it has received will be honored, and these cases fit comfortably within the doctrine of promissory estoppel. But in other situations it may be hard to see that the charity or its other donors changed position in any meaningful way on account of the reneging donor's pledge.

The Restatement, Second, Contracts § 90(2) simply treats charitable subscriptions as *sui generis* and provides for their enforcement without regard to reliance, bargained-for or not: "A charitable subscription ... is binding ... without proof that the promise induced action or forbearance." Some jurisdictions have adopted the more forthright Restatement position; others cling to the older approach of purporting to find consideration or reliance where there is little or none; and a few continue to deny enforcement of the pledge when they cannot find substantial detrimental reliance by the disappointed charity.

■ LEARNED HAND, J., in *James Baird Co. v. Gimbel Bros.*, 64 F.2d 344, 346 (2d Cir. 1933):

But the plaintiff says that even though no bilateral contract was made, the defendant should be held under the doctrine of "promissory estoppel." This is to be chiefly found in those cases where persons subscribe to a venture, usually charitable, and are held to their promises after it has been completed. It has been applied much more broadly, however, and has now been generalized in section 90, of the Restatement of Contracts. We may arguendo accept it as it there reads, for it does not apply to the case at bar [in which general contractor Baird claimed that merchant Gimbel Bros. had breached a contract to furnish linoleum]. Offers are ordinarily made in exchange for a consideration, either a counter-promise or some other act which the promisor wishes to secure. In such cases they propose bargains; they presuppose that each promise or performance is an inducement to the other. But a man may make a promise without expecting an equivalent; a donative promise, conditional or absolute. The common law provided for such by sealed instruments, and it is unfortunate that these are no longer generally available. The doctrine of "promissory estoppel" is to avoid the harsh results of allowing the promisor in such a case to repudiate, when the promisee has acted in reliance upon the promise. But an offer for an exchange is not meant to become a promise until a consideration has been received, either a counter-promise or whatever else is stipulated. To extend it would be to hold the offeror regardless of the stipulated condition of his offer. In the case at bar the defendant offered to deliver the linoleum in exchange for the plaintiff's acceptance.... That offer could become a promise to deliver only when the equivalent was received; that is, when the plaintiff promised to take and pay for it. There is no room in such a situation for the doctrine of "promissory estoppel."

Clausen & Sons v. Theo. Hamm Brewing Co.

United States Court of Appeals, Eighth Circuit, 1968.
395 F.2d 388.

■ LAY, J. Clausen & Sons brings a suit in two counts against Theo. Hamm Brewing Co. Count I relates to a treble damage action based upon the Sherman Act §§ 1 and 2 and the Clayton Act §§ 2 and 3. Count II, with which we are concerned here, relates to an alleged breach of contract. Hamm sought a summary judgment dismissal of both counts under Fed.R.Civ.P. 56. The trial court overruled defendant's motion as to the antitrust claim but sustained its motion as to Count II....

We reverse and remand to the district court with directions to reinstate Count II.

Plaintiff alleges that it had been a wholesale distributor of defendant's products since 1911. Clausen states that in 1950 an oral contract was made with Hamm to become an exclusive Hamm's beer distributor for an area defined as Southern Minneapolis and contiguous suburbs. In reliance upon said contract Clausen alleges (1) they discontinued all competitors' products; (2) purchased and maintained inventories, sales, advertising, warehouse space, personnel and facilities as a Hamm's exclusive distributor; (3) that Clausen was to remain the exclusive distributor as long as Clausen performed its undertaking. It is alleged that in April 1963 Hamm terminated its oral agreement.

The trial court sustained Hamm's motion for summary judgment on the ground that the contract pleaded was terminable at will since on its face there existed a "lack of mutuality of obligation."

We need not repeat in detail our concern of summary dismissal under Rule 56. If there exists the slightest doubt as to a factual dispute or "genuine issue of fact" summary judgment should be denied.

Hamm does not dispute this rule but nevertheless urges that under the pleadings and Minnesota law there exists no doubt that it is entitled to a summary judgment. We disagree.

"Mutuality of obligation" is only a semantical exercise surrounding the real determinant of a contract, namely, consideration. The Minnesota Supreme Court has acknowledged this:

> Defendant contends that there is such a lack of mutuality that the contract is unenforceable. * * *

> Use of the term "mutuality" often leads to confusion in that the word may have several meanings in dealing with contracts. As used here, the essence of defendant's argument is that, inasmuch as defendant could not demand that plaintiff deliver any quantity of material or recover damages if he failed to do so under exhibit 1, it must follow that the contract is unenforceable. The rule relied upon by defendant is often stated in the axiom that the promise of both parties is binding or neither is binding.

> "What the argument really amounts to is that the contract is lacking in consideration." (Emphasis ours.) Noreen v. Park Construction Co., 255 Minn. 187 (1959).

See also *Reichert v. Pure Oil Co.*, 164 Minn. 252 (1925), discussing mutuality of obligation (consideration) as opposed to mutuality of remedy (a prerequisite for specific performance).

But Hamm argues under the facts pleaded that consideration is totally lacking and cannot possibly be proved under the facts alleged. Analysis disputes this.

First, Minnesota has long recognized the principle that consideration may be a detriment incurred, and that it is *not* required that consideration pass from the promisee to the promisor to be valid. The court in *Home Supply Co. v. Ostrom*, 204 N.W. at 647, stated:

> Even though no consideration passed to the plaintiff at the time of its agreement and waiver of the lien right, yet Lindahl's reliance and action on such waiver should be treated as sufficient consideration. There is a consideration if the promisee, being induced by the agreement, does anything legal which he is not bound to do or refrains from doing anything which he has a right to do—it is sufficient that something valuable flows from him, or that he suffers some prejudice or inconvenience, and that the agreement is the inducement to the transaction.

*Could
be
considered*

Thus, Clausen's theory that it *was* obligated to invest substantially in Hamm's advertising, products, sales personnel, buildings, etc. was not considered by the lower court in his opinion....

*could
be
estoppel*

Secondly, it may be that the trial court upon proof will find sufficient evidence to justify contractual liability by way of promissory estoppel. Under this theory liability may ensue even if the detriment incurred by one party is not bargained for, if it can be shown that the promisor should reasonably have expected its promise to induce another's detrimental action.

argument

Because of the indefiniteness of the duration of Clausen's alleged obligations, the lower court found the contract to be terminable at will.[3] Even assuming the evidence would show an unqualified unilateral right by Clausen to terminate this would not necessarily deprive the agreement of its essential consideration. Minnesota has long recognized the principle that where a contract is supported by valuable consideration (such as a detriment incurred in exchange for a promise, as in the instant case), then a right of one party to terminate it at will does not render it invalid for lack of mutuality....

Thus we feel that under Minnesota law where an exclusive franchise dealer under an implied contract, terminable on notice, has at the instance of a manufacturer or supplier invested his resources and credit in establishment of a costly distribution facility for the supplier's product, and the supplier thereafter unreasonably terminates the contract and dealership without giving the dealer an opportunity to recoup his investment, a claim may be stated. Hamm in effect argues that even if the court can find consideration, plaintiff cannot prove any causal damages. But this is not our concern now. The fact that a plaintiff may have assumed an almost insurmountable burden to prove his alleged claim is a problem often faced by many pleaders. Yet the law must recognize the right to try.

Reversed and remanded with directions to reinstate Count II for a plenary trial.

QUESTIONS AND NOTES

1. Is it clear that Clausen & Sons made no promise in return for Theo. Hamm Brewing Company's promise to make it its exclusive distributor?

2. What action did Clausen & Sons take in reliance on Theo. Hamm Brewing Company's promise to make it its exclusive distributor? Was it bargained-for action?

---

3. However, a hearing of the evidence may be required to determine whether the alleged contract is in fact terminable at will. A provision which would limit the termination rights of a party may be implied into the bargain under some circumstances.

3. If Clausen & Sons' action was not bargained-for, will Theo. Hamm Brewing Company be bound by its promise forever?

Garwood Packaging v. Allen & Co.

United States Court of Appeals, Seventh Circuit, 2004.
378 F.3d 698.

■ POSNER, J.

This is a diversity suit, governed by Indiana law, in which substantial damages are sought on the basis of promissory estoppel. The suit pits Garwood Packaging, Inc., which created a packaging system designed to increase the shelf life of fresh meat, and its two principals, Garwood and McNamara, against Allen & Company (an investment company) and a vice-president of Allen named Martin. We shall refer to the plaintiffs collectively as "GPI" and the defendants collectively as "Allen." The district court granted summary judgment in favor of Allen and dismissed the suit.

...

GPI had flopped in marketing its food-packaging system and by 1993 had run up debts of $3 million and was broke. It engaged Martin to help find investors. After an initial search turned up nothing, Martin told GPI that Allen (Martin's employer, remember) would consider investing $2 million of its own money in GPI if another investor could be found who would make a comparable investment. The presence of the other investor would reduce the risk to Allen not only by augmenting GPI's assets but also by validating Allen's judgment that GPI might be salvageable, because it would show that someone else was also willing to bet a substantial sum of money on GPI's salvation. To further reduce its risk Allen decided to off-load half its projected $2 million investment on other investors.

Martin located a company named Hobart Corporation that was prepared to manufacture $2 million worth of GPI packaging machines in return for equity in the company. Negotiations with Hobart proved arduous, however. There were two sticking points: the amount of equity that Hobart would receive and the obtaining of releases from GPI's creditors. Hobart may have been concerned that unless the creditors released GPI the company would fail and Hobart wouldn't be able to sell the packaging systems that it manufactured. Or it may have feared that the creditors would assert liens in the systems. All that is clear is that Hobart insisted on releases. They were also important to the other investors whom Allen wanted to bring into the deal, the ones who would contribute half of Allen's offered $2 million.

Martin told Garwood and McNamara (GPI's principals) that he would see that the deal went through "come hell or high water." Eventually, however, Allen decided not to invest, the deal collapsed, and GPI was forced to declare bankruptcy. The reason for Allen's change of heart was that the investors who it thought had agreed to put up half of "Allen's" $2 million had gotten cold feet. When Allen withdrew from the deal, no contract had been signed and no agreement had been reached on how much stock either Allen or Hobart would receive in exchange for their contributions to GPI. Nor had releases been obtained from the creditors.

GPI's principal claim on appeal, and the only one we need to discuss (the others fall with it), is that Martin's unequivocal promise to see the deal through to completion bound Allen by the doctrine of promissory estoppel, which makes a promise that induces reasonable reliance legally enforceable. *Restatement (Second) of Contracts* § 90(1) (1981); 1 E. Allan Farnsworth, *Farnsworth on Contracts* § 2.19 (3d ed.2004). If noncontractual promises were never enforced, reliance on their being enforceable would never be reasonable, so let us consider why the law might want to allow people to rely on promises that do not create actual contracts and whether the answer can help GPI.

The simplest answer to the "why" question is that the doctrine merely allows reliance to be substituted for consideration as the basis for making a promise enforceable. On this view promissory estoppel is really just a doctrine of contract law. The most persuasive reason for the requirement of consideration in the law of contracts is that in a system in which oral contracts are enforceable—and by juries, to boot—the requirement provides some evidence that there really *was* a promise that was intended to be relied on as a real commitment. Lon L. Fuller, "Consideration and Form," 41 *Colum. L.Rev.* 799, 799-801 (1941). Actual reliance, in the sense of a costly change of position that cannot be recouped if the reliance turns out to have been misplaced, is substitute evidence that there may well have been such a promise. The inference is especially plausible in a commercial setting, because most business-people would be reluctant to incur costs in reliance on a promise that they believed the promisor didn't consider himself legally bound to perform.

In other words, reasonable reliance is seen as nearly as good a reason for thinking there really was a promise as bargained-for reliance is. In many such cases, it is true, no promise was intended, or intended to be legally enforceable; in those cases the application of the doctrine penalizes the defendant for inducing the plaintiff to incur costs of reliance. The penalty is withheld if the reliance was unreasonable; for then the plaintiff's wound was self-inflicted—he should have known better than to rely.

A relevant though puzzling difference between breach of contract and promissory estoppel as grounds for legal relief is that while the promise relied on to trigger an estoppel must be definite in the sense of being clearly a promise and not just a statement of intentions, its terms need not be as clear as a contractual promise would have to be in order to be enforceable. Indiana may go furthest in this direction: "Even though there were insufficient terms for the enforcement of an express oral contract, and unfulfilled pre-existing conditions prohibiting recovery for breach of a written contract ..., we are not precluded from finding a promise under these circumstances. Indeed, it is precisely under such circumstances, where a promise is made but which is not enforceable as a 'contract,' that the doctrine of promissory estoppel is recognized." *First National Bank of Logansport v. Logan Mfg. Co.*

The reason for this difference between breach of contract and promissory estoppel is unclear. A stab at an explanation is found in *Rosnick v. Dinsmore* (Neb. 1990), where the court said that "promissory estoppel only provides for damages as justice requires and does not attempt to provide the plaintiff damages based upon the benefit of the bargain. The usual measure of damages under a theory of promissory estoppel is the loss incurred by the promisee in reasonable reliance on the promise, or 'reliance damages.' Reliance damages are relatively easy to determine, whereas the determination of 'expectation' or 'benefit of the bargain' damages available in a contract action requires more detailed proof of the terms of the contract." The only problem with this explanation is that its premise is mistaken; if the promise giving rise to an estoppel is clear, the plaintiff will usually be awarded its value, which would be the equivalent of the expectation measure of damages in an ordinary breach of contract case. *Restatement, supra,* § 90 comment d. The rationale in both cases is that the benefit of the contract to the promisee is a good proxy for the opportunities that he forewent in making the contract. L.L. Fuller & William R. Perdue, Jr., "The Reliance Interest in Contract Damages 1," 46 *Yale L.J.* 52, 60 (1936) ("physicians with an extensive practice often charge their patients the full office call fee for broken appointments. Such a charge looks on the face of things like a claim to the promised fee; it seems to be based on the 'expectation interest.' Yet the physician making the charge will quite justifiably regard it as compensation for the loss of the opportunity to gain a similar fee from a different patient"). Of course, if the promise is unclear, damages will be limited to expenses incurred in reasonable reliance on the vague promise, *First National Bank of Logansport v. Logan Mfg. Co.,* but that would be equally true in a breach of contract case in which the promise that the defendant had broken was unclear.

But even though the court is "not precluded from finding a promise" by its vagueness, the vaguer the alleged promise the less likely it is to be found to *be* a promise. *Restatement* § 33(3) and comment *f.* And if it is *really* vague, the promisee would be imprudent to rely on it—he wouldn't know whether reliance was worthwhile. The broader principle, which the requirement that the promise be definite and at least minimally clear instantiates, is that the promisee's reliance must be reasonable; if it is not, then not only is he the gratuitous author of his own disappointment, but probably there wasn't really a promise, or at least a promise intended or likely to induce reliance. The "promise" would have been in the nature of a hope or possibly a prediction rather than a commitment to do something within the "promisor's" power to do ("I promise it will rain tomorrow"); and the "promisee" would, if sensible, understand this. He would rely or not as he chose but he would know that he would have to bear the cost of any disappointment.

We note, returning to the facts of this case, that there was costly reliance by GPI, which forewent other opportunities for salvation, and by Garwood and McNamara, who moved from Indiana to Ohio to be near Hobart's plant where they expected their food-packaging system to be manufactured, and who forgave their personal loans to GPI and incurred other costs as well. The reliance was on statements by Martin, of which "come hell or high water" was the high water mark but is by no means an isolated example. If GPI's evidence is credited, as it must be in the procedural posture of the case, Martin repeatedly confirmed to GPI that the deal would go through, that Allen's commitment to invest $2 million was unconditional, that the funding would be forthcoming, and so on; and these statements induced the plaintiffs to incur costs they would otherwise not have done.

But were these real promises, and likely to be understood as such? Those are two different questions. A person may say something that he intends as merely a prediction, or as a signal of his hopes or intentions, but that is reasonably understood as a promise, and if so, as we know (this is the penal or deterrent function of promissory estoppel), he is bound. But what is a reasonable, and indeed actual, understanding will often depend on the knowledge that the promisee brings to the table. McNamara, with whom Martin primarily dealt, is a former investment banker, not a rube. He knew that in putting together a deal to salvage a failing company there is many a slip 'twixt cup and lips. Unless blinded by optimism or desperation he *had* to know that Martin could not mean *literally* that the deal would go through "come hell or high water," since if Satan or a tsunami obliterated Ohio that would kill the deal. Even if Allen had dug into its pockets for the full $2 million after the investors who it had hoped would put up half the amount defected, the deal might well not have gone through because of Hobart's demands and because of the creditors. GPI acknowledges that the Internal Revenue Service, one of its largest creditors, wouldn't give a release until paid in full. Some of GPI's other creditors also intended to fight rather than to accept a pittance in exchange for a release. Nothing is more common than for a deal to rescue a failing company to fall apart because all the creditors' consent to the deal cannot be obtained—that is one of the reasons for bankruptcy law. Again these were things of which McNamara was perfectly aware.

The problem, thus, is not that Martin's promises were indefinite, which they were not if GPI's evidence is credited, but that they could not have been reasonably understood by the persons to whom they were addressed (mainly McNamara, the financial partner in GPI) to *be* promises rather than expressions of optimism and determination. To move to Ohio, to forgive personal loans, to forgo other searches for possible investors, and so forth were in the nature of gambles on the part of GPI and its principals. They may have been reasonable gambles, in the sense that the prospects for a successful salvage operation were good enough that taking immediate, even if irrevocable, steps to facilitate and take advantage of the expected happy outcome was prudent. But we often reasonably rely on things that are not promises. A farmer plants his crops in the spring in reasonable reliance that spring will be followed by summer rather than by winter. There can be reasonable reliance on statements as well as on the regularities of nature, but if the statements are not reasonably understood as legally enforceable promises there can be no action for promissory estoppel.

Suppose McNamara thought that there was a 50 percent chance that the deal would go through and believed that reliance on that prospect would cost him $100,000, but also believed that by relying he could expect either to increase the likelihood that the deal would go through or to make more money if it did by being able to start production sooner and that in either event the expected benefit of reliance would exceed $100,000. Then his reliance would be reasonable even if not induced by enforceable promises. The numbers are arbitrary but the example apt. GPI and its principals relied, and may have relied reasonably, but they didn't rely on Martin's "promises" because those were not promises reasonably understood as such by so financially sophisticated a businessman as McNarama. So we see now that the essence of the doctrine of promissory estoppel is not that the plaintiff have reasonably relied on the defendant's promise, but that he have reasonably relied on its *being* a promise in the sense of a legal commitment, and not a mere prediction or aspiration or bit of puffery.

One last point. Ordinarily the question whether a plaintiff reasonably understood a statement to be a promise is a question of fact and so cannot be resolved in summary judgment proceedings. But if it is clear that the question can be answered in only one way, there is no occasion to submit the question to a jury. This, we believe, is such a case.

AFFIRMED.

NOTE ON SECTION 90—HANDLE WITH CARE

Two things must be kept in mind when dealing with unbargained-for reliance upon promises. The first is that the unbargained-for reliance doctrine bears down more heavily on the adequacy notion than does the consideration doctrine. The law may not question the adequacy of consideration but it must (by definition) question the adequacy of reliance. The second is that the measure of recovery available to the injured party in order to avoid injustice is often more properly measured by the cost of the reliance than by the value of the unperformed promise.

That different legal consequences will flow depending on whether the consideration (bargained-for reliance) label or the unrequested reliance label is attached to a promise makes the distinction between the two categories more than just an interesting intellectual exercise. Section 90 recognizes promises that are relied upon as enforceable, but different in major respects from promises that are truly bargained-for. It furnishes the law of contract with a way to protect an innocent party against loss suffered because of her understandable reliance on what is essentially a gift promise without overcompensating her by converting a gift into a bargain.

VII. FORM AND ENFORCEABILITY

The complexity of the doctrine of consideration is an objection to using it as the basic mark of the enforceable contract. The doctrine does not always permit a person to look at an agreement and readily declare with confidence whether it is an enforceable contract. Contract law would be much less confusing if there were a clear and simple method to determine whether a promise is binding.

One way to tell whether a promise merits reliance by others and enforcement by the law is to look at the seriousness with which it is made. If the promisor takes special steps to indicate that he considers his obligation to be serious, we are more ready to make him keep it. On the other hand, we are not always impressed with the importance (or the fairness) of enforcing a chance or casual statement that the parties didn't seem to treat as important when made.

Intuitively, the *form* of the promise is a significant indication of its seriousness and thus its enforceability. As Professor Ames wrote in *Law and Morals*, 22 HARV. L. REV. 97, 101 (1908):

> I asked [my twelve year old son] one day about his plans for the afternoon, and he told me he was to play tennis with his friend John. In the evening, when asked if he had had a good afternoon with John, he said, "Oh, I haven't been with him. I thought I would rather play with Willie." "But didn't John expect you?" "Yes, I suppose he did." "Was it quite right, after you had led him to expect you, to disappoint him?" "Oh, but I didn't promise him that I would come."

At the twelve-year-old level, adding "cross my heart" or "scout's honor" is apt to convert an off-hand statement into a binding promise enforceable in a twelve-year-old's court. Various similar formalities have been common in a broad range of adult societies down to the present time. One is the oath: the promise for which divine sanction and enforcement are invoked. Another is the promise marked by a tangible gift, pledge or ceremonial act. The token exchange, such as the gift of a golden ring in our marriage ceremony, has been used at various times throughout the world to mark the solemn promise. Shaking hands or having a drink together is another common ceremony to bind promisor to promisee. Sometimes a formula of words is used, as in Roman law. The pledge of a valuable possession as security for a promise is a formality that has provided one root for our modern doctrine of consideration; it can be found both in the simple legal systems of primitive tribes and in medieval Frankish law. Most of us still carry around with us some belief in the efficacy of such formalities. Imagine how you feel when the other person breaks her word after you had shaken hands on the deal. But by and large, modern American law claims to be free of formalities.

Consideration itself can come to resemble a formality, particularly when it is most stubbornly insisted that the law will not question the adequacy of consideration. When one dollar is recited to be the consideration given in exchange for a six-month option to purchase a large office building or some other very valuable right, the "exchange" is a ceremony, not a bargain.

Formalities may serve a variety of useful functions, including "evidentiary," "cautionary," and "channeling" functions. Most forms provide reliable evidence that the transaction occurred and that an agreement was made. These evidentiary tracks may be the writing indicating the content of the agreement, the testimony of the required witness before whom it was made, or the promisee's possession of the formal token (the ring, the cup). We have already suggested a second "cautionary" function of formality: it is likely to require that the promisor go to some trouble to perform it, and in doing so there is an opportunity for reflection and caution.

Finally, by creating a formality, the law tells the person who wants to be sure that she receives an enforceable promise how to ensure that result. Contract behavior is channeled in directions set by the formality. If the law would prefer written promises, a rule that unwritten promises are not enforceable will lead people to behave in the desired way.

A. THE SEAL

In medieval times, when few could write their names, documents were commonly authenticated by affixing the wax impression of a seal to important papers. In the beginning, seals were reserved for royalty and very important personages. The impression of the seal on the paper was a sure sign that a powerful person had agreed to it and had gone to the trouble of melting the wax to show that he meant it. The sealed document was of itself treated as unimpeachable proof of the act by the law for centuries. In those times, a seal "imported its own consideration," that is, no independent consideration requirement applied to promises made under seal.

As seals became more and more common, scrawls or pre-printed marks were accepted as seals, and the seal's importance declined. About half of the American states have abolished all legal significance of the seal by statute beginning a century ago. In a few states, a document is still recognized as enforceable merely because it bears a seal. In others, the statute of limitations is longer for a document under seal. But in such major commercial states as California, Illinois, New York, Ohio, and Texas, statutes have abolished practically all distinctions between sealed and un-sealed documents. This means that a document is not enforceable because it is under seal if it is not enforceable without the seal. UCC § 2-203 has similarly rendered seals of no effect in connection with contracts for the sale of goods in all the states.

B.   FORMAL WRITING AS A
BASIS FOR ENFORCEABILITY

In the eighteenth century, the common law flirted with the idea that all written promises ought to be enforceable, but this was soon rejected and since then the law has clung to the general attitude that written promises (at least those not under seal) are no more deserving of legal enforcement than oral promises. To a degree this offends commonly held attitudes that the writing is more important than the oral conversation. Certainly, the carefully written out agreement often marks the seriously considered, solemnly assumed obligation most deserving of the law's sanction. Moreover, there are situations in which lawyers for all parties would, for sound reasons, like a promise to be enforceable even though it doesn't meet common law standards. In such a situation, it would be very convenient to have some formality like the seal or the writing available to make the agreement legally binding. To fill this "unfortunate gap" in the law, the Commissioners on Uniform State Laws in 1925 proposed the Uniform Written Obligations Act:

> A written release or promise, hereafter made and signed by the person releasing or promising, shall not be invalid or unenforceable for lack of

consideration, if the writing also contains an additional express statement, in any form of language, that the signer intends to be legally bound.

This innovation was received with a staggering lack of enthusiasm. Only Pennsylvania (in 1927) and Utah (in 1929) ever adopted it, and Utah repealed it four years later.

Despite the lack of success of the Uniform Written Obligations Act, a number of statutes more or less along the same lines—though much more limited—have been adopted. A strong argument in favor of developing a simple formality, such as the writing, is that it would clarify the enforceability of promises to make donative transfers (mostly gifts within a family or other intimate association) and substantially reduce the significance of the doctrine of consideration in these marginal areas.

Drafters have been using a comparable device for a long time. They seek to obviate issues of consideration by reciting the payment of a nominal sum as consideration in the contract. The sums recited are virtually never actually paid. We will return to a special case giving effect to the false recital of nominal consideration in *Marsh v. Lott,* p. 647. Such recitals, if given effect, reduce consideration to a formality. The Restatement, Second, Contracts, however, generally refuses to give effect to false recitals of consideration except in certain special situations. Section 218 provides:

§ 218. Untrue Recitals; Evidence of Consideration.

(1) A recital of a fact in an integrated agreement may be shown to be untrue.

(2) Evidence is admissible to prove whether or not there is consideration for a promise, even though the parties have reduced their agreement to a writing which appears to be a completely integrated agreement.

And Comment e explains this:

> Where consideration is required, the requirement is not satisfied by a false recital of consideration, although in some circumstances a recital of consideration may make a promise binding without consideration. See §§ 71, 87, 88. An incorrect statement of a consideration does not prevent proof either that there was no consideration or that there was a consideration different from that stated. In some such cases the recital may imply a promise not explicitly stated.

The reference to § 71 apparently is to Comment b that says in part:

> But it is not enough that the promise induces the conduct of the promisee or that the conduct of the promisee induces the making of the promise; both elements must be present, or there is no bargain. Moreover, a mere pretense of bargain does not suffice, as where there is a false recital of consideration or where the purported consideration is merely nominal. In such cases there is no

consideration and the promise is enforced, if at all, as a promise binding without consideration under §§ 82–94....

The other references in this Comment to § 71 are to sections dealing with options and guaranties where the Restatement explicitly declares binding a writing that recites "a purported consideration" and the Comments make clear that the enforceability of the option or guaranty is not diminished if the recital is of merely nominal consideration or is false.

The experience of continental civil law systems suggests that a single formality cannot resolve all the problems surrounding gift promises. In both French and German law, for instance, consideration as we know it is not required, but as Professor Melvin Eisenberg indicates, clarifying the possibility of enforceable gift promises is not the end of the matter:

Under the German Civil Code, a donative promise is normally enforceable to its full extent only if it is in writing and authenticated by a notary. Under French law a donative promise is normally enforceable to its full extent only if it is executed in writing before two notaries, or a notary and two witnesses, and formally accepted by the promisee, or is cast in the form known as disguised donation (a transaction that falsely appears to be something other than a gift, such as a pretended bargain or the acknowledgment of a nonexistent debt). A major aim of these formalities, like the intended effect of the Written Obligations Act, is to bring home to the promisor that he is entering into a transaction with legal implications. In the case of notarial authentication, this is accomplished by involving a specifically legal figure: the French notary has traditionally combined the roles of official, family counselor, and legal specialist in the drafting of personal instruments such as conveyances and wills; the German notary plays similar roles. In the case of a disguised donation, the legal implications of the promisor's acts are brought home by the fact that he "must so arrange the contract containing the gift as to give it the appearance of an onerous judicial act. The donor is thus clearly aware of the scope of his obligation."

Such formalities certainly address the problems of deliberative intent and evidentiary security. Form alone, however, cannot meet the problems of improvidence and ingratitude. Accordingly, the French and German Civil Codes do not stop their treatment of donative promises at the formal level, but instead go on to provide extensive treatment of circumstances arising after the promise has been made. For example, under article 519 of the German Civil Code, "[a] donor is entitled to refuse fulfillment of a promise made gratuitously insofar as, having regard to his other obligations, he is not in a position to fulfill the promise without endangering his own reasonable maintenance or the fulfillment of obligations imposed upon him by law to furnish maintenance to others." Under article 530(1), a donative promise may be revoked "if the donee, by any serious misconduct towards the donor or a close relative of the donor shows himself guilty of gross ingratitude." Under the French Civil Code, a donative promise made by a person with no living descendants is normally revoked by operation of law upon the birth of a child, and a donative promise can be revoked on the ground of ingratitude involving such matters as serious cruelty, wrongs, or injuries (*sévices, délits ou injures grave*). Both Codes carry this approach to its logical conclusion by making even completed gifts revocable under comparable circumstances, and both Codes place substantial limits on the power of an individual to disenfranchise his immediate family by either gift or will.

As these rules suggest, our legal system could not appropriately follow the lead of the civil law by making donative promises enforceable on the basis of their form—as through recognition of nominal consideration—unless we were also prepared to follow the civil law by developing and administering a body of rules dealing with the problems of improvidence and ingratitude. Certainly such an enterprise is possible. It may be questioned, however, whether the game would be worth the candle. An inquiry into improvidence involves the measurement of wealth, lifestyle, dependents' needs, and even personal utilities. An inquiry into ingratitude involves the measurement of a maelstrom, since many or most donative promises arise in an intimate context in which emotions, motives, and cues are invariably complex and highly interrelated. Perhaps the civil-law style of adjudication is suited to wrestling with these kinds of inquiries, but they have held little appeal for common-law courts, which have traditionally been oriented toward inquiry into acts rather than into personal characteristics.

Melvin A. Eisenberg, *Donative Promises,* 47 U. CHI. L. REV. 1, 12–16 (1979).

C. THE STATUTE OF FRAUDS

Throughout the United States, state statutes define specific kinds of contracts that must be in writing to be enforceable. All of these statutes are descendants of the English Statute of Frauds. This area of law can be studied in detail only in the context of the specific statute in force in a given state. It is important to remember here that the writing doesn't make the agreement enforceable; it keeps it from being *unenforceable.* And that's very different from the old effect of a seal—or the Uniform Written Obligations Act.

WEST'S ANN. CALIFORNIA CIVIL CODE:

§ 1624. Statute of Frauds.

(a) The following contracts are invalid, unless they, or some note or memorandum thereof, are in writing and subscribed by the party to be charged or by the party's agent:

(1) An agreement that by its terms is not to be performed within a year from the making thereof.

(2) A special promise to answer for the debt, default, or miscarriage of another.

(3) An agreement for the leasing for a longer period than one year, or for the sale of real property, or of an interest therein; such an agreement, if made by an agent of the party sought to be charged, is invalid, unless the authority of the agent is in writing, subscribed by the party sought to be charged.

(4) An agreement authorizing or employing an agent, broker, or any other person to purchase or sell real estate, or to lease real estate for a longer period than one year, or to procure, introduce, or find a purchaser or seller of real estate or a lessee or lessor of real estate where the lease is for a longer period than one year, for compensation or a commission.

(5) An agreement which by its terms is not to be performed during the lifetime of the promisor.

(6) An agreement by a purchaser of real property to pay an indebtedness secured by a mortgage or deed of trust upon the property purchased, unless assumption of the indebtedness by the purchaser is specifically provided for in the conveyance of the property.

(7) A contract, promise, undertaking, or commitment to loan money or to grant or extend credit, in an amount greater than one hundred thousand dollars ($100,000), not primarily for personal, family, or household purposes, made by a person engaged in the business of lending or arranging for the lending of money or extending credit. For purposes of this section, a contract, promise, undertaking, or commitment to loan money secured solely by residential property consisting of one to four dwelling units shall be deemed to be for personal, family, or household purposes.

(b) Notwithstanding paragraph (1) of subdivision (a):

(1)-(4) [Specifies an exception to the statute of frauds for certain qualified financial contracts that permits party admissions, written confirmations and electronic communications to satisfy the requirement of a writing.]

Additional Statute of Frauds provisions are now apt to be scattered through a state's statute books. Thus, when California adopted the UCC, its writing requirement for sales of goods contracts was relocated from Civil Code § 1624 to the Commercial Code and conformed to the UCC:

§ 2-201. Formal Requirements; Statute of Frauds.

(1) Except as otherwise provided in this section a contract for the sale of goods for the price of $500 or more is not enforceable by way of action or defense unless there is some writing sufficient to indicate that a contract for sale has been made between the parties and signed by the party against whom enforcement is sought or by his authorized agent or broker. A writing is not insufficient because it omits or incorrectly states a term agreed upon but the contract is not enforceable under this paragraph beyond the quantity of goods shown in such writing.

(2) Between merchants if within a reasonable time a writing in confirmation of the contract and sufficient against the sender is received and the party receiving it has reason to know its contents, it satisfies the requirements of subdivision (1) against such party unless written notice of objection to its contents is given within 10 days after it is received.

(3) A contract which does not satisfy the requirements of subdivision (1) but which is valid in other respects is enforceable

(a) If the goods are to be specially manufactured for the buyer and are not suitable for sale to others in the ordinary course of the seller's business and the seller, before notice of repudiation is received and under circumstances which reasonably indicate that the goods are for the buyer, has made either a substantial beginning of their manufacture or commitments for their procurement;

(b) If the party against whom enforcement is sought admits in his pleading, testimony or otherwise in court that a contract for sale was made, but the contract is not enforceable under this provision beyond the quantity of goods admitted; or

(c) With respect to goods for which payment has been made and accepted or which have been received and accepted (Section 2-606).

QUESTIONS AND NOTES

1. In applying UCC § 2-201 in *Am. Iron & Metal Co. v. U.S. Ferrous Trading Div.*, 2007 U. S. Dist. LEXIS 27847 (D. Conn. Apr. 16, 2007), the Court was faced with an agreement evidenced by emails regarding a domestic sale of goods that omitted material terms and signatures. AIM claimed Tube had breached a contract to purchase scrap metal from AIM for resale to an Egyptian buyer. Two e-mails evidenced this transaction. A June 23 e-mail from Tube's managing director to AIM's CEO stated:

> "Thanks for your offer per phone earlier today, i.e,. about 25–30,000 MT HSMI, your option, about 10-5000 MT P&S your option, about 30–35,000 MT total, your option for shipment anytime August 2006, your option- Price: HMS-USD 300/MT-P&S USD 305/MT-The Egyptians said they'd open their L/C within 5 working days. We'd expect to pay you out of that L/C, without any out-of-pocket expenses against our small commission (which we'd have to share with the Egyptian agent), e.g., banking expenses, survey fees. Thanks for your support. Let's keep our fingers crossed for our joint efforts to be successful."

A June 26 e-mail from the same sender to the same recipient read:

> "Following our telecon earlier today, we hereby confirm that the Egyptians accepted your/our firm counter as per our [June 23, 2006] email. They require, however, that 97% of the cargo value is payable against shipping documents under their L/C and the balance after completion of discharge and draft survey there by SGS at both ends (also for quality inspection at loadport and final there!) with average of both SGS surveys to be the final weight. This is standard in Egypt and we hope acceptable to you too.... . If you have any further questions, please let me know. Otherwise please o.k. and we'll proceed issuing the corresponding contract."

Subsequently, the market price dropped. Tube repudiated the contract and defended on the ground that the agreement was not sufficiently memorialized in a writing. The Court found the statute of frauds was satisfied, noting that UCC § 2-201 does not even require the parties to be identified as buyer or seller, or the writing to be complete or include certain terms such as the price term. It must only manifest the intention of the parties to be bound. Extrinsic evidence clarified the meaning of the shorthand expressions used in the email. Moreover, UCC § 2-201(2) does not require a signature of the party to be charged where the agreement is between merchants. An otherwise sufficient writing sent by one merchant to another binds the non-signing merchant unless that merchant objects to the writing within ten days of its receipt. The only required term in the writing is the quantity term. Stating the quantity in "ranges" qualified by "about" met the UCC requirement.

2. An important change in the Statute of Frauds occurred in 1986 when the United States acceded to the United Nations Convention on Contracts for the International Sale of Goods, effective January 1, 1988. Article 11 of the CISG provides:

> A contract of sale need not be concluded in or evidenced by writing and is not subject to any other requirements as to form. It may be proved by any means, including witnesses.

Article 12 of the convention allows nations that are party to it to make a formal declaration that Article 11 does not apply when any party to the contract has its place of business in that nation but the United States has not made that declaration. Under the federal Constitution, treaties, like federal statutes, are the supreme law of the land and preempt inconsistent state statutes. The law of all fifty states on a subject that had been a matter of quite uniform state law for several centuries has therefore been displaced with respect to transactions between Americans and persons with a place of business in another nation signatory to the convention.

Sterling v. Taylor
California Supreme Court, 2007.
40 Cal.4th 757.

■ CORRIGAN, J. delivered the Opinion of the Court

...

I. FACTUAL AND PROCEDURAL BACKGROUND

In January 2000, defendant Lawrence Taylor and plaintiff Donald Sterling discussed the sale of three apartment buildings in Santa Monica owned by the Santa Monica Collection partnership (SMC). Defendant was a general partner in SMC. Plaintiff and defendant, both experienced real estate investors, met on March 13,

2000 and discussed a series of transactions including the purchase of the SMC properties. At this meeting, plaintiff drafted a handwritten memorandum entitled "Contract for Sale of Real Property."[1]

The memorandum encompasses the sale of five properties; only the SMC properties are involved here. They are identified in the memorandum as "808 4th St.," "843 4th St.," and "1251 14th St.," with an aggregate price term of "approx. 10.468 X gross income[,] estimated income 1.600.000, *Price $16,750*.00." Although defendant had given plaintiff rent rolls showing the income from the properties, neither man brought these documents to the March 13 meeting. Plaintiff dated and initialed the memorandum as "Buyer," but the line he provided for "Seller" was left blank. Plaintiff contends the omission was inadvertent. Defendant, however, asserts he did not sign the document because he needed approval from a majority of SMC's limited partners.

On March 15, 2000, plaintiff wrote to defendant, referring to the properties by street address only, and stating "[t]his letter will confirm our contract of sale of the above buildings." The letter discussed deposits plaintiff had given to defendant, and

---

1. The memorandum may be rendered in typescript as follows:

"*Contract for Sale of Real Property*

"Seller Larry Taylor, & Christina Development, and Buyer Donald T. Sterling, Trustee of Sterling Family Trust, agree to the following terms and conditions;

	D.P.	
"1. Fox Plaza		
	3 000,000 [sic]	
	3,000,000 (cash to loan)	Price $31,000,000
"2. Barrington Bldg.		
	2,000,000 D.P.	
	6 000,000 D.P.	Price $12,700,000
"3. 808 4th St. }	approx 10.468 X gross income	
"4. 843 4th St. }	income	
"5. 1251 14th St.}	estimated 1.600.000,	Price $ 16,750.00
	escrow 30 days. Brentwood scrow. [Sic.]	

"Cash to loan.
"Contract to be completed within 30 days.
"Date 3/13/2000   Seller _____

                                                                   "Buyer DTS"

In the handwritten original, a single bracket links items 3, 4, and 5 (the SMC properties) to the notations on the right. In those notations, though the word "income" appears on a separate line above "estimated 1.600.000," it is closer to the line below it than to the line above it, and the parties agree the intended phrasing was "estimated income 1.600.000."

The parties do not explain the association between defendant and Christina Development, or the inclusion of Christina Development in the memorandum.

noted "our agreement that the depreciation allocation and tax benefits will be given to me no later than April 1, 2000, since I now have equitable tittle [*sic*]." Price terms were not mentioned. Both parties signed the letter, defendant beneath the handwritten notation "Agreed, Accepted, & Approved."

Plaintiff claims the March 13 memorandum was attached to the March 15 letter, which defendant annotated and signed in his presence. Defendant insists nothing was attached to the March 15 letter, which he did not sign until March 30. According to defendant, his signature reflected only an accommodation to acknowledge the deposits he had received from plaintiff.

On April 4, 2000, defendant sent plaintiff three formal purchase agreements with escrow instructions, identifying the properties by their legal descriptions. SMC was named as the seller and the Sterling Family Trust as the buyer. The price terms totalled $16,750,000. Defendant signed the agreements as a general partner of SMC. Plaintiff refused to sign. Defendant claims plaintiff telephoned on April 28, saying the purchase price was unacceptable. Plaintiff asserts that after reviewing the rent rolls, he determined the actual rental income from the SMC buildings was $1,375,404, not $1,600,000 as estimated on the March 13 memorandum. Plaintiff claims he tried to have defendant correct the escrow instructions, but defendant did not return his calls. Plaintiff wanted to lower the price to $14,404,841, based on the actual rental income figure and the 10.468 multiplier noted in the memorandum.[2]

Plaintiff did not ask for the $16,750.00 purchase price stated in the memorandum. He admits that he "accidentally left off one zero" when he wrote down that figure. Defendant also acknowledges that the price recorded on the memorandum was meant to be $16,750,000.[3]

Defendant returned plaintiff's uncashed deposit checks on May 23. The parties conducted further negotiations in December 2000 and January 2001. Defendant provided additional rent rolls, but no agreement was reached.

In March 2001 the trustees of the Sterling Family Trust sued Taylor, SMC, and related entities, alleging breach of a written contract to sell the properties for a total price of $14,404,841. The March 13 memorandum and the March 15 letter were attached to the complaint as the "Purchase Agreement." The complaint included causes of action for breach of the implied covenant of good faith and fair dealing,

[handwritten margin note: P's desired price]

---

2. The formula does not yield the plaintiff's modified price: $1,375,404 multiplied by 10.468 is $14,397,729. In a declaration filed in the trial court, plaintiff explained that he made two mistakes in arriving at the figure of $14,404,841, one in the rental income calculation and another in the multiplier he applied to that figure.

3. Given the superscript notation employed by plaintiff when he wrote "$16,750.00," it might be said that *three* zeros were omitted from the price. However, the characterization of the error is immaterial in light of the parties' agreement that the intended figure was $16,750,000.

specific performance, declaratory relief, an accounting, intentional misrepresentation, and imposition of a constructive trust.

Defendants sought summary judgment, claiming that no contract was formed,
the alleged contract violated the statute of frauds, and plaintiffs could not prove
fraud. Defendants contended the memorandum and letter did not satisfy the statute
because they established no agreement on price, failed to sufficiently identify either
the contracting parties or the properties, and were not signed by Taylor and Christina Development. The trial court granted summary judgment. It ruled that the
price term was too uncertain to be enforced and the writings did not comply with
the statute of frauds. The court also concluded that the undisputed facts disclosed
neither a fraudulent intent on defendant's part nor damages to plaintiff, thus fore-
closing the misrepresentation claim.

The Court of Appeal reversed as to the contract causes of action, but remanded
for entry of summary adjudication in defendants' favor on the fraud claim. The
court held that Taylor's name and signature on the writings submitted by plaintiffs
satisfied the statute of frauds. It also deemed the identification of the properties by
street address sufficient, in light of extrinsic evidence specifying the city and state.
Likewise, the court held that the price terms in the March 13 memorandum, while
ambiguous, could be clarified by examining extrinsic evidence. It concluded that defendants' evidence raised a triable issue as to whether the parties had agreed on a
formula for determining the purchase price. The court further ruled that the fraud
claim failed because plaintiffs could not prove damages. Only the contract claims are
at issue in this appeal.

II. DISCUSSION

Defendants contend the Court of Appeal improperly considered extrinsic evidence to establish essential contract terms. They insist the statute of frauds requires
a memorandum that, standing alone, supplies all material elements of the contract.
Plaintiffs, on the other hand, argue that extrinsic evidence is routinely admitted for
the purpose of determining whether memoranda comply with the statute of frauds.[4]

Both sides of this debate find support in California case law, sometimes in the
same opinion. Part A of our discussion explains that plaintiffs' view is correct. The

---

4. Defendants' argument is supported by amicus curiae Professor Richard A. Lord, current editor of the fourth edition of Williston on Contracts. The Apartment Association of Greater Los
Angeles has also contributed an amicus curiae brief, urging us in cursory fashion to reverse the
Court of Appeal's decision in order to discourage "dishonest dealing and sharp real estate practice."

Amicus curiae California Association of Realtors favors plaintiffs' position, arguing that ambiguities are not unusual in real estate transactions and resort to extrinsic evidence is required to
prevent parties who have second thoughts from escaping their contractual obligations.

statute of frauds does not preclude the admission of evidence in any form; it imposes a writing requirement, but not a comprehensive one. In part B, however, we conclude that defendants are nevertheless entitled to judgment. The Court of Appeal properly considered the parties' extrinsic evidence, but erroneously deemed it legally sufficient under the statute of frauds to establish the price sought by plaintiffs.

A. The Memorandum Requirement of the Statute of Frauds

The statute of frauds does not require a written contract; a "note or memorandum ... subscribed by the party to be charged" is adequate. (Civ.Code, § 1624, subd. (a.).)[5] In *Crowley v. Modern Faucet Mfg. Co.* (1955), we observed that "[a] written memorandum is not identical with a written contract [citation]; it is merely evidence of it and usually does not contain all of the terms." Indeed, in most instances it is not even necessary that the parties intended the memorandum to serve a contractual purpose. (Rest.2d Contracts, § 133; 1 Witkin, Summary of Cal. Law, *supra*.)

A memorandum satisfies the statute of frauds if it identifies the subject of the parties' agreement, shows that they made a contract, and states the essential contract terms with reasonable certainty. "Only the essential terms must be stated, details or particulars need not [be]. What is essential depends on the agreement and its context and also on the subsequent conduct of the parties...." (Rest.2d Contracts, § 131, com. *g*).

This court recently observed that the writing requirement of the statute of frauds "serves only to prevent the contract from being unenforceable; it does not necessarily establish the terms of the parties' contract." (*Casa Herrera, Inc. v. Beydoun* (2004). Unlike the parol evidence rule, which "determines the enforceable and incontrovertible terms of an integrated written agreement," the statute of frauds "merely serve[s] an evidentiary purpose." (*Ibid.*) As the drafters of the Second Restatement of Contracts explained: "The primary purpose of the Statute is evidentiary, to require reliable evidence of the existence and terms of the contract and to prevent enforcement through fraud or perjury of contracts never in fact made. The contents of the writing must be such as to make successful fraud unlikely, but the possibility need not be excluded that some other subject matter or person than those intended will also fall within the words of the writing. Where only an evidentiary purpose is served, *the requirement of a memorandum is read in the light of the dispute which arises and the admissions of the party to be charged;* there is no need for evidence on points not in dispute." (Rest.2d Contracts, § 131, com. *c*, italics added).

---

5. Civil Code section 1624, subdivision (a) states: "The following contracts are invalid, unless they, or some note or memorandum thereof, are in writing and subscribed by the party to be charged or by the party's agent[.]" Subdivision (a)(3) of section 1624 includes agreements for the sale of real property. ...

Thus, when ambiguous terms in a memorandum are disputed, extrinsic evidence is admissible to resolve the uncertainty. Extrinsic evidence can also support reformation of a memorandum to correct a mistake. (Rest.2d Contracts, § 131, com. *g*)

Because the memorandum itself must include the essential contractual terms, it is clear that extrinsic evidence cannot *supply* those required terms. It can, however, be used to *explain* essential terms that were understood by the parties but would otherwise be unintelligible to others. Two early cases from this court demonstrate that a memorandum can satisfy the statute of frauds, even if its terms are too uncertain to be enforceable when considered by themselves.

In *Preble v. Abrahams* (1891), a written agreement for the sale of land described the property to be sold as "forty acres of the eighty-acre tract at Biggs."[7] The court observed: "An agreement not in writing for the sale and purchase of real estate is void. And the description of the property in the written agreement is so entirely uncertain as to render the instrument inoperative and void, unless we can go beyond the face of it to ascertain its meaning."

To give effect to the agreement, the *Preble* court relied on extrinsic evidence that another buyer had purchased one 40–acre tract and the defendant had agreed to purchase the remainder. "We think the evidence makes the subject-matter sufficiently certain, and that is all that is necessary. Professor Pomeroy says: 'It is not strictly accurate to say that the subject-matter must be absolutely certain from the writing itself, or by reference to some other writing. The true rule is, that the situation of the parties and the surrounding circumstances, when the contract was made, can be shown by parol evidence, so that the court may be placed in the position of the parties themselves; and if *then* the subject-matter is identified, and the terms appear reasonably certain, it is enough.' (Pomeroy on Contracts, sec. 227, note.)"

In *Brewer v. Horst–Lachmund Co.* (1900), a contract was memorialized by two telegrams employing a form of shorthand notation so arcane that "[i]f there were nothing to look to but the telegrams, the court might find it difficult, if not impossible, to determine the nature of the contract, or that any contract was entered into between the parties." The defendant contended the telegrams were an insufficient "note or memorandum" to satisfy the statute of frauds. The *Brewer* court disagreed, stating: "[T]he court is permitted to interpret the memorandum (consisting of the two telegrams) by the light of all the circumstances under which it was made; and if, when the court is put into possession of all the knowledge which the parties to the

---

7. The document in question was referred to by the *Preble* court variously as an "agreement," a "contract," and a "memorandum." The brevity and informality of the writing are such that, at least by modern standards, it can properly be considered only a "memorandum" for purposes of the statute of frauds.

transaction had at the time, it can be plainly seen from the memorandum who the parties to the contract were, what the subject of the contract was, and what were its terms, then the court should not hesitate to hold the memorandum sufficient. Oral evidence may be received to show in what sense figures or abbreviations were used; and their meaning may be explained as it was understood between the parties." (*Ibid.*)

Reading the telegrams "by the light of the circumstances surrounding the parties," the *Brewer* court concluded it was clear that they referred to a contract for the purchase of 296 bales of hops on terms understood by the parties. The facts of *Brewer* were adapted by the drafters of the Restatements as an illustration of a sufficient memorandum for purposes of the statute of frauds. (Rest.2d Contracts, § 131, com. *e*, illus. 7; and see *id.*, Reptr.'s Note.)

Despite this venerable authority, conflicting statements appear in other California cases.... Defendants rely on these and similar cases to argue that the Court of Appeal improperly considered extrinsic evidence to determine the meaning of essential but imperfectly stated terms in the memorandum drafted by plaintiff Sterling.

To clarify the law on this point, we disapprove the statements in California cases barring consideration of extrinsic evidence to determine the sufficiency of a memorandum under the statute of frauds. The purposes of the statute are not served by such a rigid rule, which has never been a consistent feature of the common law. Corbin observes: "Judicial dicta abound to the effect that the writing must contain all of the 'essential terms and conditions' of the contract, and it is often said that these must be so clear as to be understood 'without any aid from parol testimony.' But the long course of judicial decision shows that 'essential terms and conditions' is itself a term of considerable flexibility and that the courts do not in fact blind themselves by excluding parol testimony when it is a necessary aid to understanding." (4 Corbin on Contracts (rev. ed.1997) § 22.2).

"Some confusion is attributable to a failure to keep clearly in mind the purpose of the statute and the informal character of the evidence that the actual words of the statute require; some is no doubt due to differences in the attitude of the judges as to the beneficence of the statute and the wisdom of its existence.[11] Further, there are differences in the strictness of judicial requirements as to the contents of the memorandum. It is believed that sometimes these apparent differences can be explained by the degree of doubt existing in the court's mind as to the actual making and performance of the alleged contract. The better and the more disinterested is the oral testimony offered by the plaintiff, the more convincing the corroboration that is found in the surrounding circumstances, and the more limited the disputed issue

---

11. This court has noted the criticism directed at the statute of frauds.

because of admissions made by the defendant, the less that should be and is required of the written memorandum." (4 Corbin on Contracts, *supra,* § 22.2).

Williston offers similar counsel: "In determining the requisites and meaning of a 'note or memorandum in writing,' courts often look to the origin and fundamental purpose of the Statute of Frauds. In fact, a failure to do so will often result in a futile preoccupation with the numerous and conflicting precepts and decisions involving the clauses providing for a note or memorandum, and a corresponding failure to see the forest for the trees.

"The Statute of Frauds was not enacted to afford persons a means of evading just obligations; nor was it intended to supply a cloak of immunity to hedging litigants lacking integrity; nor was it adopted to enable defendants to interpose the Statute as a bar to a contract fairly, and admittedly, made. In brief, the Statute 'was intended to guard against the perils of perjury and error in the spoken word.' Therefore, if after a consideration of the surrounding circumstances, the pertinent facts and all the evidence in a particular case, the court concludes that enforcement of the agreement will not subject the defendant to fraudulent claims, the purpose of the Statute will best be served by holding the note or memorandum sufficient even though it is ambiguous or incomplete." (10 Williston on Contracts (4th ed.1999) § 29:4).[12]

The governing principle is: "That is certain which can be made certain." (Civ.Code, § 3538) We hold that if a memorandum includes the essential terms of the parties' agreement, but the meaning of those terms is unclear, the memorandum is sufficient under the statute of frauds if extrinsic evidence clarifies the terms with reasonable certainty and the evidence as a whole demonstrates that the parties intended to be bound. Conflicts in the extrinsic evidence are for the trier of fact to resolve, but whether the evidence meets the standard of reasonable certainty is a question of law for the court.[13]

We emphasize that a memorandum of the parties' agreement is *controlling* evidence under the statute of frauds. Thus, extrinsic evidence cannot be employed to prove an agreement at odds with the terms of the memorandum. This point was made in *Beazell v. Schrader* (1963). There, the plaintiff sought to recover a 5 percent

---

12. Williston, like this court in *Franklin v. Hansen*, has embraced conflicting views. ...

13. We note that a flexible, pragmatic view of the statute of frauds has deep roots in the common law. In 1747, Lord Hardwicke, sitting as Lord Chancellor, observed: "The meaning of the statute is to reduce contracts to a certainty, in order to avoid perjury on the one hand, and fraud on the other, and therefore, both in this court and the courts of common law, when an agreement has been reduced to such a certainty, and the substance of the statute has been complied with in the material part, the forms have never been insisted upon." (*Welford v. Beazely* (1747) 26 Eng.Rep. 1090 (Ch.); accord, *Moss v. Atkinson, supra,* 44 Cal. 3, 16; *Clason's Ex'rs v. Bailey* (N.Y.Sup.Ct.1817) 14 Johns 484; *Higdon v. Thomas* (Md.1827) 1 H. & G. 139.)

real estate broker's commission under an oral agreement. The escrow instructions, which specified a 1.25 percent commission, were the "memorandum" on which the plaintiff relied to comply with the statute. However, he contended the instructions incorrectly reflected the parties' actual agreement, as shown by extrinsic evidence. The *Beazell* court rejected this argument, holding that under the statute of frauds, "the parol agreement of which the writing is a memorandum must be one whose terms are consistent with the terms of the memorandum." Thus, in determining whether extrinsic evidence provides the certainty required by the statute, courts must bear in mind that the evidence cannot contradict the terms of the writing.

B. The Sufficiency of This Memorandum

As noted above, it is a question of law whether a memorandum, considered in light of the circumstances surrounding its making, complies with the statute of frauds. Accordingly, the issue is generally amenable to resolution by summary judgment. We independently review the record to determine whether a triable issue of fact might defeat the statute of frauds defense in this case.

A memorandum of a contract for the sale of real property must identify the buyer, the seller, the price, and the property.[14] (*King v. Stanley* (1948). Defendants contend the memorandum drafted by plaintiff Sterling fails to adequately specify the seller, the property, or the price.[15]

The Court of Appeal correctly held that the seller and the properties were sufficiently identified. The parties themselves displayed no uncertainty as to those terms before their dispute over the price arose. It is a "cardinal rule of construction that when a contract is ambiguous or uncertain the practical construction placed upon it by the parties before any controversy arises as to its meaning affords one of the most reliable means of determining the intent of the parties." (*Bohman v. Berg* (1960)) The same rule governs the interpretation of a memorandum under the statute of frauds. (See Rest.2d Contracts, § 131, com. *g*)[16]

---

14. The traditional formulation of essential terms also included the time and manner of payment, factors not at issue in this case. In H*ouse of Prayer v. Evangelical Assn. for India* (2003), the court reasoned that because contracts for the sale of real property are enforceable without specification of a time of performance, that term is not essential under the statute of frauds.

15. Defendants do not here challenge the sufficiency of Taylor's signature on the March 15 letter to meet the subscription requirement of the statute of frauds. Both the letter and the March 13 memorandum may be considered together to satisfy the statute. The parties' dispute concerns only the terms of the memorandum.

16. This rule of construction undermines the contention in Professor Lord's amicus curiae brief that the multiple ambiguities in the memorandum before us, considered together in the abstract, render it insufficient under the statute of frauds. A skillful attorney can conjure ambiguities from nearly any document, but such hypothetical difficulties often disappear when the surrounding circumstances are considered.

The memorandum referred to "Seller Larry Taylor, & Christina Development." Defendants argue that the omission of the actual owner of the properties, SMC, is fatal. However, they do not dispute Taylor's authorization to act as SMC's agent, or his actual performance of that role. A contract made in the name of an agent may be enforced against an undisclosed principal, and extrinsic evidence is admissible to identify the principal. If a term is stated in a memorandum with sufficient certainty to be enforced, it satisfies the statute of frauds. Therefore, the reference to Taylor was adequate, regardless of the apparently mistaken inclusion of Christina Development.

Similarly, while the properties were identified in the memorandum only by street address, neither party displayed any confusion over their actual location. The purchase agreements Taylor prepared included full legal descriptions, and when Sterling received those agreements he did not object that he wanted to buy buildings on 4th and 14th Streets in Manhattan rather than Santa Monica. In any event, the better view has long been that extrinsic evidence may be consulted to locate property described in imprecise terms, even though a memorandum with a more complete description would be preferable.

As defendants forthrightly conceded in the trial court, "[t]he problem here is the price term." The Court of Appeal concluded that the lines in the memorandum stating "approx. 10.468 X gross income[,] estimated income 1.600.000, *Price $16,750*.00 " were ambiguous, given the use of the modifier "approx." before the multiplier, the omitted zero in the price, and the uncertain meaning of "gross income." The court then considered Sterling's testimony that "approx." was meant to modify the total price, not the multiplier; that the missing zero was merely an error; and that "gross income" was used by the parties to refer to actual gross annual income. It decided that this evidence, if accepted by the trier of fact, could establish an agreement to determine the price based on a formula, which would be binding under *Carver v. Teitsworth* (1991). In *Carver,* a bid for either a specified price or $1,000 over any higher bid was deemed sufficiently certain.

In this court, plaintiffs also cite *Cal. Lettuce Growers v. Union Sugar Co.* (1955), to show that a price term may be calculated from a formula. There, a price formula was derived from industry custom and the parties' past practice. Plaintiffs contend the parties here negotiated a 10.468 multiplier to be applied to the actual gross rental income from the buildings in March 2000, as indicated by the fact that Taylor gave Sterling rent rolls before their March 13 meeting.

The Court of Appeal erred by deeming Sterling's testimony sufficient to establish his interpretation of the memorandum for purposes of the statute of frauds. Had Taylor testified that the parties meant to leave the price open to determination based on a rental income figure that was yet to be determined, this would be a different case. Then, the "admissions of the party to be charged" might have supported a reasonably certain price term derived from a negotiated formula. (Rest.2d Contracts, § 131, com. c.) Here, however, Taylor insists the price was meant to be $16,750,000, and Sterling agrees that was the number he intended to write down, underlined, as the "Price."

$16,750,000 is clearly an approximate product of the formula specified in the memorandum, applied to the income figure stated there.[17] On the other hand, Sterling's asserted price of $14,404,841 cannot reasonably be considered an approximation of $16,750,000. It is instead an approximate product of the formula applied to an actual income figure not found in the memorandum. The writing does not include the term "actual gross income," nor does it state that the price term will vary depending on proof or later agreement regarding the actual rental income from the buildings. In effect, Sterling would employ only the first part of the price term ("approx. 10.468 X gross income") and ignore the last parts ("estimated income 1.600.000, *Price $16,750*.00 "). He would hold Taylor to a price that is 10.468 times the actual rental income figure gleaned from the rent rolls, but only "approximately" so because of Sterling's computational errors.

Thus, two competing interpretations of the memorandum were before the court. Taylor's is consistent with the figures provided in the memorandum, requiring only the correction of the price by reference to undisputed extrinsic evidence. Sterling's price is not stated in the memorandum, and depends on extrinsic evidence in the form of his own testimony, disputed by Taylor, that the parties intended to apply the formula to actual gross rental income instead of the estimated income noted in the memorandum. Even if the trier of fact were to accept Sterling's version of the parties' negotiations, the price he seeks is not reflected in the memorandum; indeed, it is inconsistent with the price term that appears in the memorandum. Under these circumstances, we conclude the evidence is insufficient to establish Sterling's price term with the reasonable certainty required by the statute of frauds.

The statute of frauds demands written evidence that reflects the parties' mutual understanding of the essential terms of their agreement, when viewed in light of the transaction at issue and the dispute before the court. The writing requirement is intended to permit the enforcement of agreements actually reached, but "to prevent enforcement through fraud or perjury of contracts never in fact made." (Rest.2d Contracts, § 131, com. c.) The sufficiency of a memorandum to fulfill this purpose may depend on the quality of the extrinsic evidence offered to explain its terms. In *Preble v. Abrahams,* the memorandum failed to describe the property to be sold with any certainty, but extrinsic evidence established that the parties could only have been referring to the portion of a tract that was not sold to another buyer. Similarly,

---

17. The actual product of $1,600,000 multiplied by 10.468 is $16,748,800.

in *Brewer v. Horst–Lachmund Co.*, telegrams that were otherwise inscrutable demonstrated an ascertainable agreement when the court considered the circumstances of the transaction and the parties' understanding of the terms employed.

Here, unlike in the *Preble* and *Brewer* cases, the extrinsic evidence offered by plaintiffs is at odds with the writing, which states a specific price and does not indicate that the parties contemplated any change based on actual rental income. Therefore, the evidence is insufficient to show with reasonable certainty that the parties understood and agreed to the price alleged by plaintiffs. The price terms stated in the memorandum, considered together with the extrinsic evidence of the contemplated price, leave a degree of doubt that the statute of frauds does not tolerate. The trial court properly granted defendants summary judgment.

■ KENNARD, J., Concurring and Dissenting.

I agree with the majority that extrinsic evidence is admissible to resolve the meaning of an ambiguity in a written memorandum required by the statute of frauds as evidence of an agreement, and that conflicts in the evidence are for the trier of fact to resolve. The majority, however, goes astray when it takes it upon itself to resolve an existing conflict in the evidence. In my view, the ambiguity in the language of the memorandum at issue should be resolved by the trier of fact.

...

II.

The parties' dispute here centers on whether the price description in the memorandum is ambiguous so that extrinsic evidence is admissible to clarify its meaning and satisfy the statute of frauds. Regarding price the memorandum states: "approx. 10.468 X gross income [¶] estimated income 1.600.000, *Price $16,750,000.*" Plaintiff claims that the word "approx." modified the entire statement, not just "10.468 X gross income," and that the parties understood the term "gross income" to mean actual annual gross rental income. In other words, plaintiff's position is that the memorandum sets forth a formula for determining the actual price—10.468 multiplied by actual annual gross rental income, which results in a price of $14,404,841— and that the reference to "*Price $16,750,000*" is an estimate of the actual price, determined by application of the formula just mentioned, albeit using a somewhat inaccurate estimate of gross annual rental income. (See e.g., *Cal. Lettuce Growers v. Union Sugar Co.* (1955) [price need not be specified if it can be objectively determined]; *Carver v. Teitsworth* (1991) [same].) Defendant disagrees, contending that the memorandum's mention of "*Price $16,750,000*" reflects the actual purchase price agreed upon by the parties. Both have a point.

As the Court of Appeal observed, the language in the memorandum is ambiguous; that is, it can reasonably be read as each party proposes. To accept plaintiff's argument would give meaning to the language in the disputed statement of "10.468 X gross income [¶] estimated 1.600.000." To accept defendant's argument would give meaning to the term *"Price $16,750,000."* Which view should be accepted is a determination to be made by the trier of fact, based on its consideration of the extrinsic evidence presented. Either way, the trier of fact's resolution would result in a specific purchase price: one arrived at through application of a formula expressed in the memorandum, the other through acceptance of the figure $16,750,000 mentioned in the memorandum.

The majority, however, simply adopts defendant's view instead of leaving it to the trier of fact to resolve the conflict in the evidence. In accepting defendant's view, the majority rejects plaintiff's view as attempting to alter rather than explain the terms of the memorandum. I disagree.

Apparently based on its own evaluation of the evidence, which as discussed above is conflicting, the majority takes it upon itself to decide that the agreed price was $16,750,000 and then concludes that any extrinsic evidence presented by plaintiff would be inconsistent with that figure. The majority reasons that plaintiff is looking only to the first part of the memorandum's price description of "approx. 10.468 X gross income," while ignoring the last part stating "estimated income 1.600.000, *Price $16,750,000.*" This is both a misapprehension of plaintiff's view and a failure to appreciate that defendant's view too is not free from ambiguity.

Plaintiff's position that the memorandum sets forth a formula for determining the price does not ignore the memorandum's reference to "estimated income 1.600.000, *Price $16,750,000.*" According to plaintiff, the memorandum's *stated* price is itself an *estimate,* for it is the product of the *estimated* income of 1.600.000 times 10.468, while the *actual* price is to be determined by using the formula 10.468 multiplied by the *actual* gross income, resulting in a price of $14,404,841. Defendant's view that the actual price is $16,750,000 finds support in the memorandum's mention of *"Price $16,750,000 "* but it ignores the memorandum's formula that plaintiff relies on. Unlike the majority, I see no reason to reject plaintiff's position as a matter of law when the purchase terms in the memorandum are ambiguous and are as reasonably susceptible to plaintiff's position as to defendant's. I would leave it to the trier of fact to resolve the ambiguity.

QUESTIONS

Can you reconcile the California Supreme Court majority opinion in this case with the decision in *Am. Iron & Metal Co. v. U.S. Ferrous Trading Div.*, discussed in Note 1 on p. 578? Is the California Supreme Court majority's underlying concern that the memorandum insufficiently evidences the agreement between Sterling and Taylor, or that there was no agreement between Sterling and Taylor on the question of price?

McIntosh v. Murphy

Hawaii Supreme Court, 1970.
52 Haw. 29, 469 P.2d 177.

■ LEVINSON, J. This case involves an oral employment contract which allegedly violates the provision of the Statute of Frauds requiring "any agreement that is not to be performed within one year from the making thereof" to be in writing in order to be enforceable. In this action the plaintiff-employee Dick McIntosh seeks to recover damages from his employer, George Murphy and Murphy Motors, Ltd., for the breach of an alleged one-year oral employment contract.

While the facts are in sharp conflict, it appears that defendant George Murphy was in southern California during March, 1964 interviewing prospective management personnel for his Chevrolet–Oldsmobile dealerships in Hawaii. He interviewed the plaintiff twice during that time. The position of sales manager for one of the dealerships was fully discussed but no contract was entered into. In April, 1964 the plaintiff received a call from the general manager of Murphy Motors informing him of possible employment within thirty days if he was still available. The plaintiff indicated his continued interest and informed the manager that he would be available. Later in April, the plaintiff sent Murphy a telegram to the effect that he would arrive in Honolulu on Sunday, April 26, 1964. Murphy then telephoned McIntosh on Saturday, April 25, 1964 to notify him that the job of assistant sales manager was open and work would begin on the following Monday, April 27, 1964. At that time McIntosh expressed surprise at the change in job title from sales manager to assistant sales manager but reconfirmed the fact that he was arriving in Honolulu the next day, Sunday. McIntosh arrived on Sunday, April 26, 1964 and began work on the following day, Monday, April 27, 1964.

As a consequence of his decision to work for Murphy, McIntosh moved some of his belongings from the mainland to Hawaii, sold other possessions, leased an apartment in Honolulu and obviously forwent any other employment opportunities. In short, the plaintiff did all those things which were incidental to changing one's residence permanently from Los Angeles to Honolulu, a distance of approximately 2200 miles. McIntosh continued working for Murphy until July 16, 1964, approximately two and one-half months, at which time he was discharged on the grounds that he was unable to close deals with prospective customers and could not train the salesmen.

At the conclusion of the trial, the defense moved for a directed verdict arguing that the oral employment agreement was in violation of the Statute of Frauds, there being no written memorandum or note thereof. The trial court ruled that as a matter of law the contract did not come within the Statute, reasoning that Murphy bargained for acceptance by the actual commencement of performance by McIntosh, so that McIntosh was not bound by a contract until he came to work on Monday, April 27, 1964. Therefore, assuming that the contract was for a year's employment, it was performable within a year exactly to the day and no writing was required for it to be enforceable. Alternatively, the court ruled that if the agreement was made final by the telephone call between the parties on Saturday, April 25, 1964, then that part of the weekend which remained would not be counted in calculating the year, thus taking the contract out of the Statute of Frauds. With commendable candor the trial judge gave as the motivating force for the decision his desire to avoid a mechanical and unjust application of the Statute.[1]

The case went to the jury on the following questions: (1) whether the contract was for a year's duration or was performable on a trial basis, thus making it terminable at the will of either party; (2) whether the plaintiff was discharged for just cause; and (3) if he was not discharged for just cause, what damages were due the plaintiff. The jury returned a verdict for the plaintiff in the sum of $12,103.40. The defendants appeal to this court on four principal grounds, three of which we find to be without merit. The remaining ground of appeal is whether the plaintiff can maintain an action on the alleged oral employment contract in light of the prohibition of the Statute of Frauds making unenforceable an oral contract that is not to be performed within one year.

I. TIME OF ACCEPTANCE OF THE EMPLOYMENT AGREEMENT

The defendants contend that the trial court erred in refusing to give an instruction to the jury that if the employment agreement was made more than one day before the plaintiff began performance, there could be no recovery by the plaintiff. The reason given was that a contract not to be performed within one year from its making is unenforceable if not in writing.

The defendants are correct in their argument that the time of acceptance of an offer is a question of fact for the jury to decide. But the trial court alternatively decided that even if the offer was accepted on the Saturday prior to the commencement of performance, the intervening Sunday and part of Saturday would

---

1. THE COURT: You make the law look ridiculous, because one day is Sunday and the man does not work on Sunday; the other day is Saturday; he is up in Fresno. He can't work down there. And he is down here Sunday night and shows up for work on Monday. To me that is a contract within a year. I don't want to make the law look ridiculous, Mr. Clause, because it is one day later, one day too much, and that one day is a Sunday, and a non working day.

not be counted in computing the year for the purposes of the Statute of Frauds. The judge stated that Sunday was a non-working day and only a fraction of Saturday was left which he would not count. In any event, there is no need to discuss the relative merits of either ruling since we base our decision in this case on the doctrine of equitable estoppel which was properly briefed and argued by both parties before this court, although not presented to the trial court.

II. ENFORCEMENT BY VIRTUE OF ACTION IN RELIANCE ON THE ORAL CONTRACT

In determining whether a rule of law can be fashioned and applied to a situation where an oral contract admittedly violates a strict interpretation of the Statute of Frauds, it is necessary to review the Statute itself together with its historical and modern functions. The Statute of Frauds, which requires that certain contracts be in writing in order to be legally enforceable, had its inception in the days of Charles II of England. Hawaii's version of the Statute is found in HRS § 656–1 and is substantially the same as the original English Statute of Frauds.

The first English Statute was enacted almost 300 years ago to prevent "many fraudulent practices, which are commonly endeavored to be upheld by perjury and subornation of perjury." 29 Car. 2, c. 3 (1677). Certainly, there were compelling reasons in those days for such a law. At the time of enactment in England, the jury system was quite unreliable, rules of evidence were few, and the complaining party was disqualified as a witness so he could neither testify on direct-examination nor, more importantly, be cross-examined. The aforementioned structural and evidentiary limitations on our system of justice no longer exist.

Retention of the Statute today has nevertheless been justified on at least three grounds: (1) the Statute still serves an evidentiary function thereby lessening the danger of perjured testimony (the original rationale); (2) the requirement of a writing has a cautionary effect which causes reflection by the parties on the importance of the agreement; and (3) the writing is an easy way to distinguish enforceable contracts from those which are not, thus channelling certain transactions into written form.

In spite of whatever utility the Statute of Frauds may still have, its applicability has been drastically limited by judicial construction over the years in order to mitigate the harshness of a mechanical application.[3] Furthermore, learned writers

---

3. Thus a promise to pay the debt of another has been construed to encompass only promises made to a creditor which do not benefit the promisor (Restatement of Contracts § 184 (1932)); 3 Williston, Contracts § 452 (Jaeger ed. 1960); a promise in consideration of marriage has been interpreted to exclude mutual promises to marry (Restatement, supra § 192; 3 Williston, supra § 485); a promise not to be performed within one year means a promise not performable within one year (Restatement, supra § 198; 3 Williston, supra § 495); a promise not to be performed within one year may be removed from the Statute of Frauds if one party has fully performed

continue to disparage the Statute regarding it as "a statute for promoting fraud" and a "legal anachronism."

Another method of judicial circumvention of the Statute of Frauds has grown out of the exercise of the equity powers of the courts. Such judicially imposed limitations or exceptions involved the traditional dispensing power of the equity courts to mitigate the "harsh" rule of law. When courts have enforced an oral contract in spite of the Statute, they have utilized the legal labels of "part performance" or "equitable estoppel" in granting relief. Both doctrines are said to be based on the concept of estoppel, which operates to avoid unconscionable injury.

Part performance has long been recognized in Hawaii as an equitable doctrine justifying the enforcement of an oral agreement for the conveyance of an interest in land where there has been substantial reliance by the party seeking to enforce the contract....

It is appropriate for modern courts to cast aside the raiments of conceptualism which cloak the true policies underlying the reasoning behind the many decisions enforcing contracts that violate the Statute of Frauds. There is certainly no need to resort to legal rubrics or meticulous legal formulas when better explanations are available. The policy behind enforcing an oral agreement which violated the Statute of Frauds, as a policy of avoiding unconscionable injury, was well set out by the California Supreme Court. In *Monarco v. LoGreco*, a case which involved an action to enforce an oral contract for the conveyance of land on the grounds of 20 years performance by the promisee, the court said:

> The doctrine of estoppel to assert the statute of frauds has been consistently applied by the courts of this state to prevent fraud that would result from refusal to enforce oral contracts in certain circumstances. Such fraud may inhere in the unconscionable injury that would result from denying enforcement of the contract after one party has been induced by the other seriously to change his position in reliance on the contract * * *.

In seeking to frame a workable test which is flexible enough to cover diverse factual situations and also provide some reviewable standards, we find very persuasive section [139] of the [Second] Restatement of Contracts. That section specifically covers those situations where there has been reliance on an oral contract which falls within the Statute of Frauds. Section [139] states:

(1) A promise which the promisor should reasonably expect to induce action or forbearance on the part of the promisee or a third person and which does induce the action or forbearance is enforceable notwithstanding the Statute

_____

(Restatement, supra § 198; 3 Williston, supra § 504); and the Statute will not be applied where all promises involved are fully performed (Restatement, supra § 219; 3 Williston, supra § 528).

of Frauds if injustice can be avoided only by enforcement of the promise. The remedy granted for breach is to be limited as justice requires.

(2) In determining whether injustice can be avoided only by enforcement of the promise, the following circumstances are significant: (a) the availability and adequacy of other remedies, particularly cancellation and restitution; (b) the definite and substantial character of the action or forbearance in relation to the remedy sought; (c) the extent to which the action or forbearance corroborates evidence of the making and terms of the promise, or the making and terms are otherwise established by clear and convincing evidence; (d) the reasonableness of the action or forbearance; (e) the extent to which the action or forbearance was foreseeable by the promisor.

We think that the approach taken in the Restatement is the proper method of giving the trial court the necessary latitude to relieve a party of the hardships of the Statute of Frauds. Other courts have used similar approaches in dealing with oral employment contracts upon which an employee had seriously relied. This is to be preferred over having the trial court bend over backwards to take the contract out of the Statute of Frauds. In the present case the trial court admitted just this inclination and forthrightly followed it.

There is no dispute that the action of the plaintiff in moving 2200 miles from Los Angeles to Hawaii was foreseeable by the defendant. In fact, it was required to perform his duties. Injustice can only be avoided by the enforcement of the contract and the granting of money damages. No other remedy is adequate. The plaintiff found himself residing in Hawaii without a job.

It is also clear that a contract of some kind did exist. The plaintiff performed the contract for two and one-half months receiving $3,484.60 for his services. The exact length of the contract, whether terminable at will as urged by the defendant, or for a year from the time when the plaintiff started working, was up to the jury to decide.

In sum, the trial court might have found that enforcement of the contract was warranted by virtue of the plaintiff's reliance on the defendant's promise. Naturally, each case turns on its own facts. Certainly there is considerable discretion for a court to implement the true policy behind the Statute of Frauds, which is to prevent fraud or any other type of unconscionable injury. We therefore affirm the judgment of the trial court on the ground that the plaintiff's reliance was such that injustice could only be avoided by enforcement of the contract.

Affirmed.

■ ABE, J., with whom KOBAYASHI, J., joins, dissenting.

The majority of the court has affirmed the judgment of the trial court; however, I respectfully dissent.

I.

As acknowledged by this court, the trial judge erred when as a matter of law he ruled that the alleged employment contract did not come within the Statute of Frauds; however, I cannot agree that this error was not prejudicial as this court intimates.

On this issue, the date that the alleged contract was entered into was all important and the date of acceptance of an offer by the plaintiff was a question of fact for the jury to decide. In other words, it was for the jury to determine when the alleged one-year employment contract was entered into and if the jury had found that the plaintiff had accepted the offer more than one day before plaintiff was to report to work, the contract would have come within the Statute of Frauds and would have been unenforceable.

II.

This court holds that though the alleged one-year employment contract came within the Statute of Frauds, nevertheless the judgment of the trial court is affirmed "on the ground that the plaintiff's reliance was such that injustice could only be avoided by enforcement of the contract."

I believe this court is begging the issue by its holding because to reach that conclusion, this court is ruling that the defendant agreed to hire the plaintiff under a one-year employment contract. The defendant has denied that the plaintiff was hired for a period of one year and has introduced into evidence testimony of witnesses that all hiring by the defendant in the past has been on a trial basis. The defendant also testified that he had hired the plaintiff on a trial basis.

Here on one hand the plaintiff claimed that he had a one-year employment contract; on the other hand, the defendant claimed that the plaintiff had not been hired for one year but on a trial basis for so long as his services were satisfactory. I believe the Statute of Frauds was enacted to avoid the consequences this court is forcing upon the defendant. In my opinion, the legislature enacted the Statute of Frauds to negate claims such as has been made by the plaintiff in this case. But this court holds that because the plaintiff in reliance of the one-year employment contract (alleged to have been entered into by the plaintiff, but denied by the defendant) has changed his position, "injustice could only be avoided by enforcement of the contract." Where is the sense of justice?

Now assuming that the defendant had agreed to hire the plaintiff under a one-year employment contract and the contract came within the Statute of Frauds, I cannot agree, as intimated by this court, that we should circumvent the Statute of Frauds by the exercise of the equity powers of courts. As to statutory law, the sole function of the judiciary is to interpret the statute and the judiciary should not usurp legislative power and enter into the legislative field. Thus, if the Statute of Frauds is too harsh as intimated by this court, and it brings about undue hardship, it is for the legislature to amend or repeal the statute and not for this court to legislate.

Long 'f to Hoeley.

QUESTIONS AND NOTES

1. Put yourself in Mr. McIntosh's shoes. Would you move 2,200 miles on the basis of a one-year employment contract without having something in writing? Why didn't McIntosh? Is it significant that McIntosh had arranged before any job offer had been made to arrive in Hawaii on April 26?

2. If a reasonable person would expect a writing to evidence a one-year employment contract, isn't McIntosh's version of the agreement dubious?

3. The jury awarded McIntosh $12,103.40, and we do not know exactly how it calculated that sum. It appears to be quite close to the unpaid salary for the unexpired term of the year-long contract. Section 90 of the Restatement, Second, Contracts recognizes that when enforcement of the promise is based on unbargained-for reliance, "the remedy granted for breach may be limited as justice requires." What is the value you would put on McIntosh's reliance if you were a judge trying this case without a jury?

4. In *Stearns v. Emery-Waterhouse Co.*, 596 A.2d 72 (Me. 1991), the court refused to apply the reliance based exception to the Statute of Frauds in a factual context similar to that in *McIntosh*. Stearns sued his former employer for breach of an oral agreement with the company's president to employ him to age 55 at an annual salary of $85,000. Stearns asserted that in reliance on this oral agreement, he left his prior employment and moved from Massachusetts to Maine, where he served as Emery-Waterhouse's director of retail sales for nearly two years. Stearns was then assigned a different job at a reduced salary of $68,000. Six months later, before he turned 55, Stearns was terminated. The court described the question before it as "whether an employee may avoid the statute of frauds based solely upon his detrimental reliance on an employer's oral promise of continued employment." The court answered no because: "[I]n the employment context [doing so] contravenes the policy of the Statute to prevent fraud. It is too easy for a disgruntled former employee to allege reliance on a promise, but difficult factually to distinguish such reliance from the ordinary preparations that attend any new employment. Thus, such pre-employment actions of reliance do not properly serve the evidentiary function of the writing required by the statute."

D.   THE PAROL EVIDENCE RULE

Agreements that need not be written in order to qualify for enforceability are often written if they involve deals of any consequence. There are, of course, several practical advantages to putting an understanding into a writing to which both parties affix their signatures, even when a writing is not essential to the agreement's enforceability. Reducing the agreement to writing will lead the parties to examine its terms and think through their bargain. A writing evidences the deal, thus reducing problems of proof at trial. It also evidences the deal to other people, such as bankers who may be asked to finance the transaction or lend money against the contract as collateral. And it limits reliance on memory and stale impressions and thus reduces—if it does not cut off—disagreement as to what was and what was not fully agreed upon at the conclusion of negotiations.

Putting the agreement in writing, however, has another effect–invoking the parol evidence rule. In contract litigation this effect is not always a desirable one. This "rule" is stated as follows in a leading treatise:

> Parol evidence. . . may not be admitted into evidence to add to or contradict the clear and unambiguous terms of a written instrument that appears, on its face, to express an agreement that is complete in all of its essential terms, in an effort to show that, at or before the signing of the document, some further or different terms were orally agreed upon by the parties.

28 Williston, Contracts § 70:135 at 12 (4th ed. 2003) (Richard A. Lord, ed.)

The idea behind the parol evidence rule so defined is commonsensical enough—if the writing is the whole contract, then it is impermissible to contradict its terms by looking outside the contract. This tight definition also contains the basis for the four major exceptions that limit the application of the rule. First, the rule is only applied to an "integrated" contract: it is always open to a party to attempt to prove by any relevant evidence that the contract is not complete. Second, while outside evidence is not permitted for certain purposes (Williston states in extreme form that the new evidence may not "add to or contradict" the terms of the agreement), the rule does not eliminate the need to interpret the agreement and give contextual meaning to its admitted terms.

The third and fourth exceptions, which are derived from a close reading of the rule, may be considered subsets of the first exception but are worthy of explicit mention. The third exception applies to all evidence of *subsequent* agreements—conversations, writings and conduct of the parties. The rule limits the applicability of only *prior* and *contemporaneous* evidence of agreements. Fourth, the rule only proscribes   evidence   of   contemporaneous   *oral*   agreements;   evidence   of contemporaneous *written* agreements and collateral deals, therefore, are still permissible under the rule.

Collectively these limitations on the rule have the capacity to swallow it up whole. Since completeness in a writing is almost impossible to achieve, the application of the rule causes big problems to judges and lawyers alike. The result is about what one would expect: judicial application of the rule ranges from very arbitrary to very relaxed.

Perhaps the major significance of the parol evidence rule is to allocate decision-making authority among the official participants in the court process. In the rare case tried before a jury, the rule determines whether the jury will hear the disputed evidence. It all boils down to a question of how much of the story the parties will be permitted to tell to the jury at trial.

In cases decided by the judge alone, the rule doesn't have this effect because the judge must hear the evidence in order to decide whether to admit it as proof. But in the case of a bench trial the rule alters the balance of authority between the trial judge and a reviewing appellate court in deciding what the terms of the contract mean. The same issue may be stated in a somewhat different way by asking whether the interpretation of a written contract is a matter of fact (to be decided by the trier of fact, a judge or jury) or is a matter of law (to be decided by the trier of law, either the trial judge or a reviewing appeals court). As Restatement, Second, Contracts § 212(2) and Comment d indicate:

§ 212. Interpretation of Integrated Agreement.

(1) The interpretation of an integrated agreement is directed to the meaning of the terms of the writing or writings in the light of the circumstances, in accordance with the rules stated in this Chapter.

(2) A question of interpretation of an integrated agreement is to be determined by the trier of fact if it depends on the credibility of extrinsic evidence or on a choice among reasonable inferences to be drawn from extrinsic evidence. Otherwise a question of interpretation of an integrated agreement is to be determined as a question of law.

COMMENT:

d. *"Question of Law."* Analytically, what meaning is attached to a word or other symbol by one or more people is a question of fact. But general usage as to the meaning of words in the English language is commonly a proper subject for judicial notice without the aid of evidence extrinsic to the writing. Historically, moreover, partly perhaps because of the fact that jurors were often illiterate, questions of interpretation of written documents have been treated as questions of law in the sense that they are decided by the trial judge rather than by the jury. Likewise, since an appellate court is commonly in as good a position to decide such questions as the trial judge, they have been treated as questions of law for purposes of appellate review. Such treatment has the effect of limiting the power of the trier of fact to exercise a dispensing power in the guise of a finding of fact, and thus contributes to the stability and predictability of contractual relations. In cases of standardized contracts such as insurance policies, it also provides a method of assuring that like cases will be decided alike.

Understood in this way, the parol evidence rule has a political significance. Its popularity in rigid form during the 19th and early 20th centuries can be interpreted as an institutional preference for the resolution of contract disputes by judges, and particularly by appellate judges. Its softening during the 20th century can be understood as indicating a greater willingness to permit lay jurors to play a determinative role in interpreting the obligations created by written contracts. As appellate judges have sought to assert more control over the resolution of disputes based on written contracts, the rule has to some degree increased in significance more recently, although it is still a rare case in which application of the parol evidence rule is case-dispositive.

Most legal scholars agree that the true rule is one of very limited application, and properly so if full effect is to be given to the principle that parties should be bound only as they actually agreed. At the same time, there is strong pressure—particularly in an economy in which written promises are used as an important source for obtaining credit and hence must be relied on by those who are strangers to it—to limit the effect of a contract to the terms found in the document alone. Trial courts generally recognize that the rule (when broadly applied) is a very handy tool for shortening trials by quickly eliminating a lot of evidence that the judge feels is highly improbable anyway. Hence, understanding how to use the parol evidence rule both as sword and as shield is of great importance to the drafting and the litigating lawyer.

ARTHUR L. CORBIN, *THE PAROL EVIDENCE RULE*, 53 YALE L.J. 603, 622 (1944):[*]

Parol Evidence Admissible for Purposes of Interpretation. No parol evidence that is offered can be said to vary or contradict a writing until by process of interpretation the meaning of the writing is determined. The "parol evidence rule" is not, and does not purport to be, a rule of interpretation or a rule as to the admission of evidence for the purpose of interpretation. Even if a written document has been

---

[*] Copyright 1944, Yale Law Journal. Reprinted by permission of The Yale Law Journal Company and Fred B. Rothman & Company.

assented to as the complete and accurate integration of the terms of a contract, it must still be interpreted and all those factors that are of assistance in this process may be proved by oral testimony.

It is true that the language of some agreements has been believed to be so plain and clear that the court needs no assistance in interpretation. Even in these cases, however, the courts seem to have had the aid of parol evidence of surrounding circumstances. The meaning to be discovered and applied is that which each party had reason to know would be given to the words by the other party. Antecedent and surrounding factors that throw light upon this question may be proved by any kind of relevant evidence.

The more bizarre and unusual an asserted interpretation is, the more convincing must be the testimony that supports it. At what point the court should cease listening to testimony that white is black and that a dollar is fifty cents is a matter for sound judicial discretion and common sense. Even these things may be true for some purposes. As long as the court is aware that there may be doubt and ambiguity and uncertainty in the meaning and application of agreed language, it will welcome testimony as to antecedent agreements, communications, and other factors that may help to decide the issue. Such testimony does not vary or contradict the written words; it determines that which cannot afterwards be varied or contradicted.

Lee v. Joseph E. Seagram & Sons

United States Court of Appeals, Second Circuit, 1977.
552 F.2d 447.

■ GURFEIN, J. This is an appeal by defendant Joseph E. Seagram & Sons, Inc. ("Seagram") from a judgment entered by the District Court, Hon. Charles H. Tenney, upon the verdict of a jury in the amount of $407,850 in favor of the plaintiffs on a claim asserting common law breach of an oral contract....

The jury could have found the following. The Lees owned a 50% interest in Capitol City Liquor Company, Inc. ("Capitol City"), a wholesale liquor distributorship located in Washington, D.C. The other 50% was owned by Harold's brother, Henry D. Lee, and his nephew, Arthur Lee. Seagram is a distiller of alcoholic beverages. Capitol City carried numerous Seagram brands and a large portion of its sales were generated by Seagram lines.

The Lees and the other owners of Capitol City wanted to sell their respective interests in the business and, in May 1970, Harold Lee, the father, discussed the possible sale of Capitol City with Jack Yogman ("Yogman"), then Executive Vice President of Seagram (and now President), whom he had known for many years. Lee offered to sell Capitol City to Seagram but conditioned the offer on Seagram's agreement to relocate Harold and his sons, the 50% owners of Capitol City, in a new distributorship of their own in a different city.

About a month later, another officer of Seagram, John Barth, an assistant to Yogman, visited the Lees and their co-owners in Washington and began negotiations for the purchase of the assets of Capitol City by Seagram on behalf of a new distributor, one Carter, who would take it over after the purchase. The purchase of the assets of Capitol City was consummated on September 30, 1970 pursuant to a written agreement. The promise to relocate the father and sons thereafter was not reduced to writing.

Harold Lee had served the Seagram organization for thirty-six years in positions of responsibility before he acquired the half interest in the Capitol City Distributorship. From 1958 to 1962, he was chief executive officer of Calvert Distillers Company, a wholly-owned subsidiary. During this long period he enjoyed the friendship and confidence of the principals of Seagram.

In 1958, Harold Lee had purchased from Seagram its holdings of Capitol City stock in order to introduce his sons into the liquor distribution business, and also to satisfy Seagram's desire to have a strong and friendly distributor for Seagram products in Washington, D.C. Harold Lee and Yogman had known each other for 13 years.

The plaintiffs claimed a breach of the oral agreement to relocate Harold Lee's sons, alleging that Seagram had had opportunities to procure another distributorship for the Lees but had refused to do so. The Lees brought this action on January 18, 1972, fifteen months after the sale of the Capitol City distributorship to Seagram. They contended that they had performed their obligation by agreeing to the sale by Capitol City of its assets to Seagram, but that Seagram had failed to perform its obligation under the separate oral contract between the Lees and Seagram. The agreement which the trial court permitted the jury to find was "an oral agreement with defendant which provided that if they agreed to sell their interest in Capitol City, defendant in return, within a reasonable time, would provide the plaintiffs a Seagram distributorship whose price would require roughly an amount equal to the capital obtained by the plaintiffs for the sale of their interest in Capitol City, and which distributorship would be in a location acceptable to plaintiffs." No specific exception was taken to this portion of the charge. By its verdict for the plaintiffs, we must assume—as Seagram notes in its brief—that this is the agreement which the jury found was made before the sale of Capitol City was agreed upon.

Appellant urges several grounds for reversal. It contends that, as a matter of law, (1) plaintiffs' proof of the alleged oral agreement is barred by the parol evidence rule; and (2) the oral agreement is too vague and indefinite to be enforceable. Appellant also contends that plaintiffs' proof of damages is speculative and incompetent.

I

The District Court, in its denial of the defendant's motion for summary judgment, treated the issue as whether the written agreement for the sale of assets was an "integrated" agreement not only of all the mutual agreements concerning the sale of Capitol City assets, but also of *all* the mutual agreements of the parties. Finding the language of the sales agreement "somewhat ambiguous," the court decided that the determination of whether the parol evidence rule applies must await the taking of evidence on the issue of whether the sales agreement was intended to be a complete and accurate integration of all of the mutual promises of the parties.

Seagram did not avail itself of this invitation. It failed to call as witnesses any of the three persons who negotiated the sales agreement on behalf of Seagram regarding the intention of the parties to integrate all mutual promises or regarding the failure of the written agreement to contain an integration clause.

Appellant contends that, as a matter of law, the oral agreement was "part and parcel" of the subject-matter of the sales contract and that failure to include it in the written contract barred proof of its existence. The position of appellant, fairly stated, is that the oral agreement was either an inducing cause for the sale or was a part of the consideration for the sale, and in either case, should have been contained in the written contract. In either case, it argues that the parol evidence rule bars its admission.

Appellees maintain, on the other hand, that the oral agreement was a collateral agreement and that, since it is not contradictory of any of the terms of the sales agreement, proof of it is not barred by the parol evidence rule. Because the case comes to us after a jury verdict we must assume that there actually was an oral contract, such as the court instructed the jury it could find. The question is whether the strong policy for avoiding fraudulent claims through application of the parol evidence rule nevertheless mandates reversal on the ground that the jury should not have been permitted to hear the evidence.

The District Court stated the cardinal issue to be whether the parties "intended" the written agreement for the sale of assets to be the complete and accurate integration of all the mutual promises of the parties. If the written contract was not a complete integration, the court held, then the parol evidence rule has no application....

The law of New York is not rigid or categorical, but is in harmony with this approach. As Judge Fuld said in *Fogelson:* "Decision in each case must, of course, turn upon the type of transaction involved, the scope of the written contract and the content of the oral agreement asserted." 300 N.Y. at 338. And the Court of Appeals wrote in *Ball v. Grady*, 267 N.Y. 470, 472 (1935): "In the end, the court must find the limits of the integration as best it may be reading the writing in the light of surrounding circumstances."

Thus, certain oral collateral agreements, even though made contemporaneously, are not within the prohibition of the parol evidence rule "because they are separate, independent, and complete contracts, although relating to the same subject. * * * [T]hey are allowed to be proved by parol, because they were made by parol, and no part thereof committed to writing."

Although there is New York authority which in general terms supports defendant's thesis that an oral contract inducing a written one or varying the consideration may be barred, the overarching question is whether, in the context of the particular setting, the oral agreement was one which the parties would ordinarily be expected to embody in the writing. For example, integration is most easily inferred in the case of real estate contracts for the sale of land. In more complex situations, in which customary business practice may be more varied, an oral agreement can be treated as separate and independent of the written agreement even though the written contract contains a strong integration clause.

Thus, as we see it, the issue is whether the oral promise to the plaintiffs, as individuals, would be an expectable term of the contract for the sale of assets by a corporation in which plaintiffs have only a 50% interest, considering as well the history of their relationship to Seagram.

Here, there are several reasons why it would *not* be expected that the oral agreement to give Harold Lee's sons another distributorship would be integrated into the sales contract. In the usual case, there is an identity of parties in both the claimed integrated instrument and in the oral agreement asserted. Here, although it would have been physically possible to insert a provision dealing with only the shareholders of a 50% interest, the transaction itself was a *corporate* sale of assets. Collateral agreements which survive the closing of a corporate deal, such as employment agreements for particular shareholders of the seller or consulting agreements, are often set forth in separate agreements. It was expectable that such an agreement as one to obtain a new distributorship for certain persons, some of whom were not even parties to the contract, would not necessarily be integrated into an instrument for the sale of *corporate* assets. As with an oral condition precedent to the legal effectiveness of an otherwise integrated written contract, which is not barred by the parol evidence rule if it is not directly contradictory of its terms.

Similarly, it is significant that there was a close relationship of confidence and friendship over many years between two old men, Harold Lee and Yogman, whose authority to bind Seagram has not been questioned. It would not be surprising that a handshake for the benefit of Harold's sons would have been thought sufficient. In point, as well, is the circumstance that the negotiations concerning the provisions of the sales agreement were not conducted by Yogman but by three other Seagram representatives, headed by John Barth. The two transactions may not have been integrated in their minds when the contract was drafted.

Finally, the written agreement does not contain the customary integration clause, even though a good part of it (relating to warranties and negative covenants) is boilerplate. The omission may, of course, have been caused by mutual trust and confidence, but in any event, there is no such strong presumption of exclusion because of the existence of a detailed integration clause, as was relied upon by the Court of Appeals in *Fogelson, supra.*

Nor do we see any contradiction of the terms of the sales agreement. The written agreement dealt with the sale of corporate assets, the oral agreement with the relocation of the Lees. Thus, the oral agreement does not vary or contradict the money consideration recited in the contract as flowing to the selling corporation. That is the only consideration recited, and it is still the only consideration to the corporation.

We affirm Judge Tenney's reception in evidence of the oral agreement and his denial of the motion under Rule 50(b) with respect to the parol evidence rule.

II

Appellant contends, however, that the jury verdict cannot stand because the oral agreement was so vague and indefinite as to be unenforceable. First, appellant argues that the failure to specify purchase price, profitability or sales volume of the distributorship to be provided, is fatal to the contract's validity. The contention is that, because the oral agreement lacks essential terms, the courts cannot determine the rights and obligations of the parties. Second, appellant contends that the agreement is unenforceable because there were no specific limits to plaintiffs' discretion in deciding whether to accept or reject a particular distributorship; and hence the agreement was illusory.

The alleged agreement, as the jury was permitted to find, was to provide the Lees with a liquor distributorship of approximately half the value and profit potential of Capitol City, within a reasonable time. The distributorship would be "in a location acceptable to plaintiffs," and the price would require roughly an amount equal to the plaintiffs' previous investment in Capitol City. The performance by plaintiffs in agreeing to the sale of Capitol City caused the counter-performance of the oral promise to mature.

Once the nature of the agreement found by the jury is recognized, it becomes clear that appellant's contentions are without merit. As for the alleged lack of essential terms, there was evidence credited by the jury, which *did* establish the purchase

price, profitability and sales volume of the distributorship with reasonable specificity. In addition to the direct testimony of the Lees, there was evidence that
distributorships were valued, as a rule of thumb, at book value plus three times the
previous year's net profit after taxes. Between this industry standard and the reference to the Capitol City transaction, there was extrinsic evidence to render the
parties' obligations reasonably definite. Professor Corbin has observed that a court
should be slow to deny enforcement "if it is convinced that the parties themselves
meant to make a 'contract' and to bind themselves to render a future performance.
Many a gap in terms can be filled, and should be, with a result that is consistent with
what the parties said and that is more just to both of them than would be a refusal of
enforcement." Corbin on Contracts § 97, at 425–26. New York courts are in accord
in hesitating to find that a contract is too indefinite for enforcement. The requirement that the alleged oral agreement be performed within a reasonable time is
particularly unobjectionable, especially in light of the fact, which Seagram knew,
that plaintiffs would have to reinvest the proceeds from the sale of Capitol City
within one year or suffer adverse tax consequences.

As for the alleged unbridled discretion which the oral agreement conferred on
the plaintiffs, we similarly conclude that there is no fatal defect. We note at the outset that the requirement that the new distributorship be "acceptable" to the Lees
did not render the agreement illusory in the sense that it is not supported by consideration; the Lee's part of the bargain was to join in the sale of Capitol City's assets
and assignment of its franchise, which they had already performed. More importantly, we do not agree that the Lees had "unbridled" discretion. New York
courts would in all events impose an obligation of good faith on the Lees' exercise
of discretion, *see e.g., Wood v. Lucy, Lady Duff-Gordon,* and there was also extrinsic
evidence of what would constitute an "acceptable distributorship," and hence constitute reasonable performance by Seagram. Seagram appears to contend that if it
had tendered reasonable performance, by offering an acceptable distributorship to
the Lees, that the Lees nevertheless could have found it not "acceptable." This is
not correct. It is true that Seagram could not have forced the Lees to *take* a distributorship, because they had not promised to do so. But Seagram's tender of
reasonable performance would discharge its obligations under the oral agreement,
whether or not the Lees "accepted." The Lees could not prevent Seagram from
fulfilling its obligations by unreasonably refusing an acceptable distributorship.
Since the obligations of the parties under the contract therefore were ascertainable,
it was not void for indefiniteness.

III

The jury awarded the two sons and the estate of the father damages in the
amount of $407,850. The essence of the court's charge on the subject was that in a
contract action the basic principle of damages "is to indemnify a plaintiff for the

gains prevented and the losses sustained by a defendant's breach, to leave him no worse but in no better position than he would have been had the breach not occurred." The court charged that the jury was to determine the reasonable value of the injury, if any. It charged further that "from the sum thus arrived at, you will then deduct such amount, if any, as from the evidence you find fairly measures the benefit to plaintiffs resulting from the fact that plaintiffs were freed to engage their services and capital in other situations during the time they would otherwise have been engaged in the management of an investment in the alleged promised distributorship."

Plaintiffs introduced testimony by Ernest L. Sommers, a certified public accountant, whom the District Court found to be qualified as an expert. Sommers compared one-half of the profits of Capitol City in its *last* fiscal year ending June 1, 1970 on the theory that profits for the past five years showed an upward trend, with the amount earned on investments in bonds by the plaintiffs in the year succeeding the sale. He found that one-half of the Capitol City pre-tax profits, based on one-half the sales price, amounted to 14.508%. The return on the bond investment was 7.977%. He then subtracted the percentage return on the investment bonds from the percentage return of the Capitol City operation, which gave him a percentage figure for the loss occasioned by the breach, of 6.531%. This figure, applied to one-half the sales price, came to $83,800 per annum before taxes. Multiplying this figure by only ten years—an assumed minimum measure for the life of the "new" distributorship—would make an $838,000 total loss. Discounting to present value, the witness reduced the figure to $549,000. The jury returned a verdict, as we have seen, for a lesser amount, $407,850. There is, therefore, no element of damage in the verdict amount for which no evidence was submitted to the jury. Appellant contends, however, that plaintiffs' proof of damages was speculative and incompetent.

Appellant's position is based in large measure on some confusion about the precise nature of the agreement found by the jury. Plaintiffs' evidence bore directly on the damages sustained by breach of a contract to provide a distributorship of one-half the cost and worth of Capitol City, and on the "fair measure" of the sums properly deducted. Appellant's contention that plaintiffs should have been required to prove, as a *sine qua non* to any damage award, that there was a Seagram distributor actually willing to sell his distributorship to them, is without merit. The oral agreement, as the jury was permitted to find, was for Seagram to *provide* a distributorship for the Lees. The jury was permitted to find that Seagram could have fulfilled this obligation by steering a voluntary sale of a distributorship to the plaintiffs or could have financed an intermediate transaction, warehousing the acquired distributorship for the plaintiffs.

Seagram contends that lost profits are not the proper measure of damages for breach of contract, and that cases allowing damages for destruction of injury to an ongoing business are not controlling. Lost profits can, however, be a proper measure of damages for breach of contract. As the Court of Appeals for the First Circuit said in *Standard Machinery Co. v. Duncan Shaw Corp.*, 208 F.2d 61, 64:

> Certainly no authority need be cited for the broad proposition that prospective profits, if proved, are an element of a plaintiff's damages for breach of contract, or for the further proposition that evidence of past profits from an established business provides a reasonable basis for estimating future profits from the business.

This is so even if the prospective business has not yet begun operation.

Seagram objects to the fact that plaintiffs' proof concerned the profit experience of Capitol City. It suggests that the best way of determining profits would be to consider the profits of an existing distributorship. But it came forward with no such proof, presumably for tactical reasons. We hold that the method of proof used by the plaintiffs was adequate in the circumstances. Since Seagram's breach has made difficult a more precise proof of damages, it must bear the risk of uncertainty created by its conduct....

———————

Recall: *Postal Instant Press v. Sealy,* p. 170.
          Eastern Air Lines v. McDonnell Douglas Corp., p. 183.

———————

PG&E v. G.W. Thomas Drayage & Rigging Co.
California Supreme Court, 1968.
69 Cal.2d 33, 442 P.2d 641, 69 Cal.Rptr. 561.

■ TRAYNOR, C.J. Defendant appeals from a judgment for plaintiff in an action for damages for injury to property under an indemnity clause of a contract.

In 1960 defendant entered into a contract with plaintiff to furnish the labor and equipment necessary to remove and replace the upper metal cover of plaintiff's steam turbine. Defendant agreed to perform the work "at [its] own risk and expense" and to "indemnify" plaintiff "against all loss, damage, expense and liability resulting from * * * injury to property, arising out of or in any way connected with the performance of this contract." Defendant also agreed to procure not less than $50,000 insurance to cover liability for injury to property. Plaintiff was to be an additional named insured, but the policy was to contain a cross-liability clause extending the coverage to plaintiff's property.

During the work the cover fell and injured the exposed rotor of the turbine. Plaintiff brought this action to recover $25,144.51, the amount it subsequently spent on repairs. During the trial it dismissed a count based on negligence and thereafter secured judgment on the theory that the indemnity provision covered injury to all property regardless of ownership.

Defendant offered to prove by admissions of plaintiff's agents, by defendant's conduct under similar contracts entered into with plaintiff, and by other proof that in the indemnity clause the parties meant to cover injury to property of third parties only and not to plaintiff's property. Although the trial court observed that the language used was "the classic language for a third party indemnity provision" and that "one could very easily conclude that * * * its whole intendment is to indemnify third parties," it nevertheless held that the "plain language" of the agreement also required defendant to indemnify plaintiff for injuries to plaintiff's property. Having determined that the contract had a plain meaning, the court refused to admit any extrinsic evidence that would contradict its interpretation.

When the court interprets a contract on this basis, it determines the meaning of the instrument in accordance with the "* * * extrinsic evidence of the judge's own linguistic education and experience." (3 Corbin on Contracts (1960 ed.) [1964 Supp. § 579].) The exclusion of testimony that might contradict the linguistic background of the judge reflects a judicial belief in the possibility of perfect verbal expression. This belief is a remnant of a primitive faith in the inherent potency[2] and inherent meaning of words.

The test of admissibility of extrinsic evidence to explain the meaning of a written instrument is not whether it appears to the court to be plain and unambiguous on its face, but whether the offered evidence is relevant to prove a meaning to which the language of the instrument is reasonably susceptible.

A rule that would limit the determination of the meaning of a written instrument to its four-corners merely because it seems to the court to be clear and unambiguous, would either deny the relevance of the intention of the parties or presuppose a degree of verbal precision and stability our language has not attained.

Some courts have expressed the opinion that contractual obligations are created by the mere use of certain words, whether or not there was any intention to incur

---

2. E.g., "The elaborate system of taboo and verbal prohibitions in primitive groups; the ancient Egyptian myth of Khern, the apotheosis of the words, and of Thoth, the Scribe of Truth, the Giver of Words and Script, the Master of Incantations; the avoidance of the name of God in Brahmanism, Judaism and Islam; totemistic and protective names in mediaeval Turkish and Finno–Ugrian languages; the misplaced verbal scruples of the 'Précieuses'; the Swedish peasant custom of curing sick cattle smitten by witchcraft, by making them swallow a page torn out of the psalter and put in dough. * * * " from Ullman, The Principles of Semantics (1963 ed.) 43. (*See also* Ogden and Richards, The Meaning of Meaning (rev. ed. 1956) pp. 24–47.)

such obligations.[4] Under this view, contractual obligations flow, not from the intention of the parties but from the fact that they used certain magic words. Evidence of the parties' intention therefore becomes irrelevant.

In this state, however, the intention of the parties as expressed in the contract is the source of contractual rights and duties.[5] A court must ascertain and give effect to this intention by determining what the parties meant by the words they used. Accordingly, the exclusion of relevant, extrinsic evidence to explain the meaning of a written instrument could be justified only if it were feasible to determine the meaning the parties gave to the words from the instrument alone.

If words had absolute and constant referents, it might be possible to discover contractual intention in the words themselves and in the manner in which they were arranged. Words, however, do not have absolute and constant referents. "A word is a symbol of thought but has no arbitrary and fixed meaning like a symbol of algebra or chemistry, * * *." (*Pearson v. State Social Welfare Board* (1960)). The meaning of particular words or groups of words varies with the "* * * verbal context and surrounding circumstances and purposes in view of the linguistic education and experience of their users, and their hearers or readers (not excluding judges). * * * A word has no meaning apart from these factors; much less does it have an objective meaning, one true meaning." (Corbin, *The Interpretation of Words and the Parol Evidence Rule* (1965) 50 Cornell L.Q. 161, 187.) Accordingly, the meaning of a writing "* * * can only be found by interpretation in the light of all the circumstances that reveal the sense in which the writer used the words. The exclusion of parol evidence regarding such circumstances merely because the words do not appear ambiguous to the reader can easily lead to the attribution to a written instrument of a meaning that was never intended."

Although extrinsic evidence is not admissible to add to, detract from, or vary the terms of a written contract, these terms must first be determined before it can be decided whether or not extrinsic evidence is being offered for a prohibited purpose. The fact that the terms of an instrument appear clear to a judge does not preclude the possibility that the parties chose the language of the instrument to express different terms. That possibility is not limited to contracts whose terms have acquired a particular meaning by trade usage, but exists whenever the parties' understanding of the words used may have differed from the judge's understanding.

---

4. "A contract has, strictly speaking, nothing to do with the personal, or individual, intent of the parties. A contract is an obligation attached by the mere force of law to certain acts of the parties, usually words, which ordinarily accompany and represent a known intent." Hotchkiss v. National City Bank of New York (S.D.N.Y.1911).

5. "A contract must be so interpreted as to give effect to the mutual intention of the parties as it existed at the time of contracting, so far as the same is ascertainable and lawful." (Civ.Code, § 1636.)

Accordingly, rational interpretation requires at least a preliminary consideration of all credible evidence offered to prove the intention of the parties.[7] Such evidence includes testimony as to the "circumstances surrounding the making of the agreement * * * including the object, nature and subject matter of the writing * * *" so that the court can "place itself in the same situation in which the parties found themselves at the time of contracting." If the court decides, after considering this evidence, that the language of a contract, in the light of all the circumstances, "is fairly susceptible of either one of the two interpretations contended for * * *" extrinsic evidence relevant to prove either of such meanings is admissible.[8]

In the present case the court erroneously refused to consider extrinsic evidence offered to show that the indemnity clause in the contract was not intended to cover injuries to plaintiff's property. Although that evidence was not necessary to show that the indemnity clause was reasonably susceptible of the meaning contended for by defendant, it was nevertheless relevant and admissible on that issue. Moreover, since that clause was reasonably susceptible of that meaning, the offered evidence was also admissible to prove that the clause had that meaning and did not cover injuries to plaintiff's property.[9] Accordingly, the judgment must be reversed.

---

7. When objection is made to any particular item of evidence offered to prove the intention of the parties, the trial court may not yet be in a position to determine whether in the light of all of the offered evidence, the item objected to will turn out to be admissible as tending to prove a meaning of which the language of the instrument is reasonably susceptible or inadmissible as tending to prove a meaning of which the language is not reasonably susceptible. In such case the court may admit the evidence conditionally by either reserving its ruling on the objection or by admitting the evidence subject to a motion to strike.

8. Extrinsic evidence has often been admitted in such cases on the stated ground that the contract was ambiguous. This statement of the rule is harmless if it is kept in mind that the ambiguity may be exposed by extrinsic evidence that reveals more than one possible meaning.

9. The court's exclusion of extrinsic evidence in this case would be error even under a rule that excluded such evidence when the instrument appeared to the court to be clear and unambiguous on its face. The controversy centers on the meaning of the word "indemnify" and the phrase "all loss, damage, expense and liability." The trial court's recognition of the language as typical of a third party indemnity clause and the double sense in which the word "indemnify" is used in statutes and defined in dictionaries demonstrate the existence of an ambiguity. (Compare Civ.Code, § 2772, "Indemnity is a contract by which one engages to save another from a legal consequence of the conduct of one of the parties, or of some other person," with Civ.Code, § 2527, "Insurance is a contract whereby one undertakes to indemnify another against loss, damage, or liability, arising from an unknown or contingent event." Black's Law Dictionary (4th ed. 1951) defines "indemnity" as "A collateral contract or assurance, by which one person engages to secure another against an anticipated loss or to prevent him from being damnified by the legal consequences of an act or forbearance on the part of one of the parties or of some third person." Stroud's Judicial Dictionary (2d ed. 1903) defines it as a "Contract * * * to indemnify against a liability.* * *" One of the definitions given to "indemnify" by Webster's Third New International Dict. (1961 ed.) is "to exempt from incurred liabilities.")

QUESTION

In light of Chief Justice Traynor's footnote 9, why did he decide the case on the basis of his far-reaching statements about the parol evidence rule?

UNIFORM COMMERCIAL CODE:

§ 2-202. Final Written Expression: Parol or Extrinsic Evidence.

Terms with respect to which the confirmatory memoranda of the parties agree or which are otherwise set forth in a writing intended by the parties as a final expression of their agreement with respect to such terms as are included therein may not be contradicted by evidence of any prior agreement or of a contemporaneous oral agreement but may be explained or supplemented

(a) by course of dealing or usage of trade (Section 1–205) or by course of performance (Section 2–208); and

(b) by evidence of consistent additional terms unless the court finds the writing to have been intended also as a complete and exclusive statement of the terms of the agreement.

DRAFTING EXERCISE

Compare the Uniform Commercial Code's statement of the parol evidence rule with Williston's statement of it on p. 599. First, list the substantive differences in

---

Plaintiff's assertion that the use of the word "all" to modify "loss, damage, expense and liability" dictates an all inclusive interpretation is not persuasive. If the word "indemnify" encompasses only third party claims, the word "all" simply refers to all such claims. The use of the words "loss," "damage," and "expense" in addition to the word "liability" is likewise inconclusive. These words do not imply an agreement to reimburse for injury to an indemnitee's property since they are commonly inserted in third party indemnity clauses, to enable an indemnitee who settles a claim to recover from his indemnitor without proving his liability. Civ.Code, § 2778, provides: "1. Upon an indemnity against liability * * * the person indemnified is entitled to recover upon becoming liable; 2. Upon an indemnity against claims, or demands, or damages, or costs * * * the person indemnified is not entitled to recover without payment thereof; * * *."

The provision that defendant perform the work, "at his own risk and expense" and the provisions relating to insurance are equally inconclusive. By agreeing to work at its own risk defendant may have released plaintiff from liability for any injuries to defendant's property arising out of the contract's performance, but this provision did not necessarily make defendant an insurer against injuries to plaintiff's property. Defendant's agreement to procure liability insurance to cover damages to plaintiff's property does not indicate whether the insurance was to cover all injuries or only injuries caused by defendant's negligence.

the two statements of the rule. Then choose the version of the rule you prefer and write a paragraph explaining why it should be adopted rather than the alternative.

Eskimo Pie Corp. v. Whitelawn Dairies

United States District Court, S.D. New York, 1968.
284 F.Supp. 987.

■ MANSFIELD, D.J.

The actions arise out of written contracts between Eskimo Pie Corporation ("Eskimo" herein), Whitelawn Dairies, Inc. ("Whitelawn" herein) and Supermarket Advisory Sales, Inc. ("SAS" herein) (Whitelawn and SAS are collectively referred to herein as "Whitelawn–SAS") entered into on or about December 30, 1960, and modified in various respects in 1961 and 1962. These contracts are referred to by the parties as the "Package Deal." All parties agree that the Package Deal is an integrated agreement setting forth in several writings all of the essential terms agreed upon by Eskimo and Whitelawn–SAS. Under the terms of the Package Deal Eskimo granted to Whitelawn, an ice cream manufacturer, the right to manufacture certain ice cream products bearing "Eskimo" wrappers and labels and to SAS the right to purchase such Eskimo-branded products from Eskimo or an Eskimo-authorized manufacturer for sale in the New York City Metropolitan Area as follows:

> During the term of this Agreement [SAS] shall have the *non-exclusive* right to purchase the Eskimo stock and stickless products listed in Exhibit A hereto, which may be amended from time to time by addition or deletion, from Eskimo or from a manufacturer authorized by Eskimo to manufacture such products within the New York City metropolitan area * * *. (emphasis supplied).

The present lawsuits were instituted after Eskimo, beginning sometime in 1962 and 1963, sold its Eskimo-branded products to others in the New York City Metropolitan Area, and entered into agreements with M.H. Renken Dairy Co. ("Renken" herein) to manufacture, and with Food Enterprises, Inc. ("Food Enterprises" herein) to sell, such products, and assisted Harry L. Darnstaedt and Imperial Ice Cream Novelties, Inc. ("Imperial" herein) in selling such products in the New York City Metropolitan Area. This led to a deterioration in the relationship between the parties to the Package Deal; a purported termination by Whitelawn and SAS of purchases and sales thereunder; and mutual claims of breach of contract, since Whitelawn and SAS appear to have refused to accept and pay for certain products.

A threshold question, which appears to be central to the entire dispute between the parties, arises out of the meaning of the word "non-exclusive" as used in the above quotation from the Package Deal, and the proposal of Whitelawn–SAS to offer parol evidence with respect to its meaning. Whitelawn and SAS contend that the word "non-exclusive" as used in the Package Deal meant that Eskimo would have the right to continue existing licenses granted by it to others in the New York City Metropolitan Area and to grant new licenses to national companies (such as the Borden Company, National Dairy Products Corporation), but not to grant licenses to so-called "independent" companies unless required to do so by order of a court or governmental agency, and that Eskimo itself was not to compete with Whitelawn and SAS in the sale of Eskimo-branded ice cream products. Eskimo denies such contentions as to the meaning of the word "non-exclusive" and asserts that it plainly meant that Eskimo was granting a bare non-exclusive right to Whitelawn and SAS to manufacture and sell Eskimo products, while retaining the unfettered right to license others as it saw fit to manufacture and sell Eskimo-branded ice cream products.

Whitelawn–SAS proposes, upon the jury trial of the issues of liability raised by the two lawsuits, to introduce not only the written agreements constituting the Package Deal, but also parol and extrinsic evidence as to what the parties understood and intended the term "non-exclusive" to mean, including earlier drafts of the Package Deal, correspondence and conversations between the parties leading up to its execution, and subsequent conduct of the parties, including a letter written by Darnstaedt on February 12, 1963 stating that the parties "had a gentlemen's agreement that Eskimo would not solicit any stick franchises in New York City except any of the national companies that Eskimo is serving around the country." More specifically, Whitelawn–SAS would offer testimony of its lawyers and others who negotiated the Package Deal on its behalf to the effect that earlier drafts, including one submitted by an Eskimo official named Gunn (now deceased) contained a clause which would have obligated Eskimo not to license or franchise the Eskimo mark, or sell Eskimo-branded ice cream products, to anyone in the New York City Metropolitan Area other than existing licensees or national dairy organizations, unless Eskimo should be required to do so by court or governmental order; that thereafter Eskimo refused to sign an agreement containing the express clause because of a fear expressed by Eskimo's counsel that the proposed clause might violate the federal antitrust laws; and that accordingly, after a series of conferences, the proposed clause was deleted on the understanding that its meaning would be deemed incorporated into the word "non-exclusive" used in the above-quoted license to Whitelawn–SAS.

Although Eskimo, if such parol evidence were admitted at the trial, would offer testimony of its officials contradicting that of the Whitelawn–SAS negotiators, it argues, that such evidence is barred by the parol evidence rule, and seeks preliminary rulings before trial is commenced.

The question of whether parol evidence should be admitted at trial is one of law to be determined and ruled upon by the Court. Normally such rulings are made when the evidence is offered during trial, with the party offering the evidence, should objection be sustained, preserving his rights through an offer of proof out of the jury's presence. In this case, however, Eskimo asserts that since the parol evidence to be offered is extensive (both parties agreeing that if the evidence is admitted several witnesses will be required to testify for at least a few days), Eskimo would be forced to engage in multiple and continuous objections to and/or motions to strike, testimony as to each of the numerous conversations between the negotiators, and proof of each item of correspondence, drafts, etc., with the result that even if the evidence should ultimately be excluded, Eskimo would be unduly prejudiced before the jury. This argument has much merit and is supported by those who follow the practice in such cases of holding a preliminary hearing for the purpose of ruling on the admissibility of such evidence. Whitelawn–SAS contends, however, that since the parol evidence should be admitted at trial, a preliminary hearing would result in needless waste and expense occasioned by duplication in testimony and proof. In view of these opposing contentions, consideration by the Court at this time of the applicable evidentiary principles seems appropriate.

All parties agree that in this diversity suit the admissibility of the parol and extrinsic evidence to be offered by Whitelawn–SAS is governed by the law of the State of New York, where Whitelawn and SAS are incorporated and have their principal places of business, where Eskimo is authorized to do business, where the agreements involved were for the most part negotiated, and where they were to be performed.

Whitelawn–SAS argues that parol evidence should be admitted on the ground that the term "non-exclusive" is ambiguous, and that even if it in fact lacks ambiguity such evidence may be received to show that the parties gave the term special or particular meaning not to be gathered from the language by a reasonably intelligent person having knowledge of the custom, usage and surrounding circumstances. In support of their position, Whitelawn–SAS relies principally on § 2–202 of the Uniform Commercial Code ("UCC" herein), Corbin on Contracts §§ 535, 536, 542, 543, 579 and decisions of the late respected Judge Frank.

The effective date of [New York's UCC section 2–202] is September 27, 1964, which postdates the Package Deal....

In any event even if § 2–202 of the UCC were applicable to the written contract here at issue, much of the proof which Whitelawn–SAS would offer to show what the parties intended the word "non-exclusive" to mean would not be admissible. Section 2–202 limits the parties, in explaining the meaning of language in a written integrated contract, to proof of a "course of dealing," "usage of the trade," and a "course of performance." None of these terms encompass testimony or other proof as to the subjective intent of the parties. The term "course of dealing" as defined in

§ 1–205(1) refers to "previous conduct between the parties" indicating a common basis for interpreting expressions used by them. In short, proof of such conduct is limited to objective facts as distinguished from oral statements of agreement. Likewise the term "usage of trade" is defined in § 1–205(2) as

> any practice or method of dealing having such regularity of observance in a place, vocation or trade as to justify an expectation that it will be observed with respect to the transaction in question. The existence and scope of such a usage are to be proved as facts. If it is established that such a usage is embodied in a written trade code or similar writing the interpretation of the writing is for the court.

The comments of the drafters as well as those of independent commentators make it clear that "usage of the trade" refers to evidence of generalized industry practice or similar recognized custom, as distinguished from particular conversations or correspondence between the parties with respect to the terms of the agreement. The same general conclusions must be reached with respect to proof of a "course of performance."

The courts of New York have never subscribed to the view that, in the absence of ambiguity, evidence as to the subjective intent of the parties may be substituted for the plain meaning that would otherwise be ascribed to the language of a written agreement by a reasonably intelligent person having knowledge of the surrounding circumstances, customs and usages. On the contrary, prior New York law adhered to time-honored objective standards to determine the meaning of language found in writings which represent as did the Package Deal here the final and complete integrated agreement reached by the parties. The cardinal principles forming the cornerstone of those standards are (1) that the meaning to be attributed to the language of such an instrument is that which a reasonably intelligent person acquainted with general usage, custom and the surrounding circumstances would attribute to it; and (2) that in the absence of ambiguity parol evidence will not be admitted to determine the meaning that is to be attributed to such language.

> The question is as to the fair and reasonable meaning that may be given to the writing sued on. Written words may have more than one meaning. "The letter killeth but the spirit giveth life." 2 Cor. 3:6. "Form should not prevail over substance and a sensible meaning of words should be sought." Atwater & Co. v. Panama R.R. Co., 246 N.Y. 519, 524. But plain meanings may not be changed by parol, and the courts will not make a new contract for the parties under the guise of interpreting the writing. "The fact that the parties intended their words to bear a certain meaning, would be immaterial were it not for the fact that the words either normally or locally might properly bear such meaning." Williston on Contracts, § 613.

Heller v. Pope, 250 N.Y. 132 (1928) (Pound, J.).

Thus the oral statements of the parties as to what they intended unambiguous language in an integrated document to mean are excluded by the parol evidence rule, because the very purpose and essence of the rule is to avoid fraud that might be perpetrated if testimony as to subjective intent could be substituted for the plain meaning, objectively interpreted in the light of surrounding circumstances, customs and usage. The effect of admitting such testimony in the absence of some showing of ambiguity would be to permit a party to substitute his view of his obligations for those clearly stated. Where—as in the present case—some of the negotiators of the written agreement have died or are unavailable, the door could be opened to fraud. Accordingly, the view of the New York courts has been that an objective standard is essential to maintain confidence in the written integrated agreement as the medium for conducting commercial relations.

The first question to be determined in the present case, therefore, is whether the term "non-exclusive" as used in the Package Deal is ambiguous, which must be decided by the Court. An "ambiguous" word or phrase is one capable of more than one meaning when viewed objectively by a reasonably intelligent person who has examined the context of the entire integrated agreement and who is cognizant of the customs, practices, usages and terminology as generally understood in the particular trade or business. In the absence of proof that the term "non-exclusive" could possibly have the meaning, among others, attributed to it by Whitelawn–SAS, parol evidence must be excluded.

Applying the foregoing principles, the word "non-exclusive" when used—as was the case here—in an integrated license agreement drafted by legal counsel, has an established legal meaning that is usually accepted in the absence of a qualifying context, custom, usage or similar surrounding circumstance. The term has repeatedly been defined as meaning that the licensee is granted a bare right to use the trademark or patent being licensed without any right to exclude others, including other licensees taking from the grantor, from utilizing the mark or invention involved....

Despite the meaning thus usually ascribed by the law to the term "non-exclusive" Whitelawn–SAS urge that here the legal draftsmen intended it to have a contrary meaning, i.e., that subject to certain detailed and specific exceptions (The Borden Company, National Dairy Products Corporation, existing licensees and existing written commitments to others), and except to the extent that Eskimo might be required to deviate therefrom by court or governmental order, the term meant "exclusive." In a business world not noted for its economy of language (the Package Deal covers 70 typewritten pages, including amendments) no business reason, custom or usage is advanced for attaching such an elaborate and paradoxical meaning to the term "non-exclusive," when legal counsel negotiating for both sides could easily have spelled out such specifics in comprehensible terms. Whitelawn–SAS's assertion that the term was used to conceal a detailed secret "gentlemen's agreement" that was feared by Eskimo to violate the antitrust laws hardly comports with the word's having a secondary meaning as a matter of generalized trade usage or custom. On the contrary, such evidence would indicate that the term, despite the definite and plain meaning usually attributed to it, was being used to express a particular, subjective meaning initially conceived by the parties solely for the purpose at hand, and not because the term would be recognized by others as having such a special meaning. Unless the language is meaningless on its face (e.g. "abracadabra") or ambiguous, however, the test for admission of parol evidence is not a secret code meaning given to it by the parties but whether it might objectively be recognized by a reasonably intelligent person acquainted with applicable customs, usages and the surrounding circumstances as having such a special meaning. For instance, would an executive in the ice cream business, who was not privy to the secret oral "gentlemen's agreement," recognize the term "non-exclusive" in this context and setting as granting an "exclusive" right, subject to certain exceptions or as having a meaning other than that usually attributed to it? If so, parol evidence would be admissible. If the law were otherwise, not only the term "non-exclusive" but every apparently clear term in a written agreement, such as a specific purchase price (e.g., "$10,000") could be changed by secret oral agreement to mean something different (e.g., "$25,000").

Nevertheless, although the term "non-exclusive" as used in the Package Deal does not on its face appear to be ambiguous, Whitelawn–SAS will be afforded the opportunity to offer proof showing that the term is ambiguous, and Eskimo the opportunity to rebut such proof. In accordance with the principles hereinabove outlined, proof on the issue of ambiguity may encompass the terms of the Package Deal itself, the surrounding circumstances, common usage and custom as to the meaning attributed to it and subsequent conduct of the parties under the Package Deal, but evidence of the subjective understanding of the parties as to the meaning attributed by them to the term "non-exclusive" will not be received.

Since the issue of ambiguity must be determined by the Court before ruling on the admission of parol evidence and since Eskimo might suffer prejudice if such rulings were made in the jury's presence, the proof with respect to ambiguity will be received at a preliminary hearing by the Court. Upon conclusion of the preliminary hearing, the Court will rule upon the issue of ambiguity, and the admissibility of the evidence at trial will be governed accordingly. Thereupon, pursuant to Rule 42(b), F.R.C.P., the Court will hold a separate jury trial of the issue of liability, to be followed by trial before the same jury of the damage issues, except with respect to issues raised by the sixth claim set forth in the Whitelawn–SAS complaint.

So ordered.

QUESTIONS AND NOTES

1. Is Judge Mansfield's approach to the parol evidence rule in the *Eskimo Pie* case reconcilable with the opinion of Chief Justice Traynor in *PG & E v. G.W. Thomas Drayage* and the opinion of Judge Gurfein in *Lee v. J.E. Seagram & Sons, Inc.*? Is the major difference among them one of attitude, or is there a substantial dispute as to what the basic legal rule is? Or do the apparent differences among the opinions demonstrate the truth of Judge Frank's suggestion on p. 61, that "perhaps nine-tenths of legal uncertainty is caused by uncertainty as to what the court will find, on conflicting evidence, to be the facts of cases"?

2. Chief Justice Traynor says, p. 612, that "rational interpretation requires at least a preliminary consideration of all credible evidence offered to prove the intention of the parties." Does Judge Mansfield give preliminary consideration to the proof Whitelawn–SAS wishes to introduce as to the meaning intended by the term "nonexclusive"?

3. Would either Chief Justice Traynor or Judge Mansfield disagree with Justice Holmes, p. 58, that a party would not be permitted to prove that the words "five hundred feet should mean one hundred inches, or that Bunker Hill Monument should signify Old South Church"?

4. Note the variety of proof that Whitelawn–SAS sought to introduce in the *Eskimo Pie* case. Does even the strictest reading of the parol evidence rule, p. 599, require exclusion of all of it? What about the subsequent communications and conduct of the parties?

5. What do you think of the behavior of the attorneys for the parties in this case? Is it appropriate for an attorney to draft a contract so as to make the transaction appear innocent, when in fact he knows that the true deal would raise eyebrows at the Antitrust Division of the Justice Department? Should an attorney who papers over a possible antitrust violation in this way be disciplined? Should the attorney be civilly liable to those who are injured by the unlawful deal? If the violation of the antitrust laws is a crime, should the attorney be subject to prosecution? What should the attorney say to his client who comes to him to draft a contract in a deal that looks unlawful? What must the attorney say to the client?

6. For an interesting comparison of the more "formalist" tendencies of the New York state courts and the more "contextualist" tendencies of the California state courts in matters of contract interpretation and enforcement see Geoffrey Miller, *Bargains Bicoastal: New Light on Contract Theory*, 31 CARDOZO L. REV. 1475 (2010). Professor Miller suggests that the fact that New York law has become a predominant choice of law in large commercial transactions suggests that the verdict of the marketplace favors formalism over contextualism.

NOTE: FORMALITIES AND INTERNATIONAL CONTRACTS

In most of the world, important contracts of all kinds and certain kinds of transactions regardless of importance (*e.g.* those involving real estate) are expected to be in writing, and a statute may even require a writing in some circumstances. Nevertheless, the Statute of Frauds or a similar broad requirement that commercial contracts be in writing is found in only a few nations. Even England repealed its Statute of Frauds in 1934. As noted above at p. 579, the CISG permits the proof of a contract "by any means, including witnesses." CISG Article 11. For sale of goods transactions between a party in the United States and a party from nation that has adopted the CISG (i.e. most of our significant trading partners), therefore, the state Statute of Frauds (typically UCC § 2–201) would presumptively not apply.

Applying the parol evidence rule to international transactions is even more problematic. The CISG has no rule similar to the parol evidence rule, and in general, in most non-English speaking legal systems, the evidentiary rules strongly favor free use of all relevant evidence. The allocation of responsibility between appellate and trial judges is quite different in most of the world, and jury trial in civil cases outside the United States is unknown or very rare, even among our common law cousins. Therefore, an American judge interpreting a written contract relating to an international sale of goods may be in an unaccustomed position, with little guidance from the CISG on how to go about the interpretive task.

MCC–Marble Ceramic Center v. Ceramica Nuova d'Agostino, S.p.A.

United States Court of Appeals, Eleventh Circuit, 1998.
144 F.3d 1384.

■ BIRCH, J. This case requires us to determine whether a court must consider parol evidence in a contract dispute governed by the United Nations Convention on Contracts for the International Sale of Goods ("CISG"). The district court granted summary judgment on behalf of the defendant-appellee, relying on certain terms and provisions that appeared on the reverse of a pre-printed form contract for the sale of ceramic tiles. The plaintiff-appellant sought to rely on a number of affidavits that tended to show both that the parties had arrived at an oral contract before memorializing their agreement in writing and that they subjectively intended not to apply the terms on the reverse of the contract to their agreements. The magistrate judge held that the affidavits did not raise an issue of material fact and recommended that the district court grant summary judgment based on the terms of the contract.

The district court agreed with the magistrate judge's reasoning and entered summary judgment in the defendant-appellee's favor. We REVERSE.

BACKGROUND

The plaintiff-appellant, MCC–Marble Ceramic, Inc. ("MCC"), is a Florida corporation engaged in the retail sale of tiles, and the defendant-appellee, Ceramica Nuova d'Agostino S.p.A. ("D'Agostino") is an Italian corporation engaged in the manufacture of ceramic tiles. In October 1990, MCC's president, Juan Carlos Monzon, met representatives of D'Agostino at a trade fair in Bologna, Italy and negotiated an agreement to purchase ceramic tiles from D'Agostino based on samples he examined at the trade fair. Monzon, who spoke no Italian, communicated with Gianni Silingardi, then D'Agostino's commercial director, through a translator, Gianfranco Copelli, who was himself an agent of D'Agostino. The parties apparently arrived at an oral agreement on the crucial terms of price, quality, quantity, delivery and payment. The parties then recorded these terms on one of D'Agostino's standard, pre-printed order forms and Monzon signed the contract on MCC's behalf. According to MCC, the parties also entered into a requirements contract in February 1991, subject to which D'Agostino agreed to supply MCC with high grade ceramic tile at specific discounts as long as MCC purchased sufficient quantities of tile. MCC completed a number of additional order forms requesting tile deliveries pursuant to that agreement.

MCC brought suit against D'Agostino claiming a breach of the February 1991 requirements contract when D'Agostino failed to satisfy orders in April, May, and August of 1991. In addition to other defenses, D'Agostino responded that it was under no obligation to fill MCC's orders because MCC had defaulted on payment for previous shipments. In support of its position, D'Agostino relied on the pre-printed terms of the contracts that MCC had executed. The executed forms were printed in Italian and contained terms and conditions on both the front and reverse. According to an English translation of the October 1990 contract,[3] the front of the order form contained the following language directly beneath Monzon's signature:

> [T]he buyer hereby states that he is aware of the sales conditions stated on the reverse and that he expressly approves of them with special reference to those numbered 1–2–3–4–5–6–7–8.

Clause 6(b), printed on the back of the form states:

> [D]efault or delay in payment within the time agreed upon gives D'Agostino the right to * * * suspend or cancel the contract itself and to cancel possible other pending contracts and the buyer does not have the right to indemnification or damages.

---

3. D'Agostino provided the translation of the contract. MCC has never contested its accuracy.

D'Agostino also brought a number of counterclaims against MCC, seeking damages for MCC's alleged nonpayment for deliveries of tile that D'Agostino had made between February 28, 1991 and July 4, 1991. MCC responded that the tile it had received was of a lower quality than contracted for, and that, pursuant to the CISG, MCC was entitled to reduce payment in proportion to the defects.[4] D'Agostino, however, noted that clause 4 on the reverse of the contract states, in pertinent part:

> Possible complaints for defects of the merchandise must be made in writing by means of a certified letter within and not later than 10 days after receipt of the merchandise * * *.

Although there is evidence to support MCC's claims that it complained about the quality of the deliveries it received, MCC never submitted any written complaints.

MCC did not dispute these underlying facts before the district court, but argued that the parties never intended the terms and conditions printed on the reverse of the order form to apply to their agreements. As evidence for this assertion, MCC submitted Monzon's affidavit, which claims that MCC had no subjective intent to be bound by those terms and that D'Agostino was aware of this intent. MCC also filed affidavits from Silingardi and Copelli, D'Agostino's representatives at the trade fair, which support Monzon's claim that the parties subjectively intended not to be bound by the terms on the reverse of the order form. The magistrate judge held that the affidavits, even if true, did not raise an issue of material fact regarding the interpretation or applicability of the terms of the written contracts and the district court accepted his recommendation to award summary judgment in D'Agostino's favor. MCC then filed this timely appeal.

DISCUSSION

We review a district court's grant of summary judgment de novo and apply the same standards as the district court. Summary judgment is appropriate when the pleadings, depositions, and affidavits reveal that no genuine issue of material fact exists and the moving party is entitled to judgment as a matter of law.

The parties to this case agree that the CISG governs their dispute because the United States, where MCC has its place of business, and Italy, where D'Agostino has its place of business, are both States Party to the Convention. Article 8 of the CISG governs the interpretation of international contracts for the sale of goods and

---

4. Article 50 of the CISG permits a buyer to reduce payment for nonconforming goods in proportion to the nonconformity under certain conditions. See CISG, art. 50.

forms the basis of MCC's appeal from the district court's grant of summary judgment in D'Agostino's favor.[7] MCC argues that the magistrate judge and the district court improperly ignored evidence that MCC submitted regarding the parties' subjective intent when they memorialized the terms of their agreement on D'Agostino's pre-printed form contract, and that the magistrate judge erred by applying the parol evidence rule in derogation of the CISG.

I. Subjective Intent Under the CISG

Contrary to what is familiar practice in United States courts, the CISG appears to permit a substantial inquiry into the parties' subjective intent, even if the parties did not engage in any objectively ascertainable means of registering this intent. Article 8(1) of the CISG instructs courts to interpret the "statements * * * and other conduct of a party * * * according to his intent" as long as the other party "knew or could not have been unaware" of that intent. The plain language of the Convention, therefore, requires an inquiry into a party's subjective intent as long as the other party to the contract was aware of that intent.

In this case, MCC has submitted three affidavits that discuss the purported subjective intent of the parties to the initial agreement concluded between MCC and D'Agostino in October 1990. All three affidavits discuss the preliminary negotiations and report that the parties arrived at an oral agreement for D'Agostino to supply quantities of a specific grade of ceramic tile to MCC at an agreed upon price. The affidavits state that the "oral agreement established the essential terms of quality, quantity, description of goods, delivery, price and payment." The affidavits also note that the parties memorialized the terms of their oral agreement on a standard D'Agostino order form, but all three affiants contend that the parties subjectively intended not to be bound by the terms on the reverse of that form despite a provision

---

7. Article 8 provides:

(1) For the purposes of this Convention statements made by and other conduct of a party are to be interpreted according to his intent where the other party knew or could not have been unaware what that intent was.

(2) If the preceding paragraph is not applicable, statements made by and conduct of a party are to be interpreted according to the understanding a reasonable person of the same kind as the other party would have had in the same circumstances.

(3) In determining the intent of a party or the understanding a reasonable person would have had, due consideration is to be given to all relevant circumstances of the case including the negotiations, any practices which the parties have established between themselves, usages and any subsequent conduct of the parties.

CISG, art. 8.

directly below the signature line that expressly and specifically incorporated those terms.[9]

The terms on the reverse of the contract give D'Agostino the right to suspend or cancel all contracts in the event of a buyer's non-payment and require a buyer to make a written report of all defects within ten days. As the magistrate judge's report and recommendation makes clear, if these terms applied to the agreements between MCC and D'Agostino, summary judgment would be appropriate because MCC failed to make any written complaints about the quality of tile it received and D'Agostino has established MCC's non-payment of a number of invoices amounting to $108,389.40 and 102,053,846.00 Italian lira.

Article 8(1) of the CISG requires a court to consider this evidence of the parties' subjective intent. Contrary to the magistrate judge's report, which the district court endorsed and adopted, article 8(1) does not focus on interpreting the parties' statements alone. Although we agree with the magistrate judge's conclusion that no "interpretation" of the contract's terms could support MCC's position, article 8(1) also requires a court to consider subjective intent while interpreting the conduct of the parties. The CISG's language, therefore, requires courts to consider evidence of a party's subjective intent when signing a contract if the other party to the contract was aware of that intent at the time. This is precisely the type of evidence that MCC has provided through the Silingardi, Copelli, and Monzon affidavits, which discuss not only Monzon's intent as MCC's representative but also discuss the intent of D'Agostino's representatives and their knowledge that Monzon did not intend to agree to the terms on the reverse of the form contract. This acknowledgment that D'Agostino's representatives were aware of Monzon's subjective intent puts this case squarely within article 8(1) of the CISG, and therefore requires the court to consider MCC's evidence as it interprets the parties' conduct.

II. Parol Evidence and the CISG

Given our determination that the magistrate judge and the district court should have considered MCC's affidavits regarding the parties' subjective intentions, we must address a question of first impression in this circuit: whether the parol evidence rule, which bars evidence of an earlier oral contract that contradicts or varies

---

9. MCC makes much of the fact that the written order form is entirely in Italian and that Monzon, who signed the contract on MCC's behalf directly below this provision incorporating the terms on the reverse of the form, neither spoke nor read Italian. This fact is of no assistance to MCC's position. We find it nothing short of astounding that an individual, purportedly experienced in commercial matters, would sign a contract in a foreign language and expect not to be bound simply because he could not comprehend its terms. We find nothing in the CISG that might counsel this type of reckless behavior and nothing that signals any retreat from the proposition that parties who sign contracts will be bound by them regardless of whether they have read them or understood them.

the terms of a subsequent or contemporaneous written contract, plays any role in cases involving the CISG. We begin by observing that the parol evidence rule, contrary to its title, is a substantive rule of law, not a rule of evidence. The rule does not purport to exclude a particular type of evidence as an "untrustworthy or undesirable" way of proving a fact, but prevents a litigant from attempting to show "the fact itself—the fact that the terms of the agreement are other than those in the writing." As such, a federal district court cannot simply apply the parol evidence rule as a procedural matter—as it might if excluding a particular type of evidence under the Federal Rules of Evidence, which apply in federal court regardless of the source of the substantive rule of decision.[13]

The CISG itself contains no express statement on the role of parol evidence. See Honnold, Uniform Law § 110 at 170. It is clear, however, that the drafters of the CISG were comfortable with the concept of permitting parties to rely on oral contracts because they eschewed any statute of frauds provision and expressly provided for the enforcement of oral contracts. Compare CISG, art. 11 (a contract of sale need not be concluded or evidenced in writing) with U.C.C. § 2–201 (precluding the enforcement of oral contracts for the sale of goods involving more than $500). Moreover, article 8(3) of the CISG expressly directs courts to give "due consideration * * * to all relevant circumstances of the case including the negotiations * * *" to determine the intent of the parties. Given article 8(1)'s directive to use the intent of the parties to interpret their statements and conduct, article 8(3) is a clear instruction to admit and consider parol evidence regarding the negotiations to the extent they reveal the parties' subjective intent.

Despite the CISG's broad scope, surprisingly few cases have applied the Convention in the United States, and only two reported decisions touch upon the parol evidence rule, both in *dicta*. One court has concluded, much as we have above, that the parol evidence rule is not viable in CISG cases in light of article 8 of the Convention....

Our reading of article 8(3) as a rejection of the parol evidence rule, however, is in accordance with the great weight of academic commentary on the issue. As one scholar has explained:

> [T]he language of Article 8(3) that "due consideration is to be given to all relevant circumstances of the case" seems adequate to override any domestic rule

---

13. An example demonstrates this point. The CISG provides that a contract for the sale of goods need not be in writing and that the parties may prove the contract "by any means, including witnesses." CISG, art. 11. Nevertheless, a party seeking to prove a contract in such a manner in federal court could not do so in a way that violated in the rule against hearsay. See Fed.R.Evid. 802 (barring hearsay evidence). A federal district court applies the Federal Rules of Evidence because these rules are considered procedural, regardless of the source of the law that governs the substantive decision.

that would bar a tribunal from considering the relevance of other agreements *
* *. Article 8(3) relieves tribunals from domestic rules that might bar them from
"considering" any evidence between the parties that is relevant. This added
flexibility for interpretation is consistent with a growing body of opinion that the
"parol evidence rule" has been an embarrassment for the administration of
modern transactions.

Honnold, Uniform Law § 110 at 170–71....

This is not to say that parties to an international contract for the sale of goods
cannot depend on written contracts or that parol evidence regarding subjective contractual intent need always prevent a party relying on a written agreement from
securing summary judgment. To the contrary, most cases will not present a situation
(as exists in this case) in which both parties to the contract acknowledge a subjective
intent not to be bound by the terms of a pre-printed writing. In most cases, therefore,
article 8(2) of the CISG will apply, and objective evidence will provide the basis for
the court's decision. Consequently, a party to a contract governed by the CISG will
not be able to avoid the terms of a contract and force a jury trial simply by submitting
an affidavit which states that he or she did not have the subjective intent to be bound
by the contract's terms. Moreover, to the extent parties wish to avoid parol evidence
problems they can do so by including a merger clause in their agreement that extinguishes any and all prior agreements and understandings not expressed in the
writing.

Considering MCC's affidavits in this case, however, we conclude that the magistrate judge and the district court improperly granted summary judgment in favor
of D'Agostino. Although the affidavits are, as D'Agostino observes, relatively conclusory and unsupported by facts that would objectively establish MCC's intent not
to be bound by the conditions on the reverse of the form, article 8(1) requires a court
to consider evidence of a party's subjective intent when the other party was aware
of it, and the Silingardi and Copelli affidavits provide that evidence. This is not to
say that the affidavits are conclusive proof of what the parties intended. A reasonable
finder of fact, for example, could disregard testimony that purportedly sophisticated
international merchants signed a contract without intending to be bound as simply
too incredible to believe and hold MCC to the conditions printed on the reverse of
the contract. Nevertheless, the affidavits raise an issue of material fact regarding the
parties' intent to incorporate the provisions on the reverse of the form contract. If
the finder of fact determines that the parties did not intend to rely on those provisions, then the more general provisions of the CISG will govern the outcome of the
dispute.

MCC's affidavits, however, do not discuss all of the transactions and orders that
MCC placed with D'Agostino. Each of the affidavits discusses the parties' subjective intent surrounding the initial order MCC placed with D'Agostino in October

1990. The Copelli affidavit also discusses a February 1991 requirements contract between the parties and reports that the parties subjectively did not intend the terms on the reverse of the D'Agostino order form to apply to that contract either. D'Agostino, however, submitted the affidavit of its chairman, Vincenzo Maselli, which describes at least three other orders from MCC on form contracts dated January 15, 1991, April 27, 1991, and May 4, 1991, in addition to the October 1990 contract. MCC's affidavits do not discuss the subjective intent of the parties to be bound by language in those contracts, and D'Agostino, therefore, argues that we should affirm summary judgment to the extent damages can be traced to those order forms. It is unclear from the record, however, whether all of these contracts contained the terms that appeared in the October 1990 contract. Moreover, because article 8 requires a court to consider any "practices which the parties have established between themselves, usages and any subsequent conduct of the parties" in interpreting contracts, CISG, art. 8(3), whether the parties intended to adhere to the ten day limit for complaints, as stated on the reverse of the initial contract, will have an impact on whether MCC was bound to adhere to the limit on subsequent deliveries. Since material issues of fact remain regarding the interpretation of the remaining contracts between MCC and D'Agostino, we cannot affirm any portion of the district court's summary judgment in D'Agostino's favor.

CONCLUSION

MCC asks us to reverse the district court's grant of summary judgment in favor of D'Agostino. The district court's decision rests on pre-printed contractual terms and conditions incorporated on the reverse of a standard order form that MCC's president signed on the company's behalf. Nevertheless, we conclude that the CISG, which governs international contracts for the sale of goods, precludes summary judgment in this case because MCC has raised an issue of material fact concerning the parties' subjective intent to be bound by the terms on the reverse of the pre-printed contract. The CISG also precludes the application of the parol evidence rule, which would otherwise bar the consideration of evidence concerning a prior or contemporaneously negotiated oral agreement. Accordingly, we REVERSE the district court's grant of summary judgment and REMAND this case for further proceedings consistent with this opinion.

QUESTIONS AND NOTES

1. On the facts of this case, would the parol evidence rule cause injustice or prevent it?

2. Why didn't the magistrate or the district court realize that the CISG allows parol evidence?

3. CISG Art. 6 provides: "The parties may ... derogate from or vary the effect of any of [the Convention's] provisions." Presumably this is the basis for the Court of Appeals' suggestion at p. 627 that even under the CISG: "to the extent parties wish to avoid parol evidence problems, they can do so by including a merger clause in their agreement that extinguishes any and all prior agreements and understandings not expressed in the writing." But is this really so? What if one of the paragraphs on the back of the D'Agostino form was a merger clause? The court in *TeeVee Toons v. Schubert*, 2006 U.S. Dist. LEXIS 59455 (S.D.N.Y. 2006), found that the validity of the merger clause itself was a question of the intent of the parties which could be proven by any relevant evidence notwithstanding the parol evidence rule. Only if the parties actually intended to incorporate the parol evidence rule into their agreement (based on all the evidence) would they be deemed to have exercised their right under CISG Art. 6 to opt out of Art. 11. If the parties in *MCC Marble* did not intend to include *any* of the boilerplate in the D'Agostino form in their agreement, what difference would it make if there is an integration clause in Italian buried in the fine print?

NOTE ON RECONSIDERING CONSIDERATION

This is probably a good time to pause and look back on the six chapters you have just completed. Reconsider *Best v. Southland*, p. 13, and the legal definition of enforceable promises. The doctrine you have learned from these chapters reflects the law as stated in statutes and judicial opinions. Yet the rules seem to have an exception available for just about every case in which a serious and sensible promise might not be enforced for lack of consideration. This is most obvious if promissory estoppel and similar ideas of unbargained-for action in reliance are carried to their logical extremes. It appears more subtly if one focuses on the outcomes of cases, rather than what the courts state to be the law.

The doctrine of consideration is often cited and saluted as a correct statement of the law, but it is only infrequently applied to throw out a serious and sensible deal. The editors of this Casebook made up *Best v. Southland* because of their frustration with the difficulty experienced in finding a real modern case that sums up and applies the law. Professor Andrew Kull states the matter boldly and provocatively:

> The modern literature on gratuitous noncommercial promises assumes the continued applicability of standard consideration doctrine to this class of cases. Yet to judge by the American decisions of the last several decades, courts are no longer willing to regard the absence of consideration as a sufficient reason to

deny the enforceability of a promise; with the result that "want of consideration" is rarely an insuperable obstacle to enforcement of a gratuitous promise
that is both unequivocal and seriously intended....

A little over a generation ago it was still possible to decry the mischief caused
by certain well-known consequences of consideration doctrine in a commercial
setting: the "preexisting duty rule" that hindered contract modifications, or the
requirement that a "firm offer" or option be supported by separate consideration. Given the far greater likelihood today that the good-faith modification will
be enforced, and that the firm offer will be honored, anyone curious about how
the law treats truly gratuitous promises must look outside the business world.
The fundamental choices for a system of contract law that have always been implicated by the doctrine of consideration are accordingly debated against a
background of gratuitous and unrelied-upon promises made by uncles to neph-
ews, by grateful beneficiaries to selfless rescuers, by charitable widows to worthy
causes. It is not always noticed—so secure are the assumptions about doctrines
in this area—that the most visible of these promises have long been enforced.

More recent cases involving gratuitous promises in noncommercial settings
suggest that the absence of consideration, in and of itself, is unlikely to constitute a bar to legal enforceability. Promises found by the courts to have been
actually made and seriously intended will typically be found either to be supported by consideration or else to have induced reliance. To meet the
requirements of doctrine in the harder cases, judges will point to "consideration" that would not satisfy the usual definition or else find "reliance" despite
the absence of any significant change of position on the part of the promisee.
Two broad categories of gift promises, charitable subscriptions and marriage
settlements, are now routinely enforced as being sui generis.

A rule denying enforceability to gift promises might be justified if it were
true that gratuitous transactions, as a class, were distinctively lacking in social
importance. While an exchange of goods, according to Fuller, is "a transaction
which conduces to the production of wealth and the division of labor," a gift—
here he quotes an otherwise forgotten set of nineteenth-century lectures on the
French Civil Code—is merely a "'sterile transmission.'"

Nothing authorizes the conjecture that a gratuitous transfer produces less
economic utility than an otherwise comparable transaction in a bargain context.
Unless a voluntary transaction is beneficial to the parties, it will not take place.
(Whether a particular gift also "conduces to the production of wealth and the
division of labor" will presumably depend on the circumstances; but the same
may be said of bargains.) Unsurprisingly, then, our legal system makes no discrimination against gratuitous transactions per se: the executed gift is enforced
on the same terms as the completed sale. The argument that gratuitous promises

do not merit enforcement cannot depend, therefore, on the proposition that the gratuitous transfer is itself unmeritorious.

Andrew Kull, *Reconsidering Gratuitous Promises*, 21 J. LEGAL STUD. 39, 39–50 (1992).

Professor Kull's critique is limited by the lesson Professor Eisenberg taught in the article excerpted on pp. 574-575: Were the common law to abandon the consideration doctrine as a limit on enforcing donative promises we would not solve, but would only shift our difficulties. For then, like the law in most of the world, typified by the French and German Civil Codes, we would have to deal under some new rubric with the possibilities of improvident donors and ungrateful recipients.

As is often the case, no one can say it better than Professor Corbin:

So far as human history has gone, the fact is that we do not wish to enforce all promises and the courts have not enforced all promises. Therefore, we must continue to determine the factors that make promises enforceable; and our legal history will compel us to do this under some such title as "consideration." Doubtless, this would not be denied by those who have suggested the abandonment of the "doctrine." It may well be that they had in mind some specific form of doctrine that, like the present author, they knew did not explain all the cases. The American Law Institute has adopted a definition of "consideration" that limits it to something that is bargained for and given in exchange for a promise; but immediately it devotes ten sections to inform us what other factors will make a promise enforceable. The term "consideration" can be totally abandoned as well as limited; we should then instantly be obliged to consider, under other descriptions, the factors that will make a promise enforceable.

However variable and widely or narrowly inclusive the usage of the term "consideration" may be, we shall have to struggle along with it in the process of differentiating between enforceable and non-enforceable promises.

1 ARTHUR L. CORBIN, CORBIN ON CONTRACTS, § 111, AT 495–96 (1963).

CHAPTER 7

FORMATION: CREATING CONTRACTUAL OBLIGATION

I. THE MOMENT WHEN A PROMISE BECOMES BINDING

Bargaining may be prolonged or fleeting, but if successful, the parties reach agreement at some time. This moment of contract formation may be difficult to identify precisely, but it is of great significance. For that is when the full legal consequences of an enforceable agreement arise. From that moment, neither party may back out of the deal without liability.

Potential liability for one or both parties may exist before contract formation is completed. In the classic analysis of contract formation, that point of potential liability is first reached when one party makes a specific proposition to the other in such form that the person who makes the proposition is legally vulnerable to being bound to that proposition. She has, in legal terms, made an *operative offer*. So long as the offer is outstanding, the party to whom it is made can bind himself and the offeror to the terms of the deal simply by manifesting assent to the terms proposed in the offer. Thereafter, neither party can withdraw or modify the deal without the consent of the other. The definition of the operative point in time may seem arid and metaphysical but it merely describes in lawyer's terms the common sense difference between just talk and meaning business.

Determining this too-late-now-to-change-your-mind point can be a very important, for a perfect defense to a contract claim is either that no operative offer was ever made or that the offer was no longer operative at the time the plaintiff claims it was accepted. A person must be able to predict with some confidence whether she is vulnerable to becoming bound by another's acceptance and whether she has the power to bind another by accepting his proposition. To sum up, in a dispute over contract formation, one begins with: (1) Was an operative offer ever made, and by whom? (2) Was that offer still operative when the claimed acceptance was given? and (3) Was there an operative acceptance?

Formation, or, as it is familiarly called, "offer and acceptance," has long been a darling of legal education and often is the first topic students study in a Contracts course. The subject is dominated by rules and doctrines that appear crisp and clear but which prove troubling when they are tested by concrete cases or when probed during a class hour filled with imaginative professorial hypothetical situations that are analyzed in detail.

The question of when an offer may be revoked leads us to the land of the wildly improbable tale. Riders gallop across the moor toward York in response to a promise of payment if they complete the ride only to be disappointed almost in sight of their goal when the offer is revoked. (*Great Northern Railway Co. v. Witham*, p. 644.) This disappointing fate is shared by athletic young men who climb almost to the gold ball at the top of the flagpole only to be similarly deprived of their promised reward. Letters are fished out of mailboxes with a wad of chewing gum attached to a long string, creating endless doctrinal puzzles. Breakfast clubbers, lingering over their morning coffee, read about rewards in newspaper advertisements, look up, see a familiar face, and run off to catch the bank robber right outside their breakfast nook window.

There is a method to this madness. You should learn how to analyze a fact situation and apply a tightly crafted rule to it. The rules of formation set out in the Restatement, Second, Contracts, the UCC and the Convention on International Sale of Goods provide perfect fodder for this exercise, and you should learn them in your first year of law study. But also know that application of these rules remains uncertain at the edges. Mastering these rules, means understanding the limits of their usefulness.

The clear and simple rules of offer and acceptance attempt to deal with an equivocal reality by imposing upon it a set of conventional rules that claim to obviate the conflict and messiness of reality by providing a positive answer to all questions. The attempt fails because the rules are reductionist. They oversimplify the problems and strip them of the crucial detail of experienced reality. For example, the rules insist that there is a precise moment when "just talk" becomes "a deal." Before that moment the parties have no obligations to each other. After that moment they are both fully bound to one another. Sometimes that is a fairly accurate picture of reality, but sometimes not. It works best in familiar transactions that are isolated deals between strangers, people who meet to "window-shop" and expect to walk away and never see each other again if it doesn't reach the clear moment of decision to buy or sell. But many of the most important deals arise out of a stream of communications between parties and often grow out of a relationship that extends over a lifetime or even generations. The Maglicas (p. 340) met, fell in love, moved in together, made love, built a business, raised kids, shared twenty years, fought, and fell apart. Try squeezing that reality into the framework of offer and acceptance.

In commercial deals, parties surf the web, read each other's promotional materials, telephone and inquire about terms, make proposals, change their terms, think it all over, and come back with a new deal. A sales representative may visit, take measurements, and dicker over price. The buyer may reach "an agreement in principle," then remember an item he forgot to mention, learn from a brother-in-law that someone he knew had a bad experience in a similar deal and that you have to insist that the other side provide for adjustments, decide he wants a blue one instead of a green one, send out a purchase order, find out that one term will have to be changed and renegotiate it. The seller may then mail out a sales invoice that has some terms different from the purchase order, discover that the warehouse won't deliver on Tuesday but will come through with the goods on Friday, deliver the goods, discover that one part is too big and the other is missing, and on and on. Picking one moment and saying that before then there was no deal and after that all the legal consequences of a contract apply is a Procrustean approach that makes the reality fit the rule only by cutting off all the pieces of the situation that do not conform to the simple model.

Imposing some form of conventional rules on contract formation may be inevitable. Reality is messy and doesn't lend itself to simple analysis. Yet there are heavy costs associated with not being sure whether there is a binding contract or not. It may be better to have a clear but imperfect rule than endless disputes and legal fees. Moreover, reasonable people will often disagree on the significance of the tangle of reality. Buyers generally believe that they are free to walk away until the last moment, while sellers usually think that fair dealing requires a commitment to negotiation leading to a deal. When a seller invests lots of time and effort in meeting a buyer's needs, he may assume the buyer is obligated to proceed in good faith to complete a deal unless there is some reason to back out. The wise guy who window shops and kicks tires all day with no intention to deal is regarded as little better than a thief. Feelings about such matters are quite situation-specific. Walking around a store and looking at price tags doesn't imply commitment, but as the seller's reliance increases, it becomes increasingly easy to find some expectation that the buyer will carry through in good faith.

You already have seen the fruits of the law's insistence on a moment of formation in the problems that result from the tendency of that insistence to create compensating doctrinal pressures. For example, *Mattei v. Hopper*, p. 31, and *Sylvan Crest Sand & Gravel Co. v. United States*, p. 36, both involved buyers who used heavily conditioned promises in an effort to stall off the moment when they would be irrevocably bound to the promise to buy. Modification cases such as *Schwartzreich v. Bauman-Basch*, p. 525, can be understood as parties continuing the negotiation process to deal with changes that arise after offer and acceptance. The subcontractor bid cases such as *Drennan v. Star Paving*, p. 659, arise because the parties have conflicting interests in defining the moment when it becomes too late to back out or to insist on different terms. These considerations also play a role in the cases you read on interpretation of incomplete agreements, such as *Lee v. Jos. E. Seagram & Sons*, p. 602.

At the root of all this is the sense that sometimes a party is bound before a contract is fully formed, bound by unbargained-for reliance, or bound by obligations of good faith and fair dealing, or bound by some other theory, but certainly bound. The theory of liability may be hard to frame, but the sense of obligation is clear. These problems are not new, nor are they unique to our legal system. You are likely to have to wrestle with them throughout your career. From the beginning, you should be aware that they are a price paid for the advantages believed to follow from the crisp approach to formation described earlier in this Note.

II.　OPERATIVE OFFER OR INVITATION TO NEGOTIATE?

Whether an offer is ripe for acceptance, or "operative," might appear to be a simple question. But all of the problems of vagueness, illusoriness, lack of capacity, fraud, and those other elements that may fatally taint a promise are present here. Moreover, if bargain is the key to contract, an offeror must ask and receive delivery of an identifiable price in order for what he promises in return to be converted into a contract.

Usually the price requested is in the form of a return promise from the person to whom the offer is addressed, but it may be a requested act, or it may be both. We shall return to the complications these possibilities can create. For now the task is to identify the earmarks of an operative offer.

Lefkowitz v. Great Minneapolis Surplus Store

Minnesota Supreme Court, 1957.
251 Minn. 188, 86 N.W.2d 689.

■ MURPHY, J. This is an appeal from an order of the Municipal Court of Minneapolis denying the motion of the defendant for amended findings of fact, or, in the alternative, for a new trial. The order for judgment awarded the plaintiff the sum of $138.50 as damages for breach of contract.

This case grows out of the alleged refusal of the defendant to sell to the plaintiff a certain fur piece which it had offered for sale in a newspaper advertisement. It appears from the record that on April 6, 1956, the defendant published the following advertisement in a Minneapolis newspaper:

Saturday 9 A.M. Sharp
3 Brand New
Fur Coats
Worth to......$100.00
First Come
First Served
$1
Each

On April 13, the defendant again published an advertisement in the same newspaper as follows:

Saturday 9 A.M.
2 Brand New Pastel
Mink 3–Skin Scarfs
Selling for $89.50
Out they go
Saturday. Each......$1.00
1 Black Lapin Stole
Beautiful
worth $139.50......$1.00
First Come
First Served

The record supports the findings of the court that on each of the Saturdays following the publication of the above-described ads the plaintiff was the first to present himself at the appropriate counter in the defendant's store and on each occasion demanded the coat and the stole so advertised and indicated his readiness to pay the sale price of $1. On both occasions, the defendant refused to sell the merchandise to the plaintiff, stating on the first occasion that by a "house rule" the offer was intended for women only and sales would not be made to men, and on the second visit that plaintiff knew defendant's house rules.

The trial court properly disallowed plaintiff's claim for the value of the fur coats since the value of these articles was speculative and uncertain. The only evidence of value was the advertisement itself to the effect that the coats were "Worth to $100.00," how much less being speculative especially in view of the price for which they were offered for sale. With reference to the offer of the defendant on April 13, 1956, to sell the "1 Black Lapin Stole * * * worth $139.50 * * *" the trial court held that the value of this article was established and granted judgment in favor of the plaintiff for that amount less the $1 quoted purchase price.

1. The defendant contends that a newspaper advertisement offering items of merchandise for sale at a named price is a "unilateral offer" which may be withdrawn without notice. He relies upon authorities which hold that, where an advertiser publishes in a newspaper that he has a certain quantity or quality of goods which he wants to dispose of at certain prices and on certain terms, such advertisements are not offers which become contracts as soon as any person to whose notice they may come signifies his acceptance by notifying the other that he will take a certain quantity of them. Such advertisements have been construed as an invitation for an offer of sale on the terms stated, which offer, when received, may be accepted or rejected and which therefore does not become a contract of sale until accepted by the seller; and until a contract has been so made, the seller may modify or revoke such prices or terms.

The defendant relies principally on *Craft v. Elder & Johnston Co.* In that case, the court discussed the legal effect of an advertisement offering for sale, as a one-day special, an electric sewing machine at a named price. The view was expressed that the advertisement was "not an offer made to any specific person but was made to the public generally. Thereby it would be properly designated as a unilateral offer and not being supported by any consideration could be withdrawn at will and without notice." It is true that such an offer may be withdrawn before acceptance. Since all offers are by their nature unilateral because they are necessarily made by one party or on one side in the negotiation of a contract, the distinction made in that decision between a unilateral offer and a unilateral contract is not clear. On the facts before us we are concerned with whether the advertisement constituted an offer, and, if so, whether the plaintiff's conduct constituted an acceptance.

There are numerous authorities which hold that a particular advertisement in a newspaper or circular letter relating to a sale of articles may be construed by the court as constituting an offer, acceptance of which would complete a contract.

The test of whether a binding obligation may originate in advertisements addressed to the general public is "whether the facts show that some performance was promised in positive terms in return for something requested." 1 Williston, Contracts (Rev. ed.) § 27.

The authorities above cited emphasize that, where the offer is clear, definite, and explicit, and leaves nothing open for negotiation, it constitutes an offer, acceptance of which will complete the contract. The most recent case on the subject is *Johnson v. Capital City Ford Co.*, in which the court pointed out that a newspaper advertisement relating to the purchase and sale of automobiles may constitute an offer, acceptance of which will consummate a contract and create an obligation in the offeror to perform according to the terms of the published offer.

Whether in any individual instance a newspaper advertisement is an offer rather than an invitation to make an offer depends on the legal intention of the parties and the surrounding circumstances. We are of the view on the facts before us that the offer by the defendant of the sale of the Lapin fur was clear, definite, and explicit, and left nothing open for negotiation. The plaintiff having successfully managed to be the first one to appear at the seller's place of business to be served, as requested by the advertisement, and having offered the stated purchase price of the article, he was entitled to performance on the part of the defendant. We think the trial court was correct in holding that there was in the conduct of the parties a sufficient mutuality of obligation to constitute a contract of sale.

2. The defendant contends that the offer was modified by a "house rule" to the effect that only women were qualified to receive the bargains advertised. The advertisement contained no such restriction. This objection may be disposed of briefly by stating that, while an advertiser has the right at any time before acceptance to modify his offer, he does not have the right, after acceptance, to impose new or arbitrary conditions not contained in the published offer.

Affirmed.

QUESTIONS AND NOTES

1. What tests would you apply to the advertisement in this case to determine its practical effect on you, the typical buyer? What would your expectations be if you trotted down to the Great Minneapolis Surplus Store and you were first in line? Fourth in line? Fortieth in line?

2. Would your expectations be different if the words about limited quantity were not in the ads? Suppose they merely read: "Fur Coats—Worth to $100—First Come, First Served—$1 each."

3. Suppose there were a sign on the door of the Great Minneapolis Surplus Store when you arrived that read as follows: "Sale offer in yesterday's paper has been withdrawn." How would you react? Would the addition of words explaining that the price in the ad was a typesetter's mistake alter your reaction?

4. Would the furs on sale have to be in new condition? Suppose all of them had stains and blemishes. Does the offer have to describe the condition of the furs to be potentially binding?

5. How (and when) would you expect your deal on the sale item to be closed? Would saying, "I'll take this one" bind the surplus store? Suppose you asked for credit on the surplus store's usual terms of 10% down and the rest in ten easy installments of 9¢ apiece? Suppose you asked to have the coat delivered?

6. Is the result in *Lefkowitz v. Great Minneapolis Surplus Store* consistent with the following Comment *b* to Restatement, Second, Contracts § 26?

b. Advertising. Business enterprises commonly secure general publicity for the goods or services they supply or purchase. Advertisements of goods by display, sign, handbill, newspaper, radio or television are not ordinarily intended or understood as offers to sell. The same is true of catalogues, price lists and circulars, even though the terms of suggested bargains may be stated in some detail. It is of course possible to make an offer by an advertisement directed to the general public, but there must ordinarily be some language of commitment or some invitation to take action without further communication.

7. Shouldn't sellers be held to sell goods at the terms they advertise? False advertising is extensively regulated by both federal and state government and is often a misdemeanor under state criminal law. It is also likely to be misrepresentation and a tort. Why the reluctance to treat it as a breach of contract?

8. Although the traditional "black-letter" rule is that an advertisement is not ordinarily an offer, Jay Feinman and Stephen Brill argue that, upon close examination, the cases, while acknowledging the traditional rule in *dicta*, actually hold that advertisements are offers in the specific cases before them. Moreover, they argue that this is the correct result as a general matter: "An advertisement is an offer because it is right for the public to expect, the legislature to dictate, and the courts to enforce standards of fairness in the marketplace." Jay M. Feinman & Stephen R. Brill, *Is an Advertisement an Offer? Why It Is, and Why It Matters*, 58 HASTINGS L.J. 61 (2006).

9. By the way, why is Mr. Lefkowitz buying ladies' clothing? Is it for his wife? Or is it for himself? Is the Great Minneapolis Surplus Store's "house rule" targeted at men generally, or men who want to purchase women's clothing? What if the advertised items were men's clothing, or gender neutral?

III. COMPLETENESS AS THE INDICATOR OF AN OPERATIVE OFFER–OPEN TERMS

UNIFORM COMMERCIAL CODE:

§ 2–204.   *Formation in General.*

(1) A contract for sale of goods may be made in any manner sufficient to show agreement, including conduct by both parties which recognizes the existence of such a contract.

(2) An agreement sufficient to constitute a contract for sale may be found even though the moment of its making is undetermined.

(3) Even though one or more terms are left open a contract for sale does not fail for indefiniteness if the parties have intended to make a contract and there is a reasonably certain basis for giving an appropriate remedy.

§ 2–305.   Open Price Term.

(1) The parties if they so intend can conclude a contract for sale even though the price is not settled. In such a case the price is a reasonable price at the time for delivery if

   (a) nothing is said as to price; or

   (b) the price is left to be agreed by the parties and they fail to agree; or

   (c) the price is to be fixed in terms of some agreed market or other standard as set or recorded by a third person or agency and it is not so set or recorded.

(2) A price to be fixed by the seller or by the buyer means a price for him to fix in good faith.

(3) When a price left to be fixed otherwise than by agreement of the parties fails to be fixed through fault of one party the other may at his option treat the contract as cancelled or himself fix a reasonable price.

(4) Where, however, the parties intend not to be bound unless the price be fixed or agreed and it is not fixed or agreed there is no contract. In such a case the buyer must return any goods already received or if unable so to do must pay their reasonable value at the time of delivery and the seller must return any portion of the price paid on account.

UN CONVENTION ON CONTRACTS FOR THE INTERNATIONAL SALE OF GOODS:

Article 55

Where a contract has been validly concluded but does not expressly or implicitly fix or make provision for determining the price, the parties are considered, in the absence of any indication to the contrary, to have impliedly made reference to the price generally charged at the time of the conclusion of the contract for such goods sold under comparable circumstances in the trade concerned.

QUESTIONS AND NOTES

1. What hallmarks turn a bargaining proposal that into an operative offer? The specificity and completeness of the negotiations leading to it are two obvious signs of its ripeness; a detailed and lengthy proposal is more likely to be considered an operative offer. But what about the converse: does the vagueness or incompleteness of a manifestation of intent prevent it from being an offer?

RESTATEMENT, SECOND, CONTRACTS § 24 provides:

> An offer is the manifestation of willingness to enter into a bargain, so made as to justify another person in understanding that his assent to that bargain is invited and will conclude it.

RESTATEMENT, SECOND, CONTRACTS § 33 provides:

> (1) Even though a manifestation of intention is intended to be understood as an offer, it cannot be accepted so as to form a contract unless the terms of the contract are reasonably certain.
>
> (2) The terms of a contract are reasonably certain if they provide a basis for determining the existence of a breach and for giving an appropriate remedy.
>
> (3) The fact that one or more terms of a proposed bargain are left open or uncertain may show that a manifestation of intention is not intended to be understood as an offer or as an acceptance.

Can you state a rule more contentful than these two sections? Is the approach taken by the Restatement consistent with UCC § 2–204? Does the total omission of some very important terms prevent the conclusion that the proposal is an offer?

2. The validity of open-price contracts under the CISG is not as obvious as a reading of Article 55 alone suggests. CISG Article 14(1) provides:

> (1) A proposal for concluding a contract addressed to one or more specific persons constitutes an offer if it is sufficiently definite and indicates the intention of the offeror to be bound in case of acceptance. A proposal is sufficiently definite if it indicates the goods and expressly or implicitly fixes or makes provision for determining the quantity and the price.

When would Article 55 apply given Article 14(1)? Some of the experts drafting the Convention have taken the view that Article 55 applies only "where a contract has been validly concluded," but that an agreement based on an open price term is not based on a valid offer because of Article 14(1). Authoritative reconciliation of these divergent strands in the CISG will require further interpretive litigation.

IV. The Duration of Offers and the Use of Options

An offeror is vulnerable to being bound to a contract by the acceptance of his offer. "Duration of the offer" refers to the time within which an offeree may bind the offeror. The offeree's power to bind arises with the making of an operative offer and continues until it is terminated. While the offeree's power may be terminated in a number of ways (some of which will be discussed later in this Chapter), two of the more important are lapse of time and revocation or withdrawal of the offer before acceptance.

The preceding four sentences highlight how confusing lawyer's vocabulary can be when it adopts the habit of describing people by attaching the endings "or" and "ee" to indicate their legal status. One who makes an offer is an offeror, and one who receives the offer is the offeree. Later you will learn about assignors and assignees, mortgagors and mortgagees, subrogors and subrogees, and on and on. The habit is too deeply engrained to be eradicated, but it is unfortunate. For one thing, many lawyers far into their careers remain confused as to who is the mortgagor and who is the mortgagee. Offeror and offeree and promisor and promisee have another vice that should lead you to avoid using this terminology if you can. Most contracts involve reciprocal negotiations leading to the exchange of promises. In such a case it is misleading and ambiguous to refer to one side as promisor (or offeror) and the other promisee (or offeree) because there are multiple promises (or multiple offers and counteroffers) made and received by each side. You can more clearly identify the parties by name or by reference to their role in the transaction (for example, buyer and seller or builder and owner).

Of course, the party making the offer may put a time limit on it, and that limit will be respected by the courts. But even if no specific time limit is set, offers eventually die of old age. The life span of an offer varies with the surrounding facts and circumstances, and the expert who ultimately determines its duration is a court.

A. REVOCATION

If a promise not supported by consideration is unenforceable, it logically follows that an offer can be withdrawn by an offeror at any time prior to the receipt of consideration by its acceptance. This is the traditional common law rule, subject as usual to several interesting variations, some logical and some not. Leaving the consideration doctrine to the side, there is nothing inevitable about the rule permitting free withdrawal of unaccepted offers. The rule could just as well be that every operative offer must be left open for a reasonable time to give the promisee a chance to consider and accept or reject it. This, too, would make sense, for in making a serious offer, the offeror must contemplate that the equally serious offeree will have a reasonable time to consider it or at least will have the amount of time stated in the operative offer itself. There are no insurmountable difficulties with this approach, and many advanced systems of law have adopted it. But the consideration concept has been too powerful in common law thinking to permit general acceptance of this alternative. So the basic approach with which we shall work is that an offeror is free to withdraw the offer at any time prior to acceptance.

Great Northern Railway Co. v. Witham

Court of Common Pleas, 1873.
L.R. 9 C.P. 16.

The cause was tried before BRETT, J., at the sittings at Westminster after the last term. The facts were as follows: In October, 1871, the plaintiffs advertised for tenders for the supply of goods (amongst other things iron) to be delivered at their station at Doncaster, according to a certain specification. The defendant sent in a tender, as follows:

> I, the undersigned, hereby undertake to supply the Great Northern Railway Company, for twelve months from November 1st, 1871, to October 31st, 1872, with such quantities of each or any of the several articles named in the attached specification as the company's storekeeper may order from time to time, at the price set opposite each article respectively, and agree to abide by the conditions stated on the other side.
>
> [Signed] Samuel Witham.

The company's officer wrote in reply, as follows:

> Mr. S. Witham:
>
> Sir: I am instructed to inform you that my directors have accepted your tender, dated, etc., to supply this company at Doncaster station any quantity they may order during the period ending October 31st, 1872, of the description of iron mentioned on the enclosed list, at the prices specified therein. The terms of the contract must be strictly adhered to. Requesting an acknowledgment of the receipt of this letter.
>
> [Signed] S. Fitch, Assistant Secretary.

To this the defendant replied:

> I beg to own receipt of your favor of 20th instant, accepting my tender for bars, for which I am obliged. Your specifications shall receive my best attention.
>
> S. Witham.

Several orders for iron were given by the company, which were from time to time duly executed by the defendant; but ultimately the defendant refused to supply any more, whereupon this action was brought.

A verdict having been found for the plaintiffs,

Digby Seymour, Q.C., moved to enter a nonsuit.

■ KEATING, J. In this case Mr. Digby Seymour moved to enter a nonsuit. The circumstances were these: The Great Northern Railway Company advertised for tenders for the supply of stores. The defendant made a tender in these words: "I hereby undertake to supply the Great Northern Railway Company, for twelve months, from etc. to etc., with such quantities of each or any of the several articles named in the attached specifications as the company's storekeeper may order from time to time, at the price set opposite each article respectively," etc. Some orders were given by the company, which were duly executed. But the order now in question was not executed; the defendant seeking to excuse himself from the performance of his agreement, because it was unilateral, the company not being bound to give the order. The ground upon which it was put by Mr. Seymour was, that there was no consideration for the defendant's promise to supply the goods; in other words, that, inasmuch as there was no obligation on the company to give an order, there was no consideration moving from the company, and therefore no obligation on the defendant to supply the goods. The case mainly relied on in support of that contention was *Burton v. Great Northern Railway Co.* But that is not an authority in the defendant's favor. It was the converse case. The Court there held that no action would lie against the company for not giving an order. If before the order was given the defendant had given notice to the company that he would not perform the agreement, it might be that he would have been justified in so doing. But here the company had given the order, and had consequently done something which amounted to a consideration for the defendant's promise. I see no ground for doubting that the verdict for the plaintiffs ought to stand.

■ BRETT, J. The company advertised for tenders for the supply of stores, such as they might think fit to order, for one year. The defendant made a tender offering to supply them for that period at certain fixed prices; and the company accepted his tender. If there were no other objection, the contract between the parties would be found in the tender and the letter accepting it. This action is brought for the defendant's refusal to deliver goods ordered by the company; and the objection to the plaintiffs' right to recover is, that the contract is unilateral. I do not, however, understand what objection that is to a contract. Many contracts are obnoxious to the same complaint. If I say to another, "If you will go to York, I will give you £100," that is in a certain sense a unilateral contract. He has not promised to go to York. But if he goes, it cannot be doubted that he will be entitled to receive the £100. His going to York at my request is a sufficient consideration for my promise. So, if one says to another, "If you will give me an order for iron, or other goods, I will supply it at a given price"; if the order is given, there is a complete contract which the seller is bound to perform. There is in such a case ample consideration for the promise. So, here, the company having given the defendant an order at his request, his acceptance of the order would bind them. If any authority could have been found to sustain Mr. Seymour's contention, I should have considered that a rule ought to be granted. But none has been cited. *Burton v. Great Northern Railway Co.* is not at all to the purpose. This is matter of every day's practice; and I think it would be wrong to countenance the notion that a man who tenders for the supply of goods in this way is not bound to deliver them when an order is given. I agree that this judgment does not decide the question whether the defendant might have absolved himself from the further performance of the contract by giving notice.

Rule refused.

QUESTIONS AND NOTES

1. What did the railroad accept by its letter of acceptance? What did the purchasing agent for the railroad think he was doing when he wrote that letter?

2. After the railroad gave Witham an order, was Witham bound to fill only that order or all orders the railroad might place during the one-year term of the blanket order agreement? In other words, weren't the parties bargaining here for a one-year assured supply rather than just a single order? Once the railroad placed an order, didn't it accept the deal proposed and bind both itself and Witham to their agreement for a one-year term?

3. Can you find a promise by implication in the railroad's letter to buy from no one else? If such a promise to buy from no one else were "made," would this bind Witham to deliver all year as ordered by the railroad?

4. Anglo–American law might have taken any one of the approaches suggested in the three preceding questions. For better or for worse, however, the dominant position is that suggested in the case itself: a continuing offer is open for its term and may be accepted by placing an order before revocation. The acceptance binds the offeror to the extent of the order but no further, i.e., the offeror can revoke to the extent the offer is not yet accepted.

B. OPTIONS

One common device that renders an offer irrevocable is to cast it as an option. An option is a promise not to revoke another promise for a period of time. The irrevocability of an offer is neatly accommodated to the consideration requirement by making the sale of the power to revoke part of a two-level bargain transaction. Level one is the basic offer, for which a price is demanded but not yet received. Level two is a collateral offer to keep the basic offer open for a specified time, but for which *another* price is demanded. Receipt of the price for irrevocability creates the option. It does not bind the other party to accept the basic offer. However, it does give that person time to consider whether or not to accept without fear that the offer will be withdrawn while it is being considered.

Marsh v. Lott

California Court of Appeals, 1908.
8 Cal.App. 384, 97 P. 163.

■ SHAW, J. Action for specific performance of a contract, whereby plaintiff asserts that in consideration of 25 cents he was given an option to purchase, for the sum of $100,000, certain real estate owned by defendant. Judgment was rendered for defendant. Plaintiff appeals from the judgment, and from an order denying his motion for a new trial.

The contract, specific performance of which is sought, is as follows:

> For and in consideration of the sum of twenty-five cents to me in hand paid I hereby give Robt. Marsh & Co. an option to purchase, at any time up to and including June 1st, 1905, with privilege of 30 days extension, from date hereof, the following described property, to wit: South ½ of lot 9 & all of lot 8, block 101, Bellevue Terrace tract, and all of the property owned by myself in above block, for the sum of one hundred thousand dollars, payable thirty thousand cash, balance on or before 4 years, 4½% net.
>
> I agree to furnish an unlimited certificate of title showing said property to be free from all incumbrance, and to convey the same in such condition by deed of grant, bargain and sale, & pay regular commission.
>
> M.A. Lott. [Seal.] Date: Feby. 25th, 1905.
>
> Property: 90-165. Building: 6 flats—2 cottages. Rents: $260.00.

On June 1, 1905, plaintiff notified defendant in writing that he exercised the right accorded by said contract regarding the extension of time therein specified, and elected to extend the same for a period of 30 days.

On June 2, 1905, defendant, by a written instrument served upon plaintiff, revoked said option, and notified him that she withdrew said property from sale.

On June 29, 1905, within the extended time, plaintiff left at the residence of defendant an instrument, of which the following is a copy:

June 29, 1905.

Mrs. M.A. Lott 507 South Olive street, City.

Dear Madame:

Referring to your agreement with me dated February 25, 1905, by which you gave me the privilege of purchasing the south half of lot nine and the whole of lot eight, in block one hundred and one, Bellevue Terrace tract, in this city, I again tender you in gold coin of the United States the sum of $30,000 as provided in said agreement, and demand of you performance on your part as in said agreement provided. This tender will also be made to your attorney, J. Wiseman MacDonald, Esq., as per request this morning when I tendered you $30,000 in gold coin at your residence on said property.

Yours truly,

Robert Marsh & Company.

The contention of appellant is that certain findings are not supported by the evidence. The findings material to a consideration of the case are as follows: The court found that the sum of 25 cents paid for the option was an inadequate and insufficient consideration for the same, and that the said option contract was not just and reasonable to defendant and no adequate consideration was paid to her for it. By finding 9 it appears that

after such revocation and withdrawal of said option, plaintiff, under the name of Robert Marsh & Co., on the 29th day of June, 1905, in an instrument left at the defendant's house, offered to pay to the defendant the sum of $30,000, and under the said name demanded from defendant a conveyance of the said property, but plaintiff did not at any time actually tender $30,000, or any sum at all in cash, to the defendant, nor did he, in his, or any other name, at any time, tender or offer to defendant any note or mortgage, or other evidence of indebtedness in the amount of $70,000, or any sum at all, either carrying interest at 4½ per cent, net, or at any rate at all, nor did he, in his own name, or any other name, at any time, offer to pay defendant the balance of $70,000, on or before four years from the date of said option, or at any time, with interest at 4½ per cent. net, or with or without interest.

And by finding 10 it appears that

plaintiff has not duly or at all performed all and every provision and thing on his part in said option agreement contained. He has made no tender or offer to defendant, save as is set forth in finding No. 9 hereof. Plaintiff is willing to perform the matters on the part of Robert Marsh & Co. to be performed according to the terms of the said option, and is able to pay the sum of thirty thousand dollars.

If there was no sufficient consideration for the option, then it was a mere nudum pactum, and defendant's revocation thereof, notwithstanding her promise to the contrary, was effectual in terminating any right of plaintiff to consummate the purchase.

If on the other hand, the offer was to remain open a fixed time and was made upon a valuable consideration, equity will ignore the attempted revocation, and treat a subsequent acceptance, made within the time defined in the option, exactly as if no attempted revocation had been made. Subdivision 1 of section 3391, of the Civil Code makes an adequate consideration for the contract one of the conditions for the specific enforcement thereof. The provision, however, has reference to the consideration to be paid for the property, the right to purchase which at a stipulated price within a given time is the subject of the option. It has no application to the sufficiency of the consideration paid for the executed contract, whereby defendant transferred to plaintiff the right to elect to purchase at the stipulated price. It is not the option which it is sought to enforce, but that which, by plaintiff's acceptance of defendant's offer, has ripened into an executory contract, whereby, for an adequate consideration, the one agrees to buy and the other agrees to sell. "The sale of an option is an executed contract; that is to say, the lands are not sold, the contract is not executed as to them, but the option is as completely sold and transferred in praesenti as a piece of personal property instantly delivered on payment of the price." *Ide v. Leiser*, 10 Mont. 5. From the very nature of the case no standard exists whereby to determine the adequate value of an option to purchase specific real estate. The land has a market value susceptible of ascertainment, but the value of an option upon a piece of real estate might, and oftentimes does, depend upon proposed or possible improvements in the particular vicinity. To illustrate: If A., having information that the erection of a gigantic department store is contemplated in a certain locality, wishes an option for a specified time to purchase property owned by B. in the vicinity of such proposed improvement, and takes the option on B.'s property at the full market price at the time, must he pay a greater sum therefor because of his knowledge and the fact of B.'s ignorance of the proposed improvement? It is not possible that B., upon learning of the proposed improvement, can, in the absence of facts constituting fraud, etc., revoke or rescind the option upon the claim that he sold and transferred the right specified therein for an inadequate consideration. In our judgment any money consideration, however small, paid and received for an option to purchase property at its adequate value is binding upon the seller thereof for the time specified therein, and is irrevocable for want of its adequacy.

The provisions of section 3391, Civ.Code, are but a codification of equitable principles that have existed from time immemorial, and the sufficiency of the price paid for an option has never been measured by its adequacy. In Warvelle on Vendors (2d Ed.) § 125, it is said: "If the option is given for a valuable consideration, whether adequate or not, it cannot be withdrawn or revoked within the time fixed, and it will be binding and obligatory upon the owner, or his assigns with notice, until it expires by its own limitation." In *Mathews Slate Co. v. New Empire Slate Co.* 122 F. 972, it is said:

> writing under seal, by which the one party, in consideration of $1, the payment of which is acknowledged, agrees to sell and convey to the other party within a specified time certain lands and premises, on payment by the other party of a specified consideration, such contract is valid and binding, and ought to be and may be specifically enforced. The seller has the right to fix his price, and covenant and agree that, on receiving that price within a certain time, he will convey the premises, and, if within that time the purchaser of the option tenders the money and demands a conveyance, he is entitled to it. To hold otherwise is to destroy the efficacy of such contracts and agreements.

Mr. Freeman in his note to the case of *Mueller v. Nortmann*, 96 Am.St.Rep. 997, says:

> "An option given by the owner of land for a valuable consideration, whether adequate or not, agreeing to sell it to another at a fixed price if accepted within a specified time, is binding upon the owner and all his successors in interest with knowledge thereof."

It therefore follows that the purported revocation made by defendant on June 2, 1905, was ineffectual for the purpose of terminating plaintiff's right to exercise the privilege of electing to accept the offer prior to the time designated therein for its expiration.

[Having thus found that the plaintiff gave sufficient consideration for the option, the court went on in the balance of the opinion to consider the terms of the land sale contract covered by the option. After discussing and dismissing various alternative interpretations of this contemplated transaction, the court denied the plaintiff specific performance, arguing somewhat tenuously that the deal would be unjust and inequitable to the defendant because it would compel her to convey title to the land without a written promise by the plaintiff to pay the $70,000 balance of the $100,000 total sales price.]

The judgment and order are affirmed.[*]

---

[*] Five weeks after this decision, Marsh tried again. He tendered cash for the full purchase price plus interest and instituted a new suit. He fared no better this time. He lost in the trial court, and the Supreme Court of California affirmed on appeal because, on the face of his new complaint, his restated claim was barred by *laches* (an equitable defense arising out of undue delay in asserting a claim), and—if the former suit could be considered by the court to avoid the *laches* defense—the judgment therein set up the bar of *res judicata*.

QUESTION

Would you reach the same conclusion that the consideration was adequate if this had been a one-cent option giving a right to purchase a twenty million dollar building anytime in five years?

Reread: *De Los Santos v. Great Western Sugar Co.,* p. 28;
Note, pp. 473–474.

RESTATEMENT, SECOND, CONTRACTS:

§ 25. Option Contracts.

An option contract is a promise which meets the requirements for the formation of a contract and limits the promisor's power to revoke an offer.

§ 87. Option Contract.

(1) An offer is binding as an option contract if it

(a) is in writing and signed by the offeror, recites a purported consideration for the making of the offer, and proposes an exchange on fair terms within a reasonable time; or

(b) is made irrevocable by statute.

(2) An offer which the offeror should reasonably expect to induce action or forbearance of a substantial character on the part of the offeree before acceptance and which does induce such action or forbearance is binding as an option contract to the extent necessary to avoid injustice.

C.   FIRM OFFER STATUTES

In many commercial transactions the parties may wish to maintain the climate for continuing negotiations by leaving offers open even though the parties fail to employ the formalism of token consideration to keep an offer open. Accordingly there has been pressure to find a way to hold an offeror to her offer during the stated period she has promised to keep the offer open, even in the absence of a delivered purchase price for the option. This has led to the enactment of firm offer statutes such as the following:

UNIFORM COMMERCIAL CODE:

§ 2-205. Firm Offers.

An offer by a merchant to buy or sell goods in a signed writing which by its terms gives assurance that it will be held open is not revocable, for lack of consideration, during the time stated or if no time is stated for a reasonable time, but in no event may such period of irrevocability exceed three months; but any such term of assurance on a form supplied by the offeree must be separately signed by the offeror.

NEW YORK GENERAL OBLIGATIONS LAW (MCKINNEY 2006):

§ 5-1109. Written Irrevocable Offer.

Except as otherwise provided in section 2-205 of the uniform commercial code with respect to an offer by a merchant to buy or sell goods, when an offer to enter into a contract is made in a writing signed by the offeror, or by his agent, which states that the offer is irrevocable during a period set forth or until a time fixed, the offer shall not be revocable during such period or until such time because of the absence of consideration for the assurance of irrevocability. When such a writing states that the offer is irrevocable but does not state any period or time of irrevocability, it shall be construed to state that the offer is irrevocable for a reasonable time.

QUESTION

If 25¢ will buy an option on a $100,000 property for five months, as was the case in *Marsh v. Lott*, doesn't consideration become a formality like the seal? Should payment of an option price of 25¢ make an offer to sell goods at a set price for two years irrevocable despite the three months limitation of UCC § 2-205?

UN CONVENTION ON CONTRACTS FOR THE INTERNATIONAL SALE OF GOODS:

Article 16

(1) Until a contract is concluded an offer may be revoked if the revocation reaches the offeree before he has dispatched an acceptance.

(2) However, an offer cannot be revoked:

(a) if it indicates, whether by stating a fixed time for acceptance or otherwise, that it is irrevocable; or

(b) if it was reasonable for the offeree to rely on the offer as being irrevocable and the offeree has acted in reliance on the offer.

Mid–South Packers v. Shoney's

United States Court of Appeals, Fifth Circuit, 1985.
761 F.2d 1117.

■ PER CURIAM. This diversity action on a Mississippi contract is before us following the district court's entry of summary judgment in favor of plaintiff Mid–South Packers, Inc., (Mid–South) and against defendant Shoney's, Inc., (Shoney's). We affirm.

I.

The facts, as viewed in the light most favorable to Shoney's, are as follows. In the spring of 1982, Mid–South and Shoney's engaged in negotiations for the sale by Mid–South to Shoney's of various pork products including bacon and ham. A business meeting was held between representatives of the two companies on April 17, 1982, at the offices of Mid–South in Tupelo, Mississippi. The discussion concerned prices and terms at which Mid–South could supply bacon and ham to Shoney's. At this meeting, Mid–South submitted a letter styled "Proposal" that set forth prices and terms at which Mid–South would supply Shoney's with various types of meat. The letter also provided that Shoney's would be informed forty-five days prior to any adjustment in price. The letter contained neither quantity nor durational terms. Shoney's expressed neither assent to nor rejection of the prices outlined in the letter. Shoney's estimated its needs from Mid–South at 80,000 pounds of meat per week. The legal effect of the letter proposal is the center of the controversy.

In July 1982, Shoney's began purchasing goods from Mid–South. The transactions were initiated by Shoney's, either through purchase orders or through telephone calls. On the day following each shipment, Mid–South sent invoices to Shoney's containing additional provisions for payment of both fifteen percent per annum interest on accounts not paid within seven days and reasonable collection costs, including attorney's fees. Shoney's bought vast quantities of bacon from Mid–South until August 12, 1982. On that date, Mid–South informed Shoney's at a meeting of their representatives that the price for future orders of bacon would be raised by $0.10 per pound, due to a previous error in computation by Mid–South. Shoney's objected to the price modification, apparently in reliance on the forty-five day notice provision contained in the disputed letter proposal. After negotiations, Mid–South agreed to increase the price by only $0.07 per pound. Shoney's neither agreed nor refused to purchase at the new price. Mid–South's new proposal was never reduced to writing.

On the first Shoney's purchase order sent after the August 12 meeting, Shoney's requested shipment at the old lower price. When Mid–South received the purchase order its representative, Morris Ates, called Shoney's representative, Ray Harmon, and advised Harmon that Mid–South would only deliver at the new higher price. The uncontradicted testimony of Ates is that Harmon told Ates to ship the bacon and to note the higher price on Shoney's purchase order. The bacon was shipped, and an invoice at the new price followed as did Shoney's payment, also at the new price.

From August 18 until October 5, 1982, Shoney's placed numerous orders for goods, including bacon, with Mid–South. Some if not all of these orders involved telephone conversations between representatives of the two companies, at which time Mid–South again quoted its increased selling price. The telephone conversations were followed by written purchase orders from Shoney's which quoted both the new price from Mid–South and a price computed at the original amount of $0.07 less per pound. In all cases, the orders were filled by Mid–South and invoiced at the new price. These invoices also included the additional terms providing for interest on delinquent accounts and reasonable collection costs. Shoney's paid Mid–South's quoted prices in all instances except the final order. On the final order before Shoney's began purchasing from another supplier, Shoney's offset the amount due on the invoice by $26,208, the amount allegedly overcharged on prior orders as a result of the $0.07 price increase.

Mid–South then brought this action to recover the amount offset plus interest and reasonable collection costs, including attorney's fees, as provided in the invoices. Shoney's admits that it owes $8,064.00 of the offset to Mid–South, inasmuch as this amount is attributable to orders placed after the expiration of the forty-five day notice period which, Shoney's contends, commenced on August 12 when Mid–South asked for the price increase.

II.

Shoney's contends that it accepted the proposal of Mid–South to supply it meat by placing orders with Mid–South, thereby forming a binding contract between the parties. Shoney's characterizes the contract as a "requirements contract" and asserts that the quantity term under the contract was that amount it reasonably and in good faith required. Accordingly, Shoney's argues that the notice provision contained in the letter proposal contractually bound Mid–South to notify Shoney's forty-five days before increasing its prices.

Mid–South asserts that the proposal was at most a "firm offer." Mid–South argues that under Uniform Commercial Code § 2–205, (hereinafter referred to as U.C.C. or the Code), a firm offer is irrevocable despite a lack of consideration "during the time stated or if no time is stated for a reasonable time; but in no event may such period of irrevocability exceed three (3) months." Thus, Mid–South contends that under any construction of the document, the offer must have expired three months after April 17, 1982, the date of the letter proposal, or on approximately July 17, 1982; therefore, it asserts the right on August 12, 1982, to increase the selling price without notice.

The district court, on consideration of cross summary judgment motions, adopted Mid–South's theory, holding that no long-term requirements contract was created and that each purchase order constituted a separate contract for the amount stated at the price required by Mid–South.

Requirements contracts are recognized in Mississippi and are not void for indefiniteness. However, an essential element of a requirements contract is the promise of the buyer to purchase exclusively from the seller either the buyer's entire requirements or up to a specified amount. Absent such a commitment, the requirements contract fails for want of consideration.

Ray Harmon, Shoney's agent in the transaction, maintained that Shoney's at all times had the right to purchase goods from suppliers other than Mid–South, that Shoney's continued to purchase from Mid–South because it was satisfied with its service and the quality of its goods, and that the purchase orders sent by Shoney's to Mid–South beginning in July 1982 "would have been the only commitment (Shoney's) would have made." Mid–South agrees that Shoney's had the right to change suppliers. Thus, by Shoney's own admission, no requirements contract could have arisen from the April 17 letter proposal and the meeting at which it was discussed.

Under the Code, the letter proposal and surrounding negotiations constituted, at most, a "firm offer" which was irrevocable, without consideration, only for a period of three months commencing on April 17 and ending on July 17, 1982. Thus, Mid–South had the right, after July 17, to raise its offered price as it did and the district court was correct in so holding.

The district court was also correct in holding that each purchase order stood on its own as a contract between Shoney's and Mid–South. More specifically, Mid–South's letter proposal was its offer in the sense that it was a promise to sell at the listed prices, justifying Shoney's in understanding that its assent, i.e., its purchase orders or telephone calls, would close the bargain. Thus, each time Shoney's manifested its assent, in telephone calls or purchase orders to Mid–South, a new and independent contract between the parties was created.

Mid–South's offer, held open in its discretion at least after July 17, was properly revoked and replaced by the offer of a seven-cent price increase at the August 12 meeting. Shoney's accepted this new offer for the first time on August 18 when Harmon, having been informed by Ates that Mid–South would not sell except at the new price, ordered shipment. Thereafter, Shoney's created separate contracts and obligated itself to pay the new price each time it mailed purchase orders with that price noted on them. Shoney's practice of also noting the old price on the purchase orders had no contractual significance since Harmon admitted that the practice was "a tracking procedure" used by Shoney's internally in order to determine the difference between the old price and the new. Ates' testimony is uncontradicted that Harmon also told him this.

In addition, Harmon admitted that Shoney's ordered at and paid the new price with the intention of causing Mid–South to believe that Shoney's had accepted the new price so that the shipments would continue; and Mid–South attached precisely that significance to Shoney's conduct. Shoney's secretly harbored intent to later deduct the difference between the old and new price could not bind Mid–South. Conduct may bind a party to a contract if it "show[s] agreement." "Agreement" of the parties must be manifested either in language or conduct in the circumstances. The only manifestations Shoney's made were those consistent with assent to Mid–South's new offer. Finally, the parties' "course of performance" is consistent only with Mid–South's expressed offer and Shoney's expressed acceptance of the new price.

Shoney's remedy under the circumstances was either to reserve whatever right it might have had to the old price by sending its purchase orders with an "explicit reservation," or to find a supplier who would sell at an acceptable price. No rational theory of the law of contracts could permit Shoney's to manifest acceptance of Mid–South's new offer, thus inducing performance, and then revoke that acceptance and demand compliance with the terms of the prior, withdrawn offer. Hence, the entire $26,208 offset by Shoney's is due and owing Mid–South and the district court's judgment, to this extent, was proper.

QUESTIONS AND NOTES

1. Did the parties ever have a contract in this case? When?

2. If Shoney's wants firm prices for more than ninety days without obligating itself to buy any certain quantity from any certain supplier, how would you suggest it obtain that result?

3. Even if this had been a binding requirements contract, wouldn't the statements and conduct of Shoney's acceding to the price increase nevertheless have been a binding good faith modification of such contract?

D.   OPTIONS PURCHASED BY
BEGINNING PERFORMANCE

When an offer proposes an exchange of promises, the general rule is that the offer may be withdrawn anytime up to the delivery of the requested return promise. So if I promise you $500 if you promise to sell me your cow, you can cut off my power to withdraw the offer by promising to sell me the cow as requested. Until you give me the promise I seek, I am free to call off the deal.

Consideration may also consist of a performance instead of a promise. At what point in time is the power to withdraw the offer terminated when a prolonged performance (rather than a promise to perform) is requested? Suppose I promise to pay you $500 if you paint my house. We might interpret this offer as calling for acceptance by delivery of a promise to paint my house (and this is the usually preferred interpretation for reasons that will become obvious when we see how complicated the alternative can be). If you start to paint (rather than expressly promise to paint), we can imply from your conduct the requested promise. If we treat the agreement this way, both sides are bound when the promises are exchanged. But we could also interpret this offer as calling for acceptance only by performance, that is, by you painting the house. If we treat it that way, must you completely paint the house to accept the offer and bind me? Can I sit by as you carry in all your paints, ladders, and drop cloths and then revoke the offer before you start to paint? Can I sit by calmly while you paint 98.7% of the house and then, as you dip your brush for the last time, notify you that I revoke my offer?

When the requested performance is prolonged in time, there is a great potential for unfairness if the offeror may revoke his offer after the other party has expended time and effort in part performance. While the inclination to bind the offeror is therefore strong, there is an understandable reluctance to bind the offeree to complete his performance. If he decides halfway through the job that he doesn't want to paint your house and isn't interested in the $500, why shouldn't he be permitted to abandon the effort? After all, he didn't *promise* to paint your house.

Binding the offeror but not the offeree offends a sense of symmetry dear to the legal mind. This sense of symmetry is embodied in a number of places in classical contract law doctrine, particularly in the concept of "mutuality of obligation" and in the distinction between "unilateral" and "bilateral" contracts. Both of these concepts are generally discredited and we avoid them in this Casebook because their use tends to create more problems than solutions. You will encounter them in many judicial opinions, however, and should be aware of the underlying problem they describe.

Basically three approaches to the problems created by an offer of a promise in exchange for performance rather than a return promise exist:

(a) The strictly logical view that if a performance and not a promise is requested, no contract is formed and neither side is bound until the requested performance is complete and both sides are bound.

(b) The view that once the requested performance has substantially begun, both offeror and offeree are bound in a complete contract to the entire undertaking. This view binds the offeree to a promise he may never have intended to make and gives little weight to the difference between an offer calling for a performance and one calling for a promise in response.

(c) The third view, embodied in Restatement, Second, Contracts § 45, treats an offer of this sort as creating an option contract when the offeree begins performance. Exercise of the option is conditioned on the completion of the performance as requested in the offer. During the course of performance the offeror cannot revoke the offer. Sometimes it is said that the offer calling for performance as the consideration implicitly contains a subsidiary promise to keep the offer open while performance is being tendered. Under this view, the offeror is bound from the time performance begins because he has received as consideration the beginning of performance by the offeree. Nonetheless, the offeree is free to withdraw anytime up to completion of performance.

RESTATEMENT, SECOND, CONTRACTS:

§ 45. *Option Contract Created by Part Performance or Tender.*

(1) Where an offer invites an offeree to accept by rendering a performance and does not invite a promissory acceptance, an option contract is created when the offeree tenders or begins the invited performance or tenders a beginning of it.

(2) The offeror's duty of performance under any option contract so created is conditional on completion or tender of the invited performance in accordance with the terms of the offer.

E.   ACTION IN RELIANCE AS AN OPTION CREATOR

In addition to firm offer statutes and consideration furnished by beginning performance, the unbargained-for action in reliance concept stated in § 90 of the

Restatement, Second, Contracts has been applied by courts to protect offerees from premature revocation of the offer.

Drennan v. Star Paving Co.
California Supreme Court, 1958.
51 Cal.2d 409, 333 P.2d 757.

■ TRAYNOR, J. Defendant appeals from a judgment for plaintiff in an action to recover damages caused by defendant's refusal to perform certain paving work according to a bid it submitted to plaintiff.

On July 28, 1955, plaintiff, a licensed general contractor, was preparing a bid on the "Monte Vista School Job" in the Lancaster school district. Bids had to be submitted before 8 p.m. Plaintiff testified that it was customary in that area for general contractors to receive the bids of subcontractors by telephone on the day set for bidding and to rely on them in computing their own bids. Thus on that day plaintiff's secretary, Mrs. Johnson, received by telephone between 50 and 75 subcontractors' bids for various parts of the school job. As each bid came in, she wrote it on a special form, which she brought into plaintiff's office. He then posted it on a master cost sheet setting forth the names and bids of all subcontractors. His own bid had to include the names of subcontractors who were to perform one-half of one per cent or more of the construction work, and he had also to provide a bidder's bond of 10 per cent of his total bid of $317,385 as a guarantee that he would enter the contract if awarded the work.

Late in the afternoon, Mrs. Johnson had a telephone conversation with Kenneth R. Moon, an estimator for defendant. He gave his name and telephone number and stated that he was bidding for defendant for the paving work at the Monte Vista School according to plans and specifications and that his bid was $7,131.60. At Mrs. Johnson's request he repeated his bid. Plaintiff listened to the bid over an extension telephone in his office and posted it on the master sheet after receiving the bid form from Mrs. Johnson. Defendant's was the lowest bid for the paving. Plaintiff computed his own bid accordingly and submitted it with the name of defendant as the subcontractor for the paving. When the bids were opened on July 28th, plaintiff's proved to be the lowest, and he was awarded the contract.

On his way to Los Angeles the next morning plaintiff stopped at defendant's office. The first person he met was defendant's construction engineer, Mr. Oppenheimer. Plaintiff testified: "I introduced myself and he immediately told me that they had made a mistake in their bid to me the night before, they couldn't do it for the price they had bid, and I told him I would expect him to carry through with their original bid because I had used it in compiling my bid and the job was being awarded them. And I would have to go and do the job according to my bid and I would expect them to do the same."

Defendant refused to do the paving work for less than $15,000. Plaintiff testified that he "got figures from other people" and after trying for several months to get as low a bid as possible engaged L & H Paving Company, a firm in Lancaster, to do the work for $10,948.60.

The trial court found on substantial evidence that defendant made a definite offer to do the paving on the Monte Vista job according to the plans and specifications for $7,131.60, and that plaintiff relied on defendant's bid in computing his own bid for the school job and naming defendant therein as the subcontractor for the paving work. Accordingly, it entered judgment for plaintiff in the amount of $3,817 (the difference between defendant's bid and the cost of the paving to plaintiff) plus costs.

Defendant contends that there was no enforceable contract between the parties on the ground that it made a revocable offer and revoked it before plaintiff communicated his acceptance to defendant.

There is no evidence that defendant offered to make its bid irrevocable in exchange for plaintiff's use of its figures in computing his bid. Nor is there evidence that would warrant interpreting plaintiff's use of defendant's bid as the acceptance thereof, binding plaintiff, on condition he received the main contract, to award the subcontract to defendant. In sum, there was neither an option supported by consideration nor a bilateral contract binding on both parties.

Plaintiff contends, however, that he relied to his detriment on defendant's offer and that defendant must therefore answer in damages for its refusal to perform. Thus the question is squarely presented: Did plaintiff's reliance make defendant's offer irrevocable?

Section 90 of the Restatement of Contracts states: "A promise which the promisor should reasonably expect to induce action or forbearance of a definite and substantial character on the part of the promisee and which does induce such action or forbearance is binding if injustice can be avoided only by enforcement of the promise." This rule applies in this state.

Defendant's offer constituted a promise to perform on such conditions as were stated expressly or by implication therein or annexed thereto by operation of law. Defendant had reason to expect that if its bid proved the lowest it would be used by plaintiff. It induced "action * * * of a definite and substantial character on the part of the promisee."

Had defendant's bid expressly stated or clearly implied that it was revocable at any time before acceptance we would treat it accordingly. It was silent on revocation, however, and we must therefore determine whether there are conditions to the right of revocation imposed by law or reasonably inferable in fact. In the analogous problem of an offer for a unilateral contract, the theory is now obsolete that the offer is revocable at any time before complete performance. Thus section 45 of the Restatement of Contracts provides:

> If an offer for unilateral contract is made, and part of the consideration requested in the offer is given or tendered by the offeree in response thereto, the offeror is bound by a contract, the duty of immediate performance of which is conditional on the full consideration being given or tendered within the time stated in the offer, or, if no time is stated therein, within a reasonable time.

In explanation, comment b states that the

> main offer includes as a subsidiary promise, necessarily implied, that if part of the requested performance is given, the offeror will not revoke his offer, and that if tender is made it will be accepted. Part performance or tender may thus furnish consideration for the subsidiary promise. Moreover, merely acting in justifiable reliance on an offer may in some cases serve as sufficient reason for making a promise binding (see § 90).

Whether implied in fact or law, the subsidiary promise serves to preclude the injustice that would result if the offer could be revoked after the offeree had acted in detrimental reliance thereon. Reasonable reliance resulting in a foreseeable prejudicial change in position affords a compelling basis also for implying a subsidiary promise not to revoke an offer for a bilateral contract.

The absence of consideration is not fatal to the enforcement of such a promise. It is true that in the case of unilateral contracts the Restatement finds consideration for the implied subsidiary promise in the part performance of the bargained-for exchange, but its reference to section 90 makes clear that consideration for such a promise is not always necessary. The very purpose of section 90 is to make a promise binding even though there was no consideration "in the sense of something that is bargained for and given in exchange." Reasonable reliance serves to hold the offeror in lieu of the consideration ordinarily required to make the offer binding. In a case involving similar facts the Supreme Court of South Dakota stated that

> we believe that reason and justice demand that the doctrine [of section 90] be applied to the present facts. We cannot believe that by accepting this doctrine as controlling in the state of facts before us we will abolish the requirement of a consideration in contract cases, in any different sense than an ordinary estoppel abolishes some legal requirement in its application. We are of the opinion, therefore, that the defendants in executing the agreement [which was not supported by consideration] made a promise which they should have reasonably expected would induce the plaintiff to submit a bid based thereon to the Government, that

such promise did induce this action, and that injustice can be avoided only by enforcement of the promise.

When plaintiff used defendant's offer in computing his own bid, he bound himself to perform in reliance on defendant's terms. Though defendant did not bargain for this use of its bid neither did defendant make it idly, indifferent to whether it would be used or not. On the contrary it is reasonable to suppose that defendant submitted its bid to obtain the subcontract. It was bound to realize the substantial possibility that its bid would be the lowest, and that it would be included by plaintiff in his bid. It was to its own interest that the contractor be awarded the general contract; the lower the subcontract bid, the lower the general contractor's bid was likely to be and the greater its chance of acceptance and hence the greater defendant's chance of getting the paving subcontract. Defendant had reason not only to expect plaintiff to rely on its bid but to want him to. Clearly defendant had a stake in plaintiff's reliance on its bid. Given this interest and the fact that plaintiff is bound by his own bid, it is only fair that plaintiff should have at least an opportunity to accept defendant's bid after the general contract has been awarded to him.

It bears noting that a general contractor is not free to delay acceptance after he has been awarded the general contract in the hope of getting a better price. Nor can he reopen bargaining with the subcontractor and at the same time claim a continuing right to accept the original offer. In the present case plaintiff promptly informed defendant that plaintiff was being awarded the job and that the subcontract was being awarded to defendant.

Defendant contends, however, that its bid was the result of mistake and that it was therefore entitled to revoke it. It relies on the rescission cases. In those cases, however, the bidder's mistake was known or should have been to the offeree, and the offeree could be placed in status quo. Of course, if plaintiff had reason to believe that defendant's bid was in error, he could not justifiably rely on it, and section 90 would afford no basis for enforcing it. Plaintiff, however, had no reason to know that defendant had made a mistake in submitting its bid, since there was usually a variance of 160 per cent between the highest and lowest bids for paving in the desert around Lancaster. He committed himself to performing the main contract in reliance on defendant's figures. Under these circumstances defendant's mistake, far from relieving it of its obligation constitutes an additional reason for enforcing it, for it misled plaintiff as to the cost of doing the paving. Even had it been clearly understood that defendant's offer was revocable until accepted, it would not necessarily follow that defendant had no duty to exercise reasonable care in preparing its bid. It presented its bid with knowledge of the substantial possibility that it would be used by plaintiff; it could foresee the harm that would ensue from an erroneous underestimate of the cost. Moreover, it was motivated by its own business interest. Whether or not these considerations alone would justify recovery for negligence had the case been tried on that theory, they are persuasive that defendant's mistake should not defeat recovery under the rule of section 90 of the Restatement of Contracts. As between the subcontractor who made the bid and the general contractor who reasonably relied on it, the loss resulting from the mistake should fall on the party who caused it.

Leo F. Piazza Paving Co. v. Bebek & Brkich and *Bard v. Kent* are not to the contrary. In the *Piazza* case the court sustained a finding that defendants intended, not to make a firm bid, but only to give the plaintiff "some kind of an idea to use" in making its bid; there was evidence that the defendants had told plaintiff they were unsure of the significance of the specifications. There was thus no offer, promise, or representation on which the defendants should reasonably have expected the plaintiff to rely. The *Bard* case held that an option not supported by consideration was revoked by the death of the optionor. The issue of recovery under the rule of section 90 was not pleaded at the trial, and it does not appear that the offeree's reliance was "of a definite and substantial character" so that injustice could be avoided "only by the enforcement of the promise."

There is no merit in defendant's contention that plaintiff failed to state a cause of action, on the ground that the complaint failed to allege that plaintiff attempted to mitigate the damages or that they could not have been mitigated. Plaintiff alleged that after defendant's default, "plaintiff had to procure the services of the L & H Co. to perform said asphaltic paving for the sum of $10,948.60." Plaintiff's uncontradicted evidence showed that he spent several months trying to get bids from other subcontractors and that he took the lowest bid. Clearly he acted reasonably to mitigate damages....

The judgment is affirmed.

QUESTIONS AND NOTES

1. Does the problem of the mistaken subcontractor's bid have to be decided on the basis of whether there was consideration? What alternative bases for decision are suggested by Chapter One? What are the advantages and disadvantages of the alternatives?

2. Do you think the problem of subcontractors' bids would be better solved by a special rule or statute for this specific problem than by reference to the general law of contract formation and consideration? If so, what should the statute provide?

3. After this decision, Star Paving executives may wonder how, in a situation when they are seeking to conclude a bargain, they can be bound if the other party relies on their offer even before there is a bargain. How would you explain this apparent paradox to the folks at Star Paving? Is the paradox avoidable? Is it in Star

Paving's best interest to avoid it? What additional information would you like in answering this last question?

4. Did Star Paving ever promise that its bid would be irrevocable? Are all subcontractors' bids in California to be interpreted as containing an implied promise of irrevocability after this case?

F.   ADDITIONAL OFFER TERMINATORS

In addition to an offer terminated by the passage of a stated period of time or, in the absence of statement, of a reasonable period and by the proper revocation before acceptance, there are several other offer-terminating events.

1.   A rejection or a counteroffer by the offeree.

2.   Death or incapacity of the offeror or offeree before acceptance.

3.   Destruction of the subject matter of the contract before acceptance.

4.   Supervening legal prohibition of the proposed bargain.

V.   THE BINDING EVENT: ACCEPTANCE

The offer can be described accurately as the statement of a promise and of the price (the consideration) which the offeror will accept for the promise. The bargain becomes binding when the price is paid, when the consideration is delivered in response to the offer. But what if payment is made before all the material terms of the offer are fully disclosed?

Hill v. Gateway 2000

United States Court of Appeals, Seventh Circuit, 1997.
105 F.3d 1147.

■ EASTERBROOK, J.

A customer picks up the phone, orders a computer, and gives a credit card number. Presently a box arrives, containing the computer and a list of terms, said to govern unless the customer returns the computer within 30 days. Are these terms effective as the parties' contract, or is the contract term-free because the order-taker did not read any terms over the phone and elicit the customer's assent?

One of the terms in the box containing a Gateway 2000 system was an arbitration clause. Rich and Enza Hill, the customers, kept the computer more than 30 days before complaining about its components and performance. They filed suit in federal court arguing, among other things, that the product's shortcomings make Gateway a racketeer (mail and wire fraud are said to be the predicate offenses), leading to treble damages under RICO for the Hills and a class of all other purchasers. Gateway asked the district court to enforce the arbitration clause; the judge refused, writing that "[t]he present record is insufficient to support a finding of a valid arbitration agreement between the parties or that the plaintiffs were given adequate notice of the arbitration clause."

The Hills say that the arbitration clause did not stand out: they concede noticing the statement of terms but deny reading it closely enough to discover the agreement to arbitrate, and they ask us to conclude that they therefore may go to court. Yet an agreement to arbitrate must be enforced "save upon such grounds as exist at law or in equity for the revocation of any contract." 9 U.S.C. § 2. *Doctor's Associates, Inc. v. Casarotto,* holds that this provision of the Federal Arbitration Act is inconsistent with any requirement that an arbitration clause be prominent. A contract need not be read to be effective; people who accept take the risk that the unread terms may in retrospect prove unwelcome. Terms inside Gateway's box stand or fall together. If they constitute the parties' contract because the Hills had an opportunity to return the computer after reading them, then all must be enforced.

ProCD, Inc. v. Zeidenberg holds that terms inside a box of software bind consumers who use the software after an opportunity to read the terms and to reject them by returning the product. Likewise, *Carnival Cruise Lines, Inc. v. Shute* enforces a forum-selection clause that was included among three pages of terms attached to a cruise ship ticket. *ProCD* and *Carnival Cruise Lines* exemplify the many commercial transactions in which people pay for products with terms to follow; *ProCD* discusses others. The district court concluded in *ProCD* that the contract is formed when the consumer pays for the software; as a result, the court held, only terms known to the consumer at that moment are part of the contract, and provisos inside the box do not count. Although this is one way a contract could be formed, it is not the only way: "A vendor, as master of the offer, may invite acceptance by conduct, and may propose limitations on the kind of conduct that constitutes acceptance. A buyer may accept by performing the acts the vendor proposes to treat as acceptance." Gateway shipped computers with the same sort of accept-or-return offer ProCD made to users of its software. *ProCD* relied on the Uniform Commercial Code rather than any peculiarities of Wisconsin law; both Illinois and South Dakota, the two states whose law might govern relations between Gateway and the Hills, have adopted the UCC;

neither side has pointed us to any atypical doctrines in those states that might be pertinent; *ProCD* therefore applies to this dispute.

Plaintiffs ask us to limit *ProCD* to software, but where's the sense in that? *ProCD* is about the law of contract, not the law of software. Payment preceding the revelation of full terms is common for air transportation, insurance, and many other endeavors. Practical considerations support allowing vendors to enclose the full legal terms with their products. Cashiers cannot be expected to read legal documents to customers before ringing up sales. If the staff at the other end of the phone for direct-sales operations such as Gateway's had to read the four-page statement of terms before taking the buyer's credit card number, the droning voice would anesthetize rather than enlighten many potential buyers. Others would hang up in a rage over the waste of their time. And oral recitation would not avoid customers' assertions (whether true or feigned) that the clerk did not read term X to them, or that they did not remember or understand it. Writing provides benefits for both sides of commercial transactions. Customers as a group are better off when vendors skip costly and ineffectual steps such as telephonic recitation, and use instead a simple approve-or-return device. Competent adults are bound by such documents, read or unread. For what little it is worth, we add that the box from Gateway was crammed with software. The computer came with an operating system, without which it was useful only as a boat anchor. Gateway also included many application programs. So the Hills' effort to limit *ProCD* to software would not avail them factually, even if it were sound legally—which it is not.

For their second sally, the Hills contend that ProCD should be limited to executory contracts (to licenses in particular), and therefore does not apply because both parties' performance of this contract was complete when the box arrived at their home. This is legally and factually wrong: legally because the question at hand concerns the *formation* of the contract rather than its *performance*, and factually because both contracts were incompletely performed. *ProCD* did not depend on the fact that the seller characterized the transaction as a license rather than as a contract; we treated it as a contract for the sale of goods and reserved the question whether for other purposes a "license" characterization might be preferable. All debates about characterization to one side, the transaction in *ProCD* was no more executory than the one here: Zeidenberg paid for the software and walked out of the store with a box under his arm, so if arrival of the box with the product ends the time for revelation of contractual terms, then the time ended in *ProCD* before Zeidenberg opened the box. But of course ProCD had not completed performance with delivery of the box, and neither had Gateway. One element of the transaction was the warranty, which obliges sellers to fix defects in their products. The Hills have invoked Gateway's warranty and are not satisfied with its response, so they are not well positioned to say that Gateway's obligations were fulfilled when the motor carrier unloaded the box. What is more, both ProCD and Gateway promised to help customers to use their products. Long-term service and information obligations are common in the computer business, on both hardware and software sides. Gateway offers "lifetime service" and has a round-the-clock telephone hotline to fulfill this promise. Some vendors spend more money helping customers use their products than on developing and manufacturing them. The document in Gateway's box includes promises of future performance that some consumers value highly; these promises bind Gateway just as the arbitration clause binds the Hills.

Next the Hills insist that *ProCD* is irrelevant because Zeidenberg was a "merchant" and they are not. Section 2-207(2) of the UCC, the infamous battle-of-the-forms section, states that "additional terms [following acceptance of an offer] are to be construed as proposals for addition to a contract. Between merchants such terms become part of the contract unless ...." Plaintiffs tell us that *ProCD* came out as it did only because Zeidenberg was a "merchant" and the terms inside ProCD's box were not excluded by the "unless" clause. This argument pays scant attention to the opinion in *ProCD,* which concluded that, when there is only one form, "sec. 2-207 is irrelevant." 86 F.3d at 1452. The question in *ProCD* was not whether terms were added to a contract after its formation, but how and when the contract was formed—in particular, whether a vendor may propose that a contract of sale be formed, not in the store (or over the phone) with the payment of money or a general "send me the product," but after the customer has had a chance to inspect both the item and the terms. *ProCD* answers "yes," for merchants and consumers alike. Yet again, for what little it is worth we observe that the Hills misunderstand the setting of *ProCD.* A "merchant" under the UCC "means a person who deals in goods of the kind or otherwise by his occupation holds himself out as having knowledge or skill peculiar to the practices or goods involved in the transaction," § 2-104(1). Zeidenberg bought the product at a retail store, an uncommon place for merchants to acquire inventory. His corporation put ProCD's database on the Internet for anyone to browse, which led to the litigation but did not make Zeidenberg a software merchant.

At oral argument the Hills propounded still another distinction: the box containing ProCD's software displayed a notice that additional terms were within, while the box containing Gateway's computer did not. The difference is functional, not legal. Consumers browsing the aisles of a store can look at the box, and if they are unwilling to deal with the prospect of additional terms can leave the box alone, avoiding the transactions costs of returning the package after reviewing its contents. Gateway's box, by contrast, is just a shipping carton; it is not on display anywhere. Its function is to protect the product during transit, and the information on its sides is for the use of handlers (Fragile! This Side Up!) rather than would-be purchasers.

Perhaps the Hills would have had a better argument if they were first alerted to the bundling of hardware and legal-ware after opening the box and wanted to return the computer in order to avoid disagreeable terms, but were dissuaded by the expense of shipping. What the remedy would be in such a case—could it exceed the shipping charges? is an interesting question, but one that need not detain us because the Hills knew before they ordered the computer that the carton would include *some* important terms, and they did not seek to discover these in advance. Gateway's ads state that their products come with limited warranties and lifetime support. How limited was the warranty: 30 days, with service contingent on shipping the computer back, or five years, with free onsite service? What sort of support was offered? Shoppers have three principal ways to discover these things. First, they can ask the vendor to send a copy before deciding whether to buy. The Magnuson-Moss Warranty Act requires firms to distribute their warranty terms on request; the Hills do not contend that Gateway would have refused to enclose the remaining terms too. Concealment would be bad for business, scaring some customers away and leading to excess returns from others. Second, shoppers can consult public sources (computer magazines, the Web sites of vendors) that may contain this information. Third, they may inspect the documents after the product's delivery. Like Zeidenberg, the Hills took the third option. By keeping the computer beyond 30 days, the Hills accepted Gateway's offer, including the arbitration clause.

The Hills' remaining arguments, including a contention that the arbitration clause is unenforceable as part of a scheme to defraud, do not require more than a citation to *Prima Paint Corp. v. Flood & Conklin Mfg. Co.*, 388 U.S. 395 (1967). Whatever may be said pro and con about the cost and efficacy of arbitration (which the Hills disparage) is for Congress and the contracting parties to consider. Claims based on RICO are no less arbitrable than those founded on the contract or the law of torts. The decision of the district court is vacated, and this case is remanded with instructions to compel the Hills to submit their dispute to arbitration.

QUESTIONS AND NOTES

1. Didn't the Hills have the legal right to retain the computer they had paid for based upon the original terms of the deal? How can Gateway turn the Hills' exercise of that right into assent to new and additional terms by delivering the new terms with the computer? Compare *Klocek v. Gateway*, 104 F. Supp. 2d 1332 (D. Kan. 2000) (holding on nearly identical facts that Gateway's standard terms did not become part of the contract on account of customer's failure to return computer). Note that CISG Art. 18(1), p. 699, appears to specifically reject Gateway's tactic of unilaterally declaring that retention of the goods amounts to affirmative consent to

new unbargained-for terms: "Silence or inactivity does not in itself amount to acceptance."

2. What if, instead of an arbitration clause, the fine print enclosed with the box said: "Unless this computer is returned to Gateway in its original packing within 30 days, Customer agrees that Gateway shall be Customer's exclusive computer supplier for 10 years. Purchase of a computer from any other source shall result in liquidated damages of $1000 to Gateway for each such instance"? Can Gateway stick any term it wants, relevant or not to the purchase of the computer, into the fine print and enforce it against the Hills based on the Hills' supposed acceptance of Gateway's "offer" manifested solely by the Hills' retention of the computer the Hills had already paid for? Lest you consider this hypothetical remote and remain confident that an efficient market will prevent such overreaching by sellers, consider the terms of the subsequent Gateway 2000 arbitration clause at issue in *Brower v. Gateway 2000*, 676 N.Y.S.2d 569 (App. Div. 1998). That clause required all United States Gateway buyers to arbitrate their claims in Chicago, Illinois under the rules of the International Chamber of Commerce (ICC). The ICC (a respected institution in international commercial arbitration) requires that all the claimant's paperwork be mailed to ICC offices in France along with a $4000 arbitration fee, only $2000 of which might be refunded if the consumer prevailed after traveling to Chicago for the arbitration hearing. Although the New York courts found that this outrageous arbitration clause buried in the boilerplate was properly assented to under the UCC, they also found the clause unconscionable and refused to enforce it. But that was before the Supreme Court of the United States decided *Concepcion*, p. 266 which has limited application of the unconscionability defense to arbitration under the Federal Arbitration Act.

3. What if, in lieu of returning the Gateway computer, the Hills had sent a letter to Gateway's customer service department stating that they rejected the additional terms set forth in the package but were otherwise satisfied with the computer and would retain it based solely on the terms originally negotiated over the phone?

4. Sellers commonly reserve to themselves the right to unilaterally modify certain contract terms by providing notice to consumers. We are all familiar with envelope stuffers disclosing new terms that purport to bind buyers of wireless services, bank customers, credit cardholders and the like. Those terms are asserted to become binding on the consumer unless the contract is terminated promptly, even if termination is costly to the consumer. Are those new terms binding or not? How can one side reserve to itself the right to unilaterally impose new or different unbargained-for terms on notice to its counterparty notwithstanding reliance? If the seller can do this does it matter at all what the original contract provides? On the other hand, don't sellers in a national marketplace need to provide goods and services on a uniform set of terms to both existing and future customers?

5. The problem of enforcing unbargained-for "standard" terms in consumer contracts is an old and universal problem that keeps re-emerging in new contexts. It is common nowadays, for example, that in order to complete a transaction over the internet, a consumer must click on a "button" that says "I Agree" to standard terms that no one reads and that the seller knows no one reads. Those terms may be reasonable or not, but invariably they are drawn with an eye towards maximizing the legal position of the seller. Although market forces and consumer protection legislation may limit how far sellers can go in imposing onerous or non-germane unbargained-for terms, as *Hill v. Gateway* illustrates, the consumer can take little comfort that traditional American contract law will protect him from such terms in all but the most egregious circumstances. The nations within the European Community seem to take a more restrictive view: Article 6 of the EUROPEAN COMMUNITY COUNCIL DIRECTIVE 93/13/EEC (Apr. 5, 1993) provides: "Member States shall lay down that unfair terms used in a contract concluded with a consumer by a seller or supplier shall ... not be binding on the consumer...." "Unfair terms" include a lengthy non-exclusive list of specific types of provisions set forth in the Directive's Annex (including certain types of mandatory arbitration provisions), as well as any "contractual term which has not been individually negotiated ... if contrary to the requirement of good faith, it causes a significant imbalance in the parties' rights and obligations arising under the contract, to the detriment of the consumer." *Id.* at Art. 3(1). The GERMAN CIVIL CODE [BGB] §§ 305-310 adopts this approach to the problem as well. An attempt to incorporate similar concepts into the proposed 2003 version of UCC Article 2 was defeated by strong opposition from certain business sectors. See UCC Art. 2 Discussion Draft § 2-206 (Nov. 1996) ("When a consumer manifests assent to a standard form, a term contained in the form which the consumer could not reasonably have expected is not part of the contract unless the consumer expressly agrees to it.").

6. Judge Easterbrook rather casually dismisses the Hills' unconscionability argument. Note that *Hill* was a consumer class action case, and the arbitration clause imposed by Gateway had the effect of precluding class-wide relief. It is hard to imagine how individual arbitrations could ever vindicate consumer claims not involving personal injuries for transactions of this type. The enforceability of arbitration clauses in such circumstances remains controversial. *See* Note, p. 264.

The P's form frames the contract as buyer's offer.
This gives P the power of acceptance.

Beard Implement Co. v. Krusa

Appellate Court of Illinois, Fourth District, 1991.
208 Ill.App.3d 953, 153 Ill.Dec. 387, 567 N.E.2d 345.

■ JUSTICE STEIGMANN delivered the opinion of the court:

This action involves an alleged breach of contract between plaintiff seller, Beard Implement Company, Inc., a farm implement dealership, and defendant buyer, Carl Krusa, a farmer, for the purchase of a 1985 Deutz–Allis N–5 combine. The dispositive issue on appeal is whether the trial court in a bench trial erred in finding a contract existed between the parties. Specifically, defendant contends that plaintiff never accepted defendant's offer to purchase the combine. We agree and reverse.   *holding*

At trial, defendant testified that between December 20 and December 23, 1985, he had several conversations with plaintiff's representatives concerning the purchase of a new combine. Defendant owned a 1980 Deutz–Allis N–5 combine at that time. In fall 1985, both spindles on his combine had broken and defendant spoke with plaintiff's representatives about repairing them.

On December 23, 1985, defendant met with plaintiff's representatives at plaintiff's office in Arenzville, Illinois. Defendant testified that one of plaintiff's representatives, either Jim Beard or Gerry Beard, filled out a purchase order for a new combine for the price of $52,800 cash and the trade-in of the combine defendant then owned. (See appendix for a copy of this order.) Defendant signed the Allis–Chalmers purchase order, which was dated December 23, 1985. None of plaintiff's representatives signed that order on December 23, 1985, or at any time thereafter. The bottom left corner of this order reads as follows:

DEALER'S SALESMAN

This order subject to acceptance by dealer.

Accepted by: _____

DEALER

At the same time defendant signed the purchase order, he also signed a counter check drawn on a local bank in the amount of $5,200. Defendant testified that because he did not have his checkbook, plaintiff provided him with the counter check. The check was undated and intended to represent a down payment on the combine. Defendant testified that the check was not dated because he was to call plaintiff later and let plaintiff know if he wanted to proceed with the transaction. At that time, plaintiff would put a date on the check.

Defendant testified that he had misgivings over the Christmas weekend and, after discussing the situation with his wife, telephoned plaintiff's manager, Duane Hess, on December 26, 1985, and told Hess that he did not wish to proceed with the

The contract makes clear that sign = acceptance

transaction. Defendant explained to Hess that defendant and his wife had determined that "the price was too high" and they "did not want to go further into debt to finance the transaction." Defendant testified that Hess told him that if defendant thought the combine was too expensive, Hess would let defendant out of the deal. Hess did not indicate whether he had signed the order.

Earlier on December 26, 1985, defendant had met with a representative of Cox Implement Company. Defendant identified a copy of the order form that one of Cox's salesman had filled out. This order was dated December 26, 1985, but was signed on December 27. Defendant testified that he told Cox's salesman that his price was too high and that defendant could not go through with either that bid or plaintiff's bid. However, after Cox's quoted price was reduced and the figures on the purchase order were scratched out, defendant signed the purchase order with Cox on December 27, 1985. Defendant stated the agreement with Cox was for the same model combine he was negotiating for with plaintiff but at a lower price. He wanted to consummate the transaction by December 31, 1985, in order to take advantage of the investment tax credit.

Defendant wrote a letter to plaintiff that was dated December 26, 1985, but sent on December 27, 1985. That letter read as follows:

> Dec. 26, '85
>
> Dear Sirs:
>
> As I told you by phone on Dec. 26, '85, I do not wish to purchase the 1985 N–5 combine we talked about so please send me the uncashed counter check on the Bank of Bluffs for the amount of $5,200. Since my "Purchase Order Sheet" had not yet been signed by the dealer rep, the check wasn't cashed before notification, & the combine wasn't picked up, the [inconvenience] should have been slight.
>
> Feel free to consult my attorney, John D. Coonrod, for details. Again, excuse these changes of events.
>
> Sincerely,
>
> Carl W. Krusa
>
> (FOR "K" FARMS)

Defendant testified that Jim Beard visited defendant at his farm around lunchtime on December 27, 1985. During this visit, Jim told defendant, "There's no problem, Carl, just please send a check to Tony Thomas for his time explaining the differences between models and options." Defendant recalled that their conversation was friendly and that Jim told him something to the effect that, "Carl, we maybe lost a little bit of commission on this, but don't worry about it. I'll make it up on the next sales." Defendant signed the contract with Cox later that afternoon.

Defendant testified that when he spoke with Hess on the evening of December 26, Hess did not indicate that he had signed the order that had been signed earlier by defendant. Defendant testified that in his letter to plaintiff, he enclosed a check for $100 made payable to Thomas for Thomas' time. Defendant believed that once this sum was paid, he was released from any obligation to plaintiff seller.

Jim Beard testified that in fall 1985, he approached defendant several times about purchasing a new combine. Jim testified that he again spoke with defendant about purchasing a new combine at plaintiff's Arenzville office at 3:30 or 4 p.m. on December 23, 1985. Gerry Beard was also present. Jim stated that he did not have the authority to sell the combine at a given price; only Gerry and Hess had that authority. The price quoted by Gerry to defendant was $52,800 and the trade-in of defendant's existing combine. Jim identified the purchase order bearing defendant's signature. Jim filled in all the other information on that order.

Jim testified that defendant did not make any statements that he was going to consider the purchase further after signing the purchase order. Jim also stated that defendant did not make any statements to the effect that the purchase order was not to be considered a completed contract.

Jim identified the counter check payable to plaintiff for $5,200. He stated that he filled out the check and defendant signed it, but that he forgot to fill in the date on the check. Jim did not recall any statement made by defendant that the check should be held. Jim recalled that the purchase order and check were signed at approximately 5:30 p.m. He stated that defendant was not threatened or told that he could not leave the office until he signed the order. Jim stated that he would not have signed the order if defendant had said anything about reserving the right to call back later and cancel the deal.

Jim next spoke with defendant on December 27, 1985. Hess told Jim that defendant did not want to buy the combine and asked Jim to visit defendant. Jim met with defendant that same day and asked defendant why he could not buy the combine. Defendant told him that he could not afford it. Jim stated that defendant did not mention that he had purchased a combine from someone else.

On cross-examination, Jim admitted that he did not sign the purchase order which defendant had signed. He testified that Gerry and Hess are authorized to accept offers on behalf of plaintiff, but that neither one signed the order.

Gerry Beard testified that defendant came to plaintiff's office in the afternoon of December 23. Gerry stated that he attempted to persuade defendant to purchase a new combine. Gerry testified that he offered to sell the new combine to defendant for $52,800 and that defendant replied, "I'll take the deal." Defendant then signed the order and counter check and left plaintiff's offices.

Gerry stated that he is authorized to accept contracts on behalf of plaintiff. He testified that he accepted the contract with defendant. Gerry stated that defendant did not indicate, after signing the counter check and purchase order, that the trans-action was not a completed deal.

On appeal, defendant argues that the trial court erred in finding that a contract existed between him and plaintiff for the purchase of a combine. Defendant argues plaintiff never accepted defendant's offer to purchase the combine because the pur-chase order defendant signed required a signature by a "dealer" on behalf of plaintiff for acceptance and none of plaintiff's representatives ever signed that or-der. Accordingly, defendant's subsequent refusal to "go through with the deal" constituted a valid revocation of his offer.

Plaintiff argues that a contract existed between the parties even before their agreement was reduced to writing. Essentially, plaintiff contends that after the ver-bal agreement was reached, the terms of that agreement were memorialized on the purchase order, which was then signed by defendant. Further, plaintiff argues that this verbal agreement was evidenced by a counter check, which was also signed by defendant and which represented a down payment on the combine. Plaintiff asserts that it accepted both the purchase order and the down payment by placing those documents in its office.

In deciding whether the offer in the present case has been accepted, this court must first identify both the offeror and the offer. A treatise on contract law provides some guidance on this issue: "A problem arises when A, through a salesman, has frequently solicited orders from B, the contract to arise when approved by A at A's home office. As we have seen in this situation, B is the offeror and A the offeree." J. Calamari & J. Perillo, Contracts § 2–18 (3d ed. 1987).

In *Foremost Pro Color. v. Eastman Kodak* the court considered whether a contract existed based on two unsigned purchase orders. The district court had concluded that no contract existed because the purchase orders were merely offers to buy, in-viting acceptance either by a prompt promise to ship or by prompt or current shipment. The court of appeals agreed and stated that the weight of authority sug-gests that purchase orders are not enforceable contracts until accepted by the offeree.

In the instant case, the purchase order form signed by defendant constitutes an offer made by defendant to plaintiff. Thus, this court needs to determine whether defendant's offer was accepted by plaintiff.

Section 2–206 of the Uniform Commercial Code—Sales (Code) states the fol-lowing:

(1) Unless otherwise unambiguously indicated by the language or circumstances

   (a) an offer to make a contract shall be construed as inviting acceptance in any manner and by any medium reasonable in the circumstances;

(b) an order or other offer to buy goods for prompt or current shipment shall be construed as inviting acceptance either by a prompt promise to ship or by the prompt or current shipment of conforming or non-conforming goods, but such a shipment of non-conforming goods does not constitute an acceptance if the seller seasonably notifies the buyer that the shipment is offered only as an accommodation to the buyer.

(2) Where the beginning of a requested performance is a reasonable mode of acceptance an offeror who is not notified of acceptance within a reasonable time may treat the offer as having lapsed before acceptance.

For the purposes of the present case, the key word in this statute is the term "unambiguously." If defendant's offer contained on the purchase order is unambiguous in inviting acceptance only by the signature of plaintiff's "dealer," no contract exists until the purchase order is signed accordingly. If, however, defendant's offer is ambiguous in inviting plaintiff's acceptance, a contract between plaintiff and defendant could be found to exist.

On appeal, defendant has cited several cases supporting the argument that the purchase order he signed unambiguously invites acceptance only by signature of plaintiff's "dealer." One such case is *Brophy v. City of Joliet* (Ill. App. 1957) which involved the sale of revenue bonds. In that case, the court stated that where an offer requires an acceptance to be made in writing, no other form of acceptance can be made. The offer in *Brophy* read as follows:

> The signed acceptance of this proposal shall constitute a contract between the undersigned and the city * * *. * * *
>
> [] Accepted for and on behalf of * * *, which is hereby acknowledged by the duly, qualified officials.
>
> [] _____
>
> Mayor
>
> [] _____
>
> City Clerk

In *La Salle National Bank v. Vega* the court dealt with a real estate sales document which was signed by the seller as offeror and clearly stated that a contract would be in full force upon execution by the purchasing trust. The court held that the document did not constitute a valid contract in the absence of acceptance by the written execution of the purchasing trust. The court noted that an offeror has complete control over his offer and its terms of acceptance, and no other mode may be used where a written acceptance is required.

In *Zinni v. Royal Lincoln–Mercury, Inc.*, the court wrote the following:

> Although the modes of a valid acceptance may be varied, the requirement of an acceptance by the offeror still exists. * * * Where an order form, containing

the buyer's offer, requires the acceptance of the seller, no contract will exist until the seller has manifested acceptance of the offer. The record before us contains no manifestation of the defendant's acceptance of the plaintiff's offer. Although the order form contains a space for the defendant's signature, defendant did not sign it. While we believe defendant's acceptance may be manifested in ways other than its signature, plaintiff's complaint fails to allege an alternative manifestation of defendant's acceptance. Absent an acceptance by the defendant, no contract existed between the parties.

In *Southwestern Stationery & Bank Supply, Inc. v. Harris Corp.*, the court held that the seller's purchase order, which provided that the order was "'subject to acceptance by Seller'" and that "'Seller shall mail to Purchaser a signed duplicate copy hereof, and the same shall constitute the entire contract between the parties,'" unambiguously specified the proper method of acceptance. Therefore, in absence of a written acceptance by the seller, there was no contract for the sale of a printing press. The face of that purchase order stated the following:

This order is hereby accepted and dated at Seller's Cleveland, Ohio, Office on

_____

HARRIS CORPORATION, a Delaware Corporation Sheet Fed Press Division, Seller

By _____

A case most like the present one is *Antonucci v. Stevens Dodge, Inc.* where the Civil Court of the City of New York wrote:

When the offeror extends a promise and asks for a promise in return, and where the offeree accepts the offer by making the requested promise, the agreement is called a bilateral contract. Where the agreement takes the form of a written instrument, the acceptance is effective only when the document has been signed and delivered, unless it was clearly the intention of the parties that the earlier verbal agreement be binding and that the writing act merely as a memorandum or better evidence of the oral contract.

The printed form agreement before the Court was drafted by the defendant and contains the following clause: "This order cancels and supersedes any prior agreement and as of the date hereof comprises the entire agreement relating to the subject matters covered hereby * * *." It is clear that the defendant, the offeree, intended that this form agreement be deemed to be the entire contract and any verbal agreements, if contrary to the terms of the written agreement, not be binding.

In the bottom lefthand corner of the agreement there is printed in large underlined type: "* * * THIS ORDER SHALL NOT BECOME BINDING UNTIL ACCEPTED BY DEALER OR HIS AUTHORIZED REPRESENTATIVE." * * * At the bottom of the paragraph containing this sentence is a blank

[handwritten annotation:] → that says this is different than P's form — no explicit requirement

line under which is printed "purchaser's signature." Plaintiff signed on this line. Below this is a blank line which has printed before it "Accepted By." Under this line is printed "Dealer or his Authorized Representative." This line bears no signature.

On the back of the agreement are printed ten conditions. * * * Paragraph 10 states: "This order is subject to acceptance by the dealer, which acceptance shall be signified by the signature of Dealer, Dealer's Manager or other authorized signature on the reverse side hereof."

It is obvious that the parties intended the agreement to be bilateral and that the offer by the plaintiff to purchase the pickup be deemed accepted by the defendant only when he or his authorized representative signed the order.

The presenting of the order by the dealer was an invitation to the plaintiff to make an offer to purchase the pickup truck. The signing of the order by the plaintiff constituted an offer by him to purchase the truck. By the printed terms of the agreement only the signature of the defendant or its authorized representatives would constitute acceptance of the plaintiff's offer and thus create a binding bilateral contract. In a bilateral contract it is essential that the fact of acceptance be communicated to the offeror. The failure of the defendant or his representative to sign the order is conclusive proof that the defendant did not accept the offer. It was the defendant who drafted the agreement and set forth the manner in which it would accept an offer. The fact that defendant ordered and accepted delivery of a pickup truck does not constitute acceptance under the terms of the agreement. By the terms of the agreement only the signature of the defendant could constitute acceptance. The plaintiff's refusal to accept the truck constituted a valid revocation of his offer. As a general rule, an offer may be revoked or withdrawn at any time before it is accepted with certain exceptions set forth in the Uniform Commercial Code. This case does not fall within any of the code exceptions.

The Court finds by a fair preponderance of the credible evidence that an enforceable bilateral contract was not formed because of defendant's failure to accept plaintiff's offer and that plaintiff validly revoked his offer.

Plaintiff counters defendant's argument by contending that plaintiff was the one to offer the combine to defendant and defendant accepted plaintiff's offer by signing a counter check and giving that check to plaintiff as a down payment on the combine. We are unpersuaded.

We construe section 2–206 of the Code as giving approval to an ancient and cardinal rule of the law of contracts: the offeror is the master of his offer. An offeror may prescribe as many conditions or terms of the method of acceptance as he may wish, including, but not limited to, the time, place, and manner. We also note that contracts are generally construed against the party who drafted the document (*see* Restatement (Second) of Contracts § 206) and that plaintiff drafted the purchase order in the present case, and then gave it to defendant to use for his offer to purchase the combine.

Based on the foregoing, we conclude that the purchase order in this case "unambiguously" required the signature by plaintiff's "dealer" in order to be a proper acceptance of defendant's offer. Because plaintiff's "dealer" never signed the purchase order, no contract ever existed.

For the reasons stated, the judgment in favor of plaintiff is reversed.

Crt doesn't like result = Δ is screwed

↳ M jury had found for P

↳ This is rare area in contracts where
Technicalities prevail

↳ we don't want to interpret someone into a contract

APPENDIX

EXHIBIT A

ALLIS-CHALMERS

FARM EQUIPMENT   ▼▼ VERSATILE
DEALER'S RETAIL PURCHASE ORDER

DATE _12 - 23_ 19_25_

PURCHASER		DEALER	
NAME _Carl Kxxxxx_		NAME _Beard Implement Co._	
ADDRESS STREET OR ROUTE		ADDRESS	
CITY _Bluff_ STATE _Ill_ ZIP		CITY IS _Arenzville,_ STATE _Ill._ ZIP	
COUNTY	PHONE _754-2225_	ORDER NUMBER	
		DELIVER ON OR ABOUT	

I (we), the undersigned, hereby order from you the Equipment described below, to be delivered as shown above. This order is subject to your ability to obtain such Equipment from the manufacturer and you shall be under no liability if delivery of the Equipment is delayed or prevented due to labor disturbances, transportation difficulties, or for any reason beyond your control.

USED MACHINERY, IF ANY, INCLUDED IN THIS ORDER MUST BE CLEARLY INDICATED AS USED

QTY	CATALOG NO.	EQUIPMENT	SERIAL NO.	AMOUNT
1		N5 Combine		
		Feed House Reverse		
		air-Bam Screen		
		Engine Block Heater		
		3" Rasher		
		H.D. Final Drive		
		Tailing Tail 2-3-4		
		Cent. Reel Speed		
		Wipers		
		Chains		
		Perforated Heads		
		Cloth Seat		
		Cab Light		
		Dual Lamps		
		20' Series VII		
		Header		
		Auto Height Control		
		30.5 x 32		
		Gauge 10' Perkarier		
		Rasp 6-30		
		Cam bird		
		AM-FM Tape		
		Radio		
		He Metric Engine + Machine		

NOTE: COMPLETE THIS SECTION WHEN NEW FARM TRACTORS ARE SOLD WITHOUT ROPS (ROLL-OVER PROTECTION). ROLL-OVER PROTECTION (CAB OR ROLL BAR) REFUSED BY PURCHASER.

SIGNATURE OF PURCHASER _____

PRICE OF MACHINERY	$
FREIGHT HANDLING	$
TOTAL CASH PURCHASE PRICE	$
TRADE-IN ALLOWANCE	$
TRADE DIFFERENCE	$52,800.00
TAX (TOTAL OR TRADE DIFFERENCE)	$
TOTAL AMOUNT DUE	$
CASH WITH ORDER	$
CASH ON DELIVERY	$
BALANCE DUE	$

PRICE OF MACHINERY | $

Check One

☐ SOLD USED AS-IS. No warranty of any kind has been given by the dealer or his agent.
☐ SOLD USED WITH 50-50 WARRANTY. The dealer hereby guarantees this (these) machine(s) for _____ hours after 19___ with the understanding that necessary repairs made within this period of time will be charged half to the buyer and half to the dealer, of total retail cost of parts and labor used.
☐ Other _____ (specify warranty used)

SPECIAL AGREEMENTS _____

BILL OF SALE FOR PROPERTY TAKEN IN TRADE

For value received I/We hereby bargain and sell, grant and deliver to DEALER named above the following listed machines and certify that such is free of encumbrance unless otherwise noted.

	Serial No.	Amount
N5 Combine		
6-30		
20' Grain Table		

ALL WARRANTY REPAIRS MADE UNDER THIS AGREEMENT must be made in dealer's shop and buyer is responsible for hauling equipment for repair. No warranty is given by the dealer for tires, batteries or accessories, and the buyer is fully responsible for repairs necessitated by accident, misuse or negligence. This guarantee is not transferable.

I hereby agree to the conditions of this order, expressed in the foregoing, constituting a purchase order contract. I hereby certify that I am 21 years of age or older and acknowledge receipt of this order.

_____
DEALER'S SALESMAN

This order subject to acceptance by dealer.

Accepted by: _____
                    DEALER

Carl W. Kxxxx
_____
(PURCHASER'S SIGNATURE)

QUESTIONS AND NOTES

1. Was a writing necessary to form a contract in this case? See the UCC § 2–201. Even if § 2–201 does require a writing as a predicate to contract enforcement, isn't it possible to have an oral contract subject to a later written confirmation under the UCC? Note that the Statute of Frauds requires only that the party to be charged sign the writing. Why is the plaintiff dealer required to sign the purchase order in this case? It is its form, and presumably it filled in all the blanks. Shouldn't the defendant buyer's signature suffice?

2. How can the UCC at once treat the Hills' failure to return the computer as a valid acceptance of the unsigned, unread, and unknown arbitration clause, but not Beard Implement's conduct in accepting Mr. Krusa's $5,200 check as a deposit against a fully negotiated purchase order?

3. What is all this business about the customer being liable for the salesman's time if the customer decides not to buy? What happened to the check Krusa gave the salesman here? If Beard accepted it, was it an accord and satisfaction barring this suit?

4. The court in this opinion recounts the testimony extensively, mentioning many details of each side's version of what happened. Do the two versions differ materially? Do the differences matter for the court's analysis of the case?

A.   THE MIRROR IMAGE RULE

If acceptance binds the offeror by delivering to him the requested exchange, what if the terms of the acceptance purport to vary the offer in some way? In the real world, commercial agreements are not the product of discrete and distinctly defined offers and acceptances, but more often emerge in the course of an ongoing relationship made up of an open-ended number of communications between the parties.

United States v. Braunstein
United States District Court, S.D. New York, 1947.
75 F.Supp. 137.

■ MEDINA, D.J. The United States has brought suit for breach of a contract whereby defendants, it is said, agreed to buy from it 9599 twenty-five pound boxes of raisins unfit for human consumption which could be converted into alcohol. The parties have stipulated that an interchange of telegrams, hereinafter referred to, constitutes the contract, if there was one, that furnishes the foundation for the suit. Defendant Sidney Braunstein asserts this interchange of telegrams did not create a contract, and moves for summary judgment.

On July 21, 1945 the Commodity Credit Corporation, an instrumentality of the United States, issued Announcement AWS–11 which invited bids for the purchase of the off-condition raisins in question and laid down requirements to which all bids must conform. Thus, all bids were required to state that they were subject to the terms and conditions of that announcement and to designate what bonded distillery the raisins would be shipped to, should the bidder be successful. The announcement also required that the raisins be paid for by check within ten days from the date of the telegram accepting the bid.

The interchange of telegrams began on August 3, 1945, when the defendant Pearl Distilling Co. sent the following telegram to David Ludlum of the Washington office of the Commodity Credit Corporation:

> David Ludlum, Contracting and Adjustment Div. Sales Branch Office of Supply US Dep of Agriculture.
>
> Offer ten cents per pound for 9599 boxes of raisins located Cleveland Ohio
>
> Pearl Distilling Co.

This telegram lacked the required reference to Announcement AWS–11 and did not designate the distillery for shipment. On receiving the telegram, David Ludlum telegraphed the Pearl Distilling Co. referring to Announcement AWS–11 and asking for shipping information. Pearl Distilling Co. supplied this information by a telegram of August 7, 1945 and inquired about shipping costs.

The Commodity Credit Corporation's telegram of August 9, 1945 is the crux of this whole interchange. It reads:

> Pearl Distilling Company
> 377–91 East 163rd Street
> New York, New York
>
> Subject terms announcement AWS 11 CCC accepts your August 3 offer to purchase and August 7 wire giving shipping instructions for 9599 boxes raisins at 10 cents per box plus freight and 3 per cent tax from Cleveland, Ohio to New Brunswick, New Jersey, at 45 cents per cwt.
>
> Forward certified check in the amount of $2,138.92. Contract AW–S(F) 31752
>
> Commodity Credit Corporation David S. Ludlum

Pearl Distilling Co. had offered ten cents a pound. The telegram of August 9th specified a price of ten cents a box. The total price of $2,138.92 appears to have been calculated on the basis of ten cents a box, although the method of calculation is not entirely clear. Since a box contained twenty-five pounds, the price was off by something like twenty-three thousand dollars. It was the Commodity Credit Corporation's intention to accept the offer of ten cents a pound, but one of its employees had made a mistake in preparing the telegram of August 9th and in calculating the price.

When the defendants received this telegram, they did nothing and no check was sent to the Commodity Credit Corporation. Ten days later, when the time for receipt of the check had expired, the Commodity Credit Corporation looked into the matter, discovered its error, and sent this telegram:

> Aug 20 PM 4:28
> Pearl Distilling Co
> 377–91 East 163 St
>
>   Reourtel August 9 contract AW–S (F)–31752 covering sale of raisins should read at 10 cents per pound instead of 10 cents per box also certified check should be in the amount of $25,176.52 instead of $2,138.92 Please confirm
>
> David S. Ludlum
> Commodity Credit Corporation

Again the defendants did nothing, and so matters stood for two months. The raisins, of course, had not been shipped to the defendants. Then, on October 19, 1945, the Commodity Credit Corporation notified the defendants that if they failed to pay for the raisins by October 25, the raisins would be sold and the defendants held for any loss. The defendants did not pay, the raisins were sold at a loss, and the United States brought suit for breach of contract.

There is a contract if the telegram of August 9 was an acceptance of the offer of August 3. If there can be an issue of fact as to whether that telegram of August 9 was an acceptance, this motion for summary judgment must be denied. To put it another way, does the mistaken substitution of "ten cents per box" for "ten cents per pound" coupled with a calculation of the total price based on the wrong figure defeat, as a matter of law, what was intended as an acceptance?

The basic principles of law involved here are simple. To create a contract, an acceptance must be "unequivocal," Restatement, Contracts § 58 (1932), "positive and unambiguous," 1 Williston, Contracts § 72 Rev.Ed.1936, and "must comply exactly with the requirements of the offer." Restatement, Contracts § 59 (1932). A reply to an offer that fails to comply with these requirements is a rejection.

Certainly no reasonable man could say that on its face the telegram of August 9 met these requirements. The mention of a price foreign to the negotiation renders the effect of the telegram uncertain and ambiguous. Furthermore, the mere use of the word "accept" does not automatically make a communication an acceptance.

The government, however, insists that the defendants knew perfectly well what the telegram of August 9 meant; that, in spite of a clerical error, it was an acceptance; for no reasonable man could think that the government was in effect rejecting an offer of ten cents a pound and making what amounted to a counter-offer of ten cents for a twenty-five pound box. The argument comes to this: that a reasonable man would disregard the error and see behind to the intention that, but for a surface obscurity, was perfectly clear.

There is limited merit to this contention. The law would not allow the defendants to treat the telegram of August 9 as a counter-offer which their acceptance could turn into a contract seriously disadvantageous to the government, since there was obviously something dubious about it. "An offeree may not snap up an offer that is on its face too good to be true." 1 Williston, Contracts § 94, Rev.Ed.1936. It is a justifiable conclusion that the defendants did not think the telegram was a counter-offer, but that they knew the Commodity Credit Corporation's intention varied from what the words of the telegram expressed. This conclusion, however, does not help the government. "If either party knows that the other does not intend what his words or other acts express, this knowledge prevents such words or other acts from being operative as an offer or acceptance." Restatement, Contracts § 71(c) (1932).

The government next urges that the court may interpret the telegrams in the interest of justice so as to make a contract out of them, citing 3 Williston, Contracts §§ 603, 605, 616, 618–620, 628, 629, Rev.Ed.1936. There it is shown that courts have disregarded clerical errors or particular words, and have supplied and interposed words in their attempt to give writings a construction which would not render them void or meaningless. This court is urged to interpret the telegram of August 9 into an acceptance on the basis of such authority.

It is true that there is much room for interpretation once the parties are inside the framework of a contract, but it seems that there is less in the field of offer and acceptance. Greater precision of expression may be required, and less help from the court given, when the parties are merely at the threshold of a contract. If a court should undertake to resolve ambiguities in the negotiations between parties, disregard clerical errors, and rearrange words, leaving out some and putting in others, it is hard to see where the line of demarcation could be drawn and the general effect would inevitably be a condition of chaos and uncertainty.

But the courts have refrained from reforming offers and acceptances. Thus, in the classic case of *Harvey v. Facey*, [1893] A.C. 552 (P.C.), it would have taken but little interpretation to construe as an offer the defendant's telegram, "Lowest price for Bumper Hall Pen £900," which was a reply to plaintiff's telegram, "Will you sell us Bumper Hall Pen? Telegraph lowest cash price." But the Judicial Committee of the Privy Council ruled otherwise.

In 1 Williston, Contracts § 72, Rev.Ed.1936, are cited several examples of communications held to be insufficient as acceptances. They too would have needed but slight interpretation to come up to the legal standard, but again the courts were reluctant to interpret parties into a contractual status. Indeed, this very reluctance may have been one of the causes for the development of the doctrine of quasi-contract. And it seems significant that the fictions indulged in that branch of the law were made only in instances of clearly defined unjust enrichment. There is nothing of that kind here.

It may be rigorous to disregard a purported acceptance because of a clerical error, but if there is any fault, it lies with the Commodity Credit Corporation. "Since one who speaks or writes, can, by exactness of expression, more easily prevent mistakes in meaning, than one with whom he is dealing, doubts arising from ambiguity of language are resolved against the former in favor of the latter." Restatement, Contracts § 236, comment *d* (1932).

A decision for defendants will not interfere with commercial dealings by requiring formality in offer and acceptance. It will merely mean that if a purported acceptance repeats the terms of the offer, the acceptor takes the risk of his own clerical error in repetition.

The government made a point in passing, without pressing it, that the telegram of August 3 in which the Commodity Credit Corporation asked the defendants for shipping instructions was itself an acceptance, since only the successful bidder would be asked for these instructions. This telegram, however, was insufficiently unequivocal to be an acceptance.

At the request of the government, and to avoid any possible misconception of the attendant facts and circumstances, an opportunity was afforded for the filing of supplemental affidavits, which were finally forthcoming. They add nothing of any relevance to the sole issue of offer and acceptance, which by the stipulation of the parties depends upon the telegrams above referred to.

Motion granted. Complaint dismissed.

QUESTIONS AND NOTES

1. In the fall of 1945 commodity prices were subject to wartime price controls, and the wholesale price ceiling on several varieties of *edible* raisins in 25–pound boxes was as low as 8 cents per pound. Does this perhaps explain why the government clerk made his mistake? Did Braunstein make the original mistake by promising too high a price for inedible raisins? Or was Braunstein's only mistake not anticipating the imminent end of World War II?

2. If the government's telegram was not a rejection, a counteroffer, or an acceptance, what was it?

3. The government appealed the above decision. The Second Circuit dismissed its appeal. Although the dismissal was based on the jurisdictional technicality that the judgment appealed from was not final since it did not dispose of all claims against all of the defendants, Judge Augustus Hand closed his opinion with these words:

> We may add, though it is by way of dictum since the appeal is not properly before us, that the district judge's disposition of the merits as between the plaintiff and Braunstein seems to us correct and we should have disposed of the case on his opinion had we not felt it necessary to raise the question of the finality of the judgment for purposes of appeal.

4. Suppose the government had refused to deliver and Braunstein sued the government. Would the court have found a contract, and, if so, what would be its terms? Would the result in such a suit depend on whether Braunstein tendered the government the contract price? How much would he have to tender?

5. Suppose the error in this case wasn't over the price term, but rather that one telegram provided that arbitration was to occur within ten days of any dispute, while the reply telegram provided that arbitration was to occur within ten months of any dispute. Still no contract?

6. At some point wasn't Braunstein bound to reply to the government or be bound to the government's revised price term in its August 20 telegram by his silence?

Recall: *Stare v. Tate*, p. 438.

B. THE UCC AND THE BATTLE OF THE FORMS

UNIFORM COMMERCIAL CODE:

§ 2–207. Additional Terms in Acceptance or Confirmation.

(1) A definite and seasonable expression of acceptance or a written confirmation which is sent within a reasonable time operates as an acceptance even though it states terms additional to or different from those offered or agreed upon, unless acceptance is expressly made conditional on assent to the additional or different terms.

(2) The additional terms are to be construed as proposals for addition to the contract. Between merchants such terms become part of the contract unless:

(a) the offer expressly limits acceptance to the terms of the offer;

(b) they materially alter it; or

(c) notification of objection to them has already been given or is given within a reasonable time after notice of them is received.

(3) Conduct by both parties which recognizes the existence of a contract is sufficient to establish a contract for sale although the writings of the parties do not otherwise establish a contract. In such case the terms of the particular contract consist of those terms on which the writings of the parties agree, together with any supplementary terms incorporated under any other provisions of this Act.

Section 2–207 has three distinct subparts that serve somewhat different functions. Subsection 1 deals with the problem discussed in *Braunstein*, whether the terms of an acceptance must perfectly match the offer in order to create a contract. This subsection takes the position that generally an acceptance is operative even if it states different or additional terms. Subsection 2 tries to deal with the content of a contract formed by offer and acceptance that do not match. Between non-merchants additional terms become proposals for modification of the contract, but between merchants they become part of the contract unless there is some objection by the other side or they materially alter the contract. Subsection 3 provides that even if the writings exchanged by the parties do not establish a contract, one may be found from their conduct, if they behaved as if a contract existed. In such a case, the content of the contract is the terms on which the parties' writings agree plus the general rules provided by the UCC.

Certain textual anomalies in § 2–207 compound the confusion arising from its complex structure. Subsection 1 talks about "additional or different" terms, while Subsection 2 talks only about "additional terms." Is this a slip of the pen, or does it suggest a substantive difference? Most (but not all) courts considering this have concluded that Subsection 2 applies to both additional and different terms. As the following case indicates, the most vexing question is what kinds of additional or different terms *materially* alter the contract. Most of the cases that have arisen involve a few situation types. The two most common are clauses that limit warranty liability for defective products and those that limit or provide special remedies, such as limitations of consequential damages or an arbitration clause. Consider the treatment of this issue in the CISG, which does not go as far as § 2–207(1) in finding a contract on the basis of nonmatching documents so long as the parties agree in fact, but provides clearer guidance on what provisions materially alter the deal.

2-207(2) essentially changes last shot rule to first shot rule

2-207 (3) = contract occurs when parties perform
↳ conduct alone

UN CONVENTION ON CONTRACTS FOR THE INTERNATIONAL SALE OF GOODS:

Article 19

(1) A reply to an offer which purports to be an acceptance but contains additions, limitations or other modifications is a rejection of the offer and constitutes a counter-offer.

(2) However, a reply to an offer which purports to be an acceptance but contains additional or different terms which do not materially alter the terms of the offer constitutes an acceptance, unless the offeror, without undue delay, objects orally to the discrepancy or dispatches a notice to that effect. If he does not so object, the terms of the contract are the terms of the offer with the modifications contained in the acceptance.

(3) Additional or different terms relating, among other things, to the price, payment, quality and quantity of the goods, place and time of delivery, extent of one party's liability to the other and or the settlement of disputes are considered to alter the terms of the offer materially.

UNIDROIT PRINCIPLES OF INTERNATIONAL COMMERCIAL CONTRACTS (2004):

Article 2.1.11
(Modified acceptance)

(1) A reply to an offer which purports to be an acceptance but contains additions, limitations or other modifications is a rejection of the offer and constitutes a counter-offer.

(2) However, a reply to an offer which purports to be an acceptance but contains additional or different terms which do not materially alter the terms of the offer constitutes an acceptance, unless the offeror, without undue delay, objects to the discrepancy. If the offeror does not object, the terms of the contract are the terms of the offer with the modifications contained in the acceptance.

Article 2.1.12
(Writings in confirmation)

If a writing which is sent within a reasonable time after the conclusion of the contract and which purports to be a confirmation of the contract contains additional or different terms, such terms become part of the contract, unless they materially alter the contract or the recipient, without undue delay, objects to the discrepancy.

When there's discrepancy, fill in will - gap rules

Article 2.1.20
(Surprising terms)

(1) No term contained in standard terms which is of such a character that the other party could not reasonably have expected it, is effective unless it has been expressly accepted by that party.

(2) In determining whether a term is of such a character regard is to be had to its content, language and presentation.

Article 2.1.22
(Battle of forms)

Where both parties use standard terms and reach agreement except on those terms, a contract is concluded on the basis of the agreed terms and of any standard terms which are common in substance unless one party clearly indicates in advance, or later and without undue delay informs the other party, that it does not intend to be bound by such a contract.

Northrop Corp. v. Litronic Industries

United States Court of Appeals, Seventh Circuit, 1994.
29 F.3d 1173.

■ POSNER, C.J.

"Battle of the forms" refers to the not uncommon situation in which one business firm makes an offer in the form of a preprinted form contract and the offeree responds with its own form contract. At common law, any discrepancy between the forms would prevent the offeree's response from operating as an acceptance. So there would be no contract in such a case. This was the "mirror image" rule, which Article 2 of the Uniform Commercial Code jettisoned by providing that "a definite and seasonable expression of acceptance or a written confirmation which is sent within a reasonable time operates as an acceptance even though it states terms additional to or different from those offered or agreed upon, unless acceptance is made conditional on assent to the additional or different terms." UCC § 2-207(1). Mischief lurks in the words "additional to or different from." The next subsection of 2-207 provides that if additional terms in the acceptance are not materially different from those in the offer, then, subject to certain other qualifications (*id.* at 1335-37), they become part of the contract, § 2-207(2), while if the additional terms are materially different they operate as proposals and so have no effect unless the offeror agrees to them, UCC § 2-207, comment 3; if the offeror does not agree to them, therefore, the terms of the contract are those in the offer. A clause providing for interest at normal rates on overdue invoices, or limiting the right to reject goods because of defects falling within customary trade tolerances for acceptance with adjustment, would be the sort of additional term that is not deemed material, and hence it would become a part of the contract even if the offeror never signified acceptance of it. *Id.,* comment 5.

The Code does not explain, however, what happens if the offeree's response contains *different* terms (rather than additional ones) within the meaning of section 2-207(1). There is no consensus on that question. See James J. White & Robert S. Summers, *Uniform Commercial Code* 33-36 (3d ed. 1988); John E. Murray, Jr., "The Chaos of the 'Battle of the Forms': Solutions," 39 *Vand.L.Rev.* 1307, 1354-65 (1986). We know there is a contract because an acceptance is effective even though it contains different terms; but what are the terms of the contract that is brought into being by the offer and acceptance? One view is that the discrepant terms in both the nonidentical offer and the acceptance drop out, and default terms found elsewhere in the Code fill the resulting gap. Another view is that the offeree's discrepant terms drop out and the offeror's become part of the contract. A third view, possibly the most sensible, equates "different" with "additional" and makes the outcome turn on whether the new terms in the acceptance are materially different from the terms in the offer in which event they operate as proposals, so that the offeror's terms prevail unless he agrees to the variant terms in the acceptance or not materially different from the terms in the offer, in which event they become part of the contract. John L. Utz, "More on the Battle of the Forms: The Treatment of 'Different' Terms Under the Uniform Commercial Code," 16 *U.C.C.L.J.* 103 (1983). This interpretation equating "different" to "additional," bolstered by drafting history which shows that the omission of "or different" from section 2-207(2) was a drafting error, substitutes a manageable inquiry into materiality, for a hair-splitting inquiry into the difference between "different" and "additional." It is hair-splitting ("metaphysical," "casuistic," "semantic," in the pejorative senses of these words) because all different terms are additional and all additional terms are different.

Unfortunately, the Illinois courts whose understanding of Article 2 of the UCC is binding on us because this is a diversity suit governed, all agree, by Illinois law have had no occasion to choose among the different positions on the consequences of an acceptance that contains "different" terms from the offer. We shall have to choose.

The battle of the forms in this case takes the form of something very like a badminton game, but we can simplify it a bit without distorting the issues. The players are Northrop, the giant defense firm, and Litronic, which manufactures electronic components, including "printed wire boards" that are incorporated into defense weapon systems. In 1987 Northrop sent several manufacturers, including Litronic, a request to submit offers to sell Northrop a customized printed wire board designated by Northrop as a "1714 Board." The request stated that any purchase would be made by means of a purchase order that would set forth terms and conditions that would override any inconsistent terms in the offer. In response, Litronic mailed an offer to sell Northrop four boards for $19,000 apiece, to be delivered within six weeks. The offer contained a 90-day warranty stated to be in lieu of any other warranties, and provided that the terms of the offer would take precedence over any terms proposed by the buyer. Lynch, a purchasing officer of Northrop, responded to the offer in a phone conversation in which he told Litronic's man, Lair, that he was accepting the offer up to the limit of his authority, which was $24,999, and that a formal purchase order for all four boards would follow. Litronic was familiar with Northrop's purchase order form, having previously done business with Northrop, which had been using the same form for some time. Had Lair referred to any of the previous orders, he would have discovered that Northrop's order form provided for a warranty that contained no time limit.

Lynch followed up the phone conversation a month later with a "turn on" letter, authorizing Litronic to begin production of all four boards (it had done so already) and repeating that a purchase order would follow. The record is unclear when the actual purchase order was mailed; it may have been as much as four months after the phone conversation and three months after the turn-on letter. The purchase order required the seller to send a written acknowledgment to Northrop. Litronic never did so, however, and Northrop did not complain; it does not bother to follow up on its requirement of a signed acknowledgment.

Although Litronic had begun manufacturing the boards immediately after the telephone call from Lynch, for reasons that are unknown but that Northrop does not contend are culpable Litronic did not deliver the first three boards until more than a year later, in July of 1988. Northrop tested the boards for conformity to its specifications. The testing was protracted, either because the boards were highly complex or because Northrop's inspectors were busy, or perhaps for both reasons. At all events it was not until December and January, five or six months after delivery, that Northrop returned the three boards (the fourth had not been delivered), claiming that they were defective. Litronic refused to accept the return of the boards, on the ground that its 90-day warranty had lapsed. Northrop's position of course is that it had an unlimited warranty, as stated in the purchase order.

As an original matter one might suppose that this dispute is not over the terms of the warranty but over whether Northrop waited more than the "reasonable time" that the Uniform Commercial Code allows the buyer of nonconforming goods to reject them. UCC § 2-602(1). That in fact is how the magistrate judge framed the issue, as we shall see. But the parties continue to treat it as a "warranty" case. Their implicit view is that Litronic's 90-day warranty, if a term of the contract, not only barred Northrop from complaining about defects that showed up more than 90 days after the delivery of the boards but also limited to 90 days the time within which Northrop was permitted to reject the boards because of defects that rendered them nonconforming. We accept this view for purposes of deciding these appeals. ...

Litronic's appeal concerns the breach of its warranty on the No. 1714 boards. It wins if the warranty really did expire after only 90 days. The parties agree that Litronic's offer to sell the No. 1714 boards to Northrop, the offer made in response to Northrop's request for bids, was the offer. So far, so good. If Northrop's Mr. Lynch accepted the offer over the phone, the parties had a contract then and there, but the question would still be on what terms. Regarding the first question, whether there was a contract, we may assume to begin with that the acceptance was sufficiently "definite" to satisfy the requirement of definiteness in section 2-207(1); after all, it impelled Litronic to begin production immediately, and there is no suggestion that it acted precipitately in doing so. We do not know whether Lynch in his conversation with Lair made acceptance of the complete contract expressly conditional on approval by Lynch's superiors at Northrop. We know that he had authority to contract only up to $24,999, but we do not know whether he told Lair what the exact limitation on his authority was or whether Litronic knew it without being told. It does not matter. The condition, if it was a condition, was satisfied and so drops out.

We do not think that Northrop's acceptance, via Lynch, of Litronic's offer could be thought conditional on Litronic's yielding to Northrop's demand for an open-ended warranty. For while Lynch's reference to the purchase order might have alerted Litronic to Northrop's desire for a warranty not limited to 90 days, Lynch did not purport to make the more extensive warranty a condition of acceptance. So the condition, if there was one, was not an express condition, as the cases insist it be.

There was a contract, therefore; further, and, as we shall note, decisive, evidence being that the parties acted as if they had a contract—the boards were shipped and paid for. The question is then what the terms of the warranty in the contract were. Lynch's reference in the phone conversation to the forthcoming purchase order shows that Northrop's acceptance contained different terms from the offer, namely the discrepant terms in the purchase order, in particular the warranty—for it is plain that the Northrop warranty was intended to be indefinite in length, so that, at least in the absence of some industry custom setting a limit on warranties that do not specify a duration (cf. UCC § 2-207, comments 4 and 5), a point not raised, any limitation on the length of the warranty in the offer would be a materially different term. Of course the fact that Northrop preferred a longer warranty than Litronic was offering does not by itself establish that Northrop's acceptance contained different terms. But Lynch did not accept Litronic's offer and leave it at that. He said that he would issue a Northrop purchase order, and both he and Lair knew (or at least should have known) that the Northrop purchase order form contained a different warranty from Litronic's sale order form. And we have already said that Lynch did not, by his oral reference to the purchase order, condition Northrop's purchase on Litronic's agreeing to comply with all the terms in the purchase order form, given the courts' insistence that any such condition be explicit. (Judges are skeptical that even businesspeople read boilerplate, so they are reluctant, rightly or wrongly, to make a contract fail on the basis of a printed condition in a form contract.) But Lynch said enough to make clear to Lair that the acceptance contained different terms from the offer.

The Uniform Commercial Code, as we have said, does not say what the terms of the contract are if the offer and acceptance contain different terms, as distinct from cases in which the acceptance merely contains additional terms to those in the offer. The majority view is that the discrepant terms fall out and are replaced by a suitable UCC gap-filler. The magistrate judge followed this approach and proceeded to section 2-309, which provides that nonconforming goods may be rejected within a "reasonable" time (see also § 2-601(1)), and she held that the six months that Northrop took to reject Litronic's boards was a reasonable time because of the complexity of the required testing. The leading minority view is that the discrepant terms *in the acceptance* are to be ignored, and that would give the palm to Litronic. Our own preferred view—the view that assimilates "different" to "additional," so that the terms in the offer prevail over the different terms in the acceptance only if the latter are materially different, has as yet been adopted by only one state, California. Under that view, as under what we are calling the "leading" minority view, the warranty in Litronic's offer, the 90-day warranty, was the contractual warranty, because the unlimited warranty contained in Northrop's acceptance was materially different.

Because Illinois in other UCC cases has tended to adopt majority rules, and because the interest in the uniform nationwide application of the Code—an interest asserted in the Code itself (see § [1-103])—argues for nudging majority views, even if imperfect (but not downright bad), toward unanimity, we start with a presumption that Illinois, whose position we are trying to predict, would adopt the majority view. We do not find the presumption rebutted. The idea behind the majority view is that the presence of different terms in the acceptance suggests that the offeree didn't *really* accede to the offeror's terms, yet both parties wanted to contract, so why not find a neutral term to govern the dispute that has arisen between them? Of course the offeree may not have had any serious objection to the terms in the offer at the time of contracting; he may have mailed a boilerplated form without giving any thought to its contents or to its suitability for the particular contract in question. But it is just as likely that the discrepant terms *in the offer* itself were the product of a thoughtless use of a boilerplate form rather than a considered condition of contracting. And if the offeror doesn't want to do business other than on the terms in the offer, he can protect himself by specifying that the offeree must accept all those terms for the parties to have a contract. UCC § 2-207(2)(a). Now as it happens Litronic did state in its offer that the terms in the offer "take precedence over terms and conditions of the buyer, unless specifically negotiated otherwise." But, for reasons that we do not and need not fathom, Litronic does not argue that this language conditioned the existence of the contract on Northrop's acceding to the 90-day warranty in the offer; any such argument is therefore waived.

It is true that the offeree likewise can protect himself by making his acceptance of the offer conditional on the offeror's acceding to any different terms in the acceptance. But so many acceptances are made over the phone by relatively junior employees, as in this case, that it may be unrealistic to expect offerees to protect themselves in this way. The offeror goes first and therefore has a little more time for careful specification of the terms on which he is willing to make a contract. What we are calling the leading minority view may tempt the offeror to spring a surprise on the offeree, hoping the latter won't read the fine print. Under the majority view, if the offeree tries to spring a surprise (the offeror can't, since his terms won't prevail if the acceptance contains different terms), the parties move to neutral ground; and the offeror can, we have suggested, more easily protect himself against being surprised than the offeree can protect *himself* against being surprised. The California rule dissolves all these problems, but has too little support to make it a plausible candidate for Illinois, or at least a plausible candidate for our guess as to Illinois's position.

There is a further wrinkle, however. The third subsection of section 2-207 provides that even if no contract is established under either of the first two subsections, it may be established by the "conduct of the parties," and in that event (as subsection (3) expressly provides) the discrepant terms vanish and are replaced by UCC gap fillers. This may seem to make it impossible for the offeror to protect himself from being contractually bound by specifying that the acceptance must mirror his offer. But subsection (3) comes into play only when the parties have by their conduct manifested the existence of a contract, as where the offeror, having specified that the acceptance must mirror the offer yet having received an acceptance that deviates from the offer, nonetheless goes ahead and performs as if there were a contract. That is one way to interpret what happened here but it leads to the same result as applying subsection (2) interpreted as the majority of states do, so we need not consider it separately.

[handwritten margin notes: 2-207(3) / looks like minority view]

Given the intricacy of the No. 1714 boards, it is unlikely that Northrop would have acceded to a 90-day limitation on its warranty protection. Litronic at argument stressed that it is a much smaller firm, hence presumably unwilling to assume burdensome warranty obligations; but it is a curious suggestion that little fellows are more likely than big ones to get their way in negotiations between firms of disparate size. And Northrop actually got only half its way, though enough for victory here; for by virtue of accepting Litronic's offer without expressly conditioning its acceptance on Litronic's acceding to Northrop's terms, Northrop got not a warranty unlimited in duration, as its purchase order provides, but (pursuant to the majority understanding of UCC § 2-207(2)) a warranty of "reasonable" duration, courtesy the court. If special circumstances made a 90-day warranty reasonable, Litronic was free to argue for it in the district court.

On the view we take, the purchase order has no significance beyond showing that Northrop's acceptance contained (albeit by reference) different terms. The fact that Litronic never signed the order, and the fact that Northrop never called this omission to Litronic's attention, also drop out of the case, along with Northrop's argument that to enforce the 90-day limitation in Litronic's warranty would be unconscionable. But for future reference we remind Northrop and companies like it that the defense of unconscionability was not invented to protect multi-billion dollar corporations against mistakes committed by their employees, and indeed has rarely succeeded outside the area of consumer contracts.

AFFIRMED.

■ RIPPLE, J., concurring. [Omitted].

QUESTIONS AND NOTES

1. Can you reconcile this case with *Hill v. Gateway*, p. 664, also a Seventh Circuit decision? Gateway (which had never done business with the Hills before) was entitled to (i) not mention arbitration when it took the order over the phone, (ii) stick its arbitration clause in the boilerplate terms enclosed with the shipment, and (iii) hold the Hills to those unbargained-for terms based on the Hills' retention of the goods. Litronic, on the other hand, can't enforce its limited warranty term despite (i) sending a form to Northrop Corporation in advance of the telephone call on which Northrop committed to buy the No. 1714 boards, (ii) a provision in the Litronic form that the terms of the offer (presumably including the limited warranty) would take precedence over any terms proposed by the buyer, and (iii) Northrop's retention of the goods. Why is Northrop Corporation being protected against unbargained-for terms buried in boilerplate forms but not the Hills? How does that result square with Chief Judge Posner's pointed reminder to Northrop "that the defense of unconscionability was not invented to protect multi-billion dollar corporations against mistakes committed by their employees"? And if the problem is the

imposition of unbargained for terms contained in unread forms, why does it matter whether there are multiple conflicting forms?

2. Isn't the lesson of this case simply that you must get your counterparty to sign your form if you want to enforce your unbargained-for boilerplate terms against him? Isn't that obvious? But, then again, why should a signature on a form that no one reads and no one is expected to read matter? Consider this passage from Lord Devlin's opinion in *McCutcheon v. David MacBrayne Ltd.*, 1 W.L.R. 125, 132-33 (H.L. 1964):

> My Lords, when a person in the Isle of Islay wishes to send goods to the mainland he goes into the office of MacBrayne (the respondents) in Port Askaig which is conveniently combined with the local post office. There he is presented with a document headed "conditions" containing three or four thousand words of small print divided into 27 paragraphs.... If it were possible for your Lordships to escape from the world of make-believe which the law has created into the real world in which transactions of this sort are actually done, the answer would be short and simple. It should make no difference whatever [whether the document was signed]. This sort of document is not meant to be read, still less to be understood. Its signature is in truth about as significant as a handshake that marks the formal conclusion of a bargain.

C.   REFORM EFFORTS AND THE FUTURE OF 2-207

Most scholarly and judicial observers would agree that the original § 2–207 is both a great advance in the law and, at the same time, unacceptably flawed. Its great value is that it makes clear that communications do not have to match perfectly to result in a contract. It is flawed in subsection (2), which fails to clearly delineate those terms that will be incorporated and those that will not. The following sections were a small part of the proposed revisions of Article 2 adopted by the American Law Institute and the Commissioners on Uniform State Laws in 2003 but later, in the face of substantial opposition in the state legislatures, withdrawn.

WITHDRAWN REVISIONS TO UNIFORM COMMERCIAL CODE:

§ 2–206. Offer and Acceptance in Formation of Contract.

(1) Unless otherwise unambiguously indicated by the language or circumstances:

(a) An offer to make a contract must be construed as inviting acceptance in any manner and by any medium reasonable under the circumstances.

(b) An order or other offer to buy goods for prompt or current shipment must be construed as inviting acceptance either by a prompt promise to ship or by the prompt or current shipment of conforming goods or non-conforming goods, but the shipment of nonconforming goods is not an acceptance if the seller seasonably notifies the buyer that the shipment is offered only as an accommodation to the buyer.

(2) If the beginning of a requested performance is a reasonable mode of acceptance, an offeror that is not notified of acceptance within a reasonable time may treat the offer as having lapsed before acceptance.

(3) A definite and seasonable expression of acceptance in a record operates as an acceptance even if it contains terms additional to or different from the offer.

§ 2–207. Terms of Contract; Effect of Confirmation.

Subject to § 2-202,

if (i) conduct by both parties recognizes the existence of a contract although their records do not otherwise establish a contract, (ii) a contract is formed by an offer and acceptance, or (iii) a contract formed in any manner is confirmed by a record that contains terms additional to or different from those in the contract being confirmed, the terms of the contract are:

(a) terms that appear in the records of both parties;

(b) terms, whether in a record or not, to which both parties agree; and

(c) terms supplied or incorporated under any provision of this Act.

QUESTIONS AND NOTES

1. How do the various existing views of § 2-207 discussed in *Northrop Corp. v. Litronic Indus.*, p. 688, differ from the unenacted 2003 version of the UCC reprinted above?

2. The Battle of the Forms has been a darling of legal education for two generations now, but modern contracting habits may render it of historical interest only. Written forms rarely cross nowadays. Given the pervasiveness of web-based contracting, orders do not generally become accepted until someone (generally the party with less bargaining power) clicks on an "I Accept" button on his counterparty's website or purchasing software, and thereby in some theoretical sense "manifests assent" to all the boilerplate terms and conditions that neither party has read or thought about. This is as true in commercial purchasing as it is in consumer transactions. In a paper world it was possible to just not sign the other guy's form

and confirm the transaction on your own form; not so, with the ubiquitous "I Accept" button if you want to actually complete the transaction. And once you click aren't both parties bound to whatever those terms are? Sending a later form would simply be a proposal for modification that if ignored by the counterparty would fall out of the analysis. In these circumstances, the Battle of the Forms collapses into the *Hill v. Gateway*, p. 664 problem, leaving one party, generally the more vulnerable one, exposed to un-bargained-for, one-sided and unfair terms. The answer of course, as suggested in the 2003 proposed revision of 2-206 and 2-207 is to police un-bargained-for terms, rejecting those that do not conform to both parties' reasonable expectations and replacing them with neutral standard terms drawn from the common law or Article 2. This in fact is the solution that most courts have groped towards notwithstanding the textual difficulties under existing 2-207. But the 2003 proposed revision which expressly adopted this solution was itself roundly rejected by the state legislatures, leaving only the (quite limited) unconscionability doctrine as a mechanism for policing unfair terms in the absence of applicable consumer protection legislation. Ironically, new technology and changed contracting habits leave businesses previously able to avoid assenting to unfair boilerplate terms in the past under 2-207 increasingly stuck with those terms, outside the scope of existing consumer protections, and generally in a poor position given their status as merchants to assert an unconscionability defense notwithstanding imbalances in bargaining power and substantive unfairness. For a thoughtful introduction to these issues see Francis J. Mootz III, *After the Battle of the Forms: Commercial Contracting in the Electronic Age*, 4 J.L. & POL'Y INFO. SOC'Y 271 (2008).

VI. BARGAINING OVER DISTANCE

Adams v. Lindsell

King's Bench, 1818.
1 Barn. & Ald. 681.

Action for non-delivery of wool according to agreement. At the trial at the last Lent assizes for the county of Worcester, before Burrough, J., it appeared that the defendants, who were dealers in wool, at St. Ives, in the county of Huntingdon, had, on Tuesday September 2d, 1817, written the following letter to the plaintiffs, who were woolen manufacturers residing in Bromsgrove, Worcestershire: "We now offer you eight hundred tods of wether fleeces, of a good fair quality of our country wool, at 35s. 6d. per tod, to be delivered at Leicester, and to be paid for by two months' bill in two months, and to be weighed up by your agent within fourteen days, receiving your answer in course of post."

This letter was misdirected by the defendants, to Bromsgrove, Leicestershire, in consequence of which it was not received by the plaintiffs in Worcestershire till 7 p.m. on Friday, September 5th. On that evening the plaintiffs wrote an answer, agreeing to accept the wool on the terms proposed. The course of the post between St. Ives and Bromsgrove is through London, and consequently this answer was not received by the defendants till Tuesday, September 9th. On the Monday September 8th, the defendants not having, as they expected, received an answer on Sunday September 7th, (which in case their letter had not been misdirected, would have been in the usual course of the post), sold the wool in question to another person. Under these circumstances, the learned judge held, that the delay having been occasioned by the neglect of the defendants, the jury must take it, that the answer did come back in due course of post; and that then the defendants were liable for the loss that had been sustained: and the plaintiffs accordingly recovered a verdict.

Jervis having in Easter Term obtained a rule *nisi* for a new trial, on the ground that there was no binding contract between the parties.

Dauncey, Puller & Richardson shewed cause. They contended, that at the moment of the acceptance of the offer of the defendants by the plaintiffs, the former became bound. And that was on the Friday evening, when there had been no change of circumstances. They were then stopped by the Court, who called upon

Jervis & Campbell in support of the rule. They relied on *Payne v. Cave*, and more particularly on *Cooke v. Oxley*. In that case, Oxley, who had proposed to sell goods to Cooke, and given him a certain time at his request, to determine whether he would buy them or not was held not liable to the performance of the contract, even though Cooke, within the specified time, had determined to buy them, and given Oxley notice to that effect. So here the defendants who had proposed by letter to sell this wool, are not to be held liable, even though it be now admitted that the answer did come back in due course of post. Till the plaintiff's answer was actually received, there could be no binding contract between the parties; and before then the defendants had retracted their offer by selling the wool to other persons. But

THE COURT said that if that were so, no contract could ever be completed by the post. For if the defendants were not bound by their offer when accepted by the plaintiffs till the answer was received, then the plaintiffs ought not to be bound till after they had received the notification that the defendants had received their answer and assented to it. And so it might go on *ad infinitum*. The defendants must be considered in law as making, during every instant of the time their letter was traveling, the same identical offer to the plaintiffs; and then the contract is completed by the acceptance of it by the latter. Then as to the delay in notifying the acceptance, that arises entirely from the mistake of the defendants, and it therefore must be taken as against them, that the plaintiffs' answer was received in course of post.

Rule discharged.

NOTE ON MAILBOX RULE: A COMPARATIVE PERSPECTIVE

The rule that an acceptance is effective when the offeree sends it off to the offeror has several curious aspects that deserve comment. First, it applies only to acceptances. The Restatement, Second, Contracts reflects the case law and the statutes that deal with these matters in some states when it provides that rejections, counteroffers, and the exercise of an option are all effective when received, rather than when transmitted.

Moreover, the "mailbox rule" making acceptances effective when sent applies only in the common law nations. In the rest of the world, acceptances are effective when received. Indeed, now that the CISG is the law of the United States, the following rules apply here to international sale of goods transactions involving nationals of other ratifying states:

UN CONVENTION ON CONTRACTS FOR THE INTERNATIONAL SALE OF GOODS:

Article 18

(1) A statement made by or other conduct of the offeree indicating assent to an offer is an acceptance. Silence or inactivity does not in itself amount to acceptance.

(2) An acceptance of an offer becomes effective at the moment the indication of assent reaches the offeror. An acceptance is not effective if the indication of assent does not reach the offeror within the time he has fixed or, if no time is fixed, within a reasonable time, due account being taken of the circumstances of the transaction, including the rapidity of the means of communication employed by the offeror. An oral offer must be accepted immediately unless the circumstances indicate otherwise.

(3) However, if, by virtue of the offer or as a result of the practices which the parties have established between themselves or of usage, the offeree may indicate assent by performing an act, such as one relating to the dispatch of the goods or payment of the price, without notice to the offeror, the acceptance is effective at the moment the act is performed, provided that the act is performed within the period of time laid down in the preceding paragraph.

Article 22

An acceptance may be withdrawn if the withdrawal reaches the offeror before or at the same time as the acceptance would have become effective.

Article 23

A contract is concluded at the moment when an acceptance of an offer becomes effective in accordance with the provisions of this Convention.

Article 24

For the purposes of this Part of the Convention, an offer, declaration of acceptance or any other indication of intention "reaches" the addressee when it is made orally to him or delivered by any other means to him personally, or to his place of business or mailing address or, if he does not have a place of business or mailing address, to his habitual residence.

UNIDROIT PRINCIPLES OF INTERNATIONAL COMMERCIAL CONTRACTS (2004):

Article 2.1.6

(Mode of acceptance)

(1) A statement made by or other conduct of the offeree indicating assent to an offer is an acceptance. Silence or inactivity does not in itself amount to acceptance.

(2) An acceptance of an offer becomes effective when the indication of assent reaches the offeror.

(3) However, if, by virtue of the offer or as a result of practices which the parties have established between themselves or of usage, the offeree may indicate assent by performing an act without notice to the offeror, the acceptance is effective when the act is performed.

Article 2.1.10

(Withdrawal of acceptance)

An acceptance may be withdrawn if the withdrawal reaches the offeror before or at the same time as the acceptance would have become effective.

QUESTION

In light of modern electronic communications, does it make any difference anymore (other than on law school examinations) whether acceptances are binding upon dispatch or receipt? Would you ever rely on the mailbox rule rather than transmit your acceptance electronically if you had any concern that the offer might be withdrawn?

VII. PRE-CONTRACTUAL LIABILITY

One situation in which it is justifiable to treat propositions that appear quite final as preliminary negotiations rather than operative offers is when the parties explicitly contemplate a final formal writing as their agreement. Then all that precedes the final formal writing can be considered talk. Yet sometimes the parties contemplate being bound by their agreement before it is reduced to a final formal writing. The formal writing is contemplated merely as a memorial or memorandum recording an agreement that the parties have already reached. In such a case, it is the talk that precedes the writing that is of primary importance. We have seen how the law, through the parol evidence rule and other devices, has sought to reduce the significance of oral negotiations when there is a final and complete written contract. But what happens if the final written agreement is never reached? Do the oral agreement and such preliminary writings as may exist constitute a contract? As has already been noted, this tension between the views that the agreement is the contract and that the writing is the contract is persistent and reappears throughout the law of contracts.

K.N. LLEWELLYN, ON OUR CASE-LAW OF CONTRACT: OFFER AND ACCEPTANCE, 48 YALE L.J. 1, 13–14 (1938):

Most so-called rules do indicate at least something about what facts they apply to, *or* something about some legal consequence; and, mostly, *something* of both. But what needs note is that until even the most precise of expressions about legal consequences is guided to the facts which may emerge, the supposed rule can acquire no meaning *in life* (as distinct from, say, a meaning in logic.)

Take, for instance, in the Offer and Acceptance field, the two current formulations on when, pending execution of an intended writing, the expressions of agreement do, and when they do not, constitute offer and acceptance. The Restatement, [Second, Contracts § 27], says, in effect, that either may be the case. This is true. Comment (a) says that it is very reasonable that sometimes one should be the case, sometimes the other. This is also true. Comment (b) says that you can also phrase the issue as one between a mere memorial and the exclusive operative consummation. And this is true. Comment (c) says that even a memorial may operate to change an agreement reached without it. True no less. But further, deponent Restatement saith not. Result: the opinion can write (and often does) in precisely the same language for any case on the problem, no matter which way the case comes out, and almost no guidance is given by "the settled rule" as to what to fill in on the one blank space: "In our opinion this case falls clearly within the * * * branch of the rule." Yet there is, and has been, good and shrewd judicial discussion of useful criteria to use—persuasive, too, I suggest, to any court to which it might be quoted—*because it helps.*

The following is the good and shrewd judicial discussion to which Professor Llewellyn refers:

■ EMERY, J., in *Mississippi and Dominion Steamship Co. v. Swift*, 86 Me. 248, 258 (1894):

[I]t is quite clear that, after all, the question is mainly one of intention. If the party sought to be charged intended to close a contract prior to the formal signing of a written draft, or if he signified such an intention to the other party, he will be bound by the contract actually made, though the signing of the written draft be omitted. If on the other hand, such party neither had nor signified such an intention to close the contract until it was fully expressed in a written instrument and attested by signatures, then he will not be bound until the signatures are affixed. The expression of the idea may be attempted in other words: if the written draft is viewed by the parties merely as a convenient memorial, or record of their previous contract, its absence does not affect the binding force of the contract; if, however, it is viewed as the consummation of the negotiation, there is no contract until the written draft is finally signed.

In determining which view is entertained in any particular case, several circumstances may be helpful, as: [1] whether the contract is of that class which are usually found to be in writing; [2] whether it is of such nature as to need a formal writing for its full expression; [3] whether it has few or many details; [4] whether the amount involved is large or small; [5] whether it is a common or unusual contract; [6] whether the negotiations themselves indicate that a written draft is contemplated as the final conclusion of the negotiations. If a written draft is proposed, suggested or referred to, during the negotiations, it is some evidence that the parties intended it to be the final closing of the contract.

Still, with the aid of all rules and suggestions, the solution of the question is often difficult, doubtful and sometimes unsatisfactory.

Empro Mfg. Co. v. Ball-Co. Mfg.

United States Court of Appeals, Seventh Circuit, 1989.
870 F.2d 423.

■ EASTERBROOK, J. We have a pattern common in commercial life. Two firms reach concord on the general terms of their transaction. They sign a document, captioned "agreement in principle" or "letter of intent," memorializing these terms but anticipating further negotiations and decisions—an appraisal of the assets, the clearing of a title, the list is endless. One of these terms proves divisive, and the deal collapses. The party that perceives itself the loser then claims that the preliminary document has legal force independent of the definitive contract. Ours is such a dispute.

Ball-Co Manufacturing, a maker of specialty valve components, floated its assets on the market. Empro Manufacturing showed interest. After some preliminary negotiations, Empro sent Ball-Co a three-page "letter of intent" to purchase the assets of Ball-Co and S.B. Leasing, a partnership holding title to the land under Ball-Co's plant. Empro proposed a price of $2.4 million, with $650,000 to be paid on closing and a 10-year promissory note for the remainder, the note to be secured by the "inventory and equipment of Ballco." The letter stated "[t]he general terms and conditions of such proposal (which will be subject to and incorporated in a formal, definitive Asset Purchase Agreement signed by both parties)." Just in case Ball-Co might suppose that Empro had committed itself to buy the assets, paragraph four of the letter stated that "Empro's purchase shall be subject to the satisfaction of certain conditions precedent to closing including, but not limited to" the definitive Asset Purchase Agreement and, among five other conditions, "[t]he approval of the shareholders and board of directors of Empro."

Although Empro left itself escape hatches, as things turned out Ball-Co was the one who balked. The parties signed the letter of intent in November 1987 and negotiated through March 1988 about many terms. Security for the note proved to be the sticking point. Ball-Co wanted a security interest in the land under the plant; Empro refused to yield.

When Empro learned that Ball-Co was negotiating with someone else, it filed this diversity suit. Contending that the letter of intent obliges Ball-Co to sell only to it, Empro asked for a temporary restraining order. The district judge set the case for a prompt hearing and, after getting a look at the letter of intent, dismissed the complaint under Fed.R.Civ.P. 12(b)(6) for failure to state a claim on which relief may be granted. Relying on *Interway, Inc. v. Alagna* (Ill. App.1980), the district judge concluded that the statement, appearing twice in the letter, that the agreement is "subject to" the execution of a definitive contract meant that the letter has no independent force.

Empro insists on appeal that the binding effect of a document depends on the parties' intent, which means that the case may not be dismissed—for Empro says that the parties intended to be bound, a factual issue. Empro treats "intent to be bound" as a matter of the parties' states of mind, but if intent were wholly subjective there would be no parol evidence rule, no contract case could be decided without a jury trial, and no one could know the effect of a commercial transaction until years after the documents were inked. That would be a devastating blow to business. Contract law gives effect to the parties' wishes, but they must express these openly. Put differently, "intent" in contract law is objective rather than subjective—a point *Interway* makes by holding that as a matter of law parties who make their pact "subject to" a later definitive agreement have manifested an (objective) intent not to be bound, which under the parol evidence rule becomes the definitive intent even if one party later says that the true intent was different. As the Supreme Court of Illinois said in *Schek v. Chicago Transit Authority* (1969), "intent must be determined solely from the language used when no ambiguity in its terms exists." Parties may decide for themselves whether the results of preliminary negotiations bind them, but they do this through their words.

Because letters of intent are written without the care that will be lavished on the definitive agreement, it may be a bit much to put dispositive weight on "subject to" in every case, and we do not read *Interway* as giving these the status of magic words. They might have been used carelessly, and if the full agreement showed that the formal contract was to be nothing but a memorial of an agreement already reached, the letter of intent would be enforceable. Conversely, Empro cannot claim comfort from the fact that the letter of intent does not contain a flat disclaimer, such as the one in *Feldman* pronouncing that the letter creates no obligations at all. The text and structure of the letter—the objective manifestations of intent—might show that the parties agreed to bind themselves to some extent immediately. *Borg-Warner* is such a case. One party issued an option, which called itself "firm and binding"; the other party accepted; the court found this a binding contract even though some terms remained open. After all, an option to purchase is nothing if not binding in advance of the definitive contract. The parties to *Borg-Warner* conceded that the option and acceptance usually would bind; the only argument in the case concerned whether the open terms were so important that a contract could not arise even if the parties wished to be bound, a subject that divided the court.

A canvass of the terms of the letter Empro sent does not assist it, however. "Subject to" a definitive agreement appears twice. The letter also recites, twice, that it contains the "general terms and conditions", implying that each side retained the right to make (and stand on) additional demands. Empro insulated itself from binding effect by listing, among the conditions to which the deal was "subject", the "approval of the shareholders and board of directors of Empro." The board could veto a deal negotiated by the firm's agents for a reason such as the belief that Ball–Co had been offered too much (otherwise the officers, not the board, would be the firm's final decisionmakers, yet state law vests major decisions in the board). The shareholders could decline to give their assent for any reason (such as distrust of new business ventures) and could not even be required to look at the documents, let alone consider the merits of the deal. Empro even took care to require the return of its $5,000 in earnest money "without set off, in the event this transaction is not closed," although the seller usually gets to keep the earnest money if the buyer changes its mind. So Empro made clear that it was free to walk.

Neither the text nor the structure of the letter suggests that it was to be a one-sided commitment, an option in Empro's favor binding only Ball–Co. From the beginning Ball–Co assumed that it could negotiate terms in addition to, or different from, those in the letter of intent. The cover letter from Ball–Co's lawyer returning the signed letter of intent to Empro stated that the "terms and conditions are generally acceptable" but that "some clarifications are needed in Paragraph 3(c) (last sentence)," the provision concerning Ball–Co's security interest. "Some clarifications are needed" is an ominous noise in a negotiation, foreboding many a stalemate. Although we do not know what "clarifications" counsel had in mind, the specifics are not important. It is enough that even on signing the letter of intent Ball–Co proposed to change the bargain, conduct consistent with the purport of the letter's text and structure.

The shoals that wrecked this deal are common hazards in business negotiations. Letters of intent and agreements in principle often, and here, do no more than set the stage for negotiations on details. Sometimes the details can be ironed out; sometimes they can't. Illinois, as *Chicago Investment*, *Interway*, and *Feldman* show, allows parties to approach agreement in stages, without fear that by reaching a preliminary understanding they have bargained away their privilege to disagree on the specifics. Approaching agreement by stages is a valuable method of doing business. So long as Illinois preserves the availability of this device, a federal court in a diversity case must send the disappointed party home empty-handed. Empro claims that it is entitled at least to recover its "reliance expenditures," but the only expenditures it has identified are those normally associated with pre-contractual efforts: its complaint mentions the expenses "in negotiating with defendants, in investigating and reviewing defendants' business, and in preparing to acquire defendants' business." Outlays of this sort cannot bind the other side any more than paying an expert to tell you whether the painting at the auction is a genuine Rembrandt compels the auctioneer to accept your bid.

Affirmed.

QUESTIONS AND NOTES

1. Is Empro arguing that it has an agreement to buy Ball–Co's assets and therefore is entitled to expectancy damages for Ball–Co's refusal to deliver? Or is it arguing that it has an agreement with Ball–Co to negotiate in good faith for the sale of assets, and Ball–Co should be prevented from negotiating with others in breach of its obligations to Empro? Although the parties may not be bound by a "definitive Asset Purchase Agreement," do they have a distinct subsidiary agreement to work together in good faith to finalize such an agreement? While that effort is going on, may Ball–Co open negotiations with others? If the parties intended to establish an exclusive negotiation period by the letter of intent why isn't that specifically provided for in the preliminary writing?

2. What specific "reliance expenditures" might Empro be seeking in this case?

3. Judge Easterbrook rejects the possibility that "paying an expert to tell you whether the painting at the auction is a genuine Rembrandt compels the auctioneer to accept your bid." Fair enough, but if, by representing that it will sell the painting on a given date, the auction house induces potential buyers to spend many thousands of dollars on experts to examine the painting and test its genuineness, might the auctioneer incur some good faith obligations? For example, if, after inducing all those reliance expenditures, the auctioneer refuses without cause to recognize the bidder or excludes a bidder from the auction unjustifiably, might there not be some liability for the reliance losses suffered?

Arcadian Phosphates v. Arcadian Corp.

United States Court of Appeals, Second Circuit, 1989.
884 F.2d 69.

■ OAKES, C.J. This appeal is from a judgment in a diversity suit involving claims for breach of contract and promissory estoppel. The claims are based on a memorandum which described the sale of a fertilizer company's phosphate fertilizer business to a joint venture. The appellants—the potential purchasers, consisting of the joint venture and two individuals involved in its formation—claim that the memorandum was a binding contract. The appellee—the potential seller, the fertilizer company—argues that the memorandum was an unenforceable "agreement to agree." We affirm on appellants' breach of contract claims. Because summary judgment was, however, inappropriate on appellants' promissory estoppel claim, we reverse and remand for further consideration of that claim.

I. FACTS

Appellee Arcadian Corporation ("Arcadian") is a New York corporation that manufactures and sells fertilizer. Appellant Arcadian Phosphates, Inc. ("API") is a Delaware corporation incorporated in 1986 by appellants Judas Azuelos and Eli Sivan as a vehicle for the purchase of Arcadian's phosphate fertilizer business. Azuelos, a citizen and resident of France, represents the Office Togolais Des Phosphates ("OTP"), the governmental entity in Togo that mines, markets, and exports phosphate rock. Sivan, a citizen of Israel and resident of the United Kingdom, was a businessman engaged in buying and selling Togolese phosphate rock on the world market, and is now the president, treasurer, and one of the directors of API.

In 1986, OTP became Arcadian's chief supplier of phosphate. At the same time Arcadian, allegedly motivated by a sharp drop in the price of fertilizer, began negotiating the sale of its phosphate fertilizer facility in Geismar, Louisiana to API. In June 1986, the parties signed a four-page memorandum of understanding outlining areas of agreement concerning the assets to be purchased, the purchase price, and an option for Arcadian to purchase up to 20% of API. The memorandum also set deadlines for further action, all subject to the approval of Arcadian's board and appellants' ability to obtain financing. After such board approval and appellants' successful but unconsummated search and after further negotiations, the parties signed a one-and-a-half page memorandum on November 6, 1986, that incorporated the June memorandum. It is this November 6 memorandum that appellants claim was a binding contract for the sale of Arcadian's phosphate fertilizer business.

The November 6 memorandum, together with the June memorandum that was incorporated by reference, was termed an "agreement" though subject to approval by the boards of both OTP and Arcadian. It specified the purchase price, the timing and amounts of the payments, the fixed assets to be purchased, and a closing date of not later than May 31, 1987. It also outlined a framework of negotiation for the purchase of Arcadian's finished product inventory at closing at a "mutually agreeable market value," with phosphate stores to be purchased at closing at Arcadian's book value. Other provisions were less definite: for example, the memorandum referred to part of the payment as "a note secured to Arcadian's satisfaction" and to additional equity participants in the proposed joint venture as "subject to mutual agreement." The November 6 memorandum provided that if negotiations for the sale failed, Arcadian would repay any capital expenditures agreed to thereafter and made by API, and if the negotiations failed through no fault of API, Arcadian would refund API's deposit. The November 6 memorandum also stated that "the service and supply agreement will be negotiated and agreed to by December 31, 1986" and "[a] binding sales agreement will be completed by December 31, 1986." Finally, both parties agreed to the memorandum "to cooperate fully and work judiciously in order to expedite the closing date and consummate the sale of the business."

By November 14, 1986, the Arcadian board unanimously approved what Arcadian's CEO then called the "proposed agreement"—though the CEO now says that the board only approved of his proceeding with negotiations. The November 6 memorandum was also approved by OTP. The parties then confirmed by Telex their respective approvals and took steps to consummate the transaction. According to the appellants, these included establishment of API offices at Arcadian headquarters; Arcadian's obtaining lenders' consents after informing them of the "agreed upon" sale with a "signed agreement"; introduction of Azuelos and Sivan to one supplier as "new owners"; and beginning the negotiation of supply contracts for API.

On November 26, API tendered a cash deposit of $687,500 as required. Arcadian executed an escrow agreement for the deposit, referring to the parties' "agreement" and pursuant to which the deposit was to be non-refundable except "because of force majeure or Sellers' default." The minutes of an Arcadian directors' meeting on December 11, 1986, reflect the deposit payment and say that "[f]inal negotiations are continuing to work out the necessary service and marketing agreements," with a closing date of the "venture" to be "no later than May 31, 1987."

On December 17, 1986, Arcadian agreed in writing that its option for 20% minority participation in API could be reduced by API to as low as 5% to enable API to secure financing. API also incurred, it is alleged, expenses of over $100,000 to install "fenders" at Arcadian docking facilities in Geismar, Louisiana, in order to permit the discharge of Togolese rock. API also obtained a bank commitment for the $7 million required for its cash payment toward the $13.75 million purchase price and allegedly entered into a long-term rock supply contract with OTP. According to appellants, Arcadian did not undertake to enter any 1987 supply contract, but merely extended its existing contract pending the closing. And in January 1987 Arcadian allegedly commissioned a survey which designated which portions of the land and buildings were to go to API and which to remain with Arcadian.

However, as the minutes of the Arcadian board meeting of February 26, 1987, reflect, the market for phosphates changed "dramatically" with market prices of diammonium phosphate, apparently the bellwether of the industry, going up 25% in four to five weeks, production levels increasing, and inventories being depleted. The same board minutes noted:

> [API] is pushing for an early closing and therefore is attempting to lock up financing as soon as possible. However, major issues and concerns still exist from Arcadian's point of view and need to be resolved. The major issues to be negotiated involve inventory

transfer, charges for SG & A expenses and insurance coverage. The concerns of Arcadian are the need for retention by Arcadian of majority ownership and control of [API] and the long-term affect [sic] on the nitrogen business. After extended discussion it was the consensus of the Board that Arcadian could not proceed with the joint venture as originally contemplated. In order to proceed with any potential joint venture of the phosphate business, it was the consensus of the Board that Arcadian must have majority ownership and management of the venture and the other open issues must be resolved to Arcadian's satisfaction.

When Arcadian informed API of its change of position—from agreeing to own 5% to 20% of the joint venture (at API's option) to wanting to own 50%–plus and returning the down payment—this suit ensued.

II. DISCUSSION

A. Breach of Contract

As appellants urge, we examine their breach of contract claims under a framework devised by Judge Leval in *Teachers Insurance & Annuity Association v. Tribune Co.*, 670 F.Supp. 491 (S.D.N.Y.1987). In *Tribune,* Judge Leval surveyed the doctrine on preliminary agreements, like the one in this case, noting that "[a] primary concern for courts in such disputes is to avoid trapping parties in surprise contractual obligations that they never intended." Therefore, the judge concluded, "[m]ore is needed than agreement on each detail [to create a binding obligation. There must be] overall agreement * * * to enter into the binding contract."

In *Tribune,* Judge Leval identified two types of preliminary agreements. In the first, the parties have reached complete agreement on all of the issues that require negotiation, but they have not yet completely formalized their agreement. In the second, the parties have committed themselves to some major terms, but some terms will remain to be negotiated—as is the case with the memorandum at issue here. "The parties can bind themselves to a concededly incomplete agreement," Judge Leval said of this second type, "in the sense that they accept a mutual commitment to negotiate together in good faith in an effort to reach final agreement within the scope that has been settled in the preliminary agreement."

To determine whether a preliminary manifestation of assent was a binding preliminary agreement of the second type, Judge Leval used a modified version of a test that this court devised for preliminary agreements that more closely resemble the first type. Judge Leval considered whether the intent to be bound was revealed by (1) the language of the agreement; (2) the context of the negotiations; (3) the existence of open terms; (4) partial performance; and (5) the necessity of putting the agreement in final form, as indicated by the customary form of such transactions. The first factor, the language of agreement, is the most important.

In applying the *Tribune* test to this case, we need look no further than the first factor. The language of the November memorandum—two references to the possibility that negotiations might fail and the reference to a binding sales agreement to be completed at some future date—shows that Arcadian did not intend to be bound.... In *Tribune,* a letter described itself as a "binding agreement," and in *Butler,* the parties agreed that their agreement was binding. This fact was critical to Judge Leval's reasoning in *Tribune:* "[A] party that does not wish to be bound," he said, "can very easily protect itself by not accepting language that indicates a 'firm commitment' or 'binding agreement.'" Conversely, a party that *wishes* to be bound can very easily protect itself by refusing to accept language that shows an intent *not* to be bound. In order to prevail on the breach of contract claims, Arcadian needed to show only that API "should have known that [Arcadian] did not intend to be bound before the [final] contract was signed." The language of the November memorandum reveals just that: API should not have believed that Arcadian intended to be bound.

As Judge Leval noted in *Tribune,* "There is a strong presumption against finding binding obligation in agreements which include open terms, call for future approvals and expressly anticipate future preparation and execution of contract documents." In *Tribune,* the language of the agreement argued persuasively for overcoming this presumption; here, the language of the agreement argues persuasively for letting the presumption stand.

Appellants argue that the question whether a contract exists is ill-suited for summary judgment. On the contrary: Where "a question of intention is determinable by written agreements, the question is one of the law, appropriately decided * * * on a motion for summary judgment." Since in this case intent can readily be determined by examining the November memorandum, summary judgment was perfectly appropriate even though there was considerable partial performance.

B. Promissory Estoppel

Summary judgment was not appropriate, however, on appellants' promissory estoppel claim. In New York, promissory estoppel has three elements: "a clear and unambiguous promise; a reasonable and foreseeable reliance by the party to whom the promise is made; and an injury sustained by the party asserting the estoppel by reason of his reliance." Prevailing on a promissory estoppel claim, however, sometimes entitles a party only to its out-of-pocket expenses, rather than to benefit-of-the-bargain damages.[2]

---

2. Out of pocket damages are particularly appropriate where, as may be the case here, the plaintiff cannot rationally calculate the benefit of the bargain. It is difficult to make this calculation rationally unless one can say that the defendant's failure to follow through on a promise is a but for cause of the loss of profits. Here, Arcadian's alleged failure to bargain in good faith is not a but

Appellants' promissory estoppel claim is based on evidence that Arcadian knew and approved of API's expenditures and collateral contracts, but Arcadian suddenly demanded a majority interest in API when the phosphate fertilizer business became "dramatically" profitable. When appellants rejected Arcadian's proposed modification of the latter's equity position, appellants say Arcadian called off negotiations—thereby violating its promise to bargain in good faith. Because appellants' allegations raise genuine issues of material fact as to whether Arcadian made a clear, unambiguous promise to negotiate in good faith, whether appellants reasonably and foreseeably relied on that promise in entering into expenditures and collateral contracts with suppliers or others, and whether appellants thereby sustained an injury, the district court erred in granting summary judgment on their promissory estoppel claim.[4]

We therefore affirm as to appellants' breach of contract claims, but reverse and remand as to their promissory estoppel claim.

QUESTIONS AND NOTES

1. This case was decided the same year as *Empro v. Ball–Co.* Are the results consistent?

2. Does it make sense to speak of the agreement in *Arcadian* as not binding when the court leaves open the possibility of reliance-based damages?

3. The court appears to be using the terminology "breach of contract" to describe API's claim to performance of the contract of sale and joint venture, and the term "promissory estoppel" to describe Arcadian's obligations to negotiate in good faith and API's claim for "out-of-pocket expenses." This appears to be a somewhat different usage of the term "promissory estoppel" than has been used in earlier cases in this Casebook. That is, usually promissory estoppel refers to promises made binding by unbargained-for action in reliance, in contrast to promises that become

---

for cause of API's lost profits, since even with the best faith on both sides the deal might not have been closed. Because attributing API's lost profits to Arcadian's bad faith may be speculative at best, the district court may decide that damages based on API's out of pocket costs are most appropriate.

4. The district court justified its decision by saying, "A claim for promissory estoppel under New York law must fall where the 'negotiations of the parties as reflected in the draft agreements made it clear that the obligations of both [were] contingent upon execution and delivery of formal contract documents.'" But the district court conflated Arcadian's substantive obligation with its obligation to bargain in good faith. Unlike Arcadian's substantive obligations, its obligation to bargain in good faith was obviously intended to begin immediately. The good faith obligation cannot, therefore, be said to be contingent upon formal contract documents.

binding because of consideration. In this case, if API is found to have relied on Arcadian's promises to negotiate a deal in good faith, wasn't that reliance bargained-for, that is, wasn't there an exchange of the promise for this action in reliance which Arcadian sought to induce API to take?

4. If API is successful at trial, what will its damages be? The court mentions out-of-pocket expenses. That probably will include the $100,000 to install fenders at the docking facility in Louisiana. Will its recovery also include API's costs of extricating itself from the arrangements it made with the bank? How about the lost opportunities to make deals with others that API gave up to invest its energies in negotiating with Arcadian?

St. Jude Medical v. Medtronic

Minnesota Court of Appeals, 1995.
536 N.W.2d 24.

■ HUSPENI, J. ...

This case arises out of the merger and acquisition of respondent Electromedics, Inc., a company which designs, manufactures, and markets medical equipment and disposable devices, focusing on blood therapy and surgical care. Both appellant St. Jude Medical, Inc., and respondent Medtronic, Inc., sought to acquire Electromedics.

Medtronic purchased 346,359 shares of Electromedics' stock between March and August 1993. In July 1993, Medtronic presented an unsolicited merger proposal of $5.50 per share; Electromedics rejected the offer outright, but realized that the company was on the market despite the fact that it had "not plan[ned] to be for sale."

Electromedics hired Dain Bosworth as its financial advisor to consider "strategic alternatives" for the company's future. Eighteen potential buyers surfaced. The Electromedics board of directors decided to auction off the company to secure the best price for the shareholders.

St. Jude hired Piper Jaffray Inc. as its financial advisor for the exclusive purpose of proposing the acquisition or merger with Electromedics. As of November 4, 1993, St. Jude was an active contender in the competition for merger. St. Jude expressed a strong interest in purchasing Electromedics under the condition that St. Jude would have an exclusive right to negotiate and would receive a termination fee, which would be $2-4 million, in the event negotiations fell through.

On November 12, Medtronic formally proposed a merger at $6.125 per share. The Electromedics board considered the offer inadequate, but did not give Medtronic an answer.

By December 6, Electromedics entered into a final agreement and merger plan with St. Jude. The exclusive agreement required Electromedics to refrain from marketing the sale of the company or contacting other "suitors." The agreement also included the following "termination fee" provision:

> In recognition of the efforts and expenses expended and incurred by [St. Jude] with respect to Electromedics and the opportunity Electromedics presents to [St. Jude], if (i) this Agreement is terminated * * *, Electromedics will pay to [St. Jude] within five business days after demand by [St. Jude] * * * a termination fee equal to $3,000,000.

No fee would be due if a court prohibited the merger, if the Electromedics board did not approve the merger, or if St. Jude breached the agreement. St. Jude's final bid was $6.375 per share.

The day after news of the merger reached the press, Medtronic sent Electromedics a new formal offer of $6.75 per share. St. Jude agreed to match that bid. Medtronic then increased its bid to $6.875 per share and put $3 million in escrow to cover the possible termination fee to St. Jude.[1] St. Jude made it clear that it expected Electromedics to pay the $3 million termination fee if it accepted Medtronic's bid.

On December 22, the Electromedics board authorized a merger with Medtronic at $6.875 per share, for a total of $97 million. When Electromedics informed St. Jude of its decision, St. Jude demanded payment of the termination fee. The merger agreement with Medtronic prohibited Electromedics from paying the fee without Medtronic's prior written consent. When Electromedics failed to pay the fee, St. Jude brought this action, alleging breach of contract, unjust enrichment, tortious interference with contract, and a claim for attorney fees and costs.

In March 1994, St. Jude moved for summary judgment and Electromedics/Medtronic moved to dismiss St. Jude's claims. In denying both motions, the district court, noting that "many [jurisdictions] have upheld termination fees," chose to use a "liquidated damages analysis to determine the validity of the fee provision in question." After addressing the factors used to determine whether a liquidated damages provision is, in fact, a penalty rather than a reasonable estimate of actual damages, the court stated: "[I]nsufficient evidence has been presented to

---

1. Dain Bosworth and counsel for Medtronic were of the opinion that the termination fee provision in the St. Jude merger was invalid and unenforceable. Medtronic wanted Electromedics to accept its offer, terminate the St. Jude merger agreement, and refuse to pay the termination fee because it was invalid. Electromedics perceived this as an agreement to breach another agreement and refused nonpayment of the termination fee. As a compromise, Medtronic agreed to deposit $3 million into an escrow account to fund any liability for the termination fee under the St. Jude agreement.

the Court to allow it to conclude, as a matter of law, that the termination fee is a penalty rather than a valid liquidated damages provision."

After a December 1994 hearing ... Electromedics/Medtronic's motion for summary judgment was granted. This court concluded:

> Electromedics did not intend to liquidate [St. Jude's] damages when they agreed to the three million dollar penalty fee. [St. Jude's] candid concession through its counsel at oral arguments is a binding judicial admission evincing the intent of the parties in regards to the liquidated damages. Accordingly, [St. Jude] cannot carry its burden of establishing the first element of its first claim for relief. Therefore, the three million dollar penalty provision is void and will not be enforced.

In the corporate world, termination fees are a common and generally accepted method to "reimburse the prospective purchaser for expenditures incurred in pursuing the transaction." *Gray v. Zondervan Corp.* (W.D.Mich.1988).

> Cancellation fee provisions typically require the [seller] to pay the bidder a specified dollar amount. * * * [T]he fee ordinarily ranges from one to five percent of the proposed acquisition price. A cancellation fee reduces the risk of entering a negotiated merger by guaranteeing the initial bidder reimbursement for the out of pocket costs associated with making the offer and, in some instances, for the bidder's lost time and opportunities. Accordingly, they are increasingly common in negotiated acquisitions.

Stephen M. Bainbridge, *Exclusive Merger Agreements and Lock–Ups in Negotiated Corporate Acquisitions*, 75 MINN.L.REV. 239, 246 (1990).

Contrary to Electromedics/Medtronic's assertion that termination fees are inherently invalid and unenforceable,[3] the law generally accepts them as long as they do not encroach upon the ultimate purpose of the acquisition process: to sell a company to the highest bidder and maximize the shareholders' profits.

State and federal courts have upheld termination fees when a well-informed board negotiated the fee in good faith, with no apparent conflict of interest, and followed responsible procedure, when the amount of the termination fee is reasonable in relation to the bidder's efforts and the magnitude of the transaction, and when the reasonable and fully-disclosed fee does not hinder a board vote on the overall merger/sales transaction.

---

3. We note that despite this argument renouncing termination fees, the Electromedics/Medtronic's merger agreement contained a $2 million termination fee provision identical to the provision at issue here. The termination fee, originally $3 million, had been reduced to $2 million when Medtronic increased its bid to $6.875 per share and put $3 million in escrow to cover the possible termination fee to St. Jude at issue in this case.

The parties here, with the benefit of legal counsel and financial advisors, negotiated the termination fee as part of the merger agreement. The $3 million fee is reasonable as it is only a small percentage of the total $90 million contract sales price. Most importantly, the termination fee provision brought St. Jude into the auction as a committed bidder for purchase, and was a catalyst for the bidding contest that ultimately resulted in Electromedics receiving a bid close to its market value. For these reasons, we conclude the termination fee provision was valid and enforceable.

The district court, however, applied a liquidated damages analysis to this case and invalidated the termination fee as an unenforceable penalty because St. Jude admitted that it never intended to liquidate damages.

We are aware that termination fee provisions have been likened to liquidated damage provisions. A liquidated damages analysis is inappropriate here, however, because this case lacks the breach of contract necessary to invoke such analysis. By definition, a party may establish a claim for liquidated damages only when it proves three essential elements: (1) the parties intended to liquidate damages; (2) at the time the parties made the contract, the amount of liquidated damages was a reasonable estimate of the presumed actual damages that the breach would cause; and (3) at the time the parties made the contract, it was difficult to determine the amount of actual damages that would result from a breach. Implicit in each of these elements is the breach of a contract. One court has aptly defined liquidated damages as

> the sum a party to a contract agrees to pay if he breaks some promise, and which, having been arrived at by a good faith effort to estimate in advance the actual damage that will probably ensue from the breach, is legally recoverable as agreed damages if the breach occurs.

Indeed, "damages," by their very nature, mean "compensation in money as a substitute for and the equivalent of the promised performance." *Westmount Country Club v. Kameny* (NJ Super. 1964); Corbin on Contracts § 990.

The parties agree that no breach occurred here when Electromedics accepted Medtronic's bid rather than St. Jude's; the merger agreement allowed Electromedics to choose a course of action: either accept St. Jude's offer or select another buyer and pay St. Jude the termination fee. Electromedics exercised a contract right when it chose to accept Medtronic's offer; that decision did not breach the merger agreement with St. Jude. Without an underlying breach of contract, the court cannot apply a liquidated damages analysis to this case. Thus, the ... district court erred when it ... applied a liquidated damages analysis to the facts of this case and interpret[ed] the candid admission of counsel for St. Jude that there was "no intention of liquidating damages" as requiring a conclusion that the termination provision must be an unenforceable penalty.

Because the merger agreement gave Electromedics a choice of performance, we believe it is appropriate to liken the termination fee provision to an alternative performance contract.

An alternative contract is one in which a party promises to render some one of two or more alternative performances either one of which is mutually agreed upon as the bargained-for-equivalent given in exchange for the return performance by the other party. Corbin at § 1079.

[S]ome alternative contracts giving the power of choice between the alternatives to the promisor can easily be confused with contracts that provide for the payment of liquidated damages in case of breach, provided that one of the alternatives is the payment of a sum of money. * * * If, upon a proper interpretation of the contract, it is found that the parties have agreed that either one of the two alternative performances is to be given by the promisor and received by the promisee as the agreed exchange and equivalent for the return performance rendered by the promisee, the contract is a true alternative contract. This is true even though one of the alternative performances is the payment of a liquidated sum of money; that fact does not make the contract one for the rendering of a single performance with a provision for liquidated damages in case of breach.

Corbin at § 1082.

Electromedics/Medtronic contend that the termination fee provision was not an alternative performance contract because St. Jude was not obligated to perform in exchange for the $3 million termination fee that Electromedics would pay. In making this argument, Electromedics and Medtronic overlook the nuances of the merger agreement and the auction process.

The record shows that the parties drafted the merger agreement to cover two stages—the auction period as well as the purchase and merger. The merger agreement committed St. Jude as a purchaser of Electromedics and, thereby, increased the stakes in the auction. When St. Jude signed the merger agreement, it presented itself as a viable contender for purchase: St. Jude had already hired financial advisors, undergone complex financial analysis and preparation, and taken the risk publicly to commit to the merger.

The history of the auction proves that St. Jude's initial bid, and later its willingness to increase the bid, caused Medtronic to increase its own bid twice and to offer a purchase price near Electromedics' actual market value. This sequence of events is remarkable, considering that Medtronic's initial unsolicited bid had been far below Electromedics' market value. Ultimately, Electromedics sold for $11 million more than it would have before St. Jude became a contender in the acquisition.

The merger agreement between Electromedics and St. Jude enhanced the bidding and maximized the shareholders' profits. The record shows the termination fee in this case worked, as St. Jude contends, "exactly as it should have." During that first stage of the contract, St. Jude performed by actively participating in the auction. Electromedics agreed to perform by paying a termination fee if the parties' negotiations ended after this first stage and never progressed to the merger with St. Jude.

In the second stage of the contract, St. Jude would have performed by purchasing Electromedics for $90 million and Electromedics would have performed by approving the sale. Implicit in the parties' agreement, however, is the fact that they would never have reached this second stage if Electromedics chose to sell to another company. The merger agreement gave Electromedics the choice to end at stage one or proceed to stage two.

When Electromedics selected Medtronic as its buyer, Electromedics terminated its merger agreement with St. Jude at stage one, after St. Jude had already provided consideration for the contract. Given that Electromedics chose to terminate the contract at that stage, Electromedics still had the duty to perform by paying St. Jude the $3 million termination fee.

The district court erred when it applied a liquidated damages analysis to this case and invalidated the termination fee as an unenforceable penalty. The termination fee provision is a valid and enforceable contract between the parties.

... We reverse summary judgment on the termination fee provision and direct the district court to enter judgment of $3 million in favor of St. Jude....

QUESTIONS AND NOTES

1. In what ways is this situation pre-contractual? In what ways is it a fully-formed contract?

2. What is the difference between an alternative contract where one alternative is a termination fee and a contract with a liquidated damages clause? How does the court decide that this is an alternative contract?

3. Given this decision, are penalty clauses now enforceable if one is careful to call them "termination fees"?

Hoffman v. Red Owl Stores
Wisconsin Supreme Court, 1965.
26 Wis.2d 683, 133 N.W.2d 267.

Action by Joseph Hoffman (hereinafter "Hoffman") and wife, plaintiffs, against defendants Red Owl Stores, Inc. (hereinafter "Red Owl") and Edward Lukowitz.

The complaint alleged that Lukowitz, as agent for Red Owl, represented to and agreed with plaintiffs that Red Owl would build a store building in Chilton and stock it with merchandise for Hoffman to operate in return for which plaintiffs were to put up and invest a total sum of $18,000; that in reliance upon the above-mentioned agreement and representations plaintiffs sold their bakery building and business and their grocery store and business; also in reliance on the agreement and representations Hoffman purchased the building site in Chilton and rented a residence for himself and his family in Chilton; plaintiffs' actions in reliance on the representations and agreement disrupted their personal and business life; plaintiffs lost substantial amounts of income and expended large sums of money as expenses. Plaintiffs demanded recovery of damages for the breach of defendants' representations and agreements.

The action was tried to a court and jury. The facts hereinafter stated are taken from the evidence adduced at the trial. Where there was a conflict in the evidence the version favorable to plaintiffs has been accepted since the verdict rendered was in favor of plaintiffs.

Hoffman assisted by his wife operated a bakery at Wautoma from 1956 until sale of the building late in 1961. The building was owned in joint tenancy by him and his wife. Red Owl is a Minnesota corporation having its home office at Hopkins, Minnesota. It owns and operates a number of grocery supermarket stores and also extends franchises to agency stores which are owned by individuals, partnerships, and corporations. Lukowitz resides at Green Bay and since September, 1960, has been divisional manager for Red Owl in a territory comprising Upper Michigan and most of Wisconsin in charge of 84 stores. Prior to September, 1960, he was district manager having charge of approximately 20 stores.

In November, 1959, Hoffman was desirous of expanding his operations by establishing a grocery store and contacted a Red Owl representative by the name of Jansen, now deceased. Numerous conversations were had in 1960 with the idea of establishing a Red Owl franchise store in Wautoma. In September, 1960, Lukowitz succeeded Jansen as Red Owl's representative in the negotiations. Hoffman mentioned that $18,000 was all the capital he had available to invest and he was repeatedly assured that this would be sufficient to set him up in business as a Red Owl store. About Christmastime, 1960, Hoffman thought it would be a good idea if he bought a small grocery store in Wautoma and operated it in order that he gain experience in the grocery business prior to operating a Red Owl store in some larger community. On February 6, 1961, on the advice of Lukowitz and Sykes, who had succeeded Lukowitz as Red Owl's district manager, Hoffman bought the inventory and fixtures of a small grocery store in Wautoma and leased the building in which it was operated.

After three months of operating this Wautoma store, the Red Owl representatives came in and took inventory and checked the operations and found the store was operating at a profit. Lukowitz advised Hoffman to sell the store to his manager, and assured him that Red Owl would find a larger store for him elsewhere. Acting on this advice and assurance, Hoffman sold the fixtures and inventory to his manager on June 6, 1961. Hoffman was reluctant to sell at that time because it meant losing the summer tourist business, but he sold on the assurance that he would be operating in a new location by fall and that he must sell this store if he wanted a bigger one. Before selling, Hoffman told the Red Owl representatives that he had $18,000 for "getting set up in business" and they assured him that there would be no problems in establishing him in a bigger operation. The makeup of the $18,000 was not discussed; it was understood plaintiff's father-in-law would furnish part of it. By June, 1961, the towns for the new grocery store had been narrowed down to two, Kewaunee and Chilton. In Kewaunee, Red Owl had an option on a building site. In Chilton, Red Owl had nothing under option, but it did select a site to which plaintiff obtained an option at Red Owl's suggestion. The option stipulated a purchase price of $6,000 with $1,000 to be paid on election to purchase and the balance to be paid within thirty days. On Lukowitz's assurance that everything was all set plaintiff paid $1,000 down on the lot on September 15th.

On September 27, 1961, plaintiff met at Chilton with Lukowitz and Mr. Reymund and Mr. Carlson from the home office who prepared a projected financial statement. Part of the funds plaintiffs were to supply as their investment in the venture were to be obtained by sale of their Wautoma bakery building.

On the basis of this meeting Lukowitz assured Hoffman: "* * * [E]verything is ready to go. Get your money together and we are set." Shortly after this meeting Lukowitz told plaintiffs that they would have to sell their bakery business and bakery building, and that their retaining this property was the only "hitch" in the entire plan. On November 6, 1961, plaintiffs sold their bakery building for $10,000. Hoffman was to retain the bakery equipment as he contemplated using it to operate a bakery in connection with his Red Owl store. After sale of the bakery Hoffman obtained employment on the night shift at an Appleton bakery.

[During the next four months there were numerous detailed meetings between the parties, at which Red Owl's agents discussed financing arrangements for the new store. A dispute developed and the negotiations broke down.]

The case was submitted to the jury on a special verdict with the first two questions answered by the court. This verdict, as returned by the jury, was as follows:

Question No. 1: Did the Red Owl Stores, Inc., and Joseph Hoffmann on or about mid-May of 1961 initiate negotiations looking to the establishment of Joseph Hoffmann as a franchise operator of a Red Owl Store in Chilton?

Answer: Yes. (Answered by the Court.)

Question No. 2: Did the parties mutually agree on all of the details of the proposal so as to reach a final agreement thereon?

Answer: No. (Answered by the Court.)

Question No. 3: Did the Red Owl Stores, Inc., in the course of said negotiations, make representations to Joseph Hoffmann that if he fulfilled certain conditions that they would establish him as a franchise operator of a Red Owl Store in Chilton?

Answer: Yes.

Question No. 4: If you have answered Question No. 3 ''Yes,' then answer this question: Did Joseph Hoffmann rely on said representations and was he induced to act thereon?

Answer: Yes.

Question No. 5: If you have answered Question No. 4 ''Yes,' then answer this question: Ought Joseph Hoffmann, in the exercise of ordinary care, to have relied on said representations?

Answer: Yes.

Question No. 6: If you have answered Question No. 3 ''Yes' then answer this question: Did Joseph Hoffmann fulfill all the conditions he was required to fulfill by the terms of the negotiations between the parties up to January 26, 1962?

Answer: Yes.

Question No. 7: What sum of money will reasonably compensate the plaintiffs for such damages as they sustained by reason of:

(a) The sale of the Wautoma store fixtures and inventory?

   Answer: $16,735.

(b) The sale of the bakery building?

   Answer: $2,000.

(c) Taking up the option of the Chilton lot?

   Answer: $1,000.

(d) Expenses of moving his family to Neenah?

   Answer: $140.

(e) House rental in Chilton?

   Answer: $125.

Plaintiffs moved for judgment on the verdict while defendants moved to change the answers to Questions 3, 4, 5, and 6 from "Yes" to "No," and in the alternative for relief from the answers to the subdivisions of Question 7 or a new trial. On March 31, 1964, the circuit court entered the following order:

It Is Ordered in accordance with said decision on motions after verdict hereby incorporated herein by reference:

1. That the answer of the jury to Question No. 7(a) be and the same is hereby vacated and set aside and that a new trial be had on the sole issue of the damages for loss, if any, on the sale of the Wautoma store, fixtures and inventory.

2. That all other portions of the verdict of the jury be and hereby are approved and confirmed and all after-verdict motions of the parties inconsistent with this order are hereby denied.

Defendants have appealed from this order and plaintiffs have cross-appealed from paragraph 1, thereof.

■ CURRIE, C.J. ...

Applicability of Doctrine to Facts of this Case

The record here discloses a number of promises and assurances given to Hoffman by Lukowitz in behalf of Red Owl upon which plaintiffs relied and acted upon to their detriment.

Foremost were the promises that for the sum of $18,000 Red Owl would establish Hoffman in a store. After Hoffman had sold his grocery store and paid the $1,000 on the Chilton lot, the $18,000 figure was changed to $24,100. Then in November, 1961, Hoffman was assured that if the $24,100 figure were increased by $2,000 the deal would go through. Hoffman was induced to sell his grocery store fixtures and inventory in June, 1961, on the promise that he would be in his new store by fall. In November, plaintiffs sold their bakery building on the urging of defendants and on the assurance that this was the last step necessary to have the deal with Red Owl go through.

We determine that there was ample evidence to sustain the answers of the jury to the questions of the verdict with respect to the promissory representations made by Red Owl, Hoffman's reliance thereon in the exercise of ordinary care, and his fulfillment of the conditions required of him by the terms of the negotiations had with Red Owl.

There remains for consideration the question of law raised by defendants that agreement was never reached on essential factors necessary to establish a contract between Hoffman and Red Owl. Among these were the size, cost, design, and layout of the store building; and the terms of the lease with respect to rent, maintenance, renewal, and purchase options. This poses the question of whether the promise necessary to sustain a cause of action for promissory estoppel must embrace all essential details of a proposed transaction between promisor and promisee so as to be the equivalent of an offer that would result in a binding contract between the parties if the promisee were to accept the same.

Originally the doctrine of promissory estoppel was invoked as a substitute for consideration rendering a gratuitous promise enforceable as a contract. In other words, the acts of reliance by the promisee to his detriment provided a substitute for consideration. If promissory estoppel were to be limited to only those situations where the promise giving rise to the cause of action must be so definite with respect to all details that a contract would result were the promise supported by consideration, then the defendants' instant promises to Hoffman would not meet this test. However, sec. 90 of Restatement, 1 Contracts, does not impose the requirement that the promise giving rise to the cause of action must be so comprehensive in scope as to meet the requirements of an offer that would ripen into a contract if accepted by the promisee. Rather the conditions imposed are:

(1) Was the promise one which the promisor should reasonably expect to induce action or forbearance of a definite and substantial character on the part of the promisee?

(2) Did the promise induce such action or forbearance?

(3) Can injustice be avoided only by enforcement of the promise?

We deem it would be a mistake to regard an action grounded on promissory estoppel as the equivalent of a breach-of-contract action. As Dean Boyer points out, it is desirable that fluidity in the application of the concept be maintained. 98 U. Pa. L. Rev. 459 (1950). While the first two of the above-listed three requirements of promissory estoppel present issues of fact which ordinarily will be resolved by a jury, the third requirement, that the remedy can only be invoked where necessary to avoid injustice, is one that involves a policy decision by the court. Such a policy decision necessarily embraces an element of discretion.

We conclude that injustice would result here if plaintiffs were not granted some relief because of the failure of defendants to keep their promises which induced plaintiffs to act to their detriment.

Damages

Defendants attack all the items of damages awarded by the jury.

The bakery building at Wautoma was sold at defendants' instigation in order that Hoffman might have the net proceeds available as part of the cash capital he was to invest in the Chilton store venture. The evidence clearly establishes that it was sold at a loss of $2,000. Defendants contend that half of this loss was sustained by Mrs. Hoffman because title stood in joint tenancy. They point out that no dealings took place between her and defendants as all negotiations were had with her husband. Ordinarily only the promisee and not third persons are entitled to enforce the remedy of promissory estoppel against the promisor. However, if the promisor actually foresees, or has reason to foresee, action by a third person in reliance on the promise, it may be quite unjust to refuse to perform the promise. Here not only did defendants foresee that it would be necessary for Mrs. Hoffman to sell her joint interest in the bakery building, but defendants actually requested that this be done. We approve the jury's award of $2,000 damages for the loss incurred by both plaintiffs in this sale.

Defendants attack on two grounds the $1,000 awarded because of Hoffman's payment of that amount on the purchase price of the Chilton lot. The first is that this $1,000 had already been lost at the time the final negotiations with Red Owl fell through in January, 1962, because the remaining $5,000 of purchase price had been due on October 15, 1961. The record does not disclose that the lot owner had foreclosed Hoffman's interest in the lot for failure to pay this $5,000. The $1,000 was not paid for the option, but had been paid as part of the purchase price at the time Hoffman elected to exercise the option. This gave him an equity in the lot which could not be legally foreclosed without affording Hoffman an opportunity to pay the balance. The second ground of attack is that the lot may have had a fair market value of $6,000, and Hoffman should have paid the remaining $5,000 of purchase price. We determine that it would be unreasonable to require Hoffman to have invested an additional $5,000 in order to protect the $1,000 he had paid. Therefore, we find no merit to defendants' attack upon this item of damages.

We also determine it was reasonable for Hoffman to have paid $125 for one month's rent of a home in Chilton after defendants assured him everything would be set when plaintiff sold the bakery building. This was a proper item of damage.

Plaintiffs never moved to Chilton because defendants suggested that Hoffman get some experience by working in a Red Owl store in the Fox River Valley. Plaintiffs, therefore, moved to Neenah instead of Chilton. After moving, Hoffman worked at night in an Appleton bakery but held himself available for work in a Red Owl store. The $140 moving expense would not have been incurred if plaintiffs had not sold their bakery building in Wautoma in reliance upon defendants' promises. We consider the $140 moving expense to be a proper item of damage.

We turn now to the damage item with respect to which the trial court granted a new trial, i.e., that arising from the sale of the Wautoma grocery-store fixtures and inventory for which the jury awarded $16,735. The trial court ruled that Hoffman could not recover for any loss of future profits for the summer months following the sale on June 6, 1961, but that damages would be limited to the difference between the sales price received and the fair market value of the assets sold, giving consideration to any goodwill attaching thereto by reason of the transfer of a going business. There was no direct evidence presented as to what this fair market value was on June 6, 1961. The evidence did disclose that Hoffman paid $9,000 for the inventory, added $1,500 to it and sold it for $10,000 or a loss of $500. His 1961 federal income-tax return showed that the grocery equipment had been purchased for $7,000 and sold for $7,955.96. Plaintiffs introduced evidence of the buyer that during the first eleven weeks of operation of the grocery store his gross sales were $44,000 and his profit was $6,000 or roughly 15 percent. On cross-examination he admitted that this was gross and not net profit. Plaintiffs contend that in a breach-of-contract action damages may include loss of profits. However, this is not a breach-of-contract action.

The only relevancy of evidence relating to profits would be with respect to proving the element of goodwill in establishing the fair market value of the grocery inventory and fixtures sold. Therefore, evidence of profits would be admissible to afford a foundation for expert opinion as to fair market value.

Where damages are awarded in promissory estoppel instead of specifically enforcing the promisor's promise, they should be only such as in the opinion of the court are necessary to prevent injustice. Mechanical or rule-of-thumb approaches to the damage problem should be avoided. In discussing remedies to be applied by courts in promissory estoppel we quote the following views of writers on the subject:

> Enforcement of a promise does not necessarily mean Specific Performance. It does not necessarily mean Damages for breach. Moreover the amount allowed as Damages may be determined by the plaintiff's expenditures or change of position in reliance as well as by the value to him of the promised performance. Restitution is also an 'enforcing' remedy, although it is often said to be based upon some kind of a rescission. In determining what justice requires, the court must remember all of its powers, derived from equity, law merchant, and other sources, as well as the common law. Its decree should be molded accordingly.

1A Corbin, Contracts, § 200.

> The wrong is not primarily in depriving the plaintiff of the promised reward but in causing the plaintiff to change position to his detriment. It would follow that the damages should not exceed the loss caused by the change of position, which would never be more in amount, but might be less, than the promised reward.

Seavey, *Reliance on Gratuitous Promises or Other Conduct*, 64 Harv. L. Rev. 913 (1951).

"There likewise seems to be no positive legal requirement, and certainly no legal policy, which dictates the allowance of contract damages in every case where the defendant's duty is consensual." Shattuck, *Gratuitous Promises—A New Writ?*, 35 Mich. L. Rev. 908 (1936).

At the time Hoffman bought the equipment and inventory of the small grocery store at Wautoma he did so in order to gain experience in the grocery-store business. At that time discussion had already been had with Red Owl representatives that Wautoma might be too small for a Red Owl operation and that a larger city might be more desirable. Thus Hoffman made this purchase more or less as a temporary experiment. Justice does not require that the damages awarded him, because of selling these assets at the behest of defendants, should exceed any actual loss sustained measured by the difference between the sales price and the fair market value.

Since the evidence does not sustain the large award of damages arising from the sale of the Wautoma grocery business, the trial court properly ordered a new trial on this issue.

QUESTIONS AND NOTES

1. Did Red Owl Stores ever promise Hoffman anything? What?

2. When the deal began to go sour before any final contract was executed, Red Owl and its lawyers probably were in substantial doubt whether they were exposed to any liability to Hoffman. What, if anything, might they have done at that point to limit their potential liability? Was there any way Red Owl could call the deal off once it began to talk to Hoffman and once he began to take it seriously?

3. If Hoffman had withdrawn from the transaction at the last minute, would Red Owl have a good cause of action? What would be the basis, and what would be the remedy?

4. The court holds that the evidence does not sustain the jury verdict of $20,000 damages made to Hoffman. On remand, what damages should the trial court award? Who really won on appeal—Hoffman or Red Owl?

5. Franchising, the marketing of goods through independent outlets under a common trademark and common business methods, has become of great economic significance throughout the world. Typically, the franchisee, like Hoffman, must make a substantial personal and financial investment in the franchise. Often he depends on the expertise and representations of the franchisor, who is supposed to know all about the business and be in a position to advise the potential franchisee which location is ideal for, say, a Red Owl market. Most franchisors are sophisticated business enterprises; many franchisees are small, independent, family-run businesses. The franchisor usually has great power over the franchisee and his operation, with continuing control over the trademark, the use of which is essential to the business. The franchisor usually retains broad powers to ensure that the franchisee maintains its standards, including the power to terminate the franchise if the franchisee does not toe the mark. The franchisee typically bears the risk of financial loss if the franchisor's rosy predictions of potential business are not borne out in experience.

Unlike some other legal systems which long have provided indemnity for terminated franchisees and other protections, our contract law has tended not to constrain the strategic and economic power of the franchisor. This has produced a variety of reactions, including legislation and Federal Trade Commission administrative rules that seek to control franchising practices and protect franchisees. Recall *Postal Instant Press v. Sealy*, p. 170 and notes following. *Hoffman v. Red Owl* is an example of the imaginative use of common law methods towards a similar end. What other theories might the court have drawn upon to protect Hoffman's reliance on what Red Owl told him? Was Red Owl's behavior a tort? Did Red Owl make misrepresentations? Did Red Owl occupy a position of trust vis-à-vis Hoffman placing it under a special duty to protect him from loss?

6. *Hoffman v. Red Owl Stores,* has drawn a large amount of scholarly attention over the years as a kind of high-water mark for the doctrine of promissory estoppel, and it continues to be controversial. Professor Robert Scott suggests that the case was wrongly decided, is an outlier, and is not generally followed. To explain the contrary jury's verdict, he suggests that Red Owl failed to adequately raise three important issues at trial: (1) Whether Lukowitz's authority to make the financial representation that $18,000 would be sufficient was limited to the sale of the grocery business and the purchase of the option in Chilton; (2) Whether Hoffman's reliance should have been measured by the standard of a reasonable person rather than from the perspective of someone of Hoffman's limited education, business experience and acumen; and (3) Whether Hoffman was conflating the amount of equity and amount of cash Red Owl was demanding. *See* Robert E. Scott, Hoffman v. Red Owl Stores *and the Myth of Precontractual Reliance*, 68 OHIO ST. L.J. 71 (2007). Conversely, Professors William Whitford and Stewart Macaulay while acknowledging Professor Scott's arguments, conclude, based on their own interview of Joe Hoffman, that the case was correctly decided. They emphasize that at the first meeting over the proposed financial plan, two people in addition to Hoffman and Lukowitz were present. These two men were Red Owl officials who worked full time on the development of new stores and they assured Hoffman during the planning seemed sufficient and that building should commence soon. Given this context, Whitford and Macaulay believe that the jury reasonably found Lukowitz's statements to be a promise upon which Hoffman reasonably relied on to his detriment. *See* William C. Whitford & Stewart Macaulay, Hoffman v. Red Owl Stores: *The Rest of the Story*, 61 HASTINGS L.J. 801 (2010).

CHAPTER 8

PERFORMANCE AND BREACH

I.   EVENTS AFTER FORMATION

In earlier Chapters we considered two central theoretical questions: what makes a promise a contract, and when is a contract formed. In practice, however, formation and enforceability issues arise rarely, and, when they do it is almost always retrospectively, when a party resisting enforcement of what both sides almost certainly considered a contract now claims that the rules of consideration or offer and acceptance were not satisfied. In other words, enforceability and formation issues are most likely to be raised by a lawyer trying to get his client out of a contract on technical grounds, not by parties to an agreement in the course of trying to work their way through the contract to performance.

In this Chapter the perspective shifts to examine how parties and their lawyers deal with the obligation of contract *during* performance. Now the parties are trying to make a contract work or to use the existence of a contract as the basis for a claim. A claim of contract breach requires proof that performance was due, and that the failure to perform caused injury of the plaintiff. To demonstrate breach, one must first determine what performance was due and that requires determining both what performance was promised and under what circumstances that performance became due. During the course of performance whether acting as counselor, advocate, or judge, the lawyer gives meaning to the obligations of the agreement by interpreting its express and implied terms in light of events subsequent to contract formation. The variety of subsequent events that may affect performance obligations is practically infinite. The goods may be late or off-grade, or only half of what was expected may arrive; the employee may not show up for work because of illness or accident; the employer may have no work because its major customer has suddenly gone out of business or because a storm has flooded the plant; the builder may be late completing the building because the architect's plans were unusual and tricky, or the basement that was supposed to be dug from easily worked soil in fact must be hewn out of solid rock; the builder may be slow getting on with the job because the owner has been slow obtaining bank credit and making the progress payments.

In each of these situations, a lawyer may be called upon to advise the client what to do next—what legal significance to give the obligation in light of the events. Or the lawyer may be called upon as a litigator to press or defend a claim of breach of contract. Or a judge may be called upon to characterize the obligations and events and determine the legal consequences for the parties.

Do not lose sight of the truth that clients make and perform contracts. Contracts are not the private preserve of their lawyers. Most contracts are made without a lawyer's involvement, and most parties prefer to work out performance problems themselves, calling on a lawyer only when the situation has become a real mess. Contract law has evolved out of the resolution of disputes that ripened into litigation. An analytic structure built in this way sees the situation long after the conflicting claims have arisen and the relationship between the parties has soured. Law may come into the picture too late, and slant in the wrong direction, to help businesspersons manage problems as they arise. In litigation, courts are engaged in salvage operations at best, seeking to raise the hulk or apportion blame for the sinking.

As you study the law governing performance disputes, consider the extent to which that study provides helpful guidance in how to head off disputes at an earlier stage and assist businesspersons in reducing and avoiding costly conflict. In most disputes there are repeated opportunities for the parties to cure defective performances, to limit the loss by covering for the lacking performance in the market, and to communicate to ameliorate and define the consequences of the failure to perform. This communication may lead the parties to modify their relationship in light of the new circumstances but keep the deal alive, or it might lead them to move quickly and relatively cleanly into alternative arrangements with other persons. In any event, good communication during performance is likely to allow both parties to more efficiently accommodate to the situation than any lawsuit could.

The conventional doctrines and techniques available to a lawyer in dealing with performance problems are the subject of this Chapter. It will come as no surprise to the student who has gotten this far that the heart of the matter is interpretation of the terms of the contract: the words and symbols used by the parties; the additional terms implied by context, custom, usage, and prior dealings; and the terms supplied constructively by the law and imposed upon the parties. All must be discovered and weighed against the others in light of the events that now give rise to a dispute threatening the transaction. Beyond interpretation as such, the events must be fitted into an analytical structure to determine the legal consequences of particular failures of performance. This Chapter introduces you to the confusing and complex vocabulary that has grown up over the centuries to describe performance terms. Behind the complexities of terminology can be found a quite clear and simple set of useful concepts. The plan of this Chapter is to start with the basic ideas here and then show how to work with the confusing labels attached to those ideas.

Promises and Conditions. A lawyer considering the legal import of a subsequent event on the contract relationship operates within a very simple system of classification. The basic distinction is that between (a) an event that is *promised* and (b) an event that *conditions* a promise.

If a party fails to do what it promised, its failure is a breach; a court may require it to pay money damages sufficient to provide the non-breaching party with the financial equivalent of performance. However, as you saw from the first cases after *Best v. Southland* in Chapter One, not all promises are absolute; most obligations are limited by their terms. The promise is likely to be *conditioned* on an event, so that until that event occurs, the obligation to perform does not arise. Thus, in *Mattei v. Hopper*, p. 31, the purchaser's obligation was conditioned on the broker "obtaining leases satisfactory to the purchaser."

The promise-condition distinction has crucial remedial implications. A failure of a party to perform a promised event is a breach of the contract, giving rise to legal remedies for breach, particularly damages. The failure of an event on which a promise is conditioned excuses performance of that promise—that is, it terminates, or at least suspends, the obligation of the contract. Breach of promise gives rise to damages; failure of a condition excuses the conditioned performance.

This simple promise-condition distinction may seem more complicated than it is because the two classifications are not mutually exclusive. An event that is a condition may also have been promised, so that its nonoccurrence may not only excuse performance of a counter-promise but also constitute a breach giving rise to damages. Conversely, the breach of a contract promise may also operate as a conditioning event terminating the obligation of further performance by the other party. Every contract term thus may be characterized in one of four ways: it may be a pure condition; it may be a pure promise; it may be both a promise and a condition; or it may be nothing, and its occurrence will have no impact on the parties' continuing obligations. Damages for breach of contract are generally conservative, and the burden on the breaching party is likely to be relatively light or at least bearable. In contrast, the result of finding a discharging condition is that one side may lose the entire benefit of the contract without any compensation whatsoever.

Consider the following illustration. On February 1, 2016, Seller agrees that for a price of $5.00 per bushel, payable September 20, 2016, he will deliver 1,000 bushels of Grade A wheat to Buyer's grain elevator on September 10, 2016, and another 1,000 bushels on October 10, 2016. Seller agrees to do this so long as (a) the U.S. Congress does not increase the existing tariff of foreign wheat prior to June 10, 2016, and (b) Seller's total 2016 crop of wheat exceeds 10,000 bushels. In return, Buyer agrees to accept the wheat and pay Seller his requested price of $5.00 per bushel.

The most obvious promises in the agreement are Seller's undertaking to sell and deliver to Buyer's grain elevator 2,000 bushels of wheat (1,000 by September 10 and

1,000 by October 10), and Buyer's agreement to accept wheat and to pay the purchase price. Whether Congress increases the existing tariff prior to June 10 and whether Seller's 2016 crop exceeds 10,000 bushels clearly appear to be conditions that will affect Seller's obligation to perform. Moreover, Buyer's promise to pay would appear conditioned by Seller's promise to deliver by September 10 and October 10. In other words, Seller's timely delivery is both a promise and a condition. Apart from these explicit promises and conditions, there may be more subtle ones as well. Congress' action on the existing tariff may well be outside the control of either party, but one may imply a promise on the part of either or both parties not to attempt to influence Congress to increase the existing tariff. And while neither party found it necessary to make explicit, one may fairly construct the condition that the promises need only be performed if Seller's crop is not destroyed by fire, or perhaps even that Buyer's access to the market is not disturbed by war, revolution, or total market collapse.

The fact that a promise is conditioned does not interfere with the application of the contract formation and enforceability doctrines with which you are familiar. A promise is no less a promise because it is conditioned, unless, of course, the limitation is so extreme as to make it illusory. Recall Chapter One, Topic II. A contract is formed when the promises are exchanged. Neither party can then change his mind and withdraw without the consent of the other. Recall Chapter Seven. But if the conditioning event does not occur, the obligation to perform never becomes due. The tariff may be increased prior to June 10, 2016, or Seller's crop may fall short of the stated 10,000 bushels. In either event, Seller doesn't have to perform because he never promised to perform under those circumstances. And if Seller doesn't have to deliver the wheat, Buyer won't have to pay because her promise to pay was, in turn, conditioned on Seller's delivery.

A closer look at the potential conditioning events underscores the centrality of interpretation:

1. Seller's duty to deliver is expressly conditioned in the agreement on the tariff level. Congressional action on tariffs is out of Seller's control, and Seller makes no *promise* what the tariff would be. If the tariff is increased and Seller doesn't deliver, Seller breaches no promise, and Buyer has no claim against Seller. An increased tariff prior to June 10, 2016, is an event that excuses Seller's obligation to deliver wheat and thus gives rise to no breach or remedial claim. Seller's obligation is conditioned on the June 10 tariff level.

2. The agreement also says Seller's duty to deliver depends on the crop size. Unlike the tariff level, crop size is largely within Seller's control. Again Seller makes no promise that the crop will exceed 10,000 bushels; if he plants a crop in good faith and it fails, Buyer can't recover damages from Seller for non-delivery because Seller never promised to deliver under such circumstances. But

might the condition be interpreted to require that Seller at least plant a crop? Perhaps. The absence of an implied promise to plant might well negate any commitment in Seller's conditional promise and render it illusory, a construction that courts often seek to avoid. Like the tariff level, crop size is a condition, but that condition may also give rise to an implied promise because Seller has some control over its occurrence.

3. Buyer's duty to pay on September 20, 2016 is not expressly made conditional on Seller's prior delivery of 1,000 bushels of Grade A wheat. But if Seller doesn't deliver any wheat, no court would find that Buyer ought to have paid Seller anyway. Seller's delivery is an implied condition to Buyer's obligation to perform her promise. If non-delivery by Seller were not excused, it would of course be a breach of Seller's promise, and Buyer would have a claim for damages against Seller. But non-delivery would also be the nonoccurrence of an event on which Buyer's promise to pay depends. Seller's timely delivery of Grade A wheat is both a promise and a condition: its unexcused nonoccurrence gives rise to a claim for damages. Even if delivery is excused by the failure of one of Seller's conditions, non-delivery excuses the Buyer's counter-performance of payment.

Merritt Hill Vineyards v. Windy Heights Vineyard

New York Court of Appeals, 1984.
61 N.Y.2d 106, 472 N.Y.S.2d 592, 460 N.E.2d 1077.

■ KAYE, J.

In September, 1981, plaintiff, Merritt Hill Vineyards, entered into a written agreement with defendants, Windy Heights Vineyard and its sole shareholder Leon Taylor, to purchase a majority stock interest in respondents' Yates County vineyard, and tendered a $15,000 deposit. The agreement provides that "[i]f the sale contemplated hereby does not close, Taylor shall retain the deposit as liquidated damages unless Taylor or Windy Heights failed to satisfy the conditions specified in Section 3 thereof." Section 3, in turn, lists several "conditions precedent" to which the obligation of purchaser to pay the purchase price and to complete the purchase is subject. Among the conditions are that, by the time of the closing, Windy Heights shall have obtained a title insurance policy in a form satisfactory to Merritt Hill, and Windy Heights and Merritt Hill shall have received confirmation from the Farmers Home Administration that certain mortgages on the vineyard are in effect and that the proposed sale does not constitute a default.

In April, 1982, at the closing, plaintiff discovered that neither the policy nor the confirmation had been issued. Plaintiff thereupon refused to close and demanded return of its deposit. When defendants did not return the deposit, plaintiff instituted this action, asserting two causes of action, one for return of the deposit, and one for approximately $26,000 in consequential damages allegedly suffered as a result of defendants' failure to perform.

Special Term denied plaintiff's motion for summary judgment on both causes of action. The Appellate Division unanimously reversed Special Term's order, granted plaintiff's motion for summary judgment as to the cause of action for return of the deposit, and ... granted summary judgment in favor of defendants, dismissing plaintiff's second cause of action for consequential damages. Both plaintiff and defendants appealed from that decision....

On the merits, plaintiff's right to return of its deposit or to consequential damages depends upon whether the undertaking to produce the policy and mortgage confirmation is a promise or a condition.

A promise is "a manifestation of intention to act or refrain from acting in a specified way, so made as to justify a promisee in understanding that a commitment has been made." (Restatement, Contracts 2d, § 2, subd. [1].) A condition, by comparison, is "an event, not certain to occur, which must occur, unless its non-occurrence is excused, before performance under a contract becomes due." (Restatement, Contracts 2d, § 224.) Here, the contract requirements of a title insurance policy and mortgage confirmation are expressed as conditions of plaintiff's performance rather than as promises by defendants. The requirements are contained in a section of the agreement entitled "Conditions Precedent to Purchaser's Obligation to Close," which provides that plaintiff's obligation to pay the purchase price and complete the purchase of the vineyard is "subject to" fulfillment of those requirements. No words of promise are employed.* Defendants' agreement to sell the stock of the vineyard, not those conditions, was the promise by defendants for which plaintiff's promise to pay the purchase price was exchanged.

Defendants' failure to fulfill the conditions of section 3 entitles plaintiff to a return of its deposit but not to consequential damages. While a contracting party's failure to fulfill a condition excuses performance by the other party whose performance is so conditioned, it is not, without an independent promise to perform the

---

* Plaintiff contends that the failure to produce the policy and confirmation is also a breach of section 5, entitled "Representations, Warranties and Agreements." A provision may be both a condition and a promise, if the parties additionally promise to perform a condition as part of their bargain. Such a promise is not present here. The only provision of section 5 conceivably relevant is that "Windy Heights has good and marketable title to the Property and all other properties and assets * * * as of December 31, 1980." But this is quite different from the conditions of section 3 that a title insurance policy and mortgage confirmation be produced at the closing, which took place in April, 1982. Both the complaint and plaintiff's affidavits are premised on nonperformance of section 3 of the agreement, not section 5.

condition, a breach of contract subjecting the nonfulfilling party to liability for damages. This is in accord with the parties' expressed intent, for section 1 of their agreement provides that if defendants fail to satisfy the conditions of section 3 plaintiff's deposit will be returned. It does not provide for payment of damages.

On the merits of this case the Appellate Division thus correctly determined that plaintiff was entitled to the return of its deposit but not to consequential damages.

Accordingly, the order of the Appellate Division should be affirmed.

QUESTIONS AND NOTES

1. The contract in this case provided that if the deal failed to close, seller would retain the deposit as its liquidated damages unless seller had failed to fulfill enumerated conditions. Buyer sues for return of deposit and for consequential damages. Judge Kaye finds that the failure to provide satisfactory title insurance was a condition on the buyer's promise to buy, and not a promise by the seller, on the basis that the contract calls for the return of the buyer's deposit if the conditions are not satisfied but does not provide for the payment of damages. She relies heavily on the absence of express words of promise. But recall *Wood v. Lucy, Lady Duff–Gordon*, p. 40.

The lower court opinion in this case suggests that seller could have met both terms but failed to, and that the buyer would not allow the seller more time to correct the defects. In other words, this decision may be understood as saying: "Buyer, you can go ahead and close by waiving the conditions or you can get out of this deal and recover your full deposit if seller fails to provide the closing documents on time. BUT you don't also get damages." Or perhaps put another way: "If buyer insists on terminating the contract on the closing date, the mitigation rule forecloses recovery of damages that could have been avoided had buyer granted seller an extension of time." Viewed this way, this case is an example of the doctrinal conflict between "time is of the essence" in real property transactions and the defaulting party's right to offer a cure of technical defects.

Do you expect that most contracts expressly provide that if a party doesn't keep its promises, it will have to pay damages? What significance do you attach to the absence of words of promise? What other factors support Judge Kaye's conclusion that she might have included in her opinion?

2. Does the court's classification of the contractual provisions regarding title insurance and mortgagee consent as conditions determine that the only consequence of the non-occurrence of these events is to permit the buyer to get out of the

deal, or does the court's sense that the only proper consequence of the non-occurrence of these events is to permit buyer to terminate (but not receive damages) determine the classification?

A.   EXPRESS CONDITIONS

Parties commonly limit their promises when the agreement is made. They may expressly provide either that the obligation of performance will not arise until an event occurs ("upon tender of the full purchase price, seller will execute and deliver a deed ...") or that performance will occur unless the obligation is extinguished by the occurrence of an event ("I promise to paint your garage tomorrow unless it rains"). The limiting event (tender of the full purchase price or rain) is defined by Restatement, Second, Contracts § 224 as a condition.

On the other hand, lawyers commonly refer to a term in an agreement that makes an event a condition as itself the condition. While most of us slip into this verbal shorthand, the distinction that the Restatement seeks to preserve between the event and the term that describes an event is significant. An event need not be expressly described in a contract in order to operate as a condition, but it may be implied by a court interpreting the deal, even though it is not necessarily mentioned by the parties. If a condition is implied by an interpreting court, it has precisely the same legal effect as a condition that the parties themselves took into account and expressly stated in the agreement.

Howard v. Federal Crop Insurance Corp.

United States Court of Appeals, Fourth Circuit, 1976.
540 F.2d 695.

■ WIDENER, J....

Federal Crop Insurance Corporation, an agency of the United States, in 1973, issued three policies to the Howards, insuring their tobacco crops, to be grown on six farms, against weather damage and other hazards.

The Howards (plaintiffs) established production of tobacco on their acreage, and have alleged that their 1973 crop was extensively damaged by heavy rains, resulting in a gross loss to the three plaintiffs in excess of $35,000. The plaintiffs harvested and sold the depleted crop and timely filed notice and proof of loss with FCIC, but, prior to inspection by the adjuster for FCIC, the Howards had either plowed or disked under the tobacco fields in question to prepare the same for sowing a cover crop of rye to preserve the soil. When the FCIC adjuster later inspected the fields, he found the stalks had been largely obscured or obliterated by plowing or disking and denied the claims, apparently on the ground that the plaintiffs had violated a portion of the policy which provides that the stalks on any acreage with respect to which a loss is claimed shall not be destroyed until the corporation makes an inspection.

The holding of the district court is best capsuled in its own words: "The inquiry here is whether compliance by the insureds with this provision of the policy was a condition precedent to the recovery. The court concludes that it was and that the failure of the insureds to comply worked a forfeiture of benefits for the alleged loss."[1]

There is no question but that apparently after notice of loss was given to defendant, but before inspection by the adjuster, plaintiffs plowed under the tobacco stalks and sowed some of the land with a cover crop, rye. The question is whether, under paragraph 5(f) of the tobacco endorsement to the policy of insurance, the act of plowing under the tobacco stalks forfeits the coverage of the policy. Paragraph 5 of the tobacco endorsement is entitled *Claims*. Pertinent to this case are subparagraphs 5(b) and 5(f), which are as follows:

> 5(b) *It shall be a condition precedent* to the payment of any loss that the insured establish the production of the insured crop on a unit and that such loss has been directly caused by one or more of the hazards insured against during the insurance period for the crop year for which the loss is claimed, and furnish any other information regarding the manner and extent of loss as may be required by the Corporation. (Emphasis added)
>
> 5(f) The tobacco stalks on any acreage of tobacco of types 11a, 11b, 12, 13, or 14 with respect to which a loss is claimed *shall not be destroyed until the Corporation makes an inspection.* (Emphasis added)

The arguments of both parties are predicated upon the same two assumptions. First, if subparagraph 5(f) creates a condition precedent, its violation caused a forfeiture of plaintiffs' coverage. Second, if subparagraph 5(f) creates an obligation (variously called a promise or covenant) upon plaintiffs not to plow under the tobacco stalks, defendant may recover from plaintiffs (either in an original action, or, in this case, by a counterclaim, or as a matter of defense) for whatever damage it

---

1. The district court also relied upon language in subparagraph 5(b), infra, which required as a condition precedent to payment that the insured, in addition to establishing his production and loss from an insured case, "furnish any other information regarding the manner and extent of loss as may be required by the Corporation." The court construed the preservation of the stalks as such "information." We see no language in the policy or connection in the record to indicate this is the case.

sustained because of the elimination of the stalks. However, a violation of subparagraph 5(f) would not, under the second premise, standing alone, cause a forfeiture of the policy.

Generally accepted law provides us with guidelines here. There is a general legal policy opposed to forfeitures. Insurance policies are generally construed most strongly against the insurer. When it is doubtful whether words create a promise or a condition precedent, they will be construed as creating a promise. The provisions of a contract will not be construed as conditions precedent in the absence of language plainly requiring such construction.

Plaintiffs rely most strongly upon the fact that the term "condition precedent" is included in subparagraph 5(b) but not in subparagraph 5(f). It is true that whether a contract provision is construed as a condition or an obligation does not depend entirely upon whether the word "condition" is expressly used. However, the persuasive force of plaintiffs' argument in this case is found in the use of the term "condition precedent" in subparagraph 5(b) but not in subparagraph 5(f). Thus, it is argued that the ancient maxim to be applied is that the expression of one thing is the exclusion of another.

The defendant places principal reliance upon the decision of this court in *Fidelity–Phenix Fire Insurance Company v. Pilot Freight Carriers*, 193 F.2d 812 (4th Cir.1952). Suit there was predicated upon a loss resulting from theft out of a truck covered by defendant's policy protecting plaintiff from such a loss. The insurance company defended upon the grounds that the plaintiff had left the truck unattended without the alarm system being on. The policy contained six paragraphs limiting coverage. Two of those imposed what was called a "condition precedent." They largely related to the installation of specified safety equipment. Several others, including paragraph 5, pertinent in that case, started with the phrase, "It is further warranted." In paragraph 5, the insured warranted that the alarm system would be on whenever the vehicle was left unattended. Paragraph 6 starts with the language: "The assured agrees, by acceptance of this policy, that the foregoing conditions precedent relate to matters material to the acceptance of the risk by the insurer." Plaintiff recovered in the district court, but judgment on its behalf was reversed because of a breach of warranty of paragraph 5, the truck had been left unattended with the alarm off. In that case, plaintiff relied upon the fact that the words "condition precedent" were used in some of the paragraphs but the word "warranted" was used in the paragraph in issue. In rejecting that contention, this court said that "warranty" and "condition precedent" are often used interchangeably to create a condition of the insured's promise, and "[m]anifestly the terms 'condition precedent' and 'warranty' were intended to have the same meaning and effect."

Fidelity–Phenix thus does not support defendant's contention here. Although there is some resemblance between the two cases, analysis shows that the issues are actually entirely different. Unlike the case at bar, each paragraph in *Fidelity–Phenix* contained either the term "condition precedent" or the term "warranted." We held that, in that situation, the two terms had the same effect in that they both involved forfeiture. That is well established law. In the case at bar, the term "warranty" or "warranted" is in no way involved, either in terms or by way of like language, as it was in *Fidelity–Phenix.* The issue upon which this case turns, then, was not involved in *Fidelity–Phenix.*

The Restatement of the Law of Contracts states:

§ 261. *Interpretation of Doubtful Words as Promise or Condition.*

Where it is doubtful whether words create a promise or an express condition, they are interpreted as creating a promise; but the same words may sometimes mean that one party promises a performance and that the other party's promise is conditional on that performance.

Two illustrations (one involving a promise, the other a condition) are used in the Restatement:

2. A, an insurance company, issues to B a policy of insurance containing promises by A that are in terms conditional on the happening of certain events. The policy contains this clause: "provided, in case differences shall arise touching any loss, *the matter shall be submitted to impartial arbitrators,* whose award shall be binding on the parties." This is a promise to arbitrate and does not make an award a condition precedent of the insurer's duty to pay.

3. A, an insurance company, issues to B an insurance policy in usual form containing this clause: "In the event of disagreement as to the amount of loss it shall be ascertained by two appraisers and an umpire. The loss shall *not be payable until 60 days after the award of the appraisers when such an appraisal is required.*" This provision is not merely a promise to arbitrate differences but makes an award a condition of the insurer's duty to pay in case of disagreement. (Emphasis added)

We believe that subparagraph 5(f) in the policy here under consideration fits illustration 2 rather than illustration 3. Illustration 2 specifies something to be done, whereas subparagraph 5(f) specifies something not to be done. Unlike illustration 3, subparagraph 5(f) does not state any conditions under which the insurance shall "not be payable," or use any words of like import. We hold that the district court erroneously held, on the motion for summary judgment, that subparagraph 5(f) established a condition precedent to plaintiffs' recovery which forfeited the coverage.

From our holding that defendant's motion for summary judgment was improperly allowed, it does not follow the plaintiffs' motion for summary judgment should have been granted, for if subparagraph 5(f) be not construed as a condition precedent, there are other questions of fact to be determined. At this point, we merely hold that the district court erred in holding, on the motion for summary judgment, that subparagraph 5(f) constituted a condition precedent with resulting forfeiture.

The explanation defendant makes for including subparagraph 5(f) in the tobacco endorsement is that it is necessary that the stalks remain standing in order for the Corporation to evaluate the extent of loss and to determine whether loss resulted from some cause not covered by the policy. However, was subparagraph 5(f) inserted because without it the Corporation's opportunities for proof would be more difficult, or because they would be impossible? Plaintiffs point out that the Tobacco Endorsement, with subparagraph 5(f), was adopted in 1970, and crop insurance goes back long before that date. Nothing is shown as to the Corporation's prior 1970 practice of evaluating losses. Such a showing might have a bearing upon establishing defendant's intention in including 5(f). Plaintiffs state, and defendant does not deny, that another division of the Department of Agriculture, or the North Carolina Department, urged that tobacco stalks be cut as soon as possible after harvesting as a means of pest control. Such an explanation might refute the idea that plaintiffs plowed under the stalks for any fraudulent purpose. Could these conflicting directives affect the reasonableness of plaintiffs' interpretation of defendant's prohibition upon plowing under the stalks prior to adjustment?

We express no opinion on these questions because they were not before the district court and are mentioned to us largely by way of argument rather than from the record. . . Nothing we say here should preclude FCIC from asserting as a defense that the plowing or disking under of the stalks caused damage to FCIC if, for example, the amount of the loss was thereby made more difficult or impossible to ascertain whether the plowing or disking under was done with bad purpose or innocently. To repeat, our narrow holding is that merely plowing or disking under the stalks does not of itself operate to forfeit coverage under the policy.

The case is remanded for further proceedings not inconsistent with this opinion.

QUESTIONS AND NOTES

1. The court decides that subparagraph 5(f) is not a condition to Howard's right to recover on his claim for crop damage. Is subparagraph 5(f) a promise? What are the insurer's damages for Howard's breach of that promise?

2. Who should have the burden of demonstrating the existence of an insured loss? Could the insurer ever disprove such a claim if it had to carry the burden of proof rather than the farmer? As a result of this decision, is the insurer liable for however many stalks of tobacco the farmer claims to have lost?

3. Does it matter if the farmer plows the field under the day after the crop is allegedly damaged by rain or if the insurer delays sending out an adjuster for two months?

4. Note that the language of subparagraph 5(f) is somewhat ambiguous. What do you advise the insurer to do to avoid these problems in the future? Suppose the insurer printed a new policy form that began every clause in the contract with the following words in large red letters: "It shall be a condition precedent to each and every one of the obligations of the company under this policy that ..."?

5. Suppose the court did find subparagraph 5(f) to be a condition but Howard has a video recording taken after the storm but before the plowing under showing each and every one of his tobacco stalks in loving detail? What arguments would you make for Howard that the condition should not bar his claim?

6. Can you reconcile *Howard* with *Merritt Hill*? Did it make sense to allow buyer to terminate in *Merritt Hill* but not get damages? Does it make sense in *Howard* to allow the insurer to receive damages but not terminate coverage?

ARTHUR L. CORBIN, *CONDITIONS IN THE LAW OF CONTRACT*, 28 YALE L.J. 739, 746 (1919):

It may be observed that both a promise and a condition are means that are used to bring about certain desired action by another person. For example, an insurance company desires the payment of premiums. One means of securing this desired object would be to obtain a promise by the insured to pay premiums; on failure to pay them an action would lie. In fact, however, insurance policies seldom contain such a promise; the payment of the premiums is secured in a more effective way than that. The insurance company makes its own duty to pay the amount of the policy expressly conditional upon the payment of premiums. Here is no express promise of the insured creating a duty to pay premiums, but ... an express condition precedent to his right to recover on the policy. Payment by the insured is obtained not by holding a lawsuit over him *in terrorem* but by hanging before him a purse of money to be reached only by climbing the ladder of premiums. Before bilateral contracts became enforceable this was the only contractual way for a promisor to secure his desired object. He might offer his promise and specify the desired performance as the one mode of acceptance; or he might deliver his own sealed promise, making it expressly conditional upon the desired performance. In either case the promisee would have no legal right against the promisor, and could not get the purse of money, unless he first performed as desired. But as soon as bilateral contracts (mutual promises creating mutual duties) became enforceable, the courts observed that a promisor now had a new remedy and a new means of securing his desired object.

Previously, in getting a return promise he got nothing; now he got a legally enforceable right. Hence, it did not appear unjust to declare mutual promises to be independent, and to compel a defendant to perform as he had agreed even though the plaintiff had failed to perform his part; the defendant had a like remedy in his turn against the plaintiff. It gradually became evident, however, that the contracting parties usually made no conscious choice of remedies, choosing the remedy on a promise rather than the advantage given by a condition. Often the remedy on a promise is very inadequate, and it is not surprising that the courts reverted to the earlier form. At first they seized upon such words as "for" and "in consideration of," construing these to create express conditions. Later, by reading wholly between the lines, they found a supposed intention of the parties that the defendant's promise should be conditional, or in the absence of any intention whatever they frankly constructed a condition in order to do justice according to the *mores* of the time. Thus grew up the rules of law concerning implied and constructive conditions.

1. Limitations on Express Conditions

When a contract expressly denominates an event as a condition of a party's obligation to perform, it gives that party very potent controls over the other—controls that in many cases are more powerful than any remedy available for breach of promise. Skillful drafters make full use of this control by incorporating in written agreements various express terms that they specify shall be conditions to their client's obligation. At first blush, one would expect that a system committed to freedom of contract would give full effect to an explicit agreement by the parties that performance by one party was not required if the other party did not first fully satisfy all the conditions. After all, conditions are intended to fix the time and order of performance and to allocate the risks. But, there are limitations on the power of even the cleverest of lawyers to control the other party by sophisticated use of express conditions. Suppose, for example, that the landowner who contracts to have a large building constructed on his lot insists upon an express provision in his contract with the builder that unless the building is completed no later than December 10th, the obligation of the owner to pay for the building will be discharged. Suppose, further, that the overanxious (and overconfident) builder agrees to the contract with this term included. If the building (with a contract price of $15,000,000) is only 95% completed on December 10th, does the owner get it for nothing?

A court is likely to be very strict with a party seeking to enforce so harsh a condition and may find waiver of the condition on rather flimsy grounds. As you have seen in *Howard v. FCIC*, the process of interpretation also provides ample opportunities to avoid injustice. Moreover, "the law abhors a forfeiture," and if the result of giving full effect to the condition is so labeled, the court will avoid enforcing it. In addition to doctrine concerning interpretation, waiver, and anti-forfeiture, the law of restitution or the distinction between entire and divisible contracts may also be drawn upon to limit the untoward consequences of enforcement of such conditions. Finally, a condition may so limit a party's obligation that it will be held to swallow up her promise and the consideration supporting enforcement of the agreement. "I will paint your house if I feel like it" is a promise so conditioned as to be illusory. *See* p. 27. Thus, although there is no general principle denying enforcement of the parties' express conditions because they operate harshly, in many instances courts find other bases to limit enforcement of a condition that appears to operate in a harsh manner.

The lines that mark these limitations may sometimes be indistinct and wavering, for they are greatly affected by the relative positions of the parties and their respective bargaining power. Many of the trapdoors that are used by courts to allow parties to escape from express conditions may swing open only when there is a sense of moral outrage at shockingly unfair terms. Courts are more apt to relieve harsh conditions imposed by powerful drafters on parties with no realistic ability to bargain.

EDWIN W. PATTERSON, *CONSTRUCTIVE CONDITIONS IN CONTRACTS,* 42 COLUM. L. REV. 903, 926 (1942):

The Prevention of Forfeitures and Unjust Enrichment. Relief against forfeitures originated, in English law, in courts of equity, which developed the mortgagor's equity of redemption and gave relief against the penalties of penal bonds. The principle that one person should not be unjustly enriched at another's expense originated partly in the equitable doctrine of constructive trusts and partly in the common law remedies for quasi contract. Avowedly and vocally the courts stay, for the most part, within these conventional lines. Yet under the guise of "interpretation" or "construction," much is done by way of relieving against express conditions which entail forfeiture—a practice now partly recognized and placed on its true ground. With respect to constructive conditions, two points may be noted: (1) That "forfeiture" is sometimes to be taken in a broader sense than unjust enrichment; (2) that unjust enrichment is an influential factor in situations where the remedy is, or is conceived to be, contractual, not quasi contractual. As to the first, the process of determining when a party's breach is sufficiently "material" to justify the other in ceasing performance is influenced by the extent to which the former has committed himself as a result of the contract, even though his commitment has not enriched the other party. Whether one calls this "hardship" or "forfeiture," the principle is clear. The second point is exemplified in several ways. The rule that substantial performance of the promise is a sufficient compliance with the constructive condition to permit recovery "on the contract," is apparently limited to cases in which the defendant has received the benefit of the performance. That "substantial performance" has been chiefly applied to building contracts merely shows that the "inarticulate and unconscious judgment" would be a better judgment if it were articulated. Another example is "severability," which divides and weakens the force of constructive conditions and which is influenced by the principle of avoiding unjust enrichment as well as by the terms of the contract. The doctrine of "waiver," which permits a partial failure of a constructive condition to be excused by loose and sometimes dubious manifestations of consent, is likewise influenced by the principle of unjust enrichment. Finally, the quasi contractual remedy for unjust enrichment has grown up alongside the contractual remedy, and even under the same procedural forms, to mitigate the hardships of constructive conditions. That it has grown sporadically and unevenly is another story.

RESTATEMENT, SECOND, CONTRACTS:

§ 229. Excuse of a Condition to Avoid Forfeiture.

To the extent that the non-occurrence of a condition would cause disproportionate forfeiture, a court may excuse the non-occurrence of that condition unless its occurrence was a material part of the agreed exchange.

Margolin v. Franklin
Illinois Appellate Court, First District, 1971.
132 Ill.App.2d 527, 270 N.E.2d 140.

■ ADESKO, PRESIDING JUSTICE. Plaintiff, Essco Motors, brought an action against defendants Melvin and Betty Franklin to confess judgment on a promissory note. Defendants petitioned to open and vacate the judgment by confession and counterclaimed for $1,500.00 by reason of plaintiff's fraudulent and wilful conversion of their automobile. The cause proceeded to trial. The court, sitting without a jury, entered judgment on the counterclaim in the amount of $921.00.

Plaintiff appeals contending (1) the finding as to a modification in terms of payment of the contract was not supported by the evidence and is contrary to the established law of Illinois; (2) the defendant failed to prove the value of the automobile at the time of the alleged conversion; and (3) the plaintiff was deprived of a fair and impartial hearing due to the bias of the trial judge.

The facts adduced at trial are as follows: On January 31, 1966, defendants entered into a retail installment contract with plaintiff Essco Motors to purchase a 1961 Ford Thunderbird. The price was $1,352.00 on which defendants paid $300.00 down leaving a balance of $1,052.00. To this balance Essco Motors added finance and insurance charges in the amount of $604.00. The Franklins signed a note in the amount of $1,656.00.

The contract called for 24 monthly payments of $69.00 due on the 15th of each month, commencing February 15, 1966. The Franklins made $69.00 payments on February 15, 1966, March 15, 1966, April 25, 1966, May 23, 1966, June 24, 1966, July 26, 1966, August 24, 1966, September 27, 1966 and October 27, 1966. On November 26, 1966, the plaintiff had the automobile repossessed and held a "technical sale" as it was described by one of plaintiff's employees, because "we can get the car back after it is sold."

The testimony of the parties differs sharply as to what transpired between April and November of 1966. Irvin Tyne, credit and collection manager of Essco Motors, testified the Franklins called and asked if they could make a late payment for the month of April. He told them it would be alright for that month. He further testified that in May the payment was not made by the 15th and he sent a reminder notice on the 17th and a final notice on the 20th. The May payment was received on the 23rd. The same situation occurred in June with the reminder and final notices being sent before payment was received. Reminder notices were also sent in the months of July, August, September and October since payment had not been made by the 15th of those months. Payments were made in those months on the 26th, 24th, 27th and 27th respectively. Tyne also testified he spoke on the phone to Mrs. Franklin in July, August and September and she stated in each instance she would make payment shortly.

In November, after the reminder notice was sent, Tyne called the Franklins at their respective places of employment and their home but could not reach them. He thought the defendants had "skipped" town and ordered a repossession of the automobile. The car was returned to the Essco Motors on November 26, 1966.

Mrs. Franklin testified she spoke with Mr. Tyne in April and explained to him her husband had changed jobs and would not get paid until later in the month. She asked that the payment date be changed from the 15th of the month to the 27th of the month and received his agreement. The April payment was made on April 25, 1966. In May she received a notice from Essco Motors before the 27th requesting payment. She called Essco Motors and asked them about the notice. The man she talked to said the notice was sent out by mistake and that she should forget about it. Mrs. Franklin further testified she had no conversations with nor did she receive any notices from Essco Motors concerning the payments after the May conversation. In November, Mrs. Franklin testified she was in New Orleans about one week before the car was repossessed. The car was repossessed on November 25, 1966, from a parking spot in front of the Franklins' apartment. The Franklins received notice that Essco Motors was going to sell the car.

Plaintiff contends the finding of the trial court as to a modification in terms of payment of the contract was not supported by the evidence and is contrary to established law in Illinois. The trial court found the Franklins had not breached the contract with Essco Motors and the taking of their automobile amounted to wrongful repossession and a breach of contract on the part of Essco. The court believed Mrs. Franklin's testimony that Essco Motors agreed to accept payments in the latter part of each month. The court stated its belief was evidenced by the exhibits at trial that showed Essco Motors accepted these payments. We agree with the trial court that the testimony and exhibits indicate a pattern of conduct on the part of Essco to accept payments from the Franklins on or before the 27th day of each month.

The law in Illinois is clear that a vendor may not establish a pattern of accepting time payments which may be slightly late and then suddenly insist on a strict compliance of the time provisions of the contract and declare a forfeiture of the merchandise. The Illinois Supreme Court has consistently held that the right to forfeit a contract is waived where the contract provides for prompt payment at fixed dates and payments are not so made and accepted after they become due. Where the parties have treated the time clause as waived with respect to some of the payments, the vendor, to avail himself of the right to forfeiture for failure to make subsequent payments on time, must give reasonable, definite and specific notice of his changed intention. The vendor in this case, Essco Motors after agreeing to a modification of the payment terms of the contract did not give the Franklins reasonable, definite and specific notice of its changed intention. Accordingly, Essco Motors could not suddenly insist on a strict literal compliance of the payment provisions of the contract and declare a forfeiture. We reject defendant's first contention.

Plaintiff-appellant next contends defendant-appellee failed to prove the value of the automobile at the time of the alleged conversion. In a conversion suit, the party alleging conversion must prove the reasonable value of the property at the time of the wrongful taking. In the instant case, on January 31, 1966, the defendants paid Essco Motors $300.00 down and executed a note for $1,656.00. The time sale price for the 1961 Thunderbird was $1,956.00. By the time of the conversion ten months later, defendants had paid Essco $921.00 of which $621.00 was in steady monthly payments. During those ten months, defendants expended $325.00 for an engine overhaul and exerted proper care and the maintenance on the automobile. On the basis of the evidence presented as to purchase price, engine overhaul, care and maintenance, period of use and depreciation, and balance due, we find that $921.00 is reasonable compensation to the defendants for damages incurred by the wrongful possession of their automobile.

Plaintiff-appellant finally contends it was deprived of a fair and impartial hearing due to the bias of the trial judge. Plaintiff cites two examples of the trial judge's prejudice: (1) The trial judge believed the testimony of Mrs. Franklin who was fabricating her story; and (2) the trial judge made remarks about car dealers and finance companies which show an attitude of distaste and prejudice towards persons in the time sale business.

As to the first example, the trier of fact is the sole judge of the credibility of the witnesses and because the judge believed the defendants does not mean he was prejudiced against the plaintiff. As to the second example, we have carefully reviewed the report of the proceedings, especially those portions cited to us by plaintiff-appellant in its brief and nowhere do we find the prejudicial statements allegedly made by the trial court. We find only allegations by trial counsel that the trial court made prejudicial statements. The trial judge himself expressed shock when counsel for the plaintiff made such charges at the presentation of the motion to amend the judgment. The trial judge denied making such statements and to emphasize his impartiality stated never before had he entered a judgment against the seller and repossessor of merchandise.

Appellant, Essco Motors, has by innuendo and inference at trial and on appeal attempted to create the impression the decision of the trial court was based on prejudice and bias instead of the facts. This contention is without foundation.

Judgment affirmed.

QUESTIONS AND NOTES

1. What, if anything, might Essco have done differently as of May 15 to protect its right to enforce the due date expressly stated in its contract? How would different behavior affect the story that could be told at trial?

2. Comment c following the Reporter's Note to Restatement, Second, Contracts § 229 states:

> COMMENT
>
> *c.* When an obligee has acquiesced in an obligor's failure strictly to adhere to a timetable of payment or performance, courts often are inhospitable to the obligee's sudden invocation of forfeiture provisions. The courts may find a "waiver"—an implicit subsequent agreement modifying the requirement of strictly timely payment or performance; it may find the obligee's acquiescence evidence that time was not of the essence; or it may treat the obligee's acquiescence as a factor, which because it induced reliance, triggers the court's power of equity.

3. Did the Court deem Essco to have waived its right, to be estopped from insisting upon its right, or to have agreed to a modification? Is there a difference?

4. Should it be assumed that every time a creditor takes a lenient attitude toward a debtor in distress, the consequence will be a waiver of the original time set for payment in the agreement? Don't people who finance cars for wage earners build in late payments as a cost of business?

5. Would it have made a difference to the court whether the contract itself stated that a history of acceptance of late payments would not constitute a waiver? In *Zinser v. Uptown Fed. Sav. & Loan*, 542 N.E.2d 87 (Ill. App. Ct. 1989), the plaintiff purchased a truck and entered into a written installment loan agreement with the car dealership which was then immediately assigned to the Bank. The installment loan agreement provided: "Waiver of any default in the payment of any installment of the total of payments when due shall not operate as a waiver of any subsequent default. No extension of the time of payment or any other modification of the terms of this contract shall be binding on holder unless written consent thereof is given." Before the first installment payment became due, the plaintiff lost his job. He promptly informed the Bank and requested a moratorium on future payments until he got another job, and the Bank orally agreed. When the plaintiff found new employment, he paid for the three months prior and for the following month. During the next six months, the plaintiff paid some of the installment payments on time and some late. Although the plaintiff believed he was current, the Bank asserted that the plaintiff was behind in three or four payments and, so, repossessed the plaintiff's truck. Among the plaintiff's claims against the Bank was "that despite the non-waiver clause in the installment contract, the repossession and retention of his truck without notice or consent constitutes an 'unfair act or practice' where the Bank has condoned past defaults." The court concluded that "[t]here is nothing in the [*Margolin*] opinion to indicate that the dealer's repossession of the automobile without notice violated public policy or constituted an 'unfair act or practice.'" But was it a breach of contract?

---

2. Conditions Precedent, Concurrent, and Subsequent

Where an event must exist or occur before a duty of immediate performance of a promise arises, the condition is said to be precedent. For instance, consider, "I promise to take your cows into shelter if it rains tomorrow." Only upon the occurrence of the conditioning event—the rain—does any obligation to perform arise. If it doesn't rain, the promisor need do nothing.

Where the occurrence of an event extinguishes an existent immediate duty to perform, the condition is said to be subsequent. So if Seller says "I will sell you my grain for $5.00 per bushel, unless Congress raises the parity support level above $4.25," the occurrence of the conditioning event—Congressional action raising the support level above $4.25—extinguishes or discharges the outstanding obligation to perform. If Congress doesn't raise the support level, the promisor must sell the grain.

The distinction between conditions precedent and subsequent is more form than substance. Words usually can be arranged in such a way as to make any condition appear to be a duty-discharging event (condition subsequent) or a duty-ripening event (condition precedent). For example, if a contract between Seller and Buyer states, "Seller agrees to perform on February 1 unless fire destroys Seller's warehouse," the destruction of the warehouse by fire appears to be a condition subsequent, discharging Seller's duty. But what if the contract states, "Seller agrees to perform on February 1 on condition that fire does not destroy Seller's warehouse." Is it, as it appears to be, a condition precedent to Seller's duty to perform, or is it only a condition precedent in form but a condition subsequent in fact?

Little consequence should be attached to such distinctions. As Holmes observed, "[I]n one sense, all conditions are subsequent; in another all are precedent." Partly on account of Holmes' criticism of this terminology, the Restatement, Second, Contracts defines conditions precedent as simply "conditions" in § 224: "A condition is an event, not certain to occur, which must occur, unless its non-occurrence is excused, before performance under a contract becomes due." Restatement, Second, Contracts also drops the use of the term condition subsequent and treats the concept in § 230 under the heading "Event that Terminates a Duty." Section 230 provides in relevant part that "if under the terms of the contract the occurrence of an event is to terminate an obligor's duty of immediate performance or one to pay damages for breach, that duty is discharged if the event occurs."

If little should turn on the distinction between conditions precedent and conditions subsequent, and if the Restatement avoids this terminology, why mention it at all? Historically, the distinction served as the basis for allocating burdens of pleading and proof in litigation. If a condition is labeled precedent, the party claiming breach must allege (and, if the allegation is challenged, ultimately prove) the occurrence of the condition as an essential element of the claim. On the other hand, if a condition is labeled a condition subsequent, the party defending against the claim must allege (and ultimately prove) the occurrence as an excuse for nonperformance.

At one time, this distinction was given great weight. Most conditions were interpreted to be precedent, and plaintiffs often found themselves pleading and proving the satisfaction of a great number of irrelevant conditions. Pleading rules required plaintiffs to allege specifically, and not generally, all facts relevant to the occurrence of all conditions. At the same time, pleading rules allowed defendant, by filing a general denial, to put these facts into issue, thereby requiring plaintiff to prove all these conditions were satisfied. The cumbersome, costly, and potentially unfair aspects of this system for allocating burdens of pleading and proof were substantial.

Modern civil procedure ameliorates these problems. Federal Rule of Civil Procedure 9(c) provides that "[i]n pleading the performance or occurrence of conditions precedent, it is sufficient to aver generally that all conditions precedent have been performed or have occurred. A denial of performance or occurrence shall be made specifically and with particularity." Similar rules govern most state courts. Complementing these changes, courts have shown an increased willingness to allocate burdens of pleading and proof without relying on the labels *condition precedent* and *condition subsequent.* They seem sensitive to the difficulty of proving negatives; that one party or the other may be the best source of information about the occurrence or nonoccurrence of the event; and the very fact that the lengthy, standardized form may have been drafted by one of the parties alone, without opportunity for negotiation or dickering on the fine points of allocating burdens of proof. Nevertheless, in at least some jurisdictions the distinction between conditions precedent and conditions subsequent still matters. If the parties in fact intend to allocate burden of pleading and proof by the use of such language as "on condition that" or "but if," no harm is done. One suspects, however, that the choice of such language is not generally consciously intended to perform this function.

Where each party's duty to perform is conditional upon a simultaneous tender of performance by the other, the conditions are often described as *conditions concurrent.* Consider, "I promise to deliver the bicycle to you if, as, and when you pay me $200, and you, in return, promise to pay me $200 if, as, and when I deliver the bicycle to you." Since nothing is said about which performance is to come first, the law requires neither party to perform unless the other performs at the same time. Performance, or a "tender" of performance (an offer to perform in accordance with the terms of the promise and a capacity to carry out the offer), by either party thus becomes a condition precedent to an immediate duty of performance by the other party. Only upon the occurrence of the conditioning event—performance or tender by one party—does any obligation to perform arise in the other party. If neither side performs or tenders performance, neither party has a duty to perform, and neither party can pursue a remedial claim. When conditions are concurrent, either party can place the other in default only by performing or tendering such performance so as to assure the other party that the exchange will be simultaneous. Put differently, where performance is promised to be concurrent, it is a condition precedent to a suit by either party that there be at least a tender of performance.

B.   IMPLIED AND CONSTRUCTIVE CONDITIONS

Some conditions unexpressed in the agreement may be fairly said to have been intended by the parties, but others are implied as a matter of justice, irrespective of actual intention. As Corbin observed, "A fact or event may be a condition of a contractual right or duty, even though the parties had no intention that it should so operate, said nothing about it in words, and did nothing from which an inference of intention could be drawn." Conditions that arise in this way are often called, at Corbin's urging, "constructive."

In this Topic we shall examine several commonly encountered constructive conditions, those that excuse performance based on impossibility, frustration of contract, and mistake.

The early position of the common law was that the occurrence of an event subsequent to contract formation was irrelevant unless the parties had expressly agreed that the event was a condition of performance. Even if an event had a devastating effect on the contractual relationship, the narrow logic of promise enforcement led the common law to stick to the letter of an agreement that made little or no sense under the unanticipated, but actual, circumstances facing the parties. Thus, judges were unwilling to excuse performance when supervening events had made performance of the agreement factually impossible. After all, liability for contract breach is not based on fault, and, hence, although it might be impossible for a party to perform, it would not be impossible to pay damages. Unless the parties expressly agreed to certain excusing conditions, therefore, they were held to virtually absolute liability in the event of nonperformance.

This narrow view was gradually abandoned, and courts became increasingly willing to read various excusing conditions based on the occurrence of supervening events into contracts, notwithstanding the parties' failure to anticipate and expressly provide for them. The controlling idea is that the parties would have included the condition if they had thought about it. The court is not rewriting the contract when it reads the condition in but is merely conforming the agreement to the imperfectly expressed intention of the parties.

---

1. Promises Implied by Social Expectations and Good Faith

When a contractual duty is conditional, it may be necessary for a court to interpret the agreement to require the promisor to cooperate by refraining from conduct that may prevent the occurrence of the condition or perhaps even to take affirmative steps to make the condition happen.

Recall: *Mattei v. Hopper*, p. 31.
            Sylvan Crest Sand and Gravel v. United States, p. 36.
            Wood v. Lucy, Lady Duff-Gordon, p. 40.
            B. Lewis Productions v. Angelou, p. 43.

QUESTION AND NOTE

Mattei's duty to purchase was made expressly dependent on his satisfaction with the leases Coldwell Banker was to obtain for him. *See Mattei v. Hopper*, p. 31. In order to conclude that Mattei had sufficiently committed himself to buy and, therefore, that there was consideration to bind Ms. Hopper to her promise to sell, the California Supreme Court interpreted the agreement to require Mattei to act in good faith in assessing whether he was satisfied with the leases. If Mattei does not act in good faith in determining whether the leases are satisfactory, the nonoccurrence of the condition to his duty to buy (that is, the absence of satisfactory leases) is "excused," and he would be obligated to buy the property despite the nonoccurrence of the condition. If Mattei does cooperate in good faith but is not satisfied with the leases, then his duty to purchase the property never arises because the lease condition is not satisfied. How much cooperation will do? What affirmative steps, if any, need Mattei take?

Broadly speaking entering into a contract is a form of cooperative behavior in which parties assume obligations to work together. Courts must consider the extent to which the contract implies a duty on one party to cooperate with the other in ways not explicitly required by the terms of the agreement. What did the agreement in *Mattei v. Hopper*, p. 31, require Mattei to do in seeking satisfactory leases, and what did the contract in *Wood v. Lucy, Lady Duff-Gordon*, p. 40, require Wood to do to satisfy his obligations under the arrangement? As these implied obligations are interpreted to require increasingly affirmative actions by a party, the interpreting court may appear to be "making a contract for the parties" rather than simply interpreting the agreement the parties made for themselves. Locating the appropriate outer boundaries of this judicial power raises difficult questions of policy and judicial competence.

Every contract contains obligations of cooperation, good faith, and fair dealing. The content of these obligations derives largely from the expectations of the community or business in which the parties are operating. The existence of these obligations is recognized by the Uniform Commercial Code. See § 1–304 ("Every contract or duty within this Act imposes an obligation of good faith in its performance or enforcement.") UCC § 1–201(20) defines good faith to mean "honesty in fact and the observance of reasonable commercial standards of fair dealing." (Unless the contracting party is a merchant, however, many states continue to use an older formulation of the good faith standard that limits the obligation of such a party to "honesty in fact.")

In accord with UCC § 1–304, the Restatement, 2(d) provides in § 205: "Every contract imposes upon each party a duty of good faith and fair dealing in its performance and its enforcement." The Comments to § 205 state:

a. Meanings of "Good Faith."... The phrase "good faith" is used in a variety of contexts, and its meaning varies somewhat with the context. Good faith performance or enforcement of a contract emphasizes faithfulness to an agreed common purpose and consistency with the justified expectations of the other party; it excludes a variety of types of conduct characterized as involving "bad faith" because they violate community standards of decency, fairness or reasonableness. The appropriate remedy for a breach of the duty of good faith also varies with the circumstances....

. . .

d. Good Faith Performance. Subterfuges and evasions violate the obligation of good faith in performance even though the actor believes his conduct to be justified. But the obligation goes further: bad faith may be overt or may consist of inaction, and fair dealing may require more than honesty. A complete catalogue of types of bad faith is impossible, but the following types are among those which have been recognized in judicial decisions: evasion of the spirit of the bargain, lack of diligence and slacking off, willful rendering of imperfect performance, abuse of a power to specify terms, and interference with or failure to cooperate in the other party's performance....

Parev Products Co. v. I. Rokeach & Sons

United States Court of Appeals, Second Circuit, 1941.
124 F.2d 147.

■ CLARK, J. This appeal involves the question whether or not an injunction should issue to enforce an asserted implied negative covenant in a contract granting an exclusive license to use a secret formula for a food product. In the District Court the complaint was dismissed on the merits on the ground that the parties to the contract did not intend a negative covenant. Although the District Court may perhaps have emphasized "intent" more than is realistic as to matters concerning which the parties have not revealed their thinking processes, it is, of course, obvious that the terms of the contract and the status arising out of those terms are of paramount importance. We turn, therefore, at once to the facts of the case.

In 1924, plaintiff, Parev Products, Co., Inc., entered into a contract with defendant, I. Rokeach & Sons, Inc. At that time, as can be reasonably inferred from some of the terms of the contract, plaintiff was not in the best of financial condition. So far as appears, its principal product of manufacture was Parev Schmaltz, a cooking oil made from coconut oil in such a way as to be Kosher, that is, usable with meat and dairy products without violation of the Jewish dietary laws. Parev Schmaltz was then supposed to be manufactured by a secret formula made by plaintiff's president,

Aaron Proser, and, as the contract warranted, known only to him, Solomon Proser, and Julius Proser, though at the time a patent had been applied for on the formula and process. Defendant, on the other hand, was a successful business house of long standing. It engaged in extensive merchandising of food and cleansing products, mostly to orthodox Jews. The purpose of the contract, so far as appears, was to enable plaintiff to get out of its difficulties and to provide defendant with a Kosher semisolid vegetable oil.

By the terms of the contract, defendant obtained the exclusive use of all the necessary secret formulae, etc., for a period of twenty-five years, with an option to renew for another twenty-five years. In return, plaintiff was to receive royalties on all sales of Parev Schmaltz. Defendant had several powers to terminate, however. It could terminate the contract at any time it found the formula not to have been secret. Up to two years after the date of the contract, it could terminate the contract without cause upon payment of $100; and after two years, upon payment of $500. If any patents were judicially declared invalid, the contract was to terminate automatically. In defending any patent actions, plaintiff was to bear the full cost if suits arose during the first two years; after that, costs were to be split.

Under the agreement defendant was privileged to use Parev Schmaltz as it should "think fit for its use and benefit absolutely." This same privilege was restated in another part of the contract with a complete specification of what was included, such as labels, trademarks, good will, and so on. For its part, plaintiff agreed not to engage or aid in the manufacture or sale of any product "similar" to Parev Schmaltz or in any business incidental thereto during the life of the contract; moreover, it agreed to deliver the agreement of the three Prosers not to "engage or aid, either severally or collectively, directly or indirectly, in the manufacture, sale or distribution of any article that might be in competition with [defendant] in the sale, manufacture and distribution of Parev Schmaltz or of any similar product." Defendant promised after termination or expiration of the contract "not to engage in, directly or indirectly, in [sic] the manufacture, sale or distribution of the product Parev Schmaltz, or any product of a similar nature." Defendant was privileged to discard the name Parev Schmaltz, however, and any name which was substituted would always remain defendant's property.

It should be noted that the contract therefore contained at least three express negative covenants, none directly applicable to the case before the court, and that the one to be made by the Prosers as individuals is the more extensive in mode of expression at least.

Thereafter defendant immediately dropped the name Parev Schmaltz, adopted Nyafat in its stead, and commenced production. From the beginning, Nyafat was a success and during the fifteen-year period from 1924 to 1939, royalties of approximately $135,000 were paid over. In 1940, however a disturbing factor entered the picture. Defendant began the distribution of Kea, a semisolid cooking oil made almost wholly from cottonseed oil. Although defendant does not manufacture Kea, it distributes it under its own label as a Kosher product to the same orthodox Jewish trade. Defendant, of course, has not paid any royalties to plaintiff on its sales of Kea. Plaintiff claims that, since the royalties on Nyafat are based on an absolute sum per ounce and since the price obtained by defendant has been falling, defendant has undertaken the sale of Kea to avoid its royalty obligation. Defendant, on the other hand, asserts that Crisco and Spry, widely selling cooking oils, were cutting into the Nyafat market. This was aggravated, defendant says, by a nationwide price war which occurred as soon as Spry went on the market. Consequently, it is urged, defendant had to obtain a new product "similar" to Spry and Crisco, and in the same price range.

In this action, plaintiff seeks an injunction against any further sales of Kea by defendant. The theory is that we should imply a negative covenant on the part of defendant not to compete with its own Nyafat, or in any other way to interfere with the sales of Nyafat. Defendant's argument is that no covenant should be implied beyond what it calls conduct on its part of a "tortious" nature, or, in the alternative, that any covenant would forbid only the sale of products of a "similar nature." Kea, it says, is not similar. One is made from coconut oil, one from cottonseed oil. One is yellow, one is white; one is neutral in flavor, the other has an onion flavor. Other, somewhat esoteric, differences can be spelled out.

Although the District Court placed considerable reliance on this argument, we do not think that this should be finally conclusive. If any covenant is to be implied, it must be one which reaches the core of this dispute, which is the claim that a directly competitive product is produced by defendant. Whatever reasons there are for imposing on defendant such a strict obligation are hardly vitiated by the difference in composition of the two products. They are used for exactly the same purpose—shortening; if any covenant is to be implied, it would be hollow unless it took note of this fact. Thus, it seems rather unlikely that had plaintiff undertaken the manufacture of Kea today a court would have been content to say, as against a suit by the defendant, that the products were not similar under plaintiff's express covenant not to distribute a similar shortening.

Should, therefore, a covenant be implied under all the present circumstances? When we turn to the precedents we are met at once with the confusion of statement whether a covenant can be implied only if it was clearly "intended" by the parties, or whether such a covenant can rest on principles of equity. Expressions can be found which insist on "intention," which seem to combine both a requirement of "intention" and of "equity and justice," and which by-pass "intention" and rely solely on equity. One may perhaps conclude that in large measure this confusion arises out of the reluctance of courts to admit that they were to a considerable extent "remaking" a contract in situations where it seemed necessary and appropriate so to do. "Intention of the parties" is a good formula by which to square doctrine with result. That this is true has long been an open secret. *See* 3 WILLISTON ON CONTRACTS, Rev.Ed.1936, § 825; Holmes, *The Path of the Law*, 10 HARV.L.REV. 457, 466; Fuller, *Legal Fictions*, 25 ILL.L.REV. 363, 369; Chafee, *The Disorderly Conduct of Words*, 41 COL.L.REV. 381, 398.[2] Of course, where intent, though obscure, is nevertheless discernible, it must be followed; but a certain sophistication must be recognized—if we are to approach the matter frankly—where we are dealing with changed circumstances, fifteen years later, with respect to a contract which does not touch this exact point and which has at most only points of departure for more or less pressing analogies.

Here defendant has a strong point in stressing the various extensive grants to it of the contract, as well as the express negative covenants which do not touch the present case. Undoubtedly extensive freedom of action was intended it. And yet that could not have been wholly unlimited, as indeed, defendant properly concedes when it admits that at least tortious competition or destruction of the Nyafat market was not open to it. And we must consider that in the period of time since the making of the contract there have been various developments which present a situation not clearly, if at all, within the contemplation of the parties at the time. Here a status exists upon which each party should be entitled to rely. What we should seek is therefore that which will most nearly preserve the status created and developed by the parties.

If we thus emphasize the situation existing today, two facts stand out. Plaintiff must clearly rely on defendant for any future benefit to be derived from its original formula; and defendant, if it is to continue to remain in the vegetable oil market, must be able to prevent the inroads of outside products, such as Crisco and Spry. So far as the plaintiff is concerned, it has long since lost its hold on its own formula. Nyafat is known to the public as a Rokeach product. Even were the defendant to release the formula, plaintiff would have some difficulty. This is not the controlling factor, for if it were, defendant might very well terminate the contract. Instead, the sales of Nyafat continue. And yet if no covenant is found, defendant to some extent can let Nyafat slip in sales, while Kea is boosted. In other words, if the defendant does not terminate the contract, it can keep Nyafat under its control until Kea is

---

2. *Cf.* Chafee, *loc. cit.*:

My first suggestion is, that we should firmly resolve never to speak of the intention of a testator or other writer on a given point except after we have carefully convinced ourselves that that point was actually in his mind when he wrote the words in question. For example, we will never say "He intended this result" when we merely think that if he had foreseen the present contingency (which he didn't) then he would have intended this result. That consideration may be helpful, but it is not his intention.

successfully built up, and then it can safely forget Nyafat. The advantage is all to defendant. But a court of equity should grant some protection to a person who parts with his formula for exploitation. Thus, a court would hardly have permitted the defendant from the inception of this contract to lock up the plaintiff's formula in a vault and freely market Kea. There is no reason to do so now.

But defendant has an equally justifiable complaint to make. Kea, it asserts, is marketed only to compete with other products; and no attempt is made to injure Nyafat's market. Certainly we cannot say that defendant must market Nyafat, come what may, down to the sale of a mere can a year, while the vegetable oil business goes to outsiders. That would as violently alter the status of the parties as would a decree of complete freedom to defendant. It is thus clear that a strict injunction against any marketing of Kea is unjustified. Yet a complete denial of relief to the plaintiff under any circumstances would not be fair either.

As we have previously suggested, defendant indirectly acknowledges the need for a middle ground when it argues that cases implying a negative covenant have as their rationale the requirement that the conduct enjoined be tortious. This, presumably, amounts to saying that so long as defendant acts in good faith in judging the extent to which Kea must be sold to meet the competition of Crisco and Spry, no cause of action lies. But this, it seems to us, is to state the rule too narrowly; a limited rule of good faith, valid so far as it goes, does not exhaust the possibilities. The really equitable solution is to permit defendant to sell Kea so long as it does not invade Nyafat's market if that point is susceptible of proof, as we think it is. Thus, assuming that defendant is correct in its assertions, Kea sells only to people who no longer buy Nyafat.[3] Hence, all the plaintiff is entitled to is the market Nyafat has created and will retain, regardless of outside competition.

An injunction to reach such a conclusion would be so vague as to be meaningless under present circumstances. Its practical effect would be to restrain defendant from any sales of Kea—which we have held to be unfair. Only by inserting "good faith" in the restraining order could defendant be protected; and this would be equivalent to the rule we have found too narrow. It follows, then, that on the present record plaintiff cannot obtain an injunction. A broad one would be unfair to defendant; a narrow one would be an empty gesture.

But plaintiff should not be denied the opportunity to show a loss of the Nyafat market as we have thus defined it. Plaintiff may be protected if it can be determined what sales of Kea represent loss to outside products, what sales represent loss to

---

3. It is only fair to state that plaintiff produced two housewives who said they had discontinued the use of Nyafat because Kea was cheaper. These witnesses did not say, however, that they would not have switched to Spry or Crisco.

Nyafat. Expert appraisal of market conditions would, it seems to us, answer this.[4] If loss were established, the measure of damages would be the amount of royalties on the displaced jars of Nyafat. On this record, the evidence is too fragmentary to be conclusive. Since an injunction was sought, the action was brought too soon to reflect the nature of the competition among the various cooking oils. If the plaintiff has further evidence of the inroads of Kea, it should be entitled to present it, either hereinafter in this case or in a later action.

Judgment affirmed, with costs to defendant and with leave to plaintiff either to move to reopen the action, or to bring a subsequent action, for relief not inconsistent with this opinion.

QUESTIONS AND NOTES

1. What is the result in this case? Does the court imply a negative covenant in this case? What are its terms? The Second Circuit may be understood as saying that the trial court was right to deny the specific injunction sought, but that the plaintiff is entitled to go back and try again. What will happen next time?

2. If cottonseed oil shortening is cheaper, looks better, and has superior cooking characteristics to coconut oil shortening and, therefore, will be preferred by 90 out of 100 consumers with a choice, how can Rokeach sell Kea without inevitably causing Nyafat to lose 90% of its market?

3. Rokeach has an option to cancel this agreement upon payment of $500. If it were to exercise this right and pay the $500, would it still be limited in its marketing of Kea? Why didn't Rokeach's lawyer tell his client to give notice of cancellation and avoid all this litigation?

4. Should a judge be as ready to imply a negative covenant after 15 years as she might be to find an obligation not to compete immediately after the contract was negotiated? The court is confronted with a contract that has been working for 15 years and has given rise to a network of relationships from which it is difficult to extract the parties. Perhaps, as suggested by Professor Michael Asimow, *Rokeach* is a case of the judge forcing the parties to go back and negotiate a settlement because he knew there was no way to determine this dispute by trial.

---

4. Assume, for example, that sales of Nyafat dropped steadily from 1933 to 1936, then from 1936 to 1939 Nyafat held its own. And assume Kea was introduced in 1939. If from 1939 on, Nyafat still held its own, Kea was not injuring Nyafat. On the other hand, if Nyafat again declined while Kea went up, Kea would be invading Nyafat's own irreducible minimum market. To be sure, this is an oversimplified example, and many extraneous factors affecting marketing would have to be eliminated. This would be the task of expert witnesses.

5. The available information on the actual outcome of this dispute is instructive, for it reminds us that eventually all disputes are resolved, sometimes by events that have little to do with the actions of the parties or their lawyers. In 1988, the retired manager of I. Rokeach & Sons informed us that after the Second Circuit decision, the product formula for Nyafat was radically changed because its major ingredient, coconut oil, became unavailable after the Japanese invasion of the Philippines in late 1941. His best recollection is that in consideration for the termination of the agreement, Rokeach paid Parev Products a small amount. In 1945, after the end of the war, the original formula was restored, but nothing more was paid to Parev. Meanwhile, the competing product, Kea, was not well accepted in the market and was dropped by Rokeach within two years of its introduction.

■ ANTONIN SCALIA, J., in *Tymshare v. Covell*, 727 F.2d 1145, 1152 (D.C. Cir. 1984): [T]he doctrine of good faith performance is a means of finding within a contract an implied obligation not to engage in the particular form of conduct which, in the case at hand, constitutes "bad faith." In other words, the authorities that invoke, with increasing frequency, an all-purpose doctrine of "good faith" are usually if not invariably performing the same function executed (with more elegance and precision) by Judge Cardozo in *Wood v. Lady Duff–Gordon*, when he found that an agreement which did not recite a particular duty was nonetheless "'instinct with an obligation imperfectly expressed.'" The new formulation may have more appeal to modern taste since it purports to rely directly upon considerations of morality and public policy, rather than achieving those objectives obliquely, by honoring the reasonable expectations created by the autonomous expressions of the contracting parties. But it seems to us that the result is, or should be, the same.

---

2. Supervening Events

Sometimes a party is unable to perform because of circumstances that could not have been reasonably anticipated or, at the very least, were unexpected. If the agreement does not expressly condition performance on a different state of affairs, the party must argue that the obligation was impliedly conditioned on the nonoccurrence of the present, unanticipated, circumstances. Even if circumstances do render performance impossible, the party's excuse will only be accepted if the court determines that the promisor has not assumed the risk of those supervening events. While actual performance may be impossible, generally there is nothing impossible or impracticable about assessing damages for nonperformance.

Thus, when a defendant claims excuse from performance because supervening events have rendered performance very difficult or impossible, courts are very likely to hold the party to its promise despite hardship. Nevertheless, there is a limit. Relief may be available in a few cases on the basis of unforeseeable changed circumstances that create palpably unfair results, do not square with general expectations, or impose staggering burdens on one party.

This tendency cannot be pushed too far, or it will protect contract breakers from liability for losses caused by market risks or by their own failure to be prudent in protecting themselves. There are cases in which somebody once could have performed or now could, but the party involved in the particular contract can't perform because it didn't do soon enough what was necessary to enable it to perform. Courts find in these cases that the nonperformer's present inability to perform is no excuse unless the parties have expressly agreed that it shall be one. Here the notion of fault obviously is a factor despite the dogma to the contrary.

Most students and some judges have trouble with the confusing vocabulary used regarding supervening events. The following cases will talk about four kinds of situations: impossibility, impracticability, frustration of contract, and mistake. There are differences between a situation in which performance is impossible and one in which it is merely so onerous that the label of impracticability applies. Frustration of contract is used to describe situations in which performance is not in any sense impossible for the party seeking excuse, but supervening events have made performance silly or futile. Overlying all these situations is the possibility that the problem is not a supervening event after formation; instead, the facts never were as the parties supposed; the contract is flawed by an essential mistake.

These terms all characterize factual situations that overlap broadly. As a result, more than one of these doctrines might fairly apply in a single case. It remains a mystery whether the problem in *Mineral Park Land v. Howard*, p. 766, is that some supervening event, heavy rains perhaps, made extraction of the earth and gravel impracticable, or whether, because of some miscalculation when the parties negotiated the deal, there never was as much earth and gravel there as the parties thought when they made the contract. Both factors might well have been present. Indeed, shifting to another example, Judge Teitelbaum in *ALCOA v. Essex*, p. 771, discusses the mess in which the parties found themselves in terms of impracticability, frustration of contract, mistake, and unconscionability. Your job in mastering this material will involve learning how events under a particular label (impossibility, impracticability, frustration, or mistake) differ from the others, while at the same time seeing the overlaps and interconnections among them.

---

3. Impossibility

The clearest category in which the excuse of impossibility is recognized includes contracts that require the personal services of an individual who is obviously unable to perform because of death or disability. It also includes contracts pertaining to specific property when the unique subject matter has been destroyed, as well as when a specified means of performance is impossible, for example, a contract requiring shipment by a specific ship which sinks before loading. Finally, it includes situations in which performance has become forbidden by law or governmental order.

Oneal v. Colton Consolidated School District No. 306

Washington Court of Appeals, 1976.
16 Wash.App. 488, 557 P.2d 11.

■ McINTURFF, C.J. Stanley Oneal appeals his discharge and denial of sick leave benefits by the Colton Consolidated School District No. 306 (District). We reverse the discharge and affirm denial of sick leave benefits.

Mr. Oneal and the District entered into a teacher employment contract in April, 1974, for the 1974–75 school year, to commence August 29, 1974. As a result of deteriorating diabetic eyesight, Mr. Oneal tendered his written resignation to the District on July 24, 1974:

> It is with great regret that I must ask to be released from my 1974–75 teaching contract after my 27½ days sick leave are used up. For personal reasons, which I have discussed with Mr. Swanson, I feel I must do this for the benefit of the students.

Though his resignation had not been accepted by the District before commencement of the school year, Mr. Oneal did not report for work. His offer of resignation, conditioned upon receipt of 27½ days accumulated sick leave benefits, was not acted upon until September 20, 1974, when the District, by letter, refused the offer. Mr. Oneal remained adamant in his demand that he receive sick leave as a condition of resignation in a letter dated September 25, 1974. The District then discharged Mr. Oneal, with notice of probable cause, at their regular meeting on October 3, 1974. The District further accepted his resignation but refused to pay accumulated sick leave benefits. We find this course of events, the coexistence of discharge and resignation, confusing, to say the least.

Mr. Oneal appealed his discharge directly to the Superior Court pursuant to RCW 28A.58.515, and sought damages including sick leave. The action of the District was upheld by the Superior Court, resulting in the present appeal.

We are asked to determine by what method the teaching contract between the parties was terminated, whether through resignation by Mr. Oneal, discharge of Mr. Oneal by the District, or discharge of the contract by operation of law. In resolving the employment relationship between this teacher and his school district, we are governed by general principles of contract law.

We hold that the contractual duty of Mr. Oneal to teach during the 1974–75 school year was discharged by operation of law through impossibility of performance. As regards impossibility, the trial court entered the following findings:

> That for several years plaintiff suffered from deteriorating eyesight which was the result of diabetes.

> That following the completion of the 1973–74 school year and prior to the 24th day of July, 1974, plaintiff became aware of the fact that his eyesight had deteriorated to a point where plaintiff believed he would be unable to perform his teaching duties during the 1974–75 school year.

That the court was finding as fact an impossibility of performance by Mr. Oneal in the 1974–75 school year, is made apparent by the court's memorandum opinion wherein the court states:

> After the completion of the spring semester in 1974, during the summer recess, plaintiff became aware that his eyesight had deteriorated to the point where he would be unable to perform his teaching duties for the following year. The deterioration of plaintiff's eyesight had reached the state where he was then physically incapacitated for teaching duties and the plaintiff knew and understood this to be a fact. * * * The plaintiff did make a final decision, prior to the beginning of the contract year, that he would not abide by the contract. It is true that he made this decision because he was physically unable to abide by the contract.

The court's findings of impossibility of performance are substantially supported by testimony in the record, and will be accepted on appeal. It was the testimony of Robert P. Reilly, Assistant Director of the Washington State Teacher's Retirement System that Mr. Oneal had been found "disabled" from teaching duties in a medical report, and that he was thus eligible for receipt of disability benefits. His diabetic eyesight was found to be a continuing and progressively deteriorating condition existing in March, 1974, onward. Mr. Oneal's difficulty with class preparation was corroborated by Darrell Woodside, a fellow teacher in the District. Mr. Oneal was forced to hold papers very close to his eyes and write in large letters. He was unable to use a regular grade book, and found it necessary to record grades on a second piece of paper to make them more easily read. Conduct of reading classes was made even more difficult by older textbooks in use at that time. Frustration with inability to prepare lesson plans during the summer of 1974 was echoed by Mrs. Oneal.

Mr. Oneal's contractual duty was thus discharged by operation of law, by virtue of impossibility of performance. For these purposes, impossibility may be defined not only as strict impossibility, but also impracticality arising from extreme and unreasonable difficulty, expense, injury, or loss involved. Here, performance was impossible through greatly deteriorated eyesight.

The court concluded there had been a breach of contract by Mr. Oneal and probable cause for his discharge. But because his duty was discharged by operation of law, there remained no contract capable of breach. Therefore, Mr. Oneal's discharge by the District was without "probable" or "sufficient" cause within the meaning of RCW 28A.58.450, and shall be expunged from his employment record.

We now turn to examine Mr. Oneal's renewed argument on appeal that he be awarded accumulated sick leave benefits for that period commencing August 29, 1974, the start of the 1974–75 school year....

A review of the present case shows Mr. Oneal's contractual duty was discharged by operation of law prior to commencement of the 1974–75 school year. The complete failure of Mr. Oneal to perform under his 1974–75 contract, though discharged by operation of law, also discharged the contractual duty of the District, including that provision in the contract for payment of sick leave. With complete discharge of the contract before time of performance, the employment relationship of the parties ceased to exist. Mr. Oneal therefore "cease[d] to be employed" within the meaning of RCW 28A.58.100(2)(f) before August 29, 1974, ending his entitlement to receipt of accumulated sick leave benefits. Sick leave benefits were properly withheld by the District and the Superior Court.

Judgment of the Superior Court affirming the discharge of Mr. Oneal is reversed, with order by this court that the discharge be expunged from his employment record. Denial of sick leave benefits to Mr. Oneal by the Superior Court is affirmed.

QUESTIONS AND NOTES

1. After receiving Mr. Oneal's letter of July 24, 1974, the school board presumably had to find a new teacher. If it had to pay the substitute more than Mr. Oneal's contract rate, should he be liable for the difference? After all, it isn't his fault that he can't perform, but contract damages don't depend on moral fault, do they? As between the School Board and Oneal, who should bear that risk?

2. Is the court's interpretation of the sick leave rules sensible? It seems to say that a sick employee is entitled to accumulated leave unless the employee is so sick that his performance of the contract is excused, in which case the employee loses accumulated leave. A bit like Catch–22, isn't it? Suggest a simple sensible way out of the mess.

3. This suit appears to be about 27½ days of sick leave benefits. Why would either Mr. Oneal or the School Board pursue this litigation on appeal after trial in the Superior Court?

4. Do disabilities that can be accommodated or ameliorated discharge the obligation of a contract if neither party wishes to accommodate? If Mr. Oneal could continue teaching if the School Board would afford him assistance with grading, does it have to do so, or be found to be in breach of the employment contract? If Mr. Oneal could undergo a risky medical procedure that might fix his eyesight, but refuses the operation, is he in breach? What if all he needs are stronger glasses?

Canadian Industrial Alcohol Co. v. Dunbar Molasses Co.

New York Court of Appeals, 1932.
258 N.Y. 194, 179 N.E. 383.

■ CARDOZO, C.J. A buyer sues a seller for breach of an executory contract of purchase and sale.

The subject-matter of the contract was "approximately 1,500,000 wine gallons Refined Blackstrap [molasses] of the usual run from the National Sugar Refinery, Yonkers, N.Y., to test around 60% sugars."

The order was given and accepted December 27, 1927, but shipments of the molasses were to begin after April 1, 1928, and were to be spread out during the warm weather.

After April 1, 1928, the defendant made delivery from time to time of 344,083 gallons. Upon its failure to deliver more, the plaintiff brought this action for the recovery of damages. The defendant takes the ground that, by an implied term of the contract, the duty to deliver was conditioned upon the production by the National Sugar Refinery at Yonkers of molasses sufficient in quantity to fill the plaintiff's order. The fact is that the output of the refinery, while the contract was in force, was 485,848 gallons, much less than its capacity, of which amount 344,083 gallons were allotted to the defendant and shipped to the defendant's customer. The argument for the defendant is that its own duty to deliver was proportionate to the refinery's willingness to supply, and that the duty was discharged when the output was reduced.

The contract, read in the light of the circumstances existing at its making, or more accurately in the light of any such circumstances apparent from this record, does not keep the defendant's duty within boundaries so narrow. We may assume, in the defendant's favor, that there would have been a discharge of its duty to deliver if the refinery had been destroyed or if the output had been curtailed by the failure of the sugar crop or conceivably in some circumstances by unavoidable strikes. We may even assume that a like result would have followed if the plaintiff had bargained not merely for a quantity of molasses to be supplied from a particular refinery, but for molasses to be supplied in accordance with a particular contract between the defendant and the refiner, and if thereafter such contract had been broken without fault on the defendant's part. The inquiry is merely this, whether the continuance of a special group of circumstances appears from the terms of the contract, interpreted in the setting of the occasion, to have been a tacit or implied presupposition in the minds of the contracting parties, conditioning their belief in a continued obligation.

Perkin's intention

Accepting that test, we ask ourselves the question: What special group of circumstances does the defendant lay before us as one of the presuppositions imminent in its bargain with the plaintiff? The defendant asks us to assume that a manufacturer, having made a contract with a middleman for a stock of molasses to be procured from a particular refinery, would expect the contract to lapse whenever the refiner chose to diminish his production, and this in the face of the middleman's omission to do anything to charge the refiner with a duty to continue. Business could not be transacted with security or smoothness if a presumption so unreasonable were at the root of its engagements. There is nothing to show that the defendant would have been unable by a timely contract with the refinery to have assured itself of a supply sufficient for its needs. There is nothing to show that the plaintiff, in giving the order for the molasses, was informed by the defendant that such a contract had not been made, or that performance would be contingent upon obtaining one thereafter. If the plaintiff had been so informed, it would very likely have preferred to deal with the refinery directly, instead of dealing with a middleman. The defendant does not even show that it tried to get a contract from the refinery during the months that intervened between the acceptance of the plaintiff's order and the time when shipments were begun. It has wholly failed to relieve itself of the imputation of contributory fault. 3 Williston on Contracts, § 1959. So far as the record shows, it put its faith in the mere chance that the output of the refinery would be the same from year to year, and finding its faith vain, it tells us that its customer must have expected to take a chance as great. We see no reason for importing into the bargain this aleatory element. The defendant is in no better position than a factor who undertakes in his own name to sell for future delivery a special grade of merchandise to be manufactured by a special mill. The duty will be discharged if the mill is destroyed before delivery is due. The duty will subsist if the output is reduced because times turn out to be hard and labor charges high.

Clearly not intended

Why didn't D contract w/ refinery

The judgment should be affirmed, with costs.

distillation

QUESTIONS AND NOTES

1. Does the fact that Dunbar Molasses might at one time have avoided the situation which eventually prevented its performance make it any less impossible for it to perform in the end? What, then, is the breach—nonperformance or action (or inaction) resulting in eventual impossibility? Is it, in other words, the fact of impossibility or the reason for the impossibility which determines whether or not a performance is excused?

2. What does impossibility excuse—the duty to perform or the duty to pay damages for breach of a duty to perform? Is "impossibility of paying damages" ever a defense to an action for breach of contract?

3. Suppose the defendant, Dunbar, had made a contract with National Sugar Refinery and that thereafter National Sugar breached that contract. Would Dunbar then be excused from its agreement with the Canadian Industrial Alcohol Company?

4. Note that in 1932 Chief Judge Cardozo was prepared to assume that the obligation to deliver the molasses would have been discharged if the particular plant from which it was to come was destroyed by fire, or if output was curtailed by failure of the sugar crop, but only conceivably in some circumstances by an unavoidable strike. It seems likely that the list of excusing causes would be longer today, but the uncertainty Cardozo expresses would persist.

Whitman v. Anglum

Connecticut Supreme Court of Errors, 1918.
92 Conn. 392, 103 A. 114.

On the 5th day of March, 1914, the plaintiff and defendant entered into a contract in writing whereby the plaintiff agreed to purchase, and the defendant agreed to sell, at least 175 quarts of milk each day from April 1, 1914, to April 1, 1915. The contract contained the following: "The said Whitman is to come and get the milk at No. 1 Wawarme avenue, in the city of Hartford."

The premises of the defendant are known as No. 1 Wawarme avenue. On the 23d day of November, 1914, by an order of the commissioner of domestic animals for the state, all the defendant's cattle and products of his farm were quarantined. The defendant was quarantined, and he was not allowed to go from the premises. Shortly after the quarantine order, all the cows on the farm were killed. The quarantine was intended as far as possible to prevent all persons and animals from going on or off the premises, as well as to prevent the removal of products of all kinds that might carry infection of the "hoof and mouth disease" then prevalent among the defendant's cattle. From November 22, 1914, the defendant failed to furnish or offer to furnish milk until March 13, 1915. From a judgment in favor of the plaintiff, the defendant has appealed.

■ SHUMWAY, J. (after stating the facts as above). This was an absolute and unconditional undertaking by the defendant to sell and deliver milk daily of the specified quality and amount. The defendant's claim is that he was excused from the performance of the contract by reason of the quarantine, which made it illegal for him to leave his premises and carry away any products of his farm or any articles that might carry infection. The quarantine order did not make it illegal to deliver milk, nor make it illegal for the defendant to procure its delivery.

This much is conceded. But the defendant contends that the clause in the contract, to wit, "The said Whitman is to come and get the milk at No. 1 Wawarme avenue," is an essential part of the contract, and, as delivery was to be made at the place named, therefore delivery under the terms of the contract was illegal. There is nothing in the record to show that the defendant could not perform his contract. While it may be true that the plaintiff could not enter the defendant's house or go upon other parts of the premises which were under quarantine, it does not follow that the contract could not be performed substantially if not literally. The contract was not to deliver milk produced on the premises. All that can be said is, the defendant was under a temporary disability to perform his contract. He is not, however, released from the obligations of his contract because it was difficult or impossible to perform them, so long as the performance was not illegal.

There is no error. The other Judges concurred.

QUESTIONS AND NOTES

1. Was Anglum a wholesaler who dealt in the distribution of raw milk to dairies, or was he a dairy farmer who sold only his own production? What did Whitman think he was buying when he contracted with Anglum: 175 quarts of milk from Anglum's cows or 175 quarts of milk?

2. Is this a question of impossibility or one of interpretation of the contract?

4. Impracticability

Performance may not be literally impossible but may nevertheless impose a disproportionately heavy burden on one of the parties. While logically these situations merge into those in which the party is stuck with a bad bargain, performance may vary so materially from the parties' expectations that it will be sensible to excuse performance in these circumstances. This approach treats impossibility as a question of interpretation, that is, did the parties contemplate performance under *these* circumstances? As is generally true in matters of interpretation, judges have a large amount of discretion to achieve what they might regard as substantial justice.

Because the law was slow and uncertain in excusing performance made onerous by supervening event, generations of contract drafters have included excusing clauses, known variously as *force majeure, vis major*, or Act of God clauses. A typical one reads:

> *Force Majeure.* Neither party shall be responsible for any resulting loss if the fulfillment of any of the terms or provisions of this agreement is delayed or prevented by revolutions, insurrections, riots, wars, acts of enemies, national emergency, strikes, floods, fires, acts of God, or by any other cause not within the control of the party whose performance is interfered with which by the exercise of reasonable diligence such party is unable to prevent, whether of the class of causes enumerated above or not.

In the course of time, the expectations of lawyers, including judges, have been influenced by the commonness of such clauses. When the clause is not present, the court is very likely to imply its presence because all decent contracts have such a clause in them. This is a striking example of how the inadequacies of the substantive law motivate drafters to find solutions that, in the course of generations, become an expected part of transactions. These solutions, in turn, are integrated into the implied conditions judges will find in every contract, thus curing the original inadequacy of the substantive law. During the past generation this expectation found its way into the UCC and later the CISG.

Mineral Park Land Co. v. Howard

California Supreme Court, 1916.
172 Cal. 289, 156 P. 458.

■ SLOSS, J. The defendants appeal from a judgment in favor of plaintiff for $3,650. The appeal is on the judgment roll alone.

The plaintiff was the owner of certain land in the ravine or wash known as the Arroyo Seco, in South Pasadena, Los Angeles county. The defendants had made a contract with the public authorities for the construction of a concrete bridge across the Arroyo Seco. In August, 1911, the parties to this action entered into a written agreement whereby the plaintiff granted to the defendants the right to haul gravel and earth from plaintiff's land, the defendants agreeing to take therefrom all of the gravel and earth necessary in the construction of the fill and cement work on the proposed bridge, the required amount being estimated at approximately 114,000 cubic yards. Defendants agreed to pay 5 cents per cubic yard for the first 80,000 yards, the next 10,000 yards were to be given free of charge, and the balance was to be paid for at the rate of 5 cents per cubic yard.

The complaint was in two counts. The first alleged that the defendants had taken 50,131 cubic yards of earth and gravel, thereby becoming indebted to plaintiff in the sum of $2,506.55, of which only $900 had been paid, leaving a balance of $1,606.55 due. The findings support plaintiff's claim in this regard, and there is no question of the propriety of so much of the judgment as responds to the first count.

The second count sought to recover damages for the defendants' failure to take from plaintiff's land any more than the 50,131 yards.

It alleged that the total amount of earth and gravel used by defendants was 101,000 cubic yards, of which they procured 50,869 cubic yards from some place other than plaintiff's premises. The amount due the plaintiff for this amount of earth and gravel would, under the terms of the contract, have been $2,043.45. The count charged that plaintiff's land contained enough earth and gravel to enable the defendants to take therefrom the entire amount required, and that the 50,869 yards not taken had no value to the plaintiff. Accordingly the plaintiff sought, under this head, to recover damages in the sum of $2,043.45.

The answer denied that the plaintiff's land contained any amount of earth and gravel in excess of the 50,131 cubic yards actually taken, and alleged that the defendants took from the said land all of the earth and gravel available for the work mentioned in the contract.

The court found that the plaintiff's land contained earth and gravel far in excess of 101,000 cubic yards of earth and gravel, but that only 50,131 cubic yards, the amount actually taken by the defendants, was above the water level. No greater quantity could have been taken "by ordinary means," or except by the use, at great expense, of a steam dredger, and the earth and gravel so taken could not have been used without first having been dried at great expense and delay. On the issue raised by the plea of defendants that they took all the earth and gravel that was available the court qualified its findings in this way: It found that the defendants did take all of the available earth and gravel from plaintiff's premises, in this, that they took and removed "all that could have been taken advantageously to defendants, or all that was practical to take and remove from a financial standpoint"; that any greater amount could have been taken only at a prohibitive cost, that is, at an expense of 10 or 12 times as much as the usual cost per yard. It is also declared that the word "available" is used in the findings to mean capable of being taken and used advantageously. It was not "advantageous or practical" to have taken more material from plaintiff's land, but it was not impossible. There is a finding that the parties were not under any mutual misunderstanding regarding the amount of available gravel, but that the contract was entered into without any calculation on the part of either of the parties with reference to the amount of available earth and gravel on the premises.

The single question is whether the facts thus found justified the defendants in their failure to take from the plaintiff's land all of the earth and gravel required. This question was answered in the negative by the court below. The case was apparently thought to be governed by the principle—established by a multitude of authorities—that where a party has agreed, without qualification, to perform an act which is not in its nature impossible of performance, he is not excused by difficulty of performance, or by the fact that he becomes unable to perform.

It is, however, equally well settled that, where performance depends upon the existence of a given thing, and such existence was assumed as the basis of the agreement, performance is excused to the extent that the thing ceases to exist or turns out to be nonexistent. Thus, where the defendants had agreed to pasture not less than 3,000 cattle on plaintiff's land, paying therefor $1 for each and every head so pastured, and it developed that the land did not furnish feed for more than 717 head, the number actually put on the land by defendant, it was held that plaintiff could not recover the stipulated sum for the difference between the cattle pastured and the minimum of 3,000 agreed to be pastured. Similarly, in *Brick Co. v. Pond*, where the plaintiff had leased all the "good No. 1 fire clay on his land," subject to the condition that the lessees should mine or pay for not less than 2,000 tons of clay every year, paying therefor 25 cents per ton, the court held that the lessees were not bound to pay for 2,000 tons per year, unless there was No. 1 clay on the land in such quantities as would justify its being taken out. In *Ridgely v. Conewago Iron Co.* the holding was that a mining lease requiring the lessee to mine 4,000 tons of ore annually, and to pay therefor a fixed sum per ton, or, failing to take out such quantity, to pay therefor, imposed no obligation on the lessee to pay for such stipulated quantity after the ore in the demised premises had become exhausted. There are many other cases dealing with mining leases of this character, and the general course of decision is to the effect that the performance of the obligation to take out a given quantity or to pay royalty thereon, if it be not taken out, is excused if it appears that the land does not contain the stipulated quantity.

We think the findings of fact make a case falling within the rule of these decisions. The parties were contracting for the right to take earth and gravel to be used in the construction of the bridge. When they stipulated that all of the earth and gravel needed for this purpose should be taken from plaintiff's land, they contemplated and assumed that the land contained the requisite quantity, available for use. The defendants were not binding themselves to take what was not there. And, in determining whether the earth and gravel were "available," we must view the conditions in a practical and reasonable way. Although there was gravel on the land, it was so situated that the defendants could not take it by ordinary means, nor except at a prohibitive cost. To all fair intents then, it was impossible for defendants to take it. "A thing is impossible in legal contemplation when it is not practicable; and a thing is impracticable when it can only be done at an excessive and unreasonable cost." 1 Beach on Contr. § 216. We do not mean to intimate that the defendants could excuse themselves by showing the existence of conditions which would make

not   just   a little   more   expensive

the performance of their obligation more expensive than they had anticipated, or which would entail a loss upon them. But, where the difference in cost is so great as here, and has the effect, as found, of making performance impracticable, the situation is not different from that of a total absence of earth and gravel.

On the facts found, there should have been no recovery on the second count.

The judgment is modified by deducting therefrom the sum of $2,043.45, and, as so modified, it stands affirmed.

QUESTIONS AND NOTES

1. Is Howard not liable for the price of underwater gravel because the high cost of procurement makes performance "impossible," or is he not liable because a reasonable person would say that his promise was to take only commercially available gravel?

2. Why was it impracticable to dig the gravel? Does it make any difference whether the gravel was flooded by an unexpected rainstorm or whether there never were 101,000 cubic yards above water? In other words, is this a case of impracticability because of supervening cause or of mistake in calculating the volume of available gravel?

3. Can you reconcile *Mineral Park Land v. Howard*, p. 766 and *Whitman v. Anglum*, p. 764? Why no excuse in *Whitman* but termination of the contract in *Mineral Park*?

————

UNIFORM COMMERCIAL CODE:

§ 2–615. *Excuse by Failure of Presupposed Conditions.*

Except so far as a seller may have assumed a greater obligation and subject to the preceding section on substituted performance:

(a) Delay in delivery or non-delivery in whole or in part by a seller who complies with paragraphs (b) and (c) is not a breach of his duty under a contract for sale if performance as agreed has been made impracticable by the occurrence of a contingency the non-occurrence of which was a basic assumption on which the contract was made or by compliance in good faith with any applicable foreign or domestic governmental regulation or order whether or not it later proves to be invalid.

(b) Where the causes mentioned in paragraph (a) affect only a part of the seller's capacity to perform, he must allocate production and deliveries among his customers but may at his option include regular customers not then under contract as well as his own requirements for further manufacture. He may so allocate in any manner which is fair and reasonable.

(c) The seller must notify the buyer seasonally that there will be delay or non-delivery and, when allocation is required under paragraph (b), of the estimated quota thus made available for the buyer.

UN CONVENTION ON CONTRACTS FOR THE INTERNATIONAL SALE OF GOODS:

Article 79

(1) A party is not liable for a failure to perform any of his obligations if he proved that the failure was due to an impediment beyond his control and that he could not reasonably be expected to have taken the impediment into account at the time of the conclusion of the contract or to have avoided or overcome it or its consequences.

(2) If the party's failure is due to the failure by a third person whom he has engaged to perform the whole or a part of the contract, that party is exempt from liability only if:

(a) he is exempt under the preceding paragraph; and

(b) the person whom he has so engaged would be so exempt if the provisions of that paragraph were applied to him.

(3) The exemption provided by this article has effect for the period during which the impediment exists.

(4) The party who fails to perform must give notice to the other party of the impediment and its effect on his ability to perform. If the notice is not received by the other party within a reasonable time after the party who fails to perform knew or ought to have known of the impediment, he is liable for damages resulting from such non-receipt.

(5) Nothing in this article prevents either party from exercising any right other than to claim damages under this Convention.

QUESTION

How would the outcome of the preceding four cases be different if UCC § 2–615 were the applicable standard of excuse? Would the outcomes be different if CISG Art. 79 were applicable?

5. Frustration of Contract

A party's performance is not literally impossible if it is merely called upon, for example, to pay money for a counterperformance which has lost all meaning because of the occurrence of a supervening event. Consider the lease of property for a service station along a busy highway in a remote area. If the State builds a highway nearby that diverts all but a small fraction of the traffic, can the lessee claim an excuse from paying high rent premised on a large volume of through traffic? The lessee still has the property, and payment is not impossible. Is the situation different if the State decides to fight global warming by outlawing gasoline-fueled motor vehicles? Must the tenant continue to pay rent if the site could still be used as rest stop for passing travelers even though it could no longer legally sell gasoline? Doesn't such change go to the heart of the transaction and suggest an implied condition of the contract that such change frustrates the contract and excuses performance?

The classic cases in this area are the so-called *Coronation Cases*, *Krell v. Henry*, 2 K.B. 740 (1903) and *Chandler v. Webster*, 1 K.B. 493 (1904). In 1902, King Edward VII was to be crowned in a spectacular ceremony at Westminster Abbey coupled with an equally spectacular parade along Pall Mall. Rooms along Pall Mall with a view of the parade route were rented for exorbitant sums. But shortly before the event the King fell ill with appendicitis and the parade was cancelled. In subsequent litigation over the room rentals on Pall Mall, the English courts held the contacts frustrated and discharged by the supervening event of the King's illness and the cancellation of the parade. Interestingly, only future performance was discharged, that is deposits paid could not be recovered but monies not yet due at the time the King fell ill did not have to be paid. This result was later codified in the United Kingdom by the Frustrated Contracts Act of 1943 (Aug. 5, 1943).

---

6. Mistake

Doctrines of impossibility, impracticability, and frustration of contract are applied when supervening events upset the expectations that the parties had or are deemed to have had when they made the contract. But what if the facts and circumstances were never as the parties assumed? From the viewpoint of the court being asked to intervene, a case in which there has been a serious mistake in the assumptions underlying the agreement is very similar to a case of impossibility caused by supervening unforeseen events. One of the parties is seeking to be relieved from a catastrophic loss because performance of the contract has turned out to be a very different thing than was originally contemplated. As in impossibility cases, those involving mistaken assumptions lend themselves to the construction of an implied condition that excuses performance or to an analysis that "the true construction of the contract" is that the parties did not intend performance under these circumstances.

Two root ideas already discussed under impossibility apply also to mistake in assumption. On the one hand, the parties have made a deal, and it should be performed. At the same time, if the mistake is sufficiently material to the deal, the agreement is unlikely to be very sensible if the assumptions turn out to be incorrect. Also arguing against enforcement is our sense that it is inequitable for a party to insist on performance of the contract when it is clear that because of a mistake—even though it was without fault—there is a gross and obvious lack of equivalence in what the parties actually exchanged. It seems unfair that a person should be able to insist on delivery of a diamond for the price of a pebble or collect the price of a diamond for a mere pebble. Sensible courts seek to avoid this kind of commercial catastrophe.

In many contract situations, however, the chance that things wouldn't work out as the parties expected was part of the deal and a factor in the negotiations. The contract price may reflect the risks assumed by one side, and the distribution of risks of different kinds may be a major function of the contract terms. When the subject of the erroneous assumptions is speculative, when a warranty is made by one side, or when the contract is aleatory in nature, there is less interest in relieving the injured party of its mistake.

This concern with placing the risk of loss on one party or the other may be the sensible part of the distinction courts often claim to draw between "mutual" and "unilateral" mistake. As often stated, relief may be granted for a mutual, but not for a unilateral, mistake. The case law in this area is confused beyond reconciliation. Courts cannot agree on what is "mutual" and what is "unilateral," and in many jurisdictions cases can be found in which relief is granted in both situations, however they are defined. But when courts talk about unilateral mistake, they often seem to be indicating that the mistake was as to a matter peculiarly the concern of one party who assumed the risk of its existence. When an assumption goes to the heart of the bargain, the parties' interest in it is mutual, and a serious mistake as to that assumption is likely to render the performance excused.

Judge Teitelbaum's famous opinion in *Aluminum Company of America v. Essex Group, Inc. ("ALCOA")* grapples with these distinctions between "mutual" and "unilateral" mistake. ALCOA and Essex were competitors in the aluminum wire and cable business. ALCOA is also a very large vertically integrated producer of aluminum products. That is, it mines, transports, smelts, processes, fabricates, and markets aluminum from ore to finished products. Essex needed a reliable source of supply for its business and originally planned simply to enter into a toll conversion contract, under which Essex would purchase ore and turn it over to ALCOA, who would convert the ore into molten aluminum that would be delivered in its molten state to Essex. This meant that Essex's plant would be next door to and physically connected to ALCOA's, so that the liquid aluminum could flow economically from one to the other. Essex shopped around for a source of aluminum ore and for a steamship company to carry the ore to the plant. It ended up buying the ore from ALCOA of Australia Proprietary Ltd., an Australian corporation, 51% of which is owned by ALCOA. All ore supplied under this contract was carried from Australia to the plant in vessels of the ALCOA Steamship Co., a wholly owned subsidiary of ALCOA. The connections between ALCOA and Essex were intimate and tangled.

Why did the parties enter into this kind of a deal? Part of the answer probably lies in the antitrust laws. Aluminum production requires a high level of specialized technical competence and a great deal of capital investment in plant and equipment. These requirements discourage potential competitors from entering this business. Historically these barriers were reinforced by industrial property rights to the central process for the electrolytic reduction of aluminum from ore. ALCOA held patents to the process of electrically smelting aluminum metal from ore and, accordingly, for many years lawfully monopolized aluminum production in the United States and a number of other countries. During the 1930's ALCOA was successfully prosecuted by the Government under the antitrust laws as a monopolist. Although ALCOA's monopoly was effectively broken during World War II, when two other independent producers were brought into the industry with Government help, it remains a dominant participant in the industry. As such, it must be very careful how it deals with customers like Essex, who are also its competitors in the sale and distribution of finished goods. It is always caught on the horns of a dilemma between treating its competitors too harshly and thus abusing its dominant market position, or cooperating rather than competing with its competitors and running the risk of being found to have conspired with its competitors to restrain trade. In its dealings with Essex, for example, several ALCOA executives who held positions both in the parent firm and in its Australian subsidiary were constrained on the advice of counsel to insulate themselves so that they would not be involved in any way in the negotiations of both the smelting deal and the ore purchase contract. Sometimes, even 600 pound gorillas have to be careful where they sit down.

With this background in mind, read Judge Teitelbaum's analysis of mistake, impracticability, and frustration in *ALCOA*. Consider also how the facts of this unique situation affect his choice of remedy.

Aluminum Co. of America v. Essex Group

United States District Court, W.D. Pennsylvania, 1980.
499 F.Supp. 53.

■ TEITELBAUM, D.J. ...

By December 26, 1967 the parties had entered into ... [a] service contract known as the Molten Metal Agreement under which Essex would supply ALCOA with alumina which ALCOA would convert by a smelting process into molten aluminum....

The price provisions of the contract contained an escalation formula which indicates that $.03 per pound of the original price escalates in accordance with changes in the Wholesale Price Index–Industrial Commodities (WPI) and $.03 per pound escalates in accordance with an index based on the average hourly labor rates paid to ALCOA employees at the Warrick plant. The portion of the pricing formula which is in issue in this case under counts one and two is the production charge which is escalated by the WPI. ALCOA contends that this charge was intended by the parties to reflect actual changes in the cost of the non-labor items utilized by ALCOA in the production of aluminum from alumina at its Warrick, Indiana smelting plant. In count one of this suit ALCOA asserts that the WPI used in the Molten Metal Agreement was in fact incapable of reasonably reflecting changes in the non-labor costs at ALCOA's Warrick, Indiana smelting plant and has in fact failed to so reflect such changes.

The Court finds, based upon consideration of all the evidence, that ALCOA is entitled to reformation of the Molten Metal Agreement....

COUNT ONE

ALCOA's first count seeks an equitable modification of the contract price for its services. The pleadings, arguments and briefs frame the issue in several forms. ALCOA seeks reformation or modification of the price on the basis of mutual mistake of fact, unilateral mistake of fact, unconscionability, frustration of purpose, and commercial impracticability.

A.

The facts pertinent to count one are few and simple. In 1967 ALCOA and Essex entered into a written contract in which ALCOA promised to convert specified amounts of alumina supplied by Essex into aluminum for Essex. The service is to be performed at the ALCOA works at Warrick, Indiana. The contract is to run until the end of 1983. Essex has the option to extend it until the end of 1988. The price for each pound of aluminum converted is calculated by a complex formula which includes three variable components based on specific indices. The initial contract price was set at fifteen cents per pound, computed as follows:

A.	Demand Charge	$ 0.05/lb.
B.	Production Charge	
	(i) Fixed component	.04/lb.
	(ii) Non-labor production cost component	.03/lb.
	(iii) Labor production cost component	.03/lb.
	Total initial charge	$ 0.15/lb.

The demand charge is to vary from its initial base in direct proportion to periodic changes in the Engineering News Record Construction Cost–20 Cities Average Index published in the Engineering News Record. The Non-labor Production Cost Component is to vary from its initial base in direct proportion to periodic changes in the Wholesale Price Index–Industrial Commodities (WPI–IC) published by the Bureau of Labor Statistics of the United States Department of Labor. The Labor Production Cost Component is to vary from its initial base in direct proportion to periodic changes in ALCOA's average hourly labor cost at the Warrick, Indiana works. The adjusted price is subject to an overall "cap" price of 65% of the price of a specified type of aluminum sold on specified terms, as published in a trade journal, American Metal Market.

The indexing system was evolved by ALCOA with the aid of the eminent economist Alan Greenspan. ALCOA examined the non-labor production cost component to assure that the WPI–IC had not tended to deviate markedly from their non-labor cost experience in the years before the contract was executed. Essex agreed to the contract including the index provisions after an examination of the past record of the indices revealed an acceptable pattern of stability.

ALCOA sought, by the indexed price agreement, to achieve a stable net income of about four cents per pound of aluminum converted. This net income represented ALCOA's return (i) on its substantial capital investment devoted to the performance of the contracted services, (ii) on its management, and (iii) on the risks of short-falls or losses it undertook over an extended period. The fact that the non-labor production cost component of ALCOA's costs was priced according to a surrogate, objective index opened the door to a foreseeable fluctuation of ALCOA's return due to deviations between ALCOA's costs and the performance of the WPI–IC. The range of foreseeable deviation was roughly three cents per pound. That is to say that in some years ALCOA's return might foreseeably (and did, in fact) rise to seven cents per pound, while in other years it might foreseeably (and did, in fact) fall to about one cent per pound.

Essex sought to assure itself of a long term supply of aluminum at a favorable price. Essex intended to and did manufacture a new line of aluminum wire products. The long term supply of aluminum was important to assure Essex of the steady use of its expensive machinery. A steady production stream was vital to preserve the market position it sought to establish. The favorable price was important to allow Essex to compete with firms like ALCOA which produced the aluminum and manufactured aluminum wire products in an efficient, integrated operation.

In the early years of the contract, the price formula yielded prices related, within the foreseeable range of deviation, to ALCOA's cost figures. Beginning in 1973, OPEC actions to increase oil prices and unanticipated pollution control costs greatly increased ALCOA's electricity costs. Electric power is the principal non-labor cost factor in aluminum conversion, and the electric power rates rose much more rapidly than did the WPI–IC. As a result, ALCOA's production costs rose greatly and unforeseeably beyond the indexed increase in the contract price....

During the most recent years, the market price of aluminum has increased even faster than the production costs. At the trial ALCOA introduced the deposition of Mr. Wilfred Jones, an Essex employee whose duties included the sale of surplus metal. Mr. Jones stated that Essex had resold some millions of pounds of aluminum which ALCOA had refined. The cost of the aluminum to Essex (including the purchase price of the alumina and its transportation) was 36.35 cents per pound around June of 1979. Mr. Jones further stated that the resale price in June 1979 at one cent per pound under the market, was 73.313 cents per pound, yielding Essex a gross profit of 37.043 cents per pound. This margin of profit shows the tremendous advantage Essex enjoys under the contract as it is written and as both parties have performed it. A significant fraction of Essex's advantage is directly attributable to the corresponding out of pocket losses ALCOA suffers. ALCOA has sufficiently shown that without judicial relief or economic changes which are not presently foreseeable, it stands to lose in excess of $75,000,000 out of pocket, during the remaining term of the contract.

* * *

C.

ALCOA initially argues that it is entitled to relief on the theory of mutual mistake. ALCOA contends that both parties were mistaken in their estimate of the suitability of the WPI–IC as an objective index of ALCOA's non-labor production costs, and that their mistake is legally sufficient to warrant modification or avoidance of ALCOA's promise. Essex appropriately raised several defenses to these claims. Essex first argues that the asserted mistake is legally insufficient because it is essentially a mistake as to future economic events rather than a mistake of fact. Essex next argues that ALCOA assumed or bore the risk of the mistake. Essex finally argues that the requested remedy of reformation is not available under Indiana law.

The late Professor Corbin wrote the best modern analysis of the doctrine of mutual mistake. Corbin took pains to show the great number and variety of factors which must be considered in resolving claims for relief founded on the doctrine of mistake, and to show the inappropriateness of any single verbal rule to govern the decision of mistake cases. Corbin on Contracts § 597 at 582–83 (1960).

The present case involves a claimed mistake in the price indexing formula. This is clearly a mistake concerning a factor affecting the value of the agreed exchange. Of such mistakes Corbin concluded that the law must consider the character of the risks assumed by the parties. He further concluded:

> In these cases, the decision involves a judgment as to the materiality of the alleged factor, and as to whether the parties made a definite assumption that it existed and made their agreement in the belief that there was *no risk* with respect to it. Opinions are almost sure to differ on both of these matters, so that decisions must be, or appear to be, conflicting. The court's judgment on each of them is a judgment on a matter of fact, not a judgment as to law. No rule of thumb should be constructed for cases of this kind.

The new Restatement 2d of Contracts follows a similar approach....

Both Professor Corbin and the Restatement emphasize the limited place of the doctrine of mistake in the law of contracts. They, along with most modern commentators, emphasize the importance of contracts as devices to allocate the risks of life's uncertainties, particularly economic uncertainties. Where parties to a contract deliberately and expressly undertake to allocate the risk of loss attendant on those uncertainties between themselves or where they enter a contract of a customary kind which by common understanding, sense, and legal doctrine has the effect of allocating such risks, the commentators and the opinions are agreed that there is little room for judicial relief from resulting losses. The new Restatement agrees, § 296. This is, in part, the function of the doctrine of assumption of the risk as a limitation of the doctrine of mistake. Whether ALCOA assumed the risk it seeks relief from is at issue in this case. The doctrine of assumption of the risk is therefore considered below. The important point to note here is that the doctrine of assumption of the risk is not the only risk allocating limitation on the doctrine of mistake. Other important risk allocating limitations are inherent in the doctrine of mistake itself. They find expression in the cases and treatises in declarations that there has been no mistake, or no legally cognizable mistake, or a mistake of the wrong sort.

ALCOA claims that there was a mutual mistake about the suitability of the WPI–IC as an index to accomplish the purposes of the parties. Essex replies that the mistake, if any, was not a mistake of *fact,* but it was rather a mistake in predicting future economic conditions. Essex asserts that such a mistake does not justify legal relief for ALCOA. The conflicting claims require the Court to resolve three questions: (1) Was the mistake one of "fact" as the cases and commentators use that word? (2) If so, was it of the sort of fact for which relief could be granted? (3) If the mistake was not one of "fact," is relief necessarily foreclosed?

The Court finds the parties' mistake in this case to be one of fact rather than one of simple prediction of future events. Plainly the mistake is not wholly isolated from predictions of the future or from the searching illuminations of painful hindsight. But this is not the legal test. At the time the contract was made both parties were aware that the future was unknown, and their agreed contract was intended to bind them for many years to come. Both knew that Essex sought an objective pricing formula and that ALCOA sought a formula which would cover its out of pocket costs over the years and which would yield it a return of around four cents a pound. Both parties to the contract carefully examined the past performance of the WPI–IC before agreeing to its use. The testimony was clear that each assumed the Index was adequate to fulfill its purpose. This mistaken assumption was essentially a present actuarial error.

The parties took pains to avoid the full risk of future economic changes when they embarked on a twenty-one year contract involving services worth hundreds of millions of dollars. To this end they employed a customary business risk limiting device—price indexing—with more than customary sophistication and care. They chose not a single index formula but a complex one with three separate indices....

The doctrine of mistake has long distinguished claims of mutual mistake from claims of unilateral mistake. The standards for judicial relief are higher where the proven mistake is unilateral than where it is mutual.

Essex asserts that ALCOA's mistake was unilateral. Mr. O'Malley, Chairman of the Board of Essex Corporation, testified at trial that he had no particular concern for ALCOA's well-being and that in the negotiations of the contract he sought only Essex's best interests. Essex claims this testimony tends to rebut any possible mutual mistake of fact between the parties. The Court disagrees.

The cases clearly establish that mutual mistake lies in error concerning mutually understood material facts. The law of mutual mistake is not addressed primarily to motivation or to desire to have a good bargain, such as that credibly testified to by Mr. O'Malley. As Mr. O'Malley struck the bargain for Essex, he understood the function of the Wholesale Price Index, as part of the pricing formula, to be the protection of ALCOA from foreseeable economic fluctuations. He further had every reason to believe that the formula was selected on the factual prediction that it would, within tolerable limits, serve its purpose. While he did not share the motive to protect ALCOA, he understood the functional purposes of the agreement. He therefore shared this mistake of fact. And his mistake was Essex's. The Court recognizes that Mr. O'Malley and Essex would cheerfully live with the benefit of their mistake, but the law provides otherwise. As a matter of law Mr. O'Malley's testimony of Essex's indifference concerning ALCOA's motivation for the use of the Wholesale Price Index as a gauge for tracking non-labor costs is immaterial.

Is it enough that one party is indifferent to avoid a mutual mistake? The Court thinks not. This situation resembles that in *Sherwood v. Walker*, the celebrated case of Rose of Aberlone. There the owner of a prize breeding cow sold her for slaughter at the going rate for good slaughter cattle. The owner had unsuccessfully tried to breed her and had erroneously concluded she was sterile. In fact she was pregnant at the time of the sale and she was much more valuable for breeding than for slaughter. There as here, the buyer was indifferent to the unknown fact; he would have been pleased to keep the unexpected profit. But he understood the bargain rested on a presumed state of facts. The court let the seller avoid the contract because of mutual mistake of fact.

In *Sherwood,* the buyer didn't know the highly pedigreed Rose was with calf. He probably could not have discovered it at the time of the sale with due diligence. Here the parties could not possibly have known of the sudden inability of the Wholesale Price Index to reflect ALCOA's non-labor costs. If, over the previous twenty years, the Wholesale Price Index had tracked, within a 5% variation, pertinent costs to ALCOA, a 500% variation of costs to Index must be deemed to be unforeseeable, within any meaningful sense of the word.

The Restatements and these cases reveal four facets of risk assumption and risk allocation under the law of mistake. First, a party to a contract may expressly assume a risk. If a contractor agrees to purchase and to remove 114,000 cubic yards of fill from a designated tract for the landowner at a set price "regardless of subsurface soil and water conditions" the contractor assumes the risk that subsurface water may make the removal unexpectedly expensive.

Customary dealing in a trade or common understanding may lead a court to impose a risk on a party where the contract is silent. Often the result corresponds to the expectation of both parties, but this will not always be true. At times legal rules may form the basis for the inferred common understanding. Equity traditionally put the risk of casualty losses on the purchaser of land while the purchase contract remained executory. This allocation was derived from the doctrine of equitable conversion. "Equity regards as done that which ought to be done." The rule could always be modified by express agreement. It survives today—where it does survive largely by reason of its acceptance as part of the common expectations of real estate traders and their advisors.

Third, where neither express words nor some particular common understanding or trade usage dictate a result, the court must allocate the risk in some reasoned way....

Fourth, where parties enter a contract in a state of conscious ignorance of the facts, they are deemed to risk the burden of having the facts turn out to be adverse, within very broad limits. Each party takes a calculated gamble in such a contract. Because information is often troublesome or costly to obtain, the law does not seek to discourage such contracts. Thus if parties agree to sell and purchase a stone which both know may be glass or diamond at a price which in some way reflects their uncertainty, the contract is enforceable whether the stone is in fact glass or diamond. If, by contrast, the parties both mistakenly believe it to be glass, the case is said not to be one of conscious ignorance but one of mutual mistake. Consequently the vendor may void the contract.

In this case Essex raises two arguments. First, it asserts that ALCOA expressly or by fair implication assumed the risk that the WPI–IC would not keep up with ALCOA's non-labor production costs. Second, it asserts that the parties made a calculated gamble with full awareness that the future was uncertain, so the contract should be enforced despite the mutual mistake. Both arguments are correct within limits, and within those limits they affect the relief ALCOA may receive. Both arguments fail as complete defenses to ALCOA's claim.

Once courts recognize that supposed specific values lie, and are commonly understood to lie, within a penumbra of uncertainty, and that the range of probability is subject to estimation, the principle of conscious uncertainty requires reformulation. The proper question is not simply whether the parties to a contract were conscious of uncertainty with respect to a vital fact, but whether they believe that uncertainty was effectively limited within a designated range so that they would deem outcomes beyond that range to be highly unlikely. In this case the answer is clear. Both parties knew that the use of an objective price index injected a limited range of uncertainty into their projected return on the contract. Both had every reason to predict that the likely range of variation would not exceed three cents per pound. That is to say both would have deemed deviations yielding ALCOA less of a return on its investment, work and risk of less than one cent a pound or of more than seven cents a pound to be highly unlikely. Both consciously undertook a closely calculated risk rather than a limitless one. Their mistake concerning its calculation is thus fundamentally unlike the limitless conscious undertaking of an unknown risk which Essex now posits.

. . .

E.

This leaves the question of framing a remedy for ALCOA. Essex argues that reformation is not available. It cites many Indiana cases declaring that reformation is only available to correct writings which, through mistake, do not reflect the agreement of the parties. The declarations to that effect are clear.

But the point is immaterial here. This case does not fall within reformation as a traditional head of equity jurisprudence. It does fall within the more general rules of equitable restitution. Courts have traditionally applied three remedial rules in cases of mistake, frustration and impracticability. In some cases courts declare that no contract ever arose because there was no true agreement between the parties, *Raffles v. Wichelhaus*, or because the parties were ignorant of existing facts which frustrated the purpose of one party or made performance impracticable. In some other cases the courts hold that a contract is voidable on one of the three theories. In these cases the customary remedy is rescission. In both classes of cases where one or both parties have performed under the supposed contract, the courts award appropriate restitution in the light of the benefits the parties have conferred on each other. The aim is to prevent unjust enrichment. The courts in such cases often call this remedy "reformation" in the loose sense of "modification." ...

... To decree rescission in this case would be to grant ALCOA a windfall gain in the current aluminum market. It would at the same time deprive Essex of the assured long term aluminum supply which it obtained under the contract and of the gains it legitimately may enforce within the scope of the risk ALCOA bears under the contract. A remedy which merely shifts the windfall gains and losses is neither required nor permitted by Indiana law.

To frame an equitable remedy where frustration, impracticability or mistake prevent strict enforcement of a long term executory contract requires a careful examination of the circumstances of the contract, the purposes of the parties, and the circumstances which upset the contract. For some long term executory contracts rescission with or without restitution will be the only sensible remedy. Where developments make performance of the contract economically senseless or purposeless, to modify the contract and to enforce it as modified would be highly inappropriate. But in cases like the present one modification and enforcement may be the only proper remedy. *Parev Products Co. v. I. Rokeach and Sons, Inc.* In this case Essex sought an assured long term supply of aluminum at a price which would let it earn a profit on its finished products. ALCOA, facing ordinary market risks in 1967, sought a long term, limited risk use for its Warrick Works. A remedy modifying the price term of the contract in light of the circumstances which upset the price formula will better preserve the purposes and expectations of the parties than any other remedy. Such a remedy is essential to avoid injustice in this case.

During the trial the parties agreed that a modification of the price term to require Essex to pay ALCOA the ceiling price specified in the contract would be an appropriate remedy if the Court held for ALCOA. The Court understands from the parties that ALCOA will continue to suffer a substantial but smaller out of pocket loss at this price level. But ALCOA has not argued that the ceiling price term is subject to the same basic assumptions about risk limitation as is the indexed price term. Accordingly the Court adopts the ceiling price term as part of the remedy it grants to ALCOA.

The Court must recognize, though, that before the contract expires economic changes may make this remedy excessively favorable to ALCOA. To deal with that possibility, the Court must frame a remedy which is suitable to the expectations and to the original agreement of the parties. A price fixed at the contract ceiling could redound to ALCOA's great profit and to Essex's great loss in changed circumstances. Therefore the Court adopts the following remedial scheme. For the duration of the contract the price for each pound of aluminum converted by ALCOA shall be the lesser of the current Price A or Price B indicated below.

Price A shall be the contract ceiling price computed periodically as specified in the contract.

Price B shall be the greater of the current Price B1 or Price B2. *Price B1* shall be the price specified in the contract, computed according to the terms of the contract. *Price B2* shall be that price which yields ALCOA a profit of one cent per pound of aluminum converted. This will generally yield Essex the benefit of its favorable bargain, and it will reduce ALCOA's disappointment to the limit of risk the parties expected in making the contract. The profit shall be computed using the same accounting methods used for the production of plaintiff's exhibit 431. The profit and the resulting price shall be computed once each calendar quarter, as soon after the close of the quarter as the necessary information may be assembled. When Price B2 applies, ALCOA shall bill Essex periodically, as specified in the contract at the price specified at the last quarterly price computation. Essex shall pay those bills according to the payment terms previously observed by the parties. When the next quarterly price computation is completed, that price shall be applied retroactively to the aluminum converted during the previous quarter. ALCOA shall refund any surplus payment by Essex upon the computation of the price or shall bill Essex for any additional money due.

ALCOA shall keep detailed records of the pertinent costs, indices and computations used to calculate Prices A, B1 and B2 and shall preserve them for two years beyond the termination of the contract. ALCOA shall send Essex, in the manner and at the times specified in the contract, the price information called for in the contract, as well as a quarterly statement of Price B2 whether or not that price then applies. The statement of Price B2 need not specify the elements from which it was calculated.

CONCLUSION

This case is novel. The sums of money involved are huge. The Court has been considerably aided by the thorough and commendable work of all of the counsel who have participated in the case. There remains a need for a few concluding remarks concerning the theory of Count One of this case and its limitations.

One of the principal themes in the development of commercial contract doctrines since the 1920's has been the need for a body of law compatible with responsible commercial practices and understandings. The old spirit of the law manifest in *Parradine v. Jane*, is gone. The new spirit of commercial law in Indiana and elsewhere appears in the Uniform Commercial Code, in new developments of implied covenants, and in the new Restatement.

At stake in this suit is the future of a commercially important device—the long term contract. Such contracts are common in many fields of commerce. Mineral leases, building and ground leases, and long term coal sales agreements are just three examples of such contracts. If the law refused an appropriate remedy when a prudently drafted long term contract goes badly awry, the risks attending such contracts would increase. Prudent business people would avoid using this sensible business tool. Or they would needlessly suffer the delay and expense of ever more detailed and sophisticated drafting in an attempt to approximate by agreement what the law could readily furnish by general rule.

Another aspect of the new spirit of commercial law is important in this case. Much of the story of modern business law and of modern management concerns deals with the problem of risk limitation. The development of the concept of limited liability in the modern corporation illustrates this development. So do the proliferation of insurance, the development of no-fault auto insurance, and the recurring analysis of a party's capacity to anticipate losses and spread them or insure against them. *Force majeur* clauses, price indexing agreements and "double net" leases all aim to clarify and to limit the risk of long term contracts. Responsible business managers are attentive to risk control.

Corporate managers are fiduciaries. Law, founded on good sense, requires them to act with care in the management of businesses owned by other people. Attention to risk limitation is essential to the fiduciary duty of corporate managers. Courts must consider the fiduciary duty of management and the established practice of risk limitation in interpreting contracts and in the application of contract doctrines such as mistake, frustration and impracticability. Corporate managers should not gamble with corporate funds. Generally they do not. Courts should not presume that they do, nor should they frame rules founded on such a presumption. Instead, courts should be alert to indications that the parties to a commercial contract sought to limit their risks, and should interpret the contracts and frame remedies to protect that purpose.

Parev Products Co. v. I. Rokeach & Sons, Inc., decided by Judges Clark, Frank and Learned Hand, illustrated an aspect of this point. There Parev, the plaintiff, by contract gave the defendant the exclusive right to produce and to market its product, Nyafat, a cooking oil, for fifty years for a specified royalty. The defendant had the option to cancel the contract at any time for a fee. The plaintiff agreed not to market the product or any similar product during the contract, and the defendant agreed not to market the product or any similar product after the end of the contract. In

1939 competitors began to sell Crisco and Spry, white semi-solid cooking oils which reduced the sales of the plaintiff's oil. The defendant responded to the falling sales by introducing a new product of its own, Kea, similar to Crisco and Spry. The plaintiff sued to enjoin this further competition with its product. Since the express negative covenants did not forbid this competition, the plaintiff argued that the court should imply a negative covenant to forbid it.

The court rejected the defendant's argument that only covenants intended by the parties may be implied. The court noted the then traditional "reluctance of courts to admit that they were to a considerable extent 'remaking' a contract in situations where it seemed necessary and appropriate to do so." The court acknowledged that a discernible intent of the parties should control the case, but it found no sufficient indication of intent respecting this problem: [Here the court quotes extensively from *Parev.*]

The court protected the "status" of both parties by implying a term requiring the defendant to compensate the plaintiff for royalties lost due to competition with the defendant's new product.

The court gave close attention to the legitimate business aims of the parties, to their purpose of avoiding the risks of great losses, and to the need to frame a remedy to preserve the essence of the agreement. To that extent the decision exemplifies the new spirit of contract law.

This attitude toward contract law and toward the work of the courts will disturb some people even at this late date. It strains against half-remembered truths and remembered half-truths from the venerated first year course in Contract Law. The core of the trouble lies in the hoary maxim that the courts will not make a contract for the parties. The maxim requires three replies. First, courts today can indeed make contracts for the parties. Given certain minimal indicators of an intent to contract, the courts are today directed to impose on the parties the necessary specific provisions to complete the process. See U.C.C. §§ 2–204, 2–207, 2–208. Second, a distinction has long been noted between judicial imposition of initial terms and judicial interpretations and implications of terms to resolve disputes concerning contracts the parties have made for themselves. The maxim bears less weight when it is applied to dispute resolution than it does when it is applied to questions of contract formation. This case is plainly one of dispute resolution. Third, the maxim rests on two sensible notions: (1) Liability under the law of contract rests on assent, not imposition. (2) Judges are seldom able business men; they seldom have the information, ability, or time to do a good job of contracting for the parties. Neither of these notions applies here. The parties have made their own contract. The Court's role here is limited to framing a remedy for a problem they did not foresee and provide for. And while the Court willingly concedes that the managements of ALCOA and Essex are better able to conduct their business than is the Court, in this dispute the Court has information from hindsight far superior to that which the parties had when they made their contract. The parties may both be better served by an informed judicial decision based on the known circumstances than by a decision wrenched from words of the contract which were not chosen with a prevision of today's circumstances. The Court gladly concedes that the parties might today evolve a better working arrangement by negotiation than the Court can impose. But they have not done so, and a rule that the Court may not act would have the perverse effect of discouraging the parties from resolving this dispute or future disputes on their own. Only a rule which permits judicial action of the kind the Court has taken in this case will provide a desirable practical incentive for businessmen to negotiate their own resolution to problems which arise in the life of long term contracts.[35]

Finally, the Court notes that this case presents a problem of the appropriate legal response to problems of inflation. There are many long term contracts extant where inflation has upset the basic equivalence of the agreement. Courts will increasingly have to attend to problems like the present one. Bearing in mind the hazards of premature generalization, the Court would suggest that four factors considered in this decision will likely prove to be of durable importance in deciding whether to modify contracts: (1) the parties' prevision of the problems which eventually upset the balance of the agreements and their allocation of the associated risks; (2) the parties' attempts at risk limitation; (3) the existence of severe out of pocket losses and (4) the customs and expectations of the particular business community.

The problem of inflation is most frequently encountered as a change in the value of money to purchase things of all sorts. Long term fixed price contracts are most apt to be deranged by the process of inflation and are most apt to require judicial remedies. But inflation is not a coherent phenomenon. Prices of different things change at different rates. The record in this case shows clearly that the price of energy-intensive services has increased since 1973 much more rapidly than has the general Wholesale Price Index. An indexed price term in a contract may prevent or minimize the hardship of inflation, but if it fails to do so, as was true in this case, a court should look beyond the fact of the parties' prevision of the general problem of inflation and should ask if the deviation between the index and the pertinent costs of the parties was adequately foreseen and its risk allocated in the contract. Indexing may speak more forcefully of a general purpose to limit the risks of a long term contract than of the prevision of the specific problem which the parties encounter.

The existence of severe out of pocket losses should be essential to the award of relief. Inflation will often increase the value of goods so that a seller could sell his

---

35. The Court is aware of the practical incentive to negotiation which lies in the delay, expense and uncertainty of litigation. This case shows that at times these burdens are insufficient to prompt settlements.

goods for more than the stipulated contract price. This causes the seller disappointment and brings the purchaser a profit. But within a broad range this sort of market risk is assumed by parties to a long term contract. It would probably be highly disruptive to commercial relations and to transaction plans to allow parties to escape their contracts generally on this ground. Only a showing of unusual circumstance strongly suggesting the parties intended to allow the seller an excuse for performing in these circumstances should justify relief. This problem is hardly fanciful. In long term leases the landlord's principal cost is the value of the land and buildings. These are settled costs fixed before the lease or early in the leasing process. The landlord's variable costs that are subject to inflation will usually be limited to maintenance, taxes, and utilities. Many leases put some or all of these costs on the lessee. Under these circumstances the landlord may suffer little or no out of pocket loss due to inflation, but he may suffer serious disappointment if his rent receipts fall greatly behind the current rental value of his property. This sort of disappointment seems less serious and relief from it seems more destructive of contract expectations than the disappointment of serious out of pocket losses and the destruction of expectations incident to their relief.

The limitation of judicial relief to cases where the parties evidence a desire to limit their risks, where one party suffers severe out of pocket losses not adequately foreseen and provided for by the parties seems adequate to prevent a general disruption of commercial life by inflation. This limitation also seems generally compatible with the fair needs and understanding of responsible businessmen. Little more can be asked of the courts in the development of the law.

The foregoing shall constitute findings of fact and conclusions of law as required by Federal Rule of Civil Procedure 52(a). An appropriate Order will issue.

QUESTIONS AND NOTES

1. This case settled on appeal after argument before the Third Circuit but before its decision.

2. These parties were locked into the very tight embrace of a seventeen-year contract from which it would be extremely difficult for them to extricate themselves. Their plants, in which each had a very heavy investment, were physically connected. They dealt in a product market with few participants or alternative sources of supply. Neither party could simply cancel the contract, pick up its marbles, and go play somewhere else. Yet most traditional contract remedies give damages on the assumption that a disappointed party after material breach or repudiation will cover in the market for the performance it will not receive from the other side. Judge Teitelbaum's remedies are unusual, but what were the practical options once he found

that the original price clause was a result of mistake or had rendered performance impracticable?

3. The core problem in this case is the price clause designed by ALCOA with the help of an eminent economist who later became Chairman of the Federal Reserve System. As events worked out, that clause was a disaster in dealing with the consequences of the machinations of another potential monopolist, OPEC, and tightening pollution control laws. Was Alan Greenspan at fault for not designing a price clause that would cover every contingency? Instead of suing Essex, should ALCOA have sued Alan Greenspan for its $75 million out of pocket losses (not to mention pain and suffering)? There are limits on what even the wealthiest contracting parties, with the best lawyers and economists, can do to price-in all the contingencies of a long-term and inherently risky deal. Perhaps this is a situation in which the opportunities to realize gains from trade are limited by the inevitable potential of catastrophe arising from unknown future events. Should a court treat such a situation the same way classical contract law deals with a prize cow thought to be sterile who turns out to be with calf?

4. Dislocation in market prices following the OPEC oil embargo in 1973 was a fertile source of litigation and a reminder of the potential for runaway hyperinflation. Many nations of the world have suffered inflation rates in excess of 1,000% a year that destroy the expectations of contract. Nations faced with that kind of catastrophe look to legislative, non-legal, or revolutionary solutions, rather than judge-made remedies. Judge Teitelbaum struggled heroically to do justice in this one case, but would his approach be much help if a party to every contract in society complained that its obligations had been rendered meaningless by inflation that made the dollar valueless?

5. Judge Teitlebaum's opinion provoked a wide range of scholarly comment. Here are two widely divergent reactions:

> In *ALCOA*, the parties, at the time of contracting, were unable to deal with certain changed circumstances over the duration of a seventeen-year contract. Yet preserving the contract was important to the parties and to third parties dependent upon its performance but not represented in the litigation. Ian Macneil has argued that in situations such as this there are relational norms that the contract should be preserved and conflict harmonized by adjustment. These norms put a high premium upon developing mechanisms for adjustment over time and good faith efforts to adjust in the light of change. Thus, if in an *ALCOA*-type case, the court concludes that the disadvantaged party is entitled to "some relief" but not discharge, and the advantaged party has refused to accept a reasonable adjustment in light of risks that the disadvantaged party did not assume, relational theory also supports a court imposed adjustment to preserve

the contract, to adjust the price and to avoid the twin devils of unbargained-for hardship and unjust enrichment.

Richard E. Speidel, *The New Spirit of Contract,* 2 J.L. & COM. 193, 208 (1982).[*]

This is, I believe the only instance in which an American court has claimed power to recast by its own direct order, without some transparent disguise like "reformation" an essential term in an exchange that was still in progress when some unforeseen external event produced major imbalance. This form of "adjustment" to govern the performances not yet rendered is the one recommended by some authors in American law reviews....

The first reason that I have urged (for me it is a sufficient reason) for judges to abstain from rewriting the contracts of other people is that they are not qualified for such tasks. Nothing in their prior training as lawyers or their experience in directing litigation and giving coherence to its results will qualify them to invent viable new designs for disrupted enterprises, now gone awry, that the persons most concerned had tried to construct but without success. As one able author has contended, judges trained as judges, are "institutionally incapable" of achieving success in such undertakings.

The second reason, however, is important enough to be stated first for it raises an issue that I regard as a major issue of civil liberty. The question that I have repeatedly raised but have not tried to answer is the question—when an unforeseen event has so drastically altered a contract that the parties to it are fully excused from its further performance, from what source does any court derive the power to impose on them a new contract without the free assent of both? Where rescission is awarded on any of the standard grounds—fraud, mistake, substantial breach, defective capacity, duress—no one has ever suggested that such a power lay hidden somewhere. For myself, I do not propose to spend time looking for the source of the power. I am convinced that it does not exist.

John P. Dawson, *Judicial Revision of Frustrated Contract: The United States*, 64 B.U. L. REV. 1, 37–38 (1984).[*]

6. Professors White and Peters assess the caselaw in the two decades following the *ALCOA* decision as follows:

American courts have not only refused to rewrite contracts, they appear to have held the line at avoiding them . . .

There is no evidence in the cases of the last two decades that the courts have become more receptive to pleas of mistake or supervening changes. If anything, the lessons of the game theorists may be sinking in. We now appreciate more

---

[*] Copyright 1982, The Journal of Law & Commerce.

[*] Copyright 1984, Boston University Law Review.

than before that parties at the time of contracting and later will respond to the events considered here . . .

[W]e see just a hint that the courts are getting harder, not softer, that they are more, not less, likely to leave the parties in their contract than formerly…[W]e see no weakening of the judicial spine …

[T]he threat to freedom of contract that Jack [Dawson] saw in *Alcoa* has receded. No courts have followed its holding and only a few judges have embraced its reasoning.

James J. White & David A. Peters, *A Footnote for Jack Dawson*, 100 MICH. L. REV. 1954, 1966, 1971-72 (2002).

II.   UNEXCUSED NONPERFORMANCE

A.   REPRISE OF THE PROMISE VS. CONDITION DISTINCTION

Labeling a contract term as a promise or condition is primarily a statement of the consequence of nonoccurrence—damages or suspension of the obligation of counter-performances. This is a nice way of saying that the definition is tautological: A promised event is a promise because its non-occurrence constitutes a breach of promise affording the injured party a right to damages, while a condition is a condition because its failure excuses counter-performance. As Holmes teaches in the quotation at the end of this Note, "You can always imply a condition in a contract. But why do you imply it?"

Consider again the hypothetical agreement between Seller and Buyer at the beginning of this Chapter that illustrated the basic contract structure. Seller agreed to sell and deliver to Buyer's grain elevator 2,000 bushels of wheat (1,000 by September 10 and 1,000 by October 10). What if, come September 10, Seller delivers 990 bushels instead of the required 1,000? Or what if it delivers 1,000 bushels but delivers a day late? In either event, unless it has a legal excuse, Seller has breached the contract; Buyer has a remedial claim. But is Seller's breach *material*, permitting Buyer to reject the shipment and abandon its own performance? Or must Buyer pay, accept the second shipment, and be satisfied with a claim for the shortage or the delay in the first shipment? The answer, we can say with confidence, depends on whether exact or literal performance by Seller is a condition of Buyer's promise to pay. If it is, the failure of Seller's performance may be variously described as a material breach, total breach, or failure of consideration. But if exact amount or specific completion date is "merely" a promise and not a condition of Buyer's promised payment, Seller's failure to perform exactly as promised will be variously described as an immaterial breach, partial breach, or partial failure of consideration. But how helpful is that in deciding which it is?

The vocabulary in this area is needlessly confusing. Courts use a wide variety of terms to describe breaches of mere promises on the one hand and failures of promissory conditions on the other:

Independent Promise and Dependent Promise: An independent promise is one whose performance is required even though a promised counter-performance is not rendered. In other words, breach of the counter-promise is merely a breach of promise and not a breach of a promissory condition. A dependent promise, on the other hand, is one which need not be performed if the counter-promise on which it is deemed to be dependent is not performed. Breach of the counter-promise, in other words, is a breach of a promissory condition.

Mere Covenant: This is just another history-laden way of saying mere promise, that is, not a promissory condition.

Immaterial Breach, Partial Breach, Partial Failure of Consideration: Breach of promise but not the nonoccurrence of a condition, that is, this event gives rise only to damages.

Material Breach, Total Breach, Failure of Consideration: Failure of promissory condition, the result of which is both a breach giving rise to damages and failure of a condition, excusing counter-performance.

These terms are essential parts of the lawyer's vocabulary (hence you should learn them), but always remember that they are only labels assigned to determinations *after* they have been made; you will find them of no help in deciding what the effect of an event should be. Despite the logical form in which the question is often put, the effect of a breach on a promised counter-performance is decided on the basis of context and an assessment of the relative importance of various performances. And this assessment presents a lawyer with some agonizing decisions in counseling clients.

As Justice Holmes put it in *The Path of the Law*, 10 HARV. L. REV. 457 (1897):

> The training of lawyers is a training in logic. The processes of analogy, discrimination, and deduction are those in which they are most at home. The language of judicial decision is mainly the language of logic. And the logical method and form flatter the longing for certainty and for repose which is in every human mind. But certainty generally is illusion and repose is not the destiny of

man. Behind the logical form lies a judgment as to the relative worth and importance of competing legislative grounds, of an inarticulate and unconscious judgment it is true, and yet the root and nerve of the whole proceeding. You can give any conclusion a logical form. You can always imply a condition in a contract. But why do you imply it? It is because of some belief as to the practice of the community or of a class, or because of some attitude of yours upon a matter not capable of exact quantitative measurement, and therefore not capable of founding exact logical conclusions. Such matters really are battlegrounds where the means do not exist for determinations that shall be good for all time, and where the decision can do no more than embody the preference of a given body in a given time and place.

B.   THE EVALUATION OF NONPERFORMANCE

The effect of a particular nonperformance on the continuing relationship of the parties may include two aspects: damages and the suspension or termination of the promisee's performance obligations. If the nonperformance is not very important, it will not disturb the promisee's security as to eventual performance, and therefore it is unlikely to suspend the obligation of counter-performance. After minor nonperformance, the disappointed party can be left to its remedy in damages, if any have been suffered. More serious breaches, however, will not only produce damages, but also threaten the security of the relationship. The disappointed party's duty of counterperformance is at least suspended until performance is assured.

If a delivery arrives an hour late, for instance, that is a breach, and the disappointed Buyer can recover damages if it has suffered any. During that hour of delay, Buyer's obligations to pay probably are suspended. But absent unusual circumstances that would make the delay of overriding significance, it is unlikely that Buyer is permanently excused or that the contract is terminated. When the goods arrive, Buyer must take and pay for them. Seen this way, the operative legal questions are (a) does the nonperformance justify the suspension of counter-performance and (b) is the nonperformance sufficiently serious to consider the contract terminated by the failure of performance. Obviously, only a serious or aggravated breach will threaten the existence of the relationship.

RESTATEMENT, SECOND, CONTRACTS:

§ 241. Circumstances Significant in Determining Whether a Failure Is Material.

In determining whether a failure to perform or to make an offer to perform is material, the following circumstances are significant:

(a) the extent to which the injured party will be deprived of the benefit which he reasonably expected;

(b) the extent to which the injured party can be adequately compensated for the part of that benefit of which he will be deprived;

(c) the extent to which the party failing to perform or to offer to perform will suffer forfeiture;

(d) the likelihood that the party failing to perform or to offer to perform will cure his failure, taking account of all the circumstances including any reasonable assurances;

(e) the extent to which the behavior of the party failing to perform or to offer to perform comports with standards of good faith and fair dealing.

§ 242. Circumstances Significant in Determining when Remaining Duties Are Discharged.

In determining the time after which a party's uncured material failure to render or to offer performance discharges the other party's remaining duties to render performance under the rules stated in §§ 237 and 238, the following circumstances are significant:

(a) those stated in § 241;

(b) the extent to which it reasonably appears to the injured party that delay may prevent or hinder him in making reasonable substitute arrangements;

(c) the extent to which the agreement provides for performance without delay, but a material failure to perform or to offer to perform on a stated day does not of itself discharge the other party's remaining duties unless the circumstances, including the language of the agreement, indicate that performance or an offer to perform by that day is important.

Walker & Co. v. Harrison

Michigan Supreme Court, 1957.
347 Mich. 630, 81 N.W.2d 352.

■ SMITH, J. This is a suit on a written contract. The defendants are in the dry-cleaning business. Walker & Company, plaintiff, sells, rents, and services advertising signs and billboards. These parties entered into an agreement pertaining to a sign. The agreement is in writing and is termed a "rental agreement." It specifies in part that:

> The lessor agrees to construct and install, at its own cost, one 18'9" high x 8'8" wide pylon type d.f. neon sign with electric clock and flashing lamps * * *. The lessor agrees to and does hereby lease or rent unto the said lessee the said SIGN for the term, use and rental and under the conditions, hereinafter set out, and the lessee agrees to pay said rental * * *.
>
> (a) The term of this lease shall be 36 months * * *.
>
> (b) The rental to be paid by lessee shall be $148.50 per month for each and every calendar month during the term of this lease; * * *.
>
> (c) *Maintenance.* Lessor at its expense agrees to maintain and service the sign together with such equipment as supplied and installed by the lessor to operate in conjunction with said sign under the terms of this lease; this service is to include cleaning and repainting of sign in original color scheme as often as deemed necessary by lessor to keep sign in first class advertising condition and make all necessary repairs to sign and equipment installed by lessor. * * *.

At the "expiration of this agreement," it was also provided, "title to this sign reverts to lessee." This clause is in addition to the printed form of agreement and was apparently added as a result of defendants' concern over title, they having expressed a desire "to buy for cash" and the salesman, at one time, having "quoted a cash price."

The sign was completed and installed in the latter part of July, 1953. The first billing of the monthly payment of $148.50 was made August 1, 1953, with payment thereof by defendants on September 3, 1953. This first payment was also the last. Shortly after the sign was installed, someone hit it with a tomato. Rust, also, was visible on the chrome, complained defendants, and in its corners were "little spider cobwebs." In addition, there were "some children's sayings written down in here." Defendant Herbert Harrison called Walker for the maintenance he believed himself entitled to under subparagraph (c) above. It was not forthcoming. He called again and again. "I was getting, you might say, sorer and sorer. * * * Occasionally, when I started calling up, I would walk around where the tomato was and get mad again. Then I would call up on the phone again." Finally, on October 8, 1953, plaintiff not having responded to his repeated calls, he telegraphed Walker that:

"You Have Continually Voided Our Rental Contract By Not Maintaining Signs As Agreed As We No Longer Have A Contract With You Do Not Expect Any Further Remuneration."

Walker's reply was in the form of a letter. After first pointing out that "your telegram does not make any specific allegations as to what the failure of maintenance comprises," and stating that "We certainly would appreciate your furnishing us with such information," the letter makes reference to a prior collateral controversy between the parties, "wondering if this refusal on our part prompted your attempt to void our rental contract," and concludes as follows:

We would like to call your attention to paragraph G in our rental contract, which covers procedures in the event of a Breach of Agreement. In the event that you carry out your threat to make no future monthly payments in accordance with the agreement, it is our intention to enforce the conditions outlined under paragraph G through the proper legal channels. We call to your attention that your monthly rental payments are due in advance at our office not later than the 10th day of each current month. You are now approximately 30 days in arrears on your September payment. Unless we receive both the September and October payments by October 25th, this entire matter will be placed in the hands of our attorney for collection in accordance with paragraph G which stipulates that the entire amount is forthwith due and payable.

No additional payments were made and Walker sued in assumpsit for the entire balance due under the contract, $5,197.50, invoking paragraph (g) of the agreement. Defendants filed answer and claim of recoupment, asserting that plaintiff's failure to perform certain maintenance services constituted a prior material breach of the agreement, thus justifying their repudiation of the contract and grounding their claim for damages. The case was tried to the court without a jury and resulted in a judgment for the plaintiff. The case is before us on a general appeal.

Defendants urge upon us again and again, in various forms, the proposition that Walker's failure to service the sign, in response to repeated requests, constituted a material breach of the contract and justified repudiation by them. Their legal proposition is undoubtedly correct. Repudiation is one of the weapons available to an injured party in event the other contractor has committed a material breach. But the injured party's determination that there has been a material breach, justifying his own repudiation, is fraught with peril, for should such determination, as viewed by a later court in the calm of its contemplation, be unwarranted, the repudiator himself will have been guilty of material breach and himself have become the aggressor, not an innocent victim.

What is our criterion for determining whether or not a breach of contract is so fatal to the undertaking of the parties that it is to be classed as "material"? There is no single touchstone. Many factors are involved. They are well stated in [the first Restatement of Contracts] section 275 in the following terms:

> In determining the materiality of a failure fully to perform a promise the following circumstances are influential:
>
> (a) The extent to which the injured party will obtain the substantial benefit which he could have reasonably anticipated;
>
> (b) The extent to which the injured party may be adequately compensated in damages for lack of complete performance;
>
> (c) The extent to which the party failing to perform has already partly performed or made preparations for performance;
>
> (d) The greater or less hardship on the party failing to perform in terminating the contract;
>
> (e) The wilful, negligent or innocent behavior of the party failing to perform;
>
> (f) The greater or less uncertainty that the party failing to perform will perform the remainder of the contract.

We will not set forth in detail the testimony offered concerning the need for servicing. Granting that Walker's delay (about a week after defendant Herbert Harrison sent his telegram of repudiation Walker sent out a crew and took care of things) in rendering the service requested was irritating, we are constrained to agree with the trial court that it was not of such materiality as to justify repudiation of the contract, and we are particularly mindful of the lack of preponderant evidence contrary to his determination. The trial court, on this phase of the case, held as follows:

> Now Mr. Harrison phoned in, so he testified, a number of times. He isn't sure of the dates but he sets the first call at about the 7th of August and he complained then of the tomato and of some rust and some cobwebs. The tomato, according to the testimony, was up on the clock; that would be outside of his reach, without a stepladder or something. The cobwebs are within easy reach of Mr. Harrison and so would the rust be. I think that Mr. Bueche's argument that these were not materially a breach would clearly be true as to the cobwebs and I really can't believe in the face of all the testimony that there was a great deal of rust seven days after the installation of this sign. And that really brings it down to the tomato. And, of course, when a tomato has been splashed all over your clock, you don't like it. But he says he kept calling their attention to it, although the rain probably washed some of the tomato off. But the stain remained, and they didn't come. I really can't find that that was such a material breach of the contract as to justify rescission. I really don't think so.

Nor, we conclude, do we. There was no valid ground for defendants' repudiation and their failure thereafter to comply with the terms of the contract was itself a material breach, entitling Walker, upon this record, to judgment.

QUESTIONS AND NOTES

1. Was it a breach for Walker not to come when Harrison called the first time? How about the second time Harrison called?

2. If it was a breach for Walker not to respond, what would Harrison's damages be? Would Harrison be entitled to any other remedies?

3. Why would Harrison buy the sign in the first place? If people laughed because this dry cleaner's shop had a sign with a tomato stain on its clock, would Harrison be getting the substantial benefit he reasonably anticipated from the contract?

4. Does the fact that it would take Harrison only three minutes to clean off the sign himself affect your decision whether Walker's failure to come was a material breach?

5. Should Walker & Co.'s damages be offset by its savings from not having to service the sign for the three-year term of the lease?

6. If Harrison came to you for advice on August 7, what would you tell him? If he came to you on September 3, when the next rent check was due, what would you advise him to do? If he came to you on October 8, before the telegram was sent, what advice would you give? If he came to you after receiving Walker's letter, what would you say?

C.   SITUATION TYPES OF NONPERFORMANCE

No simple rules predict the legal consequence of every conceivable breach, but common breach situations do usually fall into identifiable patterns. Most partial failures in performance are of two types: (i) late performances and (ii) defective performances that vary in quality or quantity from what the contract calls for. Late performances, in turn, fall into two subcategories: failure to make timely payment of money and failure to timely deliver goods or services. There is a practical difference in the treatment courts give these two subcategories: late payment is less likely to be a material breach than late delivery of goods or services.

1. Late Performance: Payment

The practical and important issue when parties fix payment terms is who is going to extend how much credit in the deal—the buyer, the seller, both, or neither. Payment may be due at some time after the delivery date of the goods or other bargained-for counterperformance or in installments. Such arrangements are common in our credit-dominated society. If payment is due after delivery, late payment forces the Seller to accept delayed repayment of the credit extended under the terms of the contract. The late paying buyer is, in effect, merely extending the due date of a loan involuntarily. But this is so common in today's economy that we tend to feel that payment exactly on time is not of great consequence so long as the buyer pays interest, the delay is not too great, and the debt is eventually paid in full.

One sense in which late payment is less disruptive than late delivery of goods is that the loss can be easily computed since the seller's loss and its compensation in damages are in the same medium: money. Moreover consequential damages or lost mitigation opportunities do not figure prominently in late payment cases though they may in the late delivery context. Unless the disappointed seller lacks sufficient capital or credit, it can be made whole by damages measured simply by the going interest rate. Hence, the seller who insists on immediate termination because of late payment is suspect unless the buyer is in serious financial trouble.

Sometimes payment is required at the time of delivery (cash-on-delivery or "COD" terms); sometimes a contract requires a downpayment or full prepayment prior to delivery. If a delay in payment is treated as a minor or immaterial breach even in these cases Seller might be obligated to deliver on credit even though it specifically bargained not to bear that credit risk. Generally the law's solution is simple: Seller is not so obligated. Seller can suspend its performance and wait for payment before further delivery. But how long must seller wait—or how many delayed payments must it tolerate—before it can terminate its contract obligation because payment is late?

———————

Foundation Dev. Corp. v. Loehmann's

Supreme Court of Arizona, 1990.
163 Ariz. 438, 788 P.2d 1189.

■ FELDMAN, VICE CHIEF JUSTICE. Loehmann's, Inc. (Loehmann's) petitions us to review a court of appeals opinion dealing with grounds for termination of a long-term commercial lease. The trial court ruled that Loehmann's delay in paying a common area charge was a trivial breach of its lease and therefore refused to permit the landlord, Foundation Development Corporation (Foundation), to re-enter and take possession of the leased premises. The court of appeals reversed....

In 1978, Loehmann's became the anchor tenant in the Lincoln View Plaza Shopping Center by entering into a twenty-year lease with Foundation's predecessor in interest. The lease contained no provision for percentage rental or rental increase during the twenty-year term. Loehmann's had an option to renew for two five-year terms. The lease therefore was potentially of thirty years' duration, expiring in 2008. Loehmann's was to operate a retail clothing store, part of its nationwide chain.

In addition to rental payments due on the first day of each month, Loehmann's was liable for common area charges based on its proportionate share of the total square footage in the shopping complex. Loehmann's customary practice was to make estimated partial payments for the common area charges at the end of each of the first three quarters of each lease year. At the end of the fourth quarter, Foundation submitted an adjusted statement itemizing its actual expenditures for the year. Loehmann's then paid the difference between the partial payments it had made and the total actual expenditures, generally paying thirty days or longer after it received the statement. Loehmann's total annual payments to Foundation were approximately $50,000 ($45,000 annual rent plus approximately $5,000 for common area charges).

The lease also contained a section describing "Conditions of Default." If Loehmann's failed "to pay any installment of minimum annual rental or additional rental or other charges [and did not cure] within ten (10) days after receipt * * * of notice of such neglect or failure," Foundation could "prior to the removal of such Condition of Default," elect to terminate the lease. The lease stipulated that "with respect to * * * [Loehmann's] obligation to pay rent, taxes and other charges * * * [or] in any case where either party * * * is required to do any act, the time for the performance thereof shall be of the essence."

On February 23, 1987, Geri Beemiller (Beemiller), an employee of Foundation's local managing agent, Rae–Marc Asset Management (Rae–Marc), sent Loehmann's the year-end statement for common area charges for the lease year ending January 31, 1987. The statement was addressed to Kevin Gaw (Gaw) at Loehmann's Halsey Street address in New York. The balance due was $3,566.44. The statement did not indicate when payment was due, and Beemiller indicated that if Gaw had any questions, he should contact her. The lease had no provision indicating a time schedule for the payment of the fourth installment of the common area charge.

Believing that Foundation had miscalculated its proration of the total square footage of the complex, Gaw sent an inquiry to Beemiller on March 18, 1987. Beemiller responded to the Halsey Street address on March 25, 1987, indicating that because a portion of the complex had been sold, Loehmann's proportionate share of the total had been increased.

On April 10, 1987, Timothy Richardson, another Rae–Marc employee in Phoenix, sent a demand letter to Loehmann's. He referred to the original February 23, 1987 statement (erroneously noting that it covered the period ending March 31, 1987 and not January 31), and appended it, but did not mention Gaw's recent inquiry to Beemiller or the latter's response. He addressed the letter to Loehmann's at the leased premises in Phoenix and at the address listed on the lease on Baychester Avenue, New York. He copied the letter to the Halsey Street address. Richardson did not address the letter to a specific individual. He further stated: "We have not yet received your payment in the amount of $3,566.44. We must reinstate time of the essence of your lease and insist that this amount be paid within ten days from the date of this letter."

Loehmann's received Richardson's letter in the Phoenix store on April 13, 1987. Because the local store was not responsible for paying rent or other charges, the letter was forwarded to the Halsey Street office. The letter sent to the Baychester Avenue address was returned to Foundation, presumably because Loehmann's no longer occupied that building.

Loehmann's Halsey Street office received the letter on Friday, April 17, 1987. Apparently because the letter was not addressed to any particular individual, the mail room personnel sent it to Loehmann's general counsel, Marvin Gardner. Mr. Gardner was not in his office that Friday, which Loehmann's notes was Good Friday. When he returned to work on Monday April 20, 1987, he sent the notice to the accounting department. A senior staff accountant marked the letter "REC'D 4-20-87." The accountant approved the original statement for common area charges on April 22, 1987 by affixing his initials, and noting the date and the store number. On Friday April 24, 1987 a check was issued. Loehmann's claims the check was mailed the next day, April 25. On Tuesday April 28, 1987, Foundation filed a complaint in superior court seeking termination of the lease, immediate possession of the leased premises, and payment of the accrued common area charges. A day later, April 29, Foundation received Loehmann's check in Phoenix.

A. The Historical Perspective

The landlord-tenant relationship had its genesis in feudal England. Most land was held through a personal relationship between a tenant and his lord, the tenant expecting to hold for a lifetime, the lord expecting to dispose of the holding as he pleased after the tenant died. As the concept of a tenancy for years first developed, the law regarded the tenant as having only contract rights. Courts, however, gradually became aware that mere contractual remedies did not protect the tenant's right to quiet enjoyment of the property. By 1235, the development of the writ *quare ejecit infra terminum* gave the tenant a remedy against those who took from the original landowner, and by the fifteenth century, the writ *de ejectione firmae* afforded him protection against third parties, not only those claiming through his landlord. The law clearly recognized that the tenant had an important property right in the leasehold that transcended his contractual relationship with the landlord.

Thus, because of its historical underpinnings, landlord-tenant law is infused with principles of both real property and contract law. Therefore, although logically and analytically it is correct to say that a lease is both a conveyance and a contract, the modern law traditionally viewed it as a conveyance.

An important consequence of recognizing a lease as a conveyance was that when contract law developed the concept of dependency of covenants and thus permitted the equitable remedy of rescission upon breach, landlords and tenants did not share in this remedy. Consequently, in the absence of a statute or lease clause authorizing it, neither landlord nor tenant was empowered to terminate a leasehold because of the other's breach, and violation of a lease covenant gave rise only to an action for the damages caused by the breach. Thus, at common law a landlord could not dispossess a tenant who failed to keep his promise to pay rent, and had to be satisfied with damages for the breach.

Moreover, even if the lease specifically gave the landlord the equitable remedy of rescission—the right to re-enter and terminate for non-payment of rent—the Court of Chancery would prevent forfeiture upon payment of the rent in arrears and costs. The court provided relief based "upon the notion that such condition and forfeiture [were] intended merely as security for payment of money." Such lease provisions were not intended to enable the landlord to obtain undue advantage of a tenant on technical and inequitable grounds. Nor were they designed to destroy the landlord-tenant relationship for "slight reason." Of course, general equitable principles applied in such situations. For the court to grant relief, the tenant must have dealt fairly and must have made an honest attempt to comply with the provisions of the lease.

Obviously, the common law traditionally sought to stabilize and maintain the landlord-tenant relationship in cases where breach had occurred. Should a different rule obtain when a landlord seeks forfeiture pursuant to statute?

B. Arizona: Statute, Lease Provision, and Case Law

In Arizona, A.R.S. § 33–361(A) confers the right of re-entry and termination to the landlord for the violation of a commercial lease. The precursor to this statute became law in 1895. Presumably, the legislature responded to burgeoning business interests in the territory by affording the landlord a right of rescission. The statute states in pertinent part that: "* * * [w]hen a tenant neglects or refuses to pay rent when due and in arrears for five days, or when tenant violates any provision of the lease, the landlord * * * may re-enter and take possession, or without formal demand or re-entry, commence an action for recovery of possession of the premises."

We join Foundation in reading the statute as expressing a legislative intent to confer on the landlord a right to terminate for breach, a right not possessed at common law in 1895 absent a contractual provision. We do not, however, necessarily read it so broadly as Foundation urges—to express a legislative intent that any breach, at any time, of "any provision" would give the landlord the right to forfeit the leasehold.

Foundation argues, however, that so long as the lease provides that violation of a covenant is grounds for termination, the court must enforce the lease according to its terms. It also contends that because the lease provides for forfeiture and A.R.S. § 33–361(A) permits the landlord to "re-enter and take possession" for "violation of any provision of the lease," the trial court has no discretion regarding the enforcement of the forfeiture.

In claiming A.R.S. § 33–361 prevents judicial consideration of equitable defenses to forfeiture of Loehmann's leasehold interest, Foundation ignores the important interplay of property and contract law that preceded the enactment of the statute. The property rights concept—that a lease was a conveyance—was essential to maintain economic equilibrium in an agrarian environment. The fact that leasehold interests now prevail in the urban, business world does not diminish their importance. Commercial tenants often make substantial investments for fixtures or for improvements to the leasehold. They hire personnel and enter into agreements (often long term) to foster the continuation of their enterprise based on the expectation that they will be able to conduct their business for the term they have leased the property. Sound public policy reasons militate in favor of assuring the stability of such economic relationships. Accordingly, absent some express statement of legislative intent, we are hesitant to believe that, in enacting A.R.S. § 33–361, the legislature intended to permit forfeitures under any and all circumstances, no matter how trivial, inadvertent, non-prejudicial, or technical the breach.

There is no basis suggested for applying a different rule for a trivial or immaterial breach. By enacting A.R.S. § 33–361, the legislature effected a change in the operation of the common law: the landlord could seek to terminate a lease for a tenant's breach even in the absence of a lease provision conferring that right. Generally, we strictly construe statutes that are in derogation of the common law. While we will uphold a forfeiture when the breach is significant, we do not believe we should so literally construe A.R.S. § 33–361 as to enable a landlord to obtain an undue advantage over his tenant by permitting forfeiture for every or any breach, no matter how trivial or technical. Given the history briefly outlined above, we believe the legislative interest in enacting the predecessor of § 33–361(A) was merely to give the lessor a right not recognized at common law—the right to terminate in the absence of a contractual provision. We do not believe the legislature intended to enact the dangerous doctrine that forfeiture was to be permitted for any breach no matter how inconsequential.

Having been squarely presented with the question for the first time, we decline to hold that any breach, no matter how trivial or insignificant, can justify a forfeiture. Nor do we believe such a rule could long survive. Trivial or not, the delay in paying the rent here was at most three days. What if the breach had been three hours instead of three days or the check had been lost in the mail and came at three minutes after midnight? The questions almost answer themselves. Therefore, we now join the overwhelming majority of jurisdictions that hold the landlord's right to terminate is not unlimited. We believe a court's decision to permit termination must be tempered by notions of equity and common sense. We thus hold a forfeiture for a trivial or immaterial breach of a commercial lease should not be enforced. Accordingly, we turn to analyze whether Loehmann's breach—a three-day delay in payment—was of such dimension so as to permit forfeiture.

D. The Standard for Evaluating the Triviality of a Breach

We agree with Foundation that the payment of the common area charge, is a material provision of the lease. Nonetheless, we believe a material provision of a lease may be breached in such a trivial manner that to enforce a forfeiture would be unconscionable and inequitable.

Courts often conclude a party has breached a lease provision in a material as opposed to trivial or immaterial manner based only on the specific facts at issue. They therefore do not identify a workable standard to evaluate the triviality of a breach. The Restatement (Second) of Property § 13.1 provides that if a tenant fails to perform a valid promise contained in the lease, the landlord may terminate if he "is deprived of a significant inducement to the making of the lease and the tenant does not perform his promise within a reasonable period of time after being requested to do so." We find this statement too general to be very helpful; we believe the Restatement (Second) of Contracts § 241[13] sets forth a more explicit analytical framework. It requires the factfinder to consider the following:

> (a) the extent to which the injured party will be deprived of the benefit which he reasonably expected;

---

13. The drafters of the Restatement (Second) of Property note that the law of the late twentieth century contains a still shifting balance of property and contract concepts, with neither clearly in control. Restatement, Introduction at 4. They opine that to the extent both concepts aid in fashioning the most realistic and equitable relationships possible, it is likely that such a mixture will remain. We thus find the rule that pertains to contracts in general regarding this issue is helpful in defining the rights of the parties in the landlord tenant context.

(b) the extent to which the injured party can be adequately compensated [by damages] for the part of that benefit of which he will be deprived;

(c) the extent to which the party failing to perform or to offer to perform will suffer forfeiture;

(d) the likelihood that the party failing to perform or to offer to perform will cure his failure, taking account of all the circumstances including any reasonable assurances;

(e) the extent to which the behavior of the party failing to perform or to offer to perform comports with standards of good faith and fair dealing.

We adopt these standards for determining the triviality or immateriality of a breach in the landlord-tenant context. We turn, then, to review the trial court's grant of summary judgment in Loehmann's favor. In doing so, we consider the facts in a light most favorable to Foundation. Applying the Restatement (Second) of Contracts standard to the facts of this case, did the trial court err in finding the breach to be trivial?

E. Was the Breach Trivial in this Case?

The court determined that if the date of the receipt of the letter at Loehmann's store, April 13, 1987, initiated the time to pay or cure, the payment made on April 25, 1987 was two days late. Therefore, as to subsections (a) and (b) supra, Foundation at most would be deprived of the benefit of its bargain only in the loss of the use of the funds for two days. Foundation makes no claim that it was damaged by the delay in payment. Furthermore, it may be adequately compensated by a judgment of damages for any loss of interest on the funds it incurred in those two days.

In applying subsection (c) of the Restatement standards, the factfinder should consider the extent to which the party failing to perform or to make an offer to perform will suffer forfeiture if the failure is treated as material. Restatement (Second) of Contracts § 241 comment d. In the general contract setting, a failure to perform will not be deemed material if it occurs "late, after [the breaching party's] substantial preparation or performance." In the present case, the trial court found: "Given the magnitude of this lease, the obvious value of the property and the lease, the approximate amount of money annually due under the lease and the history of the performance under the lease, the Court finds the breach in this case to be trivial * * * * ."

The facts in the record regarding the tenant's investment (preparation), the tenant's lack of history as to previous breach during almost ten years of occupancy (performance), and the size of the breach relative to the entire amount of money annually due, support the trial judge's finding that this breach was trivial. As for subsection (d), Loehmann's has already cured its failure to perform and never indicated it was unwilling to do so.

Additionally, Loehmann's behavior comports with standards of good faith and fair dealing. The breach was not willful or persistent. The fact that the breach occurred at all was arguably due to Loehmann's belief that the time for payment was initiated upon its receipt of the demand letter and statement at the Halsey Street address in New York, not the store address in Phoenix. Furthermore, the demand letter was not addressed to a particular individual, while the previous statements and correspondence were addressed to Gaw. Lastly, the letter did not reference the previous correspondence regarding the disputed amount and in fact misstated the time period the statement covered. The fact that Loehmann's personnel engaged in responsible business practices by insuring that the payment was indeed due and the amount correct certainly does not indicate bad faith or a desire not to comply with the request for payment. The trial court's implicit finding that Loehmann's dealt in good faith and made an honest attempt to comply with the provisions of the lease is well supported in the record.

In the present case, the lease did not provide a specific due date for the payment of the common area charges. Loehmann's had paid the entire annual rent and approximately fifty to seventy-five percent of the common area charge amount due and had reasonable questions about the accuracy of the final account. While Loehmann's customary practice was to pay the final common area charge in thirty days or longer, Foundation sent its demand letter—addressed to no particular individual—only sixteen days after its agent had explained the assessment and had verified that the statement was correct. Foundation did not allege that Loehmann's had been an uncooperative tenant in any other respect or that it had indicated it was not ready, able and willing to make payment. In response to a question at oral argument as to why Foundation did not simply telephone Loehmann's to inquire as to the status of the payment, Foundation responded only that it had the right to enforce the lease as written.

Having determined that the trial court did not err in holding the breach at issue was so trivial that to enforce a forfeiture would be unjust, we must turn to Foundation's final argument: does the time of the essence clause render a trivial breach material?

F. The Time of the Essence Clause

Foundation urges us to sustain the court of appeals holding that the time of the essence provision of the lease, reinstated by the demand letter, had the effect of rendering an otherwise trivial breach, by untimely performance, material....

Professor Corbin refutes the statement that common law judges rigidly adhered to the rule that "time is of the essence" in all contracts at common law, explaining that to determine if untimely performance is a material breach, there must be weighing "of the importance of many factors in each particular case." Even if the parties include a time of the essence provision, "[i]f the enforcement of such an express provision will have the effect of enforcing an excessive penalty or an unjust forfeiture, equity will prevent such enforcement."

We believe we would be hard pressed to discover a commercial lease that did not include the condition that "time is of the essence" for payment of rent or other charges. Considering such provisions may be more appropriately included in contracts for the sale of goods where a party's performance may be conditioned on the promisor's timely performance, it is questionable whether such "stock phrases" add much to the parties' obligations in cases such as this. We do not write such words out of every contract. In contracts between a vendor and purchaser, a purchaser's failure to make timely payment may be held to go to the essence and justify the seller in refusing to convey if values are rapidly fluctuating and because of the delay the purchaser would profit by the transaction. Similarly, timely conveyance may be of the essence when a vendor is aware a buyer intends to continue a business that is already a going concern or make improvements and start a new business.

If failure of payment at the exact time will not cause injury, time cannot be absolutely "of the essence," even though, technically, delay will be a breach. The inquiry must always involve the facts of the individual case and the effect of the breach on the injured party.

We thus hold that a time of the essence provision is merely one factor to be considered when determining if a breach is material. The mere incantation that "time is of the essence" works no magic to transform trivial untimeliness into a material breach; rather, the same factors we delineated in determining general materiality apply to evaluating the effect of a particular "time of the essence" provision.

QUESTIONS AND NOTES

1. This case involved a long-term lease implicating substantial commercial interests between sophisticated parties. The Arizona Supreme Court, in affirming the trial court's refusal to declare the breach material, must address the Arizona statute and the contractual "time of the essence" condition in the lease. The court applies traditional concepts in narrowly reading the statute, which operates in derogation of the common law, in order to avoid a forfeiture of the tenant's leasehold. This analysis may provide an adequate basis for interpreting the statute as exempting minor breaches. But on what basis does the court limit the contractual "time of the essence" clause? After all, these sophisticated parties had lawyers who drafted an elaborate lease and can be presumed to have meant what they said.

2. What would be the consequence of finding this breach material? What economic loss would be realized by the breaching tenant? What loss was realized by the landlord from the breach?

3. In *Mining Investment Group LLC v. Roberts*, 177 P.3d 1207 (Ariz.App. 2008), the court distinguished *Loehmann's* in a case involved a sale of real estate rather than a long-term lease. The parties had agreed that the sale would close on October 14. The buyer was required to come up with $30,000 to close the transaction. The sellers arrived at the escrow office at 1 pm and waited for two hours for confirmation of receipt of the wire. No wire was received that day and at 5:30 pm the sellers faxed a letter to the buyer terminating the sale contract. The seller also kept the buyer's $10,000 deposit as liquidated damages. The buyer's wire came through the next business day, but the seller refused to accept it having terminated the sale contract at the close of business on the scheduled closing date. The court noting that the contract expressly provided that the failure to close by October 14 would be material breach entitling the seller to cancel the agreement and retain the deposit. It enforced the agreement as written, notwithstanding the buyer's resulting forfeiture of both its deposit and any equitable interest in the land. Right result? Different from *Loehmann's* or not? If so why?

---

2.   Late Performance: Delivery

Damages for late payment are usually easy to compute and recover, but the opposite is the case where the delay is in delivery of product or services. Conversion of loss for late delivery into money recovery is apt to be very difficult. Recall the difficulty the shipper in *Hadley v. Baxendale*, p. 160, had in recovering for the late delivery of his millshaft. In short, the definition of contract damages is too narrow to cover the hard-to-compute expense of idle workers and machinery, commercial dislocation, and lost opportunities that may follow from a delay in delivery. The result is that courts tend to deny recovery for such losses. The reason given for denying such damages may be that compensation for losses of such magnitude were not contemplated by the parties; that the losses were not foreseeable; that they are remote or too speculative. Whatever the reasons for denying them (and denied they frequently are), the uncertainty of their availability ought to be good reason for permitting prompt cancellation by a buyer who is actually faced with such losses so that he can safely cover elsewhere and thus avoid them. Where such losses do not appear to be imminent, more latitude is (and ought to be) permitted to the defaulting seller.

3.   Defective Performance: Payment

Defective payment is seldom a problem. When it arises, it involves such matters as the tender of a check when cash was specified or a tender of the wrong amount. Such error can usually be speedily corrected, and it is hard to see why the question of the extent to which a seller may immediately terminate ought not to be governed by the same considerations as those governing a late payment. Typically, there is the same—if not more—judicial reluctance to permit immediate cancellation for a defective tender of payment as there is when no payment at all is tendered. If the fault is not promptly corrected, of course, we have the same problem as in nonpayment: for how long and for how much should this seller be expected to extend credit that he may not originally have contemplated?

UNIFORM COMMERCIAL CODE:

§ 2-511. Tender of Payment by Buyer; Payment by Check.

(2) Tender of payment is sufficient when made by any means or in any manner current in the ordinary course of business unless the seller demands payment in legal tender and gives any extension of time reasonably necessary to procure it.

4. Defective Performance: Delivery

The effect of a delivery of goods or services that varies in quality or quantity from the contract specifications is a much more difficult and subtle problem. For here, as in the case of late delivery, the question of when the injured party can terminate is tied to the avoidable consequences rule. Hence, the injured buyer may lose his chance to recover for losses suffered if he does not "cover" when he should. RECALL: Chapter Two, Topic III, Section B. If the performance is grossly defective in either quality or quantity, it may, of course, be considered no performance at all. This situation resembles that of a total non-delivery on the day on which performance was called for. But can a buyer reject a slightly defective performance and cancel?

Keep in mind that our concern here is solely with the availability of the cancellation power after a defective performance. A faulty performance entitles the injured party to some compensation for the resulting damages. The question is: should the injured party *also* be entitled to terminate the contract because of faulty performance?

Simple arithmetic demonstrates why this is an important question. If Buyer has agreed to pay $5.00 per bushel for 1,000 bushels of wheat, and if the market on such wheat has dropped to $3.00 per bushel on the day on which Seller delivers only 900 bushels, how much money is Buyer ahead if he can reject the whole shipment and cancel rather than accept the goods? On the other hand, how much is he actually damaged by the shortage? If punitive damages are not recognized in the law of contracts, why should punitive cancellation be permitted? But why should the non-breaching party be required to accept less than the performance he bargained for just to protect the breaching party's windfall profit resulting from market change?

The law is caught in this dilemma: it wants to reinforce reliance on contract by not showing too much tenderness to contract breakers, but it also must avoid the senseless economic dislocation, disregard of commercial realities, and disappointment of normal expectations that would follow if it were too quick to permit a cancellation because of less than complete performance. This dilemma injects questions of "fault" and "windfall" into this area of contract law—questions that we have seen are supposed to be irrelevant or nonexistent in determining damages. Unfortunately, a court's actual weighting of these competing factors is seldom expressed in the reported opinions. Each case tends to depend on its special facts; and typically it is hard to pinpoint the decisive fact in any given case.

Admittedly, it is of small help to a lawyer to know that the client's power to cancel depends on the facts and circumstances of the particular case. The lawyer cannot be content to say: "That's a very interesting problem." The lawyer must advise the client what to do or not do. Look at the dilemma for the lawyer asked by the client for advice on how to act immediately following a breach by the client's promisor: if the default is treated as minor or immaterial, the client may be stuck with a sick contract that is unlikely to work its problems out and which might more advantageously be replaced by a new deal with someone else. Relief for the breach through damages—though theoretically available—may be lost because of his failure to terminate and cover promptly enough and, even if not lost, may prove illusory. On the other hand, if the client treats the failure of performance as a contract-terminating event, he will be in very serious trouble if the court disagrees with his estimate of the significance of the breach. For in that unhappy event, the court is likely to treat the non-breaching party's termination as a material breach in itself and require the wronged client to pay damages. Our present task is to find some helpful guidelines if we can.

Hope's Architectural Products v. Lundy's Construction

U.S. District Court, D. Kansas, 1991.
781 F.Supp. 711.

■ LUNGSTRUM, D.J. This case presents a familiar situation in the field of construction contracts. Two parties, who disagreed over the meaning of their contract, held their positions to the brink, with litigation and loss the predictable result of the dispute. What is rarely predictable, however, (and what leads to a compromise resolution of many construction disputes when cool heads hold sway) is which party will ultimately prevail. The stakes become winner-take-all.

Plaintiff Hope's Architectural Products (Hope's) is a New York corporation that manufactures and installs custom window fixtures. Defendant Lundy's Construction (Lundy's) is a Kansas corporation that contracted to buy windows from Hope's for a school remodeling project. Defendant Bank IV Olathe (Bank IV) is a national banking organization with its principal place of business in Kansas. Bank IV acted as surety for a statutory bond obtained by Lundy's for the remodeling project.

Hope's contends that Lundy's breached the contract to buy windows, entitling Hope's to damages in the amount of the contract price of $55,000. Hope's also contends that Bank IV wrongfully refused to pay Hope's on the bond when Lundy's breached the contract. Hope's has sued for breach of contract, and in the alternative, for recovery under the theory of quantum meruit....

Plaintiff Hope's is a manufacturer of custom-built windows. The initial contact between Hope's and Lundy's occurred through Mr. Richard Odor, a regional agent for Hope's in Kansas City. On June 29, 1988, Hope's contracted with Lundy's to manufacture ninety-three windows for the Rushton project. The contract price, including the cost of labor and materials for the windows, was $55,000.

Although the contract included a term pertaining to the time for delivering the windows, there is some controversy over the meaning of this provision. Even under the most favorable interpretation to Hope's, however, delivery was due twelve to fourteen weeks after Hope's received approved shop drawings from Lundy's on July 18. Thus, delivery was due no later than October 24, 1988.

During the late summer and fall of 1988, several discussions took place between Hope's and Lundy's concerning when the windows would be delivered to the job site. Production of the windows was delayed by events that, according to the testimony of Mr. Odor, were not the fault of Lundy's. On September 27, 1988, Mark Hannah, vice president of Lundy's, wrote to Hope's requesting that installation of the windows begin by October 19, and be completed by October 26. On October 14 Hannah again wrote to Hope's, threatening to withhold "liquidated damages" from the contract price if Hope's did not comply with these deadlines. Although there was no provision in the contract for liquidated damages, Hope's did not make any response to the October 14 letter.

The windows were shipped from Hope's New York plant to Kansas City on October 28. Delivery to the Rushton site was anticipated on November 4. On November 1, Hannah called Hope's office in New York to inquire about the windows. He spoke to Kathy Anderson, Hope's customer service manager. The substance of this conversation is disputed. Hope's claims that Hannah threatened a back charge of $11,000 (20% of the contract price) for late delivery of the windows. Hannah testified, however, that although the possibility of a back charge was discussed, no specific dollar amount was mentioned. Hannah specifically denies that he threatened to withhold $11,000 from the contract.

After her conversation with Hannah, Anderson immediately informed Chris Arvantinos, vice president of Hope's, of the threatened back charge. Arvantinos called Hannah to discuss the back charge, but he does not recall hearing Hannah mention the $11,000 figure. Arvantinos requested that Hannah provide assurances that Lundy's would not back charge Hope's, but Hannah was unwilling to provide such assurances.

In a letter written on November 2, Arvantinos informed Hannah that Hope's was suspending delivery of the windows until Lundy's provided assurances that there would be no back charge. Hannah received this letter on the morning of November 3, shortly before Mr. Odor visited Hannah at Lundy's. Odor, who had spoken with Arvantinos about the back charge, issued a new demand that Lundy's had to meet before Hope's would deliver the windows. He gave Hannah an invoice for the full amount of the contract price, demanding prepayment before the windows would be delivered.

Odor set out three ways that Lundy's could meet this demand: (1) payment of the contract price in full by cashier's check; (2) placement of the full contract price in an escrow account until the windows were installed; or (3) delivery of the full contract amount to the architect to hold until the windows were installed. All three options required Lundy's to come up with $55,000 before the windows would be delivered. Hannah believed that the demand presented by Odor superseded the letter from Arvantinos he received earlier that morning.

Hannah informed Odor that there was no way for Lundy's to get an advance from the school district at that time to comply with Hope's request. The meeting ended, Lundy's did not prepay, and Hope's did not deliver the windows. On November 7, 1988, Lundy's terminated the contract with Hope's. Thereafter, Lundy's obtained an alternate supplier of the windows.

On February 15, 1989, Hope's notified defendant Bank IV of Lundy's failure to pay the contract price and demanded payment from Bank IV on the public works bond. Bank IV refused to pay Hope's claim....

At the outset, the Court concludes that the Uniform Commercial Code (UCC) governs this transaction. Article 2 of the UCC applies to transactions in goods. The contract at issue in this case involved a mixed goods/services transaction. Whether the UCC applies to hybrid transactions such as this depends upon "'whether their predominant factor, their thrust, their purpose, reasonably stated, is the rendition of service, with goods incidentally involved * * * or is a transaction of sale, with labor incidentally involved.'" If the UCC applies, it applies to all facets of the transaction. The transaction at issue in this case primarily involved a sale of windows, with installation and manufacturing services provided as an incidental component. Therefore, the UCC applies.

two questions

A. Plaintiff's Contract Claim Against Defendant Lundy's

This case turns on the resolution of two central and interrelated issues: (1) when was delivery due under the contract, and (2) could Hope's lawfully demand the assurances it demanded from Lundy's under K.S.A. § 84–2–609. If the demands for assurances were proper, then Hope's would have been justified in suspending its performance and withholding delivery and Lundy's failure to provide assurances and subsequent termination of the contract amounted to a total breach. If, however, the demands for assurances were not proper under 84–2–609 then Hope's breached the contract by wrongfully withholding delivery of the windows and Lundy's was entitled to cancel the contract. The delivery date issue is addressed first because the matter of whether or not Hope's was already in breach for late delivery goes directly to the propriety of its demand for assurances.

1. Delivery Date

Delivery not timely

Even under Hope's interpretation of the delivery term, delivery of the windows was not timely. At trial, Chris Arvantinos, Hope's vice president, testified that Hope's committed to deliver the windows twelve to fourteen weeks after July 18, 1988, the day Hope's received approved shop drawings. This would make delivery due between October 10 and October 24. In fact, the windows did not arrive in Kansas City until November 4, fifteen and one-half weeks after July 18. Hope's claims that this delay was "immaterial" and did not excuse Lundy's from its duties under the contract. Hope's is unable to cite any controlling authority to support this argument, however. Moreover, this argument misses the point. Even if an "immaterial" delay did not excuse future performance by Lundy's, no performance was due from Lundy's until the windows were delivered to the job site, which never occurred.

Hope's also argues, almost in passing, that the delay was caused by problems that were outside of its control, thus excusing Hope's from responsibility for the late delivery. Under a clause in the contract, Hope's disclaimed responsibility "for delayed shipments and deliveries occasioned by strikes, fires, accidents, delays of common carriers or other causes beyond our control...." During the course of production, Hope's experienced problems with its "bonderizing" and prime paint system, which resulted in a delay in production of approximately two weeks. Hope's produced no evidence at trial, however, to show that this was a matter which was beyond its control. Moreover, it is interesting to note that Hope's did not contemporaneously seek from Lundy's any extension of the delivery date under this provision or notify Lundy's that it might result in a delay beyond October 24. It appears that reference to this clause is more of an afterthought born of litigation than a bona fide excuse for modifying the delivery date.

Hope's also contends that a three to four day delay resulted when Lundy's asked for a change in the design of the windows to include "weep holes" after production had already begun. However, Hope's representative, Odor, testified that nothing Lundy's did delayed Hope's manufacturing. Moreover, even accounting for this delay, Hope's was a week late delivering the windows.

2. Section 2–609 Demand for Assurances

Although nothing in the record indicates that Hope's expressly claimed any rights under 84–2–609 during the course of this transaction, Hope's asserted at trial that the October 14 letter from Lundy's demanding delivery by October 16 and threatening liquidated damages gave Hope's reasonable grounds for insecurity. Delivery was not due until October 24 under Hope's version of the parties' agreement, and Lundy's had no right to demand performance early, let alone broach the withholding of liquidated damages. This letter might have justified a demand for assurances under 84–2–609. However, Hope's made no such demand after receiving the letter. Instead of invoking its rights under 84–2–609, Hope's chose not to respond at all to Lundy's threat of liquidated damages. This event merely came and went without any legal consequence.

Hope's in effect invoked its rights under 84–2–609 in response to Lundy's threat of a back charge during the November 1 phone conversations. Two separate demands for assurances were made in response to this threat. Initially, Chris Arvantinos demanded assurances that Lundy's would not back charge Hope's for the delayed shipment in a telephone conversation with Mark Hannah later in the day on November 1. Arvantinos memorialized this demand in a letter composed on that day and mailed on the second of November. In their telephone conversation, Hannah refused to provide assurances that Lundy's would not back charge Hope's.

Hope's made a second demand for assurances on November 3, when Richard Odor presented Hope's invoice to Hannah demanding payment in full. Thus, Hope's demanded assurances that it would not be back charged on November 1, and when that demand was refused, Hope's made a second demand on November 3. The Court finds that Hope's was not entitled to invoke 84–2–609 on either occasion.

When Hope's made its first demand for assurances on November 1, it was already in breach of the parties' agreement. Delivery of the windows was due by October 24, but the windows did not arrive in Kansas City until November 4. A party already in breach is not entitled to invoke section 2–609 by demanding assurances. To hold otherwise would allow a party to avoid liability for breaching its contract by invoking 2–609 to extract from the nonbreaching party an assurance that no damages will be sought for the breach. A nonbreaching party in need of prompt performance could be coerced into giving up its right to damages for the breach by giving in to the demands in order to receive the needed performance. This Court refuses to endorse such a result.

Lundy's argues that Hope's demand for assurances in the November 2 letter from Arvantinos was overly broad and unreasonable. The letter informed Lundy's that Hope's would not deliver the windows to the job site until it received assurances that it would not "be backcharged or otherwise held responsible for liquidated damages, delay charges or any extra costs on account of time of delivery of the windows." When this demand was made, the windows had not yet arrived in Kansas City. Therefore, the parties did not know at this time whether the proper quantity of windows had been shipped, whether the windows were the correct size, or whether they otherwise met Lundy's specifications. If there were any nonconformities in the shipment, there could have been another delay in the time of delivery while Hope's corrected the problem. Yet, Hope's demanded a blanket assurance that it would not be held responsible for any extra costs incurred because of "time of delivery of the windows." This demand was overly broad on its face and unreasonable under 84-2-609.

The assurances Hope's demanded on November 3 were also excessive. In his meeting with Mark Hannah, Richard Odor insisted that Lundy's prepay the contract price, deliver a cashier's check to the architect, or place the full contract price in an escrow account before the windows would be delivered. Yet, Lundy's never gave any indication that it was unable or unwilling to pay the amount it owed to Hope's when the windows were delivered and the bond stood as security for Lundy's obligation. Such a demand was unreasonable and amounted to a breach by Hope's. *See Pittsburgh-Des Moines Steel v. Brookhaven Manor Water Co.* (demanding under 2-609 a personal guarantee of payment from a shareholder, or that other party escrow the entire amount of the contract price before it was due, absent any showing of an inability to pay, was unreasonable); *Scott v. Crown* (demanding payment in full before it was due was unreasonable demand under 2-609 and amounted to anticipatory breach). The payment terms under the contract were "Progress payments by the 10th of each month covering 90% of the total value of materials delivered and installation performed during the previous month with final payment upon completion of our [Hope's] work." By demanding prepayment, Hope's essentially attempted to rewrite this term of the contract.

Although Hope's contends that a threatened back charge of $11,000 for a one week delay in shipment justified its demand for prepayment, the Court is not persuaded that Lundy's made any specific demand for $11,000. The testimony on this issue was controverted, but only Kathy Anderson, Hope's customer service manager, testified, in a perfunctory manner, that an $11,000 back charge was threatened.

Mark Hannah specifically denied making such a demand. Neither Chris Arvantinos nor Richard Odor testified to recalling receiving such a demand. There was also testimony at trial from one witness for Hope's that the threatened back charge was in the amount of $5,000. The Court is not persuaded that Lundy's went beyond making unspecified threats of a back charge for possible damages it would incur because of Hope's delay.

By threatening to withhold damages from the contract price, Lundy's was merely exercising its rights under K.S.A. § 84–2–717,[4] which entitles a buyer to deduct from the amount owing on the contract any damages from the seller's breach. Giving notice of its intention to avail itself of a legal right did not indicate that Lundy's was unwilling or unable to perform under the contract. Indeed, the very nature of the right invoked by Lundy's manifests an intention that it would continue performing and pay the contract price due, less damages caused by Hope's delay. Thus, the demand for prepayment was unreasonably excessive when there was no indication that Lundy's would not pay Hope's when performance was due.

Both Hope's delay in delivering the windows and Hope's excessive demands entitled Lundy's to treat Hope's as in breach and to cancel the contract, which it did on November 7, 1988. K.S.A. § 84–2–711 (1983) ("Where the seller fails to make delivery or repudiates * * * the buyer may cancel * * *."). Thus, Hope's is not entitled to recover under its claim for breach of contract.

B. Plaintiff's Quantum Meruit Claim

Hope's also claims that it is entitled to compensation from Lundy's under the theory of quantum meruit. "Quantum meruit," which literally means "as much as he deserves," is a phrase used often in older cases to describe an equitable doctrine premised on the theories of unjust enrichment and restitution. Recovery was allowed under this theory when a benefit had been received by a party and it would be inequitable to allow the party to retain it. Instead of labeling it quantum meruit, courts today speak in terms of restitution.

To recover in restitution, a breaching plaintiff must have conferred a benefit on the nonbreaching party. The burden is on the breaching party to prove the extent of the benefit conferred, and doubts will be resolved against him.

In this case, Hope's conferred no benefit on Lundy's. The windows manufactured by Hope's were never used in the Rushton project, and the Court is not persuaded that the installation advice provided by Christiansen Steel Erection for Hope's improved the project. Hope's admits that the only labor it claims to have

---

4. "*Deduction of damages from the price.* The buyer on notifying the seller of his intentions to do so may deduct all or any part of the damages resulting from any breach of the contract from any part of the price still due under the same contract."

provided at the Rushton job site was consultation work performed by Christiansen Steel Erection, a company Hope's subcontracted with to install the windows. Mike and John Christiansen visited the job site on several occasions to advise Lundy's on how to prepare the window openings for installation. The advice they provided, however, related to the installation of windows that were never used on the project. When Lundy's canceled its contract with Hope's, it obtained an alternate supplier of a different type of windows. These windows did not require the same careful preparation of the window openings as the Hope's windows. Lundy's job foreman testified that the Christiansens' advice became moot when the alternate supplier was obtained. "[A] party's expenditures in preparation for performance that do not confer a benefit on the other party do not give rise to a restitution interest." Restatement (Second) of Contracts § 370 comment a (1977). Thus, because no benefit was conferred upon Lundy's, Hope's has no valid claim to restitution.

III. CONCLUSION

After careful consideration of the facts and law, this Court holds that Hope's breached the contract in question. Therefore, defendant Lundy's was entitled to cancel its performance and defendant Bank IV was not obligated to pay Hope's under the statutory bond.

QUESTIONS AND NOTES

1. Hope's is not entitled to damages because it is the party in breach, and it is not entitled to restitution because Lundy's never accepted the windows and, therefore, Hope's conferred no benefit. In the end it is stuck with $55,000 in custom windows that probably cannot be resold on the market. All because it was a week-and-a-half late in making delivery on a fourteen-week contract!

2. What would you advise Hope's to do when it became clear to it that the windows would not be in Kansas City by October 19? What advice would you give on October 14 after it received the letter from Lundy's vice president threatening to withhold "liquidated damages"?

3. As the problems escalated, why didn't the parties realize it might be in their interests to accommodate the other at least a little bit? The court seems to suggest that once it was clear that Hope's' delivery was going to be late, it lost all claims to demand assurances from Lundy's that there would not be an extortionate back charge on the money due it.

4. Notwithstanding its real insecurity, wouldn't Hope's have been better off to go forward with delivery and install the windows and then assert its claim for the price? How big a factor was the concern that it might cost more than the amount at stake for a New York company to litigate in Kansas?

D.   ADJUSTING THE LOSS FROM BREACH—RESTITUTION, INSTALLMENT CONTRACTS, AND DIVISIBLE CONTRACT ANALYSIS

A decision that a breach is material and therefore a terminating condition can produce harsh results. If the parties are aware of the potential problem at the time of contract formation, they can plan for the contingency and avoid it by carefully defining the requirements of performance and the consequences of default. However, parties tend to be optimistic at the time of contract formation; they hope for the best and assume that the contract will be performed, not breached. When a difficulty arises during performance and the parties are unable to resolve it, litigation may ensue. If the breach is very serious, the court will have no difficulty in finding it material and casting the entire loss on the breaching party. Conversely, if the breach is minor, a finding that it is immaterial and therefore not a condition leaves the injured party to his remedy at damages and the obligations of further performance undisturbed. But in many commonly encountered situations, neither extreme seems appropriate. In such a case the court may turn instead to familiar notions of restitution to provide the party in breach with some relief.

Many commercial contracts call for a series of deliveries for performance in return for a corresponding series of payments. As the seller ships goods in installments, the buyer is obligated to pay. As the worker performs services, the employer is obligated to make periodic wage or salary payments. As the builder completes each phase of the construction project, the owner becomes obligated to make a partial payment. There is a single contract, but many of its obligations are divisible into segments as performance proceeds.

Other transactions seem better analyzed as a series of free standing transactions, with each delivery and its matching payment forming a separate deal. The breach of one part, although serious, does not necessarily affect the other transactions between the parties. But when there is a long-term arrangement for continuing deliveries and related payments, it may be more realistic to treat the deal as one transaction, although divided into installments.

The concept of the divisible or installment contract has developed in a way that enables courts to do substantial justice. The breaching seller can bring a price action for the installments satisfactorily completed. A disappointed buyer's obligation to pay for a nonconforming installment is at least suspended, and he can sue for damages as to that installment. The basic material-immaterial breach distinction remains available to the court in deciding when to treat the entire contract as terminated to protect the seller against undue credit risk when the buyer doesn't pay and to protect the buyer against an untrustworthy seller who has shown that it cannot be relied upon to make proper delivery.

National Knitting Co. v. Bouton & Germain Co.
Wisconsin Supreme Court, 1909.
141 Wis. 63, 123 N.W. 624.

The plaintiff corporation is a manufacturer and dealer in knitted goods at Milwaukee, and the defendant corporation is a jobber in the same line of goods at Ripon. In November, 1905, the defendant ordered of the plaintiff, in writing, a quantity of gloves of different kinds at fixed prices, aggregating $322.86, delivery to be made in the following May, bill to be dated as of November 1, 1906, payable in 30 days. The order was accepted, and in April the plaintiff delivered the greater part of the goods ordered, but never delivered one item of 18 dozen gloves, and another item of 6 dozen gloves. The plaintiff sues to recover for the goods actually delivered at contract prices. The defendant contends that the contract is entire, and hence that nothing is due, because the contract has never been fully performed. The defendant also sets up a counterclaim for damages because of nondelivery of said two items, in case the court should hold the contract to be severable. The trial court held the contract to be severable, and awarded judgment for the plaintiff for the contract price of the items delivered, less damages, consisting of the loss of profits, on the items not delivered. From this judgment, defendant appeals.

■ WINSLOW, C.J. (after stating the facts as above). We think that the business world would be astonished to learn that whenever an order for a bill of merchandise is accepted the contract thus made is entire, and requires delivery of every article before there can be recovery of any part of the purchase price. Such would be the practical effect of the defendant's contention here, if it should be upheld. We cannot so hold. The question of entirety is a question of intention. Severability of the subject-matter and measurement of consideration by units may assist in determining, but do not of themselves necessarily determine, the question. In case of a contract naturally and accurately severable (such as a contract for the sale of a bill of goods at certain prices for each article), courts incline to hold the contract severable, and to grant a recovery for that portion of the goods actually delivered, less damages for the nondelivery of any portion not delivered. Under all ordinary circumstances, this course will result in exact justice. The vendor will receive pay for his goods, which the vendee has retained, and the vendee will receive compensation for any damage which he has actually suffered.

If, however, it appears by express terms or by necessary implication from the terms of a contract that the intention of the parties was to make payment of the consideration depend upon delivery of all the articles, the contract will be held entire, though the consideration may be measured in units and be actually severable. Thus, when a contract required the delivery of 2,000 yards of crushed stone for the purpose of building a bridge, it was held to be entire, notwithstanding the payment was to be at a certain rate per yard. So contracts to tow a given quantity of logs at so much per 1,000 feet, and to carry 5,000 barrels of salt at so much per barrel, have been held entire, upon the idea that the terms of the contract, in the light of the surrounding facts, showed that the parties evidently intended to contract for one entire job, and only used the unit of measurement of the consideration for convenience, and not as indicating any contemplation of severability.

The principle here decided is that contracts for the sale of goods like the present, which are naturally severable, will not be held entire contracts, in the absence of express or implied provision to that effect in the contract, or persuasive circumstances showing the intention of the parties to make it entire.

Judgment affirmed.

QUESTIONS AND NOTES

1. Did the court here find that the plaintiff's breach was immaterial? What was the plaintiff suing for?

2. If the market price of gloves had fallen, what advantage would it have been to the defendant to have the contract called entire? Would the plaintiff have been able to recover nothing? What—if anything—would it have recovered? What does it recover under the finding of divisibility?

3. Compare:

(a) Furniture Company agrees to sell a dining room set of a table, a chest, and six chairs for a price of $2000 for the table, $1000 for the chest, and $200 each for the chairs. Delivery of the chairs but non-delivery of the table. Seller later tenders the chest, and buyer refuses to take it. Entire or divisible contract? Will your answer vary depending on whether the buyer wants to keep the chairs or to return them? Does buyer's right to refuse the chest depend on whether the contract is entire or divisible?

(b) Furniture Company agrees to sell a refrigerator, a desk, and a carpet for a price of $800 for the refrigerator, $400 for the desk, and $400 for the carpet. Delivery of the refrigerator but non-delivery of the desk. Seller later tenders the carpet, and buyer refuses to take it. Entire or divisible contract? Will your answer again vary depending on whether the buyer wants to keep the refrigerator or to return it? Will this fact influence your decision as much as it would in (a)?

(c) Suppose that the contract in (b) were for a "total price" of $1600 without itemization of the separate prices. What result?

(d) Suppose that the buyer bought the items in (a) on separate days. What result? Suppose that he bought the items in (b) on separate days?

UNIFORM COMMERCIAL CODE:

§ 2–307. Delivery in Single Lot or Several Lots.

Unless otherwise agreed all goods called for by a contract for sale must be tendered in a single delivery and payment is due only on such tender but where the circumstances give either party the right to make or demand delivery in lots the price if it can be apportioned may be demanded for each lot.

§ 2–612. "Installment Contract"; Breach.

(1) An "installment contract" is one which requires or authorizes the delivery of goods in separate lots to be separately accepted, even though the contract contains a clause "each delivery is a separate contract" or its equivalent.

(2) The buyer may reject any installment which is non-conforming if the non-conformity substantially impairs the value of that installment and cannot be cured or if the non-conformity is a defect in the required documents; but if the non-conformity does not fall within subsection (3) and the seller gives adequate assurance of its cure the buyer must accept that installment.

(3) Whenever non-conformity or default with respect to one or more installments substantially impairs the value of the whole contract there is a breach of the whole. But the aggrieved party reinstates the contract if he accepts a non-conforming installment without seasonably notifying of cancellation or if he brings an action with respect only to past installments or demands performance as to future installments.

Graulich Caterer v. Hans Holterbosch

New Jersey Superior Court, Appellate Division, 1968.
101 N.J.Super. 61, 243 A.2d 253.

■ FOLEY, J.A.D. Plaintiff, caterers, take this appeal from a judgment for defendant rejecting plaintiff's suit sounding in contract.* * *

Contact between the litigants sprung from the turmoil surrounding the preparations for the opening of the 1964 New York World's Fair. Holterbosch, an American importer and distributor of Lowenbrau beer, was granted the franchise to operate the Lowenbrau Pavilion at the Fair. Final approval of this award was given on or about January 15, 1964 and contemplated an April 15, 1964 opening. This was the last major pavilion awarded, making time essential in all of defendant's considerations.

In aid of this enterprise defendant engaged a metropolitan-based industrial design consultant, Becker & Becker Associates, to formulate a feasible production plan for serving the required beer and, as a desired adjunct, platters of German food. As stated by defendant, the goal of both Lowenbrau and Holterbosch was the "quality concept of merchandising."

The Raytheon Corporation, knowing the Becker firm's privy role and eager to market their microwave concept of cooking, suggested plaintiff's name to Becker as one able to discharge the culinary requirements of the Lowenbrau Pavilion. Thus approached by Becker, plaintiff on March 10, 1964 entered into preliminary negotiations with the consultant regarding the feasibility of the Raytheon Microwave cooking concept as related to the superior quality of food desired by defendant....

At the March 10, 1964 meeting Becker and another employee of the planning firm reviewed with approval ten general food samples submitted by Graulich. Defendant Holterbosch did not personally attend this initial meeting. Informed of defendant's needs, plaintiff redesigned the samples and presented eight platters at a second meeting held on March 17, 1964....

The samples presented and approved on March 17, 1964, were prepared in the Graulich commissary at Port Elizabeth, New Jersey, by plaintiff's employees and were presented to defendant at the Raytheon office in New York City. The operation was agreed upon, with the initial delivery set for April 15, 1964....

The delayed and muddled opening of the Fair brought the parties into daily, and at times even hourly, contact. Postponements followed premature orders until a firm order for April 23, 1964 was placed by Mr. Leigh, an employee of Becker & Becker. Upon delivery the members of defendant's organization were stunned by the product and complained immediately that the tendered units did not, in any way, match the contract samples. Rejecting this 955–unit installment as unacceptable, defendant described the food as "bland," unpresentable, tasteless and "just wasn't the type of food that we could sell." Notwithstanding this low grade delivery, defendant, obligated to the Fair to serve food and committed in theory to the Raytheon ovens, conferred with the equally dissatisfied plaintiff in seeking to improve the quality standard of the product to the point where it would be acceptable....

The second delivery, made on April 25, 1964, was likewise unacceptable. Of the 2520 units delivered, between 500 to 700 were distributed among the employees and patrons of the exhibit for a fast reaction. The complaints in response to the food were many and varied. Defendant, describing the sources of unfavorable comment, stated that the sauerbraten was dry and the gravy, pasty and unpalatably "gooey," surrounded rather than enveloped the meat. The knockwurst platter suffered similarly, being dry and comparing unfavorably with the standards established by the samples. Generally, defendant complained that the food was simply not "German food" and as such was unacceptable for the Lowenbrau Pavilion.

Giving due regard to the original trier's opportunity to observe the demeanor and to judge the credibility of the witnesses, we find as a matter of fact that the deliveries of April 23 and 25, 1964 did not conform to the samples originally presented and approved. Since warranties of sample and description are characterized as "express warranties," the "whole of the goods shall conform to the sample or model." § 2–313(1)(c). The "goods" to "conform" to the sample or model must be "in accordance with the obligations under the contract" § 2–106(2); here, to comply with the standards established by the March 17 taste-test of the samples. Any distinguishing language would be controlled by the sample as presented on March 17. Additionally, the implied warranty of fitness for purpose attaches to contracts of this type, where, as here, they are not specifically excluded. A breach of these warranties triggers a buyer's rights following seller's breach as catalogued in § 2–711. These remedies include, but are not limited to, cancellation §§ 2–711(1), 2–106(4). "if the breach goes to the whole of the contract." § 2–612(3).

Here, Holterbosch had the right to reject any installment that was nonconforming, provided that the nonconformity substantially impaired the value of that installment and could not be cured. "Cure," novel to New Jersey's jurisprudence, permits the seller to cure a defective tender through repair, replacement or price allowance if he reasonably notifies the buyer of his curative intention and, in effecting the cure, makes a timely conforming delivery.

The effect of the installment contract section, § 2–612(2), is to extend the time for cure past the contract delivery date for that nonconforming installment, provided the nonconformity does not "substantially [impair] the value of that installment" and can be cured. We find that Holterbosch was justified in rejecting Graulich's tender of the April 23 initial installment since the nonconformity of the tendered goods with the accepted sample was incurable, and thus substantially impaired the value of that installment.

Replacing considerations of anticipatory repudiation and the material injury with the test of substantial impairment, § 2–612, adopts a more restrictive seller-oriented approach favoring "the continuance of the contract in the absence of an overt cancellation." To allow an aggrieved party to cancel an installment contract, § 2–612(3), requires (1) the breach be of the whole contract which occurs when the non-conformity of "one or more installments substantially impairs the value of the whole contract;" and (2) that seasonable notification of cancellation has been given if the buyer has accepted a nonconforming installment.

What amounts to substantial impairment presents a question of fact. Analyzing this factual question, the New Jersey commentators counsel that the test as to whether the nonconformity in any given installment justifies cancelling the entire contract depends on whether the nonconformity substantially impairs the value of the whole contract, and not on whether it indicates an intent or likelihood that the future deliveries also will be defective. Continuing, the Comment relates the intent underlying a breach to insecurity and those sections of the Code providing buyer with adequate assurance of performance, § 2–609, and anticipatory repudiation, § 2–610. More practical in its treatment of "substantial impairment," the official Comment states that "substantial impairment of the value of an installment can turn not only on the quality of the goods but also on such factors as time, quantity, assortment and the like. It must be judged in terms of the normal or specifically known purposes of the contract." Comment to § 2–612, ¶ 4.

At the Lowenbrau Pavilion on April 23, 1964 plaintiff Graulich, timely noticed of the nonconforming initial tender, gave assurance that future tenders would be cured to match the original samples. Unequivocally committed to the microwave kitchen method, defendant lent plaintiff three members from its staff in aid of this adjustment. Since plaintiff was given the opportunity to cure, there is no need to touch upon the substantiality of the initial nonconforming installment.

The second installment tender was as unsatisfactory as the first. The meat was dry, the gravy "gooey" and the complaints abundant. After the nonconforming second delivery it became apparent that eleventh-hour efforts attempting to rework and adjust the platters failed. Translating this into legal parlance, there was a nonconforming tender of the initial installment on a contract for the sale of goods; upon tender the buyer Holterbosch notified the seller Graulich of the nonconformity and unacceptable nature of the platters tendered; the failure of the cure assured by plaintiff, seller, was evidenced by a subsequently defective nonconforming delivery. The second unacceptable delivery and the failure of plaintiff's additional curative efforts left defendant in a position for one week without food. Time was critical. Plaintiff knew that platters of maximum quality were required on a daily installment basis. Because of defendant's immediate need for quality food and plaintiff's failure to cure, we find that the nonconformity of the second delivery, projected upon the circumstances of this case, "substantially impair[ed] the value of the whole contract [and resulted in] a breach of the whole." § 2–612(3). If the breach goes to the whole contract the buyer may cancel the whole contract. § 2–711(1). Accordingly, we find that Holterbosch was justified in cancelling the installment agreement signed on April 1, 1964.

Since defendant's counterclaim was withdrawn it is unnecessary to treat of the right retained by a cancelling party to press any remedy for breach of the whole contract. § 2–106(4).

Judgment in favor of defendant for the reasons herein stated. Costs to defendant.

QUESTIONS AND NOTES

1. If Graulich shows up the first time with gooey sauerbraten, does Holterbosch have to accept it? If it does take the sauerbraten, but it is not a perfect tender, does it have to pay for what it takes? If so, at what rate must it pay?

2. Is Holterbosch entitled to damages every time Graulich shows up with gooey sauerbraten? Does the answer depend on whether Holterbosch accepts the delivery? How would the damages be measured? If Holterbosch really needs the sauerbraten badly to meet the demands of customers and cannot find a substitute on the market, will a court award it specific performance?

3. Does Holterbosch have to give Graulich another chance and let it cure the defects in its sauerbraten the first time even if the stuff is terrible and not even close to what was called for by the contract? When can it stop giving Graulich another chance? Does there come a time when it must stop letting Graulich have any more chances? When is that?

4. The court in this case gives great emphasis to continuing, if possible, the relationship created by the contract. This approach is consistent with the dominant attitude of the UCC and makes sense if the problem is a little defect which can certainly be cured. But if this is terrible sauerbraten, produced by a unique and novel process how likely is it that Graulich will ever be able to make conforming deliveries? If it is not likely, why keep the sick relationship alive?

E.   THE PERFECT TENDER RULE

The perfect tender doctrine states that full tender of perfectly conforming goods is a condition precedent to the purchaser's obligation to pay under the contract. Why must a buyer take the goods if they aren't what was ordered? If a buyer does accept the goods, or any part of them, does buyer lose any claim for damages arising from the nonconformity to contract terms? Does the buyer have to pay at the contract rate for what is received?

The perfect tender rule logically flows from commitment to freedom of contract and the enforceability of promises. No one compelled the promisor to make any particular promise, but having made the promise, the promisor has no complaint if he is held to the precise performance promised. The other party should not have to pay the promised price for something other than what he bargained for.

If our concern were limited to the parties, then strict observance of a perfect tender rule might be justifiable. But what of the broader social interests in the transaction? In addition to the personal hardships involved, contract termination for imperfect tender is socially expensive and is likely to result in significant economic dislocation. The social interest is usually to keep the deal going if possible and to redress losses by awarding damages without cancelling the contract. To this end, the UCC imports concepts of cure, partial acceptance, and installment contracts to mitigate the rigors of a perfect tender rule. These, it should be noted, are all mitigating notions taken from the common law, where they are sometimes obscured in the double talk of courts straining for a just result without doing apparent violence to a rigid rule.

Printing Center of Texas v. Supermind Publishing Co.

Texas Court of Appeals, Houston, 1984.
669 S.W.2d 779.

■ CANNON, J. Appellee sued appellant for refund of a deposit made under a written contract to print 5000 books entitled *Supermind Supermemory*. Appellee alleged that it rightfully rejected the books upon delivery under Tex.Bus. & Com.Code Ann. § 2.601 and that it has a right to cancel the contract and recover the part of the purchase price paid under Tex.Bus. & Com.Code Ann. § 2.711. The trial court awarded appellee refund of its $2900 deposit and $3000 as reasonable attorney's fees on the verdict of the jury.

We note that appellee may have tried this suit on the wrong legal theory and if so, the judgment of the trial court is not supported by the jury findings. The parties tried this suit on the assumption that the provisions of the Texas Uniform Commercial Code governed their contract for the printing of books. Chapter 2 of the Code is limited to transactions involving the sale of goods. A contract to print books involves the sale of both goods and services. The printer sells goods which consist of paper and ink and services consisting of binding, typesetting, proofing, etc. "In such hybrid transactions, the question becomes whether the dominant factor or essence of the transaction is the sale of materials or of services."

It appears to us that the services are the essence or the dominant factor of a printing contract; therefore, Chapter 2 of the Code would not apply. Special issue number one inquired of the jury whether the books delivered to appellee failed in any respect to conform to the contract. The affirmative answer to this issue does not give the purchaser a right to reject and to recover a refund of the purchase price under the common law of contracts as it would under Chapter 2 of the Code. The buyer's remedy in that case would be damages for breach of contract. The equitable relief of rescission of the contract will not be granted for breach of the contract.

Appellant has not assigned a point of error as to whether the trial court's judgment is supported by the verdict of the jury. Therefore any error concerning this point is waived. We indulge in the doubtful assumption that Chapter 2 of the Code governs the contract between parties to enable us to adequately consider appellant's points of error.

Appellant contends in its second point of error that jury finding that the books failed to conform to the contract is so against the great weight and preponderance of the evidence as to be manifestly unjust. This finding is related to whether appellee had a right to reject the books under § 2.601 which states in part: "* * * if the goods or tender of delivery fail in any respect to conform to the contract, the buyer may (1) reject the whole * * *."

This provision has been called the perfect tender rule because it supposedly allows a buyer to reject whenever the goods are less than perfect. This statement is not quite accurate; under section 2.601 the tender must be perfect only in the sense that the proffered goods must conform to the contract in every respect. Conformity does not mean substantial performance; it means complete performance. The long standing doctrine of sales law that "there is no room in commercial contracts for the doctrine of substantial performance" is carried forward into section 2.601. Substantial compliance is not the legal equivalent of conformity with the contract under section 2.601.

In analyzing whether tendered goods are conforming, the contract of the parties must first be determined. "Conform" is defined in § 2.106(b), as "in accordance with the obligations under the contract." The contract of the parties includes more than the words used by the parties. It encompasses "the bargain of the parties in fact as found in their language or by implication from other circumstances including course of dealing or usage of trade or course of performance as provided in the Code." § 1.201(11) and § 1.201(3). Thus, the terms of a contract may be explained and supplemented through trade usage, but it may not be used to contradict an express term. § 2.202. The existence and scope of trade usage must be proved as facts. § 1.205(b). A buyer has a right to reject goods under section 2.601 if the goods fail to conform to either the express or implied terms of the contract.

Once the contract of the parties has been determined, the evidence must be reviewed to see if the right goods were tendered at the right time and place. If the evidence does establish nonconformity in some respect, the buyer is entitled to reject if he rejects in good faith. § 1.203 provides that, "Every contract or duty within this Act imposes an obligation of good faith in its performance or enforcement." Since the rejection of goods is a matter of performance, the buyer is obligated to act in good faith when he rejects the goods. Where the buyer is a merchant, his standard of good faith rejection requires honesty in fact and observance of reasonable commercial standards of fair dealing in the trade. § 2.103(a)(2). If the seller alleges that the buyer rejected in bad faith, the seller has the burden of proof on this issue. Evidence of circumstances which indicate that the buyer's motivation in rejecting the goods was to escape the bargain, rather than to avoid acceptance of a tender which in some respect impairs the value of the bargain to him, would support a finding of rejection in bad faith. Thus, evidence of rejection of the goods on account of a minor defect in a falling market would in some instances be sufficient to support a finding that the buyer acted in bad faith when he rejected the goods.

The written contract between the parties which is expressed in a bid proposal dated July 31, 1981 covers only essential terms such as quantity, trim size, and type of paper and cover. The type of paper specified in the contract was thirty pound white newsprint. Appellee's witness testified that he was shown a sample of the newsprint to be used and that the tendered books were not the same color as the sample. The witness stated the pages of the books were gray while the sample was white. This testimony is evidence of nonconformity because any sample which is made part of the basis of the bargain creates an express warranty that the whole of the goods shall conform to the sample. § 2.313(a)(3).

Other nonconformities which appellee alleges and offers proof of are off center cover art, crooked pages, wrinkled pages and inadequate perforation on a pull out page. The contract does not expressly address any of these matters. Although evidence of trade usage may have indicated that these conditions are contrary to the standards of commercial practice within the publishing industry, appellant failed to offer evidence of trade usage to supplement the contract. However, appellant knew that appellee wanted the books printed for sale to the public. In these circumstances, it is implied in the contract that the books be commercially acceptable and appealing to the public. Section 2.314 states that a warranty that the goods shall be merchantable is implied in a contract for their sale and that for goods to be merchantable, they must pass without objection in the trade and be fit for the ordinary purposes for which such goods are used. A jury could reasonably conclude that books with crooked and wrinkled pages, off center cover art, and inadequate perforation are not fit for sale to the public. We find sufficient evidence to support the jury's finding that the books did not conform to the contract.

Appellant contends that if nonconformities exist, they are minor and that appellee rejected the books in bad faith. Appellant has failed to carry its burden to prove that appellee rejected the books in bad faith. First, we do not agree with appellant's contention that the alleged nonconformities should be classified as minor. Second, there is no evidence which indicates that appellee's primary motivation in rejection of the books was to escape a bad bargain. We also note that appellant has waived its defense of rejection in bad faith by its failure to request an issue on this defense, because it has not conclusively established it under the evidence.

Appellant's second point of error is overruled.

QUESTIONS AND NOTES

1. What is the printer supposed to do with all these copies of *Supermind Supermemory*?

2. Does the printer get a chance to cure the defects before the contract is terminated? *See* UCC § 2–508:

> (1) Where any tender or delivery by the seller is rejected because nonconforming and the time for performance has not yet expired, the seller may seasonably notify the buyer of his intention to cure and may then within the contract time make a conforming delivery.

F. SUBSTANTIAL PERFORMANCE OF CONSTRUCTION CONTRACTS AND SPECIALLY MANUFACTURED GOODS

Deciding when a defective performance should be a contract-terminating event is particularly troublesome when the goods are specially manufactured or are structures built on land. In these situations, the disappointed buyer has limited opportunities to cover for her losses in the market, and the disappointed seller is likely to have even more limited opportunities to resell the goods to others in the market. Losses can quickly rise to catastrophic levels when these factors are present.

The doctrine of substantial performance has developed to deal with these special problems.

As is so often the case, the origins of this doctrine are connected with a procedural problem. To plead a cause of action for contract damages the plaintiff must allege that she has performed all of her obligations under the contract. In theory at least, a party in breach may not bring an action for damages, even if the breach is slight and damages suffered by the other side's failure to perform are great. The builder may have produced the whole office building, but if the tile in the restroom on the 14th floor does not match contract specifications, relief based on the contract price will be denied. Of course, in jurisdictions that recognize a restitutionary action by parties in breach, the builder may be able to recover *quantum meruit* for the benefit conferred, but in a number of jurisdictions this remedy is unavailable. One important motive in the early cases recognizing substantial performance was the desire to allow a builder to allege a claim in contract by stating that the construction project was substantially, if not perfectly, performed. After all, what construction project is perfectly performed? When used in this way, "substantial performance" means full performance. When a builder substantially performs, she has performed.

Over time this procedural concern merged with a more substantive concern for allowing the builder to recover based on the contract price despite immaterial breaches. Allowing an action based on contract price avoids all of the inherent uncertainties of measurement of restitutionary relief. Substantial performance came to be recognized as a rough equivalent of performance subject to immaterial breach.

In some cases, most famously *Jacob & Youngs v. Kent*, p. 833, substantial performance came to have an even broader meaning. Now substantial performance becomes the basis for granting recovery to the builder even though the project deviates significantly from the contract terms. By use of a special "diminished value" basis for measuring owner's damages, the doctrine may require owners to pay for performances that are quite different from what was agreed to, so long as the market value of the final product has not been diminished by the variation.

Manitowoc Steam Boiler Works v. Manitowoc Glue Co.
Wisconsin Supreme Court, 1903.
120 Wis. 1, 97 N.W. 515.

Action to recover the contract price and enforce a lien for supplying a steam boiler to the defendant. The evidence disclosed that the defendant operated a glue factory, requiring a large amount of steam, not only for power, but also for heating and drying; that it had an old tubular boiler, which had been manufactured by the plaintiff, and with which and its use the plaintiff was entirely familiar; that in such situation the parties negotiated for a new boiler, the defendant stating to the plaintiff that the old boiler was inadequate—that it had a commercial rating of about 80 horse power, and that one was needed of about 100 horse power. The plaintiff's manager counseled one still larger, namely, to rate about 125 horse power, as compared with the old one, 80 horse power. The agreement finally reached was that the new one should be substantially of 50 per cent. more capacity than the old, but was to be of the Scotch type, instead of the tubular type. Plaintiff constructed a boiler of the Scotch type, put it in place in a building and upon brick foundation constructed by the defendant for that purpose. After it was connected up, it was found disappointing in capacity, and not up to the old boiler, but was used, in connection with the old one, to furnish the steam necessary for the factory, while efforts were made both by plaintiff and defendant to make it work more efficiently. These efforts being still unsatisfactory, the defendant complained of the boiler as not satisfying the contract, and, as the defendant's manager testifies, desired to have it taken away. The plaintiff's manager testifies that thereupon he proposed to have a test made, and, if it did not satisfy the contract, he would either take it out and put in a new one, or enlarge it so as to make it of the necessary capacity. That test was made, the plaintiff contending that it showed the boiler to satisfy the contract, the defendant contending that it did not, but meanwhile using the boiler to supply in part the steam needed to keep its factory running. The date of this test is not disclosed, but it was some time in the autumn of 1898, and this suit was commenced on the 31st day of January, 1899. The defendant's original answer set up by way of defense the failure to perform the contract, and by way of counterclaim sought to recover $1,100 which it had paid upon the price thereof, certain additional expense occasioned by delay in the delivery of the boiler, and additional expense for wages and fuel by reason of the necessity of running two boilers. In the course of the trial defendant announced that it preferred to stand simply upon its defense that plaintiff had not performed its contract, and therefore asked leave to withdraw its counterclaims, which was granted by the court. At the close of the evidence the court made findings to the effect that the contract was as above stated, and that the boiler put in, instead of being 50 per cent. greater capacity than the old one, was about 20 per cent. less capacity, and announced that upon the then state of the pleadings the defendant would be entitled to a judgment dismissing the complaint, but, on the theory that the defendant had offered some evidence of the reasonable value of the boiler and had accepted the same, the court entered an order that the plaintiff might amend his complaint by adding a count in *quantum meruit*, and that the defendant might answer thereto simply by general denial, and could introduce no other defense, and that, when such pleadings were in, the action be postponed to the ensuing term, in order that evidence might be taken upon the new issue. To these orders the defendant took exception. The plaintiff did amend in the manner indicated, and the defendant introduced the only answer permitted—that of a general denial. Thereupon, at the ensuing term, the plaintiff introduced evidence of experts of what it would cost to build such a boiler as that supplied to the defendant. Defendant offered no further evidence, except by way of cross-examination, to show by these experts that the boiler supplied would be worth approximately $1,800 less than a boiler of the capacity found to have been contracted for. Thereupon the court made findings that the plaintiff had substantially performed its contract, except that, instead of a boiler 50 per cent. greater than the old one, it had supplied one of about 20 per cent. less capacity; that defendant had accepted the boiler; and that the reasonable value thereof was the original contract price of $2,035, for which, less the payments, judgment was rendered, from which the defendant brings this appeal.

■ DODGE, J. (after stating the facts). The result of this action, whereby the defendant is required to pay the full contract price for a boiler of only about one-half the capacity or value of that for which it agreed to pay, is somewhat startling, especially in view of the consideration, understood by both parties, that its only reason for buying a new boiler at all was that the operation of the factory required more steam than the old one could supply. Before reaching such a result, a court should pause to re-examine the rules of law or processes of reasoning upon which it is based. If the law warrants it, the force or value of a contract seems to have vanished. The contractor receives the same compensation for nonperformance as for performance. The general rule of law is firmly established that he who makes an entire contract can recover no pay unless he performs it entirely and according to its terms. This general rule has, with considerable hesitation, been relaxed for equitable considerations in certain exceptional situations where it is believed to work hardship: First, in favor of laborers who contract to perform personal services, and without fault of either party fail to complete performance; secondly, in building contracts, where the contractor constructs something on the land of another which by oversight, but in good-faith effort to perform fails to entirely satisfy the contract, but is so substantially in compliance therewith that the structure fully accomplishes the purpose of that contracted for, and the other party voluntarily accepts the benefit thereof, or where the failure is mere inconsiderable incompleteness, and the expense of completion is easy of ascertainment; and, thirdly, where the contractor supplies an article different from or inferior to that promised, and the recipient, having full opportunity to reject without loss or injury, decides to accept and retain the thing furnished. This third phase is hardly an exception, for such voluntary acceptance may well be deemed the making of a new contract to take and pay reasonably for the article which does not satisfy the original contract. In case of either of these exceptions, great caution is due in order that the innocent purchaser shall not suffer. If loss must fall anywhere, it should rest on him who breaks the contract. As said in *Allen v. McKibbin*, and quoted approvingly in *Walsh v. Fisher*, "the party in default can never gain by his default, and the other party can never be permitted to lose by it." The question, therefore, in such cases, is never what will reasonably compensate the contractor, but what can the purchaser pay without being put in worse position than if the contract had been performed? The recovery is quantum valebant from the innocent purchaser's point of view.

Proceeding to ascertain how far these principles are applicable to the situation at bar, we are confronted by the fact that substantial performance of the express contract is wholly wanting. The finding is that the boiler furnished was about 82 per cent. of the capacity of the old one, instead of 150 per cent., and that the increase of capacity was the vital and essential part of the contract. This is in no sense substantial performance. The boiler does not serve at all the purpose which the larger one would have served, and for which it was purchased. Defendant can obtain that for which it contracted, and for which it agreed to pay $2,035, and which is necessary to the purpose which induced the contract, in only one of two ways: either it can remove this boiler from its premises at large expense, if plaintiff does not remove it, and purchase and put in place another of the required size; or it can retain it, and put in another of substantially equal capacity as auxiliary to it, and at a cost equal to or greater than the original contract price, and probably necessitating reconstruction of his boiler house. One in such predicament cannot be said to have received in substance that for which he contracted. Neither do we discover either finding or proof that defendant had accepted the boiler, had decided to keep it, and use it so far as it will go toward supplying the needed steam. True, the trial court argues that it would be inequitable to allow defendant to keep the boiler and pay nothing for it, but does not find that it has elected to do so. The only finding is that it is not shown by a preponderance of the evidence that defendant rejected the boiler, or demanded its removal, though he did protest that it did not satisfy the contract. The evidence is that defendant never in words ordered plaintiff to remove the boiler, but from the testimony of the same witness (plaintiff's manager) it appears that defendant, at the time of protesting the insufficiency, did convey to defendant its wish and expectation that it be removed. That witness testified that upon such protest he agreed that he would remove the boiler if on test it did not come up to contract requirement. The test was made, the capacity ascertained, but the plaintiff's contention thereafter was that the contract was other than it is now found to have been, and for that reason did not remove it. This testimony fully confirms that of defendant's manager that he desired to have the boiler removed, and negatives any inference that it remained on defendant's premises pursuant to an election on its part to keep it.... Doubtless the fact, unexplained, that defendant made use of the boiler, which had been built into its boiler house and connected with the steam pipes in its factory, is an evidentiary circumstance having some tendency to show acceptance, but such conduct is by no means conclusive when a party cannot forego use of the appliance without at the same time giving up the use of his own premises. Thus one whose land has been plowed by another cannot be said to accept that plowing as a service merely because he sows seed and raises a crop on the land. Nor because a city runs sewerage through filter beds at its sewer outlet does it necessarily accept them. Nor because the owner lives in his house, and uses the defective furnace therein, does he necessarily accept the latter. Nor because one takes his own logs does he accept the cutting and driving done upon them by another. In *Smith v. School Dist.*, it was held sufficient to negative inference of acceptance of a school house that the district had "done nothing to prevent its removal by the builder." From such considerations it is clear that the mere use of this boiler in connection with its own premises, with which it had been connected, is not enough to overcome the foregoing evidence that defendant up to the time of the trial had elected not to accept or retain the boiler, but wished it removed, and that plaintiff fully understood such election, and had allowed said boiler to remain in breach of its agreement to remove it, because of an erroneous construction of the contract. Further, at the close of the trial, before the amendments changing the cause of action, no evidence of the value of the boiler, in the sense above defined, had been received in evidence. The trial court seemed to hold that the contract price was prima facie proof of the value. We can hardly conceive a more complete solecism than the doctrine that the contract price of a 250 horse power boiler is presumptively the value of one of 140 horse power. If the contract price proves anything, it proves that the actual boiler was not worth $2,035, but some less sum....

The result is that at the close of the trial there was no evidence to support a recovery on the contract, and the court should have rendered judgment dismissing the complaint. Neither was there evidence to support a cause of action *quantum meruit*, to accord with which amendment by the court is authorized by section 2830, Rev.St.1898. True, the court might conceive that acts subsequent to those disclosed by the proofs might take place, and might constitute acceptance; but could that justify an entire change of issues? The real controversy had been as to the capacity of the boiler contracted for. That issue being decided against it, different courses were open both to plaintiff and defendant. The former might decide to take it away and replace it by one up to the contract requirement, as it had promised to do; or perhaps it might enlarge this particular boiler, as suggested by the evidence; or it might take it away entirely, and stand its liability for damages for entire breach of the contract. The defendant might consent to any of these steps, or it might resist them in such a way as to effectively work an acceptance so as to be liable *quantum meruit*. Indeed, so far as the record discloses, these options are still open to the parties, if not foreclosed by the judgment appealed from....

Judgment reversed, and cause remanded, with directions to enter judgment dismissing the complaint.

QUESTIONS AND NOTES

1. What was the condition precedent to the defendant's duty to take and pay for the new boiler? Was it an express or an implied condition?

2. If plaintiff had been held entitled to recover the fair value of the boiler (or even the contract price) less damages to the defendant, what would it have recovered in view of the fact that "defendant can now obtain that for which it contracted" only by putting in "another boiler of substantially equal capacity at a cost equal to or greater than the original contract price?" Should the defendant have stuck to its original demand for the repayment of the $1,100 it had already paid, even without offering the boiler back to the plaintiff?

3. If the Glue Company had removed the boiler and tendered it back, would this have reduced the Boiler Company's loss?

Jacob & Youngs v. Kent

New York Court of Appeals, 1921.
230 N.Y. 239, 129 N.E. 889.

■ CARDOZO, J. The plaintiff built a country residence for the defendant at a cost of upwards of $77,000, and now sues to recover a balance of $3,483.46, remaining unpaid. The work of construction ceased in June, 1914, and the defendant then began to occupy the dwelling. There was no complaint of defective performance until March, 1915. One of the specifications for the plumbing work provides that—

> All wrought-iron pipe must be well galvanized, lap welded pipe of the grade known as "standard pipe" of Reading manufacture.

The defendant learned in March, 1915, that some of the pipe, instead of being made in Reading, was the product of other factories. The plaintiff was accordingly directed by the architect to do the work anew. The plumbing was then encased within the walls except in a few places where it had to be exposed. Obedience to the order meant more than the substitution of other pipe. It meant the demolition at great expense of substantial parts of the completed structure. The plaintiff left the work untouched and asked for a certificate that the final payment was due. Refusal of the certificate was followed by this suit.

The evidence sustains a finding that the omission of the prescribed brand of pipe was neither fraudulent nor willful. It was the result of the oversight and inattention of the plaintiff's subcontractor. Reading pipe is distinguished from Cohoes pipe and other brands only by the name of the manufacturer stamped upon it at intervals of between six and seven feet. Even the defendant's architect, though he inspected the pipe upon arrival, failed to notice the discrepancy. The plaintiff tried to show that the brands installed, though made by other manufacturers, were the same in quality, in appearance, in market value, and in cost as the brand stated in the contract—that they were, indeed, the same thing, though manufactured in another place. The evidence was excluded, and a verdict directed for the defendant. The Appellate Division reversed, and granted a new trial.

We think the evidence, if admitted, would have supplied some basis for the inference that the defect was insignificant in its relation to the project. The courts never say that one who makes a contract fills the measure of his duty by less than full performance. They do say, however, that an omission, both trivial and innocent, will sometimes be atoned for by allowance of the resulting damage, and will not always be the breach of a condition to be followed by a forfeiture. The distinction is akin to that between dependent and independent promises, or between promises and conditions. Anson on Contracts (Corbin's Ed.) § 367; 2 Williston on Contracts, § 842. Some promises are so plainly independent that they can never by fair construction be conditions of one another. Others are so plainly dependent that they must always be conditions. Others, though dependent and thus conditions when there is departure in point of substance, will be viewed as independent and collateral when the departure is insignificant. Considerations partly of justice and partly of presumable intention are to tell us whether this or that promise shall be placed in one class or in another. The simple and the uniform will call for different remedies from the multifarious and the intricate. The margin of departure within the range of normal expectation upon a sale of common chattels will vary from the margin to be expected upon a contract for the construction of a mansion or a "skyscraper." There will be harshness sometimes and oppression in the implication of a condition when the thing upon which labor has been expended is incapable of surrender because united to the land, and equity and reason in the implication of a like condition when the subject-matter, if defective, is in shape to be returned. From the conclusion that promises may not be treated as dependent to the extent of their uttermost minutiae without a sacrifice of justice, the progress is a short one to the conclusion that they may not be so treated without a perversion of intention. Intention not otherwise revealed may be presumed to hold in contemplation the reasonable and probable. If something else is in view, it must not be left to implication. There will be no assumption of a purpose to visit venial faults with oppressive retribution.

Those who think more of symmetry and logic in the development of legal rules than of practical adaption to the attainment of a just result will be troubled by a classification where the lines of division are so wavering and blurred. Something, doubtless, may be said on the score of consistency and certainty in favor of a stricter standard. The courts have balanced such considerations against those of equity and fairness, and found the latter to be the weightier. The decisions in this state commit us to the liberal view, which is making its way, nowadays, in jurisdictions slow to welcome it. Where the line is to be drawn between the important and the trivial cannot be settled by a formula. "In the nature of the case precise boundaries are impossible." 2 Williston on Contracts, § 841. The same omission may take on one aspect or another according to its setting. Substitution of equivalents may not have the same significance in fields of art on the one side and in those of mere utility on the other. Nowhere will change be tolerated, however, if it is so dominant or pervasive as in any real or substantial measure to frustrate the purpose of the contract. There is no general license to install whatever, in the builder's judgment, may be regarded as "just as good." The question is one of degree, to be answered, if there is doubt, by the triers of the facts, and, if the inferences are certain, by the judges of the law. We must weigh the purpose to be served, the desire to be gratified, the excuse for deviation from the letter, the cruelty of enforced adherence. Then only can we tell whether literal fulfillment is to be implied by law as a condition. This is not to say that the parties are not free by apt and certain words to effectuate a purpose that performance of every term shall be a condition of recovery. That question is not here. This is merely to say that the law will be slow to impute the purpose, in the silence of the parties, where the significance of the default is grievously out of proportion to the oppression of the forfeiture. The willful transgressor must accept the penalty of his transgression. For him there is no occasion to mitigate the rigor of implied conditions. The transgressor whose default is unintentional and trivial may hope for mercy if he will offer atonement for his wrong.

In the circumstances of this case, we think the measure of the allowance is not the cost of replacement, which would be great, but the difference in value, which would be either nominal or nothing. Some of the exposed sections might perhaps have been replaced at moderate expense. The defendant did not limit his demand to them, but treated the plumbing as a unit to be corrected from cellar to roof. In point of fact, the plaintiff never reached the stage at which evidence of the extent of the allowance became necessary. The trial court had excluded evidence that the defect was unsubstantial, and in view of that ruling there was no occasion for the plaintiff to go farther with an offer of proof. We think, however, that the offer, if it had been made, would not of necessity have been defective because directed to difference in value. It is true that in most cases the cost of replacement is the measure. The owner is entitled to the money which will permit him to complete, unless the cost of completion is grossly and unfairly out of proportion to the good to be attained. When that is true, the measure is the difference in value. Specifications call, let us say, for a foundation built of granite quarried in Vermont. On the completion of the building, the owner learns that through the blunder of a subcontractor part of the foundation has been built of granite of the same quality quarried in New Hampshire. The measure of allowance is not the cost of reconstruction.

There may be omissions of that which could not afterwards be supplied exactly as called for by the contract without taking down the building to its foundations, and at the same time the omission may not affect the value of the building for use or otherwise, except so slightly as to be hardly appreciable.

Handy v. Bliss, 204 Mass. 513. The rule that gives a remedy in cases of substantial performance with compensation for defects of trivial or inappreciable importance has been developed by the courts as an instrument of justice. The measure of the allowance must be shaped to the same end.

The order should be affirmed, and judgment absolute directed in favor of the plaintiff upon the stipulation, with costs in all courts.

■ McLAUGHLIN, J. I dissent. The plaintiff did not perform its contract. Its failure to do so was either intentional or due to gross neglect which, under the uncontradicted facts, amounted to the same thing, nor did it make any proof of the cost of compliance, where compliance was possible.

Under its contract it obligated itself to use in the plumbing only pipe (between 2,000 and 2,500 feet) made by the Reading Manufacturing Company. The first pipe delivered was about 1,000 feet and the plaintiff's superintendent then called the attention of the foreman of the subcontractor, who was doing the plumbing, to the fact that the specifications annexed to the contract required all pipe used in the plumbing to be of the Reading Manufacturing Company. They then examined it for the purpose of ascertaining whether this delivery was of that manufacture and found it was. Thereafter, as pipe was required in the progress of the work, the foreman of the subcontractor would leave word at its shop that he wanted a specified number of feet of pipe, without in any way indicating of what manufacture. Pipe would thereafter be delivered and installed in the building, without any examination whatever. Indeed, no examination, so far as appears, was made by the plaintiff, the subcontractor, defendant's architect, or any one else, of any of the pipe except the first delivery, until after the building had been completed. Defendant's architect then refused to give the certificate of completion, upon which the final payment depended, because all of the pipe used in the plumbing was not of the kind called for by the contract. After such refusal, the subcontractor removed the covering or insulation from about 900 feet of pipe which was exposed in the basement, cellar, and attic, and all but 70 feet was found to have been manufactured, not by the Reading Company, but by other manufacturers, some by the Cohoes Rolling Mill Company, some by the National Steel Works, some by the South Chester Tubing Company, and some which bore no manufacturer's mark at all. The balance of the pipe had been so installed in the building that an inspection of it could not be had without demolishing, in part at least, the building itself.

I am of the opinion the trial court was right in directing a verdict for the defendant. The plaintiff agreed that all the pipe used should be of the Reading Manufacturing Company. Only about two-fifths of it, so far as appears, was of that kind. If more were used, then the burden of proving that fact was upon the plaintiff, which it could easily have done, since it knew where the pipe was obtained. The question of substantial performance of a contract of the character of the one under consideration depends in no small degree upon the good faith of the contractor. If the plaintiff had intended to, and had, complied with the terms of the contract except as to minor omissions, due to inadvertence, then he might be allowed to recover the contract price, less the amount necessary to fully compensate the defendant for damages caused by such omissions. But that is not this case. It installed between 2,000 and 2,500 feet of pipe, of which only 1,000 feet at most complied with the contract. No explanation was given why pipe called for by the contract was not used, nor that any effort made to show what it would cost to remove the pipe of other manufacturers and install that of the Reading Manufacturing Company. The defendant had a right to contract for what he wanted. He had a right before making payment to get what the contract called for. It is no answer to this suggestion to say that the pipe put in was just as good as that made by the Reading Manufacturing Company, or that the difference in value between such pipe and the pipe made by the Reading Manufacturing Company would be either "nominal or nothing." Defendant contracted for pipe made by the Reading Manufacturing Company. What his reason was for requiring this kind of pipe is of no importance. He wanted that and was entitled to it. It may have been a mere whim on his part, but even so, he had a right to this kind of pipe, regardless of whether some other kind, according to the opinion of the contractor or experts, would have been "just as good, better, or done just as well." He agreed to pay only upon condition that the pipe installed were made by that company and he ought not to be compelled to pay unless that condition be performed. The rule, therefore, of substantial performance, with damages for unsubstantial omissions, has no application.

What was said by this court in *Smith v. Brady*, is quite applicable here:

I suppose it will be conceded that every one has a right to build his house, his cottage or his store after such a model and in such style as shall best accord with his notions of utility or be most agreeable to his fancy. The specifications of the contract become the law between the parties until voluntarily changed. If the owner prefers a plain and simple Doric column, and has so provided in the agreement, the contractor has no right to put in its place the more costly and elegant Corinthian. If the owner, having regard to strength and durability, has contracted for walls of specified materials to be laid in a particular manner, or for a given number of joists and beams, the builder has no right to substitute his own judgment or that of others. Having departed from the agreement, if performance has not been waived by the other party, the law will not allow him to allege that he has made as good a building as the one he engaged to erect. He can demand payment only upon and according to the terms of his contract, and if the conditions on which payment is due have not been performed, then the right to demand it does not exist. To hold a different doctrine would be simply to make another contract, and would be giving to parties an encouragement to violate their engagements, which the just policy of the law does not permit.

I am of the opinion the trial court did not err in ruling on the admission of evidence or in directing a verdict for the defendant.

For the foregoing reasons I think the judgment of the Appellate Division should be reversed and the judgment of the Trial Term affirmed.

QUESTIONS AND NOTES

1. On what theory was the plaintiff's recovery based?

2. Conceding that the plaintiff was entitled to his contract price less damages, why weren't the defendant's damages measured by the cost to him of getting what his contract called for? Was substantial performance full performance here?

3. If this had been a sales contract instead of a construction contract, with the plaintiff the seller and the defendant the buyer, and the seller had delivered Cohoes pipe instead of Reading, could the buyer have refused to take it? Would it have mattered that Cohoes pipe was "just as good" as Reading? Would the expense to the seller of delivering the wrong pipe have been considered relevant? If the buyer had taken it, what would he have had to pay for it? Why did buyer Kent have to pay for it here? Had he "taken" it?

4. If Kent had been an officer of the Reading Manufacturing Company, same result?

5. Did the contractor know that he was installing the wrong pipe? Was his breach willful?

6. If Cohoes pipe had not been "just as good" as Reading but had been serviceable pipe, would the court have reached the same result on the ground that the pipe installed in the house was "good enough"? Is 1½" of terrazzo "just as good" as 2" of terrazzo? Is it "good enough"? Good enough for what?

7. If the only thing wrong with the house was the color of the paint—cream instead of the white that the owner wanted—would builder be entitled to his full price because a cream colored house was just as valuable in the market as a white colored house?

8. If defaulting contractors may pursue a claim on the basis of *quantum meruit* for partial performance, is there any need for the doctrine of substantial performance? Consider the court's statement in *Kreyer v. Driscoll*, 159 N.W.2d 680 (Wis. 1968).

> To recover on an uncompleted construction contract on a claim of having substantially, but not fully, performed it, the contractor must make a good faith effort to perform and substantially perform his agreement . . . .
>
> [A] dispensation in favor of the contractor on the theory of substantial performance should be granted in cases of incompleteness only when such details are inconsiderable and not the fault of the contractor.

Finding that the contractor did not "substantially compl[y] with his contract to completely build a home according to plans and specifications," the court concluded that the contractor is nevertheless entitled to be reimbursed for his services and materials on the basis of *quantum meruit. See also Gentry v. Squires Constr.*, 188 S.W.3d 396, 404 (Tex. App. 2006) (holding that even though contractor did not substantially perform, he did partially perform, and homeowners benefited from that partial performance, so contractor could recover under *quantum meruit*). Note that the availability of the *quantum meruit* remedy for the defaulting contractor minimizes any unfairness that otherwise might result from a narrow view of substantial performance. Thus, substantial performance tends to assume more doctrinal significance in the minority-rule jurisdictions that refuse to recognize party-in-breach claims for restitution. On the other hand, in jurisdictions like California that liberally make available restitutionary remedies for defaulting parties, there is little reliance on the substantial performance doctrine.

Plante v. Jacobs

Wisconsin Supreme Court, 1960.
10 Wis.2d 567, 103 N.W.2d 296.

■ HALLOWS, J. The defendants argue the plaintiff cannot recover any amount because he has failed to substantially perform the contract. The plaintiff conceded he failed to furnish the kitchen cabinets, gutters and downspouts, sidewalk, closet clothes poles, and entrance seat amounting to $1,601.95. This amount was allowed to the defendants. The defendants claim some 20 other items of incomplete or faulty performance by the plaintiff and no substantial performance because the cost of completing the house in strict compliance with the plans and specifications would amount to 25 or 30 per cent of the contract price. The defendants especially stress the misplacing of the wall between the living room and the kitchen, which narrowed the living room in excess of one foot. The cost of tearing down this wall and rebuilding it would be approximately $4,000. The record is not clear why and when this wall was misplaced, but the wall is completely built and the house decorated and the defendants are living therein. Real estate experts testified that the smaller width of the living room would not affect the market price of the house.

The defendants rely on *Manitowoc Steam Boiler Works v. Manitowoc Glue Co.* for the proposition there can be no recovery on the contract as distinguished from *quantum meruit* unless there is substantial performance. This is undoubtedly the correct rule at common law. For recovery on *quantum meruit*, see *Valentine v. Patrick Warren Construction Co.* The question here is whether there has been substantial performance. The test of what amounts to substantial performance seems to be whether the performance meets the essential purpose of the contract. In the *Manitowoc* case the contract called for a boiler having a capacity of 150 per cent of the existing boiler. The court held there was no substantial performance because the boiler furnished had a capacity of only 82 per cent of the old boiler and only approximately one-half of the boiler capacity contemplated by the contract. In *Houlahan v. Clark* the contract provided the plaintiff was to drive pilings in the lake and place a boat house thereon parallel and in line with a neighbor's dock. This was not done and the contractor so positioned the boat house that it was practically useless to the owner. *Manthey v. Stock* involved a contract to paint a house and to do a good job, including the removal of the old paint where necessary. The plaintiff did not remove the old paint, and blistering and roughness of the new paint resulted. The court held that the plaintiff failed to show substantial performance. The defendants also cite *Manning v. School District No. 6.* However, this case involved a contract to install a heating and ventilating plant in the school building which would meet certain tests which the heating apparatus failed to do. The heating plant was practically a total failure to accomplish the purposes of the contract.

Substantial performance as applied to construction of a house does not mean that every detail must be in strict compliance with the specifications and the plans. Something less than perfection is the test of specific performance unless all details are made the essence of the contract. This was not done here. There may be situations in which features or details of construction of special or of great personal importance, which is not performed, would prevent a finding of substantial performance of the contract. In this case the plan was a stock floor plan. No detailed construction of the house was shown on the plan. There were no blueprints. The specifications were standard printed forms with some modifications and additions written in by the parties. Many of the problems that arose during the construction had to be solved on the basis of practical experience. No mathematical rule relating to the percentage of the price, of cost of completion or of completeness can be laid down to determine substantial performance of a building contract. Although the defendants received a house with which they are dissatisfied in many respects, the trial court was not in error in finding the contract was substantially performed.

The next question is what is the amount of recovery when the plaintiff has substantially, but incompletely, performed. For substantial performance the plaintiff should recover the contract price less the damages caused the defendant by the incomplete performance. Both parties agree. *Venzke v. Magdanz*, states the correct rule for damages due to faulty construction amounting to such incomplete performance, which is the difference between the value of the house as it stands with faulty and incomplete construction and the value of the house if it had been constructed in strict accordance with the plans and specifications. This is the diminished-value rule. The cost of replacement or repair is not the measure of such damage, but is an element to take into consideration in arriving at value under some circumstances. The cost of replacement or the cost to make whole the omissions may equal or be less than the difference in value in some cases and, likewise, the cost to rectify a defect may greatly exceed the added value to the structure as corrected. The defendants argue that under the *Venzke* rule their damages are $10,000. The plaintiff on review argues the defendants' damages are only $650. Both parties agree the trial court applied the wrong rule to the facts.

The trial court applied the cost-of-repair or replacement rule as to several items, relying on *Stern v. Schlafer* wherein it was stated that when there are a number of small items of defect or omission which can be remedied without the reconstruction of a substantial part of the building or a great sacrifice of work or material already wrought in the building, the reasonable cost of correcting the defect should be allowed. However, in *Mohs v. Quarton*, the court held when the separation of defects would lead to confusion, the rule of diminished value could apply to all defects.

In this case no such confusion arises in separating the defects. The trial court disallowed certain claimed defects because they were not proven. This finding was not against the great weight and clear preponderance of the evidence and will not be disturbed on appeal. Of the remaining defects claimed by the defendants, the court allowed the cost of replacement or repair except as to the misplacement of the living-room wall. Whether a defect should fall under the cost-of-replacement rule or be considered under the diminished-value rule depends upon the nature and magnitude of the defect. This court has not allowed items of such magnitude under the cost-of-repair rule as the trial court did. Viewing the construction of the house as a whole and its cost we cannot say, however, that the trial court was in error in allowing the cost of repairing the plaster cracks in the ceilings, the cost of mud jacking and repairing the patio floor, and the cost of reconstructing the non-weight-bearing and nonstructural patio wall. Such reconstruction did not involve an unreasonable economic waste.

The item of misplacing the living room wall under the facts of this case was clearly under the diminished-value rule. There is no evidence that defendants requested or demanded the replacement of the wall in the place called for by the specifications during the course of construction. To tear down the wall now and rebuild it in its proper place would involve a substantial destruction of the work, if not all of it, which was put into the wall and would cause additional damage to other parts of the house and require replastering and redecorating the walls and ceilings of at least two rooms. Such economic waste is unreasonable and unjustified. The rule of diminished value contemplates the wall is not going to be moved. Expert witnesses for both parties, testifying as to the value of the house, agreed that the misplacement of the wall had no effect on the market price. The trial court properly found that the defendants suffered no legal damage, although the defendants' particular desire for specified room size was not satisfied. For a discussion of these rules of damages for defective or unfinished construction and their application see Restatement, Contracts, sec. 346(1)(a) and illustrations.

Judgment affirmed.

III. REPUDIATION

In many deals that go sour, the non-breaching party gets clear notice in advance that it is not going to get the future performance it bargained for. Sometimes this notice comes in the form of an express statement by the promisor. Sometimes—as in the case of installment contracts—the party gets that "notice" by a breach of an early installment so material that he is justified in inferring that the breaching party has no intention of properly performing future duties or no ability to do so.

What effect should be given to an advance notice of intention not to perform? This event is usually labeled "anticipatory repudiation."* How can there be a breach of a duty before it is due?

---

* It is also frequently mislabeled "anticipatory breach." Since its occurrence immediately creates legal rights in the non-breaching party, there is nothing anticipatory about its effect as a breach. What it amounts to is a breach by an anticipatory repudiation in contrast to a breach by failure to perform when due.

■ JOHNSEN, J., in *Hawkinson v. Johnston*, 122 F.2d 724, 729–30 (8th Cir. 1941):

The real sanctity of any contract rests only in the mutual willingness of the parties to perform. Where this willingness ceases to exist, any attempt to prolong or preserve the status between them will usually be unsatisfactory and mechanical. Generally speaking, it is far better in such a situation, for the individuals and for society, that the rights and obligations between them should be promptly and definitely settled, if the injured party so desires, unless there is some provision in the contract that, as a matter of mutual intention, can be said to prevent this from being done. The commercial world has long since learned the desirability of fixing its liabilities and losses as quickly as possible, and the law similarly needs to remind itself that, to be useful, it too must seek to be practical.

LAWRENCE VOLD, *REPUDIATION OF CONTRACTS,* 5 NEB. L. BULL. 269, 279–85 (1927).

The substantial practical reason for permitting the aggrieved promisee to sue at once for anticipatory repudiation is that allowing an action at once tends to conserve available resources and prevent waste. If no legal recognition is extended to the promisee's valuable contractual relation pending performance, if no cause of action is recognized until there is a failure to perform at the time for performance, large losses may be incurred which suing promptly might avoid. Merely recognizing repudiation as an excuse to the aggrieved party for future non-performance is not enough since frequently there is a dispute over who is in the wrong which only litigation can settle. Unless the aggrieved promisee can at once come to court in an action for anticipatory repudiation he must either struggle on with hostile or possibly insolvent parties, incurring expense and loss of time in preparations which may be of no use to anybody, or he must cease such further preparations for performance at the peril of being found in default after all in later litigation at the time for performance. In long-time contracts which now in the business world are becoming more and more important, the importance of getting a reasonably prompt settlement of controversies over repudiation is hard to exaggerate. Very often by such settlement through litigation, the controversy can be adjusted and the productive work of the business in hand continued without serious interruption.

Even should the law's delays through appeals to the higher courts absorb more than the time outstanding between repudiation and the date for performance the general consideration of conserving available resources and avoiding waste continues applicable in favor of an immediate action for the repudiation. The sooner the controversy can be disposed of the sooner the parties can know their obligations and the sooner they can in accordance therewith adjust their affairs to practical productive efforts, instead of remaining idle or engaging in misdirected futile activity while awaiting the results of distant future litigation.

Hochster v. De La Tour

Queen's Bench, 1853.
2 Ellis & Bl. 678, 118 Eng.Rep. 922.

Action of assumpsit.

On the trial before Erle, J., at the London sittings in last Easter Term, it appeared that plaintiff was a courier, who in April, 1852, was engaged by defendant to accompany him on a tour, to commence on 1st June, 1852, on the terms mentioned in the declaration. On the 11th May, 1852, defendant wrote to plaintiff that he had changed his mind, and declined his services. He refused to make him any compensation. The action was commenced on 22d May. The plaintiff, between the commencement of the action and the 1st of June, obtained an engagement with Lord Ashburton, on equally good terms, but not commencing till July 4th. The defendant's counsel objected that there could be no breach of the contract before the 1st of June. The learned judge was of a contrary opinion, but reserved leave to enter a nonsuit on this objection. The other questions were left to the jury, who found for plaintiff.

Hugh Hill, in the same term, obtained a rule nisi to enter a nonsuit or arrest the judgment.

. . .

■ LORD CAMPBELL, C.J., now delivered the judgment of the Court.

On this motion in arrest of judgment, the question arises, Whether, if there be an agreement between A and B, whereby B engages to employ A on and from a future day for a given period of time, to travel with him into a foreign country as a courier, and to start with him in that capacity on that day, A being to receive a monthly salary during the continuance of such service, B may, before the day, refuse to perform the agreement and break and renounce it, so as to entitle A before the day to commence an action against B to recover damages for breach of the agreement; A having been ready and willing to perform it, till it was broken and renounced by B. The defendant's counsel very powerfully contended that, if the plaintiff was not contented to dissolve the contract and to abandon all remedy upon it, he was bound to remain ready and willing to perform it till the day when the actual employment as courier in the service of the defendant was to begin; and that there could be no breach of the agreement before that day to give a right of action. But it cannot be laid down as a universal rule that, whereby agreement an act is to be done on a future day, no action can be brought for a breach of the agreement till the day for doing the act has arrived. If a man promises to marry a woman on a future day, and before that day marries another woman, he is instantly liable to an action for breach of promise of marriage.

If a man contracts to execute a lease on and from a future day for a certain term, and before that day executes a lease to another for the same term, he may be immediately sued for breaking the contract. So, if a man contracts to sell and deliver specific goods on a future day, and before the day he sells and delivers them to another, he is immediately liable to an action at the suit of the person with whom he first contracted to sell and deliver them. One reason alleged in support of such an action is, that the defendant has, before the day, rendered it impossible for him to perform the contract at the day, but this does not necessarily follow; for prior to the day fixed for doing the act, the first wife may have died, a surrender of the lease executed might be obtained, and the defendant might have repurchased the goods so as to be in a situation to sell and deliver them to the plaintiff. Another reason may be that, where there is a contract to do an act on a future day, there is a relation constituted between the parties in the meantime by the contract, and that they impliedly promise that in the meantime neither will do anything to the prejudice of the other inconsistent with that relation. As for example, a man and woman engaged to marry are affianced to one another during the period between the time of the engagement and the celebration of the marriage. In this very case of traveller and courier, from the day of the hiring till the day when the employment was to begin, they were engaged to each other; and it seems to be a breach of an implied contract if either of them renounces the engagement. This reasoning seems in accordance with the unanimous decision of the Exchequer Chamber in *Elderton v. Emmens*, which we have followed in subsequent cases in this court.

The declaration in the present case, in alleging a breach, states a great deal more than a passing intention on the part of the defendant which he may repent of, and could only be proved by evidence that he had utterly renounced the contract, or done some act which rendered it impossible for him to perform it. If the plaintiff has no remedy for breach of the contract unless he treats the contract as in force, and acts upon it down to June 1st, 1852, it follows that, till then, he must enter into no employment which will interfere with his promise "to start with the defendant on such travels on the day and year," and that he must then be properly equipped in all respects as a courier for a three months' tour on the continent of Europe. But it is surely much more rational, and more for the benefit of both parties, that, after the renunciation of the agreement by the defendant, the plaintiff should be at liberty to consider himself absolved from any future performance of it, retaining his right to sue for any damage he has suffered from the breach of it. Thus, instead of remaining idle and laying out money in preparations which must be useless, he is at liberty to seek service under another employer, which would go in mitigation of the damages to which he would otherwise be entitled for a breach of the contract. It seems strange that the defendant, after renouncing the contract, and absolutely declaring that he will never act under it, should be permitted to object that faith is given to his assertion, and that an opportunity is not left to him of changing his mind.

If the plaintiff is barred of any remedy by entering into an engagement inconsistent with starting as a courier with the defendant on the 1st June, he is prejudiced by putting faith in the defendant's assertion; and it would be more consistent with principle, if the defendant were precluded from saying that he had not broken the contract when he declared that he entirely renounced it.

Suppose that the defendant, at the time of his renunciation, had embarked on a voyage for Australia, so as to render it physically impossible for him to employ the plaintiff as a courier on the continent of Europe in the months of June, July and August, 1852; according to decided cases, the action might have been brought before the 1st June; but the renunciation may have been founded on other facts, to be given in evidence, which would equally have rendered the defendant's performance of the contract impossible. The man who wrongfully renounces a contract into which he has deliberately entered cannot justly complain if he is immediately sued for a compensation in damages by the man whom he has injured; and it seems reasonable to allow an option to the injured party, either to sue immediately, or to wait till the time when the act was to be done, still holding it as prospectively binding for the exercise of this option, which may be advantageous to the innocent party, and cannot be prejudicial to the wrong-doer. An argument against the action before the 1st of June is urged from the difficulty of calculating the damages; but this argument is equally strong against an action before the 1st of September, when the three months would expire. In either case, the jury in assessing the damages would be justified in looking to all that happened, or was likely to happen, to increase or mitigate the loss of the plaintiff down to the day of trial. We do not find any decision contrary to the view we are taking of this case....

The only other case cited in the argument which we think it necessary to notice is *Planchè v. Colburn*, which appears to be an authority for the plaintiff. There the defendants had engaged the plaintiff to write a treatise for a periodical publication. The plaintiff commenced the composition of the treatise; but, before he had completed it, and before the time when in the course of conducting the publication it would have appeared in print, the publication was abandoned. The plaintiff thereupon, without completing the treatise, brought an action for breach of contract. Objection was made that the plaintiff could not recover on the special contract for want of having completed, tendered, and delivered the treatise, according to the contract. Tindal, C.J., said: "The fact was, that the defendants not only suspended, but actually put an end to, 'The Juvenile Library'; they had broken their contract with the plaintiff." The declaration contained counts for work and labour: but the plaintiff appears to have retained his verdict on the count framed on the special contract, thus showing that, in the opinion of the court, the plaintiff might treat the renunciation of the contract by the defendants as a breach, and maintain an action for that breach, without considering that it remained in force so as to bind him to perform his part of it before bringing an action for the breach of it. If it should be held that, upon a contract to do an act on a future day, a renunciation of the contract by one party dispenses with a condition to be performed in the meantime by the other, there seems no reason for requiring that other to wait till the day arrives before seeking his remedy by action, and the only ground on which the condition can be dispensed with seems to be that the renunciation may be treated as a breach of the contract.

Upon the whole, we think that the declaration in this case is sufficient. It gives us great satisfaction to reflect that, the question being on the record, our opinion may be reviewed in a court of error. In the meantime we must give judgment for the plaintiff.

QUESTIONS AND NOTES

1. If Hochster had died on May 20, after De La Tour's anticipatory repudiation of May 11, would his estate have been entitled to the contract price for his services? Would it have been entitled to damages? What if he had died on June 20? Suppose that De La Tour had discharged him without cause on June 2, and he died on June 20. What then?

2. If early in a contract, one party plainly repudiates his total duty, as Baron De La Tour did, there is no doubt that the repudiation can be safely treated as a total breach. But what if the Baron had merely notified Hochster in advance that—contrary to the contract's terms—he would have to provide his own horse. If this would not be a material breach if the notice were given when Hochster first appeared for work (and it might well not be so considered), would it still be an anticipatory repudiation if given two weeks in advance? Could Hochster refuse to report for work? Could he take another job?

UNIFORM COMMERCIAL CODE:

§ 2–610. *Anticipatory Repudiation.*

When either party repudiates the contract with respect to a performance not yet due the loss of which will substantially impair the value of the contract to the other, the aggrieved party may

(a) for a commercially reasonable time await performance by the repudiating party; or

(b) resort to any remedy for breach (Section 2–703 or Section 2–711), even though he has notified the repudiating party that he would await the latter's performance and has urged retraction; and

(c) in either case suspend his own performance or proceed in accordance with the provisions of this Article on the seller's right to identify goods to the contract notwithstanding breach or to salvage unfinished goods (Section 2–704).

COMMENTS:

1. With the problem of insecurity taken care of by the preceding section and with provision being made in this Article as to the effect of a defective delivery under an installment contract, anticipatory repudiation centers upon an overt communication of intention or an action which renders performance impossible or demonstrates a clear determination not to continue with performance.

4. After repudiation, the aggrieved party may immediately resort to any remedy he chooses provided he moves in good faith (see Section [1–304]). Inaction and silence by the aggrieved party may leave the matter open but it cannot be regarded as misleading the repudiating party. Therefore the aggrieved party is left free to proceed at any time with his options under this section, unless he has taken some positive action which in good faith requires notification to the other party before the remedy is pursued.

———

PHILLIPS, J., in *Bu–Vi–Bar Petroleum Corp. v. Krow,* 40 F.2d 488, 492 (10th Cir. 1930):

The situation of the injured party, where there has been a breach which does not indicate an intention to repudiate the remainder of the contract, and the situation of the injured party, where there has been a total renunciation of the contract, differs in important particulars. In the former case, the injured party has a genuine election either of continuing performance or ceasing to perform. Any act, indicating an intent to continue, will operate as a conclusive election. On the other hand, where the contract is wholly renounced, there can be no real election between continuation and cessation of performance, because, after notice of renunciation, the other party cannot go on and complete an executory contract and sue for any increased damages resulting from his continuing to perform.

A continued willingness upon the part of the injured party to receive performance is an indication that, if the repudiator will withdraw his repudiation, but not otherwise, the contract may proceed. It is not an irrevocable election not to treat the renunciation as a breach. The refusal to retract amounts to a continuation of such renunciation....

We are not unmindful that the above statement is contrary to the English doctrine, which is that if the promisee, after receiving the repudiation, demands or manifests a willingness to receive performance "he keeps the contract alive for the benefit of the others as well as his own; he remains subject to all his own obligations and liabilities under it, and enables the other party not only to complete the contract, if so advised, notwithstanding his previous repudiation of it, but also to take advantage of any supervening circumstance which would justify him in declining to complete it." *Frost v. Knight*, L.R. 7 Ex. 111, 112; Williston on Contracts, vol. III, pp. 2386, 2387.

But this harsh and unreasonable doctrine is modified by the American authorities, at least to the extent that so long as the party who has repudiated, notwithstanding requests for retraction and performance upon the part of the other party, refuses to retract and thus continues his repudiation without justification, the latter, if not in default himself, may still elect to treat the repudiation as a breach.

Recall: *Rockingham County v. Luten Bridge Co.*, p. 139.

QUESTION

How could the Luten Bridge Co. in the *Rockingham County* case have kept the contract alive? For how long? How long could Hochster have kept his employment contract with De La Tour alive? When, in other words, does the avoidable consequence rule enter the picture to cut off the injured party's power to continue to hold himself ready to perform for the entire contract and thus claim the contract price as his damage?

Taylor v. Johnston

California Supreme Court, 1975.
15 Cal.3d 130, 123 Cal.Rptr. 641, 539 P.2d 425.

■ SULLIVAN, J. In this action for damages for breach of contract defendants Elizabeth and Ellwood Johnston, individually and as copartners doing business as Old English Rancho, appeal from a judgment entered after a nonjury trial in favor of plaintiff H.B. Taylor and against them in the amount of $132,778.05 and costs.

Plaintiff was engaged in the business of owning, breeding, raising and racing thoroughbred horses in Los Angeles County. Defendants were engaged in a similar business, and operated a horse farm in Ontario, California, where they furnished stallion stud services. In January 1965 plaintiff sought to breed his two thoroughbred mares, Sunday Slippers and Sandy Fork to defendants' stallion Fleet Nasrullah. To that end, on January 19 plaintiff and defendants entered into two separate written contracts—one pertaining to Sunday Slippers and the other to Sandy Fork. Except for the mare involved the contracts were identical. We set forth in the margin the contract covering Sunday Slippers.[1]

---

1. "Original
        IMPORTANT PLEASE SIGN ORIGINAL AND
         RETURN AS QUICKLY AS POSSIBLE RETAINING
       DUPLICATE FOR YOUR OWN FILE."OLD ENGLISH RANCHO
Route 1, Box 224-A   January 8, 1965
Ontario, California 91761
 "Gentlemen:
 "I hereby confirm my reservation for one services to the stallion FLEET NASRULLAH for the year 1966.
 "TERMS: $3,500.00—GUARANTEE LIVE FOAL.
 "FEE is due and payable on or before Sept. 1, 1966.
 "IF stud fee is paid in full, and mare fails to produce a live foal (one that stands and nurses without assistance) from this breeding, a return, breeding the following year to said mare will be granted at no additional stallion fee.
 "FEE is due and payable prior to sale of mare or prior to her departure from the state. If mare is sold or leaves the state, no return breeding will be granted.
 "STUD CERTIFICATE to be given in exchange for fees paid.
 "VETERINARIAN CERTIFICATE due in lieu of payment if mare is barren.
 "I hereby agree that OLD ENGLISH RANCHO shall in no way be held responsible for accidents of any kind or disease.
 "Mare: SUNDAY SLIPPERS
Roan filly 1959
MOOLAH BUX–MAOLI–ORMESBY   Mr. H.B. Taylor
                                               112 North Evergreen St
                                               Burbank, California 91505
  "(Veterinary certificate must accompany all barren mares.)
  "Stakes winner of $64,000.00 last raced in 1962
                       /s/ H.B. Taylor"

The contract provided that Fleet Nasrullah was to perform breeding services upon the respective mares in the year 1966 for a fee of $3,500, payable on or before September 1, 1966. If the stud fee was paid in full and the mares failed to produce a live foal (one that stands and nurses without assistance) from the breeding a return breeding would be provided the following year without additional fee.

On October 4, 1965, defendants sold Fleet Nasrullah to Dr. A.G. Pessin and Leslie Combs II for $1,000,000 cash and shipped the stallion to Kentucky. Subsequently Combs and Pessin syndicated the sire by selling various individuals 36 or 38 shares, each share entitling the holder to breed one mare each season to Fleet Nasrullah. Combs and Pessin each reserved three shares.

On the same day defendants wrote to plaintiff advising the latter of the sale and that he was "released" from his "reservations" for Fleet Nasrullah. Unable to reach defendants by telephone, plaintiff had his attorney write to them on October 8, 1965, insisting on performance of the contracts. Receiving no answer, plaintiff's attorney on October 19 wrote a second letter threatening suit. On October 27, defendants advised plaintiff by letter that arrangements had been made to breed the two mares to Fleet Nasrullah in Kentucky. However, plaintiff later learned that the mares could not be boarded at Spendthrift Farm where Fleet Nasrullah was standing stud and accordingly arranged with Clinton Frazier of Elmhurst Farm to board the mares and take care of the breeding.

In January 1966 plaintiff shipped Sunday Slippers and Sandy Fork to Elmhurst Farm. At that time, however, both mares were in foal and could not be bred, since this can occur only during the five-day period in which they are in heat. The first heat period normally occurs nine days, and the second heat period thirty days, after foaling. Succeeding heat periods occur every 21 days.

On April 17, 1966, Sunday Slippers foaled and Frazier immediately notified Dr. Pessin. The latter assured Frazier that he would make the necessary arrangements to breed the mare to Fleet Nasrullah. On April 26, the ninth day after the foaling, Frazier, upon further inquiry, was told by Dr. Pessin to contact Mrs. Judy who had charge of booking the breedings and had handled these matters with Frazier in the past. Mrs. Judy, however, informed Frazier that the stallion was booked for that day but would be available on any day not booked by a shareholder. She indicated that she was acting under instructions but suggested that he keep in touch with her while the mare was in heat.

Sunday Slippers came into heat again on May 13, 1966. Frazier telephoned Mrs. Judy and attempted to book the breeding for May 16.[4] She informed him that Fleet

---

4. Frazier did not seek to breed Sunday Slippers on May 13, 1966, because the mare's follicle had not yet ruptured; conception can occur up to 12 hours after rupture of the follicle. Accordingly, Frazier normally tried to book a breeding for three days after the onset of heat.

Nasrullah had been reserved by one of the shareholders for that day, but that Frazier should keep in touch with her in the event the reservation was cancelled. On May 14 and May 15 Frazier tried again but without success; on the latter date, Sunday Slippers went out of heat.

On June 4, the mare went into heat again. Frazier again tried to book a reservation with Fleet Nasrullah but was told that all dates during the heat period had been already booked. He made no further efforts but on June 7, on plaintiff's instructions, bred Sunday Slippers to a Kentucky Derby winner named Chateaugay for a stud fee of $10,000.

Sandy Fork, plaintiff's other mare awaiting the stud services of Fleet Nasrullah, foaled on June 5, 1966. Frazier telephoned Mrs. Judy the next day and received a booking to breed the mare on June 14, the ninth day after foaling. On June 13, 1966, however, she cancelled the reservation because of the prior claim of a shareholder. Frazier made no further attempts and on June 14 bred Sandy Fork to Chateaugay.

Shortly after their breeding, it was discovered that both mares were pregnant with twins. In thoroughbred racing twins are considered undesirable since they endanger the mare and are themselves seldom valuable for racing. Both mares were therefore aborted. However, plaintiff was not required to pay the $20,000 stud fees for Chateaugay's services because neither mare delivered a live foal.

The instant action for breach of contract proceeded to trial on plaintiff's fourth amended complaint, which alleged two causes of action, the first for breach of the two written contracts, the second for breach of an oral agreement. Defendants' cross-complained for the stud fees. The court found the facts to be substantially as stated above and further found and concluded that by selling Fleet Nasrullah defendants had "put it out of their power to perform properly their contracts," that the conduct of defendants and their agents Dr. Pessin and Mrs. Judy up to and including June 13, 1966, constituted a breach[5] and plaintiff "was then justified in treating it as a breach and repudiation of their contractual obligations to him," and

---

5. We set forth the significant paragraph of the findings at length: "When defendants sold Fleet Nasrullah in 1965 to a purchaser who shipped him to Kentucky, defendants put it out of their power to perform properly their contracts with plaintiff. Those contracts did not require that plaintiff's rights to the breeding services of Fleet Nasrullah should be relegated to a secondary or subordinate position to that of any other person, whether he be a holder of shares in the stallion or not. No such conditions were stated in the contracts and none can be inferred therefrom. From the conduct of the defendants, their agent Dr. Pessin, and their subagent Mrs. Judy, plaintiff was justified in concluding that the defendants were just giving him the run around and had no intention of performing their contract in the manner required by its terms and as required by the covenant of good faith and fair dealing. Their conduct and that of their agent Dr. Pessin, and their subagent Mrs. Judy up to and including June 13, 1966 constituted a breach of defendants' breeding contracts with plaintiff and plaintiff was then justified in treating it as a breach and repudiation of their contractual obligation to him."

that defendants unjustifiably breached the contracts but plaintiff did not.[6] The court awarded plaintiff damages for defendants' breach in the sum of $103,122.50 ($99,800 net damage directly sustained plus $3,322.50 for reasonable costs and expenses for mitigation of damages). "Because of defendants' wholly unwarranted, high-handed, and oppressive breach of their contractual obligation to plaintiff, the plaintiff is entitled to recover from the defendants pre-judgment interest at the rate of 7% per annum on the sum of $99,800.00 from August 1, 1968 * * *." It was concluded that defendants should take nothing on their cross-complaint. Judgment was entered accordingly. This appeal followed.

Defendants' main attack on the judgment is two-pronged. They contend: first, that they did not at any time repudiate the contracts; and second, that they did not otherwise breach the contracts because performance was made impossible by plaintiff's own actions. To put it another way, defendants argue in effect that the finding that they breached the contracts is without any support in the evidence. Essentially they take the position that on the uncontradicted evidence in the record, as a matter of law there was neither anticipatory nor actual breach. As will appear, we conclude that the trial court's decision was based solely on findings of anticipatory breach and that we must determine whether such decision is supported by the evidence.

Nevertheless both aspects of defendants' argument require us at the outset to examine the specifications for performance contained in the contracts. (*See* fn. 1, *ante*.) We note that the reservation for "one services" for Fleet Nasrullah was "for the year 1966." As the evidence showed, a breeding is biologically possible throughout the calendar year, since mares regularly come into heat every 21 days, unless they are pregnant. The contracts therefore appear to contemplate breeding with Fleet Nasrullah at any time during the calendar year 1966. The trial court made no finding as to the time of performance called for by the contracts.[7] There was testimony to the effect that by custom in the thoroughbred racing business the breeding is consummated in a "breeding season" which normally extends from January until early July, although some breeding continues through August. It is possible that the parties intended that the mares be bred to Fleet Nasrullah during the 1966 breeding season rather than the calendar year 1966.[8]

---

6. The court concluded that "The defendants unjustifiably breached these contracts; the plaintiff did not breach these contracts."

7. The trial court was not compelled to specify the exact time for performance because it concluded that defendants had breached the contracts by anticipatory repudiation, i.e., a breach which occurs prior to the time for performance.

8. Perhaps the fact that the stud fees were due to be paid September 1, 1966, at the close of the breeding season supports such a conclusion. Moreover, defendants concede without argument that the trial court impliedly found the time of performance to be the breeding season.

However, in our view, it is immaterial whether the contract phrase "for the year 1966" is taken to mean the above breeding season or the full calendar year since in either event the contract period had not expired by June 7 and June 14, 1966, the dates on which Sunday Slippers and Sandy Fork respectively were bred to Chateaugay[9] and by which time, according to the findings defendants had repudiated the contracts. There can be no *actual* breach of a contract until the time specified therein for performance has arrived. Although there may be a *breach by anticipatory repudiation:* "[b]y its very name an essential element of a true anticipatory breach of a contract is that the repudiation by the promisor occur before his performance is due under the contract." In the instant case, because under either of the above interpretations the time for performance has not yet arrived, defendants' breach as found by the trial court was of necessity an anticipatory breach and must be analyzed in accordance with the principles governing such type of breach. To these principles we now direct our attention.

Anticipatory breach occurs when one of the parties to a bilateral contract repudiates the contract. The repudiation may be express or implied. An express repudiation is a clear, positive, unequivocal refusal to perform; an implied repudiation results from conduct where the promisor puts it out of his power to perform so as to make substantial performance of his promise impossible.

When a promisor repudiates a contract, the injured party faces an election of remedies: he can treat the repudiation as an anticipatory breach and immediately seek damages for breach of contract, thereby terminating the contractual relation between the parties, or he can treat the repudiation as an empty threat, wait until the time for performance arrives and exercise his remedies for actual breach if a breach does in fact occur at such time. However, if the injured party disregards the repudiation and treats the contract as still in force, and the repudiation is retracted prior to the time of performance, then the repudiation is nullified and the injured party is left with his remedies, if any, invocable at the time of performance.

As we have pointed out, the trial court found that the whole course of conduct of defendants and their agents Dr. Pessin and Mrs. Judy from the time of the sale of Fleet Nasrullah up to and including June 13, 1966, amounted to a repudiation which plaintiff was justified in treating as an anticipatory breach. However, when the principles of law governing repudiation just described are applied to the facts constituting this course of conduct as found by the trial court, it is manifest that such conduct cannot be treated as an undifferentiated continuum amounting to a single repudiation but must be divided into two separate repudiations.

---

9. Both Sunday Slippers and Sandy Fork would have had at least one more heat during the 1966 breeding season—that of Sunday Slippers commencing on June 26, 1966, and that of Sandy Fork commencing on July 7, 1966.

First, defendants clearly repudiated the contracts when, after selling Fleet Nasrullah and shipping him to Kentucky, they informed plaintiff "[y]ou are, therefore, released from your reservations made to the stallion." However, the trial court additionally found that "[p]laintiff did not wish to be 'released' from his 'reservations' * * * insist[ed] on performance of the stud service agreements * * * [and] threaten[ed] litigation if the contracts were not honored by defendants * * *." Accordingly defendants arranged for performance of the contracts by making Fleet Nasrullah available for stud service to plaintiff in Kentucky through their agents Dr. Pessin and Mrs. Judy. Plaintiff elected to treat the contracts as in force and shipped the mares to Kentucky to effect the desired performance. The foregoing facts lead us to conclude that the subsequent arrangements by defendants to make Fleet Nasrullah available to service plaintiff's mares in Kentucky constituted a retraction of the repudiation. Since at this time plaintiff had not elected to treat the repudiation as an anticipatory breach[10] and in fact had shipped the mares to Kentucky in reliance on defendants' arrangements, this retraction nullified the repudiation. Thus, plaintiff was then left with his remedies that might arise at the time of performance.

The trial court found that after the mares had arrived in Kentucky, had delivered the foals they were then carrying and were ready for servicing by Fleet Nasrullah, plaintiff was justified in concluding from the conduct of defendants, their agent Dr. Pessin, and their subagent Mrs. Judy, that "defendants were just giving him the runaround and had no intention of performing their contract in the manner required by its terms" and in treating such conduct "as a breach and repudiation of their contractual obligation to him." Since, as we have explained, defendants retracted their original repudiation, this subsequent conduct amounts to a finding of a second repudiation.

There is no evidence in the record that defendants or their agents Dr. Pessin and Mrs. Judy ever stated that Sunday Slippers and Sandy Fork would not be serviced by Fleet Nasrullah during the 1966 breeding season or that they ever refused to perform. Frazier, plaintiff's agent who made arrangements for the breeding of the mares admitted that they had never made such a statement to him.[11] Accordingly, there was no *express* repudiation or unequivocal refusal to perform.

The trial court's finding of repudiation, expressly based on the "conduct of the defendants" and their agents suggests that the court found an implied repudiation. However, there is no implied repudiation, i.e., by conduct equivalent to unequivocal refusal to perform, unless "the promisor *puts it out of his power to perform.*" Once the

---

10. Plaintiff concedes that the repudiation was not "accepted by plaintiff."

11. Q. * * * At any time, did Mrs. Judy or anyone else ever tell you that she could not or would not breed either mare to Fleet Nasrullah before the end of 1966? * * *

THE WITNESS: No.

mares arrived in Kentucky, defendants had the power to perform the contracts; Fleet Nasrullah could breed with the mares. No subsequent conduct occurred to render this performance impossible. Although plaintiff was subordinated to the shareholders with respect to the priority of reserving a breeding time with Fleet Nasrullah, there is no evidence in the record that this subordination of reservation rights rendered performance impossible. Rather it acted to postpone the time of performance, which still remained within the limits prescribed by the contracts. It rendered performance more difficult to achieve; it may even have cast doubt upon the eventual accomplishment of performance; it did not render performance impossible.[12]

Because there was no repudiation, express or implied, there was no anticipatory breach. Plaintiff contends that defendants' conduct, as found by the trial court, indicated that "defendants were just giving him the runaround and had no intention of performing their contract" and therefore that this conduct was the equivalent of an express and unequivocal refusal to perform. Plaintiff has not presented to the court any authority in California in support of his proposition that conduct which has not met the test for an implied repudiation, i.e. conduct which removed the power to perform, may nonetheless be held to amount to the equivalent of an express repudiation and thus constitute an anticipatory breach. Without addressing ourselves to the question whether some conduct could ever be found equal to an express repudiation, we hold that defendants' conduct in this case as a matter of law did not constitute an anticipatory breach.

To constitute an express repudiation, the promisor's statement, or in this case conduct, must amount to an unequivocal refusal to perform: "A mere declaration, however, of a party of an intention not to be bound will not of itself amount to a breach, so as to create an effectual renunciation of the contract; for one party cannot by any act or declaration destroy the binding force and efficacy of the contract. To justify the adverse party in treating the renunciation as a breach, the refusal to perform must be of the whole contract * * * and must be distinct, unequivocal and absolute."

---

12. Plaintiff suggests that this conduct, namely delaying plaintiff's breeding until a day not reserved by a shareholder, amounted to an anticipatory breach because Mrs. Judy inserted a condition to defendants' performance, which as the trial court found was not contemplated by the contracts. Assuming arguendo that this conduct might have amounted to a breach of contract by improperly delaying performance, at most it would have constituted only a partial breach—insufficiently material to terminate the contracts. It did not constitute a repudiation of the contracts which was the sole basis of the trial court's decision since "[t]o justify the adverse party in treating the renunciation as a breach, the refusal to perform must be of the whole contract or of a covenant going to the whole consideration * * *." (*Atkinson v. District Bond Co.*, 5 Cal.App.2d 738, 743.)

To recapitulate, Sandy Fork was in foal in January 1966, the commencement of the 1966 breeding season, and remained so until June 5, 1966. Throughout this period Fleet Nasrullah could not perform his services as contracted due solely to the conduct of plaintiff in breeding Sandy Fork in 1965. Biologically the first opportunity to breed Sandy Fork was on June 14, 1966, nine days after foaling. Frazier telephoned Mrs. Judy on June 6, 1966, and received a booking with Fleet Nasrullah for June 14, 1966. On June 13 Mrs. Judy telephoned Frazier and informed him she would have to cancel Sandy Fork's reservation for the following day because one of the shareholders insisted on using that day. Mrs. Judy gave no indication whatsoever that she could not or would not breed Sandy Fork on any of the following days in that heat period or subsequent heat periods. Frazier made no further attempts to breed Sandy Fork with Fleet Nasrullah. Thus, plaintiff, who delayed the possibility of performance for five months, asserts that the delay of performance occasioned by defendants' cancellation of a reservation on the first day during the six-month period that plaintiff made performance possible amounts to an unequivocal refusal to perform, even though there was adequate opportunity for Fleet Nasrullah to perform within the period for performance specified in the contract and even though defendants never stated any intention not to perform. We conclude that as a matter of law this conduct did not amount to an unequivocal refusal to perform and therefore did not constitute an anticipatory breach of the contract covering Sandy Fork.

Sunday Slippers foaled on April 17, 1966, first came into heat on April 26 and then successively on May 13 and June 4, 1966. Mrs. Judy informed Frazier that she would breed Sunday Slippers on any day that one of the shareholders did not want to use the stallion. Frazier unsuccessfully sought to breed the mare on April 26, May 14, May 15 and June 4, 1966, Fleet Nasrullah being reserved on those dates. Mrs. Judy continued to assure Frazier that the breeding would occur. Sunday Slippers was due to come into heat again twice during the breeding season: June 25 and July 16, 1966. At most this conduct amounts to delay of performance and a warning that performance might altogether be precluded if a shareholder were to desire Fleet Nasrullah's services on all the remaining days within the period specified for performance in which Sunday Slippers was in heat. We conclude that as a matter of law this conduct did not amount to an unequivocal refusal to perform and therefore did not constitute an anticipatory breach of the contract covering Sunday Slippers.

QUESTIONS AND NOTES

1. Could the agreement of the owner of the mares to send them to Kentucky for breeding be construed as an accord executory? If the substituted arrangement were analyzed that way, wouldn't Taylor have the right to sue under either the original

or substituted performance when the stallion was not made available? What difference would it make?

2. Is a temporizing contractor who never manages to get going on performance, but never concedes that he won't or can't perform, safe until the period of possible performance expires? How many times was Taylor required to ask for service before he was safe in concluding that he was getting the runaround?

3. In light of the court's decision that the contract set forth in footnote 1 was not repudiated, can Taylor bring his mares around the next year for stud services?

4. If the court were to find repudiation in this case, how would Taylor's damages be measured?

NOTE ON FLEET NASRULLAH

A first-year law student may find it hard to be aware of the life behind the cold print of a case report. The racing and romantic life of Fleet Nasrullah, the stallion in *Taylor v. Johnston*, was summarized in an obituary of this remarkable creature by Leon Rasmussen in the *Daily Racing Form* of February 3, 1979:

> Fleet Nasrullah, who passed away in his paddock at Spendthrift the other day at age 24, was one of this observer's all-time favorite race horses and sires. He was practically invincible while sprinting, and yet he had enough speed to stay 1⅛ miles on the grass in American record time. He lost the 1¼–mile Santa Anita Handicap in a photo while never changing leads throughout the race. At stud he sired 41 stakes winners (SWs) and his runners are closing in on $10,000,000 in purse earnings.
>
> . . .
>
> Unquestionably, Fleet Nasrullah's name is destined to live on in quality pedigrees on both sides of the family.
>
> That is the way it should be because he was some kind of horse.
>
> * I remember Ellwood Johnston saying after Fleet Nasrullah captured the 1 1/16 mile San Pasqual Handicap at Santa Anita in 1:41⅖, the fastest time at the distance at the track in three years, "he has more sheer speed than any Nasrullah alive. I wouldn't sell him for a million dollars (this was 1960)."
>
> Eddie Arcaro was one dissenter regarding Fleet Nasrullah being the fastest son of Nasrullah, insisting, "I don't know of any Nasrullah that had more speed than Bold Ruler."
>
> The comparison hardly belittles either horse and since Bold Ruler went on to become our premier sire on eight occasions, Arcaro's opinion must be given

the edge. In any case it makes a good case for speed in the sire as both these brilliant sons of Nasrullah made lasting names for themselves at stud.

Johnston obtained Fleet Nasrullah from John Hertz for a bargain-basement price of $150,000. This reporter remembers telling him that the price was ridiculously low. He replied: "In my many years of racing I've only had one losing season. If I sell Fleet Nasrullah I'll assure myself of another year in the black."

After Fleet Nasrullah added the Gr. I Californian to his stakes pelt, along with a Hollywood Premiere victory under the conditioning of Nazworthy, who had been retained by Johnston, even Hertz tried to buy him back for $500,000 but, Johnston, who had bought him primarily as a potential sire for his Old English Rancho, had a "no" reply ready. Pin Oak Farm in Kentucky offered $650,000, but Johnston kept his word that he wouldn't sell him for a million.

Finally, after using him for three years in California to large books at $6,500 a season, Johnston did sell him—for well over a million.

It was a big loss to the state's breeding program but, fortunately, and oddly enough, he sired his best breeding sons, Gummo and Don B., before becoming a "hard boot."

Fleet Nasrullah's dam, the unraced Happy Go Fleet, by Count Fleet, was foaled by Draeh, a winning, full sister to the "futurity specialists," Occupy and Occupation.

As a 2–year–old, Fleet Nasrullah was a brilliant, speed-crazy colt, exploding his tremendous speed all at once and leaving nothing for later. He didn't race at 3 because of a bleeding problem, but then, after 16 months, he came into the hands of Nazworthy who, with limitless patience and perseverance, made him one of the glamour horses in California racing.

Fleet Nasrullah was headstrong, but he was not mean. He was colorful, he was flamboyant and he did everything with a flair and a flourish. He wouldn't go to the post with a substitute pony; he would buckjump his way to the gate and he was a handful to load. However, once in his stall, he was a statue, waiting like a cat watching a bird for the bell. Rarely, if ever, did any horse outbreak him.

John Longden was Fleet Nasrullah's regular rider and while he never said he was a Count Fleet (Fleet Nasrullah's maternal grandsire who won a Triple Crown under Longden), he did consider him at least the best miler of his time. More than once getting off the colt after a winning performance, Longden would exclaim, "Man, he's fast."

Shoemaker was another admirer of Fleet Nasrullah. The only time he rode him and the only time the horse raced on the turf, Fleet Nasrullah changed leads at every turn and set a new American record for 1⅛ miles at Santa Anita.

Privately, he always felt that if he had ridden him in the Santa Anita Handicap, his (Shoe's) ability to make him change leads, where other jockeys failed, would have made the difference.

There is another interesting sidelight to the saga of Fleet Nasrullah.

After he had won his second Premiere Handicap practically eased up in 1:08⅕, one horseman, greatly impressed, asked Nazworthy, "What do you feed that big son of a gun."

"Sex," replied Jim. "He won his first distance stakes (the San Pasqual) five days after covering his first mare, and he runs faster than any horse I ever saw 28 days after covering a dozen mares."

Oak Ridge Construction v. Tolley
Superior Court of Pennsylvania, 1985.
351 Pa.Super. 32, 504 A.2d 1343.

■ HOFFMAN, J.

In June, 1982, the Tolleys and Oak Ridge entered into a contract pursuant to which Oak Ridge agreed to construct a residence on the Tolleys' property for $64,500. The Tolleys provided Oak Ridge with specifications, which were incorporated into the contract, and a plot plan. The specifications contained, inter alia, the following provision:

> 20. Water Supply Drill well 150' deep with 40' of 6' casing, ⅓ H.P. submersible pump and a 21 gallon storage tank. Should well be more than 150' a charge of $6.50 per ft. will be made. Should casing be over 40' a charge of $7.00 per ft. will be made. Should well depth require a deep lift pump, extra cost to be borne by owner. Well depth over 100' may require a larger pump.

Before drilling began, Oak Ridge warned the Tolleys that the well might be very deep because other wells in the area had been drilled to depths of 760 and 975 feet. Oak Ridge then drilled the well at a place indicated by one of the Tolleys' employees after referring to the plot plan. It was completed on August 24, 1982, after being drilled to a depth of 800 feet. On August 27, Oak Ridge sent the Tolleys an invoice including charges of $4225 for the extra 650 feet of drilling and $616 for an extra 88 feet of casing, amounts computed using the rates specified in the contract. On September 2, Mr. Tolley wrote Oak Ridge stating that those charges were "in dispute or disagreement. All work under item 20 (Water Supply) * * * are [sic] to cease pending satisfactory resolution or settlement under item 13 (Arbitration) of our construction agreement." Oak Ridge replied on September 7, stating that it believed that the Tolleys had breached the contract by refusing to pay the invoice and that it was giving them ten days notice under paragraph seven of the contract (Termination by Contractor), which provides as follows:

> Should owner in any manner, by act or omission, violate or breach any covenant herein, then CONTRACTOR may, at his option, terminate this agreement, upon ten (10) days written notice to OWNER of any such violation or breach. Upon failure of OWNER to correct the same within the ten (10) day period, then, and in such event of termination, CONTRACTOR shall be entitled to receive payment for all unpaid materials, labor, and work of sub-contractors, for work and materials completed, installed, delivered on site, and ordered but undelivered and not installed, plus 20% of the total contract price as liquidated damages. In the event CONTRACTOR shall stop work hereunder, he shall in no way be liable for any loss or damage whatsoever as a result thereof.

Oak Ridge also notified the Tolleys that it was stopping work on the house and named an arbitrator in response to Mr. Tolley's letter and pursuant to paragraph thirteen of the contract.[3] On September 10, Mr. Tolley responded, stating, "arbitration under our contract is not advised at this time."

Based upon these facts, the court below found that the Tolleys had committed an anticipatory breach of the contract justifying Oak Ridge's termination. We disagree.

> An anticipatory breach of a contract occurs whenever there has been a definite and unconditional repudiation of a contract by one party communicated to another. A statement by a party that he will not or cannot perform in accordance with agreement creates such a breach.

> In order to constitute a repudiation, a party's language must be sufficiently positive to be reasonably interpreted to mean that the party will not or cannot perform. Mere expression of doubt as to his willingness or ability to perform is not enough to constitute a repudiation, although such an expression may give an obligee reasonable grounds to believe that the obligor will commit a serious breach and may ultimately result in a repudiation * * *. However, language that

---

3. Paragraph 13 of the contract provides as follows: The parties agree, in the event of any dispute or disagreement hereafter arising between them under this contract, or any other matter in connection herewith, the same shall be referred to three arbitrators, one to be selected by OWNER, one to be selected by CONTRACTOR, and a third to be selected by appointee of OWNER and CONTRACTOR, and the decision of the majority shall be final and binding upon the parties, hereto. All appointments hereunder shall be made within ten (10) days after notice from either party that a dispute exists. If for any reason said appointments are not made within the time allowed, then either party shall have the right to their remedies at law. The cost of said arbitration (herein defined as the record costs and the fees of arbitrators) shall be equally borne between OWNER and CONTRACTOR, each to pay his own expenses and attorney's fees.

under a fair reading "amounts to a statement of intention not to perform except on conditions which go beyond the contract" constitutes a repudiation.

Comment 2 to Uniform Commercial Code § 2–610. Restatement, supra § 250 comment b.

In the instant case, we cannot say that the language in Mr. Tolley's letter constituted a "definite and unconditional repudiation" of the contract which "amounts to a statement of intention not to perform except on conditions which go beyond the contract." The letter merely stated that the charges for work performed under item twenty of the contract's specifications were "in dispute or disagreement" and requested resolution of the dispute under the arbitration clause of the contract. The letter did not contain an unequivocal refusal to pay the drilling charges or a repudiation of the entire contract. Thus, when Oak Ridge gave the Tolleys ten days' notice that it was terminating the contract, the Tolleys had not committed an anticipatory breach.

We must therefore turn to the Tolleys' contention that Oak Ridge breached the contract either by (1) drilling the well to the allegedly unreasonable depth of 800 feet or (2) stopping work on the house. In connection with their first allegation, the Tolleys argue that the lower court erred in striking testimony concerning the reasonableness of drilling a well to that depth. We disagree.

Questions of the admission and exclusion of evidence are within the sound discretion of the trial court and will not be reversed on appeal absent an abuse of discretion. The court may exclude evidence that is irrelevant or merely cumulative of other evidence. At trial, the Tolleys sought to introduce testimony to show that it was unreasonable for Oak Ridge to drill an 800 foot well because (1) most wells in the area were not that deep and (2) water found in wells of that depth may be of poor quality. However, item twenty of the contract specifications required Oak Ridge to drill a well 150 feet deep, unless a deeper well was necessary to ensure an adequate water supply, and the well location was established by the plot plan provided by the Tolleys. Furthermore, Oak Ridge warned the Tolleys that other wells in the area had been drilled to depths as great as 975 feet and that a deep well might be necessary to achieve an adequate water supply. Under these circumstances, where the contract required Oak Ridge to dig a well at the site specified by the Tolleys and they had been warned that a deep well might result, we find that evidence concerning the depth of other wells in the area was irrelevant and the lower court did not abuse its discretion in excluding it. In addition, it is well settled law that a contract to dig a well presents a different question from that presented in contracts by manufacturers or builders * * *. While there is an implied understanding in the contracts of manufacturers and builders that the completed subject of the contract shall be reasonably suitable for its purpose, this implication is based upon the supposed superior knowledge of the manufacturer or builder. However, since the quantity, if any, and the quality of water a well will furnish is unknown to both parties, there is no implication, if the contract is silent in these respects, that the well when completed will be a producing well; or, if it is productive, there is no implication as to the quantity or quality of water to be obtained therefrom. *no warranty for fitness*

In the instant case, the contract was silent as to the quality of the water to be produced. We therefore find that the lower court did not abuse its discretion in striking testimony concerning the quality of the water in this well and others of its depth when such quality was not properly at issue.

The Tolleys also allege that Oak Ridge breached the contract by stopping work on the house on September 7. "When performance of a duty under a contract was due, any nonperformance is a breach." Restatement supra § 235(2). If a breach constitutes a material failure of performance, then the non-breaching party is discharged from all liability under the contract. In determining whether a failure of performance is material, we consider the following factors:

a) the extent to which the injured party will be deprived of the benefit which he reasonably expected;

b) the extent to which the injured party can be adequately compensated for that part of that benefit of which he will be deprived;

c) the extent to which the party failing to perform or to offer to perform will suffer forfeiture;

d) the likelihood that the party failing to perform or offer to perform will cure his failure, taking account of all the circumstances including any reasonable assurances;

e) the extent to which the behavior of the party failing to perform or offer to perform comports with standards of good faith and fair dealing.

Restatement, supra, § 241.

material breach?

Here, having found that the Tolleys did not anticipatorily breach the contract, we must find that Oak Ridge breached it by stopping work on the house on September 7 without justification. We must therefore consider whether that breach was material in light of the factors enumerated above. The Tolleys, as the injured party, were deprived of the expected benefits of their contract (i.e., receiving a completed home) by Oak Ridge's work stoppage, and could not be adequately compensated for that deprivation by an award of damages. Furthermore, Oak Ridge's letter of September 7 gave no indication that the company would cure its failure to perform, and, in fact, the record indicates that Oak Ridge never did so act. Of course, a finding of material breach will result in forfeiture for Oak Ridge (i.e., the Tolleys will be discharged from all liability on the contract), however Oak Ridge will be entitled to restitution for any benefit conferred upon the Tolleys by part performance or reliance (i.e., the cost of digging the well) in excess of the loss Oak Ridge caused by its

P breached. material?

own breach. We note that the record contains no evidence concerning whether Oak Ridge's conduct "comports with standards of good faith and fair dealing." Under these circumstances, we find that Oak Ridge's breach constituted a material failure of performance thereby discharging the Tolleys from all liability under the contract.

Finally, the Tolleys contend that the lower court erred in awarding damages to Oak Ridge for the Tolleys' anticipatory breach of the contract. In view of our holding that Oak Ridge, rather than the Tolleys, breached the contract, we agree and remand the case to the lower court for a determination of damages.

———

UNIFORM COMMERCIAL CODE:

§ 2–609. Right to Adequate Assurance of Performance.

(1) A contract for sale imposes an obligation on each party that the other's expectation of receiving due performance will not be impaired. When reasonable grounds for insecurity arise with respect to the performance of either party the other may in writing demand adequate assurance of due performance and until he receives such assurance may if commercially reasonable suspend any performance for which he has not already received the agreed return.

(2) Between merchants the reasonableness of grounds for insecurity and the adequacy of any assurance offered shall be determined according to commercial standards.

(3) Acceptance of any improper delivery or payment does not prejudice the aggrieved party's right to demand adequate assurance of future performance.

(4) After receipt of a justified demand failure to provide within a reasonable time not exceeding thirty days such assurance of due performance as is adequate under the circumstances of the particular case is a repudiation of the contract.

COMMENTS:

1. The section rests on the recognition of the fact that the essential purpose of a contract between commercial men is actual performance and they do not bargain merely for a promise, or for a promise plus the right to win a law suit, and that a continuing sense of reliance and security that the promised performance will be forthcoming when due is an important feature of the bargain. If either the willingness or the ability of a party to perform declines materially between the time of contracting and the time for performance, the other party is threatened with the loss of a substantial part of what he has bargained for. A seller needs protection not merely against

having to deliver on credit to a shaky buyer, but also against having to procure and manufacture the goods, perhaps turning down other customers. Once he has been given reason to believe that the buyer's performance has become uncertain, it is an undue hardship to force him to continue his own performance. Similarly, a buyer who believes that the seller's deliveries have become uncertain cannot safely wait for the due date of performance when he has been buying to assure himself of materials for his current manufacturing or to replenish his stock of merchandise.

4. What constitutes "adequate" assurance of due performance is subject to the same test of factual conditions. For example, where the buyer can make use of a defective delivery, a mere promise by a seller of good repute that he is giving the matter his attention and that the defect will not be repeated, is normally sufficient. Under the same circumstances, however, a similar statement by a known corner-cutter might well be considered insufficient without the posting of a guaranty or, if so demanded by the buyer, a speedy replacement of the delivery involved. By the same token where a delivery has defects, even though easily curable, which interfere with easy use by the buyer, no verbal assurance can be deemed adequate which is not accompanied by replacement, repair, money-allowance or other commercially reasonable cure.

The adequacy of the assurance given is not measured as in the type of "satisfaction" situation affected with intangibles, such as in personal service cases, cases involving a third party's judgment as final, or cases in which the whole contract is dependent on one party's satisfaction, as in a sale on approval. Here, the seller must exercise good faith and observe commercial standards....

The entire foregoing discussion as to adequacy of assurance by way of explanation is subject to qualification when repeated occasions for the application of this section arise. This Act recognizes that repeated delinquencies must be viewed as cumulative. On the other hand, commercial sense also requires that if repeated claims for assurance are made under this section, the basis for these claims must be increasingly obvious.

QUESTIONS AND NOTES

1. Does the UCC entitle an injured party to adequate assurance of future performance after an immaterial breach? How about a material breach? Or is a material breach necessarily also a repudiation which does not require a demand for assurance of performance before taking legal action on it?

2. Is the real test of materiality of a breach of an installment whether or not it is of such a nature as reasonably to destroy confidence in the party who has breached? If it is, should not "retraction" of a material breach before the injured party changes his position always be permitted if such retraction is accompanied by adequate guarantees of performance?

3. Should retraction by the breaching party be necessary after a true immaterial breach? Is it? But after even an immaterial breach, shouldn't the non-breaching party nonetheless be entitled to adequate assurance of performance within thirty days if he requests it as provided in § 2–609? Why should the breaching party object to such a procedure if his breach is truly immaterial?

Pittsburgh–Des Moines Steel Co. v. Brookhaven Manor Water Co.

United States Court of Appeals, Seventh Circuit, 1976.
532 F.2d 572.

■ PELL, J.

The record discloses the following series of events. On July 24, 1968, PDM, a designer, fabricator, and engineer of steel products, submitted a proposal to Brookhaven for the construction of a one-million-gallon water tank for $175,000. The original proposal incorporated, as terms of payment, 60 percent upon receipt of materials in PDM's plant, 30 percent upon completion of erection, and 10 percent upon completion of testing, or within 30 days after the tank had been made ready for testing. The original terms were not satisfactory to Brookhaven's president, Irving Betke, and were subsequently changed. The altered payment term provided that 100% of the contract price was due and payable within 30 days after the tank had been tested and accepted. The altered proposal was signed and accepted by Brookhaven on November 26, 1968.

Sometime during the following month Norman Knuttel, PDM's district manager who had prepared and signed the original and revised proposals, talked to a representative of the Arbanas Construction Company which company had contracted with Brookhaven for the construction of the tank foundation. Knuttel was informed that Brookhaven had received a loan from Diversified Finance Corporation. Although this information as to the receipt of the loan was incorrect, Brookhaven had negotiated with Diversified for a loan for the purpose of the construction which negotiations continued into the following year. Under date of January 3, 1969, PDM's credit manager wrote Diversified with a copy to Betke which letter in part was as follows:

[W]e hereby request a letter assuring that $175,000.00 for payment of the referenced project will be held in escrow and fully committed to payment to us upon completion of referenced elevated tank.

As a matter of good business we are holding this order in abeyance until receipt of such notification.

The contract contained no provision for escrow financing. Brookhaven, through Betke, took no action upon the receipt of the copy of the letter. Subsequently, after further correspondence and meetings, resulting primarily from Brookhaven's not having secured a planned loan of $275,000.00 from Diversified Finance, PDM's credit manager sent an air mail, special delivery letter to Betke, dated March 19, 1969, which suggested that Betke "mail us your personal guarantee of payment of $175,000.00 as per the contract, to protect us in the interim between now and the time your loan is completed."

While the contract specified the payment of the amount mentioned no later than 30 days after completion of the tank, it was silent as to any reference to a personal guarantee by Betke. The letter concluded as follows:

Upon receipt of such guarantee, we could immediately set in motion our shop fabrication which would result in earlier completion of your new tank.

When your loan is completed we will still require a letter of instructions to be forwarded from you to your bank, or other financial institution which extends this loan, that $175,000.00 is to be held in escrow for disbursement only to Pittsburgh–Des Moines Steel Company in accordance with our contract.

The construction of the water tower was scheduled to begin on April 15, 1969. A crew had been scheduled for the site three months previously, and a crew was ready to appear there on April 15, 1969. As matters transpired, however, the tank was never installed at Brookhaven's site. On March 31, 1969, Betke sent PDM Comptroller Harry Kelly his personal financial statement, but he did not send PDM his personal guarantee for the loan. After Betke failed to provide his personal guarantee of the $175,000.00 contract price, PDM took no further steps toward performance.[1] On April 22, 1969, Kelly, PDM Secretary-Treasurer Tom Morris, PDM Sales Manager Dwight Long, and Betke attended a meeting on the Brookhaven premises. Although the record reveals somewhat inconsistent versions of the details of that meeting, it appears that Morris told Betke that PDM would

---

1. The record indicates that as of April 22, 1969, the foundation, the construction of which was the obligation of Brookhaven, had been completed and two thirds of the required tankage parts, which were the obligation of PDM, had been fabricated. However, it is also noted that as late as March 19, 1969, PDM had written Betke that upon the receipt of the guarantee, the shop could immediately set in motion fabrication. It is not clear whether PDM did anything to dispel the clear inference to Betke that there would be no fabrication, or at least further fabrication, until the guarantee had been received.

complete the fabrication of the tank and deliver it to the job site within a matter of weeks but that Betke replied that he had no need for the tank until the following year.

Further efforts to implement the contract broke down completely after April 22, 1969. Brookhaven's installation of the reinforced concrete foundation for the tank had been accomplished at a cost to it of $18,895. Subsequent to the March meeting, Brookhaven purchased additional land and developed two wells which provided an adequate water supply. Brookhaven later sold all its assets, including both equipment and land, to the City of Darien. At the trial of the damages issue, an expert in demolition testified that the cost of removing the reinforced concrete foundation would be about $7,000. On the basis of this testimony, which was proffered upon the legal theory that Brookhaven had a right to recover the cost of the removal, the district court found that the total amount of damages sustained by Brookhaven was the sum of $25,895.00 and entered judgment in its favor for that amount.

II. Claimed Bases of Liability

Under the contract as executed, into which prior negotiations had been merged, Brookhaven's performance of its principal obligation to pay the purchase price was not due until after the completion of construction. Nevertheless within a period of time shortly more than one month after the contract became effective, PDM was requesting that a prospective lender of the funds to Brookhaven should hold the entire $175,000.00 in escrow. This was not a request that a lending institution give a letter of intent or otherwise confirm that it would make a particular loan when the payment became due after completion of construction. Instead the letter explicitly would, if honored, have required Brookhaven to complete all necessary loan papers and to arrange for the consummation of the loan, the proceeds of which would then be held by Diversified for some months until the work was completed. It is no answer to say that perhaps Brookhaven could have arranged for the escrowed fund to have been invested in some safe, readily liquidable form which might offset in part at least the loss to Brookhaven resulting from having to pay interest on money already borrowed. PDM having purported to agree not to ask for progress payments during the course of construction, more than half of which would have been due before the first act took place by PDM on the construction site, it now was substituting another requirement clearly beyond any requirement contemplated in the contract which would not have put the purchase price in hand but would nevertheless have it where it could be available for the picking at the appropriate time. The contract is silent as to any right of PDM to insist Brookhaven provide any such guarantee during the period before completion of construction. Further, PDM made it quite clear that it was "holding this order in abeyance until receipt of" notification that the money was being so held. We find no basis for an inference that at this time Brookhaven was not ready, willing and able to perform its obligations under the contract nor that it would not be able to pay when it owed. The fact that there had been negotiations for a loan of money that would not be needed for some months, which negotiations had not come to fruition, does not support such an inference. Two months after the letter to Diversified, PDM reaffirmed its lack of retreat from the position of requiring assurance that the money would be forthcoming.

PDM argues that its position was in accordance with Section 2–609 of the Uniform Commercial Code (UCC) enacted into law in Illinois. That section which "creates a new contract enforcement procedure for the situation where one party feels insecure as to the other's performance" reads in pertinent portion as follows:

[UCC § 2–609, quoted here, is reprinted at p. 864]

There appears to be considerable doubt that a seller was entitled to this protection prior to the adoption of the UCC; therefore before deciding that question we address ourselves to whether the UCC is applicable to the present transaction. That determination is primarily dependent upon whether the one-million gallon water tank constitutes "goods" within the meaning of the UCC which defines the term in § 2–105(1) as: "'Goods' means all things, including specially manufactured goods, which are movable at the time of identification to the contract for sale other than the money in which the price is to be paid, investment securities (Article 8) and things in action."

. . .

The district court apparently regarded the matter as being the not entirely unfamiliar situation of a corporate credit department not viewing a contract of sale with the same *joie de vivre* as did the sales department; but the court thought that the sales department had legally committed the firm and that the credit department had gone beyond the grounds for actuating the assurance provided by the statute.

We find ample support in the cases arising under the UCC itself that the scope of coverage of "goods" is not to be given a narrow construction but instead should be viewed as being broad in scope so as to carry out the underlying purpose of the Code of achieving uniformity in commercial transactions. The Code, which by its own terms, § 1–102, is to be liberally construed, should be uniformly applied to achieve its purposes. We believe Illinois would so decide. In the present case, while the finished tank was scarcely one to be taken off the shelf, we are unaware of any authority that specially manufactured small dies should be goods and a very large tank not so classified. In the words of the UCC this was a "movable" "thing" "specially manufactured." That which PDM agreed to sell and Brookhaven agreed to buy was not services but goods as defined in the UCC.

That determination, however, is not dispositive of the ultimate issue. The question remaining is whether PDM's actions subsequent to the execution of the contract were within the protection provided by § 2–609. We hold that they were not.

The performance to which PDM was entitled was the full payment of the purchase price within a specified time after the completion of the tank. While we have a substantial question as to whether PDM made a written demand as required by the statute, in keeping with our concept that the UCC should be liberally construed, we do not desire to rest our decision on a formalistic approach. Letters were written which conveyed what PDM wanted done before they would pursue their obligations under the contract. The fundamental problem is that these letters, if they be deemed to be in the nature of a demand, demanded more than that to which PDM was entitled and the demand was not founded upon what in our opinion was an actuating basis for the statute's applicability.

We do not construe § 2–609 as being a vehicle without more for an implied term being inserted in a contract when a substantially equivalent term was expressly waived in the contract. The something more to trigger applicability of the statute is that the expectation of due performance on the part of the other party entertained at contracting time no longer exists because of "reasonable grounds for insecurity" arising. We find that PDM's actions in demanding either the escrowing of the purchase price or a personal guarantee lacked the necessary predicate of reasonable grounds for insecurity having arisen. The contract negates the existence of any basis for insecurity at the time of the contract when PDM was willing to wait 30 days beyond completion for payment. The fact that Brookhaven had not completed its loan negotiations does not constitute reasonable grounds for insecurity when the money in question was not to be needed for some months. Reasonable business men prefer in the absence of some compulsive reason not to commence paying interest on borrowed money until the time for the use for that money is at hand. The credit manager's January letter that the order was being held in abeyance until receipt of notification of escrowing was based upon a "matter of good business," but not upon any change of condition bearing upon Brookhaven's ability to discharge its payment obligation under the contract. With regard to the later request for a personal guarantee, it is not uncommon for an individual to decline assuming obligations of a corporation in which he is a shareholder. Indeed, the use of the corporate device frequently has as a principal purpose the limitation on individual exposure to liability. If an unfavorable risk in dealing with a corporation exists at contracting time, good business judgment may well indicate that an assurance be secured before contracting that there will be individual shareholder backup. None of this occurred and the record is silent as to any reasonable grounds for insecurity arising thereafter.

It is true that one officer of PDM testified that the company did not send a crew because we questioned whether we might be paid for the project "at that time." Some more objective factual basis than a subjective questioning, in our opinion, is needed to demonstrate reasonable grounds for insecurity. Likewise, another PDM officer testified that it was the company's normal and regular procedure not to erect a structure "until we have reason to believe that the funds to pay for the structure are available." The time of which he was speaking was a time at which there was no contractual requirement that the funds be available. The funds were only required to be available after completion of installation. He testified further that the normal procedure was not to erect until satisfactory arrangements were made. None of this subjectively normal procedure was imposed as a provision in the contract which in view of the withdrawn provision for progress payments showed reasonably to Brookhaven that not only payment, but arrangements for payment, would not be necessary until after completion.

We, of course, would not deprive PDM of resort to § 2-609 if there had been a demonstration that reasonable grounds for insecurity had arisen. The proof in that respect was lacking. The comptroller and supervisor of PDM's credit department testified that he had access to all of the credit information that the company had regarding Brookhaven, that he had reviewed that information, and that he was unaware of any change in the financial condition of Brookhaven between November of 1968 and the end of 1969. Finally, we note that despite the professed subjective questioning in April as to whether PDM might be paid, the credit manager as early as January had said that the job would be held in abeyance until arrangements had been made for escrowing and a month after the questioning, the questioning officer had offered to proceed with construction in exchange for an interest in Brookhaven, an unlikely course if Brookhaven were financially in a questionable condition. There was also testimony with the same inference that PDM was not fearful of Brookhaven's financial stability or ability to pay in connection with PDM lending to Brookhaven the amount involved at an interest rate of 9½% which rate was then unacceptable to Brookhaven. If the buyer was unable to pay for the performance of the contract, it is difficult to see that it was better able to pay a promissory note. We do not fault Brookhaven for its rejection of various proposals advanced by PDM each of which amounted to a rewriting of the contract in the absence of a proper § 2-609 basis. The fact, if it were a fact, that Brookhaven may not have had a large amount of cash lying in the bank in a checking account, not an unusual situation for a real estate developer, does not support the belief that it, as a company with substantial assets, would fail to meet its obligations as they fell due. Section 2-609 is a protective device when reasonable grounds for insecurity arise; it is not a pen for rewriting a contract in the absence of those reasonable grounds having arisen, particularly when the proposed rewriting involves the very factors which had been waived by the one now attempting to wield the pen. The situation is made no more persuasive for PDM when it is recalled that that company was the original scrivener.

Brookhaven's request to put off the contract for a year clearly came after PDM's repudiation of the contract and was indicative of nothing more than that Brookhaven was willing to undertake a new arrangement with PDM a year hence. Pursuant to § 2–610 of the UCC, Brookhaven was entitled to suspend its own performance by virtue of the anticipatory repudiation by PDM and to resort to available remedies, including damages pursuant to § 2–711 of the Code.

Affirmed.

■ CUMMINGS, J., concurring.

Although I agree with the result reached in the majority opinion, I differ with the reasoning. Reasonable men could certainly conclude that PDM had legitimate grounds to question Brookhaven's ability to pay for the water tank. When the contract was signed, the parties understood that Brookhaven would obtain a loan to help pay for the project. When the loan failed to materialize, a prudent businessman would have "reasonable grounds for insecurity." I disagree that there must be a fundamental change in the financial position of the buyer before the seller can invoke the protection of UCC § 2–609. Rather, I believe that the Section was designed to cover instances where an underlying condition of the contract, even if not expressly incorporated into the written document, fails to occur. See Comment 3 to UCC § 2–609. Whether, in a specific case, the breach of the condition gives a party "reasonable grounds for insecurity" is a question of fact for the jury.

UCC § 2–609, however, does not give the alarmed party a right to redraft the contract. Whether the party invoking that provision is merely requesting an assurance that performance will be forthcoming or whether he is attempting to alter the contract is a mixed question of law and fact, depending in part upon the court's interpretation of the obligations imposed on the parties. In this case, PDM would have been assured only if significant changes in the contract were made, either by receiving Betke's personal guarantee, by attaining escrow financing or by purchasing an interest in Brookhaven. The district court could properly conclude as a matter of law that these requests by PDM demanded more than a commercially "adequate assurance of due performance."

QUESTIONS AND NOTES

1. This case illustrates a classic conflict between the corporate sales and credit departments. The world looks very rosy to salespersons; it is optimism that makes sales. The world looks very risky to credit managers; you never can tell when the healthiest of debtors will suddenly go belly up or the most saintly appearing debtor will turn out to be a crook who has run off with the security. Judges in contract cases like to talk about the intent of the parties. When the parties are corporations that

intent is especially problematic. Where does one look to discover the intention of a corporation, into the vast, sunny chambers of the salesman's cheery heart or into the dark, fear-constricted cells of the credit manager's mind?

2. Under its original proposal PDM would have received 90% of the purchase price by completion of the job, but under the modified deal they would receive nothing until 30 days after "testing and acceptance." Can you think of a sensible reason why Brookhaven would require these terms? After all, water tank construction would not appear a very risky business, no one suggests that the Pittsburgh–Des Moines Steel Company is not fully solvent, and water tank technology has been around a long time.

3. This deal fell apart when it became clear that Brookhaven's anticipated bank loan "had failed to materialize." What would you advise PDM to do when that happened? Do you think it should have continued with the project? What were its alternatives?

4. Is any request for modification potentially a material breach? How should PDM handle this situation next time? Perhaps all sales invoices should bear in large type the legend, "ALL ORDERS ACCEPTED SUBJECT TO APPROVAL BY THE CREDIT DEPARTMENT."

5. Compare the approach taken in this case to the question whether this contract was a sale of goods governed by the UCC with that taken in *Printing Center of Texas v. Supermind Publishing*, p. 824.

■ LEARNED HAND, J., in *New York Trust Co. v. Island Oil & Transport Corp.*, 34 F.2d 653, 654 (2d Cir. 1929):

It is, indeed, one of the consequences of the doctrine of anticipatory breach that, if damages are assessed before the time of performance has expired, the court must take the chance of forecasting the future as best it can. That does not mean that it will ignore what has happened, when the period of performance has already expired. Damages never do more than restore the injured party to the position he would have been in, had the promisor performed; this is not a rule peculiar to anticipatory breach, though that is an instance. Hence it is always an answer, in that or other similar situations, to show that, had the contract continued, the promisee would not have been entitled to the performance, though he was apparently so entitled when the promisor disabled himself or repudiated.

Model Vending v. Stanisci

New Jersey Superior Court, Law Div., 1962.
74 N.J.Super. 12, 180 A.2d 393.

■ RIZZI, J.D.C. (temporarily assigned). This is an action for breach of contract by the defendant in which plaintiff seeks damages for loss of profits under a written contract entered into between the parties under date of August 15, 1958. Plaintiff is in the business of leasing various types of merchandise machines, and on the above date the parties entered into a written agreement whereby machines were to be placed by plaintiff into defendant's bowling alley premises for a period of five years. This contract gave plaintiff the exclusive privilege of placing its machines for the purpose of selling the merchandise described therein at defendant's location during the existence of the contract. The case was tried by the court without a jury and, after the trial was completed, the court pronounced its findings of fact and conclusions of law which included, *inter alia,* that defendant had breached the contract on or about July 28, 1959 by having closed down plaintiff's machines and having commenced the sale of various items of merchandise through other methods on the premises in question. There was also the finding of fact that defendant's bowling alley premises had been completely destroyed by fire on March 24, 1961 and had never been reconstructed thereafter. Plaintiff claimed damages for loss of profits that he would have enjoyed during the five-year period commencing on August 15, 1958 and continuing until August 15, 1963.

The issues remaining to be decided were whether the contract became impossible of performance by the fire of March 24, 1961, and if so, whether such impossibility, in the face of the prior breach of the said contract, would disentitle plaintiff to damages for the full five-year period or until August 15, 1963, or whether such damages would be limited to the time before the fire.

It is defendant's contention that the destruction of the premises on which the contract was to be performed thereby made the contract impossible of performance as of that date, and that plaintiff is only entitled to collect damages for loss of profits from the date of the contract to the date of the fire. Plaintiff contends that at the time of the fire defendant had already breached the contract, and therefore defendant's liability would continue during the full life of the contract, namely, until August 15, 1963, notwithstanding the destruction of the premises aforesaid. It has been conceded by the parties that if plaintiff is entitled to recover damages for the full five-year period, he will obtain a judgment for the sum of $7,924.21; but if plaintiff is limited in damages to the date of the fire aforesaid, he will be entitled to a judgment in the amount of $2,507.27.

I ... find no difficulty in concluding as a matter of law that the destruction of the bowling alley premises on March 24, 1961 made the contract impossible of performance on that date.

Plaintiff urges, however, that the contract was already in breach on the day of the fire and that its damages should be measured during the entire five-year life of the contract. The court has already concluded that such breach occurred on or about July 28, 1959, when defendant had ceased the use of plaintiff's machines and had commenced the use of other facilities for the sale of merchandise described in the contract. The diligent research of counsel has failed to produce any precedent by the courts of the State of New Jersey that deal directly with the factual situation herein described....

A reasonable analogy to the problem of supervening impossibility is found in the law of contracts concerning illegality as a defense, and particularly in situations where a contract was legal when made and an anticipatory repudiation of the contract followed by the promisor and thereafter the performance of the acts contracted for had become illegal. This type of a situation is treated in 6 Williston, Contracts (rev. ed. 1938), § 1759, p. 4996, wherein the author states the following to be the law:

> Where there has been an anticipatory repudiation of the contract and subsequently, but before the date when the promised performance becomes due, that performance is made illegal, a practical defect in the doctrine of anticipatory breach is illustrated. The difficulty is not peculiar to cases of supervening illegality but is involved in every other case where, after an anticipatory breach, supervening impossibility occurs which would in any event prevent and excuse performance of the contract. The situation differs, also, in only a slight particular, hereafter referred to, from one where it appears after the anticipatory breach that though there were no legal excuse the return performance could not or would not have been rendered to the repudiator. In each of these cases, if all the facts could have been known or foreseen at the time of the repudiation, no cause of action on the contract would have arisen. It is a practical disadvantage of the doctrine of anticipatory breach that an action may be brought and perhaps judgment obtained before the facts occur which prove that there should have been no recovery. Fortunately in most cases this evidence, though not available at the time of the repudiation, becomes available before judgment can be obtained.

> It seems clear that if the evidence thus becomes available the plaintiff can recover no substantial damages, and in the case of supervening illegality which is not due to the defendant's fault, there seems no reason to allow even nominal damages. The loss should rest where chance has placed it; and the same should be true in case of any supervening excusable impossibility.

Restatement, Contracts, § 457, p. 849 (1932), discusses the effect of supervening impossibility in the following language:

> Except as stated in § 455, where, after the formation of a contract facts that a promisor had no reason to anticipate, and for the occurrence of which he is not in contributing fault, render performance of the promise impossible, the duty of the promisor is discharged, unless a contrary intention has been manifested, even though he has already committed a breach by anticipatory repudiation; but where such facts occur after the time when performance of a promise is due, they do not discharge a duty to make compensation for a breach of contract.

Following the above statement of law, various comments appear. Comment (d) appears to be particularly appropriate to the issue here involved and is stated as follows:

> Impossibility on the part of a promisor occurring after he has committed a breach does not ordinarily discharge him, but it will do so if the breach consists merely of an anticipatory repudiation. After a breach of any other kind impossibility supervening before the time for full performance has elapsed will limit the damages recoverable if the impossibility would have occurred had there been no breach. Thus if an employer or employee who breaks his contract becomes so ill shortly afterwards that the contract could not have been performed, recovery will be limited.

The weight of authority leads the court to the view that upon breach of contract by a promisor, supervening impossibility occurring through destruction of the subject matter without the fault of the promisor will limit the damages recoverable to the time before the impossibility has taken place.

Judgment will be entered for the plaintiff in the sum of $2,507.27 and costs.

QUESTION AND NOTE

This decision is a clear statement of a generally accepted rule in cases of anticipatory repudiation, that is when the obligation is repudiated before performance is due. When the only breach is a repudiation, a court in assessing damages will take into account supervening events between breach and trial. Implicit in that doctrine is the idea that if the contract is terminated by a present material breach by nonperformance, rather than a repudiation, the disappointed party's rights are fixed as of the date of the breach, and its claim to the full expectancy is not diminished by later events. The only remaining question in this case is whether Stanisci closing down Model Vending's machines was merely an anticipatory repudiation or a present material breach by nonperformance. While you are worrying about that, consider again *Taylor v. Johnston,* p. 850. Was the breach there present or anticipatory?

CHAPTER 9

EFFECTS OF CONTRACT ON NONPARTIES

Up to this point, we have examined the effect of an agreement on the legal relations between the persons who made it. This Chapter examines the problems that arise when the community of the agreement expands to include or otherwise affect others.

Contracting parties create a special legal status for themselves: They invoke the law to lend force to *their* claims. The first two topics of this Chapter examine the traditional legal rights and obligations arising out of a contract with respect to two types of nonparties. We shall be looking at two interrelated questions: (a) who, besides parties to a contract, can claim its benefits and enforce its obligations; and (b) when can the benefits and burdens of contractual obligation be transferred from a contracting party to a third person. The first issue is labeled "rights of third-party beneficiaries," and the second usually discussed under the heading "assignment of contract." The final topic in this Chapter will examine how the existence of a contract may create obligations on nonparties to respect it.

Much of contract law is grounded on unrealistically individualistic assumptions about human interactions. Contracting parties are treated as if the contract is exclusively their private concern and as if society exists solely to support and enforce their autonomous undertakings. In fact, complex societies are extremely and persistently interdependent, and that interdependency and the relationships that arise out of it are both related to and independent of particular contracts.

The performance of an agreement to supply a manufacturer with raw materials will determine the price, availability and quality of its product to its customers and ultimately to individual consumers. It also will affect the manufacturer's workers, the truckers that carry its goods to market, and the retailers that sell goods to individuals, including perhaps the manufacturer's own workers and those of its supplier. Breach of the agreement will affect not only the immediate parties to the agreement, but a whole community of persons, some of whose vital interests will be at stake. We usually think of the contract as an exercise of private autonomy, as the creature of the parties who made it. To what extent does the law also recognize that the contract "belongs" to a larger community?

The issues discussed in this Chapter are vital to the usefulness of contract in a modern economy. By recognizing the rights of third-party beneficiaries, the ambit of private lawmaking is enlarged. Enforcement of collective bargaining agreements, consumer warranties, and creditor rights all depend on this. And when the law allows contracts to be freely assigned to third parties, it converts contract from a personal promise to a commodity that may be traded in the market.

Note the interaction between jurisprudential rationales for legal doctrine and social and economic factors. For example, the difficulties the law had in accepting the transferability of intangible contract rights could be understood as a purely conceptual hang-up of a simpler age based on the "strictly personal" nature of the relationship between contracting parties. But you will miss the most important lessons to be learned if you stop there without examining the social and economic effects of this doctrine at the time it developed. The doctrine loses its air of arid scholasticism when you consider it in the light of a 17th century decision by Lord Coke suggesting that the non-assignability of intangibles prevents the social and economic positions of landed gentry and nobles from passing to their creditors by assignment. Viewed in this light, we can follow Professor Gilmore's suggestion that "the results Coke feared were perhaps of the same order as those which have prompted modern legislation prohibiting or restricting the assignment of wage claims." GRANT GILMORE, SECURITY INTERESTS IN PERSONAL PROPERTY § 7.3 (1965).

I.   THIRD-PARTY BENEFICIARIES

Does the benefit of a contract inhere only in the parties, or may others generally claim damages by showing an interest in performance or injury by a breach? The answer, of course, lies between these two extremes. Long before the modern law of contract developed, the common law enforced a variety of agreements made for the benefit of a third party. For example, the courts very early recognized that the beneficiary of a trust can legally enforce the trustee's obligations, although the beneficiary is not a party to the transaction creating the trust. Similarly, the relationship of principal and agent was developed at an early stage to the point where persons doing business with the agent, but having no direct contact with his principal, could enforce obligations against the principal.

The difficulty with third-party beneficiary rights in contract arose in the 19th century as the concept of consideration rigidified into hard doctrine. Enforcement by the beneficiary would be challenged on the ground that there was "no mutuality of obligation," citing the English doctrine of that time that consideration must be given by the plaintiff who seeks to enforce the promise. Sometimes this requirement would be characterized as conditioning enforcement on showing "privity of contract."

Under this rigid approach, the practical result was that a contracting party could be quite sure that its legal liability under the agreement was limited to claims by the other contracting parties. It was relatively secure from finding itself in a position where it had to answer to "strangers" for the adequacy of its performance. Creation of a third-party relationship expands the community of the contract by admitting a new party to it. It does not displace the relationship between the original parties; they remain tied to each other and add the new party to their group.

A.   ENFORCEMENT BY A BENEFICIARY

Lawrence v. Fox
New York Court of Appeals, 1859.
20 N.Y. 268.

Appeal from the Superior Court of the City of Buffalo. On the trial before Mr. Justice Masten, it appeared by the evidence of a by-stander that one Holly in November, 1857, at the request of the defendant, loaned and advanced to him $300, stating at the time that he owed that sum to the plaintiff for money borrowed of him, and had agreed to pay it to him the then next day; that the defendant, in consideration thereof, at the time of receiving the money promised to pay it to the plaintiff the then next day. Upon this state of facts the defendant moved for a nonsuit, upon three several grounds, viz.: That there was no proof tending to show that Holly was indebted to the plaintiff, that the agreement by the defendant with Holly to pay the plaintiff was void for want of consideration, and that there was no privity between the plaintiff and defendant. The court overruled the motion, and the counsel for the defendant excepted. The cause was then submitted to the jury, and they found a verdict for the plaintiff for the amount of the loan and interest, $344.66, upon which judgment was entered, from which the defendant appealed to the Superior Court, at General Term, where the judgment was affirmed, and the defendant appealed to this court. The cause was submitted on printed arguments.

■ H. GRAY, J. ....

[It] is claimed that notwithstanding this promise was established by competent evidence, it was void for the want of consideration. It is now more than a quarter of a century since it was settled by the supreme court of this state—in an able and painstaking opinion by the late Chief Justice Savage, in which the authorities were fully examined and carefully analyzed—that a promise in all material respects like the one under consideration was valid; and the judgment of that court was unanimously affirmed by the court for the correction of errors. Farley v. Cleveland, 4 Cow. 432, 15 Am.Dec. 387; s.c. in error, 9 Cow. 639. In that case one Moon owed Farley and sold to Cleveland a quantity of hay, in consideration of which Cleveland promised to pay Moon's debt to Farley; and the decision in favor of Farley's right to recover was placed upon the ground that the hay received by Cleveland from Moon was a valid consideration for Cleveland's promise to pay Farley, and that the subsisting liability of Moon to pay Farley was no objection to the recovery. The fact that the money advanced by Holly to the defendant was a loan to him for a day, and that it thereby became the property of the defendant, seemed to impress the defendant's counsel with the idea that because the defendant's promise was not a trust fund placed by the plaintiff in the defendant's hands, out of which he was to realize money as from the sale of a chattel or the collection of a debt, the promise although made for the benefit of the plaintiff could not inure to his benefit. The hay which Cleveland bought of Moon was not to be paid to Farley, but the debt incurred by Cleveland for the purchase of the hay, like the debt incurred by the defendant for money borrowed, was what was to be paid.

That case has been often referred to by the courts of this state, and has never been doubted as sound authority for the principle upheld by it. It puts to rest the objection that the defendant's promise was void for want of consideration. The report of that case shows that the promise was not only made to Moon but to the plaintiff Farley. In this case the promise was made to Holly and not expressly to the plaintiff; and this difference between the two cases presents the question, raised by the defendant's objection, as to the want of privity between the plaintiff and defendant. As early as 1806 it was announced by the supreme court of this state, upon what was then regarded as the settled law of England, "That where one person makes a promise to another for the benefit of a third person, that third person may maintain an action upon it." *Schemerhorn v. Vanderheyden*, has often been reasserted by our courts and never departed from....

But it is urged that because the defendant was not in any sense a trustee of the property of Holly for the benefit of the plaintiff, the law will not imply a promise. I agree that many of the cases where a promise was implied were cases of trusts, created for the benefit of the promisor. The case of *Felton v. Dickinson*, and others that might be cited are of that class; but concede them all to have been cases of trusts, and it proves nothing against the application of the rule of this case. The duty of the trustee to pay the cestui que trust, according to the terms of the trust, implies his promise to the latter to do so. In this case the defendant, upon ample consideration received from Holly, promised Holly to pay his debt to the plaintiff; the consideration received and the promise to Holly made it as plainly his duty to pay the plaintiff as if the money had been remitted to him for that purpose, and as well implied a promise to do so as if he had been made a trustee of property to be converted into cash with which to pay. The fact that a breach of the duty imposed in the one case may be visited, and justly, with more serious consequences than in the other, by no means disproves the payment to be a duty in both. The principle illustrated by the example so frequently quoted (which concisely states the case in hand) "that a promise made to one for the benefit of another, he for whose benefit it is made may bring an action for its breach," has been applied to trust cases, not because it was exclusively applicable to those cases, but because it was a principle of law, and as such applicable to those cases.

It was also insisted that Holly could have discharged the defendant from his promise, though it was intended by both parties for the benefit of the plaintiff, and, therefore, the plaintiff was not entitled to maintain this suit for the recovery of a demand over which he had no control. It is enough that the plaintiff did not release the defendant from his promise, and whether he could or not is a question not now necessarily involved; but if it was, I think it would be found difficult to maintain the right of Holly to discharge a judgment recovered by the plaintiff upon confession or otherwise, for the breach of the defendant's promise; and if he could not, how could he discharge the suit before judgment, or the promise before suit, made as it was for the plaintiff's benefit and in accordance with legal presumption accepted by him, until his dissent was shown?

The cases cited and especially that of *Farley v. Cleveland*, established the validity of a parol promise; it stands then upon the footing of a written one. Suppose the defendant had given his note in which for value received of Holly, he had promised to pay the plaintiff and the plaintiff had accepted the promise, retaining Holly's liability. Very clearly Holly could not have discharged that promise, be the right to release the defendant as it may. No one can doubt that he owes the sum of money demanded of him, or that in accordance with his promise it was his duty to have paid it to the plaintiff; nor can it be doubted that whatever may be the diversity of opinion elsewhere, the adjudications in this state, from a very early period, approved by experience, have established the defendant's liability; if, therefore it could be shown that a more strict and technically accurate application of the rules applied, would lead to a different result (which I by no means concede), the effort should not be made in the face of manifest justice.

The judgment should be affirmed.

■ JOHNSON, C.J., and DENIO, J., based their judgment upon the ground that the promise was to be regarded as made to the plaintiff through the medium of his agent, whose action he could ratify when it came to his knowledge, though taken without his being privy thereto.

■ COMSTOCK, J. (dissenting). The plaintiff had nothing to do with the promise on which he brought this action. It was not made to him, nor did the consideration proceed from him. If he can maintain the suit, it is because an anomaly has found its way into the law on this subject. In general, there must be privity of contract. The party who sues upon a promise must be the promisee, or he must have some legal interest in the undertaking. In this case, it is plain that Holly, who loaned the money to the defendant, and to whom the promise in question was made, could at any time have claimed that it should be performed to himself personally. He had lent the money to the defendant, and at the same time directed the latter to pay the sum to the plaintiff. This direction he could countermand, and if he had done so, manifestly the defendant's promise to pay according to the direction would have ceased to exist. The plaintiff would receive a benefit by a complete execution of the arrangement, but the arrangement itself was between other parties, and was under their exclusive control. If the defendant had paid the money to Holly, his debt would have been discharged thereby. So Holly might have released the demand or assigned it to another person, or the parties might have annulled the promise now in question, and designated some other creditor of Holly as the party to whom the money should be paid. It has never been claimed that in a case thus situated the right of a third person to sue upon the promise rested on any sound principle of law. We are to inquire whether the rule has been so established by positive authority....

The cases in which some trust was involved are ... frequently referred to as authority for the doctrine now in question, but they do not sustain it. If A. delivers money or property to B., which the latter accepts upon a trust for the benefit of C., the latter can enforce the trust by an appropriate action for that purpose. If the trust be of money, I think the beneficiary may assent to it and bring the action for money had and received to his use. If it be of something else than money, the trustee must account for it according to the terms of the trust, and upon principles of equity. There is some authority even for saying that an express promise founded on the possession of a trust fund may be enforced by an action at law in the name of the beneficiary, although it was made to the creator of the trust. Thus, in Comyn, Dig. "Action on the Case upon Assumpsit," B. 15, it is laid down that if a man promise a pig of lead to A., and his executor give lead to make a pig to B., who assumes to deliver it to A., an assumpsit lies by A. against him. The case of *Delaware & H. Canal Co. v. Westchester County Bank* involved a trust because the defendants had received from a third party a bill of exchange under an agreement that they would endeavor to collect it, and would pay over the proceeds when collected to the plaintiffs. A fund received under such an agreement does not belong to the person who receives it. He must account for it specifically; and perhaps there is no gross violation of principle in permitting the equitable owner of it to sue upon an express promise to pay it over. Having a specific interest in the thing, the undertaking to account for it may be regarded as in some sense made with him through the author of the trust. But further than this we cannot go without violating plain rules of law. In the case before us there was nothing in the nature of a trust or agency. The defendant borrowed the money of Holly and received it as his own. The plaintiff had no right in the fund, legal or equitable. The promise to repay the money created an obligation in favor of the lender to whom it was made and not in favor of any one else.

The judgment of the court below should, therefore, be reversed, and a new trial granted.

QUESTIONS AND NOTES

1. What consideration did Fox get from the plaintiff? Was Lawrence a "promisee"? If Fox had promised Holly that he would promise Lawrence to pay Holly's debt, and he had done so the same day, would there have been "privity" between Lawrence and Fox?

2. Could Lawrence have sued both Holly and Fox? Could he have recovered against both? Could Holly now sue Fox? For what damages?

3. Judge Gray treats this problem as a general one of the enforceability of promises, while four of his colleagues consider the issue more appropriately decided in terms of agency or trust concepts. How should a judge decide which legal category applies? Aren't all agencies and trusts essentially third-party beneficiary situations? Don't most commercial contract beneficiary situations involve elements resembling agencies and trusts? As we will see later in this Chapter, our tendency to divide problems into conventional categories like contract, tort, and trusts, often causes more trouble than it helps. Given this tendency, how should a lawyer with a problem decide which category the particular problem fits in? Consider the question from the position of advocate, counselor with a client, and judge.

4. *Lawrence v. Fox* is a classic case in the law. Yet of the eight judges who sat in the New York Court of Appeals on the case, only three joined Judge Gray in his opinion. Of the remaining four, two flatly dissented, and the other two—although joining Gray for affirmance—did so for reasons other than his. What do you think would be the result if you argued to a court that Judge Gray's opinion is not the law because it is not a statement by a majority of the court?

5. Professor Anthony Jon Waters has written a comprehensive and provocative review of the historical records in this case. His article connects the rule in *Lawrence v. Fox* with special characteristics of the contractual "common counts" at common law and with the procedural code reform that was occurring in New York at the time of the case, as well as with the emergence during the 1960's and 1970's of the theory that members of benefitted groups have an enforceable right in claims to government service and welfare programs. We shall return to the contemporary aspects of Professor Waters's argument later in this Chapter. Now for the true story of *Lawrence v. Fox*:

From the records of the case, we learn that "Holly" was in fact one Hawley, referred to in the complaint as Samuel Hawley. The Buffalo census of 1855 lists no Samuel Hawley, but of the eighteen Hawleys who are listed, only one appears to have had sufficient means to have been involved in a three hundred dollar cash transaction. He was Merwin Spencer Hawley, a prominent merchant. In 1856, Hawley was President of the Buffalo Board of Trade, an organization with which Fox, at some point, was also connected.... The assumption that Hawley was affluent and available in Buffalo when Lawrence sued Fox does nothing, however, to solve the mystery of why Lawrence chose not to sue him. The solution to that mystery lies in the nature of Lawrence's transaction with Hawley, of which Hawley's dealings with Fox on the next day are highly suggestive.

In 1854, when the transaction took place, three hundred dollars was a very large amount of money. Even among successful entrepreneurs, a loan the size of Hawley's to Fox, to be repaid a day later, must have been out of the ordinary.... At trial in the Superior Court in Buffalo, Fox's attorney, Jared Torrance, shed some light on the nature of that transaction. The only witness in the case was William Riley, by whom Lawrence's attorney, Edward Chapin, had proved that Hawley paid three hundred dollars to Fox; that Hawley told Fox that he, Hawley, owed that amount to Lawrence; and that Fox promised Hawley that he would repay that amount to Lawrence. On cross-examination, Torrance elicited four facts: that Lawrence was not present when Hawley made the loan to Fox; that the deal took place at Mr. Purdy Merritt's on Washington Street; that there were "two or three persons present * * * doing nothing but standing near them"; and that Hawley counted out the money as he handed it to Fox.

The first fact, that Lawrence was not present, formed the basis of Fox's privity defense. This defense makes sense only in an action based on contract, a point to which we shall return. For now, it is the other three facts—the location, the bystanders, and the cash being counted out—that are noteworthy, for they suggest the milieu in which the transaction took place, and help to explain its character.

William Riley, the witness, was a horse dealer. He did his business near the canal, the life line of Buffalo's then-thriving commerce. Not many steps away was Mr. Purdy Merritt's establishment, where the transaction took place; Merritt was also a horse dealer. Torrance's cross-examination presented a more complete picture: two well-to-do merchants in a horse dealer's establishment down by the canal; a large amount of cash changing hands; and several other people present, loitering. Of these facts, not the least significant was the location:

Canal Street was more than a street. It was the name of a district, a small and sinful neighborhood * * *. As late as the 1800's, there were ninety-three saloons there, among which were sprinkled fifteen other dives known as concert halls plus sundry establishments designed to separate the sucker from his money as swiftly as possible, painlessly by preference, but painfully if necessary * * *. It must have been an eternal mystery to the clergy and the good people of the town why the Lord never wiped out this nineteenth century example of Sodom and Gamorrah with a storm or a great wave from Lake Erie.

In his cross-examination of Riley, Attorney Torrance had gone as far as he could go to set the scene for what he then sought to prove directly, also by William Riley: that Hawley lent the money to Fox for Fox to gamble with it, and that this unlawful purpose was known to Hawley.

Trial Judge Joseph Masten did not, however, permit Riley to testify to the alleged link with gambling. Attorney Chapin, for Lawrence, successfully objected on two grounds, neither of which bears upon the probable truth or untruth of the evidence that Riley was prepared to give. As to that question, the facts that Torrance had already elicited do suggest a setting in which gambling could have been taking place. But there is one more fact, this one uncontroverted, that is entirely consistent with the allegation of a connection with gambling and is difficult to explain otherwise. That fact—the central mystery of this case—is that Lawrence chose to sue not his debtor, Hawley, but his debtor's debtor, Fox. If, as seems to be the fact, Hawley was a person of considerable wealth in Buffalo, and if, as alleged, he owed three hundred dollars to Lawrence, then Lawrence must have had compelling reason to neglect the obvious action—suing Hawley—in favor of the much more difficult task of seeking recovery from Fox. A gambling debt would have presented just such a reason. If Hawley's debt to Lawrence from the day before, in the round sum of three hundred dollars, was itself the outcome of gambling and thus unenforceable at law, Lawrence was well advised to look for someone other than Hawley to sue. Furthermore, if we look to the law of gamblers rather than the law of commerce, it is clear that Fox, and not Hawley, was both the villain and the obvious person to pursue.

Commercial transactions were not then and are not now structured in such a way as to leave a creditor with no better means of recovery than to sue his debtor's debtor. The series of events described in *Lawrence v. Fox* makes no commercial sense.... had Lawrence's dealings with Hawley been of a kind condoned and upheld by the law of the land, then Lawrence would surely have sued

Hawley, and not Fox. It is not surprising, therefore, that there was no theory of recovery in the law of contracts by which Lawrence could collect from Fox.

Anthony Jon Waters, *The Property in the Promise: A Study of the Third Party Beneficiary Rule*, 98 HARV. L. REV. 1109, 1123–27 (1985).[*]

B.   WHO IS A BENEFICIARY?

Lawrence v. Fox leaves unsettled what kinds of beneficiaries could enforce any particular obligation. A broad grant of power to claim under the contract to everyone who could show that they would have been benefitted by a performance, and hence had lost by a breach, would have made a shambles of the law. A long-term manufacturing agreement between industrial giants will benefit not only the parties, but may also provide employment to a whole community. In the event of breach, may any employee, citizen, property owner, taxing authority, taxpayer, or shopkeeper sue to enforce the agreement or for the damages he suffers from its breach? Or consider an agreement to build a wonderful museum expected to enrich the cultural life of the community as well as raise neighboring property values. Can disappointed art lovers or neighbors sue for breach and collect damages for the injuries suffered by their souls and their pocketbooks respectively?

The law calls those beneficiaries who cannot claim "incidental beneficiaries" — a label that again neatly states a legal conclusion but is of no help in identifying such a beneficiary. Nor is the oft-stated test of "intent to benefit" of much help, except in the negative sense that there cannot be an intent to benefit anyone not explicitly identified in the contract, either by name or by membership in a well-defined class.

Historically, beneficiaries who *can* claim (i.e., who are not incidental beneficiaries) have been divided into donee (or sole) and creditor beneficiaries. Donees had the easier time getting judicial support. A typical donee might be the beneficiary of a life insurance policy who has trouble collecting from an intransigent insurer and finds that the deceased insured's executor won't sue on his behalf because the estate, after all, has nothing to gain by such action! In such a case, of course, the insured's intent to benefit the beneficiary named by her in the insurance policy is clear.

The creditor cases, of which *Lawrence v. Fox* is the classic example, were (and are) more difficult to justify because discerning an "intent to benefit" the creditor requires a considerable amount of imagination. It takes a lot of double talk to convince anyone that Holly's primary intent in making his deal with Fox was to benefit

---

[*] Copyright 1985, The Harvard Law Review.

his *creditor,* Lawrence. He intended to benefit *himself.* In this sense, intent to benefit is often a fiction—but one that works.

Restatement, Second, Contracts has adopted the label "intended beneficiary" to cover both donee and creditor beneficiaries; and it has retained the label "incidental beneficiary" to cover all those who, unlike the intended beneficiaries, cannot enforce the contract.

————

RESTATEMENT, SECOND, CONTRACTS:

§ 302. Intended and Incidental Beneficiaries.

(1) Unless otherwise agreed between promisor and promisee, a beneficiary of a promise is an intended beneficiary if recognition of a right to performance in the beneficiary is appropriate to effectuate the intention of the parties and either

    (a) the performance of the promise will satisfy an obligation of the promisee to pay money to the beneficiary; or

    (b) the circumstances indicate that the promisee intends to give the beneficiary the benefit of the promised performance.

(2) An incidental beneficiary is a beneficiary who is not an intended beneficiary.

————

Hale v. Groce
Oregon Supreme Court, 1987.
304 Or. 281, 744 P.2d 1289.

■ LINDE, J. Defendant, who is an attorney, was directed by a client to prepare testamentary instruments and to include a bequest of a specified sum to plaintiff. After the client's death, it was discovered that the gift was not included either in the will or in a related trust instrument. After an unsuccessful attempt to obtain judicial reformation of the will and trust, plaintiff brought the present action for damages against the attorney.

The complaint alleged as two separate claims, first, that defendant was negligent in a number of particulars and, second, that he failed to carry out a contractual promise to his client, the decedent, which the decedent had intended specifically for the benefit of plaintiff. In other states plaintiffs in such cases have sometimes been allowed to recover on one or both of these theories, as negligently injured parties or as third-party beneficiaries under a contract. It is a new question in this court.

Defendant moved to dismiss the complaint on grounds that the stated facts did not constitute a claim under either theory and that, at least as to the tort theory, the action was not commenced within the time limited by the applicable statute. The circuit court held that the action was not time-barred but allowed defendant's motion to dismiss both claims. On plaintiff's appeal, the Court of Appeals reinstated plaintiff's negligence claim, and it also remanded for trial her allegations that defendant was estopped from invoking the statute of limitations.

Both parties petitioned this court for review. Defendant asserts that a lawyer owes a professional duty of care only to his client and cannot be sued for malpractice by others who are injured by the way he performs that duty. Plaintiff asks us to reinstate her contract claim as a third-party beneficiary. We hold that the complaint states claims for damages under both theories, a claim as the intended beneficiary of defendant's professional contract with the decedent and a derivative tort claim based on breach of the duty created by that contract to the plaintiff as its intended beneficiary.

The two claims are related, but they differ in important respects. Standing alone, without a duty to plaintiff derived from defendant's contractual undertaking, plaintiff's tort claim would confront the rule that one ordinarily is not liable for negligently causing a stranger's purely economic loss without injuring his person or property. It does not suffice that the harm is a foreseeable consequence of negligent conduct that may make one liable to someone else, for instance to a client. Some source of a duty outside the common law of negligence is required. Even then, tort rules such as comparative fault may apply that do not apply to contract claims. A contract claim, on the other hand, does not necessarily depend on showing negligence.

Similar claims were made in *Currey v. Butcher*, in which attorneys were charged with a faulty search of a title. This court held that they were entitled to an instruction that they would not be liable to a person for whom their client may have acted unbeknownst to them. A chief precedent for *Currey* was *Buckley v. Gray*, which the court cited for the proposition that "an attorney employed to draw a will is not liable to a person who, through the attorney's ignorance or negligence in the discharge of his professional duties, was deprived of the portion of the estate which the testator instructed the attorney should be given such person by the will." *Currey*, 37 Or. at 389.

Since 1900, many courts have reconsidered that proposition, some preferring a contract analysis, some negligence, and at least one "a definite maybe." *Buckley v. Gray* itself was overruled in *Lucas v. Hamm*. The California Supreme Court stated that a lawyer might be liable to an intended testamentary beneficiary either for negligence or for breach of the lawyer's contract with the testator, though the court balked at recognizing professional negligence in a lawyer's failure to meet the state's rule against perpetuities and restraints on alienation.[1] After *Lucas*, the California court treated contract liability as superfluous and settled on negligence theory, which in California calls for applying "public policy" by "balancing" half a dozen "factors" in each case.

The Pennsylvania Supreme Court chose the contrary course in *Guy v. Liederbach*, a claim by a beneficiary who lost a legacy because the testator's lawyer let her subscribe as a witness to the will. The court rejected both open-ended tort liability to foreseeably injured third parties and what it considered the "unworkable" California standard noting that: "* * * although a plaintiff on a third party beneficiary theory in contract may in some cases have to show a deviation from the standard of care, as in negligence, to establish breach, the class of persons to whom the defendant may be liable is restricted by principles of contract law, not negligence principles relating to foreseeability or scope of the risk." Citing *dictum* in an early Pennsylvania decision, *Lawall v. Groman*, the court settled instead on liability to the intended beneficiary under Restatement (Second) Contracts section 302(1) (1981).

The Connecticut Supreme Court similarly allowed a disappointed beneficiary of a testamentary trust to proceed against the testatrix's lawyer on a contract theory over an objection that the lawyer's promise obligated him only to the client and not to the intended beneficiary, because the benefit to the plaintiff also was the essence of the benefit promised to the testatrix.

We agree that the beneficiary in these cases is not only a plausible but a classic "intended" third-party beneficiary of the lawyer's promise to his client within the rule of Restatement section 302(1)(b) and may enforce the duty so created, as stated id. section 304. The promise, of course, was not that the lawyer would pay plaintiff the stipulated sum, and it is too late for the lawyer to perform the promise that he did make, but this does not preclude an action for damages for the nonperformance. In principle, such an action is available to one in plaintiff's position.

Because under third-party analysis the contract creates a "duty" not only to the promisee, the client, but also to the intended beneficiary, negligent nonperformance may give rise to a negligence action as well. Not every such contract will support either claim. A contract to prepare a will or other instrument may promise different things. It may undertake to make a particular disposition by means specified by the client (for instance, in trust, or by a gift of identified property), or to accomplish the intended gift by specified means of the lawyer's choosing. Failure to do what was

---

1. The court stated:

> In view of the state of the law relating to perpetuities and restraints on alienation and the nature of the error, if any, assertedly made by defendant in preparing the instrument, it would not be proper to hold that defendant failed to use such skill, prudence, and diligence as lawyers of ordinary skill and capacity commonly exercise.

promised then would be a breach of contract regardless of any negligence. On the other hand, the lawyer's promise might be to use his best professional efforts to accomplish the specified result with the skill and care customary among lawyers in the relevant community. Because negligence liability of this kind arises only from the professional obligation to the client, it does not threaten to divide a lawyer's loyalty between the client and a potentially injured third party, as defendant argues.

Whether breach of that kind of promise is properly characterized as a breach of contract or as negligence, we have said, depends on the legal rule for which its character is at issue. *Securities–Intermountain v. Sunset Fuel*. That case, like this one, involved an issue whether the action was commenced in time....

The pertinent allegations of the contract claim were:

18. Relying on defendant's promise to select a better legal mechanism by which to give plaintiff the gift, Rogers refrained during his lifetime from giving plaintiff his Cooper Industries stock. Defendant specifically told Rogers that defendant would prepare a trust document wherein Rogers and plaintiff would be co-trustees and through which plaintiff would receive the gift Rogers' [sic] intended her to have. Rogers specifically directed defendant to draft the trust and to include plaintiff's $300,000 gift.

19. On March 8, 1982, defendant presented a trust document to Rogers for Rogers to execute. Defendant told Rogers and plaintiff, who were co-trustees of the trust, that the document included the $300,000 gift to plaintiff. Relying on defendant's representations, Rogers and plaintiff executed the trust without reading it.

20. Defendant and Rogers specifically contracted for defendant to draft the trust document with plaintiff's gift in it. Defendant breached that contract by failing to include the provision for plaintiff to receive the $300,000 gift.

These paragraphs allege breach of a specific promise "that defendant would prepare a trust document wherein Rogers and plaintiff would be co-trustees and through which plaintiff would receive the gift Rogers intended her to have," a "trust document with plaintiff's gift in it." They allege, not that defendant performed this promise negligently, but that he did not perform it at all. As far as these allegations went, he might have broken the promise purposely, or under circumstances that might be a partial or entire defense to a negligence claim.

The allegations of the terms of the contract are not as detailed as those in the architect's contract annexed to the complaint in *Securities–Intermountain*. Whether this agreement in fact was sufficiently specific to go beyond a general promise by defendant to use his professional skills to carry out the assigned project is a matter for proof. Lacking a detailed written contract like that in *Securities–Intermountain*, it may depend on correspondence, memoranda, or testimony. When an alleged contract does not lend itself to incorporation of a writing in the complaint, the issue at least may have to await affidavits and possible counteraffidavits on motion for summary judgment. It should not have been decided on a motion under ORCP 21 to dismiss the complaint....

Pierce Associates v. The Nemours Foundation

United States Court of Appeals, Third Circuit, 1988.
865 F.2d 530.

■ DEBEVOISE, D.J.

I. THE PARTIES AND THE PROCEEDINGS

The Nemours Foundation ("Nemours") owns the Alfred I. duPont Institute Children's Hospital in Wilmington, Delaware. In January 1980 Nemours entered into a general contract with Gilbane Building Company ("Gilbane") for completion of the interior of the Hospital. The Aetna Casualty & Surety Company ("Aetna") became surety on a performance bond which named Gilbane as principal and Nemours as obligee.

Gilbane entered into a number of subcontracts, including a $35.9 million fixed-price subcontract with Pierce Associates, Inc. ("Pierce") pursuant to which Pierce agreed to perform the mechanical work on the project (the heating, ventilation, air-conditioning, plumbing and fire-protection systems). Federal Insurance Company ("Federal") became surety on a performance bond which named Pierce as principal and Gilbane as obligee.

Disputes arose about performance under the general contract and under the subcontracts, and complex multi-party litigation ensued. During pretrial proceedings there were various changes in the parties' positions and realignments of adversaries which resulted in a trial at which Nemours and its general contractor Gilbane (joined by its surety Aetna) were plaintiffs seeking damages against Gilbane's subcontractor Pierce and Pierce's surety Federal.

After a 79 day trial the jury found in favor of Nemours and Gilbane on all their claims against Pierce and Federal and found against Pierce on its counterclaims. On September 15, 1986 final judgment was entered awarding $26,017,411 in damages and pre-judgment interest to Nemours and $3,018,372 in damages and pre-judgment interest to Gilbane....

These appeals do not challenge the sufficiency of the evidence. Rather, they challenge the legal sufficiency of the claims submitted to the jury and concern legal rulings of the trial court. The facts upon which these rulings were based are not in dispute.

... [I]n January 1980 Nemours entered into a general contract with Gilbane to complete the interior of its Children's Hospital. This contract includes the American Institute of Architects' "General Conditions of the Contract of Construction" (1976 ed.) (the "AIA General Conditions"). Article 1.1.2 of the AIA General conditions states: Nothing contained in the Contract Documents shall create any contractual relationship between the Owner [Nemours] or the Architect and any Subcontractor or Sub-subcontractor.

Gilbane in turn entered into a number of subcontracts. The largest was its $35.9 million fixed-price subcontract with Pierce, executed in June 1980 which called for Pierce to perform the mechanical work on the project. Gilbane entered into other subcontracts including a $19.7 million subcontract with Dynalectric Company ("Dynalectric") for electrical work and an $8.6 million subcontract with Honeywell, Inc. ("Honeywell") for installation of the building management systems.

Section 1 of the Gilbane–Pierce subcontract provided that Pierce would "furnish all materials and perform all work as described in Section 2 hereof for Phase 5B: A.I. duPont Institute for the Nemours Foundation Hospital Building * * * all in accordance with the Drawings and Specifications * * * and subject in every detail to the supervision and satisfaction of [Gilbane] and of [Nemours] or his duly authorized representative."

The subcontract provided in Section 6 that "[Pierce] agrees to be bound to [Gilbane] by the terms and conditions of this Agreement, the Drawings and Specifications, the General Contract and the General Conditions for construction * * *, and to assume toward [Gilbane] all the obligations and responsibilities that [Gilbane], by these documents, assumes toward [Nemours]." The General Conditions, of course, contained the provision that nothing contained in the "Contract Documents" shall create any contractual relationship between Nemours and any subcontractor.

A number of provisions in the subcontract, particularly those found in Section 7, imposed upon Pierce specific obligations vis-a-vis Nemours. For example: Section 7(a) requires Pierce to "furnish Shop Drawings, Erection Drawings, Details, Samples, etc.," for Nemours' approval. Section 7(b) bestowed upon Nemours the right to agree on lump sum pricing of changes to Pierce's work. Section 7(c) gave Nemours the right to inspect and condemn Pierce's work and required Pierce to "make good" the condemned work at its own expense. Section 7(e) required Pierce to "indemnify and save harmless" Nemours from any expenses, liability or loss arising from patent, copyright or trademark infringement.

After the terms of the Gilbane–Pierce subcontract were agreed upon, Gilbane sent it to Nemours for approval. By letter dated September 9, 1980 Nemours approved the subcontract and also stated, "[b]y this approval, The Nemours Foundation does not waive, and expressly reserves all of its rights and remedies under said contract and nothing herein shall be deemed or construed to create any contractual relationship between The Nemours Foundation and said subcontractor." At the foot of the letter Gilbane executed the following: "Receipt and Acceptance acknowledged this 19th day of September, 1980."

Pursuant to the requirements of the subcontract Pierce furnished Gilbane a performance bond naming Pierce as principal, Federal as surety and Gilbane as obligee. Two provisions are pertinent to the present case. The bond provides, "No right of action shall accrue on this bond to or for the use of any person or corporation other than the Obligee named herein or the heirs, executors, administrators or successors of the Obligee." Immediately after that provision there appears the following: "Provided, however, that this Performance Bond issued on behalf of the named Principal may not be assigned to any party other than the Owner, The Nemours Foundation, without the consent of the Sureties." The bond was never assigned to Nemours.

Gilbane and its subcontractors commenced performance under their respective contracts. Serious delays ensued, the causes of which were the subject of vigorous disagreement. The delays and disputes over contract plans and specifications, design revisions, job progress schedules, progress payments and change orders resulted in Nemours withholding payments. In response, in April 1983 Pierce suspended performance under the subcontract. Although the other subcontractors asserted claims against Gilbane and Nemours, they stayed on the job.

To meet the situation created by Pierce's abandonment of the job, Nemours hired contractors to correct and finish Pierce's work under the direction of Turner Construction Company ("Turner"). Gilbane and its other subcontractors coordinated with Turner and the completion contractors to finish the Hospital. Substantial completion took place by December 1984 twenty-one months late.

Not surprisingly, litigation ensued....

III. Third Party Beneficiary Claims

It must first be determined whether the district court erred as a matter of law by holding that Nemours was a third party beneficiary of the Gilbane–Pierce subcontract. Since this issue involves only a question of law the standard of review is plenary....

"It is well settled in Delaware that a third-party may recover on a contract made for his benefit * * *. But in order for there to be a third party beneficiary, the contracting parties must intend to confer the benefit." The intent to confer a third party beneficiary benefit is to be determined from the language of the contract.

Thus in the present case an intent to confer third party beneficiary status on Nemours must be gleaned from the language of the Gilbane–Pierce subcontract. The language of a contract, however, cannot be divorced from the context in which it was written. Here, we are dealing with a general contract and a subcontract in the construction industry.

Typically when major construction is involved an owner has neither the desire nor the ability to negotiate with and supervise the multitude of trades and skills required to complete a project. Consequently an owner will engage a general contractor. The general contractor will retain, coordinate and supervise subcontractors. The owner looks to the general contractor, not the subcontractors, both for performance of the total construction project and for any damages or other relief if there is a default in performance. Performance and the payment of damages are normally assured by the bond of a surety on which the general contractor is principal and the owner is the obligee.

The general contractor, in turn, who is responsible for the performance of the subcontractors, has a right of action against any subcontractor which defaults. Performance and payment of damages by a subcontractor are normally assured by the bond of a surety on which the subcontractor is principal and the general contractor is the obligee.

Thus the typical owner is insulated from the subcontractors both during the course of construction and during the pursuit of remedies in the event of a default. Conversely, the subcontractors are insulated from the owner. The owner deals with and, if necessary, sues the general contractor, and the general contractor deals with and, if necessary, sues the subcontractors.

These typical construction contract relationships have long been recognized:

[Contracts between a principal building contractor and subcontractors] are made to enable the principal contractor to perform; and their performance by the subcontractor does not in itself discharge the principal contractor's duty to the owner with whom he has contracted. The installation of plumbing fixtures or the construction of cement floors by a subcontractor is not a discharge of the principal contractor's duty to the owner to deliver a finished building containing those items; and if after their installation the undelivered building is destroyed by fire, the principal contractor must replace them for the owner, even though he must pay the subcontractor in full and has no right that the latter shall replace them. It seems, therefore, that the owner has no right against the subcontractor, in the absence of clear words to the contrary. The owner is neither a creditor beneficiary nor a donee beneficiary; the benefit that he receives from performance must be regarded as merely incidental.

A contractor entered into a contract with the Government, the latter promising to pay the cost plus a fixed fee and assenting to the letting of subcontracts. In such a case it is clear, in the absence of evidence of a different intention, that the subcontractor is not a beneficiary of the Government's promise to the contractor to pay the cost, even though the amount payable to the subcontractor is reckoned as part of the cost. The Government made no promise to pay anything to the subcontractors. For similar reasons, the Government is not a beneficiary of a subcontractor's promise to the contractor, even though the performance promised may enable the contractor to perform his contractual duty to the Government.

4 Corbin on Contracts § 779D (1951 ed.) at 46, 47.

These typical construction relationships are also recognized in Delaware law. In *Cannon*, the Delaware Supreme Court referred to the "buffer zone" which a general contract creates between the owner and a subcontractor, although in that case it found that the language of the subcontract evidenced an intent to extinguish the buffer zone.

There is nothing to prevent a departure from the typical pattern, and, as was the case in *Cannon*, a contractor and subcontractor may agree to confer upon an owner rights which are enforceable directly against the subcontractor. However, an intent to do so must be found in the contract documents. Thus in the present case it must be determined whether the Gilbane–Pierce subcontract evidences an intent on the part of both Pierce and Gilbane to depart from the typical owner-general contractor and general contractor-subcontractor relationships to confer upon Nemours a direct right of action against Pierce.

The overall structure of the contractual relationships in this case falls into the traditional mold. Nemours as owner entered into a general contract with Gilbane. Gilbane's obligations were assured by a performance bond issued by Aetna. Gilbane entered into a number of subcontracts, including the one with Pierce. Each subcontractor's obligations were assured by a performance bond, a performance bond issued by Federal in the case of Pierce. If indeed Gilbane intended that the subcontract create an obligation running directly from Pierce to Nemours, it is curious that it accepted (in fact, prescribed) a performance bond which provided that no right of action would accrue on it to or for the use of any person other than Gilbane.

The language of the Gilbane–Pierce subcontract suggests that Gilbane and Pierce contemplated that Pierce was to be obligated to Gilbane, not to Nemours.

The subcontract is between Pierce, as subcontractor, and Gilbane as the contractor. Section 6 specified Gilbane as the entity to which Pierce was to be responsible: "The Subcontractor agrees to be bound to the Contractor by the terms and conditions of the Agreement * * * and to assume toward the Contractor all the obligations and responsibilities that the Contractor, by these documents, assumes toward the Owner."

Of significance is the incorporation of the standard AIA General Conditions of the Contract for Construction into both the general contract and the subcontract. Article 1.1.2 of the General Conditions provides: "Nothing contained in the Contract Documents shall create any contractual relationship between the Owner or the Architect and any Subcontractor or Sub-subcontractor."

Nemours urges that in light of the definition of "Contract Documents" in Article 1.1.1, the Article 1.1.2 language serves only to preclude the general contract from creating a contractual relationship between Nemours as owner and Pierce as subcontractor but does not preclude the subcontract from creating such a relationship. Article 1.1.2 provides that "[n]othing contained in the Contract Documents shall create any contractual relationship between the Owner * * * and any Subcontractor * * *." As defined in Article 1.1.1, however, "Contract Documents" does not include the subcontract and, therefore, Nemours argues, there is no prohibition against the subcontract creating a third party beneficiary relationship between Nemours and Pierce.

If the Article 1.1.2 language appeared only in the general contract, Nemours' argument might be persuasive. However, there was repeated incorporation of the General Conditions and its Article 1.1.2 language into the subcontract.

At page 1A of the subcontract it is provided that all work thereunder shall be in accordance with "General Conditions of the Contract for Construction, in (sic) Specifications, (AIA Document A201—1976 Edition)." In Section 6, referred to above, Pierce as subcontractor agrees to be bound by the General Contract and the General Conditions for Construction. Section 7(g) provides that "[t]he Terms and Provisions herein contained and the General Conditions For Construction (AIA Document A201—1976 Edition) * * * shall supersede all previous communications, representations, or agreements, either oral or written, between the parties hereto with respect to the subject matter hereof."

This repeated incorporation of the General Conditions and its Article 1.1.2 no contractual relationship language is a strong indication of an intent on Gilbane's and Pierce's part to maintain the separate owner-general contractor and general contractor-subcontractor relationships.

No Delaware court appears to have construed general contracts or subcontracts which contain Article 1.1.2 of the AIA General Conditions or comparable language. Decisions in other jurisdictions, however, have held that this provision (or like language) prevents an owner from maintaining a breach of contract action against a subcontractor on a third party beneficiary theory, or prevents a subcontractor from maintaining a breach of contract action against an owner on such a theory. Thus the buffer is preserved by Article 1.1.2 or its equivalent.

Nemours' principal argument in support of its third party beneficiary theory is that the Gilbane–Pierce subcontract contains numerous provisions which evidence an intent that Nemours be benefited by Pierce's performance. The description of Pierce's work in Section 1 provides that it shall be subject to the supervision and satisfaction of the contractor and the owner. There are a number of other provisions which impose obligations on Pierce vis-a-vis Nemours, such as an obligation to furnish Shop Drawings, Erection Drawings, etc. for Nemours' approval, the requirement that Pierce indemnify and save harmless Nemours from any expense, liability or loss arising from patent, copyright or trademark infringement.

In every construction subcontract the owner is the one which ultimately benefits from its performance. However, this does not create a third party beneficiary relationship.

We conclude that the subcontract does not manifest an intent by Pierce and Gilbane to confer third party beneficiary status upon Nemours. In fact, the subcontract evidences an intent to preclude such a status. Nemours and Gilbane were but two of three parties in a relationship carefully structured by contract (the general contract and the subcontract). Pierce was the third party in that relationship. By means of the settlement agreement Nemours and Gilbane, in effect, sought to change that relationship to give Nemours a previously non-existent direct cause of action against Pierce. Without Pierce's participation that was not possible. Contractual rights cannot be so casually disregarded.

Thus to the extent that the judgment of the trial court rests upon Nemours' third party beneficiary claim it must be reversed.

QUESTION

What is gained by insisting that Nemours sue Gilbane and then have Gilbane sue Pierce, rather than allowing Nemours to sue Pierce directly? Isn't Nemours the truly injured party and Pierce the party whose breach has caused Nemours' damages?

II.   Assignment of Contract

A.   History

Recognizing a third-party beneficiary expands the community of the agreement to include a third person, who has rights but no duties. The beneficiary shares in the continuing relationship and has concurrent claims against both of the original parties. In contrast, finding an assignment transfers contractual rights and obligations in an already-formed agreement from a contracting party to a third party.

The rights and expectations of a party to a contract are likely to be valuable; commonly they will entail the right to payment of money or the receipt of goods or services. A legal mechanism for the transfer of the right to receive a promised performance effectively converts a promise into a form of property that can be traded to form new and hopefully more efficient economic combinations of resources. In short, transferability of contract rights is a key ingredient in the development of a mercantile, industrial, and, ultimately, a credit economy.

As you learn in your Property course, a major feature of the legal emergence from medieval times was the increasingly free alienability, or transfer, of land held in forms of feudal tenure. As the law faced the need to make the major form of wealth—land—freely transferable, it came also to recognize the need to make transferable the intangible rights created by contract.

This recognition did not result in an immediate outright repudiation of the old view in favor of a new one favoring transferability. Instead, by a series of devices that are used again and again by lawyers, the old rule continued to be recognized in principle while it was abandoned in practice.

First came a group of procedural gimmicks, referred to in the preceding readings, by which the transferee might sue and enforce the right under the fiction that he was acting as attorney for the original holder. This legal fiction persisted well into the 20th century in many states and is still found in a few today.

A second device was the carving of exceptions to the general rule in particular compelling cases. The assignment of foreign bills of exchange was recognized as early as the 14th century since the negotiability of these bills was a precondition of foreign commerce on any basis other than barter. Gradually the assignability of all commercial paper was recognized, first in the courts of equity and ultimately at law. As has happened in contemporary efforts to expand consumer protection, the claim against strict application of "the law" at this stage is couched in terms of fairness, consciionability, and commercial necessity. When this stage was reached, all that was left was the substanceless shadow of the old rule; but not until it had been completely eroded by exceptions and fictions was the non-assignability rule swept away formally by statute and judicial decision.

Today in most states there are comprehensive statutes dealing with assignment problems in the special context of security interests; accounts receivable; negotiable instruments and other commercial paper; consumer credit; wage assignments; small loans; and government contracts. The area, therefore, is one in which general contract doctrine has been supplanted in many vital respects by special statutory rules and policies. While in most commercial contexts assignment is now free of its medieval restraints, analogous concerns to those that limited the transfer of real property 700 years ago now motivate statutes protecting wage earners and consumers purchasing on credit from the oppression that can flow from overly free contractual assignment.

B.   ASSIGNMENT OF RIGHTS AND DELEGATION OF DUTIES

To understand the transfer of contractual interests and the effects of such a transfer, one must distinguish the rights arising from a contract from its obligations.

Assignment should be distinguished from the third-party beneficiary situation in that the rights of the assignee are sequential and to the exclusion of the original party to the contract, while the beneficiary's rights are concurrent and exist alongside those of the parties. After an assignment, the assignor retains no rights against the obligor, and the obligor cannot relieve himself of his duty by paying the assignor, at least not after he learns of the assignment.

Most contract rights are to receive performance in the form of money, goods, or services. Certainly as to money, it generally makes no difference to the obligor *whom* she pays, so long as that is the *only* variation. One person is as good as another, and the substitution of a party has little impact on the promisor's undertaking. This is not as certainly so if the performance in question is delivery of goods, and even less so in the case of services, for these may be personal in nature. It may make a big difference whom the obligor has to satisfy as a customer, and even more so under whom she must work as an employee.

Delegation of a contractual obligation is even more problematic, for now the original party is not merely designating a substitute to receive performance; he is now hiring someone to do the job for him. This is far more likely to place the obligee (the contracting party entitled to performance) in a materially different transaction than he bargained for.

UNIFORM COMMERCIAL CODE:

§ 2–210. Delegation of Performance; Assignment of Rights.

(1) A party may perform his duty through a delegate unless otherwise agreed or unless the other party has a substantial interest in having his original promisor perform or control the acts required by the contract. No delegation of performance relieves the party delegating of any duty to perform or any liability for breach.

(2) Except as otherwise provided in Section 9-406, unless otherwise agreed, all rights of either seller or buyer can be assigned except where the assignment would materially change the duty of the other party, or increase materially the burden or risk imposed on him by his contract, or impair materially his chance of obtaining return performance. A right to damages for breach of the whole contract or a right arising out of the assignor's due performance of his entire obligation can be assigned despite agreement otherwise.

(3) The creation, attachment, perfection or enforcement of a security interest in the seller's interest under a contract is not a transfer that materially changes the duty of or increases materially the burden or risk imposed on the buyer or impairs materially the buyer's chance of obtaining return performance within the purview of subsection (2) unless, and then only to the extent that, enforcement actually results in a delegation of material performance of the seller. Even in that event, the creation, attachment, perfection, and enforcement of the security interest remains effective, but (i) the seller is liable to the buyer for damages caused by the delegation to the extent that the damages could not reasonably be prevented by the buyer, and (ii) a court having jurisdiction may grant other appropriate relief, including cancellation of the contract for sale or an injunction against enforcement of the security interest or consummation of the enforcement.

(4) Unless the circumstances indicate the contrary a prohibition of assignment of "the contract" is to be construed as barring only the delegation to the assignee of the assignor's performance.

(5) An assignment of "the contract" or of "all my rights under the contract" or an assignment in similar general terms is an assignment of rights and unless the language or the circumstances (as in an assignment for security) indicate the contrary, it is a delegation of performance of the duties of the assignor and its acceptance by the assignee constitutes a promise by him to perform

those duties. This promise is enforceable by either the assignor or the other party to the original contract.

(6) The other party may treat any assignment which delegates performance as creating reasonable grounds for insecurity and may without prejudice to his rights against the assignor demand assurances from the assignee (§ 2-609).

QUESTIONS AND NOTES

1. Consistent use of the terminology ("assignment" applying to contract rights and "delegation" applying to contract obligations) is helpful to prevent confusion. But all lawyers and judges are not always so precise. Sometimes "assignment" is used to cover both assignment and delegation. Can you reword UCC § 2-210 to make it consistent with these definitions and less confusing?

2. Suppose that Barber enters into a contract with Cleanly to cut Cleanly's hair once a week for a year in return for Cleanly's promise to clean Barber's shop once a week. Compare:

(a) Cleanly "assigns" this contract to Filthy, and Filthy demands haircuts in return for his weekly cleanings.

(b) Cleanly assigns his right to haircuts to Filthy but continues to tender performance of the cleaning job himself.

(c) Barber breaches his contract with Cleanly, and Cleanly assigns his right of action against Barber to Filthy.

Even if you think that Barber can insist that "the contract" in (a) isn't assignable, can he equally insist under (b) that he doesn't have to cut Filthy's hair? If you think that he can refuse to cut Filthy's hair, is it because he depended on Cleanly's character, skill, etc.? Is either objection applicable to (c)?

3. Was the early common law right after all in its determination that contracts created strictly personal relations, and, therefore, even unconditional money rights arising out of them were unassignable? If A owes B, and B assigns A's debt to C, why should debtor A be required to pay C—someone with whom it has never "done business"? Doesn't this subject A, perhaps against its will, to a different duty than it originally undertook?

4. Assume that Jones agrees to sell his pet dog to Kindly. Can Kindly assign her claim to Cruel? Suppose that Jones doesn't want his dog in Cruel's hands? Could Kindly have taken delivery of the dog, paid for it, and then sold it to Cruel if the contract of purchase didn't restrict her future conduct with respect to the dog? Any

difference? If Jones breached his contract with Kindly, could Kindly assign her right of action against Jones to Cruel? Any difference?

————————

Herzog v. Irace

Maine Supreme Judicial Court, 1991.
594 A.2d 1106.

■ BRODY, J. ...

The facts of this case are not disputed. Gary Jones was injured in a motorcycle accident and retained Irace and Lowry to represent him in a personal injury action. Soon thereafter, Jones dislocated his shoulder, twice, in incidents unrelated to the motorcycle accident. Dr. Herzog examined Jones's shoulder and concluded that he needed surgery. At the time, however, Jones was unable to pay for the surgery and in consideration for the performance of the surgery by the doctor, he signed a letter dated June 14, 1988, written on Dr. Herzog's letterhead stating: "I, Gary Jones, request that payment be made directly from settlement of a claim currently pending for an unrelated incident, to John Herzog, D.O., for treatment of a shoulder injury which occurred at a different time." Dr. Herzog notified Irace and Lowry that Jones had signed an "assignment of benefits" from the motorcycle personal injury action to cover the cost of surgery on his shoulder and was informed by an employee of Irace and Lowry that the assignment was sufficient to allow the firm to pay Dr. Herzog's bills at the conclusion of the case. Dr. Herzog performed the surgery and continued to treat Jones for approximately one year.

In May, 1989, Jones received a $20,000 settlement in the motorcycle personal injury action. He instructed Irace and Lowry not to disburse any funds to Dr. Herzog indicating that he would make the payments himself. Irace and Lowry informed Dr. Herzog that Jones had revoked his permission to have the bill paid by them directly and indicated that they would follow Jones's directions. Irace and Lowry issued a check to Jones for $10,027 and disbursed the remaining funds to Jones's other creditors. Jones did send a check to Dr. Herzog but the check was returned by the bank for insufficient funds and Dr. Herzog was never paid.

Dr. Herzog filed a complaint in District Court against Irace and Lowry seeking to enforce the June 14, 1988 "assignment of benefits." The matter was tried before the court on the basis of a joint stipulation of facts. The court entered a judgment in favor of Dr. Herzog finding that the June 14, 1988 letter constituted a valid assignment of the settlement proceeds enforceable against Irace and Lowry. Following an unsuccessful appeal to the Superior Court, Irace and Lowry appealed to this court. Because the Superior Court acted as an intermediate appellate court, we review the District Court's decision directly.

An assignment is an act or manifestation by the owner of a right (the assignor) indicating his intent to transfer that right to another person (the assignee). For an assignment to be valid and enforceable against the assignor's creditor (the obligor), the assignor must make clear his intent to relinquish the right to the assignee and must not retain any control over the right assigned or any power of revocation. The assignment takes effect through the actions of the assignor and assignee and the obligor need not accept the assignment to render it valid. Once the obligor has notice of the assignment, the fund is "from that time forward impressed with a trust; it is * * * impounded in the [obligor's] hands, and must be held by him not for the original creditor, the assignor, but for the substituted creditor, the assignee." After receiving notice of the assignment, the obligor cannot lawfully pay the amount assigned either to the assignor or to his other creditors and if the obligor does make such a payment, he does so at his peril because the assignee may enforce his rights against the obligor directly.

Ordinary rights, including future rights, are freely assignable unless the assignment would materially change the duty of the obligor, materially increase the burden or risk imposed upon the obligor by his contract, impair the obligor's chance of obtaining return performance, or materially reduce the value of the return performance to the obligor, and unless the law restricts the assignability of the specific right involved. See Restatement (Second) Contracts § 317(2)(a) (1982). In Maine, the transfer of a future right to proceeds from pending litigation has been recognized as a valid and enforceable equitable assignment. An equitable assignment need not transfer the entire future right but rather may be a partial assignment of that right. We reaffirm these well established principles.

Relying primarily upon the Federal District Court's decision in *Shiro*, 174 F.Supp. 495, a bankruptcy case involving the trustee's power to avoid a preferential transfer by assignment, Irace and Lowry contend that Jones's June 14, 1988 letter is invalid and unenforceable as an assignment because it fails to manifest Jones's intent to permanently relinquish all control over the assigned funds and does nothing more than request payment from a specific fund. We disagree. The June 14, 1988 letter gives no indication that Jones attempted to retain any control over the funds he assigned to Dr. Herzog. Taken in context, the use of the word "request" did not give the court reason to question Jones's intent to complete the assignment and, although no specific amount was stated, the parties do not dispute that the services provided by Dr. Herzog and the amounts that he charged for those services were reasonable and necessary to the treatment of the shoulder injury referred to in the June 14 letter. Irace and Lowry had adequate funds to satisfy all of Jones's creditors, including Dr. Herzog, with funds left over for disbursement to Jones himself. Thus, this case simply does not present a situation analogous to *Shiro* because Dr. Herzog was [not] given preference over Jones's other creditors by operation of the assignment. Given that Irace and Lowry do not dispute that they had ample notice of the assignment, the court's finding on the validity of the assignment is fully supported by the evidence and will not be disturbed on appeal.

Ethical Obligations

Next, Irace and Lowry contend that the assignment, if enforceable against them, would interfere with their ethical obligation to honor their client's instruction in disbursing funds. Again, we disagree.

Under the Maine Bar Rules, an attorney generally may not place a lien on a client's file for a third party. M.Bar R. 3.7(c). The Bar Rules further require that an attorney "promptly pay or deliver to the client, as requested by the client, the funds, securities, or other properties in the possession of the lawyer which the client is entitled to receive." M.Bar R. 3.6(f)(2)(iv). The rules say nothing, however, about a client's power to assign his right to proceeds from a pending lawsuit to third parties. Because the client has the power to assign his right to funds held by his attorney, it follows that a valid assignment must be honored by the attorney in disbursing the funds on the client's behalf. The assignment does not create a conflict under Rule 3.6(f)(2)(iv) because the client is not entitled to receive funds once he has assigned them to a third party. Nor does the assignment violate Rule 3.7(c), because the client, not the attorney, is responsible for placing the incumbrance upon the funds. Irace and Lowry were under no ethical obligation, and the record gives no indication that they were under a contractual obligation, to honor their client's instruction to disregard a valid assignment. The District Court correctly concluded that the assignment is valid and enforceable against Irace and Lowry.

The entry is:

Judgment affirmed.

NOTES

1. This case involves an "assignment for security," which is a secured transaction subject to UCC Article 9. That is Dr. Herzog took the assignment only to secure payment of his fees, and his property interest in the proceeds of the lawsuit was accordingly limited to the extent of the secured obligation, i.e. the amount of the fees owed. Article 9 covers almost all transactions in which the parties intend to create a security interest in personal property. While a discussion of Article 9 is outside the scope of a first year Contracts course, one noteworthy aspect of Article 9 is the concept of "perfection." Perfection of a security interest provides the secured party with legal protection against competing claims of third parties. Typically this is accomplished by filing a "financing statement" with the appropriate government

agency, obtaining "control" over certain types of intangible property, or in the case of tangible property or negotiable instruments, perhaps by taking physical possession of the collateral. In certain situations perfection may be automatic upon the creation of the security interest. Absent perfection, the secured transaction is enforceable as between the debtor-assignor and the secured party, but the secured party's unperfected security interest is subordinate to the rights of bona fide purchasers (or assignees) for value, other perfected secured parties, lien creditors of the debtor-assignor or the debtor-assignor's bankruptcy trustee.

2. The common law traditionally resisted the idea that litigation claims might be freely transferred from injured parties to those willing to finance litigation or bear litigation risk. Rules against maintenance and champerty limited the ability of plaintiffs to transfer their claims to third parties, purportedly to prevent speculation in ill-founded litigation claims. In the United States the institution of the contingent fee has long allowed lawyers to partner-up with their clients in financing the client's litigation by taking an interest in the proceeds, but in general third parties were not permitted to do so. These traditional prohibitions appear to be relaxing in the face of modern free-market ideology, and increasingly third-party private investors are looking to acquire interests in litigation claims in exchange for providing financing and liquidity to injured plaintiffs holding unliquidated and disputed litigation claims. Professor Jonathan Molot, *A Market in Litigation Risk*, 76 U. CHI. L. REV. 367 (2009), discusses this trend and posits a brave new world where lawyers assume the role of traders, brokers, and investors in litigation claims:

> Client service need not be the defining feature of lawyering. A lawyer may use the same skills and engage in the same predictive enterprise whether he is advising a client appearing before a judge, advising a hedge fund buying stock in that company, or making an investment in the company for his own account. Moreover, a lawyer who uses his legal skills to transfer legal risk from risk-averse litigants to profit-seeking investors or insurers may serve the litigants (and society) just as effectively as those lawyers who perform the traditional professional function of advising clients. The legal profession should embrace lawyers who choose to work as principals or brokers in a market for legal risk just as much as it embraces lawyers who cling to their traditional role as agents for clients.

> Molot concludes by stating his aim in writing the article was "to expand the legal profession's self-conception so that lawyers consider it within their professional role not only to advise clients on litigation risk but also in some cases to relieve legal-risk bearers of risk."

Even if we are prepared to consign the maintenance and champerty doctrines to the dustbin of history, however, there remain, difficult barriers in transferring unliquidated litigation claims. Not only is the value of such claims uncommonly difficult to assess, but the plaintiff's lawyer's professional obligations of loyalty, zealous representation, and confidentiality may constrain the ability of a third party investor to obtain the information and control over the claim that it will seek if it is to bear the risk.

The Macke Co. v. Pizza of Gaithersburg

Maryland Court of Appeals, 1970.
259 Md. 479, 270 A.2d 645.

■ SINGLEY, J. The appellees and defendants below, Pizza of Gaithersburg, Inc.; Pizzeria, Inc.; The Pizza Pie Corp., Inc. and Pizza Oven, Inc., four corporations under the common ownership of Sidney Ansell, Thomas S. Sherwood and Eugene Early and the same individuals as partners or proprietors (the Pizza Shops) operated at six locations in Montgomery and Prince George's Counties. The appellees had arranged to have installed in each of their locations cold drink vending machines owned by Virginia Coffee Service, Inc., and on 30 December 1966, this arrangement was formalized at five of the locations, by contracts for terms of one year, automatically renewable for a like term in the absence of 30 days' written notice. A similar contract for the sixth location, operated by Pizza of Gaithersburg, Inc., was entered into on 25 July 1967.

On 30 December 1967, Virginia's assets were purchased by The Macke Company (Macke) and the six contracts were assigned to Macke by Virginia. In January, 1968, the Pizza Shops attempted to terminate the five contracts having the December anniversary date, and in February, the contract which had the July anniversary date.

Macke brought suit in the Circuit Court for Montgomery County against each of the Pizza Shops for damages for breach of contract. From judgments for the defendants, Macke has appealed.

The lower court based the result which it reached on two grounds: first, that the Pizza Shops, when they contracted with Virginia, relied on its skill, judgment and reputation, which made impossible a delegation of Virginia's duties to Macke; and second, that the damages claimed could not be shown with reasonable certainty. These conclusions are challenged by Macke.

In the absence of a contrary provision—and there was none here—rights and duties under an executory bilateral contract may be assigned and delegated, subject to the exception that duties under a contract to provide personal services may never be delegated, nor rights be assigned under a contract where *delectus personae* was an ingredient of the bargain.[1] 4 Corbin on Contracts § 865 (1951) at 434; 6 Am.Jur.2d, Assignments § 11 (1963) at 196. *Crane Ice Cream Co. v. Terminal Freezing & Heating Co.* held that the right of an individual to purchase ice under a contract which by its terms reflected a knowledge of the individual's needs and reliance on his credit and responsibility could not be assigned to the corporation which purchased his business. In *Eastern Advertising Co. v. McGaw & Co.*, our predecessors held that an advertising agency could not delegate its duties under a contract which had been entered into by an advertiser who had relied on the agency's skill, judgment and taste.

The six machines were placed on the appellees' premises under a printed "Agreement–Contract" which identified the "customer," gave its place of business, described the vending machine, and then provided:

TERMS

1. The Company will install on the Customer's premises the above listed equipment and will maintain the equipment in good operating order and stocked with merchandise.

2. The location of this equipment will be such as to permit accessibility to persons desiring use of same. This equipment shall remain the property of the Company and shall not be moved from the location at which installed, except by the Company.

3. For equipment requiring electricity and water, the Customer is responsible for electrical receptacle and water outlet within ten (10) feet of the equipment location. The Customer is also responsible to supply the Electrical Power and Water needed.

4. The Customer will exercise every effort to protect this equipment from abuse or damage.

5. The Company will be responsible for all licenses and taxes on the equipment and sale of products.

6. This Agreement–Contract is for a term of one (1) year from the date indicated herein and will be automatically renewed for a like period, unless thirty (30) day written notice is given by either party to terminate service.

7. Commission on monthly sales will be paid by the Company to the Customer at the following rate: * * *."

The rate provided in each of the agreements was "30% of Gross Receipts to $300.00 monthly[,] 35% over [$]300.00," except for the agreement with Pizza of Gaithersburg, Inc., which called for "40% of Gross Receipts."

We cannot regard the agreements as contracts for personal services. They were either a license or concession granted Virginia by the appellees, or a lease of a portion of the appellees' premises, with Virginia agreeing to pay a percentage of gross

---

1. Like all generalizations, this one is subject to an important exception. Uniform Commercial Code § [9-406(f)] makes ineffective a term in any contract prohibiting the assignment of a [particular] contract right: i.e., a right to payment.

sales as a license or concession fee or as rent, and were assignable by Virginia unless they imposed on Virginia duties of a personal or unique character which could not be delegated.

The appellees earnestly argue that they had dealt with Macke before and had chosen Virginia because they preferred the way it conducted its business. Specifically, they say that service was more personalized, since the president of Virginia kept the machines in working order, that commissions were paid in cash, and that Virginia permitted them to keep keys to the machines so that minor adjustments could be made when needed. Even if we assume all this to be true, the agreements with Virginia were silent as to the details of the working arrangements and contained only a provision requiring Virginia to "install * * * the above listed equipment and * * * maintain the equipment in good operating order and stocked with merchandise." We think the Supreme Court of California put the problem of personal service in proper focus a century ago when it upheld the assignment of a contract to grade a San Francisco street:

> All painters do not paint portraits like Sir Joshua Reynolds, nor landscapes like Claude Lorraine, nor do all writers write dramas like Shakespeare or fiction like Dickens. Rare genius and extraordinary skill are not transferable, and contracts for their employment are therefore personal, and cannot be assigned. But rare genius and extraordinary skill are not indispensable to the workmanlike digging down of a sand hill or the filling up of a depression to a given level, or the construction of brick sewers with manholes and covers, and contracts for such work are not personal, and may be assigned.

Taylor v. Palmer, 31 Cal. 240 at 247–248 (1866).

Moreover, the difference between the service the Pizza Shops happened to be getting from Virginia and what they expected to get from Macke did not mount up to such a material change in the performance of obligations under the agreements as would justify the appellees' refusal to recognize the assignment.

Restatement, Contracts, § 160(3) (1932) reads, in part:

> Performance or offer of performance by a person delegated has the same legal effect as performance or offer of performance by the person named in the contract, unless,
>
> (a) performance by the person delegated varies or would vary materially from performance by the person named in the contract as the one to perform, and there has been no * * * assent to the delegation * * *.

In cases involving the sale of goods, the Restatement rule respecting delegation of duties has been amplified by Uniform Commercial Code § 2–210(6), which permits a promisee to demand assurances from the party to whom duties have been delegated.

As we see it, the delegation of duty by Virginia to Macke was entirely permissible under the terms of the agreements. In so holding, we do not put ourselves at odds with *Eastern Advertising Co. v. McGaw*, for in that case, the agreement with the agency contained a provision that "the advertising cards were to be 'subject to the approval of Eastern Advertising Company as to style and contents,'" which the court found to import that reliance was being placed on the agency's skill, judgment and taste.

Having concluded that the Pizza Shops had no right to rescind the agreements, we turn to the question of damages.

[In an omitted portion of the opinion, the court finds that damages for lost profits might be able to be determined with reasonably certainty.]

Judgment reversed as to liability; judgment entered for appellant for costs, on appeal and below; case remanded for a new trial on the question of damages.

QUESTIONS AND NOTES

1. What story does Pizza Shops' counsel try to tell through his witnesses in order to convince the court that the duties were not to be delegated? Why doesn't the story work?

2. Why did the trial court or the Court of Appeals even listen to evidence of the nature of the relationship? Wouldn't the parol evidence rule bar its admission? If not, why?

3. What is the effect, if any, of the assignment on Virginia's obligations? Was it a breach for Virginia to assign its contract and go out of business?

4. Could Pizza Shops recover damages from Virginia when Macke failed to service its machines?

5. How much variation must Pizza Shops tolerate before there is a material variation of its expectation of performance? What did the Court of Appeals think was intolerable about the assignment of rights and delegation of duties in *Crane Ice Cream* and in *Eastern Advertising Co.*?

C. CONTRACTUAL LIMITATIONS ON ASSIGNMENT

RESTATEMENT, SECOND, CONTRACTS:

§ 322. Contractual Prohibition of Assignment.

(1) Unless the circumstances indicate the contrary, a contract term prohibiting assignment of "the contract" bars only the delegation to an assignee of the performance by the assignor of a duty or condition.

(2) A contract term prohibiting assignment of rights under the contract, unless a different intention is manifested,

   (a) does not forbid assignment of a right to damages for breach of the whole contract or a right arising out of the assignor's due performance of his entire obligation;

   (b) gives the obligor a right to damages for breach of the terms forbidding assignment but does not render the assignment ineffective;

   (c) is for the benefit of the obligor, and does not prevent the assignee from acquiring rights against the assignor or the obligor from discharging his duty as if there were no such prohibition.

§ 326. Partial Assignment.

(1) Except as stated in Subsection (2), an assignment of a part of a right, whether the part is specified as a fraction, as an amount, or otherwise, is operative as to that part to the same extent and in the same manner as if the part had been a separate right.

(2) If the obligor has not contracted to perform separately the assigned part of a right, no legal proceeding can be maintained by the assignor or assignee against the obligor over his objection, unless all the persons entitled to the promised performance are joined in the proceeding, or unless joinder is not feasible and it is equitable to proceed without joinder.

COMMENT:

   b. Partial Assignment. The distinguishing feature of a partial assignment is a manifestation of intention to make an immediate transfer of part but not all of the assignor's right, and to confer on the assignee a direct right against the obligor to the performance of that part. Historically, the right of a partial assignee could be enforced only by a suit in a court of equity, and it was therefore sometimes described as an "equitable" right. But the right of a total assignee also had historically an "equitable" character. Under the rule stated in Subsection (1), a partial assignment and a total assignment are equally effective, subject to the protection of the obligor under the rule stated in Subsection (2).

NOTE ON PARTIAL ASSIGNMENT

An obligor may challenge the partial assignment of the obligation to a number of assignees on grounds that it substantially varies its undertaking. Instead of being able to discharge its obligation by one payment to one person or in one lawsuit, the obligor must now deal with a number of claimants. Since the assignor-obligee could bring only one action at common law to enforce its claim, the partial assignees could enforce their claims only by joining all interested parties in an equitable action. Under modern pleading rules, such as Federal Rule of Civil Procedure 19, a partial assignee can maintain an action over the objection of the obligor only by joining all persons entitled to the promised total performance or, if joinder is not feasible, only if certain equitable criteria are met—for example, if relief can be shaped without the absent parties and if alternative remedies are not available.

This problem arises frequently in the construction industry. A general contractor may assign one part of a payment due from an owner to the contractor's bank as security for operating loans to meet the payroll, another part to material suppliers, and yet another to subcontractors in payment for the work they do on the job. Normally, the owner will include a non-assignability clause in the construction contract in order to better control the contractor through the partial payments. Owners suspect that contractors may lose enthusiasm for a job if they can relieve themselves of pressing obligations by partial assignment of the right to payment. As § 322 of the Restatement, Second, Contracts indicates, general contractual prohibition of assignments of money claims are of limited efficacy. Traditional common law attitudes, hostile toward partial assignments, however, put the owner in a stronger position to prevent partial assignments without her consent.

In addition to the defenses of non-assignability by express or implied agreement or because of the nature of the duty "assigned," the rights of the assignee are subject to any defenses the obligor might have had against the assignor under the assigned contract.

UNIFORM COMMERCIAL CODE ARTICLE 9:

§ 9-404. Rights Acquired by Assignee; Claims and Defenses Against Assignee.

(a) Unless an account debtor has made an enforceable agreement not to assert defenses or claims, and subject to subsections (b) to (e), inclusive, the rights of an assignee are subject to:

(1) All terms of the agreement between the account debtor and assignor and any defense or claim in recoupment arising from the transaction that gave rise to the contract; and

(2) Any other defense or claim of the account debtor against the assignor which accrues before the account debtor receives a notification of the assignment authenticated by the assignor or the assignee.

...

§ 9-405. Modification of Assigned Contract.

(a) A modification of or substitution for an assigned contract is effective against an assignee if made in good faith. The assignee acquires corresponding rights under the modified or substituted contract. The assignment may provide that the modification or substitution is a breach of contract by the assignor. This subsection is subject to subsections (b) to (d).

(b) Subsection (a) applies to the extent that:

(1) The right to payment or a part thereof under an assigned contract has not been fully earned by performance; or

(2) The right to payment or a part thereof has been fully earned by performance and the account debtor has not received notification of the assignment under Section 9-406(a).

...

§ 9-406. Discharge of account debtor; Notification of Assignment; Identification and Proof of Assignment; Restrictions on Assignment of Accounts, Chattel Paper, Payment Intangibles, and Promissory Notes Ineffective.

(a) Subject to subsections (b) to (i), an account debtor on an account, chattel paper, or a payment intangible may discharge its obligation by paying the assignor until, but not after, the account debtor receives a notification, authenticated by the assignor or the assignee, that the amount due or to become due has been assigned and that payment is to be made to the assignee. After receipt of the notification, the account debtor may discharge its obligation by paying the assignee and may not discharge the obligation by paying the assignor.

(b) Subject to subsection (h), notification is ineffective under subsection (a):

(1) if it does not reasonably identify the rights assigned;

(2) to the extent that an agreement between an account debtor and a seller of a payment intangible limits the account debtor's duty to pay a person other than the seller and the limitation is effective under law other than this article; or

(3) at the option of an account debtor, if the notification notifies the account debtor to make less than the full amount of any installment or other periodic payment to the assignee, even if:

(A) only a portion of the account, chattel paper, or payment intangible has been assigned to that assignee.

(B) a portion has been assigned to another assignee; or

(C) the account debtor knows that the assignment to that assignee is limited.

(c) Subject to subsection (h), if requested by the account debtor, an assignee shall seasonably furnish reasonable proof that the assignment has been made. Unless the assignee complies, the account debtor may discharge its obligation by paying the assignor, even if the account debtor has received a notification under subsection (a).

(d) Except as otherwise provided in subsection (e) and in Sections 2A-303 and 9-407, and subject to subsection (h), a term in an agreement between an account debtor and an assignor or in a promissory note is ineffective to the extent that it:

(1) prohibits, restricts, or requires the consent of the account debtor or person obligated on the promissory note to the assignment or transfer of, or the creation, attachment, perfection, or enforcement of a security interest in, the account, chattel paper, payment intangible, or promissory note; or

(2) provides that the assignment or transfer or the creation, attachment, perfection, or enforcement of the security interest may give rise to a default, breach, right of recoupment, claim, defense, termination, right of termination, or remedy under the account, chattel paper, payment intangible, or promissory note.

(e) Subsection (d) does not apply to the sale of a payment intangible or promissory note.

(f) Except as otherwise provided in Sections 2A-303 and 9-407, and subject to subsections (h) and (i), a rule of law, statute, or regulation, that prohibits, restricts, or requires the consent of a government, governmental body or official, or account debtor to the assignment or transfer of, or creation of a security interest in, an account or chattel paper is ineffective to the extent that the rule of law, statute, or regulation:

(1) prohibits, restricts, or requires the consent of the government, governmental body or official, or account debtor to the assignment or transfer of, or the creation, attachment, perfection, or enforcement of a security interest in, the account or chattel paper; or

(2) provides that the creation, attachment, perfection, or enforcement of the security interest may give rise to a default, breach, right of recoupment, claim, defense, termination, right of termination, or remedy under the account or chattel paper.

...

Larese v. Creamland Dairies

United States Court of Appeals, Tenth Circuit, 1985.
767 F.2d 716.

■ McKay, C. J. ... Plaintiffs entered into a 10–year franchise agreement with defendant, Creamland Dairies, in 1974. The franchise agreement provided that the franchisee "shall not assign, transfer or sublet this franchise, or any of [the] rights under this agreement, without the prior written consent of Area Franchisor [Creamland] and Baskin Robbins, any such unauthorized assignment, transfer or subletting being null and without effect." The plaintiffs attempted to sell their franchise rights in February and August of 1979, but Creamland refused to consent to the sales. Plaintiffs brought suit, alleging that Creamland had interfered with their contractual relations with the prospective buyers by unreasonably withholding its consent. The district court granted summary judgment for the defendant on the ground that the contract gave the defendant an absolute, unqualified right to refuse to consent to proposed sales of the franchise rights. Plaintiffs appeal, claiming that defendant franchisor has a duty to act in good faith and in a commercially reasonable manner when a franchisee seeks to transfer its rights under the franchise agreement.

The Colorado courts have never addressed the question of whether a franchisor has a duty to act reasonably in deciding whether to consent to a proposed transfer. The Colorado courts have, however, imposed a reasonableness requirement on consent to transfer clauses in other types of contracts. In *Basnett v. Vista Village Mobile Home Park*, the Colorado appellate court held that a landlord cannot unreasonably refuse to consent to assignment or subleasing by a tenant. While the court indicated that the courts would enforce a provision expressly granting the landlord an absolute right to consent if such a provision was freely negotiated, it refused to find such an absolute right in a provision which provided simply that the landlord must consent to assignment. The question before us, therefore, is whether the Colorado courts would impose a similar requirement of reasonableness on restraint on alienation clauses in franchise agreements.

Counsel for both parties have argued that the franchisor-franchisee relationship is a special one which is not directly analogous to that of a landlord and tenant. As the Supreme Court of Pennsylvania has noted, "[u]nlike a tenant pursuing his own interests while occupying a landlord's property, a franchisee * * * builds the good will of both his own business and [the franchisor]." *Atlantic Richfield v. Razumic.* This aspect of the relationship has led a number of courts to hold that the franchise relationship imposes a duty upon franchisors not to act unreasonably or arbitrarily in terminating the franchise. As did these courts, we find that the franchisor-franchisee relationship is one which requires the parties to deal with one another in good faith and in a commercially reasonable manner.

Defendants argue that the franchise assignment situation differs from the franchise termination situation in that the franchisor must work with the person to whom the franchise is assigned. To impose a duty of reasonableness, they argue, would violate the rule of *United States v. Colgate & Co,* that a manufacturer engaged in private business has the right "freely to exercise his own independent discretion as to parties with whom he will deal." This right, however, must be balanced against the rights of the franchisees. As is true in the termination cases, the franchisee has invested time and money into the franchise and, in doing so, has created benefits for the franchisor. We do not find it an excessive infringement of the franchisor's rights to require that the franchisor act reasonably when the franchisee has decided that it wants out of the relationship. The franchisee should not be forced to choose between losing its investment or remaining in the relationship unwillingly when it has provided a reasonable alternative franchisee.

We do not hold that a provision which expressly grants to the franchisor an absolute right to refuse to consent is unenforceable when such an agreement was freely negotiated. We do not believe the Colorado courts would find such an absolute right, however, in a provision such as the one involved in this case which provides simply that the franchisee must obtain franchisor consent prior to transfer. Rather, the franchisor must bargain for a provision expressly granting the right to withhold consent unreasonably, to insure that the franchisee is put on notice. Since, in this case, the contracts stated only that consent must be obtained, Creamland did not have the right to withhold consent unreasonably.

Reversed and remanded for further proceedings consistent with this opinion.

QUESTIONS AND NOTES

1. Can Creamland avoid the outcome above in future contracts simply by modifying the wording of the non-assignment clause to include the sentence, "Creamland has the right to refuse consent to assignment of the franchise, reasonably or unreasonably"?

2. Is it unreasonable for Creamland to object to assignment if it would have obtained fees from new franchisees that will be paid to Larese as consideration for assignment rather than to it, if assignment is permitted?

NOTE ON RESTRICTIONS ON FRANCHISE ASSIGNMENTS

In relationships between franchisees and franchisors, "the franchisee's ability to transfer or assign its franchise rights to a third party is a crucial element . . . . Most franchisors want as much control over the transfer process as possible while most franchisees want to convey their rights as freely as possible." Terrence M. Dunn, *The Franchisor's Control Over the Transfer of a Franchise*, 27 FRANCHISE L.J. 233, 233 (2008).

While courts impose certain standards on the franchisor's ability to restrict the franchisee's right to assign as a matter of general contract law, this power is also more directly and more stringently regulated by statute in certain industries. For example, the Petroleum Marketing Practices Act (PMPA), 15 U.S.C. §§ 2801-2807, controls the termination and nonrenewal of franchises for gas stations notwithstanding the terms of the particular franchise agreement promulgated by the franchisor oil company. Similarly, most states, and to a lesser extent the federal government, regulate the power of automobile manufacturers to terminate, refuse to renew, or limit assignment under automobile dealer franchise agreements. In these industries, the economic power of the (often out-of-state or foreign) franchisor has been significantly circumscribed by legislation protecting politically influential local franchisees.

D. CONTINUING OBLIGATIONS AFTER DELEGATION: NOVATION

An obligor under a contract cannot free himself of his obligation by simply delegating his duty to another. If the rule were otherwise, it would be a handy device, indeed, for getting oneself out of debt.

The right to receive payment can usually be assigned by a creditor without the consent of the party who is obligated to pay. Such an assignment cuts off the assigning creditor's right to receive payment. Delegation of the duty to pay, in contrast, never cuts off the delegating obligor's promissory duty, unless the creditor entitled to payment agrees that it will be a release. If such consent is not received, the delegation of duty creates a third-party beneficiary relationship. Recall Topic I in this Chapter. If the creditor does consent, in effect a new contract is formed between the original obligee and the third party delagatee; this transaction and its result are usually called a novation.

RESTATEMENT, SECOND, CONTRACTS:

§ 280. Novation.

A novation is a substituted contract that includes as a party one who was neither the obligor nor the obligee of the original duty.

COMMENT:

b. Effect of novation. A novation discharges the original duty, just as any other substituted contract does, so that breach of the new duty gives no right of action on the old duty. Most novations simply substitute a new obligor for an old obligor or, less commonly, a new obligee for an old obligee. Sometimes these are termed simple novations, to distinguish them from more complex transactions that are termed compound novations.

d. Substitution of obligor. A simple novation involving substitution of obligors results when an obligee promises the obligor that he will discharge the obligor's duty in consideration for a third person's promise to pay the obligee . . . A substitution of obligors may also result when an obligee promises a third person that he will discharge the obligor's duty in consideration for the third person's promise to render either the performance that was due from the obligor or some other performance. Even a promise to render part performance is consideration in that situation . . . [A] novation also results when a third person promises an obligor to assume, immediately and in substitution for the obligor's duty, a duty to the obligee to render the performance that was due from the obligor or some other performance, and the obligee agrees with the obligor or with the third person to that situation. The third person then comes under a new duty to the obligee, who is an intended beneficiary of his promise to assume, and this is consideration for the obligee's arrangement to discharge the original obligor . . . However, a mere promise by a third party to assume the obligor's duty, not offered in substitution for that duty, does not result in a novation, and the new duty that the third party may owe to the obligee as an intended beneficiary is in addition to and not in substitution for the obligor's original duty. For a novation to take place, the obligee must assent to the discharge of the obligor's duty in consideration for the promise of the third party to undertake that duty.

ILLUSTRATIONS:

1. A owes B $1,000. B promises A that he will discharge the debt immediately if C will promise B to pay B $1,000. C so promises. There is a novation under which B's and C's promises are consideration for each other and A is discharged.

3. A owes B a duty to service B's machine for a year. A sells part of his business to C, who promises A that he will assume A's duty to B if B promises to accept it immediately and in substitution for A's duty. B so promises A. There is a novation under which B's and C's promises are consideration for each other, and A's duty to service B's machine is discharged.

III. TORTIOUS INTERFERENCE WITH CONTRACT

The parties to a contract are bound to respect it in the sense that they are liable for damages or other judicial action if they breach. Beneficiaries or assignees may be granted the benefits or assume the obligations of the agreement. In these cases the parties to the agreement have chosen to deliberately expand their contractual community to encompass another. But sometimes strangers are obligated to respect the contract by not dealing with one of the parties in a manner inconsistent with that party's duties under the agreement. If the interest of the party in the contract is like property, should it be entitled to compensation if a third party trespasses on its interests as it would if the stranger walked on its grass or converted its personal property? Is a potential employer foreclosed from hiring a skilled worker if the worker is under contract to another? Should the second employer be liable in damages to the first for its losses, or should the first employer be left to its remedies against the worker it contracted with? May a manufacturer sell goods to a buyer it knows has a long-term requirements contract with a competitor?

By creating a temporary island of stability in a fluid competitive system, the commercial contract protects the expectations which are necessary to all but the simplest competitive activity * * *. Despite Justice Holmes' view that the payment of damages is an acceptable alternative to performance, the law's preference of performance to payment justifies deterring third parties from interference. * * *

Developments in the Law: Competitive Torts, 77 HARV. L. REV. 888, 959 (1964).

The extent of the law's protection in this area is shadowy, particularly when the stranger's activity consists of no more than offering the party it knows is otherwise bound the economic benefit of a more lucrative deal—activity upon which the Great American Way of Life is built.

Mitchell v. Aldrich
Vermont Supreme Court, 1960.
122 Vt. 19, 163 A.2d 833.

■ HOLDEN, J. The plaintiffs seek recovery for wrongful interference with contract relations. They claim the defendants deprived them of an advantageous agreement to purchase a herd of dairy cattle. The trial court withheld the case from the jury by directing a verdict of no liability. The plaintiffs appeal from the judgment for the defendants that was entered on this ruling.

Prior to the sale of the cattle in question, the seller, William Comette, had procured several loans from the Chittenden Trust Company. His obligations were secured by mortgages on real and personal property. The chattel mortgage included farm machinery and the dairy herd, consisting of 102 cows. In August 1947 Comette decided to sell his entire herd and to this end obtained general permission from the mortgagee. He then called the plaintiff Mitchell, informed him of his intention to sell and sought to interest Mitchell in the purchase. The following morning, Mitchell and his associate, the plaintiff Albie, visited the Comette farm and inspected the cattle. After looking over the cattle, the plaintiffs made an offer to purchase the herd for $7,800. This offer was accepted by Comette. The terms of the sale provided for the payment of $100 at that time, $900 to be paid the following day and the balance of the purchase price became due on the removal of the cattle from Comette's barn, in no event later than ten days hence. Comette informed the plaintiffs of the mortgage lien of the Chittenden Trust Company and it was understood by the buyers that approval of the bank was necessary to complete the transaction. Upon the payment of the $100, a written memorandum of the agreement was signed by Comette which set forth the terms of the sale and specified the sale was subject to the approval of the bank.

Comette communicated with his mortgagee on the same day and was advised by the bank that a Mr. Aldrich would call at his farm. The bank had made a prior arrangement with Aldrich to appraise the cattle which Comette sought to sell. It appeared that the Chittenden Trust Company had from time to time called upon Aldrich to make such appraisals. Aldrich was not in the employ of the bank and received no compensation for making the valuations. After Comette's telephone message on August 15, the bank requested Aldrich to make his appraisal right away.

The bank's loan officer, responsible for servicing the Comette obligations, was called as a witness for the defendant Aldrich and gave this testimony concerning Aldrich's authority:

A. We asked Mr. Aldrich to make an appraisal of the cattle as to determine the value of them.

Q. And did you ask him to do anything whatsoever in regard to the sale of them?

A. Other than if he wanted to buy them he had that privilege.

Q. And did you ask him, did you say anything to him in regard to interesting other people in regard to it?

A. No, sir.

After telephoning the bank, Comette informed the plaintiffs that Aldrich had been sent to look at the cows. The plaintiffs went to Aldrich and informed him of their agreement to purchase the Comette cattle. Aldrich disclaimed any interest in the property but added that he would fulfill an appointment with Drew to look at the cattle.

When Aldrich and Drew arrived at the Comette farm, Comette informed them of his undertaking with the plaintiffs, and that he had received $100 in part payment of the price agreed upon. Aldrich replied by saying the plaintiff Mitchell was a "tough fellow to do business with and that I (Comette) probably would never get my money after the cows left the barn." Aldrich went on to say that it would be impossible for Mitchell to get the bank's approval of his purchase. Drew and Aldrich then offered Comette $8,100 for the herd and Aldrich stated there would be no doubt of the bank's approval of that offer. Comette's testimony continued to the effect that he relied on Aldrich's statements for he believed him to be a representative of the bank.

The sale to Drew was completed with the approval of the mortgagee. Drew derived a net profit from the resale of the cattle. Aldrich received compensation from Drew for assistance in getting the cattle ready for auction.

Except for special justification, the law has long recognized liability against one who intentionally intrudes to disrupt an existing contract relation. The interest protected is the right of the individual to security in his business relations. He has a right to preserve the undertakings of persons with whom he has commercial dealings.

The remedy afforded is not restricted to definite and enforceable contracts. Protection is appropriate against unjustified interference with reasonable expectancies of profit though the contract is terminable at will or unenforceable against the promisor in an adversary proceeding. The added element of a definite contract may be the basis for greater protection but it is not an essential requirement.

The promise of the seller, Comette, was a valid undertaking, made with proper reference to the security interest of his mortgagee in accordance with the requirement of 9 V.S.A. § 1763. The approval of the mortgagee, although not a certainty, was anticipated and expected. Save for the consent of the bank, the plaintiffs had a rightful interest in having the seller's promise performed free from other outside interference which might make performance more difficult or impossible.

The purpose of the consent requirement was solely for the protection of the mortgagee. Clearly, if the loan was adequately safeguarded, the mortgagor was not at liberty to abrogate his promise to the buyer in order to gain a higher price. The seller's promise remained in force until such time as it was disapproved for reasons connected with the impairment of the mortgagee's interest.

There is substantial evidence to support the conclusion that the defendants intruded upon this relationship to intercept the prospective gain for themselves by procuring a breach of the seller's undertaking to the plaintiffs before the approval of the bank could be invoked. In any event, the seller broke away from his original undertaking with the plaintiffs and the evidence permitted the jury to conclude that Comette's promise to the plaintiffs would have been fulfilled according to its terms had it not been for the participation of either or both of the defendants. It was for the jury to say whether the plaintiffs' loss of the Comette agreement was caused by the defendants.

The next question is whether the interference was justified as a matter of law. If so the verdict directed by the court may be vindicated.

Justification for interference in the business relations of another is an affirmative defense, and the intruder has the burden of proving his privilege to intervene. Whether an occasion exists which justifies the invasion of another's contract or business relations by the defendant is generally a question for the jury.

The law has crystallized relatively few concrete rules to determine the existence or want of privilege. All the circumstances must be analyzed and considered with reference to the type of relation disrupted, the means employed and the purpose of the actor's interference.

It is only when the actor participated in the exercise of an absolute right equal or superior to the right invaded, that interference can be justified as a matter of law, and the issue withheld from the jury. Such a situation was found to prevail in *Raycroft v. Tayntor*. The defendant threatened to revoke a license to quarry, granted to the plaintiff's employer, unless the employer terminated the plaintiff's employment. The decision points out that the defendant was clothed with all the right and power of the owner of the quarry,—that it was the defendant's right and privilege to determine who might remain at work there. The Court concluded that the defendant was acting in response to a right, equal or superior to that of the plaintiff and there could be no liability.

But there is no legal right to knowingly invade the contract relation of others solely to promote the intervenor's financial interest. And an outsider, with knowledge of a sales agreement who prevents performance by offering a better price, may be held liable to the promisee who has suffered from the intervention. Thus the financial gain derived by the defendants from knowingly ousting the plaintiffs from their bargain with Comette, in itself affords no legal excuse.

The defendants seek refuge in the authority conferred on the Chittenden Trust Company, by statute and contract, to disapprove the plaintiffs' trade as justification for their interdiction of Comette's engagement. The authority which Aldrich derived from the bank was restricted to appraising the Comette herd. There is nothing to indicate the privilege to veto the proposed sale of the mortgaged property was delegated to Aldrich. Herein lies the principal distinction between the facts of this appeal and those that controlled in *Raycroft v. Tayntor*. In the *Raycroft* case the privilege of interference was exercised by a defendant who was clothed with all the right and power of one legally justified to intrude.

It is the defendants' position that the authority to interfere, although originally wanting, was supplied by ratification when the bank approved the sale to the defendant Drew. Whether the bank knowingly ratified the excessive acts of its appraiser in this instance is open to serious question. We are not required to settle that issue to dispose of this appeal. Even if it could be said that Aldrich acted with all the authority of the bank, the privilege of the bank to disrupt the agreement was not absolute, on the facts presented.

The mortgage from Comette to the bank transferred ownership of the mortgaged property to the mortgagee. However ownership of the mortgagee in the encumbered property is subject to the mortgagor's equity and right to redeem. And here the mortgagee had fully recognized Comette's right to redeem and had granted him general permission to offer the mortgaged property for sale. Comette's undertaking with the plaintiffs was consistent with the mortgagee's knowledge and permission, and subject to the mortgagee's final approval.

The mortgagee's right to defeat the proposed agreement to sell was limited by the nature of security required to protect the mortgage loan. In those instances where it might conclude by fair and honest judgment that the proposed sale would dissipate or jeopardize the security of the loan, a clear right to forbid the sale would exist. But where the integrity of the seller's obligation would not be affected, the mortgagee has no absolute right to prohibit the sale or disrupt the bargain.

The security available to the Chittenden Trust Company to protect Comette's obligations was not limited to the dairy herd. The bank had a mortgage on other personal property, including farm machinery and a real estate mortgage as well. The extent of Comette's indebtedness to the Chittenden Trust Company on the date of the proposed sale was not stated in the evidence. It does appear that the chattel mortgage was satisfied and discharged in 1957 by the payment of $6,692. Whether the proposed sale of the cattle to the plaintiffs at the price of $7,800 would imperil the mortgagee's security in such a way as to justify the interference and disapproval by the bank's proper representative framed an issue of fact in this controversy.

It was for the jury to say whether the defendants' interference had the consequence of destroying Comette's promise to the plaintiffs. If the jury reached an affirmative answer to this question, they were required to determine whether the defendants established that the occasion of their interference was authorized by the bank and justified by a present danger to the bank's mortgage security.

The presence of these issues of fact required that the cause be submitted to the jury for decision. It was error to grant the defendants' motion for verdict.

By the same token and for equivalent considerations the plaintiffs' motion for verdict was properly denied. The plaintiffs' assignment of error on this point is without merit.

Judgment reversed and cause remanded.

QUESTIONS AND NOTES

1. Did Comette and Mitchell have a contract before the bank approved? What is the meaning of the phrase, "it was understood by the buyers that approval of the bank was necessary to complete the transaction"?

2. Was Aldrich liable because he induced Comette to break his contract with Mitchell or because he (as an insider) manipulated the condition on which Mitchell's purchase depended?

3. If owner of newly built Apartment House A writes to all tenants of neighboring old Apartment House B offering them very attractive lease terms although knowing that many of them are under long-term leases on their present apartments, and in response some of those tenants break their leases and move into Apartment A, is the owner of Apartment A liable to the owner of Apartment B?

Della Penna v. Toyota Motor Sales, U.S.A.

California Supreme Court, 1995.
11 Cal.4th 376, 902 P.2d 740, 45 Cal.Rptr.2d 436.

■ ARABIAN, J. ...

John Della Penna, an automobile wholesaler doing business as Pacific Motors, brought this action for damages against Toyota Motor Sales, U.S.A., Inc., and its Lexus division, alleging that certain business conduct of defendants both violated provisions of the Cartwright Act, California's state antitrust statute, and constituted an intentional interference with his economic relations. The impetus for Della Penna's suit arose out of the 1989 introduction into the American luxury car market of Toyota's Lexus automobile. Prior to introducing the Lexus, the evidence at trial showed, both the manufacturer, Toyota Motor Corporation, and defendant, the American distributor, had been concerned at the possibility that a resale market might develop for the Lexus in Japan. Even though the car was manufactured in Japan, Toyota's marketing strategy was to bar the vehicle's sale on the Japanese domestic market until after the American roll-out; even then, sales in Japan would only be under a different brand name, the "Celsior." Fearing that auto wholesalers in the United States might re-export Lexus models back to Japan for resale, and concerned that, with production and the availability of Lexus models in the American market limited, re-exports would jeopardize its fledgling network of American Lexus dealers, Toyota inserted in its dealership agreements a "no export" clause....

Following the introduction into the American market, it soon became apparent that some domestic Lexus units were being diverted for foreign sales, principally to Japan. To counter this effect, Toyota managers wrote to their retail dealers, reminding them of the "no-export" policy and explaining that exports for foreign resale could jeopardize the supply of Lexus automobiles available for the United States market. In addition, Toyota compiled a list of "offenders"—dealers and others believed by Toyota to be involved heavily in the developing Lexus foreign resale market—which it distributed to Lexus dealers in the United States. American Lexus dealers were also warned that doing business with those whose names appeared on the "offenders" list might lead to a series of graduated sanctions, from reducing a dealer's allocation to possible reevaluation of the dealer's franchise agreement.

During the years 1989 and 1990, plaintiff Della Penna did a profitable business as an auto wholesaler purchasing Lexus automobiles, chiefly from the Lexus of Stevens Creek retail outlet, at near retail price and exporting them to Japan for resale. By late 1990, however, plaintiff's sources began to dry up, primarily as a result of the "offenders list." Stevens Creek ceased selling models to plaintiff; gradually other sources declined to sell to him as well.

In February 1991, plaintiff filed this lawsuit against Toyota Motors, U.S.A., Inc., alleging both state antitrust claims under the Cartwright Act and interference with his economic relationship with Lexus retail dealers. At the close of plaintiff's case-in-chief, the trial court granted Toyota's motion for nonsuit with respect to the remaining Cartwright Act claim (plaintiff had previously abandoned a related claim—unfair competition—prior to trial). The tort cause of action went to the jury, however, under the standard BAJI instructions applicable to such claims with one significant exception. At the request of defendant and over plaintiff's objection, the trial judge modified BAJI No. 7.82—the basic instruction identifying the elements of the tort and indicating the burden of proof—to require plaintiff to prove that defendant's alleged interfering conduct was "wrongful."

The jury returned a divided verdict, nine to three, in favor of Toyota. After Della Penna's motion for a new trial was denied, he appealed. In an unpublished disposition, the Court of Appeal unanimously reversed the trial court's judgment, ruling that a plaintiff alleging intentional interference with economic relations is not required to establish "wrongfulness" as an element of its prima facie case, and that it was prejudicial error for the trial court to have read the jury an amended instruction to that effect. The Court of Appeal remanded the case to the trial court for a new trial; we then granted Toyota's petition for review and now reverse.

II—A

Although legal historians have traced the origins of the so-called "interference torts" as far back as the Roman law, the proximate historical impetus for their modern development lay in mid–19th century English common law. The opinion of the Queen's Bench in *Lumley v. Gye* (1853) 2 El. & Bl. 216, a case that has become a standard in torts casebooks, is widely cited as the origin of the two torts—interference with contract and its sibling, interference with prospective economic relations[2]—in the form in which they have come down to us. The plaintiff owned the Queen's Theatre, at which operas were presented. He contracted for the services of a soprano, Johanna Wagner, to perform in various entertainments between April 15 and July 15, with the stipulation that Miss Wagner would not perform elsewhere during that time without his permission.

In an action on the case, the theater owner alleged that Gye, the owner of a rival theater, knowing of the Wagner–Lumley agreement, "maliciously" interfered with the contract by "enticing" Wagner to abandon her agreement with Lumley and appear at Gye's theater. Gye's demurrer to the complaint was overruled by the trial

---

2. Throughout this opinion, in an effort to avoid both cumbersome locutions and clumsy acronyms ("IIPEA"), we use the phrase "interference with economic relations" to refer to the tort generally known as "intentional interference with prospective contractual or economic relations" and to distinguish it from the cognate form, "intentional interference with contract."

court, a ruling that was affirmed by the justices of the Queen's Bench on the then somewhat novel grounds that (1) "enticing" someone to leave his or her employment was not limited to disrupting the relationship between master and servant but applied to a "dramatic artiste" such as Miss Wagner, and (2) "wrongfully and maliciously, or, which is the same thing, with notice, interrupt[ing]" a personal service contract, regardless of the means the defendant employed, was an actionable wrong.

The opinion in *Lumley* dealt, of course, with conduct intended to induce the breach of an existing contract, not conduct intended to prevent or persuade others not to contract with the plaintiff. That such an interference with prospective economic relations might itself be tortious was confirmed by the Queen's Bench over the next 40 years. In *Temperton v. Russell*, a labor union, embroiled in a dispute with a firm of builders, announced what today would be called a secondary boycott, intended to force a resolution of the union's grievances by pressuring suppliers of the builder to cease furnishing him construction materials. A failure to comply with the union's boycott demands, suppliers were warned, would result in union pressure on those who bought their supplies not to deal with them.

One such supplier of the builder, Temperton, sued the union's leadership, alleging that his business had been injured by breaches of supply contracts and the refusal of others to do business with him, all as a result of the union's threats. A unanimous Queen's Bench upheld the jury's verdict for the plaintiff, reasoning in part on the authority of *Lumley v. Gye*, that in the words of Lord Esher, the Master of the Rolls, "the distinction * * * between the claim for inducing persons to break contracts already entered into * * * and * * * inducing persons not to enter into contracts * * * can [not] prevail."

"There was the same wrongful intent in both cases, wrongful because malicious," Lord Esher wrote. "There was the same kind of injury to the plaintiff. It seems rather a fine distinction to say that, where a defendant maliciously induces a person not to carry out a contract already made with the plaintiff and so injures the plaintiff, it is actionable, but where he injures the plaintiff by maliciously preventing a person from entering into a contract with the plaintiff, which he would otherwise have entered into, it is not actionable."

As a number of courts and commentators have observed, the keystone of the liability imposed in *Lumley* and *Temperton*, to judge from the opinions of the justices, appears to have been the "malicious" intent of a defendant.... While some have doubted whether the use of the word "malicious" amounted to anything more than an intent to commit an act, knowing it would harm the plaintiff, Dean Keeton, assessing the state of the tort as late as 1984, remarked that "[w]ith intent to interfere as the usual basis of the action, the cases have turned almost entirely upon the defendant's motive or purpose and the means by which he has sought to accomplish it. As in the cases of interference with contract, any manner of intentional invasion of the plaintiff's interests may be sufficient if the purpose is not a proper one."

It was, legal historians have suggested, this early accent on the defendant's "intentionality" that was responsible for allying the interference torts with their remote relatives, intentional torts of a quite different order—battery, for example, or false imprisonment....

One consequence of this superficial kinship was the assimilation to the interference torts of the pleading and burden of proof requirements of the "true" intentional torts: the requirement that the plaintiff need only allege a so-called "prima facie tort" by showing the defendant's awareness of the economic relation, a deliberate interference with it, and the plaintiff's resulting injury. By this account of the matter—the traditional view of the torts and the one adopted by the first Restatement of Torts—the burden then passed to the defendant to demonstrate that its conduct was privileged, that is, "justified" by a recognized defense such as the protection of others or, more likely in this context, the defendant's own competitive business interests.

Because the plaintiff's initial burden of proof was such a slender one, amounting to no more than showing the defendant's conscious act and plaintiff's economic injury, critics argued that legitimate business competition could lead to time consuming and expensive lawsuits (not to speak of potential liability) by a rival, based on conduct that was regarded by the commercial world as both commonplace and appropriate. The "black letter" rules of the Restatement of Torts surrounding the elements and proof of the tort, some complained, might even suggest to "foreign lawyers reading the Restatement as an original matter [that] the whole competitive order of American industry is prima facie illegal."

... Acknowledging [this] criticism, the American Law Institute discarded the prima facie tort requirement of the first Restatement. A new provision, section 766B, required that the defendant's conduct be "improper," and adopted a multifactor "balancing" approach, identifying seven factors for the trier of fact to weigh in determining a defendant's liability. The Restatement Second of Torts, however, declined to take a position on the issue of which of the parties bore the burden of proof, relying on the "considerable disagreement on who has the burden of pleading and proving certain matters" and the observation that "the law in this area has not fully congealed but is still in a formative stage." In addition, the Restatement Second provided that a defendant might escape liability by showing that his conduct was justifiable and did not include the use of "wrongful means."

II-B

[In this omitted portion of the opinion, the court reviewed the addition of a "wrongful," "improper," "illegal," "independently tortious," or some other variant element to the interference with economic relations tort in many other states.]

III

[In this omitted portion of the opinion, the court reviewed the development of the economic relations tort in California Supreme Court cases, paralleling the evolution in other jurisdictions, but not yet adding a "wrongful" conduct element.]

Meanwhile, developments in the Court of Appeal and in the practical administration of such claims in the trial courts had, if anything, outdistanced our own formulations of the elements of the tort and the allocation of the burden of proof in at least two respects. First, several Court of Appeal opinions appeared to engraft onto the elements of the plaintiff's cause of action allegations and proof that the defendant's conduct was "wrongful" or, as the Court of Appeal said in *Tri-Growth Centre City, Ltd. v. Silldorf, Burdman, Duignan & Eisenberg*, was "based on facts that take the defendant's actions out of the realm of legitimate business transactions."

Second, in 1990, BAJI, the Book of Approved Jury Instructions widely used by trial judges in civil cases, relying on the Restatement Second of Torts and Mr. Witkin's account of the tort, included an instruction providing that a defendant in an economic relations tort case could defeat liability by showing that its conduct was not independently "wrongful."

These developments, of course, closely reflect a nearly concurrent change in views both within the American Law Institute and in other jurisdictions. In the face of those twin lines of development, we are thus presented with the opportunity to consider whether to expressly reconstruct the formal elements of the interference with economic relations tort to achieve a closer alignment with the practice of the trial courts, emerging views within the Court of Appeal, the rulings of many other state high courts, and the critiques of leading commentators. We believe that we should.

IV

In searching for a means to recast the elements of the economic relations tort and allocate the associated burdens of proof, we are guided by an overmastering concern articulated by high courts of other jurisdictions and legal commentators: The need to draw and enforce a sharpened distinction between claims for the tortious disruption of an existing contract and claims that a prospective contractual or economic relationship has been interfered with by the defendant....

The courts provide a damage remedy against third party conduct intended to disrupt an existing contract precisely because the exchange of promises resulting in such a formally cemented economic relationship is deemed worthy of protection from interference by a stranger to the agreement. Economic relationships short of contractual, however, should stand on a different legal footing as far as the potential for tort liability is reckoned. Because ours is a culture firmly wedded to the social rewards of commercial contests, the law usually takes care to draw lines of legal liability in a way that maximizes areas of competition free of legal penalties.

A doctrine that blurs the analytical line between interference with an existing business contract and interference with commercial relations less than contractual is one that invites both uncertainty in conduct and unpredictability of its legal effect. The notion that inducing the breach of an existing contract is simply a subevent of the "more inclusive" class of acts that interfere with economic relations, while perhaps theoretically unobjectionable, has been mischievous as a practical matter. Our courts should, in short, firmly distinguish the two kinds of business contexts, bringing a greater solicitude to those relationships that have ripened into agreements, while recognizing that relationships short of that subsist in a zone where the rewards and risks of competition are dominant.

Beyond that, we need not tread today. It is sufficient to dispose of the issue before us in this case by holding that a plaintiff seeking to recover for alleged interference with prospective economic relations has the burden of pleading and proving that the defendant's interference was wrongful "by some measure beyond the fact of the interference itself." ...

CONCLUSION

We hold that a plaintiff seeking to recover for an alleged interference with prospective contractual or economic relations must plead and prove as part of its case-in-chief that the defendant not only knowingly interfered with the plaintiff's expectancy, but engaged in conduct that was wrongful by some legal measure other than the fact of interference itself. The judgment of the Court of Appeal is reversed and the cause is remanded with directions to affirm the judgment of the trial court.

■ MOSK, J., concurring in the judgment. [Omitted].

QUESTIONS AND NOTES

1. Three of the twelve jurors found for Della Penna. To them, what was Toyota's "wrongful" act? Is aggressive competition in a capitalist economy "wrongful"?

2. What if Della Penna did not export any Lexuses back to Japan, and Toyota put Della Penna on the "offenders" list by accident? What if Toyota just didn't like Della Penna and put him on the list for that reason? What if Della Penna did export

Lexuses to Japan until Toyota put him on the list and then Della Penna contritely went before the president of Toyota and swore on a stack of bibles that he would export no more, but Toyota would not take Della Penna off the "offenders" list?

3. Can Toyota dictate to their dealers to whom they may sell Lexuses? Can Toyota then refuse to allow its dealers to sell Lexuses in the South? Or in Detroit?

4. Recall the facts in *Best v. Southland*, p. 13. Coastal Lumber Company buys the lumber that Southland was going to loan Best. What result if Best sues Coastal for tortious interference? What result if Coastal Lumber knew about the loan arrangement between Best and Southland? What result if Coastal was the secondary contractor on the Security Bank job and stood to take over the entire project if Best could not perform?

5. Suppose that Della Penna was in the process of negotiating a contract with Lexus of Stevens Creek, and a binding preliminary agreement (an agreement on all terms that require negotiation but which has not been completely formalized) was made before Toyota made threats of graduated sanctions against dealers that sold cars to those on the "offenders" list. Lexus of Stevens Creek stops selling Lexus cars to Della Penna. On what cause of action can Della Penna sue Toyota? What result? What if the negotiations had produced a binding preliminary commitment (an agreement with open terms but parties bound to continue negotiations with duty of good faith and fair dealing)? Same result?

6. Suppose that Della Penna had a contract with the Lexus of Stevens Creek retail outlet to supply him with one hundred Lexus cars a year for a term of ten years before Toyota made its threats to take graduated sanctions against dealers selling to those on the "offenders" list. Lexus of Stevens Creek stops selling Lexus cars to Della Penna, and Della Penna sues Toyota for tortious interference with contract. What result?

7. The central question what is "wrongful" or "improper" in these situations is not easily determined. Consider the following disclaimer in the Restatement of Torts, before it attempts to define "improper":

> The tort of interference with existing or prospective contractual relations ... is an intentional tort. It does not, however, fully fit the pattern for other intentional torts, especially those involving physical harm to person or property.... Initial liability depends upon the interplay of several factors and is not reducible to a single rule; and privileges, too, are not clearly established but depend upon a consideration of much the same factors. Moreover, there is considerable disagreement on who has the burden of pleading and proving certain matters, such, for example, as the existence and effect of competition for prospective business.

This has occurred for two reasons. First, the law in this area has not fully congealed but is still in a formative stage. The several forms of the tort [(1) intentional interference with performance of a contract by third person, (2) intentional interference with another's performance of his own contract, and (3) intentional interference with prospective contractual relation] are often not distinguished by the courts.... This has produced a blurring of the significance of the factors involved in determining liability. These factors are stated and described in § 767.

The second reason grows out of use of the term "malicious" in *Lumley v. Gye* (1853) and other early cases. It soon came to be realized that the term was not being used in a literal sense, requiring ill will toward the plaintiff as a requirement for imposing liability. Many courts came to call this "legal malice," and to hold that in this sense the requirement means that the infliction of the harm must be intentional and "without justification." "Justification" is a broader and looser term than "privilege," and the consequence has been that its meaning has not been very clear....

The word adopted for use in this Chapter, neutral enough to acquire a specialized meaning of its own for the purposes of the Chapter, is "improper." ... Each of [the three forms of this tort] provides that the interference must be improper. Section 767 specifies and analyzes the factors to be taken into consideration in determining whether the interference is improper, and must therefore be read and applied to each of the earlier sections. The determination of whether an interference is improper depends upon a comparative appraisal of these factors. And the decision is, whether it was improper under the circumstances—that is under the particular facts of the individual case, not in terms of rules of law or generalizations....

RESTATEMENT, SECOND, TORTS, Div. 9, Ch. 37, Introductory Note.

Does the California Supreme Court give us any direction on what is "wrongful" or "improper" in this case? How would you define "wrongful" or "improper" for the purposes of tortious interference?

8. Professor Harvey Perlman suggests "that the interference tort should be limited to cases in which the defendant's acts are independently unlawful and that if improper motivation is to give rise to liability, it should be based only on objective indicia of activity producing social loss." Perlman noted that in addition to tort law, courts have also relied on other sources to define the lawfulness of a defendant's behavior. He supported the incorporation of such sources so that "the focus will be, as it should, on the economic effects of the defendant's act." In summing up his argument, he wrote:

Where the defendant's act of interference is independently unlawful, tort objectives predominate; where the defendant's behavior is lawful except for the resulting interference, tort theory should reflect and remain consistent with contract policies. In cases of unlawful acts, the issue is viewed more properly as the scope of liability for unlawful behavior; the interference tort, with its requirement that the defendant's intention focus on the plaintiff's relationship, provides a convenient method of limiting liability to a narrow range of economic harm. In cases of otherwise lawful acts, tort liability works at cross-purposes with contract policies. Contract remedies seem to promote efficiency, whereas the addition of inducer liability inhibits effective outcomes . . . By confining the tort to cases of independently unlawful acts or cases where improper motive can be discerned from objective facts, social welfare can be enhanced . . .

[A]doption of an unlawful means test has two advantages. First, it will reduce the number of cases that actually diverge from the analysis. Second, and perhaps more significantly, it will reduce the chilling effect that the current ambiguously stated doctrine must have on socially beneficial activity.

Harvey S. Perlman, *Interference with Contract and Other Economic Expectancies: A Clash of Tort and Contract Doctrine*, 49 U. CHI. L. REV. 61, 128-29 (1982).

Adler, Barish, Daniels, Levin and Creskoff v. Epstein

Pennsylvania Supreme Court, 1978.
482 Pa. 416, 393 A.2d 1175, 1 A.L.R. 4th 1144.

■ ROBERTS, J. ...

I. BACKGROUND

From the formation of Adler Barish in February, 1976, through March of the next year, appellees were salaried associates of Adler Barish.[3] Appellees were under

---

3. In establishing Adler Barish, its partners brought with them approximately 1300 cases from their old law firm, Freedman, Borowsky and Lorry, in which they shared approximately half the profits, losses, and assets. The two firms later signed a writing whose terms gave Adler Barish custody and control over the 1300 files transferred, and preserved the financial interest partners of Adler Barish had before leaving the Freedman firm. Clients whose files were transferred became clients of Adler Barish. From March, 1976 to April, 1977, Adler Barish opened over six hundred new case files.

Appellees were salaried employees of the Freedman firm at the time Adler Barish was formed. Appellees left Freedman and went to work for Adler Barish.

We take our statement of facts from the findings of fact of the court of common pleas, sitting in equity....

the supervision of Adler Barish partners, who directed appellees' work on cases which clients brought to the firm.

While still working for Adler Barish, appellees decided to form their own law firm and took several steps toward achieving their goal. They retained counsel to advise them concerning their business venture, sought and found office space, and early in March, 1977, signed a lease.

Shortly before leaving Adler Barish, appellees procured a line of $150,000 from First Pennsylvania Bank. As security, appellees furnished bank officials with a list of eighty-eight cases and their anticipated legal fees, several of which were higher than $25,000, and together exceeded $500,000. No case on the list, however, was appellees'. Rather, each case was an Adler Barish case on which appellees were working.

Appellee Alan Epstein's employment relationship with Adler Barish terminated on March 10, 1977.[5] At his request, Epstein continued to use offices of Adler Barish until March 19. During this time, and through April 4, when Adler Barish filed its complaint, Epstein was engaged in an active campaign to procure business for his new law firm. He initiated contacts by phone and in person, with clients of Adler Barish with open cases on which he had worked while a salaried employee. Epstein advised the Adler Barish clients that he was leaving the firm and that they could choose to be represented by him, Adler Barish, or any other firm or attorney.

Epstein's attempt to procure business on behalf of the firm did not stop with these contacts. He mailed to the clients form letters which could be used to discharge Adler Barish as counsel, name Epstein the client's new counsel and create a contingent fee agreement. Epstein also provided clients with a stamped envelope addressed to Epstein. Appellees Richard Weisbord, Arnold Wolf, and Sanford Jablon, who left Adler Barish on April 1, 1977, were aware of Epstein's efforts to procure this business on behalf of their new firm and did not attempt to curtail them. Indeed, Weisbord and Wolf, upon leaving Adler Barish, also immediately began to seek business, as did Epstein, for the new firm. They too informed clients of Adler Barish of their plans and that the clients were free to discharge Adler Barish and retain Weisbord and Wolf in its stead. Their efforts continued until Adler Barish filed its complaint.

---

5. The firm received documents relating to cases for which it apparently had no file. Contrary to the firm's procedure, Epstein personally maintained files for some cases. Likewise, Epstein did not adhere to Adler Barish policy concerning certain fees. Adler Barish obtained a case which was assigned to Epstein. He sent the file to an out of state attorney for further handling. Instead of turning over the forwarding fee to the firm, Epstein kept it for himself. It appears that these events led to termination of Epstein's employment.

On April 4, the court of common pleas granted Adler Barish preliminary relief, enjoining appellees' campaign to obtain the business of Adler Barish clients. One month later, on May 5, the court entered its final decree, which provided:

[T]he defendants, ALAN B. EPSTEIN, RICHARD A. WEISBORD, ARNOLD J. WOLF and SANFORD I. JABLON, and all persons acting in concert with them or otherwise participating with them or acting in their aid or behalf, are permanently enjoined and restrained from contacting and/or communicating with those persons who up to and including April 1, 1977, had active legal matters pending with and were represented by the law firm of ADLER, BARISH, DANIELS, LEVIN and CRESKOFF, except that:

1. Nothing in this Final Decree shall be construed to preclude the defendants from announcing the formation of their new professional relationship in accordance with the requirements of DR 2-102 of the Code of Professional Responsibility.

2. Nothing in this Final Decree shall preclude those persons who, up to and including April 1, 1977, had active legal matters pending with and had been represented by the law firm of ADLER, BARISH, DANIELS, LEVIN and CRESKOFF from voluntarily discharging their present attorney and selecting any of the defendants, or any other attorney, to represent them.

The court concluded that appellees "engaged in illegal solicitation in complete and total disregard for the Code of Professional Responsibility" and thereby "tortiously interfered with the contractual and business relations that exist between Adler Barish and its clients." It found equitable relief appropriate in view of appellees' "avowed intentions * * * to continue their illegal solicitation."

Appellees appealed to the Superior Court, which reversed. In addition to granting Adler Barish's petition for allowance of appeal, we granted a stay and expedited argument.

II. APPELLEES' CONSTITUTIONAL CLAIM

The facts found by the court of common pleas, which appellees do not dispute and the Superior Court did not disturb, demonstrate that, while leaving Adler Barish, appellees made numerous contacts with Adler Barish clients on whose active cases appellees were working before leaving Adler Barish. Adler Barish argues that appellees' conduct constitutes an intentional interference with existing contractual relationships between Adler Barish and its clients. According to Adler Barish, appellees' conduct is "deserving of censure, not encouragement." Appellees on the other hand, contend that their conduct was "privileged," and that therefore no right of action for intentional interference lies. Moreover, they argue that their conduct is protected under the first and fourteenth amendments to the Constitution of the United States.

"[S]peech which does 'no more than propose a commercial transaction'" is no longer outside the protection of the first and fourteenth amendments to the Constitution of the United States. *Virginia Pharmacy Board v. Virginia Consumer Council.* Accordingly, states are barred from imposing blanket prohibitions against truthful advertising of "routine" legal services. Such a blanket prohibition "serves to inhibit the free flow of commercial information and to keep the public in ignorance."

Nothing in the challenged decree prohibited appellees from engaging in the truthful advertising protected under *Bates.* Appellees could inform the general public, including clients of Adler Barish, of the availability of their legal services, and thus the "free flow of commercial information" to the public is unimpaired. Moreover, the injunction expressly permitted appellees to announce "formation of their new professional relationship in accordance with the requirements of DR 2–102 of the Code of Professional Responsibility." Appellees therefore were permitted to mail announcements to "lawyers, clients, former clients, personal friends, and relatives." This would include the very clients of Adler Barish whose business appellees sought.

What the injunction did proscribe was appellees' "contacting and/or communicating with those persons who up to and including April 1, 1977, had active legal matters pending with and were represented by the law firm of ADLER, BARISH, DANIELS, LEVIN and CRESKOFF." Our task is to decide whether the conduct of appellees is constitutionally subject to sanction.

The Code of Professional Responsibility, DR 2–103(A) (as adopted, 1974), provides: "A lawyer shall not recommend employment, as a private practitioner, of himself, his partner, or associate to a non-lawyer who has not sought his advice regarding employment of a lawyer." Appellees clearly violated this "proscription against self-recommendation." They recommended their own employment, even though clients of Adler Barish did not seek appellees' advice "regarding employment of a lawyer."

Ohralik v. Ohio State Bar Association, makes plain that, after *Bates,* states may constitutionally impose sanctions upon attorneys engaging in conduct which violates these disciplinary rules, even though the conduct involves "commercial speech." In *Ohralik,* the state bar association suspended an attorney who "solicited" persons injured in an automobile accident by making visits to the hospital room where the persons were recovering. Mr. Justice Powell, speaking for the Court, emphasized that commercial speech does not enjoy the same constitutional protections traditionally afforded other forms of speech....

Just as in *Ohralik,* appellees' conduct frustrates, rather than advances, Adler Barish clients' "informed and reliable decisionmaking." After making Adler Barish clients expressly aware that appellees' new firm was interested in procuring their active cases, Epstein provided the clients the forms that would sever one attorney-client relationship and create another. Epstein's aim was to encourage speedy, simple action by the client. All the client needed to do was to "sign on the dotted line" and mail the forms in the self-addressed, stamped envelopes....[8]

Thus, appellees were actively attempting to induce the clients to change law firms in the middle of their active cases. Appellees' concern for their line of credit and the success of their new law firm gave them an immediate, personally created financial interest in the clients' decisions. In this atmosphere, appellees' contacts posed too great a risk that clients would not have the opportunity to make a careful, informed decision. "[T]o reduce the likelihood of overreaching and the exertion of undue influence on lay persons; to protect the privacy of individuals; and to avoid situations where the lawyer's exercise of judgment on behalf of the client will be clouded by his own pecuniary self-interest," *Ohralik v. Ohio State Bar Association*, 436 U.S. at 461, we must reject appellees' argument and conclude that, just as in *Ohralik,* the Constitution permits regulation of their conduct.[9]

III. THE RIGHT OF ACTION

Thus, we turn to whether the court of common pleas properly concluded that Adler Barish is entitled to relief. In *Birl v. Philadelphia Electric Co.* (1960), this Court adopted Section 766 of Restatement of Torts and its definition of the right of action for intentional interference with existing contractual relations....

An examination of this case in light of Restatement (Second) of Torts, § 766, reveals that the sole dispute is whether appellees' conduct is "improper." There is no doubt that appellees intentionally sought to interfere with performance of the contractual relations between Adler Barish and its clients. While still at Adler Barish, appellees' behavior, particularly their use of expected fees from Adler Barish clients' cases, indicates appellees' desire to gain a segment of the firm's business. This pattern of conduct continued until the court of common pleas enjoined it. Indeed, appellees' intentional efforts to obtain a share of Adler Barish's business were successful. The record reveals that several clients signed the forms Epstein prepared

---

8. Appellees' contacts pose consequences more serious than mailing of announcements in conformity with DR 2-102 and as allowed by the decree of the court of common pleas. Appellees' contacts make express their interest in Adler Barish clients' cases, while announcements, at most, only suggest the same. Moreover, appellees' form letters and self addressed envelopes, unlike announcements, provide appellees a means of benefiting from a clients' immediate, perhaps ill considered, response to the circumstances.

9. We also recognize that *In re Primus* forbids governmental sanctioning of an attorney who, in pursuit of ideological goals, advises a prospective client of legal rights and offers the free legal assistance of a nonprofit organization of which the attorney is a member. But appellees' goals were vastly different. Appellees were interested not in any particular client or the specific issues the cases they sought might raise, but rather their own financial gain.

on behalf of appellees notifying Adler Barish that the clients no longer wished the services of Adler Barish. Likewise, the record reveals that Adler Barish and its clients were parties to valid, existing contracts.

In assessing whether appellees' conduct is "improper," we bear in mind what this Court stated in *Glenn v. Point Park College*, where we analyzed "privileges" in conjunction with the closely related right of action for intentional interference with prospective contract relations:

> The absence of privilege or justification in the tort under discussion is closely related to the element of intent. As stated by Harper & James, The Law of Torts, § 6.11: "* * * where, as in most cases, the defendant acts at least in part for the purpose of protecting some legitimate interest which conflicts with that of the plaintiff, a line must be drawn and the interests evaluated. This process results in according or denying a privilege which, in turn, determines liability." What is or is not privileged conduct in a given situation is not susceptible of precise definition. Harper & James refer in general to interferences which "are sanctioned by the 'rules of the game' which society has adopted", and to "the area of socially acceptable conduct which the law regards as privileged" * * *.

We are guided, too, by Section 767 of Restatement (Second) of Torts, which focuses on what factors should be considered in determining whether conduct is "improper":

> In determining whether an actor's conduct in intentionally interfering with an existing contract or a prospective contractual relation of another is improper or not, consideration is given to the following factors:
>
> (a) The nature of the actor's conduct,
>
> (b) The actor's motive,
>
> (c) The interests of the other with which the actor's conduct interferes,
>
> (d) The interests sought to be advanced by the actor,
>
> (e) The proximity or remoteness of the actor's conduct to the interference and
>
> (f) The relations between the parties.[17]

---

17. Thus, new Restatement (Second) of Torts focuses upon whether conduct is "proper," rather than "privileged." Compare Restatement of Torts, § 766 (1939) ("[e]xcept as stated in Section 698 [(relating to contracts to marry)], *one who without a privilege to do so*, induces or otherwise purposely causes a third person not to (a) perform a contract with another, or (b) enter into or continue a business relation with another is liable to the other for the harm caused thereby"). Comment b to Restatement (Second) of Torts, supra at § 767, explains the shift in inquiry:

> *Privilege to Interfere, or Interference Not Improper.* Unlike other intentional torts such as intentional injury to person or property, or defamation, this branch of tort law has not developed a crystallized set of definite rules as to the existence or nonexistence of a privilege

We find nothing in the "'rules of the game' which society has adopted" which sanctions appellees' conduct. Indeed, the rules which apply to those who enjoy the privilege of practicing law in this Commonwealth expressly disapprove appellees' method of obtaining clients. We find such a departure from "[r]ecognized ethical codes" "significant in evaluating the nature of [appellees'] conduct." All the reasons underlying our Disciplinary Rules' "proscription against [appellees'] self-recommendation," especially the concern that appellees' contacts too easily could overreach and unduly influence Adler Barish clients with active cases, are relevant here.

Appellees' conduct adversely affected more than the informed and reliable decisionmaking of Adler Barish clients with active cases. Their conduct also had an immediate impact upon Adler Barish. Adler Barish was prepared to continue to perform services for its clients and therefore could anticipate receiving compensation for the value of its efforts. Moreover, Adler Barish's fee agreements with clients were a source of anticipated revenue protected from outside interference.[20]

---

to act in the manner stated in §§ 766, 766A or 766B. Because of this fact, this Section is expressed in terms of whether the interference is improper or not rather than in terms of a specific privilege to act in the manner specified. The issue in each case is whether the interference is improper or not under the circumstances; whether, upon a consideration of the relative significance of the factors involved, the conduct should be permitted without liability, despite its effect of harm to another.

20. In *Richette*, an attorney representing an employee of the defendant railroad company and member of the defendant union, brought suit charging that defendants improperly interfered with a fee agreement between plaintiff and the employee. The employee, injured at work, had retained plaintiff, but later discharged him. In upholding the jury's award of compensatory damages for plaintiff, this Court concluded:

> The jury was warranted in finding from the evidence presented that the named defendants coordinated, through wile, stratagem and deception to separate an attorney from his client. It could not be said, as a matter of the law, that the jury went astray when they concluded, as they must have, that [the employee] did not voluntarily write a letter revoking his power of attorney to [plaintiff]. Logic, sequence of events, and palpable circumstances justify their conclusion that the railroad company representatives prepared a letter of revocation, that they employed a maneuver to have [the employee] copy that letter outside the railroad company office, thinking that this would wipe away their participation in the affair; that they supplied [the employee] with the paper on which he was to copy the letter of revocation; that [a union official], working with the railroad, supervised the copying, and supplied the envelope, in which he placed the letter, which he consigned to the United States mails. The jury were warranted in concluding that all the named defendants were a part of this plan and participated fully in the enterprise which finally resulted in depriving a member of the Philadelphia bar from legal business properly his.

First Pennsylvania Bank's willingness to extend appellees credit on the basis of expected fees from cases confirms the financial significance of Adler Barish's fee agreements.

It is true that, upon termination of their employment relationship with Adler Barish, appellees were free to engage in their own business venture. But appellees' right to pursue their own business interests is not absolute. "[U]nless otherwise agreed, after the termination of the agency, the agent * * * has a duty to the principal not to take advantage of a still subsisting confidential relation created during the prior agency relation." Restatement (Second) of Agency, § 396(d).

Appellees' contacts were possible because Adler Barish partners trusted appellees with the high responsibility of developing its clients' cases. From the position of trust and responsibility, appellees were able to gain knowledge of the details, and status, of each case to which appellees had been assigned. In the atmosphere surrounding appellees' departure, appellees' contacts unduly suggested a course of action for Adler Barish clients and unfairly prejudiced Adler Barish. No public interest is served in condoning use of confidential information which has these effects. Clients too easily may suffer in the end.

Order of the Superior Court reversed and court of common pleas directed to reinstate its final decree. Each party pay own costs.

APPENDIX

Epstein sent the following cover letter:

404 South Camac Street
Philadelphia, Pennsylvania 19147
March 25, 1977

Re:

Dear

In confirmation of our recent conversation, I have terminated my association with the offices of Adler, Barish, Daniels, Levin and Creskoff and will be continuing in the practice of law in center city Philadelphia. As I explained, you have the right to determine who shall represent your interests and handle the above-captioned matter in the future. You may elect to be represented by my former office, me or any other attorney permitted to practice in this jurisdiction.

During our conversation, you expressed a desire to have me continue as your legal representative, and in recognition of your choice in this regard, I have enclosed two documents which must be signed and returned to me in the enclosed stamped, addressed envelope to effect this end. Copies of these documents are also enclosed for your records.

If you have any questions regarding these matters or any other matter, feel free to call me at KI 6–5223.

Sincerely,

Alan B. Epstein
ABE/ete
Enclosure

The Form discharging Adler Barish provides:

> Messrs. Adler, Barish, Daniels, Levin & Creskoff
> 2nd Floor, Rohm & Haas Building
> Sixth & Market Streets
> Philadelphia, PA 19106
>
> Re:
> Gentlemen:
>
> I have been advised that Alan B. Epstein, Esquire has terminated his association with your firm of attorneys and it has been carefully explained to me that I have the right to determine who shall represent me and handle the above-captioned matter.
>
> This correspondence is to serve notice I hereby discharge the office of Adler, Barish, Daniels, Levin & Creskoff from any further representation of me whatsoever and request that the members of your firm and/or your employees or agents refrain from acting against my wishes in this regard or my interests in any way whatsoever.
>
> This letter is to also serve as my notice and request that I want Alan B. Epstein to be my attorney in this matter, to keep or secure my file and all allied papers, and to handle this matter and represent me.
>
> I further direct you to deliver immediately to my attorney, Alan B. Epstein, my entire file and all allied papers and to refrain further from any actions contrary to my attorney's wishes or directions in connection with this matter.
>
> Very truly yours,

The following fee agreement was also sent to Adler Barish clients:

CONTINGENT FEE AGREEMENT

> Date _____
>
> I (we) hereby constitute and appoint ALAN EPSTEIN as my (our) attorney to prosecute a claim for me (us) for _____ against all responsible parties, including, but not limited to _____ . The claimant (deceased) is _____ , and the cause of action arose on _____ .
>
> I (we) hereby agree that the compensation of my (our) attorney for services shall be determined as follows: _____ .
>
> I (we) hereby acknowledge receipt of a duplicate copy of this Contingent Fee Agreement.
>
> _____   _____
> Name   Name
>
> _____   _____
> Address   Address

■ MANDERINO, J., dissenting....

One need not be a legal scholar to see the distinction for First Amendment purposes between the ambulance-chasing tactics used by the lawyer in *Ohralik* and the written communications which appellees mailed to the clients of Adler, Barish. The letters sent to prospective clients which would discharge Adler, Barish should the client sign on the dotted line contained no arm-twisting device pressuring clients to make an immediate response. Nor were these clients uninformed about the choices they could make in either retaining or discharging Adler, Barish as legal counsel. Additionally, appellees' communication contained *no* false and misleading statements which would confuse, deceive, or mislead prospective clients. More importantly, appellees did not attempt to motivate these clients to stir up litigation as was done in *Ohralik*.

This Court today misuses its injunctive powers to prohibit not only what is a protected form of direct solicitation under the First Amendment but to prohibit an attorney from truthfully informing a client about the client's legal rights. The Order of the Superior Court should therefore be affirmed.

QUESTIONS AND NOTES

1. Client retains Attorney A to institute a lawsuit. Client loses confidence in Attorney A and consults Attorney B about the handling of the matter. Attorney B tells Client that she does not agree with the way that Attorney A is proceeding and further tells Client of his right to discharge his attorney without paying contract damages. Client discharges Attorney A and retains Attorney X. Attorney A sues Attorney B for interference with his contract. What result?

2. Seller confers with Attorney regarding a sales agreement he finds onerous to perform. Attorney advises Seller that contract breach is not a crime and that, under the rule of *Hadley v. Baxendale,* Buyer's damages will be very limited and probably not worth the bother of litigation to collect. Seller breaches the agreement, and Buyer sues Attorney in tort for interference. What result? If Buyer has a valid claim, how will her damages be measured?

3. Don't the clients of Adler, Barish have the right to terminate that relationship and hire a new lawyer? Is Epstein's tort that he explained to the clients their legal rights?

4. Are the Restatement factors helpful in determining what is "improper"? Can you think of a better way?

Dowd and Dowd v. Gleason

Appellate Court of Illinois, First District, First Division (2004).
816 N.E.2d 754, 352 Ill.App.3d 365.

■ JUSTICE O'MALLEY delivered the opinion of the court:

Plaintiff, Dowd & Dowd, Ltd. (Dowd), filed suit against Nancy J. Gleason and Douglas G. Shreffler (defendants), after they resigned as shareholders (partners) of Dowd and opened a new law firm, Gleason, McGuire and Shreffler (GMS). While working at Dowd, Nancy Gleason managed the Allstate Insurance Company (Allstate) account. When the new firm was formed, Allstate moved its business to the new law firm. Dowd filed suit against defendants, alleging breach of fiduciary duty, breach of employment contract, tortious interference with prospective economic advantage and civil conspiracy.

The case was heard in a bench trial. In February 2001, the court entered a judgment in favor of Dowd and denied defendants' mistrial motion. In March 2001, the court found that there was no reason to delay enforcement or appeal. Defendants now appeal.

BACKGROUND

Dowd & Dowd is a law firm. In 1975 or 1976, Northbrook Excess and Surplus Insurance Company, a subsidiary of Allstate, retained Dowd for advice on insurance coverage of claims that were being made against Allstate's policyholders for injuries arising from exposure to asbestos products. Nancy Gleason, one of the defendants here, joined Dowd in 1977 as an attorney and for the next 13 years became the primary person handling the Allstate account. Lynn Crim was the head of Allstate's claims department and supervisor to George Riley, a manager in the claims department. Between 1987 and December 1990, Crim spoke with Nancy Gleason on a daily basis and spoke with Mike Dowd, the senior partner, "[r]arely."

On August 7, 1990, Dowd paralegal Leslie Henkels met with Judy Gleason (an attorney at Dowd and wife of Douglas Shreffler), Nancy Gleason (an attorney and niece of principal partner Mike Dowd), and Maureen Henegan (a Dowd secretary). During that meeting, Judy Gleason indicated that Patrick Dowd (son of Mike Dowd) was being promoted to partnership status and that she and the others were leaving the firm. On or about September 25, there was a partners meeting and Patrick's appointment was announced. Following the appointment of Patrick Dowd to partner, Nancy Gleason, Douglas Shreffler and Judith Gleason began investigating the possibility of establishing a new, separate law firm. They decided to take preliminary steps to form that firm and by December 1990, GMS had located office space, ordered furniture and equipment and initiated a banking relationship with the Harris Bank.

On December 31, 1990, Nancy Gleason and Shreffler resigned from Dowd and with Philip McGuire and Judith Gleason, started the GMS law firm. On December 31, 1990, Nancy Gleason and Shreffler went to Mike Dowd's home "in the late morning" to inform him of their resignations as officers and directors of Dowd. Crim of Allstate gave Gleason the charge of moving Allstate's cases that were currently with Dowd to the new firm. Crim testified that he learned of Gleason's new firm on December 31, 1990, "first thing in the morning."

ANALYSIS

I. STATUS OF CLIENTS

Defendants' initial contention is that the trial court's reasoning in the breach of fiduciary duty section of its order essentially reduces the status of clients to chattel and the decision deprives clients of their choice of counsel by prohibiting the mobility of lawyers. A full reading of the court's written order shows that defendants' assertion is an overstatement of the court's findings and an exaggeration of the impact of those findings.

In its written order, the trial court discussed the broad guidelines regarding the standards and obligations used to determine whether a departing partner's actions prior to leaving a firm constitute a breach of fiduciary duty. In citing an article from the Michigan Bar Journal (A. Goetz, *Break Away Lawyers,* 77 Mich. B.J. 1078 (1998)), the trial court noted that when attorneys leave a law firm to establish their own firm, it is appropriate to consider the clients as property of the firm and not property of the individual members of the firm. The trial court went on to explain that, accordingly, the lawyers may not solicit the firm's clients on company time nor may they use the firm's resources to establish their own, competing firm, particularly until proper notice has been given. While defendants were free to set up a new law firm, the question became whether any of the steps taken in connection with such action breached the fiduciary duty that the defendants owed to Dowd. On the other hand, the current firm has a duty not to interfere with the departing attorneys' continued right to practice law. The trial court noted that it is not improper for the lawyer to notify the client of his impending departure provided that he makes it clear that legal representation is the client's choice. In our view, the court's discussion encourages departing attorneys to give clients an informed choice as to who will manage their business in light of changes in employment or business structure. The court's order also reminds current firms to allow attorneys to move freely without hindrance from them.

In fact, the supreme court noted in its review of this matter that the case law supports the view that while lawyers who are planning to leave a firm may take preliminary, logical steps of obtaining office space and supplies, they may not solicit clients for their new venture. *Dowd,* 181 Ill.2d at 475 (citing *Graubard Mollen Dannett & Horowitz v. Moskovitz* (N.Y.1995). The *Graubard* court noted:

> "'[A]s a matter of principle, preresignation surreptitious "solicitation" of firm clients for a partner's personal gain * * * is actionable. Such conduct exceeds what is necessary to protect the important value of client freedom of choice in legal representation, and thoroughly undermines another important value-the loyalty owed partners (including law partners), which distinguishes partnerships (including law partnerships) from bazaars.'"

Defendants here rely on *Corti v. Fleishe* (1981), an inapposite case, for the proposition that clients may not be reduced to chattel. The appellate court in *Corti* held that the employment agreement there, which provided for the transfer of client files from defendants to plaintiff without permission from clients, was void and contrary to public policy in that it deprived clients of the right to be represented by counsel of their own choice. The *Corti* case is inapposite because that case dealt with a written agreement to transfer clients' files without permission from clients. In the instant case, there is no such agreement, oral or written. Here, we are dealing with the alleged improper solicitation of Dowd's largest client and the duty defendants owed to their former firm.

We are by no means asserting that clients of a law firm are the property of the firm in terms of "chattel," but we are reaffirming the tenet that preresignation solicitation of firm clients for a partner's personal gain is a breach of the partner's fiduciary duty to the firm.

II. BREACH OF FIDUCIARY DUTY

The supreme court opinion in this case's procedural history noted that "[t]his is a fact-intensive inquiry, and on remand the finder of fact will have to resolve a number of factual disputes before determining whether the defendants breached their fiduciary duty." *Dowd,* 181 Ill.2d at 477, 230 Ill.Dec. 229, 693 N.E.2d 358.

On remand, the trial court made several findings of fact as to defendants' breach of fiduciary duty to Dowd. Some of those findings included: failing to disclose certain facts that threatened the economic existence of Dowd, such as obtaining a $400,000 line of credit and $100,000 checking account from Harris Bank using Dowd's confidential information; paying down more than $186,000 of Dowd's line of credit to American National Bank without authorization, in order to present a better financial statement for themselves when obtaining a line of credit for GMS; soliciting Allstate's business prior to resigning from Dowd; arranging for a mass exodus of firm employees prior to December 31, 1990; downloading Allstate case service lists and mailing labels for substitution of counsel; and using of confidential information.

A. Pretermination Solicitation

One of the major questions in this case was whether defendants solicited Allstate as a client for their new firm before they left Dowd, thereby breaching their fiduciary duty to the firm. Defendants assert that Dowd's proof of solicitation was based on allegations of obtaining office space, credit, and equipment and using Dowd resources, all of which the Illinois Supreme Court has already deemed proper.

The trial court in the instant case observed that in Illinois, the breach of fiduciary duty among law partners has often been examined in connection with business partners. For instance, in *Dowell v. Bitner* (1995), the appellate court there noted that "employees may plan, form and outfit a competing corporation while still working for the employer, but they may not commence competition." (Emphasis is omitted.) Further, former employees may compete with their former corporate employer and solicit former customers as long as there was no business activity prior to termination of employment. Although the Illinois Supreme Court pointed out that lawyers are not bound by the same fiduciary duties as those of nonlawyer corporate officers and directors, the principles are similar. In its review of this case, the supreme court found the following comments from *Graubard,* a New York Court of Appeals case, relevant: secretly attempting to lure firm clients to the new association, lying to partners about plans to leave, and abandoning the firm on short notice and taking clients and files would not be consistent with a partner's fiduciary duties.

One item of evidence that supports a finding of breach of fiduciary duty based on pretermination solicitation in this case is Leslie Henkels' testimony. Henkels, a former legal assistant/paralegal at Dowd, testified that she was told in mid-December 1990 by Nancy Gleason that GMS had secured the Allstate business for the new firm. The trial court found her testimony to be credible. Ultimately, it is for the trial judge to determine the credibility of the witnesses, to weigh the evidence and draw reasonable inferences therefrom, and to resolve any conflicts in the evidentiary record.

The trial court also relied on the testimony of Leslie Henkels regarding the events of December 31, 1990. Henkels testified that on December 31, 1990, shortly before noon, Nancy Gleason called her and told her that she was faxing a letter to her to be put on the desks of the partners at Dowd. Henkels recalled that the letter was on Allstate letterhead and signed by George Riley. Nancy Gleason called back shortly thereafter and told Henkels to retrieve the faxes and destroy them, on the advice of "their counsel." Nancy then called a third time indicating that she was on her way to Mike Dowd's house to resign. The time between the first call and the third call was approximately 30 to 45 minutes. When shown Nancy Gleason's resignation letter at trial, Henkels stated that the letter was not the document she received via fax from Nancy and had not seen it before.

In contrast, Nancy Gleason testified that she told Henkels that she was sending a fax, but testified that it was not a fax from Allstate. She stated that it was her letter of resignation. Nancy testified that after speaking with Mike Dowd on December 31, 1990, she proceeded to the Allstate offices. Nancy Gleason recalled telling Crim and Riley that a new firm was being formed and certain associates would be extended offers.

The trial court expressly believed Henkels version of the December 31 events, including the content of the letter, and we will not disturb such a finding of credibility.

Timothy Nolan, an attorney that began working for GMS in July or August 1991, testified that Virginia Vermillion, an associate at Dowd prior to December 31, who joined GMS in January 1991, told him that Nancy Gleason had George Riley's commitment long before defendants left Dowd and that "they had a lock on the business long before they left." Nolan further testified that Vermillion told him that they were able to transfer the files so easily because, "[w]e knew which files were coming. We knew which attorneys were coming. We knew who was coming."

At trial, Virginia Vermillion denied telling Timothy Nolan that she knew about the new firm before January 1, 1991, or that defendants solicited the Allstate business prior to December 31. She also testified that she did not tell William Kreese, a candidate for an associate position at Dowd, that he was actually interviewing for the new law firm.

Another item of evidence that supports the finding of pretermination solicitation is the November 1990 credit memorandum created by David J. Varnerin, a relationship manager in the private banking group at Harris Bank. The November 28, 1990, memorandum that Varnerin prepared for his supervisors indicated that "[d]iscussions have been held with their principal client Allstate. The firm has been assured that their invoices will be paid promptly within 30 days. And, since the firm will have the prior firm's office administrator, we can reasonably assume that bills will be generated and sent in a very prompt manner." Also in the memorandum, business reference D. Paterson Gloor told Varnerin that "Nancy Gleason's group has a real lock on the Allstate business and he believes this client relationship will last for years." The reasonable inference from Varnerin's memorandum is that defendants made contact with and solicited Allstate's business prior to resigning from Dowd. Circumstantial evidence will suffice whenever an inference may reasonably be drawn therefrom.

We note that the supreme court stated in its prior opinion in this case that departing lawyers are permitted to prepare lists of clients *expected to leave the firm* and obtain financing based on the lists. That expectation is distinctly different from what happened in this case, where the evidence leads to the reasonable inference that the partners actually solicited the Allstate business, secured a commitment from All-state for future business and obtained financing based on that commitment, not a mere expectation.

In contrast, Lynn Crim and George Riley both testified that they had not been solicited by defendant to move their business to the new firm prior to Nancy Gleason's resignation. As stated earlier, it is for the trial judge to determine the credibility of the witnesses, to weigh the evidence and draw reasonable inferences therefrom, and to resolve any conflicts in the evidentiary record. Thus, we affirm the court's finding that Dowd met its burden of showing that defendants breached their fiduciary duty to Dowd by soliciting Allstate prior to the termination of their employment contracts.

B. Manner of Leaving Dowd

Although we have found that the trial court did not abuse its discretion in holding that defendants breached their fiduciary duty by committing pretermination solicitation, the evidence in the instant case also supports a finding that defendants breached their fiduciary duty in the manner in which they left Dowd.

The court held that "voting and accepting large bonuses for themselves and their friends and family without disclosure that they would be leaving and again stripping D & D of cash reserves" was a breach of defendants' fiduciary duty to Dowd. This was evidenced by Nancy Gleason's testimony that she received a $62,500 bonus in October 1990 based on August 1990 discussions with the other shareholders/partners to issue bonuses and a $100,000 bonus on or about December 21, 1990, despite her plans to leave Dowd on December 31, 1990. The evidence also demonstrated that defendants' discussions of forming the new firm also began in August 1990. Therefore, the court's decision to include bonuses in its award to Dowd is not an abuse of discretion. Even though we may have held differently in light of the testimony that bonuses were based, in part, on past performance and service to the firm, a reviewing court will not overturn a circuit court's findings merely because it does not agree with the lower court or because it might have reached a different conclusion had it been the trier of fact.

The trial court here also held that defendants breached their fiduciary duty by arranging for the mass exodus of firm employees before December 31, 1990. See *Veco Corp. v. Babcock* (1993) (held that actions constituted breach of fiduciary duty where defendants secretly solicited Veco employees for new company and orchestrated a mass exodus following defendants' resignation). This was evidenced by the matching of Dowd associates who eventually joined GMS and the furniture invoice providing the names of the persons using the new furniture created prior to defendants' resignations. The evidence regarding the premade furniture labels leads to the reasonable inference that defendants went so far as to solicit many Dowd attorneys who worked on the Allstate files to leave Dowd prior to their resignation. Additionally, paralegal Leslie Henkels testified that on the evening of December 31, she received a call from Judy Gleason asking her to join the firm-though it was "basically a formality since I had already been asked to join the firm months before." The circuit court's determination is not against the manifest weight of the evidence.

The trial court here heard ample amounts of testimony as to defendants' actions prior to their resignation and based on that testimony and its credibility assessments, the court determined that the manner in which defendants left Dowd was improper and a breach of their fiduciary duty. We will not disturb those determinations. A reviewing court may not overturn a trial court's findings merely because it does not agree with the lower court or because it might have reached a different conclusion.

Defendants here also contend that the trial court's finding that defendants were competing with Dowd "in their own minds" before resignation has no support in the record. Defendants are referring to the portion of the trial court's written order that stated:

"* * *The evidence shows that *in their own minds,* the firm of GMS was in business prior to the date of resignation as shown from the employer identification number application and the Professional Liability Insurance Policy Declarations effective 12/1/90, which listed 14 D & D employees for GMS, as well as the revenue projections to Harris Bank." (Emphasis added.)

The December 1, 1990, start date for GMS's professional liability insurance, compared to defendants' December 31, 1990, actual resignation date, supports the trial court's finding. Even if this finding was not supported by the record, as a reviewing court, we can sustain the decision of a lower court on any grounds that are called for by the record, regardless of whether the lower court relied on those grounds and regardless of whether the lower court's reasoning was correct. Here, we have already affirmed the trial court's finding that defendants breached their fiduciary duty to Dowd by soliciting Allstate's business prior to their resignation and the trial court's breach of fiduciary duty decision may stand on that finding alone.

C. Use of Confidential Information

Defendants also assert that the court's finding as to the use of confidential information is "flatly contradicted" by the record and the court never identifies what was considered "confidential information." The trial court, however, specifically states that it was a breach of fiduciary duty when "Nancy Gleason and Douglas Shreffler breached the agreement not to use confidential information, time and billing information and information from the financial statements of D & D for their own personal gain." In its order, the trial court cites the testimony of Maureen Gleason as evidence of defendants' use of confidential information.

Maureen Gleason testified, as an adverse witness, that in late October 1990 she and her husband prepared a projected profit and loss statement[4] for the new firm, with a start date of November 1990. It was prepared for submission to three banks, including Harris Bank. Maureen said that the unspecified associates listed therein were based on a projection of the number of associates GMS needed "to handle the business that [they] hoped to get," but no specific associates were in mind. She stated that the estimated 2,250 billable hours per associate was based on the average expectancy at law firms. She explained that the experience level and billable hours expectancy descriptions of the unspecified associates was based on who they "hope[d] to bring with [them] if [they] left." Though she had access to confidential information like this, Maureen denied using Dowd's confidential information to obtain GMS' projected figures. Maureen testified that the figures were based upon numerous publications that indicated what was the accepted amount of billable hours for associates.

The trial court believed that confidential information was in fact used to defendants' benefit in creating this projection. However, the Illinois Supreme Court stated in its prior opinion in this case that departing lawyers are permitted to prepare lists of clients expected to leave the firm and obtain financing based on the lists. Therefore, the trial court's finding is in error. Nonetheless, the finding of breach of fiduciary duty is supported on other grounds and does not change the outcome of this case.

The court also found that it was an improper use of confidential information for defendants to make payments to Dowd's line of credit with American National Bank to secure its own line of credit without authorization to do so. Defendants assert that David Varnerin, Dowd's witness, obviated such a claim and thus, the court's decision is unfounded. Varnerin testified that in considering the application for a line of credit with Harris Bank, he did not inquire as to whether Dowd's line of credit obligation had been paid off and affirmed that the decision to approve defendants' line of credit was independent of that obligation. However, Kenneth Gurber, a nondeparting partner at Dowd, testified that under normal circumstances, he would have been consulted about the American National Bank payoff, but was not, and Maureen Gleason did not have the authority to write a check for $187,000 without approval from the board of directors. Because credibility and conflicts in testimony are for the fact finder to determine, we leave the credibility assessment at the discretion of the trial court. The court was in the best position to determine whether it believed that Varnerin used the payoff information in his evaluation. Regardless of whether the court considered the payoff, the evidence demonstrates that defendants used confidential information and covert action to pay off this line of credit. As guarantors of

---

4. The projected profit and loss statement for the new firm is not cited to in the briefs.

Dowd's line of credit, paying the sum off would make them more attractive to Harris Bank officials in the position to extend a line of credit to them for the new firm.

There was also ample evidence of defendants' use of Dowd confidential records in preparation for taking Allstate with them to the new firm. Leslie Henkels testified that between August 1990 and December 31, 1990, she was directed by either Judy Gleason, Maureen Gleason or Maureen Henegan to update the service lists in order to move the Allstate business to GMS. On December 28, 1990, Henkels made sure that the service lists were up to date and the mailings lists were with them so that they could notify counsel of substitution of attorney. On December 31, 1990, between 2 p.m. and 3 p.m., Henkels took the service list binders to GMS's offices, at the instruction of Doug Shreffler.

Mary Judson, a former Dowd legal secretary, testified that on December 28, 1990, prior to defendants' resignations, she was instructed by Leslie Henkels and Maureen Henegan to update and download the Allstate service lists and mailing labels to disks. She was told that the project had to be completed that day.

In contrast, Maureen Henegan (Nancy Gleason's secretary at Dowd and GMS) testified that she did not instruct anyone at Dowd to update service lists so that they may taken to the new firm. In light of the conflicting testimony, we will not disturb the fact finder's decision as to the credibility of these witnesses. *Kalata v. Anheuser-Busch Co.* (1991). Moreover, the court's finding of use of confidential information is well supported by the record.

III. TORTIOUS INTERFERENCE

In focusing on the conduct of the defendants, the trial court here determined that Dowd proved defendants' actions constituted tortious interference with a prospective economic advantage. We agree, as shown below in our discussion of each element. Defendants, however, assert that the trial court's personal assertions of business expectations prejudiced their case and, further, that the trial court had no evidence that Dowd had a valid business expectation that they would be the recipient of Allstate's business after Nancy Gleason's departure.

To establish a cause of action for the tort of intentional interference with a prospective economic advantage, Illinois law requires that the following four elements must be proven: (1) the existence of a valid business relationship or expectancy; (2) the defendants' knowledge of plaintiff's relationship or expectancy; (3) purposeful interference by the defendants that prevents the plaintiff's legitimate expectancy from ripening into a valid business relationship or termination of the relationship; and (4) damages to plaintiff resulting from such interference.

A. Existence of a Valid Business Relationship or Expectancy

Defendants contend that Dowd did not offer any evidence that it had an expectancy to keep Allstate's business after the departure of Gleason and reminds this court that the relationship between an attorney and his client is terminable at will. While this is true, until terminated, the relationship created by an at-will contract will presumptively continue in effect so long as the parties are satisfied, and, therefore, such a relationship is sufficient to support an action for tortious interference.

The fact that the relationship between an attorney and her client is terminable at will does not of itself defeat an action for tortious interference because the action is not dependent upon an enforceable contract but, rather, upon an existing relationship. Until terminated, the relationship created by a contract terminable at will is subsisting and will presumptively continue in effect so long as the parties are satisfied. Such a relationship is sufficient to support an action for tortious interference.

The focus here is not on the conduct of the client in terminating the relationship, but on the conduct of the party inducing the breach or interfering with the expectancy. Moreover, to prevail on the claim, a plaintiff must show not merely that the defendant has succeeded in ending the relationship or interfering with the expectancy, but " 'purposeful interference,' " meaning the defendant has committed some impropriety in doing so. *Dowd* (quoting Restatement (Second) of Torts § 766B, Comment *a* (1979) ("'In order for the actor to be held liable, this Section requires that his interference be improper'")).

Defendants assert that the trial court had no evidence that Dowd had a valid business expectation that it would be the recipient of Allstate's business after Nancy Gleason's departure. They complain that following Dowd's objection during trial, George Riley from Allstate was not allowed to testify that the 200 files handled by Nancy Gleason at Dowd would have gone with her had she been fired by Dowd. We first note that a trial court's ruling on an objection to evidence will not be reversed absent an abuse of discretion.

The question posed to Riley during trial was: "If Mike Dowd had fired Nancy Gleason in 1990, would you have left the files that she was working on for you with Mike Dowd?" Following an objection, the court stated that the answer would call for speculation. Defense counsel argued that it spoke to the "missing gap" in Dowd's reasonable expectation issue. The court then allowed counsel to ask a series of questions of Riley as an offer of proof. Riley was asked what effect Nancy Gleason's termination would have had on the handling of Allstate's files. Riley responded, "Disaster," because "Nancy was an integral part of this operation." Riley was also asked if he would have allowed the 200 Allstate files to remain at Dowd absent Nancy Gleason, to which he answered, "No."

Riley's answers, in defendants' view, would support the conclusion that Dowd did not have a legitimate expectancy of continued business in the event that Gleason left Dowd. We find it important that there was no evidence that Dowd had any indication from Riley prior to December 31, 1990, that its continued business relationship was dependent upon Nancy Gleason's continued employment with

Dowd. Even if Dowd had that understanding, Dowd was unaware of Nancy Gleason's intention to leave the firm. There was also no indication that Allstate was in any way dissatisfied with the services received from Dowd. More importantly, as we have already affirmed the finding that defendants succeeded in ending the relationship, their "purposeful interference" was committed in an unseemly manner. In our view, the trial court's order does not offend the well-established rule that a client may discharge an attorney at any time, for any reason, or for no reason.

B. Knowledge of Plaintiff's Relationship or Expectancy

Dowd enjoyed a 15-year business relationship with Allstate. As partners and shareholders, defendants were undeniably aware of this relationship and its lucrative benefit to Dowd.

C. Purposeful Interference

Support for the trial court's purposeful-interference finding is found within the breach of fiduciary duty discussion of this opinion. Defendant's actions, or "impropriety" as the trial court put it, established a purposeful interference with Dowd's prospective economic advantage. The reasonable inference from the evidence discussed earlier and the court's credibility findings demonstrate that defendants covertly solicited the Allstate account prior to terminating their employment with Dowd. The covert steps taken by Nancy Gleason, Shreffler and GMS, individually and collectively, seemingly caused Dowd's largest client to make a commitment to cease doing business with Dowd. Defendants' actions, in the trial court's view, prevented Dowd from enjoying a continuing relationship with Allstate and, more importantly, precluded Allstate from having a free and unfettered choice regarding keeping its business with Dowd. Cases have recognized that pretermination solicitation of clients by members of an existing firm for the benefit of a new firm rises to a breach of a fiduciary duty.

There was no evidence introduced, for example, that Dowd was given any time to attempt to salvage its long-standing business relationship. If given the opportunity, Allstate may have remained with Dowd if offered more attractive fee arrangements (no fees for research, no second chairs at trial, and lower hourly rates are usually accorded government bodies). The latter, in the long run, might have proven more appealing to this insurer than simply having only Gleason in charge of their files. However, due to the secretiveness and abruptness of defendants' ultimate departure, the securing of the Allstate business was a feat accomplished at least by January 1, if not months earlier as the trial court believed. This alone represents some interference with Dowd's legitimate business expectation vis-a-*vis* Allstate and more importantly, casts doubt on how free and unfettered Allstate's decision to leave Dowd really was, absent a viable and familiar alternative (continuing to do business with Dowd at more advantageous terms). It also renders the pronounce-ments of Riley and Crim, as the trial court said, closer to speculation than fact, as they insist.

Defendants contend that the trial court ignored the testimony of the Allstate representatives, Crim and Riley, that they were not aware of the new firm prior to December 31 and unjustifiably credited the conflicting testimony of former Dowd paralegal Leslie Henkels that she was told that defendants had secured Allstate's commitment prior to December 31. Defendants also disagreed with the court's reli-ance on GMS associate Timothy Nolan's testimony that Virginia Vermillion told him that Allstate's commitment was secured before defendants' resignations. How-ever, these contentions are based on credibility assessments. Absent a showing of an abuse of its discretion, we will not reverse a trial court's determination on the issue.

Moreover, we hold that the trial court's purposeful-interference finding is sup-ported by the evidence and the reasonable inferences therefrom.

D. Damages

1. Compensatory Damages

Defendants also assert that because Riley from Allstate testified that Allstate would have followed Gleason in any event there can be no damages. A plaintiff must prove damages to a reasonable degree of certainty, and evidence cannot be remote, speculative, or uncertain. The trial court specifically held that "Plaintiff has proved damages with a reasonable degree of certainty." Even when the appellate court would have been better satisfied with different findings, we generally will not inter-fere with a trial court award supported by the evidence.

Here, the compensatory damages award against Nancy Gleason, Douglas Shref-fler and GMS for count III (tortious interference with prospective economic advantage) in the amount of $2,464,889.46, was based on the evidence presented by Dowd's damages opinion witness, Todd Lundy. Lundy is a certified public account-ant. The trial court specifically found that the evidence presented by Lundy, including his report, established certain damages. In preparing his report, Lundy testified that he read the pleadings, depositions, various financial documents from Dowd (such as paid bills, records of invoice collections) and some tax returns of GMS. His opinions were generally categorized as compensation and bonus-related damages, out-of-pocket damages and lost profit. The damage period was calculated beginning August 7, 1990, based on Leslie Henkels' testimony that on that date some of the defendants discussed their plan to leave Dowd. He noted that there was some dispute as to when the damage period was to begin (August 7 or September 25), so some calculations were computed based on both dates and listed separately.

Lundy testified in detail as to the amounts he calculated and the supporting information for those amounts.

For instance, Lundy testified that it was his opinion that the total damages incurred in this case amounted to $2,591,605.54. Lundy determined that the compensation and bonus-related monies issued to Nancy Gleason, Maureen Gleason, Douglas Shreffler and Judith Gleason totaled $440,274. The lost profits totaled $871,199.75. Lundy testified that he used a two-year period for the lost profits because of the manner in which law firms perform their accounting and because the information provided to Harris Bank by defendants for GMS's line of credit included a two-year projection. Lundy's calculations also included, but are not limited to, the following: Gleason and Shreffler's salaries for the period August 7, 1990, to December 31, 1990, totaling $110,999.89; a $9,719.81 construction expense in Dowd's sublease; $5,817.35 for the reinsurance conference held in Bermuda in November 1990 attended by, among others, Virginia Vermillion, Nancy Gleason, and Allstate's Riley; $5,624 Allstate lawyers' section Christmas party; total compensation, bonus-related and out-of-pocket damages in the amount of $849,206.04; and $871,199.75 in lost profit damages for years' end December 31, 1991, and December 31, 1992.

The court held that the damages, as a result of defendants' breach of fiduciary duty and tortious interference with prospective economic advantage, totaled $2,464,889.46. This was based on the total compensation/bonus payments and out-of-pocket damages of $812,859.90 incurred between August 7, 1990, to December 31, 1992, minus salaries and bonuses paid to nonparties Judy Gleason and Maureen Gleason, plus two years of lost profits. The court did not include the costs of the trip to Bermuda or the Allstate lawyers' section Christmas party because "there is no way to determine whether or not the GMS firm benefitted from those matters, or if Plaintiff would have had them in any event, even if it had known that Gleason was leaving."

The assessment of damages by a trial court sitting without a jury will not be set aside unless it is manifestly erroneous. In the instant case, the damages award is based on the detailed testimony and exhibits provided by Dowd's expert witness. The forfeiture of salary represented a period of time beginning with the breach of defendants' fiduciary duty and ends with an allowance of damages for Dowd's lost profits for a two-year period. Illinois law permits a complete forfeiture of any salary paid by a corporation to its fiduciary during a time when the fiduciary was breaching his duty to the corporation. Though there was no indication that defendants did not work at the efficiency level or with the diligence that they had prior to deciding to leave Dowd, they cannot claim a right to retain the compensation earned while breaching their fiduciary duty to Dowd.

Defendants next assert that the trial court erroneously required the forfeiture of bonuses Gleason received as a part of her compensation prior to her resignation because all partners agreed sometime in August 1990 to issue bonuses and all partners received bonuses.

Ken Gurber, a nondeparting partner at Dowd, testified that bonuses were paid for past performance and service to the firm, based on individuals' performance history and work that was done that year. Gurber also testified that the amounts were tied to the amount of income that the firm had during the year and were an inducement for future performance and to keep qualified individuals at the firm. He testified that the pay out of bonuses left the firm "cash poor." Bob Yelton, another nondeparting partner, testified that bonuses were predicated upon past performance and an inducement for future performance. Even Michael Dowd, by way of deposition, testified that in 1990, year-end bonuses were distributed because they "made some money" and they "had some to distribute." The idea that Mike Dowd would not have approved bonuses had he known that defendants were intending to leave and form their own firm has no bearing on the fact that the bonuses were approved based, at least in part, on past performance.

Although the bonuses were based in part on work performed antecedent to the period of breach (established here as beginning on August 7, 1990), they were properly included in the damages award in that the departing partners had already contemplated and discussed leaving the firm by the time the bonuses were voted upon. Nonetheless, they did not notify the firm of their intentions until after both bonuses had been issued. Because the bonuses issued here appear to be based on both past performance and as an inducement to perform well in the future, we cannot say that it was an abuse of discretion for defendants to have to forfeit those amounts. In our view, similar to the appropriateness of forfeiting salaries for the period of the breach of one's fiduciary duty, the forfeiture of bonuses during that same period may be included in the damages calculation if supported by the record. Moreover, the trial court held that Dowd proved damages with a reasonable degree of certainty, and based on the evidence, we cannot say that the holding was manifestly erroneous.

Defendants further postulate that the damages improperly reflect fees generated by work done on files that were opened at Dowd and transferred to GMS and fees on every new assignment given to Gleason at her new firm in 1991 and 1992. In defendants's view, the trial court's decision and award of damages "effectively negates Rules 1.5 and 5.6 of the Rules of Professional Conduct as promulgated by the Supreme Court."

Rule 1.5 of the Rules of Professional Conduct (134 Ill.2d R. 1.5(f)) states that a lawyer shall not divide a fee for legal services with another lawyer who is not in the same firm, unless the client consents to employment of the other lawyer by signing a disclosure. Rule 5.6 (134 Ill.2d R. 5.6) provides that a lawyer shall not participate in offering or making a partnership or employment agreement that restricts the rights of a lawyer to practice after termination of the relationship, except an agreement concerning benefits upon retirement, or an agreement in which a restriction on the lawyer's right to practice is part of the settlement of a controversy between private parties.

We do not believe that the court's ruling for damages violates either of these rules of professional conduct, as the court did not include fees for services rendered in 1991 and 1992 at GMS, but for *profits* that resulted from their misconduct. A "fee" is defined as a "charge for labor or services, esp. professional services" (Black's Law Dictionary 629 (7th ed.1999)) and fee-splitting is "[t]he division of attorney's fees between the lawyer who handles a matter and the lawyer who referred the matter" (Black's Law Dictionary 631 (7th ed.1999)). A profit is defined as "the excess of revenues over expenditure in a business transaction." Black's Law Dictionary 1226 (7th ed.1999). This case involves a breach of fiduciary duty, and the law clearly states that a defendant should not be permitted to retain any profits from such a breach.

Generally, a plaintiff must present competent proof of lost profits from which a reasonable basis of computation can be derived. Since lost profits are determined by many factors, it must be shown with a reasonable degree of certainty that defendants breached caused a specific portion of the lost profits. Here, plaintiffs' expert provided a report and explanation of how he arrived at the lost profits included in his damages opinion. The inclusion of lost profits represents the monies Dowd would have earned had Allstate remained with the firm. The trial court found the exhibit and accompanying testimony to be calculated to a reasonable degree of certainty and defendants do not even raise such an issue.

V. CONCLUSION

For the forgoing reasons, we affirm the trial court's rulings and award of damages.

Affirmed.

QUESTIONS AND NOTES

1. *Fred Siegel Co. v. Arter & Hadden*, 707 N.E.2d 853 (Ohio 1999), involved an employee who had worked with the plaintiffs until she resigned to join the defendant law firm. During the defendant's ten-year employ with the plaintiffs, she had full "access to information regarding the identity and addresses of Siegel clients and contact persons, and fee agreements." She also maintained a Rolodex containing information about personal and professional acquaintances. When the defendant

left the plaintiff firm, she took her Rolodex with her and also had a Siegel client list. The defendant then wrote letters to Siegel clients informing them that she was now at Arter & Hadden and that she "would like . . . to continue [her] professional relationship [with them]." The court held that "[i]n her letters to Siegel clients she not only provided information as to her change of law firms, but also expressed a willingness to continue providing legal services at the new firm. She thereby solicited Siegel clients to change legal representation." The court employed Section 767 of the Restatement in determining whether "an actor's interference with another's contract is improper." Turning to Section 768 of the Restatement, the court held that "establishment of the privilege of fair competition . . . will defeat a claim of tortious interference with contract where the contract is terminable at will." However, finding that "[t]he evidence is ambiguous as to whether [defendant attorney] and [defendant law firm] used information acquired through improper means in their competitive efforts," the court refused to defeat plaintiff's claim for tortious interference.

2. In *Binns v. Greenberg*, 480 F.Supp.2d 773 (E.D. Pa. 2007), the defendant law firm consulted with the plaintiff regarding a client the defendant represented. The plaintiff was referred to as "of counsel," but the plaintiff never entered into a separate agreement with the client. Faced with low funds, the defendant terminated the plaintiff. Subsequently, the plaintiff attempted to convince the client to "transfer his representation to [the plaintiff] or demand that [the plaintiff] remain fully involved through [the defendant]." Once the defendant became aware of this, the defendant "remind[ed] [the plaintiff] that he was not authorized to represent [the client]." The plaintiff then initiated suit against the defendant for tortious interference. Because no express or implied contract existed between the plaintiff and the client and because there was no evidence that the defendant acted unreasonably, the court found that no jury could find that the defendant's conduct was improper.

3. Cases like *Adler Barish* and *Dowd & Dowd* are set in the context of a traditional model of law practice that is waning, one where there is an underlying assumption of long-term exclusive and often life-long relationships of trust among the lawyers of law firm, and between the firm and its clients. Daniel J. Bussel, *No Conflict*, 25 GEORGETOWN J.L.E. 207, 227-28 (2012), contrasts this older model with the brave new world of modern law practice:

> The legal marketplace of 2012 is vastly different. Many law firms today employ hundreds or thousands of lawyers located in offices throughout the world, many of whom barely (if at all) know one another, engaged in all sorts of diverse practices. In 2011, the largest law firm in the American Lawyer's AMLAW 100 was Baker & McKenzie, with $2.27 billion in annual revenue and 3,800 attorneys practicing in seventy offices located in forty-two countries on every continent

save Antarctica. The smallest AMLAW 100 firm was McKenna Long & Aldridge, with $276.5 million in annual revenue and 425 lawyers located in nine United States offices and one in Europe. ... Such firms naturally represent thousands of clients at any one time. Lawyers at all levels from senior partner to junior partner to associate change firms regularly. The anomaly today is the lawyer who, having joined a firm as an associate upon graduation from law school and become a partner in that firm, retires from that same firm forty or fifty years later. Huge international firms with diverse practices also commonly merge.

Moreover, the stability and exclusivity that characterized most lawyer-institutional client relationships in the past has been greatly eroded. In-house legal staffs have increased in size and status, and the practice in engaging outside counsel now is to "spread it around," engaging the best lawyers for the particular matter based on a net-work of relationships with individual and often mobile partners at multiple firms.

How do these massive structural changes in the market for legal services and lawyers affect the analysis regarding the potential liability of departing partners who seek to transfer their existing client relationships ("book of business") to competitors who recruit them away from their firms? Should they?

4. One set of issues of major concern facing departing partners from dissolving law firms have been so-called "unfinished business," or "*Jewel v. Boxer,*" claims against departing lawyers and the new law firms that substitute in as counsel in the dissolving firm's ongoing client matters. Bankruptcy trustees and creditors of the dissolving firm viewed these ongoing matters as an asset of the dissolving firm and sued the successor firms for profits earned on the matters post-dissolution. Most of these unfinished business claims were settled, but in a few well-known cases the departing lawyers and their new firms refused to pay up. In an influential opinion arising out of the dissolution of Heller Ehrman LLP, Judge Charles Breyer found that at least in the case of hourly fee matters that the successor firms had no liability to the dissolving firm because the clients had an absolute right to discharge their old lawyers and hire new ones:

> The Trustee argues instead that the former Heller Shareholders had a fiduciary duty to account to Heller's estate for profits their new firms earned from work on former Heller matters. However, the fiduciary duty to account is limited to partnership property. Cal. Corp. Code § 16404(b)(1). If the profits Defendants earned are not derived from Heller partnership property, then there is no duty to account. A few basic principles demonstrate why the equities do not favor finding a property interest here.
>
> A law firm never owns its client matters. The client always owns the matter, and the most the law firm can be said to have is an expectation of future business.

At the motion hearing the Trustee was unable to articulate a basis for calculating the value of this expected future business. The Trustee suggested that the value at issue here is "good will," which does not ordinarily appear on law firm balance sheets which are on a modified cash basis. In California, and beyond, professional law partnerships do not have a "good will" asset. "The 'good will' which plaintiff claims—the expectation of future business—is personal and confidential and attaches to the individual partners of the firm, thus, no monetary value can be attributed to it and there is nothing to sell." The good will the Trustee discussed may be real in one sense: certainly a firm's reputation is a crucial part of its ability to obtain work. However, good will is not an asset to which a property interest attaches. Moreover, Heller's bankruptcy did much to undermine the firm's otherwise stellar reputation and to eviscerate any reasonable expectation of future business.

Obviously, the expectation of future business—if it is "good will"—would disappear as soon as either (1) the client removes business, which it can do at will, or (2) the law firm ceases to be able to perform the work to generate those expected future profits. "It has long been recognized in [California] that the client's power to discharge an attorney, with or without cause, is absolute." *Fracasse v. Brent* (Cal. 1972). When a client exercises "the unilateral right to discharge his or her attorney," the party discharged "only has a right to quantum meruit recovery" for the value of work already done on the matter. *Jalali v. Root* (Cal. App. 2003). Here, the client matters at issue ceased to be Heller's partnership business and became the Defendants' partnership business when the clients terminated Heller and retained new, third-party counsel.

Heller Ehrman LLP v. Davis, Wright, Tremaine LLP, 527 B.R. 24, 30-31 (N.D.Cal. 2014).

APPENDIX I. UNIFORM COMMERCIAL CODE ARTICLES 1 & 2: SELECTED SECTIONS

ARTICLE 1—GENERAL PROVISIONS
2010 OFFICIAL TEXT

PART 1
SHORT TITLE, CONSTRUCTION, APPLICATION AND SUBJECT MATTER
OF THE ACT

§ 1-101. Short Titles.

(a) This Act may be cited as the Uniform Commercial Code.

(b) This article may be cited as Uniform Commercial Code—General Provisions.

§ 1-102. Scope of Article.

This article applies to a transaction to the extent that it is governed by another article of this Act.

§ 1-103. Construction of this Act to Promote its Purposes and Policies; Applicability of Supplemental Principles of Law.

(a) This Act must be liberally construed and applied to promote its underlying purposes and policies, which are:

(1) to simplify, clarify, and modernize the law governing commercial transactions;

(2) to permit the continued expansion of commercial practices through custom, usage, and agreement of the parties; and

(3) to make uniform the law among the various jurisdictions

(b) Unless displaced by the particular provisions of this Act, the principles of law and equity, including the law merchant and the law relative to capacity to contract, principal and agent, estoppel, fraud, misrepresentation, duress, coercion, mistake, bankruptcy, and other validating or invalidating cause supplement its provisions.

961

§ 1-106.   Use of Singular and Plural; Gender.

In this Act, unless the statutory context otherwise requires:

(1) words in the singular number include the plural, and those in the plural include the singular; and

(2) words of any gender also refer to any other gender.

PART 2.
GENERAL DEFINITIONS AND PRINCIPLES OF INTERPRETATION

§ 1-201.   General Definitions.

(a) Unless the context otherwise requires, words or phrases defined in this section, or in the additional definitions contained in other articles of this Act that apply to particular articles or parts thereof, have the meanings stated.

(b) Subject to definitions contained in other articles of this Act that apply to particular articles or parts thereof:

(1) "Action", in the sense of a judicial proceeding, includes recoupment, counterclaim, set-off, suit in equity, and any other proceeding in which rights are determined.

(2) "Aggrieved party" means a party entitled to pursue a remedy.

(3) "Agreement", as distinguished from "contract", means the bargain of the parties in fact, as found in their language of inferred from other circumstances, including course of performance, course of dealing, or usage of trade as provided in Section 1-303.

(9) "Buyer in ordinary course of business" means a person that buys goods in good faith, without knowledge that the sale violates the rights of another person in the goods, and in the ordinary course from a person, other than a pawnbroker, in the business of selling goods of that kind. A person buys goods in the ordinary course if the sale to the person comports with the usual or customary practices in the kind of business in which the seller is engaged or with the seller's own usual or customary practices. A person that sells oil, gas, or other minerals at the wellhead or minehead is a person in the business of selling goods of that kind. A buyer in ordinary course of business may buy for cash, by exchange of other property, or on secured or unsecured credit, and may acquire goods or documents of title under preexisting contract for sale. Only a buyer that takes possession of the goods or has a right to recover the goods from the seller under Article 2 may be a buyer in ordinary course of business. "Buyer in ordinary course of business" does not include a person that acquires goods in a transfer in bulk or as security for or in total or partial satisfaction of a money debt.

(10) "Conspicuous", with reference to a term, means so written, displayed, or presented that a reasonable person against which it is to operate ought to have noticed it. Whether a term is "conspicuous" or is not is a decision for the court. Conspicuous terms include the following:

(A)   a heading in capitals equal to or greater in size than the surrounding text, or in contrasting type, font, or color to the surrounding text of the same or lesser size; and

(B)   language in the body of a record or display in larger type than the surrounding text, or in contrasting type, font, or color to the surrounding text of the same size, or set off from surrounding text of the same size by symbols or other marks that call attention to the language.

(11) "Consumer" means an individual who enters into a transaction primarily for personal, family, or household purposes.

(12) "Contract", as distinguished from "agreement", means the total legal obligation that results from the parties' agreement as determined by this Act as supplemented by any other applicable laws.

(17) "Fault" means a default, breach, or wrongful act or omission.

(18) "Fungible goods" means:

(A)   goods of which any unit, by nature or usage of trade, is the equivalent of any other like unit; or

(B)   goods that by agreement are treated as equivalent.

(19) "Genuine" means free of forgery or counterfeiting.

(20)   "Good faith", except as otherwise provided in Article 5, means honesty in fact and the observance of reasonable commercial standards of fair dealing.

(23) "Insolvent" means:

(A)   having generally ceased to pay debts in the ordinary course of business other than as a result of bona fide dispute;

(B)   being unable to pay debts as they become due; or

(C)   being insolvent within the meaning of federal bankruptcy law.

(24) "Money" means a medium of exchange currently authorized or adopted by a domestic or foreign government. The term includes a monetary unit of account established by an intergovernmental organization or by agreement between two or more countries.

(25) "Organization" means a person other than an individual.

(27) "Person" means an individual, corporation, business trust, estate, trust, partnership, limited liability company, association, joint venture, government, governmental subdivision, agency, or instrumentality, public corporation, or any other legal or commercial entity.

(32) "Remedy" means any remedial right to which an aggrieved party is entitled with or without resort to a tribunal.

(33) "Representative" means a person empowered to act for another, including an agent, an officer or a corporation or association, and a trustee, executor, or administrator of an estate.

(34) "Right" includes remedy.

(35) "Security interest" means an interest in personal property or fixtures which secures payment or performance of an obligation. "Security interest" includes any interest of a consignor and a buyer of accounts, chattel paper, a payment

intangible, or a promissory note in a transaction that is subject to Article 9. "Security interest" does not include the special property interest of a buyer of goods on identification of those goods to a contract for sale under Section 2-401, but a buyer may also acquire a "security interest" by complying with Article 9. Except as otherwise provided in Section 2-505, the right of a seller or lessor of goods under Article 2 or 2A to retain or acquire possession of the goods is not a "security interest", but a seller or lessor may also acquire a "security interest" by complying with Article 9. The retention or reservation of title by a seller of goods notwithstanding shipment or delivery to the buyer under Section 2-401 is limited in effect to a reservation of a "security interest." Whether a transaction in the form of a lease creates a "security interest" is determined pursuant to Section 1-203.

(36) "Send" in connection with a writing, record, or notice means:

    (A) to deposit in the mail or deliver for transmission by any other usual means of communication with postage or cost of transmission provided for and properly addressed and, in the case of an instrument, to an address specified thereon or otherwise agreed, or if there be none to any address reasonable under the circumstances; or

    (B) in any other way to cause to be received any record or notice within the time it would have arrived if properly sent.

(37) "Signed" includes any symbol executed or adopted with present intention to adopt or accept a writing.

(39) "Surety" includes a guarantor or other secondary obligor.

(40)   "Term" means a portion of an agreement that relates to a particular matter.

(41) "Unauthorized signature" means a signature made without actual, implied, or apparent authority. The term includes a forgery.

(42) "Warehouse receipt" means a receipt issued by a person engaged in the business of storing goods for hire.

(43) "Writing" includes printing, typewriting, or any other intentional reduction to tangible form. "Written" has a corresponding meaning.

§ 1-202. Notice; Knowledge.

(a) Subject to subsection (f), a person has "notice" of a fact if the person:

    (1) has actual knowledge of it;

    (2) has received a notice or notification of it; or

    (3) from all the facts and circumstances known to the person at the time in question, has reason to know that is exists.

(b) "Knowledge" means actual knowledge. "Knows" has a corresponding meaning.

(c) "Discover", "learn", or words of similar import refer to knowledge rather than to reason to know.

(d) A person "notifies" or "gives" a notice or notification to another person by taking such steps as may be reasonably required to inform the other person in ordinary course, whether or not the other person actually comes to know of it.

(e) Subject to subsection (f), a person "receives" a notice or notification when:

    (1) it comes to that person's attention; or

    (2) it is duly delivered in a form reasonable under the circumstances at the place of business through which the contract was made or at another location held out by that person as the place for receipt of its communications

(f) Notice, knowledge, or a notice or notification received by an organization is effective for a particular transaction from the time it is brought to the attention of the individual conducting that transaction and, in any event, from the time it would have been brought to the individual's attention if the organization had exercised due diligence. An organization exercises due diligence if it maintains reasonable routines for communicating significant information to the person conducting the transaction and there is reasonable compliance with the routines. Due diligence does not require an individual acting for the organization to communicate information unless the communication is part of the individual's regular duties or the individual has reason to know of the transaction and that the transaction would be materially affected by the information.

§ 1-204.   Value.

Except as otherwise provided in Articles 3, 4, 5, and 6, a person gives value for rights if the person acquires them:

(1) in return for a binding commitment to extend credit or for the extension of immediately available credit, whether or not drawn upon and whether or not a charge-back is provided for in the event of difficulties in collection;

(2) as security for, or in total or partial satisfaction of, a preexisting claim;

(3) by accepting delivery under a preexisting contract for purchase; or

(4) in return for any consideration sufficient to support a simple contract.

§ 1-205.   Reasonable Time; Seasonableness.

(a) Whether a time for taking an action required by this Act is reasonable depends on the nature, purpose, and circumstances of the action.

(b) An action is taken seasonably if it is taken at or within the time agreed or, if no time is agreed, at or within a reasonable time.

PART 3
TERRITORIAL APPLICABILITY AND GENERAL; RULES

§ 1-302.   *Variation by Agreement.*

(a) Except as otherwise provided in subsection (b) or elsewhere in this Act, the effect of provisions of this Act may be varied by agreement.

(b) The obligations of good faith, diligence, reasonableness, and care prescribed by this Act may not be disclaimed by agreement. The parties, by agreement, may determine the standards by which the performance of those obligations is to be measured if those standards are not manifestly unreasonable. Whenever this Act requires an action to be taken within a reasonable time, a time that is not manifestly unreasonable may be fixed by agreement.

(c) The presence in certain provisions of this Act of the phrase "unless otherwise agreed", or words of similar import, does not imply that the effect of other provisions may not be varied by agreement under this section.

§ 1-303.   *Course of Performance, Course of Dealing, and Usage of Trade.*

(a) A "course of performance" is a sequence of conduct between parties to a particular transaction that exists if:

    (1) the agreement of the parties with respect to the transaction involves repeated occasions for performance by a party; and

    (2) the other party, with knowledge of the nature of the performance and opportunity for objection to it, accepts the performance or acquiesces in it without objection.

(b) A "course of dealing" is a sequence of conduct concerning previous transactions between the parties to a particular transaction that is fairly to be regarded as establishing a common basis of understanding for interpreting their expressions and other conduct.

(c) A "usage of trade" is any practice or method of dealing having such regularity of observance in a place, vocation, or trade as to justify an expectation that it will be observed with respect to the transaction in question. The existence and scope of such a usage must be proved as facts. If it is established that such a usage is embodied in a trade code or similar record, the interpretation of the record is a question of law.

(d) A course of performance or course of dealing between the parties or usage of trade in the vocation or trade in which they are engaged or of which they are or should be aware is relevant in ascertaining the meaning of the parties' agreement, may give particular meaning to specific terms of the agreement, and may supplement or qualify the terms of the agreement. A usage of trade applicable in the place in which part of the performance under the agreement is to occur may be so utilized as to that part of the performance.

(e) Except as otherwise provided in subsection (f), the express terms of an agreement and any applicable course of performance, course of dealing, or usage of trade must be construed whenever reasonable as consistent with each other. If such a construction is unreasonable:

(1) express terms prevail over course of performance, course of dealing, and usage of trade;

(2) course of performance prevails over course of dealing and usage of trade; and

(3) course of dealing prevails over usage of trade.

(f) Subject to Section 2-209, a course of performance is relevant to show a waiver or modification of any term inconsistent with the course of performance.

(g) Evidence of a relevant usage of trade offered by one party is not admissible unless that party has given the other party notice that the court finds sufficient to prevent unfair surprise to the other party.

§ 1-304.   Obligation of Good Faith.

Every contract or duty within this Act implies an obligation of good faith in its performance and enforcement.

§ 1-305.   Remedies to be Liberally Administered.

(a) The remedies provided by this Act must be liberally administered to the end that the aggrieved party may be put in as good a position as if the other party had fully performed but neither consequential or special damages nor penal damages may be had except as specifically provided in this Act or by other rule of law.

(b) Any right or obligation declared by this Act is enforceable by action unless the provision declaring it specifies a different and limited effect.

§ 1-306.   Waiver or Renunciation of Claim or Right After Breach.

A claim or right arising out of an alleged breach may be discharged in whole or in part without consideration by agreement of the aggrieved party in an authenticated record.

§ 1-308.   Performance or Acceptance Under Reservation of Rights.

(a) A party that with explicit reservation of rights performs or promises performance or assents to performance in a manner demanded or offered by the other party does not thereby prejudice the rights reserved. Such words as "without prejudice", "under protest", or the like are sufficient.

(b) Subsection (a) does not apply to an accord and satisfaction.

ARTICLE 2—SALES
2000 OFFICIAL TEXT

PART 1
SHORT TITLE, GENERAL CONSTRUCTION AND SUBJECT MATTER

§ 2-101.   *Short Title.*

This Article shall be known and may be cited as Uniform Commercial Code—Sales.

§ 2-102.   *Scope; Certain Security and Other Transactions Excluded From This Article.*

Unless the context otherwise requires, this Article applies to transactions in goods; it does not apply to any transaction which although in the form of an unconditional contract to sell or present sale is intended to operate only as a security transaction nor does this Article impair or repeal any statute regulating sales to consumers, farmers or other specified classes of buyers.

§ 2-103.   *Definitions and Index of Definitions.*

(1) In this Article unless the context otherwise requires
   (a) "Buyer" means a person who buys or contracts to buy goods.
   (b) "Good faith" in the case of a merchant means honesty in fact and the observance of reasonable commercial standards of fair dealing in the trade.
   (c) "Receipt" of goods means taking physical possession of them.
   (d) "Seller" means a person who sells or contracts to sell goods....

§ 2-104.   *Definitions: "Merchant"; "Between Merchants"; "Financing Agency."*

(1) "Merchant" means a person who deals in goods of the kind or otherwise by his occupation holds himself out as having knowledge or skill peculiar to the practices or goods involved in the transaction or to whom such knowledge or skill may be attributed by his employment of an agent or broker or other intermediary who by his occupation holds himself out as having such knowledge or skill....
(3) "Between merchants" means in any transaction with respect to which both parties are chargeable with the knowledge or skill of merchants.

§ 2-105.   *Definitions: Transferability; "Goods"; "Future" Goods; "Lot"; "Commercial Unit."*

(1) "Goods" means all things (including specially manufactured goods) which are movable at the time of identification to the contract for sale other than the money in which the price is to be paid, investment securities (Article 8) and things in action. "Goods" also includes the unborn young of animals and growing crops and other identified things attached to realty as described in the section on goods to be severed from realty (Section 2-107).

(2) Goods must be both existing and identified before any interest in them can pass. Goods which are not both existing and identified are "future" goods. A purported present sale of future goods or of any interest therein operates as a contract to sell.

(3) There may be a sale of a part interest in existing identified goods.

(4) An undivided share in an identified bulk of fungible goods is sufficiently identified to be sold although the quantity of the bulk is not determined. Any agreed proportion of such a bulk or any quantity thereof agreed upon by number, weight or other measure may to the extent of the seller's interest in the bulk be sold to the buyer who then becomes an owner in common.

(5) "Lot" means a parcel or a single article which is the subject matter of a separate sale or delivery, whether or not it is sufficient to perform the contract.

(6) "Commercial unit" means such a unit of goods as by commercial usage is a single whole for purposes of sale and division of which materially impairs its character or value on the market or in use. A commercial unit may be a single article (as a machine) or a set of articles (as a suite of furniture or an assortment of sizes) or a quantity (as a bale, gross, or carload) or any other unit treated in use or in the relevant market as a single whole.

§ 2–106.   Definitions: "Contract"; "Agreement"; "Contract for Sale"; "Sale"; "Present Sale"; "Conforming" to Contract; "Termination"; "Cancellation."

(1) In this Article unless the context otherwise requires "contract" and "agreement" are limited to those relating to the present or future sale of goods. "Contract for sale" includes both a present sale of goods and a contract to sell goods at a future time. A "sale" consists in the passing of title from the seller to the buyer for a price (Section 2–401). A "present sale" means a sale which is accomplished by the making of the contract.

(2) Goods or conduct including any part of a performance are "conforming" or conform to the contract when they are in accordance with the obligations under the contract.

(3) "Termination" occurs when either party pursuant to a power created by agreement or law puts an end to the contract otherwise than for its breach. On "termination" all obligations which are still executory on both sides are discharged but any right based on prior breach or performance survives....

(4) "Cancellation" occurs when either party puts an end to the contract for breach by the other and its effect is the same as that of "termination" except that the cancelling party also retains any remedy for breach of the whole contract or any unperformed balance.

PART 2
FORM, FORMATION AND READJUSTMENT OF CONTRACT

§ 2-201.   *Formal Requirements; Statute of Frauds.*

(1) Except as otherwise provided in this section a contract for the sale of goods for the price of $500 or more is not enforceable by way of action or defense unless there is some writing sufficient to indicate that a contract for sale has been made between the parties and signed by the party against whom enforcement is sought or by his authorized agent or broker. A writing is not insufficient because it omits or incorrectly states a term agreed upon but the contract is not enforceable under this paragraph beyond the quantity of goods shown in such writing.

(2) Between merchants if within a reasonable time a writing in confirmation of the contract and sufficient against the sender is received and the party receiving it has reason to know its contents, it satisfies the requirements of subsection (1) against such party unless written notice of objection to its contents is given within 10 days after it is received.

(3) A contract which does not satisfy the requirements of subsection (1) but which is valid in other respects is enforceable

   (a) if the goods are to be specially manufactured for the buyer and are not suitable for sale to others in the ordinary course of the seller's business and the seller, before notice of repudiation is received and under circumstances which reasonably indicate that the goods are for the buyer, has made either a substantial beginning of their manufacture or commitments for their procurement; or

   (b) if the party against whom enforcement is sought admits in his pleading, testimony or otherwise in court that a contract for sale was made, but the contract is not enforceable under this provision beyond the quantity of goods admitted; or

   (c) with respect to goods for which payment has been made and accepted or which have been received and accepted (Sec. 2-606).

§ 2-202.   *Final Written Expression: Parol or Extrinsic Evidence.*

Terms with respect to which the confirmatory memoranda of the parties agree or which are otherwise set forth in a writing intended by the parties as a final expression of their agreement with respect to such terms as are included therein may not be contradicted by evidence of any prior agreement or of a contemporaneous oral agreement but may be explained or supplemented

(a) by course of dealing or usage of trade (Section 1-303); and

(b) by evidence of consistent additional terms unless the court finds the writing to have been intended also as a complete and exclusive statement of the terms of the agreement.

§ 2-203. Seals Inoperative.

The affixing of a seal to a writing evidencing a contract for sale or an offer to buy or sell goods does not constitute the writing a sealed instrument and the law with respect to sealed instruments does not apply to such a contract or offer.

§ 2-204. Formation in General.

(1) A contract for sale of goods may be made in any manner sufficient to show agreement, including conduct by both parties which recognizes the existence of such a contract.

(2) An agreement sufficient to constitute a contract for sale may be found even though the moment of its making is undetermined.

(3) Even though one or more terms are left open a contract for sale does not fail for indefiniteness if the parties have intended to make a contract and there is a reasonably certain basis for giving an appropriate remedy.

§ 2-205. Firm Offers.

An offer by a merchant to buy or sell goods in a signed writing which by its terms gives assurance that it will be held open is not revocable, for lack of consideration, during the time stated or if no time is stated for a reasonable time, but in no event may such period of irrevocability exceed three months; but any such term of assurance on a form supplied by the offeree must be separately signed by the offeror.

§ 2-206. Offer and Acceptance in Formation of Contract.

(1) Unless otherwise unambiguously indicated by the language or circumstances
   (a) an offer to make a contract shall be construed as inviting acceptance in any manner and by any medium reasonable in the circumstances;
   (b) an order or other offer to buy goods for prompt or current shipment shall be construed as inviting acceptance either by a prompt promise to ship or by the prompt or current shipment of conforming or non-conforming goods, but such a shipment of non-conforming goods does not constitute an acceptance if the seller seasonably notifies the buyer that the shipment is offered only as an accommodation to the buyer.

(2) Where the beginning of a requested performance is a reasonable mode of acceptance an offeror who is not notified of acceptance within a reasonable time may treat the offer as having lapsed before acceptance.

§ 2-207. Additional Terms in Acceptance or Confirmation.

(1) A definite and seasonable expression of acceptance or a written confirmation which is sent within a reasonable time operates as an acceptance even though it states terms additional to or different from those offered or agreed upon, unless acceptance is expressly made conditional on assent to the additional or different terms.

(2) The additional terms are to be construed as proposals for addition to the contract. Between merchants such terms become part of the contract unless:
   (a) the offer expressly limits acceptance to the terms of the offer;
   (b) they materially alter it; or
   (c) notification of objection to them has already been given or is given within a reasonable time after notice of them is received.

(3) Conduct by both parties which recognizes the existence of a contract is sufficient to establish a contract for sale although the writings of the parties do not otherwise establish a contract. In such case the terms of the particular contract consist of those terms on which the writings of the parties agree, together with any supplementary terms incorporated under any other provisions of this Act.

§ 2-208.   Course of Performance or Practical Construction.

(1) Where the contract for sale involves repeated occasions for performance by either party with knowledge of the nature of the performance and opportunity for objection to it by the other, any course of performance accepted or acquiesced in without objection shall be relevant to determine the meaning of the agreement.

(2) The express terms of the agreement and any such course of performance, as well as any course of dealing and usage of trade, shall be construed whenever reasonable as consistent with each other; but when such construction is unreasonable, express terms shall control course of performance and course of performance shall control both course of dealing and usage of trade (Section 1-205).

(3) Subject to the provisions of the next section on modification and waiver, such course of performance shall be relevant to show a waiver or modification of any term inconsistent with such course of performance.

§ 2-209.   Modification, Rescission and Waiver.

(1) An agreement modifying a contract within this Article needs no consideration to be binding.

(2) A signed agreement which excludes modification or rescission except by a signed writing cannot be otherwise modified or rescinded, but except as between merchants such a requirement on a form supplied by the merchant must be separately signed by the other party.

(3) The requirements of the statute of frauds section of this Article (Section 2-201) must be satisfied if the contract as modified is within its provisions.

(4) Although an attempt at modification or rescission does not satisfy the requirements of subsection (2) or (3) it can operate as a waiver.

(5) A party who has made a waiver affecting an executory portion of the contract may retract the waiver by reasonable notification received by the other party that strict performance will be required of any term waived, unless the retraction would be unjust in view of a material change of position in reliance on the waiver.

§ 2–210.   Delegation of Performance; Assignment of Rights.

(1) A party may perform his duty through a delegate unless otherwise agreed or unless the other party has a substantial interest in having his original promisor perform or control the acts required by the contract. No delegation of performance relieves the party delegating of any duty to perform or any liability for breach.

(2) Except as otherwise provided in Section 9-406, unless otherwise agreed, all rights of either seller or buyer can be assigned except where the assignment would materially change the duty of the other party, or increase materially the burden or risk imposed on him by his contract, or impair materially his chance of obtaining return performance. A right to damages for breach of the whole contract or a right arising out of the assignor's due performance of his entire obligation can be assigned despite agreement otherwise.

(3) The creation, attachment, perfection or enforcement of a security interest in the seller's interest under a contract is not a transfer that materially changes the duty of or increases materially the burden or risk imposed on the buyer or impairs materially the buyer's chance of obtaining return performance within the purview of subsection (2) unless, and then only to the extent that, enforcement actually results in a delegation of material performance of the seller. Even in that event, the creation, attachment, perfection, and enforcement of the security interest remains effective, but (i) the seller is liable to the buyer for damages caused by the delegation to the extent that the damages could not reasonably be prevented by the buyer, and (ii) a court having jurisdiction may grant other appropriate relief, including cancellation of the contract for sale or an injunction against enforcement of the security interest or consummation of the enforcement.

(4) Unless the circumstances indicate the contrary a prohibition of assignment of "the contract" is to be construed as barring only the delegation to the assignee of the assignor's performance.

(5) An assignment of "the contract" or of "all my rights under the contract" or an assignment in similar general terms is an assignment of rights and unless the language or the circumstances (as in an assignment for security) indicate the contrary, it is a delegation of performance of the duties of the assignor and its acceptance by the assignee constitutes a promise by him to perform those duties. This promise is enforceable by either the assignor or the other party to the original contract.

(6) The other party may treat any assignment which delegates performance as creating reasonable grounds for insecurity and may without prejudice to his rights against the assignor demand assurances from the assignee (Section 2-609).

PART 3
GENERAL OBLIGATION AND CONSTRUCTION OF CONTRACT

§ 2-301.   General Obligations of Parties.

The obligation of the seller is to transfer and deliver and that of the buyer is to accept and pay in accordance with the contract.

§ 2-302.   Unconscionable Contract or Clause.

(1) If the court as a matter of law finds the contract or any clause of the contract to have been unconscionable at the time it was made the court may refuse to enforce the contract, or it may enforce the remainder of the contract without the unconscionable clause, or it may so limit the application of any unconscionable clause as to avoid any unconscionable result.

(2) When it is claimed or appears to the court that the contract or any clause thereof may be unconscionable the parties shall be afforded a reasonable opportunity to present evidence as to its commercial setting, purpose and effect to aid the court in making the determination.

§ 2-305.   Open Price Term.

(1) The parties if they so intend can conclude a contract for sale even though the price is not settled. In such a case the price is a reasonable price at the time for delivery if
  (a) nothing is said as to price; or
  (b) the price is left to be agreed by the parties and they fail to agree; or
  (c) the price is to be fixed in terms of some agreed market or other standard as set or recorded by a third person or agency and it is not so set or recorded.

(2) A price to be fixed by the seller or by the buyer means a price for him to fix in good faith.

(3) When a price left to be fixed otherwise than by agreement of the parties fails to be fixed through fault of one party the other may at his option treat the contract as cancelled or himself fix a reasonable price.

(4) Where, however, the parties intend not to be bound unless the price be fixed or agreed and it is not fixed or agreed there is no contract. In such a case the buyer must return any goods already received or if unable so to do must pay their reasonable value at the time of delivery and the seller must return any portion of the price paid on account.

§ 2-306.   Output, Requirements and Exclusive Dealings.

(1) A term which measures the quantity by the output of the seller or the requirements of the buyer means such actual output or requirements as may occur in good faith, except that no quantity unreasonably disproportionate to any stated estimate or in the absence of a stated estimate to any normal or otherwise comparable prior output or requirements may be tendered or demanded.

(2) A lawful agreement by either the seller or the buyer for exclusive dealing in the kind of goods concerned imposes unless otherwise agreed an obligation by the seller to use best efforts to supply the goods and by the buyer to use best efforts to promote their sale.

§ 2-307. Delivery in Single Lot or Several Lots.

Unless otherwise agreed all goods called for by a contract for sale must be tendered in a single delivery and payment is due only on such tender but where the circumstances give either party the right to make or demand delivery in lots the price if it can be apportioned may be demanded for each lot.

§ 2-308. Absence of Specified Place for Delivery.

Unless otherwise agreed

    (a) the place for delivery of goods is the seller's place of business or if he has none his residence; but

    (b) in a contract for sale of identified goods which to the knowledge of the parties at the time of contracting are in some other place, that place is the place for their delivery; and

    (c) documents of title may be delivered through customary banking channels.

§ 2-309. Absence of Specific Time Provisions; Notice of Termination.

(1) The time for shipment or delivery or any other action under a contract if not provided in this Article or agreed upon shall be a reasonable time.

(2) Where the contract provides for successive performances but is indefinite in duration it is valid for a reasonable time but unless otherwise agreed may be terminated at any time by either party.

(3) Termination of a contract by one party except on the happening of an agreed event requires that reasonable notification be received by the other party and an agreement dispensing with notification is invalid if its operation would be unconscionable.

§ 2-310. Open Time for Payment or Running of Credit; Authority to Ship Under Reservation.

Unless otherwise agreed

    (a) payment is due at the time and place at which the buyer is to receive the goods even though the place of shipment is the place of delivery; and

    (b) if the seller is authorized to send the goods he may ship them under reservation, and may tender the documents of title, but the buyer may inspect the goods after their arrival before payment is due unless such inspection is inconsistent with the terms of the contract (Section 2-513); ...

§ 2–311. Options and Cooperation Respecting Performance.

(1) An agreement for sale which is otherwise sufficiently definite (subsection (3) of Section 2-204) to be a contract is not made invalid by the fact that it leaves particulars of performance to be specified by one of the parties. Any such specification must be made in good faith and within limits set by commercial reasonableness.

(2) Unless otherwise agreed specifications relating to assortment of the goods are at the buyer's option and except as otherwise provided in subsections (1)(c) and (3) of Section 2-319 specifications or arrangements relating to shipment are at the seller's option.

(3) Where such specification would materially affect the other party's performance but is not seasonably made or where one party's cooperation is necessary to the agreed performance of the other but is not seasonably forthcoming, the other party in addition to all other remedies

  (a) is excused for any resulting delay in his own performance; and

  (b) may also either proceed to perform in any reasonable manner or after the time for a material part of his own performance treat the failure to specify or to cooperate as a breach by failure to deliver or accept the goods.

§ 2–312. Warranty of Title and Against Infringement; Buyer's Obligation Against Infringement.

(1) Subject to subsection (2) there is in a contract for sale a warranty by the seller that

  (a) the title conveyed shall be good, and its transfer rightful; and

  (b) the goods shall be delivered free from any security interest or other lien or encumbrance of which the buyer at the time of contracting has no knowledge.

(2) A warranty under subsection (1) will be excluded or modified only by specific language or by circumstances which give the buyer reason to know that the person selling does not claim title in himself or that he is purporting to sell only such right or title as he or a third person may have.

(3) Unless otherwise agreed a seller who is a merchant regularly dealing in goods of the kind warrants that the goods shall be delivered free of the rightful claim of any third person by way of infringement or the like but a buyer who furnishes specifications to the seller must hold the seller harmless against any such claim which arises out of compliance with the specifications.

§ 2–313. Express Warranties by Affirmation, Promise, Description, Sample.

(1) Express warranties by the seller are created as follows:

  (a) Any affirmation of fact or promise made by the seller to the buyer which relates to the goods and becomes part of the basis of the bargain creates an express warranty that the goods shall conform to the affirmation or promise.

  (b) Any description of the goods which is made part of the basis of the bargain creates an express warranty that the goods shall conform to the description.

(c) Any sample or model which is made part of the basis of the bargain creates an express warranty that the whole of the goods shall conform to the sample or model.

(2) It is not necessary to the creation of an express warranty that the seller use formal words such as "warrant" or "guarantee" or that he have a specific intention to make a warranty, but an affirmation merely of the value of the goods or a statement purporting to be merely the seller's opinion or commendation of the goods does not create a warranty.

§ 2–314. Implied Warranty: Merchantability; Usage of Trade.

(1) Unless excluded or modified (Section 2–316), a warranty that the goods shall be merchantable is implied in a contract for their sale if the seller is a merchant with respect to goods of that kind. Under this section the serving for value of food or drink to be consumed either on the premises or elsewhere is a sale.

(2) Goods to be merchantable must be at least such as

(a) pass without objection in the trade under the contract description; and

(b) in the case of fungible goods, are of fair average quality within the description; and

(c) are fit for the ordinary purposes for which such goods are used; and

(d) run, within the variations permitted by the agreement, of even kind, quality and quantity within each unit and among all units involved; and

(e) are adequately contained, packaged, and labeled as the agreement may require; and

(f) conform to the promises or affirmations of fact made on the container or label if any.

(3) Unless excluded or modified (Section 2–316) other implied warranties may arise from course of dealing or usage of trade.

§ 2–315. Implied Warranty: Fitness for Particular Purpose.

Where the seller at the time of contracting has reason to know any particular purpose for which the goods are required and that the buyer is relying on the seller's skill or judgment to select or furnish suitable goods, there is unless excluded or modified under the next section an implied warranty that the goods shall be fit for such purpose.

§ 2–316. Exclusion or Modification of Warranties.

(1) Words or conduct relevant to the creation of an express warranty and words or conduct tending to negate or limit warranty shall be construed wherever reasonable as consistent with each other; but subject to the provisions of this Article on parol or extrinsic evidence (Section 2–202) negation or limitation is inoperative to the extent that such construction is unreasonable.

(2) Subject to subsection (3), to exclude or modify the implied warranty of merchantability or any part of it the language must mention merchantability and in case of a

writing must be conspicuous, and to exclude or modify any implied warranty of fitness the exclusion must be by a writing and conspicuous. Language to exclude all implied warranties of fitness is sufficient if it states, for example, that "There are no warranties which extend beyond the description on the face hereof."

(3) Notwithstanding subsection (2)

    (a) unless the circumstances indicate otherwise, all implied warranties are excluded by expressions like "as is", "with all faults" or other language which in common understanding calls the buyer's attention to the exclusion of warranties and makes plain that there is no implied warranty; and

    (b) when the buyer before entering into the contract has examined the goods or the sample or model as fully as he desired or has refused to examine the goods there is no implied warranty with regard to defects which an examination ought in the circumstances to have revealed to him; and

    (c) an implied warranty can also be excluded or modified by course of dealing or course of performance or usage of trade.

(4) Remedies for breach of warranty can be limited in accordance with the provisions of this Article on liquidation or limitation of damages and on contractual modification of remedy (Sections 2-718 and 2-719).

§ 2-317.   *Cumulation and Conflict of Warranties Express or Implied.*

Warranties whether express or implied shall be construed as consistent with each other and as cumulative, but if such construction is unreasonable the intention of the parties shall determine which warranty is dominant. In ascertaining that intention the following rules apply:

    (a) Exact or technical specifications displace an inconsistent sample or model or general language of description.

    (b) A sample from an existing bulk displaces inconsistent general language of description.

    (c) Express warranties displace inconsistent implied warranties other than an implied warranty of fitness for a particular purpose.

§ 2-318.   *Third Party Beneficiaries of Warranties Express or Implied.*

A seller's warranty whether express or implied extends to any natural person who is in the family or household of his buyer or who is a guest in his home if it is reasonable to expect that such person may use, consume or be affected by the goods and who is injured in person by breach of the warranty. A seller may not exclude or limit the operation of this section.

§ 2-319.   *F.O.B. and F.A.S. Terms.*

(1) Unless otherwise agreed the term F.O.B. (which means "free on board") at a named place, even though used only in connection with the stated price, is a delivery term under which

(a) when the term is F.O.B. the place of shipment, the seller must at that place ship the goods in the manner provided in this Article (Section 2-504) and bear the expense and risk of putting them into the possession of the carrier; or

(b) when the term is F.O.B. the place of destination, the seller must at his own expense and risk transport the goods to that place and there tender delivery of them in the manner provided in this Article (Section 2-503);

(c) when under either (a) or (b) the term is also F.O.B. vessel, car or other vehicle, the seller must in addition at his own expense and risk load the goods on board. If the term is F.O.B. vessel the buyer must name the vessel and in an appropriate case the seller must comply with the provisions of this Article on the form of bill of lading (Section 2-323).

(2) Unless otherwise agreed the term F.A.S. vessel (which means "free alongside") at a named port, even though used only in connection with the stated price, is a delivery term under which the seller must

(a) at his own expense and risk deliver the goods alongside the vessel in the manner usual in that port or on a dock designated and provided by the buyer; and

(b) obtain and tender a receipt for the goods in exchange for which the carrier is under a duty to issue a bill of lading.

(3) Unless otherwise agreed in any case falling within subsection (1)(a) or (c) or subsection (2) the buyer must seasonably give any needed instructions for making delivery, including when the term is F.A.S. or F.O.B. the loading berth of the vessel and in an appropriate case its name and sailing date. The seller may treat the failure of needed instructions as a failure of cooperation under this Article (Section 2-311). He may also at his option move the goods in any reasonable manner preparatory to delivery or shipment.

(4) Under the term F.O.B. vessel or F.A.S. unless otherwise agreed the buyer must make payment against tender of the required documents and the seller may not tender nor the buyer demand delivery of the goods in substitution for the documents.

§ 2-320.   C.I.F. and C. & F. Terms.

(1) The term C.I.F. means that the price includes in a lump sum the cost of the goods and the insurance and freight to the named destination. The term C. & F. or C.F. means that the price so includes cost and freight to the named destination.

(2) Unless otherwise agreed and even though used only in connection with the stated price and destination, the term C.I.F. destination or its equivalent requires the seller at his own expense and risk to

(a) put the goods into the possession of a carrier at the port for shipment and obtain a negotiable bill or bills of lading covering the entire transportation to the named destination; and

(b) load the goods and obtain a receipt from the carrier (which may be contained in the bill of lading) showing that the freight has been paid or provided for; and

(c) obtain a policy or certificate of insurance, including any war risk insurance, of a kind and on terms then current at the port of shipment in the usual amount, in the currency of the contract, shown to cover the same goods covered by the bill of lading and providing for payment of loss to the order of the buyer or for the account of whom it may concern; but the seller may add to the price the amount of the premium for any such war risk insurance; and

(d) prepare an invoice of the goods and procure any other documents required to effect shipment or to comply with the contract; and

(e) forward and tender with commercial promptness all the documents in due form and with any indorsement necessary to perfect the buyer's rights.

(3) Unless otherwise agreed the term C. & F. or its equivalent has the same effect and imposes upon the seller the same obligations and risks as a C.I.F. term except the obligation as to insurance.

(4) Under the term C.I.F. or C. & F. unless otherwise agreed the buyer must make payment against tender of the required documents and the seller may not tender nor the buyer demand delivery of the goods in substitution for the documents.

§ 2–328.   Sale by Auction.

(1) In a sale by auction if goods are put up in lots each lot is the subject of a separate sale.

(2) A sale by auction is complete when the auctioneer so announces by the fall of the hammer or in other customary manner. Where a bid is made while the hammer is falling in acceptance of a prior bid the auctioneer may in his discretion reopen the bidding or declare the goods sold under the bid on which the hammer was falling.

(3) Such a sale is with reserve unless the goods are in explicit terms put up without reserve. In an auction with reserve the auctioneer may withdraw the goods at any time until he announces completion of the sale. In an auction without reserve, after the auctioneer calls for bids on an article or lot, that article or lot cannot be withdrawn unless no bid is made within a reasonable time. In either case a bidder may retract his bid until the auctioneer's announcement of completion of the sale, but a bidder's retraction does not revive any previous bid.

(4) If the auctioneer knowingly receives a bid on the seller's behalf or the seller makes or procures such a bid, and notice has not been given that liberty for such bidding is reserved, the buyer may at his option avoid the sale or take the goods at the price of the last good faith bid prior to the completion of the sale. This subsection shall not apply to any bid at a forced sale.

PART 5
PERFORMANCE

§ 2–501.   Insurable Interest in Goods; Manner of Identification of Goods.

(1) The buyer obtains a special property and an insurable interest in goods by identification of existing goods as goods to which the contract refers even though the goods so identified are non-conforming and he has an option to return or reject them. Such

identification can be made at any time and in any manner explicitly agreed to by the parties. In the absence of explicit agreement identification occurs

(a) when the contract is made if it is for the sale of goods already existing and identified;

(b) if the contract is for the sale of future goods other than those described in paragraph (c), when goods are shipped, marked or otherwise designated by the seller as goods to which the contract refers;

(c) when the crops are planted or otherwise become growing crops or the young are conceived if the contract is for the sale of unborn young to be born within twelve months after contracting or for the sale of crops to be harvested within twelve months or the next normal harvest season after contracting whichever is longer.

(2) The seller retains an insurable interest in goods so long as title to or any security interest in the goods remains in him and where the identification is by the seller alone he may until default or insolvency or notification to the buyer that the identification is final substitute other goods for those identified.

(3) Nothing in this section impairs any insurable interest recognized under any other statute or rule of law.

§ 2-503. Manner of Seller's Tender of Delivery.

(1) Tender of delivery requires that the seller put and hold conforming goods at the buyer's disposition and give the buyer any notification reasonably necessary to enable him to take delivery. The manner, time and place for tender are determined by the agreement and this Article, and in particular

(a) tender must be at a reasonable hour, and if it is of goods they must be kept available for the period reasonably necessary to enable the buyer to take possession; but

(b) unless otherwise agreed the buyer must furnish facilities reasonably suited to the receipt of the goods.

(2) Where the case is within the next section respecting shipment tender requires that the seller comply with its provisions.

(3) Where the seller is required to deliver at a particular destination tender requires that he comply with subsection (1) and also in any appropriate case tender documents as described in subsections (4) and (5) of this section....

§ 2-507. Effect of Seller's Tender; Delivery on Condition.

(1) Tender of delivery is a condition to the buyer's duty to accept the goods and, unless otherwise agreed, to his duty to pay for them. Tender entitles the seller to acceptance of the goods and to payment according to the contract.

(2) Where payment is due and demanded on the delivery to the buyer of goods or documents of title, his right as against the seller to retain or dispose of them is conditional upon his making the payment due.

§ 2–508. *Cure by Seller of Improper Tender or Delivery; Replacement.*

(1) Where any tender or delivery by the seller is rejected because non-conforming and the time for performance has not yet expired, the seller may seasonably notify the buyer of his intention to cure and may then within the contract time make a conforming delivery.

(2) Where the buyer rejects a non-conforming tender which the seller had reasonable grounds to believe would be acceptable with or without money allowance the seller may if he seasonably notifies the buyer have a further reasonable time to substitute a conforming tender.

§ 2–511. *Tender of Payment by Buyer; Payment by Check.*

(1) Unless otherwise agreed tender of payment is a condition to the seller's duty to tender and complete any delivery.

(2) Tender of payment is sufficient when made by any means or in any manner current in the ordinary course of business unless the seller demands payment in legal tender and gives any extension of time reasonably necessary to procure it.

(3) Subject to the provisions of this Act on the effect of an instrument on an obligation (Section 3–310), payment by check is conditional and is defeated as between the parties by dishonor of the check on due presentment.

§ 2–513. *Buyer's Right to Inspection of Goods.*

(1) Unless otherwise agreed and subject to subsection (3), where goods are tendered or delivered or identified to the contract for sale, the buyer has a right before payment or acceptance to inspect them at any reasonable place and time and in any reasonable manner. When the seller is required or authorized to send the goods to the buyer, the inspection may be after their arrival.

(2) Expenses of inspection must be borne by the buyer but may be recovered from the seller if the goods do not conform and are rejected.

(3) Unless otherwise agreed and subject to the provisions of this Article on C.I.F. contracts (subsection (3) of Section 2–321), the buyer is not entitled to inspect the goods before payment of the price when the contract provides

   (a) for delivery "C.O.D." or on other like terms; or

   (b) for payment against documents of title, except where such payment is due only after the goods are to become available for inspection.

(4) A place or method of inspection fixed by the parties is presumed to be exclusive but unless otherwise expressly agreed it does not postpone identification or shift the place for delivery or for passing the risk of loss. If compliance becomes impossible, inspection shall be as provided in this section unless the place or method fixed was clearly intended as an indispensable condition failure of which avoids the contract.

PART 6
BREACH, REPUDIATION AND EXCUSE

§ 2-601.   *Buyer's Rights on Improper Delivery.*

Subject to the provisions of this Article on breach in installment contracts (Section 2–612) and unless otherwise agreed under the sections on contractual limitations of remedy (Sections 2–718 and 2–719), if the goods or the tender of delivery fail in any respect to conform to the contract, the buyer may

(a) reject the whole; or

(b) accept the whole; or

(c) accept any commercial unit or units and reject the rest.

§ 2-602.   *Manner and Effect of Rightful Rejection.*

(1) Rejection of goods must be within a reasonable time after their delivery or tender. It is ineffective unless the buyer seasonably notifies the seller.

(2) Subject to the provisions of the two following sections on rejected goods (Sections 2–603 and 2–604),

    (a) after rejection any exercise of ownership by the buyer with respect to any commercial unit is wrongful as against the seller; and

    (b) if the buyer has before rejection taken physical possession of goods in which he does not have a security interest under the provisions of this Article (subsection (3) of Section 2–711), he is under a duty after rejection to hold them with reasonable care at the seller's disposition for a time sufficient to permit the seller to remove them; but

    (c) the buyer has no further obligations with regard to goods rightfully rejected.

(3) The seller's rights with respect to goods wrongfully rejected are governed by the provisions of this Article on Seller's remedies in general (Section 2–703).

§ 2-605.   *Waiver of Buyer's Objections by Failure to Particularize.*

(1) The buyer's failure to state in connection with rejection a particular defect which is ascertainable by reasonable inspection precludes him from relying on the unstated defect to justify rejection or to establish breach

    (a) where the seller could have cured it if stated seasonably; or

    (b) between merchants when the seller has after rejection made a request in writing for a full and final written statement of all defects on which the buyer proposes to rely.

(2) Payment against documents made without reservation of rights precludes recovery of the payment for defects apparent on the face of the documents.

§ 2-606. What Constitutes Acceptance of Goods.

(1) Acceptance of goods occurs when the buyer

    (a) after a reasonable opportunity to inspect the goods signifies to the seller that the goods are conforming or that he will take or retain them in spite of their non-conformity; or

    (b) fails to make an effective rejection (subsection (1) of Section 2–602), but such acceptance does not occur until the buyer has had a reasonable opportunity to inspect them; or

    (c) does any act inconsistent with the seller's ownership; but if such act is wrongful as against the seller it is an acceptance only if ratified by him.

(2) Acceptance of a part of any commercial unit is acceptance of that entire unit.

§ 2-607. Effect of Acceptance; Notice of Breach; Burden of Establishing Breach After Acceptance; Notice of Claim or Litigation to Person Answerable Over.

(1) The buyer must pay at the contract rate for any goods accepted.

(2) Acceptance of goods by the buyer precludes rejection of the goods accepted and if made with knowledge of a non-conformity cannot be revoked because of it unless the acceptance was on the reasonable assumption that the non-conformity would be seasonably cured but acceptance does not of itself impair any other remedy provided by this Article for non-conformity.

(3) Where a tender has been accepted

    (a) the buyer must within a reasonable time after he discovers or should have discovered any breach notify the seller of breach or be barred from any remedy; ...

§ 2-608. Revocation of Acceptance in Whole or in Part.

(1) The buyer may revoke his acceptance of a lot or commercial unit whose non-conformity substantially impairs its value to him if he has accepted it

    (a) on the reasonable assumption that its non-conformity would be cured and it has not been seasonably cured; or

    (b) without discovery of such non-conformity if his acceptance was reasonably induced either by the difficulty of discovery before acceptance or by the seller's assurances.

(2) Revocation of acceptance must occur within a reasonable time after the buyer discovers or should have discovered the ground for it and before any substantial change in condition of the goods which is not caused by their own defects. It is not effective until the buyer notifies the seller of it.

(3) A buyer who so revokes has the same rights and duties with regard to the goods involved as if he had rejected them.

§ 2-609. Right to Adequate Assurance of Performance.

(1) A contract for sale imposes an obligation on each party that the other's expectation of receiving due performance will not be impaired. When reasonable grounds for insecurity arise with respect to the performance of either party the other may in

writing demand adequate assurance of due performance and until he receives such assurance may if commercially reasonable suspend any performance for which he has not already received the agreed return.

(2) Between merchants the reasonableness of grounds for insecurity and the adequacy of any assurance offered shall be determined according to commercial standards.

(3) Acceptance of any improper delivery or payment does not prejudice the aggrieved party's right to demand adequate assurance of future performance.

(4) After receipt of a justified demand failure to provide within a reasonable time not exceeding thirty days such assurance of due performance as is adequate under the circumstances of the particular case is a repudiation of the contract.

§ 2-610. *Anticipatory Repudiation.*

When either party repudiates the contract with respect to a performance not yet due the loss of which will substantially impair the value of the contract to the other, the aggrieved party may

    (a) for a commercially reasonable time await performance by the repudiating party; or

    (b) resort to any remedy for breach (Section 2-703 or Section 2-711), even though he has notified the repudiating party that he would await the latter's performance and has urged retraction; and

    (c) in either case suspend his own performance or proceed in accordance with the provisions of this Article on the seller's right to identify goods to the contract notwithstanding breach or to salvage unfinished goods (Section 2-704).

§ 2-611. *Retraction of Anticipatory Repudiation.*

(1) Until the repudiating party's next performance is due he can retract his repudiation unless the aggrieved party has since the repudiation cancelled or materially changed his position or otherwise indicated that he considers the repudiation final.

(2) Retraction may be by any method which clearly indicates to the aggrieved party that the repudiating party intends to perform, but must include any assurance justifiably demanded under the provisions of this Article (Section 2-609).

(3) Retraction reinstates the repudiating party's rights under the contract with due excuse and allowance to the aggrieved party for any delay occasioned by the repudiation.

§ 2-612. *"Installment Contract"; Breach.*

(1) An "installment contract" is one which requires or authorizes the delivery of goods in separate lots to be separately accepted, even though the contract contains a clause "each delivery is a separate contract" or its equivalent.

(2) The buyer may reject any installment which is non-conforming if the non-conformity substantially impairs the value of that installment and cannot be cured or if the non-conformity is a defect in the required documents; but if the non-conformity does not fall within subsection (3) and the seller gives adequate assurance of its cure the buyer must accept that installment.

(3) Whenever non-conformity or default with respect to one or more installments substantially impairs the value of the whole contract there is a breach of the whole. But the aggrieved party reinstates the contract if he accepts a non-conforming installment without seasonably notifying of cancellation or if he brings an action with respect only to past installments or demands performance as to future installments.

§ 2-613.   Casualty to Identified Goods.

Where the contract requires for its performance goods identified when the contract is made, and the goods suffer casualty without fault of either party before the risk of loss passes to the buyer, or in a proper case under a "no arrival, no sale" term (Section 2–324) then

(a) if the loss is total the contract is avoided; and

(b) if the loss is partial or the goods have so deteriorated as no longer to conform to the contract the buyer may nevertheless demand inspection and at his option either treat the contract as avoided or accept the goods with due allowance from the contract price for the deterioration or the deficiency in quantity but without further right against the seller.

§ 2-614.   Substituted Performance.

(1) Where without fault of either party the agreed berthing, loading, or unloading facilities fail or an agreed type of carrier becomes unavailable or the agreed manner of delivery otherwise becomes commercially impracticable but a commercially reasonable substitute is available, such substitute performance must be tendered and accepted.

(2) If the agreed means or manner of payment fails because of domestic or foreign governmental regulation, the seller may withhold or stop delivery unless the buyer provides a means or manner of payment which is commercially a substantial equivalent. If delivery has already been taken, payment by the means or in the manner provided by the regulation discharges the buyer's obligation unless the regulation is discriminatory, oppressive or predatory.

§ 2-615.   Excuse by Failure of Presupposed Conditions.

Except so far as a seller may have assumed a greater obligation and subject to the preceding section on substituted performance:

(a) Delay in delivery or non-delivery in whole or in part by a seller who complies with paragraphs (b) and (c) is not a breach of his duty under a contract for sale if performance as agreed has been made impracticable by the occurrence of a contingency the non-occurrence of which was a basic assumption on which the contract was made or by compliance in good faith with any applicable foreign or domestic governmental regulation or order whether or not it later proves to be invalid.

(b) Where the causes mentioned in paragraph (a) affect only a part of the seller's capacity to perform, he must allocate production and deliveries among his customers but may at his option include regular customers not then under contract as well as his own requirements for further manufacture. He may so allocate in any manner which is fair and reasonable.

(c) The seller must notify the buyer seasonably that there will be delay or non-delivery and, when allocation is required under paragraph (b), of the estimated quota thus made available for the buyer.

§ 2–616. Procedure on Notice Claiming Excuse.

(1) Where the buyer receives notification of a material or indefinite delay or an allocation justified under the preceding section he may by written notification to the seller as to any delivery concerned, and where the prospective deficiency substantially impairs the value of the whole contract under the provisions of this Article relating to breach of installment contracts (Section 2–612), then also as to the whole,

(a) terminate and thereby discharge any unexecuted portion of the contract; or

(b) modify the contract by agreeing to take his available quota in substitution.

(2) If after receipt of such notification from the seller the buyer fails so to modify the contract within a reasonable time not exceeding thirty days the contract lapses with respect to any deliveries affected.

(3) The provisions of this section may not be negated by agreement except in so far as the seller has assumed a greater obligation under the preceding section.

PART 7
REMEDIES

§ 2–702. Seller's Remedies on Discovery of Buyer's Insolvency.

(1) Where the seller discovers the buyer to be insolvent he may refuse delivery except for cash including payment for all goods theretofore delivered under the contract, and stop delivery under this Article (Section 2–705)....

§ 2–703. Seller's Remedies in General.

Where the buyer wrongfully rejects or revokes acceptance of goods or fails to make a payment due on or before delivery or repudiates with respect to a part or the whole, then with respect to any goods directly affected and, if the breach is of the whole contract (Section 2–612), then also with respect to the whole undelivered balance, the aggrieved seller may

(a) withhold delivery of such goods;

(b) stop delivery by any bailee as hereafter provided (Section 2–705);

(c) proceed under the next section respecting goods still unidentified to the contract;

(d) resell and recover damages as hereafter provided (Section 2–706);

(e) recover damages for non-acceptance (Section 2–708) or in a proper case the price (Section 2–709);

(f) cancel.

§ 2-704. Seller's Right to Identify Goods to the Contract Notwithstanding Breach or to Salvage Unfinished Goods.

(1) An aggrieved seller under the preceding section may

    (a) identify to the contract conforming goods not already identified if at the time he learned of the breach they are in his possession or control;

    (b) treat as the subject of resale goods which have demonstrably been intended for the particular contract even though those goods are unfinished.

(2) Where the goods are unfinished an aggrieved seller may in the exercise of reasonable commercial judgment for the purposes of avoiding loss and of effective realization either complete the manufacture and wholly identify the goods to the contract or cease manufacture and resell for scrap or salvage value or proceed in any other reasonable manner.

§ 2-706. Seller's Resale Including Contract for Resale.

(1) Under the conditions stated in Section 2-703 on seller's remedies, the seller may resell the goods concerned or the undelivered balance thereof. Where the resale is made in good faith and in a commercially reasonable manner the seller may recover the difference between the resale price and the contract price together with any incidental damages allowed under the provisions of this Article (Section 2-710), but less expenses saved in consequence of the buyer's breach.

(2) Except as otherwise provided in subsection (3) or unless otherwise agreed resale may be at public or private sale including sale by way of one or more contracts to sell or of identification to an existing contract of the seller. Sale may be as a unit or in parcels and at any time and place and on any terms but every aspect of the sale including the method, manner, time, place and terms must be commercially reasonable. The resale must be reasonably identified as referring to the broken contract, but it is not necessary that the goods be in existence or that any or all of them have been identified to the contract before the breach.

(3) Where the resale is at private sale the seller must give the buyer reasonable notification of his intention to resell.

(4) Where the resale is at public sale

    (a) only identified goods can be sold except where there is a recognized market for a public sale of futures in goods of the kind; and

    (b) it must be made at a usual place or market for public sale if one is reasonably available and except in the case of goods which are perishable or threaten to decline in value speedily the seller must give the buyer reasonable notice of the time and place of the resale; and

    (c) if the goods are not to be within the view of those attending the sale the notification of sale must state the place where the goods are located and provide for their reasonable inspection by prospective bidders; and

    (d) the seller may buy.

(5) A purchaser who buys in good faith at a resale takes the goods free of any rights of the original buyer even though the seller fails to comply with one or more of the requirements of this section.

(6) The seller is not accountable to the buyer for any profit made on any resale. A person in the position of a seller (Section 2–707) or a buyer who has rightfully rejected or justifiably revoked acceptance must account for any excess over the amount of his security interest, as hereinafter defined (subsection (3) of Section 2–711).

§ 2–708.   Seller's Damages for Non-acceptance or Repudiation.

(1) Subject to subsection (2) and to the provisions of this Article with respect to proof of market price (Section 2–723), the measure of damages for non-acceptance or repudiation by the buyer is the difference between the market price at the time and place for tender and the unpaid contract price together with any incidental damages provided in this Article (Section 2–710), but less expenses saved in consequence of the buyer's breach.

(2) If the measure of damages provided in subsection (1) is inadequate to put the seller in as good a position as performance would have done then the measure of damages is the profit (including reasonable overhead) which the seller would have made from full performance by the buyer, together with any incidental damages provided in this Article (Section 2–710), due allowance for costs reasonably incurred and due credit for payments or proceeds of resale.

§ 2–709.   Action for the Price.

(1) When the buyer fails to pay the price as it becomes due the seller may recover, together with any incidental damages under the next section, the price
  (a) of goods accepted or of conforming goods lost or damaged within a commercially reasonable time after risk of their loss has passed to the buyer; and
  (b) of goods identified to the contract if the seller is unable after reasonable effort to resell them at a reasonable price or the circumstances reasonably indicate that such effort will be unavailing.

(2) Where the seller sues for the price he must hold for the buyer any goods which have been identified to the contract and are still in his control except that if resale becomes possible he may resell them at any time prior to the collection of the judgment. The net proceeds of any such resale must be credited to the buyer and payment of the judgment entitles him to any goods not resold.

(3) After the buyer has wrongfully rejected or revoked acceptance of the goods or has failed to make a payment due or has repudiated (Section 2–610), a seller who is held not entitled to the price under this section shall nevertheless be awarded damages for non-acceptance under the preceding section.

§ 2-710.   Seller's Incidental Damages.

Incidental damages to an aggrieved seller include any commercially reasonable charges, expenses or commissions incurred in stopping delivery, in the transportation, care and custody of goods after the buyer's breach, in connection with return or resale of the goods or otherwise resulting from the breach.

§ 2-711.   Buyer's Remedies in General; Buyer's Security Interest in Rejected Goods.

(1) Where the seller fails to make delivery or repudiates or the buyer rightfully rejects or justifiably revokes acceptance then with respect to any goods involved, and with respect to the whole if the breach goes to the whole contract (Section 2-612), the buyer may cancel and whether or not he has done so may in addition to recovering so much of the price as has been paid

    (a) "cover" and have damages under the next section as to all the goods affected whether or not they have been identified to the contract; or

    (b) recover damages for non-delivery as provided in this Article (Section 2-713).

(2) Where the seller fails to deliver or repudiates the buyer may also

    (a) if the goods have been identified recover them as provided in this Article (Section 2-502); or

    (b) in a proper case obtain specific performance or replevy the goods as provided in this Article (Section 2-716).

(3) On rightful rejection or justifiable revocation of acceptance a buyer has a security interest in goods in his possession or control for any payments made on their price and any expenses reasonably incurred in their inspection, receipt, transportation, care and custody and may hold such goods and resell them in like manner as an aggrieved seller (Section 2-706).

§ 2-712.   "Cover"; Buyer's Procurement of Substitute Goods.

(1) After a breach within the preceding section the buyer may "cover" by making in good faith and without unreasonable delay any reasonable purchase of or contract to purchase goods in substitution for those due from the seller.

(2) The buyer may recover from the seller as damages the difference between the cost of cover and the contract price together with any incidental or consequential damages as hereinafter defined (Section 2-715), but less expenses saved in consequence of the seller's breach.

(3) Failure of the buyer to effect cover within this section does not bar him from any other remedy.

§ 2-713.   Buyer's Damages for Non-Delivery or Repudiation.

(1) Subject to the provisions of this Article with respect to proof of market price (Section 2-723), the measure of damages for non-delivery or repudiation by the seller is the difference between the market price at the time when the buyer learned of the breach and the contract price together with any incidental and consequential damages provided in this Article (Section 2-715), but less expenses saved in consequence of the seller's breach.

(2) Market price is to be determined as of the place for tender or, in cases of rejection after arrival or revocation of acceptance, as of the place of arrival.

§ 2-714.   Buyer's Damages for Breach in Regard to Accepted Goods.

(1) Where the buyer has accepted goods and given notification (subsection (3) of Section 2-607) he may recover as damages for any non-conformity of tender the loss resulting in the ordinary course of events from the seller's breach as determined in any manner which is reasonable.

(2) The measure of damages for breach of warranty is the difference at the time and place of acceptance between the value of the goods accepted and the value they would have had if they had been as warranted, unless special circumstances show proximate damages of a different amount.

(3) In a proper case any incidental and consequential damages under the next section may also be recovered.

§ 2-715.   Buyer's Incidental and Consequential Damages.

(1) Incidental damages resulting from the seller's breach include expenses reasonably incurred in inspection, receipt, transportation and care and custody of goods rightfully rejected, any commercially reasonable charges, expenses or commissions in connection with effecting cover and any other reasonable expense incident to the delay or other breach.

(2) Consequential damages resulting from the seller's breach include
   (a) any loss resulting from general or particular requirements and needs of which the seller at the time of contracting had reason to know and which could not reasonably be prevented by cover or otherwise; and
   (b) injury to person or property proximately resulting from any breach of warranty.

§ 2-716.   Buyer's Right to Specific Performance or Replevin.

(1) Specific performance may be decreed where the goods are unique or in other proper circumstances.

(2) The decree for specific performance may include such terms and conditions as to payment of the price, damages, or other relief as the court may deem just.

(3) The buyer has a right of replevin for goods identified to the contract if after reasonable effort he is unable to effect cover for such goods or the circumstances reasonably indicate that such effort will be unavailing or if the goods have been shipped under reservation and satisfaction of the security interest in them has been made or tendered. In the case of goods bought for personal, family, or household purposes, the buyer's right of replevin vests upon acquisition of a special property, even if the seller had not then repudiated or failed to deliver.

§ 2-717.   Deduction of Damages From the Price.

The buyer on notifying the seller of his intention to do so may deduct all or any part of the damages resulting from any breach of the contract from any part of the price still due under the same contract.

§ 2-718.   *Liquidation or Limitation of Damages; Deposits.*

(1) Damages for breach by either party may be liquidated in the agreement but only at an amount which is reasonable in the light of the anticipated or actual harm caused by the breach, the difficulties of proof of loss, and the inconvenience or nonfeasibility of otherwise obtaining an adequate remedy. A term fixing unreasonably large liquidated damages is void as a penalty.

(2) Where the seller justifiably withholds delivery of goods because of the buyer's breach, the buyer is entitled to restitution of any amount by which the sum of his payments exceeds

    (a) the amount to which the seller is entitled by virtue of terms liquidating the seller's damages in accordance with subsection (1), or

    (b) in the absence of such terms, twenty per cent of the value of the total performance for which the buyer is obligated under the contract or $500, whichever is smaller.

(3) The buyer's right to restitution under subsection (2) is subject to offset to the extent that the seller establishes

    (a) a right to recover damages under the provisions of this Article other than subsection (1), and

    (b) the amount or value of any benefits received by the buyer directly or indirectly by reason of the contract.

(4) Where a seller has received payment in goods their reasonable value or the proceeds of their resale shall be treated as payments for the purposes of subsection (2); but if the seller has notice of the buyer's breach before reselling goods received in part performance, his resale is subject to the conditions laid down in this Article on resale by an aggrieved seller (Section 2-706).

§ 2-719.   *Contractual Modification or Limitation of Remedy.*

(1) Subject to the provisions of subsections (2) and (3) of this section and of the preceding section on liquidation and limitation of damages,

    (a) the agreement may provide for remedies in addition to or in substitution for those provided in this Article and may limit or alter the measure of damages recoverable under this Article, as by limiting the buyer's remedies to return of the goods and repayment of the price or to repair and replacement of non-conforming goods or parts; and

    (b) resort to a remedy as provided is optional unless the remedy is expressly agreed to be exclusive, in which case it is the sole remedy.

(2) Where circumstances cause an exclusive or limited remedy to fail of its essential purpose, remedy may be had as provided in this Act.

(3) Consequential damages may be limited or excluded unless the limitation or exclusion is unconscionable. Limitation of consequential damages for injury to the person in the case of consumer goods is prima facie unconscionable but limitation of damages where the loss is commercial is not.

§ 2-721. Remedies for Fraud.

Remedies for material misrepresentation or fraud include all remedies available under this Article for non-fraudulent breach. Neither rescission or a claim for rescission of the contract for sale nor rejection or return of the goods shall bar or be deemed inconsistent with a claim for damages or other remedy.

§ 2-723. Proof of Market Price: Time and Place.

(1) If an action based on anticipatory repudiation comes to trial before the time for performance with respect to some or all of the goods, any damages based on market price (Section 2-708 or Section 2-713) shall be determined according to the price of such goods prevailing at the time when the aggrieved party learned of the repudiation.

(2) If evidence of a price prevailing at the times or places described in this Article is not readily available the price prevailing within any reasonable time before or after the time described or at any other place which in commercial judgment or under usage of trade would serve as a reasonable substitute for the one described may be used, making any proper allowance for the cost of transporting the goods to or from such other place.

(3) Evidence of a relevant price prevailing at a time or place other than the one described in this Article offered by one party is not admissible unless and until he has given the other party such notice as the court finds sufficient to prevent unfair surprise.

§ 2-724. Admissibility of Market Quotations.

Whenever the prevailing price or value of any goods regularly bought and sold in any established commodity market is in issue, reports in official publications or trade journals or in newspapers or periodicals of general circulation published as the reports of such market shall be admissible in evidence. The circumstances of the preparation of such a report may be shown to affect its weight but not its admissibility.

§ 2-725. Statute of Limitations in Contracts for Sale.

(1) An action for breach of any contract for sale must be commenced within four years after the cause of action has accrued. By the original agreement the parties may reduce the period of limitation to not less than one year but may not extend it.

(2) A cause of action accrues when the breach occurs, regardless of the aggrieved party's lack of knowledge of the breach. A breach of warranty occurs when tender of delivery is made, except that where a warranty explicitly extends to future performance of the goods and discovery of the breach must await the time of such performance the cause of action accrues when the breach is or should have been discovered.

(3) Where an action commenced within the time limited by subsection (1) is so terminated as to leave available a remedy by another action for the same breach such other action may be commenced after the expiration of the time limited and within

six months after the termination of the first action unless the termination resulted from voluntary discontinuance or from dismissal for failure or neglect to prosecute.

(4) This section does not alter the law on tolling of the statute of limitations nor does it apply to causes of action which have accrued before this Act becomes effective.

APPENDIX II. RESTATEMENT, SECOND, CONTRACTS: SELECTED SECTIONS

§ 1. Contract Defined.

A contract is a promise or a set of promises for the breach of which the law gives a remedy, or the performance of which the law in some way recognizes as a duty.

§ 2. Promise; Promisor; Promisee; Beneficiary.

(1) A promise is a manifestation of intention to act or refrain from acting in a specified way, so made as to justify a promisee in understanding that a commitment has been made.

(2) The person manifesting the intention is the promisor.

(3) The person to whom the manifestation is addressed is the promisee.

(4) Where performance will benefit a person other than the promisee, that person is a beneficiary.

§ 3. Agreement Defined; Bargain Defined.

An agreement is a manifestation of mutual assent on the part of two or more persons. A bargain is an agreement to exchange promises or to exchange a promise for a performance or to exchange performances.

§ 4. How a Promise May Be Made.

A promise may be stated in words either oral or written, or may be inferred wholly or partly from conduct.

§ 5. Terms of Promise, Agreement, or Contract.

(1) A term of a promise or agreement is that portion of the intention or assent manifested which relates to a particular matter.

(2) A term of a contract is that portion of the legal relations resulting from the promise or set of promises which relates to a particular matter, whether or not the parties manifest an intention to create those relations.

§ 7. Voidable Contracts.

A voidable contract is one where one or more parties have the power, by a manifestation of election to do so, to avoid the legal relations created by the contract, or by ratification of the contract to extinguish the power of avoidance.

§ 8. Unenforceable Contracts.

An unenforceable contract is one for the breach of which neither the remedy of damages nor the remedy of specific performance is available, but which is recognized in some other way as creating a duty of performance, though there has been no ratification.

§ 12. Capacity to Contract.

(1) No one can be bound by contract who has not legal capacity to incur at least voidable contractual duties. Capacity to contract may be partial and its existence in respect of a particular transaction may depend upon the nature of the transaction or upon other circumstances.

(2) A natural person who manifests assent to a transaction has full legal capacity to incur contractual duties thereby unless he is
   (a) under guardianship, or
   (b) an infant, or
   (c) mentally ill or defective, or
   (d) intoxicated.

§ 13. Persons Affected by Guardianship.

A person has no capacity to incur contractual duties if his property is under guardianship by reason of an adjudication of mental illness or defect.

§ 14. Infants.

Unless a statute provides otherwise, a natural person has the capacity to incur only voidable contractual duties until the beginning of the day before the person's eighteenth birthday.

§ 15. Mental Illness or Defect.

(1) A person incurs only voidable contractual duties by entering into a transaction if by reason of mental illness or defect
   (a) he is unable to understand in a reasonable manner the nature and consequences of the transaction, or
   (b) he is unable to act in a reasonable manner in relation to the transaction and the other party has reason to know of his condition.

(2) Where the contract is made on fair terms and the other party is without knowledge of the mental illness or defect, the power of avoidance under Subsection (1) terminates to the extent that the contract has been so performed in whole or in part or the circumstances have so changed that avoidance would be unjust. In such a case a court may grant relief as justice requires.

§ 16. Intoxicated Persons.

A person incurs only voidable contractual duties by entering into a transaction if the other party has reason to know that by reason of intoxication
   (a) he is unable to understand in a reasonable manner the nature and consequences of the transaction, or
   (b) he is unable to act in a reasonable manner in relation to the transaction.

§ 17. Requirement of a Bargain.

(1) Except as stated in Subsection (2), the formation of a contract requires a bargain in which there is a manifestation of mutual assent to the exchange and a consideration.

(2) Whether or not there is a bargain a contract may be formed under special rules applicable to formal contracts or under the rules stated in §§ 82-94.

§ 18. Manifestation of Mutual Assent.

Manifestation of mutual assent to an exchange requires that each party either make a promise or begin or render a performance.

§ 19. Conduct as Manifestation of Assent.

(1) The manifestation of assent may be made wholly or partly by written or spoken words or by other acts or by failure to act.

(2) The conduct of a party is not effective as a manifestation of his assent unless he intends to engage in the conduct and knows or has reason to know that the other party may infer from his conduct that he assents.

(3) The conduct of a party may manifest assent even though he does not in fact assent. In such cases a resulting contract may be voidable because of fraud, duress, mistake, or other invalidating cause.

§ 20. Effect of Misunderstanding.

(1) There is no manifestation of mutual assent to an exchange if the parties attach materially different meanings to their manifestations and

   (a) neither party knows or has reason to know the meaning attached by the other; or

   (b) each party knows or each party has reason to know the meaning attached by the other.

(2) The manifestations of the parties are operative in accordance with the meaning attached to them by one of the parties if

   (a) that party does not know of any different meaning attached by the other, and the other knows the meaning attached by the first party; or

   (b) that party has no reason to know of any different meaning attached by the other, and the other has reason to know the meaning attached by the first party.

§ 21. Intention to Be Legally Bound.

Neither real nor apparent intention that a promise be legally binding is essential to the formation of a contract, but a manifestation of intention that a promise shall not affect legal relations may prevent the formation of a contract.

§ 22. Mode of Assent: Offer and Acceptance.

(1) The manifestation of mutual assent to an exchange ordinarily takes the form of an offer or proposal by one party followed by an acceptance by the other party or parties.

(2) A manifestation of mutual assent may be made even though neither offer nor acceptance can be identified and even though the moment of formation cannot be determined.

§ 24. Offer Defined.

An offer is the manifestation of willingness to enter into a bargain, so made as to justify another person in understanding that his assent to that bargain is invited and will conclude it.

§ 25. Option Contracts.

An option contract is a promise which meets the requirements for the formation of a contract and limits the promisor's power to revoke an offer.

§ 26. Preliminary Negotiations.

A manifestation of willingness to enter into a bargain is not an offer if the person to whom it is addressed knows or has reason to know that the person making it does not intend to conclude a bargain until he has made a further manifestation of assent.

§ 27. Existence of Contract Where Written Memorial Is Contemplated.

Manifestations of assent that are in themselves sufficient to conclude a contract will not be prevented from so operating by the fact that the parties also manifest an intention to prepare and adopt a written memorial thereof; but the circumstances may show that the agreements are preliminary negotiations.

§ 30. Form of Acceptance Invited.

(1) An offer may invite or require acceptance to be made by an affirmative answer in words, or by performing or refraining from performing a specified act, or may empower the offeree to make a selection of terms in his acceptance.

(2) Unless otherwise indicated by the language or the circumstances, an offer invites acceptance in any manner and by any medium reasonable in the circumstances.

§ 32. Invitation of Promise or Performance.

In case of doubt an offer is interpreted as inviting the offeree to accept either by promising to perform what the offerrequests or by rendering the performance, as the offeree chooses.

§ 33. Certainty.

(1) Even though a manifestation of intention is intended to be understood as an offer, it cannot be accepted so as to form a contract unless the terms of the contract are reasonably certain.

(2) The terms of a contract are reasonably certain if they provide a basis for determining the existence of a breach and for giving an appropriate remedy.

(3) The fact that one or more terms of a proposed bargain are left open or uncertain may show that a manifestation of intention is not intended to be understood as an offer or as an acceptance.

§ 34. Certainty and Choice of Terms; Effect of Performance or Reliance.

(1) The terms of a contract may be reasonably certain even though it empowers one or both parties to make a selection of terms in the course of performance.

(2) Part performance under an agreement may remove uncertainty and establish that a contract enforceable as a bargain has been formed.

(3) Action in reliance on an agreement may make a contractual remedy appropriate even though uncertainty is not removed.

§ 35. The Offeree's Power of Acceptance.

(1) An offer gives to the offeree a continuing power to complete the manifestation of mutual assent by acceptance of the offer.

(2) A contract cannot be created by acceptance of an offer after the power of acceptance has been terminated in one of the ways listed in § 36.

§ 36. Methods of Termination of the Power of Acceptance.

(1) An offeree's power of acceptance may be terminated by
    (a) rejection or counter-offer by the offeree, or
    (b) lapse of time, or
    (c) revocation by the offeror, or
    (d) death or incapacity of the offeror or offeree.

(2) In addition, an offeree's power of acceptance is terminated by the non-occurrence of any condition of acceptance under the terms of the offer.

§ 37. Termination of Power of Acceptance Under Option Contract.

Notwithstanding §§ 38-49, the power of acceptance under an option contract is not terminated by rejection or counter-offer, by revocation, or by death or incapacity of the offeror, unless the requirements are met for the discharge of a contractual duty.

§ 38. Rejection.

(1) An offeree's power of acceptance is terminated by his rejection of the offer, unless the offeror has manifested a contrary intention.

(2) A manifestation of intention not to accept an offer is a rejection unless the offeree manifests an intention to take it under further advisement.

§ 39. Counter-Offers.

(1) A counter-offer is an offer made by an offeree to his offeror relating to the same matter as the original offer and proposing a substituted bargain differing from that proposed by the original offer.

(2) An offeree's power of acceptance is terminated by his making of a counter-offer, unless the offeror has manifested a contrary intention or unless the counter-offer manifests a contrary intention of the offeree.

§ 40. Time When Rejection or Counter-Offer Terminates the Power of Acceptance.

Rejection or counter-offer by mail or telegram does not terminate the power of acceptance until received by the offeror, but limits the power so that a letter or telegram of acceptance started after the sending of an otherwise effective rejection or counter-offer is only a counter-offer unless the acceptance is received by the offeror before he receives the rejection or counter-offer.

§ 41. Lapse of Time.

(1) An offeree's power of acceptance is terminated at the time specified in the offer, or, if no time is specified, at the end of a reasonable time.

(2) What is a reasonable time is a question of fact, depending on all the circumstances existing when the offer and attempted acceptance are made.

(3) Unless otherwise indicated by the language or the circumstances, and subject to the rule stated in § 49, an offer sent by mail is seasonably accepted if an acceptance is mailed at any time before midnight on the day on which the offer is received.

§ 42. Revocation by Communication From Offeror Received by Offeree.

An offeree's power of acceptance is terminated when the offeree receives from the offeror a manifestation of an intention not to enter into the proposed contract.

§ 43. Indirect Communication of Revocation.

An offeree's power of acceptance is terminated when the offeror takes definite action inconsistent with an intention to enter into the proposed contract and the offeree acquires reliable information to that effect.

§ 45. Option Contract Created by Part Performance or Tender.

(1) Where an offer invites an offeree to accept by rendering a performance and does not invite a promissory acceptance, an option contract is created when the offeree tenders or begins the invited performance or tenders a beginning of it.

(2) The offeror's duty of performance under any option contract so created is conditional on completion or tender of the invited performance in accordance with the terms of the offer.

§ 46. Revocation of General Offer.

Where an offer is made by advertisement in a newspaper or other general notification to the public or to a number of persons whose identity is unknown to the offeror, the offeree's power of acceptance is terminated when a notice of termination is given publicity by advertisement or other general notification equal to that given to the offer and no better means of notification is reasonably available.

§ 47. Revocation of Divisible Offer.

An offer contemplating a series of independent contracts by separate acceptances may be effectively revoked so as to terminate the power to create future contracts, though one or more of the proposed contracts have already been formed by the offeree's acceptance.

§ 48. Death or Incapacity of Offeror or Offeree.

An offeree's power of acceptance is terminated when the offeree or offeror dies or is deprived of legal capacity to enter into the proposed contract.

§ 50. Acceptance of Offer Defined; Acceptance by Performance; Acceptance by Promise.

(1) Acceptance of an offer is a manifestation of assent to the terms thereof made by the offeree in a manner invited or required by the offer.

(2) Acceptance by performance requires that at least part of what the offer requests be performed or tendered and includes acceptance by a performance which operates as a return promise.

(3) Acceptance by a promise requires that the offeree complete every act essential to the making of the promise.

§ 54. Acceptance by Performance; Necessity of Notification to Offeror.

(1) Where an offer invites an offeree to accept by rendering a performance, no notification is necessary to make such an acceptance effective unless the offer requests such a notification.

(2) If an offeree who accepts by rendering a performance has reason to know that the offeror has no adequate means of learning of the performance with reasonable promptness and certainty, the contractual duty of the offeror is discharged unless

   (a) the offeree exercises reasonable diligence to notify the offeror of acceptance, or

   (b) the offeror learns of the performance within a reasonable time, or

   (c) the offer indicates that notification of acceptance is not required.

§ 59. Purported Acceptance Which Adds Qualifications.

A reply to an offer which purports to accept it but is conditional on the offeror's asssent to terms additional to or different from those offered is not an acceptance but is a counter-offer.

§ 60. Acceptance of Offer Which States Place, Time or Manner of Acceptance.

If an offer prescribes the place, time or manner of acceptance its terms in this respect must be complied with in order to create a contract. If an offer merely suggests a permitted place, time or manner of acceptance, another method of acceptance is not precluded.

§ 61. Acceptance Which Requests Change of Terms.

An acceptance which requests a change or addition to the terms of the offer is not thereby invalidated unless the acceptance is made to depend on an assent to the changed or added terms.

§ 62. Effect of Performance by Offeree Where Offer Invites Either Performance or Promise.

(1) Where an offer invites an offeree to choose between acceptance by promise and acceptance by performance, the tender or beginning of the invited performance or a tender of a beginning of it is an acceptance by performance.

(2) Such an acceptance operates as a promise to render complete performance.

§ 63. Time When Acceptance Takes Effect.

Unless the offer provides otherwise,

(a) an acceptance made in a manner and by a medium invited by an offer is operative and completes the manifestation of mutual assent as soon as put out of the offeree's possession, without regard to whether it ever reaches the offeror; but

(b) an acceptance under an option contract is not operative until received by the offeror.

§ 66. Acceptance Must Be Properly Dispatched.

An acceptance sent by mail or otherwise from a distance is not operative when dispatched, unless it is properly addressed and such other precautions taken as are ordinarily observed to insure safe transmission of similar messages.

§ 67. Effect of Receipt of Acceptance Improperly Dispatched.

Where an acceptance is seasonably dispatched but the offeree uses means of transmission not invited by the offer or fails to exercise reasonable diligence to insure safe transmission, it is treated as operative upon dispatch if received within the time in which a properly dispatched acceptance would normally have arrived.

§ 68. What Constitutes Receipt of Revocation, Rejection, or Acceptance.

A written revocation, rejection, or acceptance is received when the writing comes into the possession of the person addressed, or of some person authorized by him to receive it for him, or when it is deposited in some place which he has authorized as the place for this or similar communications to be deposited for him.

§ 69. Acceptance by Silence or Exercise of Dominion.

(1) Where an offeree fails to reply to an offer, his silence and inaction operate as an acceptance in the following cases only:

    (a) Where an offeree takes the benefit of offered services with reasonable opportunity to reject them and reason to know that they were offered with the expectation of compensation.

    (b) Where the offeror has stated or given the offeree reason to understand that assent may be manifested by silence or inaction, and the offeree in remaining silent and inactive intends to accept the offer.

    (c) Where because of previous dealings or otherwise, it is reasonable that the offeree should notify the offeror if he does not intend to accept.

(2) An offeree who does any act inconsistent with the offeror's ownership of offered property is bound in accordance with the offered terms unless they are manifestly unreasonable. But if the act is wrongful as against the offeror it is an acceptance only if ratified by him.

§ 71. Requirement of Exchange; Types of Exchange.

(1) To constitute consideration, a performance or a return promise must be bargained for.

(2) A performance or return promise is bargained for if it is sought by the promisor in exchange for his promise and is given by the promisee in exchange for that promise.

(3) The performance may consist of

    (a) an act other than a promise, or

    (b) a forbearance, or

    (c) the creation, modification, or destruction of a legal relation.

(4) The performance or return promise may be given to the promisor or to some other person. It may be given by the promisee or by some other person.

§ 72. Exchange of Promise for Performance.

Except as stated in §§ 73 and 74, any performance which is bargained for is consideration.

§ 73. Performance of Legal Duty.

Performance of a legal duty owed to a promisor which is neither doubtful nor the subject of honest dispute is not consideration; but a similar performance is consideration if it differs from what was required by the duty in a way which reflects more than a pretense of bargain.

§ 74. Settlement of Claims.

(1) Forbearance to assert or the surrender of a claim or defense which proves to be invalid is not consideration unless

    (a) the claim or defense is in fact doubtful because of uncertainty as to the facts or the law, or

(b) the forbearing or surrendering party believes that the claim or defense may be fairly determined to be valid.

(2) The execution of a written instrument surrendering a claim or defense by one who is under no duty to execute it is consideration if the execution of the written instrument is bargained for even though he is not asserting the claim or defense and believes that no valid claim or defense exists.

§ 75. Exchange of Promise for Promise.

Except as stated in §§ 76 and 77, a promise which is bargained for is consideration if, but only if, the promised performance would be consideration.

§ 76. Conditional Promise.

(1) A conditional promise is not consideration if the promisor knows at the time of making the promise that the condition cannot occur.

(2) A promise conditional on a performance by the promisor is a promise of alternative performances within § 77 unless occurrence of the condition is also promised.

§ 77. Illusory and Alternative Promises.

A promise or apparent promise is not consideration if by its terms the promisor or purported promisor reserves a choice of alternative performances unless
    (a) each of the alternative performances would have been consideration if it alone had been bargained for; or
    (b) one of the alternative performances would have been consideration and there is or appears to the parties to be a substantial possibility that before the promisor exercises his choice events may eliminate the alternatives which would not have been consideration.

§ 78. Voidable and Unenforceable Promises.

The fact that a rule of law renders a promise voidable or unenforceable does not prevent it from being consideration.

§ 79. Adequacy of Consideration; Mutuality of Obligation.

If the requirement of consideration is met, there is no additional requirement of
    (a) a gain, advantage, or benefit to the promisor or a loss, disadvantage, or detriment to the promisee; or
    (b) equivalence in the values exchanged; or
    (c) "mutuality of obligation."

§ 82. Promise to Pay Indebtedness; Effect on the Statute of Limitations.

(1) A promise to pay all or part of an antecedent contractual or quasi-contractual indebtedness owed by the promisor is binding if the indebtedness is still enforceable or would be except for the effect of a statute of limitations.

(2) The following facts operate as such a promise unless other facts indicate a different intention:

   (a) A voluntary acknowledgment to the obligee, admitting the present existence of the antecedent indebtedness; or

   (b) A voluntary transfer of money, a negotiable instrument, or other thing by the obligor to the obligee, made as interest on or part payment of or collateral security for the antecedent indebtedness; or

   (c) A statement to the obligee that the statute of limitations will not be pleaded as a defense.

§ 83. Promise to Pay Indebtedness Discharged in Bankruptcy.

An express promise to pay all or part of an indebtedness of the promisor, discharged or dischargeable in bankruptcy proceedings begun before the promise is made, is binding.

§ 84. Promise to Perform a Duty in Spite of Non-Occurrence of a Condition.

(1) Except as stated in Subsection (2), a promise to perform all or part of a conditional duty under an antecedent contract in spite of the non-occurrence of the condition is binding, whether the promise is made before or after the time for the condition to occur, unless

   (a) occurrence of the condition was a material part of the agreed exchange for the performance of the duty and the promisee was under no duty that it occur; or

   (b) uncertainty of the occurrence of the condition was an element of the risk assumed by the promisor.

(2) If such a promise is made before the time for the occurrence of the condition has expired and the condition is within the control of the promisee or a beneficiary, the promisor can make his duty again subject to the condition by notifying the promisee or beneficiary of his intention to do so if

   (a) the notification is received while there is still a reasonable time to cause the condition to occur under the antecedent terms or an extension given by the promisor; and

   (b) reinstatement of the requirement of the condition is not unjust because of a material change of position by the promisee or beneficiary; and

   (c) the promise is not binding apart from the rule stated in Subsection (1).

§ 85. Promise to Perform a Voidable Duty.

Except as stated in § 93, a promise to perform all or part of an antecedent contract of the promisor, previously voidable by him, but not avoided prior to the making of the promise, is binding.

§ 86. Promise for Benefit Received.

(1) A promise made in recognition of a benefit previously received by the promisor from the promisee is binding to the extent necessary to prevent injustice.

(2) A promise is not binding under Subsection (1)

(a) if the promisee conferred the benefit as a gift or for other reasons the promisor has not been unjustly enriched; or

(b) to the extent that its value is disproportionate to the benefit.

§ 87. Option Contract.

(1) An offer is binding as an option contract if it
   (a) is in writing and signed by the offeror, recites a purported consideration for the making of the offer, and proposes an exchange on fair terms within a reasonable time; or
   (b) is made irrevocable by statute.
(2) An offer which the offeror should reasonably expect to induce action or forbearance of a substantial character on the part of the offeree before acceptance and which does induce such action or forbearance is binding as an option contract to the extent necessary to avoid injustice.

§ 88. Guaranty.

A promise to be surety for the performance of a contractual obligation, made to the obligee, is binding if
   (a) the promise is in writing and signed by the promisor and recites a purported consideration; or
   (b) the promise is made binding by statute; or
   (c) the promisor should reasonably expect the promise to induce action or forbearance of a substantial character on the part of the promisee or a third person, and the promise does induce such action or forbearance.

§ 89. Modification of Executory Contract.

A promise modifying a duty under a contract not fully performed on either side is binding
   (a) if the modification is fair and equitable in view of circumstances not anticipated by the parties when the contract was made; or
   (b) to the extent provided by statute; or
   (c) to the extent that justice requires enforcement in view of material change of position in reliance on the promise.

§ 90. Promise Reasonably Inducing Action or Forbearance.

(1) A promise which the promisor should reasonably expect to induce action or forbearance on the part of the promisee or a third person and which does induce such action or forbearance is binding if injustice can be avoided only by enforcement of the promise. The remedy granted for breach may be limited as justice requires.
(2) A charitable subscription or a marriage settlement is binding under Subsection (1) without proof that the promise induced action or forbearance.

§ 94. Stipulations.

A promise or agreement with reference to a pending judicial proceeding, made by a party to the proceeding or his attorney, is binding without consideration. By statute or rule of court such an agreement is generally binding only

    (a) if it is in writing and signed by the party or attorney, or

    (b) if it is made or admitted in the presence of the court, or

    (c) to the extent that justice requires enforcement in view of material change of position in reliance on the promise or agreement.

§ 95. Requirements for Sealed Contract or Written Contract or Instrument.

(1) In the absence of statute a promise is binding without consideration if

    (a) it is in writing and sealed; and

    (b) the document containing the promise is delivered; and

    (c) the promisor and promisee are named in the document or so described as to be capable of identification when it is delivered.

(2) When a statute provides in effect that a written contract or instrument is binding without consideration or that lack of consideration is an affirmative defense to an action on a written contract or instrument, in order to be subject to the statute a promise must either

    (a) be expressed in a document signed or otherwise assented to by the promisor and delivered; or

    (b) be expressed in a writing or writings to which both promisor and promisee manifest assent.

§ 110. Classes of Contracts Covered.

(1) The following classes of contracts are subject to a statute, commonly called the Statute of Frauds, forbidding enforcement unless there is a written memorandum or an applicable exception:

    (a) a contract of an executor or administrator to answer for a duty of his decedent (the executoradministrator provision);

    (b) a contract to answer for the duty of another (the suretyship provision);

    (c) a contract made upon consideration of marriage (the marriage provision);

    (d) a contract for the sale of an interest in land (the land contract provision);

    (e) a contract that is not to be performed within one year from the making thereof (the one-year provision).

(2) The following classes of contracts, which were traditionally subject to the Statute of Frauds, are now governed by Statute of Frauds provisions of the Uniform Commercial Code:

    (a) a contract for the sale of goods for the price of $ 500 or more (Uniform Commercial Code § 2-201);

    (b) a contract for the sale of securities (Uniform Commercial Code § 8-319);

(c) a contract for the sale of personal property not otherwise covered, to the extent of enforcement by way of action or defense beyond $ 5,000 in amount or value of remedy (Uniform Commercial Code § 1-206).

(3) In addition the Uniform Commercial Code requires a writing signed by the debtor for an agreement which creates or provides for a security interest in personal property or fixtures not in the possession of the secured party.

(4) Statutes in most states provide that no acknowledgment or promise is sufficient evidence of a new or continuing contract to take a case out of the operation of a statute of limitations unless made in some writing signed by the party to be charged, but that the statute does not alter the effect of any payment of principal or interest.

(5) In many states other classes of contracts are subject to a requirement of a writing.

§ 111. Contract of Executor or Administrator.

A contract of an executor or administrator to answer personally for a duty of his decedent is within the Statute of Frauds if a similar contract to answer for the duty of a living person would be within the Statute as a contract to answer for the duty of another.

§ 112. Requirement of Suretyship.

A contract is not within the Statute of Frauds as a contract to answer for the duty of another unless the promisee is an obligee of the other's duty, the promisor is a surety for the other, and the promisee knows or has reason to know of the suretyship relation.

§ 124. Contract Made Upon Consideration of Marriage.

A promise for which all or part of the consideration is either marriage or a promise to marry is within the Statute of Frauds, except in the case of an agreement which consists only of mutual promises of two persons to marry each other.

§ 125. Contract to Transfer, Buy, or Pay for an Interest in Land.

(1) A promise to transfer to any person any interest in land is within the Statute of Frauds.

(2) A promise to buy any interest in land is within the Statute of Frauds, irrespective of the person to whom the transfer is to be made.

(3) When a transfer of an interest in land has been made, a promise to pay the price, if originally within the Statute of Frauds, ceases to be within it unless the promised price is itself in whole or in part an interest in land.

(4) Statutes in most states except from the land contract and one-year provisions of the Statute of Frauds short-term leases and contracts to lease, usually for a term not longer than one year.

§ 129. Action in Reliance; Specific Performance.

A contract for the transfer of an interest in land may be specifically enforced notwithstanding failure to comply with the Statute of Frauds if it is established that the party seeking enforcement, in reasonable reliance on the contract and on the continuing assent of the party against whom enforcement is sought, has so changed his position that injustice can be avoided only by specific enforcement.

§ 130. Contract Not to Be Performed Within a Year.

(1) Where any promise in a contract cannot be fully performed within a year from the time the contract is made, all promises in the contract are within the Statute of Frauds until one party to the contract completes his performance.

(2) When one party to a contract has completed his performance, the one-year provision of the Statute does not prevent enforcement of the promises of other parties.

§ 131. General Requisites of a Memorandum.

Unless additional requirements are prescribed by the particular statute, a contract within the Statute of Frauds is enforceable if it is evidenced by any writing, signed by or on behalf of the party to be charged, which

(a) reasonably identifies the subject matter of the contract,

(b) is sufficient to indicate that a contract with respect thereto has been made between the parties or offered by the signer to the other party, and

(c) states with reasonable certainty the essential terms of the unperformed promises in the contract.

§ 132. Several Writings.

The memorandum may consist of several writings if one of the writings is signed and the writings in the circumstances clearly indicate that they relate to the same transaction.

§ 136. Time of Memorandum.

A memorandum sufficient to satisfy the Statute may be made or signed at any time before or after the formation of the contract.

§ 138. Unenforceability.

Where a contract within the Statute of Frauds is not enforceable against the party to be charged by an action against him, it is not enforceable by a set-off or counterclaim in an action brought by him, or as a defense to a claim by him.

§ 139. Enforcement by Virtue of Action in Reliance.

(1) A promise which the promisor should reasonably expect to induce action or forbearance on the part of the promisee or a third person and which does induce the action or forbearance is enforceable notwithstanding the Statute of Frauds if injustice can be avoided only by enforcement of the promise. The remedy granted for breach is to be limited as justice requires.

(2) In determining whether injustice can be avoided only by enforcement of the promise, the following circumstances are significant:
  (a) the availability and adequacy of other remedies, particularly cancellation and
       restitution;
  (b) the definite and substantial character of the action or forbearance in relation to
       the remedy sought;
  (c) the extent to which the action or forbearance corroborates evidence of the mak-
       ing and terms of the promise, or the making and terms are otherwise
       established by clear and convincing evidence;
  (d) the reasonableness of the action or forbearance;
  (e) the extent to which the action or forbearance was foreseeable by the promisor.

§ 145. Effect of Full Performance.

Where the promises in a contract have been fully performed by all parties, the Statute
of Frauds does not affect the legal relations of the parties.

§ 148. Rescission by Oral Agreement.

Notwithstanding the Statute of Frauds, all unperformed duties under an enforceable
contract may be discharged by an oral agreement of rescission. The Statute may, however, apply to a contract to rescind a transfer of property.

§ 149. Oral Modification.

(1) For the purpose of determining whether the Statute of Frauds applies to a contract
     modifying but not rescinding a prior contract, the second contract is treated as con-
     taining the originally agreed terms as modified. The Statute may, however, apply
     independently of the original terms to a contract to modify a transfer of property.
(2) Where the second contract is unenforceable by virtue of the Statute of Frauds and
     there has been no material change of position in reliance on it, the prior contract is
     not modified.

§ 150. Reliance on Oral Modification.

Where the parties to an enforceable contract subsequently agree that all or part of a duty
need not be performed or of a condition need not occur, the Statute of Frauds does not
prevent enforcement of the subsequent agreement if reinstatement of the original terms
would be unjust in view of a material change of position in reliance on the subsequent
agreement.

§ 151. Mistake Defined.

A mistake is a belief that is not in accord with the facts.

§ 152. When Mistake of Both Parties Makes a Contract Voidable.

(1) Where a mistake of both parties at the time a contract was made as to a basic as-
     sumption on which the contract was made has a material effect on the agreed

exchange of performances, the contract is voidable by the adversely affected party unless he bears the risk of the mistake under the rule stated in § 154.

(2) In determining whether the mistake has a material effect on the agreed exchange of performances, account is taken of any relief by way of reformation, restitution, or otherwise.

§ 153. When Mistake of One Party Makes a Contract Voidable.

Where a mistake of one party at the time a contract was made as to a basic assumption on which he made the contract has a material effect on the agreed exchange of performances that is adverse to him, the contract is voidable by him if he does not bear the risk of the mistake under the rule stated in § 154, and

(a) the effect of the mistake is such that enforcement of the contract would be unconscionable, or

(b) the other party had reason to know of the mistake or his fault caused the mistake.

§ 154. When a Party Bears the Risk of a Mistake.

A party bears the risk of a mistake when

(a) the risk is allocated to him by agreement of the parties, or

(b) he is aware, at the time the contract is made, that he has only limited knowledge with respect to the facts to which the mistake relates but treats his limited knowledge as sufficient, or

(c) the risk is allocated to him by the court on the ground that it is reasonable in the circumstances to do so.

§ 155. When Mistake of Both Parties as to Written Expression Justifies Reformation.

Where a writing that evidences or embodies an agreement in whole or in part fails to express the agreement because of a mistake of both parties as to the contents or effect of the writing, the court may at the request of a party reform the writing to express the agreement, except to the extent that rights of third parties such as good faith purchasers for value will be unfairly affected.

§ 157. Effect of Fault of Party Seeking Relief.

A mistaken party's fault in failing to know or discover the facts before making the contract does not bar him from avoidance or reformation under the rules stated in this Chapter, unless his fault amounts to a failure to act in good faith and in accordance with reasonable standards of fair dealing.

§ 158. Relief Including Restitution.

(1) In any case governed by the rules stated in this Chapter, either party may have a claim for relief including restitution under the rules stated in §§ 240 and 376.

(2) In any case governed by the rules stated in this Chapter, if those rules together with the rules stated in Chapter 16 will not avoid injustice, the court may grant relief on such terms as justice requires including protection of the parties' reliance interests.

§ 159. *Misrepresentation Defined.*

A misrepresentation is an assertion that is not in accord with the facts.

§ 160. *When Action Is Equivalent to an Assertion (Concealment).*

Action intended or known to be likely to prevent another from learning a fact is equivalent to an assertion that the fact does not exist.

§ 161. *When Non-Disclosure Is Equivalent to an Assertion.*

A person's non-disclosure of a fact known to him is equivalent to an assertion that the fact does not exist in the following cases only:

(a) where he knows that disclosure of the fact is necessary to prevent some previous assertion from being a misrepresentation or from being fraudulent or material.

(b) where he knows that disclosure of the fact would correct a mistake of the other party as to a basic assumption on which that party is making the contract and if non-disclosure of the fact amounts to a failure to act in good faith and in accordance with reasonable standards of fair dealing.

(c) where he knows that disclosure of the fact would correct a mistake of the other party as to the contents or effect of a writing, evidencing or embodying an agreement in whole or in part.

(d) where the other person is entitled to know the fact because of a relation of trust and confidence between them.

§ 162. *When a Misrepresentation Is Fraudulent or Material.*

(1) A misrepresentation is fraudulent if the maker intends his assertion to induce a party to manifest his assent and the maker
   (a) knows or believes that the assertion is not in accord with the facts, or
   (b) does not have the confidence that he states or implies in the truth of the assertion, or
   (c) knows that he does not have the basis that he states or implies for the assertion.

(2) A misrepresentation is material if it would be likely to induce a reasonable person to manifest his assent, or if the maker knows that it would be likely to induce the recipient to do so.

§ 163. *When a Misrepresentation Prevents Formation of a Contract.*

If a misrepresentation as to the character or essential terms of a proposed contract induces conduct that appears to be a manifestation of assent by one who neither knows nor has reasonable opportunity to know of the character or essential terms of the proposed contract, his conduct is not effective as a manifestation of assent.

§ 164. *When a Misrepresentation Makes a Contract Voidable.*

(1) If a party's manifestation of assent is induced by either a fraudulent or a material misrepresentation by the other party upon which the recipient is justified in relying, the contract is voidable by the recipient.

(2) If a party's manifestation of assent is induced by either a fraudulent or a material misrepresentation by one who is not a party to the transaction upon which the recipient is justified in relying, the contract is voidable by the recipient, unless the other party to the transaction in good faith and without reason to know of the misrepresentation either gives value or relies materially on the transaction.

§ 166. When a Misrepresentation as to a Writing Justifies Reformation.

If a party's manifestation of assent is induced by the other party's fraudulent misrepresentation as to the contents or effect of a writing evidencing or embodying in whole or in part an agreement, the court at the request of the recipient may reform the writing to express the terms of the agreement as asserted,

(a) if the recipient was justified in relying on the misrepresentation, and

(b) except to the extent that rights of third parties such as good faith purchasers for value will be unfairly affected.

§ 167. When a Misrepresentation Is an Inducing Cause.

A misrepresentation induces a party's manifestation of assent if it substantially contributes to his decision to manifest his assent.

§ 168. Reliance on Assertions of Opinion.

(1) An assertion is one of opinion if it expresses only a belief, without certainty, as to the existence of a fact or expresses only a judgment as to quality, value, authenticity, or similar matters.

(2) If it is reasonable to do so, the recipient of an assertion of a person's opinion as to facts not disclosed and not otherwise known to the recipient may properly interpret it as an assertion

(a) that the facts known to that person are not incompatible with his opinion, or

(b) that he knows facts sufficient to justify him in forming it.

§ 169. When Reliance on an Assertion of Opinion Is Not Justified.

To the extent that an assertion is one of opinion only, the recipient is not justified in relying on it unless the recipient

(a) stands in such a relation of trust and confidence to the person whose opinion is asserted that the recipient is reasonable in relying on it, or

(b) reasonably believes that, as compared with himself, the person whose opinion is asserted has special skill, judgment or objectivity with respect to the subject matter, or

(c) is for some other special reason particularly susceptible to a misrepresentation of the type involved.

§ 171. When Reliance on an Assertion of Intention Is Not Justified.

(1) to the extent that an assertion is one of intention only, the recipient is not justified in relying on it if in the circumstances a misrepresentation of intention is consistent with reasonable standards of dealing.

(2) If it is reasonable to do so, the promisee may properly interpret a promise as an assertion that the promisor intends to perform the promise.

§ 172. *When Fault Makes Reliance Unjustified.*

A recipient's fault in not knowing or discovering the facts before making the contract does not make his reliance unjustified unless it amounts to a failure to act in good faith and in accordance with reasonable standards of fair dealing.

§ 173. *When Abuse of a Fiduciary Relation Makes a Contract Voidable.*

If a fiduciary makes a contract with his beneficiary relating to matters within the scope of the fiduciary relation, the contract is voidable by the beneficiary, unless

(a) it is on fair terms, and

(b) all parties beneficially interested manifest assent with full understanding of their legal rights and of all relevant facts that the fiduciary knows or should know.

§ 174. *When Duress by Physical Compulsion Prevents Formation of a Contract.*

If conduct that appears to be a manifestation of assent by a party who does not intend to engage in that conduct is physically compelled by duress, the conduct is not effective as a manifestation of assent.

§ 175. *When Duress by Threat Makes a Contract Voidable.*

(1) If a party's manifestation of assent is induced by an improper threat by the other party that leaves the victim no reasonable alternative, the contract is voidable by the victim.

(2) If a party's manifestation of assent is induced by one who is not a party to the transaction, the contract is voidable by the victim unless the other party to the transaction in good faith and without reason to know of the duress either gives value or relies materially on the transaction.

§ 176. *When a Threat Is Improper.*

(1) A threat is improper if
  (a) what is threatened is a crime or a tort, or the threat itself would be a crime or a tort if it resulted in obtaining property,
  (b) what is threatened is a criminal prosecution,
  (c) what is threatened is the use of civil process and the threat is made in bad faith, or
  (d) the threat is a breach of the duty of good faith and fair dealing under a contract with the recipient.

(2) A threat is improper if the resulting exchange is not on fair terms, and
  (a) the threatened act would harm the recipient and would not significantly benefit the party making the threat,
  (b) the effectiveness of the threat in inducing the manifestation of assent is significantly increased by prior unfair dealing by the party making the threat, or

(c) what is threatened is otherwise a use of power for illegitimate ends.

§ 177. When Undue Influence Makes a Contract Voidable.

(1) Undue influence is unfair persuasion of a party who is under the domination of the person exercising the persuasion or who by virtue of the relation between them is justified in assuming that that person will not act in a manner inconsistent with his welfare.

(2) If a party's manifestation of assent is induced by undue influence by the other party, the contract is voidable by the victim.

(3) If a party's manifestation of assent is induced by one who is not a party to the transaction, the contract is voidable by the victim unless the other party to the transaction in good faith and without reason to know of the undue influence either gives value or relies materially on the transaction.

§ 178. When a Term Is Unenforceable on Grounds of Public Policy.

(1) A promise or other term of an agreement is unenforceable on grounds of public policy if legislation provides that it is unenforceable or the interest in its enforcement is clearly outweighed in the circumstances by a public policy against the enforcement of such terms.

(2) In weighing the interest in the enforcement of a term, account is taken of
  (a) the parties' justified expectations,
  (b) any forfeiture that would result if enforcement were denied, and
  (c) any special public interest in the enforcement of the particular term.

(3) In weighing a public policy against enforcement of a term, account is taken of
  (a) the strength of that policy as manifested by legislation or judicial decisions,
  (b) the likelihood that a refusal to enforce the term will further that policy,
  (c) the seriousness of any misconduct involved and the extent to which it was deliberate, and
  (d) the directness of the connection between that misconduct and the term.

§ 179. Bases of Public Policies Against Enforcement.

A public policy against the enforcement of promises or other terms may be derived by the court from
  (a) legislation relevant to such a policy, or
  (b) the need to protect some aspect of the public welfare, as is the case for the judicial policies against, for example,
    (i)   restraint of trade (§§ 186-188),
    (ii)   impairment of family relations (§§ 189-191), and
    (iii) interference with other protected interests (§§ 192-196, 356).

§ 181. Effect of Failure to Comply with Licensing or Similar Requirement.

If a party is prohibited from doing an act because of his failure to comply with a licensing, registration or similar requirement, a promise in consideration of his doing that act or of his promise to do it is unenforceable on grounds of public policy if

(a) the requirement has a regulatory purpose, and

(b) the interest in the enforcement of the promise is clearly outweighed by the public policy behind the requirement.

§ 183. When Agreement Is Enforceable as to Agreed Equivalents.

If the parties' performances can be apportioned into corresponding pairs of part performances so that the parts of each pair are properly regarded as agreed equivalents and one pair is not offensive to public policy, that portion of the agreement is enforceable by a party who did not engage in serious misconduct.

§ 184. When Rest of Agreement Is Enforceable.

(1) If less than all of an agreement is unenforceable under the rule stated in § 178, a court may nevertheless enforce the rest of the agreement in favor of a party who did not engage in serious misconduct if the performance as to which the agreement is unenforceable is not an essential part of the agreed exchange.

(2) A court may treat only part of a term as unenforceable under the rule stated in Subsection (1) if the party who seeks to enforce the term obtained it in good faith and in accordance with reasonable standards of fair dealing.

§ 185. Excuse of a Condition on Grounds of Public Policy.

To the extent that a term requiring the occurrence of a condition is unenforceable under the rule stated in § 178, a court may excuse the non-occurrence of the condition unless its occurrence was an essential part of the agreed exchange.

§ 186. Promise in Restraint of Trade.

(1) A promise is unenforceable on grounds of public policy if it is unreasonably in restraint of trade.

(2) A promise is in restraint of trade if its performance would limit competition in any business or restrict the promisor in the exercise of a gainful occupation.

§ 187. Non-Ancillary Restraints on Competition.

A promise to refrain from competition that imposes a restraint that is not ancillary to an otherwise valid transaction or relationship is unreasonably in restraint of trade.

§ 188. Ancillary Restraints on Competition.

(1) A promise to refrain from competition that imposes a restraint that is ancillary to an otherwise valid transaction or relationship is unreasonably in restraint of trade if

(a) the restraint is greater than is needed to protect the promisee's legitimate interest, or

(b) the promisee's need is outweighed by the hardship to the promisor and the likely injury to the public.

(2) Promises imposing restraints that are ancillary to a valid transaction or relationship include the following:

(a) a promise by the seller of a business not to compete with the buyer in such a way as to injure the value of the business sold;

(b) a promise by an employee or other agent not to compete with his employer or other principal;

(c) a promise by a partner not to compete with the partnership.

§ 189. Promise in Restraint of Marriage.

A promise is unenforceable on grounds of public policy if it is unreasonably in restraint of marriage.

§ 190. Promise Detrimental to Marital Relationship.

(1) A promise by a person contemplating marriage or by a married person, other than as part of an enforceable separation agreement, is unenforceable on grounds of public policy if it would change some essential incident of the marital relationship in a way detrimental to the public interest in the marriage relationship. A separation agreement is unenforceable on grounds of public policy unless it is made after separation or in contemplation of an immediate separation and is fair in the circumstances.

(2) A promise that tends unreasonably to encourage divorce or separation is unenforceable on grounds of public policy.

§ 191. Promise Affecting Custody.

A promise affecting the right of custody of a minor child is unenforceable on grounds of public policy unless the disposition as to custody is consistent with the best interest of the child.

§ 192. Promise Involving Commission of a Tort.

A promise to commit a tort or to induce the commission of a tort is unenforceable on grounds of public policy.

§ 193. Promise Inducing Violation of Fiduciary Duty.

A promise by a fiduciary to violate his fiduciary duty or a promise that tends to induce such a violation is unenforceable on grounds of public policy.

§ 194. Promise Interfering with Contract with Another.

A promise that tortiously interferes with performance of a contract with a third person or a tortiously induced promise to commit a breach of contract is unenforceable on grounds of public policy.

§ 195. Term Exempting From Liability for Harm Caused Intentionally, Recklessly or Negligently.

(1) A term exempting a party from tort liability for harm caused intentionally or recklessly is unenforceable on grounds of public policy.

(2) A term exempting a party from tort liability for harm caused negligently is unenforceable on grounds of public policy if

    (a) the term exempts an employer from liability to an employee for injury in the course of his employment;

    (b) the term exempts one charged with a duty of public service from liability to one to whom that duty is owed for compensation for breach of that duty, or

    (c) the other party is similarly a member of a class protected against the class to which the first party belongs.

(3) A term exempting a seller of a product from his special tort liability for physical harm to a user or consumer is unenforceable on grounds of public policy unless the term is fairly bargained for and is consistent with the policy underlying that liability.

§ 196. Term Exempting From Consequences of Misrepresentation.

A term unreasonably exempting a party from the legal consequences of a misrepresentation is unenforceable on grounds of public policy.

§ 197. Restitution Generally Unavailable.

Except as stated in §§ 198 and 199, a party has no claim in restitution for performance that he has rendered under or in return for a promise that is unenforceable on grounds of public policy unless denial of restitution would cause disproportionate forfeiture.

§ 200. Interpretation of Promise or Agreement.

Interpretation of a promise or agreement or a term thereof is the ascertainment of its meaning.

§ 201. Whose Meaning Prevails.

(1) Where the parties have attached the same meaning to a promise or agreement or a term thereof, it is interpreted in accordance with that meaning.

(2) Where the parties have attached different meanings to a promise or agreement or a term thereof, it is interpreted in accordance with the meaning attached by one of them if at the time the agreement was made

    (a) that party did not know of any different meaning attached by the other, and the other knew the meaning attached by the first party; or

    (b) that party had no reason to know of any different meaning attached by the other, and the other had reason to know the meaning attached by the first party.

(3) Except as stated in this Section, neither party is bound by the meaning attached by the other, even though the result may be a failure of mutual assent.

§ 202. Rules in Aid of Interpretation.

(1) Words and other conduct are interpreted in the light of all the circumstances, and if the principal purpose of the parties is ascertainable it is given great weight.

(2) A writing is interpreted as a whole, and all writings that are part of the same transaction are interpreted together.

(3) Unless a different intention is manifested,

   (a) where language has a generally prevailing meaning, it is interpreted in accordance with that meaning;

   (b) technical terms and words of art are given their technical meaning when used in a transaction within their technical field.

(4) Where an agreement involves repeated occasions for performance by either party with knowledge of the nature of the performance and opportunity for objection to it by the other, any course of performance accepted or acquiesced in without objection is given great weight in the interpretation of the agreement.

(5) Wherever reasonable, the manifestations of intention of the parties to a promise or agreement are interpreted as consistent with each other and with any relevant course of performance, course of dealing, or usage of trade.

§ 203. Standards of Preference in Interpretation.

In the interpretation of a promise or agreement or a term thereof, the following standards of preference are generally applicable:

(a) an interpretation which gives a reasonable, lawful, and effective meaning to all the terms is preferred to an interpretation which leaves a part unreasonable, unlawful, or of no effect;

(b) express terms are given greater weight than course of performance, course of dealing, and usage of trade, course of performance is given greater weight than course of dealing or usage of trade, and course of dealing is given greater weight than usage of trade;

(c) specific terms and exact terms are given greater weight than general language;

(d) separately negotiated or added terms are given greater weight than standardized terms or other terms not separately negotiated.

§ 204. Supplying an Omitted Essential Term.

When the parties to a bargain sufficiently defined to be a contract have not agreed with respect to a term which is essential to a determination of their rights and duties, a term which is reasonable in the circumstances is supplied by the court.

§ 205. Duty of Good Faith and Fair Dealing.

Every contract imposes upon each party a duty of good faith and fair dealing in its performance and its enforcement.

§ 206. Interpretation Against the Draftsman.

In choosing among the reasonable meanings of a promise or agreement or a term thereof, that meaning is generally preferred which operates against the party who supplies the words or from whom a writing otherwise proceeds.

§ 207. Interpretation Favoring the Public.

In choosing among the reasonable meanings of a promise or agreement or a term thereof, a meaning that serves the public interest is generally preferred.

§ 208. Unconscionable Contract or Term.

If a contract or term thereof is unconscionable at the time the contract is made a court may refuse to enforce the contract, or may enforce the remainder of the contract without the unconscionable term, or may so limit the application of any unconscionable term as to avoid any unconscionable result.

§ 209. Integrated Agreements.

(1) An integrated agreement is a writing or writings constituting a final expression of one or more terms of an agreement.

(2) Whether there is an integrated agreement is to be determined by the court as a question preliminary to determination of a question of interpretation or to application of the parol evidence rule.

(3) Where the parties reduce an agreement to a writing which in view of its completeness and specificity reasonably appears to be a complete agreement, it is taken to be an integrated agreement unless it is established by other evidence that the writing did not constitute a final expression.

§ 210. Completely and Partially Integrated Agreements.

(1) A completely integrated agreement is an integrated agreement adopted by the parties as a complete and exclusive statement of the terms of the agreement.

(2) A partially integrated agreement is an integrated agreement other than a completely integrated agreement.

(3) Whether an agreement is completely or partially integrated is to be determined by the court as a question preliminary to determination of a question of interpretation or to application of the parol evidence rule.

§ 211. Standardized Agreements.

(1) Except as stated in Subsection (3), where a party to an agreement signs or otherwise manifests assent to a writing and has reason to believe that like writings are regularly used to embody terms of agreements of the same type, he adopts the writing as an integrated agreement with respect to the terms included in the writing.

(2) Such a writing is interpreted wherever reasonable as treating alike all those similarly situated, without regard to their knowledge or understanding of the standard terms of the writing.

(3) Where theother party has reason to believe that the party manifesting such assent would not do so if he knew that the writing contained a particular term, the term is not part of the agreement.

§ 212. Interpretation of Integrated Agreement.

(1) The interpretation of an integrated agreement is directed to the meaning of the terms of the writing or writings in the light of the circumstances, in accordance with the rules stated in this Chapter.

(2) A question of interpretation of an integrated agreement is to be determined by the trier of fact if it depends on the credibility of extrinsic evidence or on a choice among reasonable inferences to be drawn from extrinsic evidence. Otherwise a question of interpretation of an integrated agreement is to be determined as a question of law.

§ 213. Effect of Integrated Agreement on Prior Agreements (Parol Evidence Rule).

(1) A binding integrated agreement discharges prior agreements to the extent that it is inconsistent with them.

(2) A binding completely integrated agreement discharges prior agreements to the extent that they are within its scope.

(3) An integrated agreement that is not binding or that is voidable and avoided does not discharge a prior agreement. But an integrated agreement, even though not binding, may be effective to render inoperative a term which would have been part of the agreement if it had not been integrated.

§ 214. Evidence of Prior or Contemporaneous Agreements and Negotiations.

Agreements and negotiations prior to or contemporaneous with the adoption of a writing are admissible in evidence to establish

(a) that the writing is or is not an integrated agreement;

(b) that the integrated agreement, if any, is completely or partially integrated;

(c) the meaning of the writing, whether or not integrated;

(d) illegality, fraud, duress, mistake, lack of consideration, or other invalidating cause;

(e) ground for granting or denying rescission, reformation, specific performance, or other remedy.

§ 215. Contradiction of Integrated Terms.

Except as stated in the preceding Section, where there is a binding agreement, either completely or partially integrated, evidence of prior or contemporaneous agreements or negotiations is not admissible in evidence to contradict a term of the writing.

§ 216. Consistent Additional Terms.

(1) Evidence of a consistent additional term is admissible to supplement an integrated agreement unless the court finds that the agreement was completely integrated.

(2) An agreement is not completely integrated if the writing omits a consistent additional agreed term which is
   (a) agreed to for separate consideration, or
   (b) such a term as in the circumstances might naturally be omitted from the writing.

§ 217. Integrated Agreement Subject to Oral Requirement of a Condition.

Where the parties to a written agreement agree orally that performance of the agreement is subject to the occurrence of a stated condition, the agreement is not integrated with respect to the oral condition.

§ 218. Untrue Recitals; Evidence of Consideration.

(1) A recital of a fact in an integrated agreement may be shown to be untrue.
(2) Evidence is admissible to prove whether or not there is consideration for a promise, even though the parties have reduced their agreement to a writing which appears to be a completely integrated agreement.

§ 219. Usage.

Usage is habitual or customary practice.

§ 220. Usage Relevant to Interpretation.

(1) An agreement is interpreted in accordance with a relevant usage if each party knew or had reason to know of the usage and neither party knew or had reason to know that the meaning attached by the other was inconsistent with the usage.
(2) When the meaning attached by one party accorded with a relevant usage and the other knew or had reason to know of the usage, the other is treated as having known or had reason to know the meaning attached by the first party.

§ 221. Usage Supplementing an Agreement.

An agreement is supplemented or qualified by a reasonable usage with respect to agreements of the same type if each party knows or has reason to know of the usage and neither party knows or has reason to know that the other party has an intention inconsistent with the usage.

§ 222. Usage of Trade.

(1) A usage of trade is a usage having such regularity of observance in a place, vocation, or trade as to justify an expectation that it will be observed with respect to a particular agreement. It may include a system of rules regularly observed even though particular rules are changed from time to time.
(2) The existence and scope of a usage of trade are to be determined as questions of fact. If a usage is embodied in a written trade code or similar writing the interpretation of the writing is to be determined by the court as a question of law.

(3) Unless otherwise agreed, a usage of trade in the vocation or trade in which the parties are engaged or a usage of trade of which they know or have reason to know gives meaning to or supplements or qualifies their agreement.

§ 223. Course of Dealing.

(1) A course of dealing is a sequence of previous conduct between the parties to an agreement which is fairly to be regarded as establishing a common basis of understanding for interpreting their expressions and other conduct.

(2) Unless otherwise agreed, a course of dealing between the parties gives meaning to or supplements or qualifies their agreement.

§ 224. Condition Defined.

A condition is an event, not certain to occur, which must occur, unless its non-occurrence is excused, before performance under a contract becomes due.

§ 225. Effects of the Non-Occurrence Of a Condition.

(1) Performance of a duty subject to a condition cannot become due unless the condition occurs or its non-occurrence is excused.

(2) Unless it has been excused, the non-occurrence of a condition discharges the duty when the condition can no longer occur.

(3) Non-occurrence of a condition is not a breach by a party unless he is under a duty that the condition occur.

§ 226. How an Event May Be Made a Condition.

An event may be made a condition either by the agreement of the parties or by a term supplied by the court.

§ 227. Standards of Preference with Regard to Conditions.

(1) In resolving doubts as to whether an event is made a condition of an obligor's duty, and as to the nature of such an event, an interpretation is preferred that will reduce the obligee's risk of forfeiture, unless the event is within the obligee's control or the circumstances indicate that he has assumed the risk.

(2) Unless the contract is of a type under which only one party generally undertakes duties, when it is doubtful whether

  (a) a duty is imposed on an obligee that an event occur, or

  (b) the event is made a condition of the obligor's duty, or

  (c) the event is made a condition of the obligor's duty and a duty is imposed on the obligee that the event occur,

  the first interpretation is preferred if the event is within the obligee's control.

(3) In case of doubt, an interpretation under which an event is a condition of an obligor's duty is preferred over an interpretation under which the non-occurrence of the event is a ground for discharge of that duty after it has become a duty to perform.

§ 228. Satisfaction of the Obligor as a Condition.

When it is a condition of an obligor's duty that he be satisfied with respect to the obligee's performance or with respect to something else, and it is practicable to determine whether a reasonable person in the position of the obligor would be satisfied, an interpretation is preferred under which the condition occurs if such a reasonable person in the position of the obligor would be satisfied.

§ 229. Excuse of a Condition to Avoid Forfeiture.

To the extent that the non-occurrence of a condition would cause disproportionate forfeiture, a court may excuse the non-occurrence of that condition unless its occurrence was a material part of the agreed exchange.

§ 230. Event That Terminates a Duty.

(1) Except as stated in Subsection (2), if under the terms of the contract the occurrence of an event is to terminate an obligor's duty of immediate performance or one to pay damages for breach, that duty is discharged if the event occurs.

(2) The obligor's duty is not discharged if occurrence of the event

    (a) is the result of a breach by the obligor of his duty of good faith and fair dealing, or

    (b) could not have been prevented because of impracticability and continuance of the duty does not subject the obligor to a materially increased burden.

(3) The obligor's duty is not discharged if, before the event occurs, the obligor promises to perform the duty even if the event occurs and does not revoke his promise before the obligee materially changes his position in reliance on it.

§ 233. Performance at One Time or in Installments.

(1) Where performances are to be exchanged under an exchange of promises, and the whole of one party's performance can be rendered at one time, it is due at one time, unless the language or the circumstances indicate the contrary.

(2) Where only a part of one party's performance is due at one time under Subsection (1), if the other party's performance can be so apportioned that there is a comparable part that can also be rendered at that time, it is due at that time, unless the language or the circumstances indicate the contrary.

§ 234. Order of Performances.

(1) Where all or part of the performances to be exchanged under an exchange of promises can be rendered simultaneously, they are to that extent due simultaneously, unless the language or the circumstances indicate the contrary.

(2) Except to the extent stated in Subsection (1), where the performance of only one party under such an exchange requires a period of time, his performance is due at an earlier time than that of the other party, unless the language or the circumstances indicate the contrary.

§ 235. Effect of Performance as Discharge and of Non-Performance As Breach.

(1) Full performance of a duty under a contract discharges the duty.

(2) When performance of a duty under a contract is due any non-performance is a breach.

§ 236. Claims for Damages for Total and for Partial Breach.

(1) A claim for damages for total breach is one for damages based on all of the injured party's remaining rights to performance.

(2) A claim for damages for partial breach is one for damages based on only part of the injured party's remaining rights to performance.

§ 237. Effect on Other Party's Duties of a Failure to Render Performance.

Except as stated in § 240, it is a condition of each party's remaining duties to render performances to be exchanged under an exchange of promises that there be no uncured material failure by the other party to render any such performance due at an earlier time.

§ 238. Effect on Other Party's Duties of a Failure to Offer Performance.

Where all or part of the performances to be exchanged under an exchange of promises are due simultaneously, it is a condition of each party's duties to render such performance that the other party either render or, with manifested present ability to do so, offer performance of his part of the simultaneous exchange.

§ 239. Effect on Other Party's Duties of a Failure Justified by Non-Occurrence Of a Condition.

(1) A party's failure to render or to offer performance may, except as stated in Subsection (2), affect the other party's duties under the rules stated in §§ 237 and 238 even though failure is justified by the non-occurrence of a condition.

(2) The rule stated in Subsection (1) does not apply if the other party assumed the risk that he would have to perform in spite of such a failure.

§ 240. Part Performances as Agreed Equivalents.

If the performances to be exchanged under an exchange of promises can be apportioned into corresponding pairs of part performances so that the parts of each pair are properly regarded as agreed equivalents, a party's performance of his part of such a pair has the same effect on the other's duties to render performance of the agreed equivalent as it would have if only that pair of performances had been promised.

§ 241. Circumstances Significant in Determining Whether a Failure Is Material.

In determining whether a failure to render or to offer performance is material, the following circumstances are significant:

(a) the extent to which the injured party will be deprived of the benefit which he reasonably expected;

(b) the extent to which the injured party can be adequately compensated for the part of that benefit of which he will be deprived;

(c) the extent to which the party failing to perform or to offer to perform will suffer forfeiture;

(d) the likelihood that the party failing to perform or to offer to perform will cure his failure, taking account of all the circumstances including any reasonable assurances;

(e) the extent to which the behavior of the party failing to perform or to offer to perform comports with standards of good faith and fair dealing.

§ 242. Circumstances Significant in Determining When Remaining Duties Are Discharged.

In determining the time after which a party's uncured material failure to render or to offer performance discharges the other party's remaining duties to render performance under the rules stated in §§ 237 and 238, the following circumstances are significant:

(a) those stated in § 241;

(b) the extent to which it reasonably appears to the injured party that delay may prevent or hinder him in making reasonable substitute arrangements;

(c) the extent to which the agreement provides for performance without delay, but a material failure to perform or to offer to perform on a stated day does not of itself discharge the other party's remaining duties unless the circumstances, including the language of the agreement, indicate that performance or an offer to perform by that day is important.

§ 243. Effect of a Breach by Non-Performance As Giving Rise to a Claim for Damages for Total Breach.

(1) With respect to performances to be exchanged under an exchange of promises, a breach by non-performance gives rise to a claim for damages for total breach only if it discharges the injured party's remaining duties to render such performance, other than a duty to render an agreed equivalent under § 240.

(2) Except as stated in Subsection (3), a breach by non-performance accompanied or followed by a repudiation gives rise to a claim for damages for total breach.

(3) Where at the time of the breach the only remaining duties of performance are those of the party in breach and are for the payment of money in installments not related to one another, his breach by non-performance as to less than the whole, whether or not accompanied or followed by a repudiation, does not give rise to a claim for damages for total breach.

(4) In any case other than those stated in the preceding subsections, a breach by non-performance gives rise to a claim for total breach only if it so substantially impairs the value of the contract to the injured party at the time of the breach that it is just in the circumstances to allow him to recover damages based on all his remaining rights to performance.

§ 244. Effect of Subsequent Events on Duty to Pay Damages.

A party's duty to pay damages for total breach by non-performance is discharged if it appears after the breach that there would have been a total failure by the injured party to perform his return promise.

§ 245. Effect of a Breach by Non-Performance As Excusing the Non-Occurrence Of a Condition.

Where a party's breach by non-performance contributes materially to the non-occurrence of a condition of one of his duties, the non-occurrence is excused.

§ 246. Effect of Acceptance as Excusing the Non-Occurrence Of a Condition.

(1) Except as stated in Subsection (2), an obligor's acceptance or his retention for an unreasonable time of the obligee's performance, with knowledge of or reason to know of the non-occurrence of a condition of the obligor's duty, operates as a promise to perform in spite of that non-occurrence, under the rules stated in § 84.

(2) If at the time of its acceptance or retention the obligee's performance involves such attachment to the obligor's property that removal would cause material loss, the obligor's acceptance or retention of that performance operates as a promise to perform in spite of the non-occurrence of the condition, under the rules stated in § 84, only if the obligor with knowledge of or reason to know of the defects manifests assent to the performance.

§ 247. Effect of Acceptance of Part Performance as Excusing the Subsequent Non-Occurrence Of a Condition.

An obligor's acceptance of part of the obligee's performance, with knowledge or reason to know of the non-occurrence of a condition of the obligor's duty, operates as a promise to perform in spite of a subsequent non-occurrence of the condition under the rules stated in § 84 to the extent that it justifies the obligee in believing that subsequent performances will be accepted in spite of that non-occurrence.

§ 248. Effect of Insufficient Reason for Rejection as Excusing the Non-Occurrence Of a Condition.

Where a party rejecting a defective performance or offer of performance gives an insufficient reason for rejection, the non-occurrence of a condition of his duty is excused only if he knew or had reason to know of that non-occurrence and then only to the extent that the giving of an insufficient reason substantially contributes to a failure by the other party to cure.

§ 250. When a Statement or an Act Is a Repudiation.

A repudiation is

(a) a statement by the obligor to the obligee indicating that the obligor will commit a breach that would of itself give the obligee a claim for damages for total breach under § 243, or

(b) a voluntary affirmative act which renders the obligor unable or apparently unable to perform without such a breach.

§ 251. When a Failure to Give Assurance May Be Treated as a Repudiation.

(1) Where reasonable grounds arise to believe that the obligor will commit a breach by non-performance that would of itself give the obligee a claim for damages for total breach under § 243, the obligee may demand adequate assurance of due performance and may, if reasonable, suspend any performance for which he has not already received the agreed exchange until he receives such assurance.

(2) The obligee may treat as a repudiation the obligor's failure to provide within a reasonable time such assurance of due performance as is adequate in the circumstances of the particular case.

§ 252. Effect of Insolvency.

(1) Where the obligor's insolvency gives the obligee reasonable grounds to believe that the obligor will commit a breach under the rule stated in § 251, the obligee may suspend any performance for which he has not already received the agreed exchange until he receives assurance in the form of performance itself, an offer of performance, or adequate security.

(2) A person is insolvent who either has ceased to pay his debts in the ordinary course of business or cannot pay his debts as they become due or is insolvent within the meaning of the federal bankruptcy law.

§ 253. Effect of a Repudiation as a Breach and on Other Party's Duties.

(1) Where an obligor repudiates a duty before he has committed a breach by non-performance and before he has received all of the agreed exchange for it, his repudiation alone gives rise to a claim for damages for total breach.

(2) Where performances are to be exchanged under an exchange of promises, one party's repudiation of a duty to render performance discharges the other party's remaining duties to render performance.

§ 254. Effect of Subsequent Events on Duty to Pay Damages.

(1) A party's duty to pay damages for total breach by repudiation is discharged if it appears after the breach that there would have been a total failure by the injured party to perform his return promise.

(2) A party's duty to pay damages for total breach by repudiation is discharged if it appears after the breach that the duty that he repudiated would have been discharged by impracticability or frustration before any breach by non-performance.

§ 255. Effect of a Repudiation as Excusing the Non-Occurrence Of a Condition.

Where a party's repudiation contributes materially to the non-occurrence of a condition of one of his duties, the non-occurrence is excused.

§ 256. Nullification of Repudiation or Basis for Repudiation.

(1) The effect of a statement as constituting a repudiation under § 250 or the basis for a repudiation under § 251 is nullified by a retraction of the statement if notification of the retraction comes to the attention of the injured party before he materially changes his position in reliance on the repudiation or indicates to the other party that he cconsiders the repudiation to be final.

(2) The effect of events other than a statement as constituting a repudiation under § 250 or the basis for a repudiation under § 251 is nullified if, to the knowledge of the injured party, those events have ceased to exist before he materially changes his position in reliance on the repudiation or indicates to the other party that he cconsiders the repudiation to be final.

§ 257. Effect of Urging Performance in Spite of Repudiation.

The injured party does not change the effect of a repudiation by urging the repudiator to perform in spite of his repudiation or to retract his repudiation.

§ 261. Discharge by Supervening Impracticability.

Where, after a contract is made, a party's performance is made impracticable without his fault by the occurrence of an event the non-occurrence of which was a basic assumption on which the contract was made, his duty to render that performance is discharged, unless the language or the circumstances indicate the contrary.

§ 262. Death or Incapacity of Person Necessary for Performance.

If the existence of a particular person is necessary for the performance of a duty, his death or such incapacity as makes performance impracticable is an event the non-occurrence of which was a basic assumption on which the contract was made.

§ 263. Destruction, Deterioration or Failure to Come Into Existence of Thing Necessary for Performance.

If the existence of a specific thing is necessary for the performance of a duty, its failure to come into existence, destruction, or such deterioration as makes performance impracticable is an event the non-occurrence of which was a basic assumption on which the contract was made.

§ 264. Prevention by Governmental Regulation or Order.

If the performance of a duty is made impracticable by having to comply with a domestic or foreign governmental regulation or order, that regulation or order is an event the non-occurrence of which was a basic assumption on which the contract was made.

§ 265. Discharge by Supervening Frustration.

Where, after a contract is made, a party's principal purpose is substantially frustrated without his fault by the occurrence of an event the non-occurrence of which was a basic assumption on which the contract was made, his remaining duties to render performance are discharged, unless the language or the circumstances indicate the contrary.

§ 266. Existing Impracticability or Frustration.

(1) Where, at the time a contract is made, a party's performance under it is impracticable without his fault because of a fact of which he has no reason to know and the non-existence of which is a basic assumption on which the contract is made, no duty to render that performance arises, unless the language or circumstances indicate the contrary.

(2) Where, at the time a contract is made, a party's principal purpose is substantially frustrated without his fault by a fact of which he has no reason to know and the non-existence of which is a basic assumption on which the contract is made, no duty of that party to render performance arises, unless the language or circumstances indicate the contrary.

§ 267. Effect on Other Party's Duties of a Failure Justified by Impracticability or Frustration.

(1) A party's failure to render or to offer performance may, except as stated in Subsection (2), affect the other party's duties under the rules stated in §§ 237 and 238 even though the failure is justified under the rules stated in this Chapter.

(2) The rule stated in Subsection (1) does not apply if the other party assumed the risk that he would have to perform despite such a failure.

§ 271. Impracticability as Excuse for Non-Occurrence Of a Condition.

Impracticability excuses the non-occurrence of a condition if the occurrence of the condition is not a material part of the agreed exchange and forfeiture would otherwise result.

§ 272. Relief Including Restitution.

(1) In any case governed by the rules stated in this Chapter, either party may have a claim for relief including restitution under the rules stated in §§ 240 and 377.

(2) In any case governed by the rules stated in this Chapter, if those rules together with the rules stated in Chapter 16 will not avoid injustice, the court may grant relief on such terms as justice requires including protection of the parties' reliance interests.

§ 274. Cancellation, Destruction or Surrender of a Writing.

An obligee's cancellation, destruction or surrender to the obligor of a writing of a type customarily accepted as a symbol or as evidence of his right discharges without consideration the obligor's duty if it is done with the manifested intention to discharge it.

§ 278. Substituted Performance.

(1) If an obligee accepts in satisfaction of the obligor's duty a performance offered by the obligor that differs from what is due, the duty is discharged.

(2) If an obligee accepts in satisfaction of the obligor's duty a performance offered by a third person, the duty is discharged, but an obligor who has not previously assented to the performance for his benefit may in a reasonable time after learning of it render the discharge inoperative from the beginning by disclaimer.

§ 279. Substituted Contract.

(1) A substituted contract is a contract that is itself accepted by the obligee in satisfaction of the obligor's existing duty.

(2) The substituted contract discharges the original duty and breach of the substituted contract by the obligor does not give the obligee a right to enforce the original duty.

§ 280. Novation.

A novation is a substituted contract that includes as a party one who was neither the obligor nor the obligee of the original duty.

§ 281. Accord and Satisfaction.

(1) An accord is a contract under which an obligee promises to accept a stated performance in satisfaction of the obligor's existing duty. Performance of the accord discharges the original duty.

(2) Until performance of the accord, the original duty is suspended unless there is such a breach of the accord by the obligor as discharges the new duty of the obligee to accept the performance in satisfaction. If there is such a breach, the obligee may enforce either the original duty or any duty under the accord.

(3) Breach of the accord by the obligee does not discharge the original duty, but the obligor may maintain a suit for specific performance of the accord, in addition to any claim for damages for partial breach.

§ 283. Agreement of Rescission.

(1) An agreement of rescission is an agreement under which each party agrees to discharge all of the other party's remaining duties of performance under an existing contract.

(2) An agreement of rescission discharges all remaining duties of performance of both parties. It is a question of interpretation whether the parties also agree to make restitution with respect to performance that has been rendered.

§ 284. Release.

(1) A release is a writing providing that a duty owed to the maker of the release is discharged immediately or on the occurrence of a condition.

(2) The release takes effect on delivery as stated in §§ 101-03 and, subject to the occurrence of any condition, discharges the duty.

§ 285. Contract Not to Sue.

(1) A contract not to sue is a contract under which the obligee of a duty promises never to sue the obligor or a third person to enforce the duty or not to do so for a limited time.

(2) Except as stated in Subsection (3), a contract never to sue discharges the duty and a contract not to sue for a limited time bars an action to enforce the duty during that time.

(3) A contract not to sue one co-obligor bars levy of execution on the property of the promisee during the agreed time but does not bar an action or the recovery of judgment against any co-obligor.

§ 289. Joint, Several, and Joint and Several Promisors of the Same Performance.

(1) Where two or more parties to a contract promise the same performance to the same promisee, each is bound for the whole performance thereof, whether his duty is joint, several, or joint and several.

(2) Where two or more parties to a contract promise the same performance to the same promisee, they incur only a joint duty unless an intention is manifested to create several duties or joint and several duties.

(3) By statute in most states some or all promises which would otherwise create only joint duties create joint and several duties.

§ 293. Effect of Performance or Satisfaction on Co-Promisors.

Full or partial performance or other satisfaction of the contractual duty of a promisor discharges the duty to the obligee of each other promisor of the same performance to the extent of the amount or value applied to the discharge of the duty of the promisor who renders it.

§ 302. Intended and Incidental Beneficiaries.

(1) Unless otherwise agreed between promisor and promisee, a beneficiary of a promise is an intended beneficiary if recognition of a right to performance in the beneficiary is appropriate to effectuate the intention of the parties and either

   (a) the performance of the promise will satisfy an obligation of the promisee to pay money to the beneficiary; or

   (b) the circumstances indicate that the promisee intends to give the beneficiary the benefit of the promised performance.

(2) An incidental beneficiary is a beneficiary who is not an intended beneficiary.

§ 304. Creation of Duty to Beneficiary.

A promise in a contract creates a duty in the promisor to any intended beneficiary to perform the promise, and the intended beneficiary may enforce the duty.

§ 305. Overlapping Duties to Beneficiary and Promisee.

(1) A promise in a contract creates a duty in the promisor to the promisee to perform the promise even though he also has a similar duty to an intended beneficiary.

(2) Whole or partial satisfaction of the promisor's duty to the beneficiary satisfies to that extent the promisor's duty to the promisee.

§ 306. Disclaimer by a Beneficiary.

A beneficiary who has not previously assented to the promise for his benefit may in a reasonable time after learning of its existence and terms render any duty to himself inoperative from the beginning by disclaimer.

§ 307. *Remedy of Specific Performance.*

Where specific performance is otherwise an appropriate remedy, either the promisee or the beneficiary may maintain a suit for specific enforcement of a duty owed to an intended beneficiary.

§ 308. *Identification of Beneficiaries.*

It is not essential to the creation of a right in an intended beneficiary that he be identified when a contract containing the promise is made.

§ 309. *Defenses Against the Beneficiary.*

(1) A promise creates no duty to a beneficiary unless a contract is formed between the promisor and the promisee; and if a contract is voidable or unenforceable at the time of its formation the right of any beneficiary is subject to the infirmity.

(2) If a contract ceases to be binding in whole or in part because of impracticability, public policy, nonoccurrence of a condition, or present or prospective failure of performance, the right of any beneficiary is to that extent discharged or modified.

(3) Except as stated in Subsections (1) and (2) and in § 311 or as provided by the contract, the right of any beneficiary against the promisor is not subject to the promisor's claims or defenses against the promisee or to the promisee's claims or defenses against the beneficiary.

(4) A beneficiary's right against the promisor is subject to any claim or defense arising from his own conduct or agreement.

§ 315. *Effect of a Promise of Incidental Benefit.*

An incidental beneficiary acquires by virtue of the promise no right against the promisor or the promisee.

§ 316. *Scope of This Chapter.*

(1) In this Chapter, references to assignment of a right or delegation of a duty or condition, to the obligee or obligor of an assigned right or delegated duty, or to an assignor or assignee, are limited to rights, duties, and conditions arising under a contract or for breach of a contract.

(2) The statements in this Chapter are qualified in some respects by statutory and other rules governing negotiable instruments and documents, relating to interests in land, and affecting other classes of contracts.

§ 317. *Assignment of a Right.*

(1) An assignment of a right is a manifestation of the assignor's intention to transfer it by virtue of which the assignor's right to performance by the obligor is extinguished in whole or in part and the assignee acquires a right to such performance.

(2) A contractual right can be assigned unless

    (a) the substitution of a right of the assignee for the right of the assignor would materially change the duty of the obligor, or materially increase the burden or risk imposed on him by his contract, or materially impair his chance of obtaining return performance, or materially reduce its value to him, or

(b) the assignment is forbidden by statute or is otherwise inoperative on grounds of public policy, or

(c) assignment is validly precluded by contract.

§ 318. Delegation of Performance of Duty.

(1) An obligor can properly delegate the performance of his duty to another unless the delegation is contrary to public policy or the terms of his promise.

(2) Unless otherwise agreed, a promise requires performance by a particular person only to the extent that the obligee has a substantial interest in having that person perform or control the acts promised.

(3) Unless the obligee agrees otherwise, neither delegation of performance nor a contract to assume the duty made with the obligor by the person delegated discharges any duty or liability of the delegating obligor.

§ 319. Delegation of Performance of Condition.

(1) Where a performance by a person is made a condition of a duty, performance by a person delegated by him satisfies that requirement unless the delegation is contrary to public policy or the terms of the agreement.

(2) Unless otherwise agreed, an agreement requires performance of a condition by a particular person only to the extent that the obligor has a substantial interest in having that person perform or control the acts required.

§ 320. Assignment of Conditional Rights.

The fact that a right is created by an option contract or is conditional on the performance of a return promise or is otherwise conditional does not prevent its assignment before the condition occurs.

§ 321. Assignment of Future Rights.

(1) Except as otherwise provided by statute, an assignment of a right to payment expected to arise out of an existing employment or other continuing business relationship is effective in the same way as an assignment of an existing right.

(2) Except as otherwise provided by statute and as stated in Subsection (1), a purported assignment of a right expected to arise under a contract not in existence operates only as a promise to assign the right when it arises and as a power to enforce it.

§ 322. Contractual Prohibition of Assignment.

(1) Unless the circumstances indicate the contrary, a contract term prohibiting assignment of "the contract" bars only the delegation to an assignee of the performance by the assignor of a duty or condition.

(2) A contract term prohibiting assignment of rights under the contract, unless a different intention is manifested,

(a) does not forbid assignment of a right to damages for breach of the whole contract or a right arising out of the assignor's due performance of his entire obligation;

(b) gives the obligor a right to damages for breach of the terms forbidding assignment but does not render the assignment ineffective;

(c) is for the benefit of the obligor, and does not prevent the assignee from acquiring rights against the assignor or the obligor from discharging his duty as if there were no such prohibition.

§ 323. Obligor's Assent to Assignment or Delegation.

(1) A term of a contract manifesting an obligor's assent to the future assignment of a right or an obligee's assent to the future delegation of the performance of a duty or condition is effective despite any subsequent objection.

(2) A manifestation of such assent after the formation of a contract is similarly effective if made for consideration or in circumstances in which a promise would be binding without consideration, or if a material change of position takes place in reliance on the manifestation.

§ 326. Partial Assignment.

(1) Except as stated in Subsection (2), an assignment of a part of a right, whether the part is specified as a fraction, as an amount, or otherwise, is operative as to that part to the same extent and in the same manner as if the part had been a separate right.

(2) If the obligor has not contracted to perform separately the assigned part of a right, no legal proceeding can be maintained by the assignor or assignee against the obligor over his objection, unless all the persons entitled to the promised performance are joined in the proceeding, or unless joinder is not feasible and it is equitable to proceed without joinder.

§ 327. Acceptance or Disclaimer by the Assignee.

(1) A manifestation of assent by an assignee to the assignment is essential to make it effective unless

(a) a third person gives consideration for the assignment, or

(b) the assignment is irrevocable by virtue of the delivery of a writing to a third person.

(2) An assignee who has not manifested assent to an assignment may, within a reasonable time after learning of its existence and terms, render it inoperative from the beginning by disclaimer.

§ 328. Interpretation of Words of Assignment; Effect of Acceptance of Assignment.

(1) Unless the language or the circumstances indicate the contrary, as in an assignment for security, an assignment of "the contract" or of "all my rights under the contract" or an assignment in similar general terms is an assignment of the assignor's rights and a delegation of his unperformed duties under the contract.

(2) Unless the language or the circumstances indicate the contrary, the acceptance by an assignee of such an assignment operates as a promise to the assignor to perform the assignor's unperformed duties, and the obligor of the assigned rights is an intended beneficiary of the promise.

§ 329. Repudiation by Assignor and Novation with Assignee.

(1) The legal effect of a repudiation by an assignor of his duty to the obligor of the assigned right is not limited by the fact that the assignee is a competent person and has promised to perform the duty.

(2) If the obligor, with knowledge of such a repudiation, accepts any performance from the assignee without reserving his rights against the assignor, a novation arises by which the duty of the assignor is discharged and a similar duty of the assignee is substituted.

§ 330. Contracts to Assign in the Future, or to Transfer Proceeds to Be Received.

(1) A contract to make a future assignment of a right, or to transfer proceeds to be received in the future by the promisor, is not an assignment.

(2) Except as provided by statute, the effect of such a contract on the rights and duties of the obligor and third persons is determined by the rules relating to specific performance of contracts.

§ 331. Partially Effective Assignments.

An assignment may be conditional, revocable, or voidable by the assignor, or unenforceable by virtue of a Statute of Frauds.

§ 336. Defenses Against an Assignee.

(1) By an assignment the assignee acquires a right against the obligor only to the extent that the obligor is under a duty to the assignor; and if the right of the assignor would be voidable by the obligor or unenforceable against him if no assignment had been made, the right of the assignee is subject to the infirmity.

(2) The right of an assignee is subject to any defense or claim of the obligor which accrues before the obligor receives notification of the assignment, but not to defenses or claims which accrue thereafter except as stated in this Section or as provided by statute.

(3) Where the right of an assignor is subject to discharge or modification in whole or in part by impracticability, public policy, non-occurrence of a condition, or present or prospective failure of performance by an obligee, the right of the assignee is to that extent subject to discharge or modification even after the obligor receives notification of the assignment.

(4) An assignee's right against the obligor is subject to any defense or claim arising from his conduct or to which he was subject as a party or a prior assignee because he had notice.

§ 337. Elimination of Defenses by Subsequent Events.

Where the right of an assignor is limited or voidable or unenforceable or subject to discharge or modification, subsequent events which would eliminate the limitation or defense have the same effect on the right of the assignee.

§ 338. Discharge of an Obligor After Assignment.

(1) Except as stated in this Section, notwithstanding an assignment, the assignor retains his power to discharge or modify the duty of the obligor to the extent that the obligor performs or otherwise gives value until but not after the obligor receives notification that the right has been assigned and that performance is to be rendered to the assignee.

(2) So far as an assigned right is conditional on the performance of a return promise, and notwithstanding notification of the assignment, any modification of or substitution for the contract made by the assignor and obligor in good faith and in accordance with reasonable commercial standards is effective against the assignee. The assignee acquires corresponding rights under the modified or substituted contract.

(3) Notwithstanding a defect in the right of an assignee, he has the same power his assignor had to discharge or modify the duty of the obligor to the extent that the obligor gives value or otherwise changes his position in good faith and without knowledge or reason to know of the defect.

(4) Where there is a writing of a type customarily accepted as a symbol or as evidence of the right assigned, a discharge or modification is not effective
   (a) against the owner or an assignor having a power of avoidance, unless given by him or by a person in possession of the writing with his consent and any necessary indorsement or assignment;
   (b) against a subsequent assignee who takes possession of the writing and gives value in good faith and without knowledge or reason to know of the discharge or modification.

§ 342. Successive Assignees From the Same Assignor.

Except as otherwise provided by statute, the right of an assignee is superior to that of a subsequent assignee of the same right from the same assignor, unless
(a) the first assignment is ineffective or revocable or is voidable by the assignor or by the subsequent assignee; or
(b) the subsequent assignee in good faith and without knowledge or reason to know of the prior assignment gives value and obtains
   (i)   payment or satisfaction of the obligation,
   (ii) jjudgment against the obligor,
   (iii) a new contract with the obligor by novation, or
   (iv) possession of a writing of a type customarily accepted as a symbol or as evidence of the right assigned.

§ 343. Latent Equities.

If an assignor's right against the obligor is held in trust or constructive trust for or subject to a right of avoidance or equitable lien of another than the obligor, an assignee does not so hold it if he gives value and becomes an assignee in good faith and without notice of the right of the other.

§ 344. Purposes of Remedies.

Judicial remedies under the rules stated in this Restatement serve to protect one or more of the following interests of a promisee:

(a) his "expectation interest," which is his interest in having the benefit of his bargain by being put in as good a position as he would have been in had the contract been performed,

(b) his "reliance interest," which is his interest in being reimbursed for loss caused by reliance on the contract by being put in as good a position as he would have been in had the contract not been made, or

(c) his "restitution interest," which is his interest in having restored to him any benefit that he has conferred on the other party.

§ 345. Judicial Remedies Available.

The judicial remedies available for the protection of the interests stated in § 344 include a judgment or order

(a) awarding a sum of money due under the contract or as damages,

(b) requiring specific performance of a contract or enjoining its non-performance,

(c) requiring restoration of a specific thing to prevent unjust enrichment,

(d) awarding a sum of money to prevent unjust enrichment,

(e) declaring the rights of the parties, and

(f) enforcing an arbitration award.

§ 346. Availability of Damages.

(1) The injured party has a right to damages for any breach by a party against whom the contract is enforceable unless the claim for damages has been suspended or discharged.

(2) If the breach caused no loss or if the amount of the loss is not proved under the rules stated in this Chapter, a small sum fixed without regard to the amount of loss will be awarded as nominal damages.

§ 347. Measure of Damages in General.

Subject to the limitations stated in §§ 350-53, the injured party has a right to damages based on his expectation interest as measured by

(a) the loss in the value to him of the other party's performance caused by its failure or deficiency, plus

(b) any other loss, including incidental or consequential loss, caused by the breach, less

(c) any cost or other loss that he has avoided by not having to perform.

§ 348. Alternatives to Loss in Value of Performance.

(1) If a breach delays the use of property and the loss in value to the injured party is not proved with reasonable certainty, he may recover damages based on the rental value of the property or on interest on the value of the property.

(2) If a breach results in defective or unfinished construction and the loss in value to the injured party is not proved with sufficient certainty, he may recover damages based on

    (a) the diminution in the market price of the property caused by the breach, or

    (b) the reasonable cost of completing performance or of remedying the defects if that cost is not clearly disproportionate to the probable loss in value to him.

(3) If a breach is of a promise conditioned on a fortuitous event and it is uncertain whether the event would have occurred had there been no breach, the injured party may recover damages based on the value of the conditional right at the time of breach.

§ 349. Damages Based on Reliance Interest.

As an alternative to the measure of damages stated in § 347, the injured party has a right to damages based on his reliance interest, including expenditures made in preparation for performance or in performance, less any loss that the party in breach can prove with reasonable certainty the injured party would have suffered had the contract been performed.

§ 350. Avoidability as a Limitation on Damages.

(1) Except as stated in Subsection (2), damages are not recoverable for loss that the injured party could have avoided without undue risk, burden or humiliation.

(2) The injured party is not precluded from recovery by the rule stated in Subsection (1) to the extent that he has made reasonable but unsuccessful efforts to avoid loss.

§ 351. Unforeseeability and Related Limitations on Damages.

(1) Damages are not recoverable for loss that the party in breach did not have reason to foresee as a probable result of the breach when the contract was made.

(2) Loss may be foreseeable as a probable result of a breach because it follows from the breach

    (a) in the ordinary course of events, or

    (b) as a result of special circumstances, beyond the ordinary course of events, that the party in breach had reason to know.

(3) A court may limit damages for foreseeable loss by excluding recovery for loss of profits, by allowing recovery only for loss incurred in reliance, or otherwise if it concludes that in the circumstances justice so requires in order to avoid disproportionate compensation.

§ 352. Uncertainty as a Limitation on Damages.

Damages are not recoverable for loss beyond an amount that the evidence permits to be established with reasonable certainty.

§ 353. Loss Due to Emotional Disturbance.

Recovery for emotional disturbance will be excluded unless the breach also caused bodily harm or the contract or the breach is of such a kind that serious emotional disturbance was a particularly likely result.

§ 354. Interest as Damages.

(1) If the breach consists of a failure to pay a definite sum in money or to render a performance with fixed or ascertainable monetary value, interest is recoverable from the time for performance on the amount due less all deductions to which the party in breach is entitled.

(2) In any other case, such interest may be allowed as justice requires on the amount that would have been just compensation had it been paid when performance was due.

§ 355. Punitive Damages.

Punitive damages are not recoverable for a breach of contract unless the conduct constituting the breach is also a tort for which punitive damages are recoverable.

§ 356. Liquidated Damages and Penalties.

(1) Damages for breach by either party may be liquidated in the agreement but only at an amount that is reasonable in the light of the anticipated or actual loss caused by the breach and the difficulties of proof of loss. A term fixing unreasonably large liquidated damages is unenforceable on grounds of public policy as a penalty.

(2) A term in a bond providing for an amount of money as a penalty for non-occurrence of the condition of the bond is unenforceable on grounds of public policy to the extent that the amount exceeds the loss caused by such non-occurrence.

§ 357. Availability of Specific Performance and Injunction.

(1) Subject to the rules stated in §§ 359-69, specific performance of a contract duty will be granted in the discretion of the court against a party who has committed or is threatening to commit a breach of the duty.

(2) Subject to the rules stated in §§ 359-69, an injunction against breach of a contract duty will be granted in the discretion of the court against a party who has committed or is threatening to commit a breach of the duty if

    (a) the duty is one of forbearance, or

    (b) the duty is one to act and specific performance would be denied only for reasons that are inapplicable to an injunction.

§ 358. Form of Order and Other Relief.

(1) An order of specific performance or an injunction will be so drawn as best to effectuate the purposes for which the contract was made and on such terms as justice requires. It need not be absolute in form and the performance that it requires need not be identical with that due under the contract.

(2) If specific performance or an injunction is denied as to part of the performance that is due, it may nevertheless be granted as to the remainder.

(3) In addition to specific performance or an injunction, damages and other relief may be awarded in the same proceeding and an indemnity against future harm may be required.

§ 359. Effect of Adequacy of Damages.

(1) Specific performance or an injunction will not be ordered if damages would be adequate to protect the expectation interest of the injured party.

(2) The adequacy of the damage remedy for failure to render one part of the performance due does not preclude specific performance or injunction as to the contract as a whole.

(3) Specific performance or an injunction will not be refused merely because there is a remedy for breach other than damages, but such a remedy may be considered in exercising discretion under the rule stated in § 357.

§ 360. Factors Affecting Adequacy of Damages.

In determining whether the remedy in damages would be adequate, the following circumstances are significant:

(a) the difficulty of proving damages with reasonable certainty,

(b) the difficulty of procuring a suitable substitute performance by means of money awarded as damages, and

(c) the likelihood that an award of damages could not be collected.

§ 361. Effect of Provision for Liquidated Damages.

Specific performance or an injunction may be granted to enforce a duty even though there is a provision for liquidated damages for breach of that duty.

§ 362. Effect of Uncertainty of Terms.

Specific performance or an injunction will not be granted unless the terms of the contract are sufficiently certain to provide a basis for an appropriate order.

§ 363. Effect of Insecurity as to the Agreed Exchange.

Specific performance or an injunction may be refused if a substantial part of the agreed exchange for the performance to be compelled is unperformed and its performance is not secured to the satisfaction of the court.

§ 364. Effect of Unfairness.

(1) Specific performance or an injunction will be refused if such relief would be unfair because

    (a) the contract was induced by mistake or by unfair practices,

    (b) the relief would cause unreasonable hardship or loss to the party in breach or to third persons, or

    (c) the exchange is grossly inadequate or the terms of the contract are otherwise unfair.

(2) Specific performance or an injunction will be granted in spite of a term of the agreement if denial of such relief would be unfair because it would cause unreasonable hardship or loss to the party seeking relief or to third persons.

§ 365. Effect of Public Policy.

Specific performance or an injunction will not be granted if the act or forbearance that would be compelled or the use of compulsion is contrary to public policy.

§ 366. Effect of Difficulty in Enforcement or Supervision.

A promise will not be specifically enforced if the character and magnitude of the performance would impose on the court burdens in enforcement or supervision that are disproportionate to the advantages to be gained from enforcement and to the harm to be suffered from its denial.

§ 367. Contracts for Personal Service or Supervision.

(1) A promise to render personal service will not be specifically enforced.

(2) A promise to render personal service exclusively for one employer will not be enforced by an injunction against serving another if its probable result will be to compel a performance involving personal relations the enforced continuance of which is undesirable or will be to leave the employee without other reasonable means of making a living.

§ 368. Effect of Power of Termination.

(1) Specific performance or an injunction will not be granted against a party who can substantially nullify the effect of the order by exercising a power of termination or avoidance.

(2) Specific performance or an injunction will not be denied merely because the party seeking relief has a power to terminate or avoid his duty unless the power could be used, in spite of the order, to deprive the other party of reasonable security for the agreed exchange for his performance.

§ 369. Effect of Breach by Party Seeking Relief.

Specific performance or an injunction may be granted in spite of a breach by the party seeking relief, unless the breach is serious enough to discharge the other party's remaining duties of performance.

§ 370. Requirement That Benefit Be Conferred.

A party is entitled to restitution under the rules stated in this Restatement only to the extent that he has conferred a benefit on the other party by way of part performance or reliance.

§ 371. Measure of Restitution Interest.

If a sum of money is awarded to protect a party's restitution interest, it may as justice requires be measured by either

(a) the reasonable value to the other party of what he received in terms of what it would have cost him to obtain it from a person in the claimant's position, or

(b) the extent to which the other party's property has been increased in value or his other interests advanced.

§ 372. Specific Restitution.

(1) Specific restitution will be granted to a party who is entitled to restitution, except that:

    (a) specific restitution based on a breach by the other party under the rule stated in § 373 may be refused in the discretion of the court if it would unduly interfere with the certainty of title to land or otherwise cause injustice, and

    (b) specific restitution in favor of the party in breach under the rule stated in § 374 will not be granted.

(2) A decree of specific restitution may be made conditional on return of or compensation for anything that the party claiming restitution has received.

(3) If specific restitution, with or without a sum of money, will be substantially as effective as restitution in money in putting the party claiming restitution in the position he was in before rendering any performance, the other party can discharge his duty by tendering such restitution before suit is brought and keeping his tender good.

§ 373. Restitution When Other Party Is in Breach.

(1) Subject to the rule stated in Subsection (2), on a breach by non-performance that gives rise to a claim for damages for total breach or on a repudiation, the injured party is entitled to restitution for any benefit that he has conferred on the other party by way of part performance or reliance.

(2) The injured party has no right to restitution if he has performed all of his duties under the contract and no performance by the other party remains due other than payment of a definite sum of money for that performance.

§ 374. Restitution in Favor of Party in Breach.

(1) Subject to the rule stated in Subsection (2), if a party justifiably refuses to perform on the ground that his remaining duties of performance have been discharged by the other party's breach, the party in breach is entitled to restitution for any benefit

that he has conferred by way of part performance or reliance in excess of the loss that he has caused by his own breach.

(2) To the extent that, under the manifested assent of the parties, a party's performance is to be retained in the case of breach, that party is not entitled to restitution if the value of the performance as liquidated damages is reasonable in the light of the anticipated or actual loss caused by the breach and the difficulties of proof of loss.

§ 375. Restitution When Contract Is Within Statute of Frauds.

A party who would otherwise have a claim in restitution under a contract is not barred from restitution for the reason that the contract is unenforceable by him because of the Statute of Frauds unless the Statute provides otherwise or its purpose would be frustrated by allowing restitution.

§ 376. Restitution When Contract Is Voidable.

A party who has avoided a contract on the ground of lack of capacity, mistake, misrepresentation, duress, undue influence or abuse of a fiduciary relation is entitled to restitution for any benefit that he has conferred on the other party by way of part performance or reliance.

§ 377. Restitution in Cases of Impracticability, Frustration, Non-Occurrence Of Condition or Disclaimer by Beneficiary.

A party whose duty of performance does not arise or is discharged as a result of impracticability of performance, frustration of purpose, non-occurrence of a condition or disclaimer by a beneficiary is entitled to restitution for any benefit that he has conferred on the other party by way of part performance or reliance.

§ 378. Election Among Remedies.

If a party has more than one remedy under the rules stated in this Chapter, his manifestation of a choice of one of them by bringing suit or otherwise is not a bar to another remedy unless the remedies are inconsistent and the other party materially changes his position in reliance on the manifestation.

§ 379. Election to Treat Duties of Performance Under Aleatory Contract as Discharged.

If a right or duty of the injured party is conditional on an event that is fortuitous or is supposed by the parties to be fortuitous, he cannot treat his remaining duties to render performance as discharged on the ground of the other party's breach by non-performance if he does not manifest to the other party his intention to do so before any adverse change in the situation of the injured party resulting from the occurrence of that event or a material change in the probability of its occurrence.

§ 380. Loss of Power of Avoidance by Affirmance.

(1) The power of a party to avoid a contract for incapacity, duress, undue influence or abuse of a fiduciary relation is lost if, after the circumstances that made the contract

voidable have ceased to exist, he manifests to the other party his intention to affirm it or acts with respect to anything that he has received in a manner inconsistent with disaffirmance.

(2) The power of a party to avoid a contract for mistake or misrepresentation is lost if after he knows or has reason to know of the mistake or of the misrepresentation if it is non-fraudulent or knows of the misrepresentation if it is fraudulent, he manifests to the other party his intention to affirm it or acts with respect to anything that he has received in a manner inconsistent with disaffirmance.

(3) If the other party rejects an offer by the party seeking avoidance to return what he has received, the party seeking avoidance if entitled to restitution can, after the lapse of a reasonable time, enforce a lien on what he has received by selling it and crediting the proceeds toward his claim in restitution.

§ 381. Loss of Power of Avoidance by Delay.

(1) The power of a party to avoid a contract for incapacity, duress, undue influence or abuse of a fiduciary relation is lost if, after the circumstances that made it voidable have ceased to exist, he does not within a reasonable time manifest to the other party his intention to avoid it.

(2) The power of a party to avoid a contract for misrepresentation or mistake is lost if after he knows of a fraudulent misrepresentation or knows or has reason to know of a non-fraudulent misrepresentation or mistake he does not within a reasonable time manifest to the other party his intention to avoid it. The power of a party to avoid a contract for non-fraudulent misrepresentation or mistake is also lost if the contract has been so far performed or the circumstances have otherwise so changed that avoidance would be inequitable and if damages will be adequate compensation.

(3) In determining what is a reasonable time, the following circumstances are significant:

(a) the extent to which the delay enabled or might have enabled the party with the power of avoidance to speculate at the other party's risk;

(b) the extent to which the delay resulted or might have resulted in justifiable reliance by the other party or by third persons;

(c) the extent to which the ground for avoidance was the result of any fault by either party; and

(d) the extent to which the other party's conduct contributed to the delay.

(4) If a right or duty of the party who has the power of avoidance for non-fraudulent misrepresentation or mistake is conditional on an event that is fortuitous or is supposed by the parties to be fortuitous, a manifestation of intention under Subsection (1) or (2) is not effective unless it is made before any adverse change in his situation resulting from the occurrence of that event or a material change in the probability of its occurrence.

§ 384. Requirement That Party Seeking Restitution Return Benefit.

(1) Except as stated in Subsection (2), a party will not be granted restitution unless
   (a) he returns or offers to return, conditional on restitution, any interest in property that he has received in exchange in substantially as good condition as when it was received by him, or
   (b) the court can assure such return in connection with the relief granted.
(2) The requirement stated in Subsection (1) does not apply to property
   (a) that was worthless when received or that has been destroyed or lost by the other party or as a result of its own defects,
   (b) that either could not from the time of receipt have been returned or has been used or disposed of without knowledge of the grounds for restitution if justice requires that compensation be accepted in its place and the payment of such compensation can be assured, or
   (c) as to which the contract apportions the price if that part of the price is not included in the claim for restitution.

* * *

INDEX

References are to pages

* * *